Applying International Accounting Standards

Applying International Accounting Standards

THIRD EDITION

David Cairns

with
Brian Creighton and Anne Daniels

Members of the LexisNexis Group worldwide

United Kingdom	LexisNexis Butterworths Tolley, a Division of Reed Elsevier (UK) Ltd, Halsbury House, 35 Chancery Lane, LONDON, WC2A 1EL, and 4 Hill Street, EDINBURGH EH2 3JZ
Argentina	LexisNexis Argentina, BUENOS AIRES
Australia	LexisNexis Butterworths, CHATSWOOD, New South Wales
Austria	LexisNexis Verlag ARD Orac GmbH & Co KG, VIENNA
Canada	LexisNexis Butterworths, MARKHAM, Ontario
Chile	LexisNexis Chile Ltda, SANTIAGO DE CHILE
Czech Republic	Nakladatelství Orac sro, PRAGUE
France	Editions du Juris-Classeur SA, PARIS
Hong Kong	LexisNexis Butterworths, HONG KONG
Hungary	HVG-Orac, BUDAPEST
India	LexisNexis Butterworths, NEW DELHI
Ireland	Butterworths (Ireland) Ltd, DUBLIN
Italy	Giuffrè Editore, MILAN
Malaysia	Malayan Law Journal Sdn Bhd, KUALA LUMPUR
New Zealand	LexisNexis Butterworths, WELLINGTON
Poland	Wydawnictwo Prawnicze LexisNexis, WARSAW
Singapore	LexisNexis Butterworths, SINGAPORE
South Africa	LexisNexis Butterworths, DURBAN
Switzerland	Stämpfli Verlag AG, BERNE
USA	LexisNexis, DAYTON, Ohio

Reprinted 2003

A CIP Catalogue record for this book is available from the British Library.

ISBN 0 406 95208-6

Typeset by Columns Design Ltd, Reading, Berkshire
Printed and bound in Great Britain by Antony Rowe Ltd, Chippenham, Wilts

Contents

About the Authors

David Cairns

David Cairns has specialised in international financial reporting for over 20 years. He was the secretary-general of the International Accounting Standards Committee (IASC) for ten years from 1985 to the end of 1994. He subsequently established a specialised consultancy business, International Financial Reporting, which provided services to companies, accounting firms, governments, government agencies and standard setting bodies around the world. He has recently been appointed to the IASB's advisory group on the application of IFRSs to small and medium entities and in emerging economies.

Prior to joining the IASC, he was a partner in Stoy Hayward and chairman of that firm's international accounting and auditing committee.

David Cairns has written and lectured extensively on international financial reporting issues. He is the author of the *International Accounting Standards Survey* (www.cairns.co.uk). He was a joint author of two *Financial Times* surveys which compared the reporting practices of large companies with IASs. He was editor of *FT World Accounting Report* from 1997 to 1999. The first edition of *A Guide to Applying International Accounting Standards* was published in 1995.

David Cairns is a senior visiting fellow at the London School of Economics and Political Science where he teaches a post-graduate course on international accounting. He is a regular visitor to other universities around the world.

In June 1995, David Cairns was appointed an OBE in recognition of his services to the accountancy profession. He was awarded a plaque by the International Federation of Accountants in recognition of his outstanding contribution to the international accountancy profession.

David Cairns is a chartered accountant and holds an MSc in accounting and finance from the London School of Economics and Political Science.

David Cairns may be contacted through www.cairns.co.uk or at the following e-mail address: david@cairns.co.uk.

Brian Creighton

Brian Creighton is a chartered accountant and a senior manager in the Financial Reporting Unit at BDO Stoy Hayward. He has previously authored/joint authored *GAAP 2001 – UK Financial Reporting and Practice*, *Reporting financial performance – A practical guide to FRS 3* and *The Rights and Duties of Company Directors*. He is a member of several committees and working parties of the Institute of Chartered Accountants in England and Wales and the London Society of Chartered Accountants.

Anne Daniels

Anne Daniels is a chartered accountant and a director in the Financial Reporting Unit at BDO Stoy Hayward. She answers technical queries on accounting standards and company law matters, carries out hot reviews accounts of public interest clients and prepares submission letters to various accountancy bodies. She is also a member of the technical committee of the London Society of Chartered Accountants and is a regular presenter at technical updates for staff and clients.

Foreword

Sir David Tweedie, Chairman, International Accounting Standards Board

The Asian financial crisis and the sudden downturn in the stock markets following the Enron collapse revealed, as perhaps never before, the central role of financial reporting in a capitalist system. Where doubts and lack of confidence exist money will not be invested. Companies wishing to borrow will be faced either with an inability to find investors or suffer from penal financing rates to account for the risk premium built in to accommodate the lack of confidence and uncertainty. As investment ceases, growth stops and unemployment rises.

Financial reporting relies on three central pillars: first sensible, robust accounting requirements that reflect the underlying financial reality; secondly, strong auditors who ensure that managers do present to investors a faithful representation of their company's interaction with its economic environment; and, thirdly, enforcement powers to back the auditor in ensuring that the accounting rules are applied properly.

The role of the IASB is to ensure that the worldwide accounting method for dealing with any particular transaction is the same whether the event takes place in Stuttgart, Seoul, Seattle or Sydney. Our mission is to produce one set of high quality, global standards. The aim is to converge on the best possible answer in producing our standards. To do that we have been charged with examining accounting standards worldwide and where a national answer is better than that of the existing international standard to adopt it. Where the international standard employs the best method then our mission is to encourage national standard setters to adopt the international proposal. For the first time it is within our grasp to ensure that investors worldwide do not struggle to comprehend the differences among national standards. Everyone could soon be using the same accounting methods.

That the IASB is in this particular position is, to a great measure, due to the work of the present author. There have been four major events which have given the IASB the opportunity to achieve its objective. The first, pioneered by David Cairns, the longest serving secretary-general in the former IASC's history, was the improvements project. When I first became chairman of the United Kingdom's Accounting Standards Board, I could have appeared on any platform worldwide and proudly have proclaimed that British accounting standards were in line with those of the IASC. This was not a particularly good boast because in the late 1980s/early 1990s international standards typically would have many options one of which, invariably, was the British method of dealing with a particular problem. The improvements project forced the IASC to choose from the competing national proposals and remove the options. Suddenly, well-established British practices were rejected by the international community and we in Britain had to think again.

The second major breakthrough occurred when the IASC made an agreement with IOSCO that, put broadly, meant that if the IASC could produce a core set of some thirty standards acceptable to the member bodies of IOSCO then any company using these standards would be able to use them to gain access to stock exchanges worldwide without reconciliation to local standards. While, through much great hard work, the IASC produced the core standards, IOSCO was not quite satisfied but a huge step forward had been made and the opportunity to re-examine the difficulties with the core standards was given to IASB.

Thirdly, the increasing professionalism of standard setting on a national basis and the growing complexity of financial transactions meant that a part-time body such as the IASC, with sixteen delegations, meeting three or four times a year for up to a week on each occasion, could no longer compete with the full-time national standard setters meeting on a much more regular basis. The danger for IASC was that it would be reduced simply to accepting the work of the national standard setters and not be a leader in its own right.

The IASC's strategy working party eventually proposed the present structure of IASB in which the fourteen man board (twelve of us full-time) would meet on a monthly basis. Seven of our Board members would liaise with the standard setters in Australasia, Canada, France, Germany, Japan, the United Kingdom and the United States – the idea being that, ideally, agendas would be aligned and thoughts passed from national standard-setter to IASB and vice versa. The idea of an international partnership to achieve the best possible solution was born.

Finally, while some twenty-four countries already accepted, without amendment, the international standards, key events over the last year have indicated increasing acceptance of international standards as the basis for financial reporting worldwide. In June 2002, the European Parliament ratified the proposal that by 2005 most, and by 2007 all, the consolidated accounts of the 7,000 listed companies of the fifteen member states of the European Union would conform to international standards.

Russia and Jamaica have also come into the fold and in July of this year it was proposed by Australia that they too would switch to international standards by 2005.

These moves have shown the IASB, as if it had not already realised it, how important it is to examine national standards and to ensure that we all converge to the best possible solution as soon as possible. To that end the Board is meeting with its partner standard setters looking at the differences among our standards and debating with our partners with the intention of ensuring that IASB's standards reflect the best possible solution by the key date of 2005.

In most situations these changes will only involve part of the standard and hence the necessity of companies and auditors worldwide to understand the existing standards. David Cairns' book is a huge help in this regard. The author's intimate knowledge of the present corpus of international standards (as already stated he was responsible for the creation of many of them) is crucial in assisting readers to understand the raison d'être of the standards.

The IASB is faced with a once in a lifetime opportunity to ensure that investors worldwide do not have to wonder what are the differences between particular national standards. In the future we should be faced with simply having one global set. The implementation of these global standards will be critical. Many companies are going to have to make the decision to move to the IASB's standards in the next few years – they (and their auditors) are going to have to become familiar with these standards in a very short period of time. This book is written by an expert author who understands these international standards exceedingly well – I commend it to you all.

Sir David Tweedie
August 2002

Preface

With the completion of the core standards, the IASC was able to say that its standards dealt with all the topics that are important in the financial statements of business enterprises. This achievement is a tribute to the many hundreds of people who, over the last 25 years, gave so much time, energy and commitment to the work and mission of the IASC. The increasing acceptance of those standards was also a tribute to the vision of those members of the accountancy profession who created the IASC and those who later saw the need for the IASC to work closely with all interested parties including the preparers and users of financial statements, regulators and national standard setting bodies.

The foundations of the core standards were laid in the 1970s and the early 1980s with the development of the first 25 IASs. These standards are often unfairly criticised. In fact, they did a great deal to improve financial reporting and often involved the IASC agreeing requirements which exceeded the equivalent national requirements. The adoption of the comparability project in March 1987 was a major turning point for the IASC and IASs. It led eventually to the adoption of ten revised IASs as well as to a new philosophy which has influenced all the IASC's later work. In the same period, the IASC completed new standards on bank disclosures, high inflation, joint ventures and the disclosure and presentation of financial instruments as well as major revisions of its standards on consolidations and associates. This period also saw a rapid expansion in the IASC's links with national standard setting bodies and other organisations, most notably IOSCO, and with business and the users of financial statements.

The list of core standards was determined by IOSCO for the specific purpose of allowing IAS financial statements to be used as a passport in multinational securities offerings and other foreign listings. In 1993 IOSCO endorsed the IAS on cash flow statements for this purpose and a few months later accepted 14 other IASs. In May 2000, IOSCO endorsed all IASs.

The completion and endorsement of the core standards is an important step but it is not the end of the journey. The IASB has already started to improve the core standards. The core standards are not the final word and should not block further improvements in financial reporting. In particular, the IOSCO endorsement of IASs standards must allow for further evolution. The IASB must avoid at all costs the risk of IASs suffering the same fate as International Standards on Auditing which were endorsed by IOSCO in 1992 only for that endorsement to lapse when the IAPC subsequently improved those standards.

The further improvement and acceptance of IASs/IFRSs requires the continuation of regular and direct links between the IASB and national standard setting bodies. The foundations of these links were laid in the early 1980s by such people as Hans Burggraaff and his immediate successors as chairman. Georges Barthes later established direct links with the European Commission and the FASB. As a result of these and other efforts, by the time I left the IASC at the end of 1994, I was in regular contact with standard setting bodies in over 20 countries and had met representatives of such bodies in another 30 countries. The IASC had launched an annual conference of standard setting bodies and was regularly seeking direct input from, or co-operation with, national bodies on IASC projects. Furthermore, about half the board delegations included people who were directly or indirectly involved in the work of national standard setting bodies.

The continuing co-operation with national standard setting bodies was strongly supported by the IASC's foundation working party which reported in 1994 and which recommended a number of specific actions to enhance that co-operation, for example an agenda for the annual meeting of standard setting bodies. The subsequent report of the strategy working party continued this theme although it painted a strange and unfamiliar picture of the IASC's past. Direct links with national standard setting bodies are now a major feature of the restructured IASB.

Recent years have seen a rapid acceleration in the use of IAS/IFRS as national standards and by companies. This process has been boosted by the decisions of the European Union and Australia to require listed companies to publish IAS/IFRS consolidated financial statements with effect from 2005. In order to help these companies, the IASB has issued proposed improvements to IASs and a proposed IFRS on first-time adoption.

This third edition of this book deals in detail with all those standards which apply in 2002 and 2003. It lists IOSCO's concerns about the standards and the actions taken by the IASC and IASB to meet those concerns.

The book also deals with some aspects of the IASC's and IASB's history and structure. It describes its evolving relationships with various national and international bodies.

In writing this book, I have drawn extensively on my experiences as the IASC's secretary-general for ten years and in my subsequent work with national standard setting bodies, companies, accounting firms, regulators and educational institutions around the world. I am indebted, therefore, to a great number of people who have made this book possible and who have taught me so much about the application of IASs. The people include many who have made an immense and unpaid contribution to the work of IASC by serving on its board, consultative group and steering committees as well as on national advisory committees and in other roles.

I was particularly fortunate to work with four outstanding chairmen – John Kirkpatrick, Georges Barthes, Arthur Wyatt and the late Eiichi Shiratori – each of whom made a very significant contribution to the work of IASC. I am grateful to them for their support, encouragement and guidance during my time at the IASC and subsequently. I also benefited greatly from listening to their predecessors and to my predecessors as secretary/secretary-general; without the resulting knowledge, I would not have been able to achieve as much as I have been credited with during my time at the IASC.

This third edition has benefited greatly from the involvement of Brian Creighton and Anne Daniels of BDO Stoy Hayward in London. They have taken responsibility for revisions of many of the existing chapters and the drafting of new chapters. They have provided invaluable input in many ways. I am grateful to my former colleagues in the firm, in particular Peter Chidgey, for making this possible.

I am also indebted to a number of people who have helped make this book a reality. Frances Roach of Buckmans helped convert my initial ideas into a realistic publishing proposal and introduced me to the publishers of both the first and second editions. Brigid Curran was a first class technical director for the IASC and she has provided invaluable help with her recollections of the debates in the improvements project. Gillian Bertol, a dedicated member of the IASC's staff for over 18 years, made sure I had the right publications, checked the further reading and dealt with the IASC's copyright. Lynette Davidson, who set up and ran IASC's library for several years, prepared the index. The preparation of the manuscript involved a team of assistants who did most of the word processing and the gathering of annual reports. They have included Louise Goldingham, Ann Lazur, Nicola Norris, Sandra Wheeler, Deborah Hainstock, Martin Roseveare, Robert Watson, Matthew Bennetts and Janet Naismith. I am very grateful to all of these people.

LexisNexis Butterworths Tolley agreed to take on the publication of the third edition and I am indebted to Andrea Oliver and Jackie Argent.

Last, but very far from least, my work for the IASC and on this book would have been impossible without the support of my wife, Stella. I am eternally grateful for her tolerance and understanding of my commitment to the international accountancy profession in general and the improvement and harmonisation of financial reporting and the IASC in particular.

I am solely responsible for errors, omissions, opinions and interpretations in the book.

Any comments or suggestions for future editions of this book and other enquiries should be sent to the following e-mail address: david@cairns.co.uk

David Cairns
September 2002

How to Use This Book

The purpose of this book is to assist those who wish to:

- apply IFRSs in the preparation of published financial statements;
- audit financial statements prepared in accordance with IFRs; and
- develop national accounting requirements which conform with IFRs.

International Financial Reporting Standards (IFRSs) encompass all existing International Accounting Standards (IASs).

This book describes and explains:

- the IASC's and IASB's organisation and due process;
- the IASC's and IASB's relationship with national standard setting bodies and other organisations;
- the requirements of each IAS and the background to, and when possible the intent of, those requirements;
- the interrelationship between the requirements of different IASs;
- the comments of the International Organization of Securities Commissions (IOSCO) on each IAS; and
- likely future developments in respect of each IAS.

The book includes examples which show the application of some of the issues in IASs and extracts from annual reports of international companies from around the world. These extracts show how such companies have complied with the accounting treatments required by IFRSs. When an extract is taken from financial statements which include a reference to IASs, the extract includes the suffix (IAS).

REFERE\NCES

References to paragraphs in the text of an IAS or IFRS are shown in parentheses with the number of the IAS or IFRS followed by the paragraph number(s). For example:

- (IAS 2, 5) refers to paragraph 5 of IAS 2 *Inventories;*
- (IAS 22, 6 and 8) refers to paragraphs 6 and 8 of IAS 22 *Business Combinations;* and
- (IAS 18, 32 and IAS 24, 17) refers to paragraph 32 of IAS 18 *Revenue* and paragraph 17 of IAS 24 *Related Party Disclosures.*

A revised IAS usually has the same number as the superseded IAS. In the interests of clarity, for any IAS which has been replaced, the date on which the IAS was published is shown in square brackets after the number. For example, IAS 21 [1983] refers to IAS 21 *Accounting for the Effects of Foreign Exchange Rates* which was published in 1983 and superseded by IAS 21 *The Effects of Changes in Foreign Exchange Rates* in 1995.

References to paragraph numbers and page numbers in exposure drafts follow the same system. For example, (E43, 3) refers to paragraph 3 of the E43 *Property, Plant and Equipment* and (E43, p3) refers to page 3 of the E43 *Property, Plant and Equipment.*

References to paragraph numbers in the *Framework for the Preparation and Presentation of Financial Statements,* draft statements of principles, discussion papers and other similar IASC/IASB papers are shown in parentheses with the summarised title of the document followed by the paragraph number(s). For example, (*Presentation,* 15) refers to paragraph 15 of the draft statement of principles on the *Presentation of Financial Statements* and (*Framework,* 87) refers to paragraph 87 of the *Framework for the Preparation and Presentation of Financial Statements.*

ABBREVIATIONS

IASB	International Accounting Standards Board
IASC	International Accounting Standards Committee
IAS(s)	International Accounting Standard(s)
E	Exposure Draft (IASC)
ED	Exposure Draft (IASB)
SOP	Statement of Principles (IASC)
DSOP	Draft Statement of Principles (IASC)
IFRS(s)	International Financial Reporting Standard(s) (IASB)
SIC	Standing Interpretations Committee (IASC) – used for both the committee itself and the interpretations issued by the committee
SIC D	Draft interpretation issued by the SIC
EU	European Union
FASB	Financial Accounting Standards Board
FAS	Statement of Financial Accounting Standard (USA)
FEE	Fédération des Experts Comptables Européens
FRS	Financial Reporting Standard (United Kingdom)

GAAP	Generally Accepted Accounting Principles
IAPC	International Auditing Practices Committee
ISA	International Standard on Auditing
ICMG	International Capital Markets Group
IFAC	International Federation of Accountants
IOSCO	International Organization of Securities Commissions
IVSC	International Valuation Standards Committee (formerly The International Assets Valuation Standards Committee – TIAVSC)
IVS(s)	International Valuation Standard(s)
SSAP	Statement of Standard Accounting Practice (United Kingdom)

CHAPTER 1

The International Accounting Standards Committee (1973–2000)

All current IASs were developed and approved by the old International Accounting Standards Committee (IASC) that was replaced by the new International Accounting Standards Board (IASB) early in 2001. This chapter describes briefly the history of the IASC, its objectives, its relationships with non-accountants, national standard setting bodies and other organisations. It concludes with a summary of the IASC's structure, funding and due process.

1.1 THE HISTORY OF THE IASC

The IASC was set up in 1973 by sixteen professional accountancy bodies in nine countries – Australia, Canada, France, Germany, Japan, Mexico, the Netherlands, the United Kingdom and Ireland, and the United States of America. The IASC's first chairman, Sir Henry Benson (later Lord Benson) has written about the period leading up to the IASC's formation and its early work[1]. Table 1.1 summarises some of the key events in the IASC's history including the major appointments within and by the IASC. A more extensive description of the IASC's history is set out in a series of working papers by the author which are available at *www.cairns.co.uk*[2]. The IASB has also commissioned an official history of the IASC which will be published during 2003.

The sixteen professional bodies which signed the 1973 agreement and the original constitution were the IASC's founder members. They were joined by other accountancy bodies who were initially called 'associate members' but distinction between 'founder members' and 'associate members' disappeared in 1977. However, the founder members retained the right to permanent seats on the board until the end of 1987.

The accountancy profession created the IASC and continued to play a very major part in the work of the IASC and the promotion of the use of IASs. The member accountancy bodies committed themselves to use their best endeavours to:

- ensure that published financial statements complied with IASs in all material respects and disclosed the fact of such compliance;
- persuade governments and standard setting bodies that published financial statements should comply with IASs;
- persuade authorities controlling securities markets and the industrial and business community that published financial statements should comply with IASs and disclose the fact of such compliance;
- ensure that auditors satisfied themselves that the financial statements complied with IASs; and
- foster acceptance and observance of IASs.

(*IASC/IFAC Mutual Commitments*, 7)

It was the accountancy bodies which first required compliance with IASs, translated and distributed IASC pronouncements, and provided the initial link between the IASC and national bodies. In many cases, the profession helped persuade other bodies, notably governments and national standard setting bodies, to support the use of IASs or base national requirements on IASs.

Since 1977, the accountancy profession has been represented at the international level by the International Federation of Accountants (IFAC).

IFAC was created in such a way that the IASC retained its autonomy, both constitutionally and in its work as a standard setter. However, some IFAC participants immediately launched a takeover bid for the IASC. A key matter – and difference among the warring parties – was the extent to which the IASC should involve non-accountants. The discussions lasted from 1977 to 1982. Integration – another word for a merger – almost succeeded but the eventual outcome was that the IASC retained its independence. The relationship between the IASC and IFAC was clarified (or at least appeared to be) and non-accountants became involved in the work of the IASC. At the 1982 world congress of accountants, the professional accountancy bodies approved the *IASC/IFAC Mutual Commitments* and the *International Accountancy Profession Agreement* as well as related changes to the IASC and IFAC constitutions. By virtue of the *Mutual Commitments*, IFAC recognised:

> '... the IASC as the sole body having the responsibility and authority to issue, in its own name, pronouncements on international accounting standards with full authority in so doing to negotiate and associate with outside bodies and to promote the worldwide acceptance and observance of those standards.'

This was not the end of the matter, however. The continuing desire of some within IFAC to take over the IASC led to the appointment in 1987 of a working party to review the aims, activities and organisation of the two bodies. The working party was under the chairmanship of John

Bishop who had represented Australia on both the IASC board and the IFAC council. The working party concluded that the existing relationship should be maintained[3].

The separate but closely linked existence of the IASC and IFAC was troublesome at times but often worked well. The IASC and IFAC recognised each other's role and responsibilities and co-operated on areas of common interest such as public sector accounting, auditing, the International Capital Markets Group (ICMG) and relationships with IOSCO and other organisations. For example, the Public Sector Committee of IFAC required the use of IASs by government business enterprises and began developing standards based on IASs for government financial reporting. The IASC and the International Auditing Practices Committee (IAPC) sought consistent solutions to related problems such as the application of the going concern assumption. The ICMG undertook a number of activities which helped promote the work of the IASC and published a useful study on accounting harmonisation.

There were also formal links between the IASC and IFAC. From 1983 IFAC appointed the thirteen countries which were represented by their professional accountancy bodies on the IASC board. IFAC made a financial contribution directly to the IASC on behalf of those countries which were not on the board and also had the power to assist the poorer countries with their financial contribution to the IASC, a power which IFAC exercised on several occasions.

The IASC also worked closely with four regional accountancy bodies:

- Confederation of Asian and Pacific Accountants (CAPA);
- East, Central and Southern African Federation of Accountants (ECSAFA);
- Fédération des Experts Comptables Européens (FEE); and
- InterAmerican Accounting Association (IAA).

Many of the changes which have taken place in the IASC's structure and relationships have been evolutionary. From time to time, however, major reviews have been carried out which have had or will have considerable importance. The approval of the IASC/IFAC mutual commitments in 1982 was one example. Another was the Bishop working party. In the early 1990s, the foundation working party pointed to further changes. It was chaired by former IASC chairman Georges Barthes and included representatives from public accounting, business and standard setting bodies. It recommended that the accountancy profession should continue to play a major part in supporting and funding the work of the IASC but that further changes should be made in order to meet the IASC's vision. In its 1994 report[4], the foundation working party recommended:

- the establishment of the advisory council to exercise oversight and raise funds;
- a proper balance on the IASC board of people from public accounting, business, other users of financial statements and national standard setting bodies; and
- the continuation and enhancement of direct links with national standard setting bodies.

The working party acknowledged that further evolution might be necessary to increase the acceptability of IASs and increase the resources available to the IASC. It identified as one possibility the replacement of the advisory council by a foundation with certain powers and responsibilities (including the selection and the appointment of the board) assigned to it by the IASC constitution. In other words, it identified the outline of the new structure which was to come into place in 2001.

1.2 THE IASC'S OBJECTIVES

The objectives of the IASC were[5]:

- to formulate and publish in the public interest accounting standards to be observed in the presentation of financial statements and to promote their worldwide acceptance and observance; and
- to work generally for the improvement and harmonisation of regulations, accounting standards and procedures relating to the presentation of financial statements.

(*IASC Constitution*, 2)

Over the years, these objectives were made operational in a number of ways. In the early years, the IASC had to develop the initial standards and work hard to get those standards accepted and used. It also made considerable efforts to persuade listed companies to disclose compliance with IASs in addition to national standards[6]. In later years, with many IASs in place, the IASC shifted its emphasis to improving those standards, filling any noticeable gaps, extending the use of IASs and narrowing the differences between IASs and national requirements.

In 1990, the IASC approved a five year plan which identified the following specific objectives:

- to develop IASs that meet the need for truly international standards of accounting and disclosure by capital markets and the international business community and which are acceptable for use in the financial statements of all issuers of equity and debt securities;

- to ensure that IASs meet the financial reporting needs of developing and newly industrialised countries and encourage the implementation of those standards;
- to develop other documents that meet other financial reporting needs that are important internationally;
- to work for greater compatibility between national accounting requirements (whatever their form) and IASs and the removal of existing differences between those requirements and International Accounting Standards; and
- to promote the use of IASs in the financial statements of all business enterprises, whether in the private sector or the public sector.

(*IASC News*, October 1990, p6)

In 1995, as part of its agreement with IOSCO (see chapter 4), the IASC focused more narrowly on the first of its 1990 objectives. It decided that it should 'reach a major milestone in a reasonably short period of time, say three or four years' and that the appropriate target was a set of core standards which would be accepted by the major stock exchanges as a basis for financial reports of foreign companies. The IASC also decided that, once it had completed the core standards, it would aim to secure uniformity in the accounting standards used by both domestic and foreign large companies in all countries (*IASC Insight*, September 1995, p3).

1.3 THE IASC AND NON-ACCOUNTANTS

The IASC concluded by the end of the 1970s that it must involve non-accountants, as well as accountants, in its work. Even by that time, interest in the international harmonisation of accounting standards had become widespread and the IASC was anxious to obtain input to its work from a wide range of users and preparers of financial statements at the formative stages of IASs.

The IASC's first response was to form the consultative group, the founder members of which were international bodies of stock exchanges, business, trades unions, financial executives and financial analysts as well as the World Bank, the OECD and the Center for Transnational Corporations of the United Nations. Subsequently IOSCO, lawyers, bankers, bank regulators, asset valuers, accounting academics and actuaries plus the FASB and the European Commission have joined the consultative group. The group has played an invaluable part in advising the board on technical and strategic issues and in supporting the IASC and the use of IASs.

In 1982, the IASC also added four places to the board for 'other organisations with an interest in financial reporting'. The financial analysts took the first place in 1986 but negotiations with the financial executives which started in the mid-1980s reached a satisfactory conclusion only in 1995 – both the financial analysts and the financial executives had been founder members of the consultative group. The Federation of Swiss Industrial Holding Companies took the third place in 1995. Discussions about board membership were also held with the International Chamber of Commerce and IOSCO but the fourth place remained empty.

Observers at board meetings are another way in which the IASC has extended the involvement of non-accountants, as well as accountants, in its work. The first observers were the FASB (1988) and the European Commission (1990) and they were followed by IOSCO (1996) and the People's Republic of China (1997).

1.4 THE IASC AND NATIONAL STANDARD SETTING BODIES

It has always been highly desirable that the IASC should work with the bodies which are responsible for setting national accounting requirements, whatever the form of those requirements and irrespective of whether the bodies are in the private sector or part of government. In the early days of the IASC, the member accountancy bodies provided the links but it was inevitable that, in due course, the IASC would establish direct links with standard setting bodies.

The IASC took a first step in 1981 when it set up a working party consisting of representatives of the standard setting bodies in the Netherlands, the UK and USA with a French chairman to seek greater harmony in the accounting rules for deferred taxes. The working party followed on from the adoption of different national standards and a flexible IAS 12 – these were the very problems which the IASC wanted to overcome (see chapter 31).

Shortly afterwards, the IASC took a second step when it decided to visit the national standard setting bodies in all board countries in order to discuss greater harmony among national and international standards. The visits were later expanded to include standard setting bodies in a number of non-board countries.

On his appointment in 1987 as chairman, Georges Barthes took a further step. He argued that the IASC should provide a focus for discussions on matters of common interest. He saw an important role for national standard setting bodies in the effort to reduce options in IASs and he sought direct links with both the European Commission and the FASB in view of their importance to international standard setting. Both were invited to join the consultative group and attend board meetings as observers (a similar invitation was extended later to Japan's standard setting body, the Business Accounting Deliberation Council, but was declined). As part of the agreement with the FASB, the IASC nominated a non-US financial executive to the Financial Accounting Standards Advisory Council, the FASB's equivalent of the IASC consultative group.

The links between the IASC and national standard setting bodies gathered pace during the consultations on E32 *Comparability of Financial Statements*. By then the IASC and the Canadian accounting standards board had also decided to work together on the development of common standards on financial instruments. The Australians had earlier played a major part in the development of the IASC framework. Later years have seen further co-operation involving more countries and further consultations on IASC projects.

In 1990, the IASC decided that an annual conference of standard setting bodies would help achieve its objective of greater compatibility of national and international standards. At the first conference, organised with considerable help from the FASB and FEE, standard setters from twenty countries debated the objectives and concepts underlying financial reporting. Subsequent conferences were held at the FASB and in London, Edinburgh, Amsterdam, Copenhagen and Hong Kong.

Three years later, G4+1 was formed. It consisted of the standard setting bodies from Australia, Canada, the UK and the USA plus the IASC – the group was later joined by New Zealand. These bodies shared similar conceptual frameworks and were keen to adopt common solutions to common problems – but the debates often reflected some major differences among group members. The group published a number of discussion papers and invitations to comment.

The IASC's growing relationship with national standard setting bodies was one of the issues considered by the foundation working party. It recommended that the IASC should work directly with other standard setting bodies in order to achieve common improvements in accounting standards as well as greater compatibility between national requirements and IASs and between national requirements of different countries. The working party identified four areas in which the IASC should continue to take direct action:

- by sponsoring an annual meeting of standard setting bodies which would, among other things, identify further areas for co-operation among standard setting bodies and identify common accounting solutions which could be considered by the IASC and national standard setting bodies;
- by encouraging co-operation among standard setting bodies on topics of mutual interest, emerging issues and other topics of mutual interest;

- by encouraging direct involvement of standard setting bodies in the work of the IASC as part of country delegations, in IASC steering committees and as commentators on IASC proposals; and
- by encouraging standard setting bodies to adopt national requirements that conform with IASs and to support the work of the IASC in their consultations with national governments, regulators, stock exchanges and other bodies.

The foundation working party focused on co-operation between the IASC and national standard setting bodies, something which had increasingly been a feature of the IASC's work in the first half of the 1990s. The November 1994 work programme, which was approved partly in response to IOSCO's comments on existing IASs, carried forward that idea. It envisaged further joint projects on interim reporting, leases, provisions, environmental accounting and discounting. At the same time, the IASC also agreed to work with national standard setting bodies to resolve the outstanding recognition and measurement issues in its financial instruments project following its decision to split that project in two.

Following the appointment of Michael Sharpe as chairman of the IASC in July 1995, competition took over from co-operation. There were numerous reports of both tension between the IASC and major standard setters and of competition between IASs and US Generally Accepted Accounting Principles (GAAP). This undoubtedly harmed the IASC more than it harmed the national bodies.

Under the leadership of Stig Enevoldsen co-operation was back as the key word (*IASC Insight*, June 1998, p17). Unlike his predecessor he has had extensive experience as a national standard setter having chaired the Danish accounting standards committee for many years and participated on behalf of Denmark in EU discussions. The IASC began to work with other national standard setters in a joint working group on financial instruments (see chapter 20).

1.5 THE IASC AND INTERGOVERNMENTAL BODIES

The IASC worked closely with several intergovernmental bodies which were concerned with the improvement and harmonisation of financial statements. These included:

- the United Nations Intergovernmental Working Group of Experts on International Standards of Accounting and Reporting (UN ISAR group);

- the Working Group on Accounting Standards of the Organisation for Economic Co-operation and Development (OECD working group); and
- the European Commission (see chapter 4).

Both the UN ISAR group and the OECD working group support the harmonisation and improvement of financial reporting but neither group saw itself as a standard setting body. The work of both groups has drawn heavily on the work of IASC; for example:

- all the UN ISAR group's conclusions on accounting issues were drawn directly from existing IASs and often the text was unchanged;
- the UN ISAR group's conclusions on the objectives and principles of financial reporting were directly based on the preliminary drafts of IASC's *Framework for the Preparation and Presentation of Financial Statements*; and
- the texts of IASs were an important source used by the OECD working group and the resulting clarifications approved by the working group were usually similar in substance to IASs.

Representatives of the UN and OECD secretariats attended meetings of the IASC consultative group. The IASC was also represented at meetings of both groups and the 1988 OECD forum on financial instruments added impetus to the IASC's financial instruments project (see chapter 20).

1.6 THE IASC'S STRUCTURE

1.6.1 Member Bodies

The members of the IASC were professional accountancy bodies. In 1982, the memberships of the IASC and IFAC were combined with the result that all the professional accountancy bodies which were members of IFAC automatically became members of the IASC and, conversely, no organisations or individuals other than the members of IFAC were members of the IASC.

The IASC member bodies met in conjunction with the general assembly of IFAC but their powers were limited to the approval of proposed amendments to the IASC constitution which had already been approved by the board of the IASC and discussed with the council of IFAC. All other responsibilities and powers were delegated to the board.

1.6.2 The IASC Board

The business of the IASC was conducted by its board which had the power to issue IASs, exposure drafts and other documents relating to its work and to consult with other bodies. Under the 1982 constitution the board consisted of:

- up to thirteen countries represented by professional accountancy bodies which were members of the IASC; and
- up to four organisations with an interest in financial reporting and co-opted by the board.

From 1 January 1988, the thirteen countries were appointed by the IFAC council (after seeking the advice of the outgoing IASC board) and the founder members lost their right to permanent seats on the board. The IASC and IFAC also agreed that the board should include:

- at least nine countries from among the most significant countries in terms of the status and development of the accountancy profession or that are of significant importance to international commerce and trade; and
- preferably not less than three developing countries.

(*IASC/IFAC Mutual Commitments*, 8)

For the term ending on 31 December 2000, the board members were: Australia, Canada, France, Germany, India and Sri Lanka, Japan, Malaysia, Mexico, Netherlands, Nordic Federation (includes Denmark, Finland, Iceland, Norway and Sweden), South Africa and Zimbabwe, UK, USA, the International Co-ordinating Committee of Financial Analysts Associations, the Swiss Federation of Industrial Holding Companies, and the International Association of Financial Executives Institutes. The European Commission, the FASB, IOSCO and China sent observers to all board meetings.

Board representatives were the people appointed to represent the board members on the board. Each board member nominated up to two representatives plus a technical adviser. The board encouraged each country to include in its delegation at least one person from business or commerce and at least one person who was directly involved in the work of the national standard setting body.

The board appointed its chairman from among its number. The board member country or organisation providing the chairman was entitled to a further representative.

Each board member had one vote at board meetings irrespective of the number of people it sent to that meeting. The chairman did not have a vote. At least three-quarters of the board had to vote in favour of publication of an IAS or an interpretation of an IAS. At least two-thirds had to vote in favour of publication of an exposure draft. An abstention had the same effect as a vote against a proposed IAS, interpretation or exposure draft.

1.6.3 Advisory Council

The advisory council was established in 1995 following the recommendations of the foundation working party. It consisted of outstanding individuals in senior positions from a variety of backgrounds. The objectives of the council were to:

- review and comment on the board's strategy and plans so as to satisfy itself that the needs of the IASC's constituencies were being met;
- prepare an annual report on the effectiveness of the board in achieving its objectives and in carrying out its due process;
- promote participation in, and acceptance of, the work of the IASC by the accountancy profession, the business community, the users of financial statements and other interested parties; and
- ensure that the IASC had the necessary level of funding.

The advisory council was not allowed to participate in, nor seek to influence, the board's technical decisions.

1.6.4 Consultative Group

The consultative group was set up in 1981 as part of the IASC's efforts to broaden the involvement of non-accountants in its work. Some of the original group members later served on the board. People from the following organisations attended meetings of the consultative group in the later years:

- Fédération Internationale des Bourses de Valeurs (FIBV) (International Federation of Stock Exchanges)
- International Chamber of Commerce (ICC)
- International Confederation of Free Trade Unions (ICFTU)
- International Organization of Securities Commissions (IOSCO)
- Basle Committee on Banking Supervision
- Fédération Bancaire de la Communauté Européenne (European Banking Federation)
- International Banking Associations
- International Bar Association (IBA)
- The International Valuation Standards Committee (IVSC)

- International Association for Accounting Education and Research (IAAER)
- The World Bank
- International Finance Corporation (IFC)
- Financial Accounting Standards Board (FASB)
- European Commission
- Organisation for Economic Co-operation and Development (OECD)
- Transnational Corporations and Management Division, United Nations

Discussions with the consultative group played an important part in the IASC's process for the setting of IASs and in gaining acceptance for the resulting standards.

1.6.5 Standing Interpretations Committee

The standing interpretations committee (SIC) was established in 1996 to review, on a timely basis and within the context of IASs and the IASC framework, accounting issues which were likely to receive divergent or unacceptable treatment in the absence of authoritative guidance. The SIC had twelve voting members appointed by the board.

1.6.6 Project Steering Committees

A steering committee was appointed by the board for each project. The role of the steering committee was to approve the draft statement of principles for publication and approve the drafts of statement of principles, exposure draft and IAS for submission to the board.

Each steering committee was chaired by a board representative and usually included representatives of the member bodies in several other countries. Steering committees also included representatives of other organisations which were represented on the board or the consultative group and other experts in the particular topic. For example, the IAS 30 steering committee involved both bankers and bank regulators. The steering committees dealing with both IAS 19 and IAS 26 consulted or involved actuaries. Valuers were consulted on the valuation aspects of IAS 16 [1993]. IOSCO appointed three people to the comparability steering committee and four people to the improvements steering committee. In November 1994, the IASC invited IOSCO to send a regulator to meetings of all steering committees, a privilege which is not shared by any other organisation.

1.6.7 IASC Staff

The IASC staff provided technical and administrative support to the board and steering committees. As the IASC's work has grown in stature so the staff has expanded both in number and in its role. The change from secretary to secretary-general in 1983 was one indication of this as was the IASC's decision to appoint a permanent secretary-general who was not on secondment from another organisation. In 1991, the IASC appointed its first technical director.

1.7 FUNDING

Until 1985, virtually the sole source of the IASC's funding was the contributions from the professional accountancy bodies on the board (90% of the then budget) and other professional accountancy bodies, directly until 1982 and then through IFAC (10%). The financial analysts started to contribute funds when they joined the board in 1986. The Federation of Swiss Holding Companies and IAFEI started to contribute funds when they joined the board in 1995 and 1996 respectively.

During its early years, the IASC received a number of small donations as well as funding from the Basel Committee of Banking Supervisors for the initial work on IAS 30. In 1990, the IASC launched its external fund-raising effort with a direct appeal to accounting firms, multinational companies and stock exchanges. In 1994, the staff obtained a grant of $500,000 from the World Bank to fund the agriculture project. In 1995, the responsibility for external fund-raising passed to the advisory council.

Another significant change in funding has been IASC publications. Prior to the late 1980s, IASs and other IASC publications were distributed by the IASC's member bodies and the IASC gained no income from the output of its efforts. The IASC launched its first annual bound volume of IASs at the world congress of accountants in October 1987. This was followed in 1988 by the first published survey on the use of IASs and, in 1991, by *IASC Insight* and *IASC Update* which replaced *IASC News*. The IASC also started to enforce its copyright over its pronouncements. Publications revenue has grown in ten years from nothing to over £1 million a year. Gillian Bertol was appointed the IASC's publications director in 1992.

1.8 THE IASC'S DUE PROCESS

The IASC developed IASs through an international due process which involved the preparers and users of financial statements, the accountancy profession and national standard setting bodies. This process helped to ensure that IASs were high quality standards that required appropriate accounting practices in particular economic circumstances. The due process also helped to ensure that IASs were acceptable to the users, preparers and auditors of financial statements.

The development of each IAS involved:

- a decision to add a project to the IASC's work programme based on a *project proposal* prepared by the staff;
- the appointment of a *steering committee* to deal with the project;
- initial *research* of the topic by the IASC staff or a consultant;
- the development, approval and publication of a *draft statement of principles* (DSOP) which sets out the underlying accounting principles which will form the basis of the proposed IAS;
- the approval of the final *statement of principles* (SOP) as the basis for the exposure draft of the proposed IAS;
- the development, approval and publication of an *exposure draft* (ED) of the proposed IAS based on the approved statement of principles ; and
- the approval and publication of the IAS.

The IASC sought the views of the consultative group, professional accountancy bodies, standard setting bodies, companies and other interested groups and individuals on a worldwide basis at each stage of the project. It also evaluated the comments received on the draft statement of principles and exposure draft before approving the final SOP and IAS.

A reduced due process was sometimes used for the revision of existing IASs. For example, the comparability and improvements project did not involve the development or issuance of a DSOP. Similarly the development of the 1998 version of IAS 19 did not involve a DSOP although the IASC did seek comments in response to a staff issues paper.

In carrying out its role, the steering committee should have:

- reviewed the issues associated with the topic along with national and regional accounting requirements and practices, existing and proposed IASC pronouncements and other relevant material;
- advised the staff on the issues to be addressed and areas for research (but this advice did not prevent the staff from addressing other issues associated with the project); and
- evaluated the comments on the DSOP and ED.

While steering committees had a considerable degree of autonomy, the board reviewed in detail all the recommendations of steering committees. An ED or IAS was published only after a line by line review by, and the approval of, the board. Furthermore, the secretary-general had to be satisfied that the steering committee had followed the requirements of the board before a DSOP was published or other steering committee proposals were submitted to the board.

The approval of an ED required the support of at least two-thirds of the board. The ED was published and comments were invited from all interested parties during the exposure period, which was usually six months but which was reduced to four months or less during the core standards project. In the core standards project, the IASC invited comments on alternative accounting treatments and indicated that the comments would help it determine its final position.

The approval of the IAS required the support of at least three-quarters of the board. Before approving the standard, the board had to decide whether any changes to the proposals in the exposure draft were so great that the board should issue another ED. In practice, the decision was often a formality because either the changes were not significant or it was clear that a further ED would be required either to seek the comments on proposed changes or to obtain the necessary degree of support.

The IASC's process for the approval of interpretations was similar to an abbreviated form of the process for the approval of IASs. The major difference was that the SIC, and not the board, approved the publication of draft interpretations. The voting arrangements in the SIC were also slightly different from those which applied in the board.

Notes

[1] Sir Henry (later Lord) Benson, 'The Story of International Accounting Standards', *Accountancy*, July 1976.

[2]The author's working papers include *The Evolution of the IASC, The Evolution of International Accounting Standards, The IASC and IOSCO* and *The Conceptual Framework: the International Experience, www.cairns.co.uk*, 2002.

[3]IFAC/IASC Working Party, *IFAC/IASC: Review of Aims, Activities and Organisation*, 1989.

[4]IASC, *Report of the International Accounting Standards Foundation Working Party*, IASC. London, 1994.

[5]See for example Stephen Elliott, 'IASC Sets Sights on Spirit of Partnership', speech to 1982 World Congress of Accountants, Mexico City, 1982 and John Kirkpatrick, 'The Case for Visible Conformity', *Accountancy*, January 1987, p17. For a report on the outcomes of these efforts, see David Cairns, *International Accounting Standards Survey 2000*, David Cairns, 2001.

[6] The original constitution referred to 'basic' standards but that idea disappeared in 1977.

Table 1.1 *Some Key Events in the IASC's History*

1973
- IASC formed – inaugural meeting on 29 June
- Sir Henry Benson appointed chairman
- Paul Rosenfield appointed secretary

1974
- First exposure draft published
- First associate members admitted (Belgium, India, Israel, New Zealand, Pakistan and Zimbabwe)
- First IAS approved

1975
- John Brennan appointed secretary

1976
- Joseph Cummings (USA) appointed chairman
- Group of Ten bank governors decides to work with the IASC on bank financial statements

1977
- Discussion paper and first IAS on inflation accounting published
- Discussion paper on acceptance and observances of IASs published
- Revised constitution adopted – board expanded to eleven countries – 'associate' members become members – reference to 'basic' standards removed
- IFAC formed – IASC continues to be autonomous but with close relationship with IFAC
- Roy Nash appointed secretary

1978
- South Africa and Nigeria join board
- John Hepworth (Australia) appointed chairman

1979
- IASC meets OECD working group on accounting standards
- Allan Cook appointed secretary

1980
- Discussion paper on bank disclosures published
- UN ISAR group meets for first time – IASC presents position paper offering co-operation
- *Financial Times* survey compares reporting practices of 200 companies with IASs
- Hans Burggraaff (Netherlands) appointed chairman

Table 1.1 *Some Key Events in the IASC's History (continued)*

1981
- Consultative group formed
- IASC commences programme of visits to national standard setting bodies with visit to the Tripartite Accounting Standards Group in the Netherlands
- Working party on deferred taxes set up with standard setters in the Netherlands, UK and USA

1982
- Geoffrey Mitchell appointed secretary
- Italy's securities regulator, CONSOB, requires listed companies to comply with IASs when no national standards
- IASC/IFAC mutual commitments and revised IASC constitution approved – board expanded to thirteen countries plus four 'other organisations with an interest in financial reporting' – all members of IFAC become members of the IASC – professional accountancy bodies recognise IASC has full and complete autonomy in the setting of IASs
- Stephen Elliott (Canada) appointed chairman

1983
- Italy joins board
- Geoffrey Mitchell appointed to new position of secretary-general

1984
- Taiwan joins board
- First formal meeting with US SEC

1985
- John Kirkpatrick (UK & Ireland) appointed chairman
- David Cairns appointed secretary-general
- OECD forum on accounting harmonisation
- IASC responds to SEC multinational prospectus proposals

1986
- Financial analysts join board
- Pakistan gives legal backing to IASs
- Dutch government proposes that IASs are equivalent to EC 7th directive
- Joint conference with New York stock exchange and International Bar Association on the globalisation of financial markets
- Accounting Society of China visits the IASC
- Framework project started

1987
- Comparability project started
- IOSCO joins consultative group and lends support to comparability project

(*Continued*)

Table 1.1 *Some Key Events in the IASC's History (continued)*

- Lawyers and bankers join consultative group
- First IASC bound volume of IASs
- First IASC annual review
- Bishop committee established to review the aims and activities of the IASC and IFAC
- Georges Barthes (France) appointed chairman

1988

- Jordan, Korea and Nordic Federation replace Mexico, Nigeria and Taiwan on the board
- IASC and CICA start joint financial instruments project
- IASC publishes survey on the use of IASs
- FASB joins consultative group and joins board as observer
- IASC nominates Derek Bonham (Hanson plc) to Financial Accounting Standards Advisory Council
- E32 *Comparability of Financial Statements* approved
- IOSCO technical committee supports the work of IASC and sees common standards as a critical goal

1989

- FEE president Herman Nordemann argues that Europe's best interests are served by international accounting standards
- *Framework for the Preparation and Presentation of Financial Statements* approved
- Review of financial reporting needs of developing and newly industrialised countries started
- IFAC public sector guideline requires government business enterprises to follow IASs
- First IASC delegation to USSR
- The World Bank reports compliance with IASs
- FEE publishes comparison of IASs and EC directives

1990

- European Commission joins consultative group and joins board as observer
- External funding launched
- Bishop committee confirms continuation of existing relationship between the IASC and IFAC
- *Statement of Intent on the Comparability of Financial Statements* approved
- IAS 30 *Disclosures in the Financial Statements of Banks and Similar Financial Institutions* approved

(Continued)

Table 1.1 *Some Key Events in the IASC's History (continued)*

- Arthur Wyatt (USA) appointed chairman
- The Asian Development Bank tells borrowers to present financial statements that conform with IASs**1991**

1991

- Brigid Curran appointed technical director
- First IASC conference of standard setting bodies (organised in conjunction with FEE and FASB)
- *IASC Insight, IASC Update* and publications subscription scheme launched
- FASB adopts international plan which supports search for international standards and close co-operation with IASC

1992

- First IASC delegation to People's Republic of China
- Gillian Bertol appointed publications director
- World standard setters meet at FASB

1993

- India replaces Korea on board
- Eiichi Shiratori (Japan) appointed chairman
- IASC attends first meeting of G4+1
- Resounding support from the accountancy profession, stock exchanges, companies and IOSCO at IASC's 20th anniversary conference
- IOSCO agrees list of core standards and endorses IAS 7 *Cash Flow Statements*
- Comparability and improvements project completed with approval of ten revised IASs
- GATS ministerial decision recognises role of IASs in removing trade barriers (Uruguay round)

1994

- Foundation working party recommends establishment of advisory council and continuation of direct links with standard setting bodies
- SEC accepts three IAS treatments plus IAS 7
- World Bank agrees to fund agriculture project
- Board meets standard setting bodies to discuss E48 *Financial Instruments*
- Liesel Knorr appointed technical director
- FASB decides to work with the IASC on earnings per share
- IOSCO accepts 14 IASs but rejects step by step endorsement of IASs ('Shiratori letters')
- G4+1 publishes first joint paper on future events

(Continued)

Table 1.1 *Some Key Events in the IASC's History (continued)*

- IASC tells IOSCO that its approach to the endorsement of IASs is unsatisfactory but agrees work programme to complete virtually all core standards by 1998
- Academics join consultative group

1995

- First German companies report under IASs
- IAS 32 *Financial Instruments: Disclosure and Presentation* approved
- Sir Bryan Carsberg appointed secretary-general
- Malaysia and Mexico replace Italy and Jordan on board – India and South Africa agree to share board seats with Sri Lanka and Zimbabwe
- Swiss holding companies join board
- Michael Sharpe (Australia) appointed chairman
- Agreement with IOSCO to complete core standards by 1999 – successful completion of IASs which are acceptable to IOSCO technical committee will allow IOSCO to endorse those IASs for use in cross-border offerings
- European Commission's harmonisation strategy supports IASC/IOSCO agreement and use of IASs by EU multinationals

1996

- Financial executives join board
- IOSCO joins board as observer
- IASC accelerates completion of core set of IASs to 1998
- Standing interpretations committee formed
- Australia sets up project to harmonise its standards with IASs
- US Congress supports need for IASs

1997

- IASC and FASB issue common standards on earnings per share
- Discussion paper on accounting for financial instruments published
- People's Republic of China joins board as observer
- Joint working group on financial instruments formed with national standard setting bodies
- IASC survey finds that 56 of 67 countries either look directly to IASs as their national standards or develop national standards based primarily on IASs
- IASC sets up its web-site

Table 1.1 *Some Key Events in the IASC's History (continued)*

1998

- Stig Enevoldsen (Nordic Federation) appointed chairman
- New laws in Belgium, France, Germany and Italy allow large companies to meet domestic requirements with IAS financial statements
- Strategy working party recommends that standing technical committee consisting mainly of national standard setters should develop IASs

1999

- IASC Board meetings are opened to public observation
- G7 Finance Ministers and IMF urge support for IASs to 'strengthen the international financial architecture'
- International Forum on Accountancy Development (IFAD) commits to support 'use of IASs as the minimum benchmark for raising national accounting standards' worldwide
- IASC Board unanimously approves restructuring into 14-member board (12 full-time) under an independent board of trustees
- Core standards completed

2000

- Basel Committee expresses support for IASs
- SEC concept release on use of IASs by foreign registrants
- IOSCO endorses use of 'IAS 2000' for use in cross-border offerings and listings
- IASC Member Bodies approve restructuring of the IASC
- European Commission announces a plan to require all EU listed companies to issue IAS consolidated financial statements from 2005
- Thomas E. Jones (IAFEI) appointed chairman

2001

- IASC replaced by IASB

CHAPTER 2

The International Accounting Standards Board

With effect from early in 2001, the IASC adopted a new structure, the main changes in which are:

- the replacement of the advisory council by a group of trustees with enhanced powers including the power to appoint the new board;
- the appointment of a new International Accounting Standards Board (IASB) consisting of 14 individuals appointed by the trustees; and
- the replacement of the consultative group by a standards advisory council.

The new structure resulted from recommendations of the IASC's strategy working party but was heavily influenced by the wishes of the US Securities and Exchange Commission (SEC) and leading standard setting bodies.

2.1 THE IASC'S STRATEGY WORKING PARTY

In 1996, the IASC set up a strategy working party to review its strategy after the completion of the IASC's core standards work programme. The working party addressed, among other things:

- the relationship between the IASC and national standard setting bodies;
- the balance between the conflicting objectives of wider board membership and of restricting the number of board participants so that the board can continue to take decisions effectively;
- whether one or more full-time board members were needed;
- whether board and other IASC meetings should be open to the public;

- what role the IASC should take in educational and training activities relating to IASs; and
- the arrangements for the funding of the IASC.

(*IASC Insight*, December 1996, p2)

The working party was chaired by Edward Waitzer, a lawyer and the former chairman of both the Ontario Securities Commission and the IOSCO technical committee. The working party included representatives from the IASC, IFAC, IOSCO, the World Bank, public accounting firms, business and standard setting bodies.

The working party addressed many of the same issues that had been considered by the foundation working party three years earlier (see chapter 1). One problem was that the foundation working party's recommendations on cooperation with national standard setting bodies, which had been approved by the board in June 1994, had not been implemented. Another problem was the rapid increase in the size of board meetings – up from 45 people to about 60 people in less than two years. Another issue was the long-term structure of the IASC. The foundation working party had acknowledged that its proposals might only be a temporary solution and that further evolution might be required[1].

The IASC published the strategy working party's initial proposals in December 1998[2]. The major recommendation was the creation of a standards development committee (SDC) that would take over many of the functions and powers of the existing IASC board but which would be subject to limited control by an enlarged IASC board. A group of trustees would appoint both the SDC and the board. The SDC and the new board formed the bicameral organisation that had been advocated by the IASC's secretary-general Sir Bryan Carsberg (*FT World Accounting Report*, January 1998, p7) and which the strategy working party had been specifically asked to consider.

The working party believed that the new structure would address three key issues:

- partnership with national standard setters so as to accelerate the convergence of national and international standards around solutions requiring high-quality, transparent and comparable information that would help participants in capital markets make economic decisions;
- wider participation in the IASC board; and
- appointment of the board by a variety of constituencies.

Under the working party's proposals, the SDC would have had eleven members including a full-time chairman and six to eight people who were voting members of national standard setting bodies with the 'technical, human and financial resources to make a significant contribution to IASC's work'. The SDC would have developed IASs but the final approval of those IASs would have rested with an expanded board of 25 members.

When the report was published, Edmund Jenkins, the then chairman of the FASB, told the *Financial Times*:

> 'The proposals mean that the technical experts who make up the standards development committee could be overridden by a board that was not as independent or objective and, arguably, less well-qualified technically.'

He and some other standard setters would have preferred a structure in which the SDC had the final say on the approval of exposure drafts and IASs.

At the end of 1998, the FASB published its vision of international standard setting[3]. It envisaged an international standard setter which would develop and promulgate international standards and which would be independent of, but supportive of and supported by, national standard setters. The FASB put forward three alternative ways in which such an international standard setter could be created, one of which was the restructuring of the IASC while another envisaged a restructured FASB taking on the role.

The proposed bicameral structure did not win support. In its final report[4], the strategy working party recommended the appointment of:

- a group of trustees who would select the board and the standards development advisory council and both exercise oversight and raise the necessary funds;
- a standard setting board of 14 individuals with the best technical skills and background experience; and
- a standards advisory council of about 40 members from diverse geographical and functional backgrounds.

The major debate during the development of the final report centred on whether the members of the new board should be selected on the basis of technical skills or geographical representation. The SEC argued forcefully both for change and for a board selected for its technical skills. The European Commission argued strongly for geographical representation. The SEC's view, supported by many other commentators, won the day.

No doubt, in time, the full story of the strategy working party will be told. There is no doubt, however, that the SEC was the major influence on the final report and that former SEC chairman David Ruder was the key member of the strategy working party from whom all other members of the working party took their instructions. The full story might also explain why the working party first recommended the bicameral structure and did not consider other possible structures (including those addressed by the foundation working party). The bicameral idea had little going for it, other than perhaps that it was the catalyst for starting the debate about the need for the radical change that some had already identified but which was likely to prove difficult to achieve.

2.2 THE IASB'S OBJECTIVES

The IASB is committed to developing, in the public interest, a single set of high quality, understandable and enforceable global accounting standards that require transparent and comparable information in general purpose financial statements. The Board cooperates with national accounting standard setters to achieve convergence in accounting standards around the world.

The IASB develops International Financial Reporting Standards (IFRSs) that set out recognition, measurement, presentation and disclosure requirements dealing with transactions and events that are important in general purpose financial statements. They may also set out such requirements for transactions and events that arise mainly in specific industries. IFRSs are based on the *Framework* which addresses the concepts underlying the information presented in general purpose financial statements (*Preface to IFRSs*, 8).

The IASB's objective is to require that like transactions and events should be accounted for and reported in a like way and unlike transactions and events to be accounted for and reported differently, both within an entity over time and among entities. Consequently, the IASB intends not to permit choices in accounting treatment (*Preface to IFRSs*, 13).

2.3 THE NEW STRUCTURE

2.3.1 Overview

In March 2001, the IASC Foundation was formed. It has the following component bodies:

- the Trustees;
- the International Accounting Standards Board (IASB);
- the Standards Advisory Council (SAC); and

- the International Financial Reporting Interpretations Committee (IFRIC).

2.3.2 Trustees

The Trustees are responsible for governance, fundraising and public awareness of the IASB. The Trustees appoint the members of the IASB, IFRIC and SAC. In addition they:

- review annually the strategy of the IASB and its effectiveness;
- approve annually the budget of the IASB and determine the basis for funding;
- review broad strategic issues affecting accounting standards, promote the IASB and its work and promote the objective of rigorous application of IFRSs;
- establish and amend operating procedures for the IASB, IFRIC and SAC;

(*IASCF Constitution*, 20)

The trustees are excluded from all technical matters relating to accounting standards. The trustees consist of 19 individuals from diverse geographical and functional backgrounds. Six trustees are appointed from North America, six from Europe, four from Asia-Pacific and three from any area. IFAC suggests five trustees. Other international organisations, preparers and users of financial statements and academics may also nominate trustees. There are eleven 'at large' trustees who bring a strong public interest, experience and background which is complementary to those of trustees nominated through the constituency process.

The trustees must show a firm commitment to the IASC Foundation and the IASB as a high quality global standard-setter, to be financially knowledgeable, and to have an ability to meet the time commitment. Each trustee must have an understanding of, and be sensitive to, international issues relevant to the success of an international organisation responsible for the development of high quality global accounting standards for use in the world's capital markets and by other users (*IASCF Constitution*, 6). An up-to-date list of the trustees can be found at *www.iasb.org.uk*.

2.3.3 International Accounting Standards Board (IASB)

The board consists of twelve full-time and two part-time members. The foremost qualification for membership is technical expertise together with experience of international business. The appointments are not based on geographical representation. A minimum of five members should have a background as practising auditors, three as preparers and three as users of financial statements, and at least one as an academic. Board members are required to act in the public interest. Full-time members are required to sever all employment relationships. Seven board members have formal liaison responsibilities with the national standard setting bodies who play a major role in the development of IFRSs and assist the IASB in achieving the convergence of accounting standards around high quality solutions. These are the standard setting bodies in Australia, Canada, France, Germany, Japan, the UK and the USA.

The board has the power to approve IFRSs, exposure drafts and interpretations of IFRSs. Each board member has one vote on such matters. At least eight members must vote in favour of publication of an IFRS, exposure draft or interpretation – this is a much smaller majority than that required of the old IASC board. The board may issue other documents with the approval of a simple majority.

The members of the new board and prior affiliations are shown in Table 2.1.

Table 2.1 *International Accounting Standards Board as at September 2002*

Member	Previous affiliation
Sir David Tweedie (chair)	UK Accounting Standards Board
Thomas E. Jones	Citicorp, USA
Mary E. Barth	Graduate School of Business, Stanford University*, USA
Hans-Georg Bruns	DaimlerChrysler, Germany
Anthony T. Cope	US Financial Accounting Standards Board
Robert P. Garnett	Anglo American, South Africa
Gilbert Gélard	KPMG, France
James J. Leisenring	US Financial Accounting Standards Board
Warren McGregor	Stevenson McGregor, Australia
Patricia O'Malley	Accounting Standards Board, Canada
Harry K. Schmid	Nestlé, Switzerland
Geoffrey Whittington	Cambridge University, UK
Tatsumi Yamada	ChuoAoyama Audit Corporation, Japan
John T. Smith	Deloitte and Touche*, USA

* continuing affiliation of part-time board member

The IASB determines the scope of any projects formally added to its agenda. During the early stages of a project, the IASB may establish an advisory committee to give advice on the issues arising in the project. Consultation with the advisory committee and the SAC occurs throughout the project. Unlike the former IASC, the board does not appoint steering committees that develop drafts for consideration by the board.

As the first stage in the development of an IFRS the IASB may publish a discussion document for public comment. It followed this process in its share based payments project when it sought comments on a position paper developed by G4+1[5].

Following the receipt and review of comments on a discussion paper, the IASB develops and publishes an exposure draft for public comment. The usual comment period is 90 days but, in exceptional circumstances, proposals may be issued with a comment period of 60 days. The IASB may also hold public hearings to discuss proposed standards and carry out field tests (both in developed countries and in emerging markets) to ensure that proposals are practical and workable around the world. Where practicable, public hearings and field tests are coordinated with national standard setters.

Following the receipt and review of comments, the IASB issues a final IFRS. The IASB also publishes a basis for conclusions to explain publicly how it reached its conclusions and to give background information that may help users of IFRSs to apply them in practice. The IASB also includes dissenting opinions in IFRSs.

Each IASB member has one vote on technical and other matters. The publication of an IFRS, exposure draft or interpretation requires approval by eight of the board's 14 members. Other decisions, including the issuance of a discussion paper and agenda decisions, require a simple majority of the board members present at a meeting attended by 50% or more of the board members. The board has full control over its technical agenda.

Meetings of IASB are open to public observation. However, certain discussions (primarily selection, appointment and other personnel issues) may be held in private.

Close coordination between the IASB's due process and that of national standard setters is important to the success of the IASB's mandate. It is likely that the due process of the IASB and national standard setting bodies will become increasingly integrated as the relationship between the IASB and national standard setters evolves. The IASB holds regular meetings with its seven liaison standard setters and uses these meetings to explore opportunities for convergence of accounting standards and cooperation in the development of national and international standards.

Cooperation is likely to include the coordination of work plans so that when the IASB starts a project, national standard setters would also add it to their own work plans and vice versa. The IASB and national standard setters have also started to review their existing standards to identify significant differences so that they can give priority in their work programmes to the areas where the differences are greatest. The process is likely to result in the IASB and national standard setters publishing their own exposure documents at approximately the same time and seeking specific comments on any significant divergences between the documents. Cooperation between the IASB and national standard setters is already evident in several IASB projects. For example, the IASB is working with the FASB on business combinations, with the UK ASB on performance reporting and the Canadian ASB on measurement. The French standard setter played a leading role in the project on first-time application.

2.3.4 Standards Advisory Council (SAC)

The SAC meets the IASB at least three times a year and those meetings are open to the public. The board is required to consult the SAC in advance of board decisions on major projects and the trustees must consult the SAC in advance of any proposed changes to the Constitution. The objectives of the SAC are to:

- give advice to the IASB on agenda decisions and priorities in the board's work;
- inform the board of the views of the organisations and individuals on the SAC on major standard setting projects; and
- give other advice to the board or the trustees.

(*IASCF Constitution*, 42)

In broad terms, the role of the SAC is similar to that of the old consultative group but there is a very important difference in membership. Whereas the consultative group consisted of organisations (who appointed their own representatives), the SAC consists of approximately 60 people from diverse geographical and functional backgrounds appointed by the trustees. It includes people from accountancy institutes, regulatory bodies, national standard setting bodies without a formal liaison relationship to the board, audit firms, companies, academic institutions, investment banks and other international groups. Members are appointed for a renewable term of three years.

The membership of the council was announced in March 2001 and an up-to-date list of members is available at *www.iasb.org.uk*.

2.3.5 International Financial Reporting Interpretations Committee (IFRIC)

IFRIC provides timely guidance on the application and interpretation of IFRSs. Its role and membership is similar to that of the former standards interpretations committee. IFRIC meets about every two months. All technical decisions are taken at sessions that are open to public observation.

IFRIC addresses issues of reasonably widespread importance, and not issues of concern to only a small set of entities. The interpretations cover both:

- newly identified financial reporting issues not specifically addressed in IFRSs; and
- issues where unsatisfactory or conflicting interpretations have developed or seem likely to develop in the absence of authoritative guidance.

In keeping with the IASB's own approach to setting standards, IFRIC applies a principles-based approach in providing interpretive guidance. To this end, IFRIC looks first to the *Framework for the Preparation and Presentation of Financial Statements* as the foundation for formulating a consensus. It then looks to the principles articulated in the applicable IFRS, if any, to develop its interpretive guidance and to determine that the proposed guidance does not conflict with provisions in the IFRS. In reaching its consensus views, IFRIC has due regard for the need for international convergence. If IFRIC concludes that the requirements of an IFRS differ from the *Framework*, it obtains direction from the IASB before providing guidance. In developing interpretations, IFRIC also works closely with similar national committees. Draft IFRIC interpretations are exposed for a 60-day comment period.

IFRIC has twelve voting members appointed by the trustees. The members are selected for their ability to maintain an awareness of current issues as they arise and the technical ability to resolve them. They include accountants in industry and public practice and users of financial statements, with a reasonably broad geographic representation. Members are appointed for fixed renewable terms of up to three years.

IFRIC is chaired by a member of the IASB, the director of technical activities or another senior member of the IASB staff or another appropriately qualified individual. The chairman is appointed by the trustees on the recommendation of the IASB and has the right to speak on technical issues but not to vote.

IFRIC also includes observers (currently from IOSCO and the European Commission) and two liaison members of the IASB. Observers and liaison IASB members have the right to speak but not to vote. Other members of the IASB may attend IFRIC meetings with the right to speak but not to vote.

A list of the current members of IFRIC and extensive details of IFRIC's due processes are available at *www.iasb.org.uk*.

2.3.6 IASB staff

The IASB operates with a significantly larger staff than that of the old IASC. The technical staff is headed by a director of technical activities (Kevin Stevenson) and director of research (Wayne Upton). There is a project director for each project.

2.4 FUNDING

The trustees are responsible for raising the funds required for the work of the IASB and the other components of the IASCF. The IASB's budget is approximately £11.5 million a year (*IASCF Annual Report 2001*, p3). The funds are provided by international financial and business firms and the IASB's commercial activities (mainly the sale of publications).

Notes

[1] IASC, *Report of the International Accounting Standards Foundation Working Party*, IASC, 1994.

[2] IASC Strategy Working Party, *Shaping IASC for the Future*, IASC, 1998.

[3] FASB, *International Accounting Standard Setting: A Vision for the Future*, FASB, 1998.

[4] IASC Strategy Working Party, *Recommendations on Shaping IASC for the Future*, IASC, 1999.

[5] G4+1, *Accounting for Share-based Payment*, G4+1 position paper, IASC and other members of G4+1, 2000.

CHAPTER 3

History of IASs

3.1 GOOD ACCOUNTING WITH SOME CHOICES

Throughout its history, the IASC has seen harmonisation as part of an improvement process and not as a lowering of standards to those of the weakest country or region. Therefore, the first aim of the IASC was always to require good accounting practices and so contribute to the improvement of financial reporting. In many instances, the IASC adopted IASs which were more extensive than existing national requirements in some board countries or elsewhere; the adoption of such IASs unquestionably contributed to the improvement of financial reporting.

In 1973, the IASC began with the idea of 'basic' standards and a commitment to fair presentation and full disclosure. The IASC also began with the notion that financial statements should provide information which is 'used by a variety of users, especially shareholders and creditors for making evaluations and financial decisions' (IAS 1(1976), 11 and 12). While the commitment to fair presentation and full disclosure was never lost, the idea of basic standards disappeared in 1977 as the IASC sought to deal with all the topics, some complex, which were important in the financial statements of business entities.

Early IASs set out the principles on each topic while avoiding the details often required for national standards. The IASC sought to filter out those practices which were unsound and so reduce the number of acceptable alternative accounting practices.

The early IASs have been criticised for being too broad and for having too many options. The criticisms have often been unfair and wrong. They sometimes ignore both the realities of getting international agreement on complex issues and the variety of acceptable practices worldwide. The criticisms also ignored what the IASC actually achieved in the early standards. In its first seven standards the IASC banned the use of inventory reserves to smooth profits, required the publication of consolidated financial statements and required the publication of a statement of changes in financial position. The IASC also signalled its intention to ban the use of hidden reserves by banks.

The early IASs allowed some choices among different acceptable accounting practices but far fewer choices than some have claimed. The choices reflected differences in national standards. For example, IAS 2 allowed a choice between FIFO and LIFO, IAS 9 allowed a choice between the capitalisation and expensing of development costs, and IAS 11 allowed a choice between the percentage of completion method and the completed contract method. These same choices were permitted by many national standards.

This first phase of international standard setting probably ended with the approval of IAS 25 *Accounting for Investments* which allowed several choices (many of the same choices are still permitted by IAS 39). The approval of IAS 25 was, however, the catalyst for change. The IASC was well aware that the early standards were a first step and that, in due course, they would have to be improved.

3.2 FRAMEWORK, COMPARABILITY AND IMPROVEMENTS PROJECTS

The beginning of the second phase can be traced to 1981 when, following the approval of IAS 12 *Accounting for Income Taxes*, the IASC set up a working party consisting of representatives of standard setting bodies to seek greater harmony in the rules for deferred taxes. The IASC also started reviewing its existing IASs and developing a series of 'building block' projects on the objectives of financial statements, liabilities, equity, assets and expenses. The reviews led to revised IASs on consolidations, associates and income taxes. The building blocks led to the IASC's *Framework for the Preparation and Presentation of Financial Statements* (see chapter 7).

The real turning point came in 1987 with the decision to start the comparability project. The IASC felt that greater acceptance of IASs would only come with a reduction in the number of permitted alternatives and, therefore, it appointed a steering committee to consider whether alternative accounting treatments allowed by IASs could be eliminated or some preference indicated.

The IASC recognised the difficulty of this task. Some alternatives reflected entrenched positions in particular countries or industries. Some were included originally to ensure the acceptability of IASs in some countries. Others reflected national laws or possibly even taxation influences. And a whole body of alternatives existed because some countries allowed the inclusion of revaluations in historical cost based financial statements.

The IASC's decision to start the comparability project was boosted by support from IOSCO later in 1987 both for the project and for the possible use of IASs in financial statements used in cross-border offerings and other foreign listings. In particular, the US SEC told the IASC in March 1987 that if it could identify a benchmark treatment in those IASs that allowed a choice of treatments, the SEC would consider requiring foreign issuers to reconcile to the IAS benchmark treatment rather than US GAAP. Representatives of IOSCO participated in all meetings of the comparability steering committee.

In January 1989, the IASC published E32 *Comparability of Financial Statements* which dealt with twenty-nine issues where existing IASs allowed a free choice of accounting treatment for like transactions and events. The IASC also published, for the first time, a glossy, executive summary of the proposals which was distributed to companies worldwide. The IASC made a special effort to consult widely on the E32 proposals, with members of the comparability steering committee and the staff participating in discussions in over a dozen countries. Gernon, Purvis and Diamond provide a detailed report[1] on one aspect of the consultations – roundtable discussions in Washington DC and Brussels with the major players in accounting standard setting, capital market regulation, business and the accounting firms.

E32 produced a record response in terms of the number and extent of comment letters. Following reconsideration of each issue in the light of the comments, the IASC approved a *Statement of Intent on the Comparability of Financial Statements* in June 1990. The statement of intent identified twenty-one issues on which the IASC decided to proceed with the E32 proposals unchanged. It also identified three issues on which the IASC decided to make substantive changes to the proposals in E32. Five E32 issues were deferred, four because they were being dealt with in the financial instruments project. The fifth issue, the recognition of finance income by a lessor on a finance lease, was dealt with in the later revision to IAS 17.

The implementation of the consequential revisions to the IASs was dealt with in the improvements project which started in June 1990. The purpose of this project was to:

- revise the IASs for the changes set out in the *Statement of Intent on the Comparability of Financial Statements*;
- ensure that the IASs were sufficiently detailed and complete, that their explanations were adequate and that they were consistent with other IASs;
- review each IAS in the context of the *Framework for the Preparation and Presentation of Financial Statements*;
- review the disclosure requirements; and
- revise the format of each IAS.

The IASC originally intended to apply this process to all existing IASs but this proved to be over-ambitious. In March 1992, the IASC recognised that the achievement of the planned programme would mean a rapid acceleration in the IASC's work and a heavy burden for those involved in the process. It also acknowledged that the programme would have raised serious doubts about the quality of the IASC's due process, both internal and external (*IASC Insight*, March 1992, p5). As a result, the IASC decided to restrict the project to the ten IASs affected by the statement of intent.

During the improvements project, the IASC issued EDs of all the revised IASs in order to allow its constituency to comment on the implementation of the statement of intent changes and the other revisions. For the twenty-one E32 issues which had been approved without substantive change, the IASC indicated that it did not intend to reconsider those issues as part of the exposure process.

For the three issues where changes had been made from the proposals in E32, the IASC said that it would reconsider them in the light of the comments on the EDs. This process resulted in the IASC reverting to the E32 proposals for two out of the three issues (inventories and borrowing costs). The controversy over LIFO is dealt with in more detail in chapter 26. It retained the statement of intent position on development costs.

In November 1993, the IASC approved the ten revised IASs which came into effect for financial statements covering periods beginning on or after 1 January 1995. Among other things, the revised IASs banned the use of the completed contract method for construction contracts, the deferral and amortisation of foreign currency gains and losses, and the immediate write-off of goodwill to equity. They included tighter requirements for the revaluation of property, the use of the pooling of interests method and the capitalisation of development and borrowing costs. The projects also identified the need for three further projects that were completed in 1997:

- an IAS on the presentation of financial statements;
- revisions to the IAS on segment reporting; and
- further improvements to the revised IAS 19 on retirement benefit costs.

In November 1994, the IASC also approved the reformatted versions of the eighteen IASs which were not revised in the comparability and improvements projects.

The improvement of, and the removal of choices in, IASs was intended to be an ongoing process. For example, the improvements project had identified the need to develop a combined IAS on the presentation of financial statements to replace IASs 1, 5 and 13. The project also pointed to the need to revise IAS 14 and identified a number of other projects which were later incorporated in the core standards programme agreed with IOSCO.

In the statement of intent, the IASC said that it would continue to consult national standard setting bodies, accountancy bodies and others on ways of eliminating the remaining free choices in IASs. It recognised, however, that it might be impracticable and inappropriate to remove some of the remaining alternative accounting treatments permitted in IASs in the foreseeable future, for example, the choice between historical cost and revaluation based carrying amounts for property, plant and equipment and for some investments. The IASC also recognised that future developments in accounting and the business environment may result in a requirement for a treatment other than that identified as the benchmark treatment, something which has now happened with negative goodwill and investment properties and may happen with joint ventures.

During this phase of its work, the IASC also completed IASs on reporting in hyperinflationary economies, bank disclosures, joint ventures and cash flow statements.

3.3 CORE STANDARDS

The core standards were identified by IOSCO in 1993 as those standards which would have to be included in a core set of IASs for those standards to be endorsed by IOSCO for use in financial statements used in cross-border offerings and other foreign listings (*IASC Insight*, December 1993, p4). Many of the core standards had been dealt with by the IASC but some of them were unacceptable to IOSCO (see chapter 4). As a result of the July 1995 agreement with IOSCO, the IASC decided to complete the core standards, an aim which was achieved at the end of 1999. IOSCO's endorsement of the core standards is dealt with in chapter 4.

The core standards programme involved the IASC completing:

- seven projects which it had already started – financial instruments, earnings per share, income taxes, intangibles, segment reporting, presentation of financial statements and employee benefits;
- two projects which it had identified as part of its future work programme – impairment and discontinued operations; and
- four new projects – interim reporting and revisions to the existing standards on research and development (IAS 9), contingencies (IAS 10) and goodwill (IAS 22).

During this phase, the IASC also continued with or started projects which would not result in core standards, notably its projects on agriculture, the extractive industries and insurance.

The IASC's work programme as at the end of 2000 immediately prior to the restructuring included:

- financial instruments – a joint project with national standard setting bodies; a draft standard was published by the IASC and the other bodies in December 2000;
- insurance – an issues paper was published in 1999;
- reporting financial performance – this project was being considered in conjunction with G4+1 – an invitation to comment was published in September 1999;
- present value – the IASC expected to publish an issues paper in 2001;
- extractive industries – an issues paper was published in November 2000;
- business combinations – a significant review, which was being carried out in conjunction with G4+1, on the use of the purchase method and the pooling of interests method; and
- bank disclosures – the review of IAS 30 was started in 2000 and will be influenced by the requirements of IAS 32 and IAS 39 plus the work of the Basel Committee.

The IASB is continuing with all these projects.

The outgoing IASC board also approved a Statement[2] in December 2000 that made suggestions about the work programme of the new board. The key recommendations were:

- the continuation of the work on business combinations, discounting, reporting financial performance, insurance, extractive industries and financial instruments;
- a review of existing national and international standards and other issues where major differences exist in order to achieve convergence of accounting standards;
- a new improvements project to deal with relatively minor improvements, transitional provisions and first-time application of IASs;
- a project on accounting for share-based payments;
- further work on intangible assets (a high priority for convergence);
- work on narrative discussion outside the notes to the financial statements;
- a comprehensive review of the *Framework*;
- a special version of IASs for small enterprises; and
- a review of IASs relating to inflation accounting.

Notes

[1] Helen Gernon, S.E.C. Purvis and Michael Diamond, *An Analysis of the IASC's Comparability Project*, Topical Issues Study 3, School of Accounting, University of Southern California, 1990.

[2] The full text of the Statement is available on the IASC's website *www.iasc.org.uk*.

CHAPTER 4

The Use of IASs and IFRSs

4.1 INTRODUCTION

This chapter describes the policies and practices adopted by national standard setting bodies[1] towards the compatibility between national requirements and IASs/IFRSs and the use of IASs/IFRSs by IOSCO and the European Union.

The *International Accounting Standards Survey 2000*[2] deals extensively with the use of IASs by national bodies and by companies. It describes the sources of national GAAP and examines whether major listed companies comply with IASs in four regions: the Americas; Europe; Asia-Pacific; Africa. The survey examines in detail the annual reports of 165 listed companies which refer to the use of IASs in their 1999/2000 financial statements focusing on:

- the approach to compliance with national GAAP and IASs;
- the level of compliance with IASs;
- the existence of 'IAS lite';
- how auditors report on compliance with IASs; and
- how auditors report on 'IAS lite'.

The survey also analyses how the companies deal with approximately 50 technical issues in IASs, including the trends in the application of IASs, possible cases of 'IAS lite' and the choices made by companies when IASs allow the use of more than one accounting treatment or presentation.

An earlier country survey was published by the IASC in 1988[3] based on responses to a questionnaire completed by the IASC's member accountancy bodies. The IASC acknowledged the limitations of its 1988 survey but it was a useful indication of the conformity between IASs and national requirements and practices before the IASC's comparability project. It also described the policies of a number of national bodies.

4.2 THE USE OF IASs AND IFRSs AS NATIONAL STANDARDS

The use of IASs and IFRSs by national standard setting bodies is driven mainly by the desire to improve financial reporting – or in the case of countries in transition from command economies, the desire to change to a system which is more appropriate for a market economy. This emphasis on the improvement of financial reporting fitted well with the IASC's long-standing view that harmonisation must be seen as part of an improvement process – harmonisation is not an end in itself.

The adoption and use of IASs and IFRSs is achieved through a variety of means. In some countries it is done through the law while in others it results from actions of independent standard setting bodies or the professional accountancy bodies. Some national standard setting bodies have adopted IASs as national accounting requirements for some or all entities (for example, Croatia, Cyprus, Kuwait, Latvia and Peru). Others have based their national requirements on IASs (for example, China, Malaysia and Singapore) or used IASs to fill gaps in their requirements or improve existing requirements (for example, Australia, Canada, France and the United States). In each case, enforcement of the standards is achieved through national processes.

While the improvement of financial reporting is the main driving force for the adoption of IASs and IFRSs, in recent years some countries have given a high priority to harmonising their standards with IASs. However, in some cases, a major obstacle has been the fear that some IAS treatments are inferior to the current national standards. For example, Australia has carried out a project to harmonise its standards with IASs but it resisted those IAS treatments which it feels are inferior to its existing requirements (for example, the use of the pooling of interests method and the fair presentation override in IAS 1).

In some cases, harmonisation efforts focus on single issues. For example, the United Kingdom accepted the IASC's treatment of warrants in the calculation of diluted earnings per share on the grounds that harmonisation should be the deciding factor when choosing between equally good, but competing, treatments.

The completion of the IASC's comparability project led some countries to reconsider those national standards which were no longer compatible with the revised IASs. For example, Canada reconsidered its foreign currencies standard following the adoption of the revised IAS 21 but, initially, it was unwilling to follow the IASC and ban the deferral and amortisation of gains and losses on long-term foreign currency items. Malaysia and Singapore, both of which have used IASs as national standards, initially resisted some of the IASC's 1993 changes.

Compatibility and convergence result not only from national bodies bringing their requirements into line with IASs and IFRSs. They also result from the IASC and now the IASB adopting IASs and IFRSs which are the same as those already in use in at least some national bodies.

It should come as no surprise that the IASC often reached agreement on the same treatment as that which had been adopted in the majority of countries. This was not a weakness on the part of the IASC; it was an inevitable consequence of the technical and political processes of standard setting and the limited number of alternative treatments available. When the IASC adopted such an approach, compatibility or convergence between IASs and national requirements was achieved in many countries without the need for additional efforts on the part of either the IASC or the national bodies. For example, the IASC's requirement to capitalise and amortise goodwill was the same requirement as that which had been adopted in the majority of countries. Therefore, no action was required by those countries to achieve compatibility or convergence with this part of IAS 22.

Compatibility and convergence among the national requirements of different countries and between national requirements and IASs also resulted from the joint efforts of national standard setting bodies and the IASC to reach common solutions on particular accounting issues. The sharing of ideas among standard setting bodies also helped to achieve a considerable degree of convergence.

Joint efforts may involve two or more national bodies, as was the case with the European Directives and the American and Canadian standards on segment reporting. They also involved the IASC, the most notable example being the IASC/Canada joint project to develop common standards on financial instruments which resulted in the adoption of virtually identical standards on presentation and disclosure (see chapter 20).

Another joint effort was that between the IASC and the FASB on earnings per share. This was particularly noteworthy for the fact that, rather than impose US GAAP on the IASC, the FASB chose to pick up and develop the IASC's initial ideas as a means of improving US GAAP. However the IASC's ideas had been influenced by existing standards in a number of countries other than the US and one of the sources of influence, the United Kingdom, has subsequently brought its existing standard into line with the common standard agreed by the IASC and the FASB.

Development banks have also played an important role in enforcing compliance with IASs. The World Bank insists that the financial statements of its borrowers conform with IASs when there are no equivalent national requirements. The International Finance Corporation adopts a similar approach in its dealings with private sector borrowers as do many of the regional development banks. For example, the Asian Development Bank prefers that financial statements conform with IASs. It points out that this is in the long-term interests of international harmonisation which will lead to easier compliance by institutions with financial reporting requirements of international financial markets (*IASC Insight*, June 1994, p12). The European Bank for Reconstruction and Development takes a similar approach.

4.3 IOSCO'S USE OF IAS/IFRS

The International Organization of Securities Commissions (IOSCO) represents the regulators of securities and futures markets. It was founded in 1974 as an inter-American organisation and adopted its worldwide focus and current name in 1986. Its resolutions are non-binding on its members. Each IOSCO member has to determine whether and how to implement an IOSCO resolution.

The IOSCO technical committee consists of sixteen agencies that regulate some of the world's larger, more developed and internationalised markets. The objectives of the committee are to:

- review major regulatory issues related to international securities and futures transactions; and
- co-ordinate practical responses to these concerns.

The committee's working party 1 deals with multinational disclosure and accounting. It is chaired by a representative of the US Securities and Exchange Commission (SEC). It is supported by an accounting and auditing sub-committee.

Direct links between the IASC and IOSCO were established in 1987 following discussions between the IASC and the SEC. IOSCO joined the IASC consultative group and immediately lent its support to the IASC's newly started comparability project. The IASC invited IOSCO to participate in meetings of the comparability steering committee and, three years later, the improvements steering committee. The IASC also offered IOSCO the opportunity of IASC board membership in 1988 but that offer was not pursued. Following the July 1995 agreement to complete the core standards, the IASC invited IOSCO to attend all board meetings as an observer. IOSCO was also an observer at meetings of the SIC. In all cases, IOSCO had the right to speak although there were recurring difficulties about whether its representatives were expressing the opinions of IOSCO or personal views.

The restructuring of the IASC does not allow for the participation of observers at meetings of the IASB but IOSCO representatives usually attend meetings as part of the public gallery.

4.3.1 Cross-border offerings and other foreign listings

At its initial meeting in June 1987, the technical committee initiated a study of cross-border securities offerings and other foreign listings, including the fact that different countries – and, hence, different IOSCO members – applied different requirements for the financial statements of foreign companies which wished to issue or list their securities. For example:

- some countries required or allowed foreign issuers to use the issuer's domestic accounting requirements, without modification or reconciliation ('mutual recognition');
- some countries allowed 'mutual recognition' but only if the domestic accounting requirements used by the foreign issuer complied with some common standards – this applied within the EU where the common standards were the Fourth and Seventh Directives;
- some countries required or allowed foreign issuers to use IASs without modification or reconciliation;
- some countries allowed foreign issuers to use the issuer's domestic accounting requirements or IASs but only if there was a reconciliation to host country GAAP – this applied in the USA where the SEC required foreign issuers to reconcile domestic GAAP/IAS financial statements to US GAAP; and
- some countries allowed a variety of approaches – for example, the UK allowed foreign issuers from other EU member states to use domestic requirements and required other foreign issuers to use UK GAAP, IASs or US GAAP.

The resulting report[4] recommended that, among other things, 'regulators be encouraged, where consistent with their legal mandate and the goal of investor protection, to facilitate the use of single disclosure documents, whether by harmonisation of standards, reciprocity or otherwise'. Subsequently the technical committee focused on three aspects of disclosure documents: accounting standards; auditing standards; and disclosure.

4.3.2 Accounting standards

The technical committee acknowledged that different accounting standards were a 'primary impediment' to cross-border offerings and that 'mutually acceptable international accounting standards [were] a critical goal because they [would] reduce the unnecessary regulatory burdens resulting from current disparities between the various national accounting standards, while protecting investors through adequate disclosure in financial statements'[5]. It looked to the IASC to provide these 'mutually acceptable standards'. At the same time, the IOSCO presidents' committee approved the following resolution[6]:

> IOSCO encourages the IASC and IAPC [International Audit Practices Committee] to act promptly to facilitate the establishment of improved international accounting and auditing standards.
> IOSCO encourages the IASC to improve international accounting standards and pursue its project to eliminate accounting alternatives and to ensure that its standards are sufficiently detailed and complete, contain adequate disclosure requirements, and are prepared with a visible commitment to the needs of the users of financial statements.
> IOSCO encourages the IAPC to improve international auditing standards including requirements on the independence of auditors and on auditors' opinions.
> IOSCO continues to strongly support the work of both the IASC and the IAPC by providing assistance through working groups in their respective projects that affect the development of common accounting and auditing standards.

This resolution contained the four ideas which dominated IOSCO's thinking during the IASC's comparability and improvements projects: the elimination of alternatives: detail and completeness; adequate disclosures; and a commitment to the needs of users of financial statements.

IOSCO representatives participated in all bar one of the meetings of the comparability steering committee. As a result, one of the criteria used by the IASC in making its choice among the alternatives allowed by the then IASs was 'the views of regulators and their representative organisations, such as the International Organization of Securities Commissions'[7]. Subsequently many of the changes made to IASs during the improvements project reflected the wishes of the IOSCO representatives – most significantly, the IASC retained LIFO as a result of IOSCO saying the IASC was going 'too far' in trying to ban it. Had IOSCO not sent that last minute message in April 1992, there is little doubt that the IASC would have banned the use of LIFO in IAS financial statements with effect from 1995.

In spite of IOSCO's involvement in the comparability and improvements projects, it was uncertain for a long time what the IASC had to do to win IOSCO's endorsement of IASs for use in cross-border offerings and foreign listings. There was an expectation that IOSCO would immediately endorse at least those IASs that had been revised as part of the comparability and improvements projects, an expectation that was fuelled by the comments of IOSCO's secretary-general at the World Congress of Accountants in October 1992 and a conference in New York a month later[8]:

> Is it necessary for all this work to be completed by the IASC before the technical committee can consider the acceptance of International Accounting Standards? In my view it is not. We could very well proceed by stages. For example, the technical committee could indicate that it accepts the Standards that were part of E32 when that work is completed. Other new or revised Standards could be accepted as soon as they have been reviewed by the [accounting and auditing] subcommittee and are considered satisfactory in the view of the technical committee.

4.3.3 Core accounting standards

In order to resolve the uncertainties, the then chairman of the technical committee – Jean Saint-Geours, the then president of the *Commission des Opérations de Bourse* (COB) in France – asked working party 1 to:

- identify those standards that comprise an acceptable comprehensive body of international accounting principles that could be used in cross-border offerings;
- advise the IASC of the working party's views on each standard as finalised – the view was to be determined by consensus and if there was not a consensus, the group would transmit to the IASC opinions expressed in the meeting; and
- upon the IASC's completion of the comprehensive body of standards to advise the Technical Committee as to the working party's recommendation with respect to the use of such standards as cross-border offerings.

In August 1993, working party 1 advised the IASC of the core standards, that is 'the necessary components of a reasonably complete set of accounting standards that would comprise a comprehensive body of principles for enterprises undertaking cross-border offerings and listings'[9]. The working party also advised the IASC that it 'was currently in the process of evaluating existing and proposed IASC accounting standards to determine their suitability as components of the core standards'.

No indication was given to the IASC at that time that all the core standards had to be completed prior to endorsement, indeed there was widespread support in IOSCO for the immediate endorsement of the ten revised IASs approved as a result of the comparability and improvements project. For example, in June 1993, Jean Saint-Geours had argued[10]:

> The results already obtained [by the IASC] were of tremendous importance and should be recognised by the IOSCO without delay.

Michael Meagher, chairman of the accounting and auditing subcommittee, took the same line at a conference in New York[11]:

> I favour a piecemeal acceptance of IASs. For example at the conclusion of the comparability project, IOSCO should consider accepting all the revised Standards from that specific project. Thereafter, as new or revised Standards are issued, these Standards should also be subject to review and acceptance by IOSCO.

Further evidence of IOSCO's support for a step by step approach came when the IOSCO presidents' committee resolved in October 1993 that IOSCO members should[12]:

> take all necessary steps to accept cash flow statements prepared in accordance with IAS 7 as an alternative to statements prepared in accordance with domestic standards in connection with cross-border offerings and continuous reporting by foreign issuers.

In April 1994, the chairman of the Ontario Securities Commission, Edward Waitzer, argued that the endorsement of IASs was 'essentially an endorsement of the processes by which those standards are created rather than an endorsement of the individual technical positions taken'[13]. He continued:

> The ten international standards recently revised by the IASC in its comparability/improvements project, with the direct involvement of IOSCO, have been subjected to appropriate due process. IOSCO should acknowledge that this task is complete and urge that other extant international standards undergo a similar revision process.

The outcome of working party 1's review of existing IASs was two letters to the IASC's then chairman, Eiichi Shiratori (hence, the 'Shiratori letters')[14], that stated:

- fourteen IASs (in addition to IAS 7), including eight of the IASs which had been revised as part of the comparability and improvements project, were acceptable to the working party;
- four IASs, including IAS 9 *Research and Development Costs* and IAS 19 *Retirement Benefit Costs* which had been revised as part of the comparability and improvements project, were unacceptable to the working party; and
- the working party supported the IASC's plans to review IASs 1, 5, 12, 13, 14 and 19.

The working party also identified a number of 'essential issues', 'suspense issues', 'other issues' and 'long-term projects':

- *essential issues* were 'matters which certain members of IOSCO believed needed to be dealt with by the IASC to obtain a reasonably comprehensive set of IASs';
- *suspense issues* were 'items that generally are encountered infrequently, often are complex, and would not need to be addressed before IOSCO would consider recommending acceptance of IASs'; and
- *other issues* and *potential long-term projects* were 'other matters that eventually should be considered by the IASC to enhance the overall comparability and transparency of financial statements'.

Most significantly, IOSCO said, for the first time, that it would not endorse any further IASs until the IASC had completed the core standards. Furthermore many of the essential and suspense issues had been considered during the comparability and improvements projects. In the circumstances, it was not surprising that Eiichi Shiratori vented the feelings of the IASC in a hard hitting speech at IOSCO's 1994 annual meeting which called on IOSCO to endorse the IASC's process for setting standards rather than review individual IASs[15]. He also questioned IOSCO proposals to reinstate accounting choices that had been eliminated during the comparability project and to allow national exemptions from the requirements of some IASs.

However, the IASC did not let its frustrations block a positive response. In November 1994, it agreed a work programme that met the substantial majority of IOSCO's needs and envisaged the completion of all the core standards (except interim reporting) by 1998. It also identified a number of issues which the IASC wanted to explore with IOSCO. In particular, the IASC hoped to persuade IOSCO to:

- accept IAS 9 which IOSCO had rejected but had indicated its wish for the IASC to allow all possible alternative accounting treatments for research and development costs;
- accept IAS 10 which IOSCO had rejected because of one sentence of implementation guidance on the measurement of provisions for contingencies; and
- deal with interim reporting separately from other topics.

In December 1994, the IASC wrote to IOSCO asking it to adopt the alternative approach put forward by Eiichi Shiratori. The IASC also set out its proposed work programme and committed to consider all IOSCO's suspense issues and other concerns as part of that programme. At the same time, the IASC invited IOSCO to participate in the work of all the IASC's steering committees (no other country or organisation had the same right).

During the ensuing negotiations, the IASC agreed to commit to consider revisions to IAS 9 and IAS 10 and carry out a project on interim reporting. It also agreed to reconsider accounting for goodwill, notwithstanding that IOSCO had found IAS 22 acceptable. As a result, in July 1995, the IASC and IOSCO announced[16]:

> The board [of the IASC] has developed a work plan that the technical committee [of IOSCO] agrees will result, upon successful completion, in IASs comprising a comprehensive core set of standards. Completion of comprehensive core standards that are acceptable to the technical committee will allow the technical committee to recommend endorsement of IASs for cross-border capital raising and listing purposes in all global markets.

The core standards work plan involved the completion of seven projects which the IASC had already started, two projects which the IASC had identified as part of its future work programme in November 1994 and four new projects.

The IASC completed the core standards in December 1999 (Table 4.1).

Table 4.1: Completion of the core standards

IOSCO core standards	IAS
General	
Disclosure of accounting policies	IAS 1
Changes in accounting policies	IAS 8
Information to be disclosed in financial statements	IAS 1
Income Statement	
Revenue recognition	IAS 18
Construction contracts	IAS 11
Production and purchase costs	IAS 2
Depreciation	IAS 16
Impairment	IAS 36
Taxes	IAS 12
Extraordinary items	IAS 8
Government grants	IAS 20
Retirement benefits	IAS 19
Employee benefits	IAS 19
Research and development	IAS 38
Interest	IAS 23
Hedging	IAS 32 and IAS 39
Balance Sheet	
Property, plant and equipment	IAS 16 and IAS 40
Leases	IAS 17
Inventories	IAS 2

Deferred taxes	IAS 12
Foreign currency	IAS 21
Investments	IAS 39 and IAS 40
Financial instruments/off balance sheet transactions	IAS 32 and IAS 39
Joint ventures	IAS 31
Contingencies	IAS 37
Events occurring after the balance sheet date	IAS 10
Current assets and current liabilities	IAS 1
Business combinations (including goodwill)	IAS 22
Other intangibles	IAS 38
Cash flow	
Cash flow	IAS 7
Other standards	
Consolidated financial statements	IAS 27
Subsidiaries operating in hyperinflationary economies	IAS 21 and IAS 29
Associates/equity accounting	IAS 28
Segments	IAS 14
Interim reporting	IAS 34
Earnings per share	IAS 33
Related party disclosures	IAS 24
Discontinued operations	IAS 35
Fundamental errors	IAS 8
Changes in estimates	IAS 8

4.3.4 IOSCO's endorsement of 'IAS 2000'

IOSCO's working party 1 commenced its evaluation of the core standards early in 1999[17]. The evaluation was based on three criteria[18]:

- how the working party's concerns had been addressed in the final standards;
- whether the IASs worked together to form an operational whole; and
- the potential impact of the standards on investors, issuers and the markets.

The working party considered over 850 issues that it had raised during the core standards project. It concluded that the majority of its concerns had been addressed. It identified about 120 outstanding substantive issues that form the basis for the 'supplemental treatments' (see below). The working party's conclusions are set out in a report published in May 2000[19].

As a result of this work and on the recommendation of the technical committee, the president's committee recommended[20]:

> IOSCO members permit incoming multinational issuers to use the 30 IASC 2000 standards to prepare their financial statements for cross-

border offerings and listings, as supplemented by the 'supplemental treatments' where necessary to address outstanding substantive issues at a national or regional level.

The supplemental treatments affect 24 of the core standards and are of four types:

Reconciliation – an IOSCO member may require reconciliation of the IAS treatment to another specified accounting treatment (which may be a host country national accounting treatment). This reconciliation would quantify the effect of applying the alternative accounting treatment. There are approximately 20 reconciliation issues affecting ten IASs (Table 4.2).

Table 4.2: IOSCO's supplemental items – reconciling items

IASC Standards	Reconciling items
IAS 12 *Income Taxes*	On subsequent recognition of tax benefits acquired in business combinations, adjust intangibles as well as goodwill
IAS 17 *Leases*	Defer gains and losses arising on sale and leaseback involving an operating lease
IAS 19 *Employee Benefits*	Recognise liability for employee termination costs when board decision taken before the balance sheet date
IAS 22 *Business Combinations*	Limit useful life of goodwill to 20 years Recognise negative goodwill on level basis
IAS 27 *Consolidated Financial Statements*	Exclude from consolidation some subsidiaries that operate in dissimilar activities
IAS 32 *Financial Instruments: Disclosure and Presentation*	Account for treasury shares repurchased for trading purposes as an asset
IAS 36 *Impairment of Assets*	Measure impairment losses based on fair value, rather than recoverable amount. Prohibit reversal of impairment losses
IAS 37 *Provisions, Contingent Liabilities and Contingent Assets*	Recognise provision for sale of assets when (*a*) there is a sale through a public offering and the enterprise is demonstrably committed no later than the publication of the prospectus and (*b*) there is a demonstrable commitment for piecemeal sales through the adoption and announcement of the plan

	Recognise provisions when event after balance sheet date but before issuance of financial statements complements board decision prior to the balance sheet date
IAS 38 *Intangible Assets*	Prohibit capitalisation of internally generated assets
	Limit useful life of intangible assets to 20 years
IAS 39 *Financial Instruments: Recognition and Measurement*	Prohibit use of non-derivative instruments as hedging instruments
	Prohibit capitalisation (basis adjustment) of accumulated gain or loss on a forecasted transaction or firm commitment
	Defer recognition of gains and losses on hedging instruments rather than include in equity
	Exclude impact of own creditworthiness on fair value of a liability

Source: IOSCO Technical Committee, *IASC Standards*, May, 2000

Supplemental Disclosure – an IOSCO member may require either more detailed disclosure than required by an IAS or additional detail on the face of the primary financial statements. There are approximately 50 supplemental disclosure issues affecting 17 IASs.

Interpretation – an IOSCO member may require a specific application of an IAS by either:

- specifying which treatment is acceptable when an IAS permits different approaches; or
- specifying a particular interpretation of an IAS when the IAS is ambiguous or silent.

There are approximately 50 interpretation issues affecting 18 IASs.

Waivers – an IOSCO member may waive particular aspects of an IAS without requiring that the effect be reconciled. The use of waivers will be restricted to exceptional circumstances such as issues identified by a domestic regulator when a specific IAS is contrary to domestic or regional regulation. There are four waiver issues (Table 4.3). Note that the resulting financial statements may not be acceptable in other jurisdictions as they do not comply with IASs.

Table 4.3: IOSCO's supplemental items – waivers

IASC Standards	Waivers
IAS 12 *Income Taxes*	Recognition of deferred tax assets based on a 'probable' test
IAS 16 *Property, Plant and Equipment*	Accounting for the effects of significant, but not hyper, inflation in the cost basis of property, plant and equipment
IAS 38 *Intangible Assets*	Provide an option to capitalise or expense the costs of internally generated assets other than goodwill and computer software provided that useful life does not exceed five years and effect of option is disclosed
IAS 39 *Financial Instruments: Recognition and Measurement*	Fair value accounting for equity instruments that do not have a quoted market price in an active market

Source: IOSCO Technical Committee, *IASC Standards*, May, 2000

The May 2000 resolution allows an IOSCO member to:

- specify how the issues outside the scope of IASs should be addressed in its jurisdiction;
- mandate specific treatments on the effective dates and transition provisions in IASs;
- supplement or waive any IAS requirements on the content, frequency and speed of publication of financial statements; and
- supplement or waive IAS requirements on the reporting currency of financial statements.

The IOSCO resolution also warned that IOSCO members may not accept:

- the use of the fair presentation override which is required by IAS 1; and
- the non-disclosure of provisions when disclosure 'can be expected to prejudice seriously the position of the enterprise in a dispute with other parties' (IAS 37, 92).

The working party also identified outstanding issues that one or more jurisdictions believe the IASC should address with future projects (either SIC interpretations or IASs/IFRSs). The working party said that it may specify supplemental treatments in future if the issues are not addressed to its satisfaction. The report includes approximately 60 future projects affecting 16 IASs.

4.3.5 Auditing standards

IOSCO wants the financial statements in a single disclosure document used in cross-border offerings and foreign listings to be audited in accordance with a comprehensive set of auditing standards. IOSCO also sees the need to consider the competence and independence of auditors. In this respect, the technical committee looked to ISAs[21]. The committee worked closely with the IAPC from 1990 to 1992. It provided commentary, critiques and proposed changes to ISAs to ensure that they adequately addressed securities regulators' concerns.

In October 1992, the technical committee concluded that the then ISAs (with the then current drafts of three standards which were expected to be finalised by early 1993) represented a comprehensive set of auditing standards and that audits conducted in accordance with these standards could be relied upon by the securities regulatory authorities for multinational reporting purposes. The presidents' committee resolved[22] that IOSCO members should:

- accept the ISAs as an acceptable basis for use in cross-border offerings and continuous reporting by foreign issuers; and
- take all steps that are necessary and appropriate in their respective jurisdictions to accept audits conducted in accordance with ISAs as an alternative to domestic auditing standards in connection with cross-border offerings and continuous reporting by foreign issuers.

The technical committee did not reach consensus on the adequacy of the ISA on the form of the audit report or the IFAC standards on auditor qualifications and independence.

At the time of the endorsement, the IAPC was working on a codification project that among other things, introduced 'blackslettering' to distinguish 'basic principles and essential procedures' from 'guidance' in ISAs. In October 1993, IOSCO advised the IAPC that the introduction of 'blacklettering' and other proposed changes to ISAs would change substantively the standards that had been endorsed and that it would not recommend the final endorsement of the ISAs if the codification was adopted in its proposed form.

The IAPC adopted the codification in June 1994, largely as proposed. Working party 1 did not recommend that the codified standards should be endorsed for use in cross-border offerings and foreign listings. IOSCO did not withdraw its 1992 resolution but that endorsement is no longer effective as the standards to which it relates no longer exist.

The IAPC and IOSCO are currently considering ways in which further progress might be made. Following its 1999 meeting, IOSCO announced:

> As the technical committee completes its work on assessment of the IASC's accounting standards it will focus greater attention on auditing issues, including interaction with the IAPC. The technical committee also is seeking to develop a process to comment on the IAPC standards, as for the IASs[23].

4.3.6 Disclosure standards

In the third area of IOSCO's work on cross-border offerings and other foreign listings – disclosure – IOSCO has developed its own standards (table 4.4). Under the disclosure standards, agreed in September 1998, companies can prepare a single non-financial statement disclosure document for cross-border offerings and listings.

According to a recent IOSCO survey[24], 16 members of working party 1 currently accept documents prepared in accordance with the disclosure standards from foreign companies or have taken steps to do so at some point. In particular:

- Spain and the UK permit optional use of the disclosure standards by foreign companies;
- Mexico requires use of the disclosure standards by both foreign and domestic companies;
- Italy's revised rules for foreign and domestic companies conform with the requirements;
- France and the USA have changed their laws or rules to permit use of the disclosure standards with effect from 2000 while Australia, Belgium, Germany, Hong Kong, Japan, Luxembourg, the Netherlands and Switzerland permit foreign companies to use the disclosure standards without the need for rule changes;
- Japan has amended its disclosures to be more comparable to the standards and will accept disclosure that complies fully; and
- Ontario and Quebec plan to reconsider their rules and currently use their discretionary authority to permit a foreign company to use the disclosure standards.

Table 4.4: IOSCO's disclosure standards – the key points

Financial data	• five most recent years (three years, if earlier information cannot be provided or restated without unreasonable effort or expense) • net sales or operating revenue • income (loss) from operations • income (loss) from continuing operations • net income (loss) • net income (loss) from operations per share • income (loss) from continuing operations per share • total assets • net assets • capital stock (excluding long-term debt/redeemable preferred stock) • number of shares as adjusted to reflect changes in capital • dividends declared per share • diluted net income per share
Capitalisation and indebtedness	• capitalisation before and after new issue • guaranteed, unguaranteed, secured and unsecured debt
Risk factors specific to company, industry or offering	• nature of the business • countries in which the company operates • absence of profitable operations in recent periods • financial position • absence of a liquid market for the company's securities • reliance on the expertise of management • potential dilution • unusual competitive conditions • expiration of material patents, trademarks or contracts • dependence on limited number of customer or suppliers
Company	• business operations • products or services • principal markets • seasonality • sources and availability of raw materials • marketing channels • patents, licences, contracts and processes • effects of government regulations • property, plant and equipment
Operating/financial review and prospects	• factors that affect financial conditions and results of operations • factors and trends expected to have a material effect in future periods

	• financial condition, changes in financial condition and results of operations (company and segment)
Operating results	• unusual or infrequent events or new developments
	• extent to which changes in sales are attributable to changes in prices, volume, products or services
	• impact of inflation
	• impact of foreign currency fluctuations
	• extent to which foreign currency net investments are hedged
	• government policies that have affected, or could affect, company's operations or investments by host country shareholders
Liquidity and capital resources	• internal and external sources of liquidity
	• sufficiency of working capital for present requirements
	• sources and amounts of cash flows
	• restrictions on the transfer of funds to the company
	• borrowings – level, seasonality, maturity profile, restrictions on use
	• financial instruments used, the maturity profile of debt, currency and interest rate structure
	• commitments for capital expenditures and sources of funding
R&D	• policies for last three years
	• expenditure on company sponsored research and development
Trend information	• production, sales and inventory, order book, costs and selling prices
	• known trends, uncertainties, demands, commitments or events likely to have material effect on net sales or revenues, income from continuing operations, profitability, liquidity or capital resources, or which would cause reported financial information not necessarily to be indicative of future operating results or financial condition
Directors and management	• experience, family relationships, qualifications and levels of compensation
	• arrangements with major shareholders, customers and suppliers
	• relationship with the company and share ownership
Major shareholders	• names, ownership interest, voting rights, etc.

Related parties	• nature and extent of transactions or proposed transactions • outstanding loans (including guarantees)
Financial information	• audited consolidated financial statements • audit reports • export sales • legal or arbitration proceedings • policy on dividend distributions • significant change since last financial statements
Memorandum and articles	• directors' voting powers • rights, preferences and restrictions for each class of the shares • annual and extraordinary general meetings of shareholders • limitations on the rights to own securities • provisions that delay, defer or prevent a change in control • the effect of law if significantly different from that in the host country • changes in capital
Material contracts	• summary of each contract outside ordinary business
Exchange controls	• regulations which may affect the import or export of capital and payments to non-resident holders of securities
Taxation	• taxes (including withholding provisions) to which shareholders in the host country may be subject
Expert statements	• name, address, qualifications and consent

IOSCO, *Disclosure Standards to Facilitate Cross-Border Offerings and Listings by Multinational Issuers*

4.3.7 The position of the US Securities and Exchange Commission

The Securities and Exchange Commission (SEC) in the United States is the most important member of IOSCO as far as the endorsement of IASs is concerned for three reasons:

- many non-US companies want to raise capital or list their securities in the USA and, if they do so, they fall within the jurisdiction of the SEC;
- the SEC currently requires foreign issuers to reconcile their domestic GAAP or IAS financial statements to US GAAP; and
- the SEC rigorously enforces compliance with the accounting standards (including IASs) used by an issuer.

The SEC has made a number of concessions to foreign issuers. For example, since 1994 it has permitted foreign issuers to use the following IAS treatments without reconciliation to US GAAP:

- a cash flow statement prepared in accordance with IAS 7 *Cash Flow Statements* (this concession reflects IOSCO's 1993 endorsement of IAS 7);
- IAS 22 *Business Combinations* insofar as it deals with the identification of a business combination as a pooling or acquisition and the determination of the period for amortisation of goodwill and negative goodwill; and
- IAS 21 *The Effects of Changes in Foreign Exchange Rates* insofar as it deals with the translation of amounts stated in a currency of a hyperinflationary economy.

The SEC also does not require reconciliation of certain inflation adjustments required by IAS 29. Foreign issuers may also use proportionate consolidation for investments in joint ventures even if the investment would be accounted for using the equity method under US GAAP; proportionate consolidation is the benchmark treatment in IAS 31.

In March 1987 (two weeks before the IASC approved the start of its comparability project), SEC representatives told the then IASC chairman and secretary-general that the number of optional accounting treatments in IASs were an obstacle to the use of IASs by SEC foreign registrants. They proposed that the IASC should identify one treatment as a 'reconciling standard' and indicated that, if consensus could be achieved on a reconciling standard, the SEC would be receptive to a proposal to allow foreign companies to reconcile to that standard rather than US GAAP. The SEC representatives also suggested that consensus on a 'reconciling standard' may be the perfect solution to international reciprocity and that the 'reconciling standard' would represent a common frame of reference for international capital markets.

Another outcome of the March 1987 meeting was the IASC's invitation to IOSCO to become a member of the IASC consultative group. SEC staff subsequently played an extensive role in IOSCO's work with the IASC. They played a critical role in the comparability and improvements project, the IASC-CICA financial instruments project, the determination of IOSCO's list of core standards and the subsequent evaluation of IASs. However the SEC's notion of IASs as a 'reconciling standard' disappeared sometime in the early 1990s. Both the SEC and IOSCO focused their later efforts on the use of full IAS financial statements – rather than a reconciliation from domestic GAAP to IASs.

In April 1996, the SEC announced that its evaluation of the IASC's core standards would be based on three key elements (Table 4.5). It accepted that IASs need not require the same accounting treatments as US GAAP but warned that any differences would be considered as part of the evaluation.

Table 4.5: The SEC's three key elements

1. The standards should include a core set of accounting pronouncements that constitute a comprehensive, generally accepted basis of accounting.
2. The standards must be of high quality – they must result in comparability and transparency, and they must provide for full disclosure. Investors must be able to meaningfully analyse performance across time periods and among companies.
3. The standards must be rigorously interpreted and applied. If accounting standards are to satisfy the objective of having similar transactions and events accounted for in similar ways – whenever and wherever they are encountered – auditors and regulators around the world must insist on rigorous interpretation and application of those standards. Otherwise, the comparability and transparency that are the objectives of common standards will be eroded.

SEC press release, April 1996

In October 1996, the US Congress passed the National Securities Markets Improvement Act of 1996 which, among other things, required the SEC to report within a year to Congress on progress in the development of IASs and the outlook for successful completion of a set of international standards that would be acceptable to the SEC for offerings and listings by foreign corporations in United States markets. In its report[25], the SEC explained:

> The Commission has made a substantial commitment of resources to the IOSCO project and, through that organisation, to the IASC's core standards project. It has done so because of the significance of the issues involved – the desire to increase the access of US investors to foreign investments in the US public markets and to improve the efficiency with which foreign companies access US capital markets. The goal must be to increase US and global capital market efficiency without unnecessary cost to US markets and US market participants – considering both the needs of investors and of those competing for capital at the lowest cost.

The SEC's report also warned that if IASs were not judged, either in principle or in application, to be of comparable quality to US standards, adoption of IASs for use by foreign issuers in the US markets may:

- lead investors to question the transparency of financial reporting in the US markets, with a resulting reduction in the stability of the

markets or efficiency of pricing of capital for both domestic and cross-border issuers; and
- put domestic registrants at a competitive disadvantage because higher disclosure requirements would be imposed on them than on foreign enterprises competing for capital in the same markets.

In February 2000, the SEC issued a concept release on International Accounting Standards[26] seeking comments on convergence towards a high quality global financial reporting framework internationally and, in particular, on whether the SEC should accept IAS financial statements of foreign issuers without a reconciliation to US GAAP.

The concept release suggests that the SEC could take one of several actions:

- maintain the current reconciliation requirements in all respects;
- remove the current reconciliation requirements for selected IASs, extending the exemption to additional IASs based on future reviews of those standards – when IASs permit alternative treatments, the SEC could also specify one treatment as acceptable while retaining the reconciliation requirement for the other treatment;
- rely on IASs for recognition and measurement principles, but require US GAAP and SEC rules for disclosures and the level of detail for the line items; or
- accept IAS financial statements without any requirement to reconcile to US GAAP.

The concept release does not indicate a preferred approach but it does indicate that, in determining what approach should be taken, the SEC will consider the outstanding issues in IOSCO's May 2000 report as well as responses to the concept release.

In response to the key question about whether IASs are of sufficiently high quality for IAS financial statements to be accepted by the SEC without reconciliation to US GAAP, US respondents generally answered 'no' whereas the European respondents answered 'yes'. Many respondents believed that there are significant variations in the way that companies apply IASs and regulators enforce compliance with IASs.

The SEC has evaluated the responses to the concept release but has not yet indicated what, if anything, it is going to do.

4.4 THE EUROPEAN UNION'S USE OF IAS/IFRS

The EU's common industrial policy calls for the creation of a unified business environment, including the harmonisation of company law and taxation. Accounting harmonisation comes under the company law harmonisation programme. The objective of the programme is to give equivalent protection throughout the EU to all third parties who have dealings with companies.

4.4.1 Accounting directives

The EU uses Directives as one of its main instruments for harmonisation in a whole range of areas including accounting. Directives instruct Member States to incorporate certain provisions in their national laws. Directives are the result of a process which begins with the European Commission and ends with approval by the Council of Ministers after consultation with the European parliament, the economic and social committee and other interested parties in Europe. As Directives determine the laws of Member States and are negotiated by representatives of the Member States, their scope is often limited to those areas on which there is agreement within, and among, the Member States and other interested parties.

The objective of the accounting Directives is to make the financial information published by companies both equivalent and comparable. It has not been the intention to develop uniform accounting standards nor to require that like transactions and events should be accounted for in a like way. The two main accounting Directives are the Fourth Company Law Directive on the annual accounts of limited companies and the Seventh Company Law Directive on consolidated accounts.

The Fourth Directive deals with most of the basic issues that are important in the presentation of annual accounts of companies. The Seventh Directive deals with the consolidated accounts of groups and certain issues that are of relevance only in such financial statements. The Seventh Directive was influenced by IAS 3; the IASC's revised standard (IAS 27) was influenced by the Seventh Directive.

While the Directives have undoubtedly contributed to the improvement and harmonisation of financial reporting in the Member States, the number of optional accounting treatments has inevitably restricted the degree of harmonisation that has been achieved. There have also been concerns that the Directives are out of date and have blocked necessary improvements in financial reporting.

The EU first addressed these concerns about the Directives in 1990. Member States and others expressed the need to take into account the harmonisation efforts at a broader international level. There was little support for reducing the number of options in the Directives or adopting new legislation. One outcome, however, was the establishment of the Commission's accounting advisory forum at which national standard setters and European organisations of users and preparers of accounts have sought solutions for accounting problems not dealt with in the Directives. Another outcome was the Commission's acceptance of the

IASC's invitation to become a member of the IASC consultative group and attend IASC board meetings as an observer.

4.4.2 Harmonisation strategies

Over the years, EU-based companies have wanted to make cross-border offerings and other foreign listings, in particular they wanted to list their securities on the New York Stock Exchange. However, many such companies were unwilling to pay the price of reconciling their domestic GAAP/IAS financial statements to US GAAP. For a time in the early 1990s, the Commission and various Member States sought to persuade the SEC to accept financial statements of EU listed companies prepared in accordance with the Directives. These efforts proved fruitless, particularly given the IASC's work with IOSCO and, ultimately, Daimler-Benz's decision in 1993 to become the first German company to comply with US GAAP as a means of listing its shares on the New York Stock Exchange.

In its 1995 strategy on accounting harmonisation[27], the European Commission finally acknowledged that financial statements prepared in accordance with the Directives did not meet the standards required by the SEC. The Commission decided to associate the EU with the efforts being undertaken by the IASC and IOSCO to reach agreement of core standards for use in cross-border offerings and other foreign listings. It recognised the need for closer co-operation within the EU in order to reach agreed positions on both international and national accounting issues. The Commission also sought to strengthen the influence of the EU in the international harmonisation debate and improve the consistency of application of agreed standards in the Member States.

As part of its strategy, the Commission agreed to make it possible for Member States to permit companies to report under IASs instead of their domestic GAAP provided that they still complied with the Directives. This led to a Commission-led comparison[28] of IASs and the Directives which identified only two relatively minor issues – the consolidation of dissimilar subsidiaries and the amortisation of negative goodwill – where conformity with IASs would conflict with the Directives. The conflict on dissimilar subsidiaries is now an IOSCO reconciling item while the conflict on negative goodwill was removed in the 1998 revisions to IAS 22.

The Commission has also published comparisons of new and revised IASs issued from 1996 onwards and the Directives. These comparisons have identified possible conflicts on:

- deferred taxes (IAS 12);
- the corridor approach to the amortisation of actuarial gains and losses (IAS 19);

- the classification of liabilities and equity (IAS 32); and
- restructuring provisions (IAS 37).

The potential conflict between IAS 39 and the Fourth Directive has been dealt with by a revision to the Fourth Directive that allows the use of fair values for certain financial assets and financial liabilities[29].

Several Member States have adopted legislation which allows, or will allow, large companies to report under IASs instead of their domestic GAAP provided that they still comply with the Directives. However, there may be more conflicts between IASs and the laws in an individual Member State than there are between IASs and the Directives. Member States may have required, or allowed, companies to follow accounting treatments which are permitted by the Directives but which conflict with IASs. For example, the bank accounts Directive allows a bank a certain amount of flexibility to use undisclosed provisions for general banking risks to smooth profits. Such provisions are not permitted by IASs and need not be used under the Directive. When, however, a Member State allows their use, a bank that makes use of such provisions will be faced with a conflict with IASs.

4.4.3 IAS regulation

In June 2000, the Commission issued an updated strategy[30] on accounting harmonisation which proposed that, by 2005, all listed EU companies (including banks and insurance companies) should publish IAS consolidated financial statements. The resulting regulation[31] was approved in June 2002. It is important to recognise that the regulation requires, rather than allows, listed companies to comply with IASs/IFRSs and that its implementation requires no action by the Member States.

Perhaps the most controversial aspect of the regulation is the endorsement mechanism. IASs/IFRSs will apply to EU listed companies only if they have been endorsed by a two tier endorsement mechanism that consists of:

- the Accounting Regulatory Committee which will operate at the political level under established EU rules for decision-making by regulatory committees and will be chaired by the Commission and composed of representatives of the Member States; and
- the European Financial Reporting Advisory Group (EFRAG) which is a private-sector initiative that includes users, preparers, the accounting profession and national standard setters and which will assess IASs/IFRSs on a timely basis and provide input into the IASB's standard setting process.

The IAS regulation identifies three criteria that must be met for the endorsement of an IAS/IFRS. They must result in a true and fair view of the financial position and performance of an entity – this principle will be considered in the light of the Fourth and Seventh Directives but does not require strict conformity with them. Second, the IAS/IFRS must be 'conducive to the European public good'. Third, the IAS/IFRS must result in financial statements that are useful to the users of those statements.

The final element of the 2000 strategy is the development of an enforcement infrastructure that will ensure rigorous application by listed EU companies of IASs confirmed by the endorsement mechanism. The key focus will be on disseminating implementation guidance, encouraging high quality audit and reinforcing coordinated regulatory oversight. There will also be an important role for EU securities regulators working through the Commission of European Securities Regulators (CESR).

Notes

1 The term 'standard setting body' is used very broadly to encompass any organisation, whether in the private sector or the public sector, which issues national accounting requirements. Such bodies may include governments, government agencies, independent standard setting bodies, and committees and boards established by the accountancy profession.

2 David Cairns, *International Accounting Standards Survey 2000*, *www.cairns.co.uk*, 2001.

3 IASC, *Survey of the Use and Application of International Accounting Standards*, IASC, 1988.

4 IOSCO, *International Equity Offerings*, IOSCO, Montreal, 1988.

5 *IASC News*, IASC, January 1989, pp2–3.

6 IOSCO, *Final Communiqué of 1988 Annual Conference*, IOSCO, Montreal, 1988.

7 E32 *Comparability of Financial Statements*, IASC, London, 1989, p12.

8 Paul, Guy, 'International Regulatory Initiatives', in Choi, F.D.S. and Levitch, R.M. (eds), *International Capital Markets in a World of Accounting Differences*, Irwin, New York, 1994.

9 Letter dated 16 August 1993 to Eiichi Shiratori, chairman of the IASC, from Linda Quinn (chairman, IOSCO working party 1) and Michael Meagher (chairman, IOSCO accounting and auditing subcommittee), IOSCO, Montreal, 1993.

10 *IASC Insight*, September 1993, p1.

11 Michael Meagher, *Dynamics of Change in Financial Reporting in the 1990s – a Securities Regulatory Perspective*, Fordham University, 1994.

12 IOSCO, *Final Communiqué of the XVIIIth Annual Conference*, IOSCO, Montreal, 1993.

13 Edward Waitzer, *International Securities Regulation – Coping with the Rashomon Effect*, 1994 annual meeting of the American Society of International Law, 17OSCB 1841, Ontario Securities Commission, 22 April 1994, pp1–189.

14 Two letters dated 17 June 1994 to Eiichi Shiratori, chairman of the IASC, from Linda Quinn (chairman, IOSCO working party 1) and Michael Meagher (chairman, IOSCO accounting and auditing subcommittee).

15 See *IASC Insight*, December 1994, pp9–12.

16 IASC, Press release, 11 July 1995.

17 IAS 40 was excluded because it had not been approved at the time of the evaluation.

18 IOSCO, *Final Communiqué of the 1999 Annual Conference*, IOSCO, May 1999.

19 IOSCO, *IASC Standards*, Report of the Technical Committee, IOSCO, May 2000.

20 IOSCO, *Final Communiqué of the 2000 Annual Conference*, IOSCO, May 2000.

21 IOSCO Technical Committee, *Report to the 1990 IOSCO Conference*, IOSCO, Montreal, 1990.

22 IOSCO Presidents Committee, *Resolution Concerning International Standards on Auditing*, IOSCO, Montreal, 1992.

23 IOSCO, *Final Communiqué of the 1999 Annual Conference*, IOSCO, May 1999.

[24] IOSCO, *Report of the Technical Committee of the IOSCO: Report on Implementation of International Disclosure Standards*, IOSCO, May 1999.
[25] Securities and Exchange Commission, *Report on Promoting Global Pre-eminence of American Securities Markets*, SEC, Washington DC, 1997.
[26] Securities and Exchange Commission, *International Accounting Standards*, Release 33-7801, 34-42430, International Series Release 1215, SEC, Washington DC, 2000.
[27] European Commission, *Accounting Harmonisation: A New Strategy vis-à-vis International Harmonisation*, European Commission (COM 95 (508)), Brussels, 1995.
[28] European Commission, *An Examination of Conformity Between the International Accounting Standards and the European Accounting Directives*, Brussels, 1995.
[29] European Commission, *Directive of the European Parliament and of the Council amending Directives 78/660/EEC, 83/349/EEC and 86/635/EEC as regards the valuation rules for the annual and consolidated accounts of certain types of companies as well as of banks and other financial institutions*, Brussels, 2001.
[30] European Commission, *EU Financial Reporting Strategy: the Way Forward*, European Commission (COM (2000) 359), Brussels, 2000.
[31] European Commission, *Regulation of the European Parliament and of the Council on the Application of International Accounting Standards*, 1606/2002 European Commission, Brussels, 2002.

CHAPTER 5

International Accounting and Financial Reporting Standards

5.1 INTRODUCTION

The IASC issued International Accounting Standards (IAS) and Interpretations of International Accounting Standards (SIC). The IASB will issue International Financial Reporting Standards (IFRS) and Interpretations of International Financial Reporting Standards (IFRIC).

The IASB uses the term IFRS to include IAS, SIC and IFRIC (*Preface*, 5). Furthermore the IASB has resolved that all IAS and SIC continue to be applicable unless and until they are amended or withdrawn (*Preface*, 5). The IASB has the power to amend or withdraw IAS and SIC.

The IASC also issued implementation guidance on IAS 39 *Financial Instruments: Recognition and Measurement* consisting of almost 230 questions and answers. This guidance was issued by the IAS 39 Implementation Guidance Committee (IGC). The guidance was not approved by the IASC board and has not been approved by the IASB. The IASB agreed that the IGC should complete its work (*IASC Update*, April 2001, p1). The IASB proposes to include much of the guidance in the revised versions of IAS 32 and IAS 39 (see chapter 20).

5.2 CURRENT IAS/IFRS

Table 5.1 lists the current IASs, other IASC pronouncements and IASB proposals.

Table 5.2 lists current SIC. The guidance issued by the IGC is dealt with in chapter 20.

Table 5.1 *International Financial Reporting Standards*

Conceptual Framework
Framework for the Preparation and Presentation of Financial Statements

Preface
Preface to International Financial Reporting Standards

IASs effective in 2002
IAS 1 *Presentation of Financial Statements*
IAS 2 *Inventories*
IAS 7 *Cash Flow Statements*
IAS 8 *Net Profit or Loss for the Period, Fundamental Errors and Changes in Accounting Policies*
IAS 10 *Events After the Balance Sheet Date*
IAS 11 *Construction Contracts*
IAS 12 *Income Taxes*
IAS 14 *Segment Reporting*
IAS 15 *Information Reflecting the Effects of Changing Prices* (non-mandatory)
IAS 16 *Property, Plant and Equipment*
IAS 17 *Leases*
IAS 18 *Revenue*
IAS 19 *Employee Benefits*
IAS 20 *Accounting for Government Grants and Disclosure of Government Assistance*
IAS 21 *The Effects of Changes in Foreign Exchange Rates*
IAS 22 *Business Combinations*
IAS 23 *Borrowing Costs*
IAS 24 *Related Party Disclosures*
IAS 26 *Accounting and Reporting by Retirement Benefit Plans*
IAS 27 *Consolidated Financial Statements and Accounting for Investments in Subsidiaries*
IAS 28 *Accounting for Investments in Associates*
IAS 29 *Financial Reporting in Hyperinflationary Economies*
IAS 30 *Disclosures in the Financial Statements of Banks and Similar Financial Institutions*
IAS 31 *Financial Reporting of Interests in Joint Ventures*
IAS 32 *Financial Instruments: Disclosure and Presentation*
IAS 33 *Earnings per Share*
IAS 34 *Interim Financial Reporting*
IAS 35 *Discontinuing Operations*
IAS 36 *Impairment of Assets*
IAS 37 *Provisions, Contingent Liabilities and Contingent Assets*
IAS 38 *Intangible Assets*
IAS 39 *Financial Instruments: Recognition and Measurement*
IAS 40 *Investment Property*
IAS 41 *Agriculture*

Table 5.1 *International Financial Reporting Standards (continued)*

Exposure drafts issued by the IASB
Improvements to International Accounting Standards
Amendments to IAS 32 Financial Instruments: Disclosure and Presentation and IAS 39 Financial Instruments: Recognition and Measurement
Improvements to IAS 22 Business Combinations
ED 1 *First-Time Application of International Financial Reporting Standards*

Table 5.2 *Interpretations*

Interpretations issued by SIC

SIC 1 *Consistency – Different Cost Formulas for Inventories*
SIC 2 *Consistency – Capitalisation of Borrowing Costs*
SIC 3 *Elimination of Unrealised Profits and Losses on Transactions with Associates*
SIC 5 *Classification of Financial Instruments – Contingent Settlement Provisions*
SIC 6 *Costs of Modifying Existing Software*
SIC 7 *Introduction of the Euro*
SIC 8 *First-Time Application of IASs as the Primary Basis of Accounting*
SIC 9 *Business Combinations – Classification either as Acquisitions or Unitings of Interests*
SIC 10 *Government Assistance – No Specific Relation to Operating Activities*
SIC 11 *Foreign Exchange – Capitalisation of Losses Resulting from Severe Currency Devaluations*
SIC 12 *Consolidation – Special Purpose Entities*
SIC 13 *Jointly Controlled Entities – Non-Monetary Contributions by Venturers*
SIC 14 *Property, Plant and Equipment – Compensation for the Impairment or Loss of Items*
SIC 15 *Incentives in an Operating Lease*
SIC 16 *Treasury Shares*
SIC 17 *Equity – Costs of an Equity Transaction*
SIC 18 *Consistency – Alternative Methods*
SIC 19 *Reporting Currency – Measurement and Presentation of Financial Statements under IAS 21 and IAS 29*
SIC 20 *Equity Accounting Method – Recognition of Losses*
SIC 21 *Income Taxes – Recovery of Revalued Non-Depreciable Assets*
SIC 22 *Business Combinations – Subsequent Adjustment of Fair Values and Goodwill Initially Reported*
SIC 23 *Property, Plant and Equipment – Major Inspection or Overhaul Costs*
SIC 24 *Earnings Per Share – Financial Instruments and Other Contracts That May Be Settled in Shares*

Table 5.2 *Interpretations (continued)*

SIC 25 *Income Taxes – Changes in the Tax Status of an Enterprise or its Shareholders*
SIC 27 *Evaluating the Substance of Transactions in the Legal Form of a Lease*
SIC 28 *Business Combinations – 'Date of Exchange' and Fair Value of Equity*
SIC 29 *Disclosure – Service Concession Arrangements*
SIC 30 *Reporting Currency – Translation from Measurement Currency to Presentation Currency*
SIC 31 *Revenue – Barter Transactions Involving Advertising Services*
SIC 32 *Intangible Assets – Web Site Costs*
SIC 33 *Consolidation and Equity Method – Potential Voting Rights and Allocation of Ownership Interests*

5.3 THE IASB'S WORK PROGRAMME

The IASB's work programme consists of active projects, active research projects and other projects. Up-to-date information about all these projects is posted at www.iasb.org.uk.

Active projects are those projects that are currently under consideration by the board (main agenda). As at September 2002, the IASB is considering the following active projects:

- business combinations (phase I) (exposure draft of improvements to IAS 22, IAS 36 and IAS 38 issued September 2002);
- business combinations (phase II) (IAS 22);
- consolidations (including special purpose entities) (IAS 27 and SIC 12);
- convergence topics on which the IASB believes that a high quality solution is available from existing international and national standards:
  - pension accounting (IAS 19);
- deposit-taking, lending and securities activities (IAS 30 and IAS 32);
- amendments to IAS 39 *Financial Instruments: Recognition and Measurement* (exposure draft issued June 2002);
- first-time application of IFRSs (ED 1 issued July 2002);
- improvements to existing IASs (exposure draft of improvements to IAS 1, IAS 2, IAS 8, IAS 10, IAS 15, IAS 16, IAS 17, IAS 21, IAS 24, IAS 27, IAS 28, IAS 33 and IAS 40 issued May 2002);
- insurance contracts (the IASC published an issues paper in November 1999);
- reporting performance (including IAS 1 and IAS 8 but raising significant new issues);

- revenue – definition and recognition – and related aspects of liabilities (including IAS 18); and
- share-based payments (IAS 19 requires some disclosure; the project will deal with significant recognition and measurement issues).

Active research projects are those projects on which the IASB has started active research, often in collaboration with others, with the intention that the projects should be moved to the main agenda when preparatory work is concluded. As at September 2002, the IASB has the following active research projects:

- the application of IFRSs to small and medium-sized entities and in emerging economies;
- lease accounting (IAS 17);
- accounting concepts, including a strategic review of the basic elements of accounting and design work on measurement, focusing initially on impairments (*Framework* and IAS 36); and
- aspects of accounting for financial instruments (IAS 32 and IAS 39).

Other topics are those topics that are being addressed by one or more national accounting standard setting partners. The IASB will be working with these partners, or at least monitoring their efforts, in order to ensure that any differences among national standard setters or with the IASB are identified and resolved as quickly as possible. Other projects as at September 2002 include:

- accounting by extractive industries (the IASC published an issues paper in November 2000);
- definitions of elements of financial statements (*Framework*);
- derecognition issues other than those addressed in IAS 39;
- impairment of assets (IAS 36);
- intangible assets (IAS 38);
- liabilities; and
- management's discussion and analysis.

5.4 APPLICATION OF IAS AND IFRS

5.4.1 Profit-oriented Entities

IFRSs are designed to apply to the general purpose financial statements of and other financial reporting by all profit-oriented entities (*Preface*, 9). This includes entities engaged in commercial, industrial, financial and similar activities.

IFRS are designed to apply whatever the legal form of an entity but national law or other requirements usually determine the application of accounting standards, including IFRS, to particular entities. For example, the EU IAS regulation applies primarily to companies listed on a stock exchange whereas some countries require all companies, but not other entities, to apply IFRS.

Occasionally the IASC has limited the application of an IAS to certain entities, as it has, for example, with IAS 14 *Segment Reporting*, IAS 33 *Earnings Per Share* and IAS 34 *Interim Reporting*.

The application of IFRS to public sector business entities is strongly supported by the IFAC public sector committee. Its guideline *Financial Reporting by Government Business Enterprises* requires that such entities should present financial statements that conform with appropriate national requirements and IASs (*IFAC Public Sector Guideline* 1, 9). This guideline was developed with considerable assistance from the IASC; the IFAC working party responsible for the guideline was chaired by the author as secretary-general of the IASC.

5.4.2 Not-for-profit Entities

IFRSs are not designed to apply to not-for-profit activities in the private sector, public sector or government (*Preface*, 9).

The IFAC public sector committee (PSC) is seeking to develop a 'coherent set of International Public Sector Accounting Standards (IPSASs), based primarily on IASs' (*IFAC Quarterly*, April 1998, p2). It has published a draft *Guideline for Government Financial Reporting* which seeks to make government more transparent and therefore more accountable. The draft considered four models of accounting: cash, modified cash, modified accrual and accrual. The project has now moved into its next phase in which the committee is developing accounting standards based on IASs for use in public sector not-for-profit activities. By September 2002, the committee had published the following IPSASs:

IPSAS 1 *Presentation of Financial Statements*
IPSAS 2 *Cash Flow Statement*
IPSAS 3 *Net Surplus or Deficit for the Period, Fundamental Errors and Changes in Accounting Policies*
IPSAS 4 *The Effects of Changes in Foreign Exchange Rates*
IPSAS 5 *Borrowing Costs*
IPSAS 6 *Consolidated Financial Statements and Accounting for Controlled Entities*
IPSAS 7 *Accounting for Investments in Associates*
IPSAS 8 *Financial Reporting of Interests in Joint Ventures*

IPSAS 9 *Revenue from Exchange Transactions*
IPSAS 10 *Financial Reporting in Hyperinflationary Economies*
IPSAS 11 *Construction Contracts*
IPSAS 12 *Inventories*
IPSAS 13 *Leases*
IPSAS 14 *Events After the Balance Sheet Date*
IPSAS 15 *Financial Instruments: Disclosure and Presentation*
IPSAS 16 *Investment Property*
IPSAS 17 *Property, Plant and Equipment*
IPSAS 18 *Segment Reporting*

The PSC has issued exposure drafts of IPSASs based on IAS 24 *Related Party Disclosures* and IAS 37 *Provisions, Contingent Liabilities and Contingent Assets* and an invitation to comment based on IAS 36 *Impairment of Assets*.

The IASC was represented on the PSC for many years from its formation in 1987.

5.4.3 Consolidated and Legal Entity Financial Statements

IFRSs apply to both the consolidated and legal entity (separate) financial statements of an entity. The legal entity financial statements alone cannot comply with IFRSs if the entity is required by IAS 27 to publish consolidated financial statements.

National law or other requirements may require or allow the application of IFRS in only consolidated financial statements. For example, the EU IAS regulation requires only that the consolidated financial statements of listed companies comply with IFRSs. It leaves to EU member states to decide whether to require or allow the use of IFRS in legal entity financial statements. Some member states are likely to continue to require or allow the use of tax rules in legal entity financial statements while requiring the entity to publish consolidated financial statements that comply with IFRSs.

The publication of legal entity financial statements by an entity that has subsidiaries is not required or may be forbidden in some jurisdictions. In such jurisdictions, the consolidated financial statements are the only published financial statements and techniques such as the equity method and proportionate consolidation may be required in those financial statements even when the entity does not have subsidiaries.

5.5 FORMAT OF IASs/IFRSs

The IASC adopted a new format for IASs in the early 1990s. This format has been used for all the new and revised IASs adopted from 1992 onwards and for all existing IASs from 1994. It will be adopted by the IASB.

The new format links the standards with the related implementation guidance. The IASC also moved footnotes into the main text (particularly footnotes to definitions) and moved explanatory material from definitions to guidance paragraphs.

IASs include paragraphs in bold italic type and IFRSs will include paragraphs in bold type. These paragraphs are the principles (or standards) in the IAS/IFRS. IASs also include, and IFRSs will also include, paragraphs in plain type. These paragraphs are implementation guidance. The different paragraphs have equal authority (*Preface*, 14).

5.5.1 Principles (Standards)

The principles use the word 'should' in IAS and 'shall' in IFRS. An entity must apply the requirements of the principles to appropriate and material items in order for its financial statements to comply with IFRSs.

For example, paragraph 7 of IAS 2 *Inventories* states:

> ***The cost of inventories should comprise all costs of purchase, costs of conversion and other costs incurred in bringing the inventories to their present location and condition.***

This means that the cost of inventories must comprise all the costs of purchase, costs of conversion and other costs incurred in bringing the inventories to their present location and condition otherwise the financial statements do not comply with IAS 2. The financial statements would not comply with IAS 2 if, for example, the entity used a marginal cost approach for the valuation of inventories.

5.5.2 Guidance Paragraphs

These paragraphs do not use the word 'should' or 'shall'. They explain how to apply the principles but are drafted to reflect the fact that the circumstances of an entity may be different from those of another entity. An entity follows the guidance paragraphs in appropriate circumstances otherwise its financial statements would not comply with IFRSs.

For example IAS 2 includes extensive implementation guidance for the principle in paragraph 7. The guidance includes the following:

> The costs of conversion of inventories include costs directly related to the units of production, such as direct labour. They also include a systematic allocation of fixed and variable production overheads that are incurred in converting materials into finished goods. Fixed production overheads are those indirect costs of production that remain relatively constant regardless of the volume of production, such as depreciation and maintenance of factory buildings and equipment, and the cost of factory management and administration. Variable production overheads are those indirect costs of production that vary directly, or nearly directly, with the volume of production, such as indirect materials and indirect labour.

This guidance explains what the IASB means by the costs of conversion. However, the guidance is flexible enough to allow for the fact that the actual costs incurred by any one entity may be different from those incurred by other entities. An entity follows the guidance but adapts it to deal with the specific costs of conversion which it incurs. However, its financial statements would not comply with IFRSs if those adaptations meant, for example, that fixed production overheads were excluded from the costs of conversion.

Another good example of the relationship between a principle and the guidance can be found in IAS 27 *Consolidated Financial Statements and Accounting for Investments in Subsidiaries*. Paragraph 11, the principle, requires the consolidation of all subsidiaries; failure to consolidate material subsidiaries would mean that the financial statements did not conform with IAS 27. Paragraph 12, the implementation guidance, helps to determine when a parent-subsidiary relationship exists; it recognises that control, the determining feature, may arise in different ways.

Guidance paragraphs also deal with the different circumstances which exist in different countries and which are important in order to ensure that like transactions and events are accounted for in a like way, no matter how they are structured. For example:

- IAS 7 explains when bank overdrafts (which arise only in some countries) are included in cash and cash equivalents in the cash flow statement notwithstanding that they are classified as liabilities in the balance sheet;
- the guidance in IAS 22 points out that legal mergers are a form of business combination and explains how the requirements of IAS 22 are applied to legal mergers; and
- IAS 19 [1993] pointed out that retirement benefit plans are set up and funded (or not) in different ways and explained how the same accounting standards were applied to these different circumstances.

5.6 TERMINOLOGY

The IASC sought to use terms consistently in different IASs whenever possible. For example, the term 'joint venture' is used in IAS 12 *Income Taxes* in the way in which it is defined in IAS 31 *Financial Reporting of Interests in Joint Ventures* and the term 'inventories' is used in IAS 22 *Business Combinations* with the same meaning as which it is defined in IAS 2 *Inventories*.

Whenever possible the IASC used the same definition in all IASs for generic terms such as 'fair value', 'control' and 'entity'. However, the term 'fair value' is used in some IASs solely in the context of assets (for example, IAS 16) but in others (for example, IAS 32 and IAS 39) it applies also to liabilities. The IASC also tried to avoid giving a technical, defined meaning to a term in one IAS if that term appears with a more general meaning in other IASs. The IASB is likely to continue with these policies.

The Framework has helped to ensure consistency of language and style. For example, all IASs refer to amounts being recognised as income or expenses rather than being included in income. The term 'income' is used, as defined in the Framework, as a gross concept and the term 'profit' (or 'loss') is used to describe the result of the period. The term 'gain' is used to describe the excess of income over expenses arising on a particular event or transaction.

The IASC used a mix of North American and British terminology (and British spellings). The following table lists IASC terminology with possible alternatives.

IASC terminology	**Possible alternatives**
Financial statements	Accounts
Income statement	Profit and loss account
Balance sheet	Statement of financial position
Net profit or loss for the period	Net income
Long-term assets	Fixed assets
Land and buildings, property	Real estate
Plant and equipment	Plant and machinery
Associates	Participating interests
Inventories	Stocks, work in progress
Receivables	Debtors
Payables	Creditors
Loans	Debt
Security (for liabilities)	Collateral
Shareholders' interest, equity	Stockholders' equity
Shares	Stock
Ordinary shares	Common stock
Revenue	Turnover
Write-downs	Reserves, value adjustments

Retirement benefit costs	Pension costs
Uniting of interests	Pooling, merger
Acquisition (business combinations)	Purchase

5.7 BENCHMARK AND ALLOWED ALTERNATIVE TREATMENTS

Some IASs include two accounting treatments for like transactions and events with one treatment specified as the benchmark treatment and the other as the allowed alternative treatment. Originally the IASC intended to use the term 'preferred' but switched to the term 'benchmark' because it reflected the intention of identifying a point of reference, rather than a preference. The IASC decided not to require a reconciliation from the allowed alternative treatments to the benchmark (preferred) treatments although certain IASs require the disclosure of the effects of using the allowed alternative treatment rather than the benchmark treatment.

It was the IASC's policy, and is the IASB's policy, to require the use of a single treatment for like transactions and events. Therefore, it is inappropriate for an entity to use the benchmark treatment for certain events and transactions and the allowed alternative for other like transactions and events. This policy was confirmed in SIC 18 but had previously been overturned in SIC 1 on the LIFO/FIFO issue (see chapter 26).

5.8 FAIR VALUE

The term 'fair value' is used extensively in IASs and in the early 1980s the IASC agreed a definition of the term which has been used in all subsequent IASs. It has been modified only to deal with liabilities as wells as assets.

'Fair value' is a generic term and is defined as the amount at which an asset could be exchanged, or a liability settled, between knowledgeable willing parties in an arm's length transaction. When an asset is exchanged in an arm's length transaction, the consideration is usually an indication of the fair value of the asset. Therefore, most business transactions are carried out at fair value. When the fair value of an asset cannot be determined for an exchange transaction, it may be estimated from the market value or some other source.

Fair value is an accountant's, rather than a valuer's, term and reflects the fact that such values may need to be determined by reference to sources other than an active market. The International Valuation

Standards explain the distinction between the accountant's notion of 'fair value' and the valuer's notion of 'market value' (IVA 1).

5.9 DISCLOSURE

IASs use the term 'disclosure' or the instruction 'disclose' in a broad sense, encompassing items presented on the face of each financial statement as well as in the notes which form part of the financial statements. Disclosures required by IASs are made in accordance with the requirements of those IASs and, unless specified to the contrary, such disclosures may be made either on the face of the relevant financial statement or in the notes.

CHAPTER 6

The Conceptual Framework

6.1 HISTORY

The IASC focused its initial efforts on the development of accounting standards which dealt with practical issues. In November 1982, the IASC added to its work programme a project on the objectives of financial statements which was intended to be 'a limited study, examining the separate roles and needs of the various publics to which International Accounting Standards are addressed' (*IASC News*, December 1982, p3). The IASC said that it did not intend to prepare an international conceptual framework. In October 1984, the IASC merged the objectives project with a review of IAS 1 [1974].

In 1984 and 1985 the IASC added to its work programme three more 'building block' projects – liabilities, equity and assets and expenses. Preliminary drafts were developed for all four projects but it became increasingly clear that there would be considerable benefits in merging the projects. In November 1986, the IASC agreed to develop a framework for financial reporting which would stand apart from IASs and which would not bind the IASC to particular accounting treatments for individual topics. The *Framework for the Preparation and Presentation of Financial Statements* (Framework) was approved in April 1989 and has been adopted by the IASB.

The Framework has not been reviewed although the IASB intends to reconsider some aspects of the Framework in the near future.

An extensive history of the IASB's conceptual framework and its use in the work of the IASC is set out in the author's 'The Conceptual Framework: the International Experience'[1].

6.2 THE FRAMEWORK IN OUTLINE

The Framework deals with:

- the users of financial statements;
- the objective of financial statements;
- the underlying assumptions of accrual and going concern;
- the qualitative characteristics – understandability, relevance, reliability and comparability;
- the definitions of assets, liabilities and equity;
- the definitions of income and expenses;
- the criteria for the recognition in the balance sheet or income statement of assets, liabilities, income and expenses;
- the bases used to measure assets, liabilities, income and expenses; and
- the concepts of capital and capital maintenance which are used to determine capital and profit.

The Framework is intended to assist:

- preparers of financial statements apply IFRSs and deal with topics which have not yet been dealt with by the IASB;
- auditors form an opinion as to whether financial statements conform with IFRSs; and
- the IASB develop future IFRSs and interpret and revise existing IASs and IFRSs.

6.3 USERS OF FINANCIAL STATEMENTS

The IASC always concerned itself with the interests of a wide range of users of financial statements. The Preface asserted that financial statements are issued to 'other persons [than management], such as shareholders, creditors, employees, and the public' (*Preface* [1982], 6). IAS 1 [1974] referred to 'a variety of users, especially shareholders and creditors (present and potential) and employees'. It also identified suppliers, customers, trade unions, financial analysts, statisticians, economists, taxation and other regulatory authorities as 'important categories of users'(IAS 1 [1974], 11).

According to the Framework, the users include present and potential investors, employees, lenders, suppliers and other trade creditors, customers, governments and their agencies and the public (*Framework*, 9). The Framework does not rank the users in order of priority, although some commentators have wrongly asserted that the Framework focuses primarily on the needs of investors.

6.4 OBJECTIVES OF FINANCIAL STATEMENTS

The objective of financial statements is to provide information about the financial position, performance and changes in financial position of an entity that is useful to a wide range of users in making economic decisions (*Framework*, 12). Such decisions include those about whether to buy, hold or sell an equity investment, the ability of the entity to pay and provide other benefits to its employees, and the security for amounts lent to the entity.

Some argue that the objective of financial statements should be to show the results of the stewardship of management, or the accountability of management for the resources entrusted to it. The IASC concluded that those users who wish to assess the stewardship or accountability of management are not interested in stewardship or accountability for its own sake but rather to decide whether to re-appoint or replace the management. Therefore the objective of decision-usefulness encompasses stewardship.

In some countries, financial statements are used to determine taxable profits, distributable profits and measures used for capital adequacy purposes. The determination of such amounts is not one of the objectives of financial statements prepared in conformity with IFRSs. Governments and regulators are free to decide, however, that such amounts should be determined using IFRSs. Indeed, bank regulators played a major part in the development of IAS 30 because they realised the importance of high quality financial statements in their assessments of capital adequacy.

Financial statements are only part of the information which flows from an entity to the users of that information. The other information includes that which is sent to all users as well as the additional specific information which some users have the power to obtain – for example, a bank may insist on additional information as a condition of granting a loan. This additional information falls outside the scope of IFRSs.

In the EU and elsewhere, financial statements of companies are required to give a true and fair view of the company's assets, liabilities, financial position and profit or loss (Fourth Directive, article 2 (3)). The application of the qualitative characteristics in the Framework and IFRSs would normally result in financial statements that give what is generally understood by a 'true and fair view'.

In North America and elsewhere, financial statements are required to 'present fairly the financial position, performance and cash flows of the entity in accordance with generally accepted accounting principles'. The application of the qualitative characteristics in the Framework and IFRSs would normally result in what is generally understood by fair presentation in accordance with generally accepted accounting principles.

The issue of fair presentation is now dealt with in IAS 1 but the IASC decided that fair presentation should be an overriding concept and not defined by reference to a particular set of accounting principles. Therefore the IASC's/IASB's approach to fair presentation is the same as the EU's approach to true and fair view and different from the US approach to fair presentation (see chapter 8).

6.5 UNDERLYING ASSUMPTIONS

6.5.1 Accrual Basis

Under the accrual basis of accounting, the effects of transactions and other events are recognised when they occur (and not as cash or cash equivalents are received or paid) and they are recorded in the accounting records and reported in the financial statements of the periods to which they relate (*Framework*, 22). There is no practical difference between the language used in IAS 1 and the Framework to define the accrual basis or assumption. The accrual basis is followed in all IASs which apply to the balance sheet and income statement. Financial statements which are prepared on some other basis, for example a cash basis, are unlikely to comply with IFRSs.

6.5.2 Going Concern

Financial statements are normally prepared on the assumption that an entity is a going concern and will continue in operation for the foreseeable future (*Framework*, 23). This approach is also reflected in IAS 1. The financial statements may need to be prepared on a different basis if the entity intends, or has a need, to liquidate or curtail materially the scale of its operations (*Framework*, 23). This issue is dealt with in IAS 1 (see chapter 8).

6.6 QUALITATIVE CHARACTERISTICS

The Framework identifies four principal qualitative characteristics – understandability, relevance, reliability and comparability – which make the financial statements useful to users (*Framework*, 24). In developing IASs, the IASC sought to achieve a balance between these qualitative characteristics. For example, IASs do not permit the recognition in the balance sheet of assets which cannot be measured reliably even though the existence of those assets may be relevant to users of the financial statements. Similarly, the IASC moved, and the IASB is moving, towards the use of more relevant, but less reliable, market values for many financial assets and financial liabilities in place of more reliable, but less relevant, historical costs.

The IASB also considers the costs which are likely to be incurred by preparers in complying with a proposed requirement and the benefits likely to be derived by users from resulting information. It is, however, inappropriate for an entity to omit certain information which is required by an IFRS on the grounds that the entity's costs exceed the benefits to the user of the financial statements.

6.6.1 Understandability

Information provided in financial statements should be readily understandable by users who are assumed to have a reasonable knowledge of business and economic activities and accounting and a willingness to study the information with reasonable diligence (*Framework*, 25). Financial statements are not directed at lay users who have no knowledge of business or accounting. It is the responsibility of entities, however, to ensure that information is understandable to those users who have the relevant knowledge to understand the information.

6.6.2 Relevance

Information must be relevant to the decision-making needs of users (*Framework*, 26). Information is relevant when it influences the economic decisions of users by helping them evaluate past, present or future events or confirming, or correcting, their past evaluations (*Framework*, 26).

The relevance of information is affected by:

- its nature, for example information about sales or related party transactions; or
- both its nature and its materiality, for example the performance of individual business segments.

In the IASC's Framework, materiality is part of relevance. Information is material if its omission or mis-statement could influence the economic decisions of users taken on the basis of the financial statements. Materiality depends on the size of the item or error judged in the particular circumstances of its omission or mis-statement (*Framework*, 30).

Financial statements should therefore disclose all items which are material enough to affect evaluations or decisions (IAS 1, 7). In contrast, financial statements need not disclose immaterial items and the IASC included a statement to this effect at the beginning of every IAS (*IASC News*, November 1983, p3).

6.6.3 Reliability

Information is reliable when:

- it is free from material error;
- it is neutral, that is free from bias; and
- it can be depended upon to represent faithfully that which it either purports to represent or could reasonably be expected to represent.

(*Framework*, 31)

An important aspect of reliability is that transactions and other events are accounted for, and presented in accordance with, their substance and economic reality and not merely their legal form (*Framework*, 35). IAS 1 [1974] identified substance over form as a consideration 'which should govern the selection of accounting policies' (IAS 1 [1974], 5). The revised IAS 1 does not include a similar requirement although it does identify substance over form as one of the factors which management should take into account in developing accounting policies for accounting issues which are not covered by IASs (IAS 1, 20 (b) (ii)).

The notion of substance over form plays an important part in a number of IASs including finance leases (IAS 17), revenue recognition (IAS 18) and liabilities and equity (IAS 32). It is also an important consideration in dealing with the recognition and derecognition of financial assets and financial liabilities, particularly in the case of securitisations and in-substance defeasance.

The Framework deals with prudence under the heading of reliability. Prudence is 'the inclusion of a degree of caution in the exercise of the judgements needed in making the estimates required under conditions of uncertainty, such that assets or income are not overstated and liabilities or expenses are not understated' (*Framework*, 37). Prudence is, however, secondary to neutrality. Therefore the exercise of prudence does not allow the creation of hidden reserves or excessive provisions, the understatement of assets or income, or the overstatement of liabilities or expenses. Such an approach would mean that the financial statements would not be neutral and, therefore, not be reliable (*Framework*, 37).

The IASC took a similar approach in IAS 1 [1974] which identified prudence as one of the three considerations which 'should govern the selection and application of accounting policies' (IAS 1 [1974], 5). The IAS explained that prudence should be exercised in recognition of the uncertainties which inevitably surround many transactions. Prudence did not justify the creation of secret or hidden reserves (IAS 1 [1974], 7(a)).

The revised IAS 1 does not include a similar requirement or similar guidance. In fact, it gives greater status than IAS 1 [1974] and the Framework to prudence albeit in the fairly limited circumstances of those accounting issues for which there are no IASs. In such circumstances, the revised IAS 1 requires that 'management should develop [accounting] policies to ensure that the financial statements provide information that is ... reliable in that they ... are prudent ...' (IAS 1, 20). It is unclear whether 'they' refers to 'accounting policies' or 'financial statements' but it would be unfortunate if the new requirement was interpreted to allow accounting policies which allowed, or financial statements which included, understated assets or overstated liabilities.

The IASC's earlier position on prudence has been consistently applied in a number of IASs. For example, IAS 10 [1978] did not permit the recognition of liabilities for general or unspecified business risks (IAS 10 [1978], 15). IAS 30 does not permit undisclosed charges for general banking risks or additional contingencies, undisclosed credits resulting from the reversal of such charges, overstated liabilities, understated assets or undisclosed accruals and provisions (IAS 30, 52).

6.6.4 Comparability

The financial effect of like transactions and other events should be measured and displayed in a consistent way:

- throughout an entity;
- over time for that entity; and
- by different entities.

(*Framework*, 39)

The need for consistency must not be confused with mere uniformity (*Framework*, 41). While recent IASC and IASB statements have referred to the desirability of uniform accounting principles, the IASC and the IASB favour uniformity of treatment only for like transactions and events. Therefore, for example, while IAS 16 requires that an item of property, plant and equipment should be depreciated over its useful life, it does not specify, nor require, a uniform life for items which are used differently. The useful life of each item should reflect the way it is used and different lives should be used for identical assets which are used differently. Similarly, IAS 19 requires that retirement benefit costs should be measured on an actuarial basis using appropriate and compatible assumptions; it does not require the use of uniform discount rates or uniform factual assumptions but a discount rate and assumptions that, within the requirements of the IAS, are appropriate for each particular entity.

6.7 BALANCE SHEET ELEMENTS

The Framework identifies three balance sheet elements – assets, liabilities and equity. It deals first with the definition of these elements and then their recognition on the balance sheet. Some items which meet the definition may not qualify for recognition on the balance sheet. Items which do not meet the definitions should not be considered for recognition and should not appear on the balance sheet.

Some have argued that the Framework gives precedence to the balance sheet by defining first the balance sheet elements and relying on those definitions to define the income statement elements. The most notable proponent of this view has been the firm of Ernst & Young (at least in the UK). It argued forcefully against the same approach in the UK's then proposed *Statement of Principles*. It argued that the approach was a 'very different approach from that which accountants have traditionally followed'[2] and the firm's senior partner complained that the ASB's proposals were 'theoretical to the point that they are scarcely comprehensible by most accountants and other businessmen' and the 'rhetoric of theorists'[3].

Ernst & Young was, and is, not alone in holding this view. In a recent study, Nobes (a former IASC board representative) describes as 'revolutionary' the Framework's approach of defining assets and liabilities first and leaving expenses and revenues as residuals, suggesting that it reverses the previous convention and will not, for example, allow the recognition of pre-opening costs as an asset or the recognition of next year's repair expenses as a liability[4].

The difference in approach can best be illustrated by a simple example, the determination of the cost of sales for a trading entity. Under the IASC's approach, cost of sales is a residual amount determined after recognising the transactions for the period and adjusting for opening and closing receivables, payables and inventories. It is the approach that virtually every accountant throughout the world uses but Ernst & Young finds it 'scarcely comprehensible' and the 'rhetoric of theorists' while Nobes thinks it 'revolutionary'.

Under the alternative approach, cost of sales is determined first and closing receivables, payables and inventories are residuals. This approach is clearly favoured by Ernst & Young and apparently supported by Nobes. Both rely on the matching principle. Neither indicates how income and expenses can be measured without, first, measuring the closing amounts of receivables, payable and inventories. The approach does have one advantage – it allows entities to choose their profit or loss for the period, something which Ernst & Young and Nobes may find attractive.

The IASC and several national standard setting bodies argue that it is impossible to define income and expenses without, first, defining assets and liabilities. In other words, it is impossible to define cost of sales without defining, first, receivables, payables and inventories. They believe that this approach gives more relevant and reliable information. They also reject the argument that it gives primacy to the balance sheet.

6.7.1 Assets

An asset is a resource controlled by the entity as a result of past events and from which future economic benefits are expected to flow to the entity (*Framework*, 49). The word 'resource' was included in the definition of an asset to help those who had difficulty with an earlier draft which defined an asset as economic benefits controlled by the enterprise. The use of the term 'resource' does not imply that assets should have a particular form.

The resource, whatever its form, must be controlled by the entity otherwise it is not an asset. Control exists when the entity owns, or has similar legal rights, to the resource unless it can be demonstrated that ownership or the existence of the legal rights does not constitute control. Control may exist when the entity does not own the resource. For example, plant and equipment held on a finance lease is an asset of the lessee which controls the benefits which are expected to flow from the plant and equipment even though the entity does not own the plant and equipment.

An asset results from a past event, such as a past transaction. Events or transactions expected to occur in the future do not in themselves give rise to assets. For example, an intention to purchase inventory does not, of itself, make that inventory an asset. Similarly, a forward contract to buy inventory does not make that inventory an asset. However, the forward contract itself is an asset if future economic benefits are expected to flow from the contract.

The future economic benefits embodied in an asset are the potential to contribute, directly or indirectly, to the flow of cash and cash equivalents to the entity (*Framework*, 53). The future economic benefits may flow to the entity in a number of ways. For example:

- inventories, property, plant and equipment, and know-how may be used in the production of goods or services to be sold by the entity;
- cash and cash equivalents, receivables or marketable securities may be exchanged for other assets;
- cash and cash equivalents may be used to settle a liability; or
- cash and cash equivalents may be distributed to the owners of the entity.

6.7.2 Liabilities

A liability is a present obligation of the entity arising from past events, the settlement of which is expected to result in an outflow from the entity of resources embodying economic benefits (*Framework*, 49).

An obligation is a duty or responsibility to act or perform in a certain way. Obligations may be legally enforceable or may arise from normal business practice, custom and a desire to maintain good business relations or act in an equitable manner (*Framework*, 60). For example, an obligation arises from the purchase of goods on credit. An obligation also arises when an entity decides, as a matter of policy, to rectify faults in products already sold; such obligations are referred to as 'constructive obligations' in IAS 37.

A present obligation is different from a commitment. A decision to acquire assets may be a commitment but it does not, of itself, give rise to a present obligation and, hence, a liability. Similarly a management decision to incur certain expenditure may be a commitment but it is not an obligation while the entity retains discretion to avoid the expenditure. An obligation arises only when the asset is delivered to the entity, when the entity enters into an irrevocable agreement to acquire the asset, or when the entity is demonstrably committed to incur expenditure. Similarly, a decision to close a factory may be a commitment but does not give rise to a present obligation and, hence, a liability until the entity is demonstrably committed to the closure.

As with an asset, a liability results from a past event such as a transaction. Events or transactions expected to occur in the future do not in themselves give rise to a liability. For example, an intention to purchase inventory or close a factory does not, of itself, meet the definition of a liability. The distinction between past events and future events is particularly important in dealing with such liabilities on provisions (see IAS 37, 17 to 22). The relationship between past events and future events is also examined in more detail in *Future Events; A Conceptual Study of Their Significance for Recognition and Measurement* published by G4+1.

The settlement of a present obligation usually involves the entity giving up assets in order to satisfy the claim of the other party. Settlement may occur in a number of ways, for example, by:

- the payment of cash or cash equivalents as is the case with most payables;
- the transfer of other assets, for example in a barter transaction or in some business combinations;
- the rendering of services to the other party as is the case with a liability for warranty repairs;
- the replacement of the obligation with another obligation; or
- the conversion of the obligation into equity.

An obligation to issue the entity's own equity securities is not a liability because the settlement of the obligation does not result in an outflow from the entity of resources embodying economic benefits (IAS 32, 16). However, when the entity has the ability to meet an obligation either by issuing its own equity securities or giving up assets, the obligation is a liability.

Some liabilities can be measured only by using a substantial degree of estimation, for example provisions (IAS 37, 10). A provision which satisfies the definition of a liability is a liability and should be recognised on the balance sheet even if the amount has to be estimated. A provision which does not meet the definition of a liability is not a liability and should not be recognised on the balance sheet.

The term 'provision' is used in some countries to cover amounts set aside for general business risks and similar items. Such provisions usually do not meet the Framework definition of a liability because they are not a present obligation nor do they arise from a past event. There is nothing in the Framework or IAS to preclude an entity from treating such items as appropriations of the net profit for the period and as part of equity; indeed, IAS 30 specifically allows banks to adopt such a practice.

The term 'provision' is sometimes used to describe the write-down of certain assets; for example, IAS 30 refers to the 'provision for losses on loans and advances' which is deducted from the total carrying amount of loans and advances (IAS 30, 45). Accumulated depreciation is sometimes referred to as a provision for depreciation. These provisions are more in the nature of measurement or value adjustments; they are not liabilities and they are not dealt with in IAS 37.

Some IASs refer to deferred income, for example, IAS 20 allows grants related to assets to be set up as deferred income (see chapter 34) and IAS 22 [1993] allowed negative goodwill to be shown as deferred income (see chapter 16). Some argue that these items do not meet the Framework definition of liabilities and therefore should be recognised immediately as income. If this argument is valid, these items are instances of where IASs depart from the Framework and they will, no doubt, be reviewed by the IASB in due course. Others argue that these items do meet the definition of a liability and that the immediate recognition as income of a grant which is intended to subsidise an entity's costs in later periods does not reflect the substance of the grant.

These items of deferred income should be distinguished from income which has been recognised as a liability (or a deduction from an asset) because the relevant service has not yet been provided. For example, a financial institution may recognise the total amount of interest receivable on a financing transaction as deferred income. Such items clearly meet the definition of a liability as the institution has an obligation to provide a service (the loan).

The IASC did consider the possibility of two more elements – deferred credits and deferred charges – during the early stages of the liabilities and assets projects but these possibilities were rejected early in the Framework project. The IASC's original ideas on deferred credits would have encompassed the types of deferred income allowed by IAS 20 and IAS 22 [1993].

6.7.3 Equity

Equity is the residual interest in the assets of the entity after deducting all its liabilities (*Framework*, 49). Therefore, a balance sheet which conforms with the Framework consists of assets, liabilities and equity; there are no other items.

Equity is usually sub-classified into various items, the nature of which often depends on the laws of the country in which the entity is registered and the actions of the entity itself. IASs require certain classifications, particularly for surpluses on the revaluation of long-term assets and deferred foreign exchange differences.

6.8 INCOME STATEMENT ELEMENTS

The Framework identifies two income statement elements – income and expenses. It deals first with the definition of the elements and then with their recognition in the income statement. Some items which meet the definitions may not qualify for recognition in the income statement. Items which do not meet the definitions should not be considered for recognition and should not be included in the income statement.

6.8.1 Income

Income is an increase in economic benefits during the accounting period in the form of inflows or enhancements of assets or decreases of liabilities that result in increases in equity, other than those relating to contributions from equity participants (*Framework*, 70).

The definition of income encompasses:

- revenue arising in the course of the ordinary activities of an entity; and
- gains, including unrealised gains, that may, or may not, arise in the course of the ordinary activities of an entity.

Provided that it meets the recognition criteria, income is usually included in the income statement. However, IFRSs may require or allow certain items that meet the definition of income to be included in equity. For example, revaluation surpluses on property, plant and equipment, all of which meet the definition of income, are included in equity. Some items that meet the definition of income, for example some unrealised gains, are not recognised as either income or equity until some future event occurs, for example the realisation of the underlying asset. Furthermore, under IAS 39, some income (unrealised gains and gains on available-for-sale financial assets and hedging instruments) may be classified as equity until some future event occurs when they are included in the income statement.

6.8.2 Expenses

Expenses are decreases in economic benefits during the accounting period in the form of outflows or depletions of assets or incurrences of liabilities that result in decreases in equity, other than those relating to distributions to equity participants (*Framework*, 70).

The definition encompasses:

- expenses that arise in the course of the ordinary activities of the entity, for example, cost of sales, wages and depreciation; and
- losses that may, or may not, arise in the course of the ordinary activities of the entity.

Provided that they meet the recognition criteria, expenses are usually included in the income statement. However, IFRSs may require or allow certain items that meet the definition of expenses to be included in equity. For example, certain revaluation deficits which meet the definition of expenses are included in equity. Under IAS 39, some expenses (for example, losses on available-for-sale financial assets and hedging instruments) may be classified as equity until some future event occurs when they are included in the income statement. Generally speaking, however, unrealised losses are usually recognised notwithstanding that the underlying asset has not been realised.

6.9 RECOGNITION CRITERIA

An item which meets the definition of an element should be recognised if:

- it is probable that any future economic benefit associated with the item will flow to or from the entity; and
- the item has a cost or value that can be measured with reliability.

(*Framework*, 83)

An item which does not meet the recognition criteria should not be recognised but may warrant disclosure when knowledge of the item is relevant to the evaluation of financial position, performance and cash flows. For example, IAS 37 requires the disclosure of certain unrecognised contingent losses and gains. Entities also often disclose information about intangible assets, such as brands, which do not qualify for recognition as assets.

6.9.1 Probability of Future Economic Benefits

An item should be recognised only if it is probable that any future economic benefits associated with the item will flow to or from the entity. The Framework provides no guidance on the meaning of 'probable'. Some argue that 'probable' means 'more likely than not' but many look to a higher threshold of perhaps 70–80% or even more, particularly in the case of assets and income. Certain IASs do provide more specific guidance. For example, IAS 18 includes three conditions for the recognition of revenue from the sale of goods which determine when it is probable that future economic benefits will flow to the entity. IAS 37 defines 'probable' as 'more likely than not' but warns that this definition does not necessarily apply in the other IASs (IAS 37, 23).

The IASC tried to avoid the use of words or phrases which may or may not have the same meaning as 'probable'. So, for example, IAS 12 uses the term 'probable' in the context of the recognition of tax assets rather than 'reasonable expectation' and 'assurance beyond any reasonable doubt', the phrases which were used in IAS 12 [1979]. This approach not only avoids confusion, it also ensures that the same test is applied for all items and that the need for different tests, when that need arises, is made clear.

6.9.2 Reliable Measurement

An item should be recognised if the item has a cost or value which can be measured with reliability. The notion of reliable measurement is less troublesome than that of probability of future economic benefits. While in many cases, cost or value must be estimated, the circumstances in which a reasonable estimate of cost or value cannot be made are rare.

IFRSs usually require initial recognition at cost. In some cases fair value is used to estimate cost as, for example, in the case of assets held under a finance lease, assets acquired in a business combination and assets exchanged for dissimilar assets. However, IAS 38 does not allow the use of fair value in place of cost for the recognition of intangible assets.

6.10 INTERRELATIONSHIP OF ELEMENTS

An item that meets the definition and recognition criteria for a particular element automatically requires the recognition or the derecognition of another (or the same) element. For example, when an entity receives cash (an asset), it must recognise income, a liability to repay the cash or supply goods or a service, or an equity contribution. Similarly, when an entity incurs expenditure, it must recognise an asset, an expense or an equity distribution. This may sound straightforward, even banal, but the notion has caused one problem – the recognition at a later date of assets which had previously failed the recognition test.

Paragraph 87 of the Framework states that an item which fails to meet the recognition criteria at one point in time 'may qualify for recognition at a later date as a result of subsequent circumstances or events'. In some cases, the later recognition of an asset which previously failed the recognition test is unavoidable. For example, claims under a lawsuit, construction contract or a tax loss carry-forward are assets but may not qualify for recognition when they first arise. However, an asset and income must be recognised on the settlement of the claims or the realisation of the tax saving.

In other cases, the later recognition of an asset which previously failed the recognition test would require the reinstatement, as an asset, of expenditure which had previously been recognised as an expense. For example, the development costs of a project are recognised as expenses when they do not meet the asset recognition criteria in IAS 38. But should this expenditure be reinstated as an asset (with a resulting credit in the income statement) at a later stage when the project is successful and the asset recognition criteria are met? IAS 38 is clear: no (IAS 38, 59). Some argue that this approach contradicts the Framework and that the entity should reinstate the asset; others argue that, once the costs have been recognised, they should not be considered again for recognition.

The IASC attempted to deal with this issue during the improvements project but could not reach agreement on an overall policy. The IASC intended to reconsider this issue but did not do so.

6.11 APPLICATION OF RECOGNITION CRITERIA

6.11.1 Executory Contracts

Obligations under contracts that are equally proportionately unperformed – executory contracts – are generally not recognised as assets and liabilities even though they meet the definition of, and recognition criteria for, assets and liabilities. Therefore, when an entity has placed an irrevocable order for inventory, it is the convention not to recognise either the liability (the obligation to acquire inventory) or the asset (inventory or the right to receive inventory) until, say, delivery has taken place. Similarly, revenue from the sale of goods is often not recognised as income and a receivable until the goods have been delivered to the customer even though the customer has placed an irrevocable order.

The non-recognition of such assets and liabilities is a matter of convention rather than the application of the underlying concepts.

6.11.2 Matching

Expenses are recognised in the income statement on the basis of a direct association between the costs incurred and the earning of specific items of income (*Framework*, 95). This process, commonly referred to as the 'matching of costs with revenues', involves the simultaneous or combined recognition of revenues and expenses that result directly and jointly from the same transactions or other events.

Matching was not a fundamental accounting assumption in IAS 1 [1974] nor was it one of the factors that governed the selection of accounting policies. Nevertheless, it is inherent in the application of the recognition criteria in most IASs. For example, expenses (including warranty and shipment costs) that relate to a particular sale of goods are recognised at the same time as the related revenue (IAS 18, 19). Similarly, current and deferred tax expense is recognised at the same time as the related taxable profit.

The application of the matching concept should not result in the recognition of items in the balance sheet which do not meet the definitions of assets or liabilities (*Framework*, 95). IASs do, however, require the spreading of certain gains and losses in order that they can be matched with associated expenses and income in circumstances which some argue result in the recognition of balance sheet items which do not meet the definitions of an asset or liability. For example:

- IAS 17 requires the deferral of gains on certain sale and leaseback transactions and the matching of the gain with the increased depreciation and interest expense (IAS 17, 52);

- IAS 20 requires that government grants related to assets should be recognised in the income statement over the periods necessary to match them with the related costs which they are intended to compensate (IAS 20, 24); and
- IAS 39 allows the use of hedge accounting because it matches income and expenses (which is usually the substance of the hedging transaction) but hedge accounting can result in balances which do not meet the definitions of assets or liabilities.

6.12 MEASUREMENT

Measurement is the process of determining the monetary amounts at which the elements of the financial statements are recognised and carried in the balance sheet and income statement (*Framework*, 99). The IASC prescribed a particular measurement basis for financial assets and financial liabilities and certain agricultural assets. It is highly unlikely, however, that the IASB will remove the cost/fair value choice for property, plant and equipment (other than, perhaps, for investment properties) or require either a historical cost or current cost approach for inventories.

IASs generally allow the common approach used around the world under which assets are measured on a recoverable historical cost basis such that:

- inventories are measured at the lower of historical cost and net realisable value; and
- property, plant and equipment are measured at the lower of depreciated historical cost and recoverable amount.

IASs also permit an alternative approach under which:

- all financial assets may be measured at fair value; and
- property, plant and equipment and other long-term assets may be measured at fair value.

6.12.1 Measurement of Assets

The following measurement bases for assets are referred to in the Framework or are used in IASs:

- historical cost;
- current cost and replacement cost;
- market value;

- net realisable value;
- recoverable amount;
- present value; and
- fair value.

The historical cost of an asset is the amount of cash or cash equivalents paid or the fair value of the consideration given to acquire it at the time of its acquisition (*Framework*, 100). Historical cost in the case of purchased assets is acquisition cost. Historical cost in the case of finished goods inventories, work in progress, other self-constructed assets and development costs is production cost. Several IASs provide standards or guidance on the determination of historical cost for relevant items.

The current cost of an asset is the amount of cash or cash equivalents that would have to be paid if the same or an equivalent asset was acquired currently (*Framework*, 100). The current costs of inventories, plant and equipment are their current replacement costs. In many cases, current cost is the entry market value.

Market value may be an exit price or an entry price. An exit price is the amount obtainable from the sale of an asset. In this case, market value is the realisable value of a marketable asset and should be determined net of transaction costs which would be incurred in selling the asset. An entry price is the amount payable on the acquisition of an asset in an active market. In this case, market value is the current cost (or replacement cost) of a marketable asset; therefore, transaction costs which would be incurred in acquiring the asset should be included. In practice, transaction costs may not be material and are sometimes ignored in both cases. The IVSC has issued guidance on the determination of market values of property, plant and equipment (see chapter 21).

The realisable value of an asset is the amount of cash or cash equivalents that could currently be obtained by selling the asset in an orderly disposal (*Framework*, 100). This measurement basis is applied as:

- net realisable value in the case of inventories (IAS 2, 4); and
- net selling price in the context of asset impairments (IAS 36).

The recoverable amount of an asset is the higher of an asset's net selling price and its value in use (IAS 36, 5).

The present value of an asset is the present discounted value of the future net cash inflows that the asset is expected to generate in the normal course of business (*Framework*, 100). Therefore, present value is either discounted realisable value or discounted recoverable amount. The present value of a receivable is the discounted value of the future net cash inflows that are expected to be received in settlement of the debt. IAS 36 requires that value in use be determined as the present value of estimated future cash flows expected to arise from the continuing use of an asset and from its disposal at the end of its useful life (IAS 36, 5).

Fair value is used in several IASs where it is defined as the amount for which an asset could be exchanged between knowledgeable willing parties in an arm's length transaction (IAS 16, 7 and IAS 22, 9). It is sometimes used as a means of determining cost, for example when allocating the cost of acquisition to identifiable assets in a business combination. In such a case, fair value is an entry price and current cost, replacement cost or market value (including acquisition transaction costs) are the most appropriate bases to use. Fair value is also used as the upper limit to carrying amount, as in the case of financial assets carried at the lower of amortised cost and fair value. In this case, fair value is an exit price and realisable value or market value (net of selling transaction costs) is the most appropriate basis to use. Fair value is also used as the basis for revalued amounts of property, plant and equipment and financial assets; in this case, market value is suggested by both IAS 16 and IAS 39.

The Framework does not refer to the principle of 'separate valuation' which is required by the EU Fourth Directive (article 31(1)(e)). However, the principle is generally applied in specific IASs, for example:

- IAS 2, IAS 16 and IAS 36 require that write-downs to net realisable value and recoverable amount should be determined on an item by item basis – they allow the grouping of similar or related items but only when they cannot be evaluated separately; and
- IAS 11 and IAS 18 require that profits and losses on construction contracts and other contracts for the rendering of services should be determined on a contract by contract basis.

IAS 39 allows (but does not require) the use of the portfolio method for held-to-maturity investments carried at amortised cost.

6.12.2 Measurement of Liabilities

The following measurement bases for liabilities are referred to in the Framework or are used in IASs:

- historical cost;
- current cost;
- amortised cost;
- settlement value;
- present value; and
- fair value.

The historical cost of a liability is the amount of proceeds received in exchange for the obligation, or in some circumstances (for example, income tax) the amount of cash or cash equivalents expected to be paid to satisfy the liability in the normal course of business (*Framework*, 100).

The current cost of a liability is the undiscounted amount of cash or cash equivalents that would be required to settle the obligations currently (*Framework*, 100).

Amortised cost is cost plus or minus the cumulative amortisation of any difference between the initial amount and the maturity amount (less any impairment write-down (IAS 39, 10)). For example, if an entity receives a loan of 100 but has to repay 110, amortised cost is 100 plus a proportion of the settlement premium.

The settlement value of a liability is the undiscounted amounts of cash or cash equivalents expected to be paid to satisfy the liabilities in the normal course of business (*Framework*, 100).

The present value of a liability is the discounted value of the future net cash outflows that are expected to be required to settle the liability in the normal course of business (*Framework*, 100).

The fair value of a liability is the amount for which the liability could be settled between knowledgeable, willing parties in an arm's length transaction (IAS 32, 5).

In practice, historical cost, current cost and settlement value are usually the same or very similar. Present value is the discounted amount of historical cost, current cost or settlement value. When settlement is deferred the fair value is likely to be a discounted amount.

IASs increasingly require that liabilities should be measured on a discounted basis unless the difference between the nominal amount of the liability and the discounted amount is not material. Therefore, discounting is required for liabilities for retirement benefit costs but it is not required for short term liabilities and is prohibited for deferred tax assets and liabilities (IAS 12, 53).

6.13 CONCEPTS OF CAPITAL AND CAPITAL MAINTENANCE

The Framework identifies two concepts of capital:

- a 'financial' concept of capital, such as invested money or invested purchasing power, under which capital is synonymous with the net assets or equity of the entity; and
- a 'physical' concept of capital, such as operating capability, under which capital is regarded as the productive capacity of the entity based, for example, on units of output per day.

(*Framework*, 102)

The concepts of capital give rise to two concepts of capital maintenance:

- financial capital maintenance, under which a profit is earned only if the financial (or money) amount of the net assets at the end of the period exceeds the financial (or money) amount of net assets at the beginning of the period, after excluding any distributions to, and contributions from, owners during the period; and
- physical capital maintenance, under which a profit is earned only if the physical productive capacity (or operating capability) of the entity (or the resources or funds needed to achieve that capacity) at the end of the period exceeds the physical productive capacity at the beginning of the period, after excluding any distributions to, and contributions from, owners during the period.

Both financial and physical capital maintenance can be measured in either nominal monetary units or units of constant purchasing power.

The physical capital maintenance concept requires the adoption of the current cost basis of measurement. The financial capital maintenance concept does not require the use of a particular basis of measurement.

It was not the IASC's intention to prescribe a particular accounting model other than in exceptional circumstances, such as for those entities reporting in the currency of a hyperinflationary economy for which either financial or physical capital must be based on units of constant purchasing power. IAS 15 required disclosures based either on a financial capital/constant purchase power approach or a physical capital approach but these disclosures are no longer mandatory and the IAS is expected to be withdrawn (see chapter 42). However, in practice a financial concept of capital is adopted by most entities.

6.14 THE IASC'S USE OF THE FRAMEWORK

The definitions of assets, liabilities, income and expenses, together with the recognition criteria, in the Framework played a major part in the work of the IASC. For example:

- the draft statement of principles on intangible assets considered first whether intangible assets were assets as defined in the Framework (*Intangible Assets* 18) and then applied the Framework recognition criteria to those intangible assets that met the asset definition (*Intangible Assets* 32) – this approach was followed through into IAS 38;
- IAS 12 seeks to recognise as assets and liabilities those tax balances that meet the definition of, and recognition criteria for, assets and liabilities;

- one of the principal concerns which led to the IASC project on employee benefit costs was that IAS 19 [1993] generated balance sheet items which may have not met the definition of assets and liabilities in the Framework (*IASC Insight*, December 1994, p16); and
- IAS 1 requires that management should use the qualitative characteristics of relevance and reliability in determining accounting policies for accounting issues not covered by IASs (IAS 1, 20).

Each IAS generally identifies the circumstances in which the Framework definition and the recognition criteria are met. For example, IAS 38 deals with whether internally generated intangible assets meet the definition of an asset (IAS 38, 8–16) and identifies the circumstances in which such costs meet the recognition criteria (IAS 38, 39–40). IAS 18 seeks to determine when certain types of revenue, which meet the Framework definition of income, meet the recognition criteria (IAS 18, objective).

The Framework does not always point to one accounting treatment for any given issue. For example, some have argued that the Framework requires the recognition of development costs as an asset (provided the costs meet all the recognition criteria) while others argued that such costs would never meet the Framework recognition criteria. Such a disagreement did not undermine the Framework or the IASC's use of the Framework; rather it focused the IASC's attention on the issue of what was an asset and when should that asset be recognised, rather than the accounting treatments adopted in particular countries.

The SIC was required to review accounting issues in the context of both existing IASs and the Framework (*SIC Operating Procedures*, 1). Most of the resulting interpretations refer to the Framework. For example, SIC 6 based its conclusion on the costs of modifying computer software on the Framework recognition criteria for liabilities and expenses (SIC 6, 6).

The IASC also used the Framework in discussions with other standard setting bodies. The first IASC conference of standard setting bodies in June 1991 dealt with the objectives and concepts underlying financial statements and considered both a discussion paper by Milburn[5] and the explicit and implicit frameworks used in a number of countries (*IASC Insight*, October 1991, p13). Subsequently, the IASC staff worked with representatives of the standard setting bodies in Australia, Canada, the UK and the USA in the preparation of *Future Events; A Conceptual Study of Their Significance for Recognition and Measurement* which was debated at the IASC conference of standard setting bodies in November 1993 and later published by G4+1.

While the IASC and the SIC used the framework in addressing projects and accounting issues, the Framework did not override the requirements of IASs. In particular, there was no requirement to depart from an IAS in order to comply with the Framework and compliance with the Framework was not necessarily a reason to depart from an IAS in accordance with the revised IAS 1 (see chapter 8). Furthermore, the Framework acknowledges that in a limited number of cases there may be a conflict between the Framework and an IAS or IFRS; in such cases the requirements of the IAS or IFRS prevail over those of the Framework (*Framework*, 3).

Notes

[1] The original article was published in Spanish as 'El Marco Conceptual: La Experiencia Internacional' in Jorge Tua (ed) *El Marco Conceptual para la Información Financiera: Analisis y Comentarios*, Asociación Española de Contabilidad y Administración de Empresas (AECA), Madrid, 2000. An English version of the article is available at www.cairns.co.uk.

[2] Ernst & Young, *The ASB's Framework – Time to Decide*, London, 1996, p4.

[3] Ibid, p1.

[4] Christopher Nobes, *Asset Measurement Bases in UK and International Standards*, ACCA, London, 2001, pp8–9.

[5] J. Alex Milburn, 'Building a Better Conceptual Framework', *CA Magazine*, December 1991, pp43–48.

CHAPTER 7

First-time Application of IFRS

7.1 RELEVANT INTERPRETATION AND EXPOSURE DRAFT

SIC 8 *First-time Application of IAS as the Primary Basis of Accounting*
ED 1 *First-time Application of International Financial Reporting Standards*

7.2 HISTORY

SIC 8 *First-time Application of IAS as the Primary Basis of Accounting* was approved in January 1998 and applied with effect from 1 August 1998. The interpretation was necessary because IAS 1 and IAS 8 did not give explicit guidance on the transition from national GAAP to IAS, a problem which an increasing number of entities were facing.

The EU's decision to require listed companies to issue IFRS consolidated financial statements with effect from 2005 and the growing number of transitional provisions in IFRS created pressure for further guidance. As a result, the IASB added a project to its work programme and issued ED 1 *First-time Application of International Financial Reporting Standards* in July 2002. Like SIC 8, ED 1 proposes retrospective application of IFRS in most areas but unlike SIC 8, ED 1 proposes 'targeted exemptions' from retrospective application and specifies that the transitional provisions in other IFRS do not apply.

The IASB proposes that an IFRS based on ED 1 should be applicable for accounting periods beginning on or after 1 January 2003. It encourages earlier application which means that any entity currently making the transition to IFRS may use the proposed IFRS. Other than in the simplest of cases, the application of ED 1 instead of SIC 8 will be simpler for all entities. As a result, this chapter does not deal in detail with the application of SIC 8.

7.3 SIC 8 IN BRIEF

When an entity applies IFRS in full for the first time, it should present its financial statements as if the IFRS effective for the period of transition had always been applied (SIC 8, 3). In other words, the entity should ignore earlier versions of IFRS and must follow the benchmark treatment for changes in accounting policies (see chapter 13). However, an entity may apply the transitional provisions in IFRS. So, for example, pre-1995 goodwill which had been written off to equity need not be reinstated. However, goodwill written off to equity in 1995 or later under national GAAP must be reinstated and dealt with in accordance with IAS 22 [1998].

Extract 7.1 *First-time application of IAS*

Bayer, Germany, 31 December 1994 (IAS)

The first-time application of the IAS affects the carrying amounts of certain items. The effect on stockholders' equity and income, however, was minimal.

Income and expenses resulting from changes were as follows:

	DM million
Difference between tax and straight-line depreciation of newly capitalized assets	236
Change in valuation method for work in process and finished goods	179
Reversal of special tax items	55
Change in currency translation method	63
Revaluation of pension commitments	(696)
Revaluation of commitments similar to pensions	160
Deferred taxes	33
	30

The change in the currency translation method with effect from 1 January 1994 decreased stockholders' equity of the Group by DM 0.4 billion. The revaluation of pension commitments is recognized in 1994 income.

Extract 7.2 *First-time application of IAS*

Danisco, Denmark, 30 April 1998 (IAS)

Compared with last year, the International Accounting Standards (IAS) have now been incorporated in the group's accounting policies which has led to a change in accounting policies in the following areas:

- Consolidated goodwill and goodwill are capitalised and amortised over expected lifetimes, however at the most 20 years.

- Production overhead is incorporated in the value of stocks.
- Deferred tax is provided for tangible assets.

In addition production is incorporated in the valuation of self-constructed tangible assets, development projects are capitalised under special conditions, the tax base of tax losses carried forward are included in the statement of deferred tax and various linguistic changes have been made to the accounting policies.

After a review of the accounts for the past 20 years comparative figures for previous years have been restated according to the changed accounting policies for consolidated goodwill and goodwill, production overhead have been incorporated in stocks, and deferred tax of fixed assets. Other changes of the accounting policies have not been incorporated in the comparative figures for previous years as the effects are immaterial.

The change of accounting policies is founded on increased international agreement on the application of the IAS for listed undertakings. At the same time the proportion of Danisco shareholders outside Denmark is increasing thus emphasising the need to be able to compare Danisco with foreign undertakings.

7.4 ED 1 IN BRIEF

ED 1 applies when an entity applies IFRS in full for the first time. Subject to certain specific exceptions, the entity should comply retrospectively with each IFRS effective at its balance sheet date. It should not use the transitional provisions in existing IFRS. It should explain how the transition affected its financial position, financial performance and cash flows.

7.5 SCOPE OF APPLICATION OF ED 1

ED 1 applies to an entity's *first IFRS financial statements*. These financial statements are the first annual financial statements in which the entity adopts IFRS as its basis of accounting by an explicit and unreserved statement of compliance with IFRS (ED 1, 2). Therefore, ED 1 does not apply when an entity presented IAS/IFRS financial statements in the previous period even though it may also have published national GAAP financial statements, disclosed compliance with national GAAP as well as IAS/IFRS or the auditors expressed a qualified opinion on those financial statements.

Companies such as Nokia and AECI which have been publishing financial statements that comply with both IAS and national GAAP[1] will not be able to use ED 1. They will be able to use IAS 1, however, if they drop the reference to IAS compliance for one year. For example, Nokia could use ED 1 in its 2003 financial statements if it removes the reference to IFRS compliance from its 2002 financial statements. Indeed, it has been suggested that French companies that used to refer to compliance with IAS have already adopted this tactic.

ED 1 can be applied by entities that have previously disclosed partial compliance with IAS/IFRS. Wienerberger has prepared its consolidated accounts 'in accordance with the principles set forth in IAS and interpretations issued by the SIC' but explains: 'In contrast to IAS, goodwill arising from the acquisition of companies up to December 31, 1996 was charged to reserves in keeping with ... the Seventh EU Directive'[2]. It will be able to use ED 1 and will, in fact, not be required to reinstate the goodwill it has written off to equity.

Similarly, Recordati will be able to use ED 1 notwithstanding that it has presented its financial statements in accordance with IAS except for IAS 12 on deferred taxation. Indeed, all the companies in compliance categories 3 to 11 in the *International Accounting Standards Survey 2000* will be able to use ED 1. It would not be surprising, therefore, if some EU companies that already disclose full compliance with IAS/IFRS find an opportunity to depart from an IAS/IFRS prior to the 2005 deadline in order that their 2005 financial statements become their 'first IFRS financial statements'.

7.6 TRANSITION TO IFRS

The *date of transition to IFRS* is the beginning of the earliest comparative period in an entity's first IFRS financial statements (ED 1, 6(b)). For example, the date of transition for an entity that presents its first IFRS financial statements for the calendar year 2005 and which is required to publish comparative information for one year is the beginning of 2004, that is 1 January 2004 (or, in effect, the end of 2003). If the entity is required to present comparative information for the income statement and cash flow statement for two years (as required by the US SEC), the date of transition is the beginning of 2003.

The date of transition to IFRS is different from the *reporting date* in an entity's first IFRS financial statements. The reporting date is the balance sheet date at the end of the reporting (not comparative) period. For example, the reporting date for an entity that presents its first IFRS financial statements for the calendar year 2005 is 31 December 2005.

The transition to IFRS involves four steps:

- the selection of accounting policies that comply with IFRS;

- the preparation of an opening IFRS balance sheet at the date of transition to IFRS;
- the determination of estimates under IFRS for the opening IFRS balance sheet and other periods presented in an entity's first IFRS financial statements; and
- the presentation and disclosure in an entity's first IFRS financial statements and interim financial reports.

7.7 IFRS ACCOUNTING POLICIES

7.7.1 The basic principles

An entity should use the same accounting policies throughout all periods presented in its first IFRS financial statements and in its opening IFRS balance sheet (ED 1, 7). This is, of course, the same requirement that applies to any IFRS financial statements.

An entity's accounting policies should comply with each IFRS effective at the reporting date for its first IFRS financial statements. Subject to the specific exemptions, the accounting policies should be applied retrospectively (ED 1, 9).

Subject to the specific exemptions in ED 1, an entity should not apply different versions of IFRS that were effective at earlier dates (ED 1, 8) nor apply any transitional provisions in those IFRS (ED 1, 9). So, for example, an entity should not apply the pre-1993 versions of the ten IAS that were revised during the comparability/improvements project. It should also not apply the earlier versions of IAS 10, IAS 12 and IAS 14 nor those IAS that were superseded by the revised IAS 1. It should also not apply the current versions of IAS if the reporting date is after the implementation of the changes proposed by the IASB in its improvements, financial instruments and business combinations exposure drafts.

Example 7.1 *Date of transition and choice of accounting policies*

The reporting date for A's first IFRS financial statements is 31 December 2005. A presents comparative information for one year only. Therefore, its date of transition to IFRS is 1 January 2004.

Continued

Continued

A applies the IFRS effective for periods ending on 31 December 2005 in:

- its opening IFRS balance sheet as at 1 January 2004;
- its balance sheet for 31 December 2005 (including comparative amounts for 2004) and its 2004 and 2005 income statement, statement of changes in equity and cash flow statement; and
- its other disclosures in those financial statements.

A is permitted, but not required, to apply in those financial statements any IFRS which is not yet effective as at 31 December 2005 but which allows early adoption.

Subject to the specific exemptions, an entity should not apply any transitional provisions in the IFRS effective at its reporting date (ED 1, 9). ED 1 prohibits the application of the transitional provisions in IAS 17, IAS 23, IAS 36, IAS 37 and IAS 38 (see also ED 1, IG11-13, 20-24 and 31-41).

The specific exemptions (see below) limit the application of the transitional provisions in IAS 19, IAS 22 and IAS 39. They continue to allow the transitional provision in IAS 21 and create new transitional provisions for IAS 16.

7.7.2 The specific exemptions

ED 1 proposes that an entity should be allowed, but not required, to take advantage of specific and targeted exemptions from retrospective application of the IFRS effective at the reporting date for its first IFRS financial statements (ED 1, 13). An entity must use all the applicable exemptions or none of them (ED 1, 14); it cannot use them selectively although it need not apply those that are not applicable in its particular case.

The exemptions relate to:

- the determination of the cost-based measurements of some assets and liabilities (IAS 16, IAS 22 and IAS 40);
- the use of valuations of assets under previous national GAAP (IAS 16 and IAS 40);
- employee benefits (IAS 19);
- business combinations (IAS 22); and
- accounting measurements reliant on designation by management (IAS 39).

Insofar as the exemptions refer to the use of fair value, an entity should apply the guidance on the determination of fair value in IAS 22 (ED 1, 15) (see chapter 16).

7.7.3 The specific exemptions – property, plant and equipment and investment property

The benchmark treatment in IAS 16 requires that property, plant and equipment should be measured at cost less depreciation and impairment losses. For several reasons, an entity may not be able to determine, without undue cost and effort, the cost of some or all its items of property, plant and equipment. For example, an entity may not have retained the necessary records such as a plant register or it may not be able to determine the amount of borrowing costs that it should, or should not, have capitalised. In such circumstances, the entity should measure such items at the date of transition to IFRS at their fair value and use that fair value as their deemed cost as at that date (ED 1, 16). Two points should be emphasised:

- the use of fair value is a means of determining (deemed) cost – it is not a revaluation that must be kept up to date under the allowed alternative treatment in IAS 16; and
- the entity need not adopt this approach if it can deal with the asset under the other IAS 16 exemption or the exemption for event-driven fair value measurements.

Using its previous national GAAP, an entity may have revalued an item of property, plant and equipment at or before the date of transition to IFRS by applying, for example, a general or specific price index to a cost that is broadly comparable to cost determined under IFRS. Alternatively it may have revalued the items to an amount that is broadly comparable to fair value determined under IFRS. Such revaluations may not comply with the allowed alternative treatment in IAS 16 (see chapter 21) or the requirements in IAS 29 for the transition from a hyperinflationary economy (see chapter 42). In such circumstances an entity may treat the revalued amounts as deemed cost under IFRS at the date of the revaluation (ED 1, 17).

The *International Accounting Standards Survey 2000* points to several instances in which this exemption may apply. For example, PKN ORLEN discloses that it revalued its fixed assets until 1995 by applying indices determined by the Central Statistical Office for individual groups of assets[3]. Several Italian survey companies retain statutory revaluations in their financial statements that refer to compliance with IAS: Algol, Banca Fideuram, Banca Popolare di Verona, Benetton, Compart, Edison, Eni,

Fiat, Italgas, L'Espresso, Montedison, Olivetti, Recordati, Saipem and Tecnost[4]. All these valuations may qualify as deemed costs under ED 1.

This exemption also applies to investment property accounted for under the cost model in IAS 40. The exemption is inappropriate for investment property accounted for using the fair value model.

In some circumstances, the previous revaluations may not be acceptable. For example, an index may have been applied to a cost that is not comparable to cost determined under IFRS. Alternatively, a revaluation may have been made to an amount that is not comparable to fair value determined under IFRS. In such circumstances, the entity must recalculate the carrying amount of the assets in accordance with either the benchmark or allowed alternative treatment in IAS 16 (see chapter 21) or use fair value at the date of transition as deemed cost (ED 1, IG 8).

7.7.4 The specific exemptions – event-driven fair values

Using its previous national GAAP, an entity may have established a deemed cost for some or all of its assets or liabilities at one particular date because of an event such as a privatisation or public offering of its securities. This practice has been common in the countries in transition, for example in China and in east and central Europe. In such circumstances, the entity may use the valuation as a deemed cost (ED 1, 19).

For example, Montedison carries property, plant and equipment affected by industrial and commercial restructuring programmes carried out prior to a 1991 decree at market values carried out by expert appraisers at the time of the restructuring[5]. The market values may qualify as deemed costs on the transition to IFRS.

7.7.5 The specific exemptions – business combinations

Retrospective application of IAS 22 would create three major problems. It would require any entity that has carried out a business combination since 1994 to reconsider whether that combination should be accounted for using the purchase method or the pooling of interests method and, when necessary, restate the accounting for that combination. It would require the reconsideration of the values attributed to the acquired assets and liabilities as at the date of any prior period acquisitions (and, hence, the determination of fair values as at that date). It may require the restatement of goodwill and negative goodwill. The IASB believes that the costs of retrospective application are likely to exceed its benefits (ED 1, BC39).

An entity that takes advantage of the specific exemptions should not, therefore, apply IAS 22 retrospectively to any business combinations that it recognised under previous GAAP before the date of transition to IFRS (ED1, 20). Therefore, for example, the entity does not restate a business combination that was accounted for using the pooling of interests method even if IAS 22/SIC 9 would have required that combination to be accounted for using the purchase method. The ban on retrospective application also has the following consequences:

- the carrying amounts determined previously immediately following the business combination are their deemed costs under IFRS at that date if IFRS require a cost-based measurement of those assets and liabilities; and
- the carrying amount of goodwill in an entity's opening IFRS balance sheet should be its carrying amount under its previous GAAP at the date of transition to IFRS after reclassifying any intangible assets that were recognised but which do not qualify for recognition under IAS 38 (see chapter 23) and after recognising any impairment loss required as at the date of transition by IAS 36 (see chapter 25).

The entity must carry out an impairment test on goodwill as at the date of transition irrespective of whether there are any indicators of impairment (ED 1, 20(b)(ii)).

The entity should not recognise any negative goodwill in its opening IFRS balance sheet (ED 1, B1(e)). This requirement reflects the proposal in the IASB's business combinations exposure draft (see chapter 16).

For those assets and liabilities acquired in a past business combination for which IFRS require a subsequent measurement that is not a cost-based measurement, the entity should restate the asset or liability on that basis. The entity recognises any resulting change in the carrying amount in equity. For example, an entity may need to restate a financial asset or investment property acquired in a past business combination from its deemed cost to fair value as at the date of transition for the purpose of applying the fair value models in IAS 39 or IAS 40. The effect of the restatement is included in equity; the effect of gains or losses subsequent to the date of transition are dealt with in accordance with IAS 39 or IAS 40.

7.7.6 The specific exemptions – employee benefits

IAS 19 includes transitional provisions that deal with the measurement and recognition of a transitional liability on defined benefit plans (see chapter 33). An entity that wishes to take advantage of the specific exemptions on first-time adoption cannot use the transitional provisions in IAS 19. Instead, it must measure and recognise net employee benefit assets or liabilities under defined benefit plans in accordance with IAS 19

(ED 1, 22 and IG 15). It should not defer any actuarial gains or losses (ED 1, 22).

Unlike the approach adopted on the exemptions relating to IAS 16 and IAS 19, this exemption removes an existing transitional provision and requires an entity to comply fully and retrospectively with the IAS immediately on transition. This means that an entity is unable to defer beyond initial adoption any deficit or other actuarial losses that arose prior to initial adoption of IFRS (IAS 19 prohibits the deferral of any surplus or other actuarial gains). In fact, the ED 1 requirement is consistent with the practice already followed by many companies when switching from national GAAP to IAS[6]. For example, MAN adopted IAS for the first time in 1998/99. It prepared an opening balance sheet as at 1 July 1997 in which it recognised a reduction in equity of DM 591 million (about 20%) attributable to the 'revaluation of pension accruals'.

An entity that wishes to take advantage of the transitional provisions in IAS 19 will not be able to use the exemptions for IAS 16 and, in particular, IAS 22. ED 1 requires than an entity must use all or none of the specific exemptions (insofar as they are applicable). Therefore, an entity that wishes to defer a deficit on its retirement benefit plan will be required to restate all its prior period business combinations.

7.7.7 The specific exemptions – foreign currencies

IAS 21 requires an entity to classify as a separate component of equity the cumulative amount of exchange differences arising on the translation of the financial statements of a foreign entity and on hedges of the net investment in that foreign entity (IAS 21, 30 and 19) (see chapter 19). IAS 21 also includes a transitional provision that allows an entity not to identify separately the amount that would have been deferred in prior periods if that amount is not reasonably determinable (IAS 21, 48).

ED 1 retains, but modifies slightly, the IAS 21 transitional provision. If the entity is unable to determine, without undue cost and effort, the amount that would have been deferred as at the date of transition, it should deem that amount to equal the equivalent amount, if any, determined under the entity's previous GAAP (ED 1, 23). Therefore, for example, an entity previously reporting under US GAAP would treat the cumulative amount deferred under US GAAP as the amount deferred under IFRS as at the date of transition. It is important to recognise, however, that this exemption applies only to the cumulative amount of the deferred exchange differences; it does not exempt the entity from restating, if necessary, the translation of financial statements from the requirements of its previous GAAP to those of IAS 21.

7.7.8 The specific exemptions – financial instruments – hedge accounting

IAS 39 requires that hedging relationships must, among other things, be designated, documented and tested for effectiveness. The IASB recognises that an entity is unlikely to have complied with these requirements prior to its adoption of IAS 39 (ED 1, BC56). Therefore, the hedging requirements in IAS 39 should be applied prospectively from the date of transition to IFRS (ED 1, 24). This requirement is intended to be consistent with the transitional provisions in IAS 39 and the related IGC Q&As. It has three consequences:

- if an entity designated a transaction as a hedge under its previous GAAP before the date of transition to IFRS, it should continue to treat that transaction as a hedge and apply the recognition, derecognition and measurement provisions of IAS 39 prospectively from the date of transition to IFRS (IAS 39, 172(b) and ED 1, C3);
- if the entity did not designate a transaction as a hedge under its previous GAAP, it should not designate that transaction as a hedge retrospectively for the purpose of applying IAS 39 (IAS 39, 172(g) and ED 1, C2); and
- if the entity designates a transaction as a hedge as at the date of transition to IFRS and it meets the other criteria in IAS 39, it is eligible for hedge accounting prospectively from that date (ED 1, C2).

The detailed application of these requirements is set out in appendix C of ED 1 and is, of course, conditional on the approval of both ED 1 as an IFRS and the improvements to IAS 39.

7.7.9 Rejected exemptions

During the development of ED 1, the IASB rejected the following exemptions from retrospective application of IFRS:

- the classification of available-for-sale financial assets (IAS 39 and ED 1, BC 54-55);
- the capitalisation of borrowing costs (IAS 23 and ED 1, BC 65 and IG 20-24);
- the recognition of decommissioning and site restoration costs (IAS 37 and ED 1, BC 66-68);
- depreciation (IAS 16 and ED 1, BC 69-70);
- the recognition of intangible assets (IAS 38 and ED 1, BC 72-76); and
- the allocation of finance lease income (IAS 17 and ED 1, BC 77-78 and IG 12).

7.8 OPENING IFRS BALANCE SHEET

An entity should prepare an opening IFRS balance sheet at the date of transition. The opening IFRS balance sheet is the starting point for the subsequent accounting period under IFRS. Subject to the specific exemptions described above, the entity should, in its opening IFRS balance sheet:

- recognise all assets and liabilities whose recognition is required by IFRS;
- not recognise items as assets or liabilities if IFRS do not permit their recognition;
- reclassify items that the entity recognised under previous GAAP as one type of asset, liability or component of equity but that are a different type of asset, liability or component of equity under IFRS; and
- apply IFRS in measuring all recognised assets and liabilities.

The entity should recognise all adjustments directly in equity.

The entity's estimates under IFRS at the date of transition should be consistent with the estimates made for the same date under previous GAAP unless there is objective evidence that those estimates were in error (ED 1, 25). In other words, the only adjustments that should be made on the transition to IFRS are adjustments arising from the change in accounting policies, the correction of errors and estimates that are inappropriate under IFRS. For example, an entity should not adjust the useful lives of property, plant and equipment if the estimates of lives used under the previous GAAP are acceptable under IFRS. It does adjust those useful lives, however, if, for example, they reflect accelerated tax depreciations and they are, as a result, unacceptable for IFRS purposes. Similarly, an entity should not change the assumptions used in determining defined benefit assets and liabilities unless those estimates were in error (ED 1, 16).

An entity may make estimates under IFRS at the date of transition that were not required at that date under previous GAAP. For example, it may be required to make estimates in its opening IFRS balance sheet with respect to provisions or the impairment of financial assets which were not required under its previous GAAP. These estimates should not reflect conditions that arose after the date of transition to IFRS (ED 1, 26 and IG 2). In other words, the entity should prepare its opening IFRS balance sheet in accordance with the requirements of IAS 10 (see chapter 39).

7.9 PRESENTATION AND DISCLOSURE

7.9.1 First IFRS financial statements

In its first IFRS financial statements, an entity should explain how the transition from previous GAAP to IFRS affected its financial position, financial performance and cash flows. The explanation should include:

- reconciliations of equity reported under previous GAAP to equity reported under IFRS for both the date of transition and at the end of the latest period presented under the entity's previous GAAP (these dates may be the same and, therefore, there may only be one reconciliation); and
- a reconciliation of the profit or loss reported under previous GAAP for the latest period in the entity's most recent annual financial statements to profit or loss under IFRS for the same period.

Extract 7.3 *Reconciliation of equity at date of transition*

Volkswagen, Germany, 31 December 2001 (IAS)

	million €
Capital and reserves according to the German Commercial Code as at January 1, 2000	9,811
Capitalization of development costs	3,982
Amended useful lives and depreciation methods in respect of tangible and intangible assets	3,483
Capitalization of overheads in inventories	653
Differing treatment of leasing contracts as lessor	1,962
Differing valuation of financial instruments	897
Effect of deferred taxes	−1,345
Elimination of special items	262
Amended valuation of pension and similar obligations	−633
Amended accounting treatment of provisions	2,022
Classification of minority interests not as part of equity	−197
Other changes	21
Capital and reserves according to IAS as at January 1, 2000	20,918

Author's note: Volkswagen's reconciliation shows the information required by ED but its transition to IAS took place before ED 1 was published and, therefore, does not necessarily reflect the accounting that ED 1 would require or allow.

If the entity recognised or reversed any impairment losses for the first time in preparing its opening IFRS balance sheet and the loss for an individual asset or cash generating unit is material, it should disclose:

- the events or circumstances that led to the recognition or reversals of the loss;
- the amount of the loss;
- the nature of the assets or cash generating unit;
- the reportable segment to which the asset or cash generating unit belongs;
- whether recoverable amount is net selling price or value in use; and
- the basis used to determine net selling price or the discount rate used to determine value in use.

(ED 1, 31(c) and IAS 37, 117)

If the entity recognised or reversed any impairment losses for the first time in preparing its opening IFRS balance sheet and the loss for an individual asset or cash generating unit is not material, it should disclose:

- the main classes of assets affected; and
- the main events and circumstances that led to the losses or reversal.

(ED 1, 31(c) and IAS 37, 118)

If an entity uses fair value as the deemed cost for some items of property, plant and equipment or investment property in its opening IFRS balance sheet (see 7.7.3), it should disclose in its first IFRS financial statements:

- the aggregate amount of those fair values;
- the aggregate adjustment to the carrying amounts reported under previous GAAP; and
- an explanation of why the measurement required by IFRS would have involved undue cost or effort.

(ED 1, 35)

These impairment disclosures are the same as those required by IAS 36 when an impairment loss is recognised or reversed in a period.

7.9.2 Interim reporting

If the entity presents an interim financial report prepared in accordance with IAS 34 for part of the period covered by its first IFRS financial statements and it also presented an interim financial report for the comparable period in the previous financial year, the current interim report should include:

- a reconciliation of equity reported under previous GAAP to equity reported under IFRS for the comparable interim period; and
- a reconciliation of the profit or loss reported under previous GAAP to profit or loss under IFRS for the comparable interim period.

Example 7.2 *Reconciliations in half yearly interim financial reports*

A is required to publish an annual report and an interim report for the first half of the year. Its year end is 31 December. It presents its first IFRS financial statements for 2003. It previously reported under French GAAP. In its interim report for the six months to 30 June 2003, it must publish:

- a reconciliation of equity as at 30 June 2002 reported under French GAAP to equity as at 30 June 2002 reported under IFRS; and
- a reconciliation of the profit or loss for the six months to 30 June 2002 reported under French GAAP to the profit or loss for the same period reported under IFRS.

The entity's first interim financial report under IAS 34 for the part of the period covered by its first IFRS financial statements should also include the reconciliations and the impairment disclosures required for the first annual financial statements.

Neither IAS 34 nor ED 1 require an entity to present an interim financial report in accordance with IAS 34 even if the entity's financial statements disclose compliance with IFRS. Furthermore, the EU IAS regulation (see chapter 4) applies only to annual financial statements; it does not require EU listed companies to publish IFRS interim financial reports. Research by the author also suggests that many entities that currently disclose IAS/IFRS compliance in their annual financial statements do not disclose IAS/IFRS compliance in their interim financial reports[7]. Therefore, an entity can avoid the proposed requirements in ED 1 by not referring to compliance with IFRS in any interim financial reports for the period covered by its first IFRS financial statements.

---

1 David Cairns, *International Accounting Standards Survey 2000*, p144 and 146.
2 ibid, p162.
3 ibid, p163.
4 ibid, p290.
5 ibid, p290.
6 ibid, p328.
7 David Cairns, *International Accounting Standards Survey – 2002 Update*.

CHAPTER 8

Financial Statements

8.1 RELEVANT STANDARD AND INTERPRETATIONS

IAS 1 *Presentation of Financial Statements*
SIC 19 *Reporting Currency – Measurement and Presentation of Financial Statements Under IAS 21 and IAS 29*
SIC 30 *Reporting Currency – Translation from Measurement Currency to Presentation Currency*

8.2 HISTORY

IAS 1 *Disclosure of Accounting Policies* (IAS 1 [1975]) was approved in 1974 and published in 1975. It required the disclosure of all significant accounting policies which had been used in the preparation of the financial statements. It also identified three fundamental accounting assumptions – going concern, consistency and accrual – and three considerations which should govern the selection and application of accounting policies – prudence, substance over form and materiality.

IAS 5 *Information to be Disclosed in Financial Statements* was approved in 1974 and published in 1975. It set out certain minimum disclosures for the balance sheet and income statement but did not propose a particular format for the financial statements.

IAS 13 *Presentation of Current Assets and Current Liabilities* was approved and published in 1977. It required each entity to determine whether or not to present current assets and current liabilities as separate classifications and specified the conventions which should be followed by those which adopted such a classification.

IAS 1 [1975] and IAS 5 were among the first batch of IASs to be reconsidered as part of the IASC's policy to review IASs once they had been in force for five years. The review of IAS 1 [1975] was integrated into the work on the objectives of financial statements (*IASC News*, November

1984, p1) and the combined project was merged into the Framework project in 1986.

In 1985, the IASC decided that substantive changes were not required to IAS 5 (*IASC News*, July 1985, p1). It acknowledged that many of the disclosures required by IAS 5 were, by then, included in other IASs but agreed to retain IAS 5 in order to keep those disclosures not dealt with elsewhere (*IASC News*, July 1985, p3).

A review of IAS 13 was carried out in 1987 but the IASC decided that a revised IAS should not be prepared.

IAS 1 [1975], IAS 5 and IAS 13 were included in the original scope of the improvements project. The IASC staff recognised that there would be considerable benefits in merging the three IASs into one IAS on the presentation of financial statements.

In March 1992, the IASC removed IAS 1 [1975], IAS 5 and IAS 13 from the scope of the improvements project but there was considerable support for the presentation project.

In March 1993, the IASC added the presentation project to its work programme. The project proposal envisaged consideration of various national standards on presentation issues, the EU Fourth Directive, the requirements of securities regulators and the practices adopted by companies. Most importantly, it intended that the project would consider fairly new ideas such as the statement of total recognised gains and losses which had recently been introduced in the United Kingdom.

The DSOP *Presentation of Financial Statements* was published in 1995 and E53 *Presentation of Financial Statements* in July 1996. The final IAS includes one substantive change from E53. Whereas E53 argued forcefully that the requirements of an IAS should not be overridden in order to achieve fair presentation, the revised IAS 1 requires an entity to depart from an IAS when compliance would be misleading (see 8.7). IAS 1 *Presentation of Financial Statements* was approved in 1997 and replaced IAS 1 [1975], IAS 5 and IAS 13 with effect from accounting periods beginning on or after 1 July 1998.

The IASB is proposing several changes to IAS 1 in its May 2002 improvements exposure draft including:

- guidance on the meaning of present fairly and further guidance on the use of the fair presentation override; and
- greater emphasis on the use of the current:non-current distinction in the balance sheet and additional guidance on the classification of long-term financial liabilities.

The IASB has an active project on reporting performance which could have a significant impact on the presentation of financial statements.

8.3 IOSCO

In June 1994, IOSCO advised the IASC that it supported the efforts to improve IAS 1, IAS 5 and IAS 13. IOSCO identified a substantial number of suspense issues in respect of IASs 1, 5 and 13 many of which were taken up in the presentation project or by the SIC. The issues which have not yet been taken up by the IASC or the IASB include:

- recognition and measurement issues for equity, for example stock dividends, stock splits, dividends in kind, increasing rate preference share and treasury stock acquisitions, reissuances and dividends;
- disclosures related to defaults under credit agreements (some aspects of this issue are dealt with in the May 2002 improvements exposure draft);
- the classification of loans payable upon demand with a specified repayment schedule or the need for disclosure in such circumstances (this was dealt with in IAS 13 but the guidance has been deleted in the revised IAS 1);
- the disclosure of reclassifications of prior period financial statement amounts;
- additional required line items such as:
  - the allowance for doubtful accounts;
  - selling, general, and administrative expenses (an optional disclosure under IAS 1);
  - bad debt expense;
  - gains and losses on disposals of assets, businesses, or financial instruments; and
- the classification of stock subscriptions receivable and similar items.

IAS 1 is included in 'IAS 2000' endorsed by IOSCO in May 2000. Among its general issues, IOSCO reports concerns about the appropriateness of overriding the fair presentation override in IAS 1 (see 8.7). Concerns have also been raised about the appropriateness of providing alternative presentations of financial information such as value added statements (it is unclear whether IOSCO members want to require or ban the publication of such information).

IOSCO points out that regulators reserve the right to specify which financial statements should be required, and the form and content of the financial statements (including minimum line items). This could have a significant effect on some IFRS financial statements and could even result in the financial statements no longer complying with IFRS.

Regulators also reserve the right to specify the frequency, period and timeliness of reporting – these issues are not dealt with in IFRSs and are beyond the IASB's powers.

IOSCO indicates that reporting currency and the manner of presentation of convenience translations will be determined by host country regulations. Such regulations may restrict the choice available in IFRSs but it is unlikely that the resulting financial statements would not comply with IFRS (see 8.13).

IOSCO's May 2000 report includes one further general issue and 16 supplemental treatments on IAS 1:

- concern that IAS 10 requires that the financial statements for a subsidiary that had been prepared on a liquidation basis should be restated on a going concern basis in the consolidated financial statements (see 8.9);
- a suggestion that the going concern assumption should be based on at least 12 months from the date of approval (rather than the balance sheet date) of the financial statements;
- an IASB project on the accounting basis to be used when the going concern assumption is not appropriate;
- further guidance on the circumstances in which management is expected to develop accounting policies that reflect the economic substance of events and not merely their legal form (see chapter 13);
- guidance on the recognition of items in equity, including enhanced guidance on disclosures of changes in equity accounts and related recognition and measurement issues (see chapters 11 and 28);
- disclosures related to defaults under credit agreements (this is dealt with in the May 2002 improvements exposure draft);
- guidance on the classification of stock subscriptions receivable;
- presentation guidance on alternative equity structures, for example partnerships, limited liability corporations, etc. (see chapter 28);
- comparative disclosures for the reconciliation of opening and closing balances of tangible and intangible assets (these are not required by IAS 16 and IAS 38);
- concerns about the appropriateness of allowing an entity to choose whether or not to present a classified balance sheet (this is dealt with in the May 2002 improvements exposure draft);
- disclosure of amounts classified as current assets that are not convertible into cash within 12 months;
- disclosure of maturities for each of the next five years and thereafter for interest-bearing liabilities, liabilities under finance leases and amounts due to related parties (IAS 17 and IAS 32 require only some of these disclosures);
- disclosure of gains and losses on investments;
- guidance on stock dividends, dividends in kind, increasing rate preferred stock, contingent warrants, greenmail transactions, forward stock transactions and hedging of an entity's equity;
- disclosure of risks and uncertainties;
- disclosure of the reliability of estimates (the May 2002 improvements exposure draft proposes disclosure of the judgements made by management in applying accounting policies); and

- disclosure of transfers from reserves to retained earnings or to net profit or loss.

8.4 IAS 1 IN BRIEF

The financial statements should include a balance sheet, an income statement, a statement of changes in equity, a cash flow statement, accounting policies and other explanatory notes. They should present fairly the financial position, financial performance and cash flows of an entity. Compliance with IFRSs usually achieves fair presentation but in extremely rare circumstances an entity may need to depart from an IFRS in order to achieve fair presentation. Financial statements should not be described as complying with IFRSs unless they comply with all IFRSs and IASB interpretations.

Financial statements should be prepared on a going concern basis and under the accrual basis using accounting policies which comply with IFRSs. Certain items should be disclosed on the face of the financial statements and other information may be disclosed either on the face of the financial statements or in the notes.

The measurement currency used to prepare the financial statements should reflect the economic substance of the underlying events and circumstances relevant to the entity. The financial statements are usually presented in the measurement currency but may be presented in another currency.

8.5 COMPONENTS OF THE FINANCIAL STATEMENTS

Financial statements consist of:

- a balance sheet;
- an income statement;
- a statement of changes in equity;
- a cash flow statement;
- accounting policies;
- other explanatory notes.

(IAS 1, 7)

The financial statements are usually included in an annual report and should be distinguished from other information in that report (IAS 1, 45). All information which is required by IFRSs should be included in the financial statements otherwise those financial statements do not comply with IFRSs.

An auditor is also required to identify the financial statements which have been subject to that report (ISA 700, 8). The necessary clarity is usually achieved if the audit report refers to specific page numbers in the annual report which are covered by the audit opinion.

IAS 1 encourages entities to present a financial review or commentary on their financial performance, financial position and the uncertainties which they face (IAS 1, 9). Some IASs recommend items which should be included in such a review or commentary, for example IAS 30 and IAS 32. However, financial statements do not include:

- reports by the board of directors or equivalent governing body;
- statements by the chairman or president of the entity; and
- discussion and analysis of the financial statements by management.

(*Framework*, 7)

IAS 1 requires that each component of the financial statements should be clearly identified with the following information prominently displayed and repeated when necessary:

- the name of the reporting entity;
- whether the financial statements cover the individual entity or a group of entities; and
- the balance sheet date and the period covered by the income statement and cash flow statement.

(IAS 1, 46)

IAS 1 also includes detailed requirements about the notes to the financial statements. They should:

- present information about the basis of preparation of the financial statements and the accounting policies;
- disclose the information required by IFRSs; and
- provide additional information which is necessary for a fair presentation.

(IAS 1, 91)

The notes include many of the disclosures required by IASs. As a matter of policy, the IASC has always interpreted 'disclosure' to mean either in the notes or on the face of the individual financial statements. However the IASB sometimes indicates whether disclosures may be made on the face of the financial statements or in the notes.

IAS 1 requires that the notes should be presented in a 'systematic manner' (IAS 1, 92). Each item on the face of the balance sheet, income statement and cash flow statement should be cross-referenced to any related information in the notes (IAS 1, 92). IAS 1 suggests (but does not require) that the notes are presented in the following order:

- the statement of compliance with IFRSs;
- statement of the measurement basis (bases) and accounting policies applied;
- supporting information for items presented on the face of each financial statement in the order in which each line item and each financial statement is presented; and
- other disclosures.

(IAS 1, 94)

8.6 FAIR PRESENTATION

Financial statements should present fairly the financial position, financial performance and cash flows of an entity (IAS 1, 10). While such a requirement had not previously been expressed in any IAS, the need for a fair presentation has always distinguished IASs from those accounting requirements which are designed to minimise taxation liabilities, maximise the protection given to creditors and protect the entity from the glare of public disclosure. Fair presentation has underpinned all IASs and played a major part in many of the IASC's efforts, for example its ban on the use of inventory reserves to smooth profits, its ban on hidden reserves in the financial statements of banks, and its requirements to disclose segment information, related party transactions and the risks associated with financial instruments.

What is new is that IAS 1 now defines fair presentation and requires, in rare circumstances, an entity to depart from an IFRS in order to achieve fair presentation. According to IAS 1, fair presentation is usually:

- the appropriate application of IFRSs, with additional disclosure when necessary (IAS 1, 10);
- the selection and application of accounting policies which comply with IFRSs (IAS 1, 15 and 20);
- when there are no IFRS requirements, the selection and application of accounting policies which provide relevant and reliable information (IAS 1, 15 and 20);
- the presentation of information in a manner which provides relevant, reliable, comparable and understandable information (IAS 1, 15); and
- additional disclosures when the requirements in IFRSs are insufficient to enable users to understand the impact of particular transactions or events on financial position and financial performance.

(IAS 1, 15)

The essence of the definition is that, for those issues covered by IFRSs, compliance with IFRSs, the interpretations of IFRSs issued by SIC/IFRIC and, when necessary, additional disclosure is virtually always essential to a fair presentation in IFRS financial statements. For those issues not covered by an IFRS, fair presentation also requires accounting policies which are based on:

- IFRSs dealing with similar and related issues;
- the framework definitions, recognition and measurement criteria for assets, liabilities, income and expenses; and
- pronouncements of other standard setting bodies and accepted industry practices but only to the extent that these are consistent with IFRSs and the Framework.

(IAS 1, 28)

> ***IASB improvements project***
>
> In its May 2002 exposure draft, the IASB proposes that fair presentation should mean that the financial statements 'represent faithfully the effects of transactions and other events in accordance with the definitions and recognition criteria for assets, liabilities, income and expenses set out in the *Framework*'. The application of IFRSs and SIC/IFRIC interpretations, with additional disclosures when necessary, is presumed to result in financial statements that achieve a fair presentation.

8.7 FAIR PRESENTATION OVERRIDE

IAS 1 treats 'fair presentation' as an overriding concept in the same way that the EU Fourth Directive treats the 'true and fair view' as an overriding concept. This approach differs markedly from the American approach to 'fair presentation' which is defined by reference to generally accepted accounting principles. There is no separate US definition of 'fair presentation' and entities following US GAAP are not allowed to depart from a particular requirement in order to achieve 'fair presentation' (although auditing standards do require a departure in certain very limited circumstances). An analysis of the approach adopted in the Fourth Directive and IAS 1 is provided by Van Hulle[1]. Alexander contrasts the EU/IASC and US approaches in his comments on E53[2].

The IASC has also taken a different approach to 'fair presentation' from the IAPC in its ISA on the audit report[3], which predates the revised IAS 1 by several years. The IAPC adopts the American approach, although there was a determined, but unsuccessful, effort by the United Kingdom's representatives to persuade the IAPC to adopt the same approach which was later adopted by the IASC[4]. The ISA requires an auditor to state whether the financial statements give a true and fair view in accordance with a specified financial reporting framework (for example, IASs) or are presented fairly in accordance with that framework (ISA 700, 17). The IAPC believes that the auditor should indicate the accounting framework in order to advise the reader of the financial statements and audit report of the context in which fairness is expressed (ISA 700, 19).

As 'fair presentation' is an overriding concept, an entity may need to depart from the requirements of a particular IFRS in order to achieve a fair presentation. Therefore IAS 1 acknowledges that, in extremely rare circumstances, compliance with an IFRS may be misleading and that in such circumstances, the entity should depart from that IFRS and adopt a treatment which achieves a fair presentation (IAS 1, 13). Such a departure from an IFRS should be made only when the treatment required by the IFRS is 'clearly inappropriate' and would not give a fair presentation even with the benefit of additional disclosure (IAS 1, 16).

8.7.1 History

The introduction of a 'fair presentation override' represented a major change of policy both from the IASC's earlier thinking and from the proposals published during the presentation project. Nothing similar had appeared in any earlier IASs. Indeed, while 'fair presentation' had underpinned earlier IASs, the IASC was very much of the view that compliance with IASs must mean compliance with all IASs.

The idea of an overriding concept such as fair presentation or a true and fair view was considered briefly during the development of the framework but rejected. The IASC limited itself to explaining that the application of the concepts in the framework and the requirements of IASs 'normally results in financial statements that convey what is generally understood as a true and fair view of, or as presenting fairly, such information' (*Framework* 46)[5]. The IASC's position was acknowledged by Koberg[6] in her research paper for the presentation project. She contrasted the approach taken in the framework with that taken in the EU Fourth Directive and argued that a change in the IASC's approach should be dealt with in the framework rather than in the proposed presentation IAS. Many, including the IASC itself, agreed with her at that time.

The concept of 'fair presentation' was not addressed in the DSOP on presentation of financial statements. It appeared for the first time in E53 but not as an overriding concept. E53 proposed that financial statements should 'present fairly the financial position, performance and cash flows of an entity' (E53, 15), something which was hardly likely to be controversial. E53 proposed to prohibit an entity from departing from the requirements of any IAS in order to give a fair presentation (E53, 15 and 17).

When it issued E53, the IASC acknowledged that an override may be necessary in individual jurisdictions, mainly to overcome less flexible legal requirements, but it could not envisage any circumstances in which compliance with 'the less rigid IAS requirements' could result in misleading financial statements (*IASC Insight*, July 1996, p16). Whatever the merits of the argument, the message was clear. It was also the first time that the IASC had admitted that IASs were 'less rigid' than the EU Fourth Directive.

The IASC also felt that it may be impossible to limit the override to the rare circumstances in which its supporters felt it was necessary (*IASC Insight*, July 1996, p16). It feared that the override might be used to apply IASs selectively and that some entities might, for example, use it to write off goodwill to equity or use the completed contract method for construction contracts, accounting treatments which the IASC had banned in IAS financial statements.

In April 1997, the IASC decided to require an override (*IASC Update*, April 1997, p2) but gave no reason for its change of mind. At that time, the IASC attached two conditions to the use of the override:

- the transaction was of a type which seemed not to have been considered when the IAS was developed; and
- compliance with the IAS would be misleading.

(*IASC Update*, April 1997, p2)

The first condition is not operational as there is no way in which an entity would know what was, and what was not, considered during the development of an IAS. Furthermore, the condition sent the very worrying message that any IAS need not be applied to items which did not exist or were not considered when that IAS was approved.

The first condition was omitted from the final version of the revised IAS 1. Its omission carries an important message. The fact that a particular event or transaction was not considered during the development of an IAS is insufficient grounds for using the override.

8.7.2 Override Conditions

The fair presentation override should be used only if compliance with the IFRS treatment would be misleading and therefore departure from that treatment is necessary to achieve a fair presentation (IAS 1, 13). IAS 1 provides some general guidance on how this requirement should be applied. First, an entity may not depart from an IFRS simply because another treatment also gives a fair presentation (IAS 1, 16). So, for example, an entity cannot use the override to write off goodwill to equity on the grounds that it believes that such a treatment gives a fair presentation. The entity must also show that the IFRS treatment – capitalisation and amortisation – would be misleading.

In reaching its conclusion that compliance with an IFRS treatment would be misleading, the entity also has to consider:

- the objective of the requirement in the IFRS and why that objective is not achieved, or is not relevant, in its particular circumstances; and
- the way in which its circumstances differ from those of other entities which follow the requirement in the IFRS.

(IAS 1, 17)

So, again using the example of goodwill, in order to use the override, an entity must show that capitalisation and amortisation is misleading in its particular case when it is not misleading for other entities.

IAS 1, rightly, does not give any examples of acceptable fair presentation overrides. Examples 8.1 and 8.2 consider cases in which the 'true and fair override' in the EU's Fourth Directive has been used. Example 8.3 considers the case in which an entity does not disclose in its IFRS financial statements some information which is required by an IFRS. In each case, the question which needs to be addressed is whether the IAS 1 'fair presentation override' could be used in the same or similar circumstances.

Example 8.1 *Fair presentation override for individual entity*

In its 2000 financial statements, Spain's electricity company Iberdrola applies the 'true and fair override' in the Fourth Directive (as incorporated in Spanish law) when reporting zero coupon debentures. Under Spanish GAAP, these debentures must be recorded as a liability at repayment value. The difference between repayment value and the amount actually received must be recorded as an asset which is amortised over the life of the debentures.

Iberdrola opts to present the zero coupon debentures at redemption value less unincurred interest from the year end to the date of maturity. Iberdrola believes that the Spanish GAAP approach 'would distort the true and fair view of the financial position' as it would lead to the reporting of liabilities at an amount higher than would have resulted 'had any other traditional financial instruments been used to provide the same financing'. Iberdrola also believes that the resulting asset 'would represent a fictitious asset' since the expenses would not have been incurred or accrued at the balance sheet date. It also argues that 'it is not advisable to present these liabilities at redemption value,

Continued

Continued

since in accordance with international practice these transactions should be recorded at the amounts received plus the accrued interest, and certain clauses and financial ratios which are mandatory in the international financial markets in which Iberdrola operates are based on this practice.'

Imagine a similar case where there is a specific requirement in an IFRS which covers the transaction or event in question and which has been developed through the IASB's due process. Can the 'fair presentation override' in IAS 1 be used to avoid that requirement in the same way that Iberdrola has used the Spanish/EU 'true and fair override' to avoid a specific requirement of Spanish law?

The answer is almost certainly 'no'. The fact that there might be a better treatment elsewhere is not a good enough reason to depart from the requirement in an IFRS. In particular, it is not appropriate to use the IAS 1 'fair presentation override' to adopt, in IFRS financial statements, an accounting treatment favoured by a national standard setting body or international practice when that treatment conflicts with that required by IFRSs.

Example 8.2 *Fair presentation override – national standard setter rejects IAS treatment*

The Fourth Directive and, hence UK company law, requires an entity to provide depreciation on any fixed asset which has a limited useful economic life. Investment properties are fixed assets and they have limited useful lives. The former ASC invoked the 'true and fair override' in order to allow such properties not to be depreciated (SSAP 19, 10 and part 4). In other words, the ASC agreed with the argument that the depreciation of such properties would not give a true and fair view.

Imagine a similar case where there is a specific requirement in an IFRS which covers the transaction or event in question and which has been developed through the IASB's due process but a national standard setting body uses a 'fair presentation' argument to adopt a different treatment. Is it permissible for a national standard setting body (rather than an individual entity) to do this? Is it permissible for entities in the country to adopt the national treatment and still claim compliance with IASs?

Continued

Continued

The answer to the first question is 'yes' but the answer to the second question is undoubtedly 'no'.

The IASB can do nothing to stop national standard setting bodies adopting accounting treatments which conflict with IFRSs or even stop them using a 'fair presentation' argument to justify their approach. However, entities which apply national treatments which conflict with IASs cannot claim compliance with IFRSs simply because their national standard setting bodies used a 'fair presentation' argument to justify those treatments.

Example 8.3 *Fair presentation override – missing IAS disclosures in IAS financial statements*

The Swiss multinational Roche stated that its 1998 consolidated financial statements 'were prepared in accordance with International Accounting Standards' but note 21 to the financial statements stated that certain geographical segment information was missing. Its auditors, Price Waterhouse, were also of the opinion that the financial statements complied with IASs and made no reference to missing segment information.

Could Roche have invoked the 'fair presentation override' to avoid disclosing information required by an IAS? The answer is almost certainly 'no'. In order to invoke the override, Roche would have had to demonstrate that the disclosure of the missing information would have been misleading. It would have had to show why its circumstances differed from those of other entities which disclosed the missing information.

The IASB intends to monitor instances of the 'fair presentation override' and will consider the need for revisions to IFRSs or interpretations (IAS 1, 18). It is also clear that some IOSCO members, particularly the SEC, will block its use. Furthermore, both the Australian accounting standards board and the Australian government have made clear that they will not allow the use of the 'fair presentation override' notwithstanding their commitment to harmonise Australian standards with IFRSs. In Europe, there is greater support for the override as the Fourth Directive includes a similar requirement.

> ***IASB improvements project***
>
> In its May 2002 exposure draft, the IASB proposes to modify the circumstances in which the fair presentation override may be used to those in which compliance with the requirements of an IAS/IFRS or SIC/IFRIC interpretation would be 'so misleading that it would conflict with the objectives of financial statements set out in the *Framework*'.
>
> The IASB also recognises that some jurisdictions may prohibit the departure from the requirements of any IAS/IFRS or SIC/IFRIC interpretation including those that are misleading. In such circumstances, the entity should, to the maximum extent possible, reduce the perceived misleading aspects of compliance by disclosing the adjustments to each item in the financial statements that would have to be made to achieve a fair presentation.

8.7.3 Override Disclosures

In the very rare circumstances in which an entity can justify the use of the 'fair presentation override', it should disclose the following information:

- that the financial statements fairly present the entity's financial position, financial performance and cash flows;
- that it has complied in all material respects with IFRSs except that it has departed from an IFRS in order to achieve a fair presentation;
- the IFRS from which it has departed and the nature of the departure;
- the treatment required by the IFRS and the reason why that treatment would be misleading;
- the treatment adopted; and
- the impact of the departure on net profit or loss, assets, liabilities, equity and cash flows for each period presented.

(IAS 1, 13)

The important and onerous parts of this requirement are the reason why the IFRS treatment would be misleading and the disclosure of the financial impact of the departure from that requirement. If an entity fails to meet these two requirements, its financial statements do not comply with IFRSs.

8.8 COMPLIANCE WITH IFRSs

Over the years, the IASC made strenuous efforts to encourage entities to disclose, when appropriate, that their financial statements comply with IASs[7]. Furthermore, one of the commitments made by the accountancy bodies to the IASC was to use their best endeavours to ensure that such disclosures were made (*IASC/IFAC Mutual Commitments*, 7). IAS 1 now requires that when financial statements comply with IFRSs, the entity should disclose that fact (IAS 1, 11). There is, of course, no sanction against an entity which does not comply with this requirement.

A much more significant new requirement is that financial statements should not be described as complying with IFRSs unless they comply with all the requirements of each IFRS and each interpretation issued by the IASB (IAS 1, 11). Some regulators will accept IFRS financial statements only on this basis. For example, Georges Barthes, the then president of the French standard setting body and a former chairman of the IASC, warned that French companies which wanted to present IAS, rather than French GAAP, consolidated financial statements must comply with the 'totality of IASs' and must not go 'standards shopping' (*FT World Accounting Report*, April 1998, p6). The SEC also requires either changes to financial statements or the removal of the reference to compliance with IFRSs when only certain IFRSs have been applied or certain information required by IFRSs has been omitted without explanation[9].

This new requirement is aimed primarily at those entities which issue financial statements which purport to comply with IFRSs but which:

- reveal that some aspects of IFRSs have not been complied with;
- fail to give certain information without any explanation; or
- adopt accounting policies which conflict with IFRSs.

The IASC's new requirement was also a warning to auditors, including international firms, who had sometimes failed to give the qualified or adverse opinions required by ISAs in cases of non-compliance with some IASs in IAS financial statements.

The IASB intends that its requirement should stop all abuses but IAS 1 may not achieve this aim. In particular, it does not deal adequately with all the different ways in which entities currently refer to compliance with IASs[8]. The new requirement deals well with those entities which issue financial statements which purport to comply with IASs but then fail to comply fully with IASs. It is less successful in dealing with those entities which currently:

- state that their financial statements are prepared in accordance with IASs but with specified exceptions;

- state that their accounting policies (rather than their financial statements) are 'based on IASs' or 'comply with IAS accounting principles'; and
- use IASs only when there are no equivalent national standards.

The *International Accounting Standards Survey 2000* shows that many companies continue to adopt such approaches. The Survey identifies 16 companies that disclose compliance with IAS with exceptions specified in the accounting policies or notes. Eight companies disclose that their accounting policies or valuation methods comply with, or are based on, IAS but four of the eight specify exceptions from full compliance. There are 12 Italian companies in the Survey that use IASs only in the absence of national standards while ING uses IASs only when possible. None of these approaches should be possible under IAS 1 although none of the companies are, of course, claiming that their financial statements comply with all IASs.

8.9 GOING CONCERN

Management is required to make an assessment of the entity's ability to continue as a going concern (IAS 1, 23). In making this assessment, management takes into account:

- all available information for the foreseeable future, that is, at least 12 months from the balance sheet date (IAS 1, 24);
- the financial history of the entity and its access to financial resources (IAS 1, 24);
- events occurring after the balance sheet date and prior to the authorisation of the financial statements (IAS 10, 13).

Examples of events occurring after the balance sheet date but before the authorisation of the financial statements which may help decide whether the going concern basis is appropriate include:

- a deterioration in operating results and financial position – this may indicate that the entity is unable to continue as a going concern even though it might have appeared to be a going concern at the balance sheet date;
- an improvement in operating results and financial position – this may indicate that the entity is able to continue as a going concern notwithstanding uncertainties which existed at the balance sheet date; and
- a business combination after the balance sheet date – this may indicate that the entity is able to continue as a going concern notwith-

standing uncertainties which existed at the balance sheet date (IAS 22, 78).

The financial statements should be prepared on the going concern basis unless management intends to liquidate the entity or cease trading, or has no alternative but to do so (IAS 1, 23). The going concern basis assumes that an entity is a going concern and will continue in operation for the foreseeable future and has, therefore, neither the intention nor the need to liquidate or curtail its operations (*Framework*, 23). As a result, the financial statements are prepared on the assumption that the entity will recover its assets and settle its liabilities under the normal terms of its operations.

When management intends to liquidate the entity or cease trading, or has no realistic alternative but to do so, IAS 1 appears to allow the use of either the going concern basis or some other basis. However, IAS 10 requires that the going concern basis should not be used when management makes its determination after the balance sheet date and before the approval of the financial statements for issuance (IAS 10, 13). In IAS 10, but not IAS 1, the IASC argues that, if the going concern assumption is no longer appropriate, the effect is so pervasive that there should be a fundamental change in the basis of accounting.

When there is significant doubt about the ability of an entity to continue as a going concern, in practice it is usual to continue to prepare the financial statements on the going concern basis. It would be unusual to change the basis until management intends to liquidate the entity or cease trading or has no realistic alternative but to do so. However, the uncertainties which cast significant doubt on the entity's ability to remain a going concern should be disclosed (IAS 1, 23). Furthermore, the doubt may indicate that assets are impaired and, therefore, that the entity should estimate the recoverable amount of those assets (IAS 36, 8 – see chapter 25).

When the financial statements are not prepared on a going concern basis, that fact should be disclosed, together with the basis on which the financial statements are prepared and the reason why the entity is not considered to be a going concern (IAS 1, 23). IFRSs provide no guidance on what other basis should be used. Many countries have special accounting requirements which must be followed in such circumstances. It is often necessary for the entity to write down all assets to the amounts which will be recovered through a forced sale and to recognise those additional liabilities which crystallise only on the cessation of trading.

In some cases, there may be significant doubt about the ability of part of an entity to continue as a going concern or management may intend to liquidate part of the entity or cease trading in part of the entity or has no realistic alternative but to do so. The IASC believed that a single set of financial statements should not mix information prepared on a going concern basis with information prepared on a different basis (E63, p6). Therefore, the financial statements of the whole entity should be prepared on a going concern basis notwithstanding that the use of the basis is inappropriate for part of the entity. However, significant doubt about the ability of part of the entity to continue as a going concern may indicate that assets are impaired and, therefore, that the entity should estimate the recoverable amount of those assets (IAS 36, 8 – see chapter 25). Similarly, a decision by management to liquidate part of the entity or to cease trading in part of the entity may also indicate that assets are impaired and that the recoverable amount of those assets should be estimated. In both cases, the application of IAS 36 may result in the recognition of impairment losses.

A decision by management to liquidate part of the entity or to cease trading in part of the entity is a restructuring as defined in IAS 37 (see chapter 27). If the decision constitutes a 'detailed formal plan' and that plan has been announced prior to the balance sheet date, the entity makes the provisions required by IAS 37. If the decision is taken after the balance sheet date – which would be the case if the events which indicate that the going concern basis is not appropriate occurred after the balance sheet date – IAS 37 prohibits the recognition of any related provisions.

A decision by management to liquidate part of the entity or to cease trading in part of the entity is also a discontinuing operation provided that the part of the entity is a separate major line of business or geographical area of operations and can be distinguished operationally (IAS 35, 2). Therefore, IAS 35 may require the separate classification of the relevant part of the entity (see chapter 37). IAS 35 also requires the use of the same recognition and measurement principles as for continuing operations (IAS 35, 17).

Following the adoption of the revised IAS 1, the IAPC reconsidered ISA 570 *Going Concern*. The revised ISA was prepared in consultation with the IASC and includes links to the standards and guidance in IAS 1[10].

8.10 ACCRUAL BASIS

Financial statements should be prepared under the accrual basis, that is, the effects of transactions and other events are recognised as they occur (and not as cash or cash equivalents are paid or received) and they are reported in the periods to which they relate (IAS 1, 25 and *Framework* 23). The accrual basis does not, of course, apply to the cash flow statement which is prepared under the cash basis. All IFRSs, except IAS 7, follow the accrual basis.

It is hard to imagine that financial statements which depart from the accrual basis would purport to, or could, conform with IFRSs.

8.11 CONSISTENCY

IAS 1 [1975] identified consistency as one of the fundamental accounting assumptions. It defined this assumption in the following way: 'It is assumed that accounting policies are consistent from one period to another' (IAS 1 [1975], 4). The Framework goes further. It suggests that the measurement and display of the financial effect of like transactions and other events must be carried out in a consistent way throughout an entity and over time for that entity (*Framework*, 39).

IAS 1 deals only with the consistency of the presentation and classification of items in the financial statements, not with the use of consistent accounting policies nor the consistent application of those policies. However, IAS 8 states that the same accounting policies are normally adopted in each period in order to help users compare the financial statements of an entity over a period of time and to identify trends in its financial position, performance and cash flows (IAS 8, 41). Furthermore, when an IAS allows the use of more than one accounting policy, an entity should choose and apply consistently one of those policies unless the IAS or an interpretation allows otherwise (SIC 18, 3). IAS 8 allows an entity to change its accounting policies but only when required by statute, a standard setting body or if the change would result in a more appropriate presentations of events and transactions (IAS 8, 42).

In its comments on E53, IOSCO emphasised the importance of consistent application of accounting policies, as well as the use of the same accounting policies. This point is dealt with in some IFRSs. For example, IAS 30 requires the management of a bank to apply its assessments of loan losses in a consistent manner from period to period (IAS 30, 45).

IOSCO's suggestion to deal more generally with the issue of consistent application was not taken up in IAS 1. It is an important point, possibly more important than the use of the same accounting policies, as changes in the application of policies can have a material effect on reported performance and financial position. Inconsistent application of accounting policies from period to period may also impair fair presentation. Therefore, it is strongly recommended that entities apply their accounting policies consistently from period to period and appropriate disclosure is made when changes in application are necessary.

> ***IASB improvements project***
>
> In its May 2002 exposure draft, the IASB proposes to amend IAS 8 to require the consistent application of accounting policies for similar transactions, similar events and other circumstances. It also proposes to incorporate the requirements of SIC 18 into IAS 8.

8.12 MATERIALITY

Each material item should be presented separately in the financial statements (IAS 1, 29). Information is material if its non-disclosure could influence the economic decisions of users taken on the basis of the financial statements (*Framework* 30 and IAS 1, 30).

Materiality depends on the size and nature of the item judged in the particular circumstances of its omission. For example, a related party transaction or the profitability of a segment are material by their nature notwithstanding that they may be small in amount when compared with, say, total revenues, profits, assets or equity. Some operating expenses may be unusually large and so warrant disclosure in order to explain the performance of an entity, or some expenses or income may be unusual in nature, rather than size, and so warrant disclosure (see IAS 8, 16).

Immaterial amounts should be aggregated with amounts of a similar nature or function and need not be presented separately (IAS 1, 29). This requirement may help to discourage excessive detail in some financial statements although the detail often reflects national requirements or even IFRSs.

8.13 PRESENTATION CURRENCY

IFRSs do not specify the currency in which an entity should present its financial statements. Virtually all entities use the currency of the country in which they are domiciled and many are required to do so by national laws.

SIC 19 acknowledges three related issues:

- the currency used to measure items in the financial statements (the measurement currency);
- the currency used to present the financial statements (presentation currency); and
- (if required) the translation of the financial statements from the measurement currency to the presentation currency.

(SIC 19, 3)

The measurement currency should provide information about the entity that is useful and reflects the economic substance of the underlying events and circumstances relevant to the entity (SIC 19, 5). It may be a currency that is used to a significant extent in, or has a significant impact on, the entity. This interpretation often allows a choice of several different currencies. As a result, the IASB is proposing further clarifications in its May 2002 improvements exposure draft. As well as changing the terminology from measurement currency to functional currency, the draft proposes that the currency should be 'the currency of the primary economic environment in which the entity operates'. The conversion of foreign currency transactions into measurement/functional currency and the translation of the foreign currency financial statements of subsidiaries, associates and joint ventures are dealt with in chapter 19.

Extract 8.1 *Non-domestic measurement currency*

Serono, Switzerland, 31 December 2001 (IAS)

In view of the international nature of the company's activities and due to the fact that more of the company's revenues are denominated in US dollars than in any other single currency, the consolidated financial statements are reported in that currency.

Author's note – the accounting policy on foreign currencies makes clear that Serono uses the US dollar as its measurement currency.

The presentation currency is usually the same as the measurement currency. When a different currency is used, as in the case of convenience translations, the translation of the financial statements from measurement to presentation currency should not change the manner in which items are reported (SIC 19, 9). In practice this means that the same method is used as for the translation of the foreign currency financial statements of a foreign entity into the measurement/functional currency of the parent (see chapter 19).

Extract 8.2 *Presentation currency differs from measurement currency*

FLV Fund, Belgium, 31 December 2001 (IAS)

As from the incorporation of the Fund until 31 December 1999 the functional currency of the Fund was the Belgian franc. During 1997, FLV Fund's major venture capital investments were made in Belgian francs. During 1998 and 1999 FLV Fund's major venture capital investments were made in Belgian francs and USD.

As from 1 January 2000 the functional currency of the Fund is the Euro-currency ('EUR'), in anticipation of a mandatory change to the EUR as of 2001. As the conversion from Belgian francs to the EUR occurs at a fixed rate of BEF 40.3399 for one EUR, the change in functional currency does not give rise to any currency gain or loss in the current or prior periods. During 2000, the majority of the Fund's investments were made in EUR or USD. For reporting purposes FLV Fund has chosen to present its financial information in USD. This is justified by the markets in which the Fund operates and by the currency used for the IPO and SPO of new shares on EASDAQ in July of 1998 and June of 2000.

The income statement and balance sheet of FLV Fund are translated into USD using the current rate method. Under the current rate method, the assets and liabilities of FLV Fund are translated at exchange rates in effect at the end of the period, and revenues and expenses are translated at the average exchange rates during each quarter. Resulting exchange differences are recorded directly in equity, in the foreign currency translation reserve.

Cash flows are translated into USD at the average exchange rates during each quarter.

Extract 8.3 *Presentation currency differs from measurement currency – convenience translation*

Matáv, Hungary, 31 December 2001 (IAS)

The consolidated financial statements are shown in millions of Hungarian Forints ('HUF'). For the convenience of the reader, the consolidated balance sheet, income statement and cash-flow statement for the year 2001 are also presented in millions of US dollars ('USD') translated at a rate of HUF 279.03 to USD 1.00 (the official rate of the National Bank of Hungary at 31 December 2001).

Entities operating in highly inflationary economies often report in a stable currency rather than the currency of their domicile (this precludes the necessity to make the restatements required by IAS 29). The same rules apply to such entities as other entities. An entity that operates in a hyperinflationary economy may use a stable currency as its measurement currency only if that currency meets the criteria in SIC 19, which is unlikely. If it uses its domestic currency as its measurement currency, it must restate its financial statements in accordance with IAS 29 (see chapter 42). If it uses its domestic currency as its measurement currency and a stable currency as its presentation currency, it must restate its financial statements in accordance with IAS 29 before translating them into the stable currency.

When an entity uses a reporting currency which is different from that of its country of domicile, it should disclose the reason for doing so (IAS 21, 43). It should also disclose the reason for any change in the reporting currency (IAS 21, 43).

IOSCO has advised the IASC that the determination of the reporting currency would remain subject to the regulations of a foreign country in which an entity wanted to offer or list its securities. In May 2000, IOSCO indicated that its members may determine the reporting currency of the financial statements and the manner of presentation of convenience translations (IOSCO, 2000, p21). So, for example, the SEC will determine any regulations about the measurement and presentation currencies of foreign companies offering or listing their securities in the United States even when those companies prepare their primary financial statements in accordance with IFRSs.

An entity should disclose its presentation currency and the level of precision used in the presentation of the figures (000s, million, billion, etc) (IAS 1, 46). Care is needed to avoid ambiguity particularly on notes which deal with fair values or with such sensitive issues as related party transactions.

8.14 COMPARATIVE INFORMATION

The Framework emphasises the importance of 'corresponding information' in helping users of the financial statements compare financial position, performance and changes in financial position over time (*Framework*, 42).

IAS 1 draws a distinction between 'numerical information' and 'narrative and descriptive information'. It requires that the financial statements should show 'comparative information' for the preceding period for all numerical information unless an IFRS permits or requires otherwise (IAS 1, 38). IFRSs currently permit few exceptions although the IASC made exceptions for:

- the reconciliation of the carrying amount of property, plant and equipment (see IAS 16, 60(e));
- movements in provisions (IAS 37, 84); and
- many of the disclosures relating to intangible assets (IAS 38, 107).

The numerical comparative information is usually the same as that reported in the prior period. It differs in the following circumstances:

- when the prior period is restated for a change in accounting policy dealt with in accordance with the benchmark treatment in IAS 8;
- when the prior period is restated for the correction of a fundamental error in accordance with the benchmark treatment in IAS 8;
- when the financial statements of the prior period have been reclassified to reflect a change in operations or a more appropriate presentation (see IAS 1, 27); and
- for discontinuing operations for which the initial disclosure event occurred after the approval of the prior period's financial statements (see IAS 35, 45 and chapter 37).

IAS 1 requires that narrative and descriptive information in the previous period's financial statements should be included in the comparative information 'when it is relevant to an understanding of the current period's financial statements' (IAS 1, 38).

When the information which was included in the previous period's financial statements has been superseded by new information, it seems appropriate that the disclosures should focus on the position at the current balance sheet date and the change in the period. For example, in the case of a legal dispute which existed at the previous balance sheet date and still exists at the current balance sheet date, it is usually sufficient to disclose:

- the financial effect of the dispute, the uncertainties relating to the amount and timing and the possibility of reimbursement as at the current balance sheet date;
- an indication that this dispute existed at the previous balance sheet date; and
- a description of the developments, if any, during the period.

Similarly, if a dispute is resolved during the period, the disclosures should concentrate on the outcome of the dispute rather than repeat the obsolete information from the prior period.

While IAS 1 requires the disclosure of the corresponding figures and narrative and descriptive information for the preceding period, it is the practice in some countries to publish figures and information for two prior periods, at least for the income statement and the cash flow statement. IFRSs do not require more than one period. Some IOSCO members may require more than one period.

When an entity changes its balance sheet date, it should disclose the period covered by the financial statements and the fact that the comparative amounts for the income statement, changes in equity, cash flows and related notes are not comparable (IAS 1, 49). Rather than disclosing the fact of non-comparability, it is usually simpler, and more helpful to readers of the financial statements, to disclose the lengths of the current period and the prior period.

Notes

1 Karel Van Hulle, 'The true and fair override in the European Union Directives', *European Accounting Review*, Vol 6 No. 4, 1997, pp711–720.

2 David Alexander, *E53 Comment Letters*, IASC, London, pp400–429.

3 *The Auditor's Report on Financial Statements* (ISA 700), International Federation of Accountants, New York.

4 Graham Stacy, 'True and fair view: a UK auditor's perspective', *European Accounting Review*, Vol 6 No. 4, pp707–8.

5 This paragraph in the Framework is frequently misquoted as saying (or implying) that the Framework requires a true and fair view or fair presentation. This was not the intention and it is not the case.

[6] Ann-Kristin Koberg, *Principles for the Preparation and Presentation of Financial Statements*, 1994 (unpublished).
[7] See, for example, John Kirkpatrick, 'The Case for Visible Conformity', *Accountancy*, January 1987, pp17–18.
[8] For a full description of the approaches to IAS compliance adopted by different companies, see David Cairns, *International Accounting Standards Survey 2000*, 2001, pp153–184.
[9] See, for example, Donald J Gannon, 'Compliance with International Accounting Standards', speech to 1998 AICPA national conference on current SEC developments (www.sec.gov).
[10] *Going Concern*, IAPC,1999.

CHAPTER 9

Balance Sheet

9.1 RELEVANT STANDARD

IAS 1 *Presentation of Financial Statements*

9.2 HISTORY

IAS 1 replaced IAS 5 *Information to be Disclosed in Financial Statements* and IAS 13 *Presentation of Current Assets and Current Liabilities* with effect for accounting periods beginning on or after 1 July 1998. The history of these IASs and the development of the revised IAS 1 are dealt with in chapter 8.

In its May 2002 improvements exposure draft, the IASB proposes several changes to IAS 1 including greater emphasis on the use of the current:non-current distinction in the balance sheet and additional guidance on the classification of long-term financial liabilities.

9.3 IOSCO

In June 1994, IOSCO advised the IASC that it supported the efforts to improve IAS 5, IAS 13 and related IASs. It identified a number of suspense issues on the presentation of the balance sheet which are described in chapter 8.

IAS 1 is included in 'IAS 2000' endorsed by IOSCO in May 2000. There are five supplemental treatments relating to the presentation of the balance sheet:

- guidance on the classification of stock subscriptions receivable;
- guidance on the presentation of alternative equity structures, for example partnerships and limited liability corporations;

- concerns about the appropriateness of allowing an entity to choose whether or not to present a classified balance sheet (this is dealt with in the May 2002 improvements exposure draft);
- disclosure of amounts classified as current assets that are not convertible into cash within 12 months; and
- disclosure of maturities for each of the next five years and thereafter for interest-bearing liabilities, liabilities under finance leases and amounts due to related parties (IAS 17 and IAS 32 require only some of these disclosures).

9.4 CONTENT AND FORMAT OF THE BALANCE SHEET

The balance sheet presents information about the financial position of the entity, including the economic resources which it controls, its financial structure and information about the liquidity and solvency of the entity (*Framework* 16). The elements – or broad classes of the financial effects of transactions and events – which relate to the measurement of financial position are assets, liabilities and equity (*Framework* 49).

IFRSs may currently allow some items which do not meet the definitions of an asset or a liability and which are not shown as part of equity to be included on the balance sheet (*Framework* 52). For example, some argue that the items of deferred income arising from the application of IAS 20 are not liabilities. Conversely there are some items which may meet the definitions of assets and liabilities but which are not recognised on the balance sheet because they do not meet the criteria for recognition, for example, some intangible assets and provisions.

The IASC was always reluctant to prescribe the format or layout of the balance sheet. That reluctance was evident throughout the presentation project but there was some support for more prescription, perhaps along the lines of the EU Fourth Directive. The eventual compromise took the form of what some described as 'mandatory flexible formats' and what IAS 1 refers to as 'structured presentation'. In other words, the requirements of IAS 1 combine compulsion and flexibility.

As a minimum the balance sheet should include the following line items:

- property, plant and equipment;
- intangible assets;
- financial assets (excluding investments accounted for using the equity method, receivables and cash and cash equivalents);
- investments accounted for using the equity method;
- inventories;
- trade and other receivables;

- cash and cash equivalents;
- trade and other payables;
- tax liabilities and assets;
- provisions;
- non-current interest-bearing liabilities;
- minority interest; and
- issued capital and reserves.

(IAS 1, 66)

> ***IASB improvements project***
>
> In its May 2002 improvements exposure draft, the IASB proposes to add the following line items to the balance sheet: investment property; biological assets; financial liabilities (instead of non-current interest bearing liabilities).

Additional line items should be presented when required by another IFRS or when necessary to present fairly the entity's financial position (IAS 1, 67). Furthermore:

- additional headings and sub-totals should be presented when necessary to present fairly the entity's financial position (IAS 1, 67) – however, IAS 1 does not specify any headings or sub totals;
- the items need not be presented in any particular order or format (IAS 1, 68) and their sequence may be amended to suit the nature of the entity and its transactions (IAS 1, 68(b));
- the descriptions of items may be amended to suit the nature of the entity and its transactions (IAS 1, 68(b));
- the line items need not be limited to items falling within the scope of other IFRSs (IAS 1, 69) (see below); and
- when different measurement bases are used for different classes of the same assets, each class should be presented as a separate line item (IAS 1, 71) (see below).

The guidance that line items need not be limited to items falling within the scope of other IFRSs stems from the IASC's reluctance to prescribe a format. It undermines the IASC's earlier efforts, particularly in the improvements project, to ensure that terms are used consistently in different IASs. In its May 2002 improvements exposure draft, the IASB proposes to delete this guidance.

It is recommended, therefore, that each line item should be limited to those items which meet the IFRS definition of that item and which are accounted for in accordance with the relevant IFRS. For example, the line item, property, plant and equipment should be limited to items which meet the IAS 16 definition of property, plant and equipment and which are accounted for in accordance with IAS 16. When items meet more than one definition, the accounting treatment adopted determines the classification.

Some items may have to be split over a number of balance sheet line items. For example, the components of cash and cash equivalents often need to be classified separately. Cash and bank balances should be classified and described as such. Financial assets, which are treated as cash equivalents, should be classified as either cash equivalents or financial assets. Bank overdrafts should be classified as liabilities.

Practical problems may also arise from the requirement that an entity should present as separate line items different classes of the same assets (but not liabilities) when different measurement bases are used for each class. The Framework identifies at least four measurement bases which are employed to different degrees and in varying combinations: historical cost; current cost; realisable or settlement value; present value (*Framework*, 100). The application of the IAS 1 requirement would mean there could be four separate line items for property, plant and equipment: cost less depreciation, fair value less subsequent depreciation, value in use and net selling price. There would be two separate line items for inventories: cost and net realisable value.

IAS 1 justifies the separate classification on the grounds that the nature or function of the assets in each class may differ (IAS 1, 71). This is often not the case. It is usually accounting standards which determine the choice of measurement basis. Furthermore, in those countries which allow a mix of historical cost and fair value based measurements, the analysis is usually given in the notes rather than by adding line items to the balance sheet.

How should an entity deal with these problems? It is suggested that the disclosures are made in the notes rather than as separate line items.

In addition to the minimum items, an entity should also disclose further sub-classifications of the line items based on the 'nature' of the items (IAS 1, 72); these disclosures may be made either on the face of the balance sheet or in the notes. The supporting guidance in IAS 1 suggests that the sub-classifications are based on the requirements of IFRSs and the 'size, nature and function of the amounts involved' (IAS 1, 73).

9.5 CURRENT ASSETS AND CURRENT LIABILITIES

An entity should determine, based on the nature of its operations, whether or not to present current and non-current assets and current and non-current liabilities as separate classifications on the face of the balance sheet (IAS 1, 53).

IAS 1 argues that the separate classification of current and non-current items is useful if the entity supplies goods or services 'within a clearly defined operating cycle' (IAS 1, 55). The operating cycle is the time between the acquisition of materials entering into a process and their realisation in cash or an instrument which is readily convertible into cash. Therefore, all manufacturing and trading and most service entities should make such a distinction. Banks and similar financial institutions do not present current and non-current items separately because most of their assets and liabilities can be settled in the near future (IAS 30, 20 – see chapter 43).

When an entity does not classify current and non-current items separately, assets and liabilities should be presented broadly in order of their liquidity (IAS 1, 53). This is the same approach as that which currently applies to banks and similar financial institutions (IAS 30, 18).

IASB improvements project

In its May 2002 improvements exposure draft, the IASB proposes to require that an entity should present current and non-current assets and current and non-current liabilities as separate classifications except when a liquidity presentation provides more relevant and reliable information. As a result, an entity that supplies goods and services within a clearly defined operating cycle will always adopt a current:non-current, rather than a liquidity, presentation.

9.5.1 Current:Non-Current Distinction

IAS 13 referred to two alternative approaches to the current:non-current distinction:

- a *liquidity approach* which was intended to give an approximate measure of an entity's ability to carry on its activities on a day to day basis without encountering financial stringencies (IAS 13, 4) – the criterion for classifying assets and liabilities as current or non-current was whether the items would be realised or liquidated in the near future (IAS 13, 5); and
- an *operating cycle approach* which was intended to identify those resources and obligations of the entity that are continuously circulating (IAS 13, 4) – the criterion for identifying assets and liabilities as circulating was whether they were consumed or settled in the production of revenue within the normal operating cycle of the entity.

IAS 13 recognised that these two approaches were to some extent incompatible and concluded that, in practice, classification was largely based on convention (IAS 13, 6). The requirements of IAS 13 followed existing convention and listed those items which were, by convention, classified as current assets or current liabilities.

IAS 1 does not follow the same convention-based approach as IAS 13. Instead, it sets out broad standards which combine the two alternative approaches. Current items include those assets and liabilities which are expected to be realised or settled within the operating cycle as well as those which are due to be settled or expected to be realised within twelve months of the balance sheet date.

9.5.2 Current Assets

An asset should be classified as a current asset when it is:

- expected to be realised in, or is held for sale or consumption in, the normal course of the entity's operating cycle; or
- held primarily for trading purposes or for the short-term and expected to be realised within twelve months of the balance sheet date; or
- cash or a cash equivalent asset which is not restricted in its use.

(IAS 1, 58)

Most, but not all, the items which were classified as current assets under IAS 13 are classified as current assets under IAS 1.

All inventories, advance payments on inventories and trade receivables are included in current assets even when they are not expected to be realised within twelve months of the balance sheet date. Those receivables and inventories which are not expected to be realised within twelve months of the balance sheet date should be separately disclosed (IAS 1, 56).

Extract 9.1 *Trade receivables due in more than one year*

Bayer, Germany, 31 December 2001 (IAS)

Trade accounts receivable [classified as current assets] as of 31 December 2001 include ... €2 million (2000: €8 million) maturing after one year.

Extract 9.2 *Long-term inventories classified as current assets*

LVMH, France, 31 December 2000 (French GAAP)

Due to the length of the ageing process for champagne and cognac, a substantial proportion of inventories will not be sold within one year. However, in accordance with industry practices, these are classified as current assets.

Financial assets that are held for trading are classified as current assets. Other financial assets are classified as current assets if they are expected to be realised within twelve months of the balance sheet date; otherwise they are classified as non-current assets.

Cash and cash equivalents which are assets are classified as current assets provided that their use is not restricted. This is a change from IAS 13 for those cash and bank balances for which their use for current operations is subject to restrictions. Under IAS 1, these balances are never classified as current assets. They are always classified as non-current assets (IAS 1, 57). The change was made at the suggestion of the SEC (*E53 Comment Letters*, p226). The requirement may lead to some misleading classifications. For example, if cash has been designated for use in the settlement of a liability which is due for settlement in three months time, IAS 1 requires the classification of the cash as a long-term asset and the liability as a current liability.

In its May 2002 improvements exposure draft, the IASB proposes to revert to the IAS 13 approach, that is a cash and cash equivalent asset should be classified as a current asset if it is not restricted in its use for at least 12 months from the balance sheet date.

9.5.3 Current Liabilities

A liability should be classified as a current liability when it is :

- expected to be settled in the normal course of the entity's operating cycle; or
- due to be settled within twelve months of the balance sheet date.

(IAS 1, 60)

Trade payables and accruals for operating costs which are expected to be settled in the normal course of the operating cycle are classified as current liabilities even if they are due to be settled after more than twelve months from the balance sheet date. Those trade payables and accruals which are not expected to be settled within twelve months of the balance sheet date should be classified as current liabilities and separately disclosed (IAS 1, 56).

Other liabilities such as loans, bank overdrafts, provisions, dividends payable, income taxes and other non-trade payables are classified as current if they are due to be settled within twelve months of the balance sheet date. Such liabilities are classified as current even when they are not expected to be settled within twelve months of the balance sheet date – note the distinction between 'expected to be settled' for operating cycle items and 'due to be settled' for other items. When non-operating cycle items are due for settlement in more than twelve months, they are classified as non-current, even when they are expected to be settled in less than twelve months.

It is usual practice to classify the current portion of long-term liabilities as current liabilities and such a practice was required by IAS 13. However, IAS 1 appears to restrict this practice to the current portion of interest-bearing liabilities. In its May 2002 improvements exposure draft, the IASB proposes to extend the requirement to all long-term financial liabilities.

A long-term interest bearing liability (but not a non-interest bearing liability) which is due to be settled within twelve months of the balance sheet date may be classified as non-current provided:

- the original term of the liability was for a period of more than twelve months;
- the entity intends to refinance the liability on a long-term basis; and
- that intention is supported by an agreement to refinance or reschedule payments, and the agreement is completed before the financial statements are approved.

(IAS 1, 63)

The IASB's May 2002 improvements exposure draft extends this approach from long-term interest bearing liabilities to all long-term financial liabilities.

The amount of any liability which has been excluded from current liabilities in accordance with this requirement, together with information in support of its presentation, should be disclosed (IAS 1, 63). The IASB's May 2002 improvements exposure draft proposes to delete this disclosure requirement.

A borrowing may become repayable on demand if certain conditions related to the entity's financial position are breached, for example if net assets fall below a certain amount or gearing exceeds a specified level. If the conditions are breached, the liability is 'due to be settled within twelve months of the balance sheet date', therefore it is classified as current. However, the liability may continue to be classified as non-current when:

- the lender has agreed, prior to the approval of the financial statements, not to demand payment as a consequence of the breach; and

- it is not probable that further breaches will occur within twelve months of the balance sheet date.

(IAS 1, 65)

For example, if an entity has exceeded its borrowing limits, with the result that a lender could demand immediate payment of loans, the entity should classify the loans as non-current only if the lender has agreed not to demand immediate payment and it is probable that the entity will not again exceed its borrowing limits within twelve months of the balance sheet date.

> ***IASB improvements project***
>
> In its May 2002 exposure draft, the IASB proposes to both amend and clarify the requirements relating to the refinancing of long-term liabilities.
>
> When the entity intends to refinance or roll over the liability for at least twelve months after the balance sheet date, the liability should be classified as a non-current liability even if it is due to be repaid within 12 months of the balance sheet date. The refinancing or roll-over must be completed before the balance sheet date.
>
> When the entity breaches an undertaking or covenant such that the liability becomes repayable on demand, the liability should be classified as a current liability unless the lender has agreed, before the balance sheet date, to allow a period of grace and not to demand payment during that period and provided that:
>
> - the breach is rectified during the period of grace; or
> - the period of grace has not ended when the financial statements are approved for issuance but it is probable that the breach will be rectified.

9.5.4 Maturity Analysis

For each asset and liability item which combines amounts expected to be recovered or settled both before and after twelve months from the balance sheet date, an entity should disclose the amount expected to be recovered or settled after more than twelve months (IAS 1, 54). The requirement applies irrespective of whether or not the entity makes a current:non-current distinction.

IAS 1 requires information about expected recovery and settlement dates for all assets and liabilities, not just financial assets and liabilities. It emphasises that the disclosure of such information about non-monetary assets and liabilities is 'useful' (IAS 1, 56). Therefore, an entity must disclose:

- the amounts included in current assets, including inventories which it does not expect to recover within twelve months of the balance sheet date;
- the amounts included in non-current assets, including property, plant and equipment and investments, which it expects to recover within twelve months of the balance sheet date;
- the amounts included in current liabilities which it expects to settle in more than twelve months from the balance sheet date; and
- the amounts included in non-current liabilities, including provisions, deferred taxes and employee benefit liabilities, which it expects to settle within twelve months of the balance sheet date.

Extract 9.3 *Maturity analysis of liabilities*

RWE, Germany, 31 December 2001 (IAS)

Liabilities

In € million	31.12.01	Remaining term < 1 year	Remaining term > 5 years
Loans	5,619	800	3,805
Loans against borrowers' notes	1,784	83	1,631
Accounts payable to banks	8,393	4,315	1,991
Accounts payable for supplies and services	5,700	5,396	1
Prepayments received	427	372	–
Accounts payable for bills accepted and drawn	19	19	–
Accounts payable to affiliates	437	403	–
Accounts payable to investees	1,270	1,199	–
Other liabilities	6,886	5,103	242
of which tax	(598)	(598)	(–)
of which under social securities	(740)	(332)	(89)
	30,535	17,690	7,670

The requirement means that an entity which manufactures goods which require more than twelve months to be ready for sale, for example some food products and beverages, must disclose the amounts of inventories which it does not expect to realise within twelve months of the balance sheet date. The amounts disclosed include those inventories which are not expected to be sold within twelve months plus those inventories which are expected to be sold within twelve months but for which the entity does not expect to receive payment (the end of the operating cycle) within twelve months of the balance sheet date.

The requirement may also affect an entity involved in construction contracts. It needs to disclose separately amounts which it expects will be payable or receivable in more than twelve months. This includes, for example, retentions by the customer which will not be settled until the completion of those contracts when completion is not expected within twelve months of the balance sheet date. It also includes:

- amounts which have been recognised as revenue but which will not be recovered within twelve months of the balance sheet date; and
- advance payments by the customer which will not be recognised as revenue within twelve months of the balance sheet date.

9.6 OFFSETTING ASSETS AND LIABILITIES

The IASC has consistently opposed the offsetting of assets and liabilities in the balance sheet except in very limited circumstances. Four IASs, developed prior to the revised IAS 1, included substantially similar requirements:

- IAS 5 required that significant items should not be offset against other items without separate identification (IAS 5, 8);
- IAS 13 required that the amount at which a current asset or current liability was stated should not be reduced by deducting another current liability or current asset unless a legal right of set-off existed and the offsetting represented the expectation as to the realisation or settlement of the asset or liability (IAS 13, 20);
- IAS 30 requires the amount at which any asset or liability is stated in the balance sheet of a bank should not be offset by the deduction of another liability or asset unless a legal right of set-off exists and the offsetting represents the expectation as to the realisation or settlement of the asset or liability (IAS 30, 23); and
- IAS 32 requires a financial asset and a financial liability should be offset when an entity has a legally enforceable right to set off the recognised amounts and intends to either settle on a net basis or to realise the asset and settle the liability simultaneously but should not be offset in other circumstances (IAS 32, 33).

IAS 1 requires that assets and liabilities should not be offset except when offsetting is required or permitted by another IFRS. The only current general requirements are those in IAS 30 and IAS 32. However, three IASs now include specific requirements on offsetting in the balance sheet:

- IAS 12 contains detailed requirements for the offsetting of tax assets and tax liabilities (see chapter 31);
- IAS 22 requires negative goodwill to be presented as a deduction from goodwill (IAS 22, 64); and
- IAS 37 restricts the circumstances in which any reimbursement by

another party in respect of expenditure covered by a provision may be recognised and requires that any amount recognised should be treated as a separate asset (IAS 37, 53).

There are two general conditions, both of which must be met, before an asset and liability may be offset:

- there must be a legal right of set-off; and
- there must be the intention to settle on a net basis or settle the asset and liability simultaneously – simultaneous settlement means that the transactions occur at the same moment with no allowance for time differences between different markets.

If there is no legal right of set-off, an asset and a liability must not be offset even if the entity intends to settle on a net basis or settle the asset and liability simultaneously. In such circumstances, the entity is exposed to credit risk and that risk would be hidden if the asset and liability were offset. If there is an intention to settle on a net basis but no legal right of set-off, the assets and liabilities must not be offset. So, for example, an entity which buys goods from, and sells goods to, another entity must not offset the payable and receivable if it intends to settle and realise on a gross basis notwithstanding that each entity may have a legal right of set-off.

Extract 9.4 *Offsetting financial assets and financial liabilities*

Iscor, South Africa, 30 June 2000 (South African GAAP and IAS)

Where a legally enforceable right of offset exists for recognised financial assets and financial liabilities, and there is an intention to settle the liability and realise the asset simultaneously, or to settle on a net basis, all related financial effects are offset.

IAS 7 allows bank overdrafts to be included in cash and cash equivalents. This has led some to infer that such overdrafts may be, or should be, offset against bank balances which are assets. IAS 14, for example, states that IAS 7 'provides guidance as to whether bank overdrafts should be presented as a component of cash or should be reported as borrowings' (IAS 14, 23). IAS 7 gives no such guidance. IAS 7 does not deal with the balance sheet classification of overdrafts nor the offsetting in the balance sheet of bank overdrafts against bank balances which are assets.

Overdrafts are presented in the balance sheet as liabilities. They are offset against other bank balances which are assets (or other financial assets) in only the limited circumstances permitted by IAS 32 for the offsetting of financial assets and financial liabilities. Furthermore, the very nature of many overdrafts is such that while there may be a legal right of set-off (to reduce the bank's credit risk), it is not the intention or practice to settle on a net basis; therefore, they cannot be offset against other bank balances or financial assets.

Extract 9.5 *Bank overdrafts in balance sheet and cash flow statement*

Hongkong Land Holdings, Hong Kong, December 2001 (IAS)

Borrowings (notes to balance sheet)

	2001 US$m	2000 US$m
Current		
Bank overdrafts	2.4	2.5
Short-term borrowings	38.4	–
Current portion of long-term borrowings	461.7	924.8
	502.5	927.3

Cash and cash equivalents (notes to the cash flow statement)

	2001 US$m	2000 US$m
Bank balances and other liquid funds	568.6	1,493.6
Bank overdrafts	(2.4)	(2.5)
	566.2	1,491.1

9.7 BALANCE SHEET FORMAT

Table 9.1 shows the format of a balance sheet based on the requirements and terminology of IFRSs and following, as closely as possible, the layout required by the EU Fourth Directive. Table 9.2 shows the format of a balance sheet based on the requirements and terminology of IFRSs using the sequence and layout which is common in North America and which is now being followed by an increasing number of European multinational companies.

Table 9.1 *Balance sheet – IFRSs and EU Fourth Directive*

Assets		
Non-current assets		
Property, plant and equipment		1,872
Investment property		250
Intangible assets		304
Investments in associates		1,118
Other financial assets		300
Non-current receivables		460
Deferred tax assets		240
		4,544
Current assets		
Inventories	643	
Current tax assets	120	
Trade receivables and prepayments	2,074	
Financial assets held for trading	440	
Cash and bank balances	202	3,479
Total assets		8,023
Equity		
Share capital	850	
Capital paid – in excess of par value	190	
Revaluation surplus	78	
Reserves	25	
Foreign exchange differences	140	
Accumulated profits	387	1,670
Minority interests		566
Non-current liabilities and deferred income		
Secured loans	838	
Unsecured loans	200	
Deferred tax liabilities	401	
Retirement benefit obligations	288	
Provisions	150	
Deferred income – government grant	80	1,957
Current liabilities		
Bank loans and overdrafts	892	
Current portion of long-term liabilities	100	
Trade and other payables	1,530	
Current tax liabilities	523	
Provisions for liabilities and charges	785	3,830
Total equity and liabilities		8,023

Table 9.2 *Balance Sheet – IFRSs and North American format*

Current assets	
Cash and bank balances	202
Financial assets held for trading	440
Trade receivables and prepayments	2,074
Current tax assets	120
Inventories	643
	3,479
Long-term assets	
Property, plant and equipment	2,594
Investment property	250
Intangible assets	384
	3,228
Accumulated depreciation and amortisation	880
	2,348
Investments in associates	1,118
Other long-term financial assets	300
Non-current receivables	460
Deferred tax assets	240
	4,466
Total assets	7,945
Current liabilities	
Bank loans	892
Current portion of long-term liabilities	100
Trade and other payables	1,530
Current tax liabilities	523
Accrued expenses	785
	3,830
Long-term liabilities and deferred income	
Secured loans	838
Unsecured loans	200
Deferred tax liabilities	401
Retirement benefit obligations	288
Accrued expenses	150
Deferred income – government grant	80
	1,957
Minority interests	566
Equity	
Share capital	850
Capital paid – in excess of par value	190
Foreign exchange differences	140
Accumulated profits	412
	1,592
Total equity and liabilities	7,945

CHAPTER 10

Income Statement

10.1 RELEVANT STANDARDS AND INTERPRETATION

IAS 1 *Presentation of Financial Statements*
IAS 8 *Net Profit or Loss for the Period, Fundamental Errors and Changes in Accounting Policies*
SIC 17 *Equity – Costs of an Equity Transaction*

10.2 HISTORY

IAS 1 replaced IAS 5 *Information to be Disclosed in Financial Statements* with effect for accounting periods beginning on or after 1 July 1998.

IAS 8 *Unusual and Prior Period Items and Changes in Accounting Policies* (IAS 8 [1978]) was approved in 1978. It required the disclosure of certain items in the income statement as well as dealing with prior period items and changes in accounting policies.

IAS 8 was reconsidered in the comparability and improvements project when a significant number of changes were made. The new requirements dealt with:

- the classification and disclosure of certain items in the income statement;
- discontinued operations (see chapter 37); and
- changes in accounting policies and corrections of fundamental errors (see chapters 13 and 14).

IAS 8 *Net Profit or Loss for the Period, Fundamental Errors and Changes in Accounting Policies* was approved in November 1993 and applied to financial statements for accounting periods beginning on or after 1 January 1995.

In its May 2002 improvements exposure draft, the IASB proposes several changes to IAS 1 and IAS 8 including some that will affect the presentation of the income statement, in particular the prohibition of extraordinary items.

The IASB has an active project on reporting performance which could have a significant impact on the presentation of the income statement.

10.3 IOSCO

In June 1994, IOSCO advised the IASC that it accepted IAS 8 for the purposes of the core standards. IOSCO identified a number of suspense issues related to IAS 5 and IAS 8 which are described in chapters 8 and 13.

IAS 1 is included in 'IAS 2000' endorsed by IOSCO in May 2000. There is one supplemental treatment relating to the presentation of the income statement: the disclosure of gains and losses on investments (IAS 32 encourages, but does not require, this disclosure).

10.4 CONTENT AND FORMAT OF THE INCOME STATEMENT

The income statement presents information about the financial performance of the entity (*Framework* 17). Profit is used as the measurement of performance in IFRSs and the elements which relate to the measurement of profit are income (which encompasses revenue and gains) and expenses (which also encompasses losses) (*Framework* 69, 74 and 78).

The IASC has always been very reluctant to prescribe the format or layout of the income statement. The reluctance to prescribe a format or layout was evident throughout the presentation project but there was some support for more prescription, perhaps along the lines of the EU Fourth Directive. The eventual compromise took the form of what some described as 'mandatory flexible formats' and what IAS 1 sometimes refers to as 'structured presentation'. In other words, the requirements of the revised IAS 1 combine compulsion and flexibility.

As a minimum, the income statement should include the following line items:

- revenue;
- the results of operating activities (see 10.6.1);
- finance costs (see 10.6.2);
- share of profits and losses of associates and joint ventures accounted for using the equity method;
- tax expense;

- profit or loss from ordinary activities (see 10.6);
- extraordinary items (see 10.7);
- minority interest; and
- net profit or loss for the period (see 10.5).

(IAS 1, 75)

Additional line items should be presented when required by another IFRS or when necessary to present fairly the entity's financial performance (IAS 1, 75).

The basic requirement to disclose, as a minimum, certain line items is supplemented by the following guidance:

- additional headings and sub-totals should be presented when required by an IFRS or when necessary to present fairly the entity's financial performance (IAS 1, 75); and
- the descriptions and sequence of items may be amended when necessary to explain the elements of performance (IAS 1, 76) – the term 'elements' is unexplained.

Unlike with the balance sheet, there is no suggestion that the line items need not be limited to, or therefore include, items falling within the scope of other IASs.

To the extent possible, it is recommended that each line item should be limited to those items which meet the IFRS definition of that item and which are accounted for in accordance with the relevant IFRS. For example, the line item 'revenue' should be limited to items which meet the IAS 18 definition of revenue and which are accounted for in accordance with IAS 18. However, some entities need to include in revenue those items which meet the definition but which are outside the scope of IAS 18 (see chapter 29). The line item 'tax expense' should be determined in accordance with IAS 12 and extraordinary items in accordance with IAS 8.

When items meet more than one definition, the accounting treatment adopted determines the classification. For example, a financial institution includes interest income in revenue whereas a trading entity classifies interest income as part of a net amount of financing costs.

10.5 NET PROFIT OR LOSS FOR THE PERIOD

All income and expenses recognised in a period should be included in the net profit or loss for the period unless an IFRS requires or permits otherwise (IAS 8, 7). Therefore, the following items should not be included in the net profit or loss for the current period:

- the amount of the correction of a fundamental error which relates to prior periods and which has been accounted for under the benchmark treatment (IAS 8, 34);
- the effect of changes in accounting policies accounted for under the benchmark treatment (IAS 8, 49);
- most surpluses and deficits arising on the revaluation of tangible assets (IAS 16, 39 and 40);
- most exchange differences arising on the translation of the financial statements of a foreign entity (IAS 21, 30) and the hedging of a net investment in a foreign entity (IAS 21, 17);
- gains and losses on financial assets when they are included in equity in accordance with the requirements of IAS 39 (see chapter 20); and
- the costs of an equity transaction (SIC 17, 6).

These items are now included in the statement of changes in equity (see chapter 11).

The net profit or loss for the period consists of two components both of which should be shown on the face of the income statement:

- the profit or loss from ordinary activities; and
- extraordinary items.

(IAS 8, 10)

Given the rarity of extraodinary items, the net profit or loss for the period is usually identical to the profit or loss from ordinary activities.

10.6 PROFIT OR LOSS FROM ORDINARY ACTIVITIES

The profit or loss from ordinary activities is the net profit or loss for the period plus extraordinary expenses and less extraordinary income – in other words it is all income and all expenses recognised in the income statement other than those items which meet the definition of extraordinary items.

The profit or loss from ordinary activities should be disclosed on the face of the income statement (IAS 8, 10). The tax expense related to the profit or loss from ordinary activities should be disclosed separately (IAS 12, 77) and is presented as a separate line item in the income statement (IAS 1, 75).

10.6.1 Operating Profit

The minimum line items for the income statement include 'the results of operating activities' ('operating profit') (IAS 1, 75). The item is not defined in IASs but the sequence of line items suggests that operating profit is the profit for the period before deducting 'financing costs' (which is also undefined – see 10.6.2 below) and before adding the share of profits less losses of associates and jointly controlled entities accounted for using the equity method.

For an entity which is not a financial institution, operating profit (results of operating activities) is all income and expenses other than:

- financing costs (appropriately defined);
- interest income and other returns on investments (insofar as they are not deducted in computing financing costs);
- equity method profits and losses of associates and jointly controlled entities;
- income taxes; and
- extraordinary items.

> *IASB improvements project*
>
> In its May 2002 improvements exposure draft, the IASB proposes to remove the requirement to disclose the results from operating activities as operating activities are not defined in IAS 1.

10.6.2 Financing Costs and Investment Income

The minimum line items for the income statement include 'financing costs' (IAS 1, 75). The item is not defined and appears nowhere else in IFRSs. The minimum line items do not include 'investment income' or 'foreign exchange differences'.

IAS 1 does not require disclosure of interest expense. The IASC's 1997 discussion paper on financial instruments did address the relevance of the disclosure of interest expense and concluded that it should be disclosed (*Accounting for Financial Assets and Financial Liabilities*, p177). The lack of the requirement was pointed out in the comment letters on E53 but no action was taken by the IASC to remedy the deficiency. It is strongly recommended that entities should disclose interest expense separately as a component of 'financing costs'.

Some have suggested that 'financing costs' should be a net item (with appropriate sub-classification in the notes) of borrowing costs, interest income, other investment income and exchange differences (and, in the case of entities adopting IAS 29, the gain or loss on the net monetary position). In many cases, it would be appropriate to present the following three line items, rather than the single item 'financing costs':

- interest expense and other borrowing costs;
- interest and other income from financial assets (insofar as it is not reported as revenue); and
- foreign exchange differences.

For entities adopting IAS 29, the gain or loss on the net monetary position is also presented on a separate line item (IAS 29, 28).

Interest expense and other borrowing costs (which could be described as 'financing costs') includes all borrowing costs, as defined in IAS 23, which are not capitalised, that is:

- interest on bank overdrafts and short-term and long-term borrowings;
- the amortisation of discounts related to borrowings;
- the amortisation of ancillary costs incurred in connection with the arrangement of borrowings; and
- finance charges on finance leases.

(IAS 23, 5)

The income statement effect of interest rate financial instruments, for example swaps, is also included with this item.

Interest income and other income from financial assets includes:

- interest income on bank deposits and other short-term and long-term advances;
- the amortisation of discounts on deposits, advances and other financial assets;
- dividend income on financial assets (usually equity instruments);
- gains less losses on financial assets; and
- the income statement effect of other financial instruments.

Such income could be presented with, or as part of, financing costs when it is incidental to the main revenue producing activities of the entity. It should be included in revenue (but separately disclosed in accordance with IAS 18) when it is part of the revenue producing activities of the entity. For example, interest and other income arising from the investment of surplus funds or other aspects of the manufacturing entity's treasury management could be presented with, or as part of, financing costs and excluded from operating profit. However, finance income arising on finance leases is part of revenue and, hence, operating profit, of a lessor. Interest and investment income of a bank or similar financial institution is presented as revenue (see chapter 43).

Exchange differences arising on foreign currency monetary items (and related financial instruments such as forward contracts and swaps) are usually part of financing costs (they are revenue for financial institutions which deal in foreign currencies). IAS 21 requires the separate disclosure of exchange differences included in the net profit or loss for the period (IAS 21, 42(a)). Exchange differences and the income statement effect of related financial instruments could be reported as a separate line or as part of a net amount of financing costs (with disclosure of the components of the net amount). The reported amount of exchange differences is, of course, a net amount and it is usually not practicable or meaningful to analyse the amount into component parts.

10.6.3 Analysis of Expenses

The operating expenses of an entity may be classified either by nature or function. Under the nature of expenses method, expenses are classified according to their nature, for example:

- raw materials and consumables;
- staff costs;
- depreciation and amortisation expense; and
- other operating expenses.

Under this method, the change in inventories during the period is usually shown separately, sometimes as an addition to (but not as part of) revenue.

Under the function of expenses method, expenses are classified according to their function, for example:

- cost of sales;
- distribution expenses;
- selling expenses; and
- administrative expenses.

Under this method, cost of sales reflects the effect of the change in inventories during the period.

It is often argued that the two methods reflect the different reporting philosophies of continental European countries (which tend to favour the nature of expenses method) and the Anglo-Saxon countries (which tend to favour the function of expenses method). The formats of the income statement in the EU Fourth Directive allow for both methods.

Extract 10.1 *Analysis of expenses by nature*

Fiat, Italy, 31 December 2000 (some IAS) (in millions of euros)	2000	1999	1998
Value of Production			
Revenues from sales and services	**57,603**	48,402	45,755
Change in work in progress, semi-finished and finished products inventories	**27**	275	(154)
Change in contract work in progress	**(48)**	(279)	14
Additions to internally produced fixed assets	**1,242**	1,107	987
Other income and revenues:			
revenue grants	**43**	33	56
other	**2,376**	1,806	1,604
Total other income and revenues	**2,419**	1,839	1,660
Total Value of Production	**61,243**	51,344	48,262
Costs of Production			
Raw materials, supplies and merchandise	**31,134**	25,720	24,102
Services	**9,042**	7,893	7,046
Leases and rentals	**409**	299	235
Personnel:			
salaries and wages	**6,140**	5,430	5,239
social security contributions	**1,710**	1,630	1,835
employee severance indemnities	**353**	333	357
employee pensions and similar obligations	**139**	59	74
other costs	**353**	196	136
Total Personnel costs	**8,695**	7,648	7,641
Amortization, depreciation and writedowns:			
amortization of intangible assets	**519**	280	238
depreciation of property, plant and equipment	**2,533**	2,074	2,072
writedown of fixed assets	**1**	5	1
writedown of receivables among current assets and liquid funds	**475**	244	253
Total Amortization, depreciation and writedowns	**3,528**	2,603	2,564
Change in raw materials, supplies and merchandise inventories	**63**	(64)	253
Provisions for risks	**1,047**	854	725
Other provisions	**7**	8	24
Other operating costs	**1,458**	1,265	1,183
Expenses of financial services companies	**983**	694	1,005
Insurance claims and other costs	**4,022**	3,636	2,738
Total Costs of Production	**60,388**	50,556	47,516
Difference between the Value and Costs of Production	**855**	788	746

During the first improvements project, the IASC expressed a clear preference for the function of expenses method; the nature of expenses method was allowed as a compromise. As a result, IAS 2 requires that an entity should disclose the cost of inventories recognised as an expense (the function of expenses method) or the operating costs applicable to revenue (the nature of expenses method). In its May 2002 improvements exposure draft, the IASB proposes to remove the disclosure requirement in IAS 2 because it is also required by IAS 1.

IAS 1 expanded on the requirements of IAS 2. It also changed the preference. An entity should present an analysis of expenses using a classification based on either the nature of expenses or their function within the entity (IAS 1, 77). Those entities which classify expenses by function (the IAS 2 preference) should also disclose the nature of expenses, including depreciation and amortisation expense, and staff costs (IAS 1, 83) but no additional disclosures are required by entities which classify expenses by nature.

No definitions or implementation guidance are provided on the various components of expenses. It is important, however, that an entity applies its own definitions consistently from period to period. For example, the components of cost of sales should be consistent from period to period. It may also be appropriate that disclosure is made of the definitions.

Extract 10.2 *Analysis of expenses by nature*

Kuoni, Switzerland, 31 December 2000 (IAS)

	2000 *CHF 1,000*	*1999* *CHF 1,000*
Turnover	**4,113,001**	**3,514,692**
Direct costs	−3,124,624	−2,664,334
Gross profit	**988,377**	**850,358**
Personnel expense	−453,749	−395,226
Lease and maintenance expense	−73,186	−61,469
Administrative expense	−91,291	−78,969
Marketing and advertising expense	−140,774	−119,338
Depreciation	−54,669	−42,529
Earnings before interest, taxes and amortisation of goodwill (EBITA)	**174,708**	**152,827**

Extract 10.3 *Analysis of expenses by function*

Schering, Germany, 31 December 2001 (IAS)

In euro m	2001	2000
Net sales	**4,842**	**4,493**
Cost of sales	−1,215	−1,089
Gross profit	**3,627**	**3,404**
Costs of		
Marketing and selling	−1,601	−1,498
Engineering and administration	−525	−456
Research and development	−864	−811
Other operating income	348	300
Other operating expenses	−317	−299
Operating profit	668	640

Extract 10.4 *Analysis of expenses by function*

Volkswagen, Germany, 31 December 2001 (IAS)

Million Euro	2001	2000
Sales revenue	88,540	83,127
Cost of sales	75,586	71,130
Gross profit Automotive Division*	+**12,954**	+**11,997**
Gross profit Financial Services Division*	+**1,328**	+**1,213**
Distribution costs	7,554	7,080
Administrative costs	2,154	2,001
Other operating income	4,118	3,656
Other operating expenses	3,268	3,761
Operating profit	+**5,424**	+**4,024**

* The result from operating leases is included in the gross profit of the Automotive Division.

10.6.4 Other Income Statement Items Requiring Disclosure

An entity should disclose (usually in the notes) the nature and amount of items of income and expense within profit or loss from ordinary activities which are of such size, nature or incidence that their disclosure is relevant to explain the performance of the entity for the period (IAS 8, 16). These items are called exceptional items in some countries but the use of such a term would have caused confusion in some languages.

Circumstances which may give rise to separate disclosure include:

- large write-downs of inventories to net realisable value;
- the write-off of a large receivable from a trade customer;
- gains or losses arising on the disposal of items of property, plant and equipment or long-term investments; and
- gains or losses arising on the settlement of lawsuits.

Extract 10.5 *Exceptional items*

Iscor, South Africa, 30 June 2000 (South African GAAP and IAS)

	Group	
	2000 Rm	1999 Rm
Surplus on sale of residential properties	48	56
Surplus on sale of investments	26	14
Restructuring costs at Vanderbijlpark Works		(64)
	74	6
Taxation effect		14
Net effect on attributable earnings	74	20

Extract 10.6 *Exceptional events*

PSA Peugeot-Citroen, France 31 December 1997 (French GAAP and US GAAP)

The exceptional events, which led to a pre-tax charge of FF 2,766 million, were as follows:

- first, in response to the risk that the British pound might weaken after its sharp rise in the second half of 1996, future sales in pounds were hedged in the first half of 1997 for a period of around twelve months. Since the pound remained high against the French franc and the hedging contracts were very expensive due to the pound/franc interest rate differential, the managing board decided to cancel the remaining contracts at the end of 1997 and to write a provision for the cost, estimated at FF 1,440 million. This provision was utilized in full and written back to the income statement in early 1998;
- second, a provision was written to cover the entire cost of Peugeot's withdrawal from the joint venture formed with PAL in India in 1994. Total provisions for Peugeot's international operations, which essentially concern the Indian project, came to FF 520 million;
- third, it was decided to charge in full to 1997 income the restructuring costs related to labor-reduction plans continuing into 1998, as well as the expenses stemming from the early retirement of the DK/DJ engine, which is being replaced by the new HDI direct injection diesel engine. Restructuring expense amounted to FF 1.467 million of which FF 610 million was for the production phase-out and FF 848 million for the labor-reduction plans. This compares with FF 318 million in 1996.

10.7 EXTRAORDINARY ITEMS

Extraordinary items are income or expenses which arise from events or transactions that are clearly distinct from the ordinary activities of the entity and therefore are not expected to recur frequently or regularly (IAS 8, 6). *Ordinary activities* are any activities which are undertaken by an entity as part of its business and such related activities in which the entity engages in furtherance of, incidental to, or arising from these activities (IAS 8, 6).

Virtually all items of income and expense arise in the course of the ordinary activities of the entity and only on rare occasions does an event or transaction give rise to an extraordinary item. IAS 8 gives two examples of events which generally give rise to extraordinary items for most entities:

- the expropriation of assets; and
- natural disasters.

The link between the two examples is that both events are outside the control of the management of the entity. The IASC considered, but eventually rejected, adding to the definition of an extraordinary item the notion that events should be outside management's control but it is implicit in the definition.

A discontinuing operation is not an extraordinary item (IAS 35, 41) because the discontinuance must be based on a single plan and is therefore within the control of management (IAS 35, 42). An expropriation of an entity's operations or part of those operations may be an extraordinary item as there is no single plan (and for this reason, the expropriation is not a discontinuing operation under IAS 35).

Events which are extraordinary for one entity may be ordinary for another. IAS 8 gives the example of an insurance entity which insures against the risks of damage caused by natural disasters. For such an entity, the claims from policyholders arising from such disasters are ordinary items. While management cannot control the occurrence of the disasters, it has made the decision to offer insurance against such occurrences and it is within management's power to remain in or abandon that business.

In the FASB's IAS/US GAAP comparison, Lopez argues that the limited list of examples of extraordinary items in IAS 8 may, in conjunction with differences in the definitions of extraordinary items in IAS 8 and US GAAP, result in the classification of a broader range of transactions and events as extraordinary under IAS 8 as compared with US GAAP[1]. It is unclear why fewer examples will result in more extraordinary items – the IASC's intention was that extraordinary items would arise 'on very rare occasions' (IAS 8, 12) and the limited number of examples reflects the rarity. Furthermore, many of the items which are classified as extraordinary under US GAAP would not qualify as extraordinary under IAS 8. For example, gains and losses from the extinguishment of debt, profits or losses on the disposal of certain assets or segments following the use of the pooling of interests method, and the gains of a debtor on a troubled debt restructuring are extraordinary items under US GAAP but they are not extraordinary items under IFRSs.

An entity should disclose the total amount of all extraordinary items on the face of the income statement (IAS 8, 10). The nature and the amount of each extraordinary item should be separately disclosed in either the income statement or notes (IAS 8, 11). It would be highly unusual for an entity to have more than one extraordinary item in the same period.

> ***IASB improvements project***
>
> In its May 2002 improvements exposure draft, the IASB proposes to eliminate the concept of extraordinary items. As a result, the revised IAS 1 will prohibit the presentation of any items of income or expense as extraordinary items on the face of the income statement or in the notes.

10.8 OFFSETTING

The offsetting of income and expenses in the income statement has not attracted the same attention as offsetting in the balance sheet. There are, however, two related issues which are sometimes confused:

- the offsetting of income and expenses so that a gain or loss, rather than the gross amounts of revenue and expenses, is reported – for example, an entity may report a gain on the disposal of an asset rather than the gross sale proceeds of the asset as income and the cost of the asset as an expense; and
- the offsetting of gains on some transactions against losses on similar transactions – for example, an entity may report an amount of profits or losses on the disposal of certain assets which is the aggregate amount of gains less the aggregate amount of losses.

IAS 1 requires that income and expenses should be offset when:

- offsetting is required or permitted by an IFRS; or
- gains, losses and related expenses arise from the same or similar transactions and events and are not material.

(IAS 1, 34)

No IFRSs require offsetting. The following are examples of income and expenses or gains and losses which may be offset:

- gains and losses on the disposal of non-current assets including property, plant and equipment, intangible assets and investments may be reported by offsetting the sale proceeds and the carrying amount of the assets (IAS 1, 36) – furthermore, aggregate gains may be offset against aggregate losses;
- expenditure reimbursed by a third party may be reported net by deducting the reimbursement from the expenditure (IAS 1, 36 and IAS 37, 54) – but if the reimbursement takes the form of a government

grant, the amount of the grants recognised in the income statement must be disclosed (IAS 20, 39(b));

- extraordinary items – income and expenses relating to the same extraordinary item may be offset but separate disclosure is required of the net amount for each extraordinary item (IAS 1, 36 and IAS 8, 11);
- the gain or loss on net monetary position in IAS 29 financial statements is a net amount of gains less losses (IAS 29, 9); and
- the share of profits or losses of associates accounted for using the equity method (IAS 28, 28) – the profits and the losses are, by definition, net amounts, and profits and losses on different associates may be offset.

10.9 INCOME STATEMENT FORMAT

Table 10.1 shows the format of an income statement based on the requirements and terminology of IFRSs and following as closely as possible the layout required by the EU Fourth Directive. Table 10.2 shows the format of an income statement based on the requirements and terminology of IFRSs using the sequence and layout which is common in North America.

Table 10.1 *Income Statement – IFRS and European Union format*

Sale of goods		14,748
Services rendered		2,956
		17,704
Cost of sales	4,870	
Cost of services rendered	2,414	
Distribution costs	3,764	
Administrative expenses	863	
Other expenses	263	12,174
Operating profit		5,530
Share of profits of associates	401	
Dividend income	30	
Interest income	46	
Royalties	50	527
		6,057
Interest and other borrowing costs	509	
Foreign exchange differences	181	690
Profit from Ordinary Activities before Income Taxes		5,367
Income taxes		2,250
Profit from Ordinary Activities		3,117
Extraordinary Items		
Extraordinary gains	600	
Extraordinary losses	–	
Income taxes on extraordinary items	240	360
Profit for the Period		3,477
Minority interest in the net profit for the period		560
Net Profit		2,917

Table 10.2 *Income Statement – IFRS and North American format*

	$	$
Revenue		
Sale of goods		14,748
Services rendered		2,956
		17,704
Other Income		
Interest		46
Royalties		50
Dividends		30
Share of profits of associates		401
		18,231
Expenses		
Cost of sales	4,870	
Cost of services rendered	2,414	
Selling and administrative expenses	4,890	
Interest and other borrowing costs	509	12,683
		5,548
Foreign exchange differences		181
Profit from Ordinary Activities before Income Taxes		5,367
Income taxes		2,250
Profit from Ordinary Activities		3,117
Extraordinary Items		
Extraordinary gains (net of income taxes of $240)	360	
Extraordinary losses (net of income taxes of $-)	–	360
Profit for the Period		3,477
Minority interest in the net profit for the period		560
Net Profit		2,917

Note

[1] G. Anthony Lopez, 'Comparative Analysis of IAS 8 Net Profit or Loss for the Period, Fundamental Errors and Changes in Accounting Policies and Related US GAAP', in *'The IASC – US GAAP Comparison Project: A Report of Similarities and Differences Between IASC standards and US GAAP'*, ed Carrie Bloomer, Norwalk, CT, FASB, 1996, p159.

CHAPTER 11

Statement of Changes in Equity

11.1 RELEVANT STANDARD AND INTERPRETATION

IAS 1 *Presentation of Financial Statements*
SIC 17 *Equity – Costs of an Equity Transaction*

11.2 HISTORY

IAS 5 *Information to be Disclosed in Financial Statements* required the disclosure of the movements in each component of equity. IAS 1 replaced IAS 5 with effect for accounting periods beginning on or after 1 July 1998. The general history of these IASs is dealt with in chapter 8.

In 1984, the IASC added a project on owners' equity to its work programme. This project was later included in the Framework project (see chapter 28).

When the proposal for the presentation of financial statements project was developed, it was envisaged that consideration would be given to existing requirements (including the disclosure of the movements in components of equity) and fairly new ideas such as the statement of total recognised gains and losses which had recently been introduced by FRS 3 in the United Kingdom. However, in the DSOP for the project, the IASC concluded that a statement of changes in equity – referred to in the DSOP as a statement of comprehensive income – should not be included in the required components of IAS financial statements because 'the concepts have as yet been insufficiently researched internationally to be included as a requirement in an IAS' (*Presentation of Financial Statements*, 19). The DSOP retained the IAS 5 requirement for disclosure of the movements in each component of equity.

After considering the comments on the DSOP, the IASC concluded that 'comprehensive income was an important issue and that financial statements should contain a statement including items of income and expense that are not recognised in the income statement' (*IASC Insight*, December 1995, p10). The IASC believed that such a statement provided the opportunity to resolve a number of emerging issues. Therefore, it proposed that the financial statements should include, as a separate component, a statement of non-owner movements in equity (E53, 9).

Before the IASC completed the revised IAS 1, it issued its 1997 discussion paper on financial instruments. This paper identified the development of an IAS requiring a statement of other comprehensive income as a 'key condition' of its proposals (*Accounting for Financial Assets and Financial Liabilities*, p187). The discussion paper also proposed that the bottom lines of the income statement and the statement of other comprehensive income should be totalled to arrive at total comprehensive income (*ibid*, p188) – E53 had not included such a proposal.

During the development of the revised IAS 1, the IASC participated in discussions at G4+1 on performance reporting. In January 1998, that group published a discussion paper, *Reporting Financial Performance: Current Developments and Future Directions*. The paper discussed the then current standards of G4+1 members and identified areas of agreement among group members about how financial performance should be measured. It also addressed some contentious issues, for example, the recycling through the income statement of gains and losses which have already been recognised in equity.

The revised IAS 1 was approved in July 1997 and requires the presentation of a statement of changes in equity as a separate component of the financial statements. It allows the statement to be presented either as a traditional equity reconciliation (in effect, what had been required by IAS 5) or as a statement of performance.

The IASB has an active project on reporting performance which could have a significant impact on the presentation of changes in equity.

11.3 IOSCO

In June 1994, IOSCO advised the IASC that it supported the efforts to improve IAS 5 and related IASs. It identified a number of suspense issues relating to equity which are described in chapter 8.

IAS 1 is included in 'IAS 2000' endorsed by IOSCO in May 2000. There are two supplemental treatments relating to the statement of changes in equity:

- a possible future project on the recognition of items in equity, including enhanced guidance on disclosures of changes in equity accounts and related recognition and measurement issues (these issues are being considered in the IASB's performance reporting project); and

- the disclosure of transfers from reserves to retained earnings or to net profit or loss (transfers from reserves to retained earnings are disclosed in the statement of change in equity; transfers from reserves to net profit or loss are allowed only in very limited cases which are likely to be reconsidered in the performance reporting project).

11.4 CONTENT AND FORMAT OF THE STATEMENT OF CHANGES IN EQUITY

An entity should present a statement showing:

- the net profit or loss for the period;
- each item of income and expense, gain or loss which is recognised directly in equity;
- the total of income, expenses, gains and losses which are recognised directly in equity; and
- the cumulative effect of changes in accounting policy and the correction of fundamental errors which are dealt with under the benchmark treatments in IAS 8 and are, therefore, adjusted against retained earnings.

(IAS 1, 86)

An entity should also present either within the above statement or in the notes:

- capital transactions with owners and distributions to owners;
- the balance of accumulated profit or loss at the beginning of the period and at the balance sheet date, and the movements for the period; and
- a reconciliation between the carrying amount of each class of equity capital, share premium and each reserve at the beginning and the end of the period, separately disclosing each movement in each class of equity capital, share premium and each reserve.

(IAS 1, 86)

Before dealing with the presentation of such information, it is important to deal with some terminology difficulties in IAS 1. According to IAS 1, the purpose of the statement of changes in equity and disclosures is to report the total gains and losses generated by the entity in the period (IAS 1, 87 and 88). However, the statement of changes in equity summarises all income and expenses – not just gains and losses – irrespective of whether they are included in the income statement or directly in equity.

The confusion results from the fact that IAS 1 uses the terms 'gains' and 'losses' differently from other IFRSs and the Framework. Furthermore, the terms are used with different meanings within IAS 1. Under the Framework, gains are part of income and losses are part of expenses; this is the usual way in which the IASB uses the terms gains and losses in other IFRSs. In IAS 1, the terms are sometimes used to mean total income and total expenses and on other occasions to mean components of income and expenses.

A further confusion is the reference to 'each reserve'. The term 'reserve' is not defined in IAS 1 nor the IASB's glossary of terms and is generally not used in other IFRSs. The term 'reserve' is used in the Framework where it means either appropriations of retained earnings or capital maintenance adjustments (*Framework*, 65). It was used in the same way in IAS 1 [1976]. In the revised IAS 1, the term 'reserve' is clearly intended to encompass every component of equity except share capital and share premium – therefore it includes retained earnings, revaluation surplus, exchange differences and the reserves envisaged by the Framework.

IAS 5 required the separate disclosure of 'retained earnings' (IAS 5, 17 (b)) and the term 'retained earnings' is used extensively throughout IFRSs. For example:

- IAS 8 requires certain adjustments to be made to retained earnings;
- IAS 16 and IAS 38 allow certain revaluation surpluses to be transferred to retained earnings;
- IAS 29 deals specifically with retained earnings when restating financial statements for the effects of hyperinflation;
- IAS 30 requires that certain amounts which are set aside for general banking risks should be treated as appropriations of retained earnings; and
- IAS 39 requires transitional adjustments to be made to retained earnings.

IAS 1 makes no reference to retained earnings but, instead, refers to 'accumulated profit or loss'.

Given all these problems with the terms used in IAS 1, what should an entity do? As the components of equity are usually determined by national laws (*Framework*, 65 to 68) or by specific IFRSs, the statement of changes in equity should show clearly the movements in each component of equity required by law or IFRSs. This will require separate presentation of movements in the following components of equity, when appropriate:

- various classes of share capital;
- capital paid in excess of share capital (share premium);
- the equity component of compound financial instruments;

- legal and other reserves which are appropriations of the accumulated profit or loss;
- capital maintenance adjustments;
- revaluation surplus;
- foreign exchange differences; and
- the accumulated profit or loss (retained earnings).

The statement of changes in equity may be presented as either:

- a reconciliation between the opening and closing balances of each component of shareholders' equity (see example 11.1); or
- a statement of total recognised gains and losses or comprehensive income which includes the net profit or loss for the period, the items which are recognised directly in equity and the adjustments resulting from changes in accounting policies or fundamental errors (see example 11.2) – the other changes in equity are shown in the notes.

(IAS 1, 89)

11.5 DIVIDENDS PAYABLE

Dividends paid or payable on the entity's share capital should be debited directly to equity (IAS 32, 30). However, dividends which relate to a financial instrument or a component part of a financial instrument, which is classified as a financial liability should be accounted for as an expense (IAS 32, 30).

The requirement to debit dividends directly to equity is understood to prohibit the deduction of dividends from the net profit for the period.

Dividends which are stated to be in respect of the period covered by the financial statements but which are not proposed or declared until after the balance sheet date are not a liability and should not be provided for (IAS 10, 11).

The amount of dividends per share, declared or proposed, for the period covered by the financial statements should be disclosed (IAS 1, 85). This amount includes both dividends paid during the period in respect of that period and dividends payable in respect of the period. No guidance is provided on the computation. IAS 33 requires that per share amounts for components of the net profit or loss for the period should be calculated using the weighted average number of shares used for basic earnings per share (IAS 33, 51). In the case of dividends per share, it is usual to use the actual number of shares (that is, the actual dividend per share) rather than the weighted average.

Example 11.1 *Statement of changes in equity – reconciliation of opening and closing balances*

	Share capital	*Share premium*	*Revaluation surplus*	*Foreign exchange differences*	*Accumulated profit*	*Total*
Balance at 1 January 1998						
– as previously reported	30,000	10,424	5,210	1,300	56,978	103,912
– effect of adopting revised IAS 12	–	–	–	–	4,413	4,413
– as restated	30,000	10,424	5,210	1,300	61,391	108,325
Revaluation of property	–	–	2,600	–	–	2,600
Foreign exchange differences	–	–	–	2,875	–	2,875
Net gains recognised directly in equity	–	–	2,600	2,875	–	5,475
Dividend paid	–	–	–	–	(15,736)	(15,736)
Net profit for the period	–	–	–	–	22,414	22,414
Issue of share capital	15,000	5,000	–	–	–	20,000
Balance at 31 December 1998	45,000	15,424	7,810	4,175	68,069	140,478

Example 11.2 *Statement of total recognised gains and losses*

	2002
Revaluation of property	2,600
Gains less losses on available-for-sale financial assets	4,215
Gains less losses on hedging instruments used to hedge firm commitments	1,030
Foreign exchange differences	2,875
Net (losses) gains recognised in equity	10,720
Net profit	22,414
Total recognised gains and losses	33,134

Extract 11.1 *Statement of changes in equity – reconciliation of opening and closing balances*

Mandarin Oriental, Hong Kong, 31 December 2001 (IAS)

	2001 US$m	2000 US$m
At 1 January		
–as previously reported	981.8	826.7
–changes in accounting policy (refer Principal Accounting Policies (E) & (F))	(389.5)	(299.1)
	592.3	527.6
–effect of adopting IAS 39 (refer Principal Accounting Policies (Q))	(2.3)	–
	590.0	527.6
Revaluation of properties		
–net revaluation (deficit)/surplus	(7.8)	15.5
–deferred tax	1.7	(2.8)
Net exchange translation differences		
–amount arising in year	(8.9)	(27.7)
Fair value gains on financial assets	0.2	–
Cash flow hedges		
–fair value losses	(2.0)	–
Net (losses)/gains not recognised in consolidated profit and loss account	(16.8)	(15.0)
Profit after tax and minority interests	3.6	13.4
Dividends	(11.5)	(10.3)
Convertible bonds issue – equity component	–	4.6
Equity rights issue	–	72.0
At 31 December	565.3	592.3

Extract 11.2 *Statement of changes in equity – reconciliation of opening and closing balances*

Erste Bank, Austria, 31 December 2001 (IAS)

In EUR million	Subscribed capital	Add. paid in capital	Retained earnings	Distributable profit	Total 2001	Total 2000
Equity as of 31 December 2000	**367**	**867**	**558**	**64**	**1,856**	–
Initial application of IAS 39	0	0	(127)	0	(127)	–
Equity as of 1 January	**367**	**867**	**431**	**64**	**1,729**	**1,436**
Translation differences	0	0	41	0	41	3
Dividends	0	0	0	(62)	(62)	(54)
Capital increase	0	0	0	0	0	275
Net profit after minority interests	0	0	162	61	223	192
Other changes	(1)	1	(27)*	0	(27)	4
Equity as of 31 December	**366**	**868**	**607**	**63**	**1,904**	**1,856**

* Thereof change caused by the cash flow hedges (EUR 19 million) plus the effect of calling in the participation capital still outstanding EUR 2 million.

CHAPTER 12

Cash Flow Statement

12.1 RELEVANT STANDARD

IAS 7 *Cash Flow Statements*

12.2 HISTORY

IAS 7 *Statement of Changes in Financial Position* (IAS 7 [1977]) was approved in 1977. It required the presentation of a statement which summarised the funds made available to finance the activities of an entity and the uses to which those funds had been put. Funds were defined either as cash, cash and cash equivalents, or working capital (IAS 7 [1977], 4).

IAS 7 [1977] was reviewed in 1985 when the IASC signalled a possible change away from the working capital approach permitted by IAS 7 to a cash and cash equivalents approach. The IASC decided that IAS 7 should not be revised at that time but noted 'with approval' the emphasis then being placed in a number of national standards on changes in cash and cash equivalents rather than changes in working capital (*IASC News*, March 1985, p3).

In 1990, the IASC decided that the time was right to commence work on a revised IAS requiring a cash and cash equivalents approach. IAS 7 *Cash Flow Statements* was approved in 1992, having then been one of the IASC's quickest and least controversial projects. IAS 7 superseded IAS 7 [1977] with effect from accounting periods beginning on or after 1 January 1994.

The May 2002 improvements exposure draft proposes consequential changes to IAS 7 as a result of proposed elimination of extraordinary items in IAS 8 (see chapter 10) and the adoption of functional currency terminology in IAS 21 (see chapter 8).

12.3 IOSCO

At its annual meeting in October 1993, IOSCO resolved that, for cross-border offerings and foreign listings, its members should 'take all steps that are necessary and appropriate in their respective home jurisdictions to accept cash flow statements prepared in accordance with IAS 7 as one alternative to the statements prepared in accordance with the regulator's domestic accounting standards relating to cash flow statements'[1]. The resolution has been signed by the substantial majority of IOSCO members but the members from Indonesia, Japan and Korea indicated their disagreement with the resolution.

Jurisdictions which have implemented the IOSCO endorsement will accept an IAS 7 cash flow statement in cross-border offerings and from other foreign issuers without reconciliation or modification of that statement. The American SEC issued proposals in April 1994 to implement the IOSCO endorsement in its rules (*IASC Insight*, June 1994, p5) and approved the final rule change later that year. IOSCO has also published a detailed report on the implementation of its endorsement[2]. This shows that 38 IOSCO members now accept IAS 7 cash flow statements.

IAS 2 is included in 'IAS 2000' endorsed by IOSCO in May 2000. There are no supplemental treatments.

12.4 IAS 7 IN BRIEF

The financial statements should include a cash flow statement which presents the changes in cash and cash equivalents classified according to operating, investing and financing activities. Operating cash flows may be presented using either the direct method or the indirect method. Non-cash transactions should be omitted from the statement.

12.5 PUBLICATION OF A CASH FLOW STATEMENT

An entity should present a cash flow statement as an integral part of its financial statements (IAS 7, 1). The requirement applies to all entities which publish IFRS financial statements.

During the development of both IAS 7 [1977] and the revised IAS 7, suggestions were made that the IAS should not apply to smaller entities. When it approved IAS 7 [1977], the IASC argued that the usefulness of statements of changes in financial position was not limited to larger entities and that smaller entities had found such information useful in presenting a clear and understandable view of their operations (*IASC News*,

November 1977, p2). The IASC maintained this view when it approved the revised IAS 7; it also recognised the practical difficulties which would arise in attempting to agree an international definition of smaller entities.

It was also suggested during the development of IAS 7 [1977], the revised IAS 7 and IAS 30 that there should be exemptions from IAS 7 for financial institutions. When the IASC approved IAS 7 [1977], it decided that a statement of changes in financial position was as necessary for financial institutions as for other entities (*IASC News*, November 1977, p3). It reached a similar conclusion during the development of IAS 30 which was approved in 1990. Several commentators on E36 *Cash Flow Statements* argued that there should be exemptions for financial institutions but, after considering the comment letters, the IASC confirmed that the IAS should apply to financial institutions (*IASC Insight*, December 1992, p12).

12.6 CASH FLOWS

The cash flow statement summarises and classifies the cash flows of an enterprise. *Cash flows* are inflows and outflows of cash and cash equivalents (IAS 7, 6). Therefore the cash flow statement does not include:

- non-cash transactions, that is transactions which do not involve the inflow or outflow of cash and cash equivalents (IAS 7, 18 and 43); and
- movements between items that constitute cash or cash equivalents (IAS 7, 9).

Non-cash transactions include:

- exchanges of non-monetary assets such as property, plant and equipment and inventories;
- the acquisition of assets by means of finance leases (but the payments of lease rentals are cash flows);
- the exchange of assets or a business in return for equity securities;
- the issuance of bonus shares to holders of the entity's equity;
- the receipt of bonus shares from another entity in which the entity holds an investment; and
- the conversion of debt securities into equity securities.

Extract 12.1 *Non-cash investing transactions*

Harmony, South Africa, 30 June 1997 (IAS)

Excluded from the statements of consolidated cash flows are the following:

- The acquisition by the company of the Vermeulenskraal Noord mineral rights for R79.1 million through the issue of shares and options.

- The acquisition by the company of Randex Limited's Weltevreden shares and other participation rights for R22.9 million through the issue of shares.
- The acquisition by the company of 90.26 per cent of the issued share capital of The Grootvlei Proprietary Mines Limited for R87.5 million through the issue of shares.
- The write-down to market value of listed investments of R13.8 million.
- The acquisition by the company of Consolidated Modderfontein Mines Limited for R89.8 million through the issue of shares.
- The acquisition by the company of Unisel Gold Mines Limited for R506.7 million through the issue of shares.

Movements between the components of cash and cash equivalents include:

- transfers between different bank accounts which are included in cash and cash equivalents; and
- the purchase or sale for cash of short term investments which are treated as cash equivalents.

12.7 CASH AND CASH EQUIVALENTS

Cash is cash on hand and demand deposits (IAS 7, 6). *Cash equivalents* are short-term, highly liquid investments which are readily convertible to known amounts of cash and which are subject to an insignificant risk of changes in value and which are held for the purpose of meeting short-term cash commitments rather than for investment or other purposes (IAS 7, 6). Cash equivalents are likely to be treated as financial assets held for trading and measured at market value under IAS 39 (see chapter 20).

The nature of cash equivalents varies from country to country depending on the particular instruments that are available and from entity to entity depending on their cash management policies. In general, however, cash equivalents may include:

- short-term bank deposits, other than those demand deposits which are included in cash;
- financial assets which have a short maturity of, say, three months or less from the date of acquisition (IAS 7, 7) notwithstanding that the original maturity of those assets may have been greater than three months; and
- equity instruments which are subject to insignificant risks of price changes, for example, redeemable preference shares acquired close to their redemption date – in practice, virtually all equity instruments are not cash equivalents.

Extract 12.2 *Cash*

Sulzer, Switzerland, 31 December 2001 (IAS)

Cash comprises bills, postal giros and bank accounts, together with sight and deposit balances. These include fixed deposits and money market papers with maturities of under 3 months.

Extract 12.3 *Cash and marketable securities*

Swisscom, Switzerland, 31 December 2001 (IAS)

Cash includes petty cash, cash at banks and cash on deposit. Cash equivalents include term deposits with financial institutions, as well as short-term money market investments with original maturity dates of three months or less.

Cash equivalents are usually assets. They are not reduced by liabilities such as bank loans and borrowings. However, an exception may be made for a bank overdraft which is repayable on demand and which forms an integral part of an enterprise's cash management (IAS 7, 8). A bank overdraft is a bank account on which at any particular point in time, the balance may be positive or negative, that is, in hand or overdrawn. The balance can be in hand (an asset) at one balance sheet date and overdrawn (a liability) at another date and may fluctuate significantly during an accounting period.

A bank overdraft account may be the only bank account which the entity uses for its day-to-day transactions. If such a bank account is not treated as a cash equivalent, the entity would have to treat:

- every payment made out of the account when it is overdrawn as a financing cash inflow as well as an operating, investing or financing outflow; and
- every receipt into the bank account when it is overdrawn as a financing cash outflow as well as an operating, investing or financing inflow.

At those times at which the balance on the bank account is in hand, the account would be cash and would, therefore, be included in cash and cash equivalents. Such an approach would be extremely complicated as well as meaningless.

In some circumstances, an overdraft account may remain overdrawn throughout an accounting period. If the account is not treated as a cash equivalent, the entity would report a financing cash inflow equal to its total payments in the period and a financing cash outflow equal to its total receipts in the period. If the account is the entity's only bank account, the only amount included in cash and cash equivalents might be the office cash balance. Again, this would be meaningless.

The IASC recognised these difficulties and concluded that a bank overdraft with the characteristics described above may be included in cash and cash equivalents, that is, deducted from those items of cash and cash equivalents which are assets. As a result, payments out of the overdraft account and receipts into that account are treated in the same way as payments out of, and receipts into, any other bank account. However, the special treatment does not apply to bank and other loans which do not have the same characteristics as overdrafts.

Two concerns have been raised about the inclusion of bank overdrafts in cash equivalents. The first is that it creates flexibility and the second is that it may result in the offsetting of assets and liabilities in the balance sheet. The first concern is valid although the flexibility reflects the reality of the different banking arrangements which exist around the world. It is better to have that flexibility than a meaningless cash flow statement.

The second concern reflects a misunderstanding of the requirements of IAS 7. IAS 7 does not deal with the balance sheet classification of cash and cash equivalents. Cash is usually classified as cash on the balance sheet. Cash equivalents are classified as bank balances (if they are bank deposits), financial assets or, in the case of bank overdrafts, as liabilities. IAS 7 does require an entity to disclose the components of cash and cash equivalents and reconcile the amounts in the cash flow statement with the equivalent items in the balance sheet (IAS 7, 45).

IAS 1 requires the presentation of 'cash and cash equivalents' on the face of the balance sheet as one of its minimum line items (IAS 1, 66). If cash equivalents for the purposes of IAS 7 include bank overdrafts, it is impossible for the line item 'cash and cash equivalents' to equate to cash and cash equivalents in the cash flow statement.

Extract 12.4 *Bank overdrafts in balance sheet and cash flow statement*

Hongkong Land Holdings, Hong Kong, December 2001 (IAS)

Borrowings (notes to balance sheet)

	2001 US$m	*2000 US$m*
...		
Current		
Bank overdrafts	2.4	2.5
Short-term borrowings	38.4	–
Current portion of long-term borrowings	461.7	924.8
	502.5	927.3

Cash and cash equivalents (notes to the cash flow statement)

	2001 *US$m*	*2000* *US$m*
Bank balances and other liquid funds	568.6	1,493.6
Bank overdrafts	(2.4)	(2.5)
	566.2	1,491.1

Extract 12.5 *Bank overdrafts included in cash and cash equivalents*

Brierley Investments, New Zealand, 30 June 2000 (IAS)

Cash and cash equivalents comprise cash balances and call deposits. For the purpose of the statement of cash flows, cash and cash equivalents are presented net of bank overdrafts.

Cash and cash equivalents	*2000* *US$m*	*1999* *US$m*
Bank balances	20.5	23.3
Call deposits	237.7	380.6
Cash and cash equivalents – balance sheet	258.2	403.9
Bank overdrafts	(2.4)	(0.6)
Cash and cash equivalents – statement of cash flows	255.8	403.3

Extract 12.6 *Bank overdrafts included in financing activities*

Lectra Systèmes, France, 31 December 2001

In thousands of euros	*2001*	*2000*
Financing activities		
Proceeds from issue of common stock	34	11,308
Purchase of treasury stock	(1,200)	(3,110)
Change in long-term and short-term debt	(5,724)	(5,765)
Change in bank overdrafts	(1,514)	(1,514)
Cash provided by (used in) financing activities	**(8,404)**	**919**

12.8 FORMAT OF CASH FLOW STATEMENT

The cash flow statement should report cash flows during the period classified by operating, investing and financing activities (IAS 7, 10). IAS 7 does not require a particular format but does include an appendix which illustrates different formats of cash flow statement. In practice, however, most cash flow statements adopt formats similar to those in the appendix of IAS 7 (see example 12.1).

A single cash flow may have elements which are classified differently. For example, the repayment of a loan may include both the repayment of principal (a financing outflow) and the payment of interest (an operating outflow or a separately reported financing outflow).

Example 12.1 *Cash flow statement*

	Year ended 31 December			
		2002		*2001*
Operating activities				
Cash generated from operations		x		x
Interest received		x		x
Interest paid		x		x
Tax paid		x		x
		–		–
Net cash from operating activities		x		x
Investing activities				
Acquisition of subsidiary, net of cash acquired	x		x	
Purchase of property, plant and equipment	x		x	
Purchase of intangible assets	x		x	
Purchase of non-current investments	x		x	
Loans made	x		x	
Disposal of current investments	x		x	
Loan and lease payments received	x		x	
Dividends received	x		x	
Government grants received	x		x	
	–		–	
Net cash in investing activities		x		x
Financing activities				
Issue of convertible bonds	x		x	
Issue of redeemable preference shares	x		x	
Issue of ordinary shares	x		x	
Purchase of treasury shares	x		x	
Proceeds from long-term borrowings	x		x	
Finance lease principal payments	x		x	
Dividends paid to group shareholders	x		x	
Dividends paid to minority interests	x		x	
	–		–	
Net cash in financing activities		x		x
		–		–
(Decrease)/Increase in cash and cash equivalents		x		x
		–		–
Movement in cash and cash equivalents				
At start of year		x		x
(Decrease)/Increase		x		x
Effects of exchange rate changes		x		x
		–		–
At end of year		x		x

Some cash flows may be classified differently according to the accounting policies adopted by an entity or by its application of these policies. For example, cash flows associated with development costs or other internally generated intangible assets which are capitalised as assets are classified as investing activities whereas the cash flows associated with similar costs which are treated as expenses are classified as operating activities.

12.9 CASH FLOWS FROM OPERATING ACTIVITIES

Operating activities are the principal revenue-producing activities of the enterprise and other activities that are not investing or financing activities (IAS 7, 6). They generally result from the transactions and other events which enter into the determination of net profit or loss but they do not include such items as the acquisition of property, plant and equipment, or capitalised intangible assets.

Cash flows from operating activities for an entity which is not a financial institution usually include:

- cash receipts from the sale of goods and the rendering of services;
- cash receipts from royalties, fees, commissions and other revenue (but sometimes not interest and dividends – see 12.11 below);
- cash payments to suppliers for goods and services;
- cash payments to, and on behalf of, employees;
- cash payments or refunds of income taxes unless they can be specifically identified with financing and investing activities (IAS 7, 35) – see 12.12 below; and
- cash receipts and payments from derivatives held for trading.

Cash flows from operating activities should be reported in the cash flow statement using either:

- the *direct method* under which the gross cash receipts and gross cash payments are disclosed (example 12.2); or
- the *indirect method* under which the net amount of receipts and payments is disclosed (example 12.3).

(IAS 7, 18)

There is an ambiguity in IAS 7 about the determination of cash flows from operating activities under the indirect method. IAS 7 defines cash flows from operating activities as the net profit or loss for the period, that is, profit after income taxes, adjusted by non-cash items (example 12.3). The example in the appendix to IAS 7 defines cash flows from operating activities as the profit before income taxes (example 12.4). This difference explains why some entities add a footnote to disclose the amount of tax paid.

Example 12.2 *Direct method of reporting cash flows from operating activities*

	$m
Cash received from customers	3,015
Cash paid to suppliers	(1,430)
Cash paid to and on behalf of employees	(950)
Tax paid	(60)
Net cash from operating activities	575

Example 12.3 *Indirect method of reporting cash flows from operating activities*

	$m
Net profit for the period	270
Adjustments for:	
Depreciation of property, plant and equipment	205
Amortisation of goodwill	80
Interest expense	140
Dividend income	(120)
Increase in receivables	(150)
Increase in inventories	(205)
Increase in payables	355
Net cash from operating activities	575

Example 12.4 *Indirect method of reporting cash flows from operating activities*

	$m
Profit from ordinary activities before income taxes	330
Adjustments for:	
Depreciation of property, plant and equipment	205
Amortisation of goodwill	80
Interest expense	140
Dividend income	(120)
Increase in receivables	(150)
Increase in inventories	(205)
Increase in payables	355
Income taxes paid	(60)
Net cash from operating activities	575

Extract 12.7 *Indirect method cash flow statement*

Nestlé, 31 December 2001 (IAS)

Consolidated cash flow statement for the year ended 31 December 2001

In millions of CHF	*Notes*	*2001*	*2000*
Operating activities			
Net profit of consolidated companies		**6,338**	5,580
Depreciation of property, plant and equipment	12	**2,581**	2,737
Impairment of property, plant and equipment	12	**222**	223
Amortisation of goodwill	15	**494**	414
Depreciation of intangible assets	16	**150**	179
Impairment of goodwill	15	**184**	230
Increase/(decrease) in provisions and deferred taxes		**(92)**	(4)
Decrease/(increase) in working capital	27	**(870)**	(368)
Other movements		**(393)**	(140)
Operating cash flow[(a)]		**8,614**	8,851
Investing activities			
Capital expenditure	12	**(3,611)**	(3,305)
Expenditure on intangible assets	16	**(288)**	(188)
Sale of property, plant and equipment		**263**	355
Acquisitions	28	**(18,766)**	(2,846)
Disposals	29	**484**	780
Income from associates		**133**	107
Other movements		**143**	39
Cash flow from investing activities		**(21,642)**	(5,058)
Financing activities			
Dividend for the previous year		**(2,127)**	(1,657)
Purchase of treasury shares		**(1,133)**	(765)
Sale of treasury shares and options		**880**	1,837
Premium on warrants issued		**209**	81
Movements with minority interests		**(172)**	(221)
Bonds issued		**3,338**	1,016
Bonds repaid		**(380)**	(1,143)
Increase/(decrease) in other medium/ long term financial liabilities		**(71)**	(155)
Increase/(decrease) in short term financing liabilities		**16,754**	921
Decrease/(increase) in marketable securities and other liquid assets		**(2,330)**	(2,788)
Decrease/(increase) in short term investments		**216**	1,452
Cash flow from financing activities		**15,184**	(1,422)
Translation differences on flows		**60**	(175)
Increase/(decrease) in cash and cash equivalents		**2,216**	2,196

In millions of CHF	*Notes*	*2001*	*2000*
Cash and cash equivalents at beginning of year		**5,451**	3,322
Effects of exchange rate changes on opening balance		**(29)**	(67)
Cash and cash equivalents retranslated at beginning of year		**5,422**	3,255
Fair-value adjustment on cash and cash equivalents		**(21)**	–
Cash and cash equivalents at end of year	8	**7,617**	5,451

(a) Taxes paid amount to CHF 2,782 million (2000: CHF 2,714 million). Interest received/paid does not differ materially from interest shown under note 2 'Net financing cost'.

IAS 7 encourages the use of the direct method as it provides information which may be useful in estimating future cash flows and which is not available under the indirect method. In particular, it shows actual amounts of cash received and paid. The direct method is favoured in some national requirements (for example, Australia and New Zealand) and is required in Japan in the cash flow statement which forms part of the securities report for individual companies. Most countries allow a choice between the two methods because of the practical difficulty faced by many entities in obtaining the information for the direct method. Practice favours the indirect method.

12.10 CASH FLOWS FROM INVESTING ACTIVITIES

Investing activities are the acquisition and disposal of long-term assets and the acquisition of other investments which are not included in cash equivalents (IAS 7, 6). Therefore, cash flows from investing activities for an entity which is not a financial institution include financial assets held to maturity and available-for-sale financial assets, for example:

- cash payments to acquire property, plant and equipment, capitalised intangible assets, and other long-term assets;
- cash payments relating to capitalised internally generated intangible assets and self-constructed property, plant and equipment;
- cash receipts from sales of property, plant and equipment, intangible assets, and other long-term assets;
- cash payments to acquire, and cash receipts from sales of, equity or debt instruments of other entities (other than payments or receipts for those instruments considered to be cash equivalents or those held for trading purposes);
- advances to, and the repayment of advances from, associates and jointly controlled entities;

- cash payments to acquire, and cash receipts from sales of, interests in joint ventures;
- cash advances and loans made to other parties;
- cash receipts from the repayment of advances and loans made to other parties; and
- cash payments for, or receipts from, derivatives except when the contracts are held for trading purposes, or the payments are classified as financing activities.

The aggregate cash flows arising from acquisitions and disposals of subsidiaries or other business units should be presented separately (IAS 7, 39).

Cash flows from investing activities are reported gross and major classes should be reported separately (IAS 7, 21). However, the following cash flows may be reported on a net basis:

- cash receipts and payments on behalf of customers when the cash flows reflect the activities of the customer rather than those of the entity (for example, rents collected by the entity on behalf of, and paid over to, the owners of properties); and
- cash receipts and payments for items in which the turnover is quick, the amounts are large, and the maturities are short (for example, advances made by the entity for, and the repayment to the entity of, principal amounts relating to credit card customers, and the purchase and sale of investments).

(IAS 7, 22)

Some investing transactions do not require the use of cash or cash equivalents, for example:

- the acquisition of long-term assets by means of a finance lease; and
- the acquisition of another business by means of an issue of shares or other equity instruments.

As with other non-cash transactions, these transactions should be excluded from the cash flow statement but should be disclosed (IAS 7, 43).

Extract 12.8 *Cash flows from investing activities*

SAS, Sweden, 31 December 2000 (IAS)

MSEK	*2000*	*1999*
Investments		
Aircraft	−5,684	−2,932
Spare parts	−504	−363
Buildings, equipment and other facilities	−687	−1,064
Shares and participations, goodwill etc.	−744	−490
Prepayments for flight equipment	−2,267	−1,133
Total investments	−9,886	−5,982
Sale of fixed assets	5,539	6,550
Translation differences, etc.	20	51
Net investments	−4,327	619

12.11 CASH FLOWS FROM FINANCING ACTIVITIES

Financing activities are activities that result in changes in the size and composition of the equity capital and borrowings of the entity (IAS 7, 6). Therefore, cash flows from financing activities for an entity which is not a financial institution include:

- cash proceeds from issuing shares or other equity instruments;
- cash payments to acquire or redeem the entity's shares;
- cash proceeds from issuing debentures, loans, notes, bonds, mortgages and other short or long-term borrowings;
- cash repayments of amounts borrowed; and
- cash payments by a lessee for the reduction of the outstanding liability relating to a finance lease.

Cash flows from financing activities are reported gross and major classes should be reported separately (IAS 7, 21). However, the following cash flows may be reported on a net basis:

- cash receipts and payments on behalf of customers when the cash flows reflect the activities of the customer rather than those of the entity (for example, the acceptance and repayment of demand deposits); and
- cash receipts and payments for items in which the turnover is quick, the amounts are large, and the maturities are short (for example, short-term borrowings which have a maturity period of three months or less).

(IAS 7, 22 and 23)

Some financing transactions do not require the use of cash or cash equivalents, for example:

- the use of a finance lease to acquire long-term assets;
- the issue of shares or other equity instruments to acquire another entity in a business combination; and
- the conversion of debt to equity.

As with other non-cash transactions, these transactions should be excluded from the cash flow statement but they should be disclosed (IAS 7, 43).

Extract 12.9 *Cash flows from financing activities*

Volkswagen, Germany, 31 December 2001 (IAS)

Million €	*2001*	*2000*
Capital contributions	135	24
Acquisition of treasury shares	–	−2,285
Dividends paid/compensation for loss	−465	−333
Other changes in equity	−345	−1,430
Take-up of bonds	4,319	2,859
Repayment of bonds	−3,232	−1,463
Change in other borrowings	6,917	7,495
Finance lease payments	−27	25
Change in loans to Group companies	−319	−141
Cash flows from financing activities	**6,983**	**4,751**

12.12 INTEREST AND DIVIDENDS

Interest and dividends received are either returns on cash and cash equivalents or returns on investments. There are arguments in favour of their being classified as cash flows from operating activities or cash flows from investing activities. Similarly, interest paid could be classified as cash flows from operating activities or financing activities. The IASC could not reach agreement on this issue in the case of an entity which is not a financial institution. Therefore, IAS 7 requires only that these cash flows should be classified in a consistent manner from period to period and disclosed separately (IAS 7, 31).

Interest and dividends received should be classified as cash flows from either operating or investing activities. Interest and dividends paid should be classified as cash flows from either operating or financing activities.

12.13 INCOME TAXES

Taxes paid should be classified as cash flows from operating activities unless they can be specifically identified with financing and investing activities (IAS 7, 35). However, while it may be possible to associate part of the tax expense for the period with investing or financing activities, it may be impracticable to identify the related tax cash flows, particularly when income taxes are paid in instalments or the payments are affected by the availability of tax loss carry forwards or other reliefs. For example, while the deductions for depreciation of property, plant and equipment permitted in determining taxable profits are associated with the investing activity of acquiring property, plant and equipment, it may be difficult to identify the related cash flows. Therefore, taxes paid are almost invariably classified as cash flows from operating activities.

The amount of taxes paid should be separately disclosed (IAS 7, 35). When tax cash flows are allocated over more than one classification, the total amount is disclosed (IAS 7, 36).

IASB improvements project

In its May 2002 improvements exposure draft, the IASB proposes to replace 'impracticability' with 'undue cost and effort'.

12.14 EXTRAORDINARY ITEMS

The cash flows associated with extraordinary items should be classified as arising from operating, investing or financing activities, as appropriate, and separately disclosed (IAS 7, 29). For example:

- any cash reimbursement arising on the appropriation of a business is classified as an investing cash flow in the same way that the proceeds of the sale of a business are classified as investing cash flows; and
- any cash received in respect of insurance claims arising from a natural disaster is classified as either operating or investing cash flow, depending on the nature of the assets for which reimbursement is obtained – for example, cash received in respect of inventories is classified as cash flow from operating activities whereas cash received in respect of plant and equipment is classified as cash flow from investing activities.

> ***IASB improvements project***
>
> In its May 2002 improvements exposure draft, the IASB proposes to prohibit the classification of income or expenses as extraordinary items (see chapter 8). If this proposal is implemented, no cash flows will be associated with extraordinary items.

12.15 FOREIGN CURRENCY CASH FLOWS

Cash flows denominated in a foreign currency should be reported in a manner consistent with IAS 21 (IAS 7, 27). Therefore:

- foreign currency cash flows should be recorded by applying to the foreign currency amount the exchange rate between the reporting currency and the foreign currency at the date of the cash flow – average rates for a period are often used (IAS 7, 25); and
- the cash flows of a foreign subsidiary should be translated at the exchange rate between the reporting currency and the foreign currencies at the date of the cash flow (IAS 7, 26) – an exchange rate that approximates the actual rate may be used, for example, a weighted average exchange rate for a period.

Unrealised exchange gains and losses, for example on monetary assets and liabilities at the balance sheet date, are not cash flows. However, unrealised gains and losses arising on the translation of foreign currency cash and cash equivalents held at the balance sheet date are reported in the cash flow statement in order to reconcile cash and cash equivalents at the beginning and the end of the period with the amounts included in the balance sheet.

> ***IASB improvements project***
>
> In its May 2000 improvements exposure draft, the IASB proposes to amend IAS 21 to refer to an entity's functional currency and make a consequential amendment to IAS 7. The overall requirements in IAS 7 for the reporting of foreign currency cash flows will remain the same.

12.16 DISCLOSURE

An entity should disclose:

- the components of cash and cash equivalents (IAS 7, 45);
- a reconciliation of the amount of cash and cash equivalents with the equivalent items reported in the balance sheet (IAS 7, 45);
- its policy for determining the composition of cash and cash equivalents and the effect of any change in that policy (IAS 7, 46);
- the amount of significant cash and cash equivalent balances held by the entity that are not available for use by the group together with a commentary by management (IAS 7, 48) – these balances may include those in a foreign country where exchange controls or other restrictions mean that the balances are not available for general use by the group.

Extract 12.10 *Reconciliation of cash and cash equivalents*

Bayer, Germany, 31 December 2001 (IAS)

Cash and cash equivalents as of 31 December 2001 amounted to €0.7 billion (2000 €0.5 billion). The liquid assets of €0.8 billion (2000 €0.7 billion) shown in the balance sheet also include marketable securities and other instruments.

Extract 12.11 *Reconciliation of cash*

S&T, Austria, 31 December 2001 (IAS)

(T€)	*2001*	*2000*
Cash at banks and in hand	30,359	12,567
Marketable securities, held for trading at fair value	5	26
	30,364	12,593

For the purpose of preparing the cash flow statement, cash and cash equivalents are derived by reducing total bank deposits and marketable securities of T€30,364 by deposits held for a period longer than three months of T€5,347 (representing net balance of T€25,017, in 2000: T€5,481). These deposits are pledged as security for long-term loans. The weighted average effective interest rate on short-term bank deposits was 4.1% (2000: 4.7%).

Extract 12.12 *Liquid assets*

Nestlé, Switzerland, 31 December 2001 (IAS)

In millions of CHF	*2001*	*2000*
Cash and cash equivalents		
Cash at bank and in hand	2,094	1,778
Cash equivalents	5,523	3,673
	7,617	5,451
Other liquid assets		
Current investments	106	326
Marketable securities and other	8,319	4,354
	8,425	4,680
Liquid assets	16,042	10,131

Liquid assets are mainly denominated in the following currencies:

In millions of CHF	*2001*	*2000*
USD	7,028	3,307
EUR	2,898	2,779
CHF	4,471	2,756
Other	1,645	1,289
	16,042	10,131

Interest rates are as follows:

In millions of CHF	*2001*	*2000*
on USD	3.2%	6.7%
on EUR	3.9%	4.8%
on CHF	2.8%	2.8%

All liquid assets have maturities of less than one year.

Liquid assets are classified as follows:

In millions of CHF	*2001*	*2000**
Available-for-sale	15,382	
Trading	660	
	16,042	

* Information not available.

Extract 12.13 *Components of, and movements in cash and cash equivalents*

Trans Zambezi Industries, Zimbabwe, 30 September 1999 (IAS)

	1999	*1998*
	Z$m	*Z$m*
At 1 October	66.7	145.6
Net cash outflow for the year	(17.7)	(123.0)
Exchange movement on cash	(7.9)	44.1
At 30 September	41.1	66.7

Movements in cash balances	*Opening*	*Closing*	*Change*
Short-term investments	104.9	152.7	47.8
Cash	138.1	166.5	28.4
Short-term loans and overdrafts	(176.3)	(278.1)	(101.8)
	66.7	41.1	(25.6)

An entity should also disclose, in aggregate, in respect of both acquisitions and disposals of subsidiaries or other business units during the period each of the following:

- the total purchase or disposal consideration;
- the portion of the purchase or disposal consideration discharged by means of cash and cash equivalents;
- the amount of cash and cash equivalents in the subsidiary or business unit acquired or disposed of; and
- the amount of the assets and liabilities other than cash or cash equivalents in the subsidiary or business unit acquired or disposed of, summarised by each major category.

(IAS 7, 40)

Extract 12.14 *Acquisition and disposal of subsidiaries*

Novartis, Switzerland, 31 December 2001 (IAS)

The following is a summary of the cash flow impact of the major divestments and acquisitions of subsidiaries:

	2001 Acquisitions CHF millions	*2001 Divestments CHF millions*	*2000 Acquisitions CHF millions*	*2000 Divestments CHF millions*
Tangible fixed assets	–52	23	–199	2,491
Other long-term assets	–61		–105	2,415
Inventories	–46		–196	2,551
Trade accounts receivable and other current assets	–73		–165	2,631
Marketable securities, cash and short-term deposits	–18		–51	–70
Long-term and short-term debt to third parties	148		200	–3,336
Trade accounts payable and other liabilities	83	2	635	–2,918
Net assets acquired/divested	**–19**	**25**	**119**	**3,764**
Less acquired /divested liquidity	18		51	70
Less decrease in investments in associated companies	111			
Sub-total	**110**	**25**	**170**	**3,834**
Goodwill	–349		–1,612	
Changes in equity and minority interests due to:				
– net assets transferred to Syngenta				–4,463
– proceeds received from Novartis shareholders in respect of Syngenta related purchase rights				687
– other				12
Divestment gains		45		1
Net Cash Flow	**–239**	**70**	**–1,442**	**71**

All acquisitions were for cash. The significant divestment in 2000 was the spin-off of Novartis Agribusiness to form Syngenta AG.

The following are the cash flows from the discontinued Agribusiness sector included in the consolidated cash flow statement.

	2000
	CHF millions
Cash flow from operating activities	1,437
Cash flow from investing activities	–166
Cash flow from financing activities	–818

Disclosure of additional information is encouraged when it may be relevant to users in understanding the entity's financial position and liquidity, for example:

- the amount of undrawn borrowing facilities that may be available for future operating activities and to settle capital commitments, indicating any restrictions on the use of these facilities;
- the aggregate amounts of the cash flows from each of the operating, investing and financing activities related to interests in joint ventures reported using proportionate consolidation;
- the aggregate amount of cash flows that represent increases in operating capacity separately from those cash flows that are required to maintain operating capacity; and
- the amount of the cash flows arising from the operating, investing and financing activities of each reported industry and geographical segment.

(IAS 7, 50)

Extract 12.15 *Unused facilities*

Czech Telecom, Czech Republic, 31 December 2000 (IAS)

At 31 December 2000 the Group had available approximately CZK 21 billion of undrawn loan facilities.

Extract 12.16 *Operating and maintenance cash flows*

Hongkong Land, Hong Kong, 31 December 2001 (IAS)

Cash flow per share is based on cash flows from operating activities less major renovations expenditure amounting to US$180.5 million (2000: US$198.2 million) ...

12.17 CASH FLOW STATEMENT OF A BANK

The basic requirements for the preparation of a cash flow statement for a bank or other financial institution are the same as those for other entities:

- the cash flow statement should present the changes in cash and cash equivalents classified according to operating, investing and financing activities;
- operating cash flows may be presented using either the direct method or the indirect method; and
- non-cash transactions should be omitted from the statement.

12.17.1 Definition of Cash and Cash Equivalents

IAS 7 does not provide any guidance on the application of the definitions of cash and cash equivalents to a bank. Furthermore, the example of a bank cash flow statement in the appendix to IAS 7 does not disclose the components of cash and cash equivalents.

An approach which is commonly adopted is to include in cash and cash equivalents:

- cash;
- balances with the central bank insofar as they are freely available; and
- money market instruments such as treasury bills and placements with other banks.

Cash equivalents also include government and other securities held for trading purposes insofar as those securities are either:

- investments which have a short maturity of, say, three months or less from the date of acquisition (IAS 7, 7) notwithstanding that the original maturity of those investments may have been greater than three months; and
- equity investments which are subject to insignificant risks of price changes, for example, redeemable preference shares acquired close to their redemption date – in practice, virtually all equity investments of a bank are not cash equivalents.

Loans and advances to, and deposits from customers are not cash and cash equivalents. Changes in such accounts are operating cash flows. Long-term deposits with the central bank are also not cash and cash equivalents, particularly if they are made in response to the efforts of the central bank to remove liquidity from financial markets or provide additional security for depositors.

Extract 12.17 *Cash and cash equivalents for a bank*

Deutsche Bank, Germany, 31 December 2000

The reported amount of cash and cash equivalents specifically comprises cash on hand, balances with central banks and debt instruments of public-sector entities, and bills of exchange eligible for refinancing at central banks.

Extract 12.18 *Cash and cash equivalents for a bank*

Gulf International Bank, Bahrain, 31 December 2000 (IAS)

	31.12.00 *US$ millions*	*31.12.99* *US$ millions*
Cash Balances with Banks	67.8	156.6
Certificates of Deposit	68.0	169.2
Treasury Bills	1.5	123.0
Securities Purchased under Agreements to Resell	–	47.3
Money Market Funds	–	6.0
	137.3	502.1

12.17.2 Classification of Cash Flows

Cash flows from the operating activities of a bank include:

- cash receipts and cash payments for interest received or paid by the bank (IAS 7, 33);
- cash receipts from fees and commissions;
- cash receipts for dividends (IAS 7, 33);
- cash receipts and payments for advances and loans to customers and the repayment of those advances and loans (IAS 7, 15 and 16);
- cash receipts and payments relating to finance leases in which the bank is the lessor;
- cash payments for the purchase of financial assets held for trading and cash receipts from the sale of such assets;
- cash receipts and payments from futures contracts, forward contracts, options contracts and swap contracts when the contracts are held for dealing or trading purposes;
- cash payments to suppliers for goods and services;
- cash payments to, and on behalf of, employees; and
- cash payments or refunds of income taxes unless they can be specifically identified with financing and investing activities (IAS 7, 35).

As with any other entity, cash flows from operating activities should be reported in the cash flow statement using either:

- the direct method; or
- the indirect method.

(IAS 7, 18)

Cash flows from investing activities include:

- cash payments to acquire property, plant and equipment and other long-term assets;
- cash receipts from sales of property, plant and equipment, intangible assets, and other long-term assets; and
- cash payments to acquire, and cash receipts from sales of, investment securities and other long-term investments.

Cash flows from the investing activities of a bank do not include those associated with dealing securities or loans and advances to customers.

Cash flows from financing activities include:

- cash proceeds from issuing shares or other equity instruments;
- cash payments to acquire or redeem the bank's shares;
- cash proceeds from issuing debentures, loans, notes, bonds, mortgages and other long-term borrowings;
- cash repayments of amounts borrowed; and
- cash payments as lessee for the reduction of the outstanding liability relating to a finance lease.

Cash flows from financing activities do not include those associated with deposits from customers.

12.17.3 Netting of Cash Flows

Cash flows arising from each of the following operating activities of a bank may be reported on a net basis:

- the acceptance and repayment of demand deposits and other deposits with a fixed maturity date (IAS 7, 24);
- placements with, and withdrawal of those placements from, other financial institutions (IAS 7, 24);
- advances and loans to customers and the repayment of those advances and loans (IAS 7, 24);
- principal amounts relating to credit card receivables (IAS 7, 24); and
- the purchase and sale of financial assets when the turnover in those assets is quick, the amounts are large and the maturities are short (IAS 7, 22 and 23).

Extract 12.19 *Cash flow statement of a bank*

UBS, Switzerland, 31 December 2001 (IAS)

CHF million *For the year ended*	*31.12.01*	*31.12.00*
Cash flow from/(used in) operating activities		
Net profit	4,973	7,792
Adjustments to reconcile net profit to cash flow from/(used in) operating activities		
Non-cash items included in net profit and other adjustments:		
Depreciation of property and equipment	1,614	1,608
Amortization of goodwill and other intangible assets	1,323	667
Credit loss expense/(recovery)	498	(130)
Equity in income of associates	(72)	(58)
Deferred tax expense	292	544
Net loss/(gain) from investing activities	513	(730)
Net (increase)/decrease in operating assets:		
Net due from/to banks	27,306	(915)
Reverse repurchase agreements, cash collateral on securities borrowed	(60,536)	(81,054)
Trading portfolio including net replacement values and securities pledged as collateral	(78,456)	(11,553)
Loans/due to customers	42,813	12,381
Accrued income, prepaid expenses and other assets	(424)	6,923
Net increase/(decrease) in operating liabilities:		
Repurchase agreements, cash collateral on securities lent	80,006	50,762
Accrued expenses and other liabilities	(5,235)	3,313
Income taxes paid	(1,742)	(959)
Net cash flow from/(used in) operating activities	12,873	11,697
Cash flow from/(used in) investing activities		
Investments in subsidiaries and associates	(467)	(9,729)
Disposal of subsidiaries and associates	95	669
Purchase of property and equipment	(2,021)	(1,640)
Disposal of property and equipment	380	335
Net (investment)/divestment in financial investments	(5,770)	(8,770)
Net cash flow from/(used in) investing activities	(7,783)	(19,135)
Cash flow from/(used in) financing activities		
Net money market paper issued	24,226	10,125
Net movements in treasury shares and treasury share contract activity	(6,038)	(647)
Capital issuance	12	15
Capital repayment by par value reduction	(683)	
Dividends paid		(3,928)
Issuance of long-term debt	18,233	14,884
Repayment of long-term debt	(18,477)	(24,640)
Issuance of trust preferred securities	1,291	2,683
Dividend payments to/and purchase from minority interests	(461)	(73)
Net cash flow from/(used in) financing activities	18,103	(1,581)
Effects of exchange rate differences	(304)	112
Net increase/(decrease) in cash equivalents	22,889	(8,907)
Cash and cash equivalents, beginning of the year	93,370	102,277
Cash and cash equivalents, end of the year	116,259	93,370
Cash and cash equivalents comprise:		
Cash and balances with central banks	20,990	2,979
Money market paper[1]	69,938	66,454
Due from banks maturing in less than three months	25,331	23,937
Total	116,259	93,370

[1] Money market paper is included in the Balance sheet under Trading portfolio assets and Financial investments.

The reporting of the purchase and sale of financial assets on a net basis does not extend to investment securities, that is, those investments which are acquired and held for yield and capital growth purposes and are usually held to maturity (IAS 30, 25). The gross amounts relating to the purchase and sale of such investments must be shown separately.

Notes

1 'Resolution Concerning Accounting Standard 7', Presidents Committee, IOSCO, October 1993.

2 'Implementation of IOSCO Resolutions', IOSCO, September 1998.

CHAPTER 13

Accounting Policies and Changes in Accounting Policies

13.1 RELEVANT STANDARDS AND INTERPRETATIONS

IAS 1 *Presentation of Financial Statements*
IAS 8 *Net Profit or Loss for the Period, Fundamental Errors and Changes in Accounting Policies*
SIC 1 *Consistency – Different Cost Formulas for Inventories*
SIC 2 *Consistency – Capitalisation of Borrowing Costs*
SIC 18 *Consistency – Alternative Methods*

13.2 HISTORY

IAS 1 replaced IAS 1 *Disclosure of Accounting Policies* (IAS 1 [1975]) with effect from accounting periods beginning on or after 1 July 1998 (see chapter 8).

IAS 8 *Unusual and Prior Period Items and Changes in Accounting Policies* (IAS 8 [1978]) was approved in 1978 and reconsidered in the comparability and improvements project when benchmark and allowed alternative treatments were identified for changes in accounting policies. IAS 8 *Net Profit or Loss for the Period, Fundamental Errors and Changes in Accounting Policies* was approved in November 1993 and applied to financial statements for accounting periods beginning on or after 1 January 1995.

In its May 2002 improvements exposure draft, the IASB proposes to transfer the text in IAS 1 relating to the selection and application of accounting policies to IAS 8. It also proposes to remove the allowed alternative treatment for changes in accounting policies (see 13.11).

13.3 IOSCO

In June 1994, IOSCO advised the IASC that it supported the efforts to improve IAS 1 and related IASs. It identified a number of suspense issues none of which related to the disclosure of accounting policies. In its comment letter on E53, IOSCO emphasised the importance of consistency in the application of accounting policies and urged the IASC to include that principle in the revised IAS 1 but this suggestion was not taken up.

In June 1994, IOSCO advised the IASC that IAS 8 was acceptable for the purposes of the IOSCO core standards. However, IOSCO identified the following suspense items:

- IOSCO will consider the transitional provisions and effective date requirements in IASs which result in changes in accounting policies or new disclosures on a case by case basis – as many IASs are being revised in a short period of time, certain IASCO members are concerned about the comparability of financial statements with prior periods; and
- some IOSCO members may not require the presentation of the pro forma information required by the allowed alternative treatment for changes in accounting policies.

IOSCO also suggested that, as a potential long-term project, the IASC should consider the accounting treatment of changes in accounting estimates, that is whether such changes should be accounted for retrospectively or prospectively. IAS 8 already requires all changes in accounting estimates to be dealt with prospectively (IAS 8, 26).

IAS 8 is included in 'IAS 2000' endorsed by IOSCO in May 2000. There is one supplemental treatment which is a concern about allowing changes in accounting policy to be accounted for as restatements of prior periods rather than as a cumulative adjustment to net profit and loss in the current period. The IASB has rejected this concern in its May 2002 improvements exposure draft.

13.4 IAS 1 AND IAS 8 IN BRIEF

Accounting policies should comply with IASs and should be disclosed.

A new accounting policy is usually applied *retrospectively*, that is to events and transactions as if the policy has always been applied. The corresponding amounts are restated (on a pro forma basis if necessary). The resulting adjustment is either:

- credited or charged to retained earnings; or
- recognised as income or expense of the current period.

Sometimes, a change in accounting policy is applied *prospectively*, that is only to those events and transactions which occur after the change in policy. In such a case, the corresponding amounts are not restated and there is no adjustment to account for.

Many new or revised IFRSs have *transitional provisions* which usually allow the IFRS to be applied only to transactions and events arising after the effective date.

13.5 ACCOUNTING POLICIES

Accounting policies are the specific principles, bases, conventions, rules and practices adopted by an entity in preparing and presenting financial statements (IAS 1, 21 and IAS 8, 6).

13.6 SELECTION OF ACCOUNTING POLICIES

IAS 1 requires that financial statements should present fairly the financial position, performance and cash flows of an entity (IAS 1, 10). In virtually all circumstances, a fair presentation requires the application of IFRSs (IAS 1, 10). When this is the case, accounting policies should be determined so that financial statements comply with IFRSs and interpretations (IAS 1, 20).

Some accounting policies are determined by the single treatment allowed by an IFRS, for example an entity must use the percentage of completion method for construction contracts and when rendering services. Other accounting treatments are determined by choosing among alternative policies allowed by IFRSs, for example an entity must base the carrying amounts of property on either historical cost or fair value at the balance sheet date.

IASB improvements project

In its May 2002 improvements exposure draft, the IASB proposes to clarify the status of its various pronouncements and authoritative non-mandatory guidance which entities need to consider when selecting accounting policies in IFRS financial statements.

When an IAS/IFRS applies to an issue, accounting policies should be determined by considering the following in order of descending importance:

- the IAS/IFRS, including any appendices that form part of the Standard;

Continued

IASB improvements project *(continued)*

- appendices to the IAS/IFRS that do not form part of the Standard; and
- implementation guidance issued in respect of the IAS/IFRS.

When a SIC/IFRIC interpretation applies to an issue, accounting policies should be determined by considering the following in order of descending importance:

- the IAS/IFRS including any appendices that form part of the Standard;
- the interpretation;
- appendices to the IAS/IFRS that do not form part of the Standard; and
- implementation guidance issued in respect of the IAS/IFRS.

13.6.1 Alternative Accounting Policies Available under an IAS

SIC 18 requires that, where more than one accounting policy is available under an IAS, an entity should select and consistently apply one of those accounting policies to similar transactions, events and circumstances. However, when an IAS or interpretation specifically requires or allows categorisation of items for which different policies may be appropriate, for example classes of fixed assets, SIC 18 requires the most appropriate accounting policy is selected and applied consistently to each of those categories.

The IASB's May 2002 improvements exposure draft proposes to include the requirements of SIC 18 within IAS 8.

13.6.2 Issues not Covered by IFRSs

An entity may have transactions and events which are not covered by an IFRS. The entity should choose accounting policies which ensure that the financial statements provide information that is:

- relevant to the decision-making needs of users; and
- reliable in that they:
  - represent faithfully the results and financial position of the entity;
  - reflect the economic substance of events and transactions and not merely their legal form;
  - are neutral, that is, free from bias;

- are prudent; and
- are complete in all material respects.

(IAS 1, 20)

This general requirement is troublesome in several respects. It is a summary of two of the qualitative characteristics in the Framework (see chapter 6) and is, therefore, not written in language appropriate for a Standard. The requirement also uses different language from the rest of IAS 1, for example, it refers to 'represent faithfully the results and financial performance' whereas IAS 1 requires that the financial statements should 'present fairly the financial position, financial performance and cash flows'. It also requires that the financial statements are 'prudent' without defining or explaining that term. In the process it elevates 'prudence' above its previous position in both IAS 1 [1975] and the Framework, a most unexpected outcome of an IASC project.

The general requirement is supported by guidance which is far more practical. It says that, when dealing with an issue not covered by IFRSs an entity should consider, among other things:

- the requirements and guidance of other IFRSs which deal with similar issues;
- the definitions of assets, liabilities, income and expenses and the recognition and measurement criteria in the Framework (but there are no measurement criteria in the Framework); and
- pronouncements of other standard setting bodies and accepted industry practices, to the extent that those are consistent with other IFRSs which deal with similar issues and the Framework.

(IAS 1, 22)

Such an approach is similar to that which the IASB would adopt in developing an IFRS on a new issue. It is also the approach which has been adopted by many entities when dealing in the past with intangible assets and financial instruments in IAS financial statements.

Many entities which report under IFRSs also report under their national accounting requirements (or, possibly, the requirements of another country) and therefore look to those requirements to determine their accounting policies for issues not covered by IFRSs. This is acceptable provided that the chosen accounting policies satisfy the criteria in IAS 1.

Extract 13.1 *Exploration and development expenditure*

Harmony, South Africa, 30 June 2000 (IAS)

Exploration costs are expensed as incurred. Costs related to property acquisitions and mineral and surface rights are capitalised.

Undeveloped properties upon which the Group has not performed sufficient exploration work to determine whether significant mineralisation exists, are carried at original cost. Where the directors consider that there is little likelihood of the properties being exploited, or the value of the exploitable rights has diminished below cost, a writedown is effected against exploration expenditure.

Development costs relating to major programmes at existing mines are capitalised. Development costs consist primarily of expenditure to expand the capacity of operating mines. Mine development costs in the ordinary cause to maintain production are expensed as incurred. Initial development and pre-production costs relating to a new ore body are capitalised until the ore body is brought into production, at which time the costs are amortised.

Extract 13.2 *Insurance*

Zurich Financial Services, Switzerland, 31 December 2001

IAS does not contain guidelines governing the accounting treatment of transactions that are specific to insurance products. In such cases, as envisioned in the IAS framework, the provisions embodied in the United States generally accepted accounting principles (US GAAP) have been applied.

13.6.3 Fair Presentation Override

As explained in chapter 8, in extremely rare circumstances an entity is required to depart from an IFRS in order to achieve fair presentation. In such circumstances, the accounting policy cannot comply with the relevant IFRS. IAS 1 provides no guidance on the selection of the appropriate accounting policy in such circumstances other than that the policy must result in 'fair presentation'.

The best approach in such circumstances is to follow the guidance for issues not covered by IASs (see 13.6.2 above). In addition, the entity should consider:

- the requirements and guidance of other IFRSs which deal with similar issues;
- the definitions of assets, liabilities, income and expenses and the recognition criteria in the Framework;
- the measurement bases permitted by the Framework and used for similar issues; and

- pronouncements of other standard setting bodies and accepted industry practices, to the extent that those are consistent with other IFRSs which deal with similar issues and the Framework.

In applying this guidance, all entities should remember that the compliance with the requirements of other standard setting bodies or industry practice is not sufficient grounds to use the fair presentation override. The use of IFRS treatment itself must be misleading before the override may be used.

13.7 CHANGES IN ACCOUNTING POLICIES

A change in accounting policy should be made only if:

- it is required by statute or an accounting standard setting body; or
- it will result in more relevant or reliable information about the financial position, performance or cash flows of the entity.

(IAS 8, 42 and 43)

A change in accounting policy arises when an entity adopts a new IFRS which requires a different accounting policy from that used in the past.

A change in accounting policy also arises when an entity switches from using one accounting treatment permitted by an IFRS to another treatment permitted by that IFRS. For example, a change in the cost formula used to assign costs to inventories from, say, LIFO to FIFO, is a change in accounting policy because it is a change from one of the treatments currently permitted by IAS 2 to another treatment permitted by IAS 2.

A decision to carry property, plant and equipment at revalued amounts rather than at amounts based on cost is a change from one treatment permitted by an IFRS to another treatment permitted by the IFRS. Therefore, it is a change in accounting policy. However, both IAS 16 and IAS 40 include specific requirements for dealing with revaluations (see chapters 21 and 22) and the revaluations are dealt with in accordance with those requirements rather than a change in accounting policy (IAS 8, 44). This means that there is no requirement for retrospective application of the change or for the restatement of the financial statements of prior periods.

A change in accounting policy needs to be distinguished from a change in the estimates which are necessary to apply that policy. For example, IAS 16 requires an entity to depreciate items of property, plant and equipment over their useful lives. Changes in useful lives are not changes in accounting policies; they are changes in accounting estimates. A change in depreciation method from, say, the declining balance method to the straight line method, is also a change in accounting estimate because the method should reflect the pattern in which the economic benefits are consumed. Similarly, as inventories are carried at the lower of cost and net realisable value, a change in net realisable value is a change in estimate and not a change in accounting policy.

13.8 IMPLEMENTATION OF REVISED ACCOUNTING STANDARDS AND LAWS

An entity publishing IFRS financial statements must change its accounting policies when required by the introduction of a new or revised IFRS. It should explain the impact of those changes in IASs which affect its financial statements. It is required to make the IAS 8 disclosures in the period of change (see below). It is also required to disclose when it has applied an IAS before its effective date (IAS 1, 19). It is also encouraged to disclose the nature and effect of a future change in accounting policy which it will have to make to comply with an IAS which it has not yet adopted but which has already been approved (IAS 8, 48).

Extract 13.3 *Early implementation of revised IASs*

Preussag, Germany, 30 September 2000 (IAS)

In addition to the binding IAS applicable for the financial year, the amendments adopted in October 2000 to IAS 12 *Income Taxes* and IAS 10 *Events After the Balance Sheet Date* were already implemented on a voluntary basis before they became effective. ...

The first-time application of the new rules led to the following substantial changes to the consolidated financial statements:

...

- The rules of IAS 12 (revised 2000) stipulate that current and deferred taxes and liabilities are measured at the tax rate applicable to undistributed profits. Thus deferred taxes for domestic companies were revalued as per 1 October 1999 on the basis of the rate of corporation tax for retained profit with an average tax rate of 52% (previously 43%). Corporate tax savings or charges reported last year and occurring in the event of future distribution of profits retained by German companies in previous years were offset against equity as per 1 October 1999 with no effect on results.
- According to the concept of fictitious profit retention stipulated in IAS 12 (revised 2000), corporation tax credits existing for German companies due to the specific features of German tax law are only taken into account once companies have taken a resolution on the appropriation of profits. For the differences from the tax balance sheet that arise from the balance sheet adjustment and revaluation of German subsidiaries

acquired after 1 October 1995, deferred taxes were calculated to apply retroactively to the time of acquisition. At the same time the goodwill of the companies in question was adjusted accordingly.

These changes [among others] resulted in equity of €278.9 million as per 1 October 1999 with no effect on results. The major changes to the individual balance sheet items are described under the respective items.

Extract 13.4 *Early implementation of revised IASs*

Hoechst, Germany, 31 December 1994 (IAS)

The annual financial statements of the Hoechst Group and Hoechst AG have been prepared in accordance with the requirements of the German Commercial Code and German Stock Corporation Law. In order to improve the international comparability of the information presented in the Group financial statements, we have applied the IASs developed by the International Accounting Standards Committee in so far as they comply with the options permitted under German commercial law. The revisions made by the IASC to existing IASs, which did not come into force until January 1 1995, have already been applied. We have however adhered to the accounting principles used in the past in cases where the application of the IASs would only result in immaterial changes.

In comparison with our prior accounting policies, material changes result from the application of the IAS in the accounting treatment of debit differences arising on consolidation (goodwill) and in the valuation of pension provisions.

Extract 13.5 *Early implementation of new and revised IASs*

Holderbank, Switzerland, 31 December 1999 (IAS)

IAS 16 (revised 1998) *Property, Plant and Equipment*; IAS 22 (revised 1998) *Business Combinations*; IAS 36 *Impairment of Assets* and IAS 38 *Intangible Assets*, have been adopted prior to their effective date as encouraged by the IASC.

Certain prior year balances have been restated according to IAS 8 to comply with current year's presentation.

Extract 13.6 *Future implementation of revised IASs*

Roche, Switzerland, 31 December 1997 (IAS)

The revision to the existing International Accounting Standard on income taxes which came into effect from 1 January 1998 is not expected to have a significant impact on recognition and measurement of current and deferred income taxes since the Group accounting policy already largely reflects the principles in the revision.

Extract 13.7 *Future implementation of revised IASs*

Lafarge, France, 31 December 1997 (IAS)

With effect from January 1, 1998, the Group will apply IAS 12 (revised) under which deferred taxes are recorded by application of the liability method to all temporary differences arising between the tax base of assets and liabilities, and their carrying amount in the balance sheets (full provision method). Goodwill, together with market shares inseparable from the companies concerned and allocated as fair value adjustments, will be excluded from the deferred tax collection base.

Even in IFRS financial statements, it is also necessary to explain the impact of changes in national accounting requirements which affect the entity's financial statements.

Extract 13.8 *Implementation of revised national requirements*

BHP, Australia, 30 June 2000 (Australian GAAP and IAS)

The policies are consistent with those applied in the prior two years except for adoption of new accounting standards:

- Revised AASB 1004 *Revenue* was first adopted for the period ended 30 June 2000. There was no material effect on profit.
- Revised 1016 *Accounting for Investments in Associates* was adopted for the period ended 30 June 2000, resulting in the application of the equity method of accounting for investments in associates. Previously the cost method was used.

Extract 13.9 *Implementation of revised national requirements*

Volvo, Sweden, 31 December 2001 (Swedish GAAP and IAS)

As of 2001, Volvo is applying the following new accounting standards issued by the Swedish Financial Accounting Standards Council: RR1:00 *Consolidated Financial Statements and Business Combinations*, RR12 *Tangible Assets*, RR14 *Joint Ventures*, RR15 *Intangible Assets*, RR16 *Provisions, Contingent Liabilities and Contingent Assets*, RR17 *Impairment of Assets*, RR18 *Income Per Share*, RR19 *Discontinuing Operations* and RR20 *Interim Financial Reporting*. All accounting standards comply in all significant respects with the corresponding accounting standard issued by the International Accounting Standards Committee (IASC).

In applying the transition rules as a consequence of the aforementioned accounting standards, there are no retroactive effects on Volvo's earlier financial statements. In applying the new standards during fiscal year 2001, RR1:00 *Consolidated Financial Statements and Business Combinations*, RR14 *Joint Ventures*, RR15 *Intangible Assets*, RR16 *Provisions, Contingent Liabilities and Contingent Assets* result in a change in Volvo's accounting policies.

IASB improvements project

In its May 2002 exposure draft, the IASB proposes to require, rather than encourage, entities to disclose the nature of a future change in accounting policy relating to a new standard which has been issued but not yet applied. Disclosure will also be required of the planned date of adoption and an estimate of the financial effect of the standard unless making such an estimate would involve undue cost or effort.

13.9 REPORTING CHANGES IN ACCOUNTING POLICIES

A change in accounting policy can be applied *retrospectively* or *prospectively*.

When a change is applied *retrospectively*, the new accounting policy is applied to events and transactions as if the new policy had always been in use. Therefore, retrospective application requires restatement for those transactions and events which would have affected the current period or earlier periods included in the comparative information.

Example 13.1 *Retrospective change in accounting policy*

On 1 January 2000, an entity decides to change its accounting policy and capitalise those borrowing costs that meet the asset recognition criteria in IAS 23. The capitalised costs relate to plant and equipment that is depreciated over a maximum of five years from the year in which the items are first used. The entity decides to apply the change retrospectively.

In order to apply the new policy retrospectively, the entity needs to ascertain what borrowing costs would have been capitalised had it applied the new accounting policy in the earlier periods – in other words, it must decide which costs would have met the IAS 23 capitalisation criteria in the year in which they were incurred. Assume that the entity concludes that the following borrowing costs would have been capitalised in each of the six years:

	Euro Millions
1995	80
1996	70
1997	90
1998	95
1999	110
2000	120

Continued

Example 13.1 *Retrospective change in accounting policy—continued*

There is no need to go back further than 1995 as any borrowing costs which would have been capitalised in earlier years relate to assets that would have been fully depreciated by 31 December 1998.

The entity then needs to calculate the increase in the carrying amount of the assets at 31 December 1998, 31 December 1999 and 31 December 2000 and the increased depreciation for 1999 and 2000 as follows:

Year in which borrowing costs incurred	Borrowing costs capitalised under new policy	Increase in carrying amount of assets	Increase in depreciation	Increase in carrying amount of assets	Increase in depreciation	Increase in carrying amount of assets
		31/12/1998	1999	31/12/1999	2000	31/12/2000
	€m	€m	€m	€m	€m	€m
1995	80	16	16	–	–	–
1996	70	28	14	14	14	–
1997	90	54	18	36	18	18
1998	95	76	19	57	19	38
1999	110	–	22	88	22	66
2000	120	–	–	–	24	96
Total		174	89	195	97	218

The change in the accounting policy is then reported in accordance with the benchmark or allowed alternative treatment (see examples 13.3 and 13.4)

When the change is applied *prospectively*, the new policy is applied only to events and transactions occurring after the date of the change; however, the new accounting policy is applied to existing balances as from the date of the change.

Example 13.2 *Prospective change in accounting policy*

The facts are the same as example 13.1 except that the entity decides to apply the change prospectively with effect from 1 January 2000.

No calculations or adjustments are necessary in respect of borrowing costs incurred prior to 1 January 2000. The new accounting policy is applied to the €120m costs which are incurred in 2000. The increased depreciation for 2000 is €24m and the increased carrying amount of assets at 31 December 2000 is €96m.

A change in accounting policy is:

- applied retrospectively or prospectively in accordance with any transitional provisions that may apply on the adoption of an IFRS (IAS 8, 46). Any such provisions are covered in the relevant chapters;
- applied retrospectively in all other cases unless the amount of any resulting adjustment that relates to previous periods is not reasonably ascertainable (IAS 8, 49 and 54); or
- applied prospectively in all remaining cases (IAS 8, 52 and 56).

13.10 CHANGES IN ACCOUNTING POLICIES – BENCHMARK TREATMENT

The adjustment resulting from retrospective application of the new accounting policy which relates to prior periods should be reported as an adjustment of the opening balance of retained earnings. In such a case, comparative information should be restated under the new accounting policy (IAS 8, 49).

Example 13.3 *Change in accounting policy – benchmark treatment*

The facts are the same as example 13.1. The application of the benchmark treatment has the following effects:

- the opening balance of retained earnings in 1999 is increased by €174m with the increase in the carrying amount of assets of the same amount;
- the income statement for 1999 is restated to show additional depreciation of €89m in place of the originally reported borrowing costs of €110m;
- the balance sheet at 31 December 1999 is restated to show an increase in the carrying amount of assets of €195m and a corresponding increase in retained earnings;
- the income statement for 2000 includes an expense of €97m for the increased depreciation. It would have included borrowing costs of €120m had the accounting policy not changed; and
- the balance sheet at 31 December 2000 includes an increase in the carrying amount of assets of €218m. Retained earnings are €218m higher than they would have been had the accounting policy not changed.

When a change in accounting policy has a material effect on the current period or any prior period presented, or may have a material effect in subsequent periods, an entity should disclose:

- the reasons for the change in policy;
- the amount of the adjustment for the current period and for each period presented;
- the amount of the adjustment relating to prior periods; and
- the fact that comparative information has been restated.

(IAS 8, 53)

Extract 13.10 *Disclosures relating to change in accounting policy dealt with under benchmark treatment*

Lundbeck, Denmark, 31 December 2000 (Danish GAAP and IAS)

There has been a change in accounting policy with respect to the recognition of sales subject to a price adjustment clause.

As from 2000, sales subject to a price adjustment clause are recognised as the price is finally determined. The change in accounting policy is in accordance with the international trend for the recognition of sales where the price has not been finally determined at the time of invoicing and delivery.

The accounting policy for the valuation of other investments comprising investments in shares and other investments has been changed, too.

As from 2000, other investments will be carried at the market price or estimated market value at the balance sheet date. The policy change is in accordance with the general trend towards value based financial statements.

As a result of the policy change, the profit for the year has been reduced by DKK 332 million before tax and DKK 164 million after tax (1999: a reduction of DKK 24 million before tax and an increase of DKK 39 million after tax) and capital and reserves at 31 December 2000 by DKK 156 million (31 December 1999: an increase of DKK 9 million).

The accumulated effect at the beginning of the year has been taken to capital and reserves. The effect of the policy change is described in greater detail in the financial review to which reference is made.

Comparative figures and financial highlights and ratios have been restated to reflect the new accounting policies. These figures are therefore comparable with the figures for the year.

In some cases, it may be difficult to disclose the amount of the adjustment for the current period because this requires the entity to recalculate the profit or loss for the current period using the old accounting policy. It may not be practicable when, for example, the financial statements have been completely recast to deal with a new accounting policy for new financial instruments.

If it is impracticable to restate the comparative information, the entity should disclose that fact (IAS 8, 53). When the comparative information is restated, it is also important to restate other prior period data, such as historical summaries, which is included in the annual report.

> ***IASB improvements project***
>
> In its May 2002 exposure draft, the IASB proposes to eliminate the allowed alternative treatment (see 13.11) for changes in accounting policies. This means that the benchmark treatment will be required in future so changes must be accounted for retrospectively as if they had always applied. As a result an entity will no longer be able to include the adjustment resulting from the retrospective application of a change in accounting policy in the profit or loss for the current period nor present comparative information as it was previously reported. This proposed change is to ensure greater comparability of financial information over time. However, a change in an accounting policy that is made on the adoption of a new IFRS should, when appropriate, be accounted for in accordance with any specific transitional provisions, which may require a treatment similar to the current allowed alternative treatment.
>
> The IASB also proposes to amend the criteria for exemption from restating comparative information on a change in accounting policy from 'impracticability' to 'undue cost or effort'.

13.11 CHANGES IN ACCOUNTING POLICIES – ALLOWED ALTERNATIVE TREATMENT

The adjustment resulting from retrospective application of the new policy which relates to prior periods should be included in the net profit or loss for the current period. Comparative information should be presented as reported in the prior period. The comparative information should also be presented on a pro forma basis as if it had been restated under the new accounting policy (IAS 8, 54).

IAS 8 does not explain what is meant by a 'pro forma basis' but the intention is that the income statement and balance sheet should be presented as if the new policy had been applied.

Example 13.4 *Change in accounting policy – allowed alternative treatment*

The facts are the same as example 13.2. The application of the allowed alternative treatment has the following effects:

- the income statement for 2000 includes income of €195m with the increase in the carrying amount of assets of the same amount as at 1 January 2000;
- the income statement for 2000 also includes an expense of €97m for the increased depreciation. It would have included borrowing costs of €120m had the accounting policy not changed;
- the balance sheet at 31 December 2000 includes an increase in the carrying amount of assets of €218m. Retained earnings are €218m higher than they would have been had the accounting policy not changed; and
- the entity publishes pro forma financial statements for 1999 showing the income statement and balance sheet as if the new policy had been applied in 1999.

When a change in accounting policy has a material effect on the current period or any prior period presented, or may have a material effect in subsequent periods, an entity should disclose:

- the reasons for the change;
- the amount of the adjustment recognised in net profit or loss in the current period; and
- the amount of the adjustment included in each period for which pro forma information is presented and the amount relating to prior periods.

(IAS 8, 57)

If it is impracticable to present pro forma information, this fact should be disclosed (IAS 8, 57). When the comparative information is restated on a pro forma basis, it is important to consider whether or not to restate other prior period data, such as historical summaries, which is included in the annual report.

Extract 13.11 *Impact of change in accounting policy dealt with in accordance with allowed alternative treatment*

BHP, Australia, 31 May 1998 (IAS)

Australian Accounting Standard AASB 1010: *Accounting for the Revaluation of Non-Current Assets* requires that the carrying value of non-current assets does not exceed recoverable amount. Recoverable amount is determined by the estimated future cash flows arising from an asset's continued use and subsequent disposal. The standard allows a test based on either discounted or undiscounted estimated cash flows. As at 31 May 1998, the BHP Group has changed its policy for determining the recoverable amount of non-current assets to a discounted cash flow basis using the weighted average pre-tax interest rate of the BHP Group's long-term borrowings. Previously, recoverable amount was determined utilising undiscounted future net cash flows. This change in accounting policy is considered appropriate given emerging trends in international accounting practice. The financial effect of this policy has been to reduce the carrying value of certain assets and reduce profit attributable to members of the BHP Entity by $2,729 million (after tax) and reduce profit attributable to outside equity interests by $17 million (no tax effect), refer note 2: Significant items. If an undiscounted basis had been applied, the reduction in profit attributable to members of the BHP Entity would have been $1,208 million (after tax) with no effect on profit attributable to outside equity interests.

13.12 DISCLOSURE

An entity should disclose:

- the measurement basis (or bases) used in preparing the financial statements; and
- each specific accounting policy which is necessary for a proper understanding of the financial statements.

(IAS 1, 97)

13.12.1 Measurement Basis

The Framework identifies at least four different measurement bases which are used in financial statements: historical cost; current cost; realisable or settlement value; and present value. If only one basis is used, which is rarely if ever the case, the disclosure is simple. When more than one measurement basis is used, IAS 1 suggests that it is sufficient to provide an indication of the categories of assets and liabilities to which each measurement basis is applied (IAS 1, 98).

13.12.2 Accounting Policies

An accounting policy is disclosed when its disclosure would assist users in understanding the way in which transactions and events are reflected in the financial statements (IAS 1, 99). This disclosure is required irrespective of whether IASs allow a choice of treatments.

CHAPTER 14

Errors

14.1 RELEVANT STANDARD

IAS 8 *Net Profit or Loss for the Period, Fundamental Errors and Changes in Accounting Policies*

14.2 HISTORY

IAS 8 *Unusual and Prior Period Items and Changes in Accounting Policies* (IAS 8 [1978]) was approved in 1978 and reconsidered in the comparability and improvements project when benchmark and allowed alternative treatments were identified for fundamental errors. IAS 8 *Net Profit or Loss for the Period, Fundamental Errors and Changes in Accounting Policies* was approved in November 1993 and applied to financial statements for accounting periods beginning on or after 1 January 1995.

In its May 2002 improvements exposure draft, the IASB proposes to remove the allowed alternative treatment for fundamental errors (see 13.11). It also proposes to remove the term 'fundamental' and require all material errors to be corrected in the same way.

14.3 IOSCO

In June 1994, IOSCO advised the IASC that IAS 8 was acceptable for the purposes of the IOSCO core standards. However, IOSCO identified the following suspense item:

- some IOSCO members may not require the presentation of the pro forma information required by the allowed alternative treatment for fundamental errors (the IASB proposes to eliminate the allowed alternative treatment).

IAS 8 is included in 'IAS 2000' endorsed by IOSCO in May 2000. IOSCO reports a concern about allowing fundamental errors to be accounted for as a cumulative adjustment to net profit and loss in the current period rather than as a restatement of the prior period. The IASB proposes to eliminate this treatment in its May 2002 improvements exposure draft.

14.4 IAS 8 IN BRIEF

Errors in prior period financial statements should be corrected unless the amounts involved do not warrant such an adjustment. When an error is of such significance that the financial statements of the prior periods were not reliable, the error should be corrected by either:

- restating the corresponding amounts so that both the current period and the prior periods are presented as if the error had not occurred; or
- recognising the correction as income or expense of the current period and presenting pro-forma statements for the current and prior periods as if the error had not occurred.

14.5 FUNDAMENTAL ERRORS

Fundamental errors are errors that are of such significance that the financial statements of one or more prior periods can no longer be considered to have been reliable at the date of their issue (IAS 8, 6). In some countries, such errors would lead to the withdrawal of the financial statements but in other countries withdrawal of the financial statements is forbidden by the law once those statements have been approved by shareholders.

The term fundamental, rather than material, is used in IAS 8 in order to emphasise that such errors have undermined, if not destroyed, the relevance and reliability of the prior period financial statements. When the term fundamental was introduced during the first improvements project, the IASC's clear intention was that such errors would be extremely rare. A fundamental error may arise, for example, when an entity discovers that its financial statements of a previous period included material amounts of worthless work in progress and receivables in respect of fraudulent contracts which cannot be enforced. A fundamental error may also arise when there has been a major breakdown in the internal accounting system and many of the reported numbers are wrong.

Fundamental errors do not include normal recurring adjustments or corrections of accounting estimates made in prior periods. For example, a change in the estimate of construction contract revenue and expenses is not a fundamental error; rather it is a change in estimate. Similarly, fundamental errors do not include changes in judgements resulting from new information. For example, the failure of a new product to meet regulatory requirements in 2001 does not mean that the entity made a fundamental error in capitalising the associated development costs in 2000.

IASB improvements project

In its May 2002 exposure draft, the IASB proposes to remove the distinction between fundamental errors and other errors. This will result in the removal of the IAS 8 distinction between:

- errors that are usually corrected in the determination of net profit or loss for the current period; and
- fundamental errors which arise only on rare occasions that have such a significant effect that the financial statements of one or more prior periods can no longer be considered reliable at their date of issue.

The IASB proposes to add a definition of errors which emphasises that the errors arise from information that was available when the prior period financial statements were prepared and could reasonably be expected to have been obtained and used.

Under the proposals in the improvements exposure draft, the correction of all (material) errors should be accounted for retrospectively, that is in accordance with the current benchmark treatment.

14.6 REPORTING CORRECTIONS OF FUNDAMENTAL ERRORS

Whereas there is some choice about whether or not to apply a change in accounting policy retrospectively or prospectively, there is little choice about fundamental errors. They must be corrected retrospectively, otherwise the financial statements will continue to be in error. However, IAS 8 allows a choice for the treatment of the resulting correction.

14.6.1 Fundamental Errors – Benchmark Treatment

The financial statements, including the comparative information for prior periods, are presented as if the error had been corrected in the period in which it arose. Therefore, the financial statements are restated so that the amount of the correction that relates to each period presented is included in the net profit or loss for that period. The amount of the correction relating to periods prior to those included in the comparative information is adjusted against the opening balance of retained earnings in the earliest period presented (IAS 8, 34).

Example 14.1 *Correction of fundamental error – benchmark treatment*

In 2001, an entity discovers that expenses and liabilities totalling $245 million had been omitted from the financial statements as at 31 December 2000. After further investigation, it discovers that $90 million of the total expenses and liabilities relates to 1999. As a result of these errors, management concludes that the 1999 and 2000 financial statements were not reliable. It decides to deal with the expenses and losses under the benchmark treatment in IAS 8. The entity publishes comparative information for the previous period.

The application of the benchmark treatment has the following effects:

- the opening balance of retained earnings in 2000 is reduced by $90 million to reflect the expenses and liabilities which occurred in 1999 – a liability of $90 million is created as at 31 December 1999;
- the income statement for 2000 is restated to show additional expenses of $155 million;
- the balance sheet at 31 December 2000 is restated to show an additional liability of $245 million and a corresponding reduction in retained earnings; and
- none of the expenses that relate to 1999 and 2000 are included in the income statement for 2001.

An entity should disclose the following information:

- the nature of the fundamental error;
- the amount of the correction for the current period and for each prior period presented;
- the amount of the correction relating to prior periods; and
- the fact that comparative information has been restated.

(IAS 8, 37)

If it is impracticable to restate the comparative information, the entity should disclose that fact (IAS 8, 37(d)). However, in such a case, the entity is actually following the allowed alternative treatment without presenting the pro forma information.

It is also important to restate other prior period data, such as historical summaries, which are included in the annual report.

> ***IASB improvements project***
>
> In its May 2002 exposure draft, the IASB proposes to amend the criteria for exemption from restating comparative information from 'impracticability' to 'undue cost or effort'.

14.6.2 Fundamental Errors – Allowed Alternative Treatment

The amount of the correction is included in the net profit or loss for the current period. Comparative information is presented as reported in the previous period. The comparative information should also be presented on a pro forma basis as if the fundamental error had been corrected in the period when it arose (IAS 8, 38). As explained in 13.11 above, IAS 8 does not explain what is meant by a 'pro forma basis' but the intention was that the income statement and the balance sheet would be presented as if the error had not occurred.

> **Example 14.2** *Correction of fundamental error – allowed alternative treatment*
>
> The facts are the same as example 14.1. The entity decides to deal with the expenses and liabilities under the allowed alternative treatment in IAS 8. The entity publishes corresponding figures for the previous period.
>
> The application of the allowed alternative treatment has the following effects:
>
> - the income statement for 2001 includes additional expenses of $245 million; and
> - the entity publishes pro forma financial statements for 2000 and 2001 showing the income statement and balance sheet as if the error had not occurred.

An entity should disclose the following information:

- the nature of the fundamental error;
- the amount of the correction recognised in net profit or loss for the current period; and
- the amount of the correction included in each period for which pro forma information is presented and the amount of the correction relating to prior period.

(IAS 8, 40)

If it is impracticable to restate the comparative information on a pro forma basis, the entity should disclose that fact (IAS 8, 40).

> *IASB improvements project*
>
> In its May 2002 exposure draft, the IASB proposes to eliminate the allowed alternative treatment.

CHAPTER 15

Consolidated Financial Statements

15.1 RELEVANT STANDARD AND INTERPRETATIONS

IAS 27 *Consolidated Financial Statements and Accounting for Investments in Subsidiaries*
SIC 12 *Consolidation of Special Purpose Entities*
SIC 33 *Consolidation and Equity Method – Potential Voting Rights and Allocation of Ownership Interests*

Four other IASs deal with issues which are important in the preparation and presentation of consolidated financial statements:

- IAS 21 *Effects of Changes in Foreign Exchange Rates* deals with the translation of the financial statements of a foreign subsidiary, associate or jointly controlled entity into the reporting currency of the parent (see chapter 19);
- IAS 22 *Business Combinations* deals with the acquisition of, and mergers with, other businesses, events which usually result in a parent-subsidiary relationship (see chapter 16);
- IAS 28 *Accounting for Investments in Associates* deals with investments in which the investor has significant influence over the investee and which are accounted for in consolidated financial statements using the equity method (see chapter 17); and
- IAS 31 *Financial Reporting of Interests in Joint Ventures* deals with interests in jointly controlled entities which are reported in consolidated financial statements using either proportionate consolidation or the equity method (see chapter 18).

15.2 HISTORY

IAS 3 *Consolidated Financial Statements* was issued in 1976. IAS 3 dealt with the presentation of consolidated financial statements and established a standard for the use of the equity method for investments in associates. The IASC approved IAS 3 before many countries, including some on the IASC board, required the presentation of consolidated financial statements. Therefore, IAS 3 was influential in improving financial reporting in many parts of the world.

IAS 3 was used in the development of the EU Seventh Directive and by many EU member states when implementing the Directive. Van Hulle and van der Tas point out that reference was often made to IAS 3 in the working party discussions on the proposed Seventh Directive and that the EU's economic and social committee explicitly referred to IAS 3 and called upon the European Commission to 'keep a watching brief' on IAS 3 and 'ensure maximum conformity between the international and European standards'[1].

IAS 3 was replaced in 1990 by IAS 27 *Consolidated Financial Statements and Accounting for Investments in Subsidiaries* and IAS 28 *Accounting for Investments in Associates*. Among other things IAS 27 reflects further improvements included in the EU Seventh Directive, in particular the Directive's notion of control, so completing a cycle of influence and co-operation between the IASC and the EU. IAS 27 also removed some of the alternative accounting treatments permitted by IAS 3, including the exemption from consolidation of a subsidiary with activities which are dissimilar from those of other entities in the group (this is one of the two conflicts between EU Directives and IASs identified by the European Commission)[2].

The May 2002 improvements exposure draft proposes several minor changes to IAS 27 that deal with:

- the exemptions from publishing consolidated financial statements;
- exemptions from consolidation;
- the use of uniform accounting policies; and
- the accounting for investments in subsidiaries in the parent entity's separate financial statements.

The IASB has an active project on consolidations, including special purpose entities, which may lead to changes to IAS 27. It is clear already, however, that the IASB intends to retain the broad approach to the definition of control that is included in IAS 27.

15.3 IOSCO

In June 1994, IOSCO advised the IASC that IAS 27 was acceptable for the purposes of the core standards. IOSCO added that it may make recommendations on the definition of a subsidiary when a majority of shares is not owned by the parent. IOSCO identified the following suspense issues:

- accounting for changes in the reporting entity, for example, spin-offs, carve-outs, and common control transactions (including simultaneous transactions and downstream mergers);
- guidance for transactions involving special purpose entities (this is dealt with in SIC 12 and is being considered further in the IASB's consolidations project);
- guidance on accounting for capital transactions by subsidiaries;
- clarification that the exemption from consolidated financial statement requirements for a wholly owned or virtually wholly owned parent should not apply in the case of that parent making a securities offering or filing (this is dealt with in the May 2002 improvements exposure draft);
- when the consolidation of subsidiaries with dissimilar activities would be incompatible with a true and fair view, some IOSCO members will accept disclosure of sub-consolidated accounts in the notes rather than consolidation (this approach is not permitted by IAS 27);
- guidance as to the type of evidence that would be necessary to apply objectively the control criteria when the parent owns one half or less of the voting power – IOSCO may recommend that its members interpret the necessary evidence required as being an irrevocable written agreement, giving the power to appoint or remove the majority of the board of directors and to cast the majority of votes; and
- guidance that if less than a majority of voting share ownership exists, it is presumed that control does not exist as a corollary to the presumption that control exists when a majority of voting power is owned – IOSCO may recommend that its members interpret IAS 27 to require a clear demonstration and evidence that this presumption has been overcome.

IOSCO also identified the following other issues:

- limitations on the treatments allowed by IAS 25 for subsidiaries excluded from consolidation and investments which cease to meet the definition of a subsidiary (this is now dealt with as a result of the adoption of IAS 39);
- 'effective control' and thus potential consolidation when stock options or other convertible securities are held and their exercise is discretionary (this is dealt with in SIC 33);
- delimiting the 'if practicable' exception for the application of uniform accounting policies (this is dealt with in the May 2002 improvements exposure draft);

- how the position of a general partner in a partnership is interpreted with regard to effective control and, thus, potential consolidation; and
- disclosure of summarised financial information for subsidiaries which are not consolidated but which are material individually or in aggregate.

IAS 27 is included in 'IAS 2000' endorsed by IOSCO in May 2000. There are seven supplemental treatments:

- the appropriateness of consolidating SPEs formed pursuant to certain national laws that specify, for example, the business purpose, business contents and the distribution of revenue (non-consolidation may not comply with IAS 27 and SIC 12);
- the appropriateness, in certain circumstances, of consolidating subsidiaries operating in dissimilar activities (consolidation is required by IAS 27);
- consideration of effective control and consolidation when share options or other convertible securities are held and exercise is discretionary;
- delimiting the 'if practicable' exception for the application of uniform accounting policies to, in any event, require the use of acceptable international standards (the first point is dealt with in the May 2002 improvements exposure draft while compliance with IFRSs already requires the use of accounting policies that comply with IFRSs);
- the position as general partner of a partnership with regard to effective control and, thus, potential consolidation;
- the disclosure of summarised financial information for subsidiaries not consolidated that are material individually or in the aggregate; and
- the creation of a rebuttable presumption that an entity should consolidate an SPE if certain of the indicators in SIC 12 are present.

15.4 IAS 27 IN BRIEF

IAS 27 is based on the entity concept under which all assets and liabilities of group entities are viewed as those of the group. Assets, liabilities, income and expense are consolidated in full and gains and losses on intra-group transactions are eliminated in full. Parent and minority shareholders are credited with their proportionate share of net assets and goodwill; minority interests are treated as an allocation of profit rather than as an expense.

The consolidated financial statements are prepared using:

- full consolidation for all subsidiaries;
- the equity method for all associates;
- proportionate consolidation or the equity method for joint venture entities;
- the purchase method for acquisitions and the pooling of interests method for unitings of interests (mergers when no acquirer can be identified); and
- the closing rate for the translation of the balance sheet, and the average rates for income statement, of a foreign entity – the translation gains and losses are included in equity until the disposal of the entity.

The group is the parent and all its subsidiaries.

A subsidiary is another entity which is controlled by the parent; control usually, but not always, results from the parent holding, directly or indirectly, more than half the voting power of the other entity.

The consolidated financial statements should report the financial position, performance and cash flows of the group as if the group were a single entity without regard for the legal boundaries of the separate legal entities. Therefore, the consolidated financial statements should:

- include all subsidiaries;
- be prepared using uniform accounting policies for like transactions and events;
- be prepared to the same reporting date; and
- exclude all intra-group transactions.

15.5 DEFINITIONS OF PARENT AND SUBSIDIARY

Consolidated financial statements deal with a parent and its subsidiaries and are sometimes referred to as group accounts. A *parent* is an entity that has one or more subsidiaries (IAS 27, 6). A *group* is a parent and all its subsidiaries (IAS 27, 6).

A *subsidiary* is an entity that is controlled by the parent (IAS 27, 6). The key to the definition of a subsidiary is the notion of control. *Control* is the power to govern the financial and operating policies of an entity so as to obtain benefits from its activities (IAS 27, 6).

Control is presumed to exist when the parent owns, directly or indirectly through subsidiaries, more than one half of the voting power of an entity unless, in exceptional circumstances, it can be clearly demonstrated that such ownership does not constitute control (IAS 27, 10). This aspect of control was included in IAS 3; however, IAS 27 goes further. Control under IAS 27 also exists when the parent owns one half or less of the voting power of an entity provided the parent has:

- power over more than one half of the voting rights by virtue of an agreement with other investors; or
- power to govern the financial and operating policies of the entity under a statute or an agreement; or
- power to appoint or remove the majority of the members of the board of directors or equivalent governing body; or
- power to cast the majority of votes at meetings of the board of directors or equivalent governing body.

(IAS 27, 12)

The change in the definition of control was potentially the most significant change in IAS 27. The change was influenced by the EU Seventh Directive (the text of IAS 27 follows closely the language of the Directive) and the thinking in a number of countries, notably Australia, as well as the concepts of assets and liabilities in the Framework. The approach is different from current US GAAP which requires the consolidation of only majority owned subsidiaries. Therefore, the scope of the consolidation under IASs and the Seventh Directive is potentially broader than that under US GAAP.

Consideration should also be given to the existence and effect of potential voting rights that are currently exercisable or convertible when assessing whether the entity controls the other entity (SIC 33, 3). Potential voting rights may arise from such instruments as share warrants, share call options, convertible debt or equity instruments that, when exercised or converted, give the entity voting power over the entity or reduce some other party's voting power over the entity. When considering the existence and effects of potential voting rights, the entity should consider all facts and circumstances except its own intentions and its financial capability to exercise or convert the instruments (SIC 33, 4). SIC 33 includes examples of the application of these requirements. The May 2002 improvements exposure draft proposes the incorporation of the requirements of SIC 33 into IAS 27.

Extract 15.1 *Control without majority ownership*

BHP, Australia, 31 May 1998 (IAS)

The BHP Group holds 50% of voting shares in Beswick Pty Ltd and its subsidiary Panary Pty Ltd which are classified as controlled entities pursuant to Australian Accounting Standard AASB 1024: *Consolidated Accounts* because of an agreement that, in substance, gives the BHP Group the capacity to enjoy the majority of the benefits and to be exposed to the majority of the risks of Beswick and Panary.

The BHP Group owns 49% in BHP Steel Building Products (Sabah) Sdn Bhd, which is classified as a controlled entity pursuant to Australian Accounting

Standard AASB 1024: *Consolidated Accounts* because the BHP Group can exercise voting control.

The tests for the existence of control in IAS 27 are virtually the same as those in the Seventh Directive. There is, however, one important difference between the Directive and IAS 27. The Directive requires that the parent should be a shareholder or member of the other entity; there is no such requirement in IAS 27. Therefore, an entity could be a subsidiary even though the parent does not own, directly or indirectly, any of the voting rights in the entity. Such circumstances are likely to be extremely rare and, in practice, this and other minor differences are unlikely to result in an entity being a subsidiary under IAS 27 but not a subsidiary under the Seventh Directive (or vice versa).

The parent-subsidiary relationship often arises as a result of a business combination and the definition of an acquisition in IAS 22 is consistent with the definition of a subsidiary in IAS 27.

The application of the control criteria in IAS 27 to so-called 'special purpose entities' is dealt with in SIC 12 (this was one of IOSCO's suspense issues). Such entities are usually set up by an entity to carry out some specific objective on its behalf. The entity should be consolidated when the substance of the relationship indicates that the parent entity controls the special purpose entity (SIC 12, 8). Control may arise through:

- the parent entity pre-determining the special purpose entity's activities;
- the special purpose entity conducting activities on behalf of the parent entity;
- the parent entity exercising decision-making powers over the special purpose entity or its assets;
- the parent entity having the rights to a majority of the benefits of the special purpose entity's activities; or
- the parent entity guaranteeing the interests of other parties involved in the special purpose entity or its activities.

(SIC 12, 10)

15.6 REQUIREMENT TO PUBLISH CONSOLIDATED FINANCIAL STATEMENTS

An entity which publishes IFRS financial statements and which is a parent should publish consolidated financial statements unless it is itself a wholly owned subsidiary or virtually wholly owned (IAS 27, 7 and 8). A parent which is itself a wholly owned subsidiary need not present consolidated financial statements because such statements may not be required by its parent and the needs of other users may be best served by the consolidated financial statements of its parent (IAS 27, 10). Virtually wholly owned is often taken to mean that the parent owns 90% or more of the voting power (IAS 27, 10) as is the case in the EU Seventh Directive.

A parent which takes advantage of these exemptions from publishing consolidated financial statements should disclose:

- the reasons why consolidated financial statements have not been published (IAS 27, 8);
- the name and registered office of its parent which publishes consolidated financial statements (IAS 27, 8); and
- the bases on which its subsidiaries are accounted for in its separate financial statements (IAS 27, 8).

> ***IASB improvements project***
>
> In its May 2002 exposure draft, the IASB proposes to restrict the exemption from publishing consolidated financial statements to parents that are either wholly owned subsidiaries or partly owned subsidiaries in which the owners of the minority interest have unanimously agreed that they need not publish consolidated financial statements. The exemption will not be available if:
>
> - the parent has securities that are publicly traded;
> - the parent is in the process of issuing securities in the public securities market; or
> - the immediate or ultimate parent does not publish IFRS financial statements.

IAS 27 refers to three ways of dealing with investments in subsidiaries in separate financial statements – cost, the equity method or available-for-sale financial assets (IAS 27, 29) – but only in the context of a parent which publishes consolidated financial statements. The same guidance can be followed by a parent which does not publish consolidated financial statements.

15.7 SCOPE OF CONSOLIDATED FINANCIAL STATEMENTS

The consolidated financial statements should include all subsidiaries except for:

- a subsidiary in which the parent's control is intended to be temporary because the subsidiary is acquired and held exclusively with a view to its subsequent disposal in the near future (temporary control); and
- a subsidiary which operates under severe long-term restrictions which significantly impair its ability to transfer funds to the parent (impaired control).

(IAS 27, 11 and 13)

A subsidiary should not be excluded from consolidation simply because its activities are dissimilar to those in the rest of the group.

Extract 15.2 *Scope of consolidation*

Nokia, Finland, 31 December 2000 (IAS)

The consolidated financial statements include the accounts of the parent company, Nokia Corporation, and each of those companies in which it owns, directly or indirectly through subsidiaries, over 50% of the voting rights. The accounts of certain companies in which Nokia has control are also consolidated. The companies acquired during the financial period have been consolidated from the date the responsibility for their operations was transferred to the Group. Similarly the result of a Group company divested during an accounting period is included in the Group accounts only to the date of disposal.

15.7.1 Temporary Control

A subsidiary should be excluded from consolidation when the parent's control of the subsidiary is intended to be temporary because the subsidiary is acquired and held exclusively with a view to its subsequent disposal in the near future. This is a stringent test. It means that the decision to dispose of the subsidiary must have been taken prior to the date of acquisition; in other words, the parent acquired the subsidiary with the intention of selling it in the near future. This may happen, for example, when the parent acquires another group of entities with the intention of disposing of one of the subsidiaries of that group. Consequently, the subsidiary is excluded from consolidation from the date of acquisition.

A subsidiary which is excluded from consolidation for this reason is accounted for as a financial asset in accordance with IAS 39 (IAS 27, 13).

> ***IASB improvements project***
>
> In its May 2002 improvements exposure draft, the IASB proposes to replace 'in the near future' with 'within 12 months from acquisition'.

15.7.2 Impaired Control

A subsidiary should be excluded from consolidation when the subsidiary operates under severe long-term restrictions which significantly impair its ability to transfer funds to the parent (IAS 27, 13). The ability to transfer funds may be impaired by, for example:

- exchange controls which block the payment of dividends or the repayment of capital to the parent; or
- statutory restriction on the distributability of profits.

Exchange controls and restrictions on the distribution of profits exist in many countries. Exclusion from consolidation is possible on these grounds only when the controls or restrictions are 'severe', 'long-term' and 'significantly impair' the transfer of funds.

A subsidiary which is excluded from consolidation for this reason is accounted for as a financial asset in accordance with IAS 39 (IAS 27, 13) (see chapter 20).

Extract 15.3 *Non-consolidated subsidiaries – impaired control*

Edcon, South Africa, 30 March 2002 (South African GAAP and IAS)

... there are currently severe restrictions on the repatriation of dividends from Zimbabwe, consequently, the results of Edgars Stores Limited Zimbabwe have not been consolidated in the year under review... Dividends from Edgars Zimbabwe will be brought to account on a cash receipt basis.

> ***IASB improvements project***
>
> In its May 2002 improvements exposure draft, the IASB proposes to remove the exemption from consolidation when a subsidiary operates under severe long-term restrictions that significantly impair its ability to transfer funds to the parent but indicate that such restrictions make it unlikely that control exists.

15.7.3 Dissimilar Activities

It is sometimes argued that a subsidiary should be excluded from consolidation when its business activities are dissimilar from those of the other entities within the group. Such an approach was permitted by IAS 3 and is required by the EU Seventh Directive when consolidation would be incompatible with the true and fair view. Some IOSCO members support this argument and intend to allow the non-consolidation of subsidiaries with dissimilar activities. The argument is often used to justify the non-consolidation of banking, finance and insurance subsidiaries by a parent when the rest of the group consists of entities which are not financial institutions.

For example the *International Accounting Standards Survey 2000* reports that:

- Benetton does not consolidate its automotive engineering operation as consolidation would have 'distorted' the consolidated financial statements; and
- Compart does not consolidate its insurance subsidiaries because they are 'different from and not complementary to' the rest of the group.

The IASC rejected such an exemption when it developed IAS 27 because consolidation of such subsidiaries is consistent with the entity concept which underpins IAS 27. The IASC believed that better information is provided by consolidating such subsidiaries, even though it may require some adaptation of the format of the balance sheet, and disclosing additional information in the consolidated financial statements about the different business activities of subsidiaries (IAS 27, 14). In particular, the segment disclosures required by IAS 14 help to explain the significance of different business activities within the group.

Extract 15.4 *Consolidation of financial services with motor vehicle manufacture*

BMW Group, Germany, 31 December 2001 (IAS)

In order to support the sale of the BMW products, the BMW Group provides various financial services – mainly loan and lease financing – to its customers. The inclusion of the financial services activities of the Group also has a significant impact on the Group financial statements. In order to provide a better insight into the assets, liabilities, financial position and performance of the Group, additional information has been presented in the BMW Group financial statements on the industrial and financial operations. Financial operations include financial services and the activities of the Group financing companies. ... These additional disclosures allow the assets, liabilities, financial position and performance of the industrial and financial operations to be presented, on an IAS basis, as if they were two separate groups.

15.7.4 Immaterial Subsidiaries

The EU Seventh Directive permits non-consolidation when a subsidiary is not material for the purposes of giving a true and fair view of the assets, liabilities, financial position and profit or loss of the group. A similar exemption exists in the national requirements of some countries; for example, in Japan a subsidiary may be excluded from consolidation if it comprises less than 10% of total group assets or sales.

There is no equivalent exemption in IAS 27. However, IFRSs do not apply to immaterial items. Therefore, it is possible to exclude from the consolidation subsidiaries which are immaterial in aggregate. In making any such decision, however, it is necessary to look at both the aggregate and individual effect of the subsidiaries on the consolidated financial statements and not just, say, total assets and sales. It is inappropriate, for example, to exclude from consolidation two subsidiaries which are individually immaterial but which are material when both are considered together.

Extract 15.5 *Non-consolidation of immaterial subsidiaries*

Bayer, Germany, 31 December 2000 (IAS)

Excluded from consolidation are 85 subsidiaries that in aggregate are immaterial to the net worth, financial position and earnings of the Bayer Group; they account for less that 1% of Group sales.

15.7.5 Disproportionate Expense and Undue Delay

The EU Seventh Directive permits non-consolidation of a subsidiary when the information necessary to prepare the consolidated financial statements cannot be obtained without disproportionate expense or undue delay. There is no equivalent exemption in IAS 27 and there was no equivalent exemption in IAS 3, which pointed out that exclusion on these grounds is often subjective and may result in variations in practice (IAS 3, 9).

It is difficult to justify non-consolidation in such circumstances. While the parent or subsidiary may believe that the costs are disproportionate, the consolidated financial statements are published for the benefit of users for whom the benefits of consolidation may be considerable.

15.8 CONSOLIDATION PROCEDURES

Consolidated financial statements present financial information about the group as if it were a single entity without regard for the legal boundaries of the separate legal entities (IAS 27, 9). In order to do this, the carrying amount of the parent's investment in each subsidiary is replaced by the identifiable asset and liabilities, goodwill or negative goodwill, and minority interest based on the procedures specified in IAS 22 (see chapter 16). In practice this is usually achieved by combining, on a line-by-line basis, like items of assets, liabilities, equity, income and expenses of the parent and subsidiaries.

Consolidation adjustments are often required to deal with:

- the fair value adjustments required on any preceding business combination (IAS 22, 32 and 34);
- the allocation of any negative goodwill arising on any preceding business combination and dealt with under the benchmark treatment in IAS 22 [1993]; and
- identifiable assets and liabilities acquired on any preceding business combination which existed at the date of the acquisition but which are not recognised in the balance sheet of the subsidiaries.

The consolidation adjustments may give rise to temporary differences which need to be dealt with in accordance with IAS 12 (see Chapter 31).

In some countries, such adjustments are sometimes incorporated in the financial statements of the subsidiaries either as a revaluation or by means of push-down accounting. Such an approach, where permitted, usually simplifies considerably the preparation of the consolidated financial statements. It is permitted by IFRSs for the purposes of the consolidated financial statements. However, such adjustments may result in the separate financial statements of the subsidiary not complying with IFRSs.

The results of operations of a subsidiary are included in the consolidated financial statements from the date of acquisition until the date of disposal. The date of acquisition is the date on which control of the net assets and operations of the subsidiary is effectively transferred to the parent (IAS 22, 9). The date of disposal is the date on which the parent ceases to have control of the subsidiary (IAS 27, 23).

15.8.1 Intra-group Balances and Transactions

The following should be eliminated in full:

- intra-group balances and intra-group transactions, including sales, expenses and dividends;
- unrealised profits resulting from intra-group transactions that are included in the carrying amount of the group's assets, such as inventory and fixed assets; and

- unrealised losses resulting from intra-group transactions that are deducted in arriving at the carrying amount of assets unless cost cannot be recovered.

(IAS 27, 17)

The elimination of unrealised profits and losses resulting from intra-group transactions may give rise to temporary differences which need to be dealt with in accordance with IAS 12 (see Chapter 31).

15.8.2 Reporting Date

The financial statements of the parent and its subsidiaries used in the preparation of the consolidated financial statements are usually drawn up to the same date. This may mean that a subsidiary must prepare, for consolidation purposes, financial statements as at the group balance sheet date; these financial statements may be different from those prepared and published by the subsidiary to meet any statutory or other requirements.

When it is impracticable for the subsidiary to prepare financial statements as at the group balance sheet date, the parent may use the financial statements of the subsidiary drawn up to a different reporting date provided the difference in dates is no greater than three months (IAS 27, 19). In such cases:

- the length of the reporting period of the subsidiary and the difference in the reporting dates should be the same from period to period (IAS 27, 20); and
- adjustments should be made for the effects of significant transactions or other events that occur between the subsidiary's balance sheet date and the group balance sheet date (IAS 27, 19).

When the parent uses the financial statements of a subsidiary drawn up to a different reporting date, the parent needs to make adjustments for the effects of significant transactions or other events that occur between the date of the subsidiary's balance sheet and the date of the consolidated balance sheet (IAS 27, 19). IAS 27 provides no guidance on the sort of significant transactions and events which would require adjustment. No adjustments are required for normal trading transactions, otherwise the financial statements would have been prepared as at the group balance sheet date. Adjustments would, perhaps, be required for major impairment write-downs or extraordinary items. When the subsidiary is a foreign entity, the parent needs to translate the assets and liabilities of the subsidiary at the exchange rate at the subsidiary's balance sheet date (IAS 21, 35). A change in the exchange rate between the date of the subsidiary's balance sheet and the date of the consolidated balance sheet could be one of the significant events for which adjustment is required. If it is, the parent adjusts for the effect of the change in exchange rate (IAS 21, 35).

15.8.3 Uniform Accounting Policies

Consolidated financial statements should be prepared using uniform accounting policies for like transactions and other events in similar circumstances (IAS 27, 21). If a subsidiary uses accounting policies other than those adopted in the consolidated financial statements for like transactions and events, appropriate adjustments are made to its financial statements before they are used to prepare the consolidated financial statements.

The accounting policies used in the separate financial statements of the parent or its subsidiaries may differ from those used in the consolidated financial statements because the separate financial statements have been prepared in accordance with national accounting requirements or tax or similar requirements which conflict with IFRSs. Even when they are prepared in accordance with IFRSs, they may follow different alternative accounting treatments permitted by IFRSs from those used in the consolidated financial statements. In all these cases, adjustments must be made when preparing the consolidated financial statements.

Extract 15.6 *Consolidation of audited accounts*

Danisco, Denmark, 30 April 2001 (IAS)

The Group accounts comprise the consolidated audited accounts of the parent company and the individual subsidiary undertakings, which have all been prepared in accordance with the Group's accounting policies.

Extract 15.7 *Adjustments to common accounting policies*

Lectra Systémes, France, 31 December 1997 (IAS)

The main differences between the rules and methods used in the consolidated statements and those applied in the annual accounts of companies in the Group concern:

- the adjustments made in order to ensure consistency of accounting principles within the Group:
  - adjustment of allowances for doubtful accounts and inventories for certain subsidiaries;
  - demonstration equipment recorded under fixed assets by certain subsidiaries which is taken to inventories;

- the adjustments required by French generally accepted consolidation principles:
  - elimination of untaxed reserves;
  - recognition of deferred taxes;
- certain adjustments left optional under French generally accepted consolidation principles:
  - finance leases have been capitalised;
  - underlying exchange gains on conversion of debts and receivables denominated in foreign currencies have been taken to the statements of income.

Extract 15.8 *Adjustments for tax driven accounting policies*

Montedison, Italy, 31 December 1997 (IAS)

The consolidation techniques require several adjustments, including in particular:

- valuation adjustments and provisions taken exclusively for tax purposes are eliminated completely.... deferred taxes payable and tax prepayments on any temporary differences between taxable income and the net income of companies included in the consolidated financial statements are computed on the basis of the tax treatment applicable to statutory financial statements.

It may be impracticable to use uniform accounting policies in preparing the consolidated financial statements although it is difficult to imagine the circumstances in which this would occur. However, if it does, the entity should disclose that fact together with the proportions of the items in the consolidated financial statements to which the different accounting policies have been applied (IAS 27, 21). The different policies should be disclosed.

> *IASB improvements project*
>
> In its May 2002 improvements exposure draft, the IASB proposes to require the use of uniform accounting policies for like transactions and events and not have a practicability exemption.

15.8.4 Minority Interests

The minority interest in the net profit or loss for the period should be separately presented as a line item in the income statement (IAS 1, 75 and IAS 27, 26).

Minority interests in the net profit or loss of consolidated subsidiaries are adjusted against the net profit or loss of the group in order to arrive at the net profit or loss attributable to the owners of the parent (IAS 27, 15(b)). It is important to determine minority interests consistently with the way in which the cost of acquisition in any preceding business combination has been allocated. For example, when the entity adopts the benchmark treatment in IAS 22, the fair value adjustments to identifiable assets and liabilities are not applied to the minority's share of those assets and liabilities. Therefore, the minority interest in the net profit or loss in subsequent periods is based on pre-acquisition carrying amounts.

The losses applicable to the minority may exceed the minority interest in the equity of the subsidiary. The excess, and any further losses applicable to the minority, are excluded from the minority interest except to the extent that the minority has a binding obligation to, and is able to, make good the losses (IAS 27, 27). If the subsidiary subsequently reports profits, the minority is not allocated an interest in such profits until its share of losses previously absorbed by the majority has been recovered (IAS 27, 27).

A subsidiary may have outstanding cumulative preferred shares which are held outside the group. The parent computes its share of profits or losses after adjusting for the subsidiary's preferred dividends, whether or not dividends have been declared (IAS 27, 28). When the dividends have not been declared, they are included in the minority interest.

Minority interests in the net assets of each consolidated subsidiary consist of:

- the amount at the date of the original combination calculated in accordance with either the benchmark or the allowed alternative treatment in IAS 22; and
- the minority's share of movements in equity since the date of the combination.

(IAS 27, 15(c))

Minority interests should be presented in the consolidated balance sheet as a line item separately from liabilities and parent shareholders' equity (IAS 1, 66 and IAS 27, 26). They may be shown either:

- between liabilities and equity; or
- as part of a total amount of equity which is sub-divided on the face of the balance sheet between parent shareholders' interests and minority shareholders' interests.

IASB improvements project

In its May 2002 improvements exposure draft, the IASB proposes that minority interests should be presented within equity but separately from shareholders' equity.

In its business combinations exposure draft, the IASB proposes to remove the benchmark treatment for the measurement of minority interests and require that all acquired identifiable assets and liabilities be measured at fair value. This will simplify the determination of minority interests in future periods.

15.9 HORIZONTAL GROUPS

IAS 27 does not require the presentation of consolidated financial statements or combined financial statements by groups of independent entities managed on a unified basis when the person or entity managing the entities is not a reporting entity and does not control the other entities. However, the general principles in IAS 27 could be followed in any such consolidated or combined financial statements.

Extract 15.9 *Combined financial statements*

Royal Dutch/Shell, Netherlands and United Kingdom, 31 December 2001

The Financial Statements reflect an aggregation in US dollars of the accounts of companies in which Royal Dutch and Shell Transport together, either directly or indirectly, have control either through a majority of the voting rights or the right to exercise a controlling interest.

15.10 DISCLOSURE

In consolidated financial statements, an entity should disclose:

- a list of significant subsidiaries including the name, country of incorporation or residence, proportion of ownership interest and, if different, proportion of voting power held;
- the reasons for not consolidating a subsidiary;
- the nature of the relationship between the parent and a subsidiary of which the parent does not own, directly or indirectly through subsidiaries, more than one half of the voting power; and
- the name of an entity in which more than one half of the voting power is owned, directly or indirectly through subsidiaries, but which, because of the absence of control, is not a subsidiary.

(IAS 27, 32)

In consolidated financial statements, an entity should also disclose the effect of the acquisition and disposal of subsidiaries on the financial position at the reporting date, the results for the reporting period and the corresponding amounts for the preceding period. This requirement was added in response to article 28 of the EU Seventh Directive which requires that, when the composition of a group has changed during a period, the consolidated financial statements must include information which makes the comparison of different periods meaningful. The impact of disposals may also be covered by the disclosures about discontinuing operations required by IAS 35 (see chapter 37).

Extract 15.10 *Impact of acquisition*

Preussag, Germany, 30 September 2000 (IAS)

The consolidation of the Thomson Travel Group produced the following significant effect on the balance sheet and on the profit and loss statement of the Preussag Group, excluding the cost of finance for the acquisition and before amortisation of goodwill:

(in mill.€)	*Prior to* consolidation of the Thomson Travel Group	*After* consolidation of the Thomson Travel Group	*Change*
Balance sheet as per 30 Sept 2000			
Tangible assets	5,504.4	6,438.8	+934.4
Current assets	4,550.4	5,643.4	+1,093.0
Provisions	3,035.8	3,289.2	+253.4
Liabilities	9,726.9	11,722.8	+1,995.9
Profit and loss statement 1999/2000			
Turnover	19,921.7	21,853.7	+1,932.0
Cost of materials	13,619.3	14,930.3	+1,311.0
Other operating expenses	3,586.1	3,846.6	+260.5

The differences resulting from the other additions to the basis of consolidation accounted for almost 3.0% of Group turnover and about 5.2% of the balance sheet total. Here, 1.1% of the increase in turnover and 2.2% of the balance sheet total was attributable to the addition of the Hebel Group alone. Where there are significant material increases in individual assets and liabilities, the differences are described separately in the notes on the respective items in the balance sheet or the profit and loss statement.

Note

1 Karel van Hulle and Leo van der Tas, 'European Union – Group Accounts', in *Transnational Accounting*, ed Ordelheide, D. and KPMG, Macmillan Press, London, 1995, p1061.

2 Contact Committee on the Accounting Directives, *An Examination of the Conformity Between the International Accounting Standards and the European Accounting Directives*, European Commission, Brussels, 1996, p13.

CHAPTER 16

Business Combinations

16.1 RELEVANT STANDARD AND INTERPRETATIONS

IAS 22 *Business Combinations*
SIC 9 *Business Combinations – Classification either as Acquisitions or Unitings of Interests*
SIC 22 *Business Combinations – Subsequent Adjustment of Fair Values and Goodwill Initially Reported*
SIC 28 *Business Combinations – 'Date of Exchange' and Fair Value of Equity Instruments*
SIC 33 *Consolidation and Equity Method – Potential Voting Rights and Allocation of Ownership Interests*

16.2 HISTORY

16.2.1 IAS 22

IAS 22 *Accounting for Business Combinations* (IAS 22 [1983]) was approved in 1983. It was reconsidered in the comparability and improvements project when a significant number of changes were made. In particular, the IASC decided that:

- the purchase method should be used for acquisitions and the pooling of interests method for uniting of interests; and
- goodwill should be capitalised and amortised over a maximum of 20 years.

The IASC also specified alternative treatments for dealing with negative goodwill and minority interests and added substantial guidance on the determination of the fair values of acquired assets and liabilities.

IAS 22 *Business Combinations* (IAS 22 [1993]) was approved in November 1993 and applied to financial statements for accounting periods beginning on or after 1 January 1995.

In July 1995, the IASC announced that, as part of a work plan agreed with IOSCO, it had decided to carry out a revision to those aspects of IAS 22 dealing with goodwill. This announcement came as a surprise given IOSCO's acceptance of IAS 22 and the SEC's acceptance of the use of goodwill amortisation requirements in IAS 22 [1993] by foreign registrants (see chapter 24).

Two other factors later affected the revisions to IAS 22 [1993]. First, the IASC started to develop its standard on provisions and decided that the requirements in IAS 22 for provisions arising on an acquisition should be dealt with in the same way as other provisions. Second, the EU contact committee identified the IAS 22 treatment of negative goodwill as one of only two conflicts between IASs and the Directives[1].

The further revised IAS 22 was approved in July 1998 and applied to accounting periods commencing on or after 1 July 1999. It includes new requirements for goodwill (which are consistent with those for intangible assets) and negative goodwill, provisions arising on business combinations and the fair value of certain acquired assets. It also includes extensive transitional provisions.

Certain consequential amendments were made to IAS 22 [1993] as a result of the adoption of the revised IAS 12.

16.2.2 G4 + 1

In November 1998, the IASC decided to seek comments on a G4 + 1 position paper on business combinations which dealt with the choice between the purchase method and the pooling of interests method[2]. The IASC appointed a steering committee to review those comments. This was the first occasion on which the IASC had dealt with a G4 + 1 paper in this way although drafts of earlier G4 + 1 papers had been considered at the IASC sponsored meetings of standard setting bodies.

The G4 + 1 position paper considered:

- whether a single method of accounting for business combinations is preferable to two or more methods;
- if so, which method should be applied to all business combinations; and
- if not, which method should be applied and when it should be applied.

The paper considered three possible methods – the purchase method, the pooling of interests method and a 'fresh-start' method which would establish a new accounting basis for all assets and liabilities being combined. The paper concluded:

- the use of a single method is preferable to two or more methods;
- the purchase method is the appropriate method to use;
- the pooling of interests method should not be used for any business combination; and
- while a case could be made for using a 'fresh-start' method for certain combinations, on balance, the use of two methods, together with the disadvantages of the 'fresh-start' method itself, outweigh the advantages of using the 'fresh-start' method for the relatively small number of business combinations to which it might apply.

The IASC considered the possibility of eliminating the pooling of interests method during the comparability project but concluded that the method should be retained for those rare circumstances in which an acquirer cannot be identified[3].

16.2.3 IASB Project on Business Combinations

The IASB is currently carrying out a two phase project to achieve convergence of existing standards on business combinations. The first phase seeks the convergence of existing standards on:

- the definition of a business combination;
- the method(s) of accounting;
- accounting for goodwill (and negative goodwill) and intangible assets acquired;
- the treatment of liabilities for terminating or reducing the activities of an acquiree;
- the initial measurement of the identifiable net assets acquired; and
- the date on which equity instruments issued as consideration should be measured.

An exposure draft for this phase is due to be published in November 2002.

The second phase may involve consideration of:

- business combinations in which separate entities or operations of entities are brought together to form a joint venture, including possible applications for 'fresh start' accounting under which the assets and liabilities of each of the combining entities are recorded by the new entity at their fair values;
- business combinations involving entities under common control;

- business combinations involving two or more mutual entities (such as mutual insurance companies or mutual co-operative entities); and
- business combinations involving the formation of a reporting entity by contract only without the obtaining of an ownership interest (for example, when separate entities are brought together by contract only to form a dual listed corporation).

Certain aspects of the second phase will be considered as part of a joint IASB/FASB project on business combinations.

16.3 IOSCO

In June 1994, IOSCO advised the IASC that IAS 22 was acceptable for the purposes of the IOSCO core standards. However, IOSCO identified the following suspense issues:

- some IOSCO members would accept the use of discounting to record acquired tax assets and liabilities only if disclosures are made providing information equivalent to recording tax assets and liabilities on an undiscounted basis (the discounting of acquired tax assets and liabilities is no longer permitted as a result of the adoption of the revised IAS 12);
- the presentation of shareholders' equity and comparative financial statements following a reverse acquisition (the IASB is dealing with reverse acquisitions in phase one of its business combinations project);
- some IOSCO members have difficulty applying the accounting treatment for reverse acquisitions due to legal constraints;
- new bases of accounting issues, including:
  - push down accounting (including push down of debt);
  - promoter and related party transactions;
  - common control transactions (including downstream mergers and simultaneous transactions);
  - joint venture formations;
  - master limited partnership formations;
  - leveraged buyouts;
  - mergers with unrelated shell corporations; and,
  - bankruptcies and reorganisations;

  The IASB plans to deal with some of these issues in the second phase of its business combinations project.
- entities without subsidiaries should follow the same accounting for legal mergers as for companies with subsidiaries but legal constraints give some IOSCO members difficulty in applying IAS 22 to legal mergers (the application of IAS 22 to legal mergers was specifically

addressed by the IASC and FEE prior to the approval of IAS 22 [1993] and some IOSCO members objected at that time to the consideration of these issues – see 16.7.2);
- limiting the scope of exclusion for 'interests in joint ventures and the financial statements of joint ventures' to 'joint venture formations'; and
- one IOSCO member believes that when the fair value of one entity or the scale of business is significantly greater than that of the other combining entity, if the shareholders of the combining entities share mutually in the risks and benefits of the combined entity, it should not be judged to be an acquisition and should be interpreted as a uniting of interests and the pooling of interest method should be allowed (this was rejected by the IASC during the development of IAS 22 [1993] and has subsequently been rejected by the SIC and the IASB).

IOSCO's suspense issues on goodwill and negative goodwill are dealt with in chapter 24.

IOSCO also proposed that the IASC should consider the following potential long-term projects:

- the bases for establishing provisions in connection with a business combination (this has been dealt with in IAS 37 and IAS 22); and
- the treatment of the related costs of the acquirer and acquiree in connection with an acquisition (the IASB is dealing with this issue in phase one of its business combinations project).

As explained in 16.6.2 below, in 1994 the SEC decided to allow foreign issuers to use IAS 22 [1993] to determine whether or not a business combination is an acquisition or a uniting of interests. An issuer which complies with IAS 22 [1993] is not required to reconcile to US GAAP for this item. However, the SEC has interpreted IAS 22 very strictly – probably far more strictly than the IASC intended – with the result that few, if any, IAS 22 unitings of interest have satisfied the SEC.

IAS 22 is included in 'IAS 2000' endorsed by IOSCO in May 2000. There are three supplemental treatments (the supplemental treatments on goodwill and negative goodwill are dealt with in chapter 24):

- guidance on the presentation of shareholders' equity and comparative financial statements following a reverse acquisition (the IASB is dealing with this issue in phase one of its business combinations project);
- reconsideration of the accounting for legal mergers due to legal constraints in certain jurisdictions; and

- reconsideration of the accounting for assumed liabilities associated with planned restructurings (the IASB is dealing with this issue in phase one of its business combinations project).

16.4 IAS 22 IN BRIEF

An entity should account for the acquisition of another business in the same way that it accounts for the acquisition of other assets and liabilities, that is, at cost which is the fair value of the purchase consideration. In consolidated financial statements, the acquisition is dealt with as follows:

- the cost of the acquisition is attributed to the identifiable assets and liabilities acquired by reference to their fair values as at the date of acquisition;
- any excess of the fair value of the purchase consideration over the amounts attributed to identifiable assets and liabilities is treated as goodwill;
- goodwill should be capitalised and amortised over its useful life with a rebuttable presumption that useful life does not exceed 20 years – pre-1995 goodwill may be written off to equity (see chapter 24);
- any excess of the amounts attributed to identifiable assets and liabilities over the fair value of the purchase consideration is treated as negative goodwill (see chapter 24); and
- negative goodwill should be recognised as income when future losses and expenses to which that negative goodwill relates are recognised – any remaining negative goodwill should be amortised over the weighted average useful lives of the identifiable, acquired depreciable and amortised assets (or in certain circumstances recognised as income immediately) (see chapter 24).

When two or more entities merge such that neither entity can be identified as the acquirer, the consolidated financial statements of the merged entities should be presented as if the merged entities had always been one entity. This method is known as the pooling of interests method and should be used only when:

- the substantial majority of the shares of the two entities are exchanged or pooled;
- the fair value of one entity is not significantly different from the fair value of the other entity; and
- the shareholders maintain substantially the same voting rights and interest in the combined entity.

16.5 DEFINITIONS OF BUSINESS COMBINATIONS

A *business combination* is the bringing together of separate entities into one economic entity as a result of one entity uniting with, or obtaining control over the net assets and operations of, another entity (IAS 22, 8). The combining entities may have the same or different legal forms. For example, both may be companies or one or both may be partnerships or unincorporated businesses. An acquisition may also involve the purchase of the net assets, including any goodwill, rather than the equity of the acquiree.

IAS 22 distinguishes between two types of business combinations:

- a *uniting of interests* (or merger) in which one entity unites with another; and
- an *acquisition* in which one entity obtains control over the net assets and operations of another entity.

All business combinations are either an acquisition or a uniting of interests (SIC 9, 7); there are no additional categories of business combinations.

16.6 ACQUISITIONS AND UNITINGS OF INTERESTS

16.6.1 The IASC's Approach

An *acquisition* is a business combination in which one entity, the *acquirer*, obtains control over the net assets and operations of another entity, the *acquiree*, in exchange for the transfer of assets, incurrence of a liability or issue of equity (IAS 22, 8). A *uniting of interests* is a business combination in which the shareholders of the combining entities combine control over the whole, or effectively the whole, of their net assets and operations to achieve a mutual sharing in the risks and the benefits attaching to the combined entity such that neither party can be identified as the acquirer (IAS 22, 8).

An acquisition can be distinguished from a uniting of interests by determining whether or not there is an acquirer. If there is an acquirer, the business combination is an acquisition. If there is not an acquirer, the business combination is a uniting of interests. In virtually all business combinations, an acquirer can be identified (IAS 22, 10 and SIC 9, 4); For example:

- when the fair value of one entity is significantly greater than that of the other, the larger entity is usually the acquirer (IAS 22, 11 (a));

- when one entity pays cash for voting ordinary shares of the other entity, the paying entity is usually the acquirer (IAS 22, 11 (b));
- when one entity pays a premium for the voting ordinary shares in the other entity, the payer of the premium is usually the acquirer – in other words, the shareholders in the acquiree receive significantly more for their shares than a pro-rata allocation would suggest;
- when the management of one entity is able to dominate the selection of the management team of the resulting combined entity, the dominant entity is usually the acquirer (IAS 22, 11(c));
- when one entity makes a take-over bid for another entity and that bid is resisted, the bidder is usually the acquirer;
- when an entity negotiates to purchase the subsidiary of another entity, the purchaser is usually the acquirer; and
- when the shareholders in one of the combining entities obtain control over the combined entity, that entity is the acquirer (SIC 9, 8).

The circumstances in which an acquirer cannot be identified are very rare (E32, 159). Furthermore, as explained below, the SEC believes that an 'exhaustive search' must be made for an acquirer although other IOSCO members may be more flexible.

The necessary mutual sharing of the risks and benefits of the combined entity for the combination to meet the definition of a uniting of interests are achieved only when:

- the substantial majority, if not all, the voting common shares of the combining entities are exchanged or pooled;
- the fair value of one entity is not significantly different from that of the other entity; and
- the shareholders of each entity maintain substantially the same voting rights and interest in the combined entity, relative to each other, after the combination as before.

(IAS 22, 16)

Even if all three characteristics are present, the combination is a uniting of interests only if an acquirer cannot be identified (SIC 9, 6).

The guidance in IAS 22 provides examples of important factors to be considered, not a comprehensive set of conditions to be met (SIC 9, 5). Therefore, single characteristics of a combined entity such as voting power or the relative fair values of the combining entities should not be evaluated in isolation in order to determine how a business combination should be accounted for (SIC 9, 5). For example, the fact that there may be a larger difference in the relative sizes of the combining entities than is usual for a uniting of interests does not preclude that combination being accounted for as a uniting of interests if the other factors are met, in particular if an acquirer cannot otherwise be identified.

While the SIC has concluded that single characteristics should not be evaluated in isolation, it has also concluded that all three criteria must be met in order to achieve mutual sharing of risks and benefits of the combined entity. Under this notion, if any one criterion is not met, a business combination is an acquisition (SIC 9, 10). For example, the fact that there may be a larger difference in the relative sizes of the combining interests means that one criterion is not met and, therefore, that the business combination is an acquisition. This appears to contradict the SIC's earlier conclusion that single characteristics should not be evaluated in isolation.

Extract 16.1 *Uniting of interests*

Novartis, Switzerland, 31 December 2001 (IAS)

The Group was formed on 20 December 1996 when all assets and liabilities of Sandoz AG and Ciba-Geigy AG were transferred by universal succession to Novartis AG. The transaction was structured as a merger of equals based on an exchange of shares, providing former Sandoz AG shareholders with 55% and former Ciba-Geigy AG shareholders with 45% of the new company. The uniting of interests method was used for this transaction. The merger was consummated before the effective date of SIC 9 on accounting for business transactions.

Extract 16.2 *Unitings of interests*

Stora Enso, Finland, 31 December 1999 (IAS)

The Stora Enso Group was formed as a combination of the Groups parented by Enso Oyj and Stora Kopparbergs Bergslags Aktiebolag (publ). Shareholders of Stora Kopparbergs Bergslags Aktiebolag (publ) converted 96.1% of their shares into shares of Enso Oyj. As a result of the merger Stora Kopparbergs Bergslags Aktiebolag is a subsidiary of Stora Enso Oyj (formerly Enso Oyj).

The Stora Enso merger conforms to the criteria for a pooling of interests under IAS 22. The historical information of the Stora Enso Group is presented as if the Group had been operative from the beginning of 1994.

16.6.2 The SEC's Interpretation

Since 1994, the SEC has allowed foreign issuers to use IAS 22 to determine whether a business combination should be accounted for under the purchase method or the pooling of interests method[4]. If a business combination is a uniting of interests under IAS 22, the foreign issuer need not reconcile to US GAAP on this issue even if the combination would be a purchase (acquisition) under US GAAP.

When the SEC made this concession, it was widely recognised that it reflected the SEC's wish that the use of the pooling of interests method should be restricted and the SEC's belief that IAS 22 adopted a more restrictive approach than that allowed by US GAAP at that time. What few realised, however, was that the SEC would interpret IAS 22 even more strictly than the IASC had contemplated.

There are two problems for foreign registrants. First, the SEC may disagree with the registrant's interpretation that a business combination is a uniting of interests under IAS 22 and so require a reconciliation to the purchase method under US GAAP. Second, if the registrant's financial statements purport to conform with IASs, the SEC may conclude that the registrant has not applied IASs properly and so require the restatement of the financial statements themselves to reflect the use of the IAS purchase method.

The SEC's current position is as follows[5]:

> 'Because of the IASC Board's clear intent to restrict uniting of interests accounting to certain limited and rare circumstances, uniting of interests should not be presumed simply because ambiguity may exist about whether one shareholder group dominates the combined entity. An exhaustive search for an acquirer must be performed that considers all the relevant facts and circumstances. The staff believes that in virtually all business combinations an acquirer can be identified.
>
> SIC 9 indicates that all relevant facts and circumstances should be considered in determining the classification of a business combination. This includes an exhaustive search for an acquirer. SIC 9 clarifies that a business combination should be classified as an acquisition unless all the characteristics in IAS 22, 15 exist and it can be demonstrated that an acquirer cannot be identified.
>
> The issuance of SIC 9 provides an important benchmark in establishing a more rigorous application of IAS 22. SIC 9 is effective for business combinations given initial accounting recognition in periods beginning on or after 1 August 1998. For 31 December year-end registrants, it applies to business combinations consummated on or after 1 January 1999.
>
> Recently, several companies seeking to enter the SEC reporting system for the first time have accounted for a previously consummated business combination as a uniting of interests in their IAS financial statements. While not yet public in the US, the companies' shares have long been publicly traded on various major stock exchanges outside the US. In each case, the business combination transaction resulted in one of the shareholder

> groups owning more than 50% but less than 60% of the combined company. Because board and management representation was divided equally, the companies believed that an acquirer could not be identified. These business combinations were consummated before the effective date of SIC 9, and the companies did not consider SIC 9 in applying the requirements of IAS 22.
>
> In each case, the staff were unable to concur that the transaction should have been accounted for as a uniting of interests under IAS 22. If SIC 9 had been effective at the time the business combination was given initial accounting recognition, restatement of the financial statements would have been required to reflect the business combination as an acquisition under IAS 22. However, the staff recognized that practice at the time of the business combination was diverse in the application of IAS 22.
>
> Therefore, the staff did not require restatement of the financial statements to be filed with the Commission. However, the companies were required to reconcile the method of accounting for the business combination to the purchase method of accounting under US GAAP. That is, the staff concluded that it was not appropriate to permit the companies to use the accommodation in Form 20-F to avoid reconciliation.
>
> Registrants that have consummated business combinations *after* the effective date of SIC 9 are expected to strictly comply with the requirements of IAS 22 and SIC 9. The staff will also challenge presentations in the primary financial statements of uniting of interests consummated *before* the effective date of SIC 9 where it appears that IAS 22 has been misapplied egregiously. Egregious misapplication may be indicated, for example, where one of the shareholder groups obtains greater than 60% of the combined voting shares, where terms of the combination or related transactions are designed to provide a relative advantage to any shareholder group, or where terms of the combination or related transactions do not result in the combination of effectively the whole of the combining companies' net assets and operations.'

The SEC's Donald Gannon provided evidence of the SEC's tough approach in the context of one European registrant[6]. He referred to a case in which a foreign entity – believed to be Novartis – was in the process of registering its shares in the US. The facts and the registrant's assertions are summarised in example 16.1.

The SEC staff disagreed with the entity's conclusion that the combination was a uniting of interests, in particular that an acquirer could not be identified. The SEC staff was also troubled by the planned disposal transactions. While the SEC had not previously addressed the issue of planned disposal transactions in the context of IAS 22, Gannon said that the SEC staff would question situations involving such transactions in the context of determining both whether any shareholder group has been provided a relative advantage and whether the shareholders of the combining entities combine control over the whole, or effectively the whole, of their net assets and operations.

The SEC decided that the registrant would have to reconcile to US GAAP on this issue (that is, it could not take advantage of the 1994 concession) if it wished to register its shares in the United States. However, the SEC did not require the registrant to restate its primary IAS financial statements because of the divergent practice in the application of IAS 22 prior to the issue of SIC 9.

Example 16.1 *Acquisition or Uniting of Interests?*

Company A and company B each contribute their separate businesses to a new company C. All existing shareholder rights in companies A and B are replaced by shareholder rights in company C. Former company A shareholders received a 45% interest in company C and former company B shareholders receive a 55% interest in company C.

The combined entities form an integrated business operated under a unified management team consisting of both former company A and B management personnel. Also, each of the predecessor entities has the same number of members on company C's board of directors.

The combination plan also includes certain planned disposal transactions. Under the terms of the merger agreement, certain business or divisions of the predecessor entities were sold or spun-off. These transactions occurred after the merger was announced and continued through periods subsequent to the consummation of the business combination.

Company C, as well as its predecessor companies A and B, prepared financial statements using IASs. In company C's financial statements, the business combination was accounted for as a uniting of interests under IAS 22.

While former company B shareholders may be presumed to control company C because of their 55% interest in the combined entity, company C asserted that this presumption had been overcome because:

- no dominant shareholder or clearly defined shareholder group existed;
- the voting shares were widely held;
- there was equal representation of the predecessor companies on company C's board; and

Continued

Continued

- the chairman and president of company C, who were from different predecessor entities, along with the board, were jointly responsible for the overall strategy and direction of company C.

Company C further asserted that former company A and B shareholders mutually shared in the risks and benefits of the combined entity because:

- all the shares of the predecessor entities were exchanged for shares of company C;
- the fair values of the combining entities were not 'significantly different'; and
- the shareholders of company A and B each maintained substantially the same voting rights and interests in the combined entity as before the merger.

Author's note – derived from Donald Gannon's paper[6].

The *International Accounting Standards Survey 2000* examines the impact of the SEC's approach in more detail. It notes that the SEC did not accept that the mergers that created Novartis and ING met the criteria in IAS 22. Subsequently, the SEC did not agree that the Stora Enso met the IAS 22 criteria. Other groups that are believed to have tried unsuccessfully to use the IAS 22 concession include AstraZeneca and Aventis.

16.6.3 The IASB's Business Combinations Project

In phase one of its business combinations project, the IASB has reached the conclusion that all business combinations should be accounted for by applying the purchase method. In other words, all business combinations are acquisitions and no combinations are unitings of interests. As a result, the use of the pooling of interests method will not be permitted for business combinations within the scope of the revised IAS 22. The IASB reached this conclusion for several reasons:

- suitable non-arbitrary criteria do not exist by which unitings of interests can be distinguished from acquisitions;
- the development of non-arbitrary criteria to distinguish unitings of interests from acquisitions would be difficult and the cost of their development would exceed the benefits;

- allowing the use of more than one method of accounting for business combinations would create incentives for businesses to structure transactions so as to achieve a particular accounting result; and
- the pooling of interests method may not be an appropriate method for mergers and other business combinations that are not acquisitions.

16.7 STRUCTURE OF BUSINESS COMBINATIONS

A business combination may be structured in a variety of ways for legal, taxation or other reasons. The requirements in IAS 22 apply whatever structure is adopted for the combination. The use of a particular structure does not determine whether or not the combination is an acquisition or a uniting of interests. For example, the creation of a new holding company to control both the combining entities is neither evidence of an acquisition nor a uniting of interests.

IAS 22 does not deal with business combinations between two entities under common control. For example, IAS 22 does not apply in the consolidated financial statements of an entity when one of its subsidiaries acquires another subsidiary or when one of its subsidiaries unites with another subsidiary. However, IAS 22 would apply in the separate financial statements of the subsidiaries which are parties to the business combination or consolidated financial statements of those subsidiaries if those financial statements purport to conform with IFRSs.

A more troublesome issue is the transfer of the net assets and operations of one entity to a second entity when that second entity is established solely for the purpose of acquiring those net assets and operations. This arises frequently on privatisations when formerly state-controlled operations are transferred to a new company in which shares will later be sold to non-government investors. Some argue that the new company should apply the purchase method in IAS 22 in respect of its acquisition of the net assets of the operations. Others argue that the transfer initially takes place between entities under common control – usually a government department and the new company which, at the time of the transfer, is initially controlled by the government (if only momentarily). The IASB is examining this issue in phase two of its current project on business combinations.

A related issue is whether the purchase method should be applied when there is a change in the ownership of the entity itself. This is required by national standards in some countries. If the purchase method is applied in such circumstances, it would resolve the issue of privatisations as they give rise to a change in the ownership of the entity. Currently, IFRSs do not require the use of the purchase method in such

Example 16.2 *Creation of new holding company*

A and B combine their net assets and operations. Under the terms of the combination, a new holding company C is formed which will hold all the shares in A and B. The former shareholders in A and B receive shares in C, in return for their shares in A and B.

While all the shares in A and B have been exchanged for shares in C, the combination may be an acquisition. It is a uniting of interests only if neither A nor B can be identified as the acquirer. If, for example, A is substantially larger than B and A's management will dominate the management of the combined entity, A is the acquirer. In such circumstances, the assets and liabilities of B are measured by reference to their fair values as at the date of the acquisition and A calculates the goodwill or negative goodwill arising on its acquisition of B. The assets and liabilities of A are recognised and measured at their carrying amounts prior to the business combination. No goodwill or negative goodwill relating to A is recognised.

Example 16.3 *Uniting of interests without creation of new holding company*

A and B combine their net assets and operations. The shareholders of B receive shares in A. The combination may be an acquisition or a uniting of interests.

The combination is a uniting of interests if the IAS 22 criteria are met notwithstanding that the net assets and operations are, in legal form, controlled by A after the combination. It is necessary to look to the substance of the combination and at such matters as the relative sizes of A and B, the relative shareholding in A after the combination of the pre-combination shareholders in A and B, and the role of A's and B's managements in the combined entity.

circumstances, but the issue may be reconsidered. It was also one of IOSCO's 1994 suspense issues but is not referred to in IOSCO's 2000 report.

One entity may acquire the net assets (including any goodwill) rather than the equity of the other entity. Such a transaction is a business combination and is dealt with in accordance with IAS 22 almost invariably as an acquisition rather than a uniting of interests. In such circumstances, the acquirer recognises the net assets (including any goodwill) acquired in its separate financial statements. No further adjustments are necessary in its consolidated financial statements.

Extract 16.3 *Common control transaction – use of pooling of interests method*

PKN ORLEN, Poland, 31 December 2000 (IAS)

In connection with the Polish Government's restructuring and privatisation program for the Polish oil sector, the Polish State Treasury, through its holding in Nafta Polska SA, reorganised the Polish oil sector in the years 1997 through 1999. The existing PKN ORLEN Group is a result of this reorganisation of several significant companies which were all under the common control of Nafta Polska SA and the Polish State Treasury. In particular, this reorganisation included the following transactions performed by the Company:

- incorporation of Centrala Produktów Naftowych 'CPN' SA – major Polish fuel retailer,
- acquisition of Rafineria Trzebinia SA – refinery,
- acquisition of Rafineria Nafty Jedicze SA – refinery,
- disposition of Dyrekcja Eksploatacji Cystern Sp. Zo.o. – major Polish rail logistics operator,
- disposition of Naftobazy Sp. Zo.o. – major Polish fuel storage farms operator.

To the extent of the Polish State Treasury's common control, this reorganisation was accounted for using the 'pooling of interests' method of accounting. As a result, the financial statements reflect this reorganisation as if it had taken place prior to 1 January 1999.

16.7.1 Reverse Acquisitions

A business combination may take the form of a reverse acquisition in which, for example, entity A obtains ownership of the shares of entity B but control of the combined entity passes to the owners of B. Legally A is the parent but, in substance, B, whose shareholders now control the combined entity, is the acquirer. Therefore it is B which applies the purchase method in its consolidated financial statements. This means that A's (and not B's) assets and liabilities are measured at fair value.

Reverse acquisitions may occur, for example, when a substantial unlisted company reverses into a dormant listed company in order to obtain, at minimum cost, the benefits of the listing. In such circumstances, it is the assets and liabilities (if any) of the dormant company which should be restated to fair values. The assets and liabilities of the unlisted company are not restated.

In some countries there are legal impediments to applying the requirements of IAS 22 in a reverse acquisition, a point acknowledged by IOSCO in its June 1994 comments on IASs.

In the exposure draft for phase one of its business combinations project, the IASB includes new guidance on the application of IAS 22 to reverse acquisitions. The guidance clarifies that, in a reverse acquisition, the cost of acquisition is deemed to have been issued by the legal subsidiary through the issue of shares to the shareholders of the legal parent. The subsequent consolidated financial statements should be issued under the name of the legal parent but should be described as a continuation of the financial statements of the legal subsidiary. In those consolidated financial statements:

- the assets and liabilities of the legal subsidiary should be recognised and measured at their pre-combination carrying amounts;
- the identifiable assets and liabilities of the legal parent should be carried at their fair values as at the date of acquisition;
- any excess of the cost of acquisition over the acquirer's interest in the fair value of the identifiable net assets of the legal parent should be accounted for as goodwill;
- the accumulated profits or losses and other equity reserves should be those of the legal subsidiary immediately prior to the business combination;
- the amount of issued capital is the sum of the issued capital of the legal subsidiary immediately prior to the business combination and the cost of acquisition;
- the capital structure should reflect that of the legal parent;
- comparative information should be that of the legal subsidiary;
- the interests of shareholders of the legal subsidiary that do not exchange their shares for shares of the legal parent should be treated as minority interests; and
- minority interests should reflect the minority shareholders' proportionate interest in the pre-combination carrying amounts of the net assets of the legal subsidiary.

16.7.2 Legal Mergers

Legal mergers represent a significant part of acquisition and merger activities in Europe, Japan and elsewhere. The IASC recognised, therefore, that any IAS on business combinations needed to deal with legal mergers. In view of the concerns raised by a number of commentators on E45 *Business Combinations* the IASC and FEE subsequently examined in detail[7]:

- the nature of legal mergers, including their substance and the circumstances in which they arise;
- whether the substance or the outcome of a legal merger is different from mergers and acquisitions which are not described as legal mergers (in the countries concerned and in other countries);

- the accounting treatments currently adopted for legal mergers and the reasons for those treatments;
- the appropriateness of the accounting treatments in IAS 22 for legal mergers; and
- whether any changes should be made to the requirements or guidance in IAS 22 and if so, why.

The work focused on legal mergers in the European Union and its conclusions may not be applicable in other environments. It recognised that, while the requirements for legal mergers differ among EU member states, a legal merger is usually a merger between two companies in which either:

- the assets and liabilities of one company are transferred to the other company and the first company is dissolved; or
- the assets and liabilities of both companies are transferred to a new company and both the original companies are dissolved.

Legal mergers are often used for tax reasons because they are usually tax neutral, that is, no tax is paid on any gain between the fair value of assets transferred and their original book value. A legal merger is also a means of transferring a loss carry forward to the acquiring company. Legal mergers may also be used to reduce administrative costs, achieve economies of scale and facilitate the restructuring of companies.

Following the IASC/FEE study, the IASC concluded that legal mergers should continue to be within the scope of IAS 22 and that the underlying business combinations should be dealt with as an acquisition or uniting of interests in accordance with the criteria in IAS 22. In particular, any legal merger which results in the two companies becoming members of the same group should be dealt with as an acquisition or as a uniting of interests in consolidated financial statements (IAS 22, 5). This view has been further reinforced by the confirmation that all business combinations are either acquisitions or uniting of interests (SIC 9, 7).

While legal mergers are within the scope of IAS 22, many arise as part of the reorganisation of the group. Such reorganisations are not dealt with in IAS 22 because they are transactions among entities under common control (IAS 22, 5 and 7). If such events are dealt with in accordance with IAS 22, any gains or losses arising on intragroup transactions should be eliminated in full (IAS 27, 17).

Notwithstanding the efforts of the IASC and FEE to deal with this issue (and the involvement of the European Commission in those efforts), IOSCO included legal mergers in its June 1994 suspense issues. As with several other such issues, IOSCO was undecided on the right approach to be adopted.

In its May 2000 supplemental treatments, IOSCO asks the IASB to revisit the issue of legal mergers because of legal constraints in some countries. This request implies that some IOSCO members wish to either:

- account for some legal mergers that are, in substance, acquisitions as unitings of interests; or
- apply the purchase method in a different manner from that required by IAS 22.

IOSCO members may also require a company without subsidiaries to follow the same accounting for a legal merger as an entity with subsidiaries. This may imply that these IOSCO members would require most legal mergers to be accounted for using the purchase method.

16.8 ACQUISITIONS AND THE PURCHASE METHOD

An acquisition usually results in a parent-subsidiary relationship in which the acquirer is the parent and the acquiree is the subsidiary of the acquirer. The acquirer includes its interest in the acquiree in its separate financial statements as an investment in a subsidiary which is initially measured at cost.

In its consolidated financial statements, the acquirer replaces the investment in subsidiary with the identifiable assets and liabilities, any goodwill or negative goodwill, and any minority interest relating to the acquisition. This is known as the purchase method. When the acquirer acquires the net assets, rather than the equity, of the acquiree, the purchase method is applied in the acquirer's separate financial statements; in effect, the transaction is treated as any other acquisition of assets and liabilities.

In order to apply the purchase method, the acquirer must determine:

- the date of the acquisition, which is the date on which the acquirer obtained control (see 16.9);
- the cost of the acquisition, which is the amount that was paid or will be paid for the other business (see 16.10);
- the assets and liabilities acquired and whether they should be recognised in the consolidated financial statements of the acquirer (see 16.11);
- the fair values of the identifiable assets and liabilities acquired as at the date of the exchange transaction or the date of acquisition (see 16.12);
- the amount at which the identifiable assets and liabilities should be measured on initial recognition in the consolidated financial statements of the acquirer (see 16.13); and

- the amount of goodwill or negative goodwill arising on the acquisition (see 16.14 and chapter 24).

16.9 DATE OF ACQUISITION

The date of acquisition is the date on which control of the acquiree's net assets and operations is effectively transferred to the acquirer (IAS 22, 20). Control is the power to govern the financial and operating policies of the acquiree so as to obtain benefits from its activities (IAS 22, 8 and IAS 27, 6). The criteria for determining control in the context of a parent/subsidiary relationship are relevant in the context of determining when control is transferred in a business combination which is an acquisition (see chapter 15).

Control is not transferred to the acquirer until all the conditions necessary to protect the interests of the parties involved have been satisfied (IAS 22, 20). However, a transaction need not be completed at law before control effectively passes to the acquirer. So, for example, the acquirer obtains control when it acquires the power to govern the financial and operating policies of the acquiree notwithstanding that the transfer of ownership of the shares in the acquiree is awaiting completion of the legal documentation.

The acquirer may obtain control before the transfer of the purchase consideration. In such circumstances, the date of acquisition remains the date on which control passes but, as explained in 16.10, the cost of acquisition is measured at the date of the exchange transaction.

The acquirer applies the purchase method in its consolidated financial statements as from the date of acquisition (unless the business is acquired and held exclusively with a view to its disposal in the near future, in which case, the business is not consolidated – see chapter 15). From that date, the acquirer should incorporate into its consolidated income statement the acquiree's results of operations and should recognise in its consolidated balance sheet the assets and liabilities of the acquiree and any goodwill, negative goodwill or minority interest arising on the acquisition (IAS 22, 19).

Extract 16.4 *Date of acquisition*

Erste Bank, Austria, 31 December 2001 (IAS)

On 11 January 2001 the papers were signed for acquisition of 87.18% of Slovenská sporitel'ňa (SLSP), the largest financial institution in the Slovak Republic. Due to contractual agreements and in observation of the applicable IAS rules, Slevenská sporitel'ňa was included in Erste Bank's consolidated financial statements as of this date.

Extract 16.5 *Date of acquisition*

HVB Group, Germany, 31 December 2000 (IAS)

During the year under review, the Bank continued to implement its Bank of the Regions strategy by merging with Bank Austria AG, Vienna. The first step was for Bank Austria to transfer its operations to a new company (Bank Austria AG) and itself then act only as a holding company (BA Holding AG, Vienna) holding the capital stock of Bank Austria AG. In a second step on 8 December 2000, BA Holding AG transferred the capital stock of Bank Austria AG to HypoVereinsbank as a non-cash contribution, for which it received 114 million new shares from the capital increase effected by the Bank to complete this transaction. The last step involved BA Holding AG being absorbed into Bank Austria AG on 2 February 2001. As part of this stage, the HypoVereinsbank shares belonging to BA Holding AG were transferred to the latter's shareholders.

The acquisition cost for the purchase of Bank Austria AG totalled €6.6 billion. The merger is accounted for using the purchase method of accounting.

16.10 COST OF ACQUISITION

An acquisition should be accounted for at its cost (IAS 22, 21) as is the case with the acquisition of all other assets. Cost is measured as at the date of the relevant exchange transactions, which is the same as the date of acquisition when the acquisition is achieved in one exchange transaction but which may be different from the date of acquisition when the acquisition is achieved in stages (SIC 28, 5). The cost of acquisition is:

- the amount of cash or cash equivalents paid or the fair value, as at the date of the exchange transaction, of the other purchase consideration given by the acquirer in exchange for control over the acquiree's net assets (IAS 22, 21); plus
- any costs directly attributable to the acquisition (IAS 22, 21), including the costs of registering and issuing equity securities, and professional fees paid to accountants, legal advisers, valuers and other consultants to effect the acquisition (IAS 22, 25).

In phase one of its business combinations project, the IASB has agreed that the cost of acquisition should not include the costs of registering and issuing equity securities or the costs of issuing liabilities. These costs of registering and issuing equity securities should be deducted from equity in accordance with SIC 17 (see chapter 28). The costs of issuing liabilities should be included in the initial measurement of the liabilities in accordance with IAS 39 (see chapter 20).

The cost of acquisition does not include general administrative costs. In particular, it does not include the costs of maintaining an acquisitions department and other costs which cannot be directly attributed to the particular acquisition (IAS 22, 25). The cost also does not include any costs of the acquiree incurred in resisting the acquisition as such costs are not directly attributable to the acquisition.

An acquisition may involve more than one exchange transaction. In such a case, the cost of acquisition is the aggregate cost of the individual transactions (IAS 22, 22) each measured as at the date on which the transactions are recognised in the financial statements (SIC 28, 5). For example, if the purchase consideration consists of equity securities issued on different dates, each tranche of securities is measured at the fair value of the securities as at the date of issuance.

When settlement of the purchase consideration is deferred, the cost of the acquisition is the present value as at the date of the exchange transaction of the consideration, taking into account any premium or discount likely to be incurred in settlement (IAS 22, 23). Therefore, it is important to distinguish between the date of the exchange transaction and the date on which the consideration is settled. For example, if the acquirer acquires ownership of equity shares in the acquiree on 1 April 2002 but payment for those shares is deferred to 31 March 2003, the date of the exchange transaction is 1 April 2002. The cost of acquisition is the present value as at 1 April 2002 of the amount to be paid on 31 March 2003.

The purchase consideration often includes marketable securities issued by the acquirer. These securities are measured at their fair value. The published price at the date of exchange is the best evidence of fair value and should be used in all except rare circumstances (IAS 22, 24 and SIC 28, 6). The published price is not a reliable indicator only when it has been affected by an undue price fluctuation or the narrowness of the market (IAS 22, 24 and SIC 28, 6). When the market price is not a reliable indicator, fair value may be determined by reference to price movements for a reasonable period before and after the announcement of the terms of the acquisition. When the market is unreliable or no quotation exists, fair value is estimated by reference to the proportional interest of the securities in the fair value of either the acquirer's entity or the entity acquired, whichever is the more clearly evident. Cash paid as an alternative to securities may also provide evidence of the total fair value given (IAS 22, 24). The IASB intends to reconsider the measurement of equity instruments that form part of the purchase consideration during phase two of its business combinations project.

The acquisition agreement may allow for adjustments to the purchase consideration in the light of one or more future events. For example, the purchase consideration may be adjusted to reflect:

- the maintenance or achievement of a specified level of earnings in future periods; or
- the maintenance of the market price of the securities issued as part of the purchase consideration.

The estimated amount of any adjustments should be included in the cost of acquisition as at the date of the exchange transaction if the adjustment is probable and the amount can be reliably estimated (IAS 22, 65). In phase one of its business combinations project, the IASB has confirmed that any additional consideration should be recognised at a later date when the adjustment becomes probable and can be measured reliably. The additional consideration should be treated as an adjustment to the cost of acquisition with a consequential adjustment to goodwill or negative goodwill (IAS 22, 68).

If the future events do not occur, or the estimate needs to be revised, the cost of the acquisition is adjusted, usually with a consequential effect on goodwill (or negative goodwill). For example, the acquisition may require that the acquirer pays an additional £1 million in cash if the profits of the acquiree in the current year exceed £5 million. At the time of the acquisition, if it is probable that this level of profits will be achieved, the additional payment of £1 million is included in the purchase consideration. If the profits of the acquiree subsequently fall short of £5 million and no payment is made, the purchase consideration must be reduced by £1 million. This will reduce goodwill by the same amount and may even convert goodwill into negative goodwill; it may also restrict the amount attributed to an acquired intangible asset (see chapters 23 and 24).

With one exception, adjustments to the cost of acquisition mean that the amounts of goodwill or negative goodwill need to be recomputed (IAS 22, 69). The one exception to the general rule is when the acquirer compensates the seller for a subsequent reduction in the value of the purchase consideration. For example, the acquirer may compensate the seller for a decline in the market price of securities given as part of the purchase consideration. In such a case, the acquirer is simply making good the value of the original consideration. Therefore, any additional consideration in the form of securities represents a reduction in the premium, or an increase in the discount, on the initial issue of those securities (IAS 22, 70). There is no increase in the cost of acquisition and, consequently, no adjustment to goodwill or negative goodwill. There is no time limit to any of these adjustments to goodwill or negative goodwill.

When the purchase consideration includes shares of the acquirer, the acquiree may also receive other securities which are designed to compensate the acquiree for any reduction in the market price of the acquirer's shares. Such securities are part of the purchase consideration and should, therefore, be measured at their fair value at the date of the exchange transaction. If the securities are a financial liability, any subsequent change in their value, redemption payment or conversion is dealt with in accordance with IAS 39. If the securities are equity, any subsequent changes in value are not recognised in the financial statements. Any payment or conversion is dealt with in the same way as other changes in equity components.

16.11 IDENTIFIABLE ASSETS AND LIABILITIES

In its consolidated financial statements, the acquirer replaces the investment in the subsidiary with those individual assets and liabilities of the acquiree which existed at the date of acquisition (plus certain other provisions) when:

- it is probable that any associated future economic benefits associated with those assets and liabilities will flow to or from the acquirer; and
- a reliable measure is available of the cost or fair value of the assets or liabilities.

(IAS 22, 26)

Assets and liabilities acquired which are recognised are described in IAS 22 as identifiable assets. Identifiable assets and liabilities may include:

- assets and liabilities which have been recognised in the balance sheet of the acquiree;
- assets and liabilities of the acquiree which had not been recognised on its balance sheet (IAS 22, 28); and
- provisions which were not liabilities of the acquiree but which relate to the acquirer's plans for the acquirer's business provided that an obligation comes into existence as a direct consequence of the acquisition (IAS 22, 30 and 31).

16.11.1 Intangible Assets

Part of the cost of acquisition may be attributable to intangible assets, such as brands, trade marks and similar items, which have not been recognised on the balance sheet of the acquiree. These assets should be recognised by the acquirer if they meet the recognition criteria; if they are not recognised, they are included in goodwill. The recognition of intangible assets acquired in a business combination is dealt with in IAS 38 (see chapter 23).

The effect of IAS 38 is that it is impossible to recognise as an intangible asset any expenditure incurred by the acquiree on start-up activities, training, advertising and promotion. It is also difficult, but not impossible, to recognise as an intangible asset such items as acquired brands and acquired in-process research and development.

In phase one of its business combinations project, the IASB has broadly confirmed the approach in IAS 22 and IAS 38. It has agreed that, with the exception of an assembled workforce, intangible assets acquired in a business combination should be recognised separately from goodwill if they arise as a result of contractual or legal rights or are separable from the business (and meet the other criteria in IAS 22 and IAS 38). Acquired in-process research and development should be recognised separately from goodwill if it meets the same criteria. However, an intangible asset such as an assembled workforce should not be recognised separately from goodwill because it cannot be measured with sufficient reliability.

One further word of warning when dealing with IAS 38 and IAS 22. IAS 38 uses the term 'identifiable' differently from the way in which it is used in IAS 22. All intangible assets, whether or not they are recognised, are 'identifiable' for the purposes of IAS 38 because the term 'identifiable' is part of the definition of an intangible asset. Only those intangible assets which are recognised as assets (which may be very few) are 'identifiable' for the purposes of IAS 22. In other words, assets which are identifiable for the purposes of IAS 38 may not be identifiable for the purposes of IAS 22.

16.11.2 Tax Assets

Some tax assets which did not qualify for recognition in the financial statements of the acquiree may qualify for recognition as a result of the business combination. For example, in some jurisdictions, it may be possible to offset previous tax losses of the acquiree against current and future taxable profits of the acquirer. Alternatively, the fact of the business combination may provide the necessary assurance that the acquiree will generate sufficient taxable profits to reap the benefits of any tax loss carry forwards. When this is the case, the tax assets should be recognised as at the date of acquisition provided that they meet the rest of the recognition criteria.

The recognition of such tax assets reduces the amount attributable to goodwill (or increases negative goodwill).

When the tax assets do not meet the recognition criteria, they should not be recognised as at the date of acquisition. Tax assets which exist at the date of acquisition but which are not recognised at that time may qualify for recognition at a later date, for example when sufficient taxable profits are earned to enable the combined entity to realise the benefits of pre-acquisition tax losses of the acquiree. In such circumstances, the recognition of the tax asset reduces goodwill in one of two ways. If the tax asset is recognised by the end of the first annual accounting period commencing after the acquisition, the full amount of the tax asset is deducted from goodwill. If the tax asset is recognised in a later period, the benefit of the tax asset is included in deferred tax income in the income statement (IAS 12, 68). At the same time, the gross carrying amount and the accumulated amortisation of goodwill are both reduced to the amounts that would have been recorded if the tax asset had been recognised at the date of the business combination. The resulting reduction in the carrying amount of goodwill is recognised as an expense in the income statement (IAS 12, 68 and IAS 22, 85).

16.11.3 Provisions

The acquirer may intend to terminate or reduce the activities of the acquiree. When that intention is an obligation at the date of acquisition, it gives rise to a liability which should be recognised as a restructuring provision by the acquirer. In practice, however, many such intentions are not obligations at the date of acquisition and should not be recognised. However, IAS 22 creates a three-month window during which the acquirer may recognise restructuring provisions which were not liabilities as at the date of acquisition. This allows the acquirer to recognise a restructuring provision which was not a liability of the acquiree at the date of acquisition if the acquirer has:

- at, or before, the date of acquisition, developed the main features of a plan which involves terminating or reducing the activities of the acquiree and that relates to:
  - compensating employees of the acquiree for termination of their employment;
  - closing facilities of the acquiree;
  - eliminating product lines of the acquiree; or
  - terminating contracts of the acquiree that have become onerous because the acquirer has communicated to the other party at, or before, the date of acquisition that the contract will be terminated;
- by announcing the main features of the plan at, or before, the date of acquisition, raised a valid expectation in those affected by the plan that it will implement the plan; and
- by the earlier of three months after the date of acquisition and the date when the annual financial statements are approved, developed those main features into a detailed formal plan identifying at least:

- the business or part of a business concerned;
- the principal locations affected;
- the location, function, and approximate number of employees who will be compensated for terminating their services;
- the expenditures that will be undertaken; and
- when the plan will be implemented.

(IAS 22, 31)

The provision should cover only the costs that relate to the plan developed at or before the date of acquisition.

The three-month window in IAS 22 is an exception to the general principle for the recognition of restructuring provisions in IAS 37 (see chapter 27).

IASB business combinations project

In phase one of its business combinations project, the IASB proposes to conform IAS 22 with IAS 37. A restructuring provision should be recognised on a business combination as an identifiable liability as at the date of acquisition only when the acquiree had at that date an existing provision recognised in accordance with IAS 37.

16.11.4 Subsequent Adjustments

The acquirer may not have recognised assets and liabilities of an acquiree at the time of acquisition because they did not meet the recognition criteria or the acquirer was unaware of their existence. Such assets and liabilities should be recognised subsequently as and when they satisfy the recognition criteria (IAS 22, 71).

If such assets and liabilities had been recognised when the acquisition was first accounted for, the amount of goodwill or negative goodwill would have been affected. Therefore, IAS 22 requires the adjustment of goodwill or negative goodwill but only if:

- in the case of a provision which was not a liability of the acquiree, the adjustment is made by the earlier of three months after the date of the acquisition (IAS 22, 31 and 71);
- in other cases, the adjustment is made by the end of the first annual accounting period commencing after acquisition (IAS 22, 71) – this time limit, while arbitrary in its length, prevents goodwill and

negative goodwill from being reassessed and adjusted indefinitely (IAS 22, 72); and

- the adjustment does not increase the carrying amount of goodwill above its recoverable amount as defined in IAS 36 (IAS 22, 72).

When these criteria are not met, any adjustments resulting from the recognition of identifiable assets or liabilities or the adjustment of the carrying amounts of existing assets or identifiable liabilities should be recognised as income or expense (IAS 22, 71). In such circumstances, it may be necessary for the entity to consider whether goodwill is impaired. In particular, when the new asset is the benefit arising from a tax loss carry forward which was not recognised at the date of acquisition, that part of the unamortised balance of goodwill arising on the acquisition which is attributable to those tax benefits should be recognised as an expense (IAS 12, 68 and IAS 22, 85).

The adjustments arising on the subsequent recognition of acquired assets and liabilities or changes to the estimates of their fair values should be calculated as if the (adjusted) fair values had been applied from the date of acquisition (SIC 22, 5). This means that both the fair value and any subsequent depreciation, amortisation or other charges are adjusted. Adjustments to depreciation, amortisation and other charges are included in the income statement in accordance with appropriate IASs.

16.12 FAIR VALUES OF IDENTIFIABLE ASSETS AND LIABILITIES

Under IAS 22 [1993], the fair values of identifiable assets and liabilities were determined by reference to their intended use by the acquirer (IAS 22 [1993], 38). Under the revised IAS 22, the fair values must be determined without regard to the acquirer's intended use of the assets. The fair values are also determined in accordance with IFRSs and the entity's accounting policies. For example, tax assets and tax liabilities are determined in accordance with the entity's policies for applying IAS 12 and employee benefit obligations are determined in accordance with the entity's policies for applying IAS 19.

Extract 16.6 *Fair values of identifiable assets and liabilities*

algroup, Switzerland, 31 December 1997 (IAS)

At the time of their initial consolidation, the assets and liabilities of consolidated subsidiaries are recorded at their estimated fair values in accordance with uniform Group principles.

Extract 16.7 *Identifiable assets and liabilities*

Danisco, Denmark, 30 April 2000 (IAS)

On the acquisition of new undertakings the purchase method is applied, according to which the assets and liabilities of newly acquired undertakings are restated at their fair value at the date of acquisition. Provision is made for obligations concerning declared restructuring in the acquired undertaking in conjunction with the acquisition. The related tax effect is taken into account. Any excess cost of acquisition over the fair value of net assets acquired is capitalised as goodwill or consolidated goodwill in the acquisition year ...

Where the fair value of the acquired assets and liabilities subsequently proves to differ from the computed values at the time of acquisition, goodwill is adjusted until the end of the financial year following the year of acquisition if the new higher value does not exceed anticipated future income. All other adjustments are charged to the profit and loss account.

IAS 22 includes detailed guidelines for arriving at the fair values of identifiable assets and liabilities acquired. The guidance is generally based on entry prices, which is consistent with the principles underlying the purchase method.

Certain of the guidelines assume that fair values are determined by the use of discounting, for example receivables, payables and net retirement benefit assets or obligations but the discounting of tax assets and tax liabilities is now prohibited by IAS 12 (see chapter 31). In other cases, discounting may be used in determining the fair values of identifiable assets and liabilities (IAS 22, 39) but it is required only when its effects would be material.

The fair value of marketable securities is their current market values (IAS 22, 39(a)). IAS 32 defines market value as the amount obtainable from the sale, or payable on the acquisition, of a financial instrument in an active market (IAS 32, 5) and provides guidance on the application of that definition (see chapter 20). In an acquisition, it is appropriate to use the amount payable on acquisition, rather than the amount obtainable from the sale, to determine the fair value of acquired marketable securities.

The fair value of non-marketable securities takes into consideration features such as price earnings ratios, dividend yields and expected growth rates of comparable securities of entities with similar characteristics (IAS 22, 39(b)). IAS 39 emphasises that it should normally be possible to estimate the fair value of a financial asset which an entity (the acquirer) has acquired from an outside party. This should be true at the time of the acquisition when the acquirer has had to consider the likely values of the assets acquired.

The fair value of receivables is the present value of the amounts to be received, determined at appropriate current interest rates, less allowances for uncollectability and collection costs, if necessary (IAS 22, 39(c)). The interest rate should be the rate of interest prevailing in the market at the time the estimate is made for receivables having substantially the same principal terms and characteristics, such as creditworthiness of the customer or borrower, the remaining term and the currency in which payments will be received. Discounting is not required for short-term receivables when the difference between the nominal amount of the receivable and the discounted amount is not material (IAS 22, 39(c)). Therefore, discounting is unnecessary for most trade receivables and other receivables classified as current assets.

The fair value of inventories of finished goods and merchandise is their selling prices less the sum of the costs of disposal and a reasonable profit allowance for the selling effort of the acquirer based on profit for similar finished goods and merchandise (IAS 22, 39 (d)). The fair value of work in progress is the selling prices of finished goods less the sum of costs to complete, costs of disposal and a reasonable profit allowance for the completing and selling effort based on profit for similar finished goods. The fair value of raw materials is current replacement costs (IAS 22, 16(d)). IAS 22 provides no guidance on what it means by a 'reasonable profit allowance'; a similar notion is included in IAS 18 when it deals with the allocation of the total selling price between the revenue for a product and the revenue for a subsequent service which will be rendered to that product (see chapter 29). IAS 18 also gives no guidance on the issue. A starting point in any assessment of a 'reasonable profit' is the normal profit on the goods.

The fair value of land and buildings is their market value (IAS 22, 39(e)). International Valuation Standards (IVSs) define market value as the estimated amount for which a property should exchange on the date of valuation between a willing buyer and a willing seller in an arm's length transaction after proper marketing wherein the parties had each acted knowledgeably, prudently and without compulsion (IVS 1, 3.1). This definition is consistent with the IAS definition of fair value. According to the IVSC, the market value of a property is based on its highest and best use (IVS 1, 4.3), which is the most probable use of the property which is physically possible, appropriately justified, legally permissible, financially feasible and which results in the highest value of the property being valued (*General Valuation Principles and Concepts*, 6.3). These notions are consistent with IAS 22.

IAS 22 [1993] required market value to be based on existing, rather than highest and best, use, a requirement that was removed in the 1998 revision. One consequence of the change is that impairment losses (see chapter 25) may be more likely under the new approach although it could always be argued that net selling price should be based on highest and best, rather than existing, use.

The fair value of items of plant and equipment is their market value determined by appraisal. When there is no evidence of market value because of the specialised nature of the plant and equipment or because the items are rarely sold, except as part of a continuing business, fair value is always depreciated replacement cost (IAS 22, 39(f)). This approach is consistent with the requirements for the revaluation of plant and equipment in IAS 16 and IVSs (see chapter 21). For accounting periods beginning before 1 July 1999, plant and equipment which is to be used temporarily or sold should be valued at net realisable value (IAS 22 [1993], 39).

The fair value of intangible assets is determined by reference to either an active market as defined in IAS 38 or, if no such market exists, on a basis which reflects the amount which the entity would have paid in an arm's length transaction between knowledgeable willing parties based on the best information available (IAS 22, 39 (g)). Further guidance is provided in IAS 38 (see chapter 23).

The fair value of net employee benefit assets or liabilities for defined benefit plans is the present value of the defined benefit obligation less the fair value of any plan assets (IAS 22, 39(h)). However, when the fair value of any plan assets exceeds the present value of the defined benefit obligation, the excess is recognised as an asset only to the extent that it is probable that it will be available to the entity in the form of refunds from the plan or reductions in future contributions – the same requirement is included in IAS 19 (IAS 22, 39(h)). In some plans, any such excess belongs to plan participants and will be paid to them in the form of increased benefits; therefore it is not recognised as an asset by the acquirer. Further guidance on the determination of the present value of the defined benefit obligation and the fair value of plan assets is provided in chapter 33.

The fair value of tax assets and liabilities is assessed from the perspective of the combined entity or group resulting from the acquisition (IAS 22, 39(i)). No adjustment is usually necessary for current tax expense already recognised by the acquiree. Adjustments to other amounts recognised by the acquiree may be required:

- when the tax benefit arising from tax loss carry forwards of the acquiree qualify for recognition as an asset as a result of the business combination – for example, when the acquirer is able to use such losses to reduce its current tax expense or that of another existing member of the acquirer's group (the use of tax losses in this way is not possible in many jurisdictions);
- when tax assets or liabilities arise from the tax treatment of the business combination; and
- for the tax effects of restating identifiable assets and liabilities to their fair values (IAS 22, 39(i)) – the restatement gives rise to temporary differences (see chapter 31).

The fair value of accounts and notes payable, long-term debt, liabilities, accruals and other claims payable is the present value of amounts to be disbursed in meeting the liabilities determined at appropriate current interest rates (IAS 22, 39(j)). The interest rate is the rate of interest prevailing in the market at the time the estimate is made for liabilities having substantially the same principal terms and characteristics, such as creditworthiness of the acquiree and acquirer, the remaining term and the currency in which payments will be made. Discounting is not required for short-term liabilities when the difference between the nominal amount of the liability and the discounted amount is not material (IAS 22, 39(j)). Therefore, discounting is unnecessary for most trade payables, short-term accruals and other items classified as current liabilities.

The fair value of onerous contracts and other identifiable liabilities of the acquiree is the present value of amounts to be disbursed in meeting the obligation determined at appropriate current interest rates (IAS 22, 39(k)). Onerous contacts might include a lease for a vacant leasehold property for which the fair value is the present value of rents and other costs to be incurred less any income and disposal proceeds. An onerous contract may be recognised as a liability only if it has been recognised as such by the acquiree or in the limited circumstances in which a restructuring provision may be recognised by the acquirer. So, for example, a leasehold property which is occupied and used profitably by the acquiree is not an onerous contract even if the acquirer intends to vacate the property. Therefore, any loss arising on the decision to vacate is a post acquisition expense unless it is covered by an acquisition provision in the limited circumstances in which such provisions are permitted.

The carrying amount of an asset or liability acquired and recognised should be adjusted when additional evidence becomes available at a later date to assist with the estimation of its fair value as at the date of acquisition (IAS 22, 71). If its carrying amount had been adjusted when the acquisition was first accounted for, the amount of goodwill or negative goodwill would have been increased or reduced. When the carrying amount is adjusted at a later date, goodwill or negative goodwill should be adjusted in accordance with the requirement for adjustments arising on the subsequent recognition of acquired assets and liabilities (see 16.11.4).

16.13 MEASUREMENT OF IDENTIFIABLE ASSETS ON INITIAL RECOGNITION

IAS 22 includes a benchmark and allowed alternative treatment for the measurement of the identifiable assets and liabilities on the initial recognition in the consolidated financial statements of the acquirer. The introduction of the benchmark treatment in IAS 22 [1993] was a substantive change from the treatment required in IAS 22 [1983].

IAS 22 [1983] required that the identifiable assets and liabilities of the acquiree should be restated to their fair values at the date of acquisition (IAS 22 [1983], 39). Under the current benchmark treatment, only the acquirer's share of the identifiable assets and liabilities of the acquiree should be restated to fair values; the minority interest is based on pre-acquisition carrying amount rather than post-acquisition fair values.

The change was made during the comparability project primarily at the insistence of the representatives of North America and IOSCO. They argued that the requirement in IAS 22 [1983] to restate assets and liabilities to fair value could be interpreted to allow only the acquirer's share to be restated. They also implied that such a treatment was the majority, if not required, practice in North America.

The proposed change was included in E32 but was opposed by a substantial number of commentators because of the conflict with the entity approach in IAS 27 (*IASC News*, July 1990, p13). It was also unanimously rejected at an IASC conference of standard setting bodies from 15 major countries in November 1993. Nevertheless, the change was incorporated in IAS 22 [1993] and retained in IAS 22 [1998].

Storey addresses this issue on the FASB's IAS/US GAAP comparison[8]. He points out:

> 'While IAS 22 turned toward what was presumed to be the majority practice in North America, it not only turned away from the earlier IAS 22 [1983] requirements and from those in IAS 27 *Consolidated Financial Statements and Accounting for Investments in Subsidiaries*, but also went counter to a developing trend among the standard-setting bodies including the FASB'.

Storey also points out that the FASB's 1995 exposure draft on consolidation policy and procedures clearly requires what is now the allowed alternative treatment in IAS 22 [1993] (which was the preferred treatment in IAS 22 [1983]).

It is easier to explain the allowed alternative treatment in IAS 22 [1993] (which was the required treatment in IAS 22 [1983]). Under this treatment, identifiable assets and liabilities should be measured at their fair values as at the date of acquisition (IAS 22, 33 and IAS 22 [1983] 39). This is a straightforward exercise (assuming that fair values can be determined). If the fair value of an identifiable asset at the date of acquisition is $1,000, the asset is measured on initial recognition at $1,000. If the fair value of an identifiable liability is $2,000, the liability is measured on initial recognition at $2,000.

The benchmark treatment is more complex but only if there is a minority interest in the acquiree or a step acquisition. Under the benchmark treatment, identifiable assets and liabilities should be measured at the aggregate of:

- the fair value of the identifiable assets and liabilities acquired as at the date of the exchange transaction to the extent of the acquirer's interest obtained in the exchange transaction; and
- the minority's proportion of the pre-acquisition carrying amounts of the assets and liabilities of the subsidiary.

(IAS 22, 32)

Therefore, there are two differences between the benchmark and allowed alternative treatments:

- the interest of any minority in the identifiable assets and liabilities of the acquiree is measured at pre-acquisition carrying amounts under the benchmark treatment but at fair value under the allowed alternative treatment; and
- fair values are determined at the date of the exchange transaction under the benchmark treatment but at the date of acquisition under the allowed alternative treatment.

Example 16.4 *Measurement of identifiable assets*

A acquires 75% of B. Among the identifiable assets is a property which was carried at cost of £8m in B's financial statements. The market value (fair value) of the property at the date of the acquisition and exchange transaction is £20m.

Under the benchmark treatment in IAS 22, the property is measured as follows:

	£m
A's interest – 75% of £20m	15
Minority interest – 25% of £8m	2
Carrying amount in A's consolidated financial statements	17

Under the allowed alternative treatment in IAS 22, the property is measured as follows:

	£m
Fair value at date of acquisition	20

The minority's interest in the asset is measured at £5m.

> ***IASB business combinations project***
>
> In phase one of its business combinations project, the IASB proposes to eliminate the benchmark treatment and require the use of the current allowed alternative treatment as it provides relevant and reliable financial information about the resources under the control of the parent. It will also bring IAS 22 into line with the entity approach in IAS 27 as well as revert to the practice required by IAS 22 [1983].

16.14 GOODWILL AND NEGATIVE GOODWILL

Any excess of the cost of the acquisition over the amount at which the identifiable assets and liabilities acquired are measured on initial recognition should be described as goodwill and recognised as an asset (IAS 22, 41). The requirements relating to goodwill, including the transitional provisions for pre-1995 goodwill, are dealt with in chapter 24.

Negative goodwill can be defined as any excess of the amount at which the identifiable assets and liabilities acquired are measured on initial recognition over the cost of the acquisition. However, as explained in chapter 24, some of the excess is not described as negative goodwill.

16.15 STEP ACQUISITIONS

An acquisition may involve more than one exchange transaction. For example, an acquisition may be achieved in stages by successive purchases on a stock exchange. In such cases, the cost of the acquisition is the aggregate cost of the individual transactions. Each significant transaction is treated separately in determining the fair values of the identifiable assets and liabilities acquired and the amount of any goodwill or negative goodwill on that transaction (IAS 22, 36).

This results in a step-by-step comparison of the cost of the individual investments with the acquirer's percentage interest in the fair values of the identifiable assets and liabilities acquired at each significant step. If all the identifiable assets and liabilities relating to an acquisition are restated to fair values at the time of successive purchases, any adjustment relating to the previously held interest of the acquirer is a revaluation and is accounted for as such in accordance with the appropriate IASs.

If the investment qualified previously as an associate and the equity method was used to account for it, the determination of fair values for the identifiable assets and liabilities acquired and the recognition of goodwill or negative goodwill occurs notionally as from the date when the equity method is applied. If the investment did not qualify previously as an associate, fair values are determined as at the date of each significant step and goodwill or negative goodwill is recognised from the date of acquisition.

16.16 UNITINGS OF INTERESTS AND THE POOLING OF INTERESTS METHOD

A uniting of interests should be accounted for using the pooling of interests method (IAS 22, 77) under which the financial statements are presented as if the combining entities had always been one entity. In other words, this method accounts for the combined entity as though the separate businesses were continuing as before, though now jointly owned and managed.

The financial statement items of the combining entities are included in the financial statements of the combined entity as if they had been combined from the beginning of the earliest period presented (IAS 22, 78). The financial statements for the period in which the combination occurs and for any comparative periods disclosed are presented in this way.

The combined entity recognises the assets, liabilities and equity of the combining entities at their existing carrying amounts adjusted only, if necessary, to conform with the accounting policies of the combined entity and apply those policies to all periods presented. Assets and liabilities are not restated to fair value and no goodwill or negative goodwill is recognised. Assets and liabilities which had not been recognised by either of the combining entities are also not recognised. The effects of all transactions between the combining entities, whether occurring before or after the uniting of interests, are eliminated.

Any difference between the amounts recorded for share capital issued on the business combination (plus any additional consideration in the form of cash or other assets) and for the share capital acquired should be adjusted against equity (IAS 22, 79).

Either or both entities may incur expenditures such as registration fees, costs of furnishing information to shareholders, finders and consultants fees, and salaries and other expenses related to services of employees involved in achieving the business combination. They may also incur costs or losses in combining the operations of the previously separate businesses. All such expenditures should be recognised as expenses in the period in which they are incurred (IAS 22, 82).

Extract 16.8 *Costs of uniting of interests*

Pharmacia & Upjohn, United States and Sweden, 31 December 1997 (US GAAP)

In 1995, the company recorded merger costs of $138 million including transaction costs of $69 million and costs to combine operations of $69 million. Transaction costs include investment banker, professional, and registration fees.

The financial statements should not incorporate a uniting of interests which occurs after the date of the most recent balance sheet included in the financial statements (IAS 22, 78).

IASB business combinations project

In phase one of its business combinations project, the IASB proposes that all business combinations should be accounted for by applying the purchase method and, therefore, that the pooling of interests method should not be permitted.

16.17 DISCLOSURE

16.17.1 All Business Combinations

In the financial statements for the period during which a business combination has taken place, an entity should disclose:

- the names and descriptions of the combining entities;
- the method of accounting for the combination;
- the effective date of the combination for accounting purposes; and
- any operations resulting from the business combination which the entity has decided to dispose of.

(IAS 22, 86)

16.17.2 Acquisitions

In the financial statements for the period during which the combination has taken place, an entity should disclose:

- the percentage of voting shares acquired; and

- the cost of acquisition and a description of the purchase consideration paid or contingently payable.

(IAS 22, 87)

Extract 16.9 *Disclosure of cost of acquisition*

Clariant, Switzerland, 31 December 1997 (IAS)

The General Meeting of Shareholders approved on April 29, 1997 to acquire the Hoechst Speciality Chemicals Business. The transaction was carried out as of July 1, 1997. The payment of the agreed purchase price of DEM 5,400 million at a rate of CHF 83.805 per DEM 100, corresponding to CHF 4,525 million, was settled by:

	CHF mio
Issuance of 3,727 million registered shares of CHF 100 par value	327
Additional paid-in surplus	1,145
Sub-total	**1,472**
Cash payment and acceptance of financial debts	3,053
Total	**4,525**

When the published price of an equity instrument that forms part of the purchase consideration is not used as its fair value, the acquirer should disclose:

- the reasons;
- the methods and assumptions used to determine fair value; and
- the difference between the published price and fair value.

(SIC 28, 7)

When an equity instrument that forms part of the purchase consideration does not have a published price, the acquirer should disclose the methods and assumptions used to determine fair value (SIC 28, 7).

When the fair values of the identifiable assets and liabilities or the purchase consideration can only be determined on a provisional basis at the end of the period in which the acquisition took place, the entity should disclose:

- the fact and reasons in the period in which the acquisition took place; and
- any subsequent adjustments to the fair values, together with an explanation, in the period in which the adjustments are made.

(IAS 22, 93)

An entity should disclose any adjustments to the carrying amounts of identifiable assets and liabilities and goodwill and negative goodwill arising as a result of the subsequent recognition of those assets and liabilities or the adjustment of estimated fair values (SIC 22, 8).

The disclosure relating to goodwill and negative goodwill are dealt with in chapter 24.

16.17.3 Uniting of Interests

In the financial statements for the period during which the uniting of interests has taken place, an entity should disclose:

- a description and the number of shares issued, together with the percentage of each entity's voting shares exchanged to effect the uniting of interests;
- amounts of assets and liabilities contributed by each entity; and
- sales revenue, other operating revenues, extraordinary items and the net profit or loss of each entity prior to the date of the combination that are included in the net profit or loss shown by the combined entity's financial statements.

(IAS 22, 94)

16.17.4 Business Combinations Effected after the Balance Sheet Date

Business combinations which have been effected after the balance sheet date and before the date on which the financial statements of one of the combining entities are authorised for issue are disclosed if they are of such importance that non-disclosure would affect the ability of the users of the financial statements to make proper evaluations and decisions (see IAS 10). An entity should disclose:

- the same information as for a business combination during or before the period; or
- the fact that it is impracticable to disclose any of this information.

(IAS 22, 96)

Notes

[1] Contact Committee on the Accounting Directives, *An Examination of the Conformity Between the International Accounting Standards and the European Accounting Directives*, European Commission, Brussels, 1996, p12.

[2] G4 + 1, *Recommendations for Achieving Convergence on the Methods of Accounting for Business Combinations*, FASB, 1998 (G4 + 1 publications are available from all members of the group – see appendix 4).

[3] The G4 + 1 position paper includes a summary of the history of the pooling of interests method in the jurisdictions of the each member organisation. The history of IAS 22 [1993] is misleading in a number of respects. In the G4 + 1 position paper, the history starts with 'an IASC board/consultative group paper dated June 1988', but the reality is that the project

started in 1987 with the IASC's decision to eliminate alternatives in IASs (the comparability project).

Between March 1987 and January 1988, the comparability steering committee considered various proposals on the choice between the purchase method and the pooling of interests method as a result of which it recommended to the IASC board in March 1988 that the use of the pooling of interests method should be required only when there was a uniting of interests and that the definition of a uniting of interests should be tightened. At its March 1988 meeting, the board supported these recommendations. It confirmed its decision in June 1988 when it also considered, but rejected, the possibility of eliminating the pooling of interests method (as the G4+1 paper acknowledges).

The exposure draft (E32 *Comparability of Financial Statements*) was approved in November 1988 and proposed that the pooling of interests method should be required but only when an acquirer could not be identified; all other business combinations should be accounted for using the purchase method. The majority of the commentators on E32 supported the proposal to restrict the use of the pooling of interests method but a number sought practical guidance on the identification of the acquirer (*IASC News*, July 1990, p12).

Following its consideration of the comments on E32 , the IASC approved the *Statement of Intent on the Comparability of Financial Statements* in July 1990. This confirmed the approach taken in E32 on this particular issue. The IASC also decided that it would not reconsider those issues which were exposed for comment in E32 and subsequently approved without substantive change. As a result, the IASC did not reconsider, between July 1990 and the approval of IAS 22 [1993] in November 1993, the choice between the purchase method and the pooling of interests method. The IASC did during that period develop the implementation guidance on the distinction between acquisitions and unitings of interests; this guidance was issued for comment in E45.

The G4 + 1 paper also refers to the change made to the definition of control in IAS 22 but does not make clear that this change was made solely as a consequence of the adoption of IAS 27 in June 1988. The definition of control in IAS 22 [1983] was identical to the definition of control in IAS 3, the IASC's original standard on consolidated financial statements. IAS 27 replaced IAS 3 and adopted a broader definition of control (see chapter 15). The definition of control in IAS 22 [1993] was identical to the definition of control in IAS 27.

[4] Securities and Exchange Commission, *Reconciliation of the Accounting by Foreign Private Issuers for Business Combinations*, International Series Release 759 (13 December 1994), Washington DC, SEC, 1994.

[5] Division of Corporate Finance, Securities and Exchange Commission, *International Financial Reporting and Disclosure Issues*, Washington DC, SEC, 2001 (obtainable from www.sec.gov).

[6] Donald J Gannon, 'Current Accounting Projects', 1998 AICPA conference on current SEC developments, 9 December 1998, Washington.

[7] Fédération des Experts Comptables Européens (FEE), *Survey on Legal Mergers in the Context of E45, Business Combinations*, Brussels: FEE, 1993.

[8] Reed K Storey, 'Comparative Analysis of IAS 22 and Related US GAAP', in *The IASC – US GAAP Comparison Project: A Report of Similarities and Differences Between IASC standards and US GAAP*, ed Carrie Bloomer, Norwalk, CT, FASB, 1996, pp 341–342.

CHAPTER 17

Associates

17.1 RELEVANT STANDARD AND INTERPRETATIONS

IAS 28 *Accounting for Investments in Associates*
SIC 3 *Elimination of Unrealised Profits and Losses on Transactions with Associates*
SIC 20 *Equity Accounting Method – Recognition of Losses*
SIC 33 *Consolidation and Equity Method – Potential Voting Rights and Allocation of Ownership Interests*

17.2 HISTORY

IAS 3 *Consolidated Financial Statements* was issued in 1976 and established a standard for the use of the equity method for investments in associates before many countries, including some on the IASC board, required the use of the equity method.

IAS 3 was replaced for accounting periods beginning on or after 1 January 1990 by IAS 27 *Consolidated Financial Statements and Accounting for Investments in Subsidiaries* and IAS 28 *Accounting for Investments in Associates*. IAS 28 provided more detailed guidance on the application of the equity method but did not adopt a substantively different approach from that in IAS 3.

The IASC revised certain paragraphs of IAS 28 in 1998 as a result of the adoption of IAS 36 *Impairment of Assets*.

The May 2002 improvements exposure draft proposes several changes to IAS 28 that deal with:

- investments held by venture capital organisations, mutual funds, unit trusts and similar entities that are measured at fair value in accordance with IAS 39 and well-established practice;

- exemptions from the application of the equity method;
- the accounting for investments in associates when the investor does not publish consolidated financial statements and in the investor's separate financial statements;
- the use of uniform accounting policies; and
- losses by the associate.

17.3 IOSCO

In June 1994, IOSCO advised the IASC that IAS 28 was acceptable for the purposes of the IOSCO core standards. However, IOSCO said that it may recommend how the 20% test for significant influence would be applied. IOSCO also identified the following suspense issues under which the IASC should consider:

- accounting for capital transactions by associates;
- eliminating alternatives to the use of the equity method for investors which do not issue consolidated financial statements, at least with respect to investors which make securities offerings and filings (this is dealt with in the May 2002 improvements exposure draft);
- providing guidance on the elimination of inter-company profits and losses on upstream and downstream transactions (this has been dealt with in SIC 3);
- disclosure of summarised financial information for material associates;
- providing guidance that it would be a rare or exceptional case when significant influence could be demonstrated below the 20% presumptive level without representation on the board of directors or equivalent governing body – IOSCO may recommend that its members interpret IAS 28 accordingly.

IOSCO also identified the following other issues under which the IASC should consider:

- delimiting the 'if practicable' exception for the application of uniform accounting policies and requiring the use of acceptable international standards (this is dealt with in the May 2002 improvements exposure draft);
- guidance on how the 20% presumption may be overcome and the disclosures when the presumption is overcome;
- the exclusion of entities which carry all investments at fair value from the scope of IAS 28, for example, investment companies (this is dealt with in the May 2002 improvements exposure draft);

- guidance as to whether potential voting interests should be considered in the 20% presumptive test (this issue is now dealt with in SIC 33);
- disclosures relating to potential material effects of possible conversions, exercises, or other contingent issuances;
- the disclosure of retained earnings attributable to equity investees;
- clarify the application of equity accounting to investments in partnerships and unincorporated entities (IAS 28 requires that the same accounting should be applied irrespective of whether the associate is a company, a partnership or an unincorporated entity); and
- the disclosure of available market values for equity investee securities owned.

IAS 28 is included in 'IAS 2000' endorsed by IOSCO in May 2000. IOSCO identifies two general issues:

- clarification of the application of the equity method to investments in partnerships and unincorporated entities (IAS 28 requires the same accounting for all associates whatever their legal form); and
- regulators may eliminate some of the alternatives to the equity method in the financial statements of investors who do not issue consolidated financial statements (this issue is dealt with in the May 2002 improvements exposure draft).

There are also four supplemental treatments:

- disclosure of summarised financial information for material equity investees;
- guidance on how the 20% presumption may be overcome and disclosures when it is overcome;
- whether potential voting interests should be considered in the determination of whether significant influence exists (this issue is dealt with in SIC 33); and
- disclosure of market values for equity investee securities owned.

17.4 IAS 28 IN BRIEF

An associate is another entity in which an investor has significant influence over that entity.

In its consolidated financial statements, an investor should include in its income statement and balance sheet its share of the profits and losses and other post-acquisition changes in the net assets of the associate (equity method).

The application of the equity method involves the same procedures as full consolidation, that is, initial recording at cost, the use of fair values for identifiable assets and liabilities, the determination of goodwill/negative goodwill, and the use of common accounting policies and reporting dates.

17.5 DEFINITIONS

An *associate* is an entity in which the investor has significant influence and which is neither a subsidiary nor a joint venture (IAS 28, 3). The entity may be a company, partnership or other entity.

The key to the definition is the notion of significant influence which is different from control (which creates a parent-subsidiary relationship) and joint control (which creates a venturer-joint venture relationship). *Significant influence* is the power to participate in the investee's financial and operating policy decisions, but is not control over those policies (IAS 28, 3). In contrast, *control* is the power to govern the financial and operating policies (IAS 27, 6) and *joint control* is the sharing of control (IAS 31, 2).

Significant influence is presumed to exist when an investor holds, directly or indirectly through subsidiaries, 20% or more of the voting power of the investee unless it can be clearly demonstrated that this is not the case (IAS 28, 4). Conversely, significant influence is presumed not to exist when the investor holds less than 20% of the voting power of the investee unless such influence can be clearly demonstrated (IAS 28, 4).

Consideration should also be given to the existence and effect of potential voting rights that are currently exercisable or convertible when assessing whether the entity has significant influence over the other entity (SIC 33, 3). Potential voting rights may arise from such instruments as share warrants, share call options, convertible debt or equity instruments that, when exercised or converted, give the entity voting power over the entity or reduce some other party's voting power over the entity. When considering the existence and effects of potential voting rights, the entity should consider all facts and circumstances except its own intentions and its financial capability to exercise or convert the instruments (SIC 33, 4). SIC 33 includes examples of the application of these requirements. The May 2002 improvements exposure draft proposes the incorporation of the requirements of SIC 33 into IAS 28.

The existence of significant influence is usually evidenced by one or more of the following:

- representation on the board of directors or equivalent governing body of the investee;
- participation in policy-making processes;
- material transactions between the entity and the investee;
- interchange of managerial personnel; or
- provision of essential technical information.

(IAS 28, 5)

A substantial or majority ownership by a second investor does not necessarily preclude an investor from having significant influence (IAS 28, 4) but the actions of the second investor may mean that the first investor does not have significant influence. For example, the second investor may be able to use its position to exclude the first investor from participation in the investee's financial and operating polices. In such circumstances, the first investor does not have significant influence over the investee.

Extract 17.1 *Associate with less than 20% interest*

LVMH, France, 31 December 1997 (IAS)

At December 31 1997, the investment in Diageo was recorded as follows in the LVMH balance sheet:

– Diageo A and B shares received in exchange for the shares held in Guinness are accounted for using the equity method, consistent with the previous treatment of the investment in Guinness;

– Diageo A shares received in exchange for the shares held in GrandMet are recorded in other investments and will be accounted for using the equity method beginning in 1998 when the merger of the two groups [Guinness and GrandMet] is finalised; Diageo B shares have been recorded as other current assets for FRF 1.6 billion.

LVMH currently holds 450.3 million shares of Diageo representing approximately 11% of the capital. Diageo is the largest wines and spirits group in the world. LVMH is the principal single shareholder of the group and LVMH's chairman and chief executive officer holds a seat on the board of directors.

Extract 17.2 *More than 20% interest not treated as an associate*

Fujitsu, Japan, 31 March 2001 (some IAS)

At March 31 2000 and 2001, the amount of ¥19,373 million representing the Company's 29.49% investment in JECC has been included in other investments and long-term loans. The Company does not regard JECC as an affiliate as it is unable to exercise significant influence over JECC's affairs.

> *IASB improvements project*
>
> In its May 2002 improvements exposure draft, the IASB proposes that IAS 28 should not apply to investments in associates held by venture capital organisations, mutual funds, unit trusts and similar entities and which are measured at fair value in accordance with IAS 39 and well-established practice. When such investments are measured at fair value, changes in fair value are included in the profit or loss for the period.

17.6 CONSOLIDATED FINANCIAL STATEMENTS

As with the acquisition of all other investments, an investment in an associate is measured on initial recognition at cost. The cost of an investment in an associate should not include any borrowing costs (IAS 23, 6).

Subsequently, an investment in an associate is reported in consolidated financial statements using either the cost method or the equity method.

> *IASB improvements project*
>
> In its May 2002 improvements exposure draft, the IASB proposes that an investor who does not issue consolidated financial statements because it does not have subsidiaries should account for investments in associates using the equity method.

17.7 COST METHOD

Under the cost method, the investment is measured at cost. The carrying amount is reduced to reflect an impairment in the value of the investment. The income statement includes distributions from accumulated net profits of the associate arising subsequent to the date of acquisition (IAS 28, 3), any write-downs to reflect an impairment in the associate and any profit or loss on the disposal of the associate.

An investment in an associate is accounted for using the cost method in only two circumstances:

- when the investment is acquired and held exclusively with a view to its disposal in the near future (IAS 28, 8); and

- from the date on which the associate operates under severe long-term restrictions that significantly impair its ability to transfer funds to the investor (IAS 28, 11).

In the first case, the cost method should be used only when the investor has made the decision to dispose of the associate prior to the date of its acquisition; in other words, the investor acquired the associate with the intention of selling it in the near future. The associate is accounted for under the cost method from the date of acquisition until the date of disposal. Consideration must be given to the need for impairment write-downs at any balance sheet date.

The cost method should also be used when the associate operates under severe long-term restrictions which significantly impair its ability to transfer funds to the entity (IAS 28, 11). Such an associate may previously have been accounted for under the equity method. In such circumstances, cost is the carrying amount of the investment at the date on which the use of the equity method becomes inappropriate (IAS 28, 11). Consideration must be also given to the need for impairment write-downs. The use of the cost method ceases when the restrictions are removed.

Extract 17.3 *Associate operating under restriction on distributions*

Anglo American Corporation, South Africa, 31 March 1995 (IAS)

Foreign associates are accounted for according to the cost method where there is uncertainty about the associate's ability to distribute earnings.

IASB improvements project

In its May 2002 improvements exposure draft, the IASB proposes to replace 'in the near future' with 'within 12 months from acquisition'. It also proposes to remove the exemption from the use of the equity method when an associate operates under severe long-term restrictions that significantly impair its ability to transfer funds to the investor but indicate that such restrictions make it unlikely that significant influence exists.

17.8 EQUITY METHOD

An investment in an associate is accounted for under the equity method in all cases other than when the use of the cost method is required. The equity method is applied form the date of acqusition of the investment until:

- the date on which the investor ceases to have significant influence; or
- the use of the method is no longer appropriate because the associate operates under severe long-term restrictions that significantly impair its ability to transfer funds to the investor.

(IAS 28, 8 and 11)

Under the equity method, the investment is initially recorded at cost and adjusted thereafter for the post-acquisition changes in the entity's share of the net assets of the associate. The income statement reflects the entity's share of the results of operations of the associate (IAS 28, 3). Other changes in the entity's share of the net assets of the associate are included in equity. Distributions received by the entity from the associate reduce the carrying amount of the investment in the associate.

Many of the concepts and procedures appropriate for the consolidation of subsidiaries and business combinations are applied in the equity method. For example:

- on acquisition of the investment, any difference between the cost of acquisition and the entity's share of the fair values of the net identifiable assets of the associate is accounted for in accordance with IAS 22 as if it were goodwill or negative goodwill (IAS 22, 17); and
- subsequently, adjustments are made to the entity's share of the profits or losses of the associate to reflect depreciation on the fair value adjustments of identifiable assets acquired and the amortisation of the goodwill or negative goodwill (IAS 28, 17).

Example 17.1 *Goodwill arising on the acquisition of an associate*

A acquires a 30% interest in B for $2 million. The book value of B's net assets in its balance sheet is $5 million. A is entitled to appoint a representative to B's management board. A decides that it has significant influence over B and that it should apply the equity method.

The investment in B is recorded in A's consolidated balance sheet at cost ($2 million). In applying the equity method, A must compare this cost with its share of the fair values of the identifiable assets and liabilities acquired. After carrying out that exercise in accordance with the procedures in IAS 22, A concludes that the fair values of B's property, plant and equipment is $0.2 million greater than its carrying amount of $2.5 million and that the carrying amounts of all B's other net assets and liabilities are equal to their fair values. A also concludes that B has an unrecorded, but identifiable, intangible asset with a fair value of $0.8 million.

Continued

Continued

A's share of the fair values of the identifiable assets and liabilities acquired is $1.8 million, that is 30% of the total of $5 million plus $0.2 million plus $0.8 million. Therefore, goodwill arising on the acquisition of the associate is $0.2 million.

In applying the equity method in subsequent periods, A must make the following adjustments to its share of B's profits as shown by B's income statement:

- increase depreciation on property, plant and equipment to reflect the fair value of $2.7 million;
- reduce any profit on the disposal of property, plant and equipment to reflect the fair value of $2.7 million and the increased depreciation;
- charge amortisation on the identifiable intangible asset acquired; and
- charge amortisation on the goodwill.

Extract 17.4 *Goodwill on investments in associates*

Jardine Matheson, Hong Kong, 31 December 2001 (IAS)

Goodwill represents the difference between the cost of acquisition and the fair value of the Group's share of the net assets of the acquired subsidiary undertaking, associate or joint venture at the effective date of acquisition.

Extract 17.5 *Goodwill on investments in associates*

Schering, Germany, 31 December 1997 (IAS)

... DM 56 million relates to the purchase of 20% of the shares in Medac GmbH, Hamburg. With Medac we cooperate in the field of oncology. The difference between the purchase price and the Group's share of the equity amounts to DM 54 million. This goodwill will be written off over 10 years.

An entity or its consolidated subsidiaries may sell assets to the associate (so-called 'downstream' transactions) or buy assets from the associate ('upstream' transactions). Unrealised profits and losses resulting from these transactions should be eliminated to the extent of the entity's interest in the associate (SIC 3, 3). Unrealised losses on these transactions should not be eliminated if the transaction provides evidence of an impairment of the asset transferred (SIC 3, 4).

This interpretation is different from the requirements for transactions between a parent and its subsidiaries but it is the same as that for transactions between a venturer and a joint venture. Unlike subsidiaries, associates are not under the control of the investor. Therefore, the IASC believed that the rationale of the requirements in IAS 31 for the proportionate elimination of profits and losses resulting from transactions between a venturer and a joint venture is also appropriate for transactions between an investor and an associate. The May 2002 improvements exposure draft proposes that SIC 3 should become part of IAS 28.

The application of the equity method also requires adjustments for the entity's proportion of those changes in the associate's equity which have not been included in the associate's income statement. For example, the entity adjusts the carrying amount for its share of any revaluation surplus arising on property, plant, equipment and available-for-sale financial assets (provided that the entity's accounting policies allow for such revaluations) and for foreign exchange translation differences.

Extract 17.6 *Application of the equity method*

Nokia, Finland, 31 December 2000 (IAS)

The Group's share of profits and losses of associated companies is included in the consolidated profit and loss account in accordance with the equity method of accounting. The Group's share of post acquisition reserves (retained earnings and other reserves) is added to the cost of associated company investments in the consolidated balance sheet.

Profits realised in connection with the sale of fixed assets between the Group and associated companies are eliminated in proportion to share ownership. Such profits are deducted from the Group's equity and fixed assets and released in the Group accounts over the same period as depreciation is charged.

Extract 17.7 *Application of the equity method*

Stora Enso, Finland, 31 December 2001 (IAS)

Associated companies, where Stora Enso holds voting rights of between 20% and 50%, are accounted for using the equity method, which involves recognising in the Income Statement the Group's share of the associate's profit or loss for the year less any amortised goodwill. ... The Group's interest in an associated company is carried in the Balance Sheet at an amount that reflects its share of the net assets of the associate together with goodwill on acquisition, as amortised, less any impairment.

Extract 17.8 *Application of the equity method*

Bayer, Germany, 31 December 2001 (IAS)

The cost of acquisition of investments in companies included at equity is adjusted annually in line with any changes in these companies' total stockholders' equity. In the first-time consolidation, differences between the cost of acquisition and the underlying equities at the date of acquisition of the investments are allocated to assets or liabilities by the same method applied to fully consolidated subsidiaries.

The most recent available financial statements of the associate should be used in applying the equity method (IAS 28, 18). When the financial statements of the associate are not drawn up to the same date as those of the entity, the associate may prepare additional financial statements or management accounts as at the same date as the financial statements of the entity. When this is impracticable, the entity may use financial statements drawn up to a different reporting date (IAS 28, 18). However, in such cases:

- the length of the reporting periods of the entity and the associate and any difference in the reporting dates should be the same from period to period; and
- the entity adjusts for the effects of any significant events or transactions between the entity and the associate that occur between the dates of the respective financial statements.

In its May 2002 improvements exposure draft, the IASB proposes that the difference between the associate's reporting date and that of the entity should not exceed three months.

Extract 17.9 *Use of published and management accounts*

Fraser and Neave, Singapore, 30 September 1997

The group's share of the results of associated companies is included in the consolidated profit statement and is based on the latest published accounts, except where the accounting periods end more than three months before 30 September, when management accounts to 30 September are used.

The entity's financial statements are usually prepared using uniform accounting policies for like transactions and events in similar circumstances. When an associate uses accounting policies which are different from those adopted by the entity, the entity makes appropriate adjustments, often with the aid of the associate. If it is not practicable for such adjustments to be calculated, that fact is disclosed (IAS 28, 20). In its May

2002 improvements exposure draft, the IASB proposes to require the use of common accounting policies.

Extract 17.10 *Uniform accounting policies*

Novartis, Switzerland, 31 December 2000 (IAS)

The recording of the results of the strategic interest in Chiron commenced on January 1, 1995. Its equity valuation is based on the Chiron equity at September 30 of each year. The amounts for Chiron incorporated in the Novartis consolidated financial statements take into account the effects stemming from differences in accounting policies between Novartis and Chiron (primarily Novartis' amortization over 10 years of in-process technology arising on Chiron's non-Ciba 1995 acquisitions which were written off by Chiron in 1995).

... The Group's associated companies utilize local accounting standards which are then adjusted to IAS.

An associate may have outstanding cumulative preferred shares, held by outside interests. The entity computes its share of profits or losses of the associate after adjusting for the preferred dividends, whether or not the dividends have been declared (IAS 28, 21).

When an entity's share of an associate's losses exceeds the carrying amount of the investment, the entity usually discontinues including its share of further losses and the investment is reported at nil value. For this purpose the carrying amount is limited to the carrying amount of instruments that provide unlimited rights to participation in the earnings or losses and a residual interest in the associate (SIC 20, 5). The carrying amount does not include other financial interests of the entity in the associate, for loans, advances, debt securities, options and trade receivables (SIC 20, 7). Additional losses are recognised only to the extent that the entity has incurred obligations or made payments on behalf of the associate to satisfy obligations of the associate that the entity has guaranteed or otherwise committed (IAS 28, 22). If the associate subsequently reports profits, the entity resumes including its share of those profits only after its share of the profits equals the share of net losses not recognised (IAS 28, 22).

Extract 17.11 *Losses of associates*

Stora Enso, Finland, 31 December 2001 (IAS)

When the Group share of losses [in an associated company] exceeds the carrying amount of an investment, the carrying amount is reduced to nil and any recognition of further losses ceases unless the Group is obliged to satisfy obligations of the investee which it has guaranteed or is otherwise committed to.

> ***IASB improvements project***
>
> In its May 2002 improvements exposure draft, the IASB proposes to withdraw SIC 20 and require that, for the purpose of recognising losses, the carrying amount of the investment in the associate should be the investment in equity shares plus other interests such as long-term receivables.

The carrying amount of an investment in an associate should be reduced in accordance with the requirements of IAS 36 to recognise an impairment loss (see chapter 25).

The gain or loss on the disposal of an investment in an associate is determined by comparing the disposal proceeds with its carrying amount. The same principle applies to a partial disposal; the entity compares the proceeds with the appropriate proportion of the carrying amount. On a partial disposal, the entity must also consider whether or not the disposal means that the investment is no longer an associate.

Extract 17.12 Disposal of investments in associates

Jardine Matheson, Hong Kong, 31 December 2001 (IAS)

The profit or loss on disposal of subsidiary undertakings, associates and joint ventures is calculated by reference to the net assets at the date of disposal including the attributable amount of goodwill which remains unamortised but does not include any attributable goodwill previously eliminated against reserves.

Partial disposals may arise from the changes in the ownership interests of the entity in relation to the interests of other investors, for example when the associate issues additional shares to other investors. IAS 28 does not give any guidance on how to work out the gain or loss on the disposal. One solution is to compare any proceeds with the change in the entity's interest in the net assets of the associate (see example 17.2).

Example 17.2 *Partial disposal as a result of a sale of rights*

A owns a 40% interest in B which A helped to establish a number of years ago. A has significant influence over B and therefore accounts for its investment using the equity method. As at 31 December 2002, B's net assets are £1 million and A's interest in B is shown as £400,000 in A's consolidated balance sheet.

Early in 2003, B makes a one-for-four rights issue which raises a total of £200,000.

If A takes up its rights at a cost of £80,000, A adds the £80,000 to the cost of its investment in B. If A sells its rights to an independent third party for £70,000, it has made a partial disposal as its interest in B has been reduced from 40% to 32%. It compares the proceeds of £80,000 with the change in its interest in B. Before the rights issue, A had 40% of £1 million (£400,000). After the rights issue A has 32% of £1.2 million (£384,000). Therefore, the gain on the partial disposal is £64,000, that is the proceeds of £80,000 less the reduction of £16,000 in A's interest.

17.9 PRESENTATION

An entity should:

- classify investments in associates accounted for using the equity method as long-term assets and as a separate item in the balance sheet;
- present its share of the profits or losses of investments in associates accounted for using the equity method as a separate item in the income statement; and
- present its share of any extraordinary items as a separate item in the income statement.

(IAS 27, 28)

'Investments accounted for using the equity method' are shown as a line item on the balance sheet (IAS 1, 66). This allows interests in associates and jointly controlled entities to be combined.

17.10 DISCLOSURE

An entity should disclose:

- an appropriate listing and description of significant associates including the proportion of ownership interest and, if different, the proportion of voting power held (IAS 28, 27);

- the methods used to account for such investments (IAS 28, 27);
- its share of the contingencies and capital commitments of an associate for which it is also contingently liable (IAS 28, 26); and
- those contingencies that arise because the entity is severally liable for all the liabilities of the associate (IAS 28, 26).

An entity which does not issue consolidated financial statements should disclose what would have been the effect had the equity method been applied to an associate if the associate is carried at cost or revalued amount in the entity's separate financial statements (IAS 28, 14).

CHAPTER 18

Joint Ventures

18.1 RELEVANT STANDARD AND INTERPRETATION

IAS 31 *Financial Reporting of Interests in Joint Ventures*
SIC 13 *Jointly Controlled Entities – Non-Monetary Contributions by Venturers*

18.2 HISTORY

IAS 31 *Financial Reporting of Interests in Joint Ventures* (IAS 31 [1993]) was approved and published in 1990 and applies to accounting periods beginning on or after 1 January 1992. The IASC revised certain paragraphs of IAS 31 in 1998 as a result of the adoption of IAS 36 *Impairment of Assets.*

The May 2002 improvements exposure draft proposes several consequential changes to IAS 31 which are similar to the equivalent changes in IAS 28 and deal with:

- interests in jointly controlled entities held by venture capital organisations, mutual funds, unit trusts and similar entities that are measured at fair value in accordance with IAS 39 and well-established practice;
- exemptions from the application of proportionate consolidation and the equity method; and
- the accounting for interests in jointly controlled entities when the venturer does not publish consolidated financial statements.

18.3 IOSCO

In June 1994, IOSCO advised the IASC that IAS 31 was acceptable for the purposes of the IOSCO core standards. IOSCO identified the following suspense issues under which the IASC should consider:

- more definitive criteria for the determination of gains and losses on transactions between a venturer and a joint venture (this issue is dealt with in SIC 13);
- the criteria for the recognition of a new basis by the venture itself for net assets sold or contributed to a joint venture (IAS 31 deals with the reporting of interests in joint ventures, not reporting by joint ventures); and
- requiring entities without subsidiaries but which make securities offerings and filings to adopt joint venture accounting rather than make disclosure in lieu of such accounting (this is dealt with in the May 2002 improvements exposure draft).

IAS 31 is included in 'IAS 2000' endorsed by IOSCO in May 2000. There are five supplemental treatments:

- the appropriateness of proportionate consolidation rather than the equity method (the IASB has indicated that it intends to consider the elimination of proportionate consolidation);
- criteria for the recognition of a new basis by the venture itself for net assets sold or contributed to the joint venture (IAS 31 does not deal with reporting by the joint venture);
- limitations on the treatments currently allowed for dealing with jointly controlled entities in separate financial statements (this is dealt with in the May 2002 improvements exposure draft);
- guidance on how any additional consideration such as cash affects the computation of the appropriate portion of the gain or loss on a contribution of assets to a joint venture; and
- the contribution to a joint venture of a 'business' and whether such a contribution is, in substance, an exchange of assets or a business combination.

18.4 IAS 31 IN BRIEF

A joint venture is a contractual arrangement whereby two or more venturers share control over an economic activity. Joint control is the contractually agreed sharing of control and is different from 'significant influence'.

A joint venture may be any one (or a combination) of:

- a jointly controlled operation in which each venturer uses its own assets and other resources and incurs its own liabilities in order to carry out the joint activity and takes an agreed share of the revenue (for example, Airbus before it was restructured);

- a jointly controlled asset in which each venturer usually owns a share of the asset, possibly incurs its own liabilities and takes/bears an agreed share of the joint revenue/output and expenses (for example, an oil pipeline or a property); or
- a jointly controlled entity in which the venturers establish a separate legal entity to carry out the joint economic activity (for example, Airbus after it was restructured as EADS).

In the case of jointly controlled operations and jointly controlled assets, a venturer should include in its financial statements its own assets, liabilities and expenses plus its share of the revenue and any jointly owned/controlled assets and any joint liabilities.

In the case of a jointly controlled entity, a venturer should include in its consolidated financial statements either:

- its proportion of the assets, liabilities, income and expenses of the jointly controlled entity (proportionate consolidation); or
- its share of the profits and losses and other post-acquisition changes in the net assets of the jointly controlled entity (equity method).

The operator (manager) of a joint venture should account for any fees, commissions etc as it provides the service.

An investor in a joint venture should account for its investment as a financial asset in accordance with IAS 39 or as an associate in accordance with IAS 28.

18.5 DEFINITION OF A JOINT VENTURE

A *joint venture* is a contractual arrangement whereby two or more parties undertake an economic activity which is subject to joint control (IAS 31, 2).

The parties to a joint venture are either:

- *venturers* who share in the control (IAS 31, 2) – there must be at least two venturers otherwise there can be no sharing of control; or
- *investors* who do not have joint control and therefore do not share in the control (IAS 31, 2) – a joint venture may have no investors.

The key to the definition of a joint venture is the notion of joint control which is different from control (which creates a parent-subsidiary relationship) and significant influence (which creates an investor-associate relationship).

Control is the power to govern the financial and operating policies of an economic activity so as to obtain benefits from it (IAS 27, 6 and IAS 31, 2).

Joint control is the contractually agreed sharing of control over the joint venture activity (IAS 31, 2). Therefore, the venturers share in the power to govern the financial and operating policies of the activity. If a party has the power to govern the financial and operating policies of the activity, that party controls the activity and the activity is a subsidiary of that party rather than a joint venture.

It is important to distinguish between the government of the financial and operating policies of the activity and the management of its day-to-day operations. It is common to appoint one or more venturers as the operator or manager of the joint venture activity. The operator or manager acts in accordance with the financial and operating policies agreed by the venturers. Therefore, an operator or manager does not control the activity solely by virtue of being its operator or manager.

The fact that the venturers share in the control of the activity does not mean that all decisions must be unanimous. The contractual arrangement usually identifies those decisions which:

- require the consent of all the venturers;
- require the consent of a specified majority of the venturers; or
- can be taken by individual venturers.

When a decision requires the unanimous approval of all the venturers, any venturer has, in effect, a right of veto. Indeed, Australia has added a paragraph to its standard based on IAS 31 which states that joint control exists when each of the venturers in a joint venture has the right to veto major decisions[1]. Some commentators on E35 felt that the holder of such a veto had control; if this is the reality in a particular case, the arrangement is not a joint venture.

The contractual arrangement which establishes the joint venture usually deals with such matters as:

- the activity and duration of the joint venture;
- the reporting obligations of the joint venture;
- the appointment of the governing body of the joint venture and each venturer's voting rights;
- the appointment of the operator or manager of the joint venture;
- capital contributions by the venturers; and
- the sharing of profits, income, expenses and output.

> ***IASB improvements project***
>
> In its May 2002 improvements exposure draft, the IASB proposes that IAS 31 should not apply to interests in joint ventures that are held by venture capital organisations, mutual funds, unit trusts and similar entities and which are measured at fair value in accordance with IAS 39 and well-established practice. When such interests are measured at fair value, changes in fair value are included in the profit or loss for the period.

Extract 18.1 *Definition of joint venture*

Iscor, South Africa, 30 June 2000 (South African GAAP and IAS)

A joint venture is an entity jointly controlled by the group and one or more other venturers in terms of a contractual agreement. It may involve a corporation, partnership or other entity in which the group has an interest.

Extract 18.2 *Definition of joint ventures*

Volkswagen, Germany, 31 December 2001 (IAS)

Joint ventures include companies where the Volkswagen Group holds the majority of voting rights but for which the articles of association or partnership agreements stipulate that important decisions can only be made on a unanimous voting basis (Minority Protection).

18.6 TYPES OF JOINT VENTURE

IAS 31 deals with three broad types of joint venture:

- jointly controlled operations;
- jointly controlled assets; and
- jointly controlled entities.

IAS 31 recognises the similarities of the different forms of joint ventures and requires accounting treatments which reflect the similarities, at least in consolidated financial statements.

The IASC's approach was new, although it did draw on the thinking being carried out in some national standard setting bodies, notably by the staff of the FASB. The approach also reflected the IASC's studies of various joint ventures and its consultations with entities involved in joint ventures. It was copied by the UN ISAR group in 1991 in its agreed conclusions on accounting for joint ventures[2].

18.7 JOINTLY CONTROLLED OPERATIONS

A *jointly controlled operation* is a joint venture which involves the use of the assets and other resources of the venturers rather than the establishment of a corporation, partnership or other entity or a financial structure which is separate from the venturers themselves (IAS 31, 8).

In a jointly controlled operation, each venturer uses its own property, plant and equipment and carries its own inventories. It also incurs its own expenses and liabilities and raises its own finance, which represent its own obligations. The contractual arrangement determines how the revenue and any expenses incurred in common are shared among the venturers.

The venturers may decide not to prepare financial statements for the joint venture; indeed, the venturers may decide not to disclose to each other the details of their own expenses.

Example 18.1 *Jointly controlled operations*

Two engineering companies, A and B, decide to produce and sell jointly an engine for use with a particular type of aircraft. A manufactures the turbines and B manufactures the rest of the engine. Each venturer bears its own manufacturing expenses and takes an agreed share of the revenue from the sale of the engine. The joint marketing and selling costs are incurred by a jointly controlled sales company and borne in equal shares by the two venturers. No financial statements are prepared for joint manufacturing activity and A and B do not disclose to each other their respective manufacturing costs; financial statements are prepared and audited for the sales company.

The manufacturing activity is a jointly controlled operation and the sales company is a jointly controlled entity (see 18.6.3 below). A and B are venturers. The accounting consequences of this joint venture are dealt with in example 18.2.

Jointly controlled operations do not create accounting or reporting problems. They could have been omitted from IAS 31 but they are included because the IASC's consultations showed that some substantial joint ventures take the form of jointly controlled operations. For example, most of the operations of Airbus Industrie (before it was restructured) were carried out by the four venturers, with each venturer incurring its own expenses and taking a share of the revenue from the sale of aircraft.

Each venturer in a jointly controlled operation records in its accounting records and, hence, in its separate financial statements:

- the assets which it controls and the liabilities which it incurs;
- the expenses which it incurs; and
- its share of the revenue which it earns from the sale of goods or services by the joint venture.

A venturer does not record a share of the other venturers' assets, liabilities, income and expenses and probably does not set up a joint venture account in its books and financial statements.

Example 18.2 *Jointly controlled operation*

In the case of the two engineering companies A and B in example 18.1 which decide to produce and sell jointly an engine for use with a particular type of aircraft, A's accounting records and separate financial statements include:

- the property, plant and equipment used to manufacture the turbines;
- inventories of raw materials and supplies for turbine manufacture, work in progress being partly completed turbines, and finished turbines awaiting despatch;
- revenue for A's share of the revenue relating to turbines that have been delivered and any resulting receivables;
- expenses for raw materials, supplies, labour and overheads related to the manufacture of turbines and any resulting payables; and
- an investment in the jointly controlled sales entity.

These items may be included with other similar items in A's financial statements particularly if A uses the same property, plant and equipment and employees to manufacture turbines for other customers.

B's accounting records and separate financial statements include similar items for its assets, liabilities, income and expenses. B does not include a share of A's assets and liabilities and A does not include a share of B's assets and liabilities.

Because the assets, liabilities, income and expenses are already recognised in the separate financial statements of the venturer, no adjustments or other consolidation procedures are required in respect of the jointly controlled operation when either venturer presents consolidated financial statements (IAS 31, 11). In example 18.2, A's consolidated financial statements include exactly the same amounts as A's separate financial statements in respect of the jointly controlled operation; the investment in the jointly controlled entity is dealt with in accordance with 18.9 below.

There have been suggestions that IAS 31 requires proportionate consolidation for jointly controlled operations. This is not the case. Similarly, there have been suggestions that some countries require or allow proportionate consolidation for jointly controlled operations. Again this cannot be the case. The reporting of interests in jointly controlled operations does not, and cannot, involve any consolidation procedures.

18.8 JOINTLY CONTROLLED ASSETS

A *jointly controlled asset* is a joint venture in which the venturers control jointly, and often own jointly, an asset contributed to, or acquired for, the purpose of the joint venture (IAS 31, 13). Each venturer may take a share of the output or the revenue from the asset and each bears an agreed share of the expenses incurred. These joint ventures do not involve the establishment of a corporation, partnership or other entity, or a financial structure separate from the venturers themselves.

The accounting records for the joint venture itself may be limited to those expenses incurred jointly by the venturers and ultimately borne by the venturers according to their agreed shares; such accounting records may be incorporated in the records of one of the venturers. The venturers may decide not to prepare financial statements for the joint venture and each venturer may withhold from the other venturers information about its expenses or revenue from the sale of its share of the output.

Example 18.3 *Jointly controlled asset*

Three oil production companies, D, E and F, jointly control, own and operate an oil pipeline which each company uses to transport its own product which it then sells for its own account. Each company has contributed one third of the cost of the pipeline; D and E have financed their shares of the cost through borrowings while F has used equity finance. E incurs all the operating expenses and invoices D and E monthly for their agreed shares of the expenses. E prepares an annual audited statement of the joint expenses but there are no financial statements of the joint venture.

The joint venture is a jointly controlled asset. D, E and F are venturers and E has a limited role as operator. The accounting consequence of this joint venture are dealt with in example 18.5.

Example 18.4 *Jointly controlled asset*

Two companies, G and H, jointly control a property which they acquired jointly and financed partly by means of a joint bank loan. G and H pay directly to the bank their respective shares of the interest and repayments of principal on the joint loan. The balance of the finance was provided in agreed shares by G and H out of their own funds. A managing agent collects the rents from tenants and deals with all expenses (other than the interest on the joint loan) in return for a commission; the agent makes a monthly net settlement with G and H. The managing agent provides G and H with an annual audited statement of the rents and joint expenses but there are no financial statements for the joint venture.

The joint venture is a jointly controlled asset and G and H are venturers. The managing agent is not a venturer as the agent does not share in the control of the activity. From the information supplied, the agent is also not an investor in the joint venture.

Jointly controlled assets rarely create accounting or reporting problems. They could also have been omitted from IAS 31 but they are included because the IASC's consultations showed that many joint ventures take the form of jointly controlled assets.

Each venturer in a joint venture which takes the form of a jointly controlled asset already has in its accounting records and in its separate financial statements:

- its share of the jointly controlled asset usually classified according to the nature of the asset rather than as an investment in a joint venture;
- any liabilities which it has incurred in respect of the joint venture, for example those liabilities incurred in financing its share of the asset;
- any revenue from the sale or use of its share of the output of the joint venture;
- any expenses which it has incurred in respect of its interest in the joint venture, for example those related to financing its interest in the assets and selling its share of the output;
- a receivable for any expenses which it has incurred in respect of the joint venture but which are recoverable from the other venturer(s);
- a liability for its share of any liabilities incurred jointly with the other venturers in relation to the joint venture; and
- a liability for any expenses incurred by the joint venture or the other venturers which are recoverable from the venturer.

Because the assets, liabilities, income and expenses are already recognised in the separate financial statements of the venturer, no adjustments or other consolidation procedures are required in respect of the jointly controlled asset when the venturer presents consolidated financial statements (IAS 31, 11). In example 18.5, D's consolidated financial statements include exactly the same amounts as D's separate financial statements in respect of the jointly controlled pipeline.

Example 18.5 *Jointly controlled asset*

In the example of the three oil production companies, D, E and F, which jointly control, own and operate an oil pipeline (see example 18.3 above), D's accounting records and separate financial statements include:

- its share of the pipeline classified as property, plant and equipment;
- a liability for the outstanding amount of its borrowing used to finance its share of the pipeline;
- its revenue from the sale of its own product;
- expenses including interest on its borrowing, its selling costs for its own product and its share of the joint operating expenses; and
- a liability for its share of operating expenses which E has incurred but has not been paid by D.

E's accounting records and separate financial statements include:

- its share of the pipeline classified as property, plant and equipment;
- a liability for the outstanding amount of its borrowing used to finance its share of the pipeline;
- its revenue from the sale of its own product;
- expenses including interest on its borrowing, its selling costs for its own product and its share of the joint operating expenses; and
- a receivable for any operating expenses which it has incurred but which are recoverable from D and F.

F's accounting records and separate financial statements include:

- its share of the pipeline classified as property, plant and equipment;
- the equity used to finance its share of the pipeline;

Continued

Continued

- its revenue from the sale of its own product;
- expenses including its selling costs for its own product and its share of the joint operating expenses;
- dividends to shareholders on the equity used to finance its share of the pipeline; and
- a payable for its share of operating expenses which E has incurred but has not been paid by F.

These items may be included with other similar items in the financial statements of D, E or F particularly if they are involved in other similar activities. Furthermore, D and E may have financed their share in the pipeline out of general borrowings and it is unlikely that F can associate specific equity finance and dividends with its share of the pipeline.

Again there have been suggestions that IAS 31 requires proportionate consolidation for jointly controlled assets and that some countries require or allow proportionate consolidation for jointly controlled assets. The misunderstanding in this case may arise because some venturers may record their interest in the asset as an investment in a joint venture.

18.9 JOINTLY CONTROLLED ENTITIES

A *jointly controlled entity* is a joint venture which involves the establishment of a corporation, partnership or other entity in which each venturer has an interest (IAS 31, 19). In some countries, it may be necessary for legal, tax or other reasons to establish all joint ventures as separate entities. In other cases, the venturers may establish a separate entity in order to limit each venturer's liability should the venture fail.

A jointly controlled entity operates in the same way as any other entity, except that there is a contractual arrangement between the venturers which establishes joint control over the entity's economic activity. The jointly controlled entity controls the assets of the joint venture, incurs liabilities and expenses and earns income. It may enter into contracts in its own name and raise finance for the purposes of the joint venture activity. Each venturer is entitled to a share of the entity's results, although some jointly controlled entities also involve a sharing of the output of the joint venture. Financial statements are usually prepared for the jointly controlled entity.

Example 18.6 *Jointly controlled entity*

Companies J and K combine their retailing activities by transferring the relevant assets, liabilities and employees into a new entity in which J and K each control 50% of the equity capital and share equally in major decisions. J and K appoint a joint governing body which is authorised to appoint senior management for the retailing activities and incur other operating expenses. J and K guarantee jointly the liabilities of the joint venture and agree to share equally in the profits of the joint venture. Audited financial statements are prepared for the new entity.

The joint venture is a jointly controlled entity and both J and K are venturers.

Example 18.7 *Jointly controlled entity*

Company L is the world's largest manufacturer and distributor of a branded consumer product. L wants to break into the market in country M in which L's products are so far unavailable. L enters into a joint venture with the government of M under which L provides expertise (including senior management) and specialist equipment. M provides the market, a ready supply of labour and finance. The joint venture is operated through a corporation under which the government of M owns 75% of the equity capital (in accordance with its foreign investment laws) and L owns the remaining 25% of the equity capital. There is a joint board of governors and the contractual arrangement provides for joint control. Audited financial statements are prepared for the corporation.

The joint venture is a jointly controlled entity and both L and the government of M are venturers. The venturers may decide (or the government or some other authority may require) the entity to present financial statements in conformity with IFRSs.

In the case of a jointly controlled entity, each venturer's interest is in another entity rather than directly in the assets, liabilities, expenses and income of the joint venture. Each venturer usually contributes cash, cash equivalents or other resources to the jointly controlled entity. These contributions are included in the venturer's accounting records and recognised in its separate financial statements as an investment in the jointly controlled entity (or as an investment in the joint venture).

Example 18.8 *Establishment of jointly controlled entity*

In example 18.6 above, J transfers to the jointly controlled entity properties with a carrying amount of £150 million, inventories of £40 million and liabilities of £25 million. Carrying amounts and fair values are identical.

J makes the following journal entry in its accounting records:

	£m	*£m*
Property	–	150
Inventories	–	40
Liabilities	25	–
Investment in jointly controlled entity	165	–
	190	190

J's separate financial statements will include an investment in the jointly controlled entity with a cost of £165 million.

18.9.1 Jointly Controlled Entities in the Separate Financial Statements of the Venturer

IAS 31 does not indicate a preference for any particular accounting treatment for reporting an interest in a jointly controlled entity in the separate financial statements of the venturer. Therefore, an interest may be reported:

- as a long-term investment at cost or revalued amount (the latter is probably rarely used in practice);
- using proportionate consolidation; or
- using the equity method.

The IASC allows a free choice in separate financial statements because such financial statements are prepared in order to meet a variety of needs with the result that different reporting practices are in use in different countries (IAS 31, 38).

IASB improvements project

In its May 2002 improvements exposure draft, the IASB proposes that an interest in a jointly controlled entity should be accounted for in the same way as in consolidated financial statements, that is by using either proportionate consolidation or the equity method.

18.9.2 Jointly Controlled Entities in the Consolidated Financial Statements of the Venturer

As far as consolidated financial statements are concerned and subject to two exceptions, IAS 31 requires the interest in the jointly controlled entity should be reported using either:

- proportionate consolidation (benchmark treatment); or
- the equity method (allowed alternative treatment).

(IAS 31, 25)

IAS 31 argues that proportionate consolidation best reflects the substance and economic reality of a venturer's interest in a jointly controlled entity, that is, control over the venturer's share of the future economic benefits (IAS 31, 26). The use of proportionate consolidation means that the venturer often reports similar amounts in its consolidated financial statements in respect of its interest in a particular joint venture irrespective of whether that joint venture is a jointly controlled operation, jointly controlled asset or jointly controlled entity.

Although IAS 31 permits the use of the equity method as an allowed alternative, the use of the method is not recommended (IAS 31, 33). IAS 31 acknowledges that the use of the equity method is supported by those who argue that it is inappropriate to combine controlled items (the assets and liabilities of the parent and subsidiaries) with jointly controlled items (the assets and liabilities of the jointly controlled entity). The equity method is also supported by those who believe that joint control and significant influence are indistinguishable from one another and, therefore, that jointly controlled entities should be reported in the same way as associates. The equity method was favoured by G4+1[3] and seems likely to be favoured by the IASB.

Proportionate consolidation or the equity method should not be used for:

- an interest in a jointly controlled entity which is acquired and held exclusively with a view to its subsequent disposal in the near future – a venturer should account for such interests as available-for-sale financial assets in accordance with IAS 39; and
- the jointly controlled entity operates under severe long-term restrictions that significantly impair its ability to transfer funds to the venturer – a venturer should account for such interests as available-for-sale financial assets in accordance with IAS 39.

Proportionate consolidation or the equity method is used, however, when the joint venture activity is of a very short duration; for example, when a jointly controlled entity is established to organise a musical event or a conference.

IASB improvements project

In its May 2002 improvements exposure draft, the IASB proposes to replace 'in the near future' with 'within 12 months from acquisition'. It also proposes to remove the exemption from the use of proportionate consolidation or the equity method when the jointly controlled entity operates under severe long-term restrictions that significantly impair its ability to transfer funds to the venturer but indicate that such restrictions make it unlikely that joint control exists.

18.9.3 Proportionate Consolidation

Proportionate consolidation is a method of reporting whereby the venturer's investment in the jointly controlled entity is replaced by the venturer's share of the assets and liabilities of the jointly controlled entity. Similarly, the venturer's income statement includes its share of the income and expenses of the jointly controlled entity. Many of the procedures applicable to full consolidation (see IAS 27 and chapter 15) are applicable to proportionate consolidation.

Example 18.9 *Jointly controlled entity – proportionate consolidation*

J and K transfer to the jointly controlled entity (see example 18.6 above) the following assets and liabilities:

Assets	*Contributed by J* £m	*Contributed by K* £m	*Jointly controlled entity* £m
Property	150	95	245
Inventories	40	60	100
Cash	–	30	30
	190	185	375
Liabilities	25	20	45
Investment in jointly controlled entity	165	165	330

In the consolidated financial statements of both J and K, the investment in the jointly controlled entity is replaced by a 50% share of the assets and liabilities of the jointly controlled entity, as follows:

Continued

Continued

	£m
Property	122.5
Inventories	50.0
Cash	15.0
	187.5
Liabilities	22.5
	165.0

IAS 31 allows a venturer to adopt one of two formats for proportionate consolidation; the venturer may either:

- combine its share of each of the assets, liabilities, income and expenses on a line-by-line basis with similar items in the venturer's financial statements; or
- include separate line items in its financial statements for its share of each of the jointly controlled entity's assets, liabilities, income and expenses – the separate line items may consist of such categories as property, plant and equipment, current assets and current liabilities.

Example 18.10 *Jointly controlled entity – proportionate consolidation*

Using the information in example 18.9 above, both J and K may either:

- combine property of £122.5 million with other property, inventories of £50 million with other inventories, cash of £15 million with other cash and liabilities of £22.5 million with other liabilities; or
- include separate line items for jointly controlled property (£122.5 million), current assets (£65 million) and current liabilities (£22.5 million).

The two formats report identical amounts of net income and of each major classification of assets, liabilities, income and expenses (IAS 31, 25 and 28). However, the two formats report different amounts for certain line items.

Whatever format is used to give effect to proportionate consolidation, it is inappropriate to offset any assets or liabilities by the deduction of other liabilities or assets, or any income or expenses by the deduction of other expenses or income, unless a legal right of set-off exists and the offsetting represents the expectation as to the realisation of the asset or the settlement of the liability (IAS 31, 29).

Extract 18.3 *Jointly controlled entities – proportionate consolidation*

Nestlé, Switzerland, 31 December 2001 (IAS)

Proportional consolidation is applied for companies over which the Group exercises joint control with partners. The individual assets, liabilities, income and expenditure are consolidated in proportion to the Nestlé participation in the equity (usually 50%).

Extract 18.4 *Jointly controlled entities – proportionate consolidation*

RTL, Luxembourg, 31 December 2000 (IAS)

A joint venture is an entity where the control of economic activity is contractually shared with one or more parties whereby no party on its own exercises effective control. Such entities are accounted for using proportionate consolidation. Under this method the Group includes its proportionate share of the joint venture's income and expenses, assets and liabilities in the relevant components of the consolidated financial statements, on a line-by-line basis.

Extract 18.5 *Jointly controlled entity – proportionate consolidation*

Czech Telecom, Czech Republic, 31 December 2000 (IAS)

The Company has a 51% interest in EuroTel providing mobile telephone services in the Czech Republic. The management and operations of EuroTel are governed by a joint venture agreement which specifies that control is exercised jointly by the Company and the other party to the joint venture. The financial results of EuroTel are included using the proportionate consolidation method and are stated in accordance with the accounting policies of the Group.

18.9.4 Equity Method

The equity method is a method of reporting whereby the venturer's interest in the jointly controlled entity is initially recorded at cost and the carrying amount is increased or decreased to recognise the venturer's share of the profits or losses of the jointly controlled entity. Similarly, the venturer's income statement includes its share of the profits or losses of the jointly controlled entity. Therefore, the venturer's consolidated balance sheet and income statement usually each include a single amount in respect of the venturer's interest in the jointly controlled entity. The equity method is described in more detail in IAS 28 (see chapter 17).

Example 18.11 *Jointly controlled entity – equity method.*

J and K transfer to the jointly controlled entity (see example 18.6 above) the following assets and liabilities:

	Contributed by J	*Contributed by K*	*Jointly controlled entity*
	£m	*£m*	*£m*
Property	150	95	245
Inventories	40	60	100
Cash	–	30	30
	190	185	375
Liabilities	25	20	45
Investment in jointly controlled entity	165	165	330

In the consolidated financial statements of both J and K, the investment in the jointly controlled entity is presented as a single line item, initially recorded at cost of £165 million.

Extract 18.6 *Jointly controlled entities – equity method*

Iscor, South Africa, 30 June 2000 (South African GAAP and IAS)

Investments in ... joint ventures are accounted for in the group financial statements using the equity method for the duration in which the group has the ability to exercise ... joint control. Equity accounted income represents the group's proportionate share of profits of these entities and the share of taxation thereon. The retained earnings net of any dividends are transferred to a non-distributable reserve. All unrealised profits and losses are eliminated. Where necessary, accounting policies are changed to ensure consistency with group policies.

The group's interest in ... joint ventures is carried in the balance sheet at an amount that reflects its share of the net assets and the unamortised portion of goodwill on acquisition. Goodwill on the acquisition of ... joint ventures is treated in accordance with the group's accounting policy for goodwill. Carrying amounts of investments in ... joint ventures are reduced to their recoverable amount where this is lower than their carrying amount.

18.10 TRANSACTIONS BETWEEN A VENTURER AND A JOINT VENTURE

A venturer may contribute or sell assets to a joint venture. Should the venturer recognise the resulting gains or losses in its income statement while the joint venture retains the assets? Similarly, a venturer may acquire assets, such as inventories, from the joint venture. Should the venturer recognise its share of the resulting gains or losses of the joint venture while the venturer retains the assets? Such gains and losses would not be recognised in consolidated financial statements if they arose on transactions between a parent and a subsidiary or among subsidiaries (see IAS 27, 17).

18.10.1 Contributions or sales by the venturer to the joint venture

IAS 31 requires that when a venturer contributes or sells assets to a joint venture, the recognition of any portion of a gain or loss from the transaction by the venturer should reflect the substance of the transaction (IAS 31, 39). The SIC relies on the requirements of IAS 16 and IAS 18 for the basis of its conclusions which imply that gains and losses would not usually be recognised (SIC 13, 5 and 6).

When the substance of the transaction justifies the recognition of the gain or loss and the venturer has transferred the significant risks and rewards of ownership, the venturer should recognise:

- all the gain or loss if the joint venture has transferred the significant risks and rewards of ownership of the asset to another party in a transaction that would qualify as a sale;
- that portion of the gain which is attributable to the interests of the other venturers if the joint venture has retained the assets; and
- the full amount of any loss when the contribution or sale provides evidence of a reduction in the net realisable value of current assets or an impairment loss.

(IAS 31, 39)

A venturer should not recognise any of the gain or loss on the transfer of non-monetary assets to a jointly controlled entity when the assets are similar to those contributed by the other venturers (which is often the case) (SIC 13, 6). This is a significant change from the requirements of IAS 31 and runs contrary to the entity approach which underpins the IASB's consolidation requirements.

When a venturer contributes or sells assets to a joint venture, no gain should be recognised if the venturer itself has retained the significant risks and rewards of ownership of those assets (IAS 31, 39). In such circumstances a sale should not be recognised whether it is made to the joint venture or any other party (IAS 18, 14 and chapter 29).

IASB improvements project

In its May 2002 improvements exposure draft, the IASB proposes to eliminate that part of SIC 13 that prohibits the recognition of the gain or loss on the transfer of non-monetary assets to a jointly controlled entity.

Example 18.12 *Contribution of an asset to a jointly controlled asset*

G and H establish a joint venture under which H acquires a 50% interest in a property already controlled and owned by G and carried in G's balance sheet at cost of £10 million. The fair value of the property is £50 million. H contributes cash of £25 million which is paid to G. Consequently, G has given up control of the property in return for joint control of the property and the receipt of £25 million cash.

If G records the transfer of the property at fair value (which is a reasonable thing to do), its income statement will show a total gain of £40 million being the fair value of the transfer to the joint venture less the carrying amount of the property. However, G is not permitted by IAS 31 to recognise that part of the gain that is attributable to its own interest in the joint venture; this part of the gain is £20 million being 50%. Subject to meeting the other conditions in IAS 31, G is permitted to recognise in its income statement that part of the gain that is attributable to H's interest in the joint venture; this part of the gain is also £20 million.

The same result is obtained if G treats the transaction as the sale of half the property to H (£25 million proceeds less £5 million carrying amount) and reclassifies the other half of the property from property to an interest in a jointly controlled property.

Example 18.13 *Transfer of assets to jointly controlled entity*

When companies J and K combine their retailing activities (see example 18.6 above), they both transfer the relevant assets and liabilities to the jointly controlled entity. The transaction is based on

Continued

Continued

an understanding of the fair values of the assets and liabilities even though those assets and liabilities were not measured at fair value in J's and K's financial statements. Sales of assets are normally measured at the fair value of the consideration received or receivable which, in this case, must reflect the fair value of the assets and liabilities contributed to the joint venture. Both J and K have, therefore, made profits but should those profits be recognised?

Under SIC 13, neither J nor K can recognise any of the gain on the transaction, notwithstanding that it was carried out at arm's length, because J and K have contributed similar assets. Under the proposals in the May 2002 improvements exposure draft, J and K may recognise that portion of the gain that is attributable to the interests of the other venturer.

18.10.2 Purchases by the venturer

When a venturer purchases assets from a joint venture, the venturer should not recognise its share of the joint venture's profits from the transaction until it resells the assets to an independent party (IAS 31, 40).

The venturer should recognise its share of the losses resulting from the purchase of assets from a joint venture in the same way as profits except that the venturer should recognise the losses immediately when they represent a reduction in the net realisable value of inventories or an impairment loss on other assets (IAS 31, 40).

Example 18.14 *Purchase of inventories from jointly controlled entity*

N and P combine their manufacturing activities in a jointly controlled entity which sells most of its output to third parties. At its balance sheet date, N's inventory includes some goods which it has bought from the jointly controlled entity for sale to N's customers. N cannot recognise its share of the jointly controlled entity's profit that relates to the inventories held by N; it reduces the carrying amount of the inventories by N's share of the joint venture's profit element. P can, of course, recognise its share of the joint venture profits relating to all sales to N, including those of goods which are included in N's inventories. When N sells the goods, it recognises both its share of the jointly controlled entity's profit plus its own profit on the sale.

Example 18.15 *Purchase of inventories from jointly controlled entity*

N and P combine their manufacturing activities in a jointly controlled entity which sells most of its output to third parties. At its balance sheet date, N's inventory includes some obsolete goods which it bought from the jointly controlled entity at a substantial discount to cost. N expects to realise the amount that it paid to the joint venture for these inventories. While there may be no need for N to write down the inventories in its financial statements, it must recognise immediately its share of the jointly controlled entity's loss on those inventories because the loss represents a reduction in the net realisable value of those inventories.

18.11 CHANGE IN STATUS OF JOINT VENTURE

The venturers may choose to change the type of joint venture for tax reasons, to attract investors or for other reasons. In the above examples:

- A and B may decide to transfer their respective manufacturing facilities to a jointly controlled entity in which A and B own, say, 75% of the equity capital and an investor contributes cash in return for the remaining 25% of the equity capital;
- D, E and F may agreed to transfer the pipeline to a jointly controlled entity in which they each own a proportion of the equity capital;
- G and H may decide to transfer the property and the related financing to a jointly controlled entity in which they each own a proportion of the equity capital; and
- J and K may decide to retain their respective retailing assets, liabilities and employees but to carry out the activities under a common name and establish a jointly controlled entity in which J and K each own a proportion of the share capital to deal with marketing, promotion and store design expenses which are shared equally.

The change in the status of a joint venture may give rise to various reporting consequences. A change may result from the actions of the venturer, the other venturers or the joint venture. A change often results from, or in, the contractual arrangement.

A venturer may acquire control, rather than have joint control, over the joint venture activity. This may occur, for example, when a venturer acquires the interests of all the other venturers and investors. In such a case, a parent/subsidiary relationship now exists which should be dealt with in accordance with IAS 27 (IAS 31, 37).

A venturer may dispose of part of its interest so that it no longer has joint control but has significant influence. A change in the contractual arrangement could have the same effect. Such a change can take place notwithstanding that the other venturers continue to have joint control. In such a case, an investor/associate relationship now exists which should be dealt with in accordance with IAS 28. If necessary, the venturer should discontinue the use of proportionate consolidation (IAS 31, 30) and start to use the equity method (IAS 28, 8).

A venturer may retain an investment in the jointly controlled entity but without having joint control or significant influence. Such a change may take place notwithstanding that the other venturers continue to have joint control. The venturer should discontinue the use of proportionate consolidation (IAS 31, 30) or the equity method (IAS 31, 34) and start to account for its interest in accordance with IAS 39.

A venturer may dispose of its interest in the jointly controlled entity. It should discontinue the use of proportionate consolidation or the equity method (IAS 31, 30 and 34) and determine the profit or loss on disposal by comparing the disposal proceeds with its share of the assets and liabilities (proportionate consolidation) or carrying amount (equity method).

18.12 DISCLOSURE

A venturer should disclose the aggregate amount of the following contingencies, unless the probability of loss is remote, separately from the amount of other contingencies:

- any contingencies that it has incurred in relation to its interests in joint ventures and its share in each of the contingencies which have been incurred jointly with other venturers;
- its share of the contingencies of the joint ventures themselves for which it is contingently liable; and
- those contingencies that arise because it is contingently liable for the liabilities of the other venturers of a joint venture.

(IAS 31, 44)

A venturer should disclose the aggregate amount of the following commitments in respect of its interests in joint ventures separately from other commitments:

- any capital commitments in relation to its interests in joint ventures and its share in the capital commitments that have been incurred jointly with other venturers; and

- its share of the capital commitments of the joint ventures themselves. (IAS 31, 45)

A venturer should disclose a listing and description of interests in significant joint ventures and the proportion of ownership interest held in jointly controlled entities (IAS 31, 46).

A venturer which reports its interests in jointly controlled entities using the line-by-line reporting format for proportionate consolidation or the equity method should disclose the aggregate amounts of each of current assets, long-term assets, current liabilities, long-term liabilities, income and expenses related to its interests in joint ventures (IAS 31, 46).

Extract 18.7 *Disclosure of aggregate amounts accounted for by proportionate consolidation*

SES, Luxembourg, 31 December 2000 (Luxembourg GAAP and IAS)

The Group's share of the assets, liabilities, revenue and expenses of the joint venture in NSAB, which are included in the consolidated accounts are as follows at 31 December 2000 and for the period then ended:

	€'000
Current assets	27,274
Non-current assets	65,327
Current liabilities	19,111
Non-current liabilities	13,706
Revenue	10,177
Operating result	4,352
Taxes	(17)
Result for period	4,148

A venturer which does not issue consolidated financial statements, because it does not have subsidiaries, should disclose the above information in its separate financial statements (IAS 31, 47). Under the proposals in the May 2002 improvements exposure draft, such a venturer will be required to use proportionate consolidation or the equity method in its separate financial statements.

Notes

1 *AASB Action Alert*, June 1998, p1, Australian Accounting Research Foundation, Melbourne.

2 *Conclusions on Accounting and Reporting by Transnational Corporations*, United Nations 1994, pp10–12.

3 *Accounting for Interests in Joint Ventures*, G4+1, 1999.

CHAPTER 19

Foreign Transactions and Operations

19.1 RELEVANT STANDARDS AND INTERPRETATIONS

IAS 21 *Effects of Changes in Foreign Exchange Rates*
IAS 39 *Financial Instruments: Recognition and Measurement*
SIC 7 *Introduction of the Euro*
SIC 11 *Foreign Exchange – Capitalisation of Losses Resulting from Severe Currency Devaluation*
SIC 19 *Reporting Currency – Measurement and Presentation of Financial Statements under IAS 21 and IAS 29*
SIC 30 *Reporting Currency – Translation from Measurement Currency to Presentation Currency*

IAS 21 does not deal with hedge accounting for foreign currency items other than the classification of exchange differences arising on a foreign currency liability accounted for as a hedge of a net investment in a foreign entity. Other aspects of hedge accounting, including the criteria to use hedge accounting, are dealt with in IAS 39 and the related implementation guidance (IGC) (see chapter 20). IAS 39 sets criteria that must be met if a hedging relationship is to qualify for special hedge accounting and these requirements apply also to hedges of net investments in foreign entities.

19.2 HISTORY

The IASC began discussing foreign currency issues in 1974 but its initial proposals were criticised for allowing too many alternatives so it decided in 1978 that it was not in a position to issue an IAS. In the ensuing years, the IASC continued to study the topic and representatives of the IASC participated in the FASB task force which was also reviewing the issue.

IAS 21 *Accounting for the Effects of Changes in Exchange Rates* (IAS 21 [1983]) was approved in 1983. It reflected developments in standard setting which had taken place around the late 1970s, in particular the use of the net investment method of dealing with foreign entities.

IAS 21 was reconsidered in the comparability and improvements project and several changes were made to the requirements dealing with foreign currency transactions. The main thrust of IAS 21 [1983] was retained with respect to the translation of the financial statements of foreign entities and other foreign operations although changes were made in respect of the translation of the income statement and the translation of the financial statements of subsidiaries reporting in the currency of a hyperinflationary economy. It also banned the deferral and amortisation of exchange differences.

IAS 21 *The Effects of Changes in Foreign Exchange Rates* was approved in November 1993 and applied to financial statements for accounting periods beginning on or after 1 January 1995. The revised IAS did not deal with hedge accounting as the IASC planned to deal with the issue in its financial instruments project. In specific circumstances that meet the criteria for hedge accounting, IAS 39 now allows the deferral of foreign currency gains and losses and, sometimes, the capitalisation of those gains and losses as part of the cost of an asset.

The May 2002 improvements exposure draft proposes several significant changes to IAS 21 that affect the translation of the foreign currency financial statements of foreign operations. In particular, the exposure draft proposes to replace the distinction between foreign entities and foreign operations that are integral to the operations of the reporting entity with a functional currency based approach. Other proposed changes deal with the translation of goodwill and fair value adjustments and the translation of the financial statements of foreign entities that operate in hyperinflationary economies. The IASB also proposes to eliminate the allowed alternative treatment that permits the capitalisation of certain exchange losses and change some of the requirements for hedge accounting.

19.3 IOSCO

In June 1994, IOSCO advised the IASC that IAS 21 was acceptable for the purposes of the IOSCO core standards. IOSCO identified the following suspense issues:

- some IOSCO members may allow goodwill and the fair value adjustments arising on the acquisition of a foreign entity to be treated as assets and liabilities of the reporting entity only if information equivalent to treating them as assets and liabilities of the foreign entity is disclosed;

- the IASC should consider foreign currency transaction hedging issues (this is now dealt with in IAS 39);
- host countries would continue to determine the measurement currency and the manner of presentation of convenience translations of financial statements (see chapter 8);
- some IOSCO members would accept the use of the allowed alternative treatment for certain exchange differences (see 19.9) only if information equivalent to the application of the benchmark treatment is disclosed (the disclosure of this information is already required by IAS 21 but the IASB now proposes to ban the treatment);
- some IOSCO members may not require the recognition of gains on long-term monetary items nor their disclosure in the notes (this is prohibited by IAS 21); and
- one member country may not require recognition of gains or losses on long-term monetary items but may instead require disclosure of those gains in the notes (this is prohibited by IAS 21).

IAS 21 is included in 'IAS 2000' endorsed by IOSCO in May 2000 when IOSCO identified the following supplemental treatments:

- concerns about the appropriateness of recognising certain exchange differences in the carrying amount of the related asset;
- concerns about the appropriateness of translating goodwill and fair value adjustments using the exchange rate at the date of the transaction (the IASB proposes to ban this treatment);
- the IASC should consider addressing the situation where forward exchange contracts are entered into to establish the amounts of the measurement currency required or available at the settlement dates of foreign currency transactions (this was dealt with in IAS 21 [1981] but, under current IAS, the transactions are recorded at the rate as at the date of the transaction whereas the forward contract is a financial instrument that is measured at fair value (see chapter 20));
- the IASC should consider addressing the apparent conflict between IAS 21 and IAS 39 in accounting for the translation of non-monetary items measured at cost;
- the IASC should consider providing guidance on how the payment of a dividend does not constitute a return of the investment; and
- the IASC should consider providing guidance on how to account for a change in the classification of a foreign operation occurring during a financial year.

19.4 IAS 21 IN BRIEF

A foreign currency transaction should be recorded in an entity's measurement currency using the exchange rate at the date of the transaction.

At subsequent balance sheet dates any resulting monetary assets or liabilities should be reported using the closing rate. Resulting exchange differences should be recognised immediately as an expense or income unless they:

- arise from a monetary item forming part of an entity's net investment in a foreign entity or a foreign currency liability accounted for as a hedge of an entity's net investment in a foreign entity and are classified as equity until the disposal of the investment; or
- arise in the restricted circumstances permitted by the allowed alternative treatment and are added to the cost of an asset.

Foreign operations are either:

- integral foreign operations whose activities are an integral part of those of the reporting entity; or
- foreign entities whose activities are not an integral part of those of the reporting entity.

The financial statements of an integral foreign operation should be translated into the measurement currency as if its transactions had been those of the reporting entity.

The balance sheet of a foreign entity should be translated into the measurement currency using the closing rate. The income statement of a foreign entity should be translated into the measurement currency using the average rate, unless the foreign entity reports in the currency of a hyperinflationary economy when it should be translated at the closing rate.

The financial statements of a foreign entity which reports in the currency of a hyperinflationary economy should be restated for the changes in the general price index in accordance with IAS 29 (see chapter 42) before they are translated into the measurement currency. If the foreign entity reports in a stable currency, no restatement is necessary.

All resulting exchange differences should be classified as equity until the disposal of the foreign entity when they should be recognised as income or expense as part of the profit or loss on disposal of the entity. Exchange differences arising on the reporting of a foreign currency item which forms part of the net investment in the foreign entity or hedges that net investment should also be included in equity until the disposal of the foreign entity.

19.5 GENERAL DEFINITIONS

Reporting currency is the currency used in presenting the financial statements of the reporting entity (IAS 21, 7).

A *foreign currency* is a currency other than the measurement currency of an entity (IAS 21, 7).

An *exchange rate* is the ratio for exchange of two currencies (IAS 21, 7). The *closing rate* is the spot exchange rate at the balance sheet date (IAS 21, 7). The *spot rate* is the exchange rate for immediate delivery (in practice, in two days) of the exchanged currencies.

An *exchange difference* is the difference resulting from reporting the same number of units of a foreign currency in the measurement currency at different exchange rates (IAS 21, 7).

Monetary items are money held and assets and liabilities to be received or paid in fixed or determinable amounts of money (IAS 21, 7).

19.6 INITIAL RECOGNITION OF FOREIGN CURRENCY TRANSACTIONS

A foreign currency transaction is usually recorded on initial recognition in the reporting currency by applying to the foreign currency amount the spot rate at the date of the transaction (IAS 21, 9). So, for example, when a German company buys goods from a British company for £10,000, the German company records the transaction using the £/€ exchange rate at the date of the transaction. For practical reasons, an entity may use a rate that approximates the actual rate at the date of the transaction. For example, it may use an average rate for a week or a month for all transactions in each foreign currency occurring during the period. Such an approach is only acceptable if exchange rates do not fluctuate significantly (IAS 21, 10).

It is no longer permissible to report a transaction using the forward rate specified in a related forward contract. Forward contracts are financial instruments and should be accounted for in accordance with IAS 39 (see chapter 20).

Extract 19.1 *Forward contracts*

Bayer, Germany, 31 December 2001 (IAS)

... foreign currency receivables and payables are translated at closing rates, irrespective of whether they are exchange-hedged. Forward contracts that, from an economic point of view, serve as a hedge against fluctuations in exchange rates are stated at fair value.

19.7 REPORTING FOREIGN CURRENCY TRANSACTIONS AT SUBSEQUENT BALANCE SHEET DATES

19.7.1 Measurement at the balance sheet date

There are three categories of foreign currency items: monetary items; non-monetary items carried at fair value; and non-monetary items carried at historical cost (IAS 21, 11).

At each balance sheet date, an entity may have foreign currency monetary items such as:

- payables or receivables in foreign currencies;
- loans and advances which are payable or receivable in a foreign currency; and
- cash and cash equivalents denominated in a foreign currency.

These should be converted into the reporting currency using the closing rate (IAS 21, 11(a)).

An entity may also have non-monetary items which are carried at fair value denominated in a foreign currency, for example a property in a foreign country which is carried at fair value or available-for-sale marketable securities listed on a foreign stock exchange which are carried at fair value in accordance with the relevant IAS. These items should be reported using the exchange rates that existed when the values were determined (IAS 21, 11(c)). So, for example, the foreign currency amount of:

- available-for-sale financial assets carried at fair value at the balance sheet date is converted using the closing rate;
- property revalued at the balance sheet date is converted using the closing rate; and
- property revalued six months before the balance sheet date is converted using the exchange rate at the date of the valuation.

> ***IASB improvements project***
>
> In its May 2002 improvements exposure draft, the IASB proposes that, when a gain or loss on a non-monetary asset is recognised directly in equity, the foreign exchange component should also be recognised directly in equity. If the gain or loss on a non-monetary asset is recognised in profit and loss, the foreign exchange component should also be recognised directly in profit and loss.

Non-monetary items which result from transactions which took place in a foreign currency but which are carried at historical cost are reported using the exchange rate at the date of the transaction (IAS 21, 11(b)). In other words, they are reported at the same amounts as they were when the transactions were initially recognised. For example, the cost of a property in a foreign country is not adjusted for subsequent changes in the exchange rate between the reporting currency and the currency of the foreign country.

Extract 19.2 *Foreign currency transactions*

CEZ, Czech Republic, 31 December 2000 (IAS)

Assets whose acquisition or construction costs were denominated in foreign currencies were translated to Czech crowns at the exchange rates prevailing at the date of each acquisition or at the date on which the related items were included in the assets.

Foreign currency on hand, bank accounts, receivables and payables denominated in foreign currencies are translated to Czech crowns at the exchange rates existing at the transaction date and are adjusted at year-end to exchange rates at that date as published by the Czech National Bank.

Exchange rate differences arising on settlement of transactions or on reporting foreign currency transactions at rates different from those at which they were originally recorded are included in the Statement of Income as they occur.

19.7.2 Recognition of Exchange Differences

An exchange difference results when there is a change in the exchange rate between the transaction date and the date of settlement of any monetary items arising from a foreign currency transaction. When the transaction is settled within the same accounting period in which the transaction occurred, all the exchange difference is recognised in that period. When the transaction is settled in a subsequent accounting period, the exchange difference is allocated among the periods in which the monetary items are outstanding.

Subject to the requirements of IAS 39 (see 19.7.3), exchange differences should be recognised as income or as expenses in the period in which they arise (IAS 21, 15). There are, however, three exceptions to this requirement:

- exchange differences arising on a monetary item that, in substance, forms part of a reporting entity's net investment in a foreign entity is included in equity;

- exchange differences arising on a foreign currency liability accounted for as a hedge of a reporting entity's net investment in a foreign entity is included in equity; and
- certain exchange differences resulting from a severe devaluation or depreciation of a currency against which there is no practical means of hedging may be added to the cost of an asset (in its May 2002 improvements exposure draft, the IASB proposes to eliminate this exception).

Extract 19.3 *Foreign currency transactions and balances*

China Petroleum & Chemical Corporation, People's Republic of China, 31 December 2001 (IAS)

The functional and reporting currency of the Group is Renminbi. Foreign currency transactions during the year are translated into Renminbi at the applicable rates of exchange quoted by the People 's Bank of China ('PBOC rates') prevailing on the transaction dates. Foreign currency monetary assets and liabilities are translated into Renminbi at the applicable PBOC rates at the balance sheet date. Exchange differences, other than those capitalised as construction in progress, are recognised as income or expense in the income statement.

Extract 19.4 *Foreign currency transactions and balances*

Jardine Matheson Holdings Limited, Hong Kong, 31 December 2001 (IAS)

Transactions in foreign currencies are accounted for at the exchange rates ruling at the transaction dates. Assets and liabilities of subsidiary undertakings, associates and joint ventures, together with all other monetary assets and liabilities expressed in foreign currencies, are translated into United States Dollars at the rates of exchange ruling at the year end. Results expressed in foreign currencies are translated into United States Dollars at the average rates of exchange ruling during the year. Exchange differences arising from the retranslation of the net investment in foreign subsidiary undertakings, associates and joint ventures and of financial instruments which are designated as and are hedges of such investments, are taken directly to exchange reserves. On the disposal of these investments, such exchange differences are recognized in the consolidated profit and loss account as part of the profit or loss on disposal. All other exchange differences are dealt with in the consolidated profit and loss account.

Extract 19.5 *Transactions in foreign currencies*

Nokia, Finland, 31 December 2001 (IAS)

Transactions in foreign currencies are recorded at the rates of exchange prevailing at the dates of the transactions. For practical reasons, a rate that approximates the actual rate at the date of the transaction is often used. At the end of the accounting period the unsettled balances on foreign currency receivables and liabilities are valued at the rates of exchange prevailing at the year end. Foreign exchange gains and losses related to normal business operations are treated as adjustments to sales or to cost of goods. Foreign exchange gains and losses associated with financing are included as a net amount under financial income and expenses.

In some cases, the balance sheet date may coincide with a major change in exchange rates. This happened in China at the end of 1993 when the existing dual rates were unified. It also happened at the end of 1998 with the introduction of the Euro with effect from 1 January 1999. In such cases, the principles of IAS 21 do not change. The closing rate should be used, notwithstanding that the rate may change significantly on the following day.

The Chinese case was complicated by a number of related facts:

- the unification of the official rate and the swap centre rate was, in effect, a devaluation of the official rate to the swap centre rate;
- many companies already made extensive use of the swap centre rate;
- the unification was announced on 28 December and the banks remained closed in order to effect the unification until the beginning of January; and
- companies had balance sheet dates of 31 December.

In such circumstances, many Chinese companies took the reasonable approach of using the 31 December swap centre rate or the unified rate. This had the effect of reflecting the devaluation in 1993.

Extract 19.6 *Unification of Chinese exchange rates*

Shanghai Petrochemical, People's Republic of China, 31 December 1993 (IAS)

Foreign currency monetary balances at the balance sheet date are translated into Renminbi at the official exchange rates set by the State Administration for Exchange Control where it is possible to determine with reasonable certainty that the equivalent amount of foreign currencies can be obtained by the Group at those rates. Any remaining foreign currency monetary balances are translated into Renminbi at rates quoted by the Shenzen Foreign Exchange Swap Centre at the balance sheet date. On 28 December 1993, the People's Bank of China announced the unification of the official and the swap centre exchange rates for the Renminbi with effect from 1 January 1994. The unified exchange rate for Renminbi will effectively be determined based on the rates prevailing at swap centres. Accordingly, in applying this policy, the Group has translated the foreign currency monetary balances at 31 December 1993 in Renminbi at rates quoted by the Shenzen Foreign Exchange Swap Centre on that date.

The requirements of IAS 21 regarding the translation of foreign currency transactions were strictly applied to the changeover to the Euro and should be similarly applied to the fixing of exchange rates when countries join EMU at later stages (SIC 7, 3).

Prior to changeover, foreign currency monetary assets and liabilities resulting from transactions continued to be translated into the reporting currency at the closing rate and the resulting exchange differences recognised as income or expense immediately (subject to the usual exceptions). Exchange differences resulting from the translation of liabilities denominated in participating currencies were not included in the carrying amount of related assets (SIC 7, 4). The start of the EMU after the balance sheet date did not change the application of these requirements at the balance sheet date. The European Commission issued a set of voluntary guidelines on the same issue[1], some of which may conflict with IASs and SIC 7.

19.7.3 Interaction between IAS 39 and IAS 21

IAS 39 interacts with IAS 21 as follows:

- exchange gains and losses on monetary assets and liabilities are reported in net profit or loss;
- any change in the fair value of a monetary asset or liability designated as a hedging instrument in a cash flow hedge, other than foreign exchange gains and losses, is accounted for in accordance with IAS 39;
- any change in the fair value of a non-monetary financial asset (for example, an equity instrument) or a non-monetary financial liability (for example, some mandatorily redeemable preference stock issued by the entity), including changes arising from foreign currency exchange rates, are accounted for in accordance with IAS 39; and
- when there is a hedge between a non-derivative monetary asset and a non-derivative monetary liability, changes in the fair value of those financial instruments are reported in net profit or loss.

The following IAS 39 *Implementation Guidance: Questions and Answers* (IGC) deal with the interaction between IAS 21 and 39:

- IGC 137-4: *Hedge accounting: hedging of future foreign currency revenue streams;*
- IGC 137-9: *Foreign currency hedge;*
- IGC 137-10: *Foreign currency cash flow hedge;*
- IGC Other-2: *IAS 21: Hedge of a net investment in a foreign entity: whether IAS 39 applies;*

- IGC Other-3: *IAS 21: Exchange differences arising on translation of foreign entities: equity or income?*
- IGC Other-4: *IAS 21: Fair value hedge of asset measured at cost*; and
- IGC Other-5: *Interaction between IAS 39 and IAS 21.*

A foreign currency borrowing may be used to hedge an expected sale in the foreign currency when the hedge meets the criteria of IAS 39, 142. In such a case the gains and losses on the effective portion of the hedge are recognised directly in equity through the statement of changes in equity in accordance with IAS 39, 158(a) and not in profit or loss as required by IAS 21 (IGC Other-4).

IGC Other-5 considers the order in which IAS 21 and IAS 39 are applied in reporting a financial asset or liability denominated in a foreign currency. It notes that, generally, the measurement of a financial asset or financial liability at fair value, cost, or amortised cost is determined first in the foreign currency in which the item is denominated. Then, the foreign currency amount is reported in the reporting currency using the closing rate or an historical rate in accordance with IAS 21. Therefore, for a financial asset or liability which is a monetary item and which is not a hedge of an unrecognised firm commitment or forecast transaction in a foreign currency, the following approach is required:

- the financial asset or liability is measured in the foreign currency in accordance with IAS 39 and any gains or losses are reported in net profit or loss or equity in accordance with IAS 39;
- the foreign currency amount of the financial asset or liability is reported in the reporting currency using the closing rate and any exchange differences are recognised in net profit and loss or equity in accordance with IAS 21.

If the financial asset or liability is a hedge of an unrecognised firm commitment or forecast transaction in a foreign currency, the gains and losses on the effective portion of the hedge are initially recognised in equity in accordance with IAS 39.

Non-monetary financial assets (for example, an investment in an equity security) should be translated at the closing rate if carried at fair value or an historical rate if carried at cost. Any changes in the carrying amount of a non-monetary item are reported in net profit or loss or in equity in accordance with IAS 39. For example, if an entity opts to report gains and losses on available-for-sale non-monetary financial assets in equity, the entity reports the entire change in the carrying amount, including any changes arising from changes in exchange rates, in equity.

19.8 NET INVESTMENT IN A FOREIGN ENTITY

Exchange differences arising on the following two items should be classified as equity until the disposal of the net investment in a foreign entity:

- on a monetary item which, in substance, forms part of a reporting entity's net investment in a foreign entity (IAS 21, 17); and
- on a foreign currency liability accounted for as a hedge of a reporting entity's net investment in a foreign entity (IAS 21, 19 and IAS 39, 142).

On disposal of the net investment in the foreign entity, the exchange differences should be recognised as income or as expenses (IAS 21, 17, 19 and 37).

This requirement is the same as the requirement for the exchange differences arising on the translation of the financial statements of the foreign entity.

A *net investment in a foreign entity* is the reporting entity's share in the net assets of that entity (IAS 21, 7). Therefore, if the foreign entity is a wholly owned subsidiary of the reporting entity, the net investment is the net assets of the foreign entity. If the reporting entity owns 75% of the foreign entity, the net investment is 75% of the net assets of the foreign entity. The net investment may include goodwill and the fair value adjustments arising on the acquisition of the foreign entity. However, in its May 2002 improvements exposure draft, the IASB proposed to require that the goodwill and fair value adjustments be treated as assets and liabilities of the foreign operation and, hence, as part of the net investment.

A monetary item that, in substance, forms part of an entity's net investment in a foreign entity is a foreign currency item for which settlement is neither planned nor likely to occur in the foreseeable future. Such an item may be an asset (which increases the net investment) or a liability (which reduces the net investment). It may be:

- a receivable such as a long-term loan to the foreign entity, but not a trade receivable; or
- a payable, but not a trade payable, to the foreign entity.

For example, a French company may lend sterling to its British subsidiary. If that loan forms part of the net investment in the British subsidiary, the French company classifies the exchange differences arising on the loan as equity until the disposal of the British subsidiary. The French company also treats exchange differences arising on the translation of the British subsidiary's financial statements into euro for the purposes of consolidation in the same way.

If the French company sells goods to its British subsidiary as part of its ordinary activities, any exchange gains and losses on any resulting receivable are recognised as income or expenses; the receivable is not part of the French company's net investment in the British subsidiary.

The same principles apply if the British subsidiary makes a sterling loan to the French parent. In the parent's financial statements, the loan reduces the net investment in the British subsidiary; therefore the resulting exchange differences are included in equity.

The same approach is adopted with a foreign currency liability which is accounted for as a hedge of a net investment in a foreign entity provided that the IAS 39 requirements on the designation of the hedge and hedge effectiveness are met (IGC Other-2). Therefore, if the French company borrows sterling and accounts for that loan as a hedge of its net investment in the British subsidiary, the French company classifies the exchange differences arising on the loan as equity until the disposal of the British subsidiary. If the loan is not accounted for as a hedge of the net investment, the exchange differences are included in the French company's income statement.

> ***IASB improvements project***
>
> In its May 2002 improvements exposure draft, the IASB proposes that exchange differences on monetary items that form part of a reporting entity's net investment in a foreign operation should be reported:
>
> - in income or expenses in the separate financial statements of the reporting entity or foreign operation; but
> - in equity in the consolidated financial statements that include the reporting entity and the foreign operation.

Extract 19.7 *Foreign currency hedging of net investments*

Nokia, Finland, 31 December 2001 (IAS)

The Group also applies hedge accounting for its foreign currency hedging on net investments. Qualifying hedges are those properly documented hedges of the foreign exchange rate risk of foreign currency-denominated net investments that meet the requirements set out in IAS 39. The hedge must be effective both prospectively and retrospectively. The Group claims hedge accounting in respect of forward foreign exchange contracts, foreign currency-denominated loans, and options, or option strategies, which have zero net premium or a net premium paid, and where the terms of the bought and sold options within a collar or zero premium structure are the same. For qualifying foreign exchange forwards the change in fair value that reflects the change in spot exchange rates is deferred in shareholders' equity. The change in fair value that reflects the change in forward exchange rates less the change in spot exchange rates is recognized in the profit and loss account. For qualifying foreign exchange options the change in intrinsic value is deferred in shareholders' equity. Changes in the time value are at all times taken directly to the profit and loss account. If a foreign currency-denominated loan is used as a hedge, all foreign exchange gains and losses arising from the transaction are recognized in shareholders' equity. Accumulated fair value changes from qualifying hedges are released from shareholders' equity into the profit and loss account only if the legal entity in the given country is sold or liquidated.

Extract 19.8 *Foreign currency hedging of net investments*

Roche, Switzerland, 31 December 2001 (IAS)

For qualifying hedges of net investment in a foreign entity, the hedging instrument is recorded at fair value. The portion of any change in fair value that is an effective hedge is included in equity. Any remaining ineffective portion is recorded in financial income (expense) where the hedging instrument is a derivative and in equity in other cases. If the entity is disposed of, then the cumulative changes of fair value of the hedging instrument that have been recorded in equity are included in financial income (expense) at the time of the disposal.

19.9 ALLOWED ALTERNATIVE TREATMENT FOR EXCHANGE DIFFERENCES

IAS 21 includes an allowed alternative treatment for certain exchange differences which arise in very limited circumstances. It is not available to any entity which is free to settle or hedge its foreign currency liabilities notwithstanding that the entity chooses not to settle or hedge.

The allowed alternative treatment deals with exchange differences which result from a severe devaluation or depreciation of a currency against which there is no practical means of hedging and which affects liabilities which cannot be settled and which arise directly on the recent acquisition of an asset invoiced in a foreign currency. These exchange differences may be included in the carrying amount of the related asset, provided that the adjusted carrying amount does not exceed the lower of the replacement cost and the amount recoverable from the sale or use of the asset (IAS 21, 21). Therefore, the cost of an asset invoiced in a foreign currency is regarded as the amount of reporting currency that the entity ultimately has to pay to settle its liabilities arising directly on the recent acquisition of the asset.

These circumstances are expected to occur only rarely, for example, when there is a shortage of foreign currency as a result of exchange control restrictions imposed by a government or a central bank and hedging instruments are not available (SIC 11, 4). Once the conditions for capitalisation of exchange losses are met, an entity should capitalise further exchange losses incurred after the first severe devaluation or depreciation of the reporting currency only to the extent that all conditions for capitalisation continue to be met (SIC 11, 5).

The SIC has concluded that 'recent' acquisitions of assets are acquisitions within twelve months prior to the severe devaluation of the reporting currency (SIC 11, 6). Twelve months is considered by the SIC to be an 'operational and economically reasonable period' for this purpose. The twelve months period refers to the date of acquisition of the asset and does not restrict the period of capitalisation of subsequent exchange losses (SIC 11, 9).

Example 19.1 *Inclusion of foreign exchange losses in the cost of equipment*

An entity imports an item of equipment into country P which has a severe shortage of foreign currency. The entity has to apply to the central bank for foreign currency funds to settle the liability for the imported equipment and has to wait several months for such funds to become available. No hedging facilities are available and without foreign funds the entity cannot settle its liability.

While the entity is awaiting funds, the country's currency depreciates so that the cost to the entity in local currency of settling the liability increases by 40%. Therefore, if the entity adopts the allowed alternative treatment in IAS 21, the increased cost of settling the liability is added to the cost of the equipment; in other words, the cost of the equipment is the amount of local currency that the entity ultimately has to pay to buy foreign currency funds to settle the liability.

If the currency depreciation occurs more than twelve months after the date of acquisition of the equipment, the increased cost of settling the liability is recognised as an expense and is not added to the cost of the equipment.

IASB improvements project

In its May 2002 improvements exposure draft, the IASB proposes to eliminate the allowed alternative treatment.

19.10 FOREIGN OPERATIONS

A *foreign operation* is a subsidiary, associate, joint venture or branch of the reporting entity, the activities of which are based or conducted in a country other than the country of the reporting entity (IAS 21, 7). A foreign operation is either:

- *a foreign operation that is integral to the operations of the reporting entity* (IAS 21, 23); or
- a *foreign entity*, that is a foreign operation, the activities of which are not an integral part of those of the reporting entity (IAS 21, 7).

A *foreign operation that is integral to the operations of the reporting entity* carries out its activities as if it were an extension of the reporting entity's operations. In such a case, a change in the exchange rate between the measurement currency and that of the country of the foreign operation has an immediate effect on the cash flows of the reporting entity. The change in exchange rate also affects any monetary items held by the foreign operation rather than the reporting entity's net investment in that operation. For example, a foreign operation may only sell goods imported from the reporting entity and remit the sale proceeds, net of local expenses, to the reporting entity. A change in the exchange rate immediately increases or reduces the sale proceeds received by the reporting entity and the value of any receivables of the foreign operation.

A *foreign entity* carries out its activities with a significant degree of autonomy from those of the reporting entity. A foreign entity accumulates cash and other monetary items, incurs expenses, generates revenue and other income and arranges borrowings, all substantially in its local currency. It may also enter into transactions in other foreign currencies and transactions in the measurement currency. The transactions of a foreign entity with the reporting entity itself are usually a small proportion of the foreign entity's activities. The activities of the foreign entity may be financed mainly from its own operations or local borrowings, rather than by the reporting entity.

In the case of a foreign entity, a change in the exchange rate between the measurement currency and that of the country of the foreign entity has little direct effect on the present and future cash flows from operations of either the foreign entity or the reporting entity. The change in the exchange rate affects the reporting entity's net investment in the foreign entity and its return on that investment rather than the individual monetary and non-monetary items held by the foreign entity.

The *net investment in a foreign entity* is the reporting entity's share in the net assets of that entity (IAS 21, 7). Therefore, if the foreign entity is a wholly owned subsidiary of the reporting entity, the net investment is the net assets of the foreign entity. If the reporting entity owns 75% of the foreign entity, the net investment is 75% of the net assets of the foreign entity. Goodwill arising on the acquisition of a foreign entity does not appear in the financial statements of the foreign entity but may be treated as an asset of the foreign entity (IAS 21, 33). Similarly, the fair value adjustments arising on the acquisition of the foreign entity may be treated as part of the net investment (IAS 21, 33).

Some national accounting standards, notably US GAAP, use a 'functional currency' approach. Although different terms are used, the standards result in the same basic approach, a fact which is acknowledged by Simpson in the FASB's IAS/US GAAP comparison[2]. The functional currency of a foreign entity is the foreign currency in which it reports (usually its local currency). The functional currency of a foreign operation that is integral to the operations of the reporting entity is the measurement currency of the reporting entity.

Extract 19.9 *Classification of foreign operations*

Bayer, Germany, 31 December 2001 (IAS)

The majority of foreign consolidated companies are to be regarded as foreign entities since they are financially, economically and organizationally autonomous. Their functional currencies according to IAS 21 are thus the respective local currencies ...

Where the operations of a foreign company are integral to those of Bayer AG, the functional currency is the euro.

Extract 19.10 *Classification of foreign operations*

BHP, Australia, 31 May 1998 (IAS)

Each foreign operation is accounted for in its functional currency, ie the currency of its primary economic environment. All foreign operations are self-sustaining operations. As such, the financial statements of these operations are translated using the current rate method.

IASB improvements project

In its May 2002 improvements exposure draft, the IASB proposes to replace the current distinction between foreign entities and integral foreign operations with a distinction based on a functional currency approach. It is expected that, in most cases, the change will not affect the classification or the accounting.

19.11 FOREIGN OPERATIONS THAT ARE INTEGRAL TO THE REPORTING ENTITY'S OPERATIONS

The financial statements of a foreign operation that is integral to the operations of the reporting entity should be translated as if the transactions of the foreign operation had been those of the reporting entity itself (IAS 21, 27). For example:

- the cost and depreciation of property, plant and equipment are translated using the exchange rate at the date of purchase of the assets (or the exchange rate that existed on the date of the valuation if the assets are carried at fair value);
- the cost of inventories is translated at the exchange rates at the date when those costs were incurred;
- the recoverable amount or realisable value of an asset is translated using the exchange rate at the date when the recoverable amount or net realisable value was determined – this is usually the closing rate; and
- resulting exchange differences are recognised by the reporting entity as income or expenses.

Example 19.2 *Translation of the financial statements of a foreign operation that is integral to the operations of the reporting entity*

A British company has a branch in the Netherlands which is integral to the operations of the British company. The balance sheet of the branch at 31 December 2002 includes the following items:

- an office building carried at market value of €50,000 less subsequent depreciation of €2,000 – the valuation was carried out as at 31 December 2001;
- fixtures, fittings and office equipment acquired in March 2001 at a cost of €10,000;
- inventory purchased from the British company for €15,000. The cost to the British company was £10,000 and the net realisable value of the inventory at 31 December 2002 is €25,000;
- receivables of €20,000; and
- a liability to the British company of £25,000.

In the financial statement of the British company:

- the market value of the office building is translated into £ sterling using the exchange rate as of 31 December 2001, that is the date of the revaluation;

(Continued)

(Continued)

- the fixtures, fittings and office equipment are translated into £ sterling using the exchange rate as of March 2001, that is the date of acquisition;
- the inventory is carried at the lower of cost to the British company (£10,000) and net realisable value (€25,000 translated using the exchange rate at 31 December 2002);
- receivables are translated into £ sterling using the exchange rate at 31 December 2002; and
- the liability to the British company should be offset against the equal amount of the receivable from the Dutch branch.

The resulting exchange differences are recognised as income or expense.

Extract 19.11 *Integral foreign operations*

Renault, France, 31 December 1999 (IAS)

For foreign companies whose activities are an extension of the parent, the historical rate method is applied for non-monetary balance sheet and income statement items and the translation adjustment is included in net income.

Extract 19.12 *Foreign branch*

Saint-Gobain, France, 31 December 1997 (IAS)

The balance sheet of the German branch is included in the balance sheet of Compagnie de Saint-Gobain [the parent].

Fixed assets in foreign currency are translated into French francs at the rate ruling at the time of acquisition or when the relevant asset was classified as fixed. Depreciation is determined on this amount.

Financial investments in foreign currency are translated at the rate ruling at the date of each transaction.

Receivables, payables and loans in foreign currency are translated at the year-end exchange rate.

A consolidation adjustment may be required to reduce the carrying amount of an asset of the foreign operation to its recoverable amount or net realisable value even when no such adjustment is necessary in any financial statements of the foreign operation. Conversely, a write-down in any financial statements of the foreign operation may need to be reversed in the consolidated financial statements of the reporting entity.

19.12 FOREIGN ENTITIES

19.12.1 Foreign Entities that do not Report in the Currency of a Hyperinflationary Economy

The financial statements of a foreign entity that does not report in the currency of a hyperinflationary economy should be translated as follows:

- the foreign entity's assets and liabilities, both monetary and non-monetary, should be translated at the closing rate; and
- the foreign entity's income and expense items should be translated at exchange rates at the dates of the transactions – an average rate is often used as an approximation of the actual rates at each transaction date.

(IAS 21, 30)

The procedures for the translation of the financial statements of a foreign entity are well known and are broadly the same as those in a number of national accounting requirements.

Goodwill arising on the acquisition of a foreign entity by the reporting entity does not appear in the financial statements of the foreign entity. It may be treated as either an asset of the reporting entity or as an asset of the foreign entity (IAS 21, 33). If goodwill is treated as an asset of the reporting entity, it is not adjusted in periods subsequent to the acquisition for changes in exchange rates. If goodwill is treated as an asset of the foreign entity, it is restated each period subsequent to the acquisition so that it is translated at the closing rate at the balance sheet date.

IAS 21 allows the same flexibility in dealing with the fair value adjustments arising on the acquisition of the foreign entity (IAS 21, 33). If the fair value adjustments are treated as assets and liabilities of the reporting entity, they are not adjusted in periods subsequent to the acquisition for changes in exchange rates. If fair value adjustments are treated as assets and liabilities of the foreign entity, they are restated each period subsequent to the acquisition so that they are translated at the closing rate at the balance sheet date.

When the financial statements of a foreign entity are drawn up to a different reporting date from that of the reporting entity, the assets and liabilities of the foreign entity are translated at the exchange rate at the balance sheet date of the foreign entity (IAS 21, 35). The reporting entity adjusts for significant movements in exchange rates up to the balance sheet date of the reporting entity in accordance with IAS 27 (IAS 21, 35).

> ***IASB improvements project***
>
> In its May 2002 exposure draft, the IASB proposes to require that both goodwill and fair value adjustments should be treated as assets and liabilities of the acquired foreign entity and, therefore, that they should be translated at the closing rate at the balance sheet date.

The translation of the financial statements of a foreign entity results in the reporting of exchange differences in the consolidated financial statements of the reporting entity arising from:

- translating income and expense items at the exchange rates at the dates of transactions and assets and liabilities at the closing rate;
- translating the opening net investment in the foreign entity at an exchange rate different from that at which it was previously reported; and
- other changes to equity in the foreign entity.

The exchange differences should be classified as equity until the disposal of the foreign entity (IAS 21, 30).

Under IAS 21 [1983], these exchange differences remained in equity even after the disposal of the foreign entity. IAS 21 now prohibits this treatment. The change from IAS 21 [1983] was made in order to bring the IAS into line with North American requirements. The proposed change attracted adverse comment from a number of sources when it was exposed in E44. Some companies were concerned about the practical difficulties of identifying the cumulative amount of exchange differences relating to a particular foreign entity; others were concerned about re-cycling prior period items through the income statement. The change also means that cumulative exchange differences are dealt with differently from cumulative revaluation surpluses on the disposal of property, plant and equipment. The re-cycling through the income statement of gains and losses initially recorded in equity is being reconsidered as part of the IASB's project on performance reporting.

The exchange differences which relate to any minority interest in the foreign entity are allocated to, and reported as, part of the minority interest in the consolidated balance sheet (IAS 21, 32).

The incorporation of the financial statements of a foreign entity into those of the reporting entity follows normal consolidation procedures, such as the elimination of intra-group balances and intra-group transactions of a subsidiary (see chapter 15). However, an exchange difference arising on an intra-group monetary item cannot be eliminated against a corresponding amount arising on other intra-group balances because the monetary item represents a commitment to convert one currency into another and exposes the reporting entity to a gain or loss through currency fluctuations. Accordingly, in the consolidated financial statements of the reporting entity, such an exchange difference continues to be recognised as income or expenses (IAS 21, 34). If, however, the difference arises from a monetary item that, in substance, forms part of the reporting entity's net investment in the foreign entity, it is classified as equity until the disposal of the net investment (IAS 21, 16 and 34).

19.12.2 Foreign Entities that Report in the Currency of a Hyperinflationary Economy

The financial statements of a foreign entity that reports in the currency of a hyperinflationary economy should be restated in accordance with IAS 29, before being translated into the measurement currency of the reporting entity (IAS 21, 36). The foreign entity's income and expense items should be translated at the closing rate (IAS 21, 30(b)). The restatement of financial statements in accordance with IAS 29 is dealt with in chapter 42.

Many foreign entities that operate in hyperinflationary economies prepare their financial statements in a stable currency. For example, many foreign entities in Latin America prepare their financial statements in US dollars. There is no need to restate these financial statements before they are translated, if necessary, into the measurement currency of the reporting entity. However, SIC 19 may preclude the use of a stable currency as the reporting currency of the foreign entity. The SIC argues that it is not appropriate that the foreign entity can avoid the requirements of IAS 29 by its choice of measurement currency. In its May 2002 improvements exposure draft, the IASB reinforces this message. When the entity's functional currency is that of a hyperinflationary economy, the entity must first apply IAS 29 and then translate the financial statements. When the foreign entity's functional currency is not that of a hyperinflationary economy, IAS 29 is not applied.

19.12.3 Disposal of Foreign Entities

The cumulative amount of exchange differences which have been included in equity should be recognised as income or an expense on disposal of that foreign entity (IAS 21, 30 and 37). The amount is recognised in the same period in which the gain or loss on disposal is recognised. When the reporting entity disposes of part of the foreign entity, the reporting entity recognises the relevant proportion of the cumulative amount of exchange differences as income or expenses; for example, the reporting entity recognises 30% of the cumulative exchange differences as income or expenses when it disposes of 30% of its investment in the foreign entity.

Under this requirement, the entity has to:

- track the cumulative amount of exchange differences that relates to each foreign entity; and
- determine when a disposal or partial disposal of the foreign entity has taken place.

A disposal of a foreign entity may result from a sale, liquidation, repayment of share capital or abandonment of the entity (IAS 21, 38). When the reporting entity sells or abandons the whole of, or liquidates, the foreign entity, all the cumulative exchange differences are recognised as income or expenses. Partial disposals create more practical difficulties particularly when the activities of the foreign entity have been reorganised within the group.

It is also important to understand what is, and what is not, a partial disposal. When the reporting entity sells or abandons part of its investment in the foreign entity, the reporting entity recognises as income or expense the appropriate proportion of the cumulative exchange differences. When the reporting entity sells, liquidates or abandons part of the operations of (rather than its investment in) the foreign entity or a subsidiary of the foreign entity, the calculations become more difficult.

The issue is more difficult to resolve when the foreign entity pays a dividend to the reporting entity. When the payment of the dividend by the foreign entity constitutes a return on the investment, the dividend is not a partial disposal (IAS 21, 38); therefore, a dividend paid out of the post-acquisition profits of the foreign entity is not a partial disposal. When the payment of the dividend by the foreign entity constitutes a return of the investment, the dividend is a partial disposal (IAS 21, 38); therefore, a dividend paid out of pre-acquisition profits, or what in some countries is called a capital dividend, may be a partial disposal. Similarly, a substantial dividend paid out of post-acquisition profits which is in substance a return of the investment is a partial disposal.

A write-down of the carrying amount of the foreign entity is not a disposal (IAS 21, 38). However, a write-down often arises on the liquidation or abandonment of a foreign entity and the liquidation or abandonment is a disposal or partial disposal (as appropriate).

Extract 19.13 *Foreign entities*

Roche, Switzerland, 31 December 2001 (IAS)

Upon consolidation assets and liabilities of Group companies using measurement currencies other than Swiss francs (foreign entities) are translated into Swiss francs using year-end rates of exchange. Sales, costs, expenses, net income and cash flows are translated at the average rates of exchange for the year. Translation differences due to the changes in exchange rates between the beginning and the end of the year and the difference between net income translated at the average and year-end exchange rates are taken directly to equity. On the divestment of a foreign entity, the identified cumulative currency translation differences relating to that foreign entity are recognised in income as part of the gain or loss on divestment.

Extract 19.14 *Foreign subsidiaries*

Renault, France, 31 December 1999 (IAS)

In general, the financial statements of foreign subsidiaries are translated as follows:

- Balance sheet items other than shareholders' equity, are translated at the year-end rate of exchange.
- Income statement items are translated at the average exchange rate for the year.
- The translation adjustment is included in consolidated shareholders' equity and has no impact on net income.

The financial statements of foreign subsidiaries with autonomous activities operating in high inflationary economies (where total inflation over three years exceeded 100%) are translated as follows:

- Balance sheet items are translated into French francs at the year-end rate used for the transfer of dividends after adjusting non-monetary items for local inflation.
- After adjustment of monetary items for inflation, items in the income statement are translated using the same year-end rate as for the balance sheet.
- The translation adjustment is included in shareholders' equity and has no impact on net income.

Extract 19.15 *Foreign subsidiaries*

Fiat, Italy, 31 December 1997 (IAS)

The balance sheets of foreign subsidiaries are translated into Italian lire applying the exchange rates in effect at the year end. The statements of operations of foreign subsidiaries are translated using the average exchange rates, except for those subsidiaries operating in high-inflation countries (cumulative inflation in excess of 100% in three years), in which case they are translated at year-end exchange rates in accordance with IAS

21. The effects of inflation on monetary assets are allocated among various income statement captions.

Exchange differences resulting from the translation of opening stockholders' equity at current exchange rates used at the end of the previous year, as well as differences between net income expressed at average exchange rates and that expressed at current exchange rates, are reflected in stockholders' equity caption 'Foreign exchange translation differences'. Such reserves relating to investments in subsidiaries or associated companies are included in the statement of operations upon the sale of the investments to third parties.

Extract 19.16 *Foreign entities*

South African Breweries, South Africa, 31 March 1998

Financial statements of foreign subsidiaries are translated into South African rand as follows:

Assets and liabilities at rates of exchange ruling at the reporting entities' financial year-end.

Income, expenditure and cash flow items at the weighted average rates of exchange during the relevant financial year.

Differences arising on translation are reflected in non-distributable reserves. Where year-ends are non-coterminous, appropriate adjustment is made for major movements in translation rates occurring in the intervening period to 31 March.

19.13 CHANGE IN CLASSIFICATION OF A FOREIGN OPERATION

A change in classification of a foreign operation is made when there is a change in the nature of the foreign operation. The change is a change in circumstances; it is not a change in accounting policy. The translation procedures applicable to the revised classification should be applied from the date of the change in the classification (IAS 21, 39).

When a foreign operation that is integral to the operations of the reporting entity is reclassified as a foreign entity, the non-monetary assets of the foreign operation are translated into the measurement currency using the exchange rate at the date of the reclassification. The resulting exchange differences are classified as equity (IAS 21, 40).

When a foreign entity is reclassified as a foreign operation that is integral to the operation of the reporting entity, the translated amounts for non-monetary items at the date of the reclassification are treated as the historical cost of those items in the period of change and subsequent periods (IAS 21, 40). Exchange differences which have been classified as equity in previous periods remain in equity until the disposal of the operation (IAS 21, 40).

19.14 DISCLOSURE

An entity should disclose the amount of exchange differences included in the net profit or loss for the period (IAS 21, 42(a)). This includes the amount recognised as income or expenses on the disposal of a foreign entity.

An entity should disclose:

- net exchange differences classified as equity as a separate component of equity; and
- a reconciliation of the amount of such exchange differences at the beginning and end of the period.

(IAS 21, 42(b))

Extract 19.17 *Reconciliation of cumulative exchange differences*

Minorco, Luxembourg, December 31, 1997 (IAS)

The adjustments arising from the translation into US dollars of the assets and the liabilities of subsidiary companies, joint ventures and equity accounted investees are as follows:

	1997	1996
Cumulative translation at the beginning of the year	**66.9**	42.1
Translation adjustment for the year	**58.6**	24.8
Cumulative translation adjustment at the end of the year	**125.5**	66.9

An entity should also disclose the amount of exchange differences arising during the period which is included in the carrying amount of an asset in accordance with the allowed alternative treatment (IAS 21, 42).

When there is a change in the classification of a significant foreign operation, an entity should disclose:

- the nature of the change in classification;
- the reason for the change;
- the impact of the change in classification on shareholders' equity; and
- the impact on net profit or loss for each prior period presented had the change in classification occurred at the beginning of the earliest period presented.

(IAS 21, 44)

An entity should disclose the method selected to translate goodwill and fair value adjustments arising on the acquisition of a foreign entity (IAS 21, 45).

An entity should disclose the effect on foreign currency monetary items or the financial statements of a foreign operation of a change in exchange rates occurring after the balance sheet date if the change is of such importance that non-disclosure would affect the ability of users of the financial statements to make proper evaluations and decisions (see IAS 10) (IAS 21, 46).

Some of the disclosures required by IAS 32 and IAS 39 relate to foreign currency transactions (see chapter 20).

Notes

1 *Accounting for the Introduction of the Euro*, European Commission, Brussels, 1997.

2 Simpson, E. Raymond, 'Comparative Analysis of IAS 21 ... and Related US GAAP', in *The IASC – US GAAP Comparison Project: A Report of Similarities and Differences Between IASC standards and US GAAP*, ed Carrie Bloomer, Norwalk, CT, FASB, 1996, pp315–6.

CHAPTER 20

Financial Assets and Financial Liabilities

20.1 RELEVANT STANDARDS AND INTERPRETATION

IAS 32 *Financial Instruments: Presentation and Disclosure*
IAS 39 *Financial Instruments: Recognition and Measurement*
SIC 5 *Classification of Financial Instruments – Contingent Settlement Provisions*
SIC 16 *Share Capital – Reacquired Own Equity Instruments (Treasury Shares)*
SIC 17 *Equity – Costs of an Equity Transaction*
SIC 33 *Consolidation and Equity Method – Potential Voting Rights and Allocation of Ownership Interest*
IAS 39 *Implementation Guidance Questions and Answers January 2002* (IGC)

Those aspects of IAS 32 dealing with the offsetting of financial assets and financial liabilities are dealt with in chapter 9 and with the classification and presentation of instruments between liabilities and equity in chapter 28.

IAS 32, IAS 39 and the questions and answers issued by the IGC total 600 pages of standards and guidance. It is not possible to deal with this amount of detail in a book of this nature. Therefore, this chapter seeks to summarise the main requirements and to indicate where further guidance, particularly the IGC questions and answers, may be obtained. The chapter also includes extracts from the annual reports of several companies. The chapter may be sufficient for those entities that have only straightforward financial instruments. The chapter inevitably includes insufficient guidance for those entities with more complex instruments. Such entities must study carefully the requirements of IAS 32, IAS 39 and the questions and answers.

All entities need to bear in mind that the IASB has proposed significant changes to some aspects of IAS 39 (see 20.2.6). The proposals do not change the fundamental accounting approach in IAS 39 but they do affect such issues as impairment, derecognition and hedge accounting.

20.2 HISTORY

20.2.1 The Early Stages

The IASC commenced its financial instruments project in 1988 (*IASC News*, September 1998, p 1). It recognised that the existence of financial instruments 'may be crucial in the assessment of the financial position and the performance of an entity'. It noted that the issues involved were attracting the attention of standard setters, regulators and the preparers and users of financial statements.

The IASC's decision followed shortly after an OECD symposium in which 200 delegates from OECD member countries, advisory bodies and observers had debated accounting for new financial instruments (*IASC News*, September 1988, p 2). The IASC's announcement of its forthcoming project was welcomed by the symposium. The IASC committed itself to take into account the many questions raised at the symposium and to work closely with national and regional standard setting bodies and experts from outside the accountancy profession. As the then IASC chairman George Barthes commented: 'It is evident that accountants alone cannot resolve all the issues which have been raised.'

The IASC decided to appoint a steering committee for this project which reflected 'a balance of backgrounds, including bankers, users of financial statements and representatives of industrial and commercial entities as well as accountants in public practice'. (*IASC News*, September 1998, p 1). This decision was overruled by the accountancy bodies which insisted on appointing six accountants from public accounting firms to the eight member steering committee – the other two members were a banker and an academic[1].

The IASC also set up a special consultative group to provide additional input from other users and preparers of financial statements (*IASC News*, June 1988, p 1). This group included representatives of bankers, businesses, financial analysts, the Basel committee, IOSCO, stock exchanges, the FASB, the European accountancy profession (FEE), auditors (IAPC) and the OECD. This was the first occasion on which the IASC had set up such a group.

Before the project started, the IASC and the accounting standards committee (AcSC)[2] of the Canadian Institute of Chartered Accountants (CICA) agreed to co-operate in the development of international and Canadian standards on financial instruments (*IASC News*, January 1989, p 4). The CICA has identified a need for standards on financial instruments and the AcSC concluded that the best way to make progress was to 'throw in its lot' with the IASC (*IASC Insight*, July 1991, pp 10-11). As the IASC's then secretary-general, I commented: 'This co-operation fits well with the IASC's belief that improvements in IASs cannot be separated from developments in national requirements' (*IASC News*, January 1989, p 4).

The intention of both the IASC and the AcSC was that they would both consider and approve the same documents. This generally proved to be the case with the DSOP, E40, E48 and IAS 32 although, as explained below, there were some differences. The procedure adopted throughout the project was that the IASC approved documents before they were submitted for approval to the AcSB although the IASC was usually aware at the time of its deliberations of the AcSB's likely views.

The CICA also agreed to provide the staff support for the project and there is no doubt that without such high level and high quality support the IASC would not have been able to carry out the project. John Carchrae, the CICA's then assistant director, accounting standards, managed the project from its inception in 1988 to 1995. Peter Martin made a significant contribution to E48 and IAS 32. Ian Hague took over responsibility for the project in 1996 and played a major part in the development of the 1997 discussion paper and supported the joint working group. The IASC staff were responsible for IAS 39 which, as explained below, was seen as an interim standard.

At its first meeting in January 1989, the steering committee agreed that the project should:

- focus on accounting for financial instruments by all types of business entities rather than just by financial institutions;
- deal with all types of financial instruments rather than a subset such as options, futures and swaps; and
- consider recognition (including derecognition), measurement and disclosure issues rather than only some issues.

(*IASC News*, April 1989, p 3)

This comprehensive approach was followed throughout the project.

20.2.2 Statement of Principles

The steering committee approved the DSOP in March 1990 and distributed it on a restricted basis for comments by June 1990[3]. The DSOP took broadly the same approach as that followed in E40, E48 and, indeed, IAS 39 but with one important exception. While the DSOP required that operating (trading) financial assets and financial liabilities should be measured at fair value, it did not permit the measurement of investing and financing items at fair value.

The IASC approved the DSOP in November 1990 but did not reach a firm conclusion on the measurement of investing and financing items. The IASC decided that, as a minimum, an entity should be allowed to measure all financial assets and financial liabilities, other than those designated as hedges, at fair value. The IASC also discussed the possibility of establishing fair value as the benchmark, rather than the allowed alternative, for non-trading financial assets and financial liabilities.

20.2.3 E40, E48 and IAS 32

In June 1991, the IASC approved E40 (*IASC Update*, June 1991, p 1); the CICA's AcSB approved a virtually identical exposure draft shortly afterwards. The IASC resolved the measurement issue by proposing:

- the use of fair value for all operating financial assets and financial liabilities (but with hedging items measured on the same basis as the positions they hedged);
- a benchmark treatment of historical cost based amounts for investing and financing financial assets and financial liabilities (again with hedging items measured on the same basis as the positions they hedged); and
- an allowed alternative treatment of fair values for non-operating financial assets and financial liabilities.

(*IASC Update*, June 1991, p 1)

The CICA's exposure draft was different from E40 in two respects:

- the CICA draft did not include the allowed alternative treatment for non-operating financial assets and financial liabilities; and
- the two drafts contained different criteria for the designation of a hedge.

The IASC and the CICA agreed to allow nine months for comments on the draft[4].

Following its review of the 192 comment letters on both exposure drafts, the IASC invited comments on its tentative conclusions through a special issue of *IASC Insight* in May 1993. The substantial majority of responses to these tentative conclusions emphasised the need for re-exposure (*IASC Update*, November 1993, p 2). While a significant minority on the IASC board favoured the immediate adoption of an IAS, the IASC decided to issue a revised exposure draft. E48 was published in January 1994. An equivalent Canadian exposure draft was published in April 1994[5].

As part of its consultations, the IASC invited representatives of standard setting bodies in twenty countries to discuss E48 with the board of the IASC in June 1994 (*IASC Insight*, September 1994, pp 5–6). The purpose of the discussion was twofold:

- to receive the comments of the standard setting bodies on the proposals in E48; and
- to learn of the experiences of the standard setting bodies in dealing with similar issues in their own countries.

While all the standard setting bodies supported the IASC's efforts and its valuable role in identifying the issues that needed to be resolved, many had serious reservations about major parts of E48. Several standard setting bodies supported splitting E48. They felt that E48's proposals on disclosure were a significant step forward and should form the basis of the first IAS. Several said that if the IASC adopted this approach they would bring their national disclosure requirements into line with the resulting IAS. They also agreed to work with the IASC to resolve the more complex issues of recognition and measurement (*IASC Insight*, September 1994, p 6).

In November 1994, following its review of the comment letters on E48 and the equivalent Canadian exposure draft, together with the input from national standard setting bodies, the IASC decided to deal with the project in two stages – presentation and disclosure in March 1995 and recognition and measurement by the end of 1995 (or 1996 if a further exposure draft was required). The decision was made in spite of considerable concern being expressed by many members of the IASC board. They favoured the adoption of an IAS based on E48 and feared that a split would delay the completion of the work on recognition and measurement. The IASC did emphasise that it would complete the recognition and measurement stage as a matter of 'high priority' (*IASC Update*, November 1994, p 1).

The presentation and disclosure stage was completed in March 1995 with the approval of IAS 32. The equivalent Canadian standard, *3860 Financial Instruments: Disclosure and Presentation* was approved early in 1995. Both standards applied to accounting periods beginning on or after 1 January 1996[6].

20.2.4 1997 Discussion Paper

The IASC's intention at the end of 1994 was to resolve the outstanding issues on recognition and measurement in conjunction with national standard setting bodies and other members of the IASC's constituency. The IASC also decided in November 1994 to reconsider the membership of the financial instruments steering committee. A new committee was formed with the aim of producing a 'progress report' to the IASC board in March 1996 (*IASC Insight*, June 1995, p 3). The new committee was supported by an advisory group which benefited from advice from representatives of major national accounting standard setters[7].

It was soon clear that the original plan to complete the project by the end of 1995 or 1996 had been replaced by a 'second phase' which would take a number of years. As John Carchrae explained[8]: 'Now is an appropriate time to stand back and re-evaluate the issues in a comprehensive and co-ordinated manner to ensure a consistent understanding among standard-setters and their constituents of the interrelationships among issues. The aim is to establish a comprehensive and harmonised framework within which measurement and recognition issues for all financial instruments can be resolved. Such a framework is more likely to withstand the test of time and avoid the inconsistencies that currently plague practice and national standards in some countries.'

The outcome of this effort was the 1997 discussion paper *Accounting for Financial Assets and Financial Liabilities* which proposed 'far reaching changes' including:

- more comprehensive balance sheet recognition of financial assets and financial liabilities from the time that an entity becomes party to a financial instrument;
- measurement of financial assets and financial liabilities at fair value regardless of management's intention to hold or trade the items;
- presentation of changes in fair value immediately as income or expense but with some provision for the presentation of some hedging gains and losses outside the income statement; and
- some modifications to the disclosure requirements in IAS 32.

(*IASC Insight*, June 1997, p 7)

In terms of quality, the discussion paper is, without doubt, the best document ever produced by the IASC. It was largely written by the chairman of the new steering committee, Alex Milburn, assisted by the CICA project director, Ian Hague[9].

The IASC again consulted extensively on these proposals. While the discussion paper was widely praised as a high-quality document, it was clear that further work was needed 'on a number of key matters, including how far a subsequent standard could practicably go in the direction of full fair value accounting' (*IASC Insight*, December 1997, p 11). Furthermore, the IASC recognised that applying the concept to traditional banking activities still presented difficulty and that there was widespread unease about including some unrealised gains in income (*IASC Insight*, October 1997, p 5). The IASC would also have faced a problem approving an IAS based on the discussion paper. During the development of both E40 and E48, less than half the board had supported a full fair value approach. In spite of the quality of the discussion paper, it was unlikely that there was the necessary three-quarters majority for such an approach.

20.2.5 An Interim Standard

Even before the IASC had time to consider the comments on the discussion paper, a new proposal emerged. The IASC's secretary-general, Sir Bryan Carsberg, announced that the IASC staff would be recommending to the IASC board at its October 1997 meeting that the IASC should:

- adopt US standards on financial instruments (including FAS 133 which was due for approval in 1998); and
- join with national standard setters, including the FASB, to work to agree a harmonised international standard.

(*IASC press release*, 8 September 1997)

It was felt that this approach would improve financial reporting throughout the world in the short term and the long term. Perhaps, more importantly, it would enable the IASC to complete the IOSCO core standards by the IASC's self-imposed deadline of April 1998. As Sir Bryan Carsberg explained[10]: 'In the view of the IASC staff, it is not acceptable to be relaxed about the possibility that the process of completing the core set of international standards will take another two or three years.' He saw the FASB's standards an as 'acceptable way forward' for an interim standard which would complete the core standards.

In making the proposal, the IASC staff did not see the FASB standards as a 'satisfactory long-term solution' – hence the proposal to work with other standard setting bodies on a long-term solution. As Sir Bryan Carsberg explained: 'The complexities and controversies of the subject mean that the best solution to accounting for financial instruments will be found only if all leading standard setters work together.' This part of the proposal was neither controversial nor new – it had been the IASC's policy throughout the financial instruments project.

What was controversial and new was the proposal to adopt US standards as IASs and to do so as an interim solution. Many IASC members did not support the idea of adopting the standards of one particular country particularly as the whole rationale of the agreement with IOSCO was to allow non-US companies to raise capital and list their securities in the United States without having to use US GAAP. There were also concerns about due process – the IASC was being asked to vote only in favour of or against the proposal without the power to amend the proposed text. To complicate matters further, even FASB members and staff were unsure how to define US standards for this purpose. IASC members were also unhappy with the attempt to integrate a different style of standards into IASs.

The IASC eventually agreed to complete an interim standard but rejected the proposal that it should adopt US standards (*IASC Update*,

November 1997, pp 1–2). It agreed that it should develop a new exposure draft although it was clear that it would be based on US standards rather than the IASC's earlier proposals in E48. The timetable for the interim standard envisaged the development and the approval of the exposure draft in six months, a comment period of three to four months and two months for the IASC to consider the comments and approve the IAS.

E62 *Financial Instruments: Recognition and Measurement* was developed by the IASC staff, approved by the board in April 1998 and published in mid July 1998. Paul Pacter, the IASC's manager on the project, provided a summary of the proposals and the reasons for them[11]. The IASC allowed only three and a half months for comments on E62 but during that time consulted extensively on the proposals. The comments were reviewed by a specially appointed steering committee; the IASC had not appointed a committee to develop E62.

IAS 39 *Financial Instruments: Recognition and Measurement* was approved at a specially scheduled meeting in December 1998 in order that the IASC could complete the core standards in accordance with its self-imposed deadline. The speed with which IAS 39 was developed and the comments on E62 were reviewed led to some criticisms. Furthermore IAS 39 incorporated a number of major changes from the proposals in E62.

IAS 39 was published in March 1999 and applied to accounting periods beginning on or after 1 January 2001. Earlier application was not permitted for accounting periods which ended prior to the publication of IAS 39.

In March 2000, the IASC appointed the IAS 39 implementation guidance committee (IGC) to develop and publish implementation guidance on IAS 39 in the form of questions and answers (Q&A). Six batches of draft Q&A were issued during 2000/2001. The final versions of the Q&As is included in *International Accounting Standards 2002*. A list of the Q&As is included in Table 20.1.

The Q&As do not have the status of a Standard or an Interpretation. They were not formally considered by the board and do not necessarily represent the views of the board, although the board was able to comments on the draft Q&As. The status of the Q&As is currently, therefore, as follows:

> Since the implementation guidance has been developed to be consistent with the requirements and guidance provided in IAS 39, other Standards, Interpretations of the Standing Interpretations Committee, and the IASB Framework, entities should consider the guidance as they select and apply accounting policies in accordance with IAS 1, 20-22.
> (*International Accounting Standards 2002*, 39 IGC-2)

It should be borne in mind, however, that the IASB proposes to incorporate virtually all the Q&As in the revised version of IAS 39 (see 20.2.6). Therefore any uncertainty about their status will be removed. A few Q&As will become redundant because of proposed changes to IAS 39 itself, for example some of those dealing with the impairment and recognition of financial assets where the underlying requirements of IAS 39 will change.

Table 20.1 *IAS 39 Implementation Guidance*

	Question
SCOPE	
Scope: financial guarantee contracts	1-1
Scope: credit derivatives	1-2
Scope: financial reinsurance	1-3-a
Scope: insurance contracts	1-3-b
Scope: investments in associates	1-4
Scope: financial guarantee contracts	1-5-a
Scope: issued financial guarantee contract	1-5-b
Scope: contracts with more than one underlying	1-6
DEFINITIONS	
From IAS 32	
Definition of a financial instrument: gold bullion	8-1
Additional definitions	
Definition of a derivative: examples of derivatives and underlyings	10-1
Definition of a derivative: settlement at a future date, interest rate swap with net or gross settlement	10-2
Definition of a derivative: gross exchange of currencies	10-3
Definition of a derivative: prepaid interest rate swap (fixed rate payment obligation prepaid at inception or subsequently)	10-4-a
Definition of a derivative: prepaid pay-variable, receive-fixed interest rate swap	10-4-b
Definition of a derivative: contract to purchase fixed rate debt	10-5
Definition of a derivative: settlement amount does not vary proportionately	10-6
Definition of originated loans and receivables: banks' deposits in other banks	10-7
Definition of a derivative: offsetting loans	10-8
Definition of trading activities: balancing a portfolio	10-9
Definition of a derivative: initial net investment	10-10
Definition of originated loans and receivables	10-11-a

Table 20.1 *IAS 39 Implementation Guidance (continued)*	**Question**
Definition of originated loans and receivables: equity security	10-11-b
Definition of amortised cost: debt instruments with stepped interest payments	10-12
Definition of amortised cost: perpetual debt instruments with fixed or market-based variable rate	10-13
Definition of amortised cost: perpetual debt instruments with decreasing interest rate	10-14
Definition of held for trading: purpose of acquisition	10-15
Definition of held-to-maturity investment: high default risk	10-16
Definition of held-to-maturity investment: fixed maturity	10-17
Definition of a derivative: option not expected to be exercised	10-18
Effective interest method: expected future cash flows	10-19
Loans and receivables originated by the enterprise: sovereign debt	10-20
Definition of held for trading: portfolio with a recent actual pattern of short term profit taking	10-21
Elaboration on the definitions	
Liability vs. equity classification	11-1
Definition of a derivative: royalty agreements	13-1
Definition of a derivative: foreign currency contract based on sales volume	13-2
Practice of settling net: forward contract to purchase a commodity	14-1
Forward contract to purchase a commodity: pattern of net settlement	14-2
Option to put a non-financial asset	14-3
Definition of a derivative: prepaid forward	15-1
Definition of a derivative: initial net investment	15-2
Regular way contracts: no established market	16-1
Regular way contracts: forward contract	16-2
Regular way contracts: which customary settlement provisions apply?	16-3
Regular way contracts: share purchase by call option	16-4
Liabilities held for trading: short sales	18-1
Liability held for trading: short sales of loan assets	18-2
Embedded derivatives	
Embedded derivatives: separation of host debt instrument	22-1
Embedded derivatives: separation of embedded option	22-2
Embedded derivatives: presentation	23-1
Embedded derivatives: accounting for convertible bond	23-2
Embedded derivatives: allocation of carrying amounts	23-3

Table 20.1 *IAS 39 Implementation Guidance (continued)*	**Question**
Separation of embedded derivatives	23-4
Commodity-indexed interest	23-5
Embedded derivatives: transferable derivative that is attached to a non-derivative financial instrument	23-6
Embedded derivatives: derivative attached to a financial instrument by a third party	23-7
Embedded derivatives: more than one embedded derivative	23-8
Embedded derivatives: equity kicker	23-9
Embedded derivatives: no reliable measurement	23-10
Embedded derivatives: issued puttable convertible debt	23-11
Embedded derivatives: debt or equity host contract	23-12
Embedded derivatives: synthetic instruments	25-1
Embedded derivatives: purchases and sales contracts in foreign currency	25-2
Embedded derivatives: dual currency bond	25-3
Embedded foreign currency derivative: unrelated foreign currency provision	25-4
Embedded foreign currency derivative: currency of international commerce	25-5
Foreign currency derivative: currency of primary economic environment	25-6
Embedded derivatives: holder permitted, but not required, to settle without recovering substantially all of its recorded investment	25-7
Embedded derivatives: purchase price subject to a cap and a floor	25-8
Embedded derivatives: hard currency supply contracts	25-9
RECOGNITION	
Initial recognition	
Recognition and derecognition of financial liabilities using trade date or settlement date accounting	27-1
Recognition: cash collateral	27-2
Trade date vs. settlement date	
Regular way transactions: loan commitments	30-1
Trade date vs. settlement date: net settlement	30-2
Trade date vs. settlement date: amounts to be recorded for a sale	34-1
Derecognition of a financial asset	
Derecognition of a portion of a loan with disproportionate risk sharing	35-1
Factors affecting derecognition of a portion of a loan	35-2
Factors affecting derecognition of financial assets transferred to a special purpose entity	35-3

Table 20.1 *IAS 39 Implementation Guidance (continued)*	**Question**
Interaction between recognition and derecognition requirements	35-4
Derecognition: wash sale transaction	35-5
Derivatives that serve as impediments to the derecognition of a financial asset	36-1
Derecognition: full recourse	37-1
Derecognition: right of first refusal	38-1
Derecognition: put option	38-2
Derecognition: repo or securities lending transaction and right of substitution	38-3
Derecognition: deep-in-the money put option held by transferee	38-4
Derecognition: clean-up call	38-5
Derecognition: call option on beneficial interest in SPE	41-1
Derecognition of part of a financial asset	
Estimating fair values when a portion of financial assets is sold – bonds	47-1
Estimating fair values when a portion of financial assets is sold – loans	47-2
Derecognition of part of a financial asset: interest-only strips and servicing assets	50-1
Derecognition of a financial liability	
Derecognition of financial liabilities: third party receives a fee to assume the obligation	57-1
Derecognition of financial liabilities: buy-back of bond obligation with intention to resell	57-2
Derecognition of a financial liability: joint responsibility for debt	57-3
Extinguishment of debt: substantially different terms	62-1
MEASUREMENT	
Initial measurement of financial assets and financial liabilities	
Initial measurement: transaction costs	66-1
Transaction costs	66-2
Initial measurement: interest-free loan	66-3
Subsequent measurement of financial assets	
Reliability of fair value measurement	70-1
Fair value measurement for an unquoted equity instrument	70-2
Reliable determination of fair value: embedded derivatives	70-3
Example of calculating amortised cost: financial asset	73-1

Table 20.1 *IAS 39 Implementation Guidance (continued)*	**Question**
Amortised cost: variable rate debt instrument	76-1
Hedge accounting: non-derivative monetary asset or non-derivative monetary liability used as a hedging instrument	78-1
Held-to-maturity investments	
Held-to-maturity financial assets: index-linked principal	80-1
Held-to-maturity financial assets: index-linked interest	80-2
Held-to-maturity financial assets: permitted sales	83-1
Held-to-maturity financial assets: change of intent or ability – permitted sales	83-2
Held-to-maturity financial assets: insignificant exercises of put options and insignificant transfers	83-3
Held-to-maturity financial assets: tainting	83-4
Held-to-maturity investments: sub-categorisation for the purposes of applying the tainting rule	83-5
Held-to-maturity investments: application of the 'tainting' rule on consolidation	83-6
Held-to-maturity financial assets: sale following rating downgrade	83-7
Held-to-maturity investments: internal downgrade	83-8
Held-to-maturity financial assets: permitted sales	86-1
Sales of held-to-maturity investments: entity-specific capital requirements	86-2
Held-to-maturity financial assets: pledged collateral, repurchase agreements (repos) and securities lending agreements	87-1
Subsequent measurement of financial liabilities	
Amortising discount and premium on liabilities	93-1
Fair value measurement considerations	
Fair value measurement considerations for investment funds	99-1
Fair value measurement: large holding	100-1
Gains and losses on remeasurement to fair value	
Amortisation of premium or discount: classification	103-1
Available-for-sale financial assets: exchange of shares	103-2
Settlement date accounting: fair value changes on sale of financial asset	106-1
Settlement date accounting: exchange of non-cash financial assets	106-2
Reclassification from available-for-sale to trading	107-1
Reclassification to trading: decision to sell	107-2
Impairment and uncollectability of financial assets	
Objective evidence of impairment	109-1
Impairment: future losses	110-1

Table 20.1 *IAS 39 Implementation Guidance (continued)*

	Question
Assessment of impairment: principal and interest	111-1
Assessment of impairment: fair value hedge	111-2
Impairment: provisioning matrix	111-3
Impairment: excess losses	111-4
Recognition of impairment on a portfolio basis	112-1
Impairment: portfolio assessment for individually impaired asset	112-2
Impairment: consideration of the value of collateral	113-1
Impairment: recognition of collateral	113-2
Impairment: observable market price	113-3
Impairment: assets carried at cost because fair value cannot be reliably measured	115-1
Impairment of available-for-sale financial assets	117-1
Impairment of non-monetary available-for-sale financial asset	117-2
Impairment: whether the available-for-sale reserve in equity can be negative	117-3
Impairment: debt instrument remeasured to fair value	118-1
Hedging	
Hedge accounting: management of interest rate risk in financial institutions	121-1
Hedge accounting considerations when interest rate risk is managed on a net basis	121-2
Hedging instruments	
Hedging instrument: hedging using more than one derivative	122-1
Hedging the fair value exposure of a bond denominated in a foreign currency	122-2
Hedging with a non-derivative financial asset or liability	122-3
Hedge accounting: use of written options in combined hedging instruments	124-1
Hedged items	
Hedge accounting: netting of assets and liabilities	127-1
Held-to-maturity investments: hedging variable rate interest rate payments	127-2
Hedged items: purchase of held-to-maturity investment	127-3
Cash flow hedges: reinvestment of funds obtained from held-to-maturity investments	127-4
Whether a derivative can be designated as a hedged item	127-5
Hedge of prepayment risk of a held-to-maturity investment	127-6
Hedge accounting: prepayable financial asset	128-1
Partial term hedging	128-2
Hedge accounting: risk components	128-3

Table 20.1 *IAS 39 Implementation Guidance (continued)*	**Question**
Hedged items: hedge of foreign currency risk of publicly traded shares	128-4
Hedges of more than one type of risk	131-1
Hedging instrument: cross-currency interest rate swap	131-2
Hedging instrument: dual foreign currency forward exchange contract	131-3
Hedge accounting: stock index	132-1
Internal hedges	134-1
Offsetting internal derivative contracts used to manage interest rate risk	134-1-a
Offsetting internal derivative contracts used to manage foreign currency risk	134-1-b
Intra-group and intra-company hedging transactions	134-2
Internal contracts: single offsetting external derivative	134-3
Internal contracts: external derivative contracts that are settled net	134-4
Hedge accounting	
Fair value hedge: risk that could affect reported income	137-1
Cash flow hedge: anticipated fixed rate debt issuance	137-2
Hedge accounting: unrecognised assets	137-3
Hedge accounting: hedging of future foreign currency revenue streams	137-4
Cash flow hedges: all in one hedge	137-5
Hedge relationships: enterprise-wide risk	137-6
Cash flow hedge: fixed interest rate cash flows	137-7
Cash flow hedge: reinvestment of fixed interest rate cash flows	137-8
Foreign currency hedge	137-9
Foreign currency cash flow hedge	137-10
Fair value hedge: variable rate debt instrument	137-11
Fair value hedge: inventory	137-12
Intra-group monetary item that will affect consolidated net income	137-13
Forecasted intra-group foreign currency transactions that will affect consolidated net income	137-14
Concurrent offsetting swaps and use of one as hedging instrument	137-15
Cash flow hedge: forecasted transaction related to an enterprise's equity	137-16
Hedge accounting: forecasted transaction	142-1
Hedging on an after-tax basis	142-2
Hedge effectiveness: assessment on cumulative basis	142-3
Retroactive designation of hedges	142-4
Hedge accounting: identification of hedged forecasted transaction	142-5

Table 20.1 *IAS 39 Implementation Guidance (continued)*	**Question**
Hedge effectiveness: counterparty credit risk	142-6
Hedge accounting: designation at the inception of the hedge	142-7
Cash flow hedge: documentation of timing of forecasted transaction	142-8
Combination of written and purchased options	144-1
Delta-neutral hedging strategy	144-2
Hedging instrument: out-of-the-money put option	144-3
Hedging instrument: proportion of the cash flows of a cash instrument	145-1
Assessing hedge effectiveness	
Hedge effectiveness: effectiveness tests	146-1
Hedge effectiveness: less than 100 per cent offset	146-2
Hedge effectiveness: under-hedging	146-3
Assuming perfect hedge effectiveness	147-1
Hedge accounting: risk of a transaction not occurring	149-1
Fair value hedges	
Fair value hedge: measurement of a non-derivative hedging instrument	153-1
Fair value hedge: amortisation of the adjustment to the carrying amount of a hedged interest bearing financial instrument	157-1
Cash flow hedges	
Cash flow hedges: performance of hedging instrument	158-1
Cash flow hedges: performance of hedging instrument	158-2
Cash flow hedges: forecasted transaction occurs prior to the specified period	158-3
Cash flow hedges: measuring effectiveness for a hedge of a forecasted transaction in a debt instrument	158-4
Cash flow hedges: firm commitment to purchase inventory in a foreign currency	158-5
Cash flow hedge: forecasted issuance of debt in foreign currency	160-1
Cash flow hedges: forecasted transaction that is not highly probable, but is expected to occur	163-1
Hedge accounting: premium or discount on forward exchange contract	164-1
DISCLOSURE	
Disclosure of changes in fair value	170-1
Presentation of interest income	170-2
EFFECTIVE DATE AND TRANSITION	
Transition rules: available-for-sale financial assets previously carried at cost	172-1
Transition rules: cash flow hedges	172-2

Table 20.1 *IAS 39 Implementation Guidance (continued)*	**Question**
Transition rules: previous revaluation under IAS 25	172-3
Transition rules: prior derecognition	172-4
Transition rules: retrospective application of hedging criteria by first-time adopters	172-5
Transition rules: fair value hedges	172-6
Transition rules: held-to-maturity financial assets	172-7
Transition rules: hedge documentation on first day of initial application	172-8
Transition rules: internal hedging derivatives	172-9
Transition: impairment	172-10
INTERACTION BETWEEN IAS 39 AND OTHER IAS	
IAS 7: Hedge accounting: cash flow statements	Other-1
IAS 21: Hedge of a net investment in a foreign entity: whether IAS 39 applies	Other-2
IAS 21: Exchange differences arising on translation of foreign entities: equity or income?	Other-3
IAS 21: Fair value hedge of asset measured at cost	Other-4
Interaction between IAS 39 and IAS 21	Other-5
Available-for-sale financial assets: separation of currency component	Other-6
APPENDICES	
Illustrative example of applying the approach in Question	121-2
Internal derivatives: examples of applying Question	134-1-6

20.2.6 Improvements to IAS 32 and IAS 39

In June 2002, the IASB issued an exposure draft of proposed amendments to IAS 32 and IAS 39 which is intended to improve the existing requirements without changing the fundamental accounting approach. The purpose of the proposed changes is to:

- promote greater consistency and clarity in reporting by allowing greater use of fair values, and underpinning this change by providing fuller guidance and more disclosure;
- provide guidance to ensure that impairment losses (write-downs) in groups of loans or other financial assets are recognised in a timely manner; and
- introduce the tough principle of 'no continuing involvement' to test asset sales (derecognition).

An entity will also be able to:

- measure any financial asset or financial liability at fair value with changes in fair value included in net profit and loss by designating it at initial recognition as held for trading; and
- classify a loan or receivable originated by the entity as an available-for-sale financial asset.

The IASB also proposes that hedges of firm commitments should be treated as fair value, rather than cash flow, hedges. It also proposes to prohibit the reclassification of the deferred gain or loss on the hedging instrument from equity to the carrying amount of the assets or liabilities resulting from the firm commitment.

The IASB will continue to consider issues relating to financial instruments but expects the basic principles of the improved IAS 32 and 39, once finalised, to remain in place for a considerable period.

20.2.7 Joint Working Group

The second part of the September 1997 proposal – to join with national standard setters, including the FASB, to agree a harmonised international standard – reflected the IASC's long standing policy. Throughout the previous nine years of the financial instruments project, right from the April 1998 OECD symposium through the meetings on E48 and the development of the 1997 discussion paper, the IASC had both recognised the importance of such co-operation and had sought to work with and learn from national bodies. Furthermore, IAS 32 had been developed in conjunction with the CICA's AcSB.

Even before the IASC could consider this part of the proposal, G4+1 decided to set up a joint working group (JWG) to complete national and international standards requiring the use of fair values for all financial instruments (*FT World Accounting Report*, October 1997, pp 3-4). The standards would be based on the IASC's discussion paper[12].

G4+1 agreed that the JWG would be chaired by Alex Milburn, the chairman of the IASC's financial instruments steering committee, and would include board members from each of the participating national bodies (Australia, Canada, New Zealand, UK and USA). It would report to G4+1, the IASC and all participating bodies. The establishment of the JWG meant that, for the first time, G4+1 would be developing a standard rather than a discussion paper.

At its October 1997 meeting, the IASC decided to participate in the joint project (*IASC Update*, November 1997, p 1). It also established an advisory group to evaluate the proposals of the JWG. Following the IASC's decision, the JWG was expanded to include representatives of France, Germany, Japan and the Nordic Federation.

In December 2000, the JWG published a draft standard and basis for conclusions which included the following 'far-reaching changes':

- measurement of virtually all financial instruments at fair value;
- recognition of virtually all gains and losses resulting from changes in fair value in the income statements in the periods in which they arise;
- prohibition of special hedge accounting for financial instruments used in hedging relationships;
- adoption of a components approach for accounting for transfers of financial assets; and
- some expansion of disclosures about financial instruments, financial risk positions and income statement effects.

(JWG, *Financial Instruments and Similar Items*, p (i))

The JWG proposals and the responses to them will be considered as part of further IASB work on financial instruments.

In August 1999, the JWG published a discussion paper on *Financial Instruments Issues Relating to Banks*. Subsequently, the Joint Working Group of Banking Associations on Financial Instruments published a paper setting out the banking community's position on the application of fair value accounting to banks[13].

20.3 IOSCO

Financial instruments and a number of related issues are among IOSCO's core standards. Furthermore, IAS 39 was developed in order to complete the core standards by the end of 1998. IOSCO participated in the IASC's financial instruments project since its inception in 1988.

IAS 32 and IAS 39 are included in 'IAS 2000' endorsed by IOSCO in May 2000. There are nine supplemental treatments relating to IAS 32. IOSCO expresses concerns about the need for the following disclosures:

- the effect of separately accounting for the components of compound financial instruments (see chapter 28);
- restrictions on disposals or utilisation of financial assets;
- the composition of financial assets;
- leverage features of certain financial instruments; and
- value at risk.

IOSCO also asks for further guidance on:

- the aggregation of similar financial instruments; and
- the computation of earnings per share when an entity has acquired shares of its own preferred stock for an amount different than the recorded book value of those shares.

IOSCO also expresses the concern that accounting for treasury shares as a deduction of equity may not be consistent with some legal requirements. It argues that shares that are repurchased for trading purposes should be presented as assets in the balance sheet, with any gain or loss on disposal included in profit and loss. It also suggests that SIC 16 should exclude from its scope transferable shares of the entity held by an employee benefit plan that is reflected in the consolidated financial statements.

There are 29 supplemental treatments relating to IAS 39. IOSCO expresses concerns about the following accounting required by IAS 39:

- the use of fair value, rather than cost, for an equity instrument that does not have a quoted market price in an active market;
- the use of non-derivative financial instruments as hedging instruments;
- the ban on the use of some non-derivatives as hedging instruments;
- the use of fair value for a contract that includes an embedded derivative if the embedded derivative cannot be measured separately;
- the inclusion of some changes in the fair value of financial assets directly in equity;
- the retention of unrealised gains in equity upon the reclassification of an asset to an amortised cost basis;
- the use of fair value for derivatives that hedge cost measured items;
- the use of cost for a liability that funds trading activities;
- the inclusion of an entity's own creditworthiness in the measurement of the fair value of a liability;
- the use of an individual item approach for the measurement of the impairment of a portfolio of homogenous assets such as loans, receivables (debtors) or securities;
- the inclusion of the accumulated gain or loss on a hedge of a forecasted transaction or firm commitment in the initial cost of the acquired asset or liability;
- the recognition of the cumulative amount of gains or losses on a hedging instrument in equity; and
- the definitions of equity instruments and liabilities.

IOSCO requests further guidance on:

- the accounting for an investment in an associate that is held but not acquired with a view to its subsequent disposal in the near future or acquired and held exclusively with a view to its disposal in the near future;
- the accounting for an investment in a subsidiary that is acquired and held exclusively with a view to the subsequent disposal in the near future;
- the derecognition principles;
- the definition of an active market;

- the effect of credit, counterparty, prepayment and liquidity risk, on the valuation of loans, bank deposits and non-traded equity securities;
- the application of the conditions for financial assets to be classified as 'held-to-maturity' to prepayment options;
- the meaning of an 'insignificant' amount of held-to-maturity investments in IAS 39, 83;
- the definition of trading activities;
- the testing for, and measurement of, impairment;
- the ability to use hedge accounting, for example whether assets, liabilities, firm commitments or forecasted transactions measured at fair value can be designated as the hedged item in a fair value or cash flow hedge;
- the application of IAS 37 to financial guarantees;
- the application of the fair value measurement principles in some financial services industries;
- the existence of impairment;
- the meaning of 'similar assets or liabilities' in the requirements for hedging instruments (IAS 39, 132); and
- possible inconsistencies between IAS 39 and IAS 21.

IOSCO also asks for the disclosure of cost information for an equity instrument that does not have a quoted market price in an active market or for which other methods of estimating fair value are clearly inappropriate or unworkable.

In addition to its work with the IASC, IOSCO has issued with the Basel Committee a series of recommendations on disclosures about trading and derivatives activities by banks and securities firms[14]. IOSCO and the Basel Committee have also published surveys of compliance with the recommendations (see also chapter 43).

20.4 IAS 32 AND IAS 39 IN BRIEF

An entity should disclose information which assists users of its financial statements to assess the extent of price risk, credit risk, liquidity risk or cash flow risk related to both recognised and unrecognised financial instruments. These disclosures should include:

- the entity's financial risk management objectives and policies, including its policy for hedging each major type of forecasted transaction for which hedge accounting is used;
- the extent and nature of financial instruments, including their significant terms and conditions which affect the amount, timing and certainty of future cash flows;

- the accounting policies and methods used in reporting financial instruments;
- the exposure to interest rate risk from financial assets and liabilities, including information about contractual repricing or maturity dates and effective interest rates;
- the exposure to credit risk, including the maximum exposure at the balance sheet date and significant concentrations of credit risk; and
- the fair value of financial instruments.

An entity is also encouraged to describe its use of financial instruments, the associated risks and the business purposes served.

IAS 32 also deals with the offsetting of financial assets and financial liabilities (see chapter 9) and the classification of a financial instrument between liabilities and equity (see chapter 28).

The main requirements of IAS 39 are summarised in table 20.2.

Table 20.2 *IAS 39 – the main requirements*

Initial recognition and measurement

All financial assets and financial liabilities, including derivatives, should be recognised on the balance sheet.

Financial assets and financial liabilities should be measured initially at cost (including transaction costs).

Subsequent measurement – assets

The following financial assets should be carried at amortised cost:

- loans and receivables originated by the entity and not held for trading;
- other fixed maturity investments, such as debt securities and mandatorily redeemable preferred shares, which the entity intends and is able to hold to maturity; and
- financial assets whose fair value cannot be reliably measured (generally limited to some equity securities with no quoted market price and forwards and options on unquoted equity securities).

All other financial assets should be measured at fair value.

Subsequent measurement – liabilities

Derivatives and liabilities held for trading (such as securities borrowed by a short seller) should be measured at fair value.

Table 20.2 *IAS 39 – the main requirements (continued)*

A guarantee recognised as a liability should be measured at fair value until it expires, or at original recorded amount if fair value cannot be measured reliably.

All other financial liabilities should be measured at original recorded amount less principal repayments and amortisation (amortised cost).

Income, expenses, gains and losses

For those financial assets and liabilities which are remeasured to fair value, an entity should either:

- recognise the entire adjustment in net profit or loss for the period; or
- recognise in net profit or loss for the period only those changes in value relating to financial assets and liabilities held for trading – other value changes should be reported in equity until the financial asset is sold, at which time the realised gain or loss is reported in net profit or loss (derivatives are always deemed held for trading unless they are designated as hedging instruments).

Transfers of financial assets and financial liabilities

Control over a financial asset has been transferred to another party if:

- the transferee has the right to sell or pledge the asset, and
- the transferor does not have the right to reacquire the transferred asset (unless either the asset is readily obtainable in the market or the reacquisition price is fair value at the time of reacquisition).

Control over a financial liability (or part thereof) has been transferred to another party if the debtor is legally released from primary responsibility for the liability.

If part of a financial asset or liability is sold or extinguished, the carrying amount is split based on relative fair values. If fair values are not determinable, a cost recovery approach to profit recognition is taken.

If a debtor delivers collateral to the creditor and the creditor is permitted to sell or repledge the collateral without constraints, the debtor should recognise the collateral given as a receivable and the creditor should recognise the collateral received as an asset and the obligation to repay the collateral as a liability.

Table 20.2 *IAS 39 – the main requirements (continued)*

Hedge accounting

Hedge accounting is permitted in certain circumstances, provided that:

- the hedging relationship is clearly defined, measurable, and actually effective; and
- the entity designates a specific hedging instrument as a hedge of a change in value or cash flow of a specific hedged item, rather than as a hedge of an overall net balance sheet position.

In the case of hedges of forecasted transactions, the carrying amount of the acquired asset or liability should be adjusted for the gain or loss on the hedging instrument.

20.5 SCOPE OF APPLICATION

Both IAS 32 and IAS 39 do not apply to some financial assets and financial liabilities but the exclusions are currently slightly different. The IASB proposes to make them the same. Table 20.3 summarises the scope exclusions.

Table 20.3 *Exclusions from scope of IAS 32 and IAS 39*

Financial Instrument	*Application of IAS 32 and IAS 39*
Interests in subsidiaries, associates, and joint ventures which are accounted for by consolidation, the equity method or proportionate consolidation in consolidated financial statements	Excluded from the scope of IAS 32 and 39 (IAS 32, 1 and IAS 39, 1). The exclusion applies also to instruments containing potential voting rights which, in substance, give access to the economic benefits associated with an ownership interest and the investment is accounted for using the consolidation or equity method of accounting (SIC 33, 11).
Investments in subsidiaries and associates and interests in joint ventures in the entity's separate financial statements	Option to treat as available-for-sale financial assets (IAS 27, 29 & 30 and IAS 28, 12 & 14).

Table 20.3 *Exclusions from scope of IAS 32 and IAS 39 (continued)*

Financial Instrument	*Application of IAS 32 and IAS 39*
Contracts for contingent purchase consideration in a business combination	Excluded from the scope of IAS 39 (IAS 39, 1).
Leases	Excluded from IAS 39 (IAS 39, 1). Not excluded from IAS 32 (IAS 32, 4). IAS 39 applies to derivatives embedded in leases and to the derecognition of lease receivables (IAS 39, 1).
Employers' assets and liabilities under employee benefit plans to which IAS 19 applies	Excluded from IAS 39 and, as regards obligations, from IAS 32. In its June 2002 exposure draft, the IASB proposes to standardise the exemption in IAS 32 and 39 to employers' rights and obligations under employee benefit plans to which IAS 19 applies.
Plan obligation for post employment benefits dealt with in IAS 26	Currently excluded from IAS 32 (IAS 32, 2) but the IASB proposes to remove this exclusion. IAS 39 does not change the IAS 26 requirements relating to employee benefit plans (IAS 39, 3).
Employers' obligations under employee stock option and stock purchase plans as described in IAS 19	Excluded from IAS 32 (IAS 32, 2) but the IASB proposes to remove this exclusion.
Rights and obligations under insurance contracts, other than contracts that principally involve the transfer of financial risk	Excluded from IAS 39 except for derivatives embedded in insurance contracts (IAS 39, 1 and 5). Obligations only are excluded from IAS 32 (IAS 32, 1 & 3). In its June 2002 exposure draft, the IASB proposes to standardise the exclusion along the lines of that currently set out in IAS 39.
Financial assets and financial liabilities of insurance companies other than rights and obligations under insurance contracts	Within the scope of both IAS 32 and IAS 39.

Table 20.3 *Exclusions from scope of IAS 32 and IAS 39 (continued)*

Financial Instrument	*Application of IAS 32 and IAS 39*
Equity instruments issued by the reporting entity (includes options, warrants and other instruments classified as shareholders' equity of the reporting entity)	*Issuer* – excluded from the scope of IAS 39 (IAS 39, 1) but included within the scope of IAS 32 (for example, on the classification between equity and liabilities and disclosure of terms, conditions and accounting policies) (IAS 32, 16, 18 & 47). *Holder* – within the scope of IAS 39.
Financial guarantee contracts, including letters of credit, that provide for payments to be made if the debtor fails to make payment when due	Currently excluded from the scope of IAS 39 (IAS 39, 1). IAS 37 deals with the recognition and measurement of financial guarantees, warranty obligations and similar instruments. The IASB proposes to limit the exclusion to measurement after initial recognition and to make other modifications.
Financial guarantee contracts that provide for payments to be made in response to changes in a specified interest rate, security price, commodity price, credit rating, foreign exchange rate, index of prices or rates, or other variable. Financial guarantees incurred or retained as a result of the derecognition standards in IAS 39	Within the scope of IAS 39 (IAS 39, 1).
Contracts that require a payment based on climatic, geological, or other physical variables	Excluded from IAS 39 except for other types of derivatives embedded in such contracts (IAS 39, 1 and IGC 1-6).
Loan commitments that are not designated as held for trading and cannot be settled net.	Currently within the scope of IAS 32 and IAS 39 but, in its June 2002 exposure draft, the IASB proposes to exclude such commitments from the scope of both IAS.

20.5.1 Insurance Contracts

IAS 32 and IAS 39 apply to:

- all the financial assets of an insurance entity including those which are held specifically to provide funds for satisfying obligations under insurance contracts; and
- financial instruments which take the form of an insurance contract but principally involve the transfer of financial risks, for example, some types of financial reinsurance and guaranteed investment contracts issued by insurance and other entities.

(IAS 32, 3 and IAS 39, 1 and 5)

IAS 32 and IAS 39 do not apply to obligations (liabilities) arising under an insurance contract which exposes the insurer to identified risks of loss from events or circumstances occurring or discovered within a specified period, including death (in the case of an annuity, the survival of the annuitant), sickness, disability, property damage, injury to others and business interruption (IAS 32, 2 and 3 and IAS 39, 1). However, entities which have such obligations are encouraged to apply the provisions of IAS 32 in presenting and disclosing information about such obligations.

20.6 DEFINITIONS

20.6.1 Financial Instruments

A *financial instrument* is any contract that gives rise to both a financial asset of one entity and a financial liability or equity instrument of another entity (IAS 32, 5 and IAS 39, 8). A contract may be in writing or may be oral. An agreement by a bank to make a loan to a customer is a contract, as is an agreement between two entities to exchange currencies.

IAS 39 applies to commodity-based contracts even though such contracts may not meet the definition of a financial instrument. However, IAS 39 does not apply to commodity-based contracts that:

- were entered into and continue to meet the entity's expected purchase, sale, or usage requirements;
- were designated for that purpose at their inception; and
- are expected to be settled by delivery.

(IAS 32, 5 and IAS 39, 6)

Therefore, for example, IAS 39 does apply to a forward contract to buy copper if the entity intends to sell the contract and does not intend to take delivery of the copper. IAS 39 does not apply to a forward contract to buy copper which will be used in the entity's manufacturing process.

Gold bullion is a commodity not a financial instrument (IGC 8-1). Therefore, it is accounted for in accordance with IAS 39 by an entity that does not expect to take delivery for its purchase, sale or usage requirements. It is not accounted for in accordance with IAS 39 by, say, the manufacturer of gold jewellery provided that the purchase is designated for its purchase, sale or usage requirements and the manufacturer expects to take delivery.

A *financial asset* is any asset that is:

- cash;
- a contractual right to receive cash or another financial asset from another entity;
- a contractual right to exchange financial instruments with another entity under conditions that are potentially favourable; or
- an equity instrument of another entity.

(IAS 32, 5 and IAS 39, 8)

Receivables are financial assets as are contracts to receive a currency or securities. The holder of a call option has a financial asset as the holder has the right to exchange financial instruments and will do so only if the exchange is favourable, that is the value of the financial instruments received exceeds the value of the financial instruments given up.

A *financial liability* is any liability that is a contractual obligation:

- to deliver cash or another financial asset to another entity; or
- to exchange financial instruments with another entity under conditions which are potentially unfavourable.

(IAS 32, 5 and IAS 39, 8)

Payables are financial liabilities as are contracts to deliver currencies or securities. The writer of a call option has a financial liability as the holder will exercise that option only if the exchange of financial instruments is favourable to the holder.

A contractual obligation which an entity can settle with its own equity securities is a financial liability if the number of equity securities to be issued varies with changes in their fair value so that the total fair value of the equity securities paid always equals the amount of the contractual obligation (IAS 39, 11). The June 2002 exposure draft includes further clarifications about the classification of such instruments.

An *equity instrument* is any contract that evidences a residual interest in the assets of an entity after deducting all of its liabilities (IAS 32, 5 and IAS 39, 8). Ordinary and certain preferred shares are examples of equity instruments as are other interests in the equity capital of the entity.

In these definitions, the term 'entity' is used to refer to any party to a contract and, therefore, includes individuals, partnerships, corporate bodies, incorporated bodies and government agencies. For example, a financial instrument may be a contract between:

- two companies as is the case with company bank accounts and most business payables, receivables and derivatives transactions;
- a company and an individual as is the case with customer receivables in a retail business or an individual's account with a bank or shareholding in a company;
- two individuals as is the case with a loan from one person to the other;
- a government agency and a company as is the case with government assistance in the form of development loans, a government's shareholding in a company and a payable/receivable resulting from the supply of goods by a company to a government department; or
- more than two parties, for instance where there is joint and several liability or a guarantee.

Financial instruments include primary instruments such as:

- cash and bank balances;
- receivables;
- equity and debt securities;
- loans, including bank loans and overdrafts; and
- payables.

Therefore, the requirements of IAS 32 and IAS 39 apply to an entity which has nothing more unusual on its balance sheet than a bank balance, some trade receivables and payables and a few marketable securities. However, the application of the requirements of IAS 32 and IAS 39 in these cases is not onerous, indeed in many cases the application of IAS 32 and IAS 39 may not require any disclosures other than those already required by existing IASs and may only require the use of fair values for the marketable securities.

20.6.2 Derivatives

Derivative financial instruments create rights and obligations which have the effect of transferring between the parties to the instrument one or more of the financial risks inherent in an underlying primary financial instrument. Financial assets and financial liabilities include assets and liabilities arising from such instruments (IAS 32, 10).

A *derivative* is a financial instrument:

- whose value changes in response to the change in a specified interest rate, security price, commodity price, foreign exchange rate, index of prices or rates, a credit rating or credit index, or similar variable (sometimes called the 'underlying');
- that requires no initial net investment or little initial net investment relative to other types of contracts that have a similar response to changes in market conditions; and
- that is settled at a future date.

(IAS 39, 10)

The key part of the definition of a derivative is the second – no or little initial investment. A financial instrument that requires a larger initial investment probably gives rise to a financial asset or a financial liability. The distinction matters because IAS 39 requires or allows specific accounting for derivatives. For example, IAS 39 allows virtually all derivatives to be used as hedging instruments. Furthermore, IAS 39 requires that all derivatives other than those used as hedging instruments should be classified as held for trading assets or liabilities and, therefore, carried at fair value with gains and losses included in the profit or loss for the period. IAS 39 requires or allows other accounting treatments for other financial assets and financial liabilities.

A derivative whose value changes in response to something other than the market price of the entity's own equity securities is a derivative and not an equity instrument even if the entity can choose or is required to settle in its own equity securities (IAS 39, 12). Derivatives include futures and forwards, swap, and option contracts. Further examples are included in IGC 10-1 to 10-6, 10-8, 10-9 and 10-18.

Derivatives do not include commitments to buy or sell non-financial assets and liabilities that are intended to be settled by making or taking delivery in the normal course of business, and for which there is no

IASB financial instruments project

In its June 2002 exposure draft, the IASB proposes to exclude from the scope of IAS 32 and IAS 39 those loan commitments that are not designated as held for trading and cannot be settled net. Such commitments meet the definition of a derivative and would be accounted for as such were it not for the proposed scope exclusion. The purpose of the proposed exclusion is to simplify the accounting for entities that grant or hold loan commitments that will result in the origination of a loan.

practice of settling net (either with the counterparty or by entering into offsetting contracts). Settling net means a cash payment based on the change in fair value (IAS 39, 1 and 14).

An *embedded derivative* is a component of a hybrid (combined) financial instrument that includes both the derivative and a host contract with the effect that some of the cash flows of the combined instrument vary in a similar way to a stand-alone derivative (IAS 39, 22). An embedded derivative should be separated from the host contract and accounted for as a derivative if all the following conditions are met:

- the economic characteristics and risks of the embedded derivative are not closely related to the economic characteristics and risks of the host contract;
- a separate instrument with the same terms as the embedded derivative would meet the definition of a derivative; and
- the hybrid (combined) instrument is not measured at fair value with changes in fair value reported in net profit or loss.

(IAS 39, 23)

IAS 39, 24 lists instances in which the economic characteristics and risks of the embedded derivative are not closely related to the economic characteristics and risks of the host contract and, therefore, in which the embedded derivative may need to be accounted for separately. IAS 39, 25 includes instances in which there is not a close relationship.

If the embedded derivative is separated from the host contract:

- the embedded derivative is measured initially at its fair value; and
- the host contract is measured initially at the cost of the hybrid instrument less the fair value of the embedded derivative.

(IGC 23.3)

Subsequently, an embedded derivative is measured at fair value in the same way as for all other derivatives. The host contract is measured in accordance with IAS 39 if it is a financial instrument (IAS 39, 23). If the embedded derivative cannot be separately measured, the entire contract should be treated as a financial instrument held for trading (IAS 39, 26) and carried at fair value.

Further guidance on the application of the requirements for embedded derivatives is included in IGC 22-1 to 25-9.

20.6.3 Risks

Transactions in financial instruments may transfer price risk, credit risk, liquidity risk or cash flow risk.

Price risk is the risk that the price (or value) of an instrument will decrease or increase. Price risk encompasses:

- *currency risk* which is the risk that the value of a financial instrument will fluctuate as a result of changes in foreign exchange rates – for example, a foreign currency receivable has the potential for gain or loss resulting from a change in the rate of exchange between the currency of the receivable and the reporting currency;
- *interest rate risk* which is the risk that the value of a financial instrument will fluctuate as a result of changes in market interest rates – for example, a fixed rate bond usually increases in value when interest rates fall and decreases in value when interest rates rise; and
- *market risk* which is the risk that the value of a financial instrument will fluctuate as a result of changes in market prices whether those changes are caused by factors specific to the individual security or its issuer, or factors affecting all securities traded in the market – for example, the value of an equity security may increase as a result of a take-over bid for the issuer or decrease on the issuer's announcement of unexpectedly poor results. Also, the value of many equity securities listed on the same market may increase or decrease on the publication of new data about the national economy.

(IAS 32, 43(a))

Price risk arises on both financial assets and financial liabilities. For example, currency risk affects both foreign currency receivables and payables, and rights and obligations under forward contracts. Changes in interest rates may affect the value of the debt securities held by an entity as an asset (an investment) and the value of debt securities issued by an entity.

Credit risk is the risk that one party to a financial instrument will fail to discharge an obligation and cause the other party to incur a financial loss (IAS 32, 43(b)). For example, credit risk arises when there is the risk that a customer may not settle an outstanding debt or that a financial institution may not be able to meet its obligations under derivatives contracts. Credit risk arises only on financial assets. An entity is not subject to credit risk on its liabilities.

Liquidity risk (or funding risk) is the risk that an entity will encounter difficulty in raising funds to meet commitments associated with financial instruments (IAS 32, 43(c)). For example, a financial institution may not be able to raise funds to meet the demands of depositors or under a call option. Liquidity risk may result from an inability to sell a financial asset quickly at close to its fair value.

Cash flow risk is the risk that future cash flows associated with a monetary financial instrument will fluctuate in amount (IAS 32, 43(d)). For example, in the case of a floating rate debt instrument, a change in interest rates affects future interest payments by the issuer and future interest receipts for the holder.

IAS 32 focuses on disclosures by an entity that assist users of its financial statements to assess the extent of these risks.

20.7 INITIAL RECOGNITION

Subject to the requirements for regular way contracts (see 20.7.1 below), an entity should recognise a financial asset or financial liability on its balance sheet when, and only when, it becomes a party to the contractual provisions of the instrument (IAS 39, 27). This is the time at which the essential conditions of an asset or liability are met, in particular control over expected future benefits (asset) or the obligation which will result in the outflow of economic benefits (liability). Therefore, for example, unconditional receivables and payables are recognised as assets or liabilities when the entity becomes a party to the contract and, as a consequence, has a legal right to receive, or a legal obligation to pay cash (IAS 39, 29(a)).

The focus on the contract is potentially different from the more traditional approach (which was proposed in E40 and E48) under which a financial asset or financial liability is recognised when all (or substantially all) the risks and benefits associated with it have been transferred to the entity (see, for example, E48, 19). However, the time at which the entity becomes a party to the contract is usually the point at which it becomes exposed to the risks and benefits inherent in the instrument. The change in approach also affects the derecognition of the asset and liability (see 20.13 and 14).

The application of this requirement requires a clear understanding of what constitutes a contract. A contract is 'an agreement between two or more parties that has clear consequences that the parties have little, if any discretion to avoid, usually because the agreement is enforceable at law' (IAS 32, 6). Contracts may take several forms and need not be in writing.

The requirement means that all contractual rights or obligations under derivatives are recognised on the balance sheet as assets or liabilities (IAS 39, 28). For example, financial options are recognised as assets or liabilities when the holder or writer becomes a party to the contract (IAS 39, 29(d)). A forward contract to purchase or sell a financial instrument is also recognised on the date on which the entity becomes a party to the contract (IAS 39, 29(c)). It is important to recognise that the contractual rights and obligations under a derivative are separate and distinct from the underlying financial assets, financial liabilities or commodity that are the subject of the derivative. The underlying asset or liability is recognised only when the derivative is exercised and the entity controls the rights to, or is obligated under the provisions of, the underlying asset or liability.

IAS 39 requires that commodity-based contracts are treated in the same way as financial instruments. Therefore, for example, a forward contract to purchase copper is recognised on the date on which the entity becomes a party to the contract provided that the copper is not required to meet the entity's purchase or usage requirements and the entity does not expect to take delivery of the copper (IAS 39, 6 and 29(c)).

In contrast to the approach for commodity-based contracts, an entity does not usually recognise assets to be acquired and liabilities to be incurred as a result of a firm commitment to purchase or sell goods or services until at least one of the parties has performed under the agreement (IAS 39, 29(b)). For example, an entity does not recognise an asset or liability as a result of placing an order for copper for use in its production process even though it becomes a party to the purchase contract when the order is placed. The copper is recognised as an asset and the obligation to the supplier is recognised as a liability usually only on delivery of the copper. Similarly, planned future transactions, no matter how likely, are not recognised as assets or liabilities since the entity is not a party to a contract requiring future receipt or delivery of benefits (IAS 39, 29(e)). A forecasted transaction or firm commitment may, however, be a hedged item (see 20.15.4) but even in such cases the entity does not recognise any asset or liability arising under the transaction or commitment until delivery.

The classification and presentation by the issuer of a financial instrument, including a compound instrument, on initial recognition is dealt with in chapter 28.

20.7.1 Regular Way Contracts

In organised securities markets, there is usually a specified period of days between the date on which a transaction is entered into and the date on which it is to be settled. Contracts entered on such markets are referred to in IAS 39 as regular way contracts.

A *regular way contract* is a contract to purchase or sell a financial asset on terms that require delivery of the asset within the time frame established generally by regulation or convention in the market place concerned (IAS 39, 16). The market place may be a formal stock exchange, futures exchange or commodities exchange, an organised over-the-counter market or some other means by which the asset is customarily exchanged (IGC 16-1).

The strict application of the recognition requirements for such contracts would result in the recognition of the contractual commitment at trade date and the exchange transaction itself at settlement date.

However, different accounting practices have developed in the securities industries for such contracts. The IASC recognised that it may be costly to change record keeping systems to conform to the letter of the recognition requirements. Therefore, for a regular way contract to purchase or sell a financial asset, an entity should use either:

- trade date accounting; or
- settlement date accounting.

The method used should be applied consistently for each of the four measurement categories of financial assets (IAS 39, 30).

Trade date accounting requires the recognition of the asset to be received and the liability to pay for it on the trade date. The *trade date* is the date that an entity commits to purchase the asset (IAS 39, 32) and is, therefore, the date on which the entity usually becomes a party to the contract. *Settlement date accounting* requires the recognition of the asset on the date the asset is transferred to the entity. The *settlement date* is the date that the asset is delivered to the entity (IAS 39, 33).

Other guidance on the application of the requirements for regular way contracts is included in IGC 16-1 to 16-4 and 30-1 to 30-3.

Extract 20.1 *Regular way contracts – trade date and settlement date*

Gulf International Bank, Bahrain, 31 December 2001 (IAS)

All regular way purchases and sales of financial assets held for trading are recognised on the trade date, i.e. the date on which the Group commits to purchase or sell the financial asset. All regular way purchases and sales of other financial assets are recognised on the settlement date, i.e. the date on which the asset is delivered to or received from the counterparty. Regular way purchases or sales are purchases or sales of financial assets that require delivery within the time frame generally established by regulation or convention in the market place.

Extract 20.2 *Regular way contracts – trade date*

Swisscom, Switzerland, 31 December 2001 (IAS)

All purchases and sales of investments are recognised on the trade date, which is the date that Swisscom commits to purchase or sell the asset.

Extract 20.3 *Regular way contracts – settlement date*

Volkswagen, Germany, 31 December 2001 (IAS)

Financial instruments are contracts that give rise to a financial asset in one company and a financial liability or in an equity instrument in another. The 'regular' purchase or sale of financial instruments is accounted for on the settlement date – that is, on the date on which the asset is delivered.

20.8 INITIAL MEASUREMENT

On initial recognition, a financial asset or financial liability should be measured at cost, which is the fair value of the consideration given (asset) or received (liability) and includes transaction costs (IAS 39, 66). When the asset arises from a forecast transaction or firm commitment which is the hedged item in a cash flow hedge, cost also includes any hedging gains and losses arising on the hedging instrument (IAS 39, 160).

Fair value is the amount for which an asset could be exchanged, or a liability settled, between knowledgeable, willing parties in an arm's length transaction (IAS 32, 5 and IAS 39, 8). It is normally determinable by reference to the transaction price or other market prices. If such prices are not reliably determinable, fair value is the sum of all future cash payments or receipts, discounted using the prevailing market rate(s) of interest for a similar instrument of an issuer with a similar credit rating (IAS 18, 11 and IAS 39, 67).

Transaction costs are incremental costs that are directly attributable to the acquisition or disposal of a financial asset or liability (IAS 39, 10). Transaction costs are part of the consideration given (received) for a financial asset (liability). Transaction costs:

- include fees and commissions paid to agents, advisers, brokers, and dealers; levies by regulatory agencies and securities exchanges; and transfer taxes and duties; and
- exclude debt premium or discount, financing costs and allocations of internal administrative or holding costs.

(IAS 39, 17).

Further guidance on transaction costs is included in IGC 66-1 and 66-2.

A financial asset or liability is measured in accordance with these requirements irrespective of whether it is measured subsequently at cost, amortised cost or fair value. In particular, the use of fair value to determine cost does not presuppose the use of fair value for subsequent measurement. Furthermore, while transaction costs are part of the cost of a financial asset or financial liability, they are excluded from the determination of fair value for the purpose of subsequent measurement.

20.9 MEASUREMENT OF FINANCIAL ASSETS SUBSEQUENT TO INITIAL RECOGNITION

20.9.1 Categorisation

For the purposes of measurement subsequent to initial recognition and the treatment of the resulting gains and losses, IAS 39 identifies four categories of financial assets:

- financial assets held for trading;
- held-to-maturity investments;
- loans and receivables originated by the entity; and
- available-for-sale financial assets.

(IAS 39, 68)

The requirements of IAS 39 for the measurement of financial assets in each category and the treatment of recognised gains and losses, before considering the impact of impairment and hedge accounting, are summarised in table 20.4. The reclassification of financial assets and the consequential treatment of gains and losses are summarised in table 20.5.

Extract 20.4 *Classification of financial assets*

Volkswagen, Germany, 31 December 2001 (IAS)

IAS 39 subdivides financial assets into the following categories: 'financial asset or liability held for trading purposes'; 'held-to-maturity investments'; 'loans and receivables originated by the enterprise'; and 'available-for-sale financial assets'.

In the Volkswagen Group financial instruments are generally classified as 'loans and receivables originated by the enterprise' or 'available-for-sale financial assets'. Financial instruments are not treated as 'held-to-maturity investments' in the Volkswagen Group.

Extract 20.5 *Classification of financial assets*

Zurich Financial Services, Switzerland, 31 December 2001 (IAS)

Fixed maturities classified as held-to-maturity are those which the Group has the ability and positive intent to hold to maturity; these investments are carried at amortized cost. Fixed maturities and equity securities which the Group buys with the intention to resell in the near term are classified as trading and are carried at fair value. The remaining fixed maturities and equity securities are classified as available-for-sale; these investments are carried at fair value.

Table 20.4 *Measurement of financial assets subsequent to initial recognition (ignoring impairment and hedge accounting)*

Category	Measurement	Recognised gains and losses
Financial assets held for trading (including all derivatives)		
• with quoted market price in an active market or when fair value can otherwise be determined	Fair value	Profit for the period
• without quoted market price in an active market *and* when fair value cannot otherwise be determined	Cost	Profit for the period in which derecognised or impaired
Loans and receivables originated by the entity		
• with fixed maturity	Amortised cost	Profit for the period in which derecognised or impaired
• without fixed maturity	Cost	
Held-to-maturity investments		
• with fixed maturity	Amortised cost	Profit for the period in which derecognised or impaired
• without fixed maturity	Cost	
Available-for-sale financial assets		
• with quoted market price in an active market or when fair value can otherwise be determined	Fair value	*Either*: • profit for the period: *or* • equity until disposal or impairment when included in profit for the period
• without quoted market price in an active market *and* when fair value cannot otherwise be determined	Cost	Profit for the period in which derecognised or impaired

Table 20.5 *Reclassification of financial assets subsequent to initial recognition*

Old category	New category	Permitted?	Recognised gains and losses
Financial assets held for trading (including all derivatives)	Loans and receivables originated by the entity	No	Not applicable
	Held-to-maturity investments	No	Not applicable
	Available-for-sale financial assets	No	Not applicable
Loans and receivables originated by the entity	Financial assets held for trading	Yes	Amortised cost to fair value – profit or loss for the period
	Held-to-maturity investments	No	Not applicable
	Available-for-sale financial assets	No (currently)	Not applicable
Held-to-maturity investments	Financial assets held for trading	Yes	Amortised cost to fair value – profit or loss for the period
	Loans and receivables originated by the entity	No	Not applicable
	Available-for-sale financial assets	Yes	Amortised cost to fair value – profit or loss for the period or equity
Available-for-sale financial assets	Financial assets held for trading	Yes	Gains and losses included in equity – left in equity until sale or other disposal
	Loans and receivables originated by the entity	No	Not applicable
	Held-to-maturity investments	No	Not applicable

20.9.2 Financial assets held for trading

Financial assets held for trading are measured subsequent to initial recognition at fair value (IAS 39, 69). IAS 39 presumes that fair value can be determined reliably for most financial assets held for trading (IAS 39, 70). The determination of fair value is dealt with in 20.11.1.

The only exception to the fair value requirement is for those financial assets held for trading that do not have a quoted market price in an active market and for which fair value cannot otherwise be determined. Fair value must be used if there is a quoted market price in an active market or fair value can be determined reliably in some other way. In the very exceptional cases in which a quoted market price is not available or fair value cannot be determined in some other way, a financial asset held for trading should be measured subsequent to initial recognition at amortised cost (if it has a fixed maturity) or cost (if it does not have a fixed maturity) less any impairment losses. The determination of amortised cost is dealt with in 20.11.2.

All recognised gains and losses on financial assets held for trading are included in the profit or loss for the period (IAS 39, 103).

A *financial asset held for trading* is a financial asset that:

- was acquired principally for the purpose of generating a profit from short-term fluctuations in price or dealer's margin (IAS 39, 10); or
- is part of a portfolio for which there is evidence of a recent actual pattern of short-term profit taking (IAS 39, 10); or
- is part of a portfolio of similar assets for which there is a pattern of trading for the purpose of generating a profit from short-term fluctuations in price or dealer's margin (IAS 39, 21).

In other words, a financial asset is classified as held for trading if either there was an intent to trade or there is recent practice of trading. If there is no intent to trade and no recent practice of trading, an acquired financial asset is either:

- a held-to-maturity investment (see 20.9.4); or
- an available-for-sale financial asset (see 20.9.5).

IGC 10-9 deals with whether the balancing of an investment portfolio requires the classification of the securities as available-for-sale or held for trading. The guidance reinforces the requirements in IAS 39.

Derivatives are always either:

- held for trading; or
- hedging instruments.

(IAS 39, 10)

If a derivative is not designated, or is ineffective, as a hedging instrument, it must be classified as held for trading.

An entity should not reclassify a financial asset held for trading after initial recognition (IAS 39, 107). Therefore, if there was intent to trade but that intent is not fulfilled, the entity should continue to classify the asset as held for trading. In particular, the requirement for intent does not limit the time period for which an instrument designated as held for trading on acquisition can be held and, therefore, classified as held for trading (IGC 10-15).

An entity should reclassify a financial asset from held-to-maturity or available-for-sale into held for trading if there is evidence of a recent actual pattern of short-term profit taking (IAS 39, 107). However, a decision to sell an asset does not, in itself, make that asset a financial asset held for trading. However, a decision to sell an asset that is part of a portfolio of similar assets for which there is a recent pattern of trading is indicative that the assets should be classified as held for trading (IGC 107-2).

Under the tainting rules for held-to-maturity investments (see 20.9.4) an entity may be required to reclassify all its held-to-maturity investments. Such assets are reclassified as held for trading only if there is evidence of a recent actual pattern of short-term profit taking. The sale, transfer or put that gave rise to the tainting may or may not provide such evidence.

On reclassification of held-to-maturity investments, the difference between carrying amount and fair value should be included in the profit or loss for the period (IAS 39, 90 and 103). On reclassification of available-for-sale financial assets, previous gains and losses included in equity are left in equity until the financial assets are sold or otherwise disposed of (IGC 107-1). Sale or disposal will often occur within a reasonably short period given that the reason for reclassification is evidence of a recent actual pattern of short-term profit taking.

IASB financial instruments project

In its June 2002 exposure draft, the IASB proposes that an entity should be able to designate any financial asset or financial liability at initial recognition as held for trading; and, therefore, carry it at fair value with changes in fair value included in net profit and loss. An entity would be precluded from reclassifying financial instruments into and out of this category while they are held.

The IASB proposes this option in order to simplify the application of IAS 39 and to facilitate consistent measurement of all financial assets and financial liabilities. Both E40 and E48 proposed a similar 'full fair value' alternative.

Extract 20.6 *Held for trading financial assets and financial liabilities*

UBS, Switzerland, 31 December 2001 (IAS)

Trading portfolio assets consist of money market paper, other debt instruments and equity instruments as well as traded loans and precious metals which are owned by the Group ('long' positions). Obligations to deliver trading securities sold but not yet purchased are reported as trading portfolio liabilities. Trading portfolio liabilities consist of money market paper, other debt instruments and equity instruments which the Group has sold to third parties but does not own ('short' positions).

The trading portfolio is carried at fair value, which includes valuation allowances for instruments, for which liquid markets do not exist, to adjust primarily for credit and settlement risks. Gains and losses realized on disposal or redemption and unrealized gains and losses from changes in the fair value of trading portfolio assets or liabilities are reported as net trading income. Interest and dividend income and expense on trading portfolio assets or liabilities are included in interest and dividend income or interest and dividend expense, respectively.

When the Group becomes party to a contract classified in its trading portfolio, it recognizes from that date (trade date) in the income statement any unrealized profits and losses arising from revaluing that contract to fair value. On a date subsequent to the trade date, the terms of spot and forward trading transactions are fulfilled (settlement date) and a resulting financial asset or liability is recognized on the balance sheet at the fair value of the consideration given or received plus the change in fair value of the contract since the trade date.

The determination of fair values of trading portfolio assets or liabilities is based on quoted market prices in active markets or dealer price quotations, pricing models (using assumptions based on market and economic conditions), or management's estimates, as applicable.

20.9.3 Loans and receivables originated by the entity

Loans and receivables originated by the entity that have a fixed maturity are measured subsequent to initial recognition at amortised cost less impairment losses. Short duration receivables with no stated interest rate, for example most trade receivables, are measured at cost, that is the amount invoiced. However, they are measured at amortised cost if the effect of imputing interest is material (IAS 18, 11 and IAS 39, 74).

Loans and receivables originated by the entity that do not have a fixed maturity are measured subsequent to initial recognition at cost less impairment losses.

Any recognised losses on loans and receivables originated by the entity are included in the profit or loss for the period. Such losses include both the effects of amortisation (including imputed interest) and impairment.

Loans and receivables originated by the entity are financial assets that are created by the entity by providing money, goods or services directly to a debtor, other than those that are originated with the intent to be sold immediately or in the short term, which should be classified as held for trading (IAS 39, 10). Originated loans and receivables should not be classified as held-to-maturity investments which means that they are measured at amortised cost irrespective of any intent to hold to maturity and they are unaffected by the tainting rules (see 20.9.4).

Examples of loans and receivables originated by the entity include:

- loans and advances made by a financial institution to its customers;
- trade receivables;
- loans and advances made to other entities;
- participation in a loan made by another lender provided that the entity funds its participation on the date that the loan is originated by the other lender (IAS 39, 19);
- a loan acquired through a syndication because each lender shares in the origination of the loan and provides money directly to the debtor (IAS 39, 19);
- a loan acquired in a business combination provided that it was similarly classified by the acquired entity (IAS 39, 19);
- deposits made by a bank to a central bank notwithstanding that the proof of deposit is negotiable (provided that the bank does not intend to sell immediately or in the short term (IGC 10.7)); and
- a debt security, or equity security that is treated as debt by the issuer, purchased at issuance when funds are transferred directly to the issuer and the investor does not intend to sell immediately or in the short term (IGC 10-11-a and 10-11-b).

The following are *not* loans and receivables originated by the entity:

- the acquisition of an interest in a pool of existing loans or receivables; and
- a transaction that is, in substance, a purchase of a loan that was previously originated.

(IAS 39, 19)

Loans or receivables that are purchased, rather than originated, are included in the appropriate one of the other three categories of financial assets (IAS 39, 20). In theory, loans and receivables originated by the entity could be reclassified as held for trading financial assets if there is a recent actual pattern of short-term profit taking.

IASB financial instruments project

In its June 2002 exposure draft, the IASB proposes that an entity should be able to classify loans and receivables originated by the entity as available-for-sale financial assets. This change would remove the anomaly whereby liquid debt securities acquired upon issue must be classified as originated loans and receivables and carried at amortised cost whereas similar securities acquired shortly afterwards may be classified as available-for-sale financial assets and carried at fair value. Under the proposed change, an entity would be required to measure an investment in a debt instrument that is quoted on an active market at fair value unless it met the definition of a held-to-maturity investment (in other words, such an investment could not be classified as an originated loan or receivable).

Extract 20.7 *Originated loans and receivables*

UBS, Switzerland, 31 December 2001 (IAS)

Loans originated by the Group include loans where money is provided directly to the borrower, other than those that are originated with the intent to be sold immediately or in the short term, which are recorded as trading portfolio assets. A participation in a loan from another lender is considered to be originated by the Group, provided it is funded on the date the loan is originated by the lender. Purchased loans are either classified as financial investments available-for-sale, or as trading portfolio assets, as appropriate.

Loans originated by the Group are recognized when cash is advanced to borrowers. They are initially recorded at cost, which is the fair value of the cash given to originate the loan, including any transaction costs, and are subsequently measured at amortized cost using the effective interest rate method.

Extract 20.8 *Originated loans and receivables*

Bulbank, Bulgaria, 31 December 2001 (IAS)

Loans originated by the bank by providing money directly to the borrower or to a sub-participant agent at draw down are categorized as loans originated by the bank and are carried at amortised cost less provisions for loan impairment.

All loans and advances are recognized when cash is advanced to borrowers.

20.9.4 Held-to-maturity investments

Held-to-maturity investments are measured subsequent to initial recognition at amortised cost less impairment losses. Any recognised losses are included in the profit or loss for the period.

The held-to-maturity classification is an exception to the general requirements in IAS 39 to use fair value for the subsequent measurement of financial assets. The IASC would have preferred to have required that such investments be measured at fair value rather than amortised cost. The category reflects an intent based approach which was criticised by some commentators and standard setting bodies when it was proposed in E48. It was also rejected in the IASC's 1997 discussion paper on financial instruments[15]. As a result, it is important to recognise that:

- an entity is not required to classify any of its financial assets as held-to-maturity investments – all held-to-maturity investments could be classified as available-for-sale financial assets or financial assets held for trading;
- the definition of held-to-maturity is very restrictive in terms of both the nature of the investments and the intent and ability of the entity with respect to those investments;
- the classification of financial assets as held-to-maturity investments must be reviewed at each balance sheet date and, if necessary, the investments must be reclassified; and
- there are penalties for those entities that sell, transfer or exercise a put option on more than an insignificant amount of held-to-maturity investments before maturity.

Held-to-maturity investments are financial assets with fixed or determinable payments and fixed maturity that an entity has the positive intent and ability to hold to maturity (IAS 39, 10). Loans and receivables originated by the entity often meet this definition but they are specifically excluded from this category of financial assets (see 20.9.3).

The definition of held-to-maturity investments includes three important elements:

- fixed or determinable payments and fixed maturity;
- the positive intent to hold to maturity; and
- the ability to hold to maturity.

Fixed or determinable payments and fixed maturity mean that the contractual arrangement defines the amounts and dates of payments to the entity as holder of the financial asset. Payments include interest and principal both during the term of the debt and on its maturity. The likelihood of the issuer defaulting in making the contractual payments is not taken into account in determining the classification of the investment by the entity as holder (IGC 10-16) but it is taken into account by the entity in measuring impairment losses.

A fixed rate debt security may be classified as a held-to-maturity investment if the amounts and dates of payment of interest and principal are fixed or determinable. A variable rate security can also be classified as a held-to-maturity investment (IAS 39, 80) as the amounts of interest are usually determinable (but not fixed), the amount of principal payments are usually fixed and the timing of both interest and principal payments are either fixed or determinable.

An equity investment is very unlikely to be a held-to-maturity investment as the amounts and timing of both dividends and capital (principal) are unlikely to be fixed or determinable. In practice, an equity investment is likely to be a held-to-maturity investment only if it meets the definition of a liability (rather than an equity instrument) of the issuer.

The fact that a financial asset has fixed or determinable payments and fixed maturity is not sufficient, however, for the entity to classify that investment as held-to-maturity. The entity must also have the positive intent to hold the financial asset to maturity. The entity does not have such an intent when:

- it has the intent to hold the investment for only an undefined period;
- it stands ready to sell the financial asset in response to changes in market interest rates or risks, liquidity needs, changes in the availability of and the yield on alternative investments, changes in financing sources and terms, or changes in foreign currency risk; or
- the issuer has a right to settle the financial asset at an amount significantly below its amortised cost.

(IAS 39, 79)

An entity has a positive intent to hold to maturity when:

- the financial asset is callable by the issuer provided that the entity intends and is able to hold the asset until it is called or until maturity and would recover substantially all of the carrying amount of the investment (IAS 39, 81);
- the financial asset is puttable (the entity has the right to require the issuer to repay or redeem the asset before maturity) provided that the entity has the positive intent and ability to hold it until maturity and does not intend to exercise the put (IAS 39, 82); and
- the financial asset is a perpetual debt instrument with no maturity date (IGC 10-17).

The fact that the entity has the positive intent to hold the investment to maturity is also not sufficient to classify the financial asset as held-to-maturity. The entity must also have the ability to hold the financial asset to maturity. It does not have that ability when it:

- does not have the financial resources available to continue to finance the investment until maturity; or
- is subject to legal or other constraint that could frustrate its intention to hold the financial asset to maturity (for example, while an issuer's call option may not frustrate the investing entity's intent to hold the asset to maturity, it may frustrate its ability to hold the asset to maturity).

(IAS 39, 87)

As mentioned earlier, there is a penalty for the misuse of the held-to-maturity category. In particular, an entity is prohibited from using the held-to-maturity category if, during the current financial year or during the two preceding financial years, it has sold, transferred or exercised a put option on more than an insignificant amount of held-to-maturity investments before maturity (IAS 39, 83). Transfers includes any reclassification out of the held-to-maturity category (IGC 83-2). Some refer to the prohibition as a 'two year sin bin'. The prohibition applies to all current and potential held-to-maturity investments, including those which are acquired within the next two years of the sale, transfer or put. The prohibition is not limited to those investments that have been sold, transferred or put (see also IGC 83-4, 5 and 6). In other words, the sale, transfer or put of some held-to-maturity investments taints other investments that are, or might be in the next two years, included in this category. At the end of the two years, the entity may again use the held-to-maturity category and may transfer financial assets into the category (IAS 39, 92).

Not all sales, transfers or puts result in the prohibition. An entity can make the following sales, transfers or puts without penalty:

- sales made close to maturity or exercised close to call date so that changes in the market rate of interest did not have a significant effect on the fair value of the investments (see also IGC 83-1);
- sales made after the entity has collected substantially all the investments' original principal through scheduled payments or prepayments (see also IGC 83-1); or
- sales made in response to an isolated event that is beyond the entity's control and that is non-recurring and could not have been reasonably anticipated by the entity.

(IAS 39, 83 and IGC 83-3)

Sales or transfers made or the exercise of put options in response to the following events do not question an entity's intent to hold to maturity and, therefore, do not result in a penalty:

- a significant deterioration in the issuer's creditworthiness that was not expected when the investments were classified as held-to-maturity (IGC 83-7 – see also IGC 83-8 for internal downgrades of credit worthiness);
- a change in tax law that eliminates or significantly reduces any tax-exempt status of interest on the held-to-maturity investments;
- a major business combination or major disposal that necessitates the sale or transfer of held-to-maturity investments to maintain the entity's interest rate risk position or credit risk policy;
- a change in statutory or regulatory requirements that significantly modifies permissible investments, the maximum level of certain kinds of investments, capital requirements or risk weights used for regulatory risk-based capital purposes;
- a significant increase by the regulator in the industry's capital requirements that causes the entity to downsize by selling held-to-maturity investments; or
- a significant increase in the risk weights of held-to-maturity investments used for regulatory risk-based capital purposes.

(IAS 39, 86)

If it is no longer appropriate to classify financial assets as held-to-maturity investments and, therefore, carry them at amortised cost, the entity should reclassify the assets as either held for trading or available-for-sale and remeasure them at fair value (IAS 39, 90). In particular, an entity should reclassify a financial asset from held-to-maturity into held for trading if there is evidence of a recent actual pattern of short-term profit taking (IAS 39, 107). If the financial assets are reclassified as held for trading, the difference between carrying amount and fair value should be included in the profit or loss for the period (IAS 39, 90 and 103). If the financial assets are reclassified as available-for-sale, the difference between carrying amount and fair value should be included in the profit or loss for the period or in equity in accordance with the entity's accounting policy for available-for sale securities (IAS 39, 90 and 103).

20.9.5 Available-for-sale financial assets

Available-for-sale financial assets are measured subsequent to initial recognition at fair value (IAS 39, 69). IAS 39 presumes that fair value can be determined reliably for most available-for-sale financial assets (IAS 39, 70). The determination of fair value is dealt with in 20.11.1.

The only exception to the fair value requirement is for those available-for-sale financial assets that do not have a quoted market price in an active market and for which fair value cannot otherwise be determined. Fair value must be used if there is a quoted market price in an active market or fair value can be determined reliably in some other way. In the very exceptional cases in which a quoted market price is not available or fair value cannot be determined in some other way, an available-for-sale financial asset should be measured subsequent to initial recognition at amortised cost (if it has a fixed maturity) or cost (if it does not have a fixed maturity) less any impairment losses. The determination of amortised cost is dealt with in 20.11.2.

Recognised gains and losses on available-for-sale financial assets are included in either:

- the profit or loss for the period; or
- equity until disposal or impairment when they are included in the profit or loss for the period.

(IAS 39, 103)

An entity should apply the same policy to all available-for-sale financial assets (IAS 39, 104). It may change that policy in a future period but the IASB believes that a change from the inclusion of gains and losses in the profit and loss account to their inclusion in equity is unlikely to meet the requirement that a voluntary change in accounting policy should be made only when it results in more appropriate presentation (IAS 8, 42 and IAS 39, 105).

Available-for-sale financial assets are the residual class of financial assets, that is they are all financial assets that are not included in one of the other three categories.

An entity should reclassify a financial asset from available-for-sale into held for trading if there is evidence of a recent actual pattern of short-term profit taking (IAS 39, 107). On reclassification, previous gains and losses included in equity are left in equity until the financial assets are sold or otherwise disposed of (IGC 107-1). Sale or disposal will often occur within a reasonably short period given that the reason for reclassification is evidence of a recent actual pattern of short-term profit taking.

Under the tainting rules for held-to-maturity investments (see 20.9.4) an entity may be required to reclassify its held-to-maturity investments to available-for-sale financial assets. The assets should be remeasured at fair value (IAS 39, 90) and the difference between carrying amount and fair value should be included in the profit or loss for the period or in equity in accordance with the entity's accounting policy for gains and losses on available-for-sale securities.

> ***IASB financial instruments project***
>
> In its June 2002 exposure draft, the IASB proposes that any financial asset can be carried at fair value with gains and losses included in net profit or loss. Therefore, the option to include recognised gains and losses on available-for-sale financial assets in the profit or loss for the period becomes redundant.

Extract 20.9 *Available-for-sale financial assets*

UBS, Switzerland, 31 December 2001 (IAS)

Financial investments are classified as available-for-sale and recorded on a settlement date basis. Management determines the appropriate classification of its investments at the time of the purchase. Financial investments consist of money market paper, other debt instruments and equity instruments, including private equity investments.

Available-for-sale financial investments may be sold in response to needs for liquidity or changes in interest rates, foreign exchange rates or equity prices.

Available-for-sale financial investments are carried at fair value. Unrealized gains or losses on available-for-sale investments are reported in shareholders' equity, net of applicable taxes, until such investment is sold, collected or otherwise disposed of, or until such investment is determined to be impaired. If an available-for-sale investment is determined to be impaired, the cumulative unrealized gain or loss previously recognized in shareholders' equity is included in net profit or loss for the period and reported in other income.

A financial investment is considered impaired if its carrying value exceeds the recoverable amount. For non-quoted investments, the recoverable amount is determined by applying recognized valuation techniques. Quoted financial investments are considered impaired if the decline in market price below cost is of such a magnitude that recovery of the cost value cannot be reasonably expected within the foreseeable future.

On disposal of an available-for-sale investment, the accumulated unrealized gain or loss included in shareholders' equity is transferred to net profit or loss for the period and reported in other income. Gains and losses on disposal are determined using the average cost method.

The determination of fair values of available-for-sale financial investments is generally based on quoted market prices in active markets, dealer price quotations, discounted expected cash flows using market rates commensurate with the credit quality and maturity of the investment or based upon review of the investee's financial results, condition and prospects including comparisons to similar companies for which quoted market prices are available.

Interest and dividend income on available-for-sale financial investments is included in interest and dividend income from financial investments.

Extract 20.10 *Available-for-sale financial assets*

Swisscom, Switzerland, 31 December 2001 (IAS)

Investments intended to be held for an indefinite period of time, which may be sold in response to needs for liquidity or changes in interest rates, are classified as available-for-sale. These investments are included in non-current financial assets unless management has the express intention of holding the investment for less than 12 months from the balance sheet date or unless they will need to be sold to raise operating capital, in which case they are included in current financial assets. Available-for-sale investments are subsequently carried at fair value. Fair value is determined by reference to stock exchange quoted bid prices or other market prices. Realized gains and losses arising from changes in the fair value of available-for-sale investments are included in the income statement in the period in which they arise. Unrealised gains and losses arising from changes in the fair value of available-for-sale investments are recorded directly to equity as fair value reserve until the investment is sold or impaired. If there is an indication that the carrying amount is greater than the recoverable amount, Swisscom estimates the recoverable amount of that asset. If the recoverable amount is below the carrying amount, Swisscom recognizes an impairment loss. The cumulative net loss that had been recognized directly in equity is removed from equity and recognized in the income statement. When available-for-sale investments are disposed of, the related accumulated fair value adjustments are included in the income statement as gains and losses from investments securities.

Extract 20.11 *Available-for-sale financial assets*

Nokia, Finland, 31 December 2001 (IAS)

Under IAS 39 the Group classifies its investments in marketable debt and equity securities and investments in unlisted equity securities into the following categories: held-to-maturity, trading, or available-for-sale depending on the purpose for acquiring the investments. All investments of the Group are currently classified as available-for-sale. Available-for-sale investments are fair valued by using quoted market rates, discounted cash flow analyses and other appropriate valuation models at the balance sheet date. Certain unlisted equities for which fair values cannot be measured reliably are reported at cost less impairment. All purchases and sales of investments are recorded on the trade date, which is the date that the Group commits to purchase or sell the asset.

The fair value changes of available-for-sale investments are recognized in shareholders' equity. When the investment is disposed of or permanently impaired the related accumulated fair value changes are recycled from shareholders' equity into the profit and loss account.

20.10 MEASUREMENT OF FINANCIAL LIABILITIES SUBSEQUENT TO INITIAL RECOGNITION

20.10.1 Categorisation

For the purposes of measurement subsequent to initial recognition and the treatment of the resulting gains and losses, IAS 39 identifies three categories of financial liabilities:

- financial liabilities held for trading;
- derivatives that are liabilities; and
- all other financial liabilities.

(IAS 39, 93)

The requirements of IAS 39, before considering the impact of the hedge accounting rules, are summarised in table 20.6.

20.10.2 Financial liabilities held for trading

Financial liabilities held for trading should be measured subsequent to initial recognition at fair value (IAS 39, 93) and gains and losses should be included in the net profit or loss for the period (IAS 39, 103). This is the same requirement as for financial assets held for trading. The determination of fair value is dealt with in 20.11.1.

A *financial liability held for trading* is one that was incurred principally for the purpose of generating a profit from short-term fluctuations in price or dealer's margin (IAS 39, 10).

The same guidance applies to financial liabilities held for trading as for financial assets held for trading (see 20.9.2).

Liabilities held for trading include:

- derivative liabilities that are not hedging instruments; and
- the obligation to deliver securities or another type of financial instrument borrowed by a short seller.

(IAS 39, 10 and IGC 18-1 & 18-2).

A liability used to fund trading activities is not necessarily a liability held for trading (IAS 39, 18). For example, a bank loan used to fund trading in equity and debt securities is a financial liability but it is not itself classified as held for trading if the entity does not intend to generate a profit from short-term fluctuations in the value of that loan or in the bank's margins for that loan.

Table 20.6 *Measurement of financial liabilities subsequent to initial recognition (ignoring hedge accounting)*

Category	Measurement	Treatment of gains and losses
Financial liabilities other than liabilities held for trading and derivatives that are liabilities	Amortised cost	Profit for the period in which derecognised or impaired
Financial liabilities held for trading including all derivatives that are liabilities (other than those derivatives dealt with below)	Fair value	Profit for the period
Derivatives that are liabilities that are linked to and must be settled by delivery of an unquoted equity instrument whose fair value cannot be reliably measured	Cost	Profit for the period

20.10.3 Derivatives that are liabilities

Derivatives that are liabilities and which are not designated, or are ineffective, as a hedging instrument should be measured subsequent to initial recognition at fair value (IAS 39, 93) and gains and losses should be included in the net profit or loss for the period (IAS 39, 103). The determination of fair value is dealt with in 20.11.1.

There is one exception to the general rule. A derivative that is a liability and which is linked to and must be settled by delivery of an unquoted equity instrument whose fair value cannot be reliably measured should be measured at cost. In such circumstances, the equity instrument itself would be measured at cost.

20.10.4 Other financial liabilities

All other financial liabilities are measured at cost which is, in appropriate cases, amortised cost.

20.11 MEASUREMENT BASES FOR FINANCIAL ASSETS AND LIABILITIES

20.11.1 Fair Value

As explained above, financial assets and liabilities held for trading and available-for-sale financial assets are usually measured subsequent to initial recognition at fair value. No deduction is made for transaction costs in determining the carrying amount of financial assets carried at fair value (IAS 39, 69).

IAS 39 presumes that fair value can be reliably determined for most financial assets held for trading and most available-for-sale financial assets (IAS 39, 70). However, IAS 39 prohibits the use of fair value when fair value cannot be reliably measured (IAS 39, 69(c) and IGC 70-2). In such circumstances, a financial asset or financial liability is measured on a cost basis.

Fair value is the amount for which an asset could be exchanged, or a liability settled, between knowledgeable, willing parties in an arm's length transaction (IAS 32, 5 and IAS 39, 8). The definition presumes that the entity is a going concern without any intention or need to liquidate, curtail materially the scale of its operations, or undertake a transaction on adverse terms (IAS 39, 98).

Fair value is usually market price and may be determined from several sources including recent transactions or published prices in an active public securities market. It may be constructed from:

- the market prices of the component parts of an instrument when markets exist only for the component parts; or
- the market price of a similar instrument when a market exists only for the similar financial instrument.

(IAS 39, 101)

When fair value is determined from a quoted market price:

- the current bid price is used for an asset held or liability to be issued;
- the current offer or asking price is used for an asset to be acquired or liability held;
- mid-market prices may be used when an entity has matching asset and liability positions; and
- the price of the most recent transaction may be used when current bid and offer prices are unavailable provided that there has not been a significant change in economic circumstances between the transaction date and the reporting date.

(IAS 39, 99)

Sometimes banking or other regulations require the use of a different measurement for specific purposes, for example capital adequacy requirements. Such regulations do not override the requirements of IAS 39 in IFRS financial statements. In particular, they do not override the general requirement to use the current bid price in the absence of a matching liability position (IGC 99-1).

Published prices may need to be adjusted in order to determine fair value when:

- the market for a financial instrument is not an active market;
- there is infrequent activity in a market;
- the market is not well established;
- small volumes are traded relative to the number of trading units of a financial instrument to be valued.

(IAS 39, 100)

Fair value may have to be estimated by:

- reference to the current market value of another instrument that is substantially the same;
- using discounted cash flow analysis; or
- using option pricing models.

(IAS 39, 100)

All these techniques are well known and frequently used in financial markets. When they are used for the purposes of IAS 39, they should incorporate the assumptions that market participants would use in their estimates of fair values, including assumptions about prepayment rates, rates of estimated credit losses, and interest or discount rates (IAS 39, 97).

As explained earlier, fair value should not be used when it cannot be reliably measured. Fair value is reliably measurable for a financial instrument when, among other things:

- there is a published price quotation in an active public securities market for that instrument;
- the instrument is a debt instrument that has been rated by an independent rating agency and the cash flows associated with the instrument can be reasonably estimated; and
- there is an appropriate valuation model for the instrument and the data inputs to that model can be measured reliably because the data come from active markets.

(IAS 39, 96)

The fair value of a financial instrument can be measured reliably if:

- the variability in the range of reasonable fair value estimates is not significant for that instrument; or
- if the probabilities of the various estimates within the range can be reasonably assessed and used in estimating fair value.

(IAS 39, 95)

Extract 20.12 *Fair values*

Nokia, Finland, 31 December 2001 (IAS)

Fair values of forward rate agreements, interest rate options and futures contracts are calculated based on quoted market rates at the balance sheet date. Interest rate and currency swaps are valued by using discounted cash flow analyses. The changes in the fair values of these contracts are reported in the profit and loss account.

Fair values of cash settled equity derivatives are calculated by revaluing the contract at year-end quoted market rates. Changes in fair value are calculated by comparing the fair value with the value calculated using the prevailing market rate at the inception of the contract. Changes in the fair value are reported in the profit and loss account.

Forward foreign exchange contracts are valued with the forward exchange rate. Changes in fair value are calculated by comparing this with the original amount calculated by using the contract forward rate prevailing at the beginning of the contract. Currency options are valued at the balance sheet date by using the Garman & Kohlhagen option valuation model. Changes in the fair value on these instruments are reported in the profit and loss account except to the extent they qualify for hedge accounting.

Embedded derivatives are identified and monitored in the Group and fair valued at the balance sheet date. The fair value changes are reported in financial income and expenses in the profit and loss account.

Extract 20.13 *Fair value of held for trading financial assets*

UBS, Switzerland, 31 December 2001 (IAS)

The determination of fair values of trading portfolio assets or liabilities is based on quoted market prices in active markets or dealer price quotations, pricing models (using assumptions based on market and economic conditions), or management's estimates, as applicable.

Extract 20.14 *Fair value of available-for-sale financial assets*

UBS, Switzerland, 31 December 2001 (IAS)

The determination of fair values of available-for-sale financial investments is generally based on quoted market prices in active markets, dealer price quotations, discounted expected cash flows using market rates commensurate with the credit quality and maturity of the investment or based upon review of the investee's financial results, condition and prospects including comparisons to similar companies for which quoted market prices are available.

20.11.2 Amortised Cost

Financial assets that have a fixed maturity should be measured at amortised cost using the effective interest rate method if they fall in the following categories:

- loans and receivables originated by the enterprise and not held for trading;
- held-to-maturity investments; and
- any financial asset that does not have a quoted market price in an active market and whose fair value cannot be reliably measured.

(IAS 39, 69 & 73)

All financial liabilities, other than liabilities held for trading and derivatives that are liabilities, should be measured subsequent to initial recognition at amortised cost (IAS 39, 93).

Amortised cost is the amount at which the financial asset or liability was measured at initial recognition minus principal repayments, plus or minus the cumulative amortisation of any difference between that initial amount and the maturity amount, and minus any write-down (directly or through the use of an allowance account) for impairment or uncollectability (IAS 39, 10). The computation of amortised cost includes all fees and points paid or received between parties to the contract (IAS 39, 10).

The calculation of amortised cost is shown in IGC 73-1.

The *effective interest method* is a method of calculating amortisation using the effective interest rate of a financial asset or financial liability (IAS 39, 10). The *effective interest rate* is the rate that exactly discounts the expected stream of future cash payments through maturity or the next market-based repricing date to the current net carrying amount of the financial asset or financial liability (IAS 39, 10).

Extract 20.15 *Amortised cost*

Volkswagen, Germany, 31 December 2001 (IAS)

Financial instruments are accounted for in the balance sheet at 'amortized cost' or at 'fair value'. The 'amortized cost' of a financial asset or liability is the amount: at which a financial asset or liability is valued when first recognized

- minus any repayments
- minus any write-down for impairment or uncollectability
- plus or minus the cumulative spread of any difference between the original amount and the amount repayable at maturity (premium), distributed using the effective interest method rather than the straight line method over the term of the financial asset or liability.

In relation to short-term receivables and payables, the amortized costs generally correspond to the nominal or repayment amount.

20.11.3 Cost

Cost is the fair value of the consideration given (asset) or received (liability) and includes transaction costs (IAS 39, 66).

20.12 IMPAIRMENT OF FINANCIAL ASSETS

20.12.1 Financial assets carried at cost or amortised cost

When an entity carries a financial asset at amortised cost or some other cost basis, it must consider the possibility that carrying amount of the assets exceeds the fair value of the asset, that is, the asset is impaired. Furthermore, the carrying amount of a financial asset that is not carried at fair value because its fair value cannot be reliably measured should be reviewed annually for impairment (IAS 39, 115).

IAS 39 adopts the same three stage approach to impairment as IAS 36:

- assess whether there is any indication that an asset may be impaired;
- if there is such an indication, estimate the recoverable amount of the asset or group of assets; and
- if recoverable amount is less than carrying amount, write down the asset to recoverable amount.

(IAS 39, 109 – see also IGC 109-1)

Objective evidence that may indicate that a financial asset or group of assets is impaired or uncollectable includes information about:

- significant financial difficulty of the issuer of the instrument;
- an actual breach of contract;
- the granting to the borrower, for economic or legal reasons relating to the borrower's financial difficulty, of a concession that the entity, as lender, would not otherwise consider;
- a high probability of bankruptcy or other financial reorganisation of the issuer;
- recognition of an impairment loss on that asset in a prior financial reporting period;
- the disappearance of an active market for that financial asset due to financial difficulties; or
- a historical pattern of collections of accounts receivable that indicates that the entire face amount of a portfolio of accounts receivable will not be collected.

(IAS 39, 110)

If it is probable that an entity will not be able to collect all amounts due according to the contractual terms, an impairment or bad debt loss has occurred (IAS 39, 111). An entity may not recognise an impairment loss for a future loss, through, for example, an allowance for future losses that is set up when a loan is given (IGC 110-1). The amount of the impairment loss should be included in net profit or loss for the period (IAS 39, 111).

The amount of the impairment loss is the difference between the asset's carrying amount and the present value of expected future cash flows discounted at the financial instrument's original effective interest rate (recoverable amount) (IAS 39, 111). If a loan, receivable, or held-to-maturity investment has a variable interest rate, the discount rate is the current effective interest rate(s) determined under the contract (IAS 39, 113).

Further guidance on the impairment requirements is included in IGC 111-1 (principal and interest on restructured loans), IGC 111-2 (fair value hedges), IGC 111-3 (use of a provisioning matrix) and IGC 111-4 (losses in excess of impairment losses – see also IAS 30, 44 and 50). The value of any collateral is taken into account in determining recoverable amount (IGC 113-1) but the collateral is not recognised as an asset (IGC 113-2). Market prices may not be used to determine an impairment loss on a fixed rate financial asset carried at amortised cost (IGC 113-3).

IASB financial instruments project

In its June 2002 financial instruments exposure draft, the IASB proposes to add further extensive guidance on the evaluation of impairment that is inherent in a group of loans, receivables and held-to-maturity investments but which cannot yet be identified with any individual asset in the group.

Impairment may be measured and recognised for financial assets individually or for a portfolio basis for a group of similar assets that are not individually identified as impaired (IAS 39, 112). The use of the portfolio approach does not allow the entity to ignore an impaired financial asset because the fair value of other financial assets in the portfolio are greater than carrying amount (IGC 112-1 and 2).

If, in a subsequent period, the amount of the impairment or bad debt loss decreases and the decrease can be objectively related to an event occurring after the write-down, the write-down should be reversed (IAS 39, 114). The reversal should not result in a carrying amount that exceeds what amortised cost would have been, had the impairment not been recognised. This is the same requirement as applies under IAS 36 for non-financial assets.

The carrying amount of a financial asset that is not carried at fair value because its fair value cannot be reliably measured should be reviewed annually for impairment (IAS 39, 115). IGC 115-1 deals with the reversal of impairment losses on financial assets carried at cost because fair value cannot be determined.

Once a financial asset has been written down to recoverable amount, interest income is based on the rate of interest used in measuring the recoverable amount (IAS 39, 116).

If a loss on a financial asset carried at fair value has been recognised directly in equity and there is objective evidence that the asset is impaired, the cumulative net loss that had been recognised directly in equity should be removed from equity and recognised in net profit or loss for the period (IAS 39, 117).

Extract 20.16 *Impairment of financial assets carried at cost or amortised cost*

Bulbank, Bulgaria, 31 December 2001 (IAS)

In 2001 the bank applied IAS 39 in assessing risks on loans and provisioning. For this purpose new internal rules and classifications were adopted. The matrix principle was abandoned and now the assessment rests on time value of money calculations, based on default probability, loan loss history and broader analysis of environment.

20.12.2 Financial assets carried at fair value

The loss on an available-for-sale financial asset may be included in equity rather than net profit or loss (see 20.9.5). The fact that the fair value of the asset is below cost is not necessarily evidence that the asset is impaired (IGC 117.1 and 3). When, however, there is objective evidence that the financial asset is impaired, the loss should be transferred from equity to net profit or loss (IAS 39, 117 and IGC 117-2).

The amount of the loss that should be removed from equity and reported in net profit or loss is the difference between the acquisition cost of the financial asset (net of any principal repayment and amortisation) and current fair value (for equity instruments) or recoverable amount (for debt instruments), less any impairment loss on that asset previously recognised in net profit or loss. The recoverable amount of a debt instrument remeasured to fair value is the present value of expected future cash flows discounted at the current market rate of interest for a similar financial asset (IAS 39, 118 and IGC 118-1).

If, in a subsequent period, the fair value or recoverable amount of the financial asset carried at fair value increases and the increase can be objectively related to an event occurring after the loss was recognised in net profit or loss, the loss should be reversed (IAS 39, 119).

Extract 20.17 *Impairment of financial assets*

Zurich Financial Services, Switzerland, 31 December 2001 (IAS)

Quoted available-for-sale securities: The Group's decision to make an impairment provision is based on an objective review of the issuer's current financial position and future prospects and an assessment of the probability that the current market price will recover to former levels. If the Group decides that an asset is impaired, the cumulative net loss previously recognized in equity is removed from equity and recognized in net income for the period.

Non-quoted available-for-sale securities: The Group takes into consideration the issuer's current financial position and future prospects in determining whether an impairment provision is required.

Held-to-maturity securities: If it is possible that the Group will not be able to collect all amounts due, principal and interest, according to the contractual terms of the security, the Group considers that impairment has taken place. The amount of the impairment loss is the difference between the asset's carrying value and the present value of expected future cash flows discounted at the security's original effective interest rate.

20.13 DERECOGNITION OF FINANCIAL ASSETS

20.13.1 General principles

An entity should derecognise (or remove from its balance sheet):

- a financial asset when, and only when, the entity loses control of the contractual rights that comprise the financial asset; or
- a portion of a financial asset when, and only when, the entity loses control of the contractual rights that comprise the portion of the financial asset.

(IAS 39, 35 – see also IGC 35-1 to 35-5)

This approach is different from the more traditional approach (which was proposed in E40 and E48) under which an asset is derecognised when all (or substantially all) the risks and benefits associated with it have been transferred to others. The change in approach is consistent with the change in approach for the recognition of the asset (see 20.7).

> ***IASB financial instruments project***
>
> In its June 2002 exposure draft, the IASB proposes to replace the approach in IAS 39 with a continuing involvement approach that disallows derecognition to the extent to which the entity, as transferor, has continuing involvement in an asset or a portion of an asset it has transferred. It will be unnecessary to consider risk retained and to use that as the basis for assessing whether derecognition is appropriate.
>
> If adopted, the new approach will lead to substantial revisions to the text of IAS 39 but the IASB believes that the results of applying the proposed requirements will be generally consistent with the guidance that already exists in IAS 39 and the related IGC Q&As.
>
> Under the new approach, a transferor has a continuing involvement when:
>
> - it could, or could be required to, reacquire control of the transferred asset; or
> - compensation based on the performance of the transferred asset will be paid.
>
> No exceptions will be made to the general principle.

Under the approach adopted in IAS 39, *control* of an asset is the power to obtain the future economic benefits that flow from the asset (IAS 39, 10). If control is not transferred, the transaction or event does not result in the derecognition of the asset – instead, the transaction or event results in the continuing recognition of the asset and, usually, the recognition of a liability (IAS 39, 36). For example, if an entity transfers control of an asset in return for cash, it recognises the cash received as income, derecognises (or removes) the asset from its balance sheet and recognises the carrying amount of the asset as an expense. On the other hand, if the sale is in substance a borrowing secured on the asset and the entity retains control of the asset, the entity recognises the receipt of cash as a liability and retains the asset on its balance sheet.

An entity loses control of the contractual rights if:

- it realises the rights to benefits specified in the contract;
- the rights expire; or
- the entity surrenders those rights.

(IAS 39, 35)

An entity generally loses control of a financial asset only if the transferee has the ability to obtain the benefits of the transferred asset (IAS 39, 37 and 41). In other words, the transferee has acquired control of the asset. Furthermore, the transaction or event should result in only one of the parties recognising the same asset (see IGC 35-4). Further guidance on the relationship between transferor and transferee is included in IGC 37-1 and 38-1 to 38-5.

For example, an entity loses control of the contractual rights in a call option and, therefore, derecognises that option if:

- it exercises the option and, therefore, replaces the option with another asset;
- the option expires unexercised; or
- it sells the option to another party and the other party acquires the contractual rights in the option.

Similarly, an entity loses control in a receivable and, therefore, derecognises that receivable if:

- it receives cash in settlement of the receivable and replaces the receivable with another asset (cash);
- it fails to collect the receivable within the statutory or contractual time limit; or
- it sells the receivable to another party and the other party acquires the contractual rights in the receivable (including the risk of non-settlement).

IAS 39 gives two examples of when an entity has lost control of a transferred financial asset and, therefore, removes that asset from its balance sheet:

- the transfer of an asset to a transferee who is free to sell or pledge approximately the full fair value of the transferred asset; and
- the transfer of an asset to a special-purpose entity (but SIC 12 may require the entity to consolidate the special-purpose entity – see chapter 15).

(IAS 39, 41 – see also IGC 35-3 and 41-1)

An entity has not lost control of a transferred financial asset when it has the right to reacquire the transferred asset unless either the asset is readily obtainable in the market or the reacquisition price is fair value at the time of reacquisition (IAS 39, 38). For example, if the entity purports to sell an equity interest in an unquoted company for cash but retains the right to reacquire the equity interest for less than fair value, the sale is accounted for as a financing – the entity retains the equity interest on its balance sheet and recognises the receipt of cash as a liability. If the right to reacquire the asset is at fair value, the sale is recognised because both the entity and the transferee are at risk for changes in the fair value of the equity interest.

An entity has also not lost control of a transferred financial asset when it is both entitled and obligated to repurchase or redeem the transferred asset on terms that effectively provide the transferee with a lender's return on the assets received in exchange for the transferred asset (IAS 39, 38). For example, if the entity purports to sell an equity interest for cash but is entitled and obligated to reacquire the equity interest for the amount paid plus a market rate of interest, the sale is accounted for as a financing – the entity retains the equity interest on its balance sheet and recognises the receipt of cash as a liability.

An entity has also not lost control of a transferred financial asset when the transferred asset is not readily obtainable in the market and the entity has retained substantially all the risks and returns of ownership through a total return swap with the transferee (IAS 39, 38). A *total return swap* provides the market returns and credit risks to one of the parties in return for an interest index to the other party, such as a LIBOR payment. Therefore, if the entity purports to sell an equity interest for cash but enters into a total return swap under which it retains the market returns and credit risk and the transferee receives a payment based on LIBOR, the sale is accounted for as a financing – the entity retains the equity interest on its balance sheet and recognises the receipt of cash as a liability.

An entity has also not lost control of a transferred financial asset when the transferred asset is not readily obtainable in the market and the entity has retained substantially all the risks and returns of ownership through an unconditional put option on the transferred asset held by the transferee (IAS 39, 38). For example, if the entity purports to sell an equity interest for cash but the transferee has an unconditional right to put the asset back to the entity and the entity has retained substantially all the risks and rewards of ownership, the sale is accounted for as a financing – the entity retains the equity interest on its balance sheet and recognises the receipt of cash as a liability.

Further guidance is included in the IAS 39 Q&As, in particular IGC 35-1 and 35-2 deal with the factors that affect the derecognition of a portion of a loan and IGC 35-5 deals with 'wash sales' in which the entity purchases an asset immediately before or soon after the sale of the same asset. IGC 38-1 to 38-5 deal with several circumstances in which the entity retains some rights, for example a right of first refusal to repurchase the asset, put options, securities lending transactions and 'clean-up calls'.

Extract 20.18 *Derecognition of financial assets*

UBS, Switzerland, 31 December 2001 (IAS)

Securities purchased under agreements to resell (reverse repurchase agreements) and securities sold under agreements to repurchase (repurchase agreements) are generally treated as collateralized financing transactions and are carried at the amounts at which the securities were acquired or sold, plus accrued interest. The Group monitors the market value of the underlying securities (which collateralize the related receivables) on a daily basis and requests additional collateral when appropriate. Interest earned on reverse repurchase agreements and interest incurred on repurchase agreements is recognized as interest income and interest expense, over the life of each agreement.

The Group offsets reverse repurchase agreements and repurchase agreements with the same counterparty for transactions covered by legally enforceable master netting agreements when net or simultaneous settlement is intended.

20.13.2 Derecognition of a portion of a financial asset

When an entity transfers part of a financial asset to another party while retaining a part, the carrying amount of the financial asset should be allocated between the part transferred and the part retained based on their relative fair values on the date of sale (IAS 39, 47). In the rare circumstance that the fair value of the part of the asset that is retained cannot be measured reliably, the entire carrying amount of the financial asset should be attributed to the portion sold (IAS 39, 47).

Examples of a partial transfer include:

- separating the principal and interest cash flows of a bond and selling some of them to another party while retaining the rest; and
- selling a portfolio of receivables while retaining the right to service the receivables profitably for a fee, resulting in an asset for the servicing.

IAS 39, 49-50 include examples of the calculations. IGC 47-1 deals with estimating fair values when a portion of an investment in bonds is sold. IGC 47-2 deals with estimating fair values when a portion of a portfolio of originated loans is sold.

Extract 20.19 *Securitisations*

UBS, Switzerland, 31 December 2001 (IAS)

The Group securitizes various consumer and commercial financial assets, which generally results in the sale of these assets to special-purpose vehicles which, in turn, issue securities to investors. Financial assets are partially or wholly derecognized when the Group gives up control of the contractual rights that comprise the financial asset.

Interests in the securitized financial assets may be retained in the form of senior or subordinated tranches, interest-only strips or other residual interests ('retained interests'). Retained interests are primarily recorded in Trading portfolio assets and carried at fair value. The determination of fair values of retained interest is generally based on listed market prices or by determining the present value of expected future cash flows using pricing models that incorporate management's best estimates of critical assumptions which may include credit losses, discount rates, yield curves and other factors.

Gains or losses on securitization depend in part on the carrying amount of the transferred financial assets, allocated between the financial assets derecognized and the retained interests based on their relative fair values at the date of the transfer. Gains or losses on securitization are recorded in net trading income.

20.13.3 Derecognition of a financial asset coupled with the recognition of a new financial asset or liability

When an entity transfers an entire financial asset but, in doing so, creates a new financial asset or assumes a new financial liability, the entity should recognise the new financial asset or financial liability at fair value (IAS 39, 51). In the rare circumstance that the fair value of the new financial asset cannot be measured reliably, its initial carrying amount should be zero (IAS 39, 54(a)) so that no gain is recognised on the transaction. If IAS 37 requires the recognition of a provision as a result of the transaction, the entity should recognise a loss (IAS 39, 54(b)).

If an entity recognises a guarantee as a liability under IAS 39, it continues to recognise the liability until it expires (IAS 39, 56). The liability is measured at its fair value (or at the greater of its original recorded amount and any provision required by IAS 37, if fair value cannot be reliably measured) (IAS 39, 56).

Examples of such a transfer include:

- selling a portfolio of receivables while assuming an obligation to compensate the purchaser of the receivables if collections are below a specified level; and
- selling a portfolio of receivables while retaining the right to service the receivables for a fee, and the fee to be received is less than the costs of servicing, thereby resulting in a liability for the servicing obligation.

20.13.4 Gain or loss on derecognition of a financial asset

The gain or loss on the derecognition of an asset is:

- the proceeds received or receivable on derecognition; *less*
- the carrying amount of the transferred asset (or the portion of that asset); *plus*
- any prior gains on that asset included in equity; and *less*
- any prior losses on that asset included in equity.

The gain or loss should be included in net profit or loss for the period (IAS 39, 43).

20.14 DERECOGNITION OF A FINANCIAL LIABILITY

20.14.1 General principles

An entity should derecognise (or remove from its balance sheet):

- a financial liability when, and only when, it is extinguished – that is, when the obligation specified in the contract is discharged, cancelled, or expires; or
- a part of a financial liability when, and only when, it is extinguished – that is, when the obligation specified in the contract for that portion is discharged, cancelled, or expires.

(IAS 39, 57)

This approach excludes the alternative approach which was proposed in E40 and E48 under which a liability is derecognised when all (or substantially all) the risks and benefits associated with it have been transferred to others. The elimination of this approach is consistent with the change in approach for the recognition of the liability (see 20.7).

A financial liability is extinguished when either:

- the entity discharges the liability by paying the creditor, normally with cash, other financial assets, goods or services; or
- the entity is legally released from primary responsibility for the liability (or part thereof) either by process of law or by the creditor.

(IAS 39, 58)

If an entity buys back its own bonds, it has discharged the liability and derecognises the liability even it intends to resell the bonds (IGC 57-2).

A payment by the entity to a third party including a payment to a trust (a so-called in-substance defeasance) does not by itself relieve the entity of its primary obligation to the creditor in the absence of a legal release (IAS 39, 59). However, when that fee does relieve the entity of the obligation, the entity derecognises the liability (IGC 57-1). An entity does not derecognise a liability when its pays another party to assume responsibility for the liability but is not legally released from its primary obligation (IGC 57-3).

When an entity exchanges an existing debt instrument for a new debt instrument with the same lender but with substantially different terms, the entity derecognises the existing debt instrument and recognises the new debt instrument (IAS 39, 61). Similarly, the debt is extinguished if the terms of an existing debt instrument are substantially modified or there is an exchange between an entity and a creditor with substantially different terms (IAS 39, 61). The terms 'substantially modified' or 'substantially different' mean that the discounted present value of the cash flows, including any fees paid net of any fees received, is at least 10 per cent different from the discounted present value of the remaining cash flows under the old terms (IAS 39, 62 and IGC 62-1).

When an entity is released by a creditor from its present obligation to make payments but assumes an obligation to pay if the party assuming primary responsibility for the obligation defaults, the entity recognises a new financial liability based on the fair value of its obligation for the guarantee (IAS 39, 64).

20.14.2 Derecognition of part of a financial liability

When an entity extinguishes part of a financial liability while retaining a part, the carrying amount of the financial liability should be allocated between the part extinguished and the part retained based on their relative fair values on the date of sale (IAS 39, 47 and 65).

In the rare circumstance that the fair value of the part of the financial liability that is retained cannot be measured reliably, the entire carrying amount of the financial liability should be attributed to the portion sold (IAS 39, 47 and 65).

20.14.3 Derecognition of a liability coupled with recognition of a new financial asset or liability

When an entity extinguishes an entire financial liability but, in doing so, creates a new financial asset or assumes a new financial liability, the entity should recognise the new financial asset or financial liability at fair value (IAS 39, 51 and 65). In the rare circumstance that the fair value of the new financial asset cannot be measured reliably, its initial carrying amount should be zero (IAS 39, 54(a) and 65).

In the rare circumstance that the fair value of the new financial liability cannot be measured reliably, its initial carrying amount should be such that no gain is recognised on the transaction. If IAS 37 requires the recognition of a provision as a result of the transaction, the entity should recognise a loss (IAS 39, 54(b)).

If an entity recognises a guarantee as a liability under IAS 39, it continues to recognise the liability until it expires (IAS 39, 56). The liability is measured at its fair value (or at the greater of its original recorded amount and any provision required by IAS 37, if fair value cannot be reliably measured) (IAS 39, 56).

While legal release, whether judicially or by the creditor, will result in derecognition of a liability, the entity may have to recognise a new liability if the derecognition criteria above are not met for the non-cash financial assets that were transferred. If those criteria are not met, the transferred assets are not removed from the entity's balance sheet, and the entity recognises a new liability relating to the transferred assets that may be equal to the derecognised liability (IAS 39, 60).

20.14.4 Gain or loss on derecognition of a financial liability

The gain or loss on derecognition is:

- the amount paid for the extinguishment of the liability; *less*
- the carrying amount (including related unamortised costs) of the derecognised liability (or the portion of that liability).

(IAS 39, 63)

The gain or loss should be included in net profit or loss for the period (IAS 39, 63).

20.15 HEDGE ACCOUNTING

Hedge accounting is a special form of accounting which changes the way that financial assets and financial liabilities are measured and the treatment of resulting gains and losses. The objective of hedge accounting is to recognise and measure the hedging instrument and the position being hedged on symmetrical bases so that they are carried on the balance sheet at the same value and offsetting gains and losses are reported in the income statement in the same periods (*Accounting for Financial Assets and Financial Liabilities*, p 134). The existing mixed attribute accounting model means that this objective is sometimes not achieved without special accounting. For example special accounting is needed to match the gain or loss on a derivative used to hedge a risk associated with an originated loan.

In its 1997 discussion paper, the IASC advocated a full fair value approach for financial assets and financial liabilities that would have reduced, but not eliminated, the mismatches. A full fair value approach does not deal with the calls for hedge accounting for hedges of expected transactions or firm commitments. At the time, the IASC argued that hedging accounting (the deferral of gains and losses) was 'not supportable within the IASC Framework and [was] not consistent with the principle proposed for recognition ... and the principle proposed for measurement on initial recognition' (*Accounting for Financial Assets and Financial Liabilities*, 4.14). Hedge accounting was also not supported by the Joint Working Group's draft standard.

IAS 39 allows a mixed attribute model for financial assets and financial liabilities which increases the calls for some form of hedge accounting. Therefore, IAS 39 allows the use of hedge accounting both when the hedging instrument and the hedged position are measured differently (for example, one at fair value and the other at amortised cost) and when they are measured in the same way but the resulting gains and losses are dealt with differently (for example, in net profit or loss for the hedging instrument and in equity for the hedged item). IAS 39 also allows the use of hedge accounting for expected transactions and firm commitments.

IAS 39 does place significant restrictions on the use of hedge accounting which means that the accounting may still be different from the intentions of management because some hedging transactions may not qualify for hedge accounting under IAS 39. In particular, IAS 39 does not allow hedge accounting for hedges of enterprise risk or internal hedges.

Hedge accounting may only be used when all the criteria in IAS 39 for hedging, hedged items, hedging instruments and a hedging relationship are met. While IAS 39 says that an entity 'should' use hedge accounting when the criteria are met (IAS 39, 121), in practice hedge accounting is optional. It is easy for management not to meet the criteria for hedge accounting, in fact it can do this simply by failing to comply with the designation or documentation requirements.

It is also worth bearing in mind that there are over 40 paragraphs of IAS 39 and over one hundred pages of IGC Q&As on hedge accounting. These requirements and guidance can be ignored by those entities that opt not to use hedge accounting.

20.15.1 Hedging, hedging instruments and hedged items

Hedging means designating of one or more hedging instruments so that their change in fair value is an offset, in whole or in part, to the change in fair value or cash flows of a hedged item (IAS 39, 10). Therefore, the use of hedge accounting requires the identification and designation of a hedging instrument and a hedged item. Furthermore, the hedge must relate to a specific identified and designated risk, and not merely to overall entity business risks, and must ultimately affect the entity's net profit or loss (IAS 39, 149).

A *hedging instrument* is a designated derivative or (in limited circumstances) another financial asset or liability whose fair value or cash flows are expected to offset changes in the fair value or cash flows of a designated hedged item (IAS 39, 10). For example, a forward contract may be a hedging instrument because its fair value or cash flows may offset changes in the fair value or cash flows of a designated hedged item.

For the purposes of IAS 39, a hedging instrument may be:

- any derivative other than a written option (IAS 39, 122) – two or more derivatives may be designated as a hedge of the same hedged item (IGC 122-1);
- a written option but only if it is designated as a hedge of a purchased option (IAS 39, 124 and IGC 124-1);
- a non-derivative financial asset or liability (including held-to-maturity investments) but only for a hedge of a foreign currency risk (IAS 39, 10 and 122 and IGC 122-2 and 122-3); or
- a non-derivative financial asset or financial liability whose fair value cannot be reliably measured but which is denominated in a foreign currency, designated as a hedge of foreign currency risk and whose foreign currency component is reliably measurable (IAS 39, 126).

An entity's own equity securities cannot be used as a hedging instrument because they are not financial assets or financial liabilities of the entity (IAS 39, 123).

A hedging instrument may be designated as a hedge of more than one type of risk provided that:

- the risks hedged can be clearly identified;
- the effectiveness of the hedge can be demonstrated; and
- it is possible to ensure that there is a specific designation of the hedging instrument and the different risk positions.

(IAS 39, 131)

A *hedged item* is an asset, liability, firm commitment, or forecasted future transaction that exposes the entity to risk of changes in fair value or changes in future cash flows (IAS 39, 10). It may be:

- a single asset, liability, firm commitment, or forecasted transaction;

- a group of assets, liabilities, firm commitments, or forecasted transactions with similar risk characteristics; or
- a held-to-maturity investment but only with respect to foreign currency exchange rates and credit risk.

(IAS 39, 127)

IGC 127-1 to 127-6 deal with several applications of the identification of a hedged item.

A financial asset or liability may be a hedged item with respect to the risks associated with either all its cash flows or fair value or for only a portion of its cash flows or fair value, if effectiveness of the portion can be measured (IAS 39, 128). IGC 128-1 to 128-4 provide further guidance.

A hedged item may be a non-financial asset or liability but only if it is designated as a hedged item for either:

- foreign currency risks; or
- its entirety for all risks.

(IAS 39, 129)

A *firm commitment* is a binding agreement for the exchange of a specified quantity of resources at a specified price on a specified future date or dates (IAS 39, 10). Such commitments are not usually recognised as assets or liabilities under the requirements of IFRSs. An entity may, however, designate such commitments as hedged items. However, it may designate a firm commitment to acquire a business in a business combination as a hedged item only with respect to foreign exchange risk (IAS 39, 135).

Designation of a firm commitment as a hedged item does not change the accounting for the commitment although it may affect the initial measurement of assets and liabilities resulting from the commitment. Designation does, however, change the accounting for the hedging instrument.

20.15.2 Hedging relationship

For the purposes of IAS 39, a hedging relationship qualifies for hedge accounting if, and only if, all of the following criteria are met:

- at the inception of the hedge there is formal documentation of the hedging relationship and the entity's risk management objective and strategy for undertaking the hedge;
- the hedge is expected to be highly effective in achieving offsetting changes in fair value or cash flows attributable to the hedged risk, consistent with the originally documented risk management strategy for that particular hedging relationship;

- for cash flow hedges, a forecasted transaction that is the subject of the hedge must be highly probable and must present an exposure to variations in cash flows that could ultimately affect reported net profit or loss;
- the effectiveness of the hedge can be reliably measured, that is, the fair value or cash flows of the hedged item and the fair value of the hedging instrument can be reliably measured; and
- the hedge was assessed on an ongoing basis and determined actually to have been highly effective throughout the financial reporting period.

(IAS 39, 142)

Designation of a hedge cannot be made retrospectively (IGC 142-4).

The formal documentation should identify:

- the hedging instrument;
- the hedged item;
- the nature of the risk being hedged; and
- how the entity will assess hedge effectiveness.

(IAS 39, 142)

IAS 39 does not specify a single method for assessing hedge effectiveness. A hedge is normally regarded as highly effective if, at inception and throughout its life, the entity can expect changes in the fair value or cash flows of the hedged item to be almost fully offset by the changes in the fair value or cash flows of the hedging instrument, and actual results are within a range of 80 per cent to 125 per cent (IAS 39, 146). What is important is that the method is specified in the formal documentation.

20.15.3 Fair value hedges

A *fair value hedge* is a hedge of the exposure to changes in the fair value of a recognised asset or liability (or an identified portion of such an asset or liability) that is attributable to a particular risk and will affect reported net income (IAS 39, 137). IGC 137-1 to 137-16 provide further guidance. Risks that can be hedged are changes in fair value caused by:

- changes in the price of the hedged item;
- some changes in interest rates;
- foreign currency rate changes; and
- some changes in counterparty credit risk.

A fair value hedge should be accounted by including both the gain or loss arising on the measurement of the hedging instrument and the gain or loss on the hedged item attributable to the hedged risk in net profit or loss (IAS 39, 153). In the case of a fair value hedge, it is the accounting for the hedged item, not the accounting for the hedging instrument, that changes.

When both the hedging instrument and the hedged item are measured at fair value and the resulting gains and losses are included in the net profit or loss for the period, hedge accounting is not needed. The gains and losses are matched at the same time. Therefore, no changes are made to the accounting. Similarly no changes are required when, for example, an entity hedges the foreign currency risk in an originated receivable with, say, a forward contract. With or without hedge accounting, the gain and matching loss are recognised at the same time in net profit or loss.

When the hedged item is carried at cost or amortised cost or the gain or loss attributable to the hedged risk is either not recognised or included in equity, the gains and losses are not matched unless hedge accounting is used. In such circumstances, IAS 39 allows the entity to change the accounting for the hedged item so as to match the gains and losses on the hedged item with those on the hedging instrument (which are already included in net profit or loss).

When the hedged item would otherwise be measured at cost or amortised cost, hedge accounting changes the measurement and the reported gains and losses on the hedged item. Under hedge accounting, the gains or losses attributable to the hedged risk in the hedged item should be :

- added to (gains)/deducted from (losses) the carrying amount of the hedged item (so changing the measurement of the hedged item); and
- recognised immediately in the net profit or loss.

(IAS 39, 153(b))

When the hedged item is measured at fair value but the resulting gains and losses would otherwise be included in equity (for example, with some available-for-sale financial assets), hedge accounting changes the accounting for the gains and losses. Under hedge accounting, the gains and losses attributable to the hedged risk should be recognised immediately in net profit or loss (IAS 39, 153(b)), instead of being included in equity.

If the hedged item is an interest-bearing financial liability, the change in carrying amount resulting from the application of hedge accounting should be amortised to net profit or loss – in other words, it becomes part of the application of amortised cost. Amortisation begins no later than when the hedged item ceases to be adjusted for changes in its fair value attributable to the risk being hedged and end no later than maturity. (IAS 39, 157).

An entity should discontinue prospectively the fair value hedge accounting when:

(a) the hedging instrument expires or is sold, terminated, or exercised; or

(b) the hedge no longer meets the criteria for qualification for hedge accounting.

(IAS 39, 156)

20.15.4 Cash flow hedges

A *cash flow hedge* is a hedge of the exposure to variability in cash flows that:

- is attributable to a particular risk associated with a recognised asset or liability or a forecasted transaction; and
- will affect reported net profit or loss.

(IAS 39, 137)

Examples of cash flow hedges include:

- a hedge of the future foreign currency risk in an unrecognised contractual commitment by an airline to purchase an aircraft for a fixed amount of a foreign currency;
- a hedge of the change in fuel price relating to an unrecognised contractual commitment to purchase fuel at a fixed price, with payment in its domestic currency; and
- use of a swap to, in effect, change floating rate debt to fixed rate debt.

A hedge of a firm commitment in an entity's own reporting currency is accounted for as a cash flow hedge notwithstanding that it is an exposure to a change in fair value (IAS 39, 137(b) and 140).

Hedge accounting for cash flow hedges affects the accounting for the gains and losses on the hedging instrument rather than the accounting for the hedged item as is the case with a fair value hedge. However, hedge accounting for cash flow hedges does affect the carrying amount of the assets and liabilities resulting from the hedged position when that position is a firm commitment or forecasted transaction (IAS 39, 158 to 162).

When the hedging instrument is a derivative:

- the portion of the gain or loss on the hedging instrument that is an effective hedge should be recognised directly in equity (rather than net profit or loss); and
- the ineffective portion should be included in net profit or loss.

(IAS 39, 158)

For example, if an entity uses a swap to change fixed rate debt into floating rate debt, hedge accounting requires that the gain or loss on the swap (the hedging instrument) is recognised in equity rather than in net profit or loss. Similarly, if an entity uses a foreign currency forward contract to hedge the foreign currency risk in a firm commitment, hedge accounting requires that the gain or loss on the forward contract is recognised in equity rather than in net profit or loss.

When the hedging instrument is not a derivative:

- the portion of the gain or loss on the hedging instrument that is an effective hedge should be recognised directly in equity; and
- the ineffective portion should be included in profit or loss or equity in accordance with the entity's policy for dealing with changes in the fair value of a financial asset or liability.

(IAS 39, 158)

When the hedged position is a firm commitment or a forecasted transaction that results in the recognition of an asset or a liability, the gains or losses on the hedging instrument that have been recognised directly in equity are included in the cost of the asset or liability (IAS 39, 160). For example, if an entity enters into a foreign currency forward contract to cover the foreign currency risk in a firm commitment to acquire an asset, under hedge accounting the gains and losses on the contract are initially included in equity. When the entity recognises the asset that was the subject of the firm commitment, it transfers the gains and losses from equity to the asset account. As a result of these so-called 'basis adjustments', the asset is recorded using the rate of exchange in the forward contract rather than the rate at the date of purchase (assuming that the forward contract covered the whole of the cost of the asset).

When the hedged position is a firm commitment or a forecasted transaction and that commitment or transaction does not result in the recognition of an asset or a liability, the gains and losses on the hedging instrument that were recognised directly in equity should be:

IASB financial instruments project

In its June 2002 exposure draft, the IASB proposes to require that hedges of firm commitments be treated as fair value hedges and to prohibit the 'basis adjustment' to the initial carrying amount of the asset or liability.

- removed from equity in the period or periods during which the commitment or forecasted transaction affects net profit or loss; and
- included in the net profit or loss for the period(s).

(IAS 39, 161)

An entity should discontinue prospectively cash flow hedge accounting when:

- the hedging instrument expires or is sold, terminated, or exercised;
- the hedge no longer meets the criteria for qualification for hedge accounting; or
- the firm commitment or forecasted transaction is no longer expected to occur.

(IAS 39, 163)

When an entity discontinues cash flow hedge accounting because a firm commitment of forecasted transaction is no longer expected to occur, it should transfer the cumulative gains or losses on the hedging instrument that were initially reported directly in equity to net profit or loss for the period (IAS 39, 163).

When an entity discontinues hedge accounting for either of the first two reasons above, the cumulative gains or losses on the hedging instrument that were initially reported directly in equity should be removed from equity when the commitment or forecasted transaction occurs. The gains or losses are included, as appropriate, in the cost of a resulting asset or liability or included in the net profit or loss for the period (IAS 39, 163, 160 and 162).

20.15.5 Hedges of a net investment in a foreign entity

A hedge of a net investment in a foreign entity is defined in IAS 21 (see chapter 19). Such hedges should be accounted for similarly to cash flow hedges:

- the portion of the gain or loss on the hedging instrument that is determined to be an effective hedge should be recognised directly in equity through the statement of changes in equity; and
- the ineffective portion should be reported immediately in net profit or loss if the hedging instrument is a derivative, or in accordance with IAS 21 in the limited circumstances in which the hedging instrument is not a derivative.

(IAS 39, 164)

The gain or loss on the hedging instrument relating to the effective portion of the hedge should be classified in the same manner as the foreign currency translation gain or loss.

Extract 20.20 *Hedge accounting*

Novartis, 31 December 2001, Switzerland (IAS)

Under IAS 39 derivative financial instruments are initially recognized in the balance sheet at cost and subsequently remeasured to their fair value. The method of recognizing the resulting gain or loss is dependent on whether the derivative contract is designed to hedge a specific risk and qualifies for hedge accounting. On the date a derivative contract is entered into, the Group designates certain derivatives as either a) a hedge of the fair value of a recognized asset or liability (fair value hedge), or b) a hedge of a forecasted transaction (cash flow hedge) or firm commitment or c) a hedge of a net investment in a foreign entity.

Changes in the fair value of derivatives which are fair value hedges and that are highly effective are recognized in the income statement, along with any changes in the fair value of the hedged asset or liability that is attributable to the hedged risk. Changes in the fair value of derivatives in cash flow hedges are recognized in equity. Where the forecasted transaction or firm commitment results in the recognition of an asset or liability, the gains and losses previously included in equity are included in the initial measurement of the asset or liability. Otherwise, amounts recorded in equity are transferred to the income statement and classified as revenue or expense in the same period in which the forecasted transaction affects the income statement.

Hedges of net investments in foreign entities are accounted for similarly to cash flow hedges. The Group hedges certain net investments in foreign entities with foreign currency borrowings. All foreign exchange gains or losses arising on translation are recognized in equity and included in cumulative translation differences.

Certain derivative instruments, while providing effective economic hedges under the Group's policies, do not qualify for hedge accounting. Changes in the fair value of any derivative instruments that do not qualify for hedge accounting under IAS 39 are recognized immediately in the income statement. When a hedging instrument expires or is sold, or when a hedge no longer meets the criteria for hedge accounting, any cumulative gain or loss existing in equity at that time remains in equity and is recognized in the income statement, when the committed or forecasted transaction is ultimately recognized in the income statement. However, if a forecasted or committed transaction is no longer expected to occur, the cumulative gain or loss that was recognized in equity is immediately transferred to the income statement.

The purpose of hedge accounting is to match the impact of the hedged item and the hedging instrument in the income statement. To qualify for hedge accounting, the hedging relationship must meet several strict conditions with respect to documentation, probability of occurrence, hedge effectiveness and reliability of measurement. At the inception of the transaction the Group documents the relationship between hedging instruments and hedged items, as well as its risk management objective and strategy for undertaking various hedge transactions. This process includes linking all derivatives designated as hedges to specific assets and liabilities or to specific firm commitments or forecasted transactions. The Group also documents its assessment, both at the hedge inception and on an ongoing basis, as to whether the derivatives that are used in hedging transactions are highly effective in offsetting changes in fair values or cash flows of hedged items.

Extract 20.21 *Hedge accounting*

Adidas, Germany, 31 December 2001 (IAS)

The Company uses derivative financial instruments, interest and currency options, as well as forward contracts, to hedge its exposure to foreign exchange and interest rate risks. In accordance with its treasury policy, the Company does not hold any derivative financial instruments for trading purposes.

Derivative financial instruments are initially recognized in the balance sheet at cost and subsequently measured at their fair value. The method of recognizing the resulting gain or loss is dependent on the nature of the item being hedged. On the date a derivative contract is entered into, the Company designates certain derivatives as either a hedge of the fair value of a recognized asset or liability (fair value hedge) or a hedge of a forecasted transaction (cash flow hedge), or a hedge of a net investment in a foreign entity. Changes in the fair value of derivatives that are designated and qualify as cash flow hedges, and that are 100% effective, are recognized in equity. If there is no 100% effectiveness, the deviating amounts are recognized in net income. Amounts deferred in equity are transferred to the income statement in the same periods during which the hedged forecasted transaction affects the income statement. For derivative instruments designated as a fair value hedge, the gain or loss on the derivative and the offsetting gain or loss on the hedged item are recognized immediately in net income.

Certain derivative transactions, while providing effective economic hedges under the Company's risk management policies, do not qualify for hedge accounting under the specific rules of IAS 39. Changes in the fair values of any derivative instruments that do not qualify for hedge accounting under IAS 39 are recognized immediately in the income statement.

Hedges of net investments in foreign entities are accounted for similarly to cash flow hedges. If the hedging instrument is a derivative (e.g. a forward contract) or for example a foreign currency borrowing, any gains and losses in the derivative and all gains and losses arising on the translation of the borrowing are recognized in equity.

The Company documents at the inception of the transaction the relationship between hedging instruments and hedged items, as well as the risk management objective and strategy for undertaking various hedge transactions. This process includes linking all derivatives designated as hedges to specific forecasted transactions. The Company also documents its assessment, both at the hedge inception and on an ongoing basis, whether the derivatives that are used in hedging transactions are highly effective in offsetting changes in cash flows of hedged items.

Extract 20.22 *Derivatives and hedge accounting*

Gulf International Bank, Bahrain, 31 December 2001 (IAS)

Derivative financial instruments are contracts the value of which is derived from one or more underlying financial instruments or indices, and include futures, forwards, swaps and options in the interest rate, foreign exchange and equity markets. On the adoption of IAS 39, the Group recognised for the first time the fair value of all derivative financial instruments in the consolidated balance sheet as either assets (positive fair values) or liabilities (negative fair values). ... Following the adoption of IAS 39, all derivative financial instruments are initially recognised in the consolidated balance sheet at cost, including transaction costs, and subsequently remeasured to fair value. Fair values are derived from prevailing market prices, discounted cash flow models or option pricing models as appropriate. In the consolidated balance sheet, derivative financial instruments with positive fair values (unrealised gains) are included in other assets and derivative financial instruments with negative fair values (unrealised losses) are included in other liabilities.

The changes in the fair values of derivative financial instruments entered into for trading purposes or to hedge other trading positions are included in other income in the consolidated statement of income.

The recognition of changes in the fair values of derivative financial instruments entered into for hedging purposes is determined by the nature of the hedging relationship. For the purposes of hedge accounting, derivative financial instruments are designated as a hedge of either: (i) the fair value of a recognised asset or liability (fair value hedge), or (ii) the future cash flows attributable to a recognised asset or liability or a firm commitment (cash flow hedge).

The Group's criteria for a derivative financial instrument to be accounted for as a hedge include:

- the hedging instrument, the related hedged item, the nature of the risk being hedged, and the risk management objective and strategy must be formally documented at the inception of the hedge,
- it must be clearly demonstrated that the hedge is expected to be highly effective in offsetting the changes in fair values or cash flows attributable to the hedged risk in the hedged item,
- the effectiveness of the hedge must be capable of being reliably measured, and
- the hedge must be assessed on an ongoing basis and determined to have actually been highly effective throughout the financial reporting period.

Changes in the fair values of derivative financial instruments that are designated, and qualify, as fair value hedges and that prove to be highly effective in relation to the hedged risk, are included in other income in the consolidated statement of income together with the corresponding change in the fair value of the hedged asset or liability that is attributable to the risk that is being hedged. Unrealised gains and losses on hedged assets or liabilities which are attributable to the hedged risk are adjusted against the carrying amounts of the hedged assets or liabilities. If the hedge no longer meets the criteria for hedge accounting, any adjustment to the carrying amount of a hedged interest-bearing financial instrument is amortised to income over the remaining period to maturity. Changes in the fair values of derivative financial instruments that are designated, and qualify, as cash flow hedges and that prove to be highly effective in relation to the hedged risk, are recognised in a separate component of shareholders' equity. Unrealised gains or losses on any ineffective portion of cash flow hedging transactions are recognised in other income in the consolidated statement of income.

The interest component of derivatives that are designated, and qualify, as fair value or cash flow hedges is recognised in interest income or interest expense over the life of the derivative instrument.

Certain derivative transactions, while providing effective economic hedges within the Group's risk management positions, do not qualify for hedge accounting under the specific rules in IAS 39. Such derivative transactions are categorised as derivatives held for trading and related fair value gains and losses included in other income in the consolidated statement of income.

Hedge accounting is discontinued when the derivative hedging instrument either expires or is sold, terminated or exercised, or no longer qualifies for hedge accounting.

Extract 20.23 *Hedge accounting*

UBS, Switzerland, 31 December 2001 (IAS)

Where the Group enters into derivatives for trading purposes, realized and unrealized gains and losses are recognized in net trading income.

The Group also uses derivative instruments as part of its asset and liability management activities to manage exposures to interest rate risks, credit risks and foreign currency risks. The Group applies either fair value or cash flow hedge accounting when it meets the specified criteria to obtain hedge accounting treatment. Derivative instruments not qualifying for hedge accounting are treated as derivative instruments used for trading purposes. The Group has entered into economic hedges of credit risk within the loan portfolio using credit default swaps to which it does not apply hedge accounting. However, in the event the Group recognizes an impairment on a loan that is economically hedged in this way, the gain on the credit default swap is offset against credit loss expense/recovery.

In a qualifying hedge of exposures to changes in fair value, the change in fair value of the hedging derivative is recognized in net profit and loss. The change in fair value of the hedged item attributable to the hedged risks adjusts the carrying value of the hedged item and is also recognized in net profit or loss. If the hedge relationship is terminated, the unamortized fair value adjustment of the hedged item is amortized to net profit or loss over the original hedge term or recognized in income if the hedged item is derecognized. In a qualifying cash flow hedge, the effective portion of the gain or loss on the hedging derivative is recognized in shareholders' equity while the ineffective portion is reported in net profit or loss. When the hedged firm commitment or forecasted transaction results in income or expense, then the associated gain or loss on the hedging derivative is removed from shareholders' equity and included in net profit or loss in the same period during which the forecasted transaction affects net profit or loss. If the forecasted transaction is no longer expected to occur, the cumulative gain or loss on the hedging derivative is recognized immediately in net profit or loss. If the hedge relationship is terminated, the cumulative gain or loss on the hedging derivative that initially had been reported in shareholders' equity when the hedge was effective, remains in shareholders' equity until the committed or forecasted transaction occurs, at which point it is reported in net profit or loss.

Extract 20.24 *Hedge accounting*

Volkswagen, Germany, 31 December 2001 (IAS)

Certain hedging instruments used by the Volkswagen Group on the basis of commercial criteria to hedge against interest or exchange rate changes, but not meeting the strict criteria of IAS 39,are classified as 'financial assets or liabilities held for trading purposes' in IAS 39 terms. They include interest limiting instruments, options or portfolio hedges. If external interest rate hedges subsequently eliminated in the consolidated financial statements are entered into in respect of loans between Group companies, such financial instruments are also assigned to this category.

...

Derivative financial instruments/hedge accounting

Volkswagen Group companies deploy derivative financial instruments to hedge balance sheet items and future cash flows.

In the case of hedging against the risk of change in value of balance sheet items (fair value hedges), both the hedge transaction and the hedged risk portion of the underlying transaction are recognized at fair value. Valuation changes are recorded in the income statement.

In the case of hedging of future cash flows (cash flow hedges), the hedge instruments are also valued at fair value. Changes in valuation are initially recognized in a special reserve and not recorded in the income statement, and are only recorded in the income statement later when the cash flow occurs.

...

1. Hedging policy and financial derivatives

In conducting its business operations the Volkswagen Group is exposed to fluctuations in prices, interest rates and exchange rates. Corporate policy is to eliminate or limit such risk by means of hedging.

All hedging operations are either centrally co-ordinated or carried out by Group Treasury.

2. Price risk

The international business operations of the Volkswagen Group expose it to fluctuations in exchange rates between foreign currencies and the Euro as well as fluctuations in interest rates on the international money and capital markets.

The general rules applicable to Group-wide exchange and interest rate hedging policy are laid down in an internal code of practice, and are oriented to the 'Minimum Requirements for Credit Institutions for the Performance of Trading Transactions' issued by the Federal Banking Supervisory Authority.

Partners in these financial transactions are top-class national and international banks, whose creditworthiness is continually assessed by the leading rating agencies.

2.1 Exchange rate risk

To avoid exchange rate risk, hedge contracts – comprising foreign exchange forward contracts, foreign exchange options and cross-currency interest rate swaps – are used. These transactions relate to the exchange rate hedging of all cash flows in foreign currency arising from operating activities (such as supplies and services rendered). The transactions also relate to hedges of intra-Group financing transactions, where the hedge and transaction are congruent in amount and term.

The Volkswagen Group hedges planned sales revenues and material purchases in foreign currency on a net basis, according to market estimates, over a period of up to 18 months by means of foreign exchange forward contracts. In 2001 hedging related primarily to the US Dollar, the British Pound and the Japanese Yen.

The currency crisis in Argentina has resulted in exchange rate risks which cannot be hedged at present.

2.2 Interest rate risk

An interest rate risk – that is, possible fluctuations in value of a financial instrument resulting from changes in market interest rates – is posed primarily in respect of medium- and long-term fixed-interest receivables and payables. The interest rate hedges and interest rate limiting instruments entered into include interest rate swaps, cross-currency interest rate swaps and other types of interest rate contracts.

In the Volkswagen Group the differing instruments are used depending on market conditions. If financial resources are passed on to subsidiaries within the Volkswagen Group, such resources are structured congruent to their refinancing.

2.3 Market risk

A market risk is posed when price changes on the financial markets positively or negatively affect the value of financial instruments. The market risk of the financial instruments shown in the balance sheet is immaterial, as they include only a small volume of quoted securities.

3. Liquidity risk

A liquidity forecast with a fixed planning horizon, unused lines of credit and globally available tap issue programs within the Volkswagen Group safeguard liquidity at all times.

4. Risk of default

The theoretical maximum risk of default in respect of the primary financial instruments corresponds to the value of all receivables less the liabilities payable to the same debtors. It is considered that the value adjustment for bad and doubtful receivables covers the effect of the actual risk involved.

The risk of default arising from financial assets involves the risk of defaulting by a contract partner, and therefore as a maximum amounts to the positive fair values relating to each contracting party. Since transactions are only entered into with top-class trading partners, and the risk management system imposes trading limits per partner, the actual risk of default is negligible.

5. Cash flow risk from financial instruments

The cash flow risk is limited by a flexible exchange and interest rate hedging strategy.

Extract 20.25 *Hedge accounting*

Nokia, Finland, 31 December 2001 (IAS)

The Group is applying hedge accounting for 'Qualifying hedges'. Qualifying hedges are those properly documented cash flow hedges of the foreign exchange rate risk of future anticipated foreign currency denominated sales and purchases that meet the requirements set out in IAS 39. The cash flow being hedged must be 'highly probable' and must ultimately impact the profit and loss account. The hedge must be highly effective both prospectively and retrospectively.

The Group claims hedge accounting in respect of forward foreign exchange contracts and options, or option strategies, which have zero net premium or a net premium paid, and where the terms of the bought and sold options within a collar or zero premium structure are the same.

For qualifying foreign exchange forwards the change in fair value is deferred in shareholders' equity to the extent that the hedge is effective. For qualifying foreign exchange options the change in intrinsic value is deferred in shareholders' equity to the extent that the hedge is effective. Changes in the time value are at all times taken directly to profit and loss account.

Accumulated fair value changes from qualifying hedges are released from shareholders' equity into the profit and loss account in the period when the hedged cash flow affects the profit and loss account. If the hedged cash flow is no longer expected to take place, all deferred gains or losses are released into the profit and loss account immediately. If the hedged cash flow ceases to be highly probable, but is still expected to take place, accumulated gains and losses remain in equity until the hedged cash flow affects the profit and loss account.

Changes in fair value of any derivative instruments that do not qualify under hedge accounting under IAS 39 are recognized immediately in the profit and loss account.

Foreign currency hedging of net investments

The Group also applies hedge accounting for its foreign currency hedging on net investments. Qualifying hedges are those properly documented hedges of the foreign exchange rate risk of foreign currency-denominated net investments that meet the requirements set out in IAS 39. The hedge must be effective both prospectively and retrospectively.

The Group claims hedge accounting in respect of forward foreign exchange contracts, foreign currency-denominated loans, and options, or option strategies, which have zero net premium or a net premium paid, and where the terms of the bought and sold options within a collar or zero premium structure are the same.

For qualifying foreign exchange forwards the change in fair value that reflects the change in spot exchange rates is deferred in shareholders' equity. The change in fair value that reflects the change in forward exchange rates less the change in spot exchange rates is recognized in the profit and loss account. For qualifying foreign exchange options the change in intrinsic value is deferred in shareholders' equity. Changes in the time value are at all times taken directly to the profit and loss account. If a foreign currency-denominated loan is used as a hedge, all foreign exchange gains and losses arising from the transaction are recognized in shareholders' equity.

Accumulated fair value changes from qualifying hedges are released from shareholders' equity into the profit and loss account only if the legal entity in the given country is sold or liquidated.

20.16 OFFSETTING OF A FINANCIAL ASSET AND A FINANCIAL LIABILITY

The general requirements for the offsetting of financial assets and financial liabilities, including the main requirements of IAS 32, are dealt with in chapter 9. Under these requirements, a financial asset and a financial liability should be offset and the net amount reported in the balance sheet when an entity:

- has a legally enforceable right to set off the recognised amounts; and
- intends either to settle on a net basis, or to realise the asset and settle the liability simultaneously.

(IAS 32, 33)

These conditions are generally not satisfied and offsetting is usually inappropriate when:

- several different financial instruments are used to emulate the features of a single financial instrument (for example, a synthetic instrument);
- financial assets and financial liabilities arise from financial instruments having the same primary risk exposure (for example, assets and liabilities within a portfolio of forward contracts or other derivative instruments) but involve different counterparties;
- financial or other assets are pledged as collateral for non-recourse financial liabilities;
- financial assets are set aside in trust by a debtor for the purpose of discharging an obligation without those assets having been accepted by the creditor in settlement of the obligation (for example, a sinking fund arrangement); or
- obligations incurred as a result of events giving rise to losses are expected to be recovered from a third party by virtue of a claim made under an insurance policy.

(IAS 32, 40)

Financial assets and financial liabilities are presented on a net basis when this reflects an entity's expected future cash flows from settling two or more separate financial instruments. When an entity has the right to receive or pay a single net amount and intends to do so, it has, in effect, only a single financial asset or financial liability. In other circumstances, financial assets and financial liabilities are presented separately from each other consistent with their characteristics as resources or obligations of the entity (IAS 32, 34). However, the existence of the right, by itself, is not a sufficient basis for offsetting. In the absence of an intention to exercise the right or to settle simultaneously, the amount and timing of an enterprise's future cash flows are not affected (IAS 32, 37).

Simultaneous settlement of two financial instruments may occur through, for example, the operation of a clearing house in an organised financial market or a face-to-face exchange. In these circumstances the cash flows are, in effect, equivalent to a single net amount and there is no exposure to credit or liquidity risk. In other circumstances, an entity may settle two instruments by receiving and paying separate amounts, becoming exposed to credit risk for the full amount of the asset or liquidity risk for the full amount of the liability. Such risk exposures may be significant even though relatively brief. Accordingly, realisation of a financial asset and settlement of a financial liability are considered simultaneous only when the transactions occur at the same moment (IAS 32, 39).

Offsetting differs from ceasing to recognise a financial asset or a financial liability. Offsetting does not give rise to recognition of a gain or a loss but ceasing to recognise a financial instrument not only results in the removal of the previously recognised item from the balance sheet but may also result in recognition of a gain or a loss – see above as regards derecognition (IAS 32, 35).

An entity may have a legal right to apply an amount due from a third party against the amount due to a creditor provided that there is an agreement among the three parties that clearly establishes the entity's right of set-off. Since the right of set-off is a legal right, the conditions supporting the right may vary from one legal jurisdiction to another and care must be taken to establish which laws apply to the relationships between the parties (IAS 32, 36).

20.17 USE OF FINANCIAL INSTRUMENTS

An entity is encouraged to disclose:

- the extent to which financial instruments are used by the entity, the associated risks and the business purposes served; and
- management's policies for controlling the risks associated with financial instruments, including policies on matters such as hedging of risk exposures, avoidance of undue concentrations of risk and requirements for collateral to mitigate credit risks.

(IAS 32, 42)

This disclosure may be made in a commentary to the financial statements. An entity should describe its financial risk management objectives and policies including its policy for hedging each major type of forecasted transaction for which hedge accounting is used (IAS 32, 43A). This is a new requirement which was introduced by the adoption of IAS 39.

20.18 NATURE, TERMS AND CONDITIONS OF FINANCIAL INSTRUMENTS

For each class of financial asset, financial liability and equity instrument, both recognised and unrecognised, an entity should disclose information about the extent and nature of the financial instruments, including significant terms and conditions that may affect the amount, timing and certainty of future cash flows (IAS 32, 47). It is also desirable for the entity to explain the nature of an instrument when the balance sheet presentation of a financial instrument differs from the instrument's legal form (IAS 32, 50), for example when an entity classifies a redeemable preferred share as a liability (see chapter 28).

IAS 32 includes a daunting list of possible disclosures about the nature and extent of the financial instruments:

(a) the principal, stated, face or other similar amount of the instrument. For some derivative instruments, such as interest rate swaps, this may be the nominal amount on which future payments are based;

(b) the date of maturity, expiry or execution;

(c) early settlement options held by either party to the instrument, including the period in which, or date at which, the options may be exercised and the exercise price or range of prices;

(d) options held by either party to the instrument to convert the instrument into, or exchange it for, another financial instrument or some other asset or liability, including the period in which, or date at which, the options may be exercised and the conversion or exchange ratio(s);

(e) the amount and timing of scheduled future cash receipts or payments of the principal amount of the instrument, including instalment repayments and any sinking fund or similar requirements;

(f) stated rate or amount of interest, dividend or other periodic return on principal and the timing of payments;

(g) collateral held, in the case of a financial asset, or pledged, in the case of a financial liability;

(h) in the case of an instrument for which cash flows are denominated in a currency other than the entity's reporting currency, the currency in which receipts or payments are required;
(i) in the case of an instrument that provides for an exchange, information described in items (a) to (h) for the instrument to be acquired in the exchange; and
(j) any condition of the instrument or an associated covenant that, if contravened, would significantly alter any of the other terms (for example, a maximum debt-to-equity ratio in a bond covenant that, if contravened, would make the full principal amount of the bond due and payable immediately).

(IAS 32, 49)

A borrower should disclose:

- the carrying amount of financial assets pledged as collateral for liabilities; and
- any significant terms and conditions relating to pledged assets. Such disclosure should be consistent with that above.

(IAS 39, 170)

A lender should disclose:

- the fair value of collateral (both financial and non-financial assets) that it has accepted and that it is permitted to sell or repledge in the absence of default;
- the fair value of collateral that it has sold or repledged; and
- any significant terms and conditions associated with its use of collateral. Such disclosure should be consistent with that above.

(IAS 39, 170)

Information about the extent and nature of financial instruments highlights any relationships between individual instruments that may affect the amount, timing or certainty of the future cash flows of an entity. The information may deal with relationships among the assets and liabilities recognised on the balance sheet as well as relationships between balance sheet items and off-balance sheet items. For example, the information includes:

- details of hedging relationships; and
- relationships between the components of synthetic instruments such as fixed rate debt created by borrowing at a floating rate and entering into a floating to fixed interest rate swap.

20.19 ACCOUNTING POLICIES

For each class of financial asset, financial liability and equity instrument, both recognised and unrecognised, an entity should disclose the accounting policies and methods adopted, including:

- the criteria for the recognition of financial assets or financial liabilities on the balance sheet (IAS 32, 47 and 52);
- the criteria for determining when to remove financial assets and financial liabilities from the balance sheet (IAS 32, 52);
- the basis of measurement applied to financial assets and financial liabilities both on initial recognition and subsequently (IAS 32, 47);
- the basis on which income and expenses arising from financial assets and financial liabilities is measured (IAS 32, 52);
- the method of applying the basis of measurement (IAS 32, 52 and 54).

An entity should also disclose:

- separately for significant classes of financial assets, the methods and significant assumptions applied in estimating fair values of financial assets and financial liabilities that are carried at fair value. This will include prepayment rates, rates of estimated credit losses, and interest or discount rates (IAS 39, 168);
- whether gains and losses arising from changes in the fair value of those available-for-sale financial assets that are measured at fair value subsequent to initial recognition are included in net profit or loss for the period or are recognised directly in equity until the financial asset is disposed of; and
- for each of the four categories of financial assets, whether regular way purchases and sales of financial assets are accounted for at trade date or settlement date.

(IAS 39, 167)

IAS 32, 46 provides guidance for determining classes of financial instruments.

IAS 32 suggests a number of specific areas for which accounting policies may need to be disclosed (table 20.7).

Table 20.7 *Suggested Accounting Policy Disclosures*

Types of transactions

- transfers of financial assets when there is a continuing interest in, or involvement with, the assets by the transferor, for example, securitisations, repurchase agreements and reverse repurchase agreements;
- transfers of financial assets to a trust for the purpose of satisfying liabilities when they mature without the obligation of the transferor being discharged at the time of the transfer, for example, an in-substance defeasance trust;
- acquisition or issuance of separate financial instruments as part of a series of transactions designed to synthesise the effect of acquiring or issuing a single instrument;
- acquisition or issuance of financial instruments as hedges of risk exposures; and
- acquisition or issuance of monetary financial instruments bearing a stated interest rate that differs from the prevailing market rate at the date of issue.

(IAS 32, 53)

Measurement – cost basis

- the costs of acquisition or issuance;
- premiums and discounts on monetary financial assets and financial liabilities;
- changes in the estimated amount of determinable future cash flows associated with a monetary financial instrument such as a bond indexed to a commodity price;
- changes in circumstances that result in significant uncertainty about the timely collection of all contractual amounts due from monetary financial assets;
- declines in the fair value of financial assets below their carrying amount; and
- restructured financial liabilities.

(IAS 32, 54)

Measurement – fair value basis

- whether carrying amounts are determined from quoted market prices, independent appraisals, discounted cash flow analysis or another appropriate method; and
- any significant assumptions made in applying those methods.

(IAS 32, 54 and 79)

Table 20.7 *Suggested Accounting Policy Disclosures (continued)*

Income and expenses

- realised and unrealised gains and losses;
- interest and other items of income and expense associated with financial assets and financial liabilities;
- income and expense arising from financial instruments held for hedging purposes; and
- the offsetting of income and expense items when the corresponding financial assets and financial liabilities on the balance sheet have not been offset.

(IAS 32, 55)

20.20 INTEREST RATE RISK

For each class of financial asset and financial liability, both recognised and unrecognised, an entity should disclose information about its exposure to interest rate risk. Therefore an entity discloses which of its financial assets and financial liabilities are:

- exposed to interest rate price risk – for example, financial assets and financial liabilities with a fixed interest rate;
- exposed to interest rate cash flow risk – for example financial assets and financial liabilities with a floating interest rate; and
- not exposed to any interest rate risk – for example investments in equity securities.

(IAS 32, 60)

The nature of an entity's business and the extent of its activity in financial instruments determines whether information about interest rate risk is presented in narrative form or tables or in a combination of both (see IAS 32, 64).

For each class of financial asset and financial liability, both recognised and unrecognised, an entity should also disclose contractual repricing or maturity dates, whichever dates are earlier (IAS 32, 56). An entity may also disclose information about expected repricing or maturity dates when those dates differ significantly from the contractual dates (IAS 32, 59). These disclosures are similar to those in IAS 30 for banks (see chapter 43).

For each class of financial asset and financial liability, both recognised and unrecognised, which create a return to the holder and a cost to the issuer reflecting the time value of money, an entity should also disclose effective interest rates when applicable (IAS 32, 56 and 62). The requirement applies to bonds, notes and similar monetary financial instruments; it does not apply to financial instruments which do not bear a determinable effective interest rate.

The effective interest rate (effective yield) is the rate which discounts the stream of future cash receipts or payments from the reporting date to the next repricing (maturity) date plus the expected carrying amount (principal amount) of the instrument at that date to the current carrying amount of the instruments. The rate is:

- a historical rate for a fixed rate instrument carried at amortised cost; and
- a current market rate for a floating rate instrument or an instrument carried at fair value.

(IAS 32, 61)

An entity may retain an exposure to the interest rate risks associated with financial assets removed from its balance sheet as a result of a transaction such as a securitisation. In such or similar circumstances, the entity normally discloses:

- the nature of the assets transferred;
- their stated principal, interest rate and term to maturity; and
- the terms of the transaction giving rise to the retained exposure to interest rate risk.

(IAS 32, 63)

An entity may become exposed to interest rate risks as a result of a transaction in which no financial asset or financial liability is currently recognised on its balance sheet. For example, an entity becomes exposed to interest rate risk when it enters into a commitment to lend funds at a fixed interest rate. In such circumstances, the entity normally discloses:

- the stated principal, interest rate and term to maturity of the amount to be lent; and
- the significant terms of the transaction giving rise to the exposure to risk.

(IAS 32, 63)

An entity may indicate the effect of a hypothetical change in the prevailing level of market interest rates on the fair value of its financial instruments and future earnings and cash flows. Such interest rate sensitivity information may be based on an assumed percentage change in market interest rates occurring at the balance sheet date. It includes the effects of changes in interest income and expense relating to floating rate financial instruments and gains or losses resulting from changes in the fair value of fixed rate instruments. When such information is disclosed, the entity discloses the basis on which it has prepared the information, including any significant assumptions.

20.21 CREDIT RISK

For each class of financial asset, both recognised and unrecognised, an entity should disclose information about its exposure to credit risk, including the amount that best represents its maximum credit risk exposure at the balance sheet date in the event that other parties fail to perform their obligations under financial instruments; the maximum exposure is calculated without taking account of the fair value of any assets pledged as security or other collateral (IAS 32, 66).

When the carrying amount of a financial asset is the maximum amount exposed to credit risk, an entity need not disclose anything further than the information on the balance sheet (IAS 32, 69). So, for example, an entity is not usually required to make additional disclosures about maximum credit risk for:

- trade receivables;
- many loans and advances; and
- interest rate swaps when the carrying amounts represent the cost, at current market rates, of replacing the swaps in the event of default.

Additional disclosure is required when the maximum potential credit loss differs significantly from the carrying amount of an asset or other amounts disclosed about the asset such as its fair value or principal amount (IAS 32, 69). This is the case when, for example, a financial asset is subject to a legally enforceable right of set-off against a financial liability or the entity has entered into master netting arrangements that do not meet the criteria for offsetting in the balance sheet (IAS 32, 70 and 71).

Additional disclosure is also required when an entity's maximum potential credit loss from an unrecognised financial asset differs significantly from its fair value, principal amount or other amounts disclosed in respect of the asset or instrument (IAS 32, 70). For example, an entity may have a right to mitigate the loss it would otherwise bear by setting off an unrecognised financial asset against an unrecognised financial liability.

An entity is exposed to credit risk when it guarantees an obligation of another party. For example, under a securitisation transaction, an entity may remain exposed to the credit risk associated with financial assets that have been removed from its balance sheet. In such circumstances, the entity discloses:

- the nature of the assets removed from its balance sheet;
- the amount and timing of the future cash flows contractually due from the assets;
- the terms of the recourse obligation; and
- the maximum loss which could arise under that obligation.

(IAS 32, 73)

An entity should also disclose significant concentrations of credit risk for each class of financial asset, both recognised and unrecognised (IAS 32, 66). Under IAS 30, banks already disclose significant concentrations of assets. Concentrations of credit risk may arise from exposures to a single debtor, groups of debtors in the same industry or geographical area or with similar levels of creditworthiness.

Information about significant concentrations is disclosed when it is not apparent from other disclosures about the business and the concentrations result in a significant exposure to loss in the event of default by other parties (IAS 32, 74). The disclosure includes:

- a description of the shared characteristic that identifies each concentration; and
- the amount of the maximum credit risk exposure associated with all recognised and unrecognised financial assets sharing that characteristic.

(IAS 32, 76)

20.22 FAIR VALUE

For each class of financial asset and financial liability, both recognised and unrecognised, an entity should disclose information about fair value (IAS 32, 77) unless the financial asset or financial liability is carried at fair value. The fair values of recognised financial assets and financial liabilities are grouped into classes and offset only to the extent that their related carrying amounts are offset (IAS 32, 87). The fair values of unrecognised financial assets and financial liabilities are presented in a class or classes separate from recognised items and are offset only to the extent that they meet the offsetting criteria for recognised financial assets and financial liabilities (IAS 32, 87).

Fair value is the amount for which an asset could be exchanged, or a liability settled, between knowledgeable, willing parties in an arm's length transaction (IAS 32, 5). In determining the fair value of its financial assets and financial liabilities, an entity takes into account:

- its current circumstances (IAS 32, 80);
- but not the costs that would be incurred to exchange or settle the underlying financial instrument (IAS 32, 83).

Therefore, the fair value of a financial asset that an entity has decided to sell for cash in the immediate future is determined by the amount that it expects to receive from such a sale without deduction of transaction costs. However, fair value is not the amount that an entity would receive or pay in a forced transaction, involuntary liquidation or distress sale. Transaction costs may include taxes and duties, fees and commissions paid to agents, advisers, brokers or dealers and levies by regulatory agencies or securities exchanges.

When a financial instrument is traded in an active and liquid market, its fair value is its quoted market price (IAS 32, 81). The current bid price is the appropriate quoted market price for an asset held or for a liability to be issued. The current offer price is the appropriate market price for an asset to be acquired or for a liability held. When current bid and offer prices are unavailable, the most recent transaction may provide evidence of the current fair value provided that there has not been a significant change in economic circumstances between the transaction date and the reporting date. When an entity has matching asset and liability positions, it may use mid-market prices as a basis for establishing fair values of both the asset and liability.

When a quoted market price is not available or when there is infrequent activity in a market, the market is not well established or small volumes are traded relative to the number of trading units of a financial instrument to be valued, techniques which may be used to determine fair value include:

- the current market value of another instrument that is substantially the same;
- discounted cash flow analysis; and
- option pricing models.

(IAS 32, 82)

When an instrument is not traded in an organised financial market, it may be appropriate for an entity to disclose a range of amounts within which the fair value of a financial instrument is reasonably believed to lie (IAS 32, 84).

When it is not practicable within constraints of timeliness or cost to determine the fair value of a financial asset or financial liability with sufficient reliability, that fact should be disclosed together with information about the principal characteristics of the underlying financial instrument that are pertinent to its fair value (IAS 32, 77). However, IAS 39 points out that an entity should always be able to estimate the fair value of a financial asset which it has acquired from a third party and that an entity is unlikely to acquire a financial instrument for which it does not expect to be able to obtain a reliable estimate of fair value after acquisition (IAS 39, 102).

20.23 FINANCIAL ASSETS CARRIED AT AN AMOUNT IN EXCESS OF FAIR VALUE

An entity may carry one or more financial assets at an amount in excess of fair value. This may happen, for example, following an increase in interest rates when fixed interest securities or loans receivable are carried at cost (or amortised cost) and are written down to market value only when the decline is other than temporary. In such circumstances the entity should disclose:

- the carrying amount and the fair value of either the individual assets or appropriate groupings of those individual assets;
- the reasons for not reducing the carrying amount; and
- the nature of the evidence that provides the basis for management's belief that the carrying amount will be recovered.

(IAS 32, 88)

The June 2002 exposure draft proposes removing the above disclosures.

20.24 DISCLOSURE OF HEDGE ACCOUNTING

An entity should describe its financial risk management objectives and policies, including its policy for hedging each major type of forecasted transaction. In the case of hedges of risks relating to future sales, that description:

- indicates the nature of the risks being hedged;
- approximately how many months or years of expected future sales have been hedged; and
- the approximate percentage of sales in those future months or years.

(IAS 39, 169)

IAS 39 identifies the following three categories of hedge:

- fair value hedges;
- cash flow hedges; and
- hedges of a net investment in a foreign entity.

(IAS 39, 169)

An entity should disclose separately for each of the above three categories:

- a description of the hedge;
- a description of the financial instruments designated as hedging instruments for the hedge and their fair values at the balance sheet date;
- the nature of the risks being hedged.

(IAS 39, 169)

For hedges of forecasted transactions, an entity should disclose for each of the above three categories:

- the periods in which the forecasted transactions are expected to occur;
- when they are expected to enter into the determination of net profit or loss; and
- a description of any forecasted transaction for which hedge accounting had previously been used but that is no longer expected to occur.

(IAS 39, 169)

If a gain or loss on derivative and non-derivative financial assets and liabilities designated as hedging instruments in cash flow hedges has been recognised directly in equity, through the statement of changes in equity, an entity should disclose:

- the amount that was so recognised in equity during the current period;
- the amount that was removed from equity and reported in net profit or loss for the period; and
- the amount that was removed from equity and added to the initial measurement of the acquisition cost or other carrying amount of the asset or liability in a hedged forecasted transaction during the current period (IAS 39, 160).

(IAS 39, 169)

20.25 OTHER IAS 32 DISCLOSURES

An entity is encouraged to disclose the total amount of the change in the fair value of financial assets and financial liabilities which has been recognised as income or expense for the period (IAS 32, 94(a)).

An entity is encouraged to disclose:

- the average aggregate carrying amount during the period of recognised financial assets and financial liabilities;
- the average aggregate principal, stated, notional or other similar amount during the period of unrecognised financial assets and financial liabilities; and
- the average aggregate fair value during the period of all financial assets and financial liabilities.

(IAS 32, 94(c))

This disclosure is particularly relevant when amounts at the balance sheet date are unrepresentative of amounts on hand during the period. IAS 30 also encourages a bank to disclose average interest rates, average interest earning assets and average interest bearing liabilities for the period (IAS 30, 17).

20.26 OTHER IAS 39 DISCLOSURES

An entity should give all of the following additional disclosures relating to financial instruments (IAS 39, 170).

If a gain or loss from remeasuring available-for-sale financial assets to fair value (other than assets relating to hedges) has been recognised directly in equity, through the statement of changes in equity:

- the amount that was so recognised in equity during the current period; and
- the amount that was removed from equity and reported in net profit or loss for the period.

If the presumption that fair value can be reliably measured for all financial assets that are available-for-sale or held for trading has been overcome (see 20.9.2 and 20.9.5) and the entity is, therefore, measuring any such financial assets at amortised cost:

- that fact;
- a description of the financial assets;
- the carrying amount of the financial assets;
- an explanation of why fair value cannot be reliably measured; and
- the range of estimates within which fair value is highly likely to lie, if possible.

If financial assets whose fair value previously could not be measured reliably are sold:

- that fact;
- the carrying amount of such financial assets at the time of sale, and
- the amount of gain or loss recognised.

Significant items of income, expense, and gains and losses resulting from financial assets and financial liabilities, whether included in net profit or loss or as a separate component of equity. In making this disclosure:

- total interest income and total interest expense (both on a historical cost basis) should be disclosed separately;
- with respect to available-for-sale financial assets that are adjusted to fair value after initial acquisition, total gains and losses from derecognition of such financial assets included in net profit or loss for the period should be reported separately from total gains and losses from fair value adjustments of recognised assets and liabilities included in net profit or loss for the period (a similar split of 'realised' versus 'unrealised' gains and losses with respect to financial assets and liabilities held for trading is not required);
- the amount of interest income that has been accrued on impaired loans and that has not yet been received in cash.

If the entity has entered into a securitisation or repurchase agreement, disclose separately for such transactions occurring in the current financial reporting period and for remaining retained interests from transactions occurring in prior financial reporting periods:

- the nature and extent of such transactions, including a description of any collateral and quantitative information about the key assumptions used in calculating the fair values of new and retained interests; and
- whether the financial assets have been derecognised.

If the entity has reclassified a financial asset as one required to be reported at amortised cost rather than at fair value disclose the reason for that reclassification.

Disclose, separately for each significant class of financial asset:

- the nature and amount of any impairment loss for a financial asset; or
- the nature and amount of any reversal of an impairment loss recognised for a financial asset.

Paragraph 46 of IAS 32 provides guidance for determining classes of financial assets.

20.27 EXAMPLES OF DISCLOSURES

Extract 20.26 *Financial asset and financial liability disclosures (extracts)*

Adidas, Germany, 31 December 2001 (IAS)

[Extracts from risk report]

Financing Risks

Interest rate changes and liquidity developments have a direct impact on the Group's consolidated financial statements. For example, the Group estimates that a 1.0 percentage point increase or decrease in interest rates would cause after-tax earnings to change by €12 million over a 12-month period. Financing as well as currency risk is centrally managed at the Group's headquarters in Germany. To ensure best response to changing market conditions, this risk is closely monitored. When a relevant risk has been identified, it is addressed with appropriately structured financing or derivative products.

Currency Risks

Due to the high share of production and sales which are denominated in different currencies, the Company is exposed to economic risks, including unexpected changes in exchange rates. The sourcing organization invoices Group companies primarily in their local currencies. As a result, the currency risk is concentrated at the sourcing level. In order to reduce exposure in these areas, natural hedges are pursued wherever possible. For additional protection, common market instruments such as options and forward contracts are used.

Extract 20.26 *(continued)*

[Extract from statement of changes in equity. Movements and columns other than in respect of fair values of financial instruments have been omitted]

	Share capital	*Capital surplus*	*Cumulative translation adjustment*	*Fair values of financial instruments*	*Retained earnings*	*Total*
Balance at 31 December 1999	116,094	7,557	(572)		556,878	679,957
Balance at 31 December 2000	116,094	7,557	(5,152)		696,825	815,324
Cumulative effect of the adoption of IAS 39, net of tax				(765)		(765)
Restated balance at 1 January 2001	116,094	7,557	(5,152)	(765)	696,825	814,559
Net gain on cash flow hedges				21,744		21,744
Net loss on net investments in foreign subsidiaries				(3,252)		(3,252)
Balance at 31 December 2001	116,094	7,557	9,638	17,727	863,597	1,014,613

Extract 20.26 *(continued)*

Accounting policies

The effects of IAS 39 are summarized in the consolidated statement of changes in equity and further information is disclosed in Notes 2 and 20.

Derivative Financial Instruments

The Company uses derivative financial instruments, interest and currency options, as well as forward contracts, to hedge its exposure to foreign exchange and interest rate risks. In accordance with its treasury policy, the Company does not hold any derivative financial instruments for trading purposes.

Derivative financial instruments are initially recognized in the balance sheet at cost and subsequently measured at their fair value. The method of recognizing the resulting gain or loss is dependent on the nature of the item being hedged. On the date a derivative contract is entered into, the Company designates certain derivatives as either a hedge of the fair value of a recognized asset or liability (fair value hedge) or a hedge of a forecasted transaction (cash flow hedge), or a hedge of a net investment in a foreign entity.

Changes in the fair value of derivatives that are designated and qualify as cash flow hedges, and that are 100% effective, are recognized in equity. If there is no 100% effectiveness, the deviating amounts are recognized in net income. Amounts deferred in equity are transferred to the income statement in the same periods during which the hedged forecasted transaction affects the income statement. For derivative instruments designated as a fair value hedge, the gain or loss on the derivative and the offsetting gain or loss on the hedged item are recognized immediately in net income.

Certain derivative transactions, while providing effective economic hedges under the Company's risk management policies, do not qualify for hedge accounting under the specific rules of IAS 39. Changes in the fair values of any derivative instruments that do not qualify for hedge accounting under IAS 39 are recognized immediately in the income statement.

Hedges of net investments in foreign entities are accounted for similarly to cash flow hedges. If the hedging instrument is a derivative (e.g. a forward contract) or for example a foreign currency borrowing, any gains and losses in the derivative and all gains and losses arising on the translation of the borrowing are recognized in equity.

The Company documents at the inception of the transaction the relationship between hedging instruments and hedged items, as well as the risk management objective and strategy for undertaking various hedge transactions. This process includes linking all derivatives designated as hedges to specific forecasted transactions. The Company also documents its assessment, both at the hedge inception and on an ongoing basis, whether the derivatives that are used in hedging transactions are highly effective in offsetting changes in cash flows of hedged items.

The fair values of forward contracts and currency options are determined on the basis of the market conditions on the reporting dates. The fair values of interest rate options on the reporting date are assessed by the financial institutions through which these options had been arranged.

Extract 20.26 *(continued)*

Investments

At 1 January 2001 the Company adopted IAS 39 and classified its investments into the following categories: trading, held-to-maturity and available-for-sale.

During the reporting period the Company did not hold any trading or held-to-maturity investments.

Investments intended to be held for an undefined period of time, which may be sold in response to needs for liquidity or changes in interest rates, are classified as available-for-sale. These are included in other non-current assets and in cash and cash equivalents.

Management determines the appropriate classification of its investments at the time of the purchase and re-evaluates such designation on a regular basis.

All purchases and sales of investments are recognized on the trade date. Cost of purchases include transaction costs. Available-for-sale investments are subsequently carried at fair value, which is based on quoted market prices at the balance sheet date. Realized and unrealized gains and losses arising from changes in the fair value of these investments are included in the income statement in the period in which they arise.

Prior to the adoption of IAS 39 the Company had recorded all of its investments at fair value.

Borrowings

Borrowings are recognized initially at the proceeds received, net of transaction costs incurred. In subsequent periods, borrowings are stated at amortized cost. Any difference between proceeds (net of transaction costs) and the redemption value is recognized in the income statement over the terms of the borrowings.

4. Cash and Cash Equivalents

Cash and cash equivalents consists of the following:

(euros in thousands)	*31 Dec 2001*	*31 Dec 2000*
Cash at banks and in hand	65,150	90,549
Marketable securities	19,845	14,157
Cash and cash equivalents	84,995	104,706

The majority of marketable securities relates to Commercial Paper and certificates of deposit in Eastern European currencies with a maximum maturity of 90 days. These marketable securities have fixed interest rates between 11.75% and 14.20% and a minimum Standard & Poor's rating of 'A1'.

In addition to short-term cash, adidas Korea has cash accounts with maturities exceeding 12 months in the amount of €2 million (2000: €1 million), which are included in other non-current assets (see also Note 11).

Extract 20.26 (*continued*)

7. Other Current Assets

Other current assets consist of the following:

(euro in thousands)	*31 Dec 2001*	*31 Dec 2000*
Prepaid expenses	73,482	88,043
Taxes receivable	75,939	83,871
Interest rate options	1,954	3,305
Currency options	6,089	12,890
Forward contracts	39,869	–
Security deposits	15,412	11,333
Receivables from affiliated companies	885	1,657
Investment property held for sale	16,923	15,926
Sundry	42,156	42,833
Other current assets, gross	272,709	259,858
Less: allowance	5,780	5,675
Other current assets, net	266,929	254,183

... With the adoption of IAS 39, the Company now states all derivative financial instruments at fair value. The prior year amount for interest rate and currency options represents capitalized premiums paid ...

11. Other Non-Current Assets

... Interest rate and currency options include the fair value of these instruments as at 31 December 2001. The prior year figure of interest rate options represents capitalized premiums paid ... Cash deposits with maturities exceeding 12 months relate to adidas Korea...

12. Borrowings and Credit Lines

In 2001, the Company has continued its diversification among different sources of financing. In addition to the arrangements of additional private placements with maturities up to six years, the Company started, in December 2001, a €250 million ABS program for the financing of trade receivables. The program, which involves five Group companies in four countries, had outstandings of €155 million at the end of the year. It runs five years, but includes a clause which permits the extension, every year, for an additional year.

As required by IAS 39 in conjunction with SIC 12, the receivables which were sold under the ABS program continue to be reported as part of the outstanding trade accounts receivables, whereas the proceeds from the sale of such receivables are included in short-term borrowings.

Short-term borrowings consist of bank borrowings, outstandings under the new ABS program, discounted trade bills and Commercial Paper. Long-term borrowings consist of bank borrowings and Private Placements.

Extract 20.26 *(continued)*

Commercial Paper was issued under a €750 million German Multi-Currency Commercial Paper Program and a €300 million Belgian Treasury Notes Program. As at 31 December 2001, Commercial Paper is outstanding in the total nominal amount of €280 million (2000: €282 million).

Borrowings are denominated in a variety of currencies in which the Company is doing business. The largest portions of net borrowings as at 31 December 2001 are denominated in euro (57.1%; 2000: 55.1%) and USD (31.0%; 2000: 32.1%).

Month-end weighted average interest rates on borrowings in all currencies range from 3.3 to 5.3% and from 4.3 to 5.7% for the years ended 31 December 2001 and 2000, respectively.

As at 31 December 2001 the Company has cash credit lines and other long-term financing arrangements in a total amount of €3.4 billion outstanding (2000: €3.6 billion); unused credit lines amount to €1.7 billion (2000: €2.0 billion). In addition, the Company has separate lines for the issuance of letters of credit in an amount of approximately €0.7 billion (2000: €0.7 billion).

The modest decline in the amount of the cash credit lines must be seen against the background of the diversification into new forms of financing, such as the introduction of the ABS program.

Short-term borrowings which are backed by committed medium-term credit lines are classified as long-term borrowings. The committed medium-term lines contain a negative-pledge clause and a minimum equity covenant. As at 31 December 2001, actual shareholders' equity is well above the amount of the minimum-equity covenant. The amounts disclosed as long-term borrowings represent outstanding borrowings under the following arrangements:

(euros in millions)	*31 Dec 2001*	*31 Dec 2000*
Committed medium-term lines	1,307	1,389
Long-term loan agreements	38	45
Private placements	225	183
Total	1,570	1,617

The above agreements have aggregated expiration dates as follows:

(euros in millions)	*31 Dec 2001*	*31 Dec 2000*
Between 1 and 3 years	628	487
Between 3 and 5 years	895	1,066
After 5 years	47	64
Total	1,570	1,617

Please refer to Note 20 for the protection against interest rate risks.

Extract 20.26 *(continued)*

14. Other Current Liabilities

... With the adoption of IAS 39, the Company now states all derivative financial instruments at fair value. Interest rate and currency options, as well as forward contracts represent negative fair values of these derivatives at the balance sheet date ...

16. Other Non-Current Liabilities

... Other non-current liabilities include mainly obligations under finance leases of €9 million ... and negative fair values of long-term interest rate options of €4 million.

Liabilities falling due after more than five years total €3 million and €5 million as at 31 December 2001 and 2000 respectively.

20. Financial Instruments

For the treatment of financial instruments, the Company adopted IAS 39 at 1 January 2001. In accordance with IAS 39, the comparative consolidated financial statements for the year ended 31 December 2000 are not restated.

In accordance with the transitional requirements of IAS 39, the Company recorded an after-tax loss of €1 million in retained earnings to recognize at fair value all derivatives designated as hedging instruments. Out of this amount a loss of €1 million is attributable to forward contracts and a gain of €4 million is relating to currency options. For interest rate options a loss of €4 million is recorded within equity.

Management of Foreign Exchange Risk

The Company is subject to currency exposure, primarily due to an imbalance of its global cash flows caused by the high share of product sourcing from suppliers in the Far East, which invoice in US dollars, while sales other than in US dollars are invoiced mainly in European currencies, but also in Japanese yen, Canadian dollars and other currencies.

It is the Company's policy to hedge identified currency risks arising from forecasted transactions when it becomes exposed. In addition, the Company hedges balance sheet risk selectively.

For the management of its currency risks the Company uses forward contracts and currency options.

In 2001, the Company incurred currency option premiums in a total amount of €3.1 million (2000: €14.0 million). The total amount of option premiums, which was charged to income in 2001, was €13.7 million (2000: €20.3 million). Paid option premiums in an amount of €2.3 million and €12.9 million were deferred as at 31 December 2001 and 2000, respectively.

The total amount of US dollar purchases against other currencies was $1.2 billion and $1.4 billion in the years ended 31 December 2001 and 2000, respectively.

Extract 20.26 (*continued*)

The notional amounts of all outstanding currency hedging instruments, which are mainly related to cash flow hedges, can be summarized as follows:

(euros in millions)	*31 Dec 2001*	*31 Dec 2000*
Forward contracts	1,372	800
Currency options	173	544
Total	1,545	1,344

Out of the total amount of outstanding hedges, the following contracts relate to the coverage of the biggest single exposure, the US dollar:

(US$ in millions)	*31 Dec 2001*	*31 Dec 2000*
Forward contracts	647	330
Currency options	131	466
Total	778	796

The fair value of the above instruments is as follows:

(euros in millions)	*31 Dec 2001*	*31 Dec 2000*
Forward contracts	28	4
Currency options	7	20
Total	35	24

Out of the fair value of €28 million for forward contracts, €24 million relate to cash flow hedges, €1 million relate to fair value hedges and €3 million are attributable to net investment hedges. The total amount shown for currency options relates to cash flow hedges.

The fair value gains as at 31 December 2001 on open cash flow hedges which hedge anticipated future foreign currency purchases will be transferred from equity to the income statement when the forecasted transaction occurs, at various dates within the next year.

In addition, fair value gains on cash flow hedges which are used to hedge an embedded derivative within a specific contract will be released from equity to the income statement at specified payment dates up to 2008 which are stated within the contract. The embedded derivative is not separated from the host contract as the economic characteristics and risk of the embedded derivative is closely related to the host contract. Other significant embedded derivatives do not exist at the balance sheet date.

The Company designated a US dollar borrowing of $250 million as a hedge of the net investment in its subsidiary adidas International BV, Amsterdam (Netherlands). The foreign exchange loss of €8 million on the translation of the borrowing was recognized in shareholders' equity.

In addition, adidas-Salomon hedges part of its net investment in Salomon & Taylor Made Co, Ltd, Tokyo (Japan) with forward contracts. The fair value gain of €3 million was recognized in equity.

Extract 20.26 (*continued*)

Management of Interest Rate Risk

Taking advantage of the declining interest rates, the Company reduced, in a zero cost strategy, the protection level for €0.4 billion of the euro interest rate hedges to a lower interest rate, with the inclusion of a floor at an average rate of 3.6%. As of the end of 2001, the outstanding interest rate hedges protect the Company's borrowings in a notional amount of €1.5 billion (2000: €1.8 billion) against a rise of the weighted average interest rate above 5.45% (2000: 6.5%). Out of this amount, the protection ends for €1.2 billion (2000: €1.6 billion) at a weighted average rate of 9.2% (2000: 8.9%).

As at 31 December 2001, the remaining life of these interest rate hedges is up to 6.0 years (2000: 6.0 years), with a weighted average of 3.1 years (2000: 3.6 years). The interest rate hedges expire as detailed below:

(euros in millions)	*31 Dec 2001*	*31 Dec 2000*
Within 1 year	230	281
Between 1 and 3 years	459	476
Between 3 and 5 years	756	435
After 5 years	50	597
Total	1,495	1,789

The fair value of the above instruments is €1 million and €5 million as at 31 December 2001 and 2000, respectively. All fair value changes are recorded directly in the income statement.

Credit Risk

The Company arranges currency and interest rate hedges, and invests cash, with major banks of a high credit standing throughout the world, and in high-quality money-market instruments.

23. Financial Expenses, net

Financial result consists of the following:

(euros in millions)	*31 Dec 2001*	*31 Dec 2000*
Interest income	11,727	12,612
Interest expense	(107,772)	(108,517)
Interest expense, net	(96,045)	(95,905)
Income from investments	334	474
Fair value gains on investments	2,181	3,126
Other – net, primarily net exchange losses	(8,348)	(1,649)
Financial expenses, net	(101,878)	(93,954)

Extract 20.27 *Financial asset and financial liability disclosures (extracts)*

Nokia, Finland, 31 December 2001 (IAS)

15. Available-for-sale investments

	2001 EURm
At 1 Jan. as originally stated (cost)	**3,111**
On adoption of IAS 39 at 1 Jan. remeasurement to fair value	**58**
Fair value at 1 Jan.	**3,169**
Additions, net	**1,581**
Revaluation surplus/(deficit)	**–**
Impairment losses (Note 7)	**–80**
Fair value at 31 Dec.	**4,670**
Non-current	**399**
Current (Note 34)	**4,271**

On the adoption of IAS 39 at 1 January 2001, all investment securities classified as available-for-sale were remeasured to fair value. The difference between their original carrying amount and their fair value at 1 January 2001 was credited to fair value and other reserves (see Consolidated statement of changes in shareholders' equity). Gains and losses arising from the change in the fair value of available-for-sale investments since that date are recognized directly in this reserve.

Available-for-sale investments, comprising marketable debt and equity securities and investments in unlisted equity shares, are fair valued, except in the case of certain unlisted equities held within Nokia Venture Funds. These investments are in immature companies, the fair values of which cannot be measured reliably. Such equities are carried at cost (EURm 153 in 2001), less impairment.

For investments traded in active markets (EURm 169 in 2001 and EURm 140 in 2000), fair value is determined by reference to exchange quoted bid prices. For other investments, fair value is estimated by reference to the current market value of similar instruments or by reference to the discounted cash flows of the underlying net assets.

Available-for-sale investments are classified as non-current, except for highly liquid, interest-bearing investments held as part of the Group's on going cash management activities and which are regarded as cash equivalents. See Note 34 for details of these investments.

16. Long-term loans receivable

These comprise loans made to customers principally to support their financing of network infrastructure, and are repayable, excluding loans which are fully written down (see Note 7), as follows:

Extract 20.27 (*continued*)

	2001 EURm	*2000 EURm*
Under 1 year	–	–
Between 1 and 2 years	**656**	–
Between 2 and 5 years	**341**	867
Over 5 years	**144**	–
Less: Provisions	**–13**	–59
	1,128	808

20. Fair value and other reserves

The Group adopted IAS 39 at 1 January 2001: the impact on shareholders' equity and on various balance sheet captions at 1 January 2001 is shown below. In accordance with IAS 39, the comparative financial statements for the year ended 31 December 2000 are not restated.

In accordance with the transitional requirements of IAS 39, the Group transferred a net loss of EUR 114 million to the hedging reserve in respect of outstanding foreign exchange forward contracts that were properly designated and highly effective as cash flow hedges of highly probable forecast foreign currency cash flows. Previously such gains and losses were reported as deferred income or expenses in the balance sheet.

Summary of impact of adopting IAS 39 at 1 January 2001:

	Hedging reserve	*Available-for-sale investments*	*Total*
Year ended 31 December 2000:			
Balance at 1 January 2001	–	–	–
Effect of adopting IAS 39			
Fair valuation of available-for-sale securities		58	58
Transfer of gains and losses on qualifying cash flow hedging derivatives	–114		–114
Balance at 1 January 2001, restated	–114	58	–56

Extract 20.27 *(continued)*

	Hedging reserve	*Available-for-sale investments*	*Total*
Year ended 31 December 2001:			
Balance at 1 January 2001, restated	−114	58	−56
Cash flow hedges			
Fair value gains/(losses) in period	76		76
Available-for-sale investments:			
Net fair value gains/(losses)		−67	−67
Transfer to profit and loss account on impairment		74	74
Transfer to profit and loss account on disposal		−7	−7
Balance at 31 December 2001	**−38**	**58**	**20**

In order to ensure that amounts deferred in the cash flow hedging reserve represent only the effective portion of gains and losses on properly designated hedges of future transactions that remain highly probable at the balance sheet date, Nokia has adopted a process under which all derivative gains and losses are initially recognized in the profit and loss account. The appropriate reserve balance is calculated at the end of each period and posted to equity.

Nokia continuously reviews the underlying and the hedges allocated thereto, to ensure that the amounts transferred to the Hedging Reserve during the year ended 31 December 2001 do not include gains/losses of forward exchange contracts that have been designated to hedge forecasted sales or purchases that are no longer expected to occur. Because of the number of transactions undertaken during each period and the process used to calculate the reserve balance, separate disclosure of the transfers of gains and losses to and from the reserve would be impractical.

All of the net fair value gains and losses at 31 December 2001 on open forward foreign exchange contracts which hedge anticipated future foreign currency sales or purchases will be transferred from the Hedging Reserve to the profit and loss account when the forecasted foreign currency cash flows occur, at various dates up to 1 year from the balance sheet date.

See Note 15 for impact of adopting IAS 39 on available-for-sale investments at 1 January 2001.

Extract 20.27 *(continued)*

23. Long-term liabilities

	Outstanding 31 Dec. 2001 EURm	*Repayment date beyond 5 years EURm*	*Outstanding 31 Dec. 2000 EURm*
Long-term loans are repayable as follows:			
Bonds	**90**	–	138
Loans from financial institutions	**76**	–	62
Loans from pension insurance companies	**25**	15	12
Other long-term finance loans	**16**	–	8
Other long-term liabilities	**76**	76	69
	283	91	289
Deferred tax liabilities	**177**	–	69
Less current portion	**–**	–	–47
Total long-term liabilities	**460**	–	311

The long-term liabilities excluding deferred tax liabilities as of 31 December 2001 mature as follows:

	EURm	*%*
2002	–	–
2003	89	31.4
2004	103	36.4
2005	–	–
2006	–	–
Thereafter	91	32.2
	283	100.0

The currency mix of the Group long-term liabilities as at 31 December 2001 was as follows:

EUR	*GBP*	*USD*	*Others*
42.18%	22.80%	7.02%	28.00%

The long-term loan portfolio includes a fixed-rate loan with a face amount of GBP 40 million that matures in 2004. The loan is callable by the creditor on a three-month notice basis beginning in 1994, although the Group does not anticipate that the creditor will request repayment prior to the final maturity. Accordingly the loan has not been classified as a current liability at 31 December 2001.

The Group has committed credit facilities totalling USD 2.6 billion and short-term uncommitted facilities. Committed credit facilities are intended to be

Extract 20.27 *(continued)*

used for U.S. and Euro Commercial Paper Programs back up purposes. Commitment fees on the facilities vary from 0.06% to 0.10% per annum.

At 31 December 2001, no Group borrowings were collateralized by assets pledged or by mortgages.

At 31 December 2001 and 2000 the weighted average interest rate on loans from financial institutions was 6.0% and 7.8%, respectively.

Bonds	*Million*	*Interest*	*2001 EURm*	*2000 EURm*
1989–2004	40.0 GBP	11.375%	**65**	66
1993–2003	150.0 FIM	Floating	**25**	25
			90	91

A bond 1996–2001, EUR 47 million, expired in 2001 and at 31 December 2000 was included in current liabilities within the current portion of long-term debt.

Extract 20.28 *Risk management*

Nokia, Finland, 31 December 2001 (IAS)

General risk management principles

Nokia's overall risk management philosophy is based on having a corporate-wide view on key risks including strategic, operational, financial and hazard risks. Risk management in Nokia means a systematic and pro-active way to analyse, review and manage all opportunities, threats and risks related to the Group's activities.

The principles documented in the Group's risk policy and accepted by the Nokia Board require that risk management is integrated into each business process. Business or function owners always have risk ownership. Key risks are reported to the Group level to enable group-wide risk management. There are specific risk management policies covering, for example, treasury and customer finance risks.

Financial risks

The key financial targets for Nokia are growth, profitability, operational efficiency and a strong balance sheet. The objective for the Treasury function is twofold: to guarantee cost-efficient funding for the Group at all times, and to identify, evaluate and hedge financial risks in close co-operation with the business groups. There is a strong focus in Nokia on creating shareholder value. The Treasury function supports this aim by minimizing the adverse effects caused by fluctuations in the financial markets on the profitability of the underlying businesses and thus on the financial performance of Nokia, and by managing the balance sheet structure of the Group.

Extract 20.28 *(continued)*

Nokia has Treasury Centers in Geneva, Singapore/Beijing and Dallas/Sao Paolo, and a Corporate Treasury unit in Espoo. This international organization enables Nokia to provide the Group companies with financial services according to local needs and requirements. The Treasury function is governed by policies approved by top management. Treasury Policy provides principles for overall financial risk management and determines the allocation of responsibilities for financial risk management in Nokia. Operating Policies cover specific areas such as foreign exchange risk, interest rate risk, use of derivative financial instruments, as well as liquidity and credit risk. The Treasury operating policy in Nokia is risk averse. Business Groups have detailed Standard Operating Procedures supplementing the Treasury policy in financial risk management related issues.

a) Market risk

Foreign exchange risk

Nokia operates globally and is thus exposed to foreign exchange risk arising from various currency combinations. Foreign currency denominated assets and liabilities together with expected cash flows from highly probable purchases and sales give rise to foreign exchange exposures. These transaction exposures are managed against various local currencies because of Nokia's substantial production and sales outside the Eurozone.

Due to the changes in the business environment, currency combinations may also change within the financial year. The most significant non-euro sales currencies during the year were U.S. dollar, British pound Sterling and Australian dollar. In general, the appreciation of the euro to other currencies has an adverse effect on Nokia's sales and operating profit in the medium to long term, while depreciation of the euro has a positive effect. The only significant non-euro purchasing currencies are Japanese yen and U.S. dollar.

Break-down by currency of the underlying foreign exchange transaction exposure 31 December 2001 – shown as a pie chart not reproduced here

According to the foreign exchange policy guidelines of the Group, material transaction foreign exchange exposures are hedged. Exposures are mainly hedged with derivative financial instruments such as forward foreign exchange contracts and foreign exchange options. The majority of financial instruments hedging foreign exchange risk have a duration of less than a year. The Group does not hedge forecasted foreign currency cash flows beyond two years. Nokia uses both fair value and cash flow foreign currency hedges to manage its exposure to foreign exchange risk.

Nokia uses the Value-at-Risk ('VaR') methodology to assess the foreign exchange risk related to the Treasury management of the Group exposures. The VaR figure represents the potential losses for a portfolio resulting from adverse changes in market factors using a specified time period and confidence level based on historical data. To correctly take into account the non-linear price function of certain derivative instruments, Nokia uses Monte Carlo simulation. Volatilities and correlations are calculated from a one-year set of daily data. The VaR figures assume that the forecasted cash flows materialize as expected. The VaR figures for transaction foreign

Extract 20.28 (*continued*)

exchange exposure including hedging transactions in Nokia Group with a one-week horizon and 95% confidence level are shown below.

Transaction foreign exchange position Value-at-Risk (EURm)

VaR	*2001*	*2000*
31 Dec.	**16.0**	12.9
Average	**20.2**	9.1
Range	**16.0–32.7**	1.8–13.7

Since Nokia has subsidiaries outside the Eurozone, the euro-denominated value of the shareholders' equity of Nokia is also exposed to fluctuations in exchange rates. Equity changes caused by movements in foreign exchange rates are shown as a translation difference in the Group consolidation. Nokia uses, from time to time, foreign exchange contracts and foreign currency denominated loans to hedge its equity exposure arising from foreign net investments.

Interest rate risk

The Group is exposed to interest rate risk either through market value fluctuations of balance sheet items (i.e. price risk) or changes in interest income or expenses (i.e. re-investment risk). Interest rate risk mainly arises through interest-bearing liabilities and assets. Estimated future changes in cash flows and balance sheet structure also expose the Group to interest rate risk.

Group companies are responsible for managing their short-term liquidity position, whereas the interest rate exposure of the Group is monitored and managed in the Treasury. Due to the current balance sheet structure of Nokia, emphasis is placed on managing the interest rate risk of investments.

Nokia uses the VaR methodology to assess and measure the interest rate risk in investment portfolios, which are benchmarked against a one-year investment horizon. The VaR figure represents the potential losses for a portfolio resulting from adverse changes in market factors using a specified time period and confidence level based on historical data. For interest rate risk Nokia uses variance-covariance methodology. Volatilities and correlations are calculated from a one-year set of daily data. The VaR-based net interest rate risk figures for financial items in Nokia Group with a one-week horizon and 95% confidence level are shown below.

Treasury investment portfolio Value-at-Risk (EURm)

VaR	*2001*	*2000*
31 Dec.	**6.4**	2.9
Average	**4.2**	3.1
Range	**1.8–8.1**	1.8–4.7

Extract 20.28 *(continued)*

Equity price risk

Nokia has certain strategic minority investments in publicly traded companies. These investments are classified as available-for-sale. The fair value of the equity investments at 31 December 2001 was EUR 169 million (EUR 140 million in 2000).

There are currently no outstanding derivative financial instruments designated as hedges of these equity investments. The VaR figures for equity investments, shown below, have been calculated using the same principles as for interest rate risk.

Equity investments Value-at-Risk (EURm)

VaR	*2001*	*2000*
31 Dec.	**8.6**	5.4
Average	**6.4**	
Range	**3.0–11.8**	

In addition to the listed equity holdings, Nokia invests in private equity through Nokia Venture Funds. The book value of these equity investments at 31 December 2001 was 130 million US dollars (121 million US dollars in 2000). Nokia is exposed to equity price risk on social security costs relating to stock option plans. Nokia hedges this risk by entering into cash settled equity swaps.

b) Credit risk

Customer Finance Credit Risk

Telecommunications network operators sometimes require their suppliers to arrange or provide term financing in relation to infrastructure projects. Nokia has maintained a financing policy aimed at close cooperation with banks, financial institutions and Export Credit Agencies to support selected customers in their financing of infrastructure investments. Nokia's intent is, market conditions permitting, to mitigate this exposure by arrangements with these institutions and investors.

Credit risks related to customer financing are systematically analyzed, monitored and managed by Nokia's Customer Finance organization, reporting to the Chief Financial Officer. Credit risks are approved and monitored by Nokia's Credit Committee along principles defined in the Company's credit policy and according to the Group's credit approval process.

Nokia's infrastructure business is concentrated amongst mobile, wireless operators. The customer finance portfolio is substantially all in this group. In keeping with the Group's financing approach, the majority of the credit risk is to i) established mobile network operators ('incumbents') with an investment grade credit rating as determined by a major credit rating agency or equivalent as determined by Nokia if no ratings are available (collectively, 'investment grade') or ii) operators supported by other investment grade telecom operators through ownership stakes and various

Extract 20.28 *(continued)*

operational and technical support ('sponsor'). However, there is no certainty that the current sponsors will continue their involvement with the operators, and the sponsors generally do not provide guarantees on the loan balances. Nokia's credit risk to start-up operators ('greenfield operators') is substantially all to operators with investment grade sponsors.

The outstanding exposures on term customer financing at 31 December 2001 were EUR 1 255 million (EUR 1 226 million in 2000) out of which EUR 1 128 million were long-term loans receivable (EUR 907 million in 2000) and EUR 127 million were contingent liabilities (EUR 319 million in 2000). For details of one-time customer finance charges see Note 7.

Term customer financing portfolio at 31 December 2001 was:

	Out-standing	*Commit-ment*	*EURm Total*	*%*
Total Portfolio	**1,255**	**2,955**	**4,210**	**100**
Incumbent, Investment Grade/				
I.G. Sponsor	376	1,191	1,568	37
Incumbent, non-I.G. Sponsor	89	470	559	13
Total Incumbent	465	1,661	2,127	51
Greenfield, I.G. Sponsor	751	1,288	2,040	48
Greenfield, non-I.G. Sponsor	39	5	44	1
Total Greenfield	790	1,293	2,083	49

Financial credit risk

Financial instruments contain an element of risk of the counterparties being unable or unwilling to meet their obligations. This risk is measured and monitored by the Treasury function. The Group minimizes financial credit risk by limiting its counterparties to a sufficient number of major banks and financial institutions.

Direct credit risk represents the risk of loss resulting from counter-party default in relation to on-balance sheet products. The fixed income and money market investment decisions are based on strict creditworthiness criteria. The outstanding investments are also constantly monitored by the Treasury. Nokia does not expect the counterparties to default given their high credit ratings.

Investments

Current Available-for-sale investments[1]	*2001 EURm*	*2000 EURm*[2]
Government, long-term (bonds)	**789**	615
Government, short-term (bills) – Corporate, long-term (bonds)	**1,475**	384
Corporate, short-term (CP)	**2,007**	1,775
Total	**4,271**	2,774

Extract 20.28 (*continued*)

1 Available-for-sale investments are carried at fair value in 2001.
2 The comparative figures for the year ended 31 December 2000 are not restated.

c) Liquidity risk

Nokia guarantees a sufficient liquidity at all times by efficient cash management and by investing in liquid interest bearing securities. Due to the dynamic nature of the underlying business Treasury also aims at maintaining flexibility in funding by keeping committed and uncommitted credit lines available. During the year Nokia further strengthened its committed funding sources with a USD 1.75 billion revolving credit facility. The committed facilities at year end totalled USD 2.6 billion.

The most significant existing funding programs include:

Revolving Credit Facility of USD 750 million, matures in 2002
Revolving Credit Facility of USD 500 million, matures in 2003
Revolving Credit Facility of USD 350 million, matures in 2004
Revolving Credit Facility of USD 1,000 million, matures in 2006
Local commercial paper program in Finland, totalling EUR 750 million
Euro Commercial Paper (ECP) program, totalling USD 500 million
US Commercial Paper (USCP) program, totalling USD 500 million
None of the above programs have been used to a significant degree in 2001.

Nokia's international creditworthiness facilitates the efficient use of international capital and loan markets. The ratings of Nokia from credit rating agencies as at 31 December 2001 were:

Short-term	Standard & Poor's	A-1
	Moody's	P-1
Long-term	Standard & Poor's	A
	Moody's	A1

Hazard risk

Nokia strives to ensure that all financial, reputation and other losses to the Group and Nokia's customers are minimized through preventive risk management measures or insurance. Insurance cover is purchased for risks which cannot be internally managed. Nokia purchases both annual insurance policies for specific risks and multi-line multi-year insurance policies where available, covering a variety of risks to decrease the likelihood of non-anticipated sudden losses. The objective is to ensure that Group's hazard risks, whether related to physical assets (e.g. buildings) or intellectual assets (e.g. brand) or liabilities (e.g. product liability) are efficiently handled through purchase of insurance cover.

Extract 20.28 *(continued)*

Notional amounts of derivative financial instruments[1]

	2001 EURm	*2000 EURm*
Foreign exchange forward contracts[2, 3]	**20,978**	10,497
Currency options bought[3]	**1,328**	2,165
Currency options sold[3]	**1,209**	2,209
Interest rate swaps	–	250
Cash settled equity swaps[4]	**182**	336

1 The notional amounts of derivatives summarized here do not represent amounts exchanged by the parties and thus are not a measure of the exposure of Nokia caused by its use of derivatives.
2 Notional amounts outstanding include positions which have been closed off.
3 As at 31 December 2001 notional amounts include contracts amounting to EUR 1.1 billion used to hedge the shareholders' equity of foreign subsidiaries (31 December 2000 EUR 0.7 billion).
4 Cash settled equity swaps can be used to hedge risk relating to incentive programs and investment activities.

Fair values of derivatives

The net fair values of derivative financial instruments at the balance sheet date were:

	2001 EURm	*2000 EURm*
Derivatives with positive fair value:[1]		
Forward foreign exchange contracts[2]	**186**	191
Currency options purchased	**11**	47
Cash settled equity swaps	**10**	-
Embedded derivatives[3]	**6**	-
Derivatives with negative fair value:[1]		
Forward foreign exchange contracts[2]	**−214**	−269
Currency options written	**−7**	−38
Cash settled equity swaps		−19

1 Out of the forward foreign exchange contracts and currency options, fair value EUR 3 million was designated for hedges of net investment in foreign subsidiaries as at 31 December 2001 (EUR −1 million in 2000) and reported in translation difference.
2 Out of the foreign exchange forward contracts, fair value EUR −38 million was designated for cash flow hedges as at 31 December 2001 (EUR −114 million in 2000) and reported in fair value and other reserves.

Extract 20.28 (*continued*)

3 Embedded derivatives are components of contracts having the characteristics of derivatives, and thus requiring fair valuing of such components. The change in the fair value is reported in other financial income and expenses.

Notes

[1] In 1992, the IASC changed the way it appointed steering committees and took control over the appointments. Therefore, the IASC had a much greater say in the membership of the steering committee appointed in 1995.

[2] Later to be replaced by the CICA's Accounting Standards Board (AcSB).

[3] At that time, it was not the IASC's practice to publish DSOPs. The practice changed in 1993 with the publication of the DSOP on earnings per share (in fact, the next DSOP after that on financial statements).

[4] See also John Carchrae, 'Financial Instruments', *IASC Insight*, July 1991, pp 10–14.

[5] For a summary of the IASC's and the CICA's response to issues raised in E40 and a comparison of E48 and the Canadian exposure draft, see John Carchrae 'Financial Instruments – New IASC and Canadian Exposure Draft', *IASC Insight*, March 1994, pp 13–17, and Peter Martin, 'Financial Instruments Re-exposed', *CA Magazine*, June/July 1994, pp 58–61.

[6] Some Canadian entities did not have to apply recommendation 3860 until a later date.

[7] See also FEE, *Accounting Treatment of Financial Instruments – A European Perspective*, FEE, Brussels, 1996.

[8] John Carchrae, 'Statement of Principles in 1996', *IASC Insight*, December 1995, pp 8–9.

[9] See also Alex Milburn and Ian Hague, 'A Need for Uniformity', *CA Magazine*, April 1997, pp 45–47 and 53.

[10] Sir Bryan Carsberg, 'IASC Staff Propose an Interim Solution on Financial Instruments, *IASC Insight*, October 1997, p 5.

[11] Paul Pacter, 'Financial Instruments: Completing the Core', *IASC Insight*, June 1998, pp 6–7.

[12] See for example: Ian Hague, 'Plans for an Integrated International Standard', *IASC Insight*, March 1998, pp 7–10; Ian Hague, 'Beyond the Exposure Draft – a Comprehensive International Standard', *IASC Insight*, June 1998, pp 8–9; Diana Willis, 'Financial Liabilities – Fair Value or Historical Cost', *IASC Insight*, October 1998, pp 8–10; and Ian Hague, 'Financial Instruments: In Pursuit of Fair Value', *IASC Insight*, December 1998, p 10.

[13] Both the JWG document and the response of the bankers are available at *www.iasb.org.uk*.

[14] *Public Disclosure of the Trading and Derivatives Activities of Banks and Securities Firms*, Basel Committee on Banking Supervision and IOSCO, 1995.

[15] For a discussion of the arguments for and against the intent based approach and, in particular, alternative measurement bases for held-to-maturity financial assets, see the IASC's 1997 discussion paper *Accounting for Financial Assets and Liabilities*, pp 96–8.

CHAPTER 21

Property, Plant and Equipment

21.1 STANDARDS AND INTERPRETATIONS

IAS 16 *Property, Plant and Equipment*

In addition to IAS 16, the following IASs and interpretations deal with specific aspects of accounting for property, plant and equipment:

IAS 17 *Leases*
IAS 20 *Accounting for Government Grants and Disclosure of Government Assistance*
IAS 23 *Borrowing Costs*
IAS 36 *Impairment of Assets*
IAS 37 *Provisions, Contingent Liabilities and Contingent Assets*
IAS 40 *Investment Property*
SIC 2 *Consistency – Capitalisation of Borrowing Costs*
SIC 14 *Property, Plant and Equipment – Compensation for the Impairment or Loss of Items*
SIC 23 *Property, Plant and Equipment – Major Inspection or Overhaul Costs*

When items of property, plant and equipment are revalued, consideration should also be given to the International Valuation Standards (IVSs) developed by the International Valuation Standards Committee (IVSC).

21.2 HISTORY

IAS 4 *Depreciation Accounting* was approved in 1974 and required the depreciation of all depreciable assets, including property, plant and equipment. IAS 16 *Accounting for Property, Plant and Equipment* (IAS 16 [1982]) was approved in 1981. It dealt mainly with the determination of cost and the revaluation of property, plant and equipment.

IAS 16 [1982] was reconsidered in the comparability and improvements project when a number of changes were made including the identification of a cost based approach as the benchmark treatment and a fair value approach as the allowed alternative treatment. The revised IAS also required significantly tighter requirements for those entities opting for a fair value approach. The IASC also took the opportunity to merge into IAS 16 those aspects of IAS 4 which deal with the depreciation of property, plant and equipment. IAS 16 *Property, Plant and Equipment* (IAS 16 [1993]) was approved in November 1993 and applied to financial statements for accounting periods beginning on or after 1 January 1995.

IAS 36 *Impairment of Assets*, which applied to accounting periods beginning on or after 1 July 1999, provides further guidance on the impairment of property, plant and equipment (see chapter 25) and led to consequential changes to IAS 16. At the same time, the IASC removed the guidance on the use of market value for existing use for many revalued items of property, plant and equipment and the link to IVSs.

In April 2000, IAS 16 was revised following the approval of IAS 40 which requires that investment property is measured in accordance with the fair value model in IAS 40 or the cost model in IAS 16 (see chapter 22).

IASB improvements project

In its May 2002 improvements exposure draft, the IASB proposes several changes to IAS 16 including:

- the measurement of exchanges of items of property, plant and equipment at fair value;
- a revised definition of residual value;
- the separate treatment of the components of an asset for the purpose of calculating depreciation;
- additional guidance on the clarification of directly attributable costs; and
- guidance on the treatment of income and expenses relating to incidental operations.

21.3 IOSCO

In June 1994, IOSCO advised the IASC that IAS 16 was acceptable for the purposes of the IOSCO core standards. However, IOSCO identified the following suspense issues:

- some IOSCO members may accept the allowed alternative treatment of fair value less subsequent accumulated depreciation dependent on the disclosure of the significant balance sheet and income statement effects of the revaluations (instead of just the balance sheet disclosure required by IAS 16);

- IOSCO may decide that disclosures of the effects of revaluations may not be required for revaluations which were required by law in some countries due to severe inflation provided that the entity discloses the year and amounts of the revaluations;
- the IASC should consider eliminating alternatives for the identification and measurement of the impairment of property, plant and equipment as IAS 16 [1993] did not provide sufficient guidance to achieve reasonably comparable results in identifying impairment or measuring the recoverable amount (this issue has been dealt with in IAS 36);
- the IASC should consider more guidance on the disposal of property, plant and equipment, in particular the evaluation of factors which may indicate whether or not a disposal has taken place and whether a gain or loss should be recognised; and
- one IOSCO member believes that the receipt of funds from customers, governments or other third parties as compensation for the loss of impairment of property, plant and equipment should be allowed to be deducted in arriving at the carrying amount of the assets or recognised fully in the income statement when received (this issue is dealt with in SIC 14 and the May 2002 improvements exposure draft).

IOSCO also identified 'environmental accounting issues' as a potential long-term IASC project; in November 1994, the IASC decided to consider a joint project with other standard setting bodies (*IASC Insight*, December 1994, p13).

IAS 16 is included in 'IAS 2000' endorsed by IOSCO in May 2000. There are five supplemental treatments:

- concerns about the acceptability of revalued amounts without disclosure of information providing significant balance sheet and income statement effects of revaluation (some information is already required by IAS 16);
- concerns about the need for more guidance on circumstances that indicate that there has been a disposal of an asset;
- concerns about accounting for the effects of significant inflation, but not hyperinflation, in the cost basis of property, plant and equipment;
- guidance on whether either a gross or net presentation should be used; and
- clarification that compensation received relating to an insurance reimbursement, an indemnity for the expropriation of assets or as a result of an involuntary conversion should be classified as extraordi-

nary when it relates to a loss reported as an extraordinary item (the IASB proposes to prohibit the presentation of extraordinary items).

21.4 IAS 16 IN BRIEF

An item of property, plant and equipment, including improvements to that item, should be recognised initially at cost. The cost of a self-constructed item is determined using the same principles as apply to inventories. Cost may include borrowing costs for those items which take a substantial period to get ready for their intended use. Government grants related to the item may be deducted from cost. Subsequent expenditure on the item which does not increase its originally assessed standard of performance should be recognised as an expense.

Subsequent to its initial recognition, an item of property, plant and equipment should be measured at either:

- cost less accumulated depreciation and any write-down for impairment; or
- fair value less any subsequent accumulated depreciation and any write-down for impairment.

Upward revaluations are permitted provided that:

- the revaluations are made to fair value;
- the revaluations are kept up to date such that carrying amount does not differ materially from fair value at the balance sheet date;
- all the items in the same class of property, plant and equipment are revalued at the same time; and
- revaluation surpluses are credited to the revaluation reserve in equity and are not included in any subsequent profit or loss on disposal.

In the case of items carried at cost less accumulated depreciation, the depreciation method should allocate the depreciable amount (cost less residual value) over the item's useful life. The method should reflect the pattern in which the asset's economic benefits are consumed. In the case of items carried at fair value less accumulated depreciation, the same rules apply except that depreciable amount is fair value less residual value and residual value is determined as at the date of the latest revaluation.

When an entity expects to recover less than its carrying amount from the future use of an item (or a group of identical items) of property, plant and equipment, the carrying amount should be reduced to recoverable amount (see chapter 25).

21.5 DEFINITION OF PROPERTY, PLANT AND EQUIPMENT

Property, plant and equipment are tangible assets that:

(a) are held by an entity for use in the production or supply of goods and services, for rental to others, or for administrative purposes; and
(b) are expected to be used during more than one period.
(IAS 16, 6)

Items of property, plant and equipment usually include land, buildings, machinery, ships, aircraft, motor vehicles, furniture and fittings, computers and office equipment.

Items of property, plant and equipment which an entity intends to sell, for example because they have reached the end of their useful lives or are surplus to requirements, are usually classified as property, plant and equipment until sold. Similar items which are acquired or produced and held for resale are classified and accounted for as inventory. So, for example, a vehicle manufacturer accounts for vehicles produced for resale as inventory but vehicles produced and held for rental under operating leases or for use by its own employees are classified as property, plant and equipment.

Property, plant and equipment includes intangible assets which are integral to an item of property, plant and equipment. For example, while computer software is, by definition, an intangible asset, it is dealt with as property, plant and equipment when it is an integral part of the related hardware or another piece of equipment (IAS 38, 3).

Each item of property, plant and equipment is usually dealt with separately although it is usual to apply the same depreciation rate to similar items. It is also usual to aggregate individually insignificant items such as moulds, tools and dies and in such cases to apply the IAS to the aggregate value of the items.

The component parts of an item of property, plant and equipment are dealt with separately when the components:

- have different useful lives (IAS 16, 12);
- provide benefits to the entity in a different pattern thus necessitating the use of different depreciation rates or methods (IAS 16, 12); or
- require the separate calculation of recoverable amount – see chapter 25.

Example of items which may need to be treated as separate items include:

- an aircraft and its engines in the financial statements of an airline;
- the land under the runway, the runway and the runway lights in the financial statements of an airport;
- the rolling stock and the track in a transit system;

- the component parts of the transmission equipment of a telephone company (see extract 21.1); and
- land and buildings on that land when the land normally has an unlimited life but the buildings have a limited life.

Extract 21.1 *Component parts of items of property, plant and equipment*

Deutsche Telekom, Germany, 31 December 2001 (German GAAP plus US GAAP)

Depreciation of non-current assets is carried out using the straight-line method over the following useful lives:

	Years
...	
Telephone facilities and terminal equipment	3 to 10
Data communications equipment, telephone network and ISDN switching equipment, radio transmission equipment, radio transmission equipment and technical equipment for broadband distribution networks	5 to 20
Broadband distribution networks, outside plant networks and cable conduit lines	15 to 20
Telecommunications power facilities and other	3 to 10

IASB improvements project

In its May 2002 improvements exposure draft, the IASB proposes to require that the components of items of property, plant and equipment with different useful lives should be accounted for separately when accounting for the replacement or renewal of those components. Each material component of an asset with a different useful economic life or a different depreciation pattern should be accounted for separately for both depreciation and capitalisation purposes.

21.6 RECOGNITION

21.6.1 Initial Recognition

An item of property, plant and equipment which is acquired or constructed should be recognised as an asset when:

- it is probable that future economic benefits associated with the asset will flow to the entity; and
- the cost of the asset to the entity can be measured reliably.

(IAS 16, 7)

The recognition standard was new to the revised IAS 16 and uses framework terminology. For all practical purposes, the standard is identical to that applying to items of property, plant and equipment acquired in a business combination (see chapter 16).

IAS 16 suggests that it is probable that the future economic benefits associated with an item of property, plant and equipment will flow to the entity only when the risks and rewards attaching to the asset have passed to the entity (IAS 16, 9). This guidance is similar to that in IAS 17 for the recognition of assets acquired under a finance lease (see chapter 32). This guidance also mirrors that given in IAS 18 for the sale of goods (see chapter 29).

The same criteria apply to items of property, plant and equipment which are being manufactured or constructed on behalf of the entity. Therefore, such items are recognised as property, plant and equipment by the entity when the risks attaching to the items have passed to the entity. For example, an entity recognises as property, the construction costs incurred as at the balance sheet date in respect of a new building if the entity has control over the partially completed building and is exposed to the risks associated with it (such as a decline in market value or physical damage through fire or some other disaster). On the other hand, an entity does not recognise as equipment a new machine which is being manufactured for it by another entity if that other entity bears all the risks and would, for example, be responsible for providing a replacement machine if the machine under construction is damaged during manufacture.

Some have interpreted the recognition criteria in IAS 16 to mean that items which have not yet been acquired but which are the subject of a binding purchase order should be recognised as property, plant and equipment. Under such an approach, for example, an airline would recognise as equipment any aircraft for which it has placed a binding order. While such an interpretation has some support, it was not the IASC's intention when it agreed the recognition criteria; such orders are treated as capital commitments and are disclosed as such.

An entity may have paid a deposit on placing an order or at some other time prior to that on which it recognises the item of property, plant and equipment on its balance sheet. The deposit is a prepayment or receivable which is classified as a non-current, rather than a current, asset. It is common practice to classify such deposits within property, plant and equipment as payments on account or assets in the course of construction. It is incorrect to classify the deposit as a current asset as it is not held for sale or consumption within the normal operating cycle nor is it held primarily for trading purposes or for the short-term (IAS 1, 57).

21.6.2 Safety and Environmental Expenditure

When an item of property, plant and equipment is acquired or constructed for safety, environmental or similar reasons, it may be difficult to establish that additional future economic benefits will flow to the entity as a result of the acquisition of the item. For example, an entity may acquire plant and equipment in order to comply with environmental regulations relating to the handling of chemicals; such expenditure may not increase the economic benefits which flow to the entity, indeed it may increase the costs of entity.

IAS 16 allows an entity to capitalise such expenditure when the item is needed to obtain the future economic benefits from other assets (IAS 16, 13). Therefore, an entity would capitalise the chemical handling equipment if the entity would not be allowed to manufacture or sell chemicals without incurring the expenditure.

When approving the revised IAS 16, the IASC recognised the limited nature of its work on safety and environmental related expenditure. It decided to include a more extensive project on environmental issues in its potential work programme but acknowledged that it was unlikely to start work on such a project for some time (*IASC Insight*, September 1993, p11). In its November 1994 review of its work programme the IASC decided to consider a joint project with other standard setting bodies (*IASC Insight*, December 1994, p13). No further work has been carried out on this project.

Clean-up costs which will be incurred at the end of the useful life of an asset are included in the costs of an asset when a provision is required for those costs (IAS 37, 20 – see chapter 27).

Extract 21.2 *Capitalisation of environmental expenditures*

Norsk Hydro, Norway, 31 December 2001 (N GAAP plus US GAAP)

Environmental expenditures which increase the life, capacity or result in improved safety or efficiency of a facility are capitalized. Expenditures that relate to an existing condition caused by past operations are expensed.

21.6.3 Subsequent Improvements

An entity may incur expenditure in order to improve a previously acquired or constructed item of property, plant and equipment. While the same recognition criteria apply to this expenditure, the entity must decide whether the expenditure should be added to the carrying amount of the existing item or treated as an expense. The expenditure should be added to the carrying amount of the existing item only when it will result in future economic benefits in excess of the originally assessed standard of performance of the existing item (IAS 16, 23). If the expenditure does not increase the originally assessed standard of performance, the expenditure is either treated as an expense or, if it is capitalised, the carrying amount of the old asset must be written off.

An asset's standard of performance can be increased, for example, by:

- extending the useful life of the asset;
- increasing the capacity of the asset;
- substantially improving the quality of the output from the asset; or
- substantially reducing operating costs.

This requirement had particular relevance in respect of expenditure incurred in order to ensure that computer and other systems were able to cope with the introduction of the euro. SIC 6 has confirmed that costs incurred in order to restore or maintain the future economic benefits that were expected from the originally assessed standard of performance of existing systems should be recognised as an expense (SIC 6, 4). While such systems may be treated as intangible assets, the same principle should apply to related items of plant and equipment, for example, the computer hardware itself. An acceptable alternative approach, which is not referred to in the interpretation, would be to write off the old systems and related hardware and capitalise the new systems and hardware.

Extract 21.3 *Capitalisation of improvements to property, plant and equipment*

Bayer, Germany, 31 December 2001 (IAS)

Expenses for the repair of property, plant and equipment are normally charged against income but they are capitalized if they result in an enlargement or substantial improvement of the respective assets.

Extract 21.4 *Capitalisation of improvements to property, plant and equipment*

Holcim, Switzerland, 31 December 2001 (IAS)

Repairs and renovation expenses are usually charged to the income statement but costs incurred are capitalized if one or more of the following conditions are satisfied: the original useful life of the asset is prolonged, the original production capacity is increased, the quality of the product is materially enhanced or production costs are reduced considerably.

Subsequent expenditure incurred as part of a regular major inspection or overhaul of an item of property, plant and equipment and which allows the continued use of the asset is expensed as incurred unless the following conditions are met (SIC 23, 5):

- a separate component of an asset has been identified which is represented by the major inspection or overhaul costs and this has already been depreciated to reflect the consumption of the benefits which are now being replaced or restored;
- it is probable that future economic benefits will flow from these costs; and
- the inspection and overhaul costs can be measured reliably.

Where the above criteria are met, the costs should be capitalised as a component of the fixed asset.

IASB improvements project

In its May 2002 improvements exposure draft, the IASB proposes to replace the notion of the 'originally assessed standard of performance' with 'standard of performance assessed immediately before the expenditure was made'. This means that subsequent expenditure on an item of property, plant and equipment should be capitalised if it increases the future economic benefits above those reflected in the most recent (and not the original) assessed standard of performance.

21.7 INITIAL MEASUREMENT

An item of property, plant and equipment which qualifies for recognition should initially be measured at its cost (IAS 16, 14). The cost of an item of property, plant and equipment which is purchased is its acquisition cost. The cost of a self-constructed item is its production cost, determined using the same principles as for inventories.

21.7.1 Cost

The acquisition cost of a purchased item of property, plant and equipment comprises its purchase price and any directly attributable costs of bringing the asset to its working condition (IAS 16, 15). Therefore, acquisition cost includes, when appropriate:

- purchase price;
- import duties;

- non-refundable purchase taxes such as any value added or similar taxes which are not recoverable by the entity from the taxing authorities;
- the costs of site preparation;
- initial delivery and handling costs;
- installation costs;
- professional fees of architects and engineers etc;
- the estimated costs of dismantling and removing the asset and restoring the site to the extent that they are recognised as a provision under IAS 37; and
- other directly attributable costs of bringing the asset to its working condition.

Trade discounts and rebates are deducted in determining the acquisition cost.

The acquisition cost of an item of property, plant and equipment acquired under a finance lease is its fair value or, if lower, the present value of the minimum lease payments (see chapter 32). The acquisition cost of an item of property, plant and equipment acquired in a business combination which is an acquisition, is determined by reference to its fair value (see chapter 16). The acquisition cost of an item of property, plant and equipment donated by a government is either its fair value or a nominal amount (see chapter 34).

The production cost of a self-constructed asset is the acquisition cost of goods, raw materials and supplies (determined as for a purchased item of property, plant and equipment), the costs of conversion and other costs incurred in bringing the asset to its working condition for its intended use. The costs of conversion are determined using the same principles that apply for inventories (see chapter 26). Therefore, such costs include:

- costs directly related to the construction of the asset, such as direct labour; and
- a systematic allocation of variable and fixed production overheads that are incurred in constructing the asset.

Other costs, such as non-production overheads and design costs, are included in production cost only to the extent that they are incurred in bringing the asset to its working condition for its intended use. Cost inefficiencies are excluded from the cost of production.

Extract 21.5 *Cost of self-constructed property, plant and equipment*

Bayer, Germany, 31 December 2001 (IAS)

The cost of construction of self-constructed property, plant and equipment comprises the direct costs of materials, direct manufacturing expenses, appropriate allocations of material and manufacturing overheads, and an appropriate share of depreciation and write-downs of assets used in construction. It includes the shares of expenses for company pension plans and discretionary employee benefits that are attributable to construction.

Extract 21.6 *Cost of self-constructed property, plant and equipment*

Schering, Germany, 31 December 2001 (IAS)

The production cost of self-manufactured assets includes, in addition to direct costs, an appropriate proportion of overheads and depreciation ... Interest on third-party borrowings is not included in production costs.

Acquisition cost or production cost includes:

- borrowing costs when the entity adopts the allowed alternative treatment under IAS 23 (see chapter 35);
- foreign exchange differences when such differences are included in borrowing costs and the entity adopts the allowed alternative treatment under IAS 23 (see chapter 35); or
- foreign exchange differences when the entity adopts the allowed alternative under IAS 21 for those differences which result from a severe devaluation or depreciation of a currency against which there is no practical means of hedging and that affects liabilities which cannot be settled and which arise directly on the recent acquisition of the item of property, plant and equipment invoiced in a foreign currency (see chapter 19).

In the circumstances permitted by IAS 39, cost also includes any deferred gains and losses on a financial instrument when that instrument has been designated as a hedge of a firm commitment or forecasted transaction to acquire the item of property, plant and equipment (see chapter 20). Such gains and losses are included in equity prior to the acquisition of the item of property, plant and equipment. On acquisition, deferred losses may be added to, and deferred gains deducted from, the cost of the item.

Acquisition cost or production cost may also include provisions for the de-commissioning, environmental and other costs which will be incurred as a result of a present obligation when such provisions are recognised as a liability and included in the cost of the related asset (IAS 37, 19 – see chapter 27). Government grants related to an item of property, plant and equipment may be deducted from acquisition cost or production cost (see chapter 34).

Acquisition cost or production cost does not include:

- start-up and similar pre-production costs unless they are necessary to bring the item to its working condition (IAS 16, 17);

- initial operating losses incurred prior to an item achieving planned performance (IAS 16, 17);
- borrowing costs incurred after the item is ready for its intended use; or
- most foreign exchange differences arising after the item is ready for its intended use.

Therefore, for example:

- the costs of the initial testing of a new item of equipment may be included in the cost of the equipment if it is necessary to bring the equipment to its working condition but costs of testing carried out after the equipment has reached its working condition should be recognised as an expense;
- the costs associated with trial production carried out after the equipment has reached its working condition should be excluded from the cost of the equipment and should be included as an expense in the income statement;
- losses incurred as a result of running a new piece of equipment at less than normal capacity should not be added to the cost of the equipment but should be included in the income statement; and
- exchange losses arising on a foreign currency loan used to acquire an aircraft should not be added to the cost of that aircraft except in the very limited circumstances permitted by the current allowed alternative treatment in IAS 21 (see chapter 19).

The payment of the acquisition cost of an item of property, plant and equipment may be deferred beyond normal credit terms. In such circumstances, the acquisition cost is the cash price equivalent or the present value of the future payments. The difference between this amount and the total payments is recognised as interest expense; it may be added to the cost of the asset as borrowing costs in the circumstances permitted by IAS 23 (IAS 16, 16).

Example 21.1 *Deferred Payment Terms*

A acquires a new building on terms under which 50% of the cost of $6 million is payable immediately and the balance is payable in a year's time. The acquisition cost is either:

- the cash price equivalent; or
- $3 million plus the present value of $3 million payable in a year's time.

Continued

Continued

Assume that the acquisition cost is $5.6 million. The initial carrying amount of the building is $5.6 million and the balance of $0.4 million is recognised as interest expense over the period in which payment is deferred. If the building is in the course of construction, the interest expense is added to the cost of the building if A adopts the allowed alternative treatment in IAS 23, the building is a qualifying asset, the same treatment is followed for other qualifying assets, and all the other requirements of IAS 23 are met.

IASB improvements project

In its May 2002 improvements exposure draft, the IASB proposes to clarify that directly attributable costs that can be included in the cost of an item of property, plant and equipment include:

- costs incurred in bringing the asset to the location and working condition necessary for it to be capable of operating in the manner intended; and
- costs reported after deducting the net proceeds from selling any items, such as samples, that are produced when bringing the asset into use.

Dismantling, removal and restoration costs recognised under IAS 37 should also be included in the cost of an item of property, plant and equipment.

The IASB proposes to require that incidental income and expenses arising during the construction or development of property, plant and equipment and before the asset is brought into working condition for its intended use should be recognised in the net profit or loss for the period and not included in the measurement of the cost of the asset.

21.7.2 Asset Exchanges

The acquisition cost of an item of property, plant and equipment acquired in exchange for another item is its fair value, which is equivalent to the fair value of the item given up adjusted by the amount of cash or cash equivalents transferred (IAS 16, 21).

The exchange should be measured at the carrying amount of the asset given up, rather than its fair value, when the item of property, plant and equipment is acquired in exchange for:

- a similar asset that has a similar use in the same line of business and which has a similar fair value; and
- an equity interest in a similar asset.

(IAS 16, 22)

Cash or cash equivalents transferred as part of the exchange transaction may indicate that the items exchanged do not have a similar value (IAS 16, 22).

The approach means that the entity does not recognise any gain on the asset given up. IAS 16 justifies this approach on the grounds that 'the earnings process is incomplete' (IAS 16, 22); that is that a transaction has not taken place. In substance, but not in form, the entity is in the same position after the exchange as it was before the exchange.

Example 21.2 *Exchange of similar assets*

A and B own adjacent properties which are identical in every other respect. A acquired its property in 1996 and its carrying amount in A's balance sheet is currently $2 million. B acquired its property in 2000 and its carrying amount in B's balance sheet is currently $3 million. A and B decide to exchange their properties, the current market value of each property being $3.5 million.

If the properties are similar assets that have a similar use in the same line of business:

- A measures the property acquired from B at $2 million, that is the carrying amount of the property transferred from A to B;
- B measures the property acquired from A at $3 million, that is the carrying amount of the property transferred from B to A; and
- neither A nor B recognises a gain on the disposal of its original property.

If the properties had not been similar assets or did not have a similar use in the same line of business:

- A would have measured the property acquired from B at $3.5 million, that is its fair value, and recognised a gain of $1.5 million on the transfer of its original property to B; and
- B would have measured the property acquired from A at $3.5 million, that is its fair value, and recognised a gain of $0.5 million on the transfer of its original property to A.

IAS 16 suggests that exchanges of 'aircraft, hotels, service stations and other real estate properties' are examples of exchanges of similar assets for which the cost of the acquired assets would be the net carrying amount of the assets given up rather than their fair value at the date of the exchange. It is not clear why these types of assets warrant special mention other than that they are exchanged in practice and that any particular asset can be often used by different entities in the same line of business.

Some take a very broad view on what is meant by a 'similar asset'. They would not recognise a gain when, for example, two airlines exchange different aircraft in an arm's length transaction or two hotel companies exchange hotel properties in an arm's length transaction. Others look more to the substance of the arrangement, in particular whether or not there has been an arm's length exchange transaction.

IASB improvements project

In its May 2002 improvements exposure draft, the IASB proposes to require that all exchanges of items of property, plant and equipment (whether similar or not) should be measured at fair value except when the fair value of neither of the assets exchanged can be determined reliably. When the fair value cannot be determined reliably, the cost of the asset acquired should be measured at the carrying amount of the asset given up.

21.8 SUBSEQUENT MEASUREMENT

Once an item of property, plant and equipment has been recognised on the balance sheet, the standards set out in IAS 16 apply to that item whether it was purchased, self-constructed, exchanged for another item, acquired in a business combination, acquired as lessee under a finance lease, donated by a government or acquired in any other way. IAS 16 includes:

- a benchmark treatment under which subsequent measurement is based on cost; and
- an allowed alternative treatment under which subsequent measurement is based on fair values.

All items in the same class of property, plant and equipment must be dealt with in the same way (IAS 16, 35). An entity may, however, use the benchmark treatment for one class of property, plant and equipment and the allowed alternative treatment for another class of property, plant and equipment. For example, an entity may use carrying amounts based on fair values for land and buildings and carrying amounts based on cost for plant and equipment.

Sometimes it is necessary to use fair value to determine the initial carrying amount of an item of property, plant and equipment. For example, when an item of property, plant and equipment is acquired:

- in exchange for another asset;
- as lessee under a finance lease;
- by means of a government grant; or
- on a business combination which is an acquisition.

This is not an application of the allowed alternative treatment. In such cases, fair value is used to establish cost rather than to revalue the asset.

Subsequent to their initial recognition, such items may be accounted for using either the benchmark treatment (with the initial carrying amount – cost – determined by reference to fair value) or the allowed alternative treatment. So, for example, an item of equipment acquired under a finance lease may be carried at either:

- cost, being fair value at the inception of the lease, less depreciation (benchmark treatment); or
- fair value at the balance sheet date less subsequent depreciation (allowed alternative treatment).

21.9 SUBSEQUENT MEASUREMENT – BENCHMARK TREATMENT

An item of property, plant and equipment should be carried at cost less any accumulated depreciation and any write-down for impairment (IAS 16, 28).

21.9.1 Depreciation

Depreciation is the systematic allocation of the depreciable amount of an item of property, plant and equipment over its useful life (IAS 16, 6). The *depreciable amount* is the cost of the item less its residual value estimated at the date of acquisition (IAS 16, 6 and 46). Cost is the amount at which the item is initially measured.

21.9.2 Residual Value

Residual value is the net amount which the entity expects to obtain for the item at the end of its useful life after deducting the expected costs of disposal (IAS 16, 6). Under the benchmark treatment, residual value is estimated at the date of acquisition and is not subsequently revised (under the allowed alternative treatment, residual value is recomputed at the time of each valuation).

Residual value is estimated by reference to the amount which the entity would obtain at the date of acquisition for similar assets which have reached the end of their useful lives and which have operated under conditions similar to those in which the item will be used (IAS 16, 46). For example, the residual value of a newly constructed building which the entity expects to use for twenty years is the amount which the entity would expect to obtain at the date of acquisition for a similar building which has been used for twenty years under conditions similar to those in which the new building will be used. Therefore, under the benchmark treatment, residual value does not take into account expected changes in prices of the item or the value of its economic benefits.

Residual value is affected by the entity's plans for the item including its policy, if any, on replacement. For example, transport companies which replace their vehicles every three or five years respectively, estimate their residual value as the amount they expect to obtain at the date of acquisition for vehicles which have been used for three or five years respectively under conditions similar to those in which the new vehicles will be used. A transport company which expects to use its vehicles until they are scrapped, estimates residual value as the scrap value of vehicles at the date of acquisition for vehicles which have reached the end of their useful lives.

Example 21.3 *Disposal Costs and Residual Value*

A acquires an item of equipment for £25 million which has a useful life of ten years, at the end of which A will have to incur dismantling and restoration costs of £5 million. A does not expect to obtain anything for equipment at the end of its useful life. A uses the straight line method to calculate depreciation and any provision for dismantling and restoration costs.

Assume that the dismantling and restoration costs meet the definition and recognition criteria for a provision when the equipment is acquired. At that time, A recognises a provision for £5 million (discounted if appropriate) and adds the amount of that provision to the cost of the equipment. Ignoring any effects of discounting, the depreciable amount of the equipment is £30 million and A charges depreciation of £3 million a year. At the end of year 1, the carrying amount of the equipment is £27 million, that is cost (£30 million) less depreciation (£3 million). At the end of year 10, the carrying amount of the equipment is zero but there is a provision of £5 million from which the dismantling and restoration costs are deducted.

IASB improvements project

In its May 2002 improvements exposure draft, the IASB proposes that residual value should be based on the current price for an asset of a similar age and condition to the estimated age and condition of the asset at the end of its useful life. It will also require that the residual value of an asset should be reviewed at each balance sheet date regardless of whether the asset has been measured under the benchmark treatment or the allowed alternative treatment. Any change in the residual value, other than a change reflected in an impairment loss, should be accounted for prospectively as an adjustment to future depreciation.

21.9.3 Useful Life

Useful life is either:

- the period of time over which an asset is expected to be used by the entity; or
- the number of production or similar units expected to be obtained from the asset by the entity.

(IAS 16, 6)

The useful life of any item of property, plant and equipment depends on the use made of that item by the entity and may be different from the useful life of identical assets held by the same or another entity. For example, the useful lives of the same aircraft vary considerably from airline to airline[1] in order to reflect the different ways in which airlines utilise their aircraft.

In practice, entities use broad estimates of useful life and the same estimate is often applied to all similar items. Useful life is determined based on a number of factors including:

- the expected usage of the asset by reference to its expected capacity or physical output;
- the expected physical wear and tear of the asset, which may be affected by such operational factors as the number of shifts for which the asset is used or the repair and maintenance programme of the entity;
- technical obsolescence arising from such factors as improvements in production, change in the market demand or the introduction of a replacement asset; and
- legal or similar limits on the use of the asset.

The useful life of an item of property, plant and equipment which is acquired under a finance lease should not exceed the lease term for that item if there is no reasonable certainty that the lessee will obtain ownership of the item by the end of the lease term (IAS 17, 19). A longer life may be used when it is reasonably certain that the entity will obtain ownership of the item at or before the end of the lease term and expects to continue to use the item for a further period.

Useful lives used for tax purposes should not be used for IFRS reporting purposes unless they reflect the period of time over which the entity expects to use the items of property, plant and equipment. When tax rules allow or require the use of so-called accelerated depreciation, it is unlikely that the rates are appropriate for IFRS reporting.

Extract 21.7 *Determination of useful life*

Holderbank, Switzerland, 31 December 2000 (IAS)

The following aspects are taken into consideration when determining the useful life of property, plant or equipment: the physical life span, the company's replacement policy, market or technological obsolescence, contractual and legal restrictions, and the remaining useful life of existing property, plant and equipment that have to be replaced as a single entity.

Extract 21.8 *Determination of useful life*

Cathay Pacific Airways, Hong Kong, 31 December 1994

Annual depreciation charges to write down the original cost of aircraft to estimated residual values are based on actual operational usage of the relevant aircraft as a proportion of its total estimated operational life. The useful operational life of an aircraft is determined by reference to its anticipated aircraft flight cycle while in service of the company. However, if the aircraft is held under a finance lease, the depreciable life of the aircraft is limited to the lease term unless a purchase option is held. A flight cycle is defined as one take-off and one landing. The residual value of aircraft and related equipment are 10% of original cost, or values guaranteed under forward sales agreements.

The useful life of an asset should be changed when expectations are significantly different from previous estimates (IAS 16, 49). The useful life may be:

- extended, for example as a result of subsequent expenditure which improves the asset's condition beyond its originally assessed standard of performance or as a result of the entity's repair and maintenance policy; or
- reduced, for example as a result of technological or market changes.

A change in useful life is accounted for as a change in accounting estimate; it is not a change in accounting policy. The depreciation charge for the current and future periods should be adjusted to reflect the new estimate of useful life (IAS 16, 49). No retrospective adjustment is made to the depreciation for prior periods.

A change in the useful life of an asset may also be an indicator that the asset is impaired. In such situations, the entity should assess whether an impairment charge is required (see chapter 25). Furthermore, the May 2002 improvements exposure draft clarifies that both the useful life and depreciation method of an item of property, plant and equipment must be reviewed at the end of each financial year.

Example 21.4 *Change in useful life*

An asset was acquired at the beginning of 1998 at a cost of £12,000. The asset is expected to have a residual value of nil and a useful life of six years. The straight-line method of depreciation is used.

		£
1998	Cost	12,000
1998	Depreciation	2,000
31/12/98	Carrying amount	10,000
1999	Depreciation	2,000
31/12/99	Carrying amount	8,000
2000	Depreciation	2,000
31/12/00	Carrying amount	6,000

In 2001, the entity recognises that changes in technology mean that the asset will reach the end of its useful life at the end of 2002. Therefore, the depreciation for 2001 and 2002 will be as follows:

		£
31/12/00	Carrying amount	6,000
2001	Depreciation	3,000
31/12/01	Carrying amount	3,000
2002	Depreciation	3,000
31/12/02	Residual value	–

Extract 21.9 *Factors leading to change in useful life*

Cathay Pacific Airways, Hong Kong, 31 December 1994

Leasehold land and buildings located at Kai Tak Airport which relate to activities which are expected to be discontinued there upon closure of the Airport in 1997 are depreciated over the period remaining to 1997. Buildings which are expected to be used after Kai Tak Airport closes are depreciated over the remaining portion of their estimated useful lives on the assumption that the relevant leases will be renewed (under the terms of the 1984 Sino-British Joint Declaration on the future of Hong Kong) either for no premium or for premiums which are commercially viable.

Extract 21.10 *Factors leading to change in useful life*

British Telecommunications, United Kingdom, 31 December 1996

Semi-electronic telephone exchange equipment is in the course of being replaced by digital equipment and will be substantially written off by 2000.

21.9.4 Depreciation Method

The depreciation method used should reflect the pattern in which the asset's economic benefits are consumed by the entity (IAS 16, 41). The straight-line method, the diminishing balance method, the sum-of-the-units method or other methods may be used (IAS 16, 47). The method used is:

- based on the asset's expected pattern of economic benefits; and
- consistently applied from period to period unless there is a significant change in the expected pattern of benefits from that asset.

(IAS 16, 50)

The depreciation method used for an asset should be changed when there has been a significant change in the expected pattern of economic benefits from the asset (IAS 16, 52). A change in method may also require a change in useful life. A change in depreciation method is accounted for as a change in accounting estimate; it is not a change in accounting policy. The depreciation charge for current and future periods should be adjusted (IAS 16, 52) to reflect the new method. No retrospective adjustment is made to the depreciation for prior periods.

Example 21.5 *Change in Depreciation Method and Useful Life*

An asset was acquired at the beginning of 1998 at a cost of £12,000. The asset is expected to have a residual value of nil and a useful life of six years. The straight-line method of depreciation is used.

		£
1998	Cost	12,000
1998	Depreciation	2,000
31/12/98	Carrying amount	10,000
1999	Depreciation	2,000
31/12/99	Carrying amount	8,000
2000	Depreciation	2,000
31/12/00	Carrying amount	6,000

In 2001, the entity decides to use the asset differently and, as a result, extend the useful life and change the depreciation method to the reducing balance method with a depreciation rate of 50%. Therefore, the depreciation for 2001, 2002 and 2003 will be as follows:

Continued

Continued

		£
31/12/00	Carrying amount	6,000
2001	Depreciation	3,000
31/12/01	Carrying amount	3,000
2002	Depreciation	1,500
31/12/02	Carrying amount	1,500
2003	Depreciation	750
31/12/03	Carrying amount	750

21.10 SUBSEQUENT MEASUREMENT – ALLOWED ALTERNATIVE TREATMENT

Under the allowed alternative treatment, an item of property, plant and equipment should be carried at revalued amount, being its fair value at the date of revaluation, less any subsequent accumulated depreciation and any accumulated impairment losses (IAS 16, 29).The use of fair value to determine the cost of an item of property, plant and equipment acquired under an asset exchange, a finance lease, on a business combination or from a government is not an application of the allowed alternative treatment.

21.10.1 International Valuation Standards

Entities adopting the allowed alternative treatment should consult the International Valuation Standards (IVSs) issued by the International Valuation Standards Committee (IVSC). The IVSC was established in 1981 and its members are the national valuation societies and institutions in more than 50 countries. The objectives of the IVSC are to:

- formulate and publish, in the public interest, valuation standards for the valuation of assets and to promote their worldwide acceptance;
- harmonise valuation standards in the world and to identify and make disclosure of differences in standards as they occur; and
- seek recognition of international valuation standards in statements of international accounting and other reporting standards.

Table 21.1 lists the current IVSs and other pronouncements issued by the IVSC.

A particular goal of the IVSC is that IVSs should be recognised in IFRSs and other reporting standards. The IVSC was a member of the IASC consultative group and was consulted extensively on the valuation aspects of IAS 16 [1993]. As a result, the guidance in IAS 16 [1993] was broadly consistent with the approach adopted in IVSs. However, the IVSC was not consulted on the 1998 changes in the guidance on the valuation of property, plant and equipment.

Table 21.1 *International Valuation Standards*

General Valuation Concepts and Principles

IVS 1 *Market Value Basis of Valuation*
IVS 2 *Valuation Bases Other Than Market Value*

International Valuation Applications (IVA)

IVA 1 *Valuation for Financial Reporting* (Exposure Draft)
IVA 2 *Valuation for Lending Purposes*

Guidance Notes (GN)

GN 1 *Real Property*
GN 2 *Valuation of Lease Interests*
GN 3 *Valuation of Plant and Equipment*
GN 4 *Intangible Assets*
GN 6 *Business Valuation*
GN 7 *Consideration of Hazardous and Toxic Substances in Valuation*
GN 8 *Depreciated Replacement Cost* (Exposure Draft)
GN 9 *Valuation Reporting* (Exposure Draft)
GN 10 *Discounted Cash Flow Analysis* (Exposure Draft)

21.10.2 Revaluations

Revaluations should be carried out with sufficient regularity such that the carrying amount of the revalued property, plant and equipment does not differ materially from fair value. Annual revaluations are necessary for those items which experience significant and volatile movements in fair value. Less frequent revaluations are necessary for items with only insignificant movements in fair value; revaluation every three or five years may be sufficient in such circumstances. Revaluations may be made on a rolling basis provided that the revaluation of the class of items is completed within a short period of time (IAS 16, 36) and the aggregate carrying amount of those items does not differ materially from fair value.

When an item is revalued, the entire class to which it belongs should be revalued (IAS 16, 34) in order to avoid both selective revaluations and the reporting of a mix of costs and fair values as at different dates. A class of assets for this purpose is a grouping of assets of a similar nature and use in an entity's operations. For example, an entity may decide to revalue all its land; alternatively, it may decide to revalue all its land and buildings or plant and machinery. It is unacceptable to revalue only some buildings or some items of plant and equipment. IAS 1 also suggests that classes of property, plant and equipment carried at fair value should be shown as a separate line item on the face of the balance sheet (IAS 1, 71).

IAS 16 requires that revaluations should be made to fair value and that the revalued assets should be carried at fair value at the date of the revaluation less any subsequent accumulated depreciation and any accumulated impairment losses (IAS 16, 29). The fair value of an asset is 'the amount for which the asset could be exchanged between knowledgeable, willing parties in an arm's length transaction' (IAS 16, 6). IAS 16 explains that the fair value of land and buildings is usually market value and that of plant equipment is either market value or depreciated replacement cost.

IVSs define market value rather than fair value. IVS 1 defines the market value of an asset as 'the estimated amount for which an asset should exchange on the date of valuation between a willing buyer and a willing seller in an arm's length transaction after proper marketing wherein the parties had each acted knowledgeably, prudently and without compulsion' (IVS 1, 3.1). Market value ignores the costs of sale and purchase and is estimated without offset of any associated taxes (IVS 1, 3.3). IVS 1 includes further guidance on the meaning of the components of its definition of market value, that is, guidance on:

- 'the estimated amount';
- 'an asset should exchange';
- 'on the date of valuations';
- 'between a willing buyer';
- 'a willing seller';
- 'in an arm's length transaction';
- 'after proper marketing';
- 'wherein the parties had each acted knowledgeably and prudently'; and
- 'and without compulsion'.

The fair value or market value of an asset may vary depending on the use to which that asset is put. IAS 16 [1993] suggested that fair value was determined on the basis of existing use (IAS 16 [1993], 33) when an asset was to be used for its existing use. The approach taken in IAS 16 [1993] was the same as that taken in the then IVSs and several national pronouncements in countries which permit the revaluation of property, plant and equipment. All these standards and pronouncements recognised that the market value of an item of property, plant and equipment (in particular, property) may depend on its use. For example, the same plot of land may have different market values for agricultural, housing, retailing or manufacturing purposes.

In the version of IAS 16 approved in 1998, the guidance on existing use was deleted. The IASC's justification was that the change was necessary to conform with IAS 36 on the impairment of assets. The IASC believed that any over-valuation resulting from the use of a higher value than an existing use value would be written back under the impairment standard. The change to IAS 16 was not included in the exposure draft on impairment. Furthermore, unlike in IAS 16 [1993], the IVSC was not consulted on the change.

Following the 1998 revision to IAS 16, the IVSC removed the concept of market value for existing use from its standards as it had been specifically developed, in conjunction with the IASC, for financial reporting purposes. However, the concept is still used by some national accounting standard setters. It is also considered to be an integral component of depreciated replacement cost methodology. IVS 1 requires that the market value of an asset is based on its highest and best use (IVS 1, 4.3). The IVSC's glossary of terms for IVSs defines the highest and best use as 'the most probable use of an asset which is physically possible, appropriately justified, legally permissible, financially feasible, and which results in the highest value of the asset valued'.

IAS 16 provides no guidance on what to do when market value is not determinable or when it might not be appropriate. On the other hand, IVS 2 includes additional guidance on the use of depreciated replacement cost for specialised properties 'which are rarely if ever sold on the open market except as part of the sale of the business in occupation'. The depreciated replacement cost of a property is based on:

- the current market value of the land for its existing use; and
- the current gross replacement (or reproduction) costs of the improvements less allowances for physical deterioration and all relevant forms of obsolescence and optimisation.

(IVS 2, 3.8)

This approach is probably consistent with the IASC's intentions as it is consistent with the IAS 16 guidance for plant and equipment. IAS 16 suggests that the fair value of plant and equipment is market value when there is evidence of market value (IAS 16, 31). When there is no evidence of market value because of the specialised nature of the plant and equipment and because such items are rarely sold, except as part of a continuing business, they are valued at depreciated replacement cost (IAS 16, 31). GN 3 issued by the IVSC adopts the same approach. It states: 'Like other tangible assets, *Plant, Machinery and Equipment* are valued at *Market Value*. When applicable a Depreciated Replacement Cost basis is applied.' (GN 3, 4.1). GN 3 suggests that plant and equipment should be separated into operational, surplus and investment property categories and valued accordingly (GN 3, 5.2).

21.10.3 Revaluation Accounting

The general rule in IAS 16 is that:

- an increase in carrying amount arising on the revaluation of an item of property, plant and equipment should be credited directly to equity under the heading of revaluation surplus (IAS 16, 37);
- a decrease in carrying amount arising on the revaluation of an item of property, plant and equipment should be recognised as an expense (IAS 16, 38);
- gains or losses on the retirement or disposal of a revalued item of property, plant and equipment are the difference between the net disposal proceeds and the carrying amount of the asset (IAS 16, 56); and
- any revaluation surplus relating to an item which has been retired or disposed of may be transferred directly to retained earnings within the equity section but it is not recycled through the income statement.

There are two exceptions to the general rule:

- an increase in carrying amount arising on the revaluation of an item of property, plant and equipment should be recognised as income to the extent that it reverses a revaluation decrease of the same asset previously recognised as an expense (IAS 16, 37); and
- a decrease in carrying amount arising on the revaluation of an item of property, plant and equipment should be charged directly against revaluation surplus to the extent that the decrease does not exceed the amount held in the revaluation surplus in respect of that same asset (IAS 16, 38).

It is important to note that:

- these two exceptions can be applied only to individual assets – it is not permitted to offset a revaluation decrease on one asset against a revaluation surplus on another asset; and
- the same exceptions apply in the case of impairment write-downs and impairment write-backs under the allowed alternative treatment.

Any accumulated depreciation relating to an asset at the date of its revaluation is either:

- restated proportionately with the change in the gross carrying amount of the asset so that the asset's carrying amount after the revaluation equals its revalued amount – this approach is usually followed when an index is used to determine depreciated replacement cost; or
- eliminated against the gross carrying amount of the asset and the net amount restated to the revalued amount of the asset – this approach is usually followed when an asset is revalued to market value determined by a valuer.

(IAS 16, 33)

21.10.4 Depreciation Of Revalued Property, Plant and Equipment

The depreciation of revalued assets is calculated and accounted for in the same way as the depreciation of assets carried on a cost basis except that depreciable amount is fair value less residual value and the residual value is based on circumstances prevailing at the date of the revaluation (IAS 16, 46). In other words:

- depreciation is based on fair value, rather than cost; and
- residual value is updated every time fair value is changed but it is still calculated as the net amount which the entity expects to obtain for the asset at the end of its useful life.

Subject to these two exceptions, an entity using the allowed alternative treatment should follow the requirements and procedures in 20.10 above.

Example 21.6 *Revaluation of building*

A building was acquired at the beginning of 1999 for £50 million. The building is expected to have a residual value of £10 million and a useful life of 40 years. The straight-line method of depreciation is used. By the end of 2001, the following entries have been made:

		Cost	*Depreciation*	*Carrying amount*
		£m	*£m*	*£m*
1999	Cost	50		
	Depreciation		1	49
2000	Depreciation		1	48
2001	Depreciation		1	47

Continued

Continued

The building is revalued at the beginning of 2002 when its market value is £55 million. The increase in carrying amount of £8 million is credited directly to equity under the heading of revaluation surplus. It is usually more meaningful to show the building at market value of £55 million rather than to restate proportionately the gross carrying amount and accumulated depreciation.

Example 21.7 *Revaluation of plant and equipment*

Plant and equipment is acquired at the beginning of 1999 for £15 million. The plant and equipment is expected to have no residual value and has a useful life of 10 years. The straight-line method of depreciation is used. By the end of 2001, the following entries have been made:

		Cost *£m*	*Depreciation* *£m*	*Carrying amount* *£m*
1999	Cost	15		
	Depreciation		1.5	13.5
2000	Depreciation		1.5	12.0
2001	Depreciation		1.5	10.5

In 2002, the plant and equipment is revalued using an index of replacement cost. The index was 110.0 when the plant and equipment was acquired in 1999 and 124.7 at the date of the revaluation. It is usual to restate both cost and accumulated depreciation by the change in the index so that the plant and equipment is shown at gross replacement cost of £17 million less accumulated depreciation of £5.1 million. The revised carrying amount is £11.9 million. The increase in carrying amount of £1.4 million is credited directly to equity under the heading of revaluation surplus.

21.10.5 Disclosures for Revalued Property, Plant and Equipment

IAS 16 requires certain additional disclosures when items of property, plant and equipment are stated at revalued amounts. The following should be disclosed:

- the basis used to revalue the assets (IAS 16, 64(a));
- the effective date of the revaluation (IAS 16, 64(b));
- whether an independent valuer was involved (IAS 16, 64(c));
- the nature of any indices used to determine replacement cost (IAS 16, 64(d));
- the carrying amount which would have been included in the financial statements for each class had the assets been carried at cost less depreciation (IAS 16, 64(e)); and
- the revaluation surplus, indicating the movement for the period and any restrictions on the distribution of the balance to shareholders (IAS 16, 64(f)).

Extract 21.11 *Revaluation of land and buildings*

Jardine Matheson, Hong Kong, 31 December 2001 (IAS)

Extract from principal accounting policies

Freehold land and buildings, and the building component of owner-occupied leasehold properties are stated at valuation. Independent valuations are performed every three years on an open market basis and in the case of the building component of leasehold properties, on the basis of depreciated replacement cost. Depreciated replacement cost used as open market value cannot be reliably allocated to the building component. In the intervening years the Directors review the carrying values and adjustment is made where there has been a material change. Revaluation surpluses and deficits are dealt with in property revaluation reserves except for movements on individual properties below depreciated cost which are dealt with in the consolidated profit and loss account. Previously the Group reflected all leasehold properties including land at valuation. Changes in IAS, which came into effect during 2001, no longer permit the valuation of leasehold interests in land. Accordingly the Group accounts for leasehold land as operating leases at amortised cost. ... Other tangible fixed assets are stated at cost less amounts provided for depreciation.

...

Where the carrying amount of a tangible fixed asset is greater than its estimated recoverable amount, it is written down immediately to its recoverable amount.

The profit or loss on disposal of tangible fixed assets is recognized by reference to their carrying amount.

Extract from notes to the financial statements

The Group's freehold properties and the building component of leasehold properties were revalued at 31 December 1999 by independent professionally qualified valuers. The Directors have reviewed the carrying values at 2000 and 2001 and, as a result, deficits on individual properties below depreciated cost of US$2 million (2000: US$5 million) and impairment losses of US$2 million (2000: US$12 million) have been charged to the consolidated profit and loss account. A net deficit of US$6 million (2000: net surplus of US$1 million) has been taken directly to property revaluation reserves. The amounts attributable to the Group, after tax and outside interests, are US$1 million, US$2 million and US$3 million respectively.

...

If the freehold properties and the building component of leasehold properties had been included in the financial statements at cost less depreciation, the carrying value would have been US$709 million (2000: US$758 million).

21.11 DISCLOSURE

An entity should disclose, in respect of each class of property, plant and equipment:

- the measurement bases used for determining the gross carrying amount and the gross carrying amount for each measurement basis used in each category;
- the depreciation methods used;
- the useful lives or the depreciation rates used; and
- the gross carrying amount and the accumulated depreciation at the beginning and end of the period.

(IAS 16, 60)

Extract 21.12 *Depreciation method*

BMW, Germany, 31 December 2001 (IAS)

All items of property, plant and equipment are considered to have finite useful lives. They are stated at acquisition of manufacturing cost less systematic depreciation based on the estimated useful lives of the assets. Depreciation on property, plant and equipment reflects the pattern of their usage and is generally computed using the straight-line method.

Expenditure on low-value non-current assets is written off in full in the year of acquisition.

Systematic depreciation is based on the following useful lives, applied throughout the Group:

	In years
Office and factory buildings, including utility distribution buildings	10 to 40
Residential buildings	40 to 50
Plant and machinery	5 to 10
Other facilities, factory and office equipment	3 to 10

Extract 21.13 *Depreciation method*

MOL, Hungary, 31 December 2000 (IAS)

Depreciation is computed on a straight-line basis over the following rates:

Buildings	2–10%
Refineries and chemicals manufacturing plants	10–25%
Gas and oil storage and transmission equipment	4–14.5%
Petrol service stations	4–20%
Telecommunication and automatisation equipment	10–33%

Depletion and depreciation of production installations and transport systems for oil and gas is calculated for each individual plant or plant-dedicated transport system using the unit of production method, based on proved, commercially recoverable reserves. Recoverable reserves are reviewed on an annual basis. Ordinary depreciation of transport systems used by several fields and of other assets is calculated on the basis of the expected useful life, using the straight-line method. Amortisation of leasehold improvements is provided using the straight-line method over the term of the respective lease or the useful life of the asset, whichever period is shorter.

The useful life and depreciation methods are reviewed periodically to ensure that the method and period of depreciation are consistent with the expected pattern of economic benefits from items of property, plant and equipment.

Extract 21.14 *Useful lives*

Bayer, Germany, 31 December 2001 (IAS)

The following depreciation periods, based on the estimated useful lives of the respective assets, are applied throughout the Group:

Buildings	20 to 50 years
Outdoor infrastructure	10 to 20 years
Plant installations	6 to 20 years
Machinery and apparatus	6 to 12 years
Laboratory and research facilities	3 to 5 years
Storage tanks and pipelines	10 to 20 years
Vehicles	4 to 8 years
Computer equipment	3 to 5 years
Furniture and fixtures	4 to 10 years

... Assets leased on terms equivalent to financing a purchase by a long-term loan (finances leases) ... are depreciated over their estimated useful life except where subsequent transfer of title is uncertain, in which case they are depreciated over their estimated useful life or the respective lease term, whichever is shorter.

An entity should also present a reconciliation of the carrying amount at the beginning and end of the period showing:

- additions;
- disposals;
- acquisitions through business combinations;
- increases or decreases resulting from revaluations;
- impairment losses;
- impairment losses reversed;
- depreciation;
- the net exchange differences arising on the translation of the financial statements of a foreign entity; and
- other movements.

(IAS 16, 60(e))

Comparative information is not currently required for this reconciliation (IAS 16, 60) but the IASB proposes in its improvements exposure draft to require disclosure.

Extract 21.15 *Reconciliation of property, plant and equipment*

Czech Telecom, Czech Republic, 31 December 2001 (IAS)

(in CZK millions)	Land and buildings	Duct, cable and other plant	Communication exchanges and related equipment	Other fixed assets	Capital work in progress	Total
YEAR ENDED 31 DECEMBER 2001						
Opening net book amount	13,566	68,297	36,791	3,734	6,617	129,005
Additions	1,100	1,476	8,858	2,109	12,791	26,334
Disposals and other movements	(270)	(4)	692	(861)	(13,543)	(13,986)
Depreciation charge	(624)	(4,558)	(8,050)	(1,491)	–	(14,723)
Closing net book amount	*13,772*	*65,211*	*38,291*	*3,491*	*5,865*	*126,630*
AT 31 DECEMBER 2001						
Cost	17,530	94,642	77,671	9,933	5,865	205,641
Accumulated depreciation	(3,758)	(29,431)	(39,380)	(6,442)	–	(79,011)
Net book amount	**13,772**	**65,211**	**38,291**	**3,491**	**5,865**	**126,630**
YEAR ENDED 31 DECEMBER 2000						
Opening net book amount	13,131	68,535	36,180	3,611	8,318	129,775
Additions	1,236	4,351	8,171	1,302	13,359	28,419
Disposals and other movements	(102)	(96)	(210)	83	(15,060)	(15,385)
Depreciation charge	(699)	(4,493)	(7,350)	(1,262)	–	(13,804)
Closing net book amount	*13,566*	*68,297*	*36,791*	*3,734*	*6,617*	*129,005*
AT 31 DECEMBER 2000						
Cost	16,887	93,535	70,401	9,344	6,617	196,784
Accumulated depreciation	(3,321)	(25,238)	(33,610)	(5,610)	–	(67,779)
Net book amount	**13,566**	**68,297**	**36,791**	**3,734**	**6,617**	**129,005**

An entity should also disclose:

- the existence and amounts of restrictions on title, and property, plant and equipment pledged as security for liabilities;
- the accounting policy for the estimated costs of restoring the site of items of property, plant or equipment;
- the amount of expenditures on account of property, plant and equipment in the course of construction (often shown as a separate class); and
- the amount of commitments for the acquisition of property, plant and equipment.

(IAS 16, 61)

Extract 21.16 *Property, plant and equipment under construction*

Nestlé, Switzerland, 31 December 2001 (IAS)

At 31 December 2001 property, plant and equipment include CHF 297 million (CHF 158 million) of assets under construction.

IAS 16 encourages, but does not require, the following disclosures:

- the carrying amount of temporarily idle property, plant and equipment;
- the gross carrying amount of any fully depreciated property, plant and equipment that is still in use;
- the carrying amount of property, plant and equipment retired from active use and held for disposal; and
- when the benchmark treatment is used, the fair value of property, plant and equipment when this is materially different from the carrying amount.

(IAS 16, 66)

Extract 21.17 *Properties held for disposal*

UBS, Switzerland, 31 December 2001 (IAS)

Property formerly bank-occupied or leased to third parties under an operating lease, which the Group has decided to dispose of and foreclosed property are defined as Properties held for resale and disclosed in Other assets. They are carried at the lower of cost or recoverable value. During 2001, properties with a carrying value of CHF 293 million (cost CHF 482 million less accumulated depreciation of CHF 189 million) have been reclassified from Investment property to Property held for resale.

Note

[1] Milne, I. R. (1994), 'Bridging the GAAP – International Airline Accounting Policies and Disclosures', *Airline Business*, Sutton, United Kingdom.

CHAPTER 22

Investment Property

22.1 RELEVANT STANDARD

IAS 40 *Investment Property*

22.2 HISTORY

IAS 25 *Accounting for Investments* was approved in 1986 and required that investment properties should be accounted for either as long-term investments in accordance with IAS 25 or as property in accordance with IAS 16. This choice meant that investment properties could be measured at cost less depreciation, fair value (or revalued amount) less depreciation or revalued amount without depreciation. This choice was considered in the comparability project but the IASC decided to defer further consideration of all the choices in IAS 25 pending further work on the financial instruments project (*Statement of Intent on the Comparability of Financial Statements*, appendix 1).

The IASC began to reconsider investment properties in November 1997, at the same time that it decided to proceed with an interim IAS on financial instruments (see chapter 20). It tentatively decided that investment property should be measured at fair value and should not be depreciated (*IASC Update*, November 1997, p2). It considered the issue again a year later (immediately prior to its approval of IAS 39) when it tentatively concluded that investment property should be measured at depreciated cost or fair value (*IASC Update*, November 1998, p1), the same approach that had been favoured in the comparability project. In March 2000, it approved IAS 40 *Investment Property* which was effective for financial statements covering periods beginning on or after 1 January 2001. IAS 40 allows a free choice between a fair value model and a cost model.

IAS 25 was superseded by IAS 38, IAS 39 and IAS 40 and ceased to have effect when IAS 40 came into force (*IASC Update*, March 2000, p2).

The IASB's May 2002 improvements project proposes to extend the definition of investment property to encompass a property interest held by a lessee under an operating lease provided that it is accounted for using the fair value model in IAS 40. The IASB also decided to continue to allow the choice between the fair value model and the cost model but to keep the matter under review with a view to reconsidering the option to use the cost model at a later date.

22.3 IOSCO

In June 1994, IOSCO advised the IASC that it had not considered IAS 25 in the context of the core standards but that it would await the IASC's work on financial instruments.

Although investment property was not specifically identified, IOSCO's 1993 list of core standards included investments and IOSCO confirmed in 1997 that this item encompassed all the issues covered by IAS 25. Therefore, the IASC was required to approve IAS 40 in order to complete the core standards. However, IAS 40 was approved and published after IOSCO had started its evaluation of the core standards. Therefore, IAS 40 is not included in 'IAS 2000' endorsed in May 2000.

22.4 IAS 40 IN BRIEF

IAS 40 permits an entity to measure investment properties at either:

- fair value, with changes in fair value recognised in the income statement; or
- cost less depreciation and any accumulated impairment losses (the benchmark treatment in IAS 16).

An entity that chooses the cost model must disclose the fair value of its investment property.

22.5 DEFINITION OF INVESTMENT PROPERTY

An *investment property* is an investment in land, a building or part of a building held by the owner (or the lessee under a finance lease) to earn rentals or for capital appreciation or both (IAS 40, 4). An investment property generates cash flows that are largely independent of the entity's other assets. This distinguishes it from an owner-occupied property which generates cash flows from both the property itself and the entity's

other assets used in the production or supply process.
Examples of investment property include:

- land held for long-term capital appreciation rather than for short-term sale in the ordinary course of business;
- land held for a currently undetermined future use (it is assumed that it is held for capital appreciation);
- a building owned by the reporting entity (or held under a finance lease) and leased out under one or more operating leases; and
- a currently vacant building which will be leased out under one or more operating leases.

(IAS 40, 6)

Extract 22.1 *Investment properties*

Hongkong Land, Hong Kong, 31 December 2001 (IAS)

Investment properties are properties which are held to earn rental income for the long term.

Investment property does not include:

- owner-occupied properties, that is those used in the production or supply of goods or services or for administrative purposes (these properties are accounted for using IAS 16);
- properties that are held for sale in the ordinary course of business, for example properties acquired exclusively with a view to their subsequent disposal in the near future or for development and resale (these properties are accounted for using IAS 2);
- properties that are being constructed or developed on behalf of third parties (these properties are accounted for using IAS 11); and
- properties that are being constructed or developed for future use as investment properties (these properties are accounted for using IAS 16 until their construction or development is complete and then accounted for in accordance with IAS 40) – existing investment properties that are being redeveloped for continued future use as investment property are accounted for under IAS 40.

(IAS 40, 7)

Sometimes an entity leases its property to its parent or another subsidiary. In the parent's consolidated financial statements, the property is not an investment property because, from the perspective of the group, it is owner-occupied. The property may be an investment property in the separate financial statements of the entity that owns the property, that is, the lessor of the property.

22.5.1 Properties held under operating leases

A property held under an operating lease is not an investment property because such interests are accounted for in accordance with IAS 17 (IAS 40, 13). The IASC recognised that, in some countries, it is common for entities to make large payments to acquire long-term leasehold interests in properties and for such interests to be, in substance, indistinguishable from ownership interests. The IASC could see no conceptual basis, however, for distinguishing these leasehold interests from other leasehold interests and concluded that such interests should continue to be accounted for in accordance with IAS 17 (IAS 40, B14-15).

In practice, long-term leasehold interests in property have, in the past, been accounted for in IAS financial statements as investment property in accordance with IAS 25 or property in accordance with IAS 16. The IASC's decision on IAS 40 prohibits such practices. The effect of the decision is twofold:

- the aggregate amount of the advance payment and any subsequent payments should be recognised as an expense in the income statement on a straight-line basis over the lease term unless another systematic basis is more representative of the time pattern of the lessee's benefits under the lease (IAS 17, 25); and
- the long-term leasehold interest may not be revalued to fair value in accordance with IAS 16 or IAS 40.

In some circumstances, it is possible to treat separately the land and buildings components in the long-term leasehold interest and account for the interest in the land as an operating lease under IAS 17 and the interest in the buildings as investment property under IAS 40 or property under IAS 16. Such an approach is possible, for example, when an entity constructs buildings on land that it has leased for a period in excess of the useful life of the buildings.

IASB improvements project

In its May 2002 improvements exposure draft, the IASB proposes to amend the definition of investment property so that a lessee's interest in property that arises under an operating lease qualifies as investment property provided that:

- the remainder of the investment property definition is met; and
- the lessee uses the fair value model.

Extracts 22.2 and 22.3 illustrate the impact on Hongkong Land of the IASC's decision on properties held under operating leases. Extract 22.2 shows the accounting required by IAS 40. Extract 22.3 shows the accounting that the company had previously followed as modified by the IAS 40 treatment of revaluation gains and losses and which the IASB now proposes to allow.

Extract 22.2 *Long-term leasehold properties – IAS 40 treatment*

Hongkong Land, Hong Kong, 31 December 2001 (IAS)

In accordance with IAS 40 and as a result of an inability to estimate reliably the element of leasehold property values attributable to the building component, leasehold land and buildings are stated at cost after deduction of depreciation and amortisation .... This is a change in accounting policy as in previous years the Group had reflected the fair value of leasehold investment properties in the financial statements and recorded fair value changes in property revaluation reserve, except for movements on individual properties below cost which were dealt with in the consolidated profit and loss account. The effect of this change has been to decrease net profit for the year ended 31st December 2000 by US$21.3 million and shareholders' funds at 1st January 2000 and 2001 by US$4,217.0 million and US$6,115.0 million respectively.

Extract 22.3 *Long-term leasehold properties – pre-IAS 40/IASB proposed treatment*

Hongkong Land, Hong Kong, 31 December 2001 (supplementary financial information prepared in accordance with IAS as modified by the revaluation of leasehold properties)

In the preparation of the supplementary financial information, properties held under long leases are included in the balance sheet at their then open market value on the basis of annual independent professional valuation. Long leases are leases with more than 20 years to run. Properties having an unexpired lease term of less than 20 years are stated at the carrying value and such provisions for impairment in value as are considered necessary by the Directors. In accordance with IAS 40, changes in fair values of investment properties which were previously taken directly to property revaluation reserve are recorded in the consolidated profit and loss account. The effect of this change has been to increase net profit for the year ended 31st December 2000 by US$1,889.7 million.

22.5.2 Investment properties held for more than one purpose

Certain properties include both a portion that is held as investment property and another portion that is held for use in the production or supply of goods or services or for administrative purposes. These portions should be accounted for separately if they can be sold separately (or leased out separately under a finance lease). If the portions cannot be sold separately, the property may be classified as an investment property only if the portion held for use in the production or supply of goods or services or for administrative purposes is insignificant. It should be noted, however, that if the entity uses the cost model for investment property and the IAS 16 benchmark treatment for other property, it applies the same accounting to both portions irrespective of whether they can be sold separately or one portion is more significant than the other.

An entity may provide ancillary services to the occupants of a property. The property may be treated as an investment property if the services are a relatively insignificant component of the whole arrangement as is the case, for example, when the entity provides only security and maintenance services to lessees in an office building owned by the entity. Conversely, the provision of services to guests are a significant component of the arrangement between a hotel guest and the owner-manager of the hotel with the result that the owner-manager should account for its interest in the hotel as owner-occupied property in accordance with IAS 16 and not as investment property – this precludes an entity from using the fair value model in IAS 40 as a means of avoiding a depreciation charge on hotel properties. Again it should be noted that if the entity uses the cost model for investment property and the IAS 16 benchmark treatment for other property, it applies the same accounting to a property irrespective of the significance of ancillary services.

In practice, there is often a distinction between the owner and the manager of a hotel. The substance of the arrangement determines whether the owner may treat the hotel property as an investment property. For example, the owner may transfer certain responsibilities to the manager under a management contract such that the owner becomes a passive investor and may be able, therefore, to treat the hotel as an investment property. Alternatively, the contract may leave the owner with a significant exposure to variations in the hotel's cash flows such that the owner must treat the hotel property as owner-occupied property.

Extract 22.4 *Investment properties held for more than one purpose*

Jelmoli, Switzerland, 31 December 2001 (Swiss law and IAS)

Investment properties also include partially owner-utilized properties as far as floor areas rented out can clearly be independently used as with apartment properties, or if it would be possible to let them out on a financial leasing basis.

22.6 RECOGNITION OF INVESTMENT PROPERTY

Investment property should be recognised as an asset only when:

- it is probable that associated future economic benefits will flow to an entity. The certainty of these flows will need to be assessed on the basis of available evidence at the time of initial recognition; and
- its cost can be measured reliably. This requirement can usually be readily satisfied on purchase.

(IAS 40, 15 and 16)

This is identical to the requirement for the recognition of other property accounted for in accordance with IAS 16.

22.7 INITIAL MEASUREMENT

An investment property is initially measured at cost. Cost is the amount of cash or cash equivalents paid or the fair value of other consideration at the time of the property's acquisition or construction. Cost comprises purchase price and any directly attributable expenditure such as professional legal fees, property transfer taxes and other transaction costs.

When payment is deferred, cost is the cash price equivalent and the difference between this amount and the total payments is recognised as an interest expense over the period of credit. All these requirements are identical to those for other property in IAS 16.

The cost of a self-constructed investment property is determined in accordance with IAS 16 (see chapter 21). It does not include any start-up costs unless they are necessary to bring the property to its working condition, initial operating losses incurred before the property achieves planned occupancy levels or abnormal amounts of wasted material, labour or other resources incurred in construction or development. Cost includes any borrowing costs capitalised in accordance with the allowed alternative treatment in IAS 23 (see chapter 35) and hedging gains and losses arising on cash flow hedges (see chapter 20).

> ***IASB improvements project***
>
> In its May 2002 improvements exposure draft, the IASB proposes to clarify that if an investment property is acquired in exchange for an equity instrument of the reporting entity then the cost of the property is the fair value of the instrument issued. The fair value of the investment property received is used to measure cost only if it is more clearly evident than the fair value of the equity instrument issued.

22.8 SUBSEQUENT EXPENDITURE

Subsequent expenditure on an investment property is capitalised only when it is probable that the resulting future economic benefits will exceed those expected based on the originally assessed standard of performance of the investment property. All other subsequent expenditure is expensed as incurred. The appropriate accounting treatment for subsequent expenditure on an investment property depends on the circumstances taken into account on its initial measurement and recognition. For instance, when the carrying amount of an investment property already takes into account a loss in future economic benefits, any subsequent expenditure incurred to restore the future economic benefits expected from the asset is capitalised. Similarly, when the purchase price of an asset reflects the entity's obligation to incur expenditure that is necessary in the future to bring the asset to its working condition the subsequent expenditure is added to the carrying amount.

Extract 22.5 *Renovations and improvements of investment property*

Hongkong Land, Hong Kong, 31 December 2001 (IAS)

The cost of maintenance repairs and minor equipment is charged to income as incurred; the cost of major renovations and improvements is capitalised.

IASB improvements project

In its May 2002 exposure draft, the IASB proposes to require that subsequent expenditure on an investment property should be capitalised only if it increases the future economic benefits embodied in the asset in excess of the standard of performance assessed immediately before the expenditure was made and can be measured reliably. This change is identical to the equivalent proposed change to IAS 16 and IAS 38.

22.9 SUBSEQUENT MEASUREMENT

IAS 40 allows an entity to measure its investment property using either:

- a fair value model; or
- a cost model.

An entity must apply the same model to all its investment properties (IAS 40, 24). It may change from one model to the other only if the change results in a more appropriate presentation.

In approving IAS 40, the IASC expressed a clear preference for the fair value model. It believed that information about the fair value and changes in the fair value of investment properties is highly relevant to users of financial statements (IAS 40, B6). It permitted the cost model only because of conceptual and practical reservations about extending the fair value model to non-financial assets and the belief among some commentators that some property markets are not yet sufficiently mature for a fair value model to work satisfactorily (IAS 40, B47-49). It follows, therefore, that once an entity has adopted IAS 40, it should not change from the fair value model to the cost model.

22.10 SUBSEQUENT MEASUREMENT – FAIR VALUE MODEL

An entity should measure all of its investment property at fair value and include any gains or losses arising from a change in fair values in the net profit or loss for the period in which they arise (IAS 40, 28). This model differs from the revaluation model in IAS 16 in which increases in the carrying amount of a property above cost are included in equity as revaluation surplus and are never included in the income statement.

Example 22.1 *Application of fair value model*

A building was acquired as an investment property at the beginning of 1998 for £50m. It is accounted for under the fair value model and revalued at the end of each year.

	Cost	*Fair value (carrying amount)*	*Income statement*
	£m	*£m*	*£m*
1998	50	55	5
1999		62	7
2000		65	3
2001		60	(5)
2002		58	(2)

The IASC believed that there is a rebuttable presumption that the fair value of an investment property can be measured reliably on a continuing basis. In exceptional circumstances, however, an entity may be unable to obtain a fair value for an investment property on a continuing basis from its initial acquisition, completion of construction or change in use. This happens only when market transactions in similar properties are infrequent and alternative measures of fair value are not available. In such rare circumstances, the entity should measure the investment property at cost less depreciation and any impairment losses, that is, using the benchmark treatment in IAS 16 (IAS 40, 47). There are two important conditions to this exception:

- it does not change the measurement of the entity's other investment properties (if any) (IAS 40, 48); and
- it does not apply after the entity has measured the property at fair value – once the property has been measured at fair value, the entity must continue to value it at fair value (IAS 40, 49).

22.10.1 Fair Value

Fair value is the amount for which the property could be exchanged between knowledgeable, willing parties in an arm's length transaction (IAS 40, 4). The fair value of investment property is usually its market value (IAS 40, 29). Fair value is not reduced by possible sale transaction costs (IAS 40, 30).

An entity adopting the fair value model should consult the International Valuation Standards (IVSs) issued by the International Valuation Standards Committee (IVSC) (see chapter 21). IVS 1 *Market Value Basis of Valuation* is particularly relevant. Its notion of market value is similar, if not identical, to the IAS 40 notion of fair value. IVS 1 defines the market value of an asset as 'the estimated amount for which an asset should exchange on the date of valuation between a willing buyer and a willing seller in an arm's length transaction after proper marketing wherein the parties had each acted knowledgeably, prudently and without compulsion' (IVS 1, 3.1). Market value ignores the costs of sale and purchase and is estimated without offset of any associated taxes (IVS 1, 3.2). IVS 1 includes further guidance on the meaning of the components of its definition of market value (see chapter 21).

IAS 40 encourages, but does not require, an entity to determine the fair value of investment property on the basis of a valuation by an independent valuer with a recognised and relevant professional qualification and who has recent experience in the location and category of the investment property being valued.

Fair value is:

- the most probable price reasonably obtainable in the market at the balance sheet date in keeping with the fair value definition; and

- the best price reasonably obtainable by the seller and the most advantageous price reasonably obtainable by the buyer.

(IAS 40, 29)

Fair value does not reflect the effects of special circumstances such as atypical financing, sale and leaseback arrangements, special considerations or concessions (IAS 40, 29). It also assumes simultaneous exchange and completion of the sale contract without any variation in price that might result when exchange and completion are not simultaneous (IAS 40, 32). The fair value of investment property should reflect the state of the market and circumstances as at the balance sheet date (IAS 40, 31). It takes into account rental income from current leases and reasonable and supportable assumptions that represent the market's view of what knowledgeable, willing parties would assume about rental income from future leases in the light of current market conditions.

The definition of fair value refers to 'knowledgeable, willing parties'. 'Knowledgeable' means that both the willing buyer and the willing seller are reasonably informed about the nature and characteristics of the property, its actual and potential uses and the state of the market as at the balance sheet date. A willing buyer is one who:

- is motivated but not compelled to buy;
- is neither over-eager nor determined to buy at any price;
- will purchase in accordance with the realities of the current market and with the current market expectations rather than an imaginary or hypothetical market that cannot be demonstrated or anticipated to exist; and
- will not pay more than the market requires.

(IAS 40, 35)

A willing seller is one who is:

- neither an over-eager nor a forced seller;
- not prepared to sell at any price;
- not prepared to hold out for an unreasonable price in the current market; and
- motivated to sell at market terms for the best price obtainable in the open market after proper marketing.

(IAS 40, 36)

Proper marketing means that the property is exposed to the market in the most appropriate manner to effect its disposal at the best price reasonably obtainable. The exposure time may vary with market conditions but must be sufficient to allow the property to be brought to the attention of an adequate number of potential purchasers and is assumed to occur before the balance sheet date.

An 'arm's length transaction' is one between parties who do not have a particular or special relationship that makes prices of transactions uncharacteristic of the market. The transaction is presumed to be between unrelated parties acting independently. Related parties may carry out transactions at an artificial price which is different from market value (IAS 24, 11-16).

The best evidence of the fair value of an investment property is normally given by current prices on an active market for similar property in the same location and condition and subject to similar lease and other contracts. However, many properties are unique so the entity must identify any differences in the nature, location or condition of the property being valued or in the contractual terms of the leases and other contracts relating to that property to derive fair value from the prices or market transactions. When there are comparable transactions on an active market when the entity acquires an investment property (or an existing property is first classified as investment property), an entity that uses the fair value model must measure that property at fair value on a continuing basis.

In the absence of current prices on an active market, an entity should consider information from a variety of sources, including:

- current prices on an active market for properties of a different nature, condition or location (or subject to different lease or other contracts) adjusted to reflect those differences;
- recent prices on less active markets with adjustments to reflect any changes in economic conditions since the date of the transactions that occurred at those prices; and
- discounted cash flow projections based on reliable estimates of future cash flows and which are supported by the terms of any existing lease and other contracts and, when possible, by external evidence such as current market rents for similar properties in the same location and condition – discount rates should reflect current market assessments of the uncertainty in the amount and timing of the cash flows.

(IAS 40, 40)

If the above sources give different fair values for an investment property but the differences lie within a reasonably narrow range, the entity should consider the reasons for the differences to derive the most reliable estimate of fair value within the range. When such an estimate can be made when the entity acquires an investment property (or an existing property is first classified as an investment property), an entity that uses the fair value model must measure that property at fair value on a continuing basis.

In exceptional cases, the range of estimates obtainable from the above sources may be so great and the probabilities of the various outcomes so difficult to assess that the usefulness of a single estimate of fair value is negated. If this arises when an entity first acquires an investment property (or when an existing property is first classified as an investment property), it may indicate that the fair value of the property cannot be determinable reliably on a continuing basis and, therefore, that the entity should measure the property at cost less depreciation and impairment losses (IAS 40, 42 and 47). If such circumstances arise after the acquisition of an investment property (or after an existing property is first classified as an investment property), the entity must continue to measure the property at fair value (IAS 40, 40).

Fair value differs from value in use as defined in IAS 36. Fair value reflects knowledge and estimates of participants in the market as well as factors that are relevant to market participants. In contrast, value in use reflects the entity's knowledge and estimates as well as entity-specific factors that may be specific to the entity and are not applicable to entities in general. For example, fair value does not reflect any of the following which may be taken into account in determining value in use:

- additional value derived from the creation of a portfolio of properties in different locations;
- synergies between an investment property and other assets of the entity;
- legal rights or legal restrictions relating to the property that are specific to the current owner and would not affect other market participants; and
- tax benefits or tax burdens that are specific to the current owner and may not be applicable to other market participants.

(IAS 40, 43)

In determining the fair value of an investment property, an entity must avoid double counting any assets or liabilities. For example:

- equipment such as elevators or air-conditioning that is an integral part of a building which is classified as an investment property but which is classified as property, plant and equipment on the entity's balance sheet – the fair value of the property should exclude the equipment;
- furniture in an office leased on a furnished basis when the rental income includes the furniture – the furniture should not be recognised as a separate asset if the fair value of the property reflects the lease of a furnished office; and
- operating lease income prepaid by the lessee of an investment property that is recognised as a liability by the entity; and

- operating lease income owing but unpaid by the lessee of an investment property that is recognised as an asset by the entity.

(IAS 40, 44)

The fair value of an investment property does not reflect any future capital expenditure that will improve or enhance the property nor does it reflect the related future benefits from this future expenditure (IAS 40, 45). This is the same requirement that applies to all other property.

An entity may expect that the present value of its payments relating to an investment property (other than payments relating to recognised financial liabilities) will exceed the present value of the related cash receipts, in other words that it will recover less from the investment property than its carrying amount. This could arise when the entity expects to incur costs that exceed the rental income that is reflected in the fair value of the property, in other words the unavoidable costs of meeting its obligations as lessor exceed the economic benefits expected to be received under the lease (see IAS 37, 66-69). In all such circumstances, the entity should apply IAS 37 to determine whether or not it should recognise a liability. This is the same requirement that applies when the amount of an impairment loss exceeds the carrying amount of an asset (see IAS 36, 61).

Extract 22.6 *Use of fair value model*

Jelmoli, Switzerland, 31 December 2001 (IAS)

In accordance with IAS 40, investment properties (rented out to third parties at no less than 80%) are booked at market value. Annual changes in market value are booked to operating income. ...

Investment properties are periodically valued by a recognized independent real estate expert (Wüest & Partner, Zurich) using the discounted cash flow (DCF) method.

Extract 22.7 *Use of fair value model*

Homburg Invest, Canada, 31 December 2000 (IAS)

... the company has adopted the fair value model for recording its property as provided for in IAS 40. In accordance with the provisions of this standard, the policy has been adopted prospectively with no restatement of prior period information. As a result of this change, the excess of fair market value over book value of property, which had previously been reported as revaluation surplus, has been transferred to retained earnings. Additionally, increases or decreases in the book value versus carrying value of assets, are reported as unrealized valuation changes in the statements of earnings under IAS 40. Change in property values in prior periods were reported as increases or decreases in the revaluation surplus account, independent of the statement of earnings. As a result of adoption of IAS 40 in the current year, earnings have increased by $30,000, future income taxes have increased by $7,500 and retained earnings have increased by $22,500 relative to unrealized valuation increases.

Extract 22.8 *Use of fair value model*

Zurich Financial Services, Switzerland, 31 December 2001 (IAS)

Real estate held for investment purposes is recorded at fair value. Fair values are determined internally by professionally qualified valuers on an annual basis with reference to current market conditions. Periodically, external valuations are performed. No depreciation is recorded for real estate held for investment. The gain or loss on disposal is based on the difference between the proceeds received and the carrying value of the investment.

22.10.2 Inability to Measure Fair Value Reliably

As explained above, IAS 40 has a rebuttable presumption that an entity is able to determine the fair value of an investment property reliably on a continuing basis. An entity that uses the fair value model may use the cost model for an investment property only in the very rare circumstances described above when, on the initial recognition of the property as an investment property, there is clear evidence that the entity will not be able to determine fair value on a continuing basis. In such rare and limited circumstances, the entity measures the property at cost less depreciation and impairment losses and assumes that the property has a residual value of zero. The entity continues to measure other investment properties at fair value (IAS 40, 48).

22.11 SUBSEQUENT MEASUREMENT – COST MODEL

An entity should measure all of its investment property using the benchmark treatment in IAS 16, that is cost less any accumulated depreciation and any accumulated impairment losses (see chapter 21). Therefore, an entity using this model accounts for investment property in the same way as other property that is accounted for using the cost model in IAS 16. However, an entity is not permitted to account for investment property using the fair value model (allowed alternative treatment) in IAS 16.

Unlike other property dealt with under the benchmark treatment in IAS 16, an entity must disclose the fair value of investment property accounted for under the cost model (IAS 40, 69). An entity determines the fair value in accordance with the fair value model and is encouraged, but not required, to use a valuation by an independent valuer with a recognised and relevant professional qualification and who has recent experience in the location and category of the investment property being valued.

In the exceptional cases in which an entity that uses the cost model cannot determine reliably the fair value of an investment property, it should disclose:

- a description of the investment property;
- an explanation of why fair value cannot be determined reliably; and
- if possible, the range of estimates within which fair value is highly likely to lie.

(IAS 40, 69)

22.12 TRANSFERS OF PROPERTY

An investment property may be transferred to inventory or property, plant and equipment. A property may also be transferred from inventory or property, plant and equipment to investment property. A transfer should only be made when there is evidence of a change in use:

- the commencement of owner-occupation (investment property to owner-occupied property);
- the commencement of development work with a view to sale (investment property to inventory);
- the end of owner-occupation (owner-occupied property to investment property);
- the commencement of an operating lease to another party (inventory to investment property); or
- the end of construction or development (assets in the course of construction or development to investment property).

(IAS 40, 51)

An entity should not transfer an investment property to inventory when it decides to dispose of the property without development. It continues to treat the property as an investment property until it is derecognised at the point of sale.

An entity does not transfer an investment property to assets in the course of construction or development when it begins to redevelop the property for its continued future use as investment property.

22.12.1 Transfers of investment property accounted for using the cost model

When an entity uses the cost model for investment property, the carrying amount of the property transferred between investment property, owner-occupied property and inventories does not change for either measurement or disclosure purposes. For example:

- the carrying amount of the investment property is cost for the purposes of IAS 2 (inventories) or IAS 16 (owner-occupied property);
- the carrying amount of a former owner-occupied property determined in accordance with IAS 16 is cost for the purposes of IAS 40; and
- the carrying amount of a property at the end of construction or development determined in accordance with IAS 16 is cost for the purposes of IAS 40.

22.12.2 Transfers of investment property accounted for using the fair value model

When an entity uses the fair value model for investment property, the property is transferred to inventory or property, plant and equipment at its fair value at the date of change in use (IAS 40, 54). This is the cost of the property for the purposes of IAS 2 or IAS 16.

22.12.3 Transfers of owner-occupied or constructed property to investment property accounted for using the fair value model

When an entity transfers an owner-occupied property to investment property that will be carried at fair value, it applies the requirements of IAS 16 up to the date of transfer. Any difference at that date of transfer between the IAS 16 carrying amount and fair value is accounted for as a revaluation under IAS 16, that is:

- any increase in the carrying amount of the property is:
  - recognised in net profit or loss for the period to the extent that it reverses a previous impairment loss for that property but only to the extent that it restores the carrying amount to what it would have been (net of depreciation) had no impairment loss been charged; and
  - credited directly to equity under the heading of revaluation surplus in all other cases;
- any decrease in the carrying amount of the property is recognised in net profit or loss for the period except to the extent that it reverses a revaluation surplus for that property included in equity.

Example 22.2 *Transfer of property carried under IAS 16 cost model to investment property carried under IAS 40 fair value model*

A building was acquired for owner occupation at the beginning of 2000 for £50m. The building was expected to have a residual value of £10m and a useful life of 40 years. The straight-line method of depreciation was used. By the end of 2002, the following entries have been made:

		Cost	*Depreciation*	*Carrying amount*
		£m	*£m*	*£m*
2000	Cost	50		
	Depreciation		1	49
2001	Depreciation		1	48
2002	Depreciation		1	47

The entity ceases to occupy the property at the beginning of 2003 when it leases the property to a third party. The fair value of the property at that date is £55m.

The increase in carrying amount of £8m is credited directly to equity under the heading of revaluation surplus. The initial carrying amount of the investment property is £55m and subsequent changes in fair value are included in the income statement.

Example 22.3 *Transfer of property carried under IAS 16 fair value model to investment property carried under IAS 40 fair value model*

The facts are the same as in example 22.2 except that the entity revalues the property to £55m at the end of 2002 in accordance with the fair value model (allowed alternative treatment) in IAS 16 and credits the surplus of £8m to equity under the heading of revaluation surplus.

The entity ceases to occupy the property at the beginning of 2003 when it leases the property to a third party. The revaluation surplus remains in equity. The initial carrying amount of the investment property is £55m and subsequent changes in fair value are included in the income statement.

When an entity completes the construction or development of a self-constructed investment property that property is transferred from property, plant and equipment to investment property. Any difference between the fair value of the property at that date and its previous carrying amount should be recognised in net profit or loss for the period. This treatment is inconsistent with the treatment of intra-group transfers of property or, indeed, a transfer of a property by one part of the entity to another part of the same entity. The inconsistency arises because the entity is changing from a cost model under IAS 16 to a fair value model under IAS 40. The entity is required to disclose the amount of transfers to and from investment property carried at fair value from and to inventories and property, plant and equipment (IAS 40, 67). Fair presentation may require separate disclosure in the income statement of material gains on the transfer of property from property, plant and equipment to investment property carried at fair value.

When an entity transfers a property from inventory to investment property that will be carried at fair value, it applies the requirements of IAS 2 up to the date of transfer. In this case, any difference between the fair value of the property at that date and its previous carrying amount should be recognised in net profit or loss for the period (IAS 40, 57). This treatment is consistent with the treatment of sales of inventories although it is inconsistent with the treatment of intra-group sales of inventories or, indeed, a sale of inventory by one part of the entity to another part of the same entity. The inconsistency arises because the entity is changing from a cost model under IAS 2 to a fair value model under IAS 40. The entity is required to disclose the amount of transfers to and from investment property carried at fair value from and to inventories and property, plant and equipment (IAS 40, 67). Fair presentation may require separate disclosure in the income statement of material gains on the transfer of property from inventories to investment property carried at fair value.

22.13 DISPOSALS OF INVESTMENT PROPERTY

An entity should derecognise an investment property on disposal or its permanent withdrawal from use when no future economic benefits are expected from its disposal. An entity determines the date of any sale of investment property in accordance with the criteria in IAS 18 for the recognition of revenue from the sale of goods (see chapter 29). An entity applies the requirements of IAS 17 to the disposal of an investment property by means of a finance lease or by a sale and leaseback transaction (see chapter 32).

The consideration receivable on the disposal of an investment property is measured at its fair value. If payment is deferred, the consideration is the cash price equivalent. The difference between the cash price equivalent and the nominal amount of the consideration is recognised as interest revenue under IAS 18 on a time proportion basis that takes into account the effective yield on the receivable.

Gains or losses arising from the disposal or retirement of an investment property are determined as the difference between the net disposal proceeds and the carrying amount of the property and are recognised as income or expense in the income statement (unless IAS 17 requires otherwise on a sale and leaseback transaction – see chapter 32). The gain or loss on disposal does not include any revaluation surplus included in equity during any period in which the property was classified as property, plant and equipment and accounted for in accordance with the fair value model (allowed alternative treatment) in IAS 16.

22.14 DISCLOSURE

22.14.1 All Investment Properties

An entity should disclose:

- the criteria used to distinguish investment property from owner-occupied property and property held for sale in the ordinary course of business when classification is difficult;
- the methods and significant assumptions applied in determining the fair value of investment property;
- whether the determination of fair value was supported by market evidence or was more heavily based on other disclosed factors because of the nature of the property and lack of comparable market data;
- the extent to which the fair value of investment property (for either measurement or disclosure purposes) is based on a valuation by an independent valuer who holds a recognised and relevant professional qualification and who has recent experience in the location and category of the investment property being valued (if there has been no such valuation, that fact should be disclosed);
- the amounts included in the income statement for:
  - rental income from investment property;
  - direct operating expenses (including repairs and maintenance) arising from investment property that generated rental income during the period; and
  - direct operating expenses (including repairs and maintenance) arising from investment property that did not generate rental income during the period;

- the existence and amounts of restrictions on the realisability of investment property or the remittance of income and proceeds of disposal; and
- material contractual obligations to purchase, construct or develop investment property or for repairs, maintenance or enhancements.

(IAS 40, 66)

22.14.2 Investment Properties Carried at Fair Value

In addition to the items in 22.14.1, an entity that applies the fair value model should disclose a reconciliation of the carrying amount of investment property at the beginning and end of the period showing the following amounts for the current period only:

- additions, disclosing separately those resulting from acquisitions and those resulting from capitalised subsequent expenditure;
- additions resulting from acquisitions through business combinations;
- disposals;
- net gains or losses from fair value adjustments;
- the net exchange differences arising on the translation of the financial statements of a foreign entity;
- transfers to and from inventories and owner-occupied property; and
- other movements.

(IAS 40, 67)

> ***IASB improvements project***
>
> In its May 2002 exposure draft, the IASB proposes to require comparative information for this reconciliation.

The reconciliation should deal separately with an investment property that, in the exceptional cases permitted by IAS 40, is measured using the benchmark treatment in IAS 16. In respect of that property, the reconciliation should also disclose:

- a description of the investment property;
- an explanation of why fair value cannot be reliably measured;
- if possible, the range of estimates within which fair value is highly likely to lie; and
- on disposal of investment property not carried at fair value:
  - the fact that the entity has disposed of investment property not carried at fair value;

  - the carrying amount of that investment property at the time of sale; and
  - the amount of gain or loss recognised.

(IAS 40, 68)

22.14.3 Investment Properties Carried at Cost

In addition to the items in 22.14.1, an entity that applies the cost model should disclose:

- the depreciation methods used;
- the useful lives or the depreciation rates used;
- the gross carrying amount and the accumulated depreciation (aggregated with accumulated impairment losses) at the beginning and end of the period;
- a reconciliation of the carrying amount of investment property at the beginning and end of the period showing the following for the current period only:
  - additions, disclosing separately those additions resulting from acquisitions and those resulting from capitalised subsequent expenditure;
  - additions resulting from acquisitions through business combinations;
  - disposals;
  - depreciation;
  - the amount of impairment losses recognised and the amount of impairment losses reversed;
  - the net exchange differences arising on the translation of the financial statements of a foreign entity;
  - transfers to and from inventories and owner-occupied property; and
  - other movements; and
- the fair value of investment property. In the exceptional cases when fair value cannot be determined reliably, disclose:
  - a description of the investment property;
  - an explanation of why fair value cannot be determined reliably; and
  - if possible, the range of estimates within which fair value is highly likely to lie.

(IAS 40, 69)

> *IASB improvements project*
>
> In its May 2002 exposure draft, the IASB proposes to require a comparative to be given for this reconciliation.

22.15 TRANSITIONAL PROVISIONS

22.15.1 Fair Value Model

Under the fair value model, an entity should report the effect of adopting IAS 40 as an adjustment to opening retained earnings for the period when it is adopted. This includes the effect of reclassifying any amount previously held for investment property in revaluation surplus. This treatment is different from the benchmark and allowed alternative treatments for changes in accounting policies under IAS 8 (IAS 40, 71) (see chapter 13).

When an entity has publicly previously disclosed the fair value of its investment property in earlier periods (determined on the same basis as IAS 40), the entity is encouraged but not required to:

- adjust the opening balance of retained earnings for the earliest period presented for which such fair value was disclosed publicly; and
- restate comparative information for those periods.

When the entity has not publicly previously disclosed such fair value information the entity should not restate comparative information and should disclose that fact.

Extract 22.9 *Transitional provisions – IAS 25 revalued amount to fair value model*

Jardine Matheson, 31 December 2001 (IAS)

In accordance with IAS 40 *Investment Property*, changes in fair values of investment properties are recorded in the consolidated profit and loss account. Previously the Group had recorded changes in fair values of investment properties in property revaluation reserves. The effect of these changes have been to decrease net profit for the year ended 31st December 2000 by US$7 million and to decrease shareholders' funds at 1st January 2000 and 1st January 2001 by US$512 million and US$1,026 million respectively. The amounts included in property revaluation reserves related to investment properties at 1st January 2000 and 2001 have been transferred to revenue reserves.

Extract 22.10 *Transitional provisions – revalued amount to fair value*

Homburg Invest, Canada, 31 December 2000 (IAS)

... the company has adopted the fair value model for recording its property as provided for in IAS 40. In accordance with the provisions of this standard, the policy has been adopted prospectively with no restatement of prior period information. As a result of this change, the excess of fair market value over book value of property, which had previously been reported as revaluation surplus, has been transferred to retained earnings. ... Change in property values in prior periods were reported as increases or decreases in the revaluation surplus account, independent of the statement of earnings.

22.15.2 Cost Model

When an entity chooses the cost model, it applies IAS 8 on the initial adoption of IAS 40. The effect of the change in accounting policy includes the reclassification of any amount previously held in revaluation surplus for investment property.

CHAPTER 23

Intangible Assets

23.1 RELEVANT STANDARD AND INTERPRETATION

IAS 38 *Intangible Assets*
SIC 32 *Intangible Assets – Web Site Costs*

23.2 HISTORY

23.2.1 Research and Development Costs (IAS 9)

IAS 9 *Accounting for Research and Development Activities* (IAS 9 [1978]) was approved and published in 1978. It required the expensing of all research costs but allowed either the capitalisation or the expensing of development costs.

The IASC reconsidered the free choice in IAS 9 [1978] in the comparability project and initially proposed that all research and development costs should be expensed (benchmark treatment) or capitalised (allowed alternative treatment) (E32, 47). Opinion among commentators on E32 was evenly divided on this issue (*IASC News*, July 1990, p9). The IASC was persuaded by the comments to change its proposals and require the capitalisation of those development costs which met certain criteria and the expensing of all other research and development costs (*Statement of Intent on the Comparability of Financial Statements*, appendix 2). This treatment was included in IAS 9 *Research and Development Costs* which was approved in November 1993 and which applied to financial statements for accounting periods beginning on or after 1 January 1995.

In November 1994, the IASC decided that it would consider during 1995 what action, if any, it should take following IOSCO's rejection of IAS 9 (*IASC Insight*, December 1994, p13). The IASC urged IOSCO to reconsider its rejection of the standard and to accept all the IASs (including IAS 9) which had been revised during the comparability and improvements project (*IASC Insight*, December 1994, p2). However, the IASC was unsuccessful in these efforts and was forced to include the revision of IAS 9 in the work plan agreed with IOSCO in July 1995.

23.2.2 Intangible Assets (IAS 38)

In April 1989, the IASC added a project on intangible assets to its work programme. After some initial work was carried out in conjunction with the accounting standards committee in the United Kingdom, the project was deferred pending completion of the improvements project. The project was restarted in 1992.

The IASC published a draft statement of principles in January 1994 shortly after the completion of the revised IAS 9, IAS 16 and IAS 22. E50 *Intangible Assets* was published in June 1995. In developing the DSOP and E50, the IASC opted, whenever possible, for the same accounting standards as those applied to property, plant and equipment, research and development, and goodwill. The IASC did not want similar items to be dealt with differently simply because they were classified differently.

E50 proposed that intangible assets should be amortised over a maximum period of 20 years. After reviewing the comment letters on E50, the IASC concluded that it could remove the 20-year ceiling if the assets were submitted to a detailed and reliable test which would detect in detail and reliably the impairment of such assets (*IASC Update*, April 1996, p2). That test was incorporated in IAS 36 (see chapter 25). Both IAS 38 and IAS 22 now require that all intangible assets and goodwill should be amortised in the same way – that is, over their useful lives (with no ceiling) and with an annual impairment test when useful life exceeds 20 years.

The IASC decided to merge the requirements on research and development with the standard on intangibles because research and development costs are intangible in nature and the physical nature of prototypes and similar assets is ancillary to the know-how embodied in them (*IASC Insight*, December 1996, p9).

IAS 38 *Intangible Assets* was approved in July 1998 and applied to accounting periods beginning on or after 1 July 1999.

IASB improvements project

In its May 2002 improvements exposure draft, the IASB proposes a number of amendments to IAS 38. These mainly relate to the:

- measurement of exchanges of intangible assets;
- definition of residual value; and
- clarification of directly attributable costs.

23.3 IOSCO

In June 1994, IOSCO advised the IASC that it had been unable to reach a consensus on the acceptability of IAS 9, particularly regarding the required capitalisation of development costs when specified criteria are met. IOSCO told the IASC that some of its members may have required disclosures providing information equivalent to the expensing of all development costs, whereas other IOSCO members may have required or allowed development costs to be expensed without such a reconciliation. One IOSCO member believed that research and development costs should not be accounted for separately and that it should be acceptable to recognise all such costs as either assets or expenses (this approach was rejected by the improvements steering committee which included four representatives of IOSCO). IOSCO also suggested that, as a potential long-term project, the IASC should reconsider the required treatment of capitalisation of development costs as an asset when specified criteria are met or consider providing more objective criteria for required capitalisation.

An IAS on intangible assets was one of IOSCO's core standards and had not been developed by the time that IOSCO carried out its June 1994 review of existing IASs.

IAS 38 is included in 'IAS 2000' endorsed by IOSCO in May 2000. There are 14 supplemental treatments:

- consideration of consistent recognition and measurement criteria with IAS 36, in particular the use of the concept of a group of assets;
- consideration of the accounting for costs incurred in issuing debt securities;
- the exclusion of certain expenses, for example preliminary studies and functional analysis, from the cost of capitalised development costs for computer software;
- concerns about the appropriateness of capitalising costs associated with the development of internally generated intangible assets – the recognition of such costs as an expense and disclosure provides more useful information to investors;
- reconsideration of the appropriateness of separability as a minimum criterion for recognition of an intangible asset (purchased or acquired);
- reconsideration of the introduction of 'the ability to restrict the access of others to future economic benefit coming from the asset' as an additional characteristic for the recognition of a purchased intangible asset;
- more guidance on whether expenses have enhanced the originally assessed standard of performance and the amortisation method for such costs;

- consideration of the capitalisation of subsequent costs if it is virtually certain that those costs will enable the asset to generate specifically attributable future economic benefits or enhance the originally assessed standard of performance and the asset is subject to an impairment test at the end of the reporting period in which capitalisation has occurred;
- concerns about the appropriateness of amortisation periods for intangibles of longer than 20 years;
- concerns about the need to disclose the reasons why a useful life of longer than five years was selected;
- consideration of an exception to the general requirement for amortisation for long-lived intangible assets;
- concerns about the appropriateness of measuring intangible assets at revalued amounts;
- concerns about the need for disclosure of the nature and amounts of expenses related to internally developed intangibles; and
- concerns about the need to provide an option to either capitalise or expense the costs for internally generated intangible assets other than goodwill and computer software.

23.4 THE STANDARD IN BRIEF

An intangible resource must meet the definition of an intangible asset before it can be considered for recognition as an asset on the balance sheet. Acquired and internally generated intangible assets should be recognised as assets provided that they meet certain tough criteria – few internally generated intangibles are expected to meet the criteria. All costs related to intangible resources which do not meet the definition of an intangible asset or the asset recognition criteria should be recognised as expenses and should not subsequently be reinstated as an asset.

Intangible assets which have been recognised as assets may subsequently be revalued to fair value but only in very limited circumstances. Other intangible assets and resources should not be revalued.

All recognised intangible assets should be amortised with the rebuttable assumption that their useful lives do not exceed 20 years. The straight-line method should normally be used and the residual value should usually be zero. An annual impairment test is required for those recognised intangibles assets which are not yet in use or which have a useful life in excess of 20 years.

23.5 DEFINITION OF INTANGIBLE ASSETS

IAS 38 draws a distinction between an intangible resource and an intangible asset. Entities have many intangible resources but few meet the definition of an intangible asset, the first hurdle which must be crossed before an intangible resource is recognised as an asset on the balance sheet.

An *intangible asset* is an identifiable non-monetary asset without physical substance held for use in the production or supply of goods or services, for rental to others, or for administrative purposes (IAS 38, 7). An *asset* is a resource:

- controlled by an entity as a result of past events; and
- from which future economic benefits are expected to flow to the entity.

(*Framework* 49 and IAS 38, 7)

Intangible resources include computer software, patents, copyrights, the development of new products and processes, films and audio recordings, customer lists, licences, quotes, franchises, brands and market share. Not all these intangible resources meet the definition of an intangible asset. If an item does not meet the definition of an intangible asset, any expenditure to acquire it or generate it internally is recognised as an expense when it is incurred (IAS 38, 9). If the item is acquired in a business combination which is an acquisition, the cost forms part of the goodwill recognised at the date of acquisition.

23.5.1 Identifiability

An intangible asset must be identifiable so as to distinguish it from goodwill. An entity is usually able to identify an asset only when:

- it could rent, sell, exchange or distribute the specific future economic benefits attributable to the asset without also disposing of future economic benefits that flow from other assets used in the same revenue earning activity; or
- it otherwise has legal rights over the economic benefits which will flow from the asset.

For example, an entity may acquire a group of assets with legal rights to exploit those assets and those legal rights may help identify the acquired intangible asset. Similarly, if an internal project aims to create legal rights for the entity, the nature of these rights may assist the entity in identifying an underlying internally generated intangible asset.

23.5.2 Control

An entity can control the future economic benefits from an intangible asset normally by means of legal rights that are enforceable in a court of law (IAS 38, 13). For example, an entity controls the benefits from market and technical knowledge if the knowledge is protected by copyright, a restraint of trade agreement or by a legal duty on employees to maintain confidentiality.

Many intangible resources fail to meet the definition of an intangible asset because an entity has insufficient control over the expected future economic benefits arising from the resource. This is usually the case with the benefits arising from research, a team of skilled staff, training, management or technical talent, a portfolio of customers, market share and advertising.

All expenditure on intangible resources which do not meet the definition of an intangible asset should be recognised as an expense in the period in which it is incurred (IAS 38, 56). Such expenditure includes that incurred on:

- start-up activities which are not included in the cost of an item of property, plant and equipment (see chapter 20);
- training;
- advertising and promotion; and
- relocating or reorganising part or all of an entity.

(IAS 38, 57)

Extract 23.1 *Advertising and promotional expenses*

Adidas-Salomon, Germany, 31 December 2001 (IAS)

Production costs for media campaigns are shown under prepaid expenses until the advertising takes place for the first time, after which they are expensed in full. Significant media buying costs (e.g. broadcasting fees) are expensed over the original duration of the campaign on a straight-line basis.

23.6 RECOGNITION OF INTANGIBLE ASSETS

Once an item has met the definition of an intangible asset, it must meet the recognition criteria before it is recognised as an asset on the balance sheet. An intangible asset should be recognised as an asset only if:

- it is probable that the future economic benefits that are attributable to the asset will flow to the entity; and
- the cost of the asset can be measured reliably.

(IAS 38, 19)

These criteria are identical to the recognition criteria in the framework except that the words 'or value' have been omitted in the second criterion. As explained below, under the requirements of IAS 38, an intangible asset may only be recognised as an asset if it has a cost.

23.6.1 Internally Generated Intangible Assets

In order to assess whether an internally generated intangible asset meets the criteria for recognition, IAS 38 distinguishes between:

- the research phase; and
- the development phase.

Research is original and planned investigation undertaken with the prospect of gaining new scientific or technical knowledge or understanding (IAS 38, 14). The 'research phase' is broader than research and includes:

- activities aimed at obtaining new knowledge;
- the search for evaluation and final selection of applications of research findings or other knowledge;
- the search for alternatives for materials, devices, products, processes, systems or services; and
- the formulation, design, evaluation and final selection of possible alternatives for new or improved materials, devices, products, processes, systems or services.

(IAS 38, 44)

Research phase costs generally comprise all costs that are directly attributable to research activities or that can be allocated on a reasonable basis to such activities. The costs include, when applicable:

- the salaries, wages and other employment related costs of personnel engaged in the research phase;
- the costs of materials and services consumed in the research phase;
- the depreciation of property, plant and equipment to the extent that these assets are used for the research phase;
- overhead costs, other than general administrative costs, related to the research phase – these costs are allocated on bases similar to those used in allocating overhead costs to inventories (see chapter 26); and
- other costs, such as the amortisation of patents and licences, to the extent that these assets are used for the research phase.

No intangible asset arising from research or the research phase should be recognised. Expenditure on research or the research phase should be recognised as an expense when it is incurred (IAS 38, 42).

Some believed that the equivalent requirement in IAS 9 conflicted with the definition of an asset in the Framework. While the argument may be correct in principle, it is highly unlikely that costs which met the IAS 9 definition or meet the IAS 38 definition of research would meet the framework definition of an asset, let alone the framework recognition criteria for an asset. Therefore, conflicts with the Framework do not arise in practice. Curran[1] addressed this problem in the context of the potential conflict between Australian standards (which require the capitalisation of research costs in certain circumstances) and IAS 9 (which banned the capitalisation of research costs):

> 'To determine whether the opportunity to capitalise research costs under the Australian Standard constitutes a real difference between the two Standards (AASB 1011 and IAS 9), and one which is likely to affect the financial statements significantly, regard must be had to the discussion in AASB 11 on the issue. The latter Standard, while not providing a separate definition of "research" and "development", states that with basic research there rarely exists any relationship between costs incurred and resulting future benefits and accordingly, the costs of basic research would normally be charged to the profit and loss account when incurred. IAS 9 then considers applied research which it broadly defines as original investigation directed primarily towards solving recognised practical problems. Even though it differs from basic research in that it is undertaken with a specific practical aim or application, when the costs are incurred any future benefits are too uncertain to warrant deferral of the costs, and they too would normally be expensed when incurred.'

If phases cannot be distinguished from one another, the entity treats all the expenditure relating to the asset as if it were incurred in the research phase (IAS 38, 41). Therefore, in practice, if an entity wishes to capitalise the development costs of an internally generated intangible asset, it must be able to identify the development phase; the research phase is the residual. Furthermore, if none of the costs associated with the asset meet the criteria for recognition as an intangible asset, there is no need to distinguish the research phase from the development phase.

Development is the application of research findings or other knowledge to a plan or design for the production of new or substantially improved materials, devices, products, processes, systems or services prior to the commencement of commercial production (IAS 38, 14). Again the 'development phase' is broader than 'development' and includes:

- the design, construction and testing of pre-production or pre-use prototypes and models;
- the design of tools, jigs, moulds and dies involving new technology;
- the design, construction and operation of a pilot plant that is not of a scale economically feasible for commercial production; and
- the design, construction and testing of a chosen alternative for new or improved materials, devices, products, processes, systems or services.

(IAS 38, 47)

Development phase costs generally comprise all costs that are directly attributable to the development phase or that can be allocated on a reasonable basis to that phase. The costs include, when applicable:

- the salaries, wages and other employment related costs of personnel engaged in the development phase;
- the costs of materials and services consumed in the development phase;
- the depreciation of property, plant and equipment to the extent that these assets are used for development activities;
- overhead costs, other than general administrative costs, related to the development phase – these costs are allocated on bases similar to those used in allocating overhead costs to inventories (see chapter 26); and
- other costs, such as the amortisation of patents and licences, to the extent that these assets are used for the development phase.

IASB improvements project

In its May 2002 improvements exposure draft, the IASB proposes to give additional guidance on directly attributable expenditure that can be included in the cost of an intangible fixed asset. It clarifies that:

- costs of employee benefits arising directly from bringing the asset to its working condition should be included in the cost; and
- costs incurred in using or redeploying intangible assets are excluded from cost as capitalisation ceases when an intangible asset is in the working condition necessary for it to be capable of operating in the manner intended. Such costs do not improve the asset's standard of performance, for example initial operating losses incurred while demand for the asset builds up.

An intangible asset arising from development or the development phase should be recognised as an asset if, and only if, the entity can demonstrate all of the following:

- the technical feasibility of completing the intangible asset so that it will be available for use or sale;
- its intention to complete the intangible asset and use or sell it;
- its ability to use or sell the intangible asset;
- how the intangible asset will generate probable future economic benefits – among other things, the entity should demonstrate the existence of a market for the output of the intangible asset or the intangible asset itself or, if it is to be used internally, the usefulness of the intangible asset;
- the availability of adequate technical, financial and other resources to complete the development and to use or sell the intangible asset; and
- its ability to measure the expenditure attributable to the intangible asset during its development reliably.

(IAS 38, 45)

These criteria determine whether it is probable that the costs will give rise to future economic benefits and so meet the criteria for the recognition of an asset (*Framework* 89). In practice the criteria severely restrict the ability of entities to recognise development phase costs as an asset and also mean that only the costs incurred in the later stages of the development phase are likely to qualify for capitalisation. For example, the development costs associated with a new pharmaceutical drug qualify for capitalisation only after the regulatory authorities have given their approval to the use of the drug. Costs incurred prior to that approval cannot be capitalised. This means that only a small proportion of total development phase costs qualify for capitalisation. In the circumstances, therefore, it is not surprising that no pharmaceutical companies presenting IFRS financial statements have capitalised any development costs.

All expenditure incurred from when the recognition criteria are met is capitalised and the entity should test for impairment at least annually during the development phase, that is, before the asset is available for use (see IAS 36 and chapter 25) (IAS 38/IAS 22 *Basis for Conclusions*, 19).

All development costs which do not meet the asset recognition criteria should be recognised as an expense in the period in which they are incurred. They should not be recognised as an asset in a subsequent period even if the criteria are met in that later period (IAS 38, 59). This is because the asset recognition test should be applied to expenditure only once, that is an entity should not be required or allowed to revisit past decisions on asset recognition.

Such intangible resources as internally generated brands, mastheads, publishing titles, customer lists and similar items should not be recognised as intangible assets on the balance sheet even if they meet the definition of an intangible asset (IAS 38, 51). All the costs associated with their development should be recognised as an expense, in the period in which they are incurred. Such items may qualify for recognition as intangible assets when they are acquired separately or they are acquired in a business combination and their fair values at the date of acquisition can be ascertained.

Extract 23.2 *Research and development costs*

Nokia, Finland, 31 December 2001 (IAS)

Research and development costs are expensed in the financial period during which they are incurred, except for certain development costs which are capitalised when it is probable that a development project will be a success, and certain criteria, including commercial and technological feasibility, have been met. Capitalised development costs are amortised on a systematic basis over their expected useful lives. The amortisation period is between 2 and 5 years.

Extract 23.3 *Research and development costs*

Schoeller Bleckmann, Austria, 31 December 2001 (IAS)

Pursuant to IAS 38 research costs are expensed as incurred. Development costs are also expensed as incurred and are not capitalised due to the uncertainties of the future economic benefits attributable. The requirements of IAS 38 for a capitalisation of development expenses are not fully met.

Extract 23.4 *Research and development costs*

Danisco, Denmark, 30 April 2001 (IAS)

Research and development costs include costs, salaries and depreciation directly or indirectly attributable to the research and development activities of the Group. Research costs are charged to the profit and loss account in the year in which they are incurred.

The main part of the Group's development costs is similarly charged to the profit and loss account in the year in which it is incurred, as it has been defrayed to sustain earnings on a continuous basis.

Clearly defined and identifiable development projects in which the technical degree of exploitation, adequate resources and potential market or development possibility in the undertaking are recognisable, and where it is the intention to produce, market or execute the project, are capitalised when a correlation exists between the costs incurred and future benefits.

Extract 23.5 *Research and development costs*

Thales, France, 31 December 2001 (French GAAP)

A significant portion of research and development expenses is funded by customers and government agencies. Internally funded research and development expenses are charged to the profit and loss account as incurred as 'Research and development expenses', except for project development costs that strictly meet the following criteria:

- the product or process is clearly defined, and costs are separately identified and measured reliably,
- the product has been shown to be technically feasible,
- the product or process will be sold or else used in-house,
- a potential market exists for the product, or its usefulness for in-house purposes has been demonstrated,
- adequate resources are available to complete the project successfully.

Such development costs are capitalised and amortised over the economic life of the product. The method of amortisation is determined according to expected future quantities or sales. The period of amortisation depends on the nature of the activity, but may not exceed 15 years.

When making an acquisition, the Group may allocate a portion of the acquisition price to R&D projects. If, at the acquisition date, these projects do not meet the criteria defined above, the value ascribed to the said projects is expensed immediately.

Extract 23.6 *Research and development costs*

Bayer, Germany, 31 December 2001 (IAS)

According to IAS 38 (Intangible Assets), research costs cannot be capitalized; development costs can only be capitalized if specific conditions are fulfilled. Development costs must be capitalized if it is sufficiently certain that the future economic benefits to the company will cover not only the usual production, selling and administrative costs but also the development costs themselves. There are also several other criteria relating to the development project and the product or process being developed, all of which have to be met to justify asset recognition. As in previous years, these conditions are not satisfied.

Extract 23.7 *Research and development costs*

Roche, Switzerland, 31 December 2001 (IAS)

Research costs are charged against income as incurred, with the exception of buildings and major items of equipment, which are capitalised and depreciated. Development costs, such as milestone payments and other similar non-refundable up-front product licence payments, are capitalised as intangible assets when it is probable that future economic benefits will flow to the Group. They are amortised on a straight-line basis over the period of the expected benefit, and are reviewed for impairment at each balance sheet date. Other development costs are charged against income as incurred since the criteria for their recognition as an asset are not met.

Extract 23.8 *Exploration, research and development costs*

Barloworld, South Africa, 30 September 2000 (IAS)

Exploration and research costs are expensed in the year in which they are incurred. Development costs are reviewed annually and are expensed if they do not qualify for capitalisation. If a project is abandoned during the development stage, the total accumulated expenditure is then written off.

Extract 23.9 *Development costs*

Adidas-Salomon, Germany, 31 December 2001 (IAS)

Research costs are expensed as incurred. Development costs are also expensed as incurred and are not capitalised due to the short product life cycle in the fashion industry.

23.6.2 Acquired Intangible Assets

When an intangible asset is acquired separately, its cost can usually be measured reliably. There is also usually evidence available from the entity's investment decisions to confirm that it is probable that future economic benefits will flow to the entity from the use of the asset.

Extract 23.10 *Acquired intangible assets*

Bayer, Germany, 31 December 2001 (IAS)

Acquired intangible assets other than goodwill are recognized at cost ...

Extract 23.11 *Acquired intangible assets*

Roche, Switzerland, 31 December 2001 (IAS)

... Patents, licences, trademarks and other intangible assets are initially recorded at fair value. Where these assets have been acquired through a business combination, this will be the fair value allocated in the acquisition accounting. Where these have been acquired other than through a business combination, the initial fair value will be cost.

23.6.3 Intangible Assets Acquired in a Business Combination

When an intangible asset is acquired in a business combination that is an acquisition, the exchange transaction usually provides evidence to confirm that it is probable that future economic benefits will flow to the entity from the use of the asset. Therefore, under IAS 22 an acquirer recognises an intangible asset that meets the recognition criteria even if that intangible asset had not been recognised in the financial statements of the acquiree. However, the acquirer should not recognise the intangible asset as an asset if its cost (that is, its fair value at the date of the exchange transaction) cannot be measured reliably; that asset is not recognised as a separate intangible asset but is included in goodwill.

23.7 COST OF INTANGIBLE ASSETS

An intangible asset should be measured initially at cost (IAS 38, 22). The guidance in IAS 38 is similar to the requirements for a tangible asset such as property, plant and equipment. The cost of an intangible asset comprises its purchase price, including any import duties and non-refundable purchase taxes, and any directly attributable expenditure on preparing the asset for its intended use. Directly attributable expenditure includes, for example, professional fees for legal services. Any trade discounts and rebates are deducted in arriving at the cost. If payment for an intangible asset is deferred beyond normal credit terms, its cost is the cash price equivalent; the difference between this amount and the total payments is recognised as interest expense over the period of credit unless it is capitalised under the allowed alternative treatment in IAS 23.

Expenditure which was initially recognised as an expense in a previous period (including a previous interim period) should not be recognised as part of the cost of an intangible asset at a later date (IAS 38, 59). For example, expenditure incurred prior to the entity establishing the technical feasibility of a process is recognised as an expense when incurred and is not reinstated as an asset when the technical feasibility of a process is established and the other criteria are met.

In the circumstances permitted by IAS 39, the cost of an intangible asset also includes any deferred gains and losses on a financial instrument when that instrument has been designated as a hedge of a firm commitment or forecasted transaction to acquire the intangible asset (see chapter 20). Such gains and losses are included in equity prior to the acquisition. On acquisition, deferred losses may be added to, and deferred gains deducted from, the cost of the asset.

23.7.1 Intangible Assets Acquired in a Business Combination

If an intangible asset is acquired in a business combination that is an acquisition, the cost of that intangible asset is its fair value at the date of acquisition (IAS 22, 39 (9)). Fair value is determined:

- by reference to an active market; or
- in the absence of such a market, on a basis which reflects the amount which the entity would have paid for the asset in an arm's length transaction between knowledgeable willing parties based on the best information available.

(IAS 22, 28 and 29)

Quoted market prices in an active market provide the most reliable measurement of fair value and the appropriate market price is usually the current bid price (IAS 38,28). If current bid prices are unavailable, the price of the most recent similar transaction may provide a basis from which to estimate fair value, provided that there has not been a significant change in economic circumstances between the transaction date and the date at which the asset's fair value is estimated.

An *active market* is a market where all the following conditions exist:

- the items traded within the market are homogenous;
- willing buyers and sellers can normally be found at any time; and
- prices are available to the public.

(IAS 38, 7)

It is uncommon for such a market to exist for many intangible assets. While transactions may occur between willing buyers and sellers, it is rare that such buyers and sellers can be found 'at any time' and it is even less likely that prices for many intangible assets are available to the public.

If no active market exists for an intangible asset, which is often the case, an entity considers the outcome of recent transactions for similar assets or uses other techniques which estimate fair value and reflect current transactions and practices in the industry to which the asset belongs (IAS 38, 29). These techniques include applying current multiples to revenue, market shares or operating profit and discounting estimated future net cash flows from the asset. These techniques are similar in substance to the method used to estimate value in use for the purposes of IAS 36 (see chapter 25).

Extract 23.12 *Cost of acquired brands*

Gucci, The Netherlands, 31 January 2000 (IAS)

The value and expected useful life of each brand acquired have been determined by the specialist brand valuation expert Interbrand Newell and Sorrell Ltd. Based on their appraisals, the Group has determined that the trademarks Yves Saint Laurent, Yves Saint Laurent Rive Gauche and Sergio Rossi will be amortized over a period of 20 years, the maximum permitted by IAS.

Acquired trademarks are amortized over their estimated useful life up to a maximum period of 20 years. Acquired trademarks, whose useful lives are estimated to be greater than 20 years, are amortized over 20 years, the maximum period permitted by IAS.

Extract 23.13 *Cost of acquired trademarks and brands*

Edcon, South Africa, 31 March 2001 (South African GAAP and IAS)

Where payments are made for the acquisition of trademarks or brand names, the amounts are capitalised and amortised over their anticipated useful lives, currently estimated to be between seven and ten years. No valuation is made of internally developed and maintained trademarks or brand names. Expenditure incurred to maintain brand names is charged in full against trading profit.

[Author's note – the trademarks represent registered rights to the exclusive use of certain trademarks and brand names.]

Extract 23.14 *Cost of acquired brands*

Hochtief, Germany, 31 December 2001 (IAS)

Intangible assets are reported at cost of acquisition or production less scheduled depreciation reflecting their useful lives. They mainly consist of the value of the 'Turner' brand capitalized at the time the Turner group was first consolidated, which is being amortized on a straight-line basis to reflect its anticipated useful life. In the prior year, future earnings implicit in Turner's order backlog were also capitalized, and subsequently recognized as income when bills were settled.

Cost is restricted to an amount which does not create or increase negative goodwill arising at the date of acquisition (IAS 22, 40).

Example 23.1 *Limitation on cost of intangible asset*

Entity A acquires entity B for \$20m. In addition to identifiable tangible assets, less liabilities, acquired amounting to \$16m, A has acquired an intangible asset for which there is no active market. A estimates the fair value of the intangible asset by applying the current multiple in the industry to the estimated future revenues which will be generated by the asset. A initially calculates that the fair value of the intangible asset is \$6m. However, the use of this fair value would result in negative goodwill of \$2m (\$20m − (\$16m + \$6m)). Therefore, the fair value of the intangible asset is restricted to \$4m.

23.7.2 Intangible Assets Acquired by a Government Grant

An intangible asset may be acquired by way of a government grant. For example, a government may grant to an entity airport landing rights, licences to operate radio or television stations, import licences or quotas or rights to access other restricted resources. The cost of these assets is determined in accordance with IAS 20 (see chapter 34). Therefore, the entity should either:

- recognise both the intangible asset and the grant at fair value; or
- recognise the asset and the grant at a nominal amount.

Example 23.2 *Grant of an intangible asset*

The government grants A the right to operate a television station. A is able to estimate that the fair value of the licence, by reference to other market transactions, is £10m. Under the requirements of IAS 20 and IAS 38, A either:

- recognises the licence as an intangible asset with a cost of £10m and sets up the grant as deferred income of £10m; or
- recognises both the licence and the grant at zero.

A may also recognise the licence and grant at £10m and deduct the grant from the cost of the asset but this is identical to the 'nominal value' approach.

23.7.3 Exchanges of Intangible Assets

The requirements in IAS 38 for exchanges of asset are identical to those in IAS 16 for the exchange of property, plant and equipment. When an intangible asset is acquired in exchange or part exchange for a dissimilar asset, the cost of the intangible asset acquired is the fair value of the asset received – this is equivalent to the fair value of the asset given up, adjusted by the amount of any cash or cash equivalents transferred (IAS 38, 34).

When an intangible asset is acquired in exchange for a similar asset that has a similar use in the same line of business and that has a similar fair value, the cost of the new asset is the carrying amount of the asset given up. Similarly, when an intangible asset is sold in exchange for an equity interest in a similar asset, the cost of the equity interest is the carrying amount of the intangible asset. In both cases, since the earnings process is incomplete, no gain or loss is recognised on the transaction.

The fair value of the asset received may provide evidence of an impairment loss in the asset given up. Under these circumstances the impairment loss is recognised for the asset given up and the carrying amount after impairment is assigned to the new asset.

> ***IASB improvements project***
>
> In its May 2002 improvements exposure draft, the IASB proposes to amend the guidance in IAS 38 on the treatment of an exchange of assets in a similar way to the proposed amendments to IAS 16 (see chapter 21).
>
> Assuming the intangible asset can be measured reliably and other recognition conditions are met, the IASB proposes that when the intangible asset is acquired in exchange for equity instruments of the reporting entity, the cost of the asset acquired is the fair value of the equity instruments issued. The fair value of the item received would only be used to measure cost if it is more clearly evident than the fair value of the equity instruments issued.
>
> Sometimes an intangible asset may be acquired in exchange or part exchange for another intangible or other asset. Generally, it is proposed that the cost of asset acquired is measured at the fair value of the asset given up, adjusted by the amount of any cash or cash equivalents transferred. Only when the fair value of the asset received is more clearly evident than the fair value of the asset given up would the cost of the asset acquired in the exchange be measured at the carrying amount of the asset given up. However, when the fair value of neither of the assets exchanged can be determined reliably, the cost of the asset acquired in exchange for a similar asset is measured at the carrying value of the asset given up.

23.7.4 Internally Generated Intangible Assets

The cost of an internally generated intangible asset is determined in the same way as the cost of any other internally generated asset (for example, inventories and plant and equipment) but with one important difference. The cost of an internally generated intangible asset is the sum of only that expenditure incurred from the date when the asset first meets the recognition criteria. Expenditure previously recognised as an expense should not be included in the cost of the asset (IAS 38, 59).

The cost of an internally generated intangible asset comprises all expenditure which can be directly attributed or allocated on a reasonable and consistent basis to creating, producing and preparing the asset for its intended use. The cost includes:

- expenditure on materials and services used or consumed in generating the intangible asset;
- the salaries, wages and other employment related costs of personnel directly engaged in generating the asset;
- any expenditure that is directly attributable to generating the asset, such as fees to register a legal right and the amortisation of patents and licences that are used to generate the asset;
- overheads which are necessary to generate the asset and which can be allocated on a reasonable and consistent basis to the asset – the allocation of overheads is made on bases similar to those used in allocating overheads to inventories (see IAS 2); and
- borrowing costs in accordance with IAS 23 (see chapter 35).

(IAS 38, 54)

> ***IASB improvements project***
>
> In its May 2002 improvements exposure draft, the IASB proposes to exclude a reasonable and consistent allocation of directly attributable costs from the cost of an internally generated intangible fixed asset.

The cost does not include:

- selling, administrative and other general overheads which are not directly attributable to the preparation of the asset for its intended use;
- inefficiencies and initial operating losses incurred before an asset achieves its planned performance; and
- costs of training staff to operate the asset.

(IAS 38, 55)

> ***IASB improvements project***
>
> In its May 2002 improvements exposure draft, the IASB proposes to add specific guidance on incidental income and expenses that arise before or during the development of an intangible asset but are not necessary to bring the asset into the working condition for its intended use. The IASB proposes that any income or expenses arising from incidental operations should be recognised in the net profit or loss for the period and not as part of the cost of the fixed asset. This is because the operations are not necessary to bring the asset into its working condition.

23.7.5 Web Site Costs

Internal costs incurred in developing and operating an entity's own web site are accounted for in accordance with the principles of IAS 38, in particular the web site should be recognised as an intangible asset only if the entity can satisfy the recognition and initial measurement requirements in IAS 38.

Typically, the development of a web site involves four stages:

- planning – including the cost of feasibility studies, defining hardware and software specifications and objectives, evaluating alternative products and suppliers and selecting preferences;
- application and infrastructure development – including the cost of obtaining a domain name, purchasing and developing hardware, developing operating software, installing developed applications on the web server and stress testing;
- graphical design development – including designing the appearance of web pages, e.g. layout and colour; and
- content development – including creating, purchasing, preparing (for example creating links and identifying tags), and uploading textual or graphical information on the web site before its completion.

(SIC 32, 2)

Costs incurred on a web site used for either internal access (for example to store customer details) or external access (for example to promote, advertise and sell products and services or provide electronic services) represent an internally generated intangible asset. The nature of any expenditure must be evaluated using the IAS 38 criteria, for example:

- planning costs are similar to research phase costs and should be expensed when incurred;
- application and infrastructure development costs, graphical design and content development costs are similar to development phase costs and may be recognised as an intangible asset; and
- any expenditure incurred in the content development stage relating to advertising and promoting an entity's own products and services should be expensed when incurred.

(SIC 32, 9)

When a web site is developed solely or primarily for advertising and promoting an entity's own products and services, the entity cannot demonstrate that future economic benefits will flow from these costs. Therefore the costs of developing such a web site must be expensed.

Any subsequent expenditure should be expensed unless it meets the criteria of subsequent expenditure in IAS 38 (see 23.7.6). Accordingly, all of the following costs would be expensed:

- selling, administrative and other general overhead expenditure (unless it can be directly attributed to preparing the web site for use);
- clearly identified inefficiencies and initial operating losses incurred before the web site achieves planned performance (for example false start testing);
- employee operational training; and
- any expenditure required to maintain the asset at its originally assessed standard of performance (IAS 38, 61).

It is unlikely that an active market will exist for web sites. Therefore, the allowed alternative treatment for measurement after initial recognition in IAS 38, 64 will not apply and the benchmark treatment must be applied (see 23.8).

When a web site is recognised as an intangible asset it is amortised over the best estimate of its useful life. This is short due to rapid changes in technology which means that many intangible assets are susceptible to technological obsolescence.

SIC 32 does not apply to expenditure incurred on:

- purchasing, developing and operating a web site's hardware as this is accounted for under IAS 16 (chapter 21);
- services from an internet service provider which are recognised as an expense when the services are received (IAS 8, 7 and the *Framework*);
- the development or operation of a web site for sale to another entity as these costs are covered by IAS 2 or IAS 11; nor
- a web site held under an operating lease.

23.7.6 Subsequent Expenditure

Subsequent expenditure on an intangible asset after its purchase or its completion should be recognised as an expense when it is incurred unless:

- it is probable that this expenditure will enable the asset to generate future economic benefits in excess of its originally assessed standard of performance; and
- this expenditure can be measured and attributed to the asset reliably.

If these conditions are met, the subsequent expenditure should be added to the cost of the intangible asset (IAS 38, 60). Again, these requirements are similar to those for property, plant and equipment.

IASB improvements project

In its improvements May 2002 exposure draft, the IASB proposes to amend the criteria in which subsequent expenditure can be capitalised. If the proposals are implemented, subsequent expenditure on an intangible asset after its purchase or completion can only be capitalised if it increases the future economic benefits embodied in the asset in excess of the standard of performance assessed immediately before the expenditure was made and it can be measured reliably.

Similarly, subsequent expenditure on an intangible asset that is already recognised will be treated as an expense if it is required to maintain the asset at the standard of performance assessed immediately before the expenditure was made. This means that the originally assessed standard of performance will no longer be relevant.

23.8 MEASUREMENT SUBSEQUENT TO INITIAL RECOGNITION

23.8.1 Benchmark Treatment

An intangible asset should be carried at its cost less any accumulated amortisation and any accumulated impairment losses (IAS 38, 63). Amortisation is dealt with in 23.9 and impairment losses are dealt with in 23.10 and chapter 25.

23.8.2 Allowed Alternative Treatment

An intangible asset should be carried at a revalued amount, being its fair value at the date of the revaluation less any subsequent accumulated amortisation and any subsequent accumulated impairment losses (IAS 38, 64). The requirements are similar to those in IAS 16 for the revaluation of property, plant and equipment except that in the case of an intangible asset fair value should be determined by reference to an active market (IAS 38, 64).

The allowed alternative treatment does not permit:

- the revaluation of intangible assets which have not previously been recognised as assets; or
- the initial recognition of intangible assets at amounts other than their cost.

(IAS 38, 65)

For example, if all costs associated with the development of an internally generated intangible asset are written off as they are incurred (because they do not meet the asset recognition criteria), that asset cannot be revalued in future periods or recognised at its fair value at some subsequent date.

If only part of the cost of an intangible asset is recognised as an asset (because the asset did not meet the criteria for recognition until part of the way through the development process), the whole of the asset may be revalued (IAS 38, 66). If an intangible asset was received by way of a government grant and recognised, it may be revalued (IAS 38, 66) – this is the case even when the asset and the grant were recognised at a nominal amount.

As explained earlier, an *active market* is a market where all the following conditions exist:

- the items traded within the market are homogenous;
- willing buyers and sellers can normally be found at any time; and
- prices are available to the public.

(IAS 38, 7)

It is uncommon for such a market to exist for many intangible assets; therefore revaluations of intangible assets are likely to be rare.

An active market may exist for such intangible assets as taxi licences, fishing licences or production quotas. However, an active market cannot exist for brands, newspaper mastheads, music and film publishing rights, patents or trademarks because such assets are unique and contracts for their sale are negotiated between individual buyers and sellers (IAS 38, 67). Therefore, such assets should not be revalued.

IAS 38 includes similar requirements about the frequency of revaluations as are included in IAS 16 for the revaluation of property, plant and equipment. Revaluations must be made with sufficient regularity that the carrying amount of the asset does not differ materially from its fair value at the balance sheet date (IAS 38, 64). The frequency of revaluations depends on the volatility of the fair values of the intangible assets being revalued which, in some cases, may mean annual revaluations.

If an intangible asset is revalued, any accumulated amortisation at the date of the revaluation is either:

- restated proportionately with the change in the gross carrying amount of the asset so that the carrying amount of the asset after revaluation equals its revalued amount; or
- eliminated against the gross carrying amount of the asset and the net amount restated to the revalued amount of the asset.

This accounting is the same as that for property, plant and equipment (see examples 21.7 and 21.8 in chapter 21).

If an intangible asset is revalued, all the other assets in its class should also be revalued, unless there is no active market for those assets (IAS 38, 70). The exception is a variation from the requirements in IAS 16 and results from the IASC's view that intangible assets should only be revalued by reference to an active market. Similarly, if the fair value of a revalued intangible asset can no longer be determined by reference to an active market, the carrying amount of the asset should be its revalued amount at the date of the last revaluation by reference to the active market less any subsequent accumulated amortisation and any subsequent accumulated impairment losses (IAS 38, 73). There are no similar requirements in IAS 16.

If an intangible asset's carrying amount is increased as a result of a revaluation, the increase should be credited directly to equity under the heading of revaluation surplus. However, a revaluation increase should be recognised as income to the extent that it reverses a revaluation decrease of the same asset and that revaluation decrease was previously recognised as an expense (IAS 38, 76).

If an asset's carrying amount is decreased as a result of a revaluation the decrease should be recognised as an expense. However, a revaluation decrease should be charged directly against any related revaluation surplus to the extent that the decrease does not exceed the amount held in the revaluation surplus in respect of the same asset (IAS 38,77).

The cumulative revaluation surplus included in equity may be transferred directly to retained earnings when the surplus is realised. The whole surplus may be realised on the retirement or disposal of the asset. However, some of the surplus may be realised as the asset is used by the entity; in such a case, the amount of the surplus realised is the difference between amortisation based on the revalued carrying amount of the asset and amortisation that would have been recognised based on the asset's historical cost. The transfer from revaluation surplus to retained earnings is not made through the income statement, but it is included in the statement of changes in equity. Again this is the same accounting as is required for revalued property, plant and equipment.

23.9 AMORTISATION

The depreciable amount of an intangible asset should be allocated on a systematic basis over the best estimate of its useful life (IAS 38, 79). There is a rebuttable presumption that the useful life of an intangible asset will not exceed twenty years from the date when the asset is available for use (IAS 38, 79). The residual value of an intangible asset is usually zero.

Many factors need to be considered in determining the useful life of an intangible asset including:

- the expected usage of the asset by the entity and whether the asset could be efficiently managed by another management team;
- typical product life cycles for the asset and public information on estimates of useful lives or similar types of assets that are used in a similar way;
- technical, technological or other types of obsolescence;
- the stability of the industry in which the asset operates and changes in the market demand for the products or services output from the asset;
- expected actions by competitors or potential competitors;
- the level of maintenance expenditure required to obtain the expected future economic benefits from the asset and the company's ability and intent to reach to such a level;
- the period of control over the asset and legal or similar limits on the use of the asset, such as the expiry dates of related leases; and
- whether the useful life of the asset is dependent on the useful life of other assets of the entity.

(IAS 38, 80)

IASB improvements project

In its May 2002 improvements exposure draft, the IASB proposes to add commercial factors alongside technical and technological ones to help determine the useful economic life of an intangible asset.

In rare cases, there may be persuasive evidence that the useful life of an intangible asset will be a specific period longer than twenty years. In these cases, the presumption that the useful life generally does not exceed twenty years is rebutted and the entity amortises the intangible asset over the best estimate of its useful life. In addition, in such circumstances, the entity should also:

- estimate the recoverable amount of the intangible asset at least annually in order to identify any impairment loss (see chapter 25); and
- disclose the reasons why the presumption is rebutted and the factor(s) that played a significant role in determining the useful life of the asset.

(IAS 38, 83)

According to IAS 38, the useful life of an intangible asset is always finite. Therefore, amortisation cannot be avoided by claiming that an intangible asset has an infinite life – in this respect, IAS 38 is different from the similar requirements for intangible assets in the United Kingdom which allow an entity to claim an infinite life (subject to certain rigorous conditions).

If control over the economic benefits from an intangible asset is achieved by means of legal rights, the useful life of the intangible asset should not exceed the period of the legal rights (IAS 38, 85). If the legal rights are renewable and renewal is virtually certain, the useful life should include the period of renewal (IAS 38, 85). The following factors may indicate that the renewal of a legal right is virtually certain:

- the fair value of the intangible asset does not reduce as the initial expiry date of the rights approaches, or does not reduce by more than the cost of renewing the underlying right;
- there is evidence (possibly based on past experience) that the legal rights will be renewed; and
- there is evidence that the conditions necessary to obtain the renewal of the legal right (if any) will be satisfied.

(IAS 38, 87)

The amortisation method used should reflect the pattern in which the asset's future economic benefits are consumed by the entity – if that pattern cannot be determined reliably, the straight-line method should be used (IAS 38, 88).

Amortisation should commence when the asset is available for use (IAS 38, 79). It is unacceptable to defer the commencement of amortisation until the period after capitalisation if the entity starts to recognise the benefits in its income statement in the period of capitalisation or the asset is ready for use by the end of that period. The IASC has rejected the suggestion of some IOSCO members that amortisation should not commence until the later period.

The residual value of an intangible asset should be assumed to be zero unless:

- there is a commitment by a third party to purchase the asset at the end of its useful life; or
- there is an active market for the asset and:
  - residual value can be determined by reference to that market; and
  - it is probable that such a market will exist at the end of the asset's useful life.

(IAS 38, 91)

There is no similar restriction in IAS 16 but IAS 16 does define residual value in terms of the amount which will be received at the end of an asset's useful life which, in the case of an intangible asset, would almost certainly be zero.

> ***IASB improvements project***
>
> In its May 2002 improvements exposure draft, the IASB proposes to revise the definition of residual value. If the proposals are implemented, residual value will be based on the price an entity would currently obtain from selling the asset, after deducting estimated costs of disposal, if the asset were of the age and condition expected at the end of its estimated useful life.
>
> It is also proposed to revise IAS 38 so that the residual value of an asset is reviewed at each balance sheet date regardless of whether the asset has been measured under the benchmark treatment or the allowed alternative treatment. Any change in the residual value, other than a change reflected in an impairment loss under IAS 36, would be accounted for prospectively as an adjustment to future amortisation.

The amortisation period and the amortisation method should be reviewed at least at each financial year end. If the expected useful life of the asset is significantly different from previous estimates, the amortisation period should be changed accordingly. If there has been a significant change in the expected pattern of economic benefits from the asset, the amortisation method should be changed to reflect the changed pattern. Such changes should be accounted for as changes in accounting estimates by adjusting the amortisation charge for the current and future periods (IAS 38, 94). This is the same approach as that in IAS 16.

> ***IASB improvements project***
>
> In its May 2002 improvements exposure draft, the IASB proposes that an entity amends the amortisation period and the expected pattern of consumption of future economic benefits where it is discovered that the expected useful life or pattern of consumption, respectively, is different to, rather than significantly different to, previous estimates. Such changes should be accounted for prospectively as changes in accounting estimates (see chapter 13).

The amortisation charge for each period should be recognised as an expense unless another IAS permits or requires it to be included in the carrying amount of another asset (IAS 38, 88). For example, the amortisation of capitalised development costs may qualify for inclusion in the costs of conversion of the related products. However, the amortisation of an acquired customer list is always recognised as an expense because selling and marketing costs are never included in the cost of inventories.

Extract 23.15 *Amortisation of intangible assets*

MAN, Germany, 31 December 2001 (IAS)

Intangible assets purchased are capitalized at cost and amortized on a straight-line basis over their useful lives, generally three to five years.

R&D costs are expensed. Excepted from this practice are the expenses incurred for the development of new products and series as from the fiscal year of their market launch: such expenses are capitalized since from that year onwards the technical completion of the new development and its future marketability are secured. Amortization is charged per unit or on a straight-line basis over the estimated useful life of four to ten years.

Extract 23.16 *Amortisation of intangible assets*

Roche, Switzerland, 31 December 2001 (IAS)

All intangible assets are amortised over their useful lives on a straight-line basis. Estimated useful lives of major classes of intangible assets are as follows:

...

Patents, licences, trademarks and other intangible assets	Lower of legal duration and economic useful life, up to a maximum of 20 years

Extract 23.17 *Amortisation of intangible assets*

Kuoni, Switzerland, 31 December 1999 (IAS)

Intangible assets comprise software acquired from third parties, licences, trademarks and similar rights. These assets are depreciated straight-line over their expected useful lives but not longer than five years.

Extract 23.18 *Amortisation of intangible assets*

Amadeus, Spain, 31 December 2000 (IAS)

... Software development projects, including e-commerce related development activities, are software applications developed by the Group which are capitalized once technical feasibility is established and where it is reasonably anticipated that the costs will be recovered through future activities or benefit future periods. These projects are being amortized applying the straight-line method over 3–5 years. Software maintenance ...

Extract 23.19 *Amortisation of intangible assets*

Petrochina, China, 31 December 2000 (IAS)

Expenditure of acquired patents, trademarks, technical know-hows and licences is capitalised and amortised using the straight-line method over their useful lives, generally over 14 to 20 years.

Extract 23.20 *Amortisation of intangible assets*

Novartis, Switzerland, 31 December 2001 (IAS)

Other acquired intangible assets are written off on a straight-line basis over the following periods:

Trademarks	10 to 15 years
Product marketing rights	6 to 20 years
Software	3 years
Others	3 to 5 years

Trademarks are amortized on a straight-line basis over their estimated economic or legal life, whichever is shorter, while the history of the Group has been to amortize product rights over estimated useful lives of 5 to 20 years. The useful lives assigned to acquired product rights are based on the maturity of the products and the estimated economic benefit that such product rights can provide. Marketing rights are amortized over their useful lives commencing in the year in which the rights are first utilized.

Extract 23.21 *Amortisation of intangible assets*

Syngenta Group, Switzerland, 31 December 2001 (IAS)

Trademarks are amortized on a straight-line basis over their estimated economic or legal life, whichever is the shorter. Useful lives assigned to acquired product rights are based on the maturity of the product and the estimated economic benefit that such product rights can provide.

Any value attributable to long-term supply agreements at preferential terms is amortized as part of cost of goods sold over the period of the supply agreement.

Extract 23.22 *Amortisation of intangible assets*

SIG, Switzerland, 31 December 2001 (IAS)

The rights to deliver packaging materials are capitalized in order to give a true and fair representation of the result situation in the systems business and are amortized using the straight-line method over the expected useful life of up to 6 years.

Extract 23.23 *Amortisation of intangible assets*

Telekomunikacja Polska SA, Poland, 31 December 2000 (IAS)

Concessions are valued at the present value of payments due plus the cost of interest and foreign exchange losses capitalised during the development period, less amortisation. The development period terminates together with a start of operational validity. The concessions are amortised over the period reflecting concession rights starting from the beginning of their operational validity.

23.10 IMPAIRMENT LOSSES

Impairment losses are dealt with in chapter 25. There are two special rules dealing with the impairment of intangible assets. First, an entity should estimate the recoverable amount at the end of each period, irrespective of whether there is an indication of impairment, for:

- an intangible asset that is not yet available for use (and which, therefore, is not being amortised);
- an intangible asset that is amortised over a period exceeding twenty years; and
- an intangible asset which has been retired from active use and is held for disposal.

(IAS 38, 99 and 106)

Extract 23.24 *Impairment of intangible assets*

Bayer, Germany, 31 December 2001 (IAS)

Write-downs are made for impairment losses. Assets are written back if the reasons for previous years' write-downs no longer apply.

In the case of an intangible asset acquired in a business combination which is an acquisition, if an impairment loss occurs before the end of the first annual accounting period commencing after the acquisition, the impairment loss is recognised as an adjustment to both the amount assigned to the intangible asset and the goodwill (negative goodwill) recognised at the date of acquisition. However, if the impairment loss relates to specific events or changes in circumstances occurring after the date of acquisition, the impairment loss is recognised as an expense under IAS 36 and not as an adjustment to the amount assigned to the goodwill (negative goodwill) recognised at the date of acquisition (IAS 38, 98).

23.11 RETIREMENTS AND DISPOSALS

An intangible asset should be derecognised (eliminated from the balance sheet) on disposal or when no future economic benefits are expected from its use and subsequent disposal (IAS 38, 103). Gains or losses arising from the retirement or disposal of an intangible asset should be determined as the difference between the net disposal proceeds and the carrying amount of the asset and should be recognised as income or expense in the income statement (IAS 38, 104). These are the same requirements as apply to the retirement of property, plant and equipment.

IASB improvements project

In its May 2002 improvements exposure draft, the IASB proposes to give additional guidance on the disposal of an intangible asset by sale or by sale and leaseback under a finance lease. The date of disposal for a sale is determined by applying the criteria in IAS 18. IAS 38 will clarify that the consideration receivable on disposal is recognised initially at fair value but if the proceeds are deferred, the consideration is initially recognised at the cash price equivalent with the difference between that amount and consideration shown as interest revenue. IAS 17 applies to the sale and leaseback.

23.12 TRANSITIONAL PROVISIONS

IAS 38 includes extensive transitional provisions. It requires retrospective application to eliminate:

- an intangible asset which had previously been capitalised but which does not qualify for recognition as an asset under IAS 38; and
- an item for which the previous measurement policies did not comply with those required by IAS 38.

The resulting adjustments should be dealt with as changes in accounting policy in accordance with IAS 8 (see chapter 13).

IASB improvements project

In its May 2002 improvements exposure draft, the IASB proposes that entities should apply the transitional rules when IAS 38 is adopted. When these rules do not apply, the IAS must be adopted retrospectively unless this would require undue cost or effort.

Continued

Continued

It also proposes that the amendments to the initial measurement of assets acquired in exchange for similar intangible assets are applied prospectively. When an exchange of assets was measured on the basis of the carrying amount of the asset given up, the entity does not need to restate the carrying amount of the asset acquired to reflect the fair value of the consideration given. This means that, on adoption of IAS 38, an entity does not apply the general rules for changes in accounting policies under IAS 8 (see chapter 13).

23.13 DISCLOSURE

For each class of intangible assets, and distinguishing between internally generated intangible assets and other intangible assets, an entity should disclose:

- the useful lives or the amortisation rates used;
- the amortisation methods used;
- the gross carrying amount and the accumulated amortisation (aggregated with accumulated impairment losses) at the beginning and end of the period; and
- the line item(s) of the income statement in which the amortisation of intangible assets is included.

(IAS 38, 107)

For each class of intangible assets, and distinguishing between internally generated intangible assets and other intangible assets, an entity should disclose a reconciliation of the carrying amount at the beginning and end of the period showing:

- additions, indicating separately those from internal development and through business combinations;
- retirement and disposals;
- increases or decreases during the period resulting from revaluations and impairment losses recognised or reversed directly in equity;
- impairment losses recognised in the income statement during the period;
- impairment losses reversed in the income statement during the period;
- amortisation recognised during the period;

- net exchange differences arising on the translation of the financial statements of a foreign entity; and
- other changes in the carrying amount.

Comparative information is not required (IAS 38, 107).

> ***IASB improvements project***
>
> In its May 2002 improvements exposure draft, the IASB proposes to require a reconciliation of the carrying amount of the intangible fixed assets at the beginning and end of the period for the comparative period. It also proposes disclosure of the methods and significant assumptions applied in estimating the asset fair values.

An entity should disclose the aggregate amount of research and development expenditure recognised as an expense during the period (IAS 38, 115).

Extract 23.25 *Reconciliation of capitalised development costs*

Nokia, Finland, 31 December 2001 (IAS)

	2001 EURm	*2000 EURm*
Capitalized development costs		
Acquisition cost Jan 1	1,097	811
Additions	431	394
Disposals	−214	−108
Accumulated amortization Dec 31	−421	−457
Net carrying amount Dec 31	893	640

Extract 23.26 *Disclosure of research and development costs*

Volkswagen, Germany, 31 December 2001 (IAS)

Of the total research and development costs incurred in 2001, €2,180 million met the criteria for capitalization as stipulated by IAS.

The following amounts were charged to cost of sales:

€ million	*2001*	*2000*
Research costs and non-capitalized development costs	1,743	2,537
Amortization of development costs	917	852
Research and development costs charged to the income statement	2,660	3,389

If an intangible asset is amortised over more than twenty years, the entity should disclose:

- the reasons why the presumption that the useful life of an intangible asset will not exceed twenty years from the date when the asset is available for use is rebutted; and
- the factor(s) which played a significant role in determining the useful life of the asset.

(IAS 38, 111)

An entity should describe any individual intangible asset which is material to the financial statements of the enterprise as a whole and disclose the carrying amount and remaining amortisation period of that asset (IAS 38, 111).

For intangible assets acquired by way of a government grant and initially recognised at fair value, an entity should disclose:

- the fair value initially recognised for these assets;
- their carrying amount; and
- whether they are carried under the benchmark or the allowed alternative treatment for subsequent measurement.

An entity should disclose:

- the existence and carrying amounts of intangible assets whose title is restricted;
- the carrying amounts of intangible assets pledged as security for liabilities; and
- the amount of commitments for the acquisition of intangible assets.

(IAS 38, 111)

If intangible assets are carried at revalued amounts, an entity should disclose by class of intangible assets:

- the effective date of revaluation;
- the carrying amount of revalued intangible assets; and
- the carrying amount that would have been included in the financial statements had the revalued intangible assets been carried under the benchmark.

(IAS 38, 113 (a))

In addition, the entity should disclose the amount of the revaluation surplus that relates to intangible assets at the beginning and end of the period, indicating the changes during the period and any restrictions on the distribution of the balance to shareholders (IAS 38, 113).

Note

1 Brigid Curran, *A Comparative Study of Australian and International Accounting Standards – Challenges for Harmonisation*, Coopers & Lybrand, Australia, 1996, p52.

CHAPTER 24

Goodwill

24.1 RELEVANT STANDARD AND INTERPRETATION

IAS 22 *Business Combinations*
SIC 22 *Business Combinations – Subsequent Adjustment of Fair Values and Goodwill Initially Reported*

24.2 HISTORY

IAS 22 *Accounting for Business Combinations* (IAS 22 [1983]) was approved in 1983. It was reconsidered in the comparability and improvements project when the IASC decided that goodwill should be capitalised and amortised over a maximum of 20 years. The IASC also specified alternative treatments for dealing with negative goodwill. IAS 22 *Business Combinations* (IAS 22 [1993]) was approved in November 1993 and applied to financial statements for accounting periods beginning on or after 1 January 1995.

In July 1995, the IASC announced that, as part of a work plan agreed with IOSCO, it had decided to carry out a revision to those aspects of IAS 22 dealing with goodwill. This announcement came as a surprise given IOSCO's acceptance of IAS 22 [1993] and the SEC's acceptance of the use of goodwill amortisation requirements in IAS 22 [1993] by foreign registrants. The reason given for the decision was the need to make the amortisation requirements for goodwill consistent with those for intangible assets. At the time, however, the IASC had proposed that the amortisation requirements for intangible assets should be consistent with those for goodwill, a long-standing policy of the IASC.

The IASC did not begin its reconsideration of goodwill until it had received the comment letters on E50 *Intangible Assets*. Following its review of the comment letters, the IASC decided that the proposed 20-year limit on the useful life of intangible assets should be removed provided that such assets were subject to a detailed and systematic impairment test. It also decided that if such a test could be developed, it would consider deleting the then 20-year restriction on the useful life of goodwill (*IASC Update*, April 1996, p2). The IASC adopted this approach because it felt that it was difficult to distinguish some intangible assets from goodwill and in order to avoid opportunities for accounting arbitrage between IAS 22 and an IAS on intangible assets (*IASC Insight*, July 1996, p6).

While the IASC was developing the revised exposure draft, the European Commission published its comparison of IASs and EU directives. The EU contact committee identified the IAS 22 treatment of negative goodwill as one of only two conflicts between IASs and the directives[1]. Whereas IAS 22 [1993] required that negative goodwill that was treated as deferred income should be recognised as income on a systematic basis, the Seventh Directive established the specific cases in which the recognition of negative goodwill may be made in the income statement. The contact committee proposed that the Seventh Directive should be amended to bring it into line with the treatment required by IAS 22. However, the IASC decided to reconsider the requirements for negative goodwill in IAS 22 and the new requirements are closer to the existing text of the Seventh Directive.

The further revised IAS 22 *Business Combinations* was approved in July 1998 and applied to accounting periods commencing on or after 1 July 1999.

As explained in Chapter 16, the IASB is currently carrying out a two-phase project to achieve convergence of existing standards on business combinations. Among other things, the first phase seeks the convergence of existing standards on accounting for goodwill (and negative goodwill) and intangible assets acquired. An exposure draft for this phase is due to be published in November 2002 and will propose several significant changes to the accounting for goodwill and negative goodwill:

- the amortisation of goodwill should be prohibited;
- there should be an annual impairment test for goodwill;
- if an impairment is identified, goodwill should be written down to its implied value, that is the difference between the recoverable amount of the relevant cash generating unit and the fair value of the net assets that would be identified if the unit was acquired at the date of the impairment test;
- the reversal of impairment write-downs for goodwill should be prohibited; and
- any negative goodwill remaining after the reassessment of the identification and measurement of the identifiable net assets should be recognised immediately in the income statement as a gain.

The new requirements will be supported by more detailed and rigorous rules for the impairment test.

The exposure draft also proposes changes to the initial measurement of net assets acquired and the recognition of intangible assets and provisions which may affect the amount attributed to goodwill or negative goodwill. It also confirms that acquired in-process research and development should be included in goodwill unless it meets the definition and recognition criteria for intangible assets.

24.3 IOSCO

In June 1994, IOSCO advised the IASC that IAS 22 was acceptable for the purposes of the IOSCO core standards. However IOSCO identified the following suspense issues relating to goodwill and negative goodwill:

- the elimination of alternatives for the identification and measurement of the impairment of goodwill (this issue has been dealt with in IAS 36 and is now reflected in IAS 22); and
- the recognition of negative goodwill in income in the year when a special cost, not recognisable as a result of the business combination, is expected to be incurred (this issue has been dealt with in the revised IAS 22).

IAS 22 is included in 'IAS 2000' endorsed by IOSCO in May 2000. There are eight supplemental treatments:

- reconsideration of the amortisation requirements for goodwill and other intangible assets, which have a different nature – the approach in IAS 22 may encourage an entity not to allocate the cost of acquisition properly which may, in turn, lead to the incorrect assessment of any impairment;
- concerns about the appropriateness of goodwill lives exceeding 20 years;
- expansion of the requirements for negative goodwill relating to expected future costs to cases where subsequent changes are made to the acquirer's plan – disclosure is essential to the application of this approach, with a requirement to explain any changes to the original restructuring plan;
- clarification of the accounting for negative goodwill if the acquired assets are all, or substantially all, non-monetary and non-depreciable or amortisable, and the appropriateness of the accounting for negative goodwill, particularly the requirement to recognise negative goodwill on a non-level basis based on expectations of future expenses.

24.3.1 SEC

In 1994, in one of its concessions, the SEC decided that a foreign issuer which complies with IAS 22 [1993] on the amortisation of goodwill or negative goodwill need not reconcile to US GAAP on this particular item[2]. The concession applies only to the period of amortisation; it does not apply to the method of amortisation, the measurement of goodwill or negative goodwill or other aspects of accounting for goodwill. Furthermore, the amount of goodwill or negative goodwill must be determined in accordance with US GAAP, not IAS 22 (SEC 2001, C3).

The 1998 change in the requirements of IAS 22 raised the question as to whether the SEC would allow the same concession to a foreign issuer which adopts the revised IAS 22. Goodwill lives of 20 years or less continue to be eligible for the 1994 concession. In the rare case in which a foreign issuer concludes that goodwill lives exceed 20 years, the need for a reconciliation adjustment to US GAAP lives will depend on the specific facts and circumstances. An entity should be prepared to justify assertions that the 20-year presumption has been rebutted. The SEC is also likely to challenge a change in estimate of the useful life of goodwill to a longer period upon adoption of the revised IAS 22 (SEC 2001, C4a).

A foreign issuer in the United States is strongly advised to consult the SEC on a pre-filing basis if it has rebutted the 20-year presumption. Such consultations are particularly important if there is any likelihood that the SEC will require the restatement of the IFRS financial statements as well as a reconciliation to US GAAP.

As far as negative goodwill is concerned, the SEC requires a reconciliation to US GAAP when an entity recognises negative goodwill in the income statement on a method other than straight-line amortisation (SEC 2001, C4b). This requirement is likely to have a bigger impact with the revised IAS 22 than it had with IAS 22 [1993], indeed it may not be possible for an entity to comply with the revised IAS 22 and take advantage of the 1994 SEC concession on the amortisation of negative goodwill.

The revised IAS 22 requires the reversal of an impairment loss on goodwill if certain conditions exist. The SEC requires a foreign issuer which reverses any prior goodwill impairments to reconcile these reversals to US GAAP (which bans such reversals) (SEC 2001, C4c).

The SEC has not updated its concession for the recent change in US GAAP under which the amortisation of goodwill is prohibited (FAS 142, 50). Foreign issuers will probably want to reconcile to the new treatment, indeed some are known to have urged the IASB to adopt the same requirement, something which it now proposes to do. It seems likely, therefore, that the SEC's 1994 concession on the amortisation of goodwill will lapse.

24.4 IAS 22 IN BRIEF

Goodwill should be capitalised and amortised over its useful life with a rebuttable presumption that useful life does not exceed 20 years – pre-1995 goodwill may be written off to equity. Any excess of the amounts attributed to identifiable assets and liabilities over the fair value of the purchase consideration is treated as negative goodwill and negative goodwill should be recognised as income when future losses and expenses to which that negative goodwill relates are recognised – any remaining negative goodwill should be amortised over the weighted average useful lives of the identifiable, acquired depreciable and amortised assets (or in certain circumstances recognised as income immediately).

24.5 RECOGNITION OF GOODWILL

Any excess of the cost of the acquisition in a business combination over the amount at which the identifiable assets and liabilities acquired are measured on initial recognition should be described as goodwill and recognised as an asset (IAS 22, 41). The measurement of the identifiable assets and liabilities is dealt with in chapter 16.

The amount attributed to goodwill includes expenditure on an intangible asset which is acquired in the acquisition but which cannot be recognised as an identifiable asset because it does not meet the recognition criteria (IAS 38, 56(b)). Therefore under IFRSs, acquired research and development is included in goodwill rather than treated as either an identifiable asset or written off as an expense as would be the case under US GAAP.

Extract 24.1 *Acquired research and development*

Hoechst, Germany, 31 December 1996, reconciliation from IASs to US GAAP

Under IAS, research-in-process and development costs are not identified as an acquired asset in connection with the allocation of the purchase price but rather capitalized as goodwill and amortized over their expected useful lives. US GAAP requires the identification of research-in-process as a component of the purchase price allocation. Such costs that have no alternative future uses must be charged as an expense at the time of acquisition.

IAS 22 does not permit goodwill to be adjusted immediately against shareholders' interests. However, under the transitional provisions, goodwill which was adjusted against shareholders' interests in accounting periods beginning before 1 January 1995 need not be reinstated as goodwill.

There may be circumstances in which the initial amount of goodwill does not reflect future economic benefits which are expected to flow to the acquirer. For example, there may have been a decline, since negotiating the purchase consideration, in the expected future cash flows from the net identifiable assets being acquired. In such circumstances, the entity tests the goodwill for impairment under IAS 36 and accounts for any impairment loss (IAS 22, 53 and IAS 36, 59) – see chapter 25. Any impairment loss reduces the initial carrying amount of goodwill and is recognised immediately as an expense.

Example 24.1 *Immediate impairment of goodwill*

On 30 September 2002, A enters into a binding purchase agreement to acquire B with effect from 1 December 2002. The agreed purchase consideration is £20m and the aggregate fair value of the identifiable net assets acquired is £16m, leaving goodwill of £4m.

On 1 November 2002, the government announces new regulations which affect adversely and significantly the business of B. A is unable to renegotiate the purchase price. The government announcement is an indication of impairment. A tests the goodwill of £4m for impairment and concludes than an impairment loss of £3m has been incurred. Immediately on the acquisition of B, A recognises the loss of £3m as a reduction in the carrying amount of goodwill and as an expense in the income statement.

24.6 AMORTISATION OF GOODWILL

Goodwill should be amortised on a systematic basis over its useful life (IAS 22, 44). The straight-line method should be used unless there is persuasive evidence that another amortisation method is more appropriate in the circumstances (IAS 22, 45). In practice, virtually all entities use the straight-line basis (some in Australia have attempted to use a reverse sum of the digits method but this method has been banned by the Australian standard setters).

As goodwill represents a payment made by the acquirer in anticipation of future economic benefits, the useful life of goodwill is the period of time over which the acquirer expects to receive the future economic benefits for which it paid. Therefore, IAS 22 requires that the amortisation period should reflect the best estimate of the period during which future economic benefits are expected to flow to the entity (IAS 22, 44).

The choice of useful life requires consideration of many factors including:

- the nature and the foreseeable life of the acquired business;
- the stability and foreseeable life of the industry to which the goodwill relates;
- the effects of product obsolescence, changes in demand and other economic factors on the acquired business;
- the service life expectancies of key individuals or groups of employees and whether the acquired business could be efficiently managed by another management team;
- the level of maintenance expenditure or funding required to obtain the expected future economic benefits from the acquired business and the company's ability and intent to reach such a level;
- expected actions by competitors or potential competitors; and
- the period of control over the acquired business and legal, regulatory or contractual provisions affecting the useful life.

(IAS 22, 48)

The useful life of goodwill should not exceed 20 years unless that presumption can be rebutted (IAS 22, 44). The presumption is likely to be rebutted only 'in rare cases' and examples are likely to be 'difficult to find' (IAS 22, 50). It may be rebutted when the goodwill is so clearly related to an identifiable asset or group of identifiable assets. When the presumption is rebutted, the entity should estimate the recoverable amount of goodwill each year even when there are no other indicators that the goodwill is impaired (IAS 22, 56) – in other words, the goodwill is subject to an annual impairment test.

The useful life of goodwill is 'always finite' (IAS 22, 51). The IASC has rejected the approach adopted in FRS 10 in the UK in which an infinite life may be used provided that the carrying amount is tested for impairment each year. The IASC believes that goodwill should always be amortised and that impairment tests should not be used as a replacement for a systematic allocation of cost (IAS 22 *Basis for Conclusions*, para 46).

IASB business combinations project

In phase one of its business combinations project, the IASB is proposing that the amortisation of goodwill should be prohibited and that there should, instead, be an annual impairment test.

Extract 24.2 *Amortisation of goodwill*

Schering, Germany, 31 December 2001 (IAS)

Goodwill is capitalised and amortized on a straight-line basis over periods of up to 15 years. In determining the economic useful life of goodwill, the Group considers contractual obligations, the period in which synergies are expected to be realized, and the strategic importance of the acquisition.

Extract 24.3 *Amortisation of goodwill*

Lonza Group, Switzerland, 31 December 2001 (IAS)

Goodwill. At the time of their initial recognition, the assets and liabilities of consolidated subsidiaries are recorded at their estimated fair value. Goodwill represents the difference between the purchase price and fair value of the net assets acquired. Goodwill is capitalized and amortized on a straight-line basis over its estimated useful life not exceeding 20 years.

Extract 24.4 *Amortisation of goodwill*

Renault, France, 31 December 2000 (some IAS)

Goodwill arising on first inclusion of subsidiaries or companies accounted for by the equity method represents the difference, at acquisition date, between the purchase cost of shares (including expenses, after income tax effect) and the proportion of assets and liabilities acquired, estimated at fair value. It is amortized on a straight-line basis over a duration specific to each company, but not longer than 20 years.

Extract 24.5 *Amortisation of goodwill*

Recordati, Italy, 31 December 2000 (IAS)

Any difference between the purchase cost of an equity investment and the subsidiary's equity at current value at the date of acquisition was debited or credited to consolidated shareholders equity until 31 December 1993; while it is accounted for among non-current intangible assets from 31 December 1994 and amortized on a straight-line basis over a period of no more than 10 years.

Extract 24.6 *Amortisation of goodwill*

Danisco, Denmark, 30 April 2001 (IAS)

Any excess cost of acquisition over the fair value of the net assets acquired is capitalised as goodwill or consolidated goodwill in the acquisition year and amortised systematically in the profit and loss account after an individual assessment of the estimated life of the asset, up to a maximum of 20 years.

...

The amortisation period of up to 20 years for goodwill and consolidated goodwill is determined on the basis of the management's experience within the group's business areas. In the opinion of the group's management it reflects the best estimate for the useful lives of the acquired undertakings.

Extract 24.7 *Amortisation of goodwill*

Interbrew, Belgium, 31 December 2000 (some IAS including IAS 22)

Goodwill represents the excess of the cost of an acquisition over the fair value of the Group's share of the net assets of the acquired subsidiary/associate at the date of acquisition. Goodwill is amortised using the straight-line method over its estimated useful life. Goodwill arising on the acquisition of breweries is generally amortised over 20 years. Goodwill arising on the acquisition of distribution companies is generally amortised over 5 years. The goodwill which arose from the acquisitions of Labatt Brewing Company Ltd, Interbrew UK Ltd (ex-Whitbread) and Bass Holdings Ltd/Bass Beers Worldwide Ltd (ex-Bass) is amortised over 40 years due to the strategic importance of these acquisitions to the long-term development of the Group, the nature and stability of the markets in which these companies operate and their position on these markets.

Extract 24.8 *Amortisation of goodwill*

Novartis, Switzerland, 31 December 2001 (IAS)

Goodwill, which is denominated in the local currency of the related acquisition, is amortized to income through administration and general overheads on a straight-line basis over its useful life. The amortization period is determined at the date of acquisition, based upon the particular circumstances, and ranges from 5 to 20 years. Goodwill relating to acquisitions arising prior to January 1 1995 has been fully written off against reserves.

Extract 24.9 *Amortisation of goodwill*

OTP Bank, Hungary, 31 December 2000 (IAS)

Goodwill, which represents the residual cost of the acquisition after recognizing the acquirer's interest in the fair value of the identifiable assets and liabilities acquired, is held as an intangible asset and amortized to the consolidated Statement of Operations, in anticipation of future economic benefits, on a straight-line basis over a period not exceeding five years or until the date of disposal of the acquired company, whichever is the shorter.

Extract 24.10 *Amortisation of goodwill*

Jardine Matheson, Hong Kong, 31 December 2001 (IAS)

Goodwill represents the difference between the cost of an acquisition and the fair value of the Group's share of the net assets of the acquired subsidiary undertaking, associate or joint venture at the effective date of acquisition. Goodwill on acquisitions occurring on or after 1st January 1995 is reported in the balance sheet as a separate asset or included within associates and joint ventures and is amortised using the straight line method over its estimated useful life which is generally between 5 and 20 years. Goodwill on acquisitions which occurred prior to 1st January 1995 was taken directly to reserves.

Extract 24.11 *Amortisation of goodwill*

Nokia, Finland, 31 December 2001 (IAS)

Goodwill is amortized on a straight-line basis over its expected useful life. Useful lives vary between two and five years depending upon the nature of the acquisition, unless a longer period not exceeding 20 years can be justified. Expected useful lives are reviewed at each balance sheet date and where these differ significantly from previous estimates, amortisation periods are changed accordingly.

24.7 IMPAIRMENT OF GOODWILL

The determination of impairment losses for goodwill is dealt with in accordance with IAS 36. When there is an indication that the goodwill is impaired (or the goodwill is being amortised over more than 20 years), the entity should estimate the recoverable amount of goodwill. In practice, this usually means estimating the recoverable amount of the cash-generating unit to which the goodwill belongs and performing the 'bottom up' and 'top down' tests in IAS 36. When the carrying amount of the cash generating unit exceeds its recoverable amount an impairment loss is recognised which is used, first, to reduce the carrying amount of

IASB business combinations project

In phase one of its business combinations project, the IASB is proposing a more detailed and rigorous impairment test for goodwill and the prohibition of the reversal of impairment write-downs of goodwill.

goodwill. An impairment loss on goodwill is reversed only if the loss was caused by a specific external event of an exceptional nature and subsequent external events have reversed the effect of that event.

Extract 24.12 *Impairment of goodwill*

Sony, Japan, 31 March 1995

Since its acquisition in November 1989, there has been slower than expected growth of the businesses of the Pictures Group, higher than expected levels of operating costs and expenses, and higher than anticipated capital investment requirements. The deterioration experienced in the year ended March 31, 1994 gave rise to a thorough internal review. Similar results experienced in the first half of the fiscal year, together with the resignation of the Pictures Group top management, caused the company to conclude that additional funding would be needed to attain acceptable levels of profitability. In light of the level of investment and likelihood of additional funding requirements, the company determined in the second quarter of the fiscal year that a discounted cash flows method provided a preferable measurement of the recoverability of its investment in acquired businesses because this method recognizes the effect of the cost of capital. The discounted future results of the Pictures Group, based on the company's forecasts, were not sufficient to justify the carrying value as of the end of the second quarter.

In formulating the financial forecasts, the company considered historical performance and the medium-term plans as well as the longer-term economic outlook. These forecasts took into consideration market conditions during the second quarter of the fiscal year as well as foreseeable opportunities for future growth in existing lines of business. Although the company believed it could fund the Pictures Group over the entire forecast period, it had not determined whether additional investments would be made in areas other than the existing lines of business.

The operating cash flows were based upon the short-term plans in effect in the second quarter of the fiscal year that called for a substantial improvement in earnings through recovered market share and cost reductions. For the longer term, it was assumed that low levels of inflation during the second quarter would continue and that the industry would grow at a slightly better rate than the economy as a whole. At the end of the forecast period a residual was included based on an appropriate multiple of the final year's results.

The company believes that the forecast results, based on the historical financial trends and market conditions during the second quarter, were the best estimate of the company's future performance. In arriving at the discounted net present value, the company used a discount rate of 9% reflecting its weighted average cost of funds, including a factor for equity allocated to the Pictures Group commensurate with the risk associated with that business as indicated by reference to comparable industry statistics.

Over the entire forecast period, after giving effect to significant additional investment required to complete the investment program contemplated during the second quarter of the fiscal year, the company forecast total operating cash flows of ¥4,166,374 million ($46,813,191 thousand). Based on such forecasts, the cumulative results of the Pictures Group's operating cash flows on a discounted net present value basis of ¥309,005 million ($3,471,966 thousand) as of September 30, 1994 were insufficient to recover a significant portion of the investment. The amount of the resultant shortfall reduced the goodwill balance arising from the Pictures Group to ¥85,197 million ($957,270 thousand) as of September 30, 1994.

Extract 24.13 *Annual assessment of goodwill*

L'Oreal, France, 31 December 1994

Each year, the Group reviews purchased goodwill on the basis of several different criteria reflecting the particularities of each sector in which it operates. These mainly concern changes in sales and profitability. At least once a year, the Group analyses changes in actual and projected sales in local currencies compared to other Group companies or similar businesses and by reference to distribution channels and different product markets. Provision is made for any permanent diminution in value, determined on the basis of these analyses in conjunction with detailed profitability analyses. This general method is applied consistently from one year to the next.

Extract 24.14 *Annual assessment of goodwill*

VA Technologie, Austria, 31 December 2001 (IAS)

In accordance with IAS 22, a maximum service life of 20 years is assumed for positive goodwill. Furthermore, remaining goodwill is examined with regard to its future economic usefulness on each balance sheet date. The discounted cash flow method is used to examine future economic usefulness on each balance sheet date. The smallest cash generating unit is identified in each case, in order to allow classification of the goodwill examined on what is probably a consistent basis.

24.8 RECOGNITION OF NEGATIVE GOODWILL

Negative goodwill can be defined as any excess of the amount at which the identifiable assets and liabilities acquired are measured on initial recognition over the cost of the acquisition. However, as explained below, some of the excess may not be described as negative goodwill in the financial statements. The IASC's requirements for negative goodwill have changed significantly in each of the different versions of IAS 24. As the transitional provisions in both IAS 22 [1993] and the revised IAS 22 do not require the restatement of prior periods, the requirements of all three IASs are described. The requirements are likely to change again as a result of phase one of the IASB's business combinations project.

24.8.1 IAS 22 [1983]

IAS 22 [1983] allowed all negative goodwill to be adjusted immediately against shareholders' interests, in practice added to those interests (IAS 22 [1983], 40(b)). However, under the transitional provisions in both IAS 22 [1993] and the revised IAS 22, negative goodwill which was added to shareholders' interests in accounting periods beginning before 1 January 1995 need not be reinstated.

IAS 22 [1983] also allowed negative goodwill to be either:

- treated as deferred income and amortised on a systematic basis; or
- allocated over individual non-monetary assets acquired in proportion to their fair values.

(IAS 22 [1983], 40 and 42)

These two treatment were, in substance, the allowed alternative and benchmark treatments in IAS 22 [1993].

24.8.2 IAS 22 [1993]

Under the benchmark treatment in IAS 22 [1993], the carrying amount of the non-monetary assets acquired were reduced proportionately until the negative goodwill was eliminated (IAS 22 [1993], 49). The effect of this treatment was twofold:

- it reduced the carrying amounts of the non-monetary assets acquired to their costs to the acquirer; and
- the discount was recognised as a reduction in expenses when the assets were sold or as the future economic benefits embodied in the assets were consumed – for example, in the case of inventories, the discount was recognised when the inventories were sold and in the case of plant and equipment, the discount was recognised through lower depreciation charges over the useful life of the plant and equipment.

To the extent that negative goodwill was deducted from the carrying amount of the identifiable assets and liabilities acquired, it was not described as negative goodwill in the financial statements.

Example 24.2 *Negative goodwill – benchmark treatment (IAS 22 [1993])*

A acquires 100% of B for $100m. The fair values of the identifiable assets are as follows:

	$m
Property	70
Inventories	50
Receivables	22
Payables	(30)
Total	112

The fair values of the identifiable net assets acquired exceed the cost of acquisition by $12m. Therefore, the carrying amounts of the non-monetary assets – property and inventories – are reduced proportionately by a total of $12m. Therefore, property is reduced to $63m and inventories to $45m.

The discount on the acquisition will be realised when the inventories are sold ($5m) and either during the useful life of the property as reduced depreciation charges or on the eventual sale of the property ($7m).

Example 24.3 *Negative goodwill – benchmark treatment (IAS 22 [1993])*

A acquires 100% of B for $80m. The fair values of the identifiable assets are as follows:

	$m
Property	10
Inventories	15
Receivables	100
Payables	(10)
Total	115

The fair values of the identifiable net assets acquired exceeds the cost of acquisition by $35m. Therefore, the carrying amounts of the non-monetary assets – property and inventories – should be reduced proportionately but they cannot be reduced below zero. Both the property and inventories are reduced to zero. This leaves a balance of $10m which is described as negative goodwill and treated as deferred income.

The discount on the acquisition will be realised when the inventories are sold ($15m) and either during the useful life of the property as reduced depreciation charges or on the eventual sale of the property ($10m). The balance of $10m will be realised through the amortisation of the negative goodwill.

Under the benchmark treatment in IAS 22 [1993], any excess which remained after reducing the carrying amount of non-monetary assets acquired to cost was described as negative goodwill and treated as deferred income (IAS 22 [1993], 49).

Example 24.4 *Negative goodwill – allowed alternative treatment (IAS 22 [1993])*

A acquires 100% of B for $100m. The fair values of the identifiable assets are as follows:

	$m
Property	70
Inventories	50
Receivables	22
Payables	(30)
Total	112

The fair values of the identifiable net assets acquired exceeds the cost of acquisition by $12m. The excess is described as negative goodwill and treated as deferred income and included in the income statement by means of the amortisation of the negative goodwill.

Under the allowed alternative treatment in IAS 22 [1993], the whole of the excess was described as negative goodwill and treated as deferred income (IAS 22 [1993], 51).

24.8.3 Revised IAS 22

The revised IAS 22 requires a new approach to negative goodwill which is a combination of the benchmark and allowed alternative treatments in IAS 22 [1993]. It is important to ensure that the initial calculation of negative goodwill does not indicate that identifiable assets have been overstated or identifiable liabilities have been omitted or understated. Therefore, the fair values attributed to the identifiable assets and liabilities should be re-evaluated and, if necessary, revised before dealing with the negative goodwill (IAS 22, 60).

The new approach reflects the entity's best estimate of the circumstances which gave rise to the negative goodwill (IAS 22 *Basis for Conclusions*, 89). The IASC identified two circumstances which may have caused the acquirer's interest in the fair values of identifiable assets and liabilities to exceed the cost of acquisition:

- the acquirer has made a bargain purchase or lucky buy; or

- the cost of acquisition was affected by the acquirer's expectations of poor trading results, or of future expenses, which cannot be recognised as identifiable liabilities under IAS 22 at the date of acquisition.

To the extent that negative goodwill relates to expectations of future losses and expenses which are identified in the acquirer's plan for the acquisition and can be measured reliably, but do not represent identifiable liabilities at the date of acquisition, that portion of negative goodwill should be recognised as income when the future losses and expenses are recognised (IAS 22, 61). So, for example, if the acquirer expects the acquiree to make a loss in the first year of its control over the acquiree and that loss is included in the acquirer's plans, the equivalent amount of negative goodwill may be recognised in the same period as the loss. Similarly, if the acquirer plans a restructuring of the acquiree but has not announced the main features of the plan in time to recognise a provision, the equivalent amount of goodwill is recognised as income in the same period in which the restructuring expenses are incurred.

To the extent that negative goodwill does not relate to such identifiable expected future losses and expenses:

- the amount of negative goodwill not exceeding the fair values of acquired identifiable non-monetary assets should be recognised as negative goodwill on the balance sheet; and

Example 24.5 *Negative goodwill*

A acquires 100% of B for $100m. The fair values of the identifiable assets are as follows:

	$m
Property	70
Inventories	50
Receivables	22
Payables	(30)
Total	112

The fair values of the identifiable net assets acquired exceed the cost of acquisition by $12m.

If A expects, and plans for, B to make a loss of $12m in the first year of control, the negative goodwill is recognised as income in that year.

If A does not expect, or plan for, B to make a loss in the first year (or the expected and planned loss does not occur), the negative goodwill is recognised as such on the balance sheet.

- the amount of negative goodwill in excess of the fair values of acquired identifiable non-monetary assets should be recognised as income immediately – this is a new possibility which was not permitted in earlier versions of IAS 22.

(IAS 22, 62)

> ***IASB business combinations project***
>
> In phase one of its business combinations project, the IASB is proposing that any negative goodwill remaining after the reassessment of the identification and measurement of the identifiable net assets should be recognised immediately in the income statement as a gain. Under this approach, negative goodwill would never be recognised on the balance sheet.

24.9 AMORTISATION OF NEGATIVE GOODWILL

24.9.1 IAS 22 [1993]

Under both the benchmark and the allowed alternative treatments in IAS 22 [1993], any amounts recognised as negative goodwill were amortised on a systematic basis over a period not exceeding 5 years unless a longer period, not exceeding 20 years from the date of acquisition, can be justified (IAS 22 [1993], 49 and 51). The arbitrary limit on the amortisation period of negative goodwill was the same as that for goodwill and the choice of the limits reflected the same considerations (although it would have been more logical to require a period of 20 years unless a shorter period, not less than 5 years, could be justified).

24.9.2 Revised IAS 22

Under the revised IAS 22, negative goodwill which is recognised as such is amortised over the remaining weighted average useful life of the identifiable acquired depreciable and amortisable assets. There is no arbitrary limit. Furthermore, while the amount recognised as negative goodwill is limited to the amount of the fair values of the acquired identifiable non-monetary assets, the amortisation period is determined by reference to the useful lives of the acquired depreciable and amortisable assets. This difference arises for practical reasons, in particular it overcomes the difficulty of estimating average useful life when some of the acquired assets have indefinite useful lives, for example land (IAS 22 *Basis for Conclusions*, para 85).

Extract 24.15 *Amortisation of negative goodwill*

MOL, Hungary, 31 December 2001 (IAS)

Negative goodwill is recognised in the accompanying consolidated statement of operations as follows:

- to the extent that negative goodwill relates to expected future losses and expenses that are identified in the Company's plan for the acquisition and can be measured reliably that portion of negative goodwill is recognised as income when the future losses and expenses are recognised.
- the amount of negative goodwill not exceeding the fair values of acquired identifiable non-monetary assets is recognised as income on a systematic basis over the remaining weighted average useful life of the identifiable acquired depreciable/amortizable assets.
- the amount of negative goodwill in excess of the fair values of acquired identifiable non-monetary assets is recognised as income immediately.

24.10 TRANSITIONAL PROVISIONS – GOODWILL

The restatement of goodwill arising prior to the effective dates of the Standards is not required by either IAS 22 [1993] or the revised IAS 22. If restatements are made, they must be made for all amounts of goodwill and negative goodwill.

24.10.1 IAS 22 [1993]

When an entity applied IAS 22 [1993] for the first time, it was encouraged, but was not required, to apply the IAS retrospectively (IAS 22 [1993], 79). An entity which did apply IAS 22 [1993] retrospectively would have had to:

- reinstate any goodwill which had previously been adjusted against shareholders' interests in accordance with IAS 22 [1983] and amortise that goodwill in accordance with IAS 22 [1993]; or
- reduce the useful life of any existing goodwill which had been recognised as an asset.

Under the transitional provisions in IAS 22 [1993], an entity which was applying the revised IAS for the first time was allowed to:

- deem that the balance of any pre-existing goodwill had been properly determined; and

- account thereafter for that pre-existing goodwill in accordance with the revised IAS [1993].

(IAS 22 [1993], 79)

An entity taking advantage of the transitional provisions was not required to reinstate goodwill which had previously been adjusted against shareholders' interests in accordance with IAS 22 [1983]. It was required, however, to amortise pre-existing goodwill which had been recognised as an asset over the shorter of the remaining life, as specified in the entity's amortisation policy, and the period specified in IAS 22 [1993].

Extract 24.16 *Use of IAS 22 [1993] transitional provisions*

Trans Zambezi, Zimbabwe, 30 September 1996 (IAS)

Goodwill arising on consolidation represents the difference (positive or negative) between the fair value of the consideration paid over the fair value of the identifiable net assets acquired at the date of acquisition. Goodwill arising on the consolidation of subsidiaries and associates acquired before 30 September 1995 has been written off against non-distributable reserves. In line with changes to International Accounting Standard 22 which came into effect in the current financial period, goodwill arising on acquisitions from 1 October 1995 is amortised through the profit and loss account on a straight line basis over the estimated economic life determined on a case by case basis (reviewed annually) but which will not exceed 20 years. Current acquisitions have been amortised over five years.

As permitted by IAS 22, the Company has elected not to apply the change in policy retrospectively. Had retrospective application been applied, the impact would have been to reduce retained profits as at 30 September 1996 by US$0.37 million and to reduce net assets by US$2.3 million.

24.10.2 Revised IAS 22

The transitional provisions in the revised IAS 22 are far more complex partly because they have to deal with goodwill which has already been accounted for under IAS 22 [1983] and IAS 22 [1993] (including the transitional provisions in IAS 22 [1993]).

Goodwill which was adjusted against shareholders' interests in accordance with IAS 22 [1983] need not be reinstated (IAS 22 [1993], 79 and IAS 22, 99, 1(a)). This is the simplest approach to adopt. If any of this goodwill is reinstated, the amount reinstated, reduced by any accumulated amortisation, should be determined in accordance with the revised IAS 24. This includes any goodwill which was reinstated following the adoption of IAS 22 [1993].

Goodwill which was recognised as an asset in accordance with IAS 22 [1983] or IAS 22 [1993] but not at the amount required by the revised

IAS 22 need not be restated. If it is restated, it must be recomputed in accordance with the revised IAS 24. If it is not restated, the amount assigned to that goodwill and the accumulated amortisation is deemed to have been properly determined (unless the previous amortisation charge was deemed to be nil). The resulting carrying amount should be amortised in accordance with the revised IAS 22.

IASB business combinations project

In phase one of its business combinations project, the IASB is proposing that the prohibition on the amortisation of goodwill and annual impairment test for goodwill should apply to goodwill arising on acquisitions for business combinations occurring both prior to, and after, the effective date of the revised IFRS. However, it is not proposing to require retrospective application with respect to goodwill arising on business combinations prior to the effective date of the revised IFRS.

24.11 TRANSITIONAL PROVISIONS – NEGATIVE GOODWILL

The restatement of negative goodwill can be extremely complex and can require judgements about decisions made several years ago. Neither IAS 22 [1993] nor the revised IAS 22 require restatement and it is recommended that restatements are not made. If restatements are made, they must be made for all amounts of goodwill and negative goodwill.

24.11.1 IAS 22 [1993]

When an entity applied IAS 22 [1993] for the first time, it was encouraged, but not required, to apply the standard retrospectively (IAS 22 [1993], 79). Retrospective application was difficult in the case of the benchmark treatment in IAS 22 [1993] as it would have meant recalculating the carrying amount of non-monetary assets and the way in which those adjusted carrying amounts would have been reflected in the income statement. In the case of the allowed alternative trea ment in IAS 22 [1993], retrospective application was broadly similar to the retrospective application of goodwill and, therefore, much easier.

Under the transitional provisions in IAS 22 [1993], an entity which was applying the revised IAS for the first time was allowed to:

- deem that the balance of any pre-existing negative goodwill had been properly determined; and

- account thereafter for that pre-existing negative goodwill in accordance with IAS 22 [1993].

(IAS 22 [1993], 79)

An entity taking advantage of the transitional provisions was not required to reinstate negative goodwill which had previously been added to shareholders' interests in accordance with IAS 22 [1983] nor to adjust the carrying amounts of non-monetary assets. It was required, however, to amortise pre-existing negative goodwill over the shorter of the remaining life, as specified in the entity's amortisation policy, and the period specified in IAS 22 [1993]. For example, an entity which had previously amortised negative goodwill over, say, 40 years had the choice between the retrospective application of IAS 22 [1993] (with a possible change in accounting policy) and writing off the unamortised balance over the shorter of its existing remaining life and 5 or 20 years (whichever is appropriate).

24.11.2 Revised IAS 22

The transitional provisions in the revised IAS 22 are far more complex partly because they have to deal with negative goodwill already accounted for under IAS 22 [1983] and IAS 22 [1993] and partly because the possible treatments have changed so much.

The reinstatement of negative goodwill which was added to shareholders' interests under IAS 22 [1983] is encouraged, but not required. If the negative goodwill is reinstated:

- the amount assigned to the negative goodwill at the date of acquisition under the revised IAS 22 should be determined and recognised as negative goodwill; and
- the accumulated amount of negative goodwill recognised as income since the date of acquisition under the revised IAS 22 should be determined and recognised.

The restatement of negative goodwill which was recognised initially as deferred income under IAS 22 [1983] is encouraged, but not required. If the negative goodwill is not restated, the amount assigned to the negative goodwill at the date of acquisition is deemed to have been properly determined.

Restatement of negative goodwill dealt with under IAS 22 [1993] is encouraged, but not required. If the negative goodwill is restated:

- the amount that would have been assigned to the negative goodwill at the date of acquisition under the revised IAS 22 should be restated and recognised;

- the related accumulated amount of negative goodwill that would have been recognised as income under IAS 22 should be restated and recognised; and
- any remaining carrying amount of the negative goodwill should be recognised as income over the remaining weighted average useful life of the identifiable depreciable/amortisable non-monetary assets acquired.

If the negative goodwill is not restated, the amount assigned to the negative goodwill (if any) at the date of acquisition is deemed to have been properly determined.

> ***IASB business combinations project***
>
> In phase one of its business combinations project, the IASB is proposing that all previously recognised negative goodwill remaining as a deferred credit in the balance sheet as at the effective date of the revised IFRS should be derecognised with a corresponding adjustment to retained earnings.

24.12 DISCLOSURE

24.12.1 Goodwill

An entity should disclose:

- the amortisation period(s) for goodwill;
- if goodwill is amortised over more than 20 years, the reason why the presumption that the useful life will not exceed 20 years has been rebutted and the factors which played a significant role in determining the useful life;
- when goodwill is not amortised on the straight-line basis, the basis used and reason why that basis is more appropriate than the straight-line basis;
- the line item in the income statement in which amortisation of goodwill is included;
- a reconciliation of the carrying amount of goodwill at the beginning and end of the period showing:
  - the gross amount and the accumulated amortisation (aggregated with accumulated impairment losses) at the beginning of the period;

- any additional goodwill received during the period;
- any adjustments resulting from subsequent identification or changes in value of identifiable assets and liabilities;
- any goodwill derecognised on the disposal of all or part of the business to which it relates during the period;
- amortisation recognised during the period;
- impairment losses recognised during the period;
- impairment losses reversed during the period;
- other changes in the carrying amount during the period; and
- the gross amount and the accumulated amortisation (aggregated with accumulated impairment losses) at the end of the period.

(IAS 22, 88)

Comparative information is currently not required for this reconciliation (IAS 22, 88) but the IASB proposes in phase one of its business combinations project to require disclosure.

24.12.2 Negative Goodwill

An entity should disclose:

- the extent to which negative goodwill is recognised as income to match losses and expenses which were identified in the entity's plan for the acquisition, together with a description of and the amount and timing of the losses and expenses;
- the amortisation period(s) for negative goodwill;
- the line item in the income statement in which amortisation of negative goodwill is included;
- a reconciliation of the carrying amount of goodwill at the beginning and end of the period showing:
  - the gross amount and the accumulated amortisation at the beginning of the period;
  - any additional negative goodwill recognised during the period;
  - any adjustments resulting from subsequent identification or changes in value of identifiable assets and liabilities;
  - any negative goodwill derecognised on the disposal of all or part of the business to which it relates during the period;
  - amortisation recognised during the period showing separately the amount recognised as income to match losses and expenses which were identified in the entity's plan for the acquisition;
  - other changes in the carrying amount during the period; and
  - the gross amount and the accumulated amortisation (aggregated with accumulated impairment losses) at the end of the period.

(IAS 22, 91)

Comparative information is not required for this reconciliation (IAS 22, 88).

Notes

[1] Contact Committee on the Accounting Directives, *An Examination of the Conformity Between International Accounting Standards and the European Accounting Directives*, European Commission, Brussels, 1996, pp12–13.

[2] Securities and Exchange Commission, *Reconciliation of the Accounting by Foreign Private Issuers for Business Combinations*, International Series Release 759 (13 December 1994), Washington, SEC.

CHAPTER 25

Impairment of Assets

25.1 RELEVANT STANDARD AND INTERPRETATION

IAS 36 *Impairment of Assets*
SIC 14 *Property, Plant and Equipment – Compensation for the Impairment or Loss of Items*

25.2 HISTORY

All IASs which have dealt with long-term assets have dealt with impairment issues. For example, IAS 16 [1993] required that the carrying amount of an item or group of identical items of property, plant and equipment should be written down to recoverable amount when that amount had declined below the carrying amount of the item or group of items. Similar requirements were included in other IASs.

25.2.1 IAS 36

During the early 1990s, both the improvements steering committee and IOSCO identified the need for more specific guidance on impairment issues. Therefore, following its review of IOSCO's comments on existing IASs, the IASC decided in November 1994 to consider a new project on the impairment of long-lived assets (*IASC Insight*, December 1994, p13). The project was included in the work programme agreed with IOSCO in July 1995 and was started in 1996.

The intention of the project was to retain the basic rule that assets should not be carried at more than they are expected to recover. Therefore the project focused on the determination of recoverable amount and whether discounting should be required, allowed or prohibited in determining that amount. The project gained increased importance as a result of the IASC's decision to remove the 20-year ceiling on the amortisation of goodwill and intangible assets if an appropriate impairment test could be developed (*IASC Update*, April 1996, p2).

The start of the impairment project coincided with the IASC's decision to accelerate its work programme so as to complete IOSCO's core standards by mid-1998. As a result, the IASC did not publish a DSOP on the impairment of assets and restricted the comment period on the exposure draft (E55) to three, rather than the usual, six months.

IAS 36 *Impairment of Assets* was approved in 1998 and applied to accounting periods beginning on or after 1 July 1999. The IASC also approved revised versions of IAS 16, IAS 28 and IAS 31 which incorporate consequential changes. In particular, they require that IAS 36 should be used for determining whether property, plant and equipment, investments in associates and interests in joint ventures have been impaired and if so, the resulting adjustments and accounting. IAS 38 and the IAS 22 rely on IAS 36 for the impairment of intangible assets and goodwill.

IASB improvements and business combinations projects

In its May 2002 improvements exposure draft, the IASB proposes several minor changes to IAS 36 dealing with internal indicators of asset impairments and the determination of value in use.

In phase one of its business combinations project, the IASB proposes to prohibit the amortisation of goodwill and require an annual impairment test. As a consequence it also proposes several changes to the application of the impairment test for goodwill.

25.2.2 G4+1

During the development of IAS 36, the IASC participated in the development of a G4+1 discussion paper on asset impairment[1]. The paper compared the actual or then proposed standards of Australia, Canada, New Zealand, the United Kingdom, the United States and the IASC. One of the interesting conclusions which can be drawn from that paper is that:

- entities reporting under US GAAP are less likely to make impairment write-downs than companies reporting under UK GAAP or IASs – US GAAP allows a higher impairment trigger point than do UK GAAP and IASs; and

- when entities reporting under US GAAP make an impairment write-down, they record bigger losses than companies reporting under UK GAAP or IASs – US GAAP requires a lower measurement of the impaired asset.

25.3 IOSCO

Impairment was included in IOSCO's list of core standards (*IASC Insight*, December 1993, p5). In June 1994, IOSCO advised the IASC that a project to eliminate alternatives for identifying and measuring impairment of the cost or carrying amount of certain assets in existing IASs was required in order to complete the core standards. IOSCO believed that the project should consider the adequacy of the existing guidance on the impairment of property, plant and equipment (IAS 16 [1993]), goodwill (IAS 22 [1993]), leases (IAS 17 [1981]) and intangible assets. IOSCO's consideration of IAS 36 is likely to be one of the more critical parts of its assessment of the core standards.

IAS 36 is included in 'IAS 2000' endorsed by IOSCO in May 2000. There are four supplemental treatments:

- concerns about the appropriateness of measuring impairment losses based on an asset's recoverable amount rather than fair value;
- concerns about the need for disclosure of how a cash generating unit (CGU) is determined and the accumulated impairment losses of tangible assets, intangible assets and goodwill – the disclosure of the carrying amount and the accumulated impairment losses of each CGU should be encouraged;
- concerns about the appropriateness of reversing impairment losses (in its business combinations exposure draft, the IASB proposes to prohibit the reversal of impairment losses on goodwill); and
- concerns about the nature, reasons for and effects of any material change in the allocation of goodwill to CGUs.

25.4 IMPACT OF IAS 36

As IASs already required that assets should not be carried in excess of recoverable amount, the adoption of IAS 36 did not give rise to a change in accounting policy and its impact should not have been as great as that of other new IASs. Experience in applying the equivalent new US standard (FAS 121) suggested that the identification of cash generating units was likely to have the greatest effect in applying IAS 36. FAS 121 forced a number of US companies, as well as some foreign issuers in the United

States, to recognise impairment losses on smaller groups of assets where previously they had made their impairment assessments on larger groups of assets.

Nurnberg and Dittmar[2] found that US oil and gas companies, restaurant chains, retail food and grocery chains, and service companies recognised more impairment losses than in the past. For example, they reported that PepsiCo had switched to determining impairment losses at the individual restaurant level which had led to a $68m write-down. Similarly, Penn Traffic reported $46.8m impairment losses after determining such losses on a supermarket by supermarket basis rather than an operating division basis.

The author's research has shown the following consequences of foreign companies applying FAS 121[3]:

- a switch from carrying out impairment tests on a country by country basis to a field by field basis which led TOTAL to recognise a loss of FFr 1,547m (FFr 758m net of taxes) for the impairment of oil and gas properties (Nurnberg and Dittmar reported that Texaco, Chevron and Phillips Petroleum were affected in the same way);
- a switch from determining impairment losses on a business by business basis to the 'lowest operational level' forced Hanson to recognise a £3.26 billion reduction in the carrying value of mineral and coal deposits; and
- the adoption of FAS 121 led Norsk Hydro to recognise in its 1995 US GAAP financial statements an impairment loss of NOK 755m as result of a decline in the expected future revenues from the Lille-Frigg oil field.

The adoption of more conservative accounting polices (even within IFRS financial statements) by some entities, particularly in continental Europe, may lessen the likelihood of their having to recognise further impairment losses on the adoption of IAS 36. It may even be the case that they will have to reverse some existing impairments with a resulting credit to the income statement.

The choice among different accounting policies allowed by IFRSs may also affect the likelihood of impairment losses, for example:

- an entity which revalues property, plant and equipment under the allowed alternative treatment in IAS 16 is more likely to have to recognise impairment losses than an entity which bases the carrying amount of property, plant and equipment on historical cost (although the revaluation exercise itself should deal with impairment issues);
- an entity which recognises assets donated by a government at fair value is more likely to have to recognise impairment losses than an entity which recognises such assets at a nominal value (see IAS 20); and

- an entity which capitalises borrowing costs under the allowed alternative treatment in IAS 23 is more likely to have to recognise impairment losses than an entity which recognises all borrowing costs as an expense.

25.5 IAS 36 IN BRIEF

IAS 36 adopts the same three-stage approach to asset impairments which entities should have been taking in the past. However, IAS 36 contains substantially more detailed requirements about the assessment of indications of impairment, the determination of recoverable amount and the subsequent accounting.

An entity should assess first whether there is any indication that an asset may be impaired, that is that the recoverable amount of the asset may be less than its carrying amount. The assessment should be carried out as at each balance sheet date. If the entity concludes that there is no indication that the asset is impaired (as is likely with many assets in profitable businesses), no further action needs to be taken (as in the past).

If there is an indication that the asset may be impaired (or, in the case of goodwill and intangible assets, useful life is more than 20 years), the entity should estimate the recoverable amount of the asset. Recoverable amount is the higher of what the entity can get for selling the asset and the present value of what it will receive from using the asset. The estimation of recoverable amount is the second stage in the IAS 36 process and often involves considering the asset in conjunction with other assets in the same cash generating unit. If the entity concludes that the recoverable amount of an asset is equal to, or exceeds, its carrying amount, no further action is required (again, as in the past).

If the entity concludes that the recoverable amount of the asset is less than its carrying amount the asset must be written down to its recoverable amount. This is the third stage and is the same action which an entity should have taken in the past. The write-down – or impairment loss – is recognised:

- as an expense in the income statement for assets carried at cost; and
- as a revaluation decrease for assets carried at revalued amounts.

Additional requirements apply to goodwill and intangible assets as well as to other assets which must be considered as part of a single cash generating unit.

An impairment loss recognised in a prior period should be reversed:

- if there has been a change in the estimates used to determine recoverable amount since the last impairment loss was recognised;

- only to the extent that it does not increase the carrying amount of an asset above the carrying amount that would have been determined for the asset had no impairment loss been recognised in prior years; and
- in the case of goodwill, the impairment loss was caused by a specific external event and subsequent external events have reversed the effect of that event.

25.6 RECOVERABLE AMOUNT

The critical issue in IAS 36 is the notion of recoverable amount. If there is an indication that an asset's recoverable amount is less than its carrying amount, the entity must estimate the asset's recoverable amount. If there is no such indication, no further action is required (other than in the case of goodwill and intangible assets which are being amortised over more than 20 years). If an entity is required to estimate recoverable amount and that amount is less than carrying amount, an impairment loss must be recognised. If recoverable amount exceeds carrying amount, as it should be in many cases in a profitable business, no adjustments are required.

Recoverable amount is the higher of an asset's net selling price and its value in use (IAS 36, 5). The definition acknowledges that the economic benefits embodied in an asset may flow to the entity in one of two ways – through the sale of the asset or through the use of that asset (and, possibly, a later sale). In developing IAS 36, the IASC rejected an alternative proposal that recoverable amount should be defined as the fair value of an asset[4]. The two approaches often lead to similar conclusions but differ when value in use exceeds the price of the asset in an active market.

It is usually unnecessary to determine both net selling price and value in use. If either one is greater than carrying amount, the asset is not impaired and the second amount need not be determined. It is necessary to estimate both amounts only when the first amount to be estimated is below carrying amount. For example, an asset cannot be impaired if the entity could sell it for more than its carrying amount; in such a case, the entity need not estimate the asset's value in use. Similarly, if an entity knows that the present value of estimated future cash flows expected to arise from continuing use of an asset exceed the asset's carrying amount, the asset is not impaired and the entity need not estimate the asset's net selling price – this is the case, for example, when the entity knows that it can continue to use the asset profitably throughout its useful life.

Recoverable amount is determined for an individual asset, unless the asset does not generate cash inflows which are largely independent of those from other assets or groups of assets. This is consistent with the approach adopted in all existing IASs. If recoverable amount cannot be determined for an individual asset, it is determined for the cash generating unit to which the asset belongs. Cash generating units are dealt with in 25.12 below. It is unnecessary, however, to look to the cash generating unit when:

- the asset's net selling price is higher than its carrying amount as in such cases no impairment loss has been incurred; or
- the asset's value in use is close to its net selling price and net selling price can be determined and used to test for impairment.

(IAS 36, 19)

The recoverable amount of an asset or a cash generating unit and the carrying amount of the asset or unit must be computed on the same basis. The recoverable amount must include all the assets (and no more) which are included in the carrying amount. The carrying amount must include all the assets which would be sold or used and which enter into the determination of recoverable amount.

25.7 NET SELLING PRICE

Net selling price is the amount obtainable from the sale of the asset in an arm's length transaction between knowledgeable, willing parties, less the costs of disposal of the asset (IAS 36, 5). *Costs of disposal* are the incremental costs directly attributable to the disposal of an asset, excluding finance costs and income tax expense (IAS 36, 5).

Net selling price is a familiar notion. The net realisable value of inventories is the net selling price of those inventories (although inventories are not dealt with in IAS 36). Similarly, the residual value of an item of property, plant and equipment is its net selling price at the end of its useful life. What is, perhaps, less familiar, is the need to reconsider the net selling price of a long-term asset at different points of time within its useful life. Furthermore, while accountants may be used to determining the residual value of an item of property, plant and equipment, such amounts are often immaterial whereas the net selling price of the same item during its useful life may be significant both in amount and in the determination of impairment losses.

As explained above, the recoverable amount and the carrying amount of the asset should be computed on the same basis. Therefore, the net selling price must include all the assets (and no more) which are included in the carrying amount and the carrying amount should include all the assets which are included in the determination of recoverable amount – in the case of a cash generating unit, some of the assets may be sold while others may be used.

A similar problem arises when the balance sheet includes a liability which is directly related to an asset. For example, the buyer of an asset may be required to take over a liability associated with that asset. If only a single net selling price is available for the asset and the liability as a package, the net selling price must be compared with the carrying amount of the property less the carrying amount of the liability. If the net selling price is compared only with the asset, any impairment loss could be overstated by up to the amount of the liability.

25.7.1 Amount Obtainable from the Sale

The best evidence of the amount obtainable from the sale of an asset is the price for that asset in a binding sale agreement in an arm's length transaction (IAS 36, 21). When such an agreement exists, recoverable amount is invariably net selling price as the asset is presumably held for disposal.

If there is no binding sale agreement for the asset but the asset is traded in an active market, the best evidence of the amount obtainable from the sale is the asset's market price (IAS 36, 22). The appropriate market price is usually the current bid price. An *active market* is a market where all the following conditions exist:

- the items traded within the market are homogenous;
- willing buyers and sellers can normally be found at any time; and
- prices are available to the public.

(IAS 38, 7)

Such markets may exist for property and some other items such as vehicles and some licences and quotas. They usually do not exist for many items of plant and equipment, most intangible assets and goodwill.

If there is no binding sale agreement or no active market for an asset, the amount obtainable from the sale of an asset is estimated by reference to recent transactions for similar assets within the same industry. So, for example, the amount obtainable from the sale of plant and equipment can often be determined from transactions made by the entity or its competitors. If there have been no recent transactions for similar assets in the same industry, or the entity cannot determine net selling price for other reasons, the recoverable amount of the asset is the asset's value in use (IAS 36, 17).

25.7.2 Costs of Disposal

Costs of disposal are deducted in determining net selling price (IAS 35, 24). Such costs include legal costs, stamp duty and similar transaction taxes, costs of removing the asset, and direct incremental costs to bring an asset into condition for its sale.

The costs of disposal do not include dismantling and similar costs which have been recognised as a liability in accordance with IAS 37 and added to the cost of the asset. The inclusion of such costs in the costs of disposal would result in their being double-counted. However, it may be simpler to include the dismantling costs in the costs of disposal and compare the resulting net selling price with the carrying amount of the asset less the carrying amount of the provision for the dismantling costs.

Employee termination benefits and costs associated with reducing or reorganising a business following the disposal of an asset are not included in the costs of disposal. These costs are dealt with in accordance with IAS 19 (see chapter 33) and IAS 37 (see chapter 27).

25.8 VALUE IN USE

Value in use is the present value of estimated future cash flows expected to arise from continuing use of the asset and from its disposal at the end of its useful life (IAS 36, 5).

The estimation of value in use is the same sort of calculation as the present value calculation which is familiar to all accountants in making capital expenditure and similar decisions. However, IAS 36 includes specific requirements about the measurement of cash flows and the rate of interest to be used in determining value in use; these requirements may lead to the use of different cash flows and a different discount rate from those used by any particular entity in capital expenditure or similar decisions. While it can argued that the same cash flows and the same discount rate should be used for both purposes, the value in use calculations are made at a later time than the capital expenditure decision; furthermore, entities are free to choose their own rules for the determination of present values in capital expenditure decisions; they do not have that flexibility when applying IAS 36. Detailed examples of the calculations are included in the appendix to IAS 36.

As explained above, the recoverable amount and the carrying amount of the asset should be computed on the same basis. Therefore, the value in use must include all the assets (and no more) which are included in the carrying amount and the carrying amount should include all the assets which are included in the determination of recoverable amount – in the case of a cash generating unit, some of the assets may be sold while others may be used.

25.8.1 Cash Flows

The estimated future cash flows expected to arise from continuing use of the asset should include:

- cash inflows which will arise from the continuing use of the asset;
- cash outflows which will be necessary to generate the cash inflows and which can be directly attributed, or allocated on a reasonable and consistent basis, to the asset; and
- net cash flows which will be received or paid for the disposal of the asset at the end of its useful life.

(IAS 36, 32)

For example, the future cash flows expected to arise from an item of equipment include the cash inflows from the sale of goods produced by the item of equipment, the labour and other costs associated with operating the equipment and the storage, distribution and selling costs associated with the goods. They also include any other cash outflows which can be allocated on a 'reasonable and consistent basis'; this would certainly include variable overheads and may include an allocation of fixed overheads.

Future cash flows include the effects of general inflation only if the discount rate includes the effect of price increases due to general inflation. If the discount rate excludes the effect of such price increases, future cash flows are estimated in real terms, that is they exclude the effects of general inflation but they do include the effects of future specific price increases or decreases.

Future cash flows exclude:

- cash inflows or outflows from financing activities because the time value of money is considered by discounting the estimated future cash flows; and
- income taxes since the discount rate is determined on a pre-tax basis and the tax effects of any impairment loss are dealt with in accordance with IAS 12 (see chapter 31).

Projections of cash inflows and outflows should be:

- based on reasonable and supportable assumptions that represent management's best estimate of the set of economic conditions which will exist over the remaining useful life of the asset;
- based on the most recent financial budgets or forecasts which have been approved by management; and
- cover a maximum period of five years, unless a longer period can be justified.

(IAS 37, 27)

Projections of cash inflows and outflows beyond the period covered by the most recent budgets and forecasts should be estimated by:

- extrapolating the projections for the period covered by these budgets and forecasts;
- using either a steady or declining growth rate unless an increasing rate can be justified; and
- using a growth rate which does not exceed the long-term average growth rate for the products, industries or country or countries in which the entity operates, or for the market in which the asset is used, unless a higher rate can be justified.

(IAS 36, 27)

A higher than average growth rate may be used in the budgets and forecasts but not in the period beyond those budgets and forecasts.

Example 25.1 *Projection of cash flows*

An entity is estimating the value in use of an item of equipment. Management has approved financial budgets and forecasts for the next two years which show a growth rate of 5%. The entity cannot justify projecting cash flows beyond five years.

Value in use is determined using the projections of cash inflows and outflows:

- for the next two years based on the financial budgets and forecasts approved by management; and
- for the ensuing three years based on an extrapolation of those budgets and forecasts and using a growth rate of not greater than 5% unless a higher rate can be justified.

Projections of future cash outflows include any further cash outflows which are expected to be incurred before the asset is ready for use or sale and which will be added to the carrying amount of the asset. For example, the value in use of a building under construction takes into account the present value of the cash flows required to complete the building. It also takes into account any fitting-out costs which will be incurred and borne by the entity in order to sell or use the building.

Future cash flows do not include cash outflows which relate to obligations which have already been recognised as liabilities (for example, payables, pensions or provisions). For example, the cash outflows do not include dismantling and similar costs which have been recognised as a liability in accordance with IAS 37 and added to the cost of the asset. The inclusion of such costs in the determination of value in use would result in their being double-counted. However, it may be simpler to include the dismantling costs in the determination of value in use and compare the resulting amount with the carrying amount of the asset less the carrying amount of the provision for the dismantling costs.

Future cash flows should be estimated for the asset in its current condition (IAS 36, 37). They should not include future cash inflows or outflows which are expected to arise from a future restructuring to which an entity is not yet committed. The inclusion of such cash inflows or outflows would be contrary to IAS 37 (see chapter 27). However, when an entity becomes committed to a restructuring, estimates of future cash flows used in determining value in use need to reflect the cost savings and other benefits from the restructuring (based on the most recent financial budgets/forecasts which have been approved by management). The future cash outflows for the restructuring itself are dealt with in accordance with IAS 37.

Estimates of future cash flows do not include cash flows arising from future capital expenditure which will improve or enhance the asset in excess of its originally assessed standard of performance and the related future benefits from this expenditure. The inclusion of these cash flows would be contrary to IAS 16 or IAS 38 (see chapters 21 and 23). These future cash flows are added to the costs of the asset only when they have been incurred. The decision to incur such cash flows often involves a calculation similar to the value in use calculation and it is unlikely that an entity would incur such costs unless the incremental value in use exceeded the amount of the costs.

The projection of net cash flows to be received (or paid) for the disposal of an asset at the end of its useful life should be the amount which an entity expects to obtain from the disposal of the asset in an arm's length transaction between knowledgeable, willing parties, after deducting the estimated costs of disposal (IAS 36, 45), that is, the asset's net selling price at the end of its useful life. The estimate reflects prices prevailing at the date of the estimate for similar assets which have reached the end of their useful lives and which have operated under conditions similar to those in which the asset will be used (this is the same approach as that used in IAS 16 to estimate residual value). However, the prices are then adjusted for the effect of future price increases due to specific price changes (this is different from the IAS 16 approach to residual value). The estimate reflects the effect of general inflation only if the discount rate includes the effect of general inflation.

Future cash flows are estimated in the currency in which they will be generated and then discounted using a discount rate appropriate for that currency. The present value is translated using the closing rate at the balance sheet date in accordance with IAS 21 (see chapter 19).

25.8.2 Discount Rate

The discount rate used to determine the present value of future cash flows should reflect current market assessments of the time value of money and the risks specific to the asset (IAS 36, 48). This rate is the return which an investor would require if it were to choose an investment which would generate cash flows of amounts, timing and risk profile equivalent to those which the entity expects to derive from the asset (IAS 36, 49).

The discount rate is independent of the entity's capital structure and the way in which the entity financed the acquisition of the asset because the future cash flows expected to arise from the asset do not depend on the way in which its purchase was financed (IAS 36, 54). This is a different approach from that followed for the capitalisation of borrowing costs in IAS 25. Therefore, the capitalisation rate used for the purposes of IAS 23 is likely to be different from, and probably lower than, the discount rate used to determine value in use.

The discount rate is estimated from the interest rate implicit in current market transactions for similar assets or from the weighted average cost of capital of a listed entity which has a single asset (or a portfolio of assets) similar in terms of service potential and risks to the asset under review. When an asset-specific rate is not directly available from the market, an entity may estimate the discount rate by taking into account:

- the entity's weighted average cost of capital determined using techniques such as the capital asset pricing model;
- the entity's incremental borrowing rate; and
- other market borrowing rates.

(IAS 36, 51)

The capital asset pricing model explains the relationship between risk and return in an efficient market and calculates the return which can be expected from an efficient portfolio investment. The model is dealt with in many text books and the academic literature on corporate finance. While the model has been criticised for not reflecting the real world, it can be adapted appropriately to suit the practical circumstance of a particular entity.

An entity normally uses a single discount rate for the estimate of an asset's value in use. However, it may use separate discount rates for different future periods when value in use is sensitive to different risks for different periods or to the term structure of interest rates (IAS 36, 56). For example, different rates may be necessary to deal with cash flows receivable or payable in different currencies. Different rates may also be needed for different assets.

The discount rate should be a pre-tax rate (IAS 36, 48) as the future cash flows exclude tax receipts and payments. The tax consequences of any impairment loss are dealt with in accordance with IAS 12 (see chapter 31).

25.9 IMPAIRMENT INDICATORS

An entity is required to assess at each balance sheet date for each asset whether there is any indication that the asset may be impaired (IAS 36, 8), that is whether there is any indication that the asset's recoverable amount is less than its carrying amount. The entity should consider both external and internal sources of information.

Extract 25.1 *Impairment indicators*

Hoechst, Germany, 31 December 1997 (IAS)

In the event that facts and circumstances indicate that the cost of the Group's long-lived assets (including intangible assets) may be impaired, an evaluation of recoverability would be performed. If an evaluation were required, the estimated future cash flows associated with the asset would be compared to the asset's carrying amount to determine if a write-down to current market value would be required.

Extract 25.2 *Impairment indicators*

Harmony, South Africa, 30 June 2000 (South African GAAP and IAS)

As a result of the significant decline in the gold price at the 1999 financial year end a number of shafts' future undiscounted cash flows were lower than their net carrying value, resulting in a number of shafts being impaired. An amount of R112 million, calculated on the discounted basis, was therefore written off.

Extract 25.3 *Impairment indicators*

Dyckerhoff, Germany, 31 December 2001 (IAS)

Primarily due to the unsatisfactory economic situation in the German market, the reported values for goodwill and also property, plant and equipment were reviewed in accordance with IAS 36.

Extract 25.4 *Impairment indicators*

Kuoni, Switzerland, 31 December 2001 (IAS)

In view of changes in the market following the events of autumn 2001, the Group was forced to reassess the value of the goodwill at a number of its acquisitions.

Extract 25.5 *Impairment indicators*

Interbrew, Belgium, 31 December 2000 (IAS accounting policies)

The main components of our goodwill are linked to the acquisitions of Labatt, Bass Brewers and Whitbread Beer Company. This goodwill is amortised over 40 years, although we recorded an exceptional write-off on the Bass goodwill, amounting to €1,234.7million, as the result of the decision of the UK Secretary of State for Trade and Industry regarding the Bass acquisition, as explained in note 20 (Important subsequent events to 31 December 2000).

[Note 20]

On 3 January 2001, the UK Secretary of State for Trade and Industry denied to Interbrew the right to merge the UK brewing operations of Bass Brewing Ltd and Whitbread Beer Company. He further decided that Interbrew should be required to divest the UK beer business of Bass Brewers. On 2 February 2001, Interbrew applied in the UK for a judicial review of the decision with the High Court of Justice Administrative Court.

If any indication of impairment exists, the entity should estimate the recoverable amount of the asset. An entity is not required to estimate the recoverable amount of any assets (other than certain goodwill and intangible assets) when there is no indication of impairment.

25.9.1 External indicators of Impairment

If an asset's market value has declined significantly more than would have been expected as a result of the passage of time or normal use, this may indicate that the asset is impaired (IAS 36, 9(a)). For example, if the market value of a building is known to have declined by more than would have been expected, the decline may indicate that the building is impaired. Such a decline may relate to an individual asset (when, for example, local circumstances impair the value of a specific building), all assets of a similar type (for example, when building values in general decline), or all assets in a particular location (for example, when building values decline in one country).

Significant changes in the technological, market, economic or legal environment in which the entity operates or in the market to which an asset is dedicated may indicate that an asset is impaired (IAS 36, 9(b)). For example, the development of new technology may reduce the demand for existing technology with the result that assets used for the old technology are impaired. Similarly, when new regulations prohibit the sale of a particular product, the plant and equipment used to produce that product may be impaired. The removal of trade barriers, such as tariffs or quotas, may indicate that assets are impaired in a country (whether importer or exporter) which has benefited from the protection previously afforded by the barriers.

Increases in market interest rates or other market rates of return on investments may affect the discount rate used in calculating an asset's value in use and so reduce the asset's recoverable amount materially (IAS 36, 9(c)). An increase in interest rates affects the recoverable amount of all assets for which value in use is critical to the determination of recoverable amount. However, an entity is not required to make a formal estimate of an asset's recoverable amount when:

- the increase in market rates does not affect the discount rate used in calculating the asset's value in use; or
- the increase in market rates affects the discount rate but previous sensitivity analysis shows that it is unlikely that there will be a material decrease in recoverable amount or that any decrease will result in a material impairment loss.

(IAS 36, 13)

As different discount rates may be used to determine the value in use of different assets, an increase in interest rates may affect the recoverable amount of some assets but not others.

If the carrying amount of the net assets of the entity is more than the market capitalisation of the entity, this may indicate that some assets are impaired (IAS 36, 9(d)). The market capitalisation is the market's estimate of the present value of the future cash flows from the entity. A decline in market capitalisation may indicate that interest rates have increased (possibly because risks associated with the assets have increased) or cash flows have decreased.

25.9.2 Internal Indicators of Impairment

Evidence of obsolescence or physical damage of an asset may indicate impairment (IAS 36, 9(e)). For example, the fact that an item of equipment is no longer in use may indicate that the item is impaired. Similarly, the fact that management thinks it is unprofitable to repair damaged equipment may indicate that the equipment is impaired.

Significant changes in the extent to which, or manner in which, an asset is used or is expected to be used and which are expected to have an adverse effect on the entity may indicate that an asset is impaired (IAS 36, 9(f)). For example, an entity may plan to discontinue or restructure a particular operation. The discontinuance or restructuring may result in a decline in the recoverable amount of some or all the assets within the operation and so indicate that the assets may be impaired. Alternatively, under IAS 16, a property may be carried at fair value based on a 'highest and best use' market value when the property is used for some other purpose; if the expected use of the asset is likely to be less profitable than the 'highest and best use', this may indicate that the asset is impaired.

The entity's internal reporting may indicate that the economic performance of an asset is, or will be, worse than expected (IAS 36, 9(g)). For example:

- the cost of acquiring an item of equipment may be significantly higher than originally budgeted – had the high cost been known before the capital investment decision was made, the equipment may not have been acquired; or
- actual net cash flows or operating profit from an item of equipment may be significantly worse than those budgeted – again, had this information been known earlier, the equipment might not have been acquired.

Previous calculations may have shown that an asset's recoverable amount is significantly greater than its carrying amount. In such a case the entity need not re-estimate the asset's recoverable amount if no events have occurred which would have eliminated that difference. Similarly, previous calculations may show that an asset's recoverable amount is not sensitive to one or more of the indications. For example, the value in use of an asset may have been determined in prior periods and shown a substantial surplus over carrying amount. If no events have occurred which would have reduced the surplus, there is no need to estimate the asset's recoverable amount.

25.10 RECOGNITION AND MEASUREMENT OF AN IMPAIRMENT LOSS

If there is an indication that an asset may be impaired, the entity should estimate the recoverable amount of the asset (IAS 36, 8). If the recoverable amount of an asset is less than its carrying amount, the carrying amount of the asset should be reduced to its recoverable amount (IAS 36, 58). No consideration should be given to whether or not the loss is permanent; the notion of recognising impairment losses only when they are 'permanent' or 'other than temporary' is not part of the requirements.

The resulting impairment loss should be recognised:

- as an expense in the income statement if the asset is carried at an amount based on cost; or
- as a revaluation decrease if the asset is carried at revalued amount to the extent that it does not exceed the amount held in the revaluation surplus for that same asset.

Example 25.2 *Recognition of impairment loss*

An asset was acquired at the beginning of 1999 at a cost of £12,000. The asset is expected to have a residual value of nil and a useful life of six years. The straight-line method of depreciation is used. By the end of 2001, there are indications that the asset's carrying amount has been impaired. The enterprise estimates that the recoverable amount of the asset is now only £2,500.

		£
1999	Cost	12,000
1999	Depreciation	2,000
31/12/99	Carrying amount	10,000
2000	Depreciation	2,000
31/12/00	Carrying amount	8,000
2001	Depreciation	2,000
2001	Impairment write down	3,500
31/12/01	Carrying amount	2,500

The write-down of £3,500 is recognised as an expense in 2001 in addition to the depreciation of £2,000 for the year.

When an impairment loss is greater than the carrying amount of the asset, the full recognition of the loss would create a liability. Such circumstances arise only when the value in use and the net selling price of the asset are both negative amounts. The entity should recognise a liability if, and only if, its recognition is required by another IAS (IAS 36, 61). In this respect, IAS 37 limits the recognition of provisions to instances in which there is an obligation or a constructive obligation (see chapter 27) and the entity may not have either an obligation or a constructive obligation to incur some or all of the net cash outflows. If the liability does not qualify for recognition as a provision under IAS 37 or any other IAS, the carrying amount of the asset is reduced to zero.

Example 25.3 *Recognition of impairment loss greater than carrying amount of the assets*

An asset was acquired at the beginning of 1999 at a cost of £12,000. The asset is expected to have a residual value of nil and a useful life of six years. The straight-line method of depreciation is used. Cost and depreciation for 1999, 2000 and 2001 are as follows:

		£
1999	Cost	12,000
1999	Depreciation	2,000
31/12/99	Carrying amount	10,000
2000	Depreciation	2,000
31/12/00	Carrying amount	8,000
2001	Depreciation	2,000
31/12/01	Carrying amount before impairment loss	6,000

At the end of 2001, there are indications that the asset's carrying amount has been impaired. The value in use of the asset is a negative amount of £1,500 because the cash outflows from the use of the asset will exceed the cash inflows. The asset's net selling price is also negative because the enterprise would have to incur substantial disposal costs. The impairment loss is restricted to £6,000 unless the negative amount qualifies for recognition as a provision in accordance with IAS 37.

After the recognition of an impairment loss, the depreciation or amortisation charge for the asset should be adjusted in future periods to allocate the asset's revised carrying amount, less its residual value (if any), on a systematic basis over its remaining useful life (IAS 36, 62). No retrospective adjustments are made; the change is a change in the estimate of the asset's carrying amount and is, therefore, dealt with in accordance with IAS 8 (see chapter 13).

Example 25.4 *Recognition of impairment loss*

An asset was acquired at the beginning of 1999 at a cost of £12,000. The asset is expected to have a residual value of nil and a useful life of six years. The straight-line method of depreciation is used. However by the end of 2001, there are indications that the asset's

(Continued)

(Continued)

carrying amount has been impaired. The enterprise estimates that the recoverable amount of the asset is now only £2,500 and that the asset will be used for a further three years.

		£
1999	Cost	12,000
1999	Depreciation	2,000
31/12/99	Carrying amount	10,000
2000	Depreciation	2,000
31/12/00	Carrying amount	8,000
2001	Depreciation	2,000
2001	Impairment write down	3,500
31/12/01	Carrying amount	2,500
2002	Depreciation	833
31/12/02	Carrying amount	1,667
2003	Depreciation	833
31/12/03	Carrying amount	834
2004	Depreciation	834
31/12/04	Carrying amount	–

In many circumstances there may be indications of impairment but the recoverable amount of the asset exceeds its carrying amount. In such circumstances, even though no impairment loss is recognised, it may be necessary to adjust the remaining useful life, the depreciation (amortisation) method or the residual value for the asset.

Example 25.5 *Change in depreciation resulting from impairment indications*

Significant future changes in regulations mean that an entity no longer expects to be able to sell certain products after a further two years. The changes are an indication of possible impairment in the equipment used to manufacture the products. Therefore, the entity must estimate the recoverable amount of the equipment. The entity concludes that the recoverable amount of the equipment exceeds its carrying amount. Therefore, no impairment loss need be recognised. However, if necessary, the remaining useful life of the equipment must be reduced to two years if there is no other use for the equipment after the end of two years.

Extract 25.6 *Impairment losses*

Bayer, Germany, 31 December 2001 (IAS)

Write-downs are made for any declines in value that go beyond the depletion reflected in depreciation. In compliance with IAS 36 (Impairment of Assets), such write-downs are measured by comparing the carrying amounts to the discounted cash flows expected to be generated by the respective assets.

Extract 25.7 *Impairment losses*

BMW, Germany, 31 December 2001 (IAS)

Sundry operating expenses contain impairment losses of euro 84 million recorded on intangible assets as a consequence of the events of 11 September 2001.

Extract 25.8 *Impairment losses*

Syngenta, Switzerland, 31 December 2001 (IAS)

Non-current assets, including recognized intangibles and goodwill, are reviewed at each balance sheet date to determine whether events or changes in circumstances indicate that the carrying amount of the asset may not be recoverable. If any such indication exists, Syngenta estimates the asset's recoverable amount as the higher of net selling price and value-in-use and recognizes an impairment loss in the income statement for the amount by which the asset's carrying value exceeds its recoverable amount. Value-in-use is estimated as the present value of future cash flows expected to result from the use of the asset and its eventual disposal, to which an appropriate discount rate is applied. ... Considerable management judgement is necessary to estimate discounted future cash flows. In 2001, the discount rate utilized was 16%. Accordingly, actual results could vary significantly from such estimates.

Extract 25.9 *Impairment losses*

Dairy Farm International, Hong Kong, 31 December 2001 (IAS)

In December 2001, the Directors reviewed the carrying value of the Group's assets and based on an assessment of their value in use, an impairment charge of US$12.9 million was recognised, principally against the IT systems assets and the equipment at the Fresh Food Processing Centre in Hong Kong. In December 2000, the Directors recognised an impairment charge of US$129.4 million against goodwill and tangible assets associated with Australia.

25.11 REASSESSMENT OF IMPAIRMENT LOSSES

When the carrying amount of an asset has been reduced to its recoverable amount, the entity follows the three-stage approach at each subsequent balance sheet date in order to assess whether the impairment loss recognised in prior years no longer exists or the amount of the loss has decreased. If there is an indication that the loss no longer exists or that the amount has reduced, the entity should estimate the recoverable amount of the asset (IAS 36, 95), that is the entity estimates again the higher of net selling price and value in use.

While IAS 36 is silent on the issue, it is also necessary to assess the asset for further impairments (unless it has been written down to zero). Therefore, when the carrying amount of an asset has been reduced to its recoverable amount, the entity must look at each balance sheet date for both indicators of impairment and indicators of the reversals of impairment.

25.11.1 Indicators of Reversal of Impairment

The indicators of a reversal of impairment are similar to the indicators of impairment except that, of course, the search is for indications of increases, rather than decreases, in recoverable amount.

If the asset's market value has increased significantly during the period, this may indicate that a previous impairment may no longer exist (IAS 36, 96). For example, local circumstances which impaired the value of a particular building may have changed for the better or building values in general or in a particular location may have increased.

Significant changes in the technological, market, economic or legal environment in which the entity operates or in the market to which the asset is dedicated may indicate that a previous impairment no longer exists. For example, delays in the implementation of new technology may have led to a resurgence in the demand for the old technology with the result that the value of the assets used for the old technology has increased.

Decreases in market interest rates or other market rates of return on investments during the period may affect the discount rate used in calculating the asset's value in use and so increase the asset's recoverable amount materially. An entity is not required to reassess recoverable amount when the decrease in rates does not affect the discount rate used in calculating the asset's value in use or previous sensitivity analysis has shown that recoverable amount will not be affected materially by the change in rates.

Significant changes in the extent to which, or manner in which, the asset is used or is expected to be used may indicate that a previous impairment no longer exists. These changes include capital expenditure which has been incurred during the period to improve or enhance an asset in excess of its originally assessed standard of performance and a commitment to discontinue or restructure the operation to which the asset belongs. Alternatively, the entity may have changed the use of land from, say, agricultural to commercial or industrial to tourist purposes with the result that the market value of the land has increased.

Evidence may be available from internal reporting that indicates that the economic performance of the asset is, or will be, better than expected (IAS 36, 96). For example, the actual cash flows or operating profit from an asset may prove to be higher than earlier forecasts.

25.11.2 Reversal of Impairment Loss

An impairment loss recognised in prior years should be reversed if, and only if, there has been a change in either:

- the estimates used to determine the asset's recoverable amount since the last impairment loss was recognised; or
- the basis used for determining recoverable amount has changed from net selling price to value in use or from value in use to net selling price.

The reversal may be made for the whole of or only part of the impairment loss.

As value in use is a discounted amount, its amount will increase the closer the future cash flows are to the present. An impairment loss is not reversed just because of this 'unwinding' of the discount even if it means that the recoverable amount of the asset becomes higher than its carrying amount (IAS 36, 101). The IASC took this approach 'for practical reasons only' and because the benefits from recognising the effects of the unwinding of the discount do not justify the costs involved (IAS 36, B113).

It is important to distinguish the unwinding of the discount from a change in the timing of the inflows and outflows of cash. An impairment loss is reversed if current estimates indicate that the cash inflows will be received earlier than previously forecast (in the same way, a delay in the receipt of forecasted cash flows may create or increase an impairment loss). An impairment loss is not reversed when there has been no change in the forecasted time of receipt of cash inflows even though the present value increases each year.

When an impairment loss is reversed, the carrying amount of the asset should be increased to what the carrying amount would have been, net of amortisation or depreciation, had no impairment loss been recognised in prior years (IAS 36, 99 and 102). Therefore, the amortisation or

Example 25.6 *Write back of previous impairment write down*

An asset was acquired at the beginning of 1999 at a cost of £12,000. The asset is expected to have a residual value of nil and a useful life of six years. The straight-line method of depreciation is used. However at the end of 2000, the entity concludes that, as a result of significant adverse changes in economic conditions, the recoverable amount of the asset is now only £2,500; the remaining useful life is four years.

		£
1999	Cost	12,000
1999	Depreciation	2,000
31/12/99	Carrying amount	10,000
2000	Depreciation	2,000
2000	Impairment loss	5,500
31/12/00	Carrying amount	2,500
2001	Depreciation	625
31/12/01	Carrying amount	1,875
2002	Depreciation	625
31/12/02	Carrying amount	1,250

At the end of 2002, the entity decides that there has been a substantial improvement in the economic conditions which led to the 2000 impairment loss and that the recoverable amount of the asset is now £5,000; the remaining useful life is two years. If the asset had not been written down in 2000, depreciation in 2001 and 2002 would have been £2,000 a year, leading to a carrying amount at the end of 2002 of £4,000. Therefore, the amount written back is limited to £2,750 in order to reinstate the carrying amount of £4,000.

Therefore, the carrying amount at 31/12/02 and the depreciation for 2003 and 2004 is as follows:

		£
31/12/02	Carrying amount before reversal of impairment loss	1,250
2002	Reversal of impairment loss	2,750
31/12/02	Carrying amount	4,000
2003	Depreciation	2,000
31/12/03	Carrying amount	2,000
2004	Depreciation	2,000
31/12/04	Carrying amount	–

depreciation of the asset must be recomputed for the periods during which the asset's carrying amount had been reduced to recoverable amount.

After the reversal of an impairment loss, the depreciation or amortisation charge for the asset should be adjusted in future periods to allocate the asset's revised carrying amount, less its residual value (if any), on a systematic basis over its remaining useful life (IAS 36, 106).

The reversal of an impairment loss for an asset should be recognised as income in the income statement in the case of an asset carried on the basis of historical cost (IAS 36, 104). It should be credited directly to equity under the heading 'revaluation surplus' in the case of an asset carried at revalued amount (IAS 36, 104). However, to the extent that an impairment loss on the same revalued asset was previously recognised as an expense in the income statement, a reversal of that impairment loss is recognised as income in the income statement.

25.12 CASH GENERATING UNITS

It is often not possible to estimate the recoverable amount of an individual asset when:

- the asset's value in use is not close to its net selling price; and
- the asset does not generate cash inflows from continuing use that are largely independent of those from other assets.

(IAS 36, 66)

For example, it is often not possible to estimate the recoverable amount of:

- individual items of equipment used in conjunction with other items in a factory, refinery or other process;
- individual aircraft, ships or vehicles in a fleet when each item in the fleet is used interchangeably and its value in use is expected to be higher than its net selling price;
- corporate assets and goodwill which do not generate, directly, any cash inflows but which are used in conjunction with other assets which do generate cash flows; and
- other assets which do not generate, directly, any cash inflows but which are used in conjunction with other assets which do generate cash flows – a free after-sales service facility or a free inter-terminal railway service at an airport are examples.

In such cases, instead of determining the recoverable amount of the individual asset, the entity should determine the recoverable amount of the cash generating unit to which the asset belongs (IAS 36, 65).

25.12.1 Definition of Cash Generating Unit

A *cash generating unit* is the smallest identifiable group of assets that generates cash inflows from continuing use that are largely independent of the cash inflows from other assets or groups of assets (IAS 36, 5). The smallest identifiable group of assets might be:

- those items of equipment used for a particular product;
- a group of wells in a single oil field ;
- a fleet of aircraft or the fleet of aircraft based at a particular airport;
- that part of the entity's operations to which goodwill is attributed;
- that part of the entity's operations which makes exclusive use of corporate assets; or
- all the passenger facilities at an single airport which includes the free inter-terminal railway service.

Cash inflows from continuing use are cash inflows from parties outside the entity (IAS 36, 68). In identifying whether cash inflows from a group of assets are largely independent of the cash inflows from other assets or groups of assets, an entity considers various factors including:

- how management monitors the entity's operations (such as by product lines, businesses, individual locations, districts or regional areas or in some other way); and
- how management makes decisions about continuing or disposing of the entity's assets and operations.

(IAS 36, 68)

If an active market exists for the output produced by an asset or a group of assets, the asset or group of assets should be identified as a cash generating unit, even if some of or all of the output is used internally (IAS 36, 69). The asset or group of assets forms a separate cash generating unit if the entity could sell this output on an active market because the asset or group of assets could generate cash inflows from continuing use which would be largely independent of the cash inflows from other assets or groups of assets.

An *active market* is a market where all the following conditions exist:

- the items traded within the market are homogenous;
- willing buyers and sellers can normally be found at any time; and
- prices are available to the public.

(IAS 38, 7)

Cash generating units should be identified consistently from period to period for the same asset or types of assets, unless a change is justified

(IAS 36, 71). If an entity determines that an asset belongs to a different cash generating unit from previous periods, or that the types of assets aggregated for the asset's cash generating unit have changed, the entity should disclose the current and former way of aggregating assets and the reasons for changing the way the cash generating unit is identified (IAS 36, 117(d)(iii)) if an impairment loss for the cash generating unit is recognised or reversed during the period.

25.12.2 Recoverable Amount

The recoverable amount of a cash generating unit is the higher of the cash generating unit's net selling price and its value in use (IAS 36, 73). Both amounts are determined in the same way as for an individual asset.

The recoverable amount and the carrying amount of the cash generating unit should be computed on the same basis. The carrying amount should be determined consistently with the way the recoverable amount is determined (IAS 36, 74). The carrying amount of a cash generating unit:

- includes the carrying amount of only those assets which can be attributed directly, or allocated on a reasonable and consistent basis, to the cash generating unit and which will generate the future cash inflows estimated in determining the cash generating unit's value in use; and
- does not include the carrying amount of any recognised liability, unless the recoverable amount of the cash generating unit cannot be determined without consideration of this liability.

(IAS 36, 75)

25.12.3 Allocation of Impairment Losses

If the recoverable amount of a cash generating unit is less than the carrying amount of the unit, the carrying amount should be reduced to its recoverable amount. The resulting impairment loss is recognised in the same way as the impairment loss for an individual asset. As with individual assets, a liability should be recognised if, and only if, it is required by other IFRSs, in particular IAS 37.

The impairment of a cash generating unit is treated as if it were the impairment of the individual assets. Therefore, it is necessary to allocate the impairment loss over the assets in the cash generating unit – it is inappropriate to treat the impairment loss as if it were a provision and classify it as a liability. The loss should be allocated to the assets in the following order:

- first, to any goodwill allocated to the cash generating unit; and
- then, to the other assets of the cash generating unit on a pro-rata basis, based on their carrying amounts.

(IAS 36, 88)

In making the allocations, the carrying amount of an individual asset should not be reduced below the highest of:

- the asset's net selling price (if determinable);
- the asset's value in use (if determinable); and
- zero.

When it is necessary to restrict the amount of the impairment loss allocated to a particular asset, the amount which would otherwise have been allocated to that asset should be allocated to the other assets on a pro-rata basis (IAS 36, 89).

25.12.4 Reversal of an Impairment Loss for a Cash Generating Unit

The reversal of an impairment loss for a cash generating unit is dealt with in the same way as the reversal of an impairment loss for an individual asset. The entity reassesses each year whether there is any indication that the impairment loss no longer exists or has been reduced. It also assesses whether there are indications of further impairment losses.

If there is an indication that the impairment loss may no longer exist or may have reduced, the entity estimates the recoverable amount of the cash generating unit. Any resulting reversal of the impairment loss should be treated as a reversal of the impairment losses for individual assets (IAS 36, 107). Therefore, any reversal is allocated to the assets of the cash generating unit in the following order:

- first, to assets other than goodwill on a pro-rata basis, based on the carrying amount of each asset in the unit; and
- then, to any goodwill allocated to the cash generating unit but only if the impairment loss was caused by a specific external event of an exceptional nature that is not expected to recur and subsequent external events have reversed the effect of that event.

In allocating a reversal of an impairment loss for a cash generating unit, the carrying amount of an asset should not be increased above the lower of:

- the recoverable amount of the asset (if determinable); and
- the carrying amount of the asset which would have been determined (net of amortisation or depreciation) had no impairment loss been recognised for the asset in prior years.

The amount of the reversal of the impairment loss that would otherwise have been allocated to the asset should be allocated to the other assets of the unit on a pro-rata basis (IAS 36, 108).

Extract 25.10 *Cash generating units*

RWE, Germany, 31 December 2001 (IAS)

Recoverability of the carrying value of intangible assets (including capitalized development costs and goodwill) as well as property, plant and equipment is regularly assessed. If the recoverable amount of an asset is less than its carrying amount, an impairment loss is recognized. If the asset is part of a unit that autonomously generates cash or cash equivalents, the depreciation is calculated based on the usage value of the unit that generates cash or cash equivalents.

Extract 25.11 *Cash generating units*

Austrian Airlines, Austria, 31 December 2001 (IAS)

According to the market value estimates produced for the aircraft stock depreciation to a lower recoverable amount is not required. In detail, calculation was made on the basis of so-called cash generating units. Since all aircraft are used to all traffic streams according to the transferral concept of the Austrian Airlines Group, the total Group fleet has been included as a single unit. An interest rate of 5.5% has been set for the purposes of calculation.

Extract 25.12 *Cash generating units*

Holcim, Switzerland, 31 December 2001 (IAS)

At each balance sheet date, the Group assesses whether there is any indication that an asset may be impaired. If any such indication exists, the recoverable amount of the asset is estimated in order to determine the extent of the impairment loss, if any. Where it is not possible to estimate the recoverable amount of an individual asset, the Group estimates the recoverable amount of the cash generating unit (defined on the basis of regional markets) to which the asset belongs.

If the recoverable amount of an asset or cash generating unit is estimated to be less than its carrying amount, the carrying amount of the asset or cash generating unit is reduced to its recoverable amount. Impairment losses are recognized immediately in the income statement.

25.13 GOODWILL

The impairment of goodwill is dealt with in the same way as the impairment of other assets except that the recoverable amount of goodwill is estimated in all periods when its useful life exceeds 20 years, irrespective of whether or not there are indications of impairment (IAS 22, 56).

Goodwill does not generate cash flows independently from other assets or groups of assets and, therefore, the recoverable amount of goodwill as an individual asset cannot be determined. If there is an indication that goodwill is impaired or goodwill is being amortised over more than 20 years, its recoverable amount is determined for the cash generating unit to which the goodwill belongs. IAS 36 requires the combination of what it describes as a 'bottom up' test and a 'top down' test.

The entity should identify first whether goodwill that relates to a cash generating unit is recognised in the financial statements. If it is, the entity should:

- identify whether the carrying amount of goodwill can be allocated on a reasonable and consistent basis to the cash generating unit;
- compare the recoverable amount of the cash generating unit to its carrying amount including goodwill; and
- recognise any resulting impairment loss.

(IAS 36, 80(a))

This test (the 'bottom up' test) ensures that an entity recognises any impairment loss that exists for the cash generating unit, including any goodwill which can be allocated on a reasonable and consistent basis. If goodwill can be allocated on a reasonable and consistent basis to a cash generating unit and the 'bottom up' test is carried out, no further testing is required.

If none of the goodwill can be allocated on a reasonable and consistent basis to the cash generating unit, the entity should first perform the 'bottom up' test for the cash generating unit. This determines whether or not any of the assets in that unit, other than goodwill, have been impaired. The entity must then perform the following 'top down' test:

- identify the smallest cash generating unit which includes the cash generating unit under review and to which the carrying amount of goodwill can be allocated on a reasonable and consistent basis (the 'larger' cash generating unit);
- compare the recoverable amount of the larger cash generating unit to its carrying amount (including the goodwill); and
- recognise any resulting impairment loss.

(IAS 36, 80(b))

The combination of the 'bottom up' and the 'top down' tests ensures that an entity recognises:

- any impairment loss that exists for the cash generating unit excluding any goodwill (the 'bottom up' test); and
- any impairment loss that exists for goodwill (the 'top down' test).

Example 25.7 *Combination of 'bottom up' and 'top down' tests*

In 2000, an entity acquired another business which operates a chain of restaurants. The application of IAS 22 to this acquisition resulted in the recognition of $50m of goodwill which is being amortised over 10 years.

By the end of 2002, it was clear that the restaurants were not producing the cash flows and operating profit which had been expected at the date of acquisition or in subsequent budgets and forecasts. Therefore, the entity is required to estimate the recoverable amount of the assets of the restaurants, including the goodwill arising on their acquisition.

The entity treats each restaurant as a cash generating unit but it cannot allocate the goodwill on a reasonable and consistent basis to individual restaurants. Therefore, the entity estimates the recoverable amount of the assets of each restaurant and compares the resulting amount with the carrying amount of those assets. This 'bottom up' test checks for any impairment in the assets of the restaurants but it provides no information about the impairment of the goodwill arising on the acquisition.

The entity decides that the smallest cash generating unit which includes the individual restaurants and the goodwill is the chain of restaurants. This is the 'larger cash generating unit'. Therefore, the entity estimates the recoverable amount of the assets of the larger cash generating unit and compares the resulting amount with the carrying amount of the assets of all the restaurants and the goodwill. This 'top down' test checks for any impairment in the goodwill (and, possibly, any corporate assets associated with the chain of restaurants) but it is insufficient on its own to check for the impairment of the assets of the individual restaurants.

Extract 25.13 *Impairment of goodwill*

Lufthansa, Germany, 31 December 2001 (IAS)

Total amortisation and depreciation amount to €1,714.1m, including exceptional amortisation of goodwill in the catering segment in the amount of €495.4m. The recoverable amount has in this connection been determined at the LSG Chefs (USA group) level; it corresponds to the value in use. The calculation was based on an interest rate before taxes of 13 per cent. The exceptional amortisation was caused by the terrorist attacks of

11 September, as a result of which the group recorded a major decline in revenue and earnings.

Extract 25.14 *Impairment of goodwill*

Beko, Austria, 31 December 2001 (IAS)

An impairment loss to the amount of 702,000.00 EUR was considered for the goodwill of the Pallas Group with effect on the net income. The write-off was necessary on account of the low recoverable value on the basis of discounted future cash-flow compared to the book value.

Extract 25.15 *Impairment of goodwill*

VA Technologie, Austria, 31 December 2001

Apart from scheduled goodwill amortisation of TEUR 28,327 (2000: 32,420 TEUR), extraordinary amortisation of TEUR 27,900 was undertaken in the Metallurgy Division as a result of the crisis in the steel industry market. This related to the goodwill derived from the purchase of the Kvaerner Group in 1999. The goodwill utility value was calculated using a model based on the discounted cash flow method with an interest rate of 8.0%. Specific company risk was taken into account in the planned cash flow. In addition, in the Transmission and Distribution Division, goodwill from VA TECH ELIN Holec High Voltage BV, amounting to TEUR 6,800 was subjected to extraordinary amortisation. This extraordinary amortisation corresponds with the reduction in value in use.

Extract 25.16 *Impairment of goodwill*

Kuoni, Switzerland, 31 December 2001 (IAS)

In view of changes in the market following the events of autumn 2001, the Group was forced to reassess the value of the goodwill at a number of its acquisitions. To provide a basis for these recalculations, business plans were produced for the next five years paying due regard to the changed market conditions. The discount rates for calculating discounted cash flow were also adjusted to reflect the higher risk levels that the market now demands. These reappraisals produced goodwill impairment (based on the value in use) of CHF 203.3 million and concerned our companies Apollo (Scandinavia), Kuoni Gastaldi (Europe), Intrav (North America) and T PRO (Incoming).

Extract 25.17 *Impairment of goodwill*

TMM, Mexico, 31 December 2000 (IAS)

The Company determined that as of 31 December 2000 goodwill related to these companies in the Land Transportation and Ports and Terminal segments had been impaired because its recoverable amount was less than its carrying amount. Management intends to dispose of their investment in these companies and made this determination upon their review of recoverability of their investment. The company does not anticipate recovering any of the goodwill.

Extract 25.18 *Impairment of goodwill*

Jardine Matheson, Hong Kong, 31 December 2001 (IAS)

In view of the continuing weakness of the Indonesian Rupiah, the Directors reviewed the carrying value of Cycle & Carriage's investment in Astra International in April 2001. This review indicated that the future cash flows from Astra International's business, when discounted at an appropriate risk-adjusted discount rate which took account of the uncertainties surrounding the Indonesian economy and its currency, were not sufficient to support the balance of goodwill arising on the acquisition of this investment. Accordingly, the balance of the goodwill was written off. The loss attributable to the Group, after tax and outside interests, amounted to US$65 million.

IASB business combinations project

In phase one of its business combinations project, the IASB proposes to prohibit the amortisation of goodwill and require an annual impairment test. As a consequence it proposes several changes to the application of the impairment test for goodwill:

- the test should be done at the smallest group of CGUs to which goodwill can be allocated on a reasonable and consistent basis and that basis should be consistent with the level at which management monitors the return on the investment made;
- there should be further guidance on the basis for estimating cash flow projections;
- if an impairment is identified, it should be measured by comparing the carrying amount of goodwill with its implied value, that is the difference between the recoverable amount of the CGU and the fair value of the net assets that would be identified and recognised if the CGU were acquired at the date of impairment;
- the gain or loss on the disposal of a business within a group of CGUs to which goodwill has been allocated should be determined after taking into account the goodwill associated with that business;

(Continued)

(Continued)

- goodwill acquired in a business combination should be tested for impairment before the end of the annual reporting period in which the combination occurred but a detailed calculation of recoverable amount is required in subsequent periods only if certain criteria are not met;
- the value in use of a CGU is the future cash flows expected to be derived by the entity from the CGU, discounted using a rate that reflects current market assessments of the time value of money and the risks specific to the asset;
- an impairment loss should not be recognised for goodwill to the extent that it arises because an intangible asset that did not meet the criteria for recognition separately from goodwill as at the date of acquisition subsequently meets these criteria and would be allocated a separate fair value when calculating the implied value of goodwill;
- the allocation of impairment losses should reflect the new method for determining impairment; and
- the reversal of impairment losses in respect of goodwill should be prohibited.

25.14 CORPORATE ASSETS

Corporate assets are assets other than goodwill that contribute to the future cash flows of both the cash generating unit under review and other cash generating units (IAS 36, 5). They include group or divisional assets such as the headquarters building, computer equipment or a research centre. The impairment of corporate assets is dealt with in the same way as the impairment of other assets.

Corporate assets do not generate cash inflows independently from other assets or groups of assets and therefore their recoverable amount cannot be determined. The approach adopted in IAS 36 is the same as that for goodwill, that is, a combination of 'bottom up' and 'top down' tests.

The entity should identify first whether any corporate assets that relate to a cash generating unit are recognised in the financial statements. If they are, the entity should:

- identify whether the carrying amount of the corporate assets can be allocated on a reasonable and consistent basis to the cash generating unit;

- compare the recoverable amount of the cash generating unit to its carrying amount including the corporate assets; and
- recognise any resulting impairment loss.

(IAS 36, 80(a))

This test (the 'bottom up' test) ensures that an entity recognises any impairment loss that exists for the cash generating unit, including any corporate assets which can be allocated on a reasonable and consistent basis. If corporate assets can be allocated on a reasonable and consistent basis to a cash generating unit and the 'bottom up' test is carried out, no further testing is required.

If none of the corporate assets can be allocated on a reasonable and consistent basis to the cash generating unit, the entity should first perform the 'bottom up' test for the cash generating unit. This determines whether or not any of the assets in that unit, other than the corporate assets, have been impaired. The entity must then perform the following 'top down' test:

- identify the smallest cash generating unit which includes the cash generating unit under review and to which the carrying amount of the corporate assets can be allocated on a reasonable and consistent basis (the 'larger' cash generating unit);
- compare the recoverable amount of the larger cash generating unit to its carrying amount (including the corporate assets); and
- recognise any resulting impairment loss.

(IAS 36, 80(b))

The combination of the 'bottom up' and the 'top down' tests ensures that an entity recognises:

- any impairment loss that exists for the cash generating unit excluding any corporate assets (the 'bottom up' test); and
- any impairment loss that exists for corporate assets (the 'top down' test).

It is frequently the case that goodwill and corporate assets are covered by the same 'top down' test. In example 25.7, the possible impairment of both goodwill and corporate assets relating to the restaurant chain are covered by the 'top down' test. However, the 'top down' test in the example does not cover, for example, corporate assets at the group level. Another 'top down' test is necessary if there are indications that group corporate assets are impaired.

25.15 DISCLOSURE

For each class of assets, the financial statements should disclose:

- the amount of impairment losses recognised in the income statement during the period and the line item(s) of the income statement in which those impairment losses are included;
- the amount of reversals of impairment losses recognised in the income statement during the period and the line item(s) of the income statement in which those impairment losses are reversed;
- the amount of impairment losses recognised directly in equity during the period; and
- the amount of reversals of impairment losses recognised directly in equity during the period.

(IAS 36, 113)

An entity should disclose the following for each reportable primary segment:

- the amount of impairment losses recognised in the income statement and directly in equity during the period; and
- the amount of reversals of impairment losses recognised in the income statement and directly in equity during the period.

(IAS 36, 116)

If an impairment loss for an individual asset or a cash generating unit is recognised or reversed during the period and is material to the financial statements of the reporting entity as a whole, an entity should disclose:

- the events and circumstances that led to the recognition or reversal of the impairment loss;
- the amount of the impairment loss recognised or reversed;
- for an individual asset:
  - the nature of the asset; and
  - the reportable segment to which the asset belongs;
- for a cash generating unit:
  - a description of the cash generating unit;
  - the amount of the impairment loss recognised or reversed by class of assets and by reportable segment based on the entity's primary format; and
  - if the aggregation of assets for identifying the cash generating unit has changed since the previous estimate of the cash generating unit's recoverable amount (if any), describe the current and former way of aggregating assets and the reasons for changing the way the cash generating unit is identified;

- whether the recoverable amount of the asset (cash generating unit) is its net selling price or its value in use;
- if recoverable amount is net selling price, the basis used to determine net selling price (such as whether selling price was determined by reference to an active market or in some other way); and
- if recoverable amount is value in use, the discount rate(s) used in the current estimate and previous estimate (if any) of value in use.

(IAS 36, 117)

If impairment losses recognised (reversed) during the period are material in aggregate to the financial statements of the reporting entity as a whole, an entity should describe briefly:

- the main classes of assets affected by impairment losses (reversals of impairment losses) for which no information is disclosed; and
- the main events and circumstances that led to the recognition (reversal) of these impairment losses for which no information is disclosed.

(IAS 36, 118)

25.16 TRANSITIONAL PROVISIONS

The adoption of IAS 36 is not a change in accounting policy for any entity which has previously been complying with IFRSs or many national accounting requirements. Therefore, impairment losses and reversals of impairment losses which result from adoption of IAS 36 should be recognised in the income statement (unless the assets concerned are carried at revalued amount) in the period in which the IAS is first applied. An impairment loss or reversal of impairment loss on a revalued asset should be treated as a revaluation decrease (increase).

Notes

1 Jim Paul (principal author), *International Review of Accounting Standards Specifying a Recoverable Amount Test for Long-Lived Assets*, G4+1, 1997 (copies of G4+1 papers may be obtained from any member of the group).

2 Hugo Nurnberg and Nelson Dittmar, 'Reporting Impairments of Long-Lived Assets: New Rules and Disclosures', *The Journal of Financial Statement Analysis*, Winter 1997.

3 David Cairns, 'Impairment of Assets', *Financial Times World Accounting Report*, June 1997, pp13-15.

4 The arguments for and against the two approaches are dealt with in detail in E55 *Impairment of Assets* (pp3-5), the basis for conclusions in IAS 36 (appendix B20 to B42) and the G4+1 discussion paper referred to above.

CHAPTER 26

Inventories

26.1 RELEVANT STANDARD AND INTERPRETATION

IAS 2 *Inventories*
SIC 1 *Consistency – Different Cost Formulas for Inventories*

26.2 HISTORY

IAS 2 *Accounting for Inventories in the Context of the Historical Cost System* (IAS 2 [1975]) was approved in 1975. While the IAS allowed a choice among different valuation formulas, 'the thrust of IAS 2 was not directed at this choice, but at getting rid of accounting treatments which, by increasing or decreasing inventory values at will, tailored profits according to what is suitable to management'[1].

IAS 2 was reviewed in 1985. Although there was 'considerable support' for outlawing LIFO and the base stock method, the IASC concluded that there was 'insufficient support internationally' for such a move at that time (*IASC News*, July 1985, p3).

IAS 2 was reconsidered in the comparability and improvements project. E32 proposed that FIFO/weighted average cost should be the preferred (benchmark) treatment and that LIFO should be the allowed alternative treatment. E32 also proposed that the base stock method should be eliminated. The IASC proposed to retain LIFO as an allowed alternative because it may 'adjust net income for the effects of some price changes' and its use was 'firmly entrenched in a number of countries, often because of the tax advantages associated with its use' (E32, 28).

Many commentators on E32 argued that the use of the LIFO method should not be permitted because:

- tax considerations do not provide an adequate conceptual basis for selecting an appropriate accounting treatment; and

- it would be inconsistent to retain LIFO in an historical cost context as a partial attempt to account for the effects of changing prices without introducing a more comprehensive method of inflation accounting.

(*IASC News*, July 1990, p8–9)

Following its reconsideration of the issues in the light of the comments on E32, the IASC concluded that LIFO should be eliminated (*Statement of Intent on the Comparability of Financial Statements*, appendix 2 and E38, p3). After reviewing the comment letters on E38, the IASC reconfirmed this position (*IASC Update*, June 1992, p2) but this decision was overturned in October 1992 when the IASC considered the final draft of the revised IAS 2. The IASC's efforts to remove LIFO were opposed on the board by Germany, Italy, Japan and Korea all of which allow, but do not require, the use of LIFO. The European financial analysts favoured elimination of LIFO but the North American analysts favoured its retention; as a single board delegation, the analysts voted in favour of elimination. Opposition to the elimination of LIFO also came from the European Commission.

Perhaps the most significant opponent of the elimination of LIFO was IOSCO (*IASC Insight*, December 1992, pp1 and 14–15). Although it had urged the IASC to eliminate alternatives in IASs, IOSCO told the IASC in April 1992 that it was going too far in seeking to eliminate LIFO. There is no doubt that had IOSCO not delivered this message, at least one of the board countries which opposed the elimination of LIFO would have changed its vote. Claims that IOSCO had advised the IASC of its view two years earlier are incorrect. IOSCO representatives had not expressed their opposition to the elimination of LIFO at meetings of the IASC consultative group, comparability steering committee or the improvements steering committee prior to April 1992.

Contrary to a growing misconception[2], the United States delegation voted in favour of the elimination of LIFO at each stage in the comparability and improvements project. While a number of American commentators favoured the retention of LIFO, that position was not shared by the board delegation. Arthur Wyatt, the IASC chairman at the time of the first improvements project, explains the US approach and what happened during the IASC's debates on LIFO[3].

> 'So after lobbying, consulting a bit with each other, the United States representatives [on the IASC board] stated that the United States was ready to give up LIFO. The United States would vote to eliminate LIFO and permit as acceptable accounting only FIFO or average cost. Well, that stunned the group. The feeling amongst the other countries had been that LIFO was not something the United States would ever concede. We also told them, of course, that we – the two United States

representatives – did not have the power to do this but that we would deal with the FASB and the SEC and urge the SEC to deal with Congress because LIFO exists in the United States, at least in part, because the Treasury Department and Congress enacted a rule that if you want to use LIFO for tax purposes, you must use it for accounting purposes as well. The LIFO conformity rule is a big hurdle in the United States to getting rid of LIFO.

So, the IASC had a discussion and we took a vote and there were two countries that voted to retain LIFO even with the United States giving it up; I cannot remember which two, but Japan was one of them and, I think, Korea was the other. So we left the meeting and LIFO was a done deal. I got back to the States and went down to see the people at the SEC and the people at the FASB. Time goes by and we have another IASC meeting – you never really decide things at one meeting. Losers always reintroduce the issue, and hence we reconsidered LIFO; and, lo and behold, Italy and Germany announced that in recent months their countries had adopted LIFO as part of their tax code and in each of these countries a company's financial statements must agree with its tax return. So, all of a sudden now we have Japan, Korea, Italy and Germany against eliminating LIFO, and as a consequence, we were unable to eliminate LIFO.'

IAS 2 *Inventories*, with LIFO as an allowed alternative treatment but with the base stock method eliminated, was approved in November 1993 and applied to financial statements for accounting periods beginning on or after 1 January 1995.

The LIFO issue continued to be troublesome. Some IASC board members argued that the revised IAS 2 should allow an entity to use LIFO for some inventories and FIFO or WAC for other similar inventories. The IASC board confirmed in a written ballot that it had not been its intention to allow such flexibility and that to do so would undermine its efforts to ensure that like transactions and events are accounted for in a like way. Therefore, it was understood at the time that an entity should use either the benchmark treatment or the allowed alternative treatment for all inventories. In its first interpretation, the SIC overturned the board's decision.

The IASB's May 2002 improvements exposure draft proposes to eliminate the use of the LIFO formula for three reasons:

- the LIFO formula does not assume a reliable representation of inventory flows;
- the use of LIFO can have 'marked distorting effects' on net profit and loss when older layers of inventories are presumed to have been used or when inventories are substantially reduced; and

- tax considerations do not provide an adequate conceptual basis for the selection of an appropriate accounting treatment and it is not acceptable to allow an accounting treatment purely because of tax regulations and advantages.

The May 2002 improvements exposure draft also proposes changes to the disclosures in IAS 2.

IAS 41 deals with inventories of biological assets and agricultural produce (see chapter 45).

26.3 IOSCO

In June 1994, IOSCO advised the IASC that IAS 2 was acceptable for the purposes of the IOSCO core standards. However, IOSCO identified the following suspense issues:

- some IOSCO members may allow inventories to be carried at a fixed quantity and value when the overall value is of secondary importance (as permitted by article 38 of the EU Fourth Directive and permitted by IAS 2 if the amounts are immaterial);
- one IOSCO member believes that measurement at cost, without a write-down to net realisable value should be allowed (this is not permitted by IAS 2);
- one IOSCO member believes that measurement at replacement cost should be allowed (IAS 2 deals only with the historical cost system);
- one IOSCO member believes that the last purchase price method should be allowed for the sake of convenience in cases where it approximates historical cost on a consistent basis (this would be permitted under IAS 2 on grounds of materiality); and
- some IOSCO members believe that those entities using LIFO should not be required to reconcile to FIFO/weighted average cost (such a reconciliation is required by IAS 2 but the IASB now proposes to eliminate LIFO and, hence, the reconciliation requirement).

IOSCO also suggested that, as a potential long-term project, the IASC should consider developing guidance on the application of the LIFO method.

IAS 2 is included in 'IAS 2000' endorsed by IOSCO in May 2000. There are no supplemental treatments.

26.4 IAS 2 IN BRIEF

Inventories should be measured at the lower of cost and net realisable value.

The cost of inventories should comprise all costs of purchase, costs of conversion and other costs incurred in bringing the inventories to their present location and condition. This includes an allocation of production overheads. Cost may include borrowing costs for those inventories which take a substantial period to get ready for their intended use. When the costs on inventories cannot be specifically identified, costs may be identified by the following formulas:

- FIFO or weighted average; or
- LIFO.

The same formula must be used for all inventories having a similar nature and use to the entity.

Inventories should be written down to net realisable value (estimated selling price less estimated costs to complete and sell) when cost exceeds net realisable value.

Inventories should be recognised as an expense when they are sold, lost or written down.

26.5 DEFINITION OF INVENTORIES

Inventories are assets:

- held for sale in the ordinary course of business;
- in the process of production for such sale; or
- in the form of materials or supplies to be consumed in the production process or in the rendering of services.

(IAS 2, 4)

Inventories include:

- goods and other assets held for resale, for example the merchandise held by a wholesaler, distributor or retailer and land and other property held by a property dealer;
- finished goods produced, or work in progress being produced, raw materials, components and other supplies awaiting use in the production process; and
- the costs incurred in rendering a service for which the entity has not yet recognised the related revenue.

The definition of inventories encompasses financial assets such as securities held for trading purposes. Such assets are specifically excluded from the scope of IAS 2 (IAS 2, 1(b)) and should be dealt with in accordance with IAS 39 (see chapter 20).

The definition of inventories encompasses inventories of biological assets and agricultural produce. Biological assets are living animals or plants (IAS 41, 5). Agricultural produce is the harvested product of an entity's biological assets (IAS 41, 5). Such inventories are accounted for in accordance with IAS 41 (see chapter 45). Product which is harvested by an entity and then held or used subsequently is accounted for in accordance with IAS 41 up to the point of harvest and IAS 2 thereafter.

The definition of inventories also encompasses producers' inventories of mineral ores. These inventories are included within the scope of IAS 2 when they are measured at the lower of cost and net realisable value. They are excluded from the scope of IAS 2 when they are measured at net realisable value in accordance with well established practices in certain industries (IAS 2, 1(c)).

26.6 RECOGNITION OF INVENTORIES AS AN ASSET

IAS 2 does not deal with the recognition of inventories as an asset. If the IASC were to develop such criteria, they would probably be similar to those for property, plant and equipment (see chapter 21). They would also probably mirror those for the sale of goods in IAS 18 (see chapter 29) which would mean that inventories should be recognised as an asset when:

- the significant risks and rewards of ownership of the goods have been transferred to the entity;
- the entity has acquired continuing managerial involvement to the degree usually associated with ownership or effective control over the goods;
- the cost of the goods can be measured reliably; and
- it is probable that the economic benefits associated with the item will flow to the entity.

(derived from IAS 18, 14)

26.7 MEASUREMENT OF INVENTORIES AS AN ASSET

Inventories should be measured at the lower of cost and net realisable value (IAS 2, 6). Therefore, inventories are not carried in excess of amounts expected to be realised from their sale or use in the ordinary course of business.

26.8 COST OF INVENTORIES

The *cost* of inventories should comprise:

- all costs of purchase of goods and other assets held for resale, raw materials, components and supplies used, or awaiting use, in production;
- the costs of conversion of finished goods and work in progress; and
- other costs incurred in bringing the inventories to their present location and condition.

(IAS 2, 7)

The cost of inventories of agricultural produce harvested from an entity's biological assets is determined in accordance with IAS 41. Up to the point of harvest, these inventories should be measured at fair value less point of sale costs (IAS 41, 13) with all gains and losses included in the income statement (IAS 41, 26). The amount determined in accordance with IAS 41 is used subsequently as cost for the purposes of IAS 2 (see chapter 45).

The costs of purchase comprise:

- the purchase price;
- import and other duties arising on the purchase of the inventories;
- non-refundable purchase taxes, such as any value added or similar taxes, which are not recoverable by the entity from the taxing authorities;
- transport and handling costs in bringing the inventories to their present location and condition; and
- other costs directly attributable to the acquisition of the inventories.

Trade discounts, rebates and other similar items are deducted in determining the costs of purchase.

Duties, purchase taxes, value added and similar taxes vary from country to country. In some cases, the duties or taxes are refunded to the entity when it sells the goods to another party. For example, in many countries, entities are able to deduct the value added tax they have paid to suppliers or customs authorities on purchases from the value added tax on sales which they charge to their customers and pay over to the authorities. Such refundable duties and taxes are not included in the costs of purchase but are included as a receivable from (or deducted from a liability owing to) the authorities. Those duties and taxes which are not refundable are included in the costs of purchase.

The costs of conversion include:

- costs directly related to the units or production, such as direct labour;
- a systematic allocation of variable production overheads that are incurred in converting materials into finished goods; and
- a systematic allocation of fixed production overheads that are incurred in converting materials into finished goods.

(IAS 2, 10)

Variable production overheads are those indirect costs of production that vary directly, or nearly directly, with the volume of production, such as indirect materials and indirect labour (IAS 2, 10). Variable production overheads are allocated to each unit of production on the basis of the actual use of the production facilities (IAS 2, 11).

Fixed production overheads are those indirect costs of production that remain relatively constant regardless of the volume of production. They include:

- depreciation of factory buildings, plant and equipment;
- the maintenance of factory buildings, plant and equipment;
- rent and property taxes for the factory buildings;
- storage and handling costs for raw materials, components, other supplies and work in progress prior to a subsequent production processes; and
- the cost of factory management and administration such as personnel and payroll costs for factory employees.

Fixed production overheads are allocated to each unit of production based on the normal capacity of the production facilities (IAS 2, 11). Normal capacity is the production expected to be achieved on average over a number of periods or seasons under normal circumstances, taking into account the loss of capacity resulting from planned maintenance (IAS 2, 11). The actual level of production may be used when it approximates normal capacity.

In periods of abnormally high production, there is the risk that inventories are carried at an amount greater than cost if fixed overheads are allocated based on normal capacity. In such circumstances, the use of normal capacity may mean that the total amount of fixed overhead allocated to inventories, both sold and on hand, in the period exceeds the total amount of fixed overheads incurred in the period. Therefore, the amount of fixed overhead allocated to each unit of production is reduced so that inventories are not measured above cost (IAS 2, 11).

No guidance is given on what is meant by abnormally high production. However, the amount of fixed overheads allocated to inventories, both sold and on hand, will exceed the total amount of fixed overheads incurred in any period in which actual production exceeds normal capacity. Therefore, the issue is really one of materiality, rather than abnormality.

Low production creates the risk that inventories are carried at an amount less than cost. In such cases, however, the amount of fixed overhead allocated to each unit of production is not increased (IAS 2, 11).

Other costs are included in the cost of inventories only to the extent that they are incurred in bringing the inventories to their present location and condition. For example, it may be appropriate to include in the cost of inventories:

- the cost of designing products for specific customers (IAS 2, 13);
- the amortisation of development costs relating to a particular product or process;
- the depreciation of a patent or licence relating to a particular product or process; and
- storage costs that are necessary in the production process prior to a further production stage (IAS 2, 14).

Extract 26.1 *Other costs included in cost of inventories*

Sulzer, Switzerland, 31 December 2001 (IAS)

Production costs include ... contract-related engineering and design costs.

Extract 26.2 *Other costs included in cost of inventories*

S&T, Austria, 31 December 2001 (IAS)

Inventories including demonstration equipment are stated at the lower of cost or net realisable value. Cost comprises all external cost including freight and duties ...

Costs which are excluded from the cost of inventories and which are recognised as an expense in the period in which they are incurred include:

- unallocated fixed production overheads (IAS 2, 11);
- abnormal amounts of wasted materials, labour, or other production costs (IAS 2, 14);
- storage costs, after production is completed (IAS 2, 14);

- administrative overheads which do not contribute to bringing inventories to their present location and condition (IAS 2, 14);
- the costs of distribution to customers; and
- selling costs (IAS 2, 14).

Borrowing costs may be included in the cost of inventories which are qualifying assets under IAS 23, that is, those which require a substantial period of time to bring them to a saleable condition (IAS 23, 6), for example wines and spirits which require time to mature. Borrowing costs should not be capitalised once the inventories are ready for their intended use. If an entity capitalises borrowing costs on some inventories, it must capitalise borrowing costs on all other inventories which are qualifying assets (SIC 2, 3).

Borrowing costs are not capitalised on inventories which are routinely manufactured or otherwise produced in large quantities on a repetitive basis over a short period of time (IAS 23, 6). In practice, therefore, the distinction between inventories which are qualifying assets and those which are not qualifying assets rests on the time taken to bring the inventories to a saleable condition. If the period is long, borrowing costs may be capitalised; if the period is short, borrowing costs should not be capitalised.

Any foreign currency transactions involved in the acquisition of inventories are recorded by applying to the foreign currency amount the exchange rate between the reporting currency and the foreign currency at the date of the transaction. The effects of subsequent changes in the exchange rate on the resulting liability are treated as exchange differences and are not included in the cost of inventories unless:

- they are included in borrowing costs and are capitalised in accordance with the allowed alternative treatment for dealing with such costs (IAS 23, 5); or
- they result from a severe devaluation or depreciation of a currency against which there is no practical means of hedging; and which affects liabilities which cannot be settled and which arise directly on the recent acquisition of the asset invoiced in a foreign currency and are capitalised under the allowed alternative treatment in IAS 21. In its May 2002 improvements exposure draft, the IASB proposes to eliminate this allowed alternative treatment (see chapter 19).

26.8.1 Cost Methods

Various costing methods have been developed for use by management for internal reporting and decision-making purposes. These methods may be used for financial reporting purposes provided that their results approximate cost as defined in IAS 2. Absorption costing methods, which incorporate an allocation of fixed overheads, may be used. Direct or marginal costing methods, however, which exclude fixed overheads are inappropriate for the purposes of applying IAS 2.

IAS 2 makes specific reference to two costing methods – the standard cost method and the retail method – both of which are acceptable for financial reporting purposes provided that their results approximate cost as defined in IAS 2. It is important to recognise, however, that the purposes of the two methods are different. The standard cost method is a management tool which may need to be adapted to produce the information required by IAS 2; the retail method is a practical means of measuring the cost of inventories for financial reporting purposes.

One definition of a standard cost is that it is the 'planned unit cost of the products, components or services produced in a period'[4]. The main uses of standard costs are in 'performance measurement, control, stock valuation and in the establishment of selling prices'[5]. Standard costs may be used to measure the cost of inventories for financial reporting purposes provided they are computed or modified in accordance with the requirements of IAS 2. In some cases, therefore, for financial reporting purposes, it may be necessary to reallocate certain costs or adjust the standard costs by some or all the variances from the standard.

Extract 26.3 *Standard costs*

Novartis, Switzerland, 31 December 2001 (IAS)

In the balance sheet inventory is primarily valued at standard cost, which approximates to historical cost determined on a first-in-first-out basis and this value is used for the cost of goods sold in the income statement.

Extract 26.4 *Standard costs*

Adidas, Germany, 31 December 2000 (IAS)

Merchandise and finished goods are valued at the lower of cost or net realizable value. Costs are determined using a standard valuation method which approximate the first-in, first-out method or the average cost method.

The retail method is often used by retailers and wholesalers for measuring the cost of inventories of large numbers of rapidly changing items that have similar margins. The method is used often because it is impracticable to use other costing methods.

Under the retail method, inventories are initially measured at selling price and then reduced to cost by applying the appropriate gross margin. As gross margins may vary significantly from product to product, it is important first to sub-divide inventories into appropriate categories with similar margins. For example, a department store needs to classify food separately from clothing and men's clothing separately from women's clothing if the margins are different in each category. An average percentage for each department can be used if the result approximates cost. However, an average for the whole store may not approximate cost and may even offset profits and losses if it results in some inventories being valued below cost and others above cost.

When the selling price of inventories has been reduced below its normal level the entity should either:

- use a reduced margin; or
- apply the normal gross margin to the normal selling price, rather than the reduced selling price.

While the retail method uses selling prices as the starting point in the calculation, it is still necessary to test that the resulting costs do not exceed the net realisable value of the inventories.

Extract 26.5 *Retail method*

Dairy Farm, Hong Kong, 31 December 2001 (IAS)

Stocks which primarily comprise goods held for resale are stated at the lower of cost and net realisable value. Cost of stock is determined using the retail inventory method which approximates to a first-in, first-out basis.

26.8.2 Cost Formulas

Cost formulas are used to assign the costs that have been incurred by the entity to inventories. IAS 2 allows the use of four formulas:

- specific identification;
- first in first out (FIFO);
- weighted average cost (WAC); and
- last in first out (LIFO).

When specific identification is not used, FIFO/WAC is the benchmark treatment and LIFO is the allowed alternative treatment.

26.8.3 Cost Formulas – Specific Identification

Specific identification means that the entity attributes the specific costs to identified items of inventories. It is required for:

- inventories which are not ordinarily interchangeable;
- goods which have been produced and segregated for specific projects; and
- services which have been carried out for specific projects.

(IAS 2, 19)

Specific identification is not a practicable means of assigning costs to inventories in many businesses. Furthermore, IAS 2 states that specific identification of costs is inappropriate when there are large numbers of items of inventory which are ordinarily interchangeable because it could be used to obtain pre-determined effects on the net profit or loss for the period (IAS 2, 20). In other words, the entity can choose those costs which it attributes to inventories and thereby pre-determine the amounts of inventories and cost of sales.

26.8.4 Cost Formulas – FIFO and WAC

Under the benchmark treatment in IAS 2, the costs of inventories for which specific identification is not required should be assigned using either FIFO or WAC (IAS 2, 21). Both the FIFO and WAC formulas assign up-to-date costs to inventories and, in practice, produce similar results when price changes are small and infrequent, and when there is a fairly rapid turnover of inventories.

FIFO assumes that the items of inventory which were purchased first are sold first, and consequently the items remaining in inventory at the end of the period are those most recently purchased or produced.

Under the WAC formula, the cost of each item is the weighted average of the cost of similar items at the beginning of a period and the cost of similar items purchased or produced during the period. The average may be calculated on a periodic basis or as each additional shipment is received.

The use of FIFO and WAC matches old costs with current revenues. In example 26.1, the revenue from the sale of 70 units on 18 February and 30 of the units sold on 20 March are matched with the cost of the opening inventories. The balance of the 20 March sale is matched with 31 January costs. In example 26.2 the revenue on 18 February is matched with the weighted average cost of the opening inventories and the purchases on 31 January.

Extract 26.6 *Weighted Average Cost*

Harmony, South Africa, 30 June 2000 (IAS)

The cost of gold produced is determined principally by the weighted average cost method using related production costs. The cost of supplies is also determined using the weighted average cost method.

Example 26.1 *FIFO*

A has the following inventory record for product X:

	Units	*Inventory Units*	*Unit Cost £*	*Total cost £*
Inventory 1/1/02	40	40	12	480
Purchases 31/1/02	50	90	15	750
Sales 18/2/02	30	60		
Purchases 1/3/02	20	80	18	360
Sales 20/3/02	15	65		
Inventory 31/3/02		65		

Applying the FIFO formula, 20 units of inventory are assumed to have been purchased on 1 March 2002 and the balance of 45 units on 31 January 2002. Therefore, the FIFO cost of inventories is assumed to be:

	£	£
20 units at £18	360	
45 units at £15	675	
Total		1,035

IASB improvements project

In its May 2002 improvements exposure draft, the IASB proposes to incorporate the requirement of SIC 1 into IAS 2, that is to require that the same cost formula should be used for all inventories having a similar nature and use to the entity. A difference in geographical location or tax rules is not sufficient to justify the use of different formulas.

26.8.5 Cost Formula – LIFO

The cost of inventories for which specific identification is not required should be assigned using LIFO (IAS 2, 23). This assumes that the items of inventory which were purchased or produced last are sold first, and consequently the items remaining in inventory at the end of the period are those first purchased or produced (IAS 2, 23 and 24).

The LIFO formula does not assign up-to-date costs to inventories but it does match up-to-date costs with revenue. In example 26.3, the revenue from the sale of 30 units on 18 February is matched with the cost of 30

Example 26.2 *Weighted average cost*

Using the same information as example 26.1, weighted average costs can be calculated as follows for product X:

	Units	*Inventory Units*	*Unit Cost*	*Total cost*	*Weighted average cost*
			£	£	£
Inventory 1/1/02	40	40		480	12.00
Purchases 31/1/02	50	90	15	750	13.67
Sales 18/2/02	30	60			13.67
Purchases 1/3/02	20	80	18	360	14.75
Sales 20/3/02	15	65			14.75
Inventory 31/3/02		65			14.75

Weighted average costs can be determined in a number of different ways. The above calculation assumes that they are recalculated every time inventory is purchased. Therefore, the 90 units held from 31 January consist of 40 units at £12 and 50 units at £15, a weighted average unit cost of £13.67. The weighted average cost is re-calculated on 1 March when the 80 units of inventory consist of 60 units at £13.67 (the former weighted average) and 20 units at £18 to give a new weighted average unit cost of £14.75. The weighted average cost of inventories at 31 March 2002 is £959. The calculation could also have been made on a quarterly basis by dividing the total cost of opening inventory and purchases (£1,590) by the total units of opening inventory and purchases (110) to give a weighted average unit cost of £14.45 and a weighted average cost of inventories of £939.

units bought on 31 January. The revenue from the sale of 15 units on 20 March is matched with the cost of 15 units bought on 1 March.

When the volume of inventories is reduced, the use of LIFO may distort the net profit or loss for the period because old costs are suddenly matched against current revenues. If, in example 26.3, A sells all its inventories of product X on 1 April at current selling prices, the revenue from the sale is matched with inventories which are carried at very old costs. In practice, inventory movements are more complex and the application of the LIFO formula requires records of the various layers of inventories that may have been created or used up.

A number of different LIFO methods are in use. In the FASB's IAS – US GAAP comparison, Upton points out: '... application of the LIFO method in the United States can be based on a wide variety of computational techniques. Two similar entities might use methods described as

Example 26.3 *LIFO*

A has the following inventory record for product X:

	Units	*Inventory Units*	*Unit Cost* £	*Total cost* £
Inventory 1/1/02	40	40	5	200
Purchases 31/1/02	50	90	15	750
Sales 18/2/02	30	60		
Purchases 1/3/02	20	80	18	360
Sales 20/3/02	15	65		
Inventory 31/3/02		65		

Applying the LIFO formula, the 65 units of inventory are assumed to be the 40 units included in the opening inventory plus 20 of the units purchased on 31 January 2002 and 5 of the units purchased on 1 March 1998. Therefore, the LIFO cost of inventories is:

	£
40 units at £5	200
20 units at £15	300
5 units at £18	90
Total	590

LIFO but produce significantly different measurements of inventories because they employed different techniques'[6].

It is often the case that tax rules, rather than accounting standards, determine the choice of method and other regulations on the application of LIFO. Indeed, few entities use LIFO unless there are related tax benefits. In the United States, tax regulations provide specific rules for the implementation of LIFO. No standards have been issued by the FASB or its predecessor bodies although the American Institute of Certified Public Accountants has issued a non-mandatory issues paper[7] which contains recommendations on LIFO inventory problems. Although IAS 2 permits the use of LIFO, the IASC has not issued any guidance on the choice of method or its application.

When the LIFO formula is used, the financial statements should disclose the difference between the amount of inventories as shown in the balance sheet and either:

- the lower of net realisable value and the amount arrived at using a FIFO or WAC formula; or

- the lower of current cost at the balance sheet date and net realisable value.

(IAS 2, 36)

This requirement ensures that the financial statements of an entity using LIFO are comparable with the financial statements of entities using FIFO or WAC. The requirement recognises, however, that some entities may not be able to calculate FIFO or WAC and may, therefore, use current costs at the balance sheet date as an approximation of FIFO or WAC.

Extract 26.7 *Impact of LIFO*

RWE, Germany, 31 December 2001 (IAS)

The market value of stocks valued using the LIFO method is €50 million (previous year: €209 million) above the carrying amounts reported in the Balance Sheet.

Extract 26.8 *Impact of LIFO*

Recordati, Italy, 31 December 2000 (IAS)

Except for work in process and promotional material, inventories are mainly valued using the LIFO cost method, by annual inventory layers. ...

Inventory values as of 31 December 2000 would have been 1,295 million lire higher if the average cost method, corresponding substantially to current costs had been applied (1,547 million lire as of 31 December 1999).

In its first interpretation[8], the SIC concluded that an entity should use the same cost formula for all inventories having a similar nature and use to the entity but that different formulas may be justified for inventories with a different nature or use (SIC 1, 3). A difference in the geographical location of the inventories and tax rules is not, by itself, sufficient to justify the use of different formulas.

IASB improvements project

In its May 2002 improvements exposure draft, the IASB proposes to eliminate LIFO as an acceptable accounting formula under IAS 2.

26.9 NET REALISABLE VALUE

The carrying amount of inventories should not exceed their net realisable value. Therefore, inventories need to be written down to net realisable value when cost exceeds that value. The need for a write-down may arise when inventories are damaged, wholly or partially obsolete or otherwise unsaleable or when their selling prices have declined. A write-down is also required when the estimated costs to complete work in progress or to make the sale are such that subsequent sales will not result in a profit.

Net realisable value is the estimated selling price in the ordinary course of business less the estimated costs of completion and the estimated costs necessary to make the sale (IAS 2, 4). Estimates of net realisable value take into consideration the purpose for which the inventory is held (IAS 2, 28). For example, the net realisable value of inventory held to satisfy contracted sales is based on the contract price. However, the net realisable value of inventories held for general sale is based on general selling prices.

Estimates of net realisable value are based on the most reliable evidence available when the estimates are made. These estimates take into consideration changes in prices or costs directly relating to events occurring after the end of the period to the extent that such events confirm conditions existing at the balance sheet date (IAS 2, 27 and IAS 10, 25). In particular, when it is known by the date on which the financial statements are authorised for issue that inventories have been, or will be, sold for less than cost after the balance sheet date, such inventories should be measured at net realisable value at the balance sheet date unless it can be clearly demonstrated that the decline in value occurred after the balance sheet date.

The net realisable value of materials and other supplies to be used in the production process is based on the selling price of the finished products less the costs of completion rather than selling price as materials and supplies. Such inventories are written down to net realisable value when the total cost of the finished products exceeds the net realisable value of the finished products. The replacement cost of materials may be the best available measure of the net realisable value of materials and supplies particularly when replacement costs fluctuate in response to the selling price of finished products (or *vice versa*). However, inventories are not written down to replacement cost when the entity expects the net realisable value of the finished products to exceed the total costs of the finished products.

Inventories are written down to net realisable value on an item by item basis (IAS 2, 26). However, items have to be grouped for practical reasons in a number of circumstances. In particular, inventories of the same product are grouped when they have similar purposes or end uses, are produced and marketed in the same geographical area, and cannot practicably be evaluated separately from other items in that product line. For example, a manufacturer or retailer might apply a global mark-down to its inventories of seasonal clothing because it cannot determine which particular garments it will sell at higher or lower than cost. A manufacturer may also apply a global write-down when it does not expect to sell all its inventory of a particular item.

It is inappropriate to group all finished goods or all inventories in a particular industry or geographical segment and determine the write-down on a global basis (IAS 2, 26). Therefore, it is inappropriate for a retailer to compare the cost of all inventories in a department store with the aggregate selling price of those inventories. Similarly, it is inappropriate for a manufacturer to determine the write-down by comparing the cost of all its inventories with their aggregate selling prices.

When inventories are written down to net realisable value, the lower net realisable value is not treated as a 'new cost' as is the case in a number of national accounting standards. If the same inventories continue to be held at the next balance sheet date (which should be a rare occurrence given the nature of inventories), the entity must compare the original cost with a new estimate of net realisable value. This may result in the reversal of the previous period's write-down (IAS 2, 30).

26.10 RECOGNITION OF INVENTORIES AS AN EXPENSE

The amount of inventories recognised as an expense in a period should comprise:

- the carrying amount of inventories sold for which revenue is recognised in the period;
- the amount of any write-downs of inventories to net realisable value which have been made in the period; and
- the carrying amount of any inventories which have been lost or destroyed during the period.

(IAS 2, 31)

The amount recognised as an expense should be reduced by the amount of any reversal of a write-down of inventories to net realisable value (IAS 2, 31).

26.11 PRACTICAL PROBLEMS

26.11.1 By-Products and Joint Products

A production process may result in joint products or a main product and a by-product. When the costs of each joint product or the main product and the by-product are not separately identifiable, the total costs are allocated between the products on a rational and consistent basis (IAS 2, 12). The allocation may be based, for example, on the relative sales value of each product either at the stage in the production process when the products become separately identifiable, or at the completion of production.

Most by-products are, by their nature, immaterial joint products. When this is the case, they are often measured at net realisable value and this value is deducted from the cost of the main product. As a result, the carrying amount of the main product is not materially different from its cost.

26.11.2 Mining Inventories

IAS 2 does not apply to mineral ores which are measured at net realisable value in accordance with well established practices in certain industries (IAS 2, 1(c) and 3). These inventories are measured at net realisable value usually because:

- sale is assured under a forward contract or a government guarantee; or
- there is a homogenous market and a negligible risk of failure to sell.

IAS 18 also does not deal with the related issue of the revenue arising from the extraction of mineral ores (IAS 18, 6 (g)).

26.12 DISCLOSURE

An entity should disclose the accounting policies adopted in measuring inventories, including the cost formula used (IAS 2, 34(a)).

Extract 26.9 *Accounting policy for inventories*

Highveld, South Africa, 31 December 2000 (IAS accounting policies)

- Finished goods and work in progress are valued at standard cost, including an appropriate apportionment of overheads. Standard cost approximates actual cost determined on the first-in, first-out basis (FIFO).

- Raw materials are valued at delivered cost determined on the FIFO basis, with appropriate reductions for handling and stockpile losses.
- Consumable stores are valued at delivered cost determined on a moving-average basis, with appropriate reductions for obsolescence and slow-moving items.
- In all cases inventories are reduced to net realisable or replacement value, if lower than cost.

Slag deposits and dumps are carried in the books at zero value. On sale of these deposits and dumps, the revenue generated is accounted for as trading profit and included in revenue.

Extract 26.10 *Accounting policy for inventories*

Sinopec, People's Republic of China, 31 December 2000 (IAS)

Inventories, other than spare parts and consumables, are carried at the lower of cost and net realisable value. Cost includes the cost of materials computed using the weighted average method and expenditure incurred in acquiring the inventories and bringing them to their existing location and condition. In the case of work in progress and finished goods, cost includes direct labour and an appropriate proportion of production overheads. Net realisable value is the estimated selling price in the ordinary course of business less the estimated costs of completion and the estimated costs necessary to make the sales.

Spare parts and consumables are stated at cost less any provision for obsolescence.

An entity should disclose:

- the total carrying amount of inventories and the carrying amount in classifications appropriate to the entity; and
- the carrying amount of inventories pledged as security for liabilities.

(IAS 2, 34)

Extract 26.11 *Classification of inventories*

Holcim, Switzerland, 31 December 2000 (IAS)

million CHF	2000	1999
Raw materials and additives	216	207
Semi-finished and finished products	612	581
Fuels	132	134
Parts and supplies	437	480
Unbilled services	26	17
Total	**1,423**	**1,419**
of which pledged/restricted	0	2

Extract 26.12 *Classification of inventories*

BHP, Australia, 30 June 2000 (IAS)

	2000 $million	1999 $million
Raw materials and stores		
At net realisable value	–	23
At cost	474	433
	474	456
Work in progress		
At net realisable value	23	197
At cost	649	617
	672	814
Finished goods		
At net realisable value	39	110
At cost	773	704
	812	814
Spares and others		
At net realisable value	–	2
At cost	180	176
	180	178
Total current inventories		
At net realisable value	62	332
At cost	2,076	1,930
	2,138	2,262

An entity should disclose the carrying amount of any inventories carried at net realisable value (IAS 2, 34). Few, if any, entities make this disclosure perhaps because the amount is usually immaterial. In its May 2002 improvements exposure draft, the IASB proposes to replace the disclosure with the disclosure of the amount of any write-downs of inventories to net realisable value, that is to require the disclosure of the income statement, rather than the balance sheet, effect of the write-downs. IAS 2 already requires the disclosure of the amount of any reversal of any write-down to net realisable value that is recognised as income in the period and the circumstances or events that led to the reversal of the write-down (IAS 2, 34).

An entity should disclose:

- the cost of inventories recognised as an expense during the period this amount is usually presented as cost of sales on the face of the income statement;
- the operating costs, applicable to revenues, recognised as an expense during the period, classified by their nature, for example raw materials

> and consumables, labour costs and other operating costs together with the amount of the net change in inventories for the period.

(IAS 2, 37)

The intention of this disclosure was to require the disclosure of the cost of goods sold but the choice of disclosures recognises that such disclosure is not relevant to all entities and is not required by some national standards (*IASC Insight*, October 1991, p10). The choice essentially allows either of the two ways of presenting expenses in the income statement formats in the EU Fourth Directive (see table 26.1). In practice, there is a growing trend for larger companies in the EU to follow the cost of sales format.

Although this new requirement came into effect only for accounting periods beginning on or after 1 January 1995, it was reconsidered in the presentation of financial statements project. Various alternative proposals were put forward during the presentation project but the end result was that IAS 1 requires similar disclosures to those required by IAS 2 but shows a preference for the 'nature of expenses' alternative (see chapter 8).

In its May 2002 improvements exposure draft, the IASB proposes to eliminate this disclosure requirement in favour of dealing with the issue in IAS 1.

Table 26.1 *Presentation of expenses based on the income statement formats in the EU Fourth Directive on annual accounts*

Articles 25 and 26 (IAS 2, 37(a))
Cost of sales
Distribution costs
Administrative expenses
Interest expense

Articles 23 and 24 (IAS 2, 37(b))
Reduction in inventories
Raw materials and consumables
Other external charges
Staff costs
Write-downs of inventories and other current assets
Other operating charges
Interest expense

Notes

1 Burggraaff, J.A., 'The Need for Standards and the Role of Standard Setting Agencies', p4, *IASC News*, October 1980.

2 See, for example, Bernard Raffournier, 'International Accounting Standards Committee'

in *International Accounting*, eds Peter Walton, Axel Haller and Bernard Raffournier, International Thomson Business Press, 1998, p55, note 8. Raffournier argues that the IASC retained LIFO because of US pressure and sees the IASC's retention of LIFO as a 'striking example' of US influence. How wrong he is! The truth, of course, is very different and would also help to disprove Raffournier's thesis that the IASC is under Anglo-Saxon influence and the views of such countries as Germany and Japan are not heard effectively (ibid, p36).

[3]Arthur Wyatt, 'Harmonization's Future' in M E Haskins, K R Ferris and T I Selling *International Financial Reporting and Analysis; A Contextual Analysis*, 4th edition, Irwin, 1996, p836.

[4] *Management Accounting Official Terminology*, Chartered Institute of Management Accountants, London, 1996, p47.

[5] Ibid, p47.

[6] Wayne S. Upton, 'Comparative Analysis of IAS 2, Inventories, and US GAAP including ARB No.43, chapter 4 'Inventory Pricing', in *The IASC – US GAAP Comparison Project: A Report of Similarities and Differences between IASC Standards and US GAAP*, ed Carrie Bloomer, Norwalk CT, FASB, 1996, p134.

[7] *Identification and Discussion of Certain Financial Accounting and Reporting Issues Concerning LIFO Inventories*, American Institute of Certified Public Accountants, New York, 1994.

[8] For a discussion of the IASC's decisions on this issue, see Cairns, D., 'Twists in the tale of the SIC's deliberations', *Accountancy* (international edition), January 1998, p65.

CHAPTER 27

Provisions and Contingencies

27.1 RELEVANT STANDARD

IAS 37 *Provisions, Contingent Liabilities and Contingent Assets*

27.2 HISTORY

27.2.1 Contingencies

IAS 10 *Contingencies and Post Balance Sheet Events* was approved and published in 1978. It dealt with those contingent losses which should be recognised as a liability and an expense, those which should only be disclosed and those which should be neither recognised nor disclosed. It prohibited the recognition of contingent assets as assets and income and allowed their disclosure in only very limited circumstances.

A standard on contingencies was included in IOSCO's original list of core standards (*IASC Insight*, December 1993, p4). In June 1994, IOSCO rejected IAS 10 because it disagreed with one sentence of implementation guidance. The IASC was unsuccessful in its effort to change IOSCO's mind. As a result, and, as part of the July 1995 agreement with IOSCO, the IASC included a project on contingencies (including a review of IAS 10) in its core standards programme (*IASC Insight*, September 1995, p4). The IASC also decided that the project should deal with provisions, a topic not on IOSCO's list of core standards.

27.2.2 Provisions

A number of early IASs referred to provisions. IAS 1 [1975] included 'liabilities and provisions' among the headings for groups of issues for which different accounting policies existed (IAS 1 [1975], 14). All the issues listed (except for commitments) were examples of items which would now be recognised as liabilities. IAS 5 included 'other liabilities and provisions' as a component of the balance sheet (IAS 5, 16) but did not define either term. IAS 12 [1979] referred to the 'provision for taxes' which was the amount of taxes payable in respect of taxable profit for the period (and, hence, a liability).

The term 'provision' was rarely used in other IASs but the IASC addressed the issue of provisions in the Framework project. The IASC confirmed that the only provisions which should be permitted in IFRS financial statements were liabilities which could be measured only by using a substantial degree of estimation (*Framework*, 64). The Framework argues that when a provision satisfies the definition of a liability, it is a liability and should be recognised as such (*Framework*, 64). The Framework maintained the long-held IASC position that provisions which do not satisfy the definition of a liability, or which do not satisfy the requirements for the write-down of an asset, are appropriations of retained earnings or some other part of equity. The use of provisions that represent secret or hidden reserves has been opposed by the IASC since IAS 1 [1975].

Shortly after approving the Framework, the IASC dealt with provisions in the context of the financial statements of banks. The IASC had much earlier indicated its opposition to the use of hidden reserves by banks, a position which the IASC reaffirmed. IAS 30 deals also with provisions for general banking risks but makes clear that many such provisions are appropriations of retained earnings and not liabilities (see chapter 43). IAS 30 also refers to the provision for losses on loans and advances which is deducted from the total carrying amount of loans and advances (IAS 30, 45) – in this case the term 'provision' means an impairment loss.

IOSCO's list of core standards did not include a standard on provisions (*IASC Insight*, December 1993, p4). When reviewing its work programme in November 1994 in the light of IOSCO's comments on existing IASs, the IASC decided to work with national standard setting bodies in order to identify possible improvements to existing IASs or the need for a new IAS on provisions (*IASC Insight*, December 1994, p13). The issue of provisions had been discussed at the 1993 IASC meeting of standard setting bodies and had already been raised in early meetings of G4+1.

As part of the agreement with IOSCO announced in July 1995, the IASC included a project on provisions in its programme (*IASC Insight*, September 1995, p4). The project would deal also with contingencies (including a review of IAS 10).

27.2.3 IAS 37

The proposal for the project was approved in March 1996. The IASC agreed that the project should be carried out jointly with the UK's

Accounting Standards Board (ASB) with the ASB's chairman, Sir David Tweedie, as chairman of the steering committee. The staff work on the project was carried out by ASB staff.

The DSOP was published in November 1996 and the exposure draft, E59, was published in August 1997. Shortly afterwards, the IASC published E61 which included proposed consequential amendments to IAS 22. IAS 37 was approved in June 1998 and applied to accounting periods beginning on or after 1 July 1999. It replaced those parts of IAS 10 which deal with contingencies. The equivalent UK standard, FRS 12 *Provisions, Contingent Liabilities and Contingent Assets*, is virtually identical to IAS 37. The IASC also approved consequential amendments to IAS 22 in respect of provisions arising on a business combination which is an acquisition but there are some inconsistencies between the two IASs which the IASB intends to remove.

27.2.4 G4+1

G4+1 published a study *Provisions: Their Recognition, Measurement, and Disclosure in Financial Statements* in 1995. The group felt that the topic was important for standard-setters worldwide because provisions are often material, there was currently little general guidance on their accounting and disclosure and it seemed likely that a common solution could be found to the issues of recognition, measurement and disclosure. The approach adopted in IAS 37 is very similar to that advocated in the G4+1 study.

27.3 IOSCO

A standard on contingencies, but not a standard on provisions, was included in IOSCO's 1993 list of core standards (*IASC Insight*, December 1993, p4). In June 1994, IOSCO advised the IASC that one essential issue had to be reviewed before it could recommend acceptance of IAS 10 for the purposes of the core standards. IOSCO argued that the possibility of recognising any amount in the range of amounts of loss, when no amount in that range is a better estimate of the loss than any other amount in the range, would lead to substantial non-comparability. This concern had clearly been raised by the American SEC; US GAAP requires the recognition of the minimum amount, rather than any amount, in the range. Other countries allow the same flexibility as was permitted by IAS 10.

In its June 1994 comments, IOSCO also identified the following suspense and other issues on IAS 10:

- deletion of the guidance on the recognition of virtually certain gains since the guidance is too general and the issues are, or should be, covered in other IASs on revenue and gain recognition (the guidance has been retained in IAS 37);
- the propriety of offsetting in the balance sheet probable losses with probable recoveries (this has been dealt with in IAS 37);
- consequential amendments to IAS 10 if impairment of financial instruments is based on discounted cash flows (the impairment of financial assets, which was dealt with in IAS 10, is now dealt with in IAS 39); and
- more guidance on, or examples of, contingencies to define more clearly their nature (this has been dealt with in IAS 37).

IOSCO also suggested that, as long-term potential projects, the IASC should consider:

- the use of, and guidance for, discounting in financial statements generally (the IASC commenced such a project); and
- more definitive guidance in applying a probability notion (this is a potential IASB project).

IAS 37 is included in 'IAS 2000' endorsed by IOSCO in May 2000. There are nine supplemental treatments:

- concerns about the appropriateness of not recognising a provision in circumstances when a board decision taken before the balance sheet date is complemented by another event occurring after the balance sheet date but before the issuance of the financial statements, for example public announcement or implementation (this concern rejects the general approach in IAS 37);
- additional disclosures for contingent assets;
- concerns about the appropriateness of not recognising a provision for the sale of assets when (1) there is a sale of a subsidiary through a public offering such that the entity would be demonstrably committed no later than the publication of the prospectus, when publication obligates the enterprise to accept offers received, and (2) for piecemeal sales when a demonstrable commitment to the restructuring occurs through the adoption of a plan and a public announcement of that plan, which may occur before any or substantially all of the assets are sold and liabilities assumed or settled;
- reconsideration of the appropriateness of using probability as a recognition criteria rather than only a measurement criteria;
- reconsideration of the appropriateness of discounting provisions;
- the issuance of additional computational guidance on discounting;
- additional guidance on the techniques to be used in determining the

best estimate, particularly when the obligation does not involve a large population of items;
- the apparent inconsistency between IAS 37 and IAS 12 regarding the anticipation of changes in regulations; and
- concerns about the appropriateness of using a risk adjusted, rather than a risk free, discount rate when computing the present value of a provision.

27.4 IAS 37 IN BRIEF

The main effects of IAS 37 are to:

- block provisions for future operating losses;
- severely limit or delay many provisions for restructuring costs; and
- accelerate the recognition in the balance sheet (but probably not in the income statement) of provisions for decommissioning costs and other environmental costs.

IAS 37 also requires several disclosures about the setting up and use of provisions.

A provision is a liability and should be recognised only when the entity has a present legal or constructive obligation arising as a result of a past event. Obligations can arise from contract, law or an entity's own actions but not simply from the intentions or a decision of management.

A provision should be measured at the best estimate of the expenditure required to settle the present obligation at the balance sheet date. Provisions should be used only for their intended purpose and should be written back to the income statement when they are no longer required. Full disclosure should be made of their nature, the amounts included in the balance sheet and the movements in the provisions.

A contingent liability should not be recognised as a liability but should be disclosed unless the possibility of loss is remote. A contingent asset should not be recognised as an asset and should not be disclosed unless the inflow of benefits is probable.

27.5 DEFINITION OF PROVISIONS

A *provision* is a liability of uncertain timing or amount (IAS 37, 10). A *liability* is a present obligation of the entity arising from past events, the settlement of which is expected to result in the outflow from the entity of resources embodying economic benefits (*Framework*, 49 and IAS 37, 10).

Therefore, a provision arises only when the entity has a present obligation arising from past events – this notion is fundamental to the approach in IAS 37 and is reinforced by the recognition criteria.

While a provision is a liability, it can be distinguished from other liabilities by the fact that there is uncertainty about the timing or amount of the future expenditure required in settlement of the obligation which gives rise to the provision. In contrast, liabilities such as trade payables and loans are usually certain as to their amount and timing while accruals are usually much less uncertain about their amount and timing than provisions.

IAS 37 also distinguishes provisions from contingent liabilities. Provisions are liabilities and are recognised as such if all the recognition criteria are met. Contingent liabilities are not recognised on the balance sheet because either:

- they are possible, rather than present, obligations – that is, they are not liabilities; or
- they are present obligations but they do not meet the recognition criteria for a provision – that is, they are liabilities but they do not meet the recognition criteria for liabilities.

Contingent liabilities are dealt with in 27.14 below.

The definition of a provision includes amounts set aside for such items as warranty repairs, legal and constructive obligations for environmental and dismantling costs and certain restructurings.

Future operating losses are not an obligation and they do not arise from a past event; therefore, they do not meet the definition of a provision. They also do not meet the recognition criteria for provisions. Therefore, provisions should not be recognised for future operating losses (IAS 37, 63). However, the expectation of future operating losses is an indication that certain assets of the operation may be impaired; the recoverable amount of those assets should be determined in accordance with IAS 36 (see chapter 25).

Example 27.1 *Future operating losses*

An entity expects that a particular factory will make operating losses for the foreseeable future. The entity does not have an obligation to incur those losses; it can, for example, avoid those losses by closing or disposing of the factory. The expected losses also do not arise from a past event; they are, by definition, a future event.

(Continued)

(Continued)

The expectation of the losses is an indication that, for example, the factory, the assets within the factory and any goodwill or corporate assets associated with the factory may be impaired. Therefore, the entity should determine the recoverable amount of the appropriate assets or cash generating unit. Recoverable amount is the higher of net selling price and value in use. The determination of value in use takes into account the expected losses. The determination of net selling price takes into account the possibility that the assets may have to be sold or scrapped.

27.6 RECOGNITION OF PROVISIONS

A provision should be recognised when:

- an entity has a present obligation (legal or constructive) as a result of a past event;
- it is probable that an outflow of resources embodying economic benefits will be required to settle the obligation; and
- a reliable estimate can be made of the amount of the obligation.

(IAS 37, 14)

If these conditions are not met, a provision should not be recognised. The entity may, however, have a contingent liability which should be disclosed (see 27.14).

The measurement of provisions is dealt with in 27.10. Except in extremely rare cases, an entity is able to make a reliable estimate of the amount of the obligation but in the extremely rare cases in which this cannot be done, a liability exists but cannot be recognised. Such a liability is disclosed as a contingent liability (see 27.14).

27.7 PRESENT OBLIGATION

The first part of the recognition criteria – a present obligation – reinforces the definition and is derived from the framework definition of liability. The existence of a present obligation is an essential characteristic of a liability (*Framework*, 60). If the entity does not have a present obligation, it does not have, and does not recognise, a liability. If the entity has a present obligation, a liability may exist and is recognised provided that the rest of the definition and all the other recognition criteria are met.

An obligation is a duty or responsibility to act or perform in a certain way (*Framework*, 60). It may be legally enforceable (a legal obligation) or arise from normal business practice, custom and a desire to maintain good business relations or act in an equitable manner (a constructive obligation).

Sometimes it is difficult to decide whether or not an entity has a present obligation. IAS 37 adopts a 'more likely than not' approach. When it is more likely than not that a present obligation exists at the balance sheet date, the entity recognises a provision (if all the recognition criteria are met). However, when it is more likely that a present obligation does not exist at the balance sheet date, the entity does not recognise a provision but may need to disclose a contingent liability (IAS 37, 15 and 16). For example, an entity has a present obligation when it is more likely than not that it will incur expenditure making warranty repairs arising from past sales or settling a legal dispute arising from a past event. It does not have a present obligation when it is more likely than not that it will not have to incur such expenditure (or any likely expenditure results from future sales or other future events).

An obligation always involves another party to whom that obligation is owed but the entity may not know the identity of that party. For example, customers are the other party for an obligation to make warranty repairs and employees are the other party for an obligation to make redundancy payments. A management or board decision to incur expenditure does not give rise to an obligation unless the decision has been communicated to those parties affected by it in such a manner that valid expectations are created that the entity will act or perform in accordance with that decision.

Extract 27.1 *Recognition*

MOL, Hungary, 31 December 2000 (IAS)

A provision is recognised when the Group has a present obligation (legal or constructive) as a result of a past event and it is probable (i.e. more likely than not) that an outflow of resources embodying economic benefits will be required to settle the obligation, and a reliable estimate can be made of the amount of the obligation.

27.7.1 Legal Obligations

A *legal obligation* is an obligation that derives from:

- a contract, through its explicit or implicit terms;
- legislation; or
- other operation of law.

(IAS 37, 10)

When a new law creates a legal obligation, that obligation arises only when the legislation is virtually certain to be enacted as drafted (IAS 37, 22). The existence of a draft law does not create either a legal or a constructive obligation because in many cases it is impossible to be virtually certain of the enactment of a law until it is enacted. This guidance in IAS 37 is similar to, but probably different from, the guidance in IAS 12 on the use of announced, but not enacted, changes in tax rates (see chapter 31).

Examples of legal obligations include the obligation to:

- repair or replace a defective product when the entity undertakes to make such repairs or replacement under the terms of a sales contract;
- make redundancy and similar payments under termination arrangements agreed with the employees concerned;
- clean up a contaminated site when the law requires such actions; and
- make good another party's losses when the entity is liable for those losses.

Extract 27.2 *Legal obligation*

Swisscom, Switzerland, 31 December 2001 (IAS)

Swisscom has a legal obligation to dismantle transmitter stations and to restore the property owned by third parties on which the stations are situated. The cost associated with the dismantlement of these sites is recorded under property, plant and equipment and depreciated over the life of the asset. The total provision required, to dismantle and restore these sites, discounted to its present value, is recorded under accrued liabilities.

27.7.2 Constructive Obligations

A *constructive obligation* is an obligation that derives from an entity's actions where:

- by an established pattern of past practice, published policies or a sufficiently specific current statement, the entity has indicated to other parties that it will accept certain responsibilities; and
- as a result, the entity has created a valid expectation on the part of those other parties that it will discharge those responsibilities.

(IAS 37, 10)

Examples of constructive obligations include:

- a policy (rather than a contractual obligation) to return the price paid for returns of goods;
- a publicly announced, detailed plan to close a factory or other part of a business's operations; and

- a policy (rather than a legal obligation) to make good environmental damage.

Extract 27.3 *Constructive obligation*

Holcim, Switzerland, 31 December 2000 (IAS) [Extract from Management Report]

IAS 37 on provisions, contingent liabilities and contingent assets was implemented in 2000. In previous years, the Group only required the raising of a provision for the costs of re-cultivating a quarry where legal or contractual obligation existed. IAS 37 expanded this to include constructive obligations. Given the Group's commitment to sustainable environmental performance, it was necessary to increase the provision.

27.7.3 Restructuring Provisions

The need for a present obligation is crucial to the recognition of provisions for restructuring costs. Under the requirements in IAS 37, restructuring provisions should be recognised only when the entity has an obligation to carry out the restructuring. The obligation is usually a constructive obligation rather than a legal obligation. It arises only when the entity has a detailed formal plan for the restructuring and has started to implement that plan or announced its main features to those affected. If there is no formal plan or the plan has not been announced, a provision should not be recognised.

In practice, IAS 37 is likely to delay the recognition of restructuring costs, in some cases to the time at which the costs are actually incurred. Most of the restructuring provisions in pre-IAS 37 financial statements were not legal obligations and many are not constructive obligations and, therefore, did not meet the IAS 37 criteria. As a result, under the transitional provisions in IAS 37, the costs associated with many pre-IAS 37 provisions will be recognised twice as an expense – once when the pre-IAS 37 provision was recognised and again when the costs are incurred.

Restructurings include:

- the sale or termination of a line of business;
- the closure of business locations in a country or region or the relocation of business activities from one country or region to another;
- changes in management structure, for example, eliminating a layer of management; and
- fundamental reorganisations which have a material effect on the nature and focus of the entity's operations.

(IAS 37, 70)

An entity should recognise a provision for restructuring costs only when the recognition criteria for provisions are met. A constructive obligation to restructure arises only when an entity:

- has a detailed formal plan for the restructuring, identifying at least:
  - the business or part of a business concerned;
  - the principal locations affected;
  - the location, function and approximate number of employees who will be compensated for terminating their services;
  - the expenditure that will be undertaken; and
  - when the plan will be implemented; and
- has raised a valid expectation in those affected that it will carry out the restructuring by starting to implement that plan or announcing its main features to those affected by it.

(IAS 37, 72)

A detailed formal plan may be evidenced by the dismantling of plant or selling assets or by the public announcement of the main features of the plan. A public announcement constitutes a constructive obligation only if it is made in such a way and in sufficient detail that it gives rise to valid expectation in other parties such as customers, suppliers and employees (or their representatives) that the entity will carry out the restructuring (IAS 37, 73). The implementation of the plan needs to begin as soon as possible and be completed within such a timeframe that significant changes to the plan are unlikely (IAS 37, 74); otherwise, it is unlikely that it will raise a valid expectation on the part of other parties.

A management or board decision to restructure taken before the balance sheet date does not give rise to a constructive obligation at the balance sheet date unless the entity has, before the balance sheet date:

- started to implement the restructuring plan; or
- announced the main features of the restructuring plan to those affected by it in a sufficiently specific manner to raise a valid expectation in them that the entity will carry out the restructuring.

Extract 27.4 *Restructuring provisions*

UBS, Switzerland, 31 December 2001 (IAS)

At the announcement of the UBS/SBC merger in December 1997, it was communicated that the merged firm's operations in various locations would be combined, resulting in vacant properties, reductions in personnel, elimination of redundancies in the information technology platforms, exit costs and other costs. As a result, a restructuring provision of CHF 7,300 million (of which CHF 7,000 million was recognised as a restructuring expense in

1997 and CHF 300 million was recognised as a component of general and administrative expense in the fourth quarter of 1999) was established, to be used over a period of four years.

The restructuring provision included approximately CHF 3,000 million employee termination benefits, CHF 1,500 million for sale and lease breakage costs associated with the closure of premises, CHF 1,650 million for IT integration projects and write-offs of equipment which management had committed to dispose of and CHF 1,150 million for other costs classified as Personal expenses, General and administrative expense or Other income.

The employee terminations affected all functional levels and all operating Business Groups. CHF 2,000 million of the provision related to employee termination benefits reflects the costs of eliminating approximately 7,800 positions, after considering attrition and redeployment within the Company. CHF 1,000 million of the provision related to payments to maintain stability in the workforce during the integration period. As of 31 December 2001, approximately 7,100 employees had been made redundant or retired early.

At 31 December 2001, the restructuring plan was completed, substantially in accordance with the above-mentioned plans. The remaining balance of the restructuring provision of CHF 21 million was recognised in the income statement.

When a restructuring involves the sale of an operation, an obligation does not arise until the entity is committed to the sale, that is it has entered into a binding sale agreement (IAS 37, 78). Prior to such an agreement, the entity may change its mind or, indeed, may not be able to find a purchaser for the operation. The intention to sell the operation may indicate that the assets of that operation are impaired and their recoverable amount (in such circumstances usually net selling price) should be determined in accordance with IAS 36 (see chapter 25). When a sale is only part of a restructuring, a constructive obligation can arise for the other parts of the restructuring before a binding sale agreement exists.

Separate requirements apply to provisions arising on a business combination which is an acquisition. Most of these provisions are restructuring provisions and while the same broad requirements apply, the revised IAS 22 allows the acquirer a three-month window of opportunity after the date of acquisition (or up to the date of the approval of the financial statements, if earlier) for a provision to be treated as an identifiable liability and, in effect, be debited to goodwill.

As explained in chapter 16, the acquirer should recognise a provision which was not a liability of the acquiree at the date of acquisition only if the acquirer has:

- at, or before, the date of acquisition, developed the main features of a plan which involves terminating or reducing the activities of the acquiree and that relates to:

- compensating employees of the acquiree for termination of their employment;
- closing facilities of the acquiree;
- eliminating product lines of the acquiree; or
- terminating contracts of the acquiree that have become onerous because the acquirer has communicated to the other party at, or before, the date of acquisition that the contract will be terminated;

- by announcing the main features of the plan at, or before, the date of acquisition, raised a valid expectation in those affected by the plan that it will implement the plan; and
- by the earlier of three months after the date of acquisition and the date when the annual financial statements are approved, developed those main features into a detailed formal plan identifying at least:
  - the business or part of a business concerned;
  - the principal locations affected;
  - the location, function, and approximate number of employees who will be compensated for terminating their services;
  - the expenditures that will be undertaken; and
  - when the plan will be implemented.

(IAS 22, 31)

The crucial difference between IAS 22 and IAS 37 is that while IAS 37 requires the announcement of the detailed formal plan before the provision is recognised, IAS 22 allows a provision to be recognised when only the main features of that plan have been developed.

> ***IASB business combinations project***
>
> In phase one of its business combinations project, the IASB proposes to conform IAS 22 with IAS 37. A restructuring provision should be recognised on a business combination as an identifiable liability as at the date of acquisition only when the acquiree had at that date an existing provision recognised in accordance with IAS 37.

27.7.4 Onerous Contracts

Many contracts, for example many routine purchase orders, can be cancelled without paying compensation to the other party; therefore there is no present obligation and no provision is recognised. Such contracts are not onerous and no provision need be recognised.

On the other hand, the present obligation under an onerous contract should be recognised as a provision (IAS 37, 66). For example, an entity may be legally obliged under a contract to take and pay for certain goods but may not be able to recover the amount paid from the sale or use of those goods. The contract is onerous and, therefore, a provision is recognised for the contract. The entity also needs to recognise any impairment loss that has occurred on assets dedicated to the contract (see chapter 25).

Extract 27.5 *Onerous contracts*

Kuoni, Switzerland, 31 December 2001 (IAS)

The provision for onerous contracts covers the loss anticipated in connection with excess flight capacity at Scandinavian charter airline Novair for the period up to the commencement of the 2005 summer season and resulting from the leasing agreement for an Airbus A-330. Until this time, the aircraft will be leased, for certain periods only, to other airlines at the current low rates prevailing in the market.

27.7.5 Decommissioning and Environmental Costs

While IAS 37 may delay the recognition of restructuring provisions, it accelerates the recognition of provisions for decommissioning and other environmental costs – at least on the balance sheet. Prior to the adoption of IAS 37, entities were allowed to build up such provisions over the useful life of the related assets. IAS 37 requires the recognition of the full amount of the provisions when a legal or constructive obligation arises which may be on the date on which the assets are acquired.

On this issue, there is an important difference between IAS 37 and FRS 12 in the UK which requires that the provisions are added to the cost of the assets. IAS 37 is silent on this issue (although E59 proposed the same treatment as that now required by FRS 12). So, for example, under both IAS 37 and FRS 12, an entity recognises as a provision the full amount of the decommissioning costs associated with an oil rig when the rig is commissioned if the entity has a present obligation to incur those costs (albeit, perhaps, a long time in the future). Under FRS 12, the costs are added to the cost of the rig because they give access to the oil reserves over the useful life of the rig. IAS 37 gives no guidance; the costs may be added to the cost of the rig but other accounting treatments are possible.

Example 27.2 *Decommissioning and environmental costs*

In the notes to its 1998 financial statements which are prepared under Australian GAAP but are consistent with IASs in all except one respect, BHP reported:

> 'Provision for restoration and rehabilitation
> Provision is made in the accounts on a progressive basis for restoration and rehabilitation costs, mainly for areas from which natural resources are extracted.
>
> Estimates are based on current costs and current technology, allowing for potential recoveries (if any), determined on an undiscounted basis encompassing the closure and removal or disposal of facilities, and site cleanup and rehabilitation. Much of the restoration and rehabilitation work can be done only after the termination of operations, which will generally be many years hence, and accordingly the consideration of work required takes into account current and anticipated legal obligations and industry best practice.
>
> The charge to income is generally determined on a units of production basis, or lease period for leased assets, so that full provision is made by the end of the asset's economic life.
> Estimates are reassessed annually and the effects of changes are recognised prospectively.'

Whereas BHP used to build up its provision for restoration and rehabilitation costs over the useful economic life of the asset, these provisions are now fully recognised in the cost of assets as it would not be able to extract the natural resources without incurring these costs. This change in policy follows the setting up of the Dual Listed Companies structure between BHP Billiton Limited and BHP Billiton Plc and the desire to align accounting policies of the BHP Billiton Limited Group with those of the BHP Billiton Plc Group to minimise differences between results reported in the UK and Australia.

The accounting policies in the BHP Billiton (formerly BHP) financial statements for the year ended 30 June 2001 include the following:

> 'Provision for restoration and rehabilitation
> In prior periods the BHP Billiton Limited Group had recognised provisions for restoration on a progressive basis over the life of each asset. At 30 June 2001, this policy was changed such that a provision for the full cost expected to be incurred at the end of

(*Continued*)

(Continued)

the life of each asset on a discounted to net present value basis is recognised at the beginning of each project and capitalised as part of the cost of the asset. The capitalised cost is amortised over the life of the operation and the annual increase in the net present value of the provision for the expected cost is included in expenses from ordinary activities. The effect of this policy change for the year ended 30 June 2001 has been an increase in net profit attributable to members of BHP Billiton Limited of $55 million.'

Extract 27.6 *Decommissioning costs*

Swisscom, Switzerland, 31 December 2001 (IAS)

The provision for dismantlement and restoration costs relates to the dismantlement of mobile stations and analogue transmitter stations and restoration of property owned by third parties on which the transmitters are situated. These costs are expected to be incurred mainly between 2005 and 2015. As a result of adopting IAS 37, Swisscom calculated the total provision required for the analogue transmitter stations discounted to its present value and recorded the cost and accumulated depreciation at 1 January 2000 under property, plant and equipment.

Extract 27.7 *Decommissioning costs*

CEZ, Czech Republic, 31 December 2001 (IAS)

CEZ's operating nuclear plant, Dukovany, consists of four 440 MW units which were placed into service from 1985 to 1987. CEZ is also finalising construction of a second nuclear power plant, Temelin. The Czech government has enacted a Nuclear Act ('Act'), which defines certain obligations for the decontamination and dismantling ('decommissioning') of the company's nuclear power plants and the final disposal of radioactive waste and spent fuel ('disposal'). The Act requires that all nuclear parts of plant and equipment be decommissioned following the end of the plant's operating life, currently 2018 for Dukovany and approximately 2033 for Temelin. A 1997 Dukovany and a 1999 Temelin decommissioning cost study estimated that nuclear decommissioning will cost CZK 12.5 billion and CZK 11.1 billion, respectively. According to the Act, an updated study is required every five years.

Pursuant to the Act, the Ministry of Industry and Trade established the Radioactive Waste Repository Authority ('RAWRA') as the central organiser and operator of facilities for the final disposal of radioactive waste and spent fuel. The RAWRA centrally organises, supervises and is responsible for all disposal facilities and for disposal of radioactive waste and spent fuel therein. The activities of the RAWRA are financed through a 'nuclear account' funded by the originators of radioactive waste (such as the

Company). Contribution to the nuclear account was stated by a government resolution in 1997, as CZK 50 per MWh produced at nuclear power plants. Since 1 October 1997, CEZ has made regular payments to the nuclear account based on its average nuclear MWh generated during the last 5 years. The originator of radioactive waste directly covers all costs associated with interim storage of radioactive waste and spent fuel. Actual costs incurred are charged against the accumulated provision for interim and long-term spent fuel storage.

Extract 27.8 *Environmental damage and site restoration costs*

Holcim, Switzerland, 31 December 2001 (IAS)

The Group provides for the costs of restoring a quarry where a legal or constructive obligation exists. The cost of raising a provision necessary before exploitation of the raw materials has commenced is included in property, plant and equipment and depreciated over the life of the quarry. Thereafter, the provision is adjusted for through operating costs over the life of the quarry and is based on the best estimate of the expenditure required to settle the obligation at balance sheet date. Where the effect of the time value of money is material, the amount of the provision is discounted based on the enterprise's long-term borrowing rate.

Extract 27.9 *Environmental damage and site restoration costs*

Türkiye Petrol Rafinerileri, Turkey, 31 December 2000 (IAS)

Independent environmental consultants were commissioned to report on the potential investment needed by the Company in respect of environmental issues. Their report, issued in March 2000, presented a preliminary identification and analysis of environmental issues and an indicative (order of magnitude) estimate of financial costs.

Financial costs in US dollars can be summarised as follows, by refinery and using the consultants' classification of the type of cost:

	Izmit	*Izmir*	*Ki ri kkale*	*Batman*	*Total*
	US$000	*US$000*	*US$000*	*US$000*	*US$000*
Provision	2,720	1,000	870	130	4,720
Contingent Liability	1,080	200	–	–	1,280
Regulatory Pollution Prevention	7,890	6,510	5,510	820	20,730
Pollution Prevention	5,330	7,380	12,440	3,980	29,130
Total	17,020	15,090	18,820	4,930	55,860

The classifications, which were intended for general guidance only, are as follows:

'Provision': obligations relating to past events, allocated to soil and groundwater issues and treatment of stockpiled wastes only.

'Contingent liability': a possible past obligation exists, but there is insufficient data, the obligation is dependent on a regulatory decision yet to be made, namely contaminated land investigation/remediation or stockpiled waste treatment requirements.

'Regulatory Pollution Prevention': any investment required arising from future obligations/emissions, for regulatory compliance.

'Pollution Prevention': any investment required arising from future obligations/emissions, from existing company commitments and non-regulatory investments ahead of regulatory pressure.

In the accompanying financial statements, provision has been made for US$ 6,000,000 (equivalent to TL 4,050,024 million at the exchange rate ruling at 31 December 2000) being the total of the two categories 'provision' and 'contingent liability'.

Since the pollution prevention measures relate to the avoidance of future pollution, and not to events that have already occurred at the balance sheet date, provision for such costs is not appropriate under IAS 37.

The consultants' report states that:

- Significant potential environmental liabilities exist for which it has not been possible to estimate costs, because of the absence of technical data.
- Significant additional provisions may be required in future to address contaminated land issues for which there is currently no regulatory requirement.

Extract 27.10 *Environmental damage and site restoration costs*

Clariant, Switzerland, 31 December 2001 (IAS)

Clariant is exposed to environmental liabilities and risk relating to its past operations, principally in respect to remediation costs. Provisions for non-recurring remediation costs are made when there is a legal or constructive obligation and the cost can be estimated reliably. The material components of the Group's potential environmental liability consist of a risk assessment based on investigation of the various sites identified by the Group as at risk for environmental exposure. Clariant believes that its provisions are adequate based upon currently available information, however, given the inherent difficulties in estimating liabilities in this area, it cannot be guaranteed that additional costs will not be incurred.

Extract 27.11 *Environmental damage and site restoration costs*

Wienerberger, Austria, 31 December 2001 (IAS)

Provisions for site restoration are created for clay pits in proportion to depletion.

27.8 PAST EVENT

Liabilities arise from past transactions or other past events (*Framework*, 63). Therefore, a provision can arise only from a past event. For example, a legal obligation arises only when the entity has sold faulty goods or agreed redundancy terms with employees. A constructive obligation arises only when, for example, the entity has announced its policy to refund the selling price of returned goods or a detailed formal plan for a restructuring.

A present obligation cannot arise from future events such as future sales or agreements. Therefore, for example, a liability cannot be recognised for warranty repairs on goods which have not yet been produced and sold or for restructurings for which there is no formal plan and no announcement of that plan.

An event that creates a legal or constructive obligation which results in the entity having no realistic alternative to settling the present obligation is called an *obligating event* (IAS 37, 10). An entity has no realistic alternative to settling the obligation created by the event only when:

- the settlement of the obligation can be enforced by law; or
- in the case of a constructive obligation, the event (which may be an action of the entity) creates valid expectations in other parties that the entity will discharge the obligation.

(IAS 37, 17)

The obligations arising from past events must exist independently of an entity's future actions. Therefore, an obligation to pay penalties or incur clean-up costs for unlawful environmental damage is a present obligation arising from a past event which does not rely on future actions by the entity (the entity has already caused the damage and cannot avoid the penalties and clean-up costs).

In contrast, expenditure which will be incurred to operate in a particular way in the future but which can be avoided by the future actions of the entity does not give rise to a provision. In such cases, the entity has no present obligation for that future expenditure, and, therefore, no provision is recognised. For example, an airline does not have a present obligation to incur expenditure on future maintenance checks of its aircraft as the expenditure can be avoided by, for example, disposing of the aircraft. This treatment may affect the way in which depreciation on the asset is calculated.

Extract 27.12 *Past event*

China Southern Airlines, China, 31 December 2000 (IAS and Hong Kong GAAP)

Previously, the cost of scheduled overhauls in respect of owned aircraft and aircraft held under finance leases was accrued to expense over the estimated overhaul cycle of the relevant aircraft. Under the new policy of the Group which complies with IAS 37 *Provisions, Contingent Liabilities and Contingent Assets*, the cost of scheduled overhauls is expensed to the profit and loss account as and when incurred.

27.9 PROBABLE OUTFLOW OF BENEFITS

A liability qualifies for recognition only when there is the probability of an outflow of resources embodying economic benefits to settle that obligation. An outflow of resources is regarded as probable if it is more likely than not to occur (IAS 37, 23). An outflow of resources is usually a payment of cash or cash equivalents but it may be the transfer of other assets. For example, in the case of warranties, the entity may incur costs in making repairs or it may replace the goods from inventory.

When there are a number of similar obligations the probability that there will be an outflow in settlement is determined for the obligations as a whole. For example, in the case of product warranties, the probability of an outflow for any one sale may be small, but it is usually more likely than not that resources will be needed to meet the cost of the warranties on all sales.

Extract 27.13 *Probable outflow of resources*

GN Store Nord, Denmark, 31 December 2000 (IAS and Danish GAAP)

Accounting Policies – A general warranty is given against defects in design, materials and workmanship for a period of one year from delivery and completion. Provisions are made for projected future warranty costs when the related income is included in net revenue.

Notes – Warranty provisions concern products sold from NetTest, GN Netcom and GN ReSound, delivered with between one and three year warranties. The provision has been calculated on the basis of historical warranty costs of the Group's products. The provision is expected to be spent within the next three years.

Extract 27.14 *Probable outflow of resources*

Heidelberg, Germany, 31 March 2001 (IAS)

The provisions for warranty obligations or obligations to undertake subsequent performance/product liability are designed to cover risks that are either not insured or which go beyond insurable risks.

Extract 27.15 *Probable outflow of resources*

Volkswagen, Germany, 31 December 2001 (IAS)

Provisions are made for warranty claims in accordance with IAS 37 based on losses to date and estimated future losses in respect of vehicles sold.

27.10 MEASUREMENT OF PROVISIONS

A provision should be measured at the best estimate of the expenditure required to settle the present obligation at the balance sheet date (IAS 37, 36). The best estimate is the amount which the entity would rationally pay to settle the obligation or transfer it to a third party (IAS 37, 37). The measurement of provisions may require reports from independent experts and use any evidence obtained from events after the balance sheet date but prior to the date on which the financial statements are approved.

While provisions arise from past events, future events are important in measuring provisions. For example, the measurement of a provision for warranty repairs may be based on the expected future costs of making those repairs or the past or future costs of replacement goods. Future events may also affect the amount required to settle an obligation. These events should be reflected in the amount of a provision when there is sufficient objective evidence that the events will occur (IAS 37, 48). For example, the amount of a provision reflects:

- an objective expectation of the technology which will be available at the time the expenditure is incurred;
- the expected cost reductions associated with increased experience in applying existing technology or the expected cost of applying existing technology to larger or more complex operations than have previously been carried out; and
- the effect of possible new legislation when sufficient objective evidence exists that the legislation is virtually certain to be enacted.

For example, a provision for the costs of repairing existing environmental damage at the end of an asset's useful life in five years' time reflects:

- the technology which will be available in five years' time; and
- the likely cost of using that technology in five years' time after taking into account the saving which will be made as a result of the knowledge gained of that technology in the next five years.

Extract 27.16 *Expected future cost*

CEZ, Czech Republic, 31 December 2001 (IAS)

In 2001 the Company revised the estimates of provisions for spent fuel storage and credited CZK 231 million to other operating expenses as a result of the change in estimate.

The current cash expenditures for the long-term storage of spent nuclear fuel represent payments to the state controlled nuclear account and the expenditures for interim storage represent mainly the purchase of interim fuel storage containers.

The actual decommissioning and spent fuel storage costs could vary substantially from the above estimates because of new regulatory requirements, changes in technology, increased costs of labour, materials, and equipment and/or the actual time required to complete all decommissioning, disposal and storage activities.

However, an entity does not anticipate the development of a completely new technology unless it is supported by sufficient objective evidence (IAS 37, 49). For example, a provision for repairing existing environmental damage in five years' time reflects only current technology and experience in applying that technology in the next five years. It does not anticipate the availability of new technology which has yet to be developed and proved successful.

Example 27.3 *Measurement of provisions for decommissioning and environmental costs*

The facts are the same as in example 27.2. The notes to BHP's 1998 financial statements state that provisions for restoration and rehabilitation are measured as follows:

> 'Estimates are based on current costs and current technology, allowing for potential recoveries (if any), determined on an

(Continued)

(Continued)

undiscounted basis encompassing the closure and removal or disposal of facilities, and site cleanup and rehabilitation.'

Compliance with IAS 37 requires BHP to take account of expected cost reductions as well as technology which it expects will be available when the costs are incurred.

27.10.1 Expected Value

A provision which involves a large population of items is measured by weighting all possible outcomes by their associated probabilities, that is by determining its 'expected value'. Each possible amount is assigned a probability, for example 60% or 90%. The sum of the probabilities must be 100%.

Example 27.4 *Expected value approach to warranty provision*

An entity sells goods with a warranty under which the entity bears the cost of repairs of any manufacturing defects which become apparent within twelve months after purchase.

If minor defects were detected in all products sold, repair costs of £2m would result. If major defects were detected in all products sold, repair costs of £6m would result.

The entity's past experience and future expectations indicate that, for the coming year, 90% of the goods sold will have no defects, 8% will have minor defects and 2% will have major defects.

The expected value of the cost of repairs is:

(90% × nil) + (8% × £2m) + (2% × £6m) = £280,000

When there is a continuous range of possible outcomes, and each point in that range is as likely as any other, the expected value is the mid-point of the range. For example, if the costs of repairing environmental damage are between $4m and $7m and probability of the costs equalling any point in the range is as likely as the probability of any other point in the range, the expected value is $5.5m, that is, the midpoint between $4m and $7m.

The DSOP that preceded IAS 37 proposed that expected values should be used to measure all provisions, including those dealing with small populations of items and one-off items. Many respondents to the DSOP argued that such provisions should be measured on other bases, such as the 'most likely outcome' (*IASC Insight*, June 1997, p18). As a result, the IASC changed the emphasis in the guidance although IAS 37 continues to imply that expected values need to be considered in all cases. For example, when a single obligation is being measured, the most likely outcome may be the best estimate of the liability, but other possible outcomes are also considered (IAS 37, 40). When other possible outcomes are either mostly higher or mostly lower than the most likely outcome, the best estimate will be a higher or lower amount than the most likely outcome.

Example 27.5 *Measurement of single obligation*

An entity has to rectify a major fault in an item of equipment which it has constructed for a customer. The most likely outcome is that the repair will succeed at a cost of $2m. There is, however, a significant chance that further work will be necessary at an additional cost of $200,000. The probability of success at the first attempt is 80% and the possibility of requiring further work is 20%. The 'most likely outcome' is that the repair will succeed at the first attempt. Therefore, a provision of $2m would be recognised.

The entity must consider, however, other possible outcomes – this leads to consideration of expected value. The expected value of the repair is:

(80% × $2m) + (20% × $200,000) = $2,040,000.

A more troublesome example is that of, say, a lawsuit in which the entity has a possibility of both winning and losing.

The risks and uncertainties that surround the events and circumstances which give rise to the provision should be taken into account in reaching the best estimate of a provision (IAS 37, 42). A risk adjustment may increase the amount at which a liability is measured.

Extract 27.17 *Probable outcomes*

Schindler, Germany, 31 December 2001 (IAS)

Provisions for product liability are based on actuarial calculations by independent experts on damage incurred but not yet reported and on cases not yet closed.

Example 27.6 *Measurement of single obligation*

A claim has been made against the entity in respect of damage allegedly caused to a certain property. If the entity wins the case, it will incur no costs. If the entity loses the case, it will have to pay damages estimated at $2m plus both parties' costs which are expected to total $400,000.

If the most likely outcome is that the entity will win the case, the best estimate of the loss is zero and, hence, no provision is required (but disclosure is required of the contingent liability). There must, however, be a probability of losing and, therefore, an expected value approach needs to be considered.

If the probability of winning is 90% and the probability of losing is 10%, the expected value of the loss is:

(90% × nil) + (10% × $2,400,000) = $240,000.

If the probability of winning is 50% and the probability of losing is 50%, the expected value of the loss is:

(50% × nil) + (50% × $2,400,000) = $1,200,000.

It may also be necessary to consider other possibilities, for example that the entity might win but have to bear its own costs.

27.10.2 Discounting

When the effect of the time value of money on a provision is material, the amount of a provision should be the present value of the expenditures expected to be required to settle the obligation (IAS 37, 45). This is consistent with the notion that the provision should be measured at the amount which the entity would rationally pay to settle the obligation. If payment is some time in the future, any payment at the balance sheet date would rationally be less than the payment at a future date. Therefore, provisions for the costs of dismantling an item of equipment in a number of years' time are usually discounted but provisions for warranty repairs carried out within 12 months of the sale of goods are not discounted.

The discount rate (or rates) should be a pre-tax rate (or rates) that reflect(s) current market assessments of the time value of money and the risks specific to the liability (IAS 37, 47). The discount rate(s) should not reflect risks for which future cash flow estimates have been adjusted (IAS 37, 47). The approach to the discounting of provisions is similar to that in IAS 36 for the impairment of assets.

Example 27.7 *Measurement of provisions for decommissioning and environmental costs*

The facts are the same as in example 27.2. The notes to BHP's 1998 financial statements state that provisions for restoration and rehabilitation are measured as follows:

> 'Estimates are based on current costs and current technology, allowing for potential recoveries (if any), determined on an undiscounted basis encompassing the closure and removal or disposal of facilities, and site cleanup and rehabilitation.'

Compliance with IAS 37 means BHP has to measure its provisions on a discounted, rather than an undiscounted, basis.

Extract 27.18 *Discounting*

MOL, Hungary, 31 December 2000 (IAS)

The amount of the provision is the present value of the risk adjusted expenditures expected to be required to settle the obligation, determined using the estimated risk free interest rate as discount rate. The reversal of such discounting in each year is recognised as an interest income. Where discounting is used, the carrying amount of provision increases in each period to reflect the unwinding of the discount by the passage of time.

Extract 27.19 *Discounting*

Preussag, Germany, 31 December 2001 (IAS)

Provisions for typical operating risks were formed in particular for recultivation and waste disposal commitments. The long-term commitments for the recultivation or restoration of locations were carried at the present value of the anticipated settlement amount. The calculation of the anticipated settlement amount was based on cost increases expected in the future. The corresponding provisions were calculated taking into account price increases of 3.5% and a discount factor of 5.5%.

Extract 27.20 *Discounting*

RWE, Germany, 31 December 2001 (IAS)

Provisions for mining damage including the corresponding provisions at RWE-DEA Upstream are long-term provisions which are recognised at their settlement value and discounted to the balance-sheet date. An interest rate of 6% was taken as the discount rate.

27.10.3 Disposals of Assets

Gains from the expected disposal of assets should not be taken into account in measuring a provision (IAS 37, 51) even if the expected disposal is closely linked to the event giving rise to the provision. An entity recognises any gains on the disposal of assets when required by other IFRSs. For example, gains on the disposal of property, plant and equipment are dealt with in accordance with IAS 16 and gains on the disposal of inventories are dealt with in accordance with IAS 2.

As explained earlier, if an entity has a contract that is onerous, the present obligation under the contract should be recognised and measured as a provision (IAS 37, 66). It would appear that, in measuring that provision, the entity cannot take into account the proceeds from the expected disposal of assets which are subject to the contract. This is inconsistent with the IASC's approach on the recognition of expected losses on construction contracts (see chapter 30) and on carrying certain financial instruments at fair value (see chapter 20).

Example 27.8 *Measurement of provisions for decommissioning and environmental costs*

The facts are the same as in example 26.4. The notes to BHP's 1998 financial statements state that provisions for restoration and rehabilitation are measured as follows:

> 'Estimates are based on current costs and current technology, allowing for potential recoveries (if any), determined on an undiscounted basis encompassing the closure and removal or disposal of facilities, and site cleanup and rehabilitation.'

Compliance with IAS 37 requires BHP to end its practice of deducting 'recoveries' from its provisions.

27.10.4 Reimbursements from Third Parties

Sometimes, an entity is able to look to another party to pay part or all of the expenditure required to settle a provision (for example, through insurance contracts, indemnity clauses or suppliers' warranties). The other party may either reimburse amounts paid by the entity or pay the amounts directly. Any such reimbursement should be recognised when, and only when, it is virtually certain that reimbursement will be received if the entity settles the obligation and the amount recognised for the reimbursement should not exceed the amount of the provision (IAS 37, 53).

In many cases the entity remains liable for the whole of the expenditure and will have to settle the full amount if the third party fails to make its reimbursement. In this situation, a provision is recognised for the full amount of the liability, and a separate asset for the expected reimbursement is recognised when it is virtually certain that the reimbursement will be received if the entity settles the liability (IAS 37, 56). If, however, the entity will not be liable for the costs if the third party fails to pay, the provision does not include the costs that are the responsibility of the third party.

When a reimbursement is recognised:

- the expense may be presented in the income statement net of the reimbursement (IAS 37, 54); and
- the provision should be recognised as a liability in the balance sheet and the reimbursement should be recognised as an asset (IAS 37, 53).

The separate classification of the liability and the asset is consistent with the normal requirements for offsetting in the balance sheet (see chapter 9).

27.10.5 Measurement of Restructuring Provisions

A restructuring provision should be measured in the same way as other provisions. It should include only the direct expenditures arising from the restructuring, which is those costs which are:

- necessarily entailed by the restructuring; and
- not associated with the ongoing activities of the entity.

(IAS 37, 80)

A restructuring provision does not include such costs as:

- retraining or relocating continuing staff;
- marketing; or
- investment in new systems and distribution networks.

(IAS 37, 81)

These expenditures relate to the future conduct of the business and are not liabilities for restructuring at the balance sheet date. Retraining, relocation and marketing costs are usually recognised as expenses when they are incurred (IAS 38 prohibits their recognition as intangible assets). The costs of new systems and distribution networks are recognised as assets in the period in which they are incurred provided that they meet the recognition criteria for property, plant and equipment in IAS 16 (usually) or for intangible assets in IAS 38.

Future operating losses up to the date of the restructuring are not included in a provision for that restructuring unless they relate to an onerous contract (IAS 37, 82). Such losses are usually recognised in the income statement as losses when they are incurred.

Gains on the expected disposal of assets are not taken into account in measuring a restructuring provision, even if the sale of assets is envisaged as part of the restructuring (IAS 37, 51 and 83).

27.11 REVIEW OF PROVISIONS

Provisions should be reviewed at each balance sheet date and adjusted to reflect the current best estimate of the expenditure required to settle the present obligation (IAS 26, 59). Any change in the provision is a change in accounting estimate; it is not a fundamental error. So, for example, if the best estimate of the cost of settling a lawsuit has increased during a period from £2m to £5m, the entity increases the provision by £3m and recognises an expense of £3m in that period. The prior period is not restated.

An event which does not give rise to an immediate legal or constructive obligation may give rise to such an obligation at a later date. For example, while a management decision does not give rise to an immediate obligation, the subsequent announcement of that decision may give rise to an obligation.

A legal obligation may arise later than the initial date of a transaction or other event. For example, an obligation to pay compensation to customers whose health was damaged as a result of using a product of the entity may arise from a change in the law whereas neither a legal nor a constructive obligation may have existed in the past (a change in the entity's public policy towards such cases would give rise to a constructive obligation). Similarly, a new law may create a legal obligation to remedy past damage caused to the environment for which the entity was not liable (again a public statement may create a constructive obligation when no such obligation existed in the past).

If it is no longer probable that an outflow of resources embodying economic benefits will be required to settle the obligation, the provision should be reversed (IAS 37, 59). If, for example, an entity had recognised in the prior period a provision of $4m for losses on settling a lawsuit but the lawsuit has been won in the current period, the provision is reversed. The reversal is recognised as income in the current period; it is, again, a change in accounting estimate. The prior period is not restated.

When discounting is used, the carrying amount of a provision increases in each period to reflect the passage of time. The increase is recognised as an interest expense (IAS 36, 60) – in contrast, IAS 19 is silent on the classification of the interest element associated with discounting employee benefit costs.

Extract 27.21 *Reviews of provisions*

CEZ, Czech Republic, 31 December 2001 (IAS)

	Nuclear Decommissioning	*Accumulated Provisions Spent Fuel Storage Interim*	*Long-term*	*Total*
Balance at 31 December 1998	2,925	2,117	12,862	17,904
Additions made during 1999				
Discount accretion	73	52	314	439
Effect of inflation	132	95	564	791
Provision	–	101	–	101
Current cash expenditures	–	(140)	(638)	(778)
Balance at 31 December 1999	3,130	2,225	13,102	18,457
Additions made during 2000				
Discount accretion	79	54	319	452
Effect of inflation	141	97	575	813
Provision	–	97	–	97
Capitalized cost of Temelin provisions	1,695	254	–	1,949
Current cash expenditures	–	(225)	(641)	(866)
Balance at 31 December 2000	5,045	2,502	13,355	20,902
Additions made during 2001				
Discount accretion	126	63	334	523
Effect of inflation	227	112	601	940
Provision	–	107	–	107
Effect of change in estimate	–	57	(288)	(231)
Current cash expenditures	–	(190)	(655)	(845)
Balance at 31 December 2001	5,398	2,651	13,347	21,396

In 2001 the Company revised the estimates of provisions for spent fuel storage and credited CZK 231 million to other operating expenses as a result of the change in estimate. The current cash expenditures for the long-term storage of spent nuclear fuel represent payments to the state controlled nuclear account and the expenditures for interim storage represent mainly the purchase of interim fuel storage containers.

The actual decommissioning and spent fuel storage costs could vary substantially from the above estimates because of new regulatory requirements, changes in technology, increased costs of labour, materials, and equipment and/or the actual time required to complete all decommissioning, disposal and storage activities.

27.12 USE OF PROVISIONS

A provision should be used only for expenditures for which the provision was originally recognised (IAS 37, 61). This requirement is an important restriction on the ability of an entity to use a provision to cover expenses for which it was not intended.

27.13 DISCLOSURE OF PROVISION

For each class of provision, an entity should disclose:

- the carrying amount at the beginning and end of the period;
- additional provisions made in the period, including increases to existing provisions;
- amounts used during the period;
- unused amounts reversed during the period; and
- the increase in the discounted amount arising from the passage of time and the effect of any change in the discount rate.

(IAS 37, 84)

Comparative information is not required for these disclosures.

For each class of provision, an entity should also disclose:

- a brief description of the nature of the obligation and the expected timing of any resulting outflows of economic benefits;
- an indication of the uncertainties about the amount or timing of those outflows, including when necessary the major assumptions made concerning future events; and
- the amount of any expected reimbursement, stating the amount of any asset that has been recognised for that expected reimbursement.

(IAS 37, 85)

Comparative information is required for those disclosures when it is relevant to an understanding of the current period's financial statements (IAS 1, 28 – see chapter 8).

Extract 27.22 *Disclosure of provisions*

Forbo, Switzerland, 31 December 2001 (IAS)

Of the specific provisions of CHF 70 million (after tax) made at the end of 1999, CHF 17.9 million were still available at the beginning of 2001. Thereof CHF 9.1 million were absorbed for the restructuring of the Vinyl Business, where the major part was used for valuation adjustments of under-utilised production facilities. Another CHF 1.5 million was used for the restructuring of the belting activities in Asia, and CHF 1.8 million was absorbed for measures in the European Adhesives Business. CHF 5.5 million were used for the divestment of the Carpet Business in 2001.

Extract 27.23 *Disclosure of provisions*

Dyckerhoff, Germany, 31 December 2001 (IAS)

The decrease in provisions for recultivation of closed quarries stemmed from the discounting (EUR 17.2 million) performed pursuant to IAS 37. The proceeds from the discounting are reported in net interest. The decrease resulting from the discounting was offset by an increase from the first-time consolidation of Suchoi Log. The decrease in supply contract commitments also resulted from the deconsolidation as of 31 December 2001. The personnel related commitments were compensated by increases owing to the restructuring measures (EUR 7.2 million). Expenses for Group restructuring (EUR 17.9 million) and losses in private companies (EUR 11.5 million) led to the increase in other uncertain commitments. They were offset in turn by decreases resulting from the change in the consolidated group as of 31 December 2001.

27.14 CONTINGENT LIABILITIES

27.14.1 Definition

Contingent losses are dealt with as either:

- provisions if they meet the definition and recognition criteria in IAS 37;
- impairments of assets under IAS 36 (for non-financial assets) or IAS 39 (for financial assets); or
- contingent liabilities when they do not qualify for recognition as a provision or the impairment of an asset.

Unrecognised contingent losses are broadly what IAS 37 defines as a contingent liability. Under IAS 37, a *contingent liability* is:

- a possible obligation that arises from past events and whose existence will be confirmed only by the occurrence or non-occurrence of one or more uncertain future events not wholly within the control of the entity; or
- a present obligation that arises from past events but which does not otherwise meet the recognition criteria for a provision.

(based on IAS 37, 10)

27.14.2 Recognition

An entity should not recognise a contingent liability as a liability (IAS 37, 27). A contingent liability is not recognised as a liability on the balance sheet because either:

- it is a possible, rather than present, obligation – that is, it is not a liability; or
- it is a present obligation but it does not meet the recognition criteria for a provision – that is, it is a liability but it does not meet the recognition criteria for a liability.

In a subsequent period, an item previously dealt with as a contingent liability may meet the definition and the recognition criteria for a provision, in which case, a provision is recognised (IAS 37, 30). For example, a possible loss on a lawsuit may become a probable loss or the amount of the loss may be capable of estimation whereas previously it could not be estimated.

27.14.3 Disclosure

When the possibility of loss is remote, no disclosure is required. In all other cases, an entity should disclose for each class of contingent liability:

- the nature of the contingent liability;
- an estimate of its financial effect;
- an indication of the uncertainties relating to the amount or timing of any outflow; and
- the possibility of any reimbursement.

(IAS 37, 86)

Many IFRSs suggest items which may need to be disclosed as contingent liabilities (see appendix 1). Many contingent liabilities are financial liabilities. Therefore, the disclosure requirements in IAS 32 also need to be considered (see chapter 20).

Extract 27.24 *Contingent liabilities*

Stora Enso, Finland, 31 December 2001 (IAS)

Group companies are parties to legal proceedings that arise in the ordinary course of business and which primarily involve claims arising out of commercial law. The Group is also involved in administrative proceedings relating primarily to competition law. The Directors do not consider that liabilities related to such proceedings, before insurance recoveries, if any, are likely to be material to the Group financial condition or results of operations.

Extract 27.25 *Contingent liabilities*

EGL, Switzerland, 31 December 2001 (IAS)

In 1998/1999 and 1997/1998, Albula-Landwasser Kraftwerke AG and Misoxer Kraftwerke AG entered into agreements under which they leased out their plants long-term and simultaneously leased them back. EGL AG has issued assurances to the American investors that it will guarantee any contractual liabilities for Albula-Landwasser Kraftwerke AG and Misoxer Kraftwerke AG arising out of these agreements. The largely theoretical risk involved with the agreements is covered by provisions with the two companies mentioned. Since the risk decreases over the life of the agreement, these provisions are dissolved by an equal amount each year.

Extract 27.26 *Contingent liabilities*

Disetronic, Switzerland, 31 December 2001 (IAS)

A warranty indemnification exists from the sale of the Pharma Packaging Systems division, which expires on 31 December 2004. There were no other guarantees to third parties outstanding at the end of the 2000/01 and 2001/02 business years. All contingent liabilities, which will probably lead to a liability, have been recorded as provisions.

27.14.4 Contingent Assets

A *contingent asset* is a possible asset that arises from past events and whose existence will be confirmed only by the occurrence or non-occurrence of one or more uncertain future events not wholly within the control of the entity (IAS 37, 10). A contingent asset is not an asset and is not, therefore, recognised as an asset on the balance sheet.

When the inflow of economic benefits is not probable, no disclosure should be made about a contingent asset. When an inflow of economic benefits is probable, an entity should disclose:

- the nature of the contingent asset; and
- an estimate of its financial effect.

(IAS 37, 89)

For example, when it is not probable that an entity will succeed in a claim against another party, the amount of the claim is not recognised as an asset or as income. It is also not disclosed. When it is probable that the claim will succeed, the nature and the amount of the likely recovery should be disclosed but the claim should not be recognised as an asset or income.

Extract 27.27 *Contingent assets*

Nestlé, Switzerland, 31 December 2001 (IAS)

Contingent assets for litigation claims in favour of the Group amount to about CHF 230 million.

Extract 27.28 *Contingent assets*

EGL, 31 December 2001 (IAS)

EGL has initiated legal proceedings against several Swiss long-distance electricity suppliers with a view to obtaining compensation for damage resulting from their unauthorised use of the Group's transmission capacity to Italy. EGL has good reason to believe that its claim will be upheld. At present, however, it is not possible to say with any degree of reliability when a legal decision will be made or how high the compensation will be.

CHAPTER 28

Equity

28.1 RELEVANT STANDARDS AND INTERPRETATIONS

IAS 1 *Presentation of Financial Statements*
IAS 32 *Financial Instruments: Disclosure and Presentation*
IAS 39 *Financial Instruments: Recognition and Measurement*
SIC 5 *Classification of Financial Instruments: Contingent Settlement Provisions*
SIC 16 *Presentation of Treasury Shares*
SIC 17 *Equity – Costs of an Equity Transaction*
IAS 39 *Implementation Guidance (IGC)*

28.2 HISTORY

IAS 5 *Information to be Disclosed in Financial Statements* was approved in 1974 and required the disclosure of certain components of equity and the movements in those components. IAS 5 was reviewed in 1985 but no changes were made.

In 1984, the IASC added a project on owners' equity to its work programme. It approved a preliminary exposure draft in March 1986 which defined equity as the residual interest in the assets less liabilities of an entity (*IASC News*, April 1986, p3). However, later that year, the IASC decided to combine into one project the then separate projects on the objectives of financial statements, assets and expenses, liabilities and equity. The outcome of the combined project was the *Framework for the Preparation and Presentation of Financial Statements* (see chapter 6).

IAS 5 has now been replaced by the revised IAS 1 which introduced the statement of changes in equity (see chapter 11). The revised IAS 1 applied to periods beginning on or after 1 July 1998.

One of the difficulties faced by the project on owners' equity was that the law in many countries determines the components of equity, the way that capital transactions are analysed between those components, and the use of those components. Provided that these laws do not affect the net profit or loss for the period or net assets, the IASC saw little benefit in dealing with the separate components of equity. IFRSs do, however, require the separate classification of certain components of equity. For example, IAS 16 and IAS 25 require the disclosure of the revaluation reserve and IAS 21 requires the disclosure of accumulated foreign exchange differences. IAS 32 requires that the equity component of compound financial instruments should be classified as equity.

The financial instrument project has dealt with the distinction between equity and liabilities in the financial statements of the issuer of equity or debt securities as well as the presentation of compound instruments, that is, those instruments which contain both an equity and a liability component. IAS 32 was approved and published in 1995 and applied to accounting periods beginning on or after 1 January 1996. IAS 39 applied to accounting periods beginning on or after 1 January 2000.

28.3 IOSCO

In June 1994, IOSCO advised the IASC that it supported efforts to improve IAS 5 and related IASs. It identified a number of suspense issues relating to equity which are described in chapter 8.

IAS 32 was approved after IOSCO completed its evaluation of the IASs in existence in 1994.

IAS 1 is included in 'IAS 2000' endorsed by IOSCO in May 2000. The following IAS 1 supplemental treatments relate to equity:

- recognition of items in equity, including enhanced guidance on disclosures of changes in equity accounts and related recognition and measurement issues (see chapter 11);
- guidance on the classification of stock subscriptions receivable;
- presentation guidance on alternative equity structures, for example partnerships, limited liability corporations, etc.;
- guidance on stock dividends, dividends in kind, increasing rate preferred stock, contingent warrants, greenmail transactions, forward stock transactions and hedging of an entity's equity; and
- disclosure of transfers from reserves to retained earnings or to net profit or loss.

IAS 32 is included in 'IAS 2000' endorsed by IOSCO in May 2000. The following IAS 32 supplemental treatments relate to equity:

- accounting for treasury shares as a deduction of equity (versus an asset) may not be consistent with certain legal environments in which those transactions are authorised and it should be possible to show shares repurchased for trading purposes as assets in the balance sheet; and

- the IASC should consider clarifying that SIC 16 excludes from its scope transferable shares of the entity held by an employee benefit plan that is reflected in the entity's consolidated financial statements.

IOSCO also asked the IASC to reconsider the definitions of equity instruments and liabilities and pointed out several possible problems (this is a current IASB project).

28.4 DEFINITIONS OF EQUITY AND EQUITY INSTRUMENT

Equity is the residual interest in the assets of the entity after deducting all its liabilities (*Framework*, 49(c)). The components of equity vary from entity to entity and from country to country but they usually include:

- funds contributed by shareholders (*Framework*, 65), for example various classes of share capital and capital paid-in in excess of par value (share premium);
- the equity component of compound financial instruments (IAS 32, 23);
- legal and other reserves which are appropriations of accumulated profit or loss or retained earnings (*Framework*, 65);
- amounts set aside for general banking risks in excess of those required by IAS 10 (IAS 30, 50) and for losses on bank loans and advances in excess of those required (IAS 30, 44);
- capital maintenance adjustments (*Framework*, 65);
- revaluation surplus (IAS 16, 39);
- foreign exchange differences (IAS 21, 42(b)); and
- the accumulated profit or loss (retained earnings) (*Framework*, 65 and IAS 1, 86(e))).

A *financial instrument* is any contract that gives rise to both a financial asset of one entity and a financial liability or equity instrument of another entity (IAS 32, 5 and IAS 39, 8). An *equity instrument* is any contract that evidences a residual interest in the assets of an entity after deducting all of its liabilities (IAS 32, 5; IAS 39, 8).

IAS 32 does not deal with the measurement of financial instruments (other than compound instruments – see 28.6.2) and equity instruments issued by an entity fall outside the scope of IAS 39 (IAS 39, 1).

Extract 28.1 *Fair value and other reserve*

Nokia, Finland, 31 December 2001 (IAS)

On the adoption of IAS 39 at 1 January 2001, all investment securities classified as available-for-sale were remeasured to fair value. The difference between their original carrying amount and their fair value at 1 January 2001 was credited to fair value and other reserves (see Consolidated statement of changes in shareholders' equity). Gains and losses arising from the change in the fair value of available-for-sale investments since that date are recognized directly in this reserve.

Extract 28.2 *Statutory reserve and welfare reserve*

China Petroleum & Chemical Corporation, People's Republic of China, 31 December 2001 (IAS)

According to the Company's Articles of Association, the Company is required to transfer 10% of its net profit, as determined in accordance with the PRC Accounting Rules and Regulations, to statutory surplus reserve until the reserve balance reaches 50% of the registered capital. The transfer to this reserve must be made before distribution of a dividend to shareholders.

...

According to the Company's Articles of Association, the Company is required to transfer 5% to 10% of its net profit, as determined in accordance with the PRC Accounting Rules and Regulations, to the statutory public welfare fund. ... This fund is non-distributable other than on liquidation. The transfer to this fund must be made before distribution of a dividend to shareholders. The directors authorised the transfer of RMB 1,402 million (2000: RMB 1,615 million) subject to shareholders' approval, being 10% of the current year's net profit determined in accordance with the PRC Accounting Rules and Regulations, to this fund.

Transaction costs incurred by an entity in issuing or acquiring its own equity instruments should be accounted for as a deduction from equity, net of related income tax benefit (SIC 17, 6). Such costs only comprise incremental external costs directly attributable to the transaction which would otherwise have been avoided (SIC 17, 5). Such costs do not include costs of issuing an equity instrument that are directly attributable to the acquisition of a business or costs relating to obligations under employee share option or share purchase plans. Costs of listing shares on a stock exchange, a secondary offering of shares, a share split or a stock dividend are not costs of an equity transaction. Nor are allocations of internal administration costs or costs of employee compensation.

The costs of a transaction that fails to be completed should be expensed (SIC 17, 6). Transaction costs that relate jointly to more than one transaction should be allocated to those transactions on a basis which is rational and consistent with similar transactions (SIC 17, 8), for example when there is a concurrent offering of some shares and stock exchange listing of other shares.

28.5 CLASSIFICATION BETWEEN LIABILITIES AND EQUITY

28.5.1 Balance Sheet Classification

An entity may issue a financial instrument which:

- takes the form of an equity instrument but which is, in substance, a financial liability; or
- takes the form of a financial liability but which is, in substance, an equity instrument.

An entity should classify such an instrument as a liability or as equity in accordance with the substance of the contractual arrangement at the time of initial recognition (IAS 32, 18). That classification continues at each subsequent reporting date until the financial instrument is removed from the entity's balance sheet (IAS 32, 19). If an entity issues a financial instrument which includes both equity and liability components, it should classify the component parts separately (IAS 32, 23 – see 28.6).

The approach adopted by IAS 32 is based on the framework definitions of a liability and equity and the related definitions of a financial liability and an equity instrument. In the *Framework*, IAS 32 and IAS 39, equity and an equity instrument are defined as residuals (see 28.4), therefore the classification of a financial instrument depends on the definitions of a liability and a financial liability.

A *financial liability* is a contractual obligation either to deliver cash or another financial asset to the holder of the instrument or to exchange another financial instrument with the holder of the instrument under conditions that are potentially unfavourable to the issuer (IAS 32, 5 and 20). When such a contractual obligation exists the instrument meets the definition of a financial liability regardless of the manner in which the contractual obligation will be settled (IAS 32, 20). So, for example, even if the issuing entity's ability to settle an obligation is restricted, say due to the lack of access to foreign currency or the need to obtain regulatory approval for a payment, the instrument is still considered a financial liability. If an instrument obliges the entity to make a cash payment (for example the repayment of a loan or interest on that loan) that instrument is a liability irrespective of the fact that it may be described as some form of equity. Similarly, if a financial instrument obliges the entity to deliver equity or debt securities of another entity, the instrument is a financial liability. However, an obligation to issue the entity's own equity instruments is not a liability but is an equity instrument since the entity is not obliged to deliver cash or another financial asset (IAS 32, 16).

A financial instrument is an equity instrument when the entity does not have a contractual obligation to deliver cash or another financial asset or to exchange another financial instrument under conditions that are potentially unfavourable (IAS 32, 21). So, for example, if an instrument entitles the holder only to a pro rata share of profits and the entity (as issuer) is not obliged to make such distributions, the instrument is an equity instrument irrespective of the fact that it may be described as some form of liability, for example as a perpetual bond.

It is relatively easy to classify certain types of financial instruments. For example, ordinary shares which represent the residual interest in the entity are equity. Similarly, options which oblige the entity to issue ordinary shares are also equity. Preferred shares are equity if the entity has no obligation to redeem them. However, a preferred share is a financial liability when:

- the entity, as issuer, is required to redeem the share for a fixed or determinable amount at a fixed or determinable future date;
- the holder has the right to require the entity to redeem the shares at or after a particular date for a fixed or determinable amount;
- there is a contractual obligation indirectly through the terms and conditions of the preferred share such that the entity, as issuer, has little discretion to avoid redeeming the instrument; or
- the holder has an option to require redemption upon the occurrence of a future event that is highly likely to occur.

(IAS 32, 22)

An entity may issue a financial instrument in which the rights and obligations regarding the manner of settlement depend on the occurrence or non-occurrence of uncertain future events or the outcome of uncertain circumstances which are beyond the control of both the issuer and the holder of the instrument. For example, an entity may issue equity shares which it is required to exchange into bonds if the entity does not achieve a specified profit level. Alternatively, an entity may issue bonds which it is required to exchange into shares if the market price of the shares reaches a specified level. The entity, as issuer, should classify such a financial instrument as a liability unless the possibility of its being required to settle in cash or another financial asset is remote at the time of issuance (SIC 5, 5 and 6).

An entity may be able to settle a contractual obligation either by a payment of financial assets (e.g. cash) or by payment in the form of its own equity securities. If the number of shares required to settle the obligation varies with changes in their fair value, so that the total fair value of the equity securities paid always equals the amount of the contractual obligation, it should be accounted for as a financial liability of the entity (IAS 32, 5 and IAS 39, 11). The holder of the obligation is not exposed to any gain or loss from fluctuations in the price of the equity securities.

IGC 11-1 considers the application of the distinction between liabilities and equity when an entity issues a put option on its own shares.

28.5.2 Dividends and Interest

Interest, dividends, losses and gains relating to a financial instrument which is classified as a liability should be recognised as an expense or income in the income statement (IAS 32, 30). When appropriate, such amounts may be included in borrowing costs which are capitalised under IAS 23 (see chapter 35).

Interest, dividends, losses and gains relating to a financial instrument which is classified as equity should be treated as appropriation of the net profit for the period and debited directly to equity (IAS 32, 30 – see chapter 11). Therefore, dividends on redeemable preference shares which are classified as a liability are recognised as an expense and not as appropriations of the net profit for the period. Dividends on that part of a convertible preference share that is classified as equity are appropriations of the net profit and are debited directly to equity.

When the balance sheet presentation of a financial instrument differs from the instrument's legal form, an entity is encouraged to explain the nature of the instrument (IAS 32, 50).

Extract 28.3 *Debt instruments*

Roche, Switzerland, 31 December 2001 (IAS)

The limited conversion preferred stock is in substance a financial liability rather than an equity instrument, and therefore it is classified as long-term debt in the balance sheet and the related dividend payments are treated as interest expense.

28.6 COMPOUND INSTRUMENTS

28.6.1 Balance Sheet Classification

An entity may issue a financial instrument which has both equity and liability components. For example, an entity may issue a bond convertible by the holder into ordinary shares of the entity. The entity should classify the component parts of a financial instrument separately as equity or liabilities as appropriate (IAS 32, 23). It classifies:

- as a financial liability, the contractual arrangement to deliver cash or other financial assets; and
- as an equity instrument, the right to ordinary shares of the entity.

(IAS 32, 25)

Therefore, in the case of a bond which is convertible into ordinary shares, the entity classifies:

- as a financial liability, the obligation to repay the bond and pay interest on the bond; and
- as an equity instrument, the call option held by the holder of the instrument to convert the bond into ordinary shares.

The classification is changed only when the liability is repaid or converted into equity. It is not changed during the life of the instrument unless it is repaid or converted (IAS 32, 26).

The holder (as opposed to the issuer) of the instrument is not required to classify separately the components of a compound instrument; the holder has an investment which is accounted for as a financial asset and an embedded derivative in accordance with IAS 39 (see chapter 20 and IGC 23-2).

28.6.2 Initial Measurement of Compound Instruments

A compound instrument is initially recognised at the fair value of the consideration received (IAS 39, 66). However, it is necessary to allocate the total amount of the consideration received between the separate equity and liability components. An entity can either:

- determine the initial carrying amount for the component that is more easily measurable (usually the liability component) and assign the residual amount to the less easily measurable component (often the equity component); or
- measure each component separately and, to the extent necessary, adjust these amounts on a pro rata basis so that the sum of the components equals total amount for the instrument

(IAS 32, 28)

Under the first approach, for a bond which is convertible into ordinary shares:

- the initial carrying amount of the liability is the present value of the stream of future payments of interest and principal – the discount rate is the prevailing market rate of interest on issue for a similar liability which does not have the conversion option; and
- the initial carrying amount of the equity instrument is the total amount of the consideration received less the initial carrying amount of the liability.

The IASC favoured this approach in its 1997 discussion paper because the fair value of the liability component is not affected by the equity component (*Accounting for Financial Assets and Financial Liabilities*, p 78). In its June 2002 improvements exposure draft, the IASB proposes to require the use of this approach.

Under the second approach, the issuer of the bond convertible into ordinary shares:

- initially measures the financial liability at the present value of the stream of future payments of interest and principal – the discount rate is the prevailing market rate of interest on issue for a similar liability that does not have the conversion option;
- initially measures the option to convert into ordinary shares by reference to the fair value of a similar option or by using an option pricing model; and
- adjusts the amounts initially determined for each component on a pro rata basis so that the sum of the initial carrying amounts of the two components equals the total amount of the consideration received.

The IASC did not favour this approach in its 1997 discussion paper and the IASB proposes to prohibit it.

The subsequent accounting for a compound instrument depends both on whether conversion takes place and the extent to which the entity measures the liability component at fair value. If full conversion takes place and the liability is measured on a cost basis, the issue of equity could be measured at the amount attributed to the equity component plus either the original amount attributed to the liability component or the fair value of that component at the date of conversion.

Transaction costs should be allocated to the liability and equity element in proportion to the allocation of proceeds. The costs allocated to the equity element are dealt with in accordance with SIC 17 (see 28.4.1 above).

Example 28.1 *Measurement of the component parts of a compound instrument*

An entity issues 2,000 convertible bonds at par with a face value of $1,000 per bond, giving total proceeds of $2,000,000. The bonds have a three-year term. Interest is payable annually in arrears at a nominal annual interest rate of 6%. Each bond is convertible at any time up to maturity into 250 ordinary shares.

When the bonds are issued:

- the prevailing market interest rate for similar debt without conversion options is 9%;
- the dividends expected over the three-year term of the bonds amount to $0.14 per share at the end of each year; and
- the risk-free annual interest rate for a three-year term is 5%.

The initial carrying amount of the liability component is calculated using a discount rate of 9% which is the market interest rate for similar bonds having no conversion rights.

	Nominal amount	*Present value*
		$
Principal	$2,000,000	1,544,367
Interest	$120,000 payable annually in arrears for three years	303,755
Total of liability component		1,848,122
Equity component (residual)		151,878
Proceeds of the bond issue		$2,000,000

The liability component is included in liabilities and the equity component is included in equity. The classification is not changed at the end of the first or second year even if the interest rates have changed or the probability of conversion has changed. The amount of the liability component is dealt with in accordance with IAS 39 after initial recognition.

Example 28.2 *Measurement of the component parts of a compound instrument*

Assume the same facts as in example 28.1 and that the financial liability is initially measured at $1,848,122 as in example 28.1. Assume that the market price of one ordinary share when the bonds are issued is $3 and that the equity component is measured using the Black-Scholes option pricing model (see paragraph A24 of IAS 32).

	$	*Pro rata valuation* $
Liability component	1,848,122	1,854,794
Option pricing model valuation of equity component	144,683	145,206
Total	1,992,805	
Proceeds of the bond issue		2,000,000

Extract 28.4 *Convertible debt instruments*

Roche, Switzerland, 31 December 2001 (IAS)

See also extract 28.6 for the statement of changes in equity.

On issue of convertible debt instruments, the cost of the liability portion is initially calculated using the market interest rate for an equivalent non-convertible instrument. The remainder of the net proceeds is allocated to the equity conversion option, which is reported in equity, and to deferred income taxes liabilities. The liability element is subsequently reported at amortised cost. Amortisation of the debt discount and release of the deferred tax liabilities are recognised in the income statement over the duration of the debt instrument. The value of the equity conversion option is not changed in future periods.

...

On 25 July 2001 the Group issued zero coupon US dollar exchangeable notes due 25 July 2021 with a principal amount of 2,051 million US dollars. The notes are exchangeable into non-voting equity securities, at any time prior to maturity. Net proceeds from the issue were 980 million US dollars (1,689 million Swiss francs). These have been initially allocated as 3,535 million Swiss francs of debt, 1,978 million Swiss francs of unamortised discount, 86 million Swiss francs of equity (in respect of the conversion option embedded in the bonds) and 46 million Swiss francs of deferred tax liability.

28.7 TREASURY SHARES

Treasury shares (or own shares) are shares of the entity acquired by the entity for the purpose of cancellation or resale. The law usually determines the powers of an entity to acquire its own shares (in some countries, the practice is forbidden) and what may be done with those shares (in some countries they must be cancelled).

If the shares are held by the entity, they should be shown as a deduction from equity (SIC 16, 4). They may be presented as a single line deduction. Alternatively, the par value (if any) may be shown as a deduction from the share capital and the balance of the consideration paid or payable for the shares is shown as a deduction from other components of equity (SIC 16, 10).

No gain or loss should be recognised in the income statement on the sale, issue or cancellation of treasury shares. The acquisition or consideration on disposal should be presented in the financial statements as a change in equity.

Costs associated with the transaction should be accounted for in accordance with SIC 17 as a deduction from equity only where they are incremental external costs directly attributable to the transaction which would otherwise have been avoided (see 28.4.1).

Extract 28.5 *Own equity instruments*

Roche, Switzerland, 31 December 2001 (IAS)

The Group's holdings in its own equity instruments are recorded as a deduction from equity. The original cost of acquisition, consideration received for subsequent resale of these equity instruments and other movements are reported as changes in equity. These instruments have been acquired primarily to meet the obligations that may arise in respect of certain of the Group's debt instruments.

28.8 DISCLOSURE

IAS 1 requires a balance sheet line item 'issued capital and reserves' (IAS 1, 66). This should be further analysed, either on the face of the balance sheet or in the notes, between the various classes of paid in capital, share premium and reserves (IAS 1, 73). In addition, the following information should be disclosed for each class of share capital:

- the number of shares authorised;
- the number of shares issued and fully paid, and issued but not fully paid;

- par value per share, or that the shares have no par value;
- a reconciliation of the number of shares outstanding at the beginning and at the end of the year;
- the rights, preferences and restrictions attaching to that class including restrictions on the distribution of dividends and the repayment of capital;
- shares in the entity held by the entity itself or by subsidiaries or associates of the entity; and
- shares reserved for issuance under options and sales contracts, including the terms and amounts.

(IAS 1, 74)

IAS 1 also requires the disclosure of:

- the nature and purpose of each reserve within equity;
- the amount of dividends which have been proposed or declared after the balance sheet date but before the financial statements are authorised; and
- the amount of cumulative preference dividends not recognised.

(IAS 1, 74)

The term 'reserve' is not defined in IAS 1 and is generally not used on other IFRSs. It is recommended that the disclosures are applied to the components of equity required by law or IFRSs.

Other IFRSs require the disclosure of:

- amounts recognised or removed from equity in the period in respect of certain financial instruments (IAS 39, 169(c), 170(a) and 170(c));
- the revaluation surplus and the movements for the period and any restrictions on its distribution to shareholders (IAS 16, 64(f)); and
- net exchange differences classified as equity and a reconciliation of the amount at the beginning and the end of the period (IAS 21, 42(b)).

In respect of treasury shares, an entity should:

- disclose the amount of reduction to equity either on the face of the balance sheet or in the notes; and
- give the related party disclosures required by IAS 24 (see chapter 38) if treasury shares are acquired from a party able to control or exercise significant influence over the reporting entity.

(SIC 16, 6 and 7)

The amount of transaction costs accounted for as a deduction from equity in the period should be disclosed separately. The related income taxes recognised directly in equity should also be included in the disclosure of the aggregate amount of current and deferred income tax credited or charged to equity (SIC 17, 9).

Extract 28.6 *Issued capital and reserves*

Roche, Switzerland, 31 December 2001 (IAS)

Extract from balance sheet in millions of CHF

Equity

	2001	2000
Share capital	160	160
Non-voting equity securities *(Genussscheine)*	–	–
Own equity instruments	(3,460)	(4,166)
Retained earnings	32,273	31,614
Total equity	28,973	27,608

Extract from consolidated statement of changes in equity in millions of CHF

	2001	2000
Share capital		
Balance at 1 January and at 31 December	160	160
Non-voting equity securities *(Genussscheine)*		
Balance at 1 January and at 31 December	–	–
Own equity instruments		
Balance at 1 January – as previously reported	(4,166)	–
Changes in accounting policies	–	(3,291)
Balance at 1 January – as restated	(4,166)	(3,291)
Movements during the year	706	(875)
Balance at 31 December	(3,460)	(4,166)
Retained earnings		
Balance at 1 January	31,614	26,794
Changes in accounting policies	382	–
Balance at 1 January – as restated	31,996	26,794
Net income	3,697	8,647
Dividends paid	(981)	(835)

Extract 28.6 *contd*

Extract from retained earnings in millions of CHF

	Accumulated profit and loss	Fair value reserve – available-for-sale investments	Fair value reserve – qualifying cash flow hedges	Equity conversion options	Currency translation reserve	2001 Total	2000 Total
At beginning of year	31,839	–	–	24	(249)	31,614	26,794
Changes in accounting policies	(283)	610	55	–	–	382	–
Net income	3,697	–	–	–	–	3,697	8,647
Dividends paid	(981)	–	–	–	–	(981)	(835)
Givaudan spin-off – special dividend and transfer of net assets	–	–	–	–	–	–	(2,642)
Changes in fair value	–	(1,077)	11	–	–	(1,066)	–
Recognised in net income	–	(613)	(53)	–	–	(666)	–
Deferred income taxes	–	(364)	(3)	–	–	(367)	–
Minority interests	–	22	(2)	–	–	20	–
Equity component of new convertible debt	–	–	–	86	–	86	24
Currency translation gains (losses)	–	–	–	–	(446)	(446)	(374)
Total	34,272	(1,422)	8	110	(695)	32,273	31,614

CHAPTER 29

Revenue

29.1 RELEVANT STANDARD AND INTERPRETATIONS

IAS 18 *Revenue*
SIC 27 *Evaluating the Substance of Transactions in the Legal Form of a Lease*
SIC 31 *Revenue – Barter Transactions Involving Advertising Services*

29.2 HISTORY

IAS 18 *Revenue Recognition* (IAS 18 [1982]) was approved in 1982 and reconsidered in the comparability and improvements project. The principal change was the deletion of the completed contract method for the recognition of revenue arising from the rendering of services. In addition a new standard on the measurement of revenue was added. IAS 18 *Revenue* was approved in November 1993 and applied to financial statements for accounting periods beginning on or after 1 January 1995.

SIC 27 was issued in February 2000 and SIC 31 in May 2001. Both became effective on 31 December 2001.

The IASB has an active project on revenue and liabilities. In the meantime, IFRIC is considering several revenue topics including:

- the reporting of gross and net revenue;
- specified trade-in rights; and
- loyalty programmes.

It is seeking to develop an overall approach for dealing with revenue recognition issues.

29.3 IOSCO

In June 1994, IOSCO advised the IASC that IAS 18 was acceptable for the purposes of the IOSCO core standards. However IOSCO identified the following suspense issues:

- the IASC should consider revenue recognition issues arising in transportation industries;
- the IASC should consider whether there is sufficient guidance in IAS 18 on real estate sales by entities in the real estate industry;
- in addition to transportation and real estate, the IASC should consider revenue recognition issues for other specialised industries such as financial institutions, insurance, oil and gas, mining, agriculture, forestry, rate-regulated utilities, commodity dealers, computer software, investment companies, broker-dealers, venture capitalists, motion picture production, broadcasting, cable television, records and music, health care providers, casinos and insurance brokers: and
- some IOSCO members may allow the use of the completed contract method (which is not permitted by IAS 18) but not require a reconciliation from that treatment to the percentage of completion method.

IAS 18 is included in 'IAS 2000' endorsed by IOSCO in May 2000. There are no supplemental treatments. However, IOSCO asked the IASB to consider accounting in the same list of specialised industries referred to in June 1994.

29.4 IAS 18 IN BRIEF

Revenue should be measured at the fair value of the consideration received or receivable. Discounting may be necessary when the receipt of the consideration is deferred (for example, when the seller provides interest free, extended credit).

Revenue from the *sale of goods* should be recognised when:

- the entity has transferred to the buyer the significant risks and rewards of ownership; and
- the entity no longer has continuing managerial involvement in, or effective control over, the goods.

Revenue from the *rendering of services* should be recognised as services are rendered provided that the outcome of the contract can be estimated reliably.

Interest should be recognised on a time proportion basis.

Royalties should be recognised on an accruals basis.

Dividend income should be recognised when the right to receive payment is established.

The recognition criteria should be applied, when appropriate, to the separate components of a transaction – for example, when a transaction involves both the sale of goods and a subsequent servicing of those goods, the revenue should be divided between the sale and the rendering of the service and each component should be accounted for separately.

Conversely, where two or more transactions are linked so that the commercial effect cannot be understood without reference to the series of transactions as a whole, then the recognition criteria should be applied to the series of transactions as a whole. For example where goods are sold and, at the same time, the seller enters into a separate repurchase agreement for the goods, the recognition criteria are applied together to the sale and repurchase agreement.

29.5 DEFINITION OF REVENUE

Revenue is the gross inflow of economic benefits during the period arising in the course of the ordinary activities of an entity when those inflows result in increases in equity, other than increases relating to contributions from equity participants (IAS 18, 7). This definition is derived from the framework's definition of income.

The *ordinary activities* of an entity are any activities which are undertaken by an entity as part of its business and such related activities in which the entity engages in furtherance of, incidental to, or arising from those activities (IAS 8, 6). Therefore, virtually all income is revenue but, as explained below, not all revenue is dealt with in IAS 18.

Revenue is normally the gross amount of, say, sales or fees. Revenue excludes amounts collected on behalf of third parties, such as certain taxes (IAS 18, 8), for instance, sales taxes, goods and services taxes and value added taxes which are collected and passed on to government authorities. The nature of such taxes varies from country to country but the entity usually gains no direct economic benefits from them (other than, perhaps, a temporary cash flow benefit). Trade discounts and volume rebates allowed by the entity are deducted from revenue (IAS 18, 10).

Extract 29.1 *Government taxes*

Stora Enso, Finland, 31 December 2001 (IAS)

Sales comprise products, raw materials, energy and services, less indirect sales tax, discounts and exchange differences on sales in foreign currency.

Extract 29.2 *Government taxes*

Telia, Sweden, 31 December 2000 (Swedish GAAP and IAS)

Sales are reported at the value of each sale less deductions for value added tax and advertising tax.

Extract 29.3 *Government taxes*

RWE, Germany, 31 December 2001 (IAS)

Net sales are recorded once the risk has been transferred to the customer ... Mineral oil tax/natural gas tax/electricity tax paid by Group companies directly is disclosed separately.

In € million	*2001 TFY*	*2000/01*
Net sales	33,301	62,878
Mineral oil tax/natural gas tax/electricity tax	3,281	6,127
Net sales (excluding mineral oil tax/natural gas tax/electricity tax)	30,020	56,751

29.5.1 Agency agreements

Amounts collected on behalf of, and passed on to, the seller in an agency relationship are not revenue of the agent (IAS 18, 8). In such a relationship, the revenue of the agent is the amount of commission which is deducted from the selling price plus any other charges made by the agent to the seller and other parties. For example, the revenue of an auctioneer is usually the commission deducted from the selling price, any commission charged to the buyer and any other fees charged by the auctioneer; amounts paid over to the seller are not revenue of the auctioneer. The revenue of a travel agent is usually the commission on ticket sales rather than the gross amount of the tickets charged to the travellers; amounts paid over to, say, an airline or shipping companies are not revenue for the travel agent. The revenue of a freight forwarding agency is the commission rather than the gross amount of freight charged by the airline, shipping or transport company.

In the case of the principal in an agency relationship, the revenue is usually the gross amount of amount charged to the ultimate customer. Any commission paid to (or deducted by) agents is accounted for as an expense. So, for example, the revenue of an airline is the gross amount charged for tickets or air freight; any commission paid to (or deducted by) travel or freight forwarding agents is an expense (this practice is required by IATA Airline Accountancy Guide 4 *Recognition of Revenue*).

Extract 29.4 *Agency relationships*

Barloworld, South Africa, 30 September 2001

Where companies act as agents and are remunerated on a commission basis, only the commission income, and not the value of the business handled, is included in revenue.

29.5.2 Scope

IAS 18 deals only with revenue arising from:

- the sale of goods;
- the rendering of services; and
- interest, royalties and dividends.

IAS 18 applies to the sale of biological assets and agricultural produce. Natural increases in herds and agricultural and forest products are also revenue but they are dealt with in IAS 41 (see chapter 45).

The extraction, rather than the sale, of ores may also give rise to revenue but IAS 18 does not apply to this revenue. This issue is being considered in the IASC's extractive industries project.

IAS 18 does not deal with revenue arising from insurance contracts of insurance companies. The IASC is currently carrying out an insurance project.

Increases in the fair value of financial assets and financial liabilities are income and, therefore, revenue but they are dealt with in accordance with IAS 39 (see chapter 20).

IAS 18 also does not apply to changes in value of other current assets or to dividends received from entities accounted for under the equity method. Lease agreements are dealt with in accordance with IAS 17 (see chapter 32).

29.6 MEASUREMENT

Revenue should be measured at the fair value of the consideration received or receivable (IAS 18, 9). Trade discounts and volume rebates allowed by the entity are deducted from revenue (IAS 18, 10).

Extract 29.5 *Measurement of revenue*

Danisco, Denmark, 30 April 2001 (IAS)

Net sales comprise sales invoiced during the year less returned goods and discounts granted in connection with sales. Refunds received from the EU are included in net sales.

Extract 29.6 *Sales to customers*

Unaxis Holding AG, Switzerland, 31 December 2001 (IAS)

Sales represent amounts invoiced for goods and services less value added tax and other openly invoiced sales taxes, as well as deductions for returns and discounts. Revenue under long-term construction and service contracts is recognised according to the percentage of completion method.

In most cases the consideration takes the form of cash or cash equivalents and the amount of revenue can be measured with ease. There are, however, three problem areas considered in turn below:

- non-cash transactions, such as barter arrangements;
- deferred payment terms which are, in substance, financing arrangements; and
- transactions which combine the sale of goods with a separately identifiable service.

29.6.1 Barter transactions

The consideration for the sale of goods or services may take the form of other goods and services as, for example, in a barter arrangement. A transaction is not regarded as generating revenue if goods or services are exchanged for goods or services of a similar nature and value. Revenue may be recognised where goods or services are exchanged for dissimilar goods and services. In such circumstances, the revenue is measured at the fair value of the goods and services received or receivable, adjusted by the amount of any cash and cash equivalents transferred (IAS 18, 12).

When the fair value of the goods and services received cannot be measured reliably, the revenue is measured by reference to the fair value of the goods sold or services provided. In practice, the latter approach may be simpler as the entity usually knows the selling price of its goods and services and may well have negotiated the deal on the basis that it receives goods or services to the value of the goods or services it has supplied. SIC 31 provides guidance in respect of barter transactions involving advertising services, when a seller provides advertising services in exchange for receiving advertising services from its customer. An exchange of similar advertising services does not generate revenue under IAS 18 (SIC 31, 3). Revenue from a barter transaction involving dissimilar advertising services cannot be measured reliably at the fair value of the services received (SIC 31, 5). Revenue can only be measured reliably by reference to non-barter advertising services rendered that:

- involve advertising similar to the advertising in the barter transaction;
- occur frequently;
- represent a predominant number of transactions and amount when compared to all transactions to provide advertising that is similar to the advertising in the barter transaction;
- involve cash and/or another form of consideration (e.g. marketable securities, non-monetary assets, and other services) that has a reliably measurable fair value; and
- do not involve the same counterparty as in the barter transaction.

(SIC 31, 5)

It is the practice in some industries for entities to exchange or swap homogeneous inventories in various locations in order to fulfil demand on a timely basis in a particular location. For example, different oil distribution companies may draw on each others' inventories as a matter of convenience. In such circumstances, it is the sale to the final customer, rather than the exchange among distributors, which is the transaction that generates revenue. The exchanges among distributors are not recorded as revenue or expenses by any of the distributors (IAS 18, 12).

29.6.2 Financing arrangements

In many business transactions, entities provide credit to those who are buying their goods or services. When, under such an arrangement, the transaction effectively constitutes a financing arrangement, the fair value of the consideration is the present value of all future receipts which is measured by discounting all future receipts using an imputed rate of interest (IAS 18, 11). In such a case, the nominal amount of the consideration consists of two components:

- revenue from the sale of goods or the rendering of a service which is recognised in accordance with the requirements for the sale of goods or the rendering of services as appropriate; and
- interest revenue which is the difference between the revenue from the sale of goods or the rendering of the service and the nominal amount

of the consideration and which is recognised using the effective interest rate method in accordance with IAS 39.
(IAS 18, 11)

The imputed rate of interest used to discount future receipts is the more clearly determinable of either:

- the prevailing interest rate for a similar instrument of an issuer with a similar credit rating; or
- a rate of interest that discounts the nominal amount of the instrument to the current cash price of the goods or services.

(IAS 18, 11)

29.6.3 Combination of sale of goods and services

The consideration may cover both the sale of goods and a separately identifiable service, for example in the following cases:

- sales of computer software which includes free after-sales technical support;
- sales of consumer products which include free servicing for an initial period;
- franchisee fees which cover both initial supplies and continuing services (IAS 18, appendix, 18);
- loan syndication fees when the lender retains a portion of the loan package at a discount to the interest rate applicable to other lenders (IAS 18, appendix, 14(c)(iii)); and
- the total income arising on a finance lease by a manufacturer or dealer when the lease gives rise to a profit or loss on the sale of goods and finance income (IAS 17, 34).

In such cases, the fair value of the consideration must be split between the two components as follows:

- revenue from the provision of the service is measured at the expected costs of that service together with a reasonable profit on that service; and
- revenue from the sale of goods is the difference between the revenue from the provision of the service and the fair value of the consideration.

(IAS 18, 13)

IAS 18 does not provide any guidance on what is meant by a 'reasonable profit' on a service. The reference to such a notion is included in examples 11 and 18 in the appendix to IAS 18 but not in the standard itself. One possible approach is to look at the profit margin on services which are rendered without the associated sale of goods. Another approach is to allocate the total consideration between the sale and service in proportion to the separate selling prices of the two components.

Extract 29.7 *Segmentation of contracts*

SAP AG, Germany, 31 December 2001 (US GAAP)

In accordance with SOP 97-2, software license fee revenues are recognized when persuasive evidence of an arrangement exists, delivery has occurred, the license fee is fixed and determinable and the collection of the fee is probable. The Company allocates a portion of its software revenues to maintenance activities or other services or products provided to the customer free of charge or at non-standard discounts when provided in conjunction with the licensing arrangement. Amounts are allocated using the residual method whereby revenue is deferred for undelivered elements based upon standard prices charged for those undelivered services or products and the residual amounts are recognized as revenue for the delivered elements. Software license fees for resellers or other members of the indirect sales channel are based on a fixed percentage of the Company's standard prices. The Company recognizes software license revenue for such contracts based upon the terms and conditions provided by the reseller to their customer. Maintenance revenues are recognized rateably over the term of the contract on a straight-line basis. Consulting and training services are generally recognized at the time the service is performed. Fees from licenses sold together with consulting services are generally recognized upon shipment provided that the SOP 97-2 criteria described above are fulfilled. In instances where the aforementioned criteria have not been met, both the license and the consulting fees are recognized under the percentage of completion method of contract accounting. The Company provides for sales returns and allowances. In limited instances, the Company will enter into fixed fee consulting arrangements. Revenues under such arrangements are generally recognized using the percentage of completion method. Provisions for estimated losses on uncompleted contracts are made in the period such losses are determined.

Extract 29.8 *Segmentation of contracts*

Technotrans, Germany, 31 December 2001 (IAS)

If a contract from a customer involves both the delivery of goods and the provision of a service, such as assembly and commissioning, revenue is realised upon acceptance by the customer.

In certain circumstances, in a departure from this principle according to IAS 18.13, individual components of a business transaction may be invoiced separately if this reflects the economic content of the business transaction more accurately. As the IAS do not make stipulations on the subdivision of a business transaction into its component parts, US EITF 00-21 *Accounting for*

Revenue Arrangements with Multiple Deliverables is used for this purpose in conjunction with IAS 1.22. It divides up a business transaction consisting of several components into goods and services elements in proportion to their respective fair value, if the latter can be determined objectively and reliably and if the service could also be procured from third parties without diminishing the practical utility of the delivered goods or their value for the customer. If these conditions are met and the significant risks of ownership for the goods have moreover passed to the buyer (IAS 18.16), the revenue from the goods is realised according to IAS 18.14 and the revenue from the services according to IAS 18.20. According to this accounting method, at 31 December 2001 revenue totalling €5,445 thousand (previous year: €1,410 thousand) had been realised from the supply of materials where their assembly or commissioning was outstanding at the balance sheet date.

29.7 RECOGNITION

Revenue is recognised when it is probable that future economic benefits will flow to the entity and these benefits can be measured reliably (*Framework*, 83). IAS 18 identifies the circumstances in which these criteria will be met for each of the three categories of revenue. The criteria are usually applied separately to each transaction. However, the recognition criteria are applied to:

- the separately identifiable components of a single transaction when the consideration covers both the sale of goods and a separately identifiable service, in which case an appropriate amount of the revenue should be deferred and recognised as the services are rendered (IAS 18, 13); and
- two or more transactions together when the transactions are linked in such a way that the commercial effect cannot be understood without reference to the series of transactions as a whole, for example when goods are sold and, at the same time, the seller enters into a separate repurchase agreement for the goods.

(IAS 18, 13)

29.8 RECOGNITION – SALE OF GOODS

Revenue from the sale of goods should be recognised when all the following conditions have been satisfied:

- the entity has transferred to the buyer the significant risks and rewards of ownership of the goods (see 29.8.1);

- the entity retains neither continuing managerial involvement to the degree usually associated with ownership nor effective control over the goods sold (see 29.8.2);
- the amount of revenue can be measured reliably (see 29.6);
- it is probable that the economic benefits associated with the transaction will flow to the entity (see 29.8.4); and
- the costs incurred or to be incurred in respect of the transaction can be measured reliably (see 29.8.5).

(IAS 18, 14)

In many cases, all these criteria are met at the same time and there is little doubt about the need to recognise revenue. For example, when goods are handed over to a customer or despatched for same day delivery, there is usually a sale and revenue should be recognised immediately. In some cases, there may be some uncertainty about whether the criteria have been met. The appendix to IAS 18 includes a number of examples which deal with such circumstances. These examples emphasise the need to apply the principles that lie behind the recognition criteria in the circumstances of each sale and to consider the law relating to the sale of goods in the country in question. The examples deal with:

- bill and hold sales;
- goods shipped subject to conditions;
- cash on delivery sales;
- lay away sales;
- orders when payment (or partial payment) is received in advance of delivery for goods not currently held in inventory;
- sale and repurchase agreements;
- sales to distributors, dealers or others for resale;
- subscriptions;
- instalment sales; and
- real estate sales.

29.8.1 Transfer of Risks and Rewards

The law in each country may determine the point in time at which the significant risks and rewards of ownership of goods are transferred. Therefore, a sale might be recognised earlier in one country than another. This does not mean that different criteria are applied in different countries but that the recognition criteria are met at different times in different countries. For example, the recognition criteria may be met on signing the contract for the sale of goods in one country but not until the transfer of possession of the goods in another country.

The risks and rewards of ownership of goods are usually transferred when either:

- legal title to the goods is transferred to the buyer; or
- possession of the goods passes to the buyer.

In many cases, both these events occur at the same time, for example with most wholesale or retail sales. In such cases, there is little practical difficulty in determining the point in time at which revenue from the sale of goods should be recognised.

In some cases, an entity may transfer legal title to, or possession of, the goods to the buyer but retain some risks and rewards of ownership. For example:

- the entity may retain an obligation for unsatisfactory performance which is not covered by normal warranty provisions (IAS 18, 16);
- the receipt of the revenue may be contingent on the buyer deriving revenue from its sale of the goods (IAS 18, 16 and appendix 2,(c) and 6);
- the goods may be shipped subject to installation and the installation is a significant part of the contract which has not yet been completed (IAS 18, 16 and appendix 2,(a));
- the buyer may have the right to rescind the purchase for a reasons specified in the sales contract and the entity is uncertain about the probability of return (IAS 18, 16 and appendix 2,(b)).

In such circumstances, it is necessary to decide whether the entity has retained significant risks and rewards – in which case, the sale and revenue are not recognised – or retained insignificant risks and rewards – in which case, the sale and the revenue are recognised.

On the other hand, the entity may transfer legal title to, or possession of, the goods and retain only insignificant risks and rewards of ownership. For example:

- the entity may retain the legal title to the goods solely to protect the collectability of the amount due (IAS 18, 17) – such an arrangement is sometimes referred to as the 'reservation of title';
- the entity may offer retail customers a refund when the customer is not satisfied with the goods but the entity can estimate reliably future returns (IAS 18, 17 and appendix 2,(b)); and
- under a bill and hold sale, delivery may be delayed at the buyer's request but the buyer takes title and accepts billing (IAS 18, appendix 1).

In such circumstances, the entity recognises the full amount of revenue but may also need to recognise a liability for the costs associated with the retained risks, for example, for expected returns (IAS 18, 17 and IAS 37, appendix C, example 4). For bill and hold sales, additional considerations apply including that delivery is probable and the goods are ready for delivery when the sale is recognised (IAS 18, appendix 1).

29.8.2 Managerial Involvement

In order to recognise a sale, an entity should not retain continuing managerial involvement in the goods to the degree usually associated with ownership. It also should not retain effective control over the goods sold. Managerial involvement and control usually pass with legal title or possession but this is not always the case.

An entity may retain some continuing managerial involvement in the goods but only to a limited extent. For example:

- a property developer may sell each apartment in a building but continue to act as managing agent for the building; or
- a franchisor may sells goods to the franchisee but limit the use of the goods to use in the franchise operations.

In such cases, the entity recognises the sale and the revenue.

29.8.3 Sales versus Leases

Care is sometimes needed in deciding whether a transaction results in a sale or a lease. Both a sale and a finance lease involve the transfer of the significant risks and rewards associated with ownership. Both also involve giving up control. However, when the transaction is such that the recipient of the asset is granted the right to use the asset for a limited period, the transaction is a lease and not a sale. SIC 27 addresses a number of issues concerning whether an arrangement between an entity and an investor involves the legal form of a lease. If an arrangement does not meet the definition of a lease, any fees are recognised in accordance with the principles of IAS 18, 20 (see 29.9 below).

29.8.4 Receipt of Consideration

Revenue is recognised only when it is probable that the consideration will be received by the entity. In practice, an entity is unlikely to transfer ownership or possession of the goods if it is unlikely, at that time, to receive the consideration. In the unlikely event that an entity does transfer ownership or possession in such circumstances, the sale and revenue are not recognised.

Uncertainty about the receipt of the consideration usually arises after the sale has taken place and has been recognised as revenue. In such cases the subsequent loss is recognised as bad debt expense. The sale is not reversed even if the loss arises during the same accounting period (IAS 18, 18).

29.8.5 Costs Incurred

Revenue is recognised only when the costs incurred, or to be incurred, in respect of the transaction can be measured reliably. This requirement ensures that revenue and expenses that relate to the same transaction are recognised simultaneously, a process which is commonly referred to as the matching of revenues and expenses. In practice, it is usually possible for the entity to estimate reliably the costs incurred, or to be incurred, and therefore to recognise the revenue.

Revenue should not be recognised in the rare circumstance in which an estimate of expenses cannot be made; any consideration already received in such circumstances is recognised as a liability or deferred income (IAS 18, 19).

29.8.6 Disclosure of Accounting Policy

An entity should disclose its accounting policy for the recognition of revenue from the sale of goods (IAS 18, 35(a)).

Extract 29.9 *Sales and warranties*

Nokia, Finland, 31 December 2001 (IAS)

Revenue recognition (extract)

Sales from the majority of the Group are recognized when persuasive evidence of an arrangement exists, delivery has occurred, the fee is fixed and determinable and collectibility is probable.

Provisions (extract)

The Group recognizes the estimated liability to repair or replace products still under warranty at the balance sheet date. The provision is calculated based on historical experience of the level of repairs and replacements.

Extract 29.10 *Sales of communications products and computer systems*

Fujitsu, Japan, 31 March 2000 (Japanese GAAP and IAS)

Revenues from sales of communications products and computer systems are generally recognized upon acceptance by the customers, whereas revenues from sales of personal computers, peripherals, other equipment and electronic devices are recognized when the products are shipped.

Extract 29.11 *Income and net sales*

Bayer, Germany, 31 December 2001 (IAS)

Sales are recognized upon delivery of goods or rendering of services to third parties and are reported net of sales taxes and rebates. Revenues from contracts that contain customer acceptance provisions are deferred until customer acceptance occurs or the contractual acceptance period has lapsed. Allocations to provisions for rebates to customers are recognized in the period in which the related sales are recorded based on the contract terms. Payments relating to the sale or outlicensing of technologies or technological expertise – once the respective agreements have become effective – are immediately recognized in income if all rights to the technologies and all obligations resulting from them have been relinquished under the contract terms. However, if rights to the technologies continue to exist or obligations resulting from them have yet to be fulfilled, the payments received are recorded in line with the actual circumstances.

Extract 29.12 *Sales*

Volkswagen, Germany, 31 December 2001 (IAS)

Sales revenue and other operating income is recognized only when the relevant service has been rendered or the goods delivered, i.e. when the risk has been transferred to the customer.

Income from assets for which a Group company has a buy-back obligation are only realized when the assets have definitively left the Group. Up to that point they are recognized in the balance sheet under inventories.

Extract 29.13 *Net sales*

Volvo, Sweden, 31 December 2001 (Swedish GAAP and IAS)

The Group's reported net sales pertain mainly to revenues from sales of goods and services. Net sales are reduced by the value of discounts granted and by returns. Income from the sale of goods is recognized when the goods are delivered to the customers. If however the sale of goods is combined with a buy-back agreement or a residual value guarantee, the sale is accounted for as an operating lease transaction if significant risks are retained in Volvo. Income from the sale of workshop services is recognized when the service is provided. Rental revenues and interest income in conjunction with financial leasing or instalment contracts is recognized over the contract period.

29.9 RECOGNITION – RENDERING OF SERVICES

The rendering of services typically involves the performance by the entity of a contractually agreed task over an agreed period of time. A construction contract is one example of the rendering of a service; other examples include contracts to install or maintain a product or to provide advertising, tuition, financial, franchise and consultancy services. IAS 11 deals with construction contracts in the financial statements of contractors; IAS 18 deals with all other services.

Both IAS 11 and IAS 18 require the same approach based on the percentage of completion method, but IAS 18 deals only with revenue whereas IAS 11 deals with revenue and expenses. However, IAS 18 states that the requirements of IAS 11 are generally applicable in all cases (IAS 18, 21).

Revenue from the rendering of a service should be recognised:

- by reference to the stage of completion of the transaction at the balance sheet date when the outcome of the transaction can be estimated reliably (IAS 18, 20); and
- only to the extent of the expenses recognised which are recoverable when the outcome of the transaction cannot be estimated reliably (IAS 18, 26). As the outcome cannot be measured reliably, no profit is recognised (IAS 18, 27).

No revenue is recognised and the costs are expensed if the outcome of a transaction cannot be estimated reliably and it is not probable that the costs incurred will be recovered. Revenue may be recognised in accordance with IAS 18, 20 once the uncertainties that prevented the outcome of the contract being estimated reliably cease to exist (IAS 18, 28).

The appendix to IAS 18 includes a number of examples which illustrate the application of the requirements. These examples deal with:

- installation fees;
- servicing fees included in the price of the product;
- advertising commissions;
- insurance agency commissions;
- financial service fees;
- admission fees;

- tuition fees;
- initiation, entrance and membership fees;
- franchise fees; and
- fees from the development of customised software.

Example 29.1 *Recognition of revenue on the rendering of services*

A consultant enters into a contract in 2000 which will take until 2002 to complete. The contract revenues and costs are as follows:

	Euro
Contract revenue	100,000
Contract costs	
2000	20,000
2001	30,000
2002	25,000

If, at the end of 2000, the consultant is able to estimate reliably the outcome of the contract it should then recognise revenue by reference to the stage of completion of the contract. If the stage of completion is determined by reference to the proportion that costs incurred to date bear to total costs, the consultant should recognise Euro 26,667 as revenue, that is 20,000/75,000 × 100,000. If the consultant had been unable to estimate reliably the outcome of the contract at the end of 2000, it recognises revenue only to the extent of costs incurred (Euro 20,000) and then only if those costs are recoverable.

29.9.1 Estimating the Outcome of the Contract

The outcome of a transaction can be estimated reliably only when all the following conditions are satisfied:

- the amount of revenue can be measured reliably (see 29.6);
- it is probable that the economic benefits associated with the transaction will flow to the entity;
- the stage of completion of the transaction at the balance sheet date can be measured reliably; and
- the costs incurred for the transaction and the costs to complete the transaction can be measured reliably.

(IAS 18, 20)

Therefore, the entity must have agreed with the other parties to the transaction:

- each party's enforceable rights regarding the service to be provided and received by the parties;
- the consideration to be exchanged; and
- the manner and terms of settlement.

(IAS 18, 23)

If the entity has agreed with the other parties their respective rights in the transaction, the consideration to be exchanged and the manner and means of settlement, it is possible to measure reliably an initial amount of revenue. This amount may change, however, as a result of variations in contract work, claims and incentive payments. The guidance in IAS 11 is helpful in determining when such amounts should be included in the revenue for the service.

A major uncertainty may exist over the costs to be incurred in carrying out the service. For example, an entity may have agreed and even received a fee for servicing a product but may not know the amount of costs that will be incurred until the contract is completed. The entity must be able to estimate the likely amount of costs, perhaps based on experience with similar contracts or from having provided the same service in the past, before it can recognise any revenue in excess of recoverable cost, i.e. before it can recognise a net profit from the service (IAS 18, 27).

In order to estimate reliably the outcome of a contract, the entity must have an effective internal financial budgeting and reporting system (IAS 18, 23). Without such a system, it is difficult to obtain reliable information to make the necessary calculations.

29.9.2 Stage of Completion

The stage of completion of a transaction may be determined by:

- surveys of the work performed;
- expressing services performed to date as a percentage of total services to be performed; or
- expressing the costs incurred for services performed to date as a percentage of the estimated total costs of services performed and to be performed.

(IAS 18, 24)

Different methods may need to be used in different circumstances. For example, when an entity enters into many annual contracts to service consumer products, a time apportionment basis may provide a reliable indication of the average stage of completion. An entity which enters into a series of unique contracts as, for example, would be the case for a consultant, needs to assess separately the stage of completion of each contract, perhaps on a proportion of costs basis.

Progress payments and advances from customers may not reflect the services performed.

29.9.3 Changes in Estimates

It is inevitable that the circumstances applying to a particular contract may change during the contract. For example:

- during the early stages of a contract the entity may not be able to estimate reliably the outcome of the contract, the total costs to be incurred or even the revenue;
- uncertainties may arise during a contract such that the entity can no longer estimate reliably the outcome of the contract as, for example, may be the case when technical problems cause a delay in a design project;
- previous uncertainties may be removed so that the outcome of the contract can be estimated reliably as, for example, when technical problems in a design project are resolved and the entity and the other party agree how the related costs are to be dealt with; or
- the estimates of revenue and costs may be revised during the contract.

When an uncertainty arises about the collectability of an amount already included in revenue, the uncollectable amount is recognised as bad debt expense rather than as an adjustment to revenue already recognised (IAS 18, 22).

29.9.4 Disclosure of Accounting Policy

An entity should disclose its accounting policy for the recognition of revenue from the rendering of services including the method used to determine the stage of completion (IAS 18, 35(a)).

Extract 29.14 *Power supplies*

CEZ, Czech Republic, 31 December 2000 (IAS)

The company bills for services rendered through the end of each month based on meter readings.

Example 29.2 *Recognition of Revenue during contract*

A consultant enters into a contract to provide certain services which start in 1999 and which are expected to be completed by the end of 2001. The total contract revenue is Euro 600,000.

At the end of 1999, the consultant is unable to estimate reliably the outcome of the contract but it is probable that all 1999 costs of Euro 75,000 will be recovered. Therefore, the consultant recognises revenue of Euro 75,000 and costs of Euro 75,000.

At the end of 2000, the consultant is able to estimate reliably the outcome of the contract. It estimates that total costs will be Euro 400,000 and that the contract is 50% complete. Therefore it recognises revenue of Euro 225,000 (50% × Euro 600,000 less Euro 75,000 recognised in 1999). It recognises costs of Euro 125,000 (50% × Euro 400,000 less Euro 75,000 recognised in 1999).

At the end of 2001, the contract is still not completed but the consultant is still able to estimate reliably the outcome of the contract. It –estimates that total costs will be Euro 420,000, total revenue will be Euro 630,000 and the contract is 90% complete. Therefore it recognises revenue of Euro 267,000 (90% × Euro 630,000 less Euro 300,000 already recognised). It recognises costs of Euro 178,000 (90% × 420,000 less Euro 200,000 already recognised).

By the end of 2002, the contract has been completed with total revenue of Euro 630,000 and total costs of Euro 415,000. It recognises revenue of Euro 63,000 in 2000.

	Revenue *Euro*	*Expenses* *Euro*	*Profit* *Euro*
1999	75,000	75,000	–
2000	225,000	125,000	100,000
2001	267,000	178,000	89,000
2002	63,000	37,000	26,000
	630,000	415,000	215,000

Extract 29.15 *Revenue recognition on contracts*

Nokia, Finland, 31 December 2001 (IAS)

Revenue recognition (extract)

Sales and cost of sales from contracts involving solutions achieved through modification of telecommunications equipment are recognized on the percentage of completion method when the outcome of the contract can be estimated reliably. Completion is measured using either the cost-to-cost input method or the milestone output method, depending upon the nature of the individual project and the most applicable measure of progress. Losses on projects in progress are recognized immediately when known and estimable. The cumulative impact of a revision in estimates is recorded in the period such revisions become known and estimable. Billings or costs incurred in excess of a project's progress to completion are recorded as unearned revenue or work-in-progress, respectively.

Extract 29.16 *Transportation revenues*

SAS, Sweden, 31 December 2000 (IAS)

Ticket sales are reported as traffic revenues only upon completion of the journey.

The value of tickets sold and still valid but not yet used on the balance sheet date is reported as unearned transportation revenue. This item is reduced either when SAS or another airline completes the air journey or when the passenger requests a refund.

A portion of unearned transportation revenue covers tickets sold that are expected to remain unutilized. An estimate of unutilized tickets' anticipated share of the unearned transportation liability is produced annually. This reserve is reported as revenue the following year in accordance with established principles.

Extract 29.17 *Telecommunications services*

Telia, Sweden, 31 December 2000 (Swedish GAAP and IAS)

Sales principally consist of traffic charges including interconnect traffic and roaming, subscription fees, hookup fees, and service charges as well as sales of customer premises equipment and advertising space in directories.

Revenue is recognized for the period in which the service is performed or the product is delivered. Subscription fees are recognized as revenue during the subscription period. Revenues from directories are reported in the period in which the directory is published. Customer cable TV hookup fees are reported as cost reductions over the depreciation schedule for the facility in question. Other hookup and installation fees are recognized as revenue as these services are rendered. In the portal operations, ad swapping with another provider is not recognized as revenue.

Sales of Indefeasible Rights of Use (IRU) regarding fiber and ducts are recognized as revenue over the period of the agreement (see also Note 28 'Leasing agreements and Contractual Obligations'). IRU swaps with other operators are not recognized as revenue.

Note 28

Telia as operating lessor

Fiber and ducts are sold as part of the operations of Telia's international carrier business. Telia has decided to view these as integral equipment.

Under the agreements, title was not transferred to the lessee. The transactions are therefore reported as operating lease agreements. Direct expenditures incurred in connection with agreements are capitalized and written off over the term of the agreement. The contracted sale price is chiefly paid in advance and is recognized as revenue during the period of the agreement. Sales not recognized as revenue are reported as long-term liabilities and prepaid income.

29.10 RECOGNITION – INTEREST

Interest revenue should be recognised when:

- it is probable that the interest will flow to the entity; and
- the amount of the interest can be measured reliably.

(IAS 18, 29 and 30)

Interest revenue should be recognised on a time proportion basis that takes into account the effective yield on the asset (IAS 18, 30(a) and IAS 39, 73).

The effective yield is the rate of interest required to discount the stream of future cash receipts expected over the asset's life to equate to the initial carrying amount of the asset (IAS 18, 31) – this is the same definition as is used in IAS 32 for the purpose of disclosures of effective interest rates (IAS 32, 61 – see chapter 20). IAS 39 requires that the same method should be used for financial assets carried on an amortised cost basis (IAS 39, 73). When this method is applied, interest revenue includes the amount of amortisation of any discount, premium or other difference between the initial carrying amount of the asset and its amount at maturity (IAS 18, 31).

Any interest which is received after the acquisition of an interest-bearing investment but which represents a recovery of acquisition cost is treated as a reduction in the cost of acquisition (IAS 18, 32). For example, when the entity acquires a government bond at a price which includes accrued interest and the bond qualifies as a held-to-maturity investment under IAS 39 and is measured at amortised cost, the appropriate part of the subsequent receipt of interest is deducted from the cost of the bond rather than included in the income statement.

Finance income arising on a finance lease is a form of interest revenue. The recognition of such income, in particular the allocation of that income over the period of the lease, is dealt with in IAS 17 (see chapter 32). The requirements are broadly similar to those which would apply under IAS 18.

IAS 18 does not apply to revenue arising from changes in the fair value of financial assets and liabilities, or their disposal (see chapter 20) or changes in value of other current assets (IAS 18, 6).

29.10.1 Disclosure of Accounting Policy

An entity should disclose its accounting policy for the recognition of interest revenue (IAS 18, 35(a) and IAS 32, 47 and 52).

Extract 29.18 *Interest income*

Böhler-Uddeholm, Austria, 31 December 2001 (IAS)

Interest income is recognized on a pro rata basis in accordance with the effective return on the asset.

Extract 29.19 *Loans to customers*

Nokia, Finland, 31 December 2001 (IAS)

Loans to customers are recorded at amortized cost. Loans are subject to regular and thorough review as to their collectibility and as to available collateral; in the event that any loan is deemed not fully recoverable, provision is made to reflect the shortfall between the carrying amount and the present value of the expected cash flows. Interest income on loans to customers is included within other operating income.

29.11 ROYALTIES

Royalties are recognised when:

- it is probable that the royalties will flow to the entity; and
- the amount of the royalties can be measured reliably.

(IAS 18, 29)

Royalties should be recognised on an accrual basis in accordance with the substance of the relevant agreement unless it is more appropriate to recognise them on some other systematic and rational basis (IAS 18, 30). This may be on a straight-line basis over the term of the agreement, for example where the licensee has the right to use certain technology for a specified time. In other cases a licensing agreement may have the substance of an outright sale as there is a fixed fee, the licensee can exploit its rights freely and the licensor has no remaining performance obligations. In such a case revenue is recognised at the time of sale. This might be the case in a licensing agreement for the use of software, where the licensor has no obligations subsequent to delivery; or where a licensee is granted rights to distribute a product in markets where the licensor has no control over the licensee and no further revenues from the licensee's sales (IAS 18, appendix).

29.11.1 Disclosure of Accounting Policy

An entity should disclose its accounting policy for the recognition of royalty revenue (IAS 18, 35(a)).

Extract 29.20 *Royalties*

adidas-Salomon, Germany, 31 December 2001 (IAS)

Royalty income is recorded based on the terms of the contracts.

Extract 29.21 *Royalties*

Roche, Switzerland, 31 December 2001 (IAS)

Royalty income is recognised on an accruals basis in accordance with the economic substance of the agreement.

29.12 DIVIDENDS

Dividends should be recognised when:

- the shareholder's right to receive payment is established;
- it is probable that the dividends will flow to the entity; and
- the amount of the dividends can be measured reliably.

(IAS 18, 29 and 30)

In practice, dividends are recognised on a cash basis or when they are declared which is usually the earliest time at which it is probable that they will flow to the holder of the investment. As most equity securities are carried at market value (or some other estimate of fair value) under IAS 39, it becomes less important for an entity to decide when to recognise dividends as expected dividends are reflected in the market value.

Dividends on equity securities declared from pre-acquisition profits are deducted from the cost of the securities. If it is difficult to make such an allocation except on an arbitrary basis, dividends are recognised as revenue unless they clearly represent a recovery of part of the cost of the equity securities (IAS 18, 32).

In consolidated financial statements, dividends from investments in associates and interests in jointly controlled entities accounted for under the equity method are deducted from the carrying amount of the investment (IAS 28, 6). The same treatment should be adopted where the investment is carried on on an equity basis in an investor's separate financial statements (IAS 18, 6 and IAS 28, 6).

29.12.1 Disclosure

An entity should disclose its accounting policy for the recognition of dividend revenue (IAS 18, 35(a) and IAS 32, 47 and 52).

Extract 29.22 *Dividends*

Volkswagen, Germany, 31 December 2001 (IAS)

Dividend income is recognized on the date on which the dividend is legally approved.

Extract 29.23 *Dividends*

Böhler-Uddeholm, Austria, 31 December 2001 (IAS)

Dividend income is recorded when a legal claim arises.

Extract 29.24 *Dividends*

Barloworld, South Africa, 30 September 2001 (IAS)

Dividend income from investments is recognised when the shareholders' rights to receive payment have been established.

29.13 DISCLOSURES

In addition to the accounting policies adopted for revenue and the method used to determine the stage of completion for contracts rendering services (see above), an entity should disclose:

- the amount of each significant category of revenue recognised during the period including revenue arising from the sale of goods; the rendering of services; interest; royalties; dividends; and
- the amount of revenue arising from exchanges of goods or services included in each significant category of revenue.

Contingent liabilities and contingent assets may arise from items such as warranty costs, claims, penalties or possible losses. Any such contingent liabilities and contingent assets should be disclosed in accordance with IAS 37 *Provisions, Contingent Liabilities and Contingent Assets* (see chapter 27).

CHAPTER 30

Construction Contracts

30.1 RELEVANT STANDARD

IAS 11 *Construction Contracts*

IAS 11 applies to the financial statements of the contractor, that is the entity which is carrying out the contract on behalf of the customer. IAS 11 does not apply to the financial statements of the customer who usually accounts for the costs as property, plant and equipment in accordance with IAS 16 or to an entity which is constructing property, plant and equipment for its own use.

IAS 18 *Revenue* deals with other contracts involving the rendering of services. Both IAS 11 and IAS 18 require the same approach based on the percentage of completion method.

30.2 HISTORY

IAS 11 *Accounting for Construction Contracts* (IAS 11 [1979]) was approved in 1979. It was reviewed in 1986 but the IASC decided that the standard should not be revised.

IAS 11 was reconsidered in the comparability and improvements project. The principal change was the elimination of the completed contract method for the recognition of revenue and profits arising from construction contracts. IAS 11 *Construction Contracts* was approved in November 1993 and applied to financial statements for accounting periods beginning on or after 1 January 1995.

30.3 IOSCO

In June 1994, IOSCO advised the IASC that IAS 11 was acceptable for the purposes of the IOSCO core standards. However, IOSCO identified the following suspense issues:

- some IOSCO members may accept IAS 11 but specify a treatment for the determination of the expected loss on a contract that would require a consistent treatment for indirect costs (see 30.7.2); and
- some IOSCO members may allow the use of the completed contract method (which is not permitted by IAS 11) but not require a reconciliation from that treatment to the percentage of completion method required by IAS 11.

IAS 11 is included in 'IAS 2000' endorsed by IOSCO in May 2000. There are no supplemental treatments.

30.4 IAS 11 IN BRIEF

When the outcome of a construction contract can be measured reliably, revenue and profits on the contract should be recognised by reference to the stage of completion of the contract (percentage of completion method). When the outcome of the contract cannot be measured reliably, revenue should be recognised to the extent that costs are recoverable. In all cases, expected losses should be recognised immediately.

The percentage of completion method is applied on a cumulative basis and the amounts of revenue and the associated estimates of total costs are revised as necessary each period.

When a contract covers a number of assets, the accounting for the construction of each asset should be dealt with separately when separate proposals have been submitted for each asset, the proposal for each asset has been separately negotiated, and the costs and revenues relating to each asset can be separately identified. An addition to a contract should be accounted for as a separate contract when the additional asset differs significantly and its price is negotiated without regard to the original contract price.

A group of contracts should be accounted for as a single contract when the contracts are negotiated as a single package, closely inter-related and performed concurrently or in a continuous sequence.

30.5 DEFINITION OF A CONSTRUCTION CONTRACT

A *construction contract* is a contract specifically negotiated for the construction of an asset or a combination of assets that are closely inter-related or inter-dependent in terms of their design, technology and function or their ultimate purpose or use (IAS 11, 3).

A construction contract may be negotiated for:

- the construction of a single asset such as a bridge, building, dam, pipeline, road, ship or tunnel;
- the construction of a number of assets which are closely inter-related or inter-dependent in terms of their design, technology and function or their ultimate purpose or use – examples include refineries and other complex pieces of plant or equipment;
- the rendering of services which are directly related to the construction of the asset or assets, for example the services of architects and project managers; or
- the demolition or restoration of assets and the restoration of the environment following the demolition of old assets.

(IAS 11, 4 and 5)

The comment letters on E42 *Construction Contracts* included a number of suggestions about ways of distinguishing construction contracts from other contracts for the sale of goods or the rendering of services. Two points are worth emphasising:

- all contracts for the rendering of services, whether or not they are construction contracts, are dealt with in the same way under IAS 11 and IAS 18; and
- the feature which distinguishes a construction contract from a contract to sell goods is that the date on which the contract activity is entered into and the date on which the contract activity is completed usually fall into different accounting periods – if the activity starts and ends in the same period, all the revenue, costs and profits are recognised in that period whatever IAS is applied.

IAS 11 classifies construction contracts as either fixed price contracts or cost plus contracts.

A *fixed price contract* is a construction contract in which the contractor agrees to a fixed contract price, or a fixed rate per unit of output, which in some cases is subject to cost escalation clauses (IAS 11, 3). In such a contract, the entity is usually able to measure contract revenue accurately; the measurement of contract costs, and hence profits, is usually far more uncertain.

A *cost plus contract* is a construction contract in which the contractor is reimbursed for allowable or otherwise defined costs, plus a percentage of these costs or a fixed fee (IAS 11, 3). In such a contract, the entity is usually able to measure reliably the expected profit even though the amounts of contract revenue and contract costs may be uncertain.

Some contracts may contain characteristics of both a fixed price contract and a cost plus contract, for example in the case of a cost plus contract with an agreed maximum price. The distinction between the different types of contracts is important in determining the expected outcome of the contract; it is unimportant in other respects.

Construction contracts are formulated in a number of ways which may have different names in different countries. For example, commentators on E42 suggested that the IAS should also deal with 'unit price contracts' and 'time and materials contracts'. The IASC considered these and other suggestions but concluded that such contracts were either 'fixed price contracts' or 'cost plus contracts' or a combination of both types. In other words, the IASC believed that all construction contracts involve either or both a fixed price or the reimbursement of costs (plus a profit margin) for all or part of the output.

30.6 COMBINING AND SEGMENTING CONTRACTS

Each construction contract is usually dealt with separately. However, in certain circumstances, IAS 11 requires contracts to be combined or segmented. The standards are derived from the guidance in *Statement of Position 81–1, Accounting for Performance of Construction-Type and Certain Production-Type Contracts* (SOP 81–1) issued by the American Institute of Certified Public Accountants. However, whereas IAS 11 requires combining or segmenting in the specified circumstances, SOP 81–1 permits combining or segmenting in those circumstances. The decision to combine or not, or segment or not, can have a significant effect on the timing of the recognition of profits and losses, particularly when some contracts are profitable and others are loss-making.

Example 30.1 *Impact of combining and segmenting contracts*

A has five contracts in progress at the end of 2002 all of which were started in 2002. The total contract revenue and total contract costs of each contract and the stage of completion at 31 December 2002 is as follows:

	1	*2*	*3*	*4*	*5*	*Total*
Total contract revenue	145	520	480	200	55	1,400
Total contract costs	110	450	350	290	85	1,285
Expected profit (loss)	35	70	130	(90)	(30)	115
Costs incurred to 31 December 2002	44	360	350	58	42	854
Stage of completion at 31 December 2002	40%	80%	100%	20%	50%	66%

Continued

Continued

If each contract is treated separately, A recognises the following profits and losses in 2002:

Contract	*Percentage complete*	*Percentage of profit (loss) recognised*	*Profit (loss)*
1	40	40	14
2	80	80	56
3	100	100	130
4	20	100	(90)
5	50	100	(30)
			80

If all the contracts are combined and treated as one contract, A recognises 66% of the expected total profit of 115, that is a profit of 76.

If contracts 3 and 4 are combined and treated as one contract but all the other contracts are dealt with separately, A recognises the following profits and losses in 2002:

Contract	*Percentage complete*	*Percentage of profit (loss) recognised*	*Profit (loss)*
1	40	40	14
2	80	80	56
3 and 4	64	64	25
5	50	100	(30)
			65

When a contract covers a number of assets, the construction of each asset should be treated as a separate construction contract when:

- separate proposals are submitted for each asset;
- each asset has been subject to separate negotiation and the contractor and customers are able to accept or reject that part of the contract relating to each asset; and
- the costs and revenues relating to each asset can be separately identified.

(IAS 11, 8)

A group of contracts, whether with a single customer or with several customers, should be treated as a single construction contract when:

- the group of contracts is negotiated as a single package;
- the contracts are so closely inter-related that they are, in effect, part of a single project with an overall profit margin; and

- the contracts are performed concurrently or in a continuous sequence.

(IAS 11, 9)

A contract to construct an additional asset at the option of the customer should be treated as a separate construction contract when:

- the asset differs significantly in design, technology or function from the asset or assets covered by the original contract; or
- the price of the asset is negotiated without regard to the original contract price.

(IAS 11, 10)

This standard may cause some practical difficulties as variations, which alter the scope of a contract, are a common feature of construction contracts. Furthermore, the price of a variation may be negotiated without regard to the original contract. If the price has been separately negotiated, the variation is accounted for as a separate contract if the additional asset is different from the asset which is the subject of the main contract.

30.7 RECOGNITION OF CONTRACT REVENUE AND CONTRACT EXPENSES

30.7.1 Revenue, Expenses and Profits

IAS 11 requires the use of the percentage of completion method under which revenue, expenses and profits are reported according to the proportion of work completed. The method may be summarised as follows:

- when the outcome of a contract can be estimated reliably, contract revenue and contract costs should be recognised as revenue and expenses in the income statement by reference to the stage of completion of the contract activity at the balance sheet date (IAS 11, 22); and
- when the outcome of a contract cannot be estimated reliably, contract revenue should be recognised as revenue in the income statement only to the extent of contract costs incurred that it is probable will be recoverable; contract costs should be recognised as an expense in the period in which they are incurred (IAS 11, 32).

The requirements of IAS 11 are applied in each accounting period on a cumulative basis to the current estimates of contract revenue and contract costs. The effect of a change in the estimate of contract revenue or contract costs, or the effect of a change in the estimate of the outcome of a contract, is accounted for as a change in accounting estimate (IAS 11, 38). The consequences of new estimates are used in the determination of the amount of revenue and expenses recognised in the income statement in the period in which the new estimate is made and in subsequent periods.

Example 30.2 *Recognition of contract revenue and expenses*

A enters into a contract to build a road for £90 million. A's initial estimate of contract costs is £74 million. The contract starts early in 2002.

If, at the end of 2002, A can estimate reliably the outcome of the contract, it recognises revenue and expenses by reference to the stage of completion of the contract activity. Therefore, if the contract is half completed, A recognises revenue of £45 million and expenses of £37 million.

On the other hand, if at the end of 2002, A is unable to estimate reliably the outcome of the contract but has incurred costs of £30 million which it is probable will be recovered, A recognises revenue of £30 million and expenses of £30 million.

Extract 30.1 *Accounting policy for long-term contracts*

Hochtief, Germany, 31 December 2001 (IAS)

Construction contracts are reported using the percentage of completion method.

Extract 30.2 *Accounting policy for long-term contracts*

VA Technologie, Austria, 31 December 2001 (IAS)

In order to reflect the contractual progress and the performance of the company for the period, pursuant to IAS 11, contracts are subjected to pro rata profit realisation in accordance with the extent of completion (percentage of completion method) on the basis of a reliable estimate of the degree of completion, total costs and income.

Extract 30.3 *Accounting policy for long-term contracts*

Sulzer, *Switzerland, 31 December 1997 (IAS)*

For major long-term customer contracts the percentage-of-completion (POC) method is used. The pro rata billings including a conservatively estimated share of profit are taken up in net sales and in trade accounts receivable after offset of advance payments is received.

Extract 30.4 *Accounting policy for long-term contracts*

Atel, Switzerland, 31 December 2001 (IAS)

Customer-specific construction contracts in the Energy Services segment have been stated using the percentage-of-completion method and the amount to be capitalized reported under receivables and sales revenue. ... Construction costs are recognised as expenses in the period in which they are incurred.

If the stage of completion or the result cannot be reliably estimated on particular contracts or contract groups, these are capitalised at contract costs that are probably collectable.

30.7.2 Expected Losses

When it is probable that total contract costs will exceed total contract revenue, the expected loss should be recognised immediately in the income statement as an expense (IAS 11, 36). The amount of the loss is determined irrespective of:

- whether or not work has commenced on the contract;
- the stage of completion of contract activity; or
- the amount of profits expected to arise on other contracts which are not treated as a single construction contract.

(IAS 11, 37)

Expected losses are determined by reference to the latest estimates of contract revenue (see 30.8), contract costs (see 30.9) and contract outcome (see 30.10). The costs include costs that relate directly to the project and indirect costs which are included in the definition of contract costs (IAS 11, 16 and 18).

Example 30.3 *Expected losses*

A enters into a contract to build a road for £90 million. A's initial estimate of contract costs is £74 million. The contract starts early in 2002.

Before the contract starts, expected contract costs increase to £95 million, with no increase in contract revenue. A recognises the expected loss of £5 million immediately.

Extract 30.5 *Expected losses*

EADS, The Netherlands, 31 December 2000 (IAS)

Contracts are reviewed for possible losses at each reporting period and provisions for estimated losses on contracts are recorded when identified.

Extract 30.6 *Expected losses*

Hochtief, Germany, 31 December 2001 (IAS)

Appropriate provisions are set aside or write-downs made, taking account of all recognizable risks, for anticipated losses on specific contracts.

A contract may be of such magnitude that it is expected to absorb a considerable part of the capacity of the entity for a substantial period. IAS 11 [1979] suggested that in such cases contract costs may include indirect costs to be incurred during the period of the contract and which would not otherwise be included in contract costs (IAS 11 [1979], 35). These indirect costs would normally be recognised as an expense in the period in which they are incurred. This guidance was deleted from IAS 11 during the first improvements project. Such indirect costs are no longer included in contract costs and therefore in the determination of any expected loss. The change was justified on the grounds that the entity is better off with the contract than without it and that such indirect costs should be recognised as expenses in the period in which they are incurred. This change does not affect the indirect costs which are attributable to contract activity, rather it deals with indirect costs which are not usually included in contract costs (see example 30.4).

30.7.3 Application of IAS 11

In order to apply the requirements of IAS 11, the entity must determine:

- the total amount of contract revenue;
- the total amount of contract costs;
- the outcome of the contract; and
- the stage of completion of the contract activity at each balance sheet date.

Only if the entity is able to determine these four things is it able to apply the percentage of completion method. Furthermore, the entity must also have an effective internal financial budgeting and reporting system (IAS 11, 29). Without such a system, it is difficult to obtain reliable information to make the calculations and, as a result, to obtain the necessary assurance about the outcome of the contract.

Example 30.4 *Expected losses*

A enters into a contract to build a road for £90 million. A's initial estimate of contract costs is £74 million. The contract will absorb all A's capacity for the next three years. A expects to incur indirect costs which are not attributable to contract activity of £5 million in each year and which do not meet the IAS 11 definition of contract costs.

At the end of the first year, A revises its estimates. Contract revenue is unchanged at £90 million. Contract costs are expected to be £80 million and indirect costs which are not attributable to contract activity are expected to be £6 million in each period.

Under IAS 11 [1979], A has an expected loss on the contract of £8 million (contract revenue of £90 million less contract costs and total indirect costs of £98 million). Therefore, A recognises immediately the expected loss of £8 million.

Under the revised IAS 11, A has an expected profit on the contract of £10 million (contract revenues of £90 million less contract costs of £80 million). A recognises the profit in each of the three years by reference to the stage of completion of the contract. A also recognises £6 million of other indirect costs in each of the three periods. Therefore, over the three years, A reports a total loss of £8 million. Depending on the stage of completion of the contract, it may report an overall profit in any one of the three years and a loss in the other periods. For example, if 70% of the work is carried out in the first year, A recognises £7 million profit on the contract and £6 million indirect costs, a profit of £1 million.

30.8 CONTRACT REVENUE

Contract revenue should comprise:

- the initial amount of revenue agreed in the contract; and
- variations in contract work, claims and incentive payments to the extent that it is probable that they will result in revenue and they are capable of being reliably measured.

(IAS 11, 11)

The total amount of contract revenue is allocated to different periods during the life of the contract in accordance with the percentage of completion method. Contract revenue is measured at the fair value of the consideration received or receivable (IAS 11, 12). In most cases, the consideration takes the form of cash or cash equivalents and the amount of revenue can be measured reliably.

Example 30.5 *Application of requirements of IAS 11*

A has a fixed price contract to build a manufacturing plant for $100 million. A's estimate of contract costs is $80 million. The contract will take 3 years starting in 2002.

By the end of 2002, A estimates that contract costs have increased to $82 million.

In 2003, the customer approves a variation resulting in an increase in contract revenue of $5 million and estimated additional contract costs of $4 million.

A determines the stage of completion of the contract by calculating the proportion that contract costs incurred for work performed to date bear to its latest estimate of total contract costs.

	2002	*2003*	*2004*
	$m	*$m*	*$m*
Initial contract price	100	100	100
Variation	–	5	5
Total contract revenue	100	105	105
Contract costs incurred to date	21	62	86
Contract costs to complete	61	24	–
Total estimated contract costs	82	86	86
Estimated profit	18	19	19
Stage of completion	25.6%	72.1%	100%

The amounts of revenue, expenses and profit recognised in the income statement are as follows:

	To date	*Prior years*	*Current year*
	$m	*$m*	*$m*
2002			
Revenue (100 × 25.6%)	25.6		25.6
Expenses (82 × 25.6%)	21.0		21.0
Profit	4.6		4.6
2003			
Revenue (105 × 72.1%)	75.7	25.6	50.1
Expenses (86 × 72.1%)	62.0	21.0	41.0
Profit	13.7	4.6	9.1
2004			
Revenue	105.0	75.7	30.3
Expenses	86.0	62.0	24.0
Profit	19.0	13.7	5.3

In practice, the measurement of contract revenue is affected by a variety of uncertainties that depend on future events. Estimates often need to be revised as events occur and uncertainties are resolved. Therefore, the total amount of contract revenue may not be known until the contract is completed. This does not prevent the entity making reliable estimates of contract revenue while the contract progresses.

30.8.1 Variations

A *variation* is an instruction by the customer for a change in scope of work to be performed under the contract (IAS 11, 12); a variation may increase or decrease contract revenue. For example, the customer may change the design of a manufacturing plant which may increase or decrease the amount of contract revenue. Alternatively, the entity and the customer may agree to extend the scope of a contract for a new highway to include an additional link road so increasing contract revenue. A variation is included in contract revenue when it is probable that the customer will approve the variation and the amount of the revenue arising from the variation and the amount of the revenue can be reliably measured.

A variation is treated as a separate contract when it relates to the construction of an additional asset and certain conditions are met (see 30.6 above). Therefore, in the case of the additional link road the entity needs to decide whether the agreement to build the link road is a variation relating to the highway contract or a separate contract. As the link road does not differ significantly in design, technology or function from the highway, the decision may depend on whether the price of the link road is negotiated separately. A number of commentators on E42 were concerned that this would lead to minor changes in contracts being treated as separate contracts particularly as the price of many variations is negotiated separately from the original contract.

30.8.2 Claims

Whereas a variation arises as a result of the initiative of the customer, a *claim* is an amount that the entity seeks to collect from the customer as reimbursement for costs not included in the contract price (IAS 11, 14); a claim, by definition, increases contract revenue.

Claims may arise from delays caused by the customer which increase contract costs. Claims may also arise from errors made by the customer in the specification or design of the project which, again, lead to increased costs not previously recognised in the contract price. Claims also arise from other disputes in the contract.

Revenue arising from claims is included in contract revenue only when the negotiations between the entity and the customer have reached such a stage that it is probable that the customer will accept the claim and the amount that the customer will reimburse to the entity can be measured reliably (IAS 11, 14). However, while there may be uncertainties over the revenue arising from claims, the additional costs which have been incurred by the entity may be certain; they are included in contract costs. Therefore, while an unresolved claim is excluded from contract revenue, the associated costs often reduce the expected profit, or increase the expected loss immediately.

30.8.3 Incentive Payments

Incentive payments are additional amounts paid to the entity if it meets or exceeds specified performance standards on the contract (IAS 11, 15); again, by definition, incentive payments increase contract revenue. For example, the entity may be entitled to an incentive payment if it completes the contract ahead of schedule. The measurement of the amount of revenue arising from incentive payments is subject to a high degree of uncertainty as it depends on future performance on the contract. Such amounts are included in contract revenue only when it is probable that the specified performance standards will be met or exceeded and that the amount of the incentive payment can be measured reliably (IAS 11, 15). Again any additional costs incurred in meeting the performance standards are included immediately in contract costs and may reduce the expected profit or increase the expected loss.

Extract 30.7 *Incentive payments and penalties*

EADS, The Netherlands, 31 December 2000 (IAS)

Incentives applicable to performance on contracts are considered in estimated profit rates and are recorded when there is sufficient information to assess anticipated contract performance. Contract penalties are charged to expense in the period it becomes probable that the Group will be subject to the penalties.

30.9 CONTRACT COSTS

Contract costs are the production costs of the contract. Therefore, they comprise:

- costs that relate directly to the specific contract;
- costs that are attributable to contract activity in general and can be allocated to the contract (for example, construction overheads); and

- such other costs as are specifically chargeable to the customer under the terms of the contract.

(IAS 11, 16 and 18)

All other costs relating to contracts are recognised as an expense in the period in which they are incurred (IAS 11, 20).

The total amount of contract costs is allocated to different periods during the life of the contract in accordance with the percentage of completion method.

Costs that relate directly to a specific contract include:

- the costs of the construction site if the costs are incurred by the entity and the site will be sold or otherwise transferred to the customer;
- site labour costs;
- site supervision costs;
- materials (less income from the sale of surplus materials);
- depreciation of plant and equipment used on the contract (less income from the disposal of plant and equipment at the end of the contract);
- costs of moving plant, equipment and materials to and from the contract site;
- costs of hiring plant and equipment used on the contract;
- costs of design and technical assistance that are directly related to the contract;
- the estimated costs of rectification and guarantee work, including expected warranty costs; and
- claims from third parties.

(IAS 11, 17)

Other incidental income is deducted from contract costs rather than treated as contract revenue (IAS 11, 17).

Costs that are attributable to contract activity in general and which are included in contract costs include:

- insurance;
- costs of design and technical assistance that are not directly related to a specific contract;
- construction overheads such as those incurred in the preparation and processing of the construction personnel payroll; and
- borrowing costs when the entity adopts the allowed alternative treatment in IAS 23 and the contract is a qualifying asset (see chapter 35).

These costs are allocated to specific contracts using methods that are systematic and rational and are applied consistently to all costs having similar characteristics. The allocation is based on the normal level of construction activity (IAS 11, 18). This approach is consistent with the allocation of fixed overheads to the cost of inventories (see chapter 26).

While IAS 11 refers to the inclusion of borrowing costs in the costs that are allocated to contracts, IAS 23 requires that the amount of borrowing costs should be reduced by the amount of any investment income arising on the temporary investment of funds borrowed specifically for the assets concerned (IAS 23, 15). This requirement has particular relevance in the context of those construction contracts which are financed, wholly or partly, by advances from the customer. In such cases, it seems appropriate that any interest income arising on the temporary investment of those advances is deducted from contract costs and so included in the profit on the contract.

Costs that relate directly to a contract and which are incurred in securing the contract are included in the contract costs if they can be separately identified and measured reliably and it is probable that the contract will be obtained (IAS 11, 21). Otherwise, costs incurred prior to securing the contract are recognised as an expense in the period in which they are incurred. While IAS 11 is silent on the issue, it would be consistent with other IFRSs (for example, IAS 9 and IAS 38) if such costs are not included in contract costs once they have been recognised as an expense; in other words, the costs should not be reinstated as contract costs when the contract is secured.

30.10 OUTCOME OF THE CONTRACT

The outcome of the contract is the profit or loss on the contract. The profit or loss is the difference between contract revenue and contract costs.

In a fixed price contract, the major uncertainty is usually total contract costs rather than contract revenue. Therefore, the outcome of a fixed price contract can be estimated reliably only when:

- total construction revenue can be measured reliably (which is usually the case);
- it is probable that the economic benefits associated with the contract will flow to the entity;
- both the costs to complete the contract and the stage of completion of the contract at the balance sheet date can be measured reliably; and
- the contract costs attributable to the contract can be clearly identified and measured reliably so that actual contract costs incurred can be compared with prior estimates.

(IAS 11, 23)

In a cost plus contract, there is less uncertainty about the outcome of the contract provided that the costs are reimbursable. The outcome of such a contract can be estimated reliably when:

- it is probable that the economic benefits associated with the contract will flow to the entity; and
- the contract costs attributable to the contract, whether or not specifically reimbursable, can be clearly identified and measured reliably.

(IAS 11, 24)

The major uncertainty in such contracts is the recoverability of contract costs and, hence, the amount of contract revenue. If profits are a fixed percentage of costs and all the costs are recoverable, the entity is able to estimate the profit on the work performed to date even though the total profit may be uncertain. However, many cost plus contracts have an agreed maximum price which sets an upper limit for revenue; in such cases, there is a risk that the contract may result in a smaller profit than expected or even a loss. For such contracts, the entity needs to estimate total contract costs that are recoverable in order to estimate the outcome of the contract.

30.11 STAGE OF COMPLETION

The stage of completion of a contract may be determined by a variety of methods, including:

- the proportion that contract costs incurred for work performed to date bear to the estimated total contract costs;
- surveys of work performed; or
- completion of a physical proportion of the contract work.

(IAS 11, 30)

When the stage of completion is determined by reference to the contract costs incurred to date, only those contract costs which reflect work already performed are included in costs incurred to date. The costs of materials that have been made specially for the contract are included in costs incurred to date irrespective of whether the materials have been installed, used or applied. Any costs which relate to future activity on the contract are excluded from costs incurred to date. They may include:

- payments to subcontractors made in advance of work performed under the subcontract; and

- the costs of materials which have been delivered to a contract site or set aside for use in a contract but not yet installed, used or applied during contract performance.

Costs which relate to future activity are included in contract work in progress.

Extract 30.8 *Stage of completion*

Preussag, Germany, 31 December 2001 (IAS)

..., the completion stage per contract was determined either by the ratio of accrued costs to expected overall costs (cost to cost method) or by the physical completion stage of the construction process.

Extract 30.9 *Stage of completion*

Atel, Switzerland, 31 December 2001 (IAS)

The stage of completion is determined by the amount of expenses already incurred.

30.12 CONSTRUCTION CONTRACT ASSETS AND LIABILITIES

The accounting for construction contracts results in various balance sheet amounts. The entity has to account for costs incurred and the profits and losses recognised on the contracts. The entity usually submits progress bills to the customer for work performed on the contract – these amounts are usually classified as receivables. The customer is often entitled to withhold payment of a certain proportion of the progress billings (retentions) until certain conditions specified in the contract (such as the rectification of defects) have been met. The customer may also make advances to the entity, that is, pay amounts in advance of work performed. IAS 11 does not deal fully with the classification of those items. However, it does require that an entity should present:

- the gross amount due from customers for contract work as an asset; and
- the gross amount due to customers for contract work as a liability.

(IAS 11, 42)

Amounts due from customers arise on contracts in progress for which costs incurred plus recognised profits (less recognised losses) exceed progress billings, that is, the contract is in a net asset position. The amount due from customers is the net amount of:

- costs incurred plus recognised profits; less
- the sum of recognised losses and progress billings.

Amounts due to customers arise on contracts for which progress billings exceed costs incurred plus recognised profits (less recognised losses), that is, the contract is in a net liability position. The amounts due to customers is the net amount of:

- costs incurred plus recognised profits; less
- the sum of recognised losses and progress billings.

Example 30.6 *Amounts due to and from customers*

Contract	1	2	3	4
	$m	$m	$m	$m
Costs incurred to date	100	100	100	100
Profits recognised to date	20	–	20	–
	120	100	120	100
Losses recognised to date	–	15	–	15
	120	85	120	85
Progress billing	90	90	140	70
Due from customers	30	–	–	15
Due to customers	–	5	20	–

Extract 30.10 *Contract work in progress*

Jardine Matheson, Hong Kong, 31 December 2001 (IAS)

Contract work in progress is valued at cost plus an appropriate portion of profit, established by reference to the percentage of completion, and after deducting progress payments and provisions for foreseeable losses.

Extract 30.11 *Contract work in progress*

Hochtief, Germany, 31 December 2001 (IAS)

Contracts in progress are reported under percentage of completion (POC) receivables or payables. In each case, if cumulative work done to date (contract costs plus contract net profit) exceeds advance payments received, the difference is posted to the assets side as a POC receivable. If the net amount after deduction of advance payments received is negative, the difference is posted to POC liabilities. Appropriate provisions are set aside or write-downs made, taking account of all recognizable risks, for anticipated losses on specific contracts.

30.13 DISCLOSURE

An entity should disclose:

- the amount of contract revenue recognised as revenue in the period;
- the methods used to determine the contract revenue recognised in the period; and
- the methods used to determine the stage of completion of contracts in progress.

(IAS 11, 39)

An entity should disclose each of the following for contracts in progress at the balance sheet date:

- the aggregate amount of costs incurred and recognised profits (less recognised losses) to date;
- the amount of advances received; and
- the amount of retentions.

(IAS 11, 40)

Contingent assets and contingent liabilities may arise from such items as warranty costs, claims, penalties or possible losses. Contingent liabilities are disclosed unless the probability of loss is remote (IAS 37, 86). Contingent assets are disclosed only when it is probable that there will be an inflow of economic benefits (IAS 37, 89). Further guidance about the disclosure of contingent liabilities and contingent assets is included in chapter 27.

CHAPTER 31

Income Taxes

31.1 RELEVANT STANDARD AND INTERPRETATIONS

IAS 12 *Income Taxes*
SIC 21 *Income Taxes – Recovery of Revalued Non-Depreciable Assets*
SIC 25 *Income Taxes – Changes in the Tax Status of an Enterprise or its Shareholders*

31.2 HISTORY

31.2.1 IAS 12

IAS 12 *Accounting for Taxes on Income* (IAS 12 [1979]) was approved and published in 1979. Deferred taxes arose only when there were timing differences between the recognition of income and expenses for accounting and tax purposes. IAS 12 [1979]:

- permitted a choice between the deferral method and the liability method of determining deferred tax balances;
- permitted a choice between comprehensive and partial application of deferred taxes; and
- allowed some flexibility on the recognition of deferred taxes on the revaluation of assets.

These choices reflected differences among national standards and which had impeded the IASC's efforts to agree a single international standard. Therefore, in 1981, the IASC set up a working party to examine the reasons underlying the differences in rules concerning deferred tax accounting in different countries and to consider whether recommendations could be developed leading to greater harmony among national standards. The working party fitted well with the notion of the IASC acting as an 'honest broker whenever serious conflicts arise or exist between the requirements of different national standard-setters'[1].

The working party consisted of representatives of the standard setting bodies in the Netherlands, the United Kingdom and the United States of America, and a French chairman. It agreed that international comparability would be helped considerably if all countries required the use of a single underlying deferred tax method. It recommended that the method that would provide the best basis for harmonisation would be the liability method (*IASC News*, November 1984, p2). The working party did not reach the same degree of consensus over the choice between comprehensive and partial application although it did suggest that international comparability would be helped considerably if those countries which required or permitted partial application were also to require the disclosure of unprovided deferred tax.

In 1987, the IASC decided to review IAS 12 [1979]. E33 *Accounting for Taxes on Income* proposed that the liability method should be the required method but that the choice between comprehensive and partial application should be retained. The IASC decided to defer further consideration because of the developments on accounting for income taxes which were then taking place in a number of countries (*IASC Annual Review* 1991/92, p10).

The project was restarted at the end of 1992. By this time, the FASB had issued FAS 109 *Accounting for Income Taxes* which required the use of a liability method in place of the deferral method. However, the FASB's liability method was different from the liability method allowed by IAS 12 [1979] and proposed by E33. The FASB's liability method focused on temporary differences between the carrying amount and tax base of assets and liabilities; hence, it is often referred to as the balance sheet liability method. In contrast, the IASC's liability method (which was widely used around the world) focused on timing differences between the recognition of income and expense and is, therefore, sometimes referred to as the income statement liability method. All timing differences are temporary differences but temporary differences also include some of the permanent differences as defined in IAS 12 [1979] and E33.

After extensive consultations and in spite of identifying a number of conceptual and practical problems, the IASC decided to adopt the balance sheet liability method but with some variations from FAS 109. The IASC published E49 and the related *Background Paper on Income Taxes* in September 1994. E49 proposed:

- the use of the balance sheet liability method;
- the use of comprehensive application; and

- the elimination of the deferral method, the income statement liability method and partial application.

IAS 12 *Income Taxes* was issued in October 1996 and applied to accounting periods beginning on or after 1 January 1998. IAS 12 was further revised in October 2000 to deal with the accounting treatment for the income tax consequences of dividends.

> ***IASB improvements project***
>
> In its May 2002 improvements exposure draft, the IASB proposes a number of changes to IAS 12 which are consequential to the proposed amendments to other existing IAS. The substance of IAS 12 will not be changed.

31.2.2 Deferred Tax Methods

The IASC has, over the years, allowed or required the use of three different methods of accounting for deferred taxes:

- the deferral method (allowed by IAS 12 [1979]);
- the income statement liability method (allowed by IAS 12 [1979] and required by E33); and
- the balance sheet liability method (required by the revised IAS 12).

In many cases, the methods result in the same amounts of deferred tax assets, liabilities, income and expenses but in some cases they result in different amounts. The similarities and differences can best be described by looking at a simple example dealing with the depreciation of an item of plant and equipment with a cost of $10,000 and a residual value of zero. Assume that accounting depreciation is 20% straight-line a year and that tax depreciation is 30% reducing balance a year. The tax rate in years 1 and 2 is 40% and in year 3 onwards is 50%. For the first four years, the depreciation and carrying amount (written down value) are as follows:

	Accounting	*Tax*	*Difference*
	$	*$*	*$*
Year 1			
Cost	10,000	10,000	–
Depreciation	2,000	3,000	(1,000)
Carrying amount	8,000	7,000	1,000

	Accounting $	*Tax* $	*Difference* $
Year 2			
Depreciation	2,000	2,100	(100)
Carrying amount	6,000	4,900	1,100
Year 3			
Depreciation	2,000	1,470	530
Carrying amount	4,000	3,430	570
Year 4			
Depreciation	2,000	1,030	970
Carrying amount	2,000	2,400	(400)

Deferral Method

Under the deferral method, the tax benefit which arises when tax depreciation exceeds accounting depreciation is deferred and is matched against the higher depreciation charge in a later period. Therefore, deferred taxes are always measured at the tax rate applying when timing differences originate. In the example, the tax benefit arising in year 1 of $1,000 is deferred and a deferred tax expense of $400 ($1,000 × 40%) is recognised. In year 2, a tax benefit of $40 is deferred. In year 3, the timing differences start to reverse as accounting depreciation exceeds tax depreciation. Deferred tax is reduced by $212; the reversal is recognised as deferred tax income so matching the benefit of the tax relief in years 1 and 2 at 40% against the higher depreciation charge in year 3. In year 4, there is a further reversal of existing deferred tax measured at the old 40% rate and the creation of a new deferred tax debit balance which is measured at the current 50% rate and recognised as income. The income statement effect in each of the four years is as follows:

	Year 1 $	*Year 2* $	*Year 3* $	*Year 4* $
Depreciation expense	2,000	2,000	2,000	2,000
Current tax expense (income)	(1,200)	(840)	(735)	(515)
Deferred tax expense (income) (40%)	400	40	(212)	(228)
Deferred tax expense (income) (50%)				(200)
	1,200	1,200	1,053	1,057

The deferral method simply matches tax expense against the related accounting income and tax income against the related accounting expense. Tax expense and tax income which is payable or recoverable before the related accounting income or accounting expense is recognised is simply deferred until the accounting income or accounting expense is recognised. Similarly, tax expense or tax income which is payable after the related accounting income or accounting expense is recognised is simply accrued when the accounting income or accounting expense is recognised. The deferral method was allowed by IAS 12 [1979][2] but was not favoured by the deferred tax working party and it was eliminated in E33, E49 and the revised IAS 12.

Income Statement Liability Method

Under the income statement liability method, a deferred tax liability is recognised when tax depreciation exceeds accounting depreciation. As the deferred tax liability represents a liability for taxes payable in the future, it is always measured at the current rate of tax and the amount is adjusted for changes in the tax rate and the imposition of new taxes (IAS 12 [1979], 15). Therefore, in the example, a deferred tax liability and deferred tax expense of $400 is recognised in year 1 and an additional deferred tax liability and deferred tax expense of $40 is recognised in year 2. In year 3, the timing differences start to reverse as accounting depreciation exceeds tax depreciation. In addition, the tax rate changes so that the accumulated deferred tax liability must be remeasured using the new 50% tax rate. Therefore, there is an additional deferred tax liability and expense of $110 (10% × ($1,000 + $100)). In addition, the revised deferred tax liability is reduced by $265 being 50% of the excess of tax depreciation over accounting depreciation. The reversal is recognised as deferred tax income. In year 4, there is a further reversal of existing deferred tax measured at the 50% rate and the creation of a new deferred tax asset which is measured at the current 50% rate and recognised as income (assuming that it qualifies for recognition). The income statement effect in each of the four years is as follows:

	Year 1	*Year 2*	*Year 3*	*Year 4*
	$	*$*	*$*	*$*
Depreciation expense	2,000	2,000	2,000	2,000
Current tax expense (income)	(1,200)	(840)	(735)	(515)
Increase in deferred tax liability to 50%			110	
Deferred tax expense (income)	400	40	(265)	(485)
	1,200	1,200	1,110	1,000

The income statement liability method recognised the increased taxes payable in future periods as a result of current timing differences as a liability and an expense; it also recognised the reduced taxes payable in future periods as a result of current timing differences as an asset and income (subject to certain restrictions). The income statement liability method was allowed by IAS 12 [1979], probably favoured by the deferred tax working party and was the required method in E33[3]. It was eliminated in E49 and the revised IAS 12.

Balance Sheet Liability Method

Under the balance sheet liability method, a deferred tax liability is recognised when the accounting carrying amount is more than the tax carrying amount and the deferred taxes are always measured at the current rate of tax. Therefore, in year 1 a deferred tax liability of $400 is recognised along with a deferred tax expense of $400. In year 2, the deferred tax liability has increased to $440 and a deferred tax expense of $40 is recognised. In year 3, there is a deferred tax liability of $285 along with deferred tax income of $155. In year 4, there is a further reversal of existing deferred tax and the creation of a new deferred tax asset which is recognised as income (assuming that it qualifies for recognition). The income statement effect in each of the four years is as follows:

	Year 1	*Year 2*	*Year 3*	*Year 4*
	$	*$*	*$*	*$*
Depreciation expense	2,000	2,000	2,000	2,000
Current tax expense (income)	(1,200)	(840)	(735)	(515)
Deferred tax expense (income)	400	40	(155)	(485)
	1,200	1,200	1,110	1,000

The balance sheet liability method recognises the increased taxes payable in future periods as a result of temporary differences as a liability and an expense; it also recognises the reduced taxes payable in future periods as a result of temporary differences as an asset and income (subject to certain restrictions). The method is, however, more complex than the income statement liability method for two reasons:

- it requires a search for differences between balance sheet carrying amounts and the tax bases of assets and liabilities, a search which is usually more demanding than the search for timing differences; and
- it sometimes results in the recognition of 'imputed' taxes which never flow to or from the tax authorities but which instead result, over a period of time, in matching tax expense and tax income – no other expenses are accounted for in this way.

The balance sheet liability method was not addressed by IAS 12 [1979], the deferred tax working party or E33. It was the required method in E49 and is the required method in the revised IAS 12[4].

Extract 31.1 *Change of deferred tax method*

Lafarge, France, 31 December 1997 (IAS)

Deferred tax is recorded under the liability method in order to allocate each year the charge to tax relating to that year, taking into account timing differences between the inclusion of expenses in accounting and tax profits (and in particular differences relating to accounting and tax depreciation). In accordance with the partial provision method, deferred taxes are accounted for to the extent that it is probable that the liability or asset will crystallise.

With effect from January 1, 1998, the Group will apply IAS 12 (revised) under which deferred taxes are recorded by application of the liability method to all temporary differences arising between the tax base of assets and liabilities, and their carrying amount in the balance sheets (full provision method). Goodwill, together with market shares inseparable from the companies concerned and allocated as fair value adjustments, will be excluded from the deferred tax collection base.

31.3 IOSCO

IOSCO's June 1994 comments on existing IASs were received by the IASC the same afternoon that the IASC approved E49 and did not include comments on IAS 12.

IAS 12 is included in 'IAS 2000' endorsed by IOSCO in May 2000. There are 17 supplemental treatments:

- the subsequent recognition of acquired tax benefits should be allocated to intangibles in addition to goodwill;
- need for additional guidance, including appropriate disclosures, on the allocation of current and deferred income taxes when the reporting entity is part of a consolidated tax return;
- concerns that deferred tax assets and liabilities derived from current assets and liabilities should be classified as current;
- reconsideration of the apparent conflict between IAS 12 and IAS 22 to measure any minority interest at the minority's proportion of the fair values of the assets and liabilities recognised;
- concerns that the recognition of deferred tax assets be made subject to very stringent conditions – the hurdle of 'more likely than not' is not sufficient;
- consideration of more guidance about the exceptions to the accounting for deferred assets and liabilities and the meaning of 'probable';
- consideration of the discounting of deferred tax assets and liabilities (discounting was addressed during the development of the revised IAS 12 and rejected);
- concerns about the need to disclose unrecognised deferred tax liabilities arising from investments in subsidiaries;
- concerns about the need for guidance on the accounting for the effects of investment tax credits;
- concerns about the need for disclosure of the treatment of significant proposed tax changes;
- concerns about the need for guidance on the meaning of 'substantive enactment';

- reconsideration of the exceptions regarding timing difference arising on investment in subsidiaries;
- concerns about the need for guidance on the treatment of a change in the tax status of an enterprise, for example whether the effects should be reported through equity or profit and loss (IAS 12 requires the effect to be reported through profit);
- concerns about the need for guidance on accounting for transactions with both income statement and equity attributes that result in disproportionate tax benefits in relation to the income statement charge;
- concerns about the need for guidance on backward tracing for an item previously charged or credited to equity;
- concerns about the need to prescribe an intra-period tax allocation method for income statement items, for example, income tax expense could first be determined for profit and loss from ordinary activities and the remainder proportionately allocated to other items; and
- concerns about the appropriateness of the deferred tax asset recognition criteria.

31.4 IAS 12 IN BRIEF

An entity should recognise all tax liabilities irrespective of when they may be paid. It should recognise tax assets only when it is probable that it will receive the related benefits. Tax liabilities and tax assets consist of both current and deferred tax liabilities and assets.

Current tax is the amount of income taxes payable (recoverable) in respect of the taxable profit (tax loss) of the current period. Current tax expense is recognised as an expense and a liability in the same period as the related accounting profit. Current tax income is recognised as income and an asset in the period of the related loss when the loss is used to recover income tax paid or payable in respect of a previous period. When the loss is used to reduce taxable profit in future periods, the recoverable tax is dealt with as a deferred tax asset.

Deferred tax usually arises only when transactions and events are dealt with differently for accounting and tax purposes. Deferred tax is the amount of income taxes payable (recoverable) in future periods in respect of taxable (deductible) temporary differences. Deferred tax liabilities arising in respect of taxable temporary differences are recognised as an expense when the temporary difference arises and as income when the temporary difference reverses. Deferred tax assets in respect of deductible temporary differences are recognised as income (subject to certain conditions) when the temporary difference arises and as an expense when the temporary difference reverses.

Deferred tax also includes income taxes recoverable in respect of tax losses used to reduce taxable profit in future periods and tax credits used to reduce income tax liabilities in future periods. This deferred tax is recognised as income when it becomes probable that future taxable profit or tax liabilities will be available against which the tax losses or tax credits can be utilised – this may occur in the period of the loss, the period in which the taxable profit or tax liability arises or an intervening period.

31.5 ACCOUNTING PROFIT AND TAXABLE PROFIT

In all countries, most transactions and events are dealt with in the same way and in the same period for both financial reporting and tax purposes. On the other hand, in most countries, some transactions and events are dealt with differently for financial reporting and tax purposes with the result that accounting profit and taxable profit are often different.

Accounting profit is the net profit or loss for a period before deducting tax expense (IAS 12, 5). In IFRS financial statements, accounting profit is determined using accounting polices which comply with IFRSs. In contrast, *taxable profit* (*tax loss*) is the profit (loss) for the period, determined in accordance with the rules established by the taxation authorities, upon which income taxes are payable (recoverable) (IAS 12, 5). Both terms cover the possibility of either profits or losses but in the interests of simplicity and clarity, the terms are used throughout the rest of this chapter to encompass both profits and losses unless the context demands otherwise.

There are differences between accounting profit and taxable profit whenever IFRS requirements differ from the tax rules used in determining taxable profit. IAS 12 [1979] categorised the differences as 'timing differences' and 'permanent differences'.

Permanent differences were differences between taxable profit and accounting profit which originated in one period but did not reverse in subsequent periods (IAS 12 [1979], 3). Permanent differences arose when items were included in the determination of accounting profit but were not included in the determination of taxable profit. For example, certain expenses may have been deducted in determining accounting profit but were not deductible in determining taxable profit; this was the case in some countries with some donations and entertaining expenses. Similarly, certain income may have been included in the determination of accounting profit but was not included in taxable profit; this was the case in some countries with interest income on government securities, interest and dividends received from other countries or trading profits from exports. Permanent differences also arose when items of income or expense were included in the determination of taxable profit but were not included in accounting profit.

Timing differences were differences between taxable profit and accounting profit which arose because items of income and expenses were included in taxable profit in a different period from that in which they were included in accounting profit (IAS 12 [1979], 3). In other words, the items of income or expense were included in the determination of both accounting profit and taxable profit but in different accounting periods. A common example of a timing difference was the depreciation of plant and equipment. While the whole of the difference between the cost of an item of plant and equipment and its disposal proceeds was recognised as an expense in determining both accounting profit and taxable profit, the deductions were often made in different periods. Another common example was employee benefit costs. While all such costs were recognised as an expense in determining both accounting profit and taxable profit, the costs were recognised as an expense under IFRSs when service was rendered but may have been deductible for tax purposes only when payments were made to employees or a fund.

IAS 12 does not refer to permanent differences or timing differences but, in practice, such differences between taxable profit and accounting profit continue to exist in most countries. However, the revised IAS 12 has changed the accounting for these differences. While all timing differences are temporary differences and continue to be accounted for in the same way as under the liability method in IAS 12 [1979], some permanent differences are temporary differences and their accounting treatment has sometimes changed.

31.6 CURRENT TAX

Current tax is the amount of income taxes payable (recoverable) in respect of the taxable profit (tax loss) for a period (IAS 12, 5). The recognition and measurement of current tax expense rarely creates any practical difficulties unless there are disputes, or the potential for disputes, with the tax authorities or the tax legislation is uncertain.

31.6.1 Recognition of Current Tax Expense

Current tax expense is recognised as an expense in the same period as the related accounting profit. Therefore, any current tax expense for the current and prior periods which is unpaid should be recognised as a liability (IAS 12, 12). If the amount already paid exceeds the amount due the excess should be recognised as an asset provided that the excess is recoverable (IAS 12, 12).

Example 31.1 *Recognition of current tax expense and liability*

A operates in a jurisdiction in which the amount of current tax for any period is payable in full 6 months after the end of that period. A's current tax for the year ended 31 December 2001 is $2m. Therefore, A recognises an expense of $2m in its income statement for the year to 31 December 2001 and a liability of $2m in its balance sheet as at 31 December 2001.

Example 31.2 *Recognition of current tax expense and liability/asset*

B operates in a jurisdiction in which estimated amounts of current tax based on the previous period's tax expense are paid during a period. Any adjustment to current tax due for the period is paid (recovered) 6 months after the end of the period. During the year ended 31 December 2001, B pays $1.5m on account of current tax for that period. The full amount of current tax due for the period is $1.8m. Therefore, B recognises an expense of $1.8m in its income statement for the year to 31 December 2001 and a liability of $0.3m in its balance sheet as at 31 December 2001.

If B had paid $2.4m on account of current tax for 2001 and the full amount due for the period was still $1.8m, B would have recognised an expense of $1.8m and an asset of $0.6m as at 31 December 2001.

31.6.2 Recognition of Current Tax Income

The recognition and measurement of current tax income is slightly more difficult. Current tax income arises when a tax loss in the current period can be used to recover income taxes paid in respect of a previous period. The use of a tax loss in this way depends on two things:

- the tax law – in many countries, it is not possible to use a loss to recover income taxes paid in respect of a previous period; and
- the existence of taxable profits and income tax liabilities in the relevant prior periods.

When an entity is allowed to use a tax loss arising in one period to recover income tax paid or payable in respect of an earlier period, the benefit is recognised as income in the period of the tax loss. Any such amount which has not been received as at the balance sheet date is either deducted from any income tax liability in respect of the earlier period or is recognised as an asset (IAS 12, 13).

Current tax income also arises when a tax loss in the current period can be used to reduce or eliminate tax expense in some or all future periods. Again, this depends on two things:

- the tax law – in many countries, the use of a tax loss to reduce future taxable profits is not allowed or is restricted in some way; and
- the existence of taxable profits and income tax liabilities in the relevant future periods.

Any recovery of income tax in this way is current tax income of the period of the loss (it is income taxes recoverable in respect of the tax loss for the period). However, IAS 12 deals with the recognition of this current tax income as if it were deferred tax income.

Example 31.3 *Tax loss carry-back*

An entity operates in a country in which it can use a tax loss arising in the current period to recover taxes paid in respect of taxable profit in the previous period. Any excess of the current period's tax loss over the previous period's taxable profit may be carried forward for a maximum of six years.

In 2001, the entity has a tax loss of $10,500; the enacted tax rate for 2001 is 40%. In 2000, the entity had a taxable profit of $6,000 and the enacted tax rate was 35%.

The entity can carry back $6,000 of the 2001 tax loss to 2000 and recover tax paid at 35%. Therefore, the entity recognises tax income of $2,100 in 2001 and either a receivable of $2,100 or a reduction of $2,100 in the liability for current tax expense on the 2000 taxable profit.

The balance of the tax loss ($4,500) may be carried forward and used to reduce the taxable profits during the next six years.

31.6.3 Measurement of Current Tax

Current tax liabilities (assets) for the current and prior periods should be measured at the amount expected to be paid to (recovered from) the taxation authorities, using the tax rates and tax laws that have been enacted or substantively enacted by the balance sheet date (IAS 12, 46).

A problem arises when a new tax rate or tax law has been announced prior to the balance sheet date but not enacted and the new tax rate or tax law would affect the amount of income tax payable or recoverable in respect of the current period. In some jurisdictions, the announcement of a new tax rate or law by the government has the substantive effect of actual enactment; this is the case, for example, in the United Kingdom where the parliamentary process is such that enactment is usually guaranteed. In such a case, tax assets and liabilities are measured using the announced tax rate and law (IAS 12, 48). In other cases where there is doubt about the enactment of the new rate or law, tax assets and liabilities must be measured using the enacted rate and law.

IAS 12 refers specifically to the tax rates and tax law enacted or substantively enacted 'at the balance sheet date' and not at the date on which the financial statements are approved for issuance. It could be argued that the enactment of a new rate or law between the balance sheet date and the date of approval of the financial statements is an event for which adjustment should be made under IAS 10, particularly if the new rate or law was announced on or before the balance sheet date. Such a possibility, while apparently reasonable, is not permitted by IAS 12.

While the guidance in IAS 12 on enacted and substantively enacted tax rates and tax law is somewhat vague, it is difficult for the IASC to issue guidance which can apply in all the particular circumstances of different countries. As it is preferable that all enterprises in the same country deal with announced changes in the same way, it is desirable that the national standard setting body or some other competent national body gives more detailed guidance when the problem arises.

Extract 31.2 *Change of tax rate*

BHP, Australia, 31 May, 1998 (IAS)

The BHP Group's deferred tax balances were restated at 31 May 1995 following the increase in the Australian company tax rate from 33% to 36% announced by the Australian Treasurer in Parliament on 19 May 1995. This increase was applicable to the BHP Group from 1 June 1995. Under Australian GAAP such an announcement is normally accepted as adequate evidence that the change will occur. Under US GAAP a change of tax rate is not recognised until it has been enacted; this occurred during 1996 and the adjustment previously made had been reversed.

31.7 DEFERRED TAX

Deferred tax usually arises only when transactions and events are dealt with differently for accounting and tax purposes. Under IAS 12, deferred tax consists of:

- the amount of income taxes payable or recoverable in future periods in respect of temporary differences; and

- the amount of income taxes recoverable in future periods from the carry forward of unused tax losses and tax credits.

Temporary differences may be either taxable temporary differences or deductible temporary differences. Taxable temporary differences give rise to deferred tax liabilities and deductible temporary differences give rise to deferred tax assets. Therefore the notion of temporary differences is critical to the balance sheet liability method. This notion, together with the related notion of tax base, is dealt with in 31.8. The recognition and measurement of the resulting deferred tax liabilities and assets is dealt with in 31.9.

Deferred tax assets and income arising from the carry forward of unused tax losses and tax credits is dealt with in 31.10. As explained earlier, these deferred tax assets and income are strictly current tax of the period in which the loss arises but they are dealt with and fit better as deferred tax.

Extract 31.3 *Deferred taxes*

Ascom, Switzerland, 31 December 2001 (IAS)

Deferred income taxes are declared in full using the liability method. Deferred income taxes arise due to temporary differences between the Group-internal and the taxable assets and liabilities. These principal temporary differences arise from depreciation on property, plant and equipment, revaluation of certain non-current assets, through provisions for pensions and other post retirement benefits and tax losses carried forward, and, in relation to acquisitions, on the difference between the fair value of the net assets acquired and their tax base.

31.8 TEMPORARY DIFFERENCES AND TAX BASE

31.8.1 Definitions

Temporary differences are differences between the carrying amount of an asset or liability in the balance sheet and its tax base (IAS 12, 5). The carrying amount of an asset or liability is determined in accordance with IASs. The tax base of an asset or liability is determined by the tax rules. Temporary differences may be taxable differences or deductible differences.

Taxable temporary differences are temporary differences which will result in taxable amounts in determining taxable profit of future periods when the carrying amount of the asset or liability is recovered or settled (IAS 12, 5). Therefore, *deferred tax liabilities* are the amounts of income taxes payable in future periods in respect of taxable temporary differences (IAS

12, 5). Taxable temporary differences and deferred tax liabilities arise when, for example, the carrying amount of an asset is greater than its tax base.

Deductible temporary differences are temporary differences that will result in amounts that are deductible in determining taxable profit of future periods when the carrying amount of the asset or liability is recovered or settled (IAS 12, 5). Therefore *deferred tax assets* include amounts of income taxes recoverable in future periods in respect of deductible temporary differences (IAS 12, 5). Deductible temporary differences and deferred tax assets arise when, for example, the carrying amount of an asset is less than its tax base.

The relationship between the carrying amount of assets and liabilities, their tax bases and deferred tax assets and liabilities can be summarised as follows:

	Balance Sheet	
	Asset	*Liability*
Carrying amount > tax base	DTL	DTA
Carrying amount < tax base	DTA	DTL
Carrying amount = tax base	None	None

DTA = deferred tax asset (deductible temporary difference)
DTL = deferred tax liability (taxable temporary difference)

31.8.2 Tax Base

The notion of tax base is critical to the determination of temporary differences. The *tax base* of an asset or liability is the amount attributed to that asset or liability for tax purposes (IAS 12, 5). The amount of the tax base depends on the tax treatment of the economic benefits which flow to the entity on the recovery of the asset or flow from the entity on the settlement of the liability.

If the flow of benefits to or from the entity is taxable or tax deductible, the tax base of the asset or liability is the amount which will be offset against the flow of benefits in determining taxable profits in the period of the flow of benefits. For example, if the flow of economic benefits to the entity from an item of plant and equipment is taxable, the tax base of the item is the amount relating to that asset which will be offset against the inflow of benefits. If the flow of benefits to or from the entity is not taxable or is not tax deductible, the tax base of the asset or liability is its accounting carrying amount.

Some items have a tax base but are not recognised as assets and liabilities in the balance sheet. For example, costs may be recognised as an expense in determining accounting profit in the period in which they are incurred but may be deductible for tax purposes over a number of periods. Similarly, income may be recognised as income for accounting purposes in one period but spread over later periods for tax purposes.

When determining the tax base of any asset or liability, the relevant tax law determines whether the inflows or outflows of economic benefits are taxable/deductible and, if they are, when they are taxable/deductible. Tax laws vary with the result that different deferred tax amounts may result from similar business events and transactions. It is important to recognise, therefore, that in the examples below the tax bases and the temporary differences may be correct only in the context of the assumptions about the tax system.

Example 31.4 *Tax base – trade receivables*

Revenue from the sale of goods is included in accounting profit and taxable profit for the same periods, that is, in the period of the sale in accordance with IAS 18. The balance sheet includes trade receivables of $1m, that is, a right to receive economic benefits of $1m. These economic benefits are not taxable when they flow to the entity (they were taxable when the sales were made). Therefore, the tax base of the receivables is their carrying amount of $1m and there is no temporary difference.

Example 31.5 *Tax base – trade receivables*

Revenue from the sale of goods is included in accounting profit in the period of the sale in accordance with IAS 18 and is included in taxable profit when the cash is received. The balance sheet includes trade receivables of $1m, that is, a right to receive economic benefits of $1m. These economic benefits are taxable when they flow to the entity (that is when the cash is received) but nothing will be offset against the taxable income. Therefore, the tax base of the receivables is zero and there is a taxable temporary difference of $1m.

In this circumstance, there will also be a deductible temporary difference on inventories if, for accounting purposes, they are recognised as an expense when the sale is made but, for tax purposes, they are deductible only when the cash is received for the sale of goods.

Example 31.6 *Tax base – plant and equipment*

A machine cost $1m. For accounting purposes, depreciation of $150,000 has been deducted in the current and prior periods giving a carrying amount of $850,000. The economic benefits flowing from the use of the machine are taxable. For tax purposes, depreciation of $400,000 has been deducted in the current and prior periods and the remaining cost will be deductible in future periods, either as depreciation or through a deduction on disposal.

The tax base of the machine is $600,000. This is the amount which will be offset against the taxable economic benefits flowing from the machine in future periods. Therefore, there is a taxable temporary difference of $250,000.

Example 31.7 *Tax base – plant and equipment*

A machine cost $1m. For accounting purposes, depreciation of $150,000 has been deducted in the current and prior periods giving a carrying amount of $850,000. The economic benefits flowing from the use of the machine are not taxable as the machine is used to produce goods for export and export sales are exempt from tax. The tax base of the machine is $850,000. Therefore, there is no temporary difference.

Example 31.8 *Tax base – plant and equipment acquired in a business combination*

B has a machine which cost $1m. For accounting purposes, B has deducted depreciation of $150,000 in the current and prior periods giving a carrying amount in B's balance sheet of $850,000. The economic benefits flowing from the use of the machine are taxable. For tax purposes, depreciation of $400,000 had been deducted in the current and prior periods and the remaining cost will be deductible in future periods, either as depreciation or through a deduction on disposal. Therefore, in B's financial statements, the tax base of the machine is $600,000. This is the amount which will be offset against the taxable economic benefits flowing from the machine in future periods. Therefore, there is a taxable temporary difference of $250,000.

A has acquired B in a business combination which is an acquisition

(Continued)

(Continued)

and has assigned a fair value of $1,300,000 to the machine. The fair value exercise does not affect the tax base of the assets; therefore, in A's consolidated financial statements the machine has a carrying amount of $1,300,000 but the machine's tax base is still $600,000. The $600,000 will be offset against the taxable economic benefits flowing from the machine in future periods. Therefore, there is a taxable temporary difference in A's consolidated financial statements of $700,000.

Example 31.9 *Tax base – trade payables*

Expenses are included in accounting profit and taxable profit for the same periods, that is, in the period in which they are incurred in accordance with IFRSs rather than in the period in which they are paid. The balance sheet includes trade payables of $1m. The outflow of economic benefits in settlement of the liability is not deductible in the period in which they occur (the expenses were deductible when they were incurred). Therefore, the tax base of the payables is their carrying amount of $1m and there is no temporary difference.

Example 31.10 *Tax base – provision for warranty costs*

Warranty costs are recognised as an expense for accounting purposes when the associated sale is made. They are deductible for tax purposes in the period in which they are paid. The balance sheet includes a provision of $1m. The outflow of economic benefits in settlement of the liability is deductible for tax purposes in the period in which it occurs. Therefore, the tax base of the provision is zero and there is a deductible temporary difference of $1m.

Example 31.11 *Tax base – accrued expenses*

Current liabilities include accrued expenses with a carrying amount of $100,000. The related expense will be deducted for tax purposes on a cash basis. Therefore, the outflow of economic benefits will be tax deductible when they occur. The tax base of the accrued expenses is zero and there is a deductible temporary difference of $100,000.

Extract 31.4 *Tax bases*

Schering, Germany, 31 December 2001 (IAS)

Deferred taxes on property, plant and equipment relate principally to lower tax bases resulting from special tax allowances for assets in certain regions of Germany.

31.8.3 Examples of Temporary Differences

The application of the definitions of temporary difference and tax base mean that many temporary differences are, in fact, also timing differences as defined in IAS 12 [1979]. However, some temporary differences are not timing differences as defined in IAS 12 [1979]. Table 31.1 deals with common examples.

31.9 RECOGNITION OF DEFERRED TAX LIABILITIES

A deferred tax liability should be recognised for all taxable temporary differences except for certain of those differences arising from:

- goodwill (see 31.9.2); or
- the initial recognition of an asset or liability (see 31.9.3); or
- investments in subsidiaries, branches and associates, and interests in joint ventures (see 31.9.4).

(IAS 12, 15)

31.9.1 The General Rule

It is inherent in the recognition of an asset that the entity will recover the carrying amount of that asset through use or sale. If this is not the case, the asset is impaired and its carrying amount should be reduced to the amount which will be recovered from use or sale. When the carrying amount of an asset exceeds its tax base, the entity will recover either through use or sale of that asset at least the amount that will be allowed as a deduction in determining taxable profit. Therefore, the entity has a present obligation to pay the resulting income taxes in future periods on the difference between carrying amount and tax base. That obligation is recognised as a deferred tax liability.

Table 31.1 *Temporary differences and timing differences*

Issue	*Accounting treatment*	*Tax treatment*	*Temporary difference (revised IAS 12)*	*Timing difference (IAS 12 [1979])*
Property, plant and equipment	Depreciation charged as economic benefits are consumed (IAS 16)	Accelerated	Taxable	✓
Property, plant and equipment	Depreciation charged as economic benefits are consumed (IAS 16)	Not deductible	Taxable	×
Property, plant and equipment	Fair value less depreciation (IAS 16)	Cost less depreciation	Taxable (if fair value greater than pre-acquisition cost)	×
Identifiable asset acquired in a business combination that is an acquisition	Fair value (IAS 22)	Pre-acquisition cost	Taxable (if fair value greater than pre-acquisition cost)	×
Goodwill	Cost less amortisation (IAS 22)	Not deductible	Taxable	×
Development costs	Capitalised and amortised (IAS 38)	Expensed when incurred	Deductible	✓
Development costs	Capitalised and amortised (IAS 38)	Accelerated depreciation	Taxable	✓
Research costs	Expensed when incurred (IAS 38)	Expensed when incurred	×	×

(*Continued*)

Table 31.1 *Temporary differences and timing differences (continued)*

Issue	*Accounting treatment*	*Tax treatment*	*Temporary difference (revised IAS 12)*	*Timing difference (IAS 12 [1979])*
Research costs	Expensed when incurred	Capitalised and amortised	✓	✓
Interest income	Time apportionment (accruals) basis (IAS 18)	Cash basis	Taxable	✓
Revenue from the sale of goods	When goods are delivered and title passes (IAS 18)	When cash is collected	Taxable	✓
Marketable securities	Carried at market value (IAS 39)	Gains or losses taxed only when the securities are sold	Taxable	✓
Retirement benefit costs	Expensed when service is rendered (IAS 19)	Expensed when payments are made to retirees, their dependants or a fund	Deductible	✓
Product warranty costs	Expensed on an accrual basis when the relevant goods are sold (IAS 18 and IAS 37)	Deducted on a cash basis	Deductible	✓
Bad debts	Recognised as an expense when the debt become uncollectible	Recognised as an expense when legal processes have been completed or if within specified monetary limits	Deductible	✓

Example 31.12 *Taxable temporary difference*

As at 31 December 2001, A has an asset which cost $10m and which has a carrying amount of $8m. Up to 31 December 2001, A has been able to deduct tax depreciation of $7m in respect of this asset in determining taxable profit for the current and prior period ends.

The tax base of the asset is $3m (cost of $10m less cumulative tax depreciation of $7m). To recover the carrying amount of the asset of $8m, the entity must earn income of $8m but will be able to deduct tax depreciation of only $3m. Consequently, A has a present obligation to pay income taxes on $5m at some future date(s) when it recovers the carrying amount of the asset. This difference between the carrying amount of $8m and the tax base of $3m is a taxable temporary difference of $5m. If the tax rate is 40%, A recognises a deferred tax liability of $2m.

31.9.2 Goodwill

Goodwill is the excess of the cost of an acquisition over the acquirer's interest in the fair value of the identifiable assets and liabilities acquired. The economic benefits flowing to the entity from goodwill are usually taxable; therefore, the tax base of goodwill is the amount which will be offset against the flow of benefits in determining taxable profits in the periods in which those benefits flow to the entity.

If the amortisation of goodwill is fully deductible for tax purposes, the tax base of goodwill is initially the amount recognised in the balance sheet. Subsequently, the tax base of goodwill is its written down amount for tax purposes. A taxable temporary difference arises when the carrying amount of the goodwill, determined in accordance with IAS 22, exceeds its tax base in the same way that a taxable temporary difference arises on any other asset when its carrying amount exceeds its tax base. A deferred tax liability should be recognised for such a temporary difference.

In many jurisdictions, however, goodwill is not deductible in determining taxable profit either as amortisation during the useful life of the goodwill or as part of the cost of the acquired business when it is sold or otherwise disposed of. If the flow of benefits to the entity from the goodwill is taxable, the tax base of the goodwill is the amount which will be offset against the flow of benefits in determining taxable profits in the period of the flow of benefits. In such jurisdictions, the amount which will be offset in this way is zero and, therefore, the tax base of the goodwill is zero which gives rise to a taxable temporary difference immediately the goodwill is recognised on the balance sheet. A deferred tax liability should not be recognised for this temporary difference (IAS 12,

15) because goodwill is a residual and the recognition of the deferred tax liability would increase the carrying amount of goodwill (IAS 12, 21).

31.9.3 Initial Recognition of Assets and Liabilities

Some assets other than goodwill may not be deductible for tax purposes either during their useful lives or when sold. If the flow of benefits to the entity from such an asset is taxable, the tax base of the asset is zero for the same reason as the tax base of non-deductible goodwill is zero. This gives rise to a taxable temporary difference immediately the asset is recognised on the balance sheet.

IAS 12 deals with three different sets of circumstances in which this situation arises:

- the recognition of the asset by means of a credit to the income statement (for example, when the asset is accrued income) when the benefits will be taxable in a later period;
- the acquisition of such an asset as part of the identifiable assets acquired in a business combination which is an acquisition; and
- the acquisition of such an asset in other circumstances.

A deferred tax liability should be recognised for this temporary difference in the first two cases but not in the third case (IAS 12, 15).

The first case is probably not controversial. The tax base of the accrued income is zero, that is the amount which will be offset against the flow of benefits in determining taxable profits. This is an example of what was a timing difference under IAS 12 [1979].

The second and third cases are more controversial not least because they deal differently with like transactions – the acquisition of assets for which the cost is not tax deductible. In both cases, there would have been a permanent difference under IAS 12 [1979]. Under the revised IAS 12 things are different. In one case but not the other the entity records notional amounts of tax.

Assuming the flow of benefits from the assets is taxable, the tax base in each case is zero. Therefore, there is a taxable temporary difference equal to the cost of the asset immediately on its recognition. If the asset is acquired in a business combination, the entity recognises the resulting deferred tax liability and increases goodwill by the same amount. In subsequent periods, as the asset is consumed, the temporary difference reduces and, as a result, the deferred tax liability reduces. The reduction in the liability is credited to the income statement as part of deferred tax expense. This accounting is pure fiction – no additional tax flows to or from the entity. The credit to the income statement results from a debit to goodwill which is usually amortised over a much longer period.

Furthermore, no other expenses associated with the earning of economic benefits from the asset are dealt with in the same way.

If the asset is acquired in any other circumstances, IAS 12 adopts a different approach. It prohibits the recognition of the resulting deferred tax liability in either the period in which the asset is acquired or in any later period (IAS 12, 15). This gets to the logically right answer but the IASC showed some reluctance to adopting such an approach. It did so only because it felt uncomfortable with either of the other two possibilities – adding the tax to the cost of the asset (which some supported and which is required by the equivalent Canadian standard) or recognising the tax as an expense immediately on the recognition of the asset.

Example 31.13 *Initial recognition of an asset*

An entity acquires an asset for $1,000 which it intends to use throughout its useful life of five years and then dispose of for a residual value of zero. The tax rate is 40%. Depreciation of the asset is not deductible for tax purposes but the economic benefits flowing from the asset are tax deductible. On disposal, any difference between disposal proceeds and cost is not taxable or deductible.

The tax base of the asset as at the date of its acquisition is zero which is the amount which will be deducted in determining taxable profits in future periods. There is, therefore, a taxable temporary difference immediately on the acquisition of the asset of $1,000. If the entity recognises the resulting deferred tax liability of $400, it has to decide what to do with the debit of $400. It could recognise the $400 as an expense, add the $400 to the cost of the asset or recognise the $400 as some other asset.

If the asset is acquired in a business combination that is an acquisition, the $400 is added to goodwill. The resulting deferred tax liability is recognised as income over the life of the asset. The addition to goodwill is recognised as an expense as part of the amortisation of goodwill over its useful life.

If the asset is acquired directly, a deferred tax liability is not recognised.

In both cases, therefore, the asset is recognised at cost ($1,000) and depreciated over its useful life. In addition, if the asset was acquired in a business combination, $400 is recognised as a deferred tax liability and as an addition to goodwill.

Extract 31.5 *Non-recognition of deferred taxes*

Groupe Bruxelles Lambert, Belgium, 31 December 2001 (IAS)

Deferred taxes are calculated in accordance with the variable carry-over method applied to the temporary differences between the book values of the assets and liabilities recorded in the balance sheet and their tax basis.

The following differences are disregarded: non-tax-deductible goodwill and initial valuations of assets and liabilities not affecting the book or taxable profit.

31.9.4 Subsidiaries, Associates and Joint Ventures

Temporary differences arise when the carrying amount of investments in subsidiaries, branches and associates or interests in joint ventures (that is the parent or investor's share of the net assets of the subsidiary, branch, associate or investee, including the carrying amount of goodwill) is different from the tax base (which is often cost) of the investment or interest. In the case of subsidiaries, the carrying amount in consolidated financial statements is represented by the carrying amounts of the various assets and liabilities.

Taxable temporary differences may arise, for example, when:

- subsidiaries, branches, associates and joint ventures have undistributed profits; or
- a parent and its subsidiary are based in different countries and changes in foreign exchanges rates affect the carrying amount of assets and liabilities.

A deferred tax liability should be recognised for such taxable temporary differences unless:

- the parent, investor or venturer is able to control the timing of the reversal of the temporary difference; and
- it is probable that the temporary differences will not reverse in the foreseeable future.

(IAS 12, 39)

A parent usually controls the dividend policy of a subsidiary and so is able to control the timing of the reversal of temporary differences. Therefore, when an entity has determined that the undistributed profits of a subsidiary or other taxable temporary differences arising in respect of that subsidiary will not be distributed in the foreseeable future, a deferred tax liability is not recognised.

The approach adopted in the revised IAS 12 is different from that in IAS 12 [1979] which focused on the taxes payable by either the parent or the subsidiary when the profits were distributed. Deferred taxes were not recognised when it was reasonable to assume that the profits would not be distributed or that a distribution would not give rise to a tax liability (IAS 12, 34).

Changes in the exchange rate affecting the translation of the financial statements of a subsidiary which is a foreign entity also give rise to temporary differences. Any resulting deferred tax liability is recognised and included in the income statement as part of deferred tax expense (IAS 12, 41).

An investor in an associate does not control the investee and usually does not determine the investee's dividend policy. Therefore, in the absence of an agreement requiring that the profits of the associate will not be distributed in the foreseeable future, an entity recognises a deferred tax liability arising from taxable temporary differences resulting from its investments in associates (IAS 12, 42).

The distribution of the profits of a joint venture is usually dealt with in the contractual arrangement (IAS 31, 5). When the entity, as a venturer, can control the sharing of profits and it is probable that the profits will not be distributed in the foreseeable future, a deferred tax liability is not recognised (IAS 12, 43).

Extract 31.6 *Non-recognition – subsidiaries*

Groupe Bruxelles Lambert, Belgium, 31 December 2001 (IAS)

Recoverable deferred taxes in respect of investments in subsidiaries are not recorded in the accounts if the group is able to control the date on which the temporary difference will reverse and if the group does not expect the temporary difference to reverse within a foreseeable future.

Extract 31.7 *Undistributed earnings of subsidiaries*

Stora Enso, Finland, 31 December 2001 (IAS)

No deferred tax liability has been recognised for the undistributed earnings of Finnish subsidiaries as, in most cases, such earnings may be transferred to the Parent Company without any tax consequences. The Group does not provide for deferred taxes on undistributed earnings of non-Finnish subsidiaries to the extent that such earnings are intended to be permanently reinvested in those operations.

Extract 31.8 *Undistributed earnings of subsidiaries, associates and joint ventures*

Ascom, Switzerland, 31 December 2001 (IAS)

Deferred income tax is provided on temporary differences arising on investments in subsidiaries, associates and joint ventures. Exceptions are temporary differences for which the timing of the reversal of the temporary difference can be controlled and it is probable that the temporary difference will not reverse in the foreseeable future.

31.9.5 Revalued Assets

In some countries, a surplus arising in the current period on certain revaluations of assets enters into the determination of tax expense for the current period. For example, in France a surplus arising on a voluntary revaluation enters into the determination of taxable profits for the current period. In such cases, the resulting current tax expense is charged to equity if the surplus is credited to equity (as it usually will be) (IAS 12, 39). In other countries or circumstances, a surplus arising in the current period on the revaluation of assets is either:

- included in taxable profit in a later period; or
- not taxed even when the asset is sold.

Revalued property, plant and equipment is dealt with under IAS 12 in the same way as other assets. When the carrying amount of a revalued asset exceeds the tax base of the asset, there is a taxable temporary difference and a deferred tax liability is recognised. The determination of the asset's tax base depends, as usual, on whether the economic benefits which will flow from the assets are taxable or not.

It is sometimes argued that a deferred tax liability need not, or should not, be recognised if the entity does not intend to sell the revalued asset. Indeed, such an approach was supported in IAS 12 [1979] and E33. The argument is no longer relevant under the revised IAS 12. It is inherent in the recognition of the asset at fair value that the entity will recover the fair value of that asset either through use or sale of the asset. If the entity does not intend to sell the asset, it can recover the fair value only through use. If the economic benefits which flow to the entity are taxable, there is a taxable temporary difference. The method of recovery does not affect the temporary difference but it may affect the tax rate which should be applied.

SIC 21 *Income Taxes – Recovery of Revalued Non-Depreciable Assets* clarifies that the deferred tax liability or asset that arises from the revaluation of a non-depreciable asset should be measured based on the tax consequences that would follow from recovery of the carrying amount of that asset through sale, regardless of the basis of measuring the carrying amount of that asset. If the tax law specifying a tax rate applicable to the taxable amount on the sale of that asset is different from the tax rate that would apply if the entity used the asset, the former rate is applied in measuring the deferred tax liability or asset related to a non-depreciable asset (SIC 21, 5).

Example 31.14 *Revalued assets*

An entity has an asset with a cost of £100,000 which is being depreciated on a straight-line basis over 10 years. For tax purposes, the asset is depreciated on a declining balance basis using a rate of 20% a year. The tax rate is 40%. Therefore after three years:

- the asset's carrying amount is £70,000;
- the asset's tax written down value is £51,200;
- there is a taxable temporary difference of £18,800; and
- there is a deferred tax liability of £7,520.

At the end of year 3, the asset is revalued to £120,000. The revaluation does not affect the tax base. Further tax depreciation will be based on the tax written down value of £51,200. Therefore, the taxable temporary difference increases to £68,800, that is by £50,000.

If the asset is used in the business, any income less further tax depreciation will be taxed at 40%. Assume that there will be no disposal/scrap proceeds. Economic benefits of (at least) £120,000 must flow to the entity against which can be offset the tax written down value of £51,200. The income will be taxed at 40% and the tax written down value will attract relief at 40%. Therefore, there is a deferred tax liability of £27,520, that is £68,800 × 40%.

If the asset is sold, assume that:

- any excess of the sale proceeds, (to the extent that the proceeds do not exceed cost) over the tax written down value is taxed at 40%; and
- any excess of the sale proceeds over the cost of the asset is taxed at 25%.

Economic benefits of (at least) £120,000 must flow to the entity against which can be offset the tax written down value of £51,200. £20,000 (the excess of the sale proceeds over cost) will be taxed at 25% and the balance of £48,800 will be taxed at 40%. Therefore, the

(Continued)

(Continued)

deferred tax liability is £24,520, that is (£20,000 × 25% + £48,800 × 40%).

The logic in each case is that by carrying the asset at £120,000, the entity is representing that it will earn £120,000 taxable income in order to recover that asset (if it does not expect to do this, the asset should not be carried at £120,000). Only £51,200 will be allowed as a tax deduction, therefore it is inevitable that the entity will have a taxable profit of £68,800. The only question to answer, therefore, is how does the entity expect to recover the asset? The answer to that question determines the tax rates to be applied.

31.10 RECOGNITION OF DEFERRED TAX ASSETS

To the extent that it is probable that taxable profit will be available against which the deductible temporary difference can be utilised, a deferred tax asset should be recognised for all deductible temporary differences except for certain of those differences arising from:

- negative goodwill which is treated as deferred income (see 31.10.2);
- the initial recognition of an asset or a liability (see 31.10.3); or
- investments in subsidiaries, branches and associates, and interests in joint ventures (see 31.10.4).

(IAS 12, 24)

30.10.1 The General Rule

It is inherent in the recognition of a liability that the entity will settle the carrying amount of that liability in future periods through an outflow of economic benefits. If this is not the case, the liability is overstated and its carrying amount should be reduced to the amount which will be settled. When the entity settles the liability, part or all of the amounts paid may be deductible in determining the taxable profit of a period later than the period in which the liability was recognised. Therefore, the entity controls a resource from which future economic benefits are expected to flow. That resource is the difference between the carrying amount of the liability and its tax base. The resource is recognised (subject to certain conditions) as a deferred tax asset.

The reversal of deductible temporary differences results in deductions in determining taxable profits of future periods. The entity benefits from those deductions in tax payments only if it earns sufficient taxable profits against which the deductions can be offset (the reversal of taxable temporary differences creates taxable profits so no similar test is needed). The entity recognises deferred tax assets only when it is probable that taxable profits will be available against which the deductible temporary differences can be utilised (IAS 12, 24). This condition is met when there are sufficient taxable temporary differences relating to the same taxation authority and the same taxable entity which are expected to reverse:

- in the same period as the expected reversal of the deductible temporary difference; or
- in periods into which a tax loss arising from the deferred tax asset can be carried back or forward.

(IAS 12, 28)

Example 31.15 *Deductible temporary difference*

An entity recognises a liability of £500,000 for accrued product warranty costs. For tax purposes, the product warranty costs are deductible when the entity pays claims or otherwise incurs the costs. The tax rate is 25%.

The tax base of the liability is nil. When the enterprise settles the liability, it reduces its taxable profit by £500,000 and, consequently, reduces its tax payments by £125,000. The difference between the carrying amount of £500,000 and the tax base of nil is a deductible temporary difference of £500,000. Therefore, the entity recognises a deferred tax asset of £125,000, provided that it is probable that the entity will earn sufficient taxable profit in future periods to benefit from a reduction in tax payments.

If the condition is not met in this way, the deferred tax asset is recognised to the extent that:

- it is probable that the entity will have sufficient taxable profit relating to the same taxation authority and the same taxable entity in the same period as the reversal of the deductible temporary difference;
- it is probable that the entity will have sufficient taxable profit relating to the same taxation authority and the same taxable entity in the same periods into which a tax loss arising from the deferred tax asset can be carried back or forward; or
- tax planning opportunities are available to the entity that will create taxable profit in appropriate periods.

(IAS 12, 29)

In making this evaluation, an entity ignores taxable amounts arising from new deductible temporary differences which are expected to originate in future periods (IAS 12, 29).

Tax planning opportunities may create or increase taxable income in a particular period and may, therefore, be used to ensure that there is sufficient taxable profit in certain periods in order to recover the tax asset. Tax planning opportunities vary from country to country but they may include:

- changing the way that income is taxed;
- deferring the claim for certain deductions;
- voluntary, taxable revaluations of assets;
- selling, and sometimes leasing back, assets; and
- selling an asset that generates non-taxable income and buying an asset that generates taxable income.

Extract 31.9 *Probability of deferred tax being realised*

Henkel, Germany, 31 December 2001 (IAS)

Any assessment of whether deferred tax assets can be recognized depends on estimating the probability that the deferred tax assets can actually be realized in future. The level of probability must be more than 50 percent and must be supported by appropriate business plans.

31.10.2 Negative Goodwill

IAS 12 adopts the same approach for negative goodwill which is treated as deferred income as for goodwill. If the amortisation of negative goodwill is fully taxable, the tax base of the negative goodwill is initially the amount recognised in the balance sheet. Subsequently, the tax base is its written down amount for tax purposes. A deductible temporary difference arises when the carrying amount of the negative goodwill, determined in accordance with IAS 22, exceeds its tax base in the same way that a deductible temporary difference arises on any other liability when its carrying amount exceeds its tax base. A deferred tax asset should be recognised for such a temporary difference (subject to the usual conditions).

In many jurisdictions, however, negative goodwill is not taxable either as amortisation during its useful life or as part of the cost of the acquired business when it is sold or otherwise disposed of. As with goodwill, in such circumstances a deferred tax asset should not be recognised because negative goodwill is a residual and the recognition of the deferred tax asset would increase the carrying amount of negative goodwill (IAS 12, 32).

31.10.3 Initial Recognition of an Asset or Liability

In the same way that a deferred tax liability is not recognised for certain temporary differences arising on the initial recognition of an asset or liability, so a deferred tax asset is not recognised in similar circumstances (see 30.9.3). The revised IAS 12 includes two examples where this problem arises:

- the receipt of a non-taxable government grant which is treated as deferred income in accordance with IAS 20; and
- a compound financial instrument in which part is classified as a liability in accordance with IAS 32.

31.10.4 Subsidiaries, Associates and Joint Ventures

Deductible temporary differences arise when the carrying amount of investments in subsidiaries, branches and associates or interests in joint ventures (that is the parent or investor's share of the net assets of the subsidiary, branch, associate or investee, including the carrying amount of goodwill) is less than the tax base (which is often cost) of the investment or interest. The same rules apply as for taxable temporary differences.

An entity should recognise a deferred tax asset for all deductible temporary differences arising from investments in subsidiaries, branches and associates, and interests in joint ventures, to the extent that, and only to the extent that, it is probable that:

- the temporary difference will reverse in the foreseeable future; and
- taxable profit will be available against which the temporary difference can be utilised.

(IAS 12, 44)

31.11 TAX LOSS CARRY FORWARDS

In some jurisdictions, a tax loss of the current period may be carried forward to reduce current tax expense in respect of some or all future periods. In most jurisdictions there is a restriction on the number of periods for which the loss can be carried forward. Similarly, unused tax credits may be carried forward in some jurisdictions to reduce future tax liabilities. These reductions in current tax expense and tax liabilities are treated as if they were deferred tax.

A deferred tax asset should be recognised for the carry-forward of unused tax losses and unused tax credits to the extent that it is probable that future taxable profit will be available against which the unused tax losses and unused tax credits can be utilised (IAS 12, 34). The criteria for recognising deferred tax assets arising from the carry-forward of unused tax losses and tax credits are the same as the criteria for recognising deferred tax assets arising from deductible temporary differences (see 30.10.1). However, the existence of unused tax losses may be strong evidence that future taxable profits may not be available. Therefore, when an entity has a history of recent losses, the entity recognises a deferred tax asset arising from unused tax losses or tax credits only to the extent that it has sufficient taxable temporary differences or there is convincing other evidence that sufficient taxable profit will be available against which the unused tax losses or unused tax credits can be utilised by the entity.

An entity considers the following criteria in assessing the probability that taxable profit will be available against which the unused tax losses or unused tax credits can be utilised:

- whether the entity has sufficient taxable temporary differences relating to the same taxation authority and the same taxable entity, which will result in taxable amounts against which the unused tax losses or unused tax credits can be utilised before they expire;
- whether it is probable that the entity will have taxable profits before the unused tax losses or unused tax credits expire;
- whether the unused tax losses result from identifiable causes which are unlikely to recur; and
- whether tax planning opportunities are available to the entity that will create taxable profit in the period in which the unused tax losses or unused tax credits can be utilised.

(IAS 12, 36)

There are two other factors which need to be taken into account:

- if the tax rules limit the period during which a tax loss may be carried forward for offset against future taxable income, only those timing differences that will reverse or can be reversed during the limited period are considered in offsetting a tax loss; and
- if the tax rules limit the types of profits against which particular tax losses can be offset, only those timing differences that will give rise to the appropriate types of profits can be considered in offsetting a tax loss.

Example 31.16 *Tax loss carry-forward*

An entity operates in a country in which it can carry forward a tax loss arising in the current period to reduce current tax expense in future periods for a maximum of six years.

As a consequence of certain non-recurring events, the entity has a tax loss of $10,500 in 2001; the enacted tax rate for 2001 is 40%. In all previous periods, the entity has had taxable profits and its budgets and plans show that it will make accounting profits and taxable profits for 2002 onwards. Therefore, it is likely that the entity will have future taxable profits that will be sufficient to allow the recognition of the benefit of the tax loss. Therefore, the entity recognises tax income of $4,200 and a tax asset (receivable) of $4,200 in 2001.

Extract 31.10 *Tax loss carry forwards*

Bank Austria, Austria, 31 December 2001 (IAS)

In respect of tax losses carried forward in the amount of €615m (2000: €663m), no deferred tax asset was recognised because, from a current perspective, a tax benefit will probably not be realisable within a reasonable period. Information in future business years may require an adjustment to deferred tax assets.

Extract 31.11 *Tax loss carry-forwards*

Beko, Austria, 31 December 2001 (IAS)

The potential tax on losses carried forward and on current losses during the year under review were carried as an asset, as this can probably be calculated against future taxable income. According to Austrian and German tax law, no time limitations apply to the recovery of losses carried forward.

Extract 31.12 *Tax loss carry-forwards*

Stora Enso, Finland, 31 December 2001 (IAS)

The Group has recognised a deferred tax asset for its net operating loss carry-forwards and established a valuation allowance against this amount based on an analysis of the probability for set-off against future profits in the relevant tax jurisdictions. At 31 December 2001 Stora Enso had losses carried forward mainly attributable to foreign subsidiaries, of EUR 890 (EUR 674) million of which some EUR 362 million had no expiry date, EUR 74 million expire during the years 2002–2006 and the remainder expire thereafter. Tax loss carry-forwards are netted against deferred tax liabilities within each jointly taxed group of companies and are only shown separately as an asset to the extent that they exceed such liabilities.

31.12 RE-ASSESSMENT OF UNRECOGNISED DEFERRED TAX ASSETS

At each balance sheet date, an entity re-assesses whether to recognise unrecognised deferred tax assets. The entity recognises a previously unrecognised deferred tax asset to the extent that it has become probable that future taxable profit will allow the deferred tax asset to be recovered. For example, an improvement in trading conditions may make it more probable that the entity will be able to generate sufficient taxable profit in the future for the deferred tax asset to meet the recognition criteria. Another example is when an entity re-assesses deferred tax assets at the date of a business combination or subsequently.

Extract 31.13 *Review of carrying amount*

Sanochemia, Austria, 30 September 2001 (IAS)

The tax relief potential of loss carry-forwards was taken into account to the extent to which taxable income can almost certainly be expected to be earned in the future in amounts sufficient to offset loss carry-forwards. The partial valuation adjustment at the balance sheet date of 30 September 2001 is due to an on-going tax audit which may annul loss carry-forwards.

31.13 BUSINESS COMBINATIONS

The benefit arising from a tax loss may be acquired on a business combination. The benefit is recognised as an asset if it meets the recognition criteria for assets acquired (IAS 22, 28 – see chapter 16). The fair value of the tax asset is assessed from the perspective of the combined entity or group resulting from the acquisition (IAS 22, 39). For example, the asset might be recognised if the parent or another existing member of the group is able to obtain the tax saving resulting from the tax loss; the asset is recognised in the consolidated balance sheet even though it has not been recognised in the separate financial statements of the acquiree. In some countries, tax rules do not permit the transfer of tax losses in such a way and, therefore, the tax asset cannot be recognised.

When the acquirer did not recognise the potential benefit of the acquired entity's tax loss carry-forwards as an identifiable asset at the date of acquisition, any such benefits realised subsequently are recognised as income in the period of realisation. In addition, the acquirer recognises as an expense that part of the unamortised balance of goodwill that is attributable to those tax benefits (IAS 22, 85).

Extract 31.14 *Assets acquired in an acquisition*

Dairy Farm International, Hong Kong, 31 December 2001 (IAS)

Provision for deferred tax is made on the revaluation of certain non-current assets and, in relation to acquisitions, on the difference between the fair values of the net assets acquired and their tax base.

31.14 MEASUREMENT OF DEFERRED TAX ASSETS AND TAX LIABILITIES

Deferred tax assets and liabilities should be measured at the tax rates that are expected to apply to the period when the asset is realised or the liability is settled, based on tax rates (and tax laws) that have been enacted or substantively enacted by the balance sheet date (IAS 12, 47). For further guidance on enacted and substantively enacted rates of tax, see 31.6.3.

When different tax rates apply to different levels of taxable income, deferred tax assets and liabilities are measured using the average rates which are expected to apply to the taxable profit of the periods in which the temporary differences are expected to reverse (IAS 12, 49).

When different tax rates apply depending on the manner in which an entity recovers the carrying amount of an asset or settles the carrying amount of a liability, deferred tax liabilities and deferred tax assets should be measured using the rate which reflects the manner in which the entity expects, at the balance sheet date, to recover or settle the carrying amount of its assets and liabilities (IAS 12, 51).

In some jurisdictions, profits are taxed at different rates depending on whether they are distributed or retained by the entity. In such circumstances, current and deferred tax assets and liabilities should be measured at the tax rate applicable to undistributed profits (IAS 12, 52A–B).

Example 31.17

An entity is in a jurisdiction where income taxes are payable at 35% on distributed profits and at 50% on undistributed profits with an amount being refundable when profits are distributed.

At 31 December 2001 the entity does not recognise a liability for dividends proposed or declared after the balance sheet date nor recognise any dividends for the year ended 31 December 2001. Taxable income for the year is €100,000 and the net taxable temporary difference is €40,000.

(Continued)

(Continued)

On 31 March 2002, the entity recognises dividends of €10,000 from previous operating profits as a liability.

Year ended 31 December 2001

The entity recognises a current income tax expense and a current tax liability of €50,000 (€100,000 × 50%). It also recognises a deferred tax expense and liability of €20,000 (€40,000 × 50%) representing the income taxes that the entity will pay when it recovers or settles the carrying amounts of its assets and liabilities (based on the tax rate applicable to undistributed profits). No asset is recognised for the amount potentially recoverable as a result of future dividends.

Year ended 31 December 2002

On 31 March 2002, the entity recognises the recovery of income taxes of €1,500 (15% × dividends recognised as a liability) as a current tax asset and as a reduction of current income tax expense for that year.

Extract 31.15 *Undistributed profits*

Lufthansa, Germany, 31 December 2001 (IAS)

IAS 12 in the version revised in the year 2000 requires the application of the corporation tax retention rate in the valuation of deferred tax differences. Consequently, deferred tax assets and liabilities respectively reported before financial year 2000 had to be released with regard to profit portions not yet distributed in financial year 2000, whereas the other deferred tax assets and liabilities recognised or carried as liability in preceding years had to be adjusted to the retention tax rate.

Deferred tax assets and liabilities should not be discounted (IAS 12, 53). Discounting would require detailed scheduling of the timing of the reversal of each temporary difference. In many cases such scheduling is impracticable or highly complex. Furthermore, temporary differences are determined by reference to the carrying amount of assets and liabilities and some carrying amounts are determined on a discounted basis, for example, assets and liabilities arising from retirement benefit obligations and asset impairments.

Example 31.18 *Different tax rates*

An asset has a carrying amount of £100,000 and a tax base of £60,000. A tax rate of 20% applies if the asset is sold, and a tax rate of 30% applies to income arising from the use of the asset.

The entity recognises a deferred tax liability of £8,000 if it expects to sell the asset without further use. It recognises a deferred tax liability of £12,000 if it expects to recover the asset's carrying amount through use.

The carrying amount of a deferred tax asset should be reviewed at each balance sheet date. An entity should reduce the carrying amount of a deferred tax asset to the extent that it is no longer probable that sufficient taxable profit will be available to allow the benefit of part or all of that deferred tax asset to be utilised. Any such reduction should be reversed to the extent that it becomes probable that sufficient taxable profit will be available (IAS 12, 56).

31.15 PRESENTATION OF CURRENT AND DEFERRED TAX

31.15.1 Current and Deferred Tax Expense (Income)

Current and deferred tax should be recognised as income or an expense and included in the net profit or loss for the period, except to the extent that the tax arises from:

- a transaction or event which is recognised, in the same or a different period, directly in equity; or
- a business combination that is an acquisition.

(IAS 12, 58)

The carrying amount of deferred tax assets and liabilities may change even though there is no change in the amount of the related temporary differences. This can result, for example, from:

- a change in tax rates or tax laws;
- a re-assessment of the recoverability of deferred tax assets; or
- a change in the expected manner of recovery of an asset.

In some jurisdictions an entity is required to pay a portion of any dividend it pays to the taxation authority on behalf of its shareholders. This is frequently known as a 'withholding tax' and should be charged to equity as part of the dividend.

Extract 31.16 *Withholding tax*

Dairy Farm International, Hong Kong, 31 December 2001 (IAS)

Provision for withholding tax which could arise on the remittance of retained earnings relating to subsidiaries is only made where there is a current intention to remit such earnings.

When it is difficult to determine the amount of current and deferred tax which relates to items credited or charged to equity, the current and deferred tax related to items that are credited or charged to equity is based on a reasonable pro rata allocation of the current and deferred tax of the entity in the tax jurisdiction concerned, or other method that achieves a more appropriate allocation in the circumstances.

When an asset is revalued for tax purposes and that revaluation is related to an accounting revaluation of an earlier period, or to one that is expected to be carried out in a future period, the tax effects of both the asset revaluation and the adjustment of the tax base are credited or charged to equity in the periods in which they occur. However, if the revaluation for tax purposes is not related to an accounting revaluation of an earlier period, or to one that is expected to be carried out in a future period, the tax effects of the adjustment of the tax base are recognised in the income statement.

A change in the tax status of an entity or its shareholders does not increase or decrease current or deferred tax liabilities and assets recognised in equity (SIC 25, 4). Instead the current and deferred tax consequences of such changes in tax status are usually included in the net profit or loss for the period. Only where they relate to transactions and events that result in a direct credit or charge to the recognised amount of equity, should they also be charged or credited directly to equity.

31.15.2 Current and Deferred Tax Assets and Liabilities

Tax assets and tax liabilities should be presented separately from other assets and liabilities in the balance sheet (IAS 12, 69). They are one of the line items which should be included on the face of the balance sheet in accordance with IAS 1. Deferred tax assets and liabilities should be distinguished from current tax assets and liabilities (IAS 12, 69).

An entity should offset current tax assets and current tax liabilities if, and only if, the entity:

- has a legally enforceable right to set off the recognised amounts; and
- intends either to settle on a net basis, or to realise the asset and settle the liability simultaneously.

(IAS 12, 71)

An entity normally has a legally enforceable right to set off a current tax asset against a current tax liability when they relate to income taxes levied by the same taxation authority and the taxation authority permits the entity to make or receive a single net payment.

An entity should offset deferred tax assets and deferred tax liabilities only if:

- the entity has a legally enforceable right to set off current tax assets against current tax liabilities; and
- the deferred tax assets and the deferred tax liabilities relate to income taxes levied by the same taxation authority on either:
  - the same taxable entity; or
  - different taxable entities which intend either to settle current tax liabilities and assets on a net basis, or to realise the assets and settle the liabilities simultaneously, in each future period in which significant amounts of deferred tax liabilities or assets are expected to be settled or recovered.

(IAS 12, 74)

In rare circumstances, an entity may have a legally enforceable right of set-off, and an intention to settle net, for some periods but not for others. In such circumstances, detailed scheduling may be required to establish reliably whether the deferred tax liability of one taxable entity will result in increased tax payments in the same period in which a deferred tax asset of another taxable entity will result in decreased payments by that second taxable entity.

Extract 31.17 *Tax assets/liabilities disclosed separately*

Dyckerhoff, Germany, 31 December 2001 (IAS)

The reported deferred tax assets which, in accordance with IAS 12, cannot be netted out against deferred tax liabilities, largely relate to anticipated tax reductions due to the lower valuation of property, plant and equipment compared to its valuation for tax purposes in Poland and due to the use of tax loss carry-forwards in Spain.

Extract 31.18 *Right to set off*

Czech Telecom, Czech Republic, 31 December 2001 (IAS)

Deferred income tax assets and liabilities are offset when there is a legally enforceable right to set off current tax assets against current tax liabilities and when the deferred income taxes relate to the same fiscal authority.

The following amounts, determined after offsetting, are shown in the consolidated balance sheet:

(In CZK millions)	*31 December 2001*	*31 December 2000*
Deferred tax assets	(1,036)	(549)
Deferred tax liabilities	12,220	10,595
	11,184	10,046

31.16 DISCLOSURE

The major components of tax expense (income) should be disclosed separately (IAS 12, 79). Components of tax expense (income) may include:

- current tax expense (income);
- any adjustments recognised in the period for current tax of prior periods;
- the amount of deferred tax expense (income) relating to the origination and reversal of temporary differences;
- the amount of deferred tax expense (income) relating to changes in tax rates or the imposition of new taxes;
- the amount of the benefit arising from a previously unrecognised tax loss, tax credit or temporary difference of a prior period that is used to reduce current tax expense;
- the amount of the benefit from a previously unrecognised tax loss, tax credit or temporary difference of a prior period that is used to reduce deferred tax expense;
- deferred tax expense arising from the write-down, or reversal of a previous write-down, of a deferred tax asset; and
- the amount of tax expense (income) relating to those changes in accounting policies and fundamental errors which are included in the determination of net profit or loss for the period in accordance with the allowed alternative treatment in IAS 8 (see chapters 13 and 14).

The following should also be disclosed separately:

- the aggregate current and deferred tax relating to items that are charged or credited to equity – this may be shown in the statement of changes in equity;
- tax expense (income) relating to extraordinary items recognised during the period – this may be disclosed in aggregate;
- an explanation of the relationship between tax expense (income) and accounting profit in either or both of the following forms:
  - a numerical reconciliation between tax expense (income) and the product of accounting profit multiplied by the applicable tax rate(s), disclosing also the basis on which the applicable tax rate(s) is (are) computed; or

  - a numerical reconciliation between the average effective tax rate and the applicable tax rate, disclosing also the basis on which the applicable tax rate is computed;
- an explanation of changes in the applicable tax rate(s) compared to the previous accounting period;
- the amount (and expiry date, if any) of deductible temporary differences, unused tax losses, and unused tax credits for which no deferred tax asset is recognised in the balance sheet;
- the aggregate amount of temporary differences associated with investments in subsidiaries, branches and associates and interests in joint ventures, for which deferred tax liabilities have not been recognised;
- in respect of each type of temporary difference, and in respect of each type of unused tax losses and unused tax credits:
  - the amount of the deferred tax assets and liabilities recognised in the balance sheet for each period presented;
  - the amount of the deferred tax income or expense recognised in the income statement, if this is not apparent from the changes in the amounts recognised in the balance sheet;
- in respect of discontinued operations, the tax expense relating to:
  - the gain or loss on discontinuance;
  - the profit or loss from the ordinary activities of the discontinued operation for the period, together with the corresponding amounts for each prior period presented; and
- dividends that were proposed or declared before the financial statements were authorised for issue but are not recognised as a liability in those financial statements.

(IAS 12, 81)

An entity should disclose the amount of a deferred tax asset and the nature of the evidence supporting its recognition, when:

- the utilisation of the deferred tax asset is dependent on future taxable profits in excess of the profits arising from the reversal of existing taxable temporary differences; and
- the entity has suffered a loss in either the current or preceding period in the tax jurisdiction to which the deferred tax asset relates.

(IAS 12, 82)

Where income taxes are payable at a higher or lower rate or are refundable or payable if part of the net profit or retained earnings is paid out as a dividend, an entity should disclose:

- the nature of the potential income tax that would result from the payment of a dividend. This would include the important features of the income tax system and the factors affecting the amount of potential income tax payable on the dividend; and

- the amounts of the potential income tax consequences practicably determinable and whether there are any such amounts that are not practicably determinable.

It may not be possible to calculate the amount of income tax payable, for example due to a large number of foreign subsidiaries. In such cases, amounts that can be determined should still be disclosed along with an explanation for any other amounts that have not been quantified (IAS 12, 82A, 87A–C).

In explaining the relationship between tax expense (income) and accounting profit, an entity uses an applicable tax rate that provides the most meaningful information to the users of its financial statements. Often, the most meaningful rate is the domestic rate of tax in the country in which the entity is domiciled. However, IAS 12 also suggests that for an entity operating in several jurisdictions, it may be more meaningful to aggregate separate reconciliations prepared using the domestic rate in each individual jurisdiction.

The average effective tax rate is the tax expense (income) divided by the accounting profit (IAS 12, 86).

An entity discloses any contingent gains and losses in accordance with IAS 37. Contingent gains and losses may arise, for example, from unresolved disputes with the taxation authorities. Similarly, when changes in tax rates or tax laws are enacted or announced after the balance sheet date, an entity discloses any significant effect of those changes on its current and deferred tax assets and liabilities in accordance with IAS 10 (see chapter 39).

Extract 31.19 *Deferred tax disclosures*

Roche, Switzerland, 31 December 2001 (IAS)

Accounting policy
Income taxes include all taxes based upon the taxable profits of the Group, including withholding taxes payable on the distribution of retained earnings within the Group. Other taxes not based on income, such as property and capital taxes, are included within operating expenses or financial expenses according to their nature.

Provision for income taxes, mainly withholding taxes, which could arise on the remittance of retained earnings, principally relating to subsidiaries, is only made where there is a current intention to remit such earnings.

Deferred income taxes are provided using the liability method, under which deferred income taxes are recognised for temporary differences between the tax bases of assets and liabilities and their carrying values for financial reporting purposes. Deferred income tax assets relating to the carry-forward of unused tax losses are recognised to the extent that it is probable that future taxable profit will be available against which the unused tax losses can be utilised.

Current and deferred income tax assets and liabilities are offset when the income taxes are levied by the same taxation authority and when there is a legally enforceable right to offset them.

Notes to the financial statements

11. Income taxes in millions of CHF

Income tax expenses
The amounts charged in the income statement are as follows:

	2001	*2000*
Current income taxes	1,335	2,913
Deferred income taxes	(297)	(641)
Total charge for income taxes	1,038	2,272

The Group's parent company, Roche Holding Ltd, and several of the Group's operating companies are domiciled in Switzerland. The maximum effective rate of all income taxes on companies domiciled in Basel, Switzerland, is 8% for holding companies and 25% for operating companies (2000: 8% and 25%).

Since the Group operates across the world, it is subject to income taxes in many different tax jurisdictions. The Group calculates its average expected tax rate as a weighted average of the tax rates in the tax jurisdictions in which the Group operates.

This rate increased during 2001 as operating income now makes up a considerably higher proportion of pre-tax income than has been the case in previous years. This leads to an increase in the Group's effective tax rate, as operating income typically occurs in jurisdictions with higher tax rates when compared to financial income.

The Group's effective tax rate differs from the Group's expected tax rate as follows:

	2001	*2000*
Group's average expected tax rate	22%	20%
Tax effect of		
–Income not taxable	−1%	−3%
–Expenses not deductible for tax purposes	+3%	+3%
–Other differences	−3%	−3%
–Gain from sale of Genentech shares	–	+8%
–Gain from sale of LabCorp shares	+2%	+2%
–Impairment of long-term assets	–	−3%
–Vitamin case	−1%	–
Group's effective tax rate	22%	24%

Income tax assets and liabilities

Amounts recognised in the balance sheet for income taxes are as follows:

	2001	*2000*
Current income taxes		
Current income tax assets	244	435
Current income tax liabilities	(716)	(882)
Net current income tax asset (liability) in the balance sheet	(472)	(447)
Deferred income taxes		
Deferred income tax assets	1,410	460
Deferred income tax liabilities	(4,162)	(2,535)
Net deferred income tax asset (liability) in the balance sheet	(2,752)	(2,075)

Amounts recognised in the balance sheet for deferred taxes are reported as long-term assets and non-current liabilities, of which approximately 40% and 15% respectively is current.

Deferred income tax assets are recognised for tax loss carry forwards only to the extent that realisation of the related tax benefit is probable. The Group has no significant unrecognised tax losses. Deferred income tax liabilities have not been established for the withholding tax and other taxes that would be payable on the unremitted earnings of certain foreign subsidiaries, as such amounts are currently regarded as permanently reinvested. These unremitted earnings totalled 27.1 billion Swiss francs at 31 December 2001 (2000: 24.8 billion Swiss francs).

The deferred income tax assets and liabilities and the deferred income tax charges (credits) are attributable to the following items:

2001	*Property, plant and equipment, and intangible assets*	*Restructuring provisions*	*Other temporary differences*	*Total*
Net deferred income tax asset (liability) at beginning of year	(3,342)	146	1,121	(2,075)
Changes in accounting policies	–	–	(561)	(561)
On issue of debt instruments	–	–	(46)	(46)
(Charged) credited to the income statement	90	21	186	297
(Charged) credited to equity	–	–	(367)	(367)
Changes in Group organisation	(22)	–	5	(17)
Currency translation effects and other	14	3	–	17
Net deferred income tax asset (liability) at end of year	(3,260)	170	338	(2,752)

2000	*Property, plant and equipment, and intangible assets*	*Restructuring provisions*	*Other temporary differences*	*Total*
Net deferred income tax asset (liability) at beginning of year	(3,128)	302	101	(2,725)
Changes in accounting policies	49	–	–	49
On issue of debt instruments	–	–	(128)	(128)
(Charged) credited to the income statement	312	(144)	473	641
Changes in Group organisation, including Givaudan spin-off	(54)	(8)	(55)	(117)
Currency translation effects and other	(521)	(4)	730	205
Net deferred income tax asset (liability) at end of year	(3,342)	146	1,121	(2,075)

Notes

1 J A Burggraaff, 'IASC: Obstacles and Opportunities', speech to the American Accounting Association, 7 August 1981.

2 IAS 12 [1979] also allowed a choice between comprehensive and partial application of deferred taxes. While this choice was allowed for the deferral method, the arguments in favour of partial application fitted better with the liability method.

3 IAS 12 [1979], the report of the deferred tax working party and E33 also allowed a choice between comprehensive and partial application of deferred taxes.

4 The revised IAS 12 does not allow partial application as it was earlier understood but it does require the recognition of only those deferred tax liabilities which meet the definition of a liability. However, proponents of partial application use a narrower definition of a liability.

CHAPTER 32

Leases

32.1 RELEVANT STANDARD AND INTERPRETATIONS

IAS 17 *Accounting for Leases*
SIC 15 *Operating Leases – Incentives*
SIC 27 *Evaluating the Substance of Transactions Involving the Legal Form of a Lease*

32.2 HISTORY

32.2.1 IAS 17

IAS 17 *Accounting for Leases* (IAS 17) [1982] was approved and published in 1982. It was, in a sense, the IASC's first joint project with a national standard setting body. The IAS was developed by a steering committee chaired by Paul Rutteman of the United Kingdom who, at the same time, chaired the working party responsible for SSAP 21 *Accounting for Leases* in the United Kingdom.

The choice between the net investment method and the net cash investment method for the allocation of finance income was reconsidered in the comparability project. The IASC concluded that further study was required (*Statement of Intent on the Comparability of Financial Statements*, appendix 3). In making this decision, the IASC confirmed that it was dealing only with the allocation of finance income to different periods; it did not intend to allow the offsetting in the balance sheet of assets and liabilities arising from leveraged leases.

As explained below, IOSCO did not accept IAS 17 when it reviewed the then existing IASs in 1994. Before committing itself to review IAS 17, the IASC decided to discuss the topic further with national standard setting bodies (*IASC Insight*, December 1994, p13). The topic had been discussed at the IASC sponsored conference of standard setting bodies in

November 1993. It has also been considered by the European Commission's accounting advisory forum[1] which had concluded that it would be difficult to agree on a uniform accounting treatment because of the different approaches towards accounting for leases based upon economic, legal or tax considerations. The forum did not recommend a preferred accounting method but, in order to establish at least the minimum level of comparability, it recommended that a lessee should disclose additional information when it did not capitalise finance leases in the balance sheet.

In July 1995, the IASC announced that, as part of the work plan agreed with IOSCO, it had decided to develop a revised IAS on leases. The project was limited to the three issues regarded as essential by IOSCO:

- enhanced disclosure by lessees;
- enhanced disclosure by lessors; and
- the allocation of finance income by lessors (the same issue as had been considered in E32).

(*IASC Insight*, March 1997, p8)

IAS 17 *Leases* was approved in 1997 and superseded IAS 17 [1982] with effect for accounting periods beginning on or after 1 January 1999.

32.2.2 G4+1 – A New Approach

The IASC signalled its intentions to 'consider a more fundamental reform' of lease accounting based on the G4+1 discussion paper[2] written by Warren McGregor, the executive director of the Australian Accounting Research Foundation and a long-serving technical advisor to Australia's delegation to the IASC. Under the new approach put forward by Warren McGregor, all material rights and obligations arising under lease contracts which meet the definitions of assets and liabilities would be recognised as assets and liabilities by the lessee. In practice, this would mean the recognition of many operating leases as assets and liabilities of the lessee. The IASC invited comments on the G4+1 paper. The project is likely to be taken up by the IASB.

32.3 IOSCO

In June 1994, IOSCO advised the IASC that there were certain essential issues which needed to be reviewed in the near term before it could recommend acceptance of IAS 17 for the purposes of the core standards. These essential issues were:

- enhanced disclosures by lessees, including disclosure of rental expenses, sublease rentals and a description of general leasing arrangements – this has been dealt with in the revised IAS 17;
- enhanced disclosures for lessors, including disclosure of information concerning future minimum rentals and amounts of contingent rentals included in income – this has been dealt with in the revised IAS 17; and
- the specification of the circumstances in which the net investment method and the net cash investment method of allocating finance income to different periods should be used – this issue had been addressed in E32 and has now been dealt with in the revised IAS 17.

In addition, IOSCO also identified the following suspense issues:

- consideration of the disclosures which should be provided when local law prohibits lease capitalisation; and
- it should be possible under IASs to account for finance leases in a manner equivalent to operating leases with disclosure of the capitalisation information.

The IASC expressed concern that both these suspense issues would have introduced a significant free choice into IAS 17 and allowed a practice which was rejected in IAS 17.

IOSCO also identified the need for:

- more definitive guidance on the identification of finance leases of lessees and lessors;
- guidance on the treatment of changes in lease provisions;
- additional guidance on real estate leases; and
- guidance on the impairment of lessee and lessor assets.

IOSCO also suggested that, as a long-term potential project, the IASC should consider new approaches for lease accounting, for example the capitalisation of all leases with a term over one year (including leases which are currently classified as operating leases). This suggestion, of course, runs counter to the request to treat finance leases in the same way as operating leases. It is also the issue which is dealt with in the G4+1 discussion paper.

IAS 17 is included in 'IAS 2000' endorsed by IOSCO in May 2000. There are 12 supplemental treatments:

- consideration of new approaches for lease capitalisation, for example the capitalisation of all leases with a term greater than one year;
- consideration of guidance on the accounting for costs incurred by a lessee in negotiating and securing either a finance lease or an operating lease;

- concerns about the need to address the accounting for any remaining deferred costs when leases are modified;
- concerns about the need for guidance on the accounting for lease renewals and extensions;
- concerns about the effect of attendant factors, such as continuing involvement, on lease classification;
- concerns about the appropriateness of immediately recognising gains resulting from sale/leaseback transactions involving an operating lease;
- concerns about the disclosure of maturities for each of the next five years and thereafter for interest-bearing liabilities, liabilities under finance leases, and amounts to related parties;
- concerns about the need for guidance on contingent lease income;
- concerns about the need for separate presentation or disclosure of income and expenses relating to rentals for significant lessor activity;
- the need for guidance on the meaning of 'reasonable certainty' as used in the definitions of a non-cancellable lease, minimum lease payments and the lease term;
- concerns about the appropriateness of recognising unearned finance income equal to the initial direct costs expensed; and
- concerns about the need to require the disclosure of the effects of sale and leaseback transactions both at the time of the transaction and on a continuing basis.

32.4 IAS 17 IN BRIEF

When an entity leases an item of property, plant and equipment such that it obtains substantially all the risks and rewards incident to ownership of the item, it should recognise the item as property, plant and equipment and the resulting obligation as a liability. The lessor should recognise the lease as a receivable and allocate the finance income over the period of the lease so as to give a constant periodic rate of return on the lessor's net investment in the lease.

32.5 LEASES

A *lease* is an agreement whereby the lessor conveys to the lessee in return for a payment or series of payments the right to use an asset for an agreed period of time (IAS 17, 3). Leases take many different forms. They range from short-term rental agreements, such as those for the hire of motor vehicles or computers for as little as a day, to long-term agreements to finance the acquisition of a fleet of aircraft. Leases also take different legal forms; for example, in France, a distinction is drawn between a *crédit-bail* and a *contrat des locations* (which is the term used in the title of the French translation of IAS 17).

Whether or not a particular agreement is a lease as defined in IAS 17 depends on the substance of the agreement rather than its form. Deciding that an agreement is a finance lease has accounting consequences as IAS 17 requires an accounting treatment for finance leases which might not otherwise be applied. Deciding that an agreement is an operating lease has fewer consequences as the requirements for operating leases are probably identical to the accounting treatment which would otherwise be applied. However, it is very important to distinguish between an operating lease and a sale.

A lease may be a finance lease or an operating lease. The distinction depends on the substance of the agreement rather than the form of the contract. Classification is made at the inception of the lease and is changed only if the lessee and lessor agree to change the provisions in a manner which would have resulted in a different classification at the inception of the lease (IAS 17, 10). In other words, if the provisions are not changed, there is no need for the lessor or the lessee to reconsider the classification of the lease in each accounting period.

IAS 17 does not apply to certain types of leases:

- lease agreements to explore for, or use, natural resources such as oil, gas, timber, metals and other mineral rights (IAS 17, 2) – this exclusion is virtually identical to a similar exclusion in FAS 13 *Accounting for Leases* in the United States; and
- licensing agreements for such items as motion picture films, video recordings, plays, manuscripts, patents and copyrights (IAS 17, 2) – again, this exclusion is virtually identical to a similar exclusion in FAS 13 *Accounting for Leases* in the United States of America – rights under such agreements are dealt with in accordance with IAS 38 (see chapter 23) (IAS 38, 5).

32.5.1 Finance Leases

A *finance lease* is a lease that transfers substantially all the risks and rewards incident to ownership of an asset – title may or may not eventually be transferred (IAS 17, 3). Finance leases are usually negotiated between an entity and a financial institution when the entity has decided, first, to acquire an item of property, plant and equipment and, second, that a finance lease is the best way of financing that acquisition. The entity has usually considered other means of financing the acquisition. In such circumstances, the entity knows the cost of the item as well as the amount of any tax credits or government grants which would be available on the acquisition.

Under a finance lease:

- the financial institution (lessor) acquires the item of property, plant and equipment and, in many jurisdictions, receives any related tax credits or government grants;
- the financial institution rents the item of property, plant and equipment to the entity (lessee) for most, if not all, of the item's useful life; and
- the entity makes a payment or series of payments to the financial institution which are sufficient for the financial institution to recover the acquisition cost of the item of property, plant and equipment plus an adequate return for the use of its funds and the risks involved.

IAS 17 suggests several factors which normally indicate that a lease is a finance lease:

- the lease transfers ownership of the asset from the lessor to the lessee by the end of the lease term (IAS 17, 8(a));
- the lessee has the option to purchase the asset at a price which is expected to be significantly lower than the fair value of the asset at the date on which the option becomes exercisable such that, at the inception of the lease, it is reasonably certain that the option will be exercised (IAS 17, 8(b));
- the lease term is for the major part of the economic life of the asset even if title is not transferred (IAS 17, 8(c));
- at the inception of the lease the present value of the minimum lease payments amounts to at least substantially all the fair value of the leased asset (IAS 17, 8(d));
- the leased assets are of a specialised nature such that only the lessee can use them (IAS 17, 8(e));
- gains and losses from the fluctuation in the fair value of the residual value belong to the lessee (IAS 17, 9(b)); and
- the lessee has the ability to continue the lease for a secondary period at a rent which is substantially lower than market rent (IAS 17, 9(c)).

Virtually all finance leases relate to items which the financial institution would otherwise not acquire. For example, a railway company may use a finance lease as the means of acquiring rolling stock; the financial institution acquires the rolling stock for which it has no use other than to lease it to the railway company. The financial institution seeks to minimise the risk that it will have to repossess, and dispose of, the rolling stock. The railway company obtains the benefits of using the rolling stock and carries the risk of, for example, changes in the demand for the use of that rolling stock and its value.

In practice, finance leases are often far more complex than described above. Some of the complexity is caused by the desire of the parties to negotiate an arrangement that results in the best deal for both parties and maximises the tax benefits. Further complexity is caused by the desire of some entities to structure leases so that they do not meet the definition of a finance lease. Such entities want the financial and commercial benefits which flow from the type of arrangement which is similar to a finance lease but without having to apply the accounting requirements which apply to finance leases. Some have opted for leasing as the means of financing the acquisition of the assets with the sole purpose of excluding the financing (and, consequently, the asset) from the balance sheet. Consequently, accounting standards which deal with leases, including IAS 17 but particularly US GAAP, have become increasingly complex.

IAS 17 [1982] suggested that a finance lease was normally non-cancellable (IAS 17 [1982], 7) but this has been deleted from the revised IAS 17. What really matters is who bears the costs of cancellation. Therefore, the revised IAS 17 states that if the lessee bears the lessor's costs associated with the cancellation by the lessee, this is a further indicator that the lease is a finance lease (IAS 17, 9(a)). In other words, while the lease may be cancellable, it is the lessee which bears the risks associated with cancellation.

32.5.2 Operating Leases

An *operating lease* is a lease other than a finance lease (IAS 17, 3). Short term leases, such as those for the hire of a motor vehicle or office equipment, are often operating leases because:

- there is no intention to transfer substantially all the risks and rewards incident to ownership from the lessor to the lessee;
- an individual lease does not secure the recovery of the lessor's capital outlay plus a return – the lessor seeks to recover its outlay and a return by a series of leases usually with different lessees; and
- the term for any individual lease is not for the major part of the useful life of the asset and the lessor often enters into many leases with different lessees for the same item of property, plant and equipment during the asset's useful life.

Operating leases may also be long-term. For example, many leases of land and buildings are long-term but the lessor retains the significant risks and rewards incident to ownership and therefore the leases are operating leases. For example:

- when the land which is the subject of the lease has an indefinite useful life and title to the land is not expected to pass from the lessor to the lessee by the end of the lease term, the lessor retains the significant risks and rewards from changes in the value of the land (IAS 17, 10);
- when the leased buildings have a useful life that is expected to extend well beyond the end of the lease term and title in the buildings is not expected to pass from the lessor to the lessee by the end of the lease term, the lessor retains the risk and rewards from changes in the value of the buildings and the use of the buildings after the end of the lease term;
- when rents on a leased building are regularly adjusted to market rates, the lessor retains a significant reward, that is the benefit of increased market rental (and, sometimes, the risks associated with downward adjustments); and
- when leases for buildings include clauses which allow the lessee to break the lease, without penalty, at specified dates, the lessor retains the risks and rewards of a break in the lease and the use of the buildings after any break.

As explained earlier, it is important to distinguish an operating lease from a sale. For example, an entity may 'sell' the right to occupy a tourist apartment for 30 years and receive a lump sum payment for that sale. The transaction, in spite of its description as a sale, is in fact a lease as the purchaser has the right to use the apartment for only an agreed period of time.

32.6 LESSEE ACCOUNTING FOR FINANCE LEASES

The substance and financial reality of a finance lease are such that:

- the lessee acquires the right to the economic benefits which are expected to flow from the leased asset for the major part of its useful life; and
- the lessee enters into an obligation to make a payment or series of payments for that right for an amount which approximates the fair value of the asset and the related finance charge.

Therefore, the lessee should recognise the finance lease as an asset and liability in its balance sheet (IAS 17, 12). The amount of the asset and the amount of the liability at the inception of the lease are equal to the fair value of the leased asset or, if lower, the present value of the minimum lease payments (IAS 17, 12). On initial recognition, the amounts recognised for the asset and for the liability are identical. However, the amount recognised for the asset is increased by any initial direct costs incurred in connection with the lease, for example, in negotiating and securing the lease (IAS 17, 17). The asset and liability are presented separately; they should not be offset (IAS 17, 15).

Example 32.1 *Lessee accounting for finance leases*

On 1 January 2002, A and B enter into an agreement under which B leases to A a machine for the whole of its useful life. The fair value of the machine is £10,000 and A will make lease payments equivalent to the fair value of the machine and interest at market rates.

At the inception of the lease, A recognises:

- the machine as plant and equipment with a cost of £10,000; and
- a liability for the obligation under the lease of £10,000.

Extract 32.1 *Leased assets*

Renault, France, 31 December 2000 (some IAS)

Equipment leased by the Group is recorded as an acquisition when the lease terms are similar to those of a purchase by credit instalments.

Extract 32.2 *Leased assets*

Preussag, Germany, 31 December 2001 (IAS)

In accordance with IAS 17, leased tangible assets in which consolidated subsidiaries carried all the risks and rewards incident to ownership of the asset (finance leasing) were valued at the cost that would have been incurred if the asset had been purchased. Scheduled depreciation was effected over the economic life or the lease term, if shorter, on the basis of the depreciation method applicable to comparable purchased or manufactured assets. The payment obligations arising from future lease payments were carried as liabilities, with no consideration of future interest expenses.

Extract 32.3 *Leased assets*

VA Technologie, Austria, 31 December 2001 (IAS)

Leasing contracts stipulating that the Group carries all the risks and opportunities related to the utilisation of the assets are treated as finance leases. The items on which the leasing contract is based are reported as assets at the current value of the capitalised lease payment and depreciated over the service life. The items reported as assets are netted against the cash value of the liability arising from future lease payments at the balance sheet date.

Extract 32.4 *Leased assets*

Schoeller-Bleckman Oil-Field Equipment, Austria, 31 December 2001 (IAS)

Where tangible assets are financed by leasing agreements which give rights approximating to ownership (finance leases), they are treated as if they were purchased outright at the lower of the fair value and the present value of the minimum lease payments and the corresponding leasing liabilities are shown in the balance sheet as finance lease obligations.

Extract 32.5 *Leased assets*

Lufthansa, Germany, 31 December 2001 (IAS)

Financial leasing
The total of leased assets to be allocated to the Group's economic ownership in accordance with IAS 17 amounts to €1,628.8m (prior year: €1,222.1m), €1,519.3m of which (prior year: €1,111.4m) relates to aircraft.

As a rule, aircraft finance lease agreements are non-terminable within the scope of a fixed basic lease term of at least four years. Their maximum term is twelve years. After expiry of the lease term, the lessee is usually entitled to acquire the asset at the respective residual value plus a mark-up of 25 per cent of the difference between the residual value as stipulated in the lease agreement and the higher market value. If this option is not exercised by the lessee, the lessor may sell the aircraft at the best possible price on the market. The lessee is entitled to 75 per cent of the sales surplus exceeding the residual value. If sales revenue is below the residual value, the difference is to be paid by the lessee. Some of these lease agreements provide for variable lease payments in so far as the included interest share is linked to the future course of market interest rates, as a rule the 6-month Libor rate.

Apart from this, there are finance lease agreements in quite different forms for buildings and parts of buildings, technical machinery and office and factory equipment.

Lease terms for buildings and parts of buildings are between 10 and 39 years. Lease agreements provide for lease payments, which are partly based on variable interest rates, partly on fixed interest rates, as well as for purchase options at the end of the contractual period. The agreements are either non-cancellable or may be cancelled upon payment of a termination penalty and the acquisition of the object of lease. Options for extensions of the agreements – if any – exist only on the part of the lessor.

Lease terms for technical equipment are between three and fifteen years. Lease agreements provide for fixed lease payments and purchase options at the end of the lease term. An extension of the lease term by the lessee is usually provided for or occurs automatically as long as there is no objection. The agreements are either non-cancellable or may be cancelled only upon payment of a termination penalty and the acquisition of the assets.

Lease terms for office and factory equipment are between three and eight years. The agreements provide for lease payments which are partly based on variable interest rates, partly on fixed interest rates as well as mainly for purchase options at the end of the contractual lease term. Some of these agreements may be extended by the lessee. The agreements are either non-cancellable or may be cancelled only upon the acquisition of the assets and payment of a termination penalty.

The *minimum lease payments* are the payments over the lease term that the lessee is, or can be required, to make excluding contingent rent, costs for services and taxes to be paid by and reimbursed to the lessor, together with any amounts guaranteed by the lessee or by a party related to the lessee (IAS 17, 3). *Contingent rent* is those lease payments which are not fixed in amount but which are based on a factor other than the passage of time, for example sales, usage etc. (IAS 17, 3).

The present value of the minimum lease payments is calculated using a discount rate which is the interest rate implicit in the lease (IAS 17, 12). If it is not practicable to determine the interest rate implicit in the lease, the lessee's incremental borrowing rate should be used (IAS 17, 12). The lessee's incremental borrowing rate is similar to, if not the same as, that which would be used to test the leased asset for impairment.

The lessee apportions lease payments between the finance charge and the reduction of the liability (IAS 17, 17). The finance charge should be allocated to periods during the lease term so as to produce a constant periodic rate of interest on the remaining balance of the liability during each period of the lease term (IAS 17, 17). The finance charge for each period is recognised as an expense of that period but may be included in borrowing costs which are capitalised (IAS 23, 5(d) – see chapter 35).

The depreciation policy for leased assets should be consistent with that for depreciable assets which are owned and the depreciation charge should be calculated in accordance with IAS 16 (IAS 17, 19). The useful life of the asset is usually limited to the lease term (IAS 16, 43 and IAS 17, 19). However, if there is reasonable certainty that the lessee will obtain ownership of the asset by the end of the lease term, the asset's useful life may exceed the lease term (IAS 17, 19).

The impairment of leased assets is dealt with in the same way as the impairment of other assets in accordance with IAS 36 (see chapter 25).

32.7 LESSOR ACCOUNTING FOR FINANCE LEASES

In the revised IAS 17, the IASC has retained the approach to lessor accounting for finance leases adopted in IAS 17 [1982] except that the choice of method for the allocation of finance income has been removed.

The substance and financial reality of a finance lease are such that the lessor acquires the right to receive a payment or series of payments for granting the lessee the right to use the item of property, plant and equipment. Therefore, the lessor's asset is a receivable. The lessor should recognise the receivable at an amount equal to the net investment in the lease (IAS 17, 28). The *net investment in the lease* is the gross investment in the lease less unearned finance income (IAS 17, 3). The *gross investment in the lease* is the aggregate of the minimum lease payments under a finance lease from the standpoint of the lessor and any unguaranteed residual value accruing to the lessor (IAS 17, 3). *Unearned finance income* is the difference between:

- the aggregate of the minimum lease payments under a finance lease from the standpoint of the lessor and any unguaranteed residual value accruing to the lessor; and
- the present value of the above amount, at the interest rate implicit in the lease (IAS 17, 3).

From the standpoint of the lessor, the minimum lease payments are the payments over the lease term which the lessee is, or can be required, to make excluding contingent rent, costs for services and taxes to be paid by and reimbursed to the lessor, together with any residual value guaranteed to the lessor by either:

- the lessee;
- a party related to the lessee; or
- an independent third party financially capable of meeting this guarantee.

If the lessee has the option to purchase the asset at a price which is expected to be sufficiently lower than the fair value at the date the option becomes exercisable that, at the inception of the lease, it is reasonably certain to be exercised, the minimum lease payments comprise the minimum payments payable over the lease term and the payment required to exercise this purchase option (IAS 17, 3). In other words, the payment required to exercise the option replaces any guaranteed residual value.

Finance income should be recognised as income (revenue) in the income statement based on a pattern reflecting a constant periodic rate of return on the lessor's net investment outstanding in respect of the finance lease (IAS 17, 30).

The lessor may need to modify the pattern of recognition of finance income (but not change the method) when there is a reduction in the estimated unguaranteed residual value. The reduction means that the lessor may receive a smaller amount of payments and, hence, a smaller amount of finance income. Any reduction in finance income in respect of amounts already recognised as income is recognised as an expense immediately (IAS 17, 32) – in practice, as a reduction in the finance income for the current period. This treatment requires, in effect, a retrospective adjustment even though a change in the residual value of an asset is usually dealt with prospectively.

Initial direct costs incurred by the lessor, such as commissions and legal fees, are either:

- recognised as an expense in the income statement immediately (IAS 17, 33); or
- allocated against finance income over the lease term – this may be achieved by recognising the costs as an expense as incurred and recognising as income in the same period a portion of the unearned finance income equal to the initial direct costs (IAS 17, 33).

Extract 32.6 *Leased assets*

S&T, Austria, 31 December 2001 (IAS)

When assets are sold under a finance lease, the present value of lease payments is recognized as a receivable. The difference between the gross receivable and the present value of the receivable is recognized as unearned finance income. Lease income is recognized over the term of the lease using the net investment method, which reflects a constant periodic rate of return.

Extract 32.7 *Leased assets*

Heidelberg Druckmaschinen, Germany, 31 March 2001 (IAS)

For installations that are leased out, which are to be regarded as sales of assets with long-term financing (finance leases) in accordance with IAS 17, receivables are shown in the amount of the discounted future lease payments.

In the framework of customer financing, the risks of credit worthiness and of default arise due to the potential danger that our customers do not comply with their payment obligations. As a consequence, assets may deteriorate in value. Recognizable risks of non-payment are taken into account through the establishment of adequate risk provisions. A summary of the overall risk of non-payment that is required for managing the portfolio is undertaken using the so-called credit at risk method. The point of departure of this method is a unified process for evaluating customer solvency (CRASH = Credit Risk Assessment Sheet). In addition to the factors financial risk and business risk, such additional aspects of the overall risk as documentary risk, contractual structure risk, and country risk are also included.

32.7.1 Manufacturers and Dealers

Some lessors are also the manufacturers of, or dealers in, the assets under the finance leases. Such lessors have revenue from both:

- the sale of the asset; and
- finance income arising under the finance lease.

The revenue from the sale of the asset is recognised in accordance with the entity's policy for the sale of goods (see IAS 18 and chapter 29). The finance income is recognised in accordance with IAS 17. The amount of the sales revenue is usually the fair value of the asset (as with other sales of goods). It is based on normal selling prices, less any applicable volume or trade discounts. The cost of the sale is the carrying amount of the asset less the present value of the unguaranteed residual value (IAS 17, 36).

A lessor which is also the manufacturer or dealer may quote artificially low rates of interest in order to attract customers. This reduces the lease payments and, hence, their present value. In such circumstances, the selling profit is restricted to that which would apply if a commercial rate of interest were charged (IAS 17, 37). This is the same approach as is implied by IAS 18 for any sale on deferred payment terms. In such cases, the amount of the sales revenue is the present value of the minimum lease payments from the standpoint of the lessor, computed at a commercial rate of interest (IAS 17, 36).

Extract 32.8 *Sales financing*

Renault, France, 31 December 2000 (IAS)

Group sales financing companies mainly finance the sale of passenger and commercial vehicles to dealers and end-users. Financing takes the form of standard loans or leasing arrangements, which may be long-term leases or include a purchase option. Unless the Group has a buy-back commitment on leased vehicles, these financing arrangements are treated as loans and posted to the balance sheet at the nominal value of outstanding capital less any provisions. Income on sales financing is calculated so as to give a constant rate over the term of the contract.

Extract 32.9 *Leased assets*

Volkswagen, Germany, 31 December 2001 (IAS)

As a lessor – generally of vehicles – in the case of finance leases, ie where essentially all risks and rewards in connection with ownership are transferred to the lessee, a receivable in the amount of the net investment in the lease is recognized. In determining the net investment in the lease all elements of the lease affecting cash flow are taken into account.

32.8 APPLYING FINANCE LEASE ACCOUNTING

A simple finance lease, from the perspective of both lessor and lessee, can be summarised as follows:

Lessor		**Lessee**	
Payments made by the lessee over the lease term	A	Payments made by the lessee over the lease term	A
Residual value guaranteed by the lessee	B	Residual value guaranteed by the lessee	B
Gross investment in the lease – minimum lease payments (A+B)	C	**Minimum lease payments (A+B)**	C
Unearned finance income	D	Finance charge	D
Net investment in the lease – acquisition cost of asset (C–D)	E	**Acquisition cost of asset (C–D)**	E

In such circumstances, the application of the requirements of IAS 17 is simple. The lessor:

- recognises the acquisition cost of the asset (E) as a receivable;
- allocates the finance income (D) over the period of the lease; and
- allocates the payments by the lessee (A) between the repayment of the receivable and the payment of finance income.

The lessee:

- recognises the acquisition cost of the asset (E) as property, plant and equipment and as a liability;
- allocates the finance charge (D) over the period of the lease;
- allocates payments to the lessor (A) between the repayment of the liability and the payment of the finance charge; and
- recognises depreciation on the item of property, plant and equipment in accordance with IAS 16.

The lessee may also need to add any initial direct costs to the cost of the asset.

In practice, finance leases are more complicated. This does not affect the principles but it does affect the amounts that are recognised by both the lessor and the lessee.

Example 32.2 *Accounting for finance leases by the lessee and the lessor*

On 1 January 1997, A and B enter into an agreement under which B leases to A a machine with a fair value and cost to B of £10,000. The lease term is 5 years and A is required to pay annual rentals, in arrears, of £3,000. The machine will have reached the end of its useful life at the end of the lease; it has no residual value. The lease is non-cancellable. There are no grants or tax credits available in respect of the machine. The lease is a finance lease with a lease term of 5 years.

The minimum lease payments from the perspective of both A and B are £15,000 which is also the gross investment in the lease. As the fair value of the machine is £10,000, the unearned finance income is £5,000.

At the inception of the lease, A recognises:

- the machine as plant and equipment with a cost of £10,000; and
- a liability for the obligation under the lease of £10,000.

At the inception of the lease, B recognises:

- a receivable of £10,000; and
- a liability to acquire the machine (or a payment) of £10,000.

A apportions each payment of £3,000 between the finance charge and the repayment of the liability. The interest rate implicit in the lease is 15.24%.

Year	*Liability at beginning of year*	*Finance charge for period*	*Payment during year*	*Liability at end of year*
	£	£	£	£
1997	10,000	1,524	3,000	8,524
1998	8,524	1,299	3,000	6,823
1999	6,823	1,040	3,000	4,863
2000	4,863	741	3,000	2,604
2001	2,604	396	3,000	–

A recognises a finance charge of £1,524 as an expense in 1997, a finance charge of £1,299 as an expense in 1998 and so on. A also recognises depreciation of £2,000 in each year.

B apportions each receipt of £3,000 between finance income and the repayment of the receivable. The interest rate implicit in the lease is 15.24%.

(*Continued*)

(Continued)

Year	*Receivable at beginning of year* £	*Finance income for period* £	*Receipt during year* £	*Receivable at end of year* £
1997	10,000	1,524	3,000	8,524
1998	8,524	1,299	3,000	6,823
1999	6,823	1,040	3,000	4,863
2000	4,863	741	3,000	2,604
2001	2,604	396	3,000	–

32.9 LESSEE ACCOUNTING FOR OPERATING LEASES

Under an operating lease, the risks and rewards incident to ownership of an asset remain with the lessor. Therefore, the lessee recognises the lease payments as an expense in the income statement on a straight-line basis over the lease term unless another systematic basis is representative of the time pattern of the lessee's benefit even if payments are not made on a straight-line basis (IAS 17, 25). The lessee does not recognise operating leases in its balance sheet as assets and liabilities, although it needs to recognise prepaid rents as an asset and accrued rents as a liability.

Under some operating leases, the lessee makes a substantial initial payment for the use of the asset for a number of years. This is the case, for example, under some leases for land and buildings when the annual rent is below market value. Such initial payments are often recognised as leasehold property, recorded at the amount of the initial payment. Such properties are dealt with in accordance with IAS 16 and may be revalued under the allowed alternative in IAS 16.

The lessee may also receive various incentives from the lessor, for example, an initial rent-free period or the reimbursement of certain costs. All such incentives should be included in the determination of the total lease payments which are then allocated over the lease term (SIC 15, 3). So, for example, the benefit of an initial rent free period of one year in a ten-year lease is recognised in the income statement over the ten years so that each year is charged with one-tenth of nine years' rent. It would be incorrect to charge no rent in the first year of the lease and a full year's rent in each of the succeeding nine years.

Extract 32.10 *Operating leases*

Volkswagen, Germany, 31 December 2001 (IAS)

Where the Company is the lessee of assets under operating leases, lease instalments and rental payments are recorded directly as expenses in the income statement.

Extract 32.11 *Operating leases*

Lufthansa, Germany, 31 December 2001 (IAS)

In addition to finance lease agreements, a considerable number of lease agreements have been concluded which, pursuant to their economic contents, qualify as operating lease agreements. Accordingly, the leased assets are to be allocated to the lessor. Apart from a further eight aircraft, these agreements mainly concern leased buildings.

The term of the operating lease agreements for aircraft is between five and ten years. Usually, the agreements are terminated automatically after expiry of the lease term, in some cases lease extension options have been agreed upon. . . .

As a rule, lease agreements for buildings have a term of five to ten years. The facilities at the Frankfurt and Munich airports have been leased for a period of 30 years.

Extract 32.12 *Operating leases*

Mandarin Oriental, Hong Kong, 31 December 2001 (IAS)

Leases of assets under which all the risks and benefits of ownership are effectively retained by the lessor are classified as operating leases.

Leasehold land payments are up-front payments to acquire long-term interests in property. Changes in IAS, which came into effect during 2001, no longer permit valuation of leasehold interests in land. These payments are stated at cost and are amortised over the period of the lease. In previous years, long-term leasehold land interests were recognised as tangible fixed assets and were stated at valuation.

Payments made under other operating leases are charged to the consolidated profit and loss account on a straight-line basis over the period of the lease. When the lease is terminated before the lease period has expired, any payment required to be made to the lessor by way of penalty is recognised as an expense in the year in which termination takes place.

32.10 LESSOR ACCOUNTING FOR OPERATING LEASES

Under an operating lease, the risks and rewards incident to ownership of an asset remain with the lessor. The asset is presented in the balance sheet of the lessor as property, plant and equipment (IAS 17, 41). The lessor should recognise depreciation on the asset on a basis consistent with its normal depreciation policy for similar assets (IAS 17, 45), that is usually in accordance with IAS 16. Any impairment of the asset is dealt with in accordance with IAS 36.

A lessor which is also the manufacturer or dealer of the asset does not recognise any selling profit on entering into an operating lease because a sale has not taken place (IAS 17, 47). The lessor has retained the significant risks and rewards of ownership and, therefore, a sale cannot be recognised under IAS 18.

The lessor should recognise operating lease income on a straight-line basis over the lease term, unless another systematic basis is more representative of the time pattern of the earnings process contained in the lease even if the lease payments are received on some other basis (IAS 17, 42). Any rents paid in advance by the lessee are recognised as a liability and any rents which are payable in arrears are recognised as a receivable.

Initial direct costs incurred to earn revenues from an operating lease are either:

- deferred and recognised as an expense over the lease term in proportion to the recognition of rental income; or
- recognised as an expense in the period in which they are incurred.

(IAS 17, 44)

The lessor may grant various incentives to the lessee, for example, an initial rent free period or the reimbursement of certain costs. All such incentives should be included in the determination of the total lease income which is allocated over the lease term (SIC 15, 4). So, for example, the cost of an initial rent free period of one year in a ten-year lease is recognised in the income statement over the ten years so that each year is credited with one-tenth of nine years' rent. It would be incorrect to credit no rent in the first year of the lease and a full year's rent in each of the succeeding nine years.

Extract 32.13 *Operating leases*

Telia, Sweden, 31 December 2000 (Swedish GAAP and IAS)

Fiber and ducts are sold as part of the operations of Telia's international carrier business. Telia has decided to view these as integral equipment. Under the agreements, title was not transferred to the lessee. The transactions are therefore reported as operating lease agreements.

Extract 32.14 *Operating leases*

BMW, Germany, 31 December 2001 (IAS)

Where Group products are recognised by BMW Group leasing companies as leased products under operating leases, they are measured at manufacturing costs. All other leased products are measured at acquisition cost. All leased products are depreciated using the straight-line method over the period of the lease to the lower of their notional residual value or estimated fair value.

Extract 32.15 *Operating leases*

Volkswagen, Germany, 31 December 2001 (IAS)

Vehicles leased out under operating leases are capitalized at cost and depreciated using the straight-line method over the term of the lease down to their estimated residual value.

32.11 SALE AND LEASEBACK

A sale and leaseback transaction usually involves:

- the sale of an asset by the entity to a financial institution; and
- the leasing of the same asset back to the entity which, as a result, becomes the lessee in the lease.

The lease payments and the sale price are usually interdependent as they are negotiated as a package and need not represent fair values. They may be affected by a number of factors. For example, tax considerations may induce the entity and the financial institution to agree to a particular sale price and rents. Alternatively, a desire to boost its annual net profits may persuade the entity as seller/lessee to accept a low selling price in return for lower rents.

Before accounting for a transaction as a sale and leaseback, it is important to confirm first that the sale qualifies for recognition as a sale. Some purported sale and leaseback transactions are, in substance, financing arrangements in which the seller/lessee retains the asset and the transaction is not, therefore, a sale.

This issue is complex, not least when the resulting lease is a finance lease, as the transaction implies that the seller has given up all the risks and rewards incident to the ownership of the asset (the sale) only to reacquire those risks and rewards (the finance lease). In such circumstances, it is necessary to look separately at the two components of the transaction – the sale and the lease. It is also appropriate to look to IAS

18, in particular the guidance on both sale and repurchase agreements for real estate (property) and the seller's continuing involvement in the property which purportedly has been sold. For example, if the seller agrees to repurchase the asset at a later date or has a call option to repurchase the asset, the seller may not, in substance, have made a sale. If the seller has retained (and never given up) the risks and rewards of ownership, even though legal title has been passed to the buyer, the transaction is a financing arrangement and not a sale (IAS 18, appendix, 5).

In the case of the Austrian company OMV, certain transactions are treated as sale and leasebacks under Austrian GAAP but as financing transactions under US GAAP (see extract 32.16). US GAAP includes extensive guidance on this issue and while the requirements of IAS 17 are much more limited, the US GAAP treatment is probably the appropriate way to deal with such transactions under IFRSs (OMV currently does not report under IFRSs).

Extract 32.16 *Sale and leaseback transactions*

OMV, Austria, 31 December 1997

In 1988 OMV Deutschland GmbH entered into two sale and leaseback transactions in respect of tank farms with an option to repurchase the assets at the end of the lease terms. ... Under Austrian GAAP gains were recognized when the agreements were signed and subsequent lease payments are charged to the income statement as incurred. Under US GAAP these have been treated as financing transactions. Accordingly, the gains on disposals have been reversed and the proceeds received have been treated as a borrowing.

Assuming that a sale is a sale, the ensuing lease in a sale and leaseback transaction may be either a finance lease or an operating lease.

32.11.1 Lessee Accounting for Sale and Leasebacks

When the ensuing lease is a finance lease, the seller/lessee has transferred, then immediately regained, the risks and rewards incident to ownership of the asset. In such circumstances, the seller/lessee should not recognise immediately as income any excess of the sale proceeds over the carrying amount of the asset. Instead, it should defer the resulting gain and recognise it as income over the lease term (IAS 17, 50). This matches the gain on the asset with the increased depreciation and the finance charge related to that asset.

When the ensuing lease is an operating lease, the seller/lessee has given up, but has not regained, the significant risks and rewards incident to ownership of the asset. A sale has taken place and should be recognised as such. However, the recognition of any profit or loss on that sale depends on whether the sale price and the lease payments have been established at fair value:

- if the sale price and the lease payments are established at fair value, any profit or loss on the sale should be recognised immediately;
- if the sale price exceeds fair value, it is likely that the lease payments are also in excess of fair value – therefore, the profit on the sale should be deferred and recognised as income over the period for which the asset is expected to be used (that is, the profit is matched against the higher rentals); and
- if the sale price is below fair value, any profit or loss should be recognised immediately except that if the loss is compensated by future lease payments below market price, the loss should be deferred and recognised as an expense in proportion to the rental payments over the period for which the asset is expected to be used.

(IAS 17, 52)

Extract 32.17 *Sale and leaseback transactions*

Holcim, Switzerland, 31 December 2001 (IAS)

In the case of sale and lease-back transactions, the book value of the related property, plant or equipment remains unchanged. Gains from a sale are included as a financing liability and the financing costs are allocated over the term of the lease in such a manner that the costs are reported over the relevant periods.

Extract 32.18 *Operating leases*

Swisscom, Switzerland, 31 December 2001 (IAS)

In March 2001 Swisscom entered into two agreements for the sale of real estate. The first relates to the sale of 30 commercial and office properties of CHF 1,272 million to a consortium led by Credit Suisse Asset Management. The second concerns the sale of 166 commercial and office properties for CHF 1,313 million to PSP Real Estate AG and WTF Holding (Switzerland) Ltd. At the same time Swisscom entered into agreements to lease back part of the sold property space.

The first transaction was completed on 1 April 2001 and the second on 19 June 2001. The total gain on the sale of the properties after transaction costs of CHF 105 million and including the reversal of environmental provisions, was CHF 807 million. A number of leaseback agreements were finance leases and the gain on the sale of these properties of CHF 239 million has been deferred and will be released to income over the individual lease terms. The remaining gain of CHF 568 million represents the gain on the sale of buildings which were either sold outright or which qualify as operating leases. The present value of the future payments under the finance lease was CHF 746 million and has been included as both a fixed asset and a lease obligation.

32.12 DISCLOSURE

32.12.1 Lessees – Finance Leases

An entity should disclose for each class of asset the net carrying amount of finance leases (IAS 17, 23(a)).

An entity should present a reconciliation between the total of minimum lease payments at the balance sheet date and their present value (IAS 17, 23(b)).

An entity should disclose the total of the minimum lease payments at the balance sheet date and their present value for each of the following periods:

- not later than one year;
- not later than one year and not later than five years; and
- later than five years.

(IAS 17, 23(b))

An entity should disclose:

- contingent rents recognised as expenses for the period (IAS 17, 23(c)) – this is a new requirement;
- the total of future minimum sublease payments expected to be received under non-cancellable sub-leases at the balance sheet date (IAS 17, 23(d));
- a general description of the lessee's significant leasing arrangements including the basis on which contingent rent payments are determined, the existence and terms of renewal or purchase options and escalation charges, and restrictions imposed by lease agreements (IAS 17, 23(e)).

Extract 32.19 *Leased assets*

SAS, Sweden, 31 December 2000 (IAS)

Of previous years' aircraft acquisitions, 16 Douglas MD-80s, 1 Boeing 767, 6 Douglas MD-90s and 1 Fokker F28 were acquired, formally via finance lease contracts, with terms of 10–17 years.

On behalf of SAS, a number of banks have agreed to pay all accruing leasing fees and an agreed residual value for 3 of the Douglas MD-80s and 1 Fokker F28 aircraft at the expiry of each leasing period. SAS has irrevocably reimbursed the banks in an amount corresponding to full settlement for these payments. The total nominal value of the banks' payment commitment on behalf of SAS on 31 December 2000, was MSEK 322 (607).

With regard to other leased aircraft, the terms of the leasing contracts (particularly pertaining to SAS's call options during the contract period and at the expiry of the leasing contract, as well as the economic risk SAS has regarding the value of the aircraft) are such that the agreements, from SAS's point of view, are comparable to a purchase.

The 24 (28) finance leased aircraft are reported in the balance sheet in the amount of MSEK 2,713 (3,089).

SAS's aircraft holding can be specified as follows:

	2000	*1999*
Owned	**11,546**	7,702
Finance leased (prepaid)	**166**	262
Other finance leased	**2,547**	2,827
Book value	**14,259**	10,791

Extract 32.20 *Finance lease obligations*

Stora Enso, Finland, 31 December 2001 (IAS)

Stora Enso has a number of finance leasing agreements for machinery and equipment maturing between 2008 and 2015 for which capital costs of EUR 818.7 (EUR 853.3) million are included in machinery and equipment; the depreciation thereon was EUR 66.7 (EUR 28.3) million. The aggregate leasing payments amounted to EUR 80.2 (EUR 54.0) million, the interest element being EUR 44.1 (EUR 14.4) million.

Leasing liabilities

	As at 31 December	
EUR million	*2000*	*2001*
Minimum lease payments		
Less than 1 year	78.5	87.2
1–5 years	344.3	325.8
Over 5 years	1,061.4	1,082.6
	1,484.2	1,495.6
Future finance charges	−703.2	−712.8
Present Value of Finance Lease Liabilities	**781.0**	**782.8**
Representing the Value of Finance Lease Liabilities		
Less than 1 year	75.0	83.3
1–5 years	265.6	243.7
Over 5 years	440.4	455.8
	781.0	**782.8**

32.12.2 Lessees – Operating Leases

In addition to the requirements of IAS 32, a lessee should disclose:

- the total of future minimum lease payments under non-cancellable operating leases for each of the following periods:
  - not later than one year;
  - later than one year and not later than five years;
  - later than five years;
- the total of future minimum sublease payments expected to be received under non-cancellable subleases at the balance sheet date;
- lease and sublease payments recognised in income for the period, with separate amounts for minimum lease payments, contingent rents, and sublease payments;
- a general description of the lessee's significant leasing arrangements including, but not limited to, the following:
  - the basis on which contingent rent payments are determined;
  - the existence and terms of renewal or purchase options and escalation clauses; and
  - restrictions imposed by lease arrangements, such as those concerning dividends, additional debt, and further leasing.

Extract 32.21 *Operating leasing commitments*

adidas-Salomon, Germany, 31 December 2001 (IAS)

The company leases offices, warehouses and equipment under leases expiring between one and ten years. Rent expenses aggregated €108 million and €99 million for the years ended 31 December 2001 and 2000, respectively.

Future minimum lease payments under non-cancellable operating leases are as follows:

(euros in millions)	*Dec 31 2001*	*Dec 31 2000*
Within 1 year	**52**	60
Between 1 and 5 years	**97**	101
After 5 years	**23**	21
Total	**172**	182

32.12.3 Lessors – Finance Leases

In addition to the requirements in IAS 32, a lessor should disclose:

- a reconciliation between the total gross investment in the lease at the balance sheet date, and the present value of minimum lease payments receivable at the balance sheet date. In addition, an entity should disclose the total gross investment in the lease and the present

value of minimum lease payments receivable at the balance sheet date, for each of the following periods:
  - not later than one year;
  - later than one year and not later than five years;
  - later than five years;
- unearned finance income;
- the unguaranteed residual values accruing to the benefit of the lessor;
- the accumulated allowance for uncollectable minimum lease payments receivable;
- contingent rents recognised in income; and
- a general description of the lessor's significant leasing arrangements.

Extract 32.22 *Leasing receivables*

Renault, France, 31 December 2000 (IAS)

	1998		*1999*		*2000*	
	€ million	*FRF million*	*€ million*	*FRF million*	*€ million*	*FRF million*
Financing for dealers	**2,619**	17,181	**3,025**	19,842	**3,129**	20,522
Financing for end-users	**5,498**	36,060	**8,752**	57,411	**8,859**	58,111
Leasing and similar operations	**3,200**	20,992	**3,847**	25,235	**4,067**	26,680
Gross value	**11,317**	**74,233**	**15,624**	**102,488**	**16,055**	**105,313**
Provisions	**(419)**	(2,750)	**(514)**	(3,372)	**(542)**	(3,552)
Net value	**10,898**	**71,483**	**15,110**	**99,116**	**15,513**	**101,761**

1999 sales financing receivables reflect the impact of the full consolidation of Nissan's European finance subsidiaries, amounting to €2,409 million (FRF 15,801 million) (note 2-D-b).

The breakdown of sales financing receivables by geographic area is as follows:

	1998		*1999*		*2000*	
	€ million	*FRF million*	*€ million*	*FRF million*	*€ million*	*FRF million*
France	**3,446**	22,603	**4,246**	27,852	**4,440**	29,128
Other European countries	**7,452**	48,880	**10,864**	71,264	**11,073**	72,633
TOTAL	**10,898**	**71,483**	**15,110**	**99,116**	**15,513**	**101,761**

These receivables mature as follows:

	1998		*1999*		*2000*	
	€ million	*FRF million*	*€ million*	*FRF million*	*€ million*	*FRF million*
Within one year	**5,823**	38,194	**7,365**	48,308	**7,823**	51,317
Between one and five years	**5,056**	33,165	**7,691**	50,449	**7,625**	50,016
Over five years	**19**	124	**54**	359	**65**	428
TOTAL	**10,898**	**71,483**	**15,110**	**99,116**	**15,513**	**101,761**

32.12.4 Lessors – Operating Leases

In addition to the requirements of IAS 32, a lessor should disclose:

- for each class of asset, the gross carrying amount, the accumulated depreciation and accumulated impairment losses at the balance sheet date:
  - the depreciation recognised in income for the period;
  - impairment losses recognised in income for the period;
  - impairment losses reversed in income for the period;
- the future minimum lease payments under non-cancellable operating leases in the aggregate and for each of the following periods:
  - not later than one year;
  - later than one year and not later than five years;
  - later than five years;
- total contingent rents recognised in income; and
- a general description of the lessor's significant leasing arrangements.

Extract 32.23 *Operating lease*

BMW, Germany, 31 December 2001 (IAS)

The BMW Group, as lessor, leases out assets (predominantly own products) as part of sales financing. Minimum lease payments of euro 3,736 million (2000: euro 3,437 million) from non-cancellable operating leases fall due as follows:

in euro million	*31.12.2001*
within one year	2,076
between one and five years	1,640
later than five years	20
	3,736

Contingent rents of euro 15 million (2000: euro 8 million), based principally on the distance driven, were recognised in income.

Changes in the estimated residual values of leased products had an impact on the result in the year of euro 65 million (2000: euro 269 million).

Changes in leased products during the year are shown in the analysis of changes in Group non-current assets on pages 48 and 49.

Notes

1 Accounting Advisory Forum, *Accounting for Lease Contracts*, European Commission, Brussels, 1995.

2 Warren McGregor (principal author), *Accounting for Leases: A New Approach*, FASB, 1996 (G4+1 publications are available from all members of the group – see appendix 4).

CHAPTER 33

Employee Benefit Costs

33.1 RELEVANT STANDARD

IAS 19 *Employee Benefits*

33.2 HISTORY

IAS 19 *Accounting for Retirement Benefit Costs* (IAS 19 [1983]) was approved in 1982 and published in 1983. Actuaries provided advice throughout the project. IAS 19 [1983] required that retirement benefit costs should be recognised as expenses when employee service was rendered. However, it allowed a choice between the accrued benefit valuation method and the projected benefit valuation method when determining the cost of defined benefit plans. It also allowed flexibility in the choice of actuarial assumptions and on the treatment of actuarial gains and losses.

In 1985, the IASC set up a joint working party of the standard setting bodies in Canada, the United Kingdom and the USA, under a Dutch chairman from the IASC board, to examine ways of mitigating conflicts between national standards on pension costs and to consider the scope for further harmonisation in the longer term (*IASC News*, November 1985, p3). The working party reported back to the IASC early in 1986. While it had been unable to resolve the conflict between the new standards issued, or under consideration, in the three countries, the IASC recognised that the working party had provided a helpful opportunity to exchange views among the bodies concerned.

IAS 19 [1983] was reconsidered in the comparability and improvements project. The principal changes related to the choice of actuarial valuation method, the treatment of past service costs, experience adjustments and the effects of changes in actuarial assumptions, and the incorporation of assumptions about future salaries in actuarial valuations.

The IASC decided to limit changes made to IAS 19 in the improvements project to the three changes required by the *Statement of Intent on the Comparability of Financial Statements*, the new format of IASs and additional guidance that was necessary to implement the statement of intent changes (E47, p3). This limit was a practical expedient made in order to complete the package of ten revised IASs by the end of 1993. However, the IASC recognised that it may have to carry out a more comprehensive review of IAS 19 in the foreseeable future (E47, p3). IAS 19 *Retirement Benefit Costs* (IAS 19 [1993]) was approved in November 1993 and applied to financial statements for accounting periods beginning on or after 1 January 1995.

Within a year, and before IAS 19 [1993] came into effect, the IASC approved a proposal for a new project on retirement benefit and other employee benefit costs (*IASC Insight*, December 1994, p2). The IASC's principal concerns at that time were that IAS 19 [1993]:

- concentrated on the income statement and gave little guidance on the balance sheet treatment of retirement benefit costs;
- generated balance sheet items which may not meet the definitions of assets and liabilities in the framework;
- may not have dealt adequately with specific types of retirement benefit plans, particularly termination indemnity plans and multi-employer hybrid plans; and
- gave only limited guidance on employment benefits other than retirement benefits.

(*IASC Insight*, December 1994, p16)

In August 1995, the IASC published a staff issues paper, *Retirement Benefit and Other Employee Benefit Costs*, which identified 20 basic issues and a further 99 sub-issues for consideration. The project was 'affected more than most' by the IASC's April 1996 decision to accelerate the completion of the core standards (*IASC Insight*, June 1996, p11). The IASC decided not to issue a DSOP and proceeded immediately to an exposure draft. The comment period on the exposure draft, which was the only opportunity for the IASC's constituency to comment on the IASC's proposals, was cut to three months. IAS 19 *Employee Benefits* was approved in January 1998 and applied to accounting periods beginning on or after 1 January 1999. It further reduced the choice of actuarial valuation methods and provided more extensive standards and guidance on employee benefits generally.

The IASC believed that the revised IAS 19 was a significant improvement over IAS 19 [1993] which was true given the limited changes made in the improvements project and the concerns expressed at the time by the IASC. The IASC indicated that even further improvement may be possible in due course. In particular, several IASC board members believed that it would be preferable to recognise all actuarial gains and losses immediately in a statement of financial performance (*IASC Insight*, January 1997, p2). This is the broadly the same view which was expressed during the comparability and improvements project and which the new project was intended to resolve.

IAS 19 was amended in 2000 to deal with the definition of scheme assets when an entity retains a legal or constructive obligation to pay benefits directly but is entitled to receive reimbursement from the plan. The resulting changes applied to accounting periods beginning on or after 1 January 2001 (see 33.13.1).

In May 2002, the IASB amended IAS 19 to deal with the interaction of the deferred recognition of actuarial gains and losses and the asset ceiling test. The revision takes effect for accounting periods ending on or after 31 May 2002 (see 33.9.3).

The IASB is developing a proposed IFRS on share based payments and expects to publish an exposure draft in 2002. IAS 19 deals only with disclosure issues. The proposed IFRS will deal with recognition and measurement issues.

The IASB has identified employee benefits as one of the convergence topics on which it believes that a high quality solution is available from existing international and national standards. The IASB's intention in starting such a project is to make changes to IAS 19, in particular to limit, if not prohibit, the deferral and amortisation of actuarial gains and losses.

33.3 IOSCO

In June 1994, IOSCO indicated its support for further revisions to IAS 19. It also said that the benchmark actuarial valuation method in IAS 19 [1993] was acceptable but that some of its members would permit the use of the allowed alternative actuarial valuation method only when the entity disclosed information based on the use of the benchmark method.

The call for this additional information surprised and disappointed the IASC on two counts. First, the IASC had rejected such a disclosure requirement following its consideration of the comments on E32 because the cost that would be involved in undertaking a second actuarial valuation may be substantial and may not be justified (*Statement of Intent on the Comparability of Financial Statements,* appendix 1). IOSCO had not dissented from this approach either at the time or subsequently during the improvements project. Second, in its June 1994 comments, IOSCO had called for the removal of similar reconciliation requirements when the allowed alternatives in IAS 2 and IAS 8 were used. It was unclear to the IASC why IOSCO supported a reconciliation on IAS 19 (the one allowed alternative for which the IASC opposed such a reconciliation) but not IAS 2 and IAS 8 (where the IASC favoured reconciliations) (*IASC Insight*, December 1994, p12).

IOSCO indicated that other required treatments, implementation guidance and disclosures in IAS 19 [1993] were generally acceptable. It believed that the following were the most significant areas requiring consideration in the further review of IAS 19:

- definitive guidance on the selection of assumptions used in actuarial valuations (this has been dealt with in the revised IAS 19);
- the recognition on the balance sheet of a minimum liability (this has been rejected – see IAS 19, appendix 3, 63 to 65);
- disclosures about entity and affiliate securities held by any retirement benefit fund and other transactions between such parties (the revised IAS 19 requires disclosure of the entity's securities held by the fund but not those of its affiliates); and
- the possibility of an exemption from the requirements of IAS 19 for welfare pension plans in Japan and the acceptance of the treatment for such plans currently adopted in Japan (this was considered and rejected by the IASC during the development of IAS 19 [1993] and has been further considered and rejected in the revised IAS 19).

While the IASC agreed with the need to address the first three of these areas, it expressed a general concern about IOSCO's proposal to allow exemptions from the requirements of IASs for certain countries.

IAS 19 is included in 'IAS 2000' endorsed by IOSCO in May 2000. There are six supplemental treatments:

- the need for the recognition of a minimum liability given the introduction of a transitional provision (the IASC rejected a general requirement for the recognition of a minimum liability);
- the need for disclosures of entity and affiliate securities held by pension funds and other transactions between such parties;
- concerns that the definition of a defined benefit plan may permit an opportunity for inappropriate accounting if the terms of a plan provide a defined level of benefit but the sponsoring entity's current obligation is limited to the amount of the legally required funding – defined benefit accounting should be applied whenever the terms of the plan provide a defined level of benefit (this is required by IAS 19);
- concerns about the appropriateness of a corridor approach under the recognition of actuarial gains and losses would not be permitted (IAS 19 allows, but does not require, the use of the corridor approach);

- concerns about the appropriateness of not recognising a liability in a balance sheet for employee termination costs in cases when a board decision is taken before the balance sheet date and the decision is confirmed before the issuance of the financial statements (the approach in IAS 19 is consistent with that taken in IAS 37 on provisions – IOSCO raised a similar concern with respect to IAS 37); and
- the need for enhanced disclosures relating to equity compensation plans (this is being dealt with in the IASB's share based payments project).

33.4 IAS 19 IN BRIEF

Employee benefit costs should be recognised as an expense as service is rendered by the relevant employees, irrespective of when the benefits are paid or when contributions are made to any separate fund. A distinction should be drawn between defined contribution and defined benefit post-employment retirement benefit plans.

The associated liabilities and expenses should be measured by reference to market prices and the liabilities should be discounted when they are due for settlement more than a year after the end of the period in which the services are rendered. The projected unit credit method should be used to determine the liability, current service cost and past service cost of defined benefit post-employment retirement benefit plans. In certain circumstances, actuarial gains and losses, past service costs and transition adjustments may be spread over a number of years.

Extract 33.1 *Accounting policy for employee benefits*

Roche, Switzerland, 31 December 2001 (IAS)

Wages, salaries, social security contributions, paid annual leave and sick leave, bonuses, and non-monetary benefits are accrued in the year in which the associated services are rendered by employees of the Group. Where the Group provides long-term employee benefits, the cost is accrued to match the rendering of the services by the employees concerned.

The Group operates a number of defined benefit and defined contribution plans throughout the world. The cost for the year for defined benefit plans is determined using the projected unit credit method. This reflects service rendered by employees to the dates of valuation and incorporates actuarial assumptions primarily regarding discount rates used in determining the present value of benefits, projected rates of remuneration growth, and long-term expected rates of return for plan assets. Discount rates are based on the market yields of high-quality corporate bonds in the country concerned.

Differences between assumptions and actual experiences, and effects of changes in actuarial assumptions are allocated over the estimated average remaining working lives of employees, where these differences exceed a defined corridor. Past service costs are allocated over the average period until the benefits become vested. Pension assets and liabilities in different defined benefit schemes are not offset unless the Group has a legally enforceable right to use the surplus in one plan to settle obligations in the other plan. Pension assets are only recognised to the extent that the Group is able to derive future economic benefits in the way of refunds from the plan or reductions of future contributions.

The Group's contributions to the defined contribution plans are charged to the income statement in the year to which they relate.

33.5 EMPLOYEE BENEFITS

Employee benefits are all forms of consideration given by an entity in exchange for service rendered by employees (IAS 19, 7). IAS 19 deals with five categories of employee benefits:

- short term benefits such as wages, annual leave and bonuses;
- post-employment benefits such as pensions and post-employment insurance and healthcare;
- other long-term benefits including long-service leave and long-term disability benefits;
- termination benefits; and
- equity compensation benefits.

IAS 19 applies to all such employee benefits, including those provided:

- under formal plans or other formal agreements between an entity and individual employees, groups of employees or their representatives and which give rise to a legal obligation;
- under legislative requirements, or through industry arrangements, whereby entities are required to contribute to national, state, industry or other multi-employer plans and which give rise to a legal obligation; and
- by those informal practices that give rise to a constructive obligation, such that the entity has no realistic alternative but to pay employee benefits.

Employee benefits may be vested or non-vested. *Vested employee benefits* are benefits which are not conditional on future employment (IAS 19, 7). For example, an employee is usually entitled to annual leave or the value of a defined contribution retirement benefit plan as service is rendered and, therefore, the benefit is said to be vested. If, however, the entitlement cannot be claimed until after a minimum period of service, the benefit is non-vested during that minimum period. For example, an employer may make contributions to a defined contribution retirement benefit plan on the basis that the employee is entitled to receive the value of the fund only after two years' employment. During the initial two years, the benefits are non-vested.

Employee benefits may be provided to the employees themselves or to their dependants. They may be settled by payments (or the provision of other assets or services) made directly to the employees, to their spouses, children or other dependants or to others. They may also be settled by payments to funds or insurance companies which take on the obligation to pay the benefits.

33.6 SHORT-TERM EMPLOYEE BENEFITS

33.6.1 Definition

Short-term employee benefits are benefits (other than termination benefits and equity compensation benefits) which fall due wholly within twelve months after the end of the period in which the employees render the related service (IAS 19, 7). Short-term employee benefits include items such as:

- wages, salaries and social security contributions;
- short-term compensated absences (such as paid annual leave and paid sick leave);
- profit sharing and bonuses; and
- non-monetary benefits such as medical care or insurance, housing, cars, free or subsidised goods or services.

33.6.2 Recognition and Measurement

An entity should recognise the undiscounted amount of short-term employee benefits expected to be paid in exchange for service in an accounting period in that period (IAS 19, 10). It should recognise:

- as a liability any amount unpaid at the balance sheet date;
- as an asset any excess at the balance sheet date of the amount paid over the undiscounted amount of the benefits (insofar as that excess is recoverable); and

- as an expense the amount of the benefits for the period.

(IAS 19, 10)

The recognition and measurement of short-term employee benefits generally does not give rise to major accounting issues. However, IAS 19 deals with two issues – compensated absences, and profit sharing and bonuses – on which problems may arise.

33.6.3 Compensated Absences

Compensated absences include paid annual leave and paid sick leave. The accounting issue which causes problems is whether or not the entity should recognise the costs of these benefits as they accrue or only when the absences arise.

Compensated absences may be either 'accumulating' or 'non-accumulating'. Accumulating compensated absences are those which can be used in future periods if the current period's entitlement is not used in full (IAS 19, 13). Non-accumulating compensated absences lapse if they are not used (IAS 19, 16). The distinction between accumulating and non-accumulating absences is important in determining whether or not the entity has a liability.

Compensated absences may also be either 'vested' or 'non-vested' (IAS 19, 13). If the benefits are vested, an employee is entitled to a cash payment for any unused entitlement on leaving the entity (or possibly earlier). If the benefits are non-vested, an employee is not entitled to a cash payment for unused entitlement. Accumulating compensated absences may be vested or non-vested. Non-accumulating absences are usually non-vested. The distinction between vested and non-vested benefits does not affect whether or not the entity has a liability but it does affect the measurement of any liability.

The expected cost of accumulating compensated absences should be recognised as an expense when the employee renders the service that increases the entitlement to future compensated absences (IAS 19, 11 (a)). The expected cost should be measured as the additional amount which the entity expects to pay as a result of the unused entitlement that has accumulated at the balance sheet date (IAS 19, 14). If the absences are vested, the obligation is met either through granting leave to the employee in a subsequent period or by making a payment to the employee. If the absences are non-vested, the measurement of the obligation must take into account the possibility that an employee may cease their employment with the entity before the leave is taken.

An entity should recognise a liability and an expense for non-accumulating absences only when the absence occurs (IAS 19, 11(b)).

Example 33.1 *Accumulating compensated absences*

An entity has 1,000 employees who are each entitled to 25 working days of holiday for each year. Unused holiday may be carried forward for one calendar year. Holiday in any year is taken first out of any balance brought forward from the previous year and then out of the current year's entitlement. At 31 December 2001, the average unused entitlement is seven days per employee. The entity expects, based on past experience which is likely to continue, that 90% of employees will take all their outstanding holidays in 2002 and that the remaining 10% will take an average of three days each. The entity recognises a liability equal to the expected cost of paying employees for (90% × 1,000 × 7) + (10% × 1,000 × 3) days, that is 6,600 days.

Example 33.2 *Non-accumulating compensated absences*

An entity has 1,000 employees who are each entitled to 25 working days of holiday for each year. Unused holiday may not be carried forward at the end of the calendar year and employees are not entitled to a cash payment for any unused entitlement on ceasing their employment.

At 31 December 2001, the average unused entitlement is seven days per employee. No liability or expense is recognised as the entity has no legal or constructive obligation to allow the leave to be taken in 2002 or later or to make related cash payments to the employees on leaving.

33.6.4 Profit Sharing and Bonuses

The accounting issue which causes problems with profit sharing and bonuses is whether or not they should be recognised as a liability and expense in the period in which the related profits are recognised or only when they are declared, announced or paid. The issue may be further complicated by the fact that some bonuses are not determined until the financial statements are finalised and some may require the approval of the same governing body which approves the financial statements.

The expected cost of profit sharing and bonus payments should be recognised as a liability and an expense (not as an appropriation of the net profit) when:

- the entity has a present legal or constructive obligation to make such payments as a result of past events; and
- a reliable estimate of the obligation can be made.

(IAS 19, 17)

A present obligation exists when the entity has no realistic alternative but to make the payments (IAS 19, 17). A constructive obligation arises when the entity's past practices, published policies or a specific current statement creates a valid expectation that a payment will be made. For example, an entity may have a practice of paying bonuses based on the year's profits. In such cases, the entity has a constructive obligation and any liability for the bonuses is recognised.

Example 33.3 *Profit sharing plans*

A profit sharing plan requires an entity to pay a specified proportion of its net profit for the year to employees who serve throughout the year. If no employees leave during the year, the total profit sharing payments for the year will be 3% of net profit. The entity estimates that staff turnover will reduce the payments to 2.5% of net profit. Therefore, the entity recognises a liability and an expense of 2.5% of net profit.

An entity can usually make a reliable estimate of its legal or constructive obligation under a profit sharing or bonus plan. For example, the estimate may be based on:

- a formula in the bonus plan;
- a decision about the amount of the profit sharing or bonus prior to the authorisation of the financial statements; or
- past practice which gives clear evidence of the amount of the constructive obligation.

The measurement of the constructive obligation reflects the possibility that some employees may lose their entitlement to the bonus, for example by leaving the employment of the entity or giving notice to leave the employment.

33.7 POST-EMPLOYMENT BENEFIT PLANS

33.7.1 Post-Employment Benefits

Post-employment benefit plans are formal or informal arrangements under which an entity provides post-employment benefits for one or more employees (IAS 19, 7). *Post-employment benefits* are employee benefits (other than termination benefits and equity compensation benefits) which are payable after the completion of employment (IAS 19, 7). Post-employment benefits can take many different forms; they include:

- certain benefits paid on or after leaving the employment of the entity irrespective of whether the employee retires from all employment or is later employed by another employer (IAS 19, 136);
- retirement benefits such as annual, monthly or weekly pensions and lump sums paid on or after employment with the entity ceases;
- post-employment life insurance; and
- post-employment medical care.

(IAS 19, 24)

Post-employment benefit plans may take several different forms which, for the purposes of IAS 19, are classified as either defined contribution plans or defined benefit plans. Post-employment benefit plans may be funded or unfunded.

The variety of different forms of post-employment plans is clearly demonstrated in table 33.1 which is derived from a FEE study of pensions and other retirement benefits in Europe. That study was prepared in the context of the variety of accounting permitted by the EU Fourth Directive. The important message in the context of all versions of IAS 19 is that the cost of providing benefits is recognised as an expense in the period in which the employee renders the service which earns those benefits and not in the period in which those benefits are paid or payable.

33.7.2 Defined Contribution Plans

A *defined contribution plan* is a post-employment benefit plan under which an entity pays fixed contributions into a separate entity (a fund) and will have no legal or constructive obligation to pay further contributions if the fund does not hold sufficient assets to pay all employee benefits relating to employee service in the current and prior periods (IAS 19, 7). Such plans are invariably funded (see below) and the fund may be held by such entities as pension or superannuation funds, a provident fund, an insurance entity or an investment company (the form of entity is often determined by local laws or regulations). The amount of the fund

Table 33.1 *Occupational retirement benefit schemes*

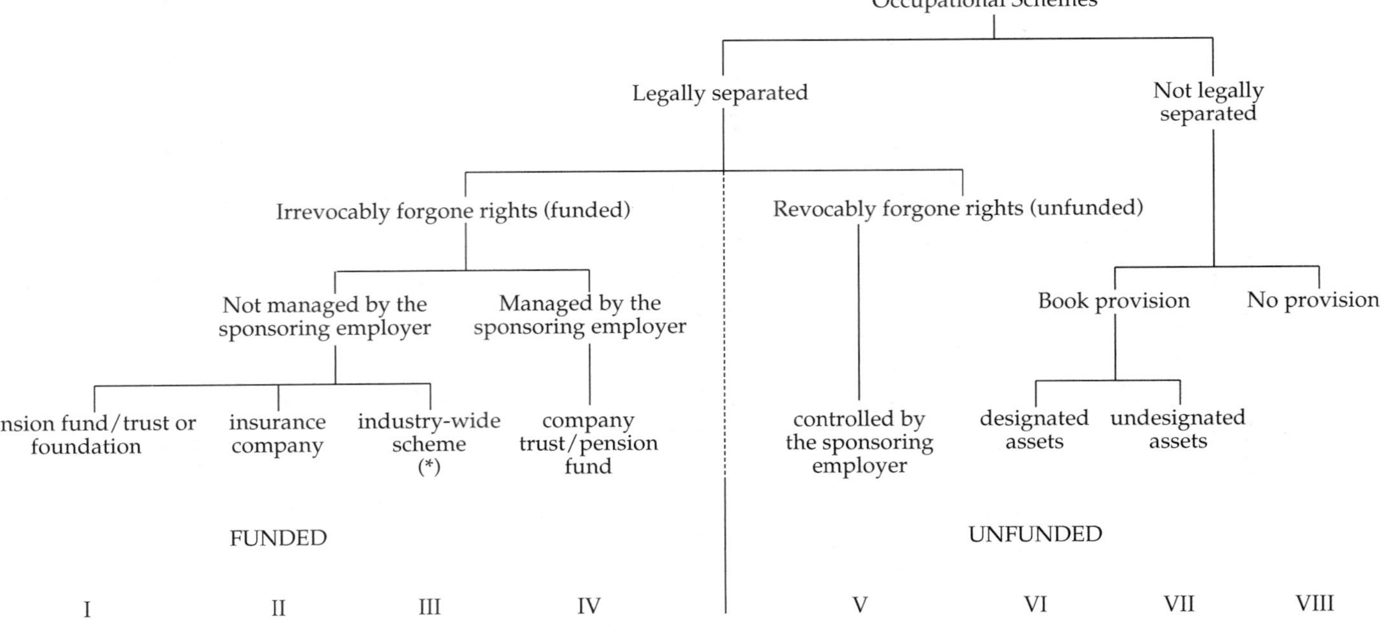

(*) An industry-wide scheme (case III) is a pension scheme not a funding system and can in theory only be set up through a funded system (I–IV). In certain countries industry-wide agreements can be set up as a book provision (system VI–VIII)

FEE, *Survey of Pensions and Other Retirement Benefits in EU and Non-EU Countries*, Routledge, London, 1995 attributable to each employee is usually separately identifiable and there may even be separate funds or accounts for each employee who is a member of such a plan.

Under a defined contribution plan:

- the entity's legal or constructive obligation is limited to the amount which it agrees to contribute to the fund; and
- actuarial risk (the risk that benefits will be less than expected) and investment risk (the risk that assets invested will be insufficient to meet expected benefits) are borne by the employee.

(IAS 19, 25)

The amount contributed is usually fixed by reference to a formula in the plan but the amount usually varies from period to period or employee to employee. For example, an entity may agree to contribute 10% of each employee's annual salary to a defined contribution plan. The contribution is a fixed percentage of salaries but the amount for each employee varies with the level of, and changes in, salaries.

33.7.3 Defined Benefit Plans

A *defined benefit plan* is a post-employment benefit plan other than a defined contribution plan (IAS 19, 7). Under a defined benefit plan:

- the entity's obligation is to provide the agreed benefits to current and former employees; and
- actuarial risk (that benefits will cost more than expected) and investment risk is borne by the entity as the employer.

(IAS 19, 27)

For example, under a defined benefit plan, a retired employee with 40 years' service may be entitled to a pension of two-thirds final salary; alternatively, an employee may be entitled on leaving to a severance payment equivalent to one month's salary for each year's service. Under such plans, the entity is obliged either to pay the specified level of retirement benefits to the employee or to make sufficient contributions to a fund so that the fund can pay the specified level of benefits to the employee. If the fund has not accumulated a sufficient amount with which to pay the benefits, the entity is obliged to make good the deficit by means of either a lump sum or increased periodic contributions.

Defined benefit plans may be funded or unfunded (see below). In some countries the plans must be funded, whereas in other countries an entity may be allowed to choose between funded and unfunded plans. Any fund may be held by such entities as pension or superannuation funds, a provident fund, an insurance entity or an investment company (the form of entity is often determined by local laws or regulations). In some cases, the fund is represented by designated assets of the entity (see table 33.1); such assets, other than qualifying insurance policies (see 33.13.1), are not plan assets for the purposes of IAS 19.

33.7.4 Multi-Employer Plans

Retirement benefit plans may take many different forms, the simplest of which is a single employer plan in which the entity provides retirement benefits for its employees only. However, many entities are members of multi-employer plans. *Multi-employer plans* are retirement benefit plans (other than state plans) that:

- pool the assets contributed by various entities that are not under common control; and
- use those assets to provide benefits to employees of more than one entity, on the basis that contribution and benefit levels are determined without regard to the identity of the entity that employs the employees concerned.

(IAS 19, 7)

Multi-employer plans do not include:

- group administration plans in which different entities pool their assets for investment purposes and to reduce management and administration costs, but the claims of different entities are segregated; and
- plans that pool the assets contributed by various entities under common control, for example a parent and its subsidiaries.

(IAS 19, 33 and 34)

In each of the above cases, an entity should account for its own plan separately as a defined contribution plan or a defined benefit plan as appropriate.

A multi-employer plan may be a defined contribution plan or a defined benefit plan. The entity must base its decision on the terms of the plan including any constructive obligation that goes beyond the formal terms.

When a multi-employer plan is a defined benefit plan, an entity should account for its proportionate share of the defined benefit obligation, plan assets and costs associated with the plan in the same way as for any other defined benefit plan and make the disclosures required by IAS 19. However, when insufficient information is available to do this, the entity should account for the plan as if it were a defined contribution plan. It should also disclose:

- the fact that the plan is a defined benefit plan;
- the reason why sufficient information is not available to account for the plan as a defined benefit plan; and
- to the extent that a surplus or deficit in the plan may affect the amount of future contributions, any available information about that surplus or deficit, the basis used to determine that surplus or deficit and the implications, if any, for the entity.

(IAS 19, 29 and 30)

Extract 33.2 *Multi-employer plan*

Roche, Switzerland, 31 December 2001 (IAS)

The Group's Japanese subsidiaries participate in the Tokyo Pharmaceutical Welfare Fund, a multi-employer plan which by its nature is a defined benefit plan. This is accounted for as a defined contribution plan in these financial statements as the Group does not have access to sufficient information about the plan to account for it as a defined benefit plan. Contributions in 2001 were 6 million Swiss francs (2000: 6 million Swiss francs).

33.7.5 State Plans

Many countries have state retirement benefit plans which are usually operated by a government or agency which is not subject to control or influence by the reporting entity. The entity decides, based on the terms of the plan, whether it is a defined contribution plan or a defined benefit plan. Most state plans are defined contribution plans as the only obligation of the entity is to pay the contributions as they fall due; there is no legal or constructive obligation to pay for future benefits.

An entity may provide post-employment benefits which substitute for benefits under a state scheme. These plans are not state plans. They are often defined benefit plans as the employer is obliged to provide benefits of a specific minimum level in order to substitute for the state benefits (IAS 19, 36 to 38).

Extract 33.3 *State plan as defined contribution plan*

China Petroleum & Chemical Corporation, People's Republic of China, 31 December 2001 (IAS)

As stipulated by the regulations of the PRC, the Group participates in various defined contribution retirement plans organised by municipal and provincial governments for its staff. The Group is required to make contributions to the retirement plans at rates ranging from 16.0% to 30.0% of the salaries, bonuses and certain allowances of its staff. A member of the plan is entitled to a pension equal to a fixed proportion of the salary prevailing at his retirement date. The Group has no other material obligation for the payment of pension benefits associated with these plans beyond the annual contributions described above. The Group's contributions for the year ended 31 December 2001 were RMB 1,358 million (2000: RMB 1,387 million).

33.7.6 Insured Plans

An entity may pay insurance premiums to fund a post-employment benefit plan. The payments as such do not determine whether the plan is a defined contribution plan or a defined benefit plan. It is necessary to look at the substance of the arrangement.

Such a plan is a defined benefit plan if the entity retains, directly or indirectly, a legal or constructive obligation to:

- pay the employee benefits directly when they fall due; or
- pay further amounts if the insurer does not pay all future employee benefits relating to employee service in the current and prior periods.

(IAS 19, 39)

In all other cases, an insured plan is a defined contribution plan. This includes plans in which the insurance policy is in the name of a plan participant (or a group of plan participants) and the entity does not have a legal or constructive obligation to cover any loss on the policy or pay benefits to the employees (IAS 19, 42).

33.7.7 Funded and Unfunded Plans

Post-employment benefit plans may be funded or unfunded. Funding is the transfer of contributions by an entity and, sometimes, its employees into an entity or fund which is legally separate from the entity and from which employee benefits are paid (IAS 19, 49). Such funds may be administered by third parties (administrators or trustees), an investment company, an insurance company or a similar entity which has discretion as to the investment of the contributions and the payment of benefits.

A defined contribution plan is, by definition, a funded plan. Many defined benefit plans are funded plans, indeed in some countries the law requires these plans to be funded. In such cases the entity makes contributions to the fund but retains the ultimate obligation to provide the specified level of retirement benefits. The entity must make good any shortfall in the fund either by means of a lump sum payment or increased contributions in future periods. The entity may also be entitled to receive any surplus in the fund by means of a refund or reduced contributions in future periods; however, the law may restrict the amount, or availability, of such refunds or reduced contributions.

In the case of a funded defined benefit plan, the amount recognised on the balance sheet is often small and may even be an asset rather than a liability. It reflects differences between funding and expense recognition and the consequences of accounting for such items as actuarial gains and losses. The payment of funded benefits when they fall due depends on the financial position and the investment performance of the fund and the entity's ability (and willingness) to make good any shortfall in the fund's assets.

In the case of an unfunded defined benefit plan, the amount recognised on the balance sheet is often substantial and may be a major source of financing for the entity. In an unfunded plan, the entity does not make contributions to a separate fund. Instead, the entity provides the specified level of benefits out of its own assets (referred to as a 'book provision' in table 33.1). The payment of unfunded benefits when they fall due depends on the financial position of the entity.

It is important to appreciate the distinction between funding and current service cost. This is particularly the case with defined benefit plans; it is less of a problem with defined contribution plans although it is still necessary to recognise the contributions as an expense of the appropriate period. Funding may be influenced by the availability of cash, tax considerations and similar factors and it may bear no resemblance to the costs associated with services rendered by the employees in the period. Therefore, the entity's contributions to a fund in a period are not necessarily the same as the current service cost which should be recognised as an expense in that period. In particular, when an entity is able to take what is sometimes described as a contribution (funding) holiday, that is make no contributions to the fund for one or more years, there is still a current service cost which must be recognised as an expense in the income statement.

Extract 33.4 *Funding of retirement benefit costs*

General Electric Company, United States of America, 31 December 2001

Funding policy for the GE pension plan is to contribute amounts sufficient to meet minimum funding requirements as set forth in employee benefit and tax laws plus such additional amounts as GE may determine to be appropriate. GE has not made contributions to the GE Pension Plan since 1987 because the fully funded status of the Plan precludes a current tax deduction and because any GE contribution would require payment of excise taxes.

Extract 33.5 *Funding of retirement benefit costs*

Roche, Switzerland, 31 December 2001 (IAS)

[Retirement] Plans are usually funded by payments from the Group and by employees to trusts independent of the Group's finances. Where a plan is unfunded, a liability for the whole obligation is recorded in the Group's balance sheet.

33.8 ACCOUNTING FOR DEFINED CONTRIBUTION PLANS

33.8.1 Recognition and Measurement

Accounting for defined contribution plans is usually very simple. When an employee has rendered service during a period, the entity should recognise the contribution payable in exchange for that service as an expense in that period; any amount unpaid at the end of the period is recognised as a liability (IAS 19, 44). Any contributions which do not fall due for payment wholly within twelve months after the end of the period should be discounted using the discount rate specified for defined benefit plans, see 33.10.3 (IAS 19, 45). If the contribution already paid exceeds the contribution due for service before the balance sheet date, the entity should recognise that excess as an asset (prepaid expense) to the extent that the prepayment is recoverable.

IAS 19 [1993] allowed for the possibility that additional contributions may be made in a period in return for service to be rendered in future periods. Such contributions were recognised as an expense systematically over the expected remaining working lives of those employees (IAS 19 [1993], 20). The IASC now believes that this issue is not relevant in a defined contribution plan (IAS 19, appendix C, 6).

Example 33.4 *Contributions to a defined contribution plan*

An entity agrees to make contributions each year of 8% of total salaries to a defined contribution post-employment benefit plan. The employees also make contributions of 3% of total salaries; these contributions are deducted from salaries and paid over to the fund.

In 2002, total salaries are €4m.

The entity recognises €320,000 as post-employment benefit expense. Any unpaid contribution at 31 December 2002 is recognised as a liability.

The entity also deducts €120,000 from salaries and pays this over to the fund. Any amount unpaid at 31 December 2002 is recognised as a liability.

33.8.2 Disclosure

An entity should disclose the amount recognised as an expense for defined contribution plans.
(IAS 19, 46)

Extract 33.6 *Defined contribution plans*

Roche, Switzerland, 31 December 2001 (IAS)

	2001	*2000*
Wages and salaries	6,026	6,156
Social security costs	719	746
Post-employment benefits: defined benefit plans	264	298
Post-employment benefits: defined contribution plans	99	58
Other employee benefits	308	325
Total employees' remuneration	7,416	7,583

The charges for employee benefits are included in the relevant expenditure line by function. The number of employees at the year-end was 63,717 (2000: 64,758). Other employee benefits consist mainly of life insurance schemes and certain other insurance schemes providing medical and dental cover.

Extract 33.7 *Defined contribution plans*

Bayer, Germany, 31 December 2001 (IAS)

In the case of defined contribution plans, the company pays contributions to publicly or privately administered pension insurance plans on a mandatory, contractual or voluntary basis. Once the contributions have been paid, the company has no further payment obligations. The regular contributions constitute net periodic costs for the year in which they are due and as such are included in the cost of goods sold, selling expenses, research and development expenses or general administration expenses, and thus in the operating result. In 2001, these expenses totalled €312 million (2000: €437 million).

33.9 ACCOUNTING FOR DEFINED BENEFIT PLANS – THE BROAD APPROACH

Accounting for defined benefit plans is more complex than accounting for defined contribution plans for several reasons:

- the entity has an obligation to provide benefits to current and former employees and the amount and timing of these benefits are usually subject to a number of major uncertainties;
- the benefits are usually payable a long time in the future and often for a long period – this adds to the uncertainties and creates the need for the discounting of the liability to make the payments;
- in the case of funded plans, the return on plan assets affects the cost of providing the benefits – the greater the return on those assets, the lower the cost of the benefits and the lower the return the higher the cost;
- the terms of the plan may be changed which may give rise to what are known as past service costs, that is, an increase or decrease in the amount of the liability;
- the assumptions made in previous periods may not be borne out by subsequent events with the result that the amount of the liability may be higher or lower than expected;
- the assumptions used for future periods may need to be changed which may increase or decrease the liability; and
- plans may be curtailed or settled before the benefits were otherwise due for payment.

There are many examples in the revised IAS 19 which explain the application of the standard and which are well worth close study by those who have to deal with the various complexities.

33.9.1 A Simple Approach

In the simple and unreal case in which everything turns out as originally estimated and there are no changes in a retirement benefit plan, accounting for a defined benefit plan involves only three basic steps:

- using actuarial assumptions to estimate the amount of benefits which employees have earned in return for their service in the current and prior periods;
- using an actuarial method and a discount rate to determine the present value of the defined benefit obligation and the current service cost; and
- determining the value of any plan assets (funded plans only).

In such a case, employee benefit expense for any period consists of:

- current service cost (which is the actuarial cost of providing benefits in respect of service rendered in the current period);

- interest (which arises as a result of the unwinding of the discount in the present value calculation); and
- the expected returns on any plan assets (funded plans only).

The amount recognised on the balance sheet is the present value of the defined benefit obligation less the fair value of plan assets (if any), both measured as at the balance sheet date. The amount recognised is a liability in the case of an unfunded plan and is either a liability or an asset in a funded plan.

33.9.2 Added Complexity

In practice, the accounting is more complex because of the complexity of the underlying transactions and events. The benefits that are eventually paid will be different in amount and timing from those assumed at an earlier date. The level of benefits will change either as a result of a conscious decision of the entity or as a result of changes in such factors as pre-retirement salaries, length of employee service, government pensions or, in the case of post-employment healthcare plans, the health of participants and medical costs. The return on any plan assets and the level of funding may vary from that assumed. There may also be a need to change the discount rate to reflect changes in market interest rates.

The accounting is made even more complex by the standards and guidance in IAS 19 (and many national standards) for dealing with the transactions and events. In particular, the resulting changes in the actuarial present value or the value of any plan assets may be spread over a number of accounting periods but the spreading is constrained in several ways (see 33.11). The transitional provisions (see 33.15) also allow the spreading of some adjustments arising on the adoption of the revised IAS 19.

Therefore, in addition to the three basic steps, the accounting for defined benefit plans also involves determining:

- the amount of any past service cost and when that cost should be recognised in the income statement;
- the amount of actuarial gains and losses (which includes gains or losses on plan assets) and when those gains and losses should be recognised in the income statement;
- the gain or loss on any curtailment or settlement of a plan and when that gain or loss should be recognised in the income statement; and
- any gain or loss dealt with under the transitional provisions in the revised IAS 19 and when that gain or loss should be recognised in the income statement.

As a result of these additional steps, the employee benefit expense (which may be negative, that is it may be income) for any period also includes:

- past service costs;
- actuarial gains and losses, which includes the difference between expected and actual returns on plan assets;
- the effect of any curtailments or settlements; and
- the amortisation of any gain or loss arising under the transitional provisions.

The additional steps also affect the amount recognised on the balance sheet. The amount recognised is the total of the present value of the defined benefit obligation at the balance sheet date plus any actuarial gains which have not been recognised less the total of:

- any actuarial losses not recognised;
- any past service cost not recognised;
- the fair value at the balance sheet date of plan assets (if any).

(IAS 19, 54)

The amount also has to be adjusted to reflect the effects, if any, of the transitional provisions in the revised IAS 19.

The amount recognised on the balance sheet is a liability in the case of an unfunded plan. The balance sheet amount could be either a liability or an asset in a funded plan. An asset would arise either as a result of the value of plan assets exceeding the obligation (that is, the plan is currently overfunded) or as a result of the spreading of actuarial gains and losses and the effects of the transitional provisions.

33.9.3 Restrictions on Assets

IAS 19 places certain restrictions on the recognition of an asset (the 'asset ceiling'). The reasoning behind the requirements is the view that an entity should not recognise as an asset an amount in excess of the present value of the future benefits that are expected to flow to the entity from that asset (IAS 19, appendix C, 76). However, the IASC also decided that this rule should not usually override the permitted deferrals of actuarial losses and past service costs (IAS 19, appendix 3, 77). Therefore, the amount recognised should be the lower of:

- the amount determined under the normal requirements of IAS 19; and
- the net total of any unrecognised actuarial losses and past service cost and the present value of any economic benefits available in the form

of refunds from the plan or reductions in future contributions to the plan.
(IAS 19, 58)

This requirement does override the transitional spreading option in IAS 19 (see 33.15). Disclosure is required of any amount not recognised as an asset because of the limit (IAS 19, 60). Therefore, when the accounting does result in an asset, an entity is encouraged to study carefully all the requirements and the interrelationships among them.

The IASC believes that the limits will come into effect only when:

- an entity has taken advantage of the transitional provisions to defer the recognition of part of the transitional liability but the obligation has been funded more quickly; or
- there is a large surplus which will eliminate the need for further contributions and cannot be returned to the entity.

(IAS 19, appendix C, 77)

In May 2002 the IASB issued an amendment to IAS 19 dealing with the interaction of deferred recognition of actuarial losses and past service costs and the asset ceiling test. The amendment overrides the permitted deferral of actuarial gains and losses and past service costs in specified instances when an entity has a surplus in a defined benefit plan that, based on current terms of the plan, cannot be fully recovered through refunds or reductions in future contributions. Without the amendment, the application of IAS 19 could have given rise to a gain solely as a result of the deferred recognition of past service cost or an actuarial loss in the current period (or to a loss solely as a result of the deferred recognition of an actuarial gain in the current period) (IAS 19, 58B).

Under the new requirements, an entity should:

- recognise immediately net actuarial losses of the current period and past service cost of the current period to the extent that they exceed any reduction in the present value of the economic benefits to be recovered through refunds or reductions in future contributions – if there is no change or an increase in the present value of the economic benefits, the entire net actuarial losses of the current period and past service cost of the current period should be recognised immediately under paragraph 54; and
- recognise immediately net actuarial gains of the current period after the deduction of past service cost of the current period to the extent that they exceed any increase in the present value of the economic benefits to be recovered through refunds or reductions in future contributions – if there is no change or a decrease in the present value

of the economic benefits, the entire net actuarial gains of the current period after the deduction of past service cost of the current period should be recognised immediately under paragraph 54.
(IAS 19, 58A)

Example 33.5 *Application of asset ceiling test*

At the end of 2001 a plan has a surplus of 60. The present value of economic benefits that will flow to the entity either from refunds or reductions in future contributions is 30. There are unrecognised actuarial gains and losses of 40. An asset of 70 (30 + 40) is recognised.

In 2002 there is an actuarial loss of 35, which increases the deferred losses to 75, and reduces the surplus to 25. The present value of economic benefits that will flow to the entity either from refunds or reductions in future contributions is 20. Under IAS 19, 58, an asset of 95 (75 + 20) would have been recognised giving rise to the recognition of a gain of 25. Under the 2002 revision to IAS 19, net actuarial gains and losses are recognised immediately to the extent they exceed any reduction in the present value of the economic benefits. This gives rise to an actuarial loss for the year of 35 analysed as follows:

Actuarial loss equal to the reduction in the economic benefits	10
Actuarial loss that exceeds the reduction in the economic benefits	25

The unrecognised actuarial gains and losses are restricted to 50 (75 – 25) which with the present value of economic benefits is now 20, which results in the recognition of an asset of 70, which is the same amount as in 2001 – hence no net gain recognised in income.

33.9.4 Business Combinations

There is one other exception to the general approach. In a business combination that is an acquisition, an entity recognises assets and liabilities arising from post-employment benefits at the present value of the obligation less the fair value of any plan assets (see chapter 16). The present value of the obligation includes:

- actuarial gains and losses that arose before the date of the acquisition;
- past service cost that arose from benefit changes, or the introduction of a plan, before the date of the acquisition; and
- amounts not recognised under the transitional provisions.

(IAS 19, 108)

In other words, in a business combination, the balance sheet amount is measured using the simple approach.

33.10 ACCOUNTING FOR DEFINED BENEFIT PLANS – ACTUARIAL PRESENT VALUE

An entity uses actuarial assumptions to estimate the amount of benefits which employees have earned in return for their service in the current and prior periods and an actuarial method and a discount rate to determine the present value of the defined benefit obligation, the current service cost and any past service cost. It should determine the present value of defined benefit obligations with sufficient regularity that the amounts recognised in the financial statements do not differ materially from the amounts that would be determined at the balance sheet date (IAS 19, 56).

The *present value of a defined benefit obligation* is the present value of expected future payments required to settle the obligation resulting from employee service in the current and prior periods (IAS 19, 7). It excludes the value of any plan assets. Therefore, all other things being equal, the actuarial value of the defined benefit obligation is the same whether or not the plan is funded.

Current service cost is the increase in the present value of the defined benefit obligation resulting from employee service in the current period (IAS 19, 7). It is the cost of providing benefits in respect of service rendered in the current period.

Past service cost is the increase in the present value of the defined benefit obligation for employee service in prior periods, resulting in the current period from the introduction of, or changes to, post-employment benefits or other long-term employee benefits. Past service cost may be either positive (when benefits are introduced or improved) or negative (when existing benefits are reduced) (IAS 19, 7).

33.10.1 Actuarial Method

There are several actuarial methods which are used to determine post-employment obligations and the funding of those obligations. IAS 19 does not deal with the funding of the obligation and it is important to recognise that the actuarial method used for funding purposes may not be appropriate for the accounting purposes of IAS 19.

In developing the revised IAS 19, the IASC reconsidered the choice of actuarial method and concluded that it should require the use of the projected unit credit method which is a form of accrued benefit method[1]. The projected unit credit method should be used to determine the present value of its defined benefit obligations, the related current service cost and any past service cost (IAS 19, 64).

The projected unit credit method should not be confused with the projected benefit methods referred to in IAS 19 [1981] and IAS 19 [1993]. The use of projected benefit methods and of forms of the accrued benefit method other than projected unit credit method is not permitted by the revised IAS 19.

The projected unit credit method (sometimes known as the accrued benefit method pro-rated on service or as the benefit/years of service method) sees each period of service as giving rise to an additional unit of benefit entitlement and measures each unit separately to build up the final obligation (IAS 19, 65). An entity should attribute benefit to periods of service under the plan's benefit formula. However, if an employee's service in later years will lead to a materially higher level of benefit than in earlier years, an entity should attribute benefit on a straight-line basis:

- from the date when service by the employee first leads to benefits under the plan (whether or not the benefits are conditional on further service);
- until the date when further service by the employee will lead to no material amount of further benefits under the plan, other than from further salary increases.

(IAS 19, 67)

Employee service gives rise to an obligation under a defined benefit plan even if the benefits are conditional on future employment, in other words, the benefits are currently non-vested. Employee service before the vesting date gives rise to a constructive obligation because, at each successive balance sheet date, the amount of future service which an employee will have to render before becoming entitled to the benefit is reduced. However, in measuring its obligation, an entity considers the probability that some employees may not satisfy any vesting requirements. For example, retirement benefits may be based on the total number of years of service but no benefits may be payable to those employees who leave before completing five years' service, that is, the first five years count towards the amount of benefits but the benefits do not vest until the completion of five years. The estimate of the obligation and current service cost include the benefits accruing in the first five years and the measurement takes into account the fact that some employees will leave during this period and not become entitled to any benefits.

Certain post-employment benefits, for example post-employment medical benefits or post-employment life assurance, become payable only if a specified event (illness or death) occurs when an employee is no longer employed. An obligation to pay such benefits is created when the employee renders service which will provide entitlement to the benefit if the specified event occurs. The probability that the specified event will occur or when it will occur affects the measurement, not the existence, of the obligation and the associated cost (IAS 19, 69).

33.10.2 Actuarial Assumptions

The amount of retirement benefits eventually payable often depends on a number of uncertain factors, for example:

- an employee's salary at, or close to, retirement;
- the employee's years of service;
- whether an employee leaves the employment of the entity voluntarily before retirement; and
- whether the employee's dependants are entitled to benefits when the employee dies.

The actuary makes assumptions about all the factors which are relevant to the particular plan. The assumptions used for accounting purposes may be different from those used for funding purposes. For example, an entity may fund a plan on the prudent basis that plan assets are always comfortably in excess of the actuarial present value of promised retirement benefits. It would be inappropriate, however, to estimate the accounting obligation or current service cost on the basis that they are materially in excess of what is required under IAS 19. Therefore, an entity may need to obtain two actuarial valuations, one using assumptions which are appropriate to meet the funding objectives and a second using assumptions which are appropriate for accounting purposes.

The assumptions used for accounting purposes need to deal with the people covered by the plan and the benefits provided by the plan. Assumptions about the people deal with such matters as:

- mortality, both during and after employment;
- rates of employee turnover, disability and early retirement;
- the proportion of plan members with dependants who will be eligible for benefits; and
- in the case of post-employment medical plans, claim rates.

Assumptions about the benefits deal with:

- future salary levels insofar as they affect the entitlement to benefits;
- future benefit levels;
- the likely mix of benefits (pensions versus lump sums, dependants' pensions, etc);

- in the case of medical benefits, future medical costs; and
- the cost of administering benefit payments claims.

IAS 19 requires that the assumptions used in measuring the obligation, current service cost and past service cost should reflect:

- estimated future salary increases arising from inflation, seniority, promotion and other relevant factors such as supply and demand in the employment market;
- the benefits set out in the terms of the plan at the balance sheet date;
- the benefits arising from any constructive obligation that goes beyond the terms of the plan at the balance sheet date;
- any changes in benefits in future periods which are required by the formal terms of a plan or a constructive obligation which goes beyond those terms;
- in the case of post-employment healthcare benefits, estimated future medical costs taking into account both inflation and specific changes in medical costs; and
- estimated future changes in the level of any state benefits which affect the benefits payable but only if those changes were enacted before the balance sheet date or past history or other reliable evidence indicates that those state benefits will change in a predictable manner (for example, in line with future changes in general price levels or salary levels).

(IAS 19, 83 to 91)

An entity may have to change future benefits when, for example:

- it has an obligation or a constructive obligation to use any surplus in the plan for the benefit of plan participants; or
- it has a past history of increasing benefits and there is no indication that practice will change in the future (hence, a constructive obligation) to increase benefits to mitigate the effects of inflation.

Such changes are reflected in the actuarial assumptions. However, the actuarial assumptions do not reflect future benefit changes which are not set out in the formal terms of the plan or which are not a constructive obligation at the balance sheet date. Such changes are accounted for when an obligation or a constructive obligation arises and may give rise to past service costs at that time.

Some post-employment benefits are linked to variables such as the level of state retirement benefits or state medical care. The measurement of such benefits reflects expected changes in such variables, based on past history and other reliable evidence.

Estimates of future medical costs are based on historical data about the entity's own experience, supplemented when necessary by historical data from other entities, insurance companies, medical providers or other sources. Estimates of future medical costs consider the effect of technological advances, changes in health care utilisation or delivery patterns and changes in the health status of plan participants. They also take account of any contributions by the employees which are required under the terms of the plan at the balance sheet date or any constructive obligation that goes beyond those terms.

Assumptions also need to be made about the expected return on any plan assets – the higher the return, the lower the cost of providing the benefits and the lower the return, the higher the cost of benefits – and the discount rate. These assumptions should be based on market expectations, at the balance sheet date, for the period over which the obligations are to be settled (IAS 19, 77). The discount rate and expected return on assets at the start of the period are also required to calculate the interest charge and expected return on assets in the income statement (see 33.10.3 and 33.13.3).

The assumptions should be 'unbiased and mutually compatible' (IAS 19, 72). Actuarial assumptions are 'unbiased' if they are neither imprudent nor excessively conservative (IAS 19, 74). Actuarial assumptions are 'mutually compatible' if they reflect consistently the economic relationships between factors such as inflation, rates of salary increase, the return on plan assets and discount rates (IAS 19, 75).

Extract 33.8 *Actuarial assumptions*

Bayer, Germany, 31 December 2001 (IAS)

All defined benefit plans necessitate actuarial computations and valuations. These are based not only on life expectancy but also on the following parameters, which vary from country to country according to economic conditions:

	Parameters	
	Dec. 31, 2001	*Dec. 31, 2000*
Discount rate	2.5% to 7.0%	3.0% to 7.3%
Projected future remuneration increases	2.0% to 4.8%	1.0% to 7.0%
Projected future pension increases	2.0% to 3.3%	1.0% to 4.5%
Projected employee turnover (according to age and gender)	Empirical data	
Projected return on plan assets	2.0% to 8.5%	3.0% to 8.5%

Extract 33.9 *Actuarial assumptions*

Roche, Switzerland, 31 December 2001 (IAS)

The Group operates defined benefit schemes in many countries and the actuarial assumptions vary based upon local economic and social conditions. The range of assumptions used in the actuarial valuations of the most significant defined benefit plans, which are in countries with stable currencies and interest rates, is as follows:

Discount rates	3 to 8%	(2000: 3 to 8%)
Projected rates of remuneration growth	2 to 9%	(2000: 2 to 9%)
Expected rates of return on plan assets	3 to 10%	(2000: 3 to 10%)
Healthcare cost trend rate	5 to 10%	(2000: 4 to 10%)

33.10.3 Discount Rate

The discount rate used to determine the present value of a defined benefit obligation, current service cost and past service cost for both funded and unfunded plans should be determined by reference to market yields at the balance sheet date on high quality corporate bonds (IAS 19, 78). The discount rate reflects the currency and estimated term of the post-employment benefit obligations (IAS 19, 78) and the estimated timing of benefit payments (IAS 19, 80).

When there is no deep market in high quality corporate bonds, the discount rate is determined by reference to the market yields at the balance sheet date on government bonds (IAS 19, 78). When there is no deep market in the relevant corporate or government bonds with a sufficiently long maturity to match the estimated maturity of all the benefit payments, an entity:

- uses current market rates of the appropriate term to discount shorter term payments; and
- estimates the discount rate for longer maturities by extrapolating current market rates along the yield curve.

(IAS 19, 81)

The discount rate and other financial assumptions are expressed in nominal (stated) terms, unless estimates in real (inflation-adjusted) terms are more reliable, for example, in a hyperinflationary economy or when the benefits are index-linked and there is a deep market in index-linked bonds of the same currency and term (IAS 19, 76).

An entity discounts the whole of a post-employment benefit obligation, even if part of the obligation falls due within twelve months of the balance sheet date (IAS 19, 66).

The fact that the obligation is measured on a discounted basis means that an entity has to recognise an interest cost as an expense. The *interest cost* is the increase during a period in the present value of a defined benefit obligation which arises because the benefits are one period closer to settlement (IAS 19, 7). In other words, the interest expense arises as a result of the unwinding of the discount.

Interest cost is computed by multiplying the discount rate at the start of the period by the present value of the defined benefit obligation throughout that period, taking account of any material changes in the obligation (IAS 19, 82). IAS 19 does not specify the classification of the interest expense. It may be included with employee benefit costs or with other interest expense.

33.11 ACCOUNTING FOR DEFINED BENEFIT PLANS – ACTUARIAL GAINS AND LOSSES

Actuarial gains and losses comprise:

- experience adjustments; and
- the effects of changes in actuarial assumptions.

(IAS 19, 7)

Actuarial variances give rise to actuarial gains when they reduce the present value of the defined benefit obligation or increase the value of the plan assets. They give rise to actuarial losses when they increase the present value of the defined benefit obligation or reduce the value of the plan assets.

Experience adjustments arise when the assumptions about the people and benefits and the financial assumptions made in the past have not been fully borne out by experience. For example, the number of employees who have left employment voluntarily before retirement may be different from the number assumed in the previous valuation, the actual level of salary increases may have been lower than assumed in the previous valuation or the return on plan assets may have been better or worse than expected.

Changes in actuarial assumptions are made when actual experience in the long-term consistently differs from that reflected in the existing assumptions. The assumptions are not changed for short-term fluctuations in economic relationships but they would be changed if those short-term fluctuations persist and prove to be long-term. For example, while higher salary increases than previously assumed give rise to an experience adjustment, the assumption about future salary increases is changed only when the higher rate of increase is expected to continue.

Actuarial gains and losses include:

- the effect of differences between actual and previously assumed salary increases on the obligation to pay benefits for service in prior years;
- under and over estimates of discretionary pension increases when an entity has a constructive obligation to grant such increases;
- estimates of benefit improvements that result from actuarial gains that have been recognised in the financial statements if the entity is obliged, by the formal terms of a plan, a constructive obligation that goes beyond those terms or legislation, to use any surplus for the benefit of plan participants;
- the increase in vested benefits when, in the absence of new or improved benefits, employees complete vesting requirements; and
- the difference between the expected return on plan assets and the actual return on plan assets (IAS 19, 105).

IAS 19 allows actuarial gains and losses to be recognised in the income statement by one of four methods but the same method must be used for both gains and losses and consistently from period to period. Two methods account for all gains and losses. Two methods account for only those gains and losses that lie outside a 10% 'corridor', that is, gains and losses are ignored if they lie within the corridor which is the greater of:

- 10% of the present value of the defined benefit obligation; and
- 10% of the fair value of any plan assets.

The four alternative methods are:

- the immediate recognition of *all* actuarial gains and losses as income or expense for the period in which they are determined;
- the deferral and amortisation of *all* actuarial gains and losses over the expected average remaining working lives of employees;
- immediate recognition of all actuarial gains and losses *outside the 10% corridor* as income or expense for the period in which they are determined; and
- the deferral and amortisation of actuarial gains and losses *outside the 10% corridor* over the expected average remaining working lives of employees.

The European Commission believes that the corridor approach conflicts with the 'basic principle in the Fourth Directive that all foreseeable liabilities must be provided for and that all charges relating to the financial year must be recognised in that year'[2]. Therefore companies that must comply with the Directives should not use the corridor approach but many, in fact, do use that approach (*International Accounting Standards Survey 2000*, pp323-6). The same argument, presumably, applies to the use of the defer and amortise approach without the corridor.

IAS 19 justifies the corridor approach because, in the long term, actuarial gains and losses may offset one another. Therefore, estimates of post-employment benefit obligations may be viewed as a range (or 'corridor') around the best estimate rather than as a precise amount. As a result, an entity is not required to recognise actuarial gains and losses that fall within a specified range or corridor as income or expenses or as adjustments to the defined benefit liability or asset. It is required to recognise as income and expenses those gains and losses which fall outside that specified range or corridor but even the recognition of these gains and losses may be spread over a period of years.

For each defined benefit plan for which it wishes to use the corridor approach, an entity should compare its net cumulative unrecognised actuarial gains and losses at the end of the previous reporting period with the greater of:

- 10% of the present value of the defined benefit obligation at that date; and
- 10% of the fair value of any plan assets at that date.

(IAS 19, 92)

In the case of an unfunded plan, only the first 10% test can be applied.

If the net cumulative unrecognised gains and losses are lower than the greater of the two amounts, no further action is required. In other words, the gains and losses are within the range or corridor and need not be recognised as income or expenditure.

If the net cumulative unrecognised gains and losses exceed the greater of the two amounts, the gains or losses are outside the range or corridor and the entity should recognise as income or expense at least a specified portion of the excess (not necessarily the total amount). The specified portion is the excess divided by the expected average remaining working lives of the employees participating in that plan (IAS 19, 93). The amount recognised is:

- added to the liability and recognised as an expense, if it is a loss; or
- deducted from the liability and recognised as income, if it is a gain.

An entity is not required to adopt the corridor approach. It may adopt any other systematic method that results in faster recognition of actuarial gains and losses as income and expenses provided that the same method is used for both gains and losses and the method is applied consistently from period to period. For example, it may recognise immediately as income or expense all the gains and losses outside the corridor. It may also opt not to use the corridor approach and either defer and amortise all actuarial gains and losses or recognise immediately all actuarial gains and losses.

The application of the corridor approach is dealt with in more detail in the examples in IAS 19.

Example 33.6 *Amortisation of actuarial loss*

In 2002, an entity carries out an actuarial valuation. Salary levels have been higher than assumed in the previous valuation with the result that the valuation of the present value of the defined benefit obligation has increased by $480,000. All the increase relates to current employees who have an average expected remaining working life of eight years.

The increase in the valuation is an actuarial loss. The entity may:

- recognise as an expense only that part of the loss which exceeds 10% of the present value of the defined benefit obligation or 10% of the fair value of the plan assets (whichever is the greater); or
- recognise the whole loss as an expense.

In either case it may recognise:

- the whole loss immediately;
- amortise the loss over the expected average working lives of the employees participating in that plan; or
- amortise the loss over a shorter period,

provided that the same method is used for both gains and losses and the method is applied consistently from period to period.

Therefore, if the part of the loss that falls outside the 10% corridor is $96,000, the entity may:

- recognise the whole loss ($480,000) immediately;
- recognise the loss that falls outside the corridor ($96,000) immediately;
- amortise the whole loss ($480,000) over eight years ($60,000 a year);
- amortise the loss that falls outside the corridor ($96,000) over eight years ($12,000 a year); or
- amortise the whole loss ($480,000) or the loss that falls outside the corridor ($96,000) over a shorter period than eight years.

Example 33.7 *Amortisation of actuarial loss*

In 2002, an entity carries out an actuarial valuation. It decides to change the assumptions about future salary and retirement benefit levels to reflect long-term changes that have taken place. As a result, the amount of the actuarial valuation increases by £5m. All the increase relates to current employees who have an average expected remaining working life of ten years.

The increase in the valuation is an actuarial loss. The entity may either:

- recognise as an expense only a portion of that part of the loss which exceeds 10% of the present value of the defined benefit obligation or 10% of the fair value of the plan assets (whichever is the greater); or
- recognise the whole loss as an expense.

In either case it may recognise:

- the whole loss immediately;
- amortise the loss over the expected average working lives of the employees participating in that plan; or
- amortise the loss over a shorter period,

provided that the same method is used for both gains and losses and the method is applied consistently from period to period.

Therefore, if the part of the loss that falls outside the 10% corridor is £2m, the entity may:

- recognise the whole loss (£5m) immediately;
- recognise the loss that falls outside the corridor (£2m) immediately;
- amortise the whole loss (£5m) over ten years (£500,000 a year);
- amortise the loss that falls outside the corridor (£2m) over ten years (£200,000 a year); or
- amortise the whole loss (£5m) or the loss that falls outside the corridor (£2m) over a shorter period than ten years.

33.12 ACCOUNTING FOR DEFINED BENEFIT PLANS – PAST SERVICE COSTS

Past service cost is the increase or decrease in the present value of the defined benefit obligation for employee service in prior periods, resulting in the current period from the introduction of, or changes to, post-employment benefits or other long-term employee benefits (IAS 19, 7).

Past service cost is an expense, that is an increase in the actuarial value, when benefits are introduced or improved. Past service cost is income, that is a reduction in the actuarial value, when existing benefits are reduced. Past service costs exclude the effect of plan amendments which reduce benefits for future service; such plan amendments are treated as a curtailment (IAS 19, 98) – see 33.14. When an entity reduces benefits payable under an existing plan but, at the same time, increases other benefits payable under the same plan for the same employees, the change is treated as a single net change (IAS 19, 101).

IAS 19 [1993] distinguished between past service costs arising in respect of changes in the benefits for existing employees and changes in benefits for those former employees who had retired. It required the immediate recognition as an expense or income of past service costs relating to retired employees and the same approach is retained in the revised IAS 19. In the case of existing employees, IAS 19 [1993] required that past service costs should be recognised as an expense or as income systematically over the expected remaining working lives of those employees or over a shorter period which reflected the receipt of economic benefits by the entity (IAS 19 [1993], 28).

The revised IAS 19 requires that past service cost which is an expense should be recognised as an expense on a straight-line basis over the average period until the benefits become vested (IAS 19, 96). The amortisation schedule should be established when the benefits are introduced or changed; it is amended only if there is a curtailment or settlement (IAS 19, 99). To the extent that the increased benefits vest immediately following the changes, the past service cost should be recognised as an expense immediately (IAS 19, 96).

Past service cost which is income should be recognised as income over the average period until the reduced portion of the benefits becomes vested (IAS 19, 100). To the extent that the reduced portion of the benefits vest immediately following the changes, the past service cost should be recognised as income immediately (IAS 19, 96).

Example 33.8 *Past service costs*

In 2002, an entity decides to enhance the retirement benefits available to its employees under a defined benefit plan. The actuarially determined cost is $500,000. $320,000 relates to current employees who have an average expected remaining working life of eight years. The balance of $180,000 relates to participating employees who have already retired.

(Continued)

(Continued)

If the enhanced benefits vest immediately, the entity recognises the increased cost of $5,000,000 immediately.

If the enhanced benefits for retired employees vest immediately but the enhanced benefits vest over five years, the entity recognises:

- the increased cost relating to retired employees ($180,000) immediately; and
- the increased cost relating to current employees ($320,000) over five years ($64,000 a year).

33.13 ACCOUNTING FOR DEFINED BENEFIT PLANS – PLAN ASSETS

33.13.1 Definition

Plan assets are:

- assets held by a long-term employee benefit fund; and
- qualifying insurance policies.

(IAS 19, 7)

Plan assets must:

- be available to be used only to pay or fund employee benefits;
- not be available to the reporting entity's own creditors (even in bankruptcy); and
- not be available to be returned or paid to the reporting entity unless either:
  - the assets or proceeds are surplus to requirements and the remaining assets of the fund or proceeds of the policy are sufficient to meet all the related employee benefit obligations of the plan or the reporting entity; or
  - the assets or proceeds are reimbursed to the reporting entity for employee benefits already paid.

Additionally, assets held by a long-term employee benefit fund must be held by an entity (a fund) that is legally separate from the reporting entity and which exists solely to pay or fund employee benefits. A qualifying insurance policy must be issued by an insurer that is not a related party of the reporting entity.

The definition of plan assets was revised in 2000 to recognise the fact that some entities may have a legal or constructive obligation to pay the employee benefits directly but with a right to be refunded by the fund. The amendment applied to periods beginning on or after 1 January 2001.

Plan assets do not include:

- the entity's own operating assets in the case of an unfunded or partially funded retirement benefit plan;
- other assets of the entity even when those assets have been segregated for the purpose of settling the employee benefit obligation;
- unpaid contributions due from the reporting entity to the fund; and
- any non-transferable financial instruments issued by the entity and held by the fund – if these instruments were included in plan assets, the entity would be able to reduce its liability simply by issuing its own non-transferable equity instruments (the issue would also increase equity).

Plan assets are reduced by any liabilities of the fund that do not relate to employee benefits, for example, liabilities arising from derivative financial instruments (IAS 19, 103).

33.13.2 Measurement

Plan assets should be measured at their fair value at the balance sheet date (IAS 19, 54 (d)). Fair value should be determined with sufficient regularity that the amounts recognised in the financial statements do not differ materially from fair values at the balance sheet date (IAS 19, 56). The fair value of an asset is the amount for which the asset could be exchanged between knowledgeable parties in an arm's length transaction (IAS 19, 7). IAS 19 provides no specific guidance on the determination of fair value although it implies that fair value is usually market value.

When no market price is available for a plan asset, fair value is estimated by, for example, discounting expected future cash flows. The discount rate is a rate that reflects both the risk associated with the asset and the maturity or expected disposal date of that asset (IAS 19, 102). Further guidance on the determination of the fair value of assets is available in IAS 39 for financial assets and in IAS 16 for property.

The only exception to the 'fair value' approach is for rights under qualifying insurance policies that exactly match the amount and timing of some or all of the benefits payable under the plan. The fair value of such qualifying insurance policies is deemed to be the present value of the related obligation, subject to any reduction if the insurance proceeds are not recoverable in full (IAS 19, 104 and 104D).

The reporting entity should recognise as a separate asset at fair value any right to a reimbursement from another party when, and only when, it is virtually certain that the other party will reimburse some or all of the expenditure required to settle a defined benefit obligation. In all other respects the reporting enterprise should treat such assets as plan assets. Insurance policies that are not qualifying insurance policies, but which give a right to reimbursements that exactly match the amount and timing of some or all of the benefits payable under the plan, should be fair valued in the same way as qualifying insurance policies (IAS 19, 104A to 104D).

33.13.3 Return on Plan Assets

The expected return on plan assets is one component of the expense recognised in the income statement. The *return on plan assets* is interest, dividends and other revenue derived from the plan assets, together with realised and unrealised gains or losses on the plan assets, less any costs of administering the plan and less any tax payable by the plan itself (IAS 19, 7).

The expected return on plan assets is based on market expectations, at the beginning of the period, for returns over the entire life of the related obligation. The expected return on plan assets reflects changes in the fair value of plan assets held during the period as a result of actual contributions paid into the fund and actual benefits paid out of the fund.

In determining the expected and actual return on plan assets, an entity deducts expected administration costs, other than those included in the actuarial assumptions used to measure the obligation (IAS 19, 107).

The difference between expected and actual return on plan assets is an actuarial gain or loss.

33.14 ACCOUNTING FOR DEFINED BENEFIT PLANS – CURTAILMENTS AND SETTLEMENTS

33.14.1 Definitions

A *curtailment* occurs when an entity either:

- is demonstrably committed to make a material reduction in the number of employees covered by a plan; or
- amends the terms of a defined benefit plan such that a material element of future service by current employees will no longer qualify for benefits, or will qualify only for reduced benefits.

(IAS 19, 111)

A *settlement* occurs when an entity enters into a transaction that eliminates all further legal or constructive obligations for part or all of the benefits provided under a plan (IAS 19, 112). For example, an entity may make a lump-sum cash payment to, or on behalf of, plan participants in exchange for their rights to receive specified post-employment benefits. However, the routine payment of benefits under a plan is not a settlement unless the payment eliminates all the legal and constructive obligations.

Both a curtailment and a settlement occur together when a plan is terminated and the obligation is settled and the plan ceases to exist. The termination of a plan is not a curtailment or settlement if the plan is replaced by a new plan that offers benefits that are, in substance, identical (IAS 19, 114).

33.14.2 Recognition and Measurement

Any gain or loss on the curtailment or settlement should be recognised when the curtailment or settlement occurs (IAS 19, 109). Curtailments are often linked with a restructuring. Therefore, an entity accounts for a curtailment at the same time as for a related restructuring (see chapter 27).

Before determining the effect of a curtailment or settlement, an entity should remeasure the obligation and any plan assets using current actuarial assumptions, current interest rates and other current market prices (IAS 19, 110). The gain or loss on a curtailment or settlement should comprise:

- any resulting change in the present value of the defined benefit obligation;
- any resulting change in the fair value of the plan assets;
- any related actuarial gains and losses, past service costs and transitional amounts which have not previously been recognised.

(IAS 19, 109 and 155)

When a curtailment relates to only some employees or only part of an obligation is settled, the gain or loss includes the proportionate share of the previously unrecognised past service cost and actuarial gains and losses and of transitional amounts remaining unrecognised.

33.15 DEFINED BENEFIT PLANS – TRANSITIONAL PROVISIONS

On the initial adoption of the revised IAS 19, all actuarial gains and losses that arose in earlier periods are dealt with as part of the effect of the change in accounting policy even if they fall inside the 10% corridor. In other words, actuarial gains and losses arising prior to the adoption of the revised IAS 19 cannot be deferred and recognised as income or expenses after the adoption of the revised IAS 19.

On first adopting the revised IAS 19, an entity should recognise as a defined benefit liability a 'transitional liability'. The transitional liability is the present value of the defined benefit obligation at the date of adoption of the revised IAS 19 less the total of:

- the fair value, at the date of adoption, of any plan assets; and
- any past service cost that should be recognised in later periods.

(IAS 19, 154)

If the transitional liability is less than the liability which had previously been recognised at the same date, the entity should recognise that decrease immediately as a change in accounting policy in accordance with IAS 8 (see chapter 13). Under the allowed alternative treatment in IAS 8, the resulting gain is included in the income statement for the period in which the change in policy is made.

If the transitional liability is more than the liability which had previously been recognised at the same date, the entity should recognise that increase:

- immediately in accordance with IAS 8; or
- as an expense on a straight-line basis over up to five years from the date of adoption of the revised IAS 19.

The choice is irrevocable which means that it cannot be changed in a subsequent period if the financial statements of that subsequent period are to comply with IFRSs. The same choice is not available when the transitional liability is less than the amount previously recognised so the transitional provisions cannot be used to create income in subsequent periods.

If the entity chooses to recognise the increase as an expense over up to five years rather than immediately, the amount of any asset recognised should not exceed the general limit for post-employment obligation assets (see 33.9.3). Disclosure is required of any amount not recognised as an asset because of this limit (IAS 19, 60). In addition, the entity should:

- disclose at each balance sheet date the amount of the increase that remains unrecognised, and the amount recognised in the current period;
- limit the recognition of subsequent actuarial gains (but not negative past service costs) by reference to the unrecognised part of the transitional liability; and

- include the related unrecognised transitional liability in determining any subsequent gain or loss on settlement or curtailment (see 33.14).

These provisions for dealing with the excess of the transitional liability over the amount previously recognised apply irrespective of whether the previous accounting policy complied with IAS 19 [1993]. In particular, subject to the provisions of SIC 8, the five year amortisation of the excess was available to any entity reporting under IFRSs for the first time and which had previously accounted for post-employment defined benefit costs on a pay-as-you-go basis. However, under the IASB's new proposals for the first-time application of IFRSs, an entity will not be able to use the IAS 19 transitional provisions. It will be required to recognise and measure the liability in accordance with IAS 19 but will be prohibited from recognising any deferred actuarial gains and losses (see chapter 7).

33.16 DEFINED BENEFIT PLANS – PRESENTATION

The net amount recognised as a defined benefit liability is presented as a liability on the balance sheet. The net amount recognised as a defined benefit asset is presented as an asset. An asset relating to one plan should be offset against a liability relating to another plan only when the entity:

- has a legally enforceable right to use the surplus on one plan to settle the obligations under the other plan; and
- intends either to settle the obligations on a net basis, or to realise the surplus in one plan and settle its obligations under the other plan simultaneously.

(IAS 19, 116)

The offsetting criteria are similar to those established in other IFRSs (see chapter 9).

33.17 DEFINED BENEFIT PLANS – DISCLOSURE

An entity should disclose:

- its accounting policy for recognising actuarial gains and losses;
- a general description of the type of plan;
- a reconciliation of the assets and liabilities recognised in the balance sheet, showing at least:

- the present value at the balance sheet date of defined benefit obligations that are wholly unfunded;
- the present value (before deducting the fair value of plan assets) at the balance sheet date of defined benefit obligations that are wholly or partly funded;
- the fair value of any plan assets at the balance sheet date;
- the net actuarial gains or losses not recognised in the balance sheet;
- the past service cost not yet recognised in the balance sheet;
- any amount not recognised as an asset, because of the limit on asset recognition;
- the fair value at the balance sheet date of any reimbursement right recognised as an asset and a description of the link to the related obligation; and
- the other amounts recognised in the balance sheet;

- the amounts included in the fair value of plan assets for:
  - each category of the reporting entity's own financial instruments; and
  - any property occupied by, or other assets used by, the reporting entity;
- a reconciliation showing the movements during the period in the net liability (or asset) recognised in the balance sheet;
- the total expense recognised in the income statement for each of the following, and the line item(s) of the income statement in which they are included:
  - current service cost;
  - interest cost;
  - expected return on plan assets;
  - expected return on any reimbursement rights recognised as an asset;
  - actuarial gains and losses;
  - past service cost; and
  - the effect of any curtailment or settlement;
- the actual return on any reimbursement rights recognised as an asset;
- the actual return on plan assets; and
- the principal actuarial assumptions used as at the balance sheet date, including, where applicable:
  - the discount rates;
  - the expected rates of return on any plan assets for the periods presented in the financial statements;
  - the expected rates of return for the periods presented in the financial statements on any reimbursement right recognised as an asset;
  - the expected rates of salary increases (and of changes in an index or other variable specified in the formal or constructive terms of a plan as the basis for future benefit increases);
  - medical cost trend rates; and
  - any other material actuarial assumptions used.

(IAS 19, 120)

An entity should disclose each actuarial assumption in absolute terms, for example as a percentage, and not just as a margin between different percentages or other variables (IAS 19, 120). Disclosures about separate plans may be made in total, separately for each plan or in such groupings as are considered to be the most useful (IAS 19, 122).

The following extracts illustrate some of these disclosures not addressed elsewhere in the chapter.

Extract 33.10 *Type of plan*

Roche, Switzerland, 31 December 2001 (IAS)

Most employees are covered by retirement benefit plans sponsored by Group companies. The nature of such plans varies according to legal regulations, fiscal requirements and economic conditions of the countries in which the employees are employed. Other post-employment benefits consist mostly of post-retirement healthcare and life insurance schemes, principally in the United States. Plans are usually funded by payments from the Group and by employees to trusts independent of the Group's finances. Where a plan is unfunded, a liability for the whole obligation is recorded in the Group's balance sheet.

Extract 33.11 *Type of plan*

Bayer, Germany, 31 December 2001 (IAS)

Group companies provide retirement benefits for most of their employees, either directly or by contributing to independently administered funds. The way these benefits are provided varies according to the legal, fiscal and economic conditions of each country, the benefits generally being based on the employees' remuneration and years of service. The obligations relate both to existing retirees' pensions and to pension entitlements of future retirees. Group companies provide retirement benefits under defined contribution and/or defined benefit plans. . . .

The pension provisions for defined benefit plans are calculated in accordance with IAS 19 (Employee Benefits) by the projected unit credit method. The future benefit obligations are valued by actuarial methods on the basis of an appropriate assessment of the relevant parameters.

Benefits expected to be payable after retirement are spread over each employee's entire period of employment, allowing for future changes in remuneration.

The legally independent fund 'Bayer Pensionskasse VvaG' (Bayer Pensionskasse) is a private insurance company and is therefore subject to the German Law on the Supervision of Private Insurance Companies. Since Bayer guarantees the commitments of the Bayer Pensionskasse, it is classified as a defined benefit plan for IAS and US GAAP purposes.

Extract 33.12 *Amount recognised in the income statement*

Roche, Switzerland, 31 December 2001 (IAS)

The amounts recognised in arriving at operating profit for post-employment defined benefit plans are as follows:

	2001	*2000*
Current service cost	362	333
Interest cost	685	675
Expected return on plan assets	(761)	(714)
Net actuarial (gains) losses recognised	(12)	2
Past service cost	5	3
(Gains) losses on curtailment	(15)	(1)
Total included in employees' remuneration	264	298

Gains on curtailment of 15 million Swiss francs relate to the 'Re-shaping for Future Growth' programme and have been included as part of 'Pharmaceuticals Division restructuring – other restructuring costs' in the income statement (see Note 6).

The actual return on plan assets was a negative return of 1,334 million Swiss francs (2000: positive return of 1,175 million Swiss francs).

Extract 33.13 *Amount recognised in the income statement*

Bayer, Germany, 31 December 2001 (IAS)

All other retirement benefit systems are defined benefit plans, which may be either unfunded, i.e. financed by provisions (accruals), or funded, i.e. financed through pension funds. In 2001, expenses for defined benefit plans amounted to €301 million (2000: €326 million). These net periodic costs – except for the interest portion – are generally included in the cost of goods sold, selling expenses, research and development expenses, general administration expenses or other operating income. For the most important defined benefit plans they are comprised as follows:

	Defined benefit plans	
€ million	*Dec. 31, 2001*	*Dec. 31, 2000*
Service cost	265	210
Past service cost	10	1
Interest cost	669	589
Return on plan assets	(640)	(526)
Amortization of actuarial amounts	(34)	(14)
	270	**260**

Extract 33.14 *Analysis of balance sheet amount*

Roche, Switzerland, 31 December 2001 (IAS)

The movements in the net asset (liability) recognised in the balance sheet for post-employment defined benefit plans are as follows:

	2001	*2000*
At beginning of year	(1,849)	(2,078)
Changes in Group organisation and Givaudan spin-off	–	84
Total expenses included in employees' remuneration (as above)	(264)	(298)
Contributions paid	177	174
Benefits paid (unfunded plans)	116	135
Currency translation effects and other	(17)	134
At end of year (as below)	(1,837)	(1,849)

Amounts recognised in the balance sheet for post-employment defined benefit plans are as follows:

	2001	*2000*
Unfunded plans		
Recognised (liability) for actuarial present value of unfunded obligations	(2,440)	(2,423)
Funded plans		
Actuarial present value of funded obligations due to past and present employees	(9,575)	(9,034)
Plan assets held in trusts at fair value	9,401	10,448
Plan assets in excess of actuarial present value of funded obligations	(174)	1,414
Less		
– unrecognised actuarial (gains) losses	731	(862)
– unrecognised past service costs	46	22
Net recognised asset (liability) for funded obligations due to past and present employees	603	574
Asset (liability) recognised		
Deficit recognised as part of liabilities for post-employment benefits	(2,610)	(2,502)
Surplus recognised as part of other long-term assets	773	653
Total net asset (liability) recognised	(1,837)	(1,849)

The above amounts include non-pension post-employment benefit schemes, principally medical plans, with an actuarial present value of obligations of 737 million Swiss francs (2000: 690 million Swiss francs) and plan assets of 530 million Swiss francs (2000: 649 million Swiss francs).

The related net liability recognised is 257 million Swiss francs (2000: 147 million Swiss francs).

Actuarial gains of 50 million Swiss francs (2000: 106 million Swiss francs) were unrecognised.

Amounts recognised in the balance sheet for post-employment defined benefit plans are predominantly non-current and are reported as long-term assets and non-current liabilities.

Included within the fair value of the assets of the funded plans are 650,000 (2000: 900,000) of the Group's non-voting equity securities with a fair value of 77 million Swiss francs (2000: 149 million Swiss francs).

Extract 33.15 *Analysis of balance sheet amount*

Bayer, Germany, 31 December 2001 (IAS)

The status of unfunded and funded defined benefit obligations, computed using the appropriate parameters, is as follows:

€ million	*Dec. 31, 2001*	*Dec. 31, 2000*
Defined benefit obligation	(11,303)	(9,535)
Fair value of plan assets	8,126	7,847
Funded status	**(3,177)**	**(1,688)**
Unrecognized transition liability (asset)	(31)	(11)
Unrecognized actuarial (gain)loss	1,366	(203)
Asset limitation due to uncertainty of obtaining future benefits	(1,215)	(1,249)
Net recognized liability	**(3,057)**	**(3,151)**

The adjustments, as yet unrecognized in the income statement, represent the difference between the defined benefit obligation – after deducting the fair value of plan assets – and the net liability recognized in the balance sheet. They arise mainly from actuarial gains or losses caused by differences between actual and previously assumed trends in employee turnover and remuneration. Pension assets in excess of the obligation are reflected in other receivables, subject to the asset limitation specified in IAS 19 (Employee Benefits). In accordance with IAS 19, the amounts reflected in the balance sheet will be recognized in the income statement over the expected average remaining working lives of existing employees. The portion of the net actuarial gain or loss to be recognized in the income statement is determined by the corridor method.

The net liability under these defined benefit plans changed as follows:

€ million	*2001*	*2000*
Net liability recognized at the beginning of the year	(3,151)	(3,191)
Pension benefit (cost)income	(270)	(260)
Employer contributions	313	255
Divestitures	87	20
Change in asset limitation	(33)	12
Changes in scope of consolidation	–	11
Changes in currency translation	(3)	2
Net liability recognized at end of year	**(3,057)**	**(3,151)**

Funds and benefit obligations are valued on a regular basis at least every three years.

For all major funds, comprehensive actuarial valuations are performed annually.

Provisions are also set up under this item for the obligations of Group companies, particularly in the United States, to provide health care to their retirees. For health care costs, the valuation is based on the assumption that they will increase at an annual rate of 5 percent in the long term. Early retirement and certain other benefits to retirees are also included, since these obligations are similar in character to pension obligations. Like pension obligations, they are valued in line with international standards. In 2001, provisions for early retirement and other post-retirement benefits amounted to €63 million (2000: €14 million), comprising €23 million (2000: €192 million) for service cost, €58 million (2000: €52 million) for interest cost, €31 million (2000: €30 million) for expected return on plan assets and €13 million (2000: €0 million) for actuarial losses.

33.18 OTHER LONG-TERM EMPLOYEE BENEFITS

33.18.1 Definition

Other long-term employee benefits are employee benefits (other than post-employment benefits, termination benefits and equity compensation benefits) which do not fall due wholly within twelve months after the end of the period in which the employees render the related service (IAS 19, 7). These benefits may include:

- long-term compensated absences such as sabbatical leave;
- jubilee or other long-service benefits;

- long-term disability benefits;
- profit sharing and bonuses; and
- other compensation paid twelve months or more after the end of the period in which it is earned.

When these benefits are payable within twelve months of the period in which the employees render the related service, the benefits are dealt with as short-term employee benefits (see 33.6).

33.18.2 Recognition and Measurement

Long-term benefits are recognised as a liability and as an expense as the related service is rendered. When the benefits are earned over an extended period, they are recognised over that period in the same way that post-employment benefits are recognised as service is rendered.

The measurement of other long-term benefits involves the same principles as the measurement of post-employment benefits. However, the benefits are not usually subject to the same degree of uncertainty as post-employment benefits and the introduction of, or changes to, the benefits rarely causes a material amount of past service cost. Therefore, IAS 19 requires (rather than allows) a simplified method of accounting for other long-term employee benefits.

The amount recognised as a liability for other long-term benefits should be the present value of the obligation at the balance sheet date minus the fair value at the balance sheet date of any plan assets out of which the obligations are to be settled directly (IAS 19, 128). All actuarial gains and losses and all past service costs are recognised immediately as income and expense. An entity should also recognise any reimbursement rights when the conditions discussed in 33.13.2 are met (IAS 19, 128). Therefore, the amount recognised as expense or income is:

- current service cost, that is the actuarial cost of benefit earned in the period;
- interest cost arising from the unwinding of the discount;
- the return on any plan assets and on any reimbursement rights recognised as an asset;
- actuarial gains and losses arising in the period;
- past service cost arising in the period; and
- the effect of any curtailments or settlements.

(IAS 19, 129)

33.19 TERMINATION BENEFITS

33.19.1 Definition

Termination benefits are employee benefits payable as a result of either:

- an entity's decision to terminate an employee's employment before the normal retirement date; or
- an employee's decision to accept voluntary redundancy in exchange for those benefits.

(IAS 19, 7)

Termination benefits are typically lump-sum payments, but sometimes also include:

- enhancement of retirement benefits or of other post-employment benefits, either indirectly through an employee benefit plan or directly; and
- salary until the end of a specified notice period if the employee renders no further service that provides economic benefits to the entity.

An entity may be committed, by legislation, by contractual or other agreements with employees or their representatives or by a constructive obligation based on business practice, custom or a desire to act equitably, to make payments (or provide other benefits) to employees when it terminates their employment. Such payments are termination benefits.

33.19.2 Recognition and Measurement

The event which gives rise to an obligation to pay termination benefits is the termination rather than employee service. Therefore, an entity should recognise termination benefits as a liability and an expense only when the entity is demonstrably committed to either:

- terminate the employment of an employee or group of employees before the normal retirement date; or
- provide termination benefits as a result of an offer made in order to encourage voluntary redundancy.

(IAS 19, 133)

An entity is demonstrably committed to a termination when, and only when, the entity has a detailed formal plan for the termination and is without realistic possibility of withdrawal. The detailed plan should include, as a minimum:

- the location, function, and approximate number of employees whose services are to be terminated;
- the termination benefits for each job classification or function; and
- the time at which the plan will be implemented. Implementation should begin as soon as possible and the period of time to complete implementation should be such that material changes to the plan are not likely.

These criteria are the same as those in IAS 37 for the recognition of provisions.

Termination benefits are measured at the amount expected to be paid in settlement of the obligation. When termination benefits fall due more than 12 months after the balance sheet date, they should be discounted using the discount rate specified for defined benefit plans. In the case of an offer made to encourage voluntary redundancy, the measurement of termination benefits should be based on the number of employees expected to accept the offer.

33.20 EQUITY COMPENSATION BENEFITS

33.20.1 Definition

Equity compensation benefits are employee benefits under which either:

- employees are entitled to receive equity financial instruments issued by the entity (or its parent); or
- the amount of the entity's obligation to employees depends on the future price of equity financial instruments issued by the entity.

(IAS 19, 7)

Equity financial instruments include shares and options to acquire shares of the entity or its parent.

Equity compensation benefits include:

- shares, share options and other equity instruments issued to employees at less than the fair value at which those instruments would be issued to a third party; and
- cash payments, the amount of which will depend on the future market price of the reporting entity's shares.

Equity compensation plans are formal or informal arrangements under which an entity provides equity compensation benefits for one or more employees (IAS 19, 7).

33.20.2 Recognition and Measurement

IAS 19 does not specify recognition and measurement requirements for equity compensation benefits.

The G4+1 issued a discussion paper *Share-based Payments* in 2000. The paper addresses the situation in which an entity obtains goods and services from other parties, including suppliers and employees, with payment taking the form of shares or share options issued by the entity to those other parties. The paper proposed that such a transaction should be recognised in the financial statements, with a corresponding charge to the income statement when those goods or services are consumed. The IASB added this subject to their agenda in 2001 and requested further comments on the G4+1 discussion paper to ensure that it had received comments from all constituents who would wish their views to be considered. The IASB expects to issue an exposure draft on the subject in late 2002 *(IASB Update,* March 2002, p4*)*.

33.20.3 Disclosure

An entity should disclose:

- the nature and terms (including any vesting provisions) of equity compensation plans;
- the accounting policy for equity compensation plans;
- the amounts recognised in the financial statements for equity compensation plans;
- the number and terms (including, where applicable, dividend and voting rights, conversion rights, exercise dates, exercise prices and expiry dates) of the entity's own equity financial instruments which are held by equity compensation plans (and, in the case of share options, by employees) at the beginning and end of the period. The extent to which employees' entitlements to those instruments are vested at the beginning and end of the period should be specified;
- the number and terms (including, where applicable, dividend and voting rights, conversion rights, exercise dates, exercise prices and expiry dates) of equity financial instruments issued by the entity to equity compensation plans or to employees (or of the entity's own equity financial instruments distributed by equity compensation plans to employees) during the period and the fair value of any consideration received from the equity compensation plans or the employees;
- the number, exercise dates and exercise prices of share options exercised under equity compensation plans during the period;

- the number of share options held by equity compensation plans, or held by employees under such plans, that lapsed during the period; and
- the amount, and principal terms, of any loans or guarantees granted by the reporting entity to, or on behalf of, equity compensation plans.

(IAS 19, 147)

An entity should also disclose:

- the fair value, at the beginning and end of the period, of the entity's own equity financial instruments (other than share options) held by equity compensation plans; and
- the fair value, at the date of issue, of the entity's own equity financial instruments (other than share options) issued by the entity to equity compensation plans or to employees, or by equity compensation plans to employees, during the period.

(IAS 19, 148)

If it is not practicable to determine the fair value of the equity financial instruments (other than share options) that fact should be disclosed.

Notes

1 For the arguments for and against the various methods, see the IASC staff issues paper *Retirement Benefit and Other Employee Benefit Costs*, IASC, 1995 and appendix C of the revised IAS 19.

2 European Commission, *Examination of the Conformity Between IAS 19 (1998) and the European Accounting Directives*, European Commission, Brussels, 1999.

CHAPTER 34

Government Grants

34.1 RELEVANT STANDARDS AND INTERPRETATION

IAS 20 *Accounting for Government Grants and Disclosure of Government Assistance*
IAS 41 *Agriculture*
SIC 10 *Government Assistance – No Specific Relation to Operating Activities*

34.2 HISTORY

IAS 20 was approved in 1982 and reformatted in 1993. It has not been reviewed. The IASC did not consider IAS 20 in the comparability project because the choice of presentation of grants related to assets does not affect net assets or the net profit or loss for the period. The IASB has no plans to review IAS 20 but the IASC acknowledged criticisms that IAS 20 allows a choice of treatments and requires a treatment of grants related to assets which may not be compatible with the framework (*IASC Insight*, June 1998, p21).

IAS 41 was issued in 2000 and applies to periods beginning on or after 1 January 2003. Government grants related to biological assets are excluded from the scope of IAS 20 and are dealt with in accordance with IAS 41 (see 34.12 and chapter 45).

34.3 IOSCO

In June 1994, IOSCO advised the IASC that IAS 20 was acceptable for the purposes of the IOSCO core standards. However, IOSCO warned that it may recommend that its members accept a different accounting treatment from that required by IAS 20 for long-term development grants such as those then being made in Italy and the former East Germany. IOSCO said that it may recommend that its members:

- consider these grants as outside the scope of IAS 20 if they were not specifically considered in the development of IAS 20; and
- allow these grants to be credited to equity – this approach is not permitted by IAS 20.

IOSCO also advised the IASC that one of its members believed that government grants related to assets should be recognised as income when received (rather over the useful life of the asset). According to this IOSCO member, immediate recognition of such grants as income was a better treatment than the treatment required by IAS 20. The immediate recognition as income of grants related to assets is not permitted by IAS 20.

In its initial response to IOSCO, the IASC expressed concern that IOSCO's proposals would:

- allow accounting treatments which had been rejected by the IASC; and
- provide exemptions for specific grants which did not exist when IAS 20 was developed.

Many of IOSCO's concerns were considered in SIC 10 which rejects the approaches put forward by IOSCO and confirms the approach adopted in IAS 20 (see 34.5).

IAS 20 is included in 'IAS 2000' endorsed by IOSCO in May 2000. There is one supplemental treatment, that is a concern about the appropriateness of recognising government grants related to assets as deferred income, rather than as a deduction from the carrying amount of the asset.

34.4 IAS 20 IN BRIEF

Government grants should be recognised as income over the periods necessary to match them with the expenses which they are intended to compensate. Grants related to assets should either be deducted from the cost of the asset or treated as deferred income; in both cases, the grant is included in the income statement as the asset is used up.

34.5 DEFINITION OF GOVERNMENT GRANTS

Government grants are assistance by governments designed to provide an economic benefit in the form of transfers of resources to an entity in return for past or future compliance with certain conditions relating to the operating activities of the entity (IAS 20, 3).

Government grants include:

- the transfer of cash or cash equivalents to the entity;
- the transfer of a non-monetary asset to the entity (IAS 20, 7);
- a reduction in a liability owing to government (IAS 20, 9) (but a reduction in a tax liability is outside the scope of IAS 20); and
- the forgiving of a loan from government.

The conditions attaching to a grant may vary considerably. For example, an entity may become entitled to a grant as a result of acquiring an asset such as an item of property, plant and equipment. In other cases, the entity may have to use an asset in a particular location. Grants may also arise on the sale of an asset, for example the sale of goods may give rise to a grant in the form of a price subsidy.

Government assistance meets the definition of a government grant even when there are no conditions specifically relating to the operating activities of the recipient entity other than the requirement to operate in certain regions or industry sectors (SIC 10, 3). This was one of the issues raised by IOSCO (see 34.3).

IAS 20 excludes from its definition of government grants those forms of government assistance which cannot reasonably have a value placed on them (IAS 20, 3). Examples include free technical or marketing advice provided by government departments and the provision of guarantees. However, an entity is required to disclose information about such assistance (see 34.11).

IAS 20 also excludes from its definition of government grants transactions with government which cannot be distinguished from the normal trading transactions of the entity. Examples include government purchases from, or sales to, the entity (IAS 20, 3) but such purchases and sales would have to be disclosed if the government and the entity are related parties (see chapter 38).

IAS 20 excludes from the definition of government assistance, and hence from the definition of government grants, benefits provided only indirectly through action affecting general trading conditions, such as the provision of infrastructure in development areas or the imposition of trading constraints on competitors (IAS 20, 3).

34.6 RECOGNITION OF GOVERNMENT GRANTS

A government grant should not be recognised unless there is reasonable assurance that:

- the entity will comply with the conditions attaching to the grant; and
- the grant will be received.

(IAS 20, 7)

In practice, most governments do not pay grants until the entity has complied with the conditions attaching to the grant. Nevertheless, receipt of a grant does not of itself provide conclusive evidence that the conditions attaching to the grant have been, or will be, fulfilled. If a grant is received by an entity but it is uncertain whether the entity will comply with the conditions attaching to it, the grant must be classified as a liability; no part of the grant should be included in income until there is reasonable assurance that the entity will comply with the conditions.

Governments often attach ongoing conditions to grants. For example, a government may make a grant towards the cost of an asset on condition that the entity uses the asset in a particular location. Such grants are recognised when received. They are included in income in accordance with IAS 20 provided the entity has complied with any pre-existing conditions and intends to comply with the ongoing conditions. The failure to comply with ongoing conditions may result in the repayment of the grant (see 34.10 below) or may prevent the entity from recognising the grant as income.

Extract 34.1 *Recognition of government grants*

Barloworld, South Africa, 30 September 2001 (IAS)

Government grants towards staff re-training costs are recognised as income over the periods necessary to match them with the related costs and are deducted in reporting the related expense. Income is not recognised until there is reasonable assurance that it will be received.

When a government forgives a loan owing to it by the entity, the amount forgiven is accounted for as a grant from the government. The grant is recognised when there is reasonable assurance that the entity will meet the terms for the forgiveness of the loan (IAS 20, 10). Such an event results in the de-recognition of the loan which is a financial liability. This approach may be distinguished from that in the IAS 39 which requires that a financial liability (the loan) should be removed from the balance sheet 'when, and only when, it is extinguished' which may be at a later time than is currently envisaged by IAS 20 (IAS 39, 57).

IAS 39 would also require that the grant should be recognised in the net profit or loss for the period in which the loan is extinguished (IAS 39, 63). IAS 20 requires that the grant is recognised as income over the periods necessary to match the grant with the costs that it is intended to compensate; this may mean spreading the grant over a number of periods (see 34.8).

34.7 MEASUREMENT OF GOVERNMENT GRANTS

A government grant which takes the form of the transfer of cash and cash equivalents is measured at the amount of the cash and cash equivalents received or receivable. When a government grant takes the form of the transfer of a non-monetary asset, the grant and the asset are measured at either:

- the fair value of the non-monetary asset; or
- a nominal amount.

(IAS 20, 23)

For example, if a government gives an entity a property with a fair value of €50 million, the entity either:

- measures both the property and the grant at €50 million; or
- measures both the property and the grant at a nominal amount, presumably zero.

IAS 20 notes that fair value is the usual approach (IAS 20, 23). The use of fair values is also consistent with IAS 18 which requires revenue to be recorded at the fair value of consideration received (IAS 18, 9).

Fair value is being used in such a case solely to measure the 'cost' of the asset and the grant; it is not being used to revalue the asset.

When the government forgives a loan, or otherwise reduces a liability owing by the entity to the government, the grant is measured at the amount forgiven or extinguished.

34.8 RECOGNITION OF GOVERNMENT GRANTS AS INCOME

A government grant should be recognised as income on a systematic basis over the periods necessary to match the grant with the related costs which it is intended to compensate (IAS 20, 12). The grant should not be credited directly to shareholders' interests. This requirement has two consequences:

- a grant which is receivable as compensation for expenses or losses already incurred or for the purpose of giving immediate financial support to the entity with no future related costs should be recognised as income immediately (IAS 20, 20); and
- a grant which is receivable as compensation for expenses or losses that will be incurred in future periods should be allocated over those future periods (IAS 20, 20).

For example:

- when an entity receives a grant in the form of a subsidy of employment costs, the grant is recognised as income in the same periods in which the employment costs are recognised as expenses;
- when an entity receives a government subsidy of £100 for each tonne of industrial output sold, the grant is recognised as income in the same period in which the sale is recognised;
- when an entity receives a grant of $10 million as compensation for losses incurred in operating in a particular location, the grant is recognised as income in the same period in which the losses are incurred;
- when a government forgives a loan of £10 million as compensation for losses incurred, the amount forgiven is recognised as income in the same period in which the losses are incurred; and
- when an entity receives a grant of €50 million in respect of a property with a useful life of 25 years, the entity recognises €2 million of the grant as income in each year (assuming that straight-line depreciation is used).

When the government makes a grant in advance of the expenses or losses being incurred, the grant is included in deferred income until the expenses or losses are recognised. When the government makes a grant in a later period than that in which the expenses or losses are incurred, the grant is recognised as a receivable in the period the expenses or losses are recognised only if the conditions in 34.6 above are met. In many cases, therefore, grants may be recognised as income in a later period than that in which the matching expenses or losses are recognised.

For example:

- when an entity receives a government subsidy of £100 for each tonne of industrial output sold in 2002 but the government does not approve the grant until after the entity has issued its 2002 financial statements, the grant is recognised as income only when there is reasonable assurance that the grant will be received which is not until 2003 or later; and
- when an entity receives a grant of $10 million in 2002 as compensation for losses incurred in operating in a particular location in 2000, the grant is recognised as a receivable and as income only when there is reasonable assurance that the grant will be received which may not be until it is received in 2002.

A grant may be received as part of a package to which a number of conditions are attached. In such circumstances, it may be appropriate to allocate parts of the grant on different bases (IAS 20, 19). For example, an entity may receive a grant which comprises part of the cost of a factory, a subsidy of borrowing costs incurred in financing the factory, and a subsidy of employment costs associated with the operation of the factory. That part of the grant which relates to the cost of the factory is recognised as income over the useful life of the factory. Those parts of the grant that relate to borrowing costs and employment costs are recognised as income in the same periods in which the costs are recognised as expenses.

A grant may relate to a non-depreciable asset such as land. For example, a government may donate a plot of land to a newly privatised entity or to an entity which agrees to operate in a particular location. If the grant is recognised at its nominal value, no income is recognised. If the asset and the grant are recognised at fair value, the grant is not usually recognised as income until the asset is sold.

The entity may be required to fulfil certain obligations as a condition of receiving the grant related to the non-depreciable asset. If so, the grant is recognised as income over the periods which bear the cost of meeting the obligations (IAS 20, 18). For example, a government may donate land to an entity on condition that the entity constructs and operates a factory on that land. If the land and the grant are measured at nominal value, no income is recognised. If the land and the grant are recognised at fair value, the grant is recognised as income over the life of the factory. If the entity buys the land and the government makes a cash grant towards its cost, the grant is recognised as income over the life of the factory.

34.9 PRESENTATION OF GRANTS

34.9.1 Grants Related to Assets

Grants related to assets should be presented in the balance sheet as either:

- deferred income; or
- a deduction in arriving at the carrying amount of the asset.

(IAS 20, 24)

For example, if an entity receives a grant of €50 million in respect of a property, the entity should either:

- credit the €50 million grant to deferred income; or
- deduct the €50 million grant in arriving at the carrying amount of the property.

This free choice was not addressed in the comparability project because it does not affect the measurement of the profit or loss for any period or the net assets (equity) of the entity. The European Commission's accounting advisory forum addressed this choice in the context of the Fourth Directive and concluded that the deferred income approach is preferable but that the deduction of grant in arriving at the carrying amount of the asset should be allowed[1].

If the grant is set up as deferred income it is recognised as income on a systematic and rational basis over the useful life of the asset (IAS 20, 26). If the grant is deducted from the carrying amount of the asset it is recognised as income over the useful life of the asset by way of a reduced depreciation charge (IAS 20, 27). IAS 20 notes that the purchase of assets and the receipt of related grants can cause major movements in the cash flow of an enterprise. These cash flows are often disclosed as separate items in the cash flow statement regardless of whether the grant and related asset are shown net or gross in the balance sheet (IAS 20, 28).

Extract 34.2 *Recognition of grants related to an asset as income*

Bayer, Germany, 31 December 2001 (IAS)

In accordance with IAS 20 (Accounting for Government Grants and Disclosure of Government Assistance), government grants and subsidies that serve to promote investment are treated as deferred income. The amounts are gradually reversed during the useful lives of the respective assets and recognised in income. The main component of deferred income as of December 31, 2001 comprises €111 million (2000: €113 million) in such grants and subsidies received from governments; the amount reversed and recognized in income was €17 million (2000: €13million).

Extract 34.3 *Recognition of grants related to assets*

Fiat, Italy, 31 December 2000 (IAS)

Capital investment grants related to investments in property, plant and equipment are recorded as deferred income when collection becomes certain and credited to income over the useful life of the related asset.

Extract 34.4 *Grants related to research and development and assets*

Danisco, Denmark, 30 April 2001 (IAS)

Government grants include grants for research and development as well as investment grants etc. Research and development grants are recorded in the profit and loss account on a systematic basis to match the related costs. Investment grants are set off against the cost of the subsidised assets.

34.9.2 Grants Related to Income

Grants related to income may be presented as either:

- a credit in the income statement, either separately or under a general heading such as other income; or
- a deduction in reporting the related expense.

(IAS 20, 29)

Example 34.1 *Repayment of government grant*

At the beginning of 1999, an entity receives a grant of £5 million towards the cost of plant on condition that it uses the plant in a development area for a minimum of five years. If the entity ceases to use the plant in the development area, it is required to repay the grant less £1 million for each completed year of use. The cost of the plant, before deducting the grant was £15 million and the plant has a useful life of ten years. The entity uses the straight-line method of depreciation.

At the beginning of 2002, following a reorganisation of its operations, the entity moves the plant to a non-development area. It is required to repay £2 million of the grant (£5 million less three years at £1 million).

If the grant had been set up as deferred income, a balance of £3.5 million would be outstanding in deferred income at the beginning of 2002 (£5 million less three years amortisation of £0.5 million). The repayment of £2 million is charged to deferred income, so reducing the balance outstanding to £1.5 million which is amortised over the remaining seven years of the useful life of the plant. No adjustment is necessary for depreciation which has been based on the cost of the plant; therefore, the annual depreciation charge remains at £1.5 million.

If the grant had been deducted in determining the carrying amount of the plant, the carrying amount of the plant at the beginning of 2002 would be £7 million (£15 million less £5 million grant less three years depreciation at £1 million). The entity adds the repayment of £2 million to the carrying amount of the plant to give a revised carrying amount of £9 million. However, IAS 20 requires that the cumulative depreciation be recalculated. The depreciable amount of the plant is now £12 million (£15 million less £3 million grant retained) so the annual depreciation charge should be £1.2 million giving a revised carrying amount at the beginning of 2002 of £8.4 million. Therefore, the entity must recognise additional depreciation of £0.6 million in 2002 (plus the £1.2 million for 2002).

34.10 REPAYMENT OF GRANTS

In certain circumstances, an entity may have to repay a government grant, for example when it fails to meet any ongoing obligations for the grant. The repayment should be accounted for as a change in an accounting estimate and not a change in accounting policy or an error.

The repayment of a grant related to expenses should be:

- applied first against any unamortised deferred income in respect of the grant; and
- recognised immediately as an expense to the extent that it exceeds any such deferred income.

(IAS 20, 32)

The repayment of a grant related to an asset should be recorded by:

- increasing the carrying amount of the asset or reducing the deferred income balance by the amount repayable; and
- recognising as an expense the cumulative additional depreciation that would have been recognised to date as an expense in the absence of the grant.

(IAS 20, 32)

The circumstances that give rise to the repayment of a grant relating to an asset may require the carrying amount of the asset to be reviewed for impairment (IAS 20, 33).

34.11 DISCLOSURE

An entity should disclose:

- the accounting policy adopted for government grants, including the methods of presentation adopted in the financial statements;
- the nature and extent of government grants recognised in the financial statements; and
- unfulfilled conditions and other contingencies attaching to government assistance that has been recognised.

(IAS 20, 39)

An entity should also indicate other forms of government assistance from which it has directly benefited (IAS 20, 39). Where such benefit is significant it may be necessary to disclose the nature, extent and duration of the assistance (IAS 20, 36). Other forms of government assistance which may require disclosure include:

- free technical and marketing advice;
- guarantees;
- government purchases; and
- the provision of infrastructure, such as transport, communications, irrigation, drainage, etc, when the provision is for the specific benefit of the entity rather than the community at large.

Loans at nil or low interest rates from government are a form of government assistance. While the terms and conditions of the loans are disclosed in accordance with IAS 32, the benefit of nil or low interest rates is not quantified by the imputation of interest (IAS 20, 37).

IAS 20 does not deal with government assistance which is provided in the form of benefits that are available in determining taxable profits or current tax expense, for example, accelerated depreciation and tax-free income or profits (IAS 20, 2). Therefore no disclosures about these items are required by IAS 20 but the effect of such items may need to be disclosed as part of the explanation of the relationship between tax expense and accounting profit (IAS 12, 81(c) – see chapter 31).

IAS 20 does not deal with government participation in the ownership of the entity (IAS 20, 2). Therefore no disclosure about such participation is required by IAS 20 but disclosures would be required under IAS 1 if the government is the parent or ultimate parent of the entity (IAS 1, 102) and under IAS 24 if the government and the entity are related parties (IAS 24, 20 and 22).

34.12 GOVERNMENT GRANTS RELATING TO BIOLOGICAL ASSETS

IAS 41 addresses government grants relating to biological assets, that is a living animal or plant, where the biological asset is measured at its fair value less estimated point-of-sale costs. IAS 41 requires a different treatment from that in IAS 20. IAS 20 must be applied where biological assets are measured at cost less accumulated depreciation and accumulated impairment losses (IAS 41, 37).

IAS 41 requires that an unconditional government grant related to a biological asset measured at its fair value less estimated point-of-sale costs should be recognised as income when, and only when, the government grant becomes receivable (IAS 41, 34). If the government grant is conditional, including where the government grant requires an entity not to engage in specified agricultural activity, the entity should recognise the government grant as income when, and only when, the conditions attaching to the grant are met (IAS 41, 35).

The two key differences from IAS 20 are that:

- the grant is recognised in income once the conditions are met and not over the life of the asset; and
- where the grant is conditional, it is recognised once conditions are met, not when there is reasonable assurance that they will be met.

The terms and conditions relating to a conditional grant may vary. If it is repayable in full and all conditions are not met then it is not recognised until all conditions are met. However, if part of the grant may be retained if some of the conditions are met, for example based on passage of time, then an appropriate amount of the grant would be recognised as income once the conditions for its retention are met.

Note

1 *Government Grants*, European Commission Accounting Advisory Forum, Brussels, 1995, p7.

CHAPTER 35

Borrowing Costs

35.1 RELEVANT STANDARD AND INTERPRETATION

IAS 23 *Borrowing Costs*
SIC 2 *Consistency – Capitalisation of Borrowing Costs*

35.2 HISTORY

IAS 23 *Capitalisation of Borrowing Costs* (IAS 23 [1984]) was approved in 1984. It allowed an entity to choose whether to expense or capitalise borrowing costs and included a limitation on the borrowing costs which could be capitalised.

The IASC reconsidered this free choice in the comparability project and initially proposed that borrowing costs should be expensed (benchmark treatment) or capitalised (allowed alternative treatment) (E32, 188). The IASC was persuaded to change its proposals and require the capitalisation of those borrowing costs that met certain criteria and the expensing of all other borrowing costs (*Statement of Intent on the Comparability of Financial Statements*, appendix 2).

The revised proposal was exposed in E39 *Borrowing Costs*. After further consideration of the issue, the IASC decided to revert to the proposals in E32, that is, the expensing of borrowing costs as the benchmark treatment and the capitalisation of those borrowing costs that meet certain criteria as the allowed alternative treatment (*IASC Update*, October 1992, p1). These treatments were included in IAS 23 *Borrowing Costs* which was approved in November 1993 and which applied to financial statements for accounting periods beginning on or after 1 January 1995.

The IASB reconsidered the choice of treatments in the second improvements project. It tentatively decided that all borrowing costs should be recognised as an expense in the period in which they are incurred and that capitalisation of borrowing costs should not be permitted (*IASB*

Update, November 2001, p4). It noted, however, that none of its partner standard setting bodies adopts such an approach. The IASB decided, therefore, to consider the issue again as part of a wider project on the amount at which an asset should initially be measured (*IASB Update*, January 2002, p3).

35.3 IOSCO

In June 1994, IOSCO advised the IASC that IAS 23 was acceptable for the purposes of the IOSCO core standards. However, IOSCO identified the following suspense issues:

- certain IOSCO members may accept the capitalisation of borrowing costs only if information equivalent to immediate expensing of those costs is disclosed – the disclosure of this information is already required by IAS 23; and
- some IOSCO members are prevented from capitalising interest with respect to mere acquisitions – IAS 23 does not allow the capitalisation of borrowing costs on 'mere acquisitions'.

IAS 23 is included in 'IAS 2000' endorsed by IOSCO in May 2000. There is one supplemental treatment. Some IOSCO members are concerned about the immediate expensing of borrowing costs (the IAS 23 benchmark treatment) and may require the use of the allowed alternative treatment (capitalisation).

35.4 IAS 23 IN BRIEF

Borrowing costs should be recognised as an expense in the period in which they are incurred (benchmark treatment).

Borrowing costs which are directly attributable to the acquisition, construction or production of qualifying assets, that is certain items of property, plant, equipment and inventories, should be capitalised (allowed alternative treatment).

35.5 DEFINITION OF BORROWING COSTS

For entities which adopt the benchmark treatment, the definition of borrowing costs is unimportant (other than for classification purposes in the income statement). There is no requirement, nor any likelihood of a requirement, that such entities should disclose the amount of borrowing costs which they would have capitalised had they adopted the allowed alternative treatment.

For those entities which opt for the allowed alternative treatment, the definition of borrowing costs is important as it sets a limit on what can be capitalised. *Borrowing costs* are defined as interest and other costs incurred by an entity in connection with the borrowing of funds (IAS 23, 4). Borrowing costs may include:

- interest on bank overdrafts and short-term and long-term borrowings;
- the amortisation of discounts or premiums relating to borrowings;
- the amortisation of ancillary costs incurred in connection with the arrangement of borrowings;
- finance charges in respect of finance leases; and
- exchange differences arising from foreign currency borrowings to the extent that they are regarded as an adjustment to interest costs.

(IAS 23, 5)

Dividends on preferred capital which is classified as a financial liability should also be treated as borrowing as IAS 32 states that the classification of a financial instrument in the balance sheet determines whether the dividends are classified as an expense or as a distribution of profits (IAS 32, 31). If the capital is classified as a liability, the dividends are classified as interest and may be included in borrowing costs for the purposes of applying IAS 23. Similarly, interest on that part of a compound instrument which is classified as equity is a distribution of profits and is not, therefore, included in borrowing costs.

One other troublesome issue is whether exchange differences arising on a foreign currency borrowing are borrowing costs. When an entity borrows in a foreign currency in order to get the benefit of lower interest rates, it is logical that any exchange loss is treated as part of the borrowing costs. It is also logical that when an entity suffers higher interest rates on a foreign currency borrowing that any resulting exchange gain is treated as a deduction from the other borrowing costs. If exchange differences are included in borrowing costs for the purposes of IAS 23, it is important to remember that capitalisation ceases when the asset is ready for its intended use and, therefore, that exchange losses are not capitalised after that time.

Extract 35.1 *Foreign exchange differences as borrowing costs*

Sinopec Shanghai Petrochemical, People's Republic of China, 31 December 2001 (IAS)

Construction in progress represents buildings, various plant and equipment under construction and pending installation, and is stated at cost less the government grants that compensate the Company for the cost of construction. Cost comprises direct costs of construction as well as interest charges, and foreign exchange differences on related borrowed funds to the extent that they are regarded as an adjustment to interest charges during the construction period, ...

Extract 35.2 *Foreign exchange differences as borrowing costs*

MOL, Hungary, 31 December 2000 (IAS)

Borrowing costs that are directly attributable to the acquisition, construction or production of a qualifying asset are capitalised. ... Borrowing costs include interest charges and other costs incurred in connection with the borrowing of funds, including exchange differences arising from foreign currency borrowings used to finance these projects to the extent that they are regarded as an adjustment to interest costs.

IAS 23 is silent on whether the interest element of retirement and other employee benefit costs may be, or should be, included in borrowing costs. IAS 19 acknowledges that interest is a component of employee benefit costs but does not specify where the interest cost should be presented in the income statement; it may be included in employee benefit costs or financing costs. For those entities which have unfunded retirement plans and those plans, in effect, provide a significant part of the funding of the entity, it seems reasonable that the interest cost should be included in borrowing costs.

35.6 RECOGNITION – BENCHMARK TREATMENT

Borrowing costs should be recognised as an expense in the period in which they are incurred (IAS 23, 7). This policy is practised by many companies that already apply IAS (*International Accounting Standards Survey 2000*, p296).

35.7 RECOGNITION – ALLOWED ALTERNATIVE TREATMENT

Borrowing costs that are directly attributable to the acquisition, construction or production of a qualifying asset should be capitalised as part of the cost of that asset (IAS 23, 11). If borrowing costs are capitalised on one qualifying asset, they must be capitalised on all qualifying assets (SIC 2, 3). All other borrowing costs should be recognised as an expense in the period in which they are incurred (IAS 23, 10).

There are two tests which must be passed before borrowing costs can be capitalised under the allowed alternative treatment:

- the costs must be directly attributable to the acquisition, construction or production of an asset; and
- the asset must be a qualifying asset.

35.7.1 Qualifying Assets

A *qualifying asset* is an asset that necessarily takes a substantial period of time to get ready for its intended use or sale (IAS 23, 4). An asset which is ready for use or sale soon after acquisition is not a qualifying asset. Similarly, capitalisation of borrowing costs on a qualifying asset ceases as soon as the asset is ready for its intended use or sale.

IAS 23 and other IASs provide some guidance on what are, and what are not, qualifying assets. They include:

- inventories that require a substantial period of time to bring them to a saleable condition (IAS 23, 6);
- construction contracts (IAS 11, 18);
- property, plant and equipment such as manufacturing plants, power generation facilities and other property in the course of construction or development (IAS 23, 6); and
- internally developed intangible assets (IAS 38, 54).

Inventories that are routinely manufactured or otherwise produced in large quantities on a repetitive basis over a short period of time are not qualifying assets. The key to the distinction is the length of time that is required to get inventories ready for use. Therefore, inventories which involve a substantial period of storage during which the production process continues are qualifying assets. Examples include wines and spirits which necessarily require time to reach maturity and timber which has to season before it is used.

IAS 23 allows investment property to be treated as a qualifying asset (IAS 23, 6). However, the definition of investment property in IAS 40 now excludes property that is being constructed or developed for future use as investment property (IAS 40, 7(d)). Such property is accounted for in accordance with IAS 16 and may, in appropriate cases, be treated as a qualifying asset for the purpose of IAS 23.

Extract 35.3 *Qualifying assets – exploration and development activities*

Anglogold, South Africa, 31 December 2000 (South African GAAP and IAS)

Capitalised mine development costs include expenditure incurred to develop new ore bodies, to define further mineralisation in existing ore bodies and to expand the capacity of a mine. Where funds have been borrowed specifically to finance a project, the amount of interest capitalised represents the actual borrowing costs incurred.

Extract 35.4 *Qualifying assets – development of hypermarkets*

Dairy Farm, Hong Kong, 31 December 2001 (IAS)

Borrowing costs relating to major development projects, mainly hypermarket properties, are capitalised during the construction period until the asset is substantially completed. Capitalised borrowing costs are included as part of the cost of the asset.

Extract 35.5 *Qualifying assets – aircraft prepayments*

SAS, Sweden, 31 December 2000 (IAS)

Interest expenses on prepayments for aircraft not yet delivered are capitalised. If it is decided to postpone delivery of aircraft for which prepayments have been made, capitalisation of interest expenses ceases.

IAS 23 [1984] allowed the capitalisation of borrowing costs for investments in other entities until the commencement of the investee's planned principal operations are in progress (see IAS 23 [1984], 9, 10 and 24). Under IAS 23 [1984], an entity could capitalise borrowing costs on, say, an investment in an associate or jointly controlled entity which was constructing a manufacturing plant but which had not yet started its operations. IAS 23 no longer permits the capitalisation of borrowing costs in such circumstances.

The transitional provisions in the revised IAS 23 do not deal with an entity which has capitalised borrowing costs on an investment in the past. Therefore, on the implementation of the revised IAS 23, an entity may treat the new IAS as a change in accounting policy and adjust the carrying amount of the investment, and follow the other procedures for a change in accounting policy in IAS 8.

35.7.2 Borrowing Costs Eligible for Capitalisation

The borrowing costs that are directly attributable to the acquisition, construction or production of a qualifying asset are those borrowing costs that would have been avoided if the expenditure on the qualifying asset had not been made (IAS 23, 13). Therefore, IAS 23 looks first to borrowings which are specific to the acquisition, construction or production of the qualifying asset and after that to general borrowings which could have been avoided.

When funds are borrowed specifically for the purpose of obtaining a qualifying asset, the amount of borrowing costs eligible for capitalisation on that asset are the actual borrowing costs incurred on the borrowing during the period, less any investment income on the temporary investment of the funds generated by those borrowings (IAS 23, 15). Investment income arises when the funds are drawn down and temporarily invested pending their expenditure on the qualifying asset. The

Example 35.1 *Specific borrowings*

A borrows $10 million in order to finance the construction of a new plant. Construction started on 1 June 2002. A is required to draw down the borrowing in three tranches – $2 million on 1 June 2002, $5 million on 1 October 2002 and the balance of $3 million on 1 December 2002.

In its 2002 financial statements, A capitalises the actual borrowing costs (subject to the other tests in IAS 23) less any investment income on the temporary investment of the three tranches pending the use of the funds for construction.

Example 35.2 *Weighted average cost of general borrowings*

A has three sources of borrowings during 2002 – a 5 year loan of £10 million with interest at 10% a year, a 20 year loan of £20 million at an interest rate of 8% and a variable rate bank overdraft. The two loans were outstanding throughout the year; the average amount of the bank overdraft was £3 million and interest on the overdraft in 2002 amounted to £450,000.

If all borrowings are used for the purpose of obtaining qualifying assets but none of the borrowings relates to a specific qualifying asset, the capitalisation rate is calculated as follows:

	Outstanding borrowing	*Interest for 2002*
	£	£
5 year loan	10,000,000	1,000,000
20 year loan	20,000,000	1,600,000
Bank overdraft	3,000,000	450,000
Total	33,000,000	3,050,000
Capitalisation rate		9.242%

amount capitalised is also restricted by the amount of expenditures on the assets which have been incurred (see 35.6 below).

When funds are borrowed generally and then used for the purpose of obtaining a qualifying asset, the amount of borrowing costs eligible for capitalisation is determined by applying a capitalisation rate to the expenditures on that asset (IAS 23, 17). The capitalisation rate is the weighted average rate on all borrowings outstanding during the period other than borrowings made specifically for the purpose of obtaining a qualifying asset (IAS 23, 17).

Example 35.3 *Weighted average cost of general borrowings*

A has the same three sources of borrowings during 2002 as in Example 35.2.

The 5 year loan of £10 million was used specifically for the purposes of acquiring a qualifying asset. Therefore it is excluded from the calculation of the weighted average which is used for other qualifying assets. The capitalisation rate for these assets is calculated as follows:

	Outstanding borrowing	*Interest for 2002*
	£	£
20 year loan	20,000,000	1,600,000
Bank overdraft	3,000,000	450,000
Total	23,000,000	2,050,000
Capitalisation rate		8.913%

When general borrowings are used for the purpose of obtaining a qualifying asset, there is no requirement to deduct any interest income on the investment of any surplus funds. The IASC did propose that such a deduction should be made (E39, 22) but withdrew the proposal when it approved the revised IAS 23. Therefore, in example 35.2, A may capitalise the full amount of £3,050,000 even if it earns interest income on the temporary investment of some of the borrowings (but the capitalisation of borrowing costs is also limited by the amount of expenditure on the asset and funds must have been used to pay for that expenditure).

In example 35.3, the position is more complicated:

- the 5 year loan is a borrowing made specifically for the purposes of acquiring a qualifying asset – therefore, any interest income on the temporary investment of the funds received on this loan restricts the amount of borrowing costs that may be capitalised on the asset concerned;

- the 20 year loan and the bank overdraft are general borrowings – therefore, the borrowing costs are not reduced by any interest income on the temporary investment of the funds.

While the distinction between specific and general borrowings has theoretical merit, a number of difficulties may arise in practice. For example, the entity may co-ordinate all its financing activities through a central treasury function so that it is unable to attribute specific borrowings to particular expenditure. Alternatively, a group may use a range of instruments to borrow funds at varying rates of interest and then lend those funds on different terms to other entities in the group.

Consolidation procedures require that any intra-group profit is eliminated and that the amounts capitalised are based on the borrowing costs incurred by the group (IAS 27, 17). However, if each subsidiary arranges its own borrowings, it uses a weighted average of its own borrowing costs which may be different from the group's weighted average rate of borrowings.

In a highly inflationary economy the impact of inflation has a significant impact on borrowing costs. It is inappropriate both to re-state the capital expenditure in accordance with IAS 29 (see chapter 42) and capitalise that part of the borrowing costs that compensates for the inflation during the same period (IAS 29, 21).

35.8 CAPITALISATION PROCEDURES

The amount of borrowing costs capitalised during a period should not exceed the lower of:

- the amount of borrowing costs incurred during that period (less interest income when appropriate) (IAS 23, 17); and
- the amount of borrowing costs that result from applying the capitalisation rate to the amount of expenditure on the qualifying asset.

Example 35.4 *Limit on capitalisation*

In example 35.2, A has incurred expenditure of £20 million on the qualifying asset during 2002. The expenditure was incurred evenly over the second half of the year. The capitalisation rate of 9.242% is applied to average expenditure of £10 million for half a year. Therefore, the amount capitalised is 9.242% × £10 million × 6/12 which is £462,100.

The expenditure on a qualifying asset includes only that expenditure which has resulted in payments of cash, transfers of other assets or the assumption of interest-bearing liabilities. It does not include amounts which have not yet been paid and which are not interest-bearing liabilities. For example, borrowing costs are not added to expenditure which has been incurred but which is included in trade payables. The expenditure on a qualifying asset includes borrowing costs which have been capitalised in a previous period. It is reduced by any progress payments received (as may be the case with a construction contract) and grants received in connection with the asset.

The capitalisation of borrowing costs should commence when:

- expenditures for the asset have been incurred;
- borrowing costs have been incurred; and
- activities that are necessary to prepare the asset for its intended use or sale are in progress.

(IAS 23, 20)

The first two criteria require little explanation as the lack of expenditures or borrowing costs would, in any event, preclude the capitalisation of borrowing costs. The third criterion is the most important. 'Activities that are necessary to prepare the asset for its intended use or sale' include:

- production or construction of the asset;
- technical and administrative work prior to the commencement of physical construction, such as that required to obtain permits prior to the commencement of the physical construction (IAS 23, 22); and
- storage which is part of a maturing process of inventories (IAS 23, 24).

For example, borrowing costs may be capitalised when:

- expenditure has been incurred in acquiring land and technical work has commenced on the design and construction of plant and equipment to be erected on the land; and
- a manufactured beverage has gone through its initial manufacturing process and is being held in storage tanks as part of a fermentation process.

Borrowing costs should not be capitalised in respect of expenditure on:

- land which is held awaiting development work; or
- raw materials which are held awaiting a manufacturing process (unless that storage is part of a maturing process).

Borrowing costs are also not capitalised:

- when no production or development is taking place (IAS 23, 22); or
- during extended periods in which active development is interrupted (IAS 23, 23).

Capitalisation continues during natural delays which are common in the location in which the asset is being constructed (IAS 23, 24). For example, capitalisation of borrowing costs continues when work is interrupted by the monsoons in countries affected by the monsoon season.

Capitalisation continues even when the carrying amount of the qualifying asset, or its expected ultimate cost, exceeds its recoverable amount or net realisable value. In such circumstances, the increased carrying amount is written down or written off in accordance with the impairment requirements of the relevant IFRSs or recognised as an expected loss in the case of a construction contract.

Capitalisation of borrowing costs should cease when substantially all the activities necessary to prepare the qualifying asset for its intended use or sale are complete (IAS 23, 25). An asset is normally ready for its intended use or sale when the physical construction of the asset is complete even though routine administrative work or minor works might still continue (IAS 23, 26). Minor works include such things as the decoration of a property to the purchaser's or user's specification.

In E39, the IASC did propose that capitalisation should continue until the actual or intended date of achieving a commercial level of use (E39, 16). So, for example, capitalisation could have continued during the period in which an entity was seeking to find tenants for a property. This guidance was deleted before the revised IAS 23 was approved. Therefore, capitalisation of borrowing costs ceases notwithstanding that the entity is not yet using the asset at a commercial level.

Some qualifying assets are completed in parts and each part is capable of being used while construction continues on other parts. For example, a property development may be completed in stages or different parts of the same inventory may reach maturity at different times. The capitalisation of borrowing costs should cease on each part of an asset when substantially all the activities necessary to prepare that part for its intended use or sale are completed (IAS 23, 27). This is achieved automatically if the asset is sold as the expenditure relating to that asset is no longer included on the balance sheet. Care is needed in the case of those assets which are retained on the balance sheet, for example, unsold properties and inventories which have completed their maturity process.

Example 35.5 *Cessation of borrowing costs*

A business park comprises several buildings, each of which can be used individually. Capitalisation of borrowing costs ceases on each building as soon as it is ready for its intended use, even if the entity is still seeking a buyer or tenant for the building. Capitalisation of borrowing costs continues on other buildings which are not yet complete.

35.9 DISCLOSURE

An entity should disclose:

- the accounting policy adopted for borrowing costs;
- the amount of borrowing costs capitalised during the period; and
- the capitalisation rate used to determine the amount of borrowing costs eligible for capitalisation.

Extract 35.6 *Accounting policy for capitalisation of borrowing costs*

Telekomunikacja Polska, Poland, 31 December 2000 (IAS)

Borrowing costs are written off to the profit and loss account as incurred net of an amount capitalised calculated using weighted average capitalisation rate. Borrowing costs are capitalised as part of the costs of the relevant fixed asset up to the date of commissioning and amortised to the profit and loss account over the period in which the asset is depreciated. Borrowing costs include interest, amortisation of discount on bonds and commercial papers issued, amortisation of ancillary costs incurred in connection with the arrangement of borrowings and foreign exchange differences.

Extract 35.7 *Accounting policy for capitalisation of borrowing costs*

CEZ, Czech Republic, 31 December 2001 (IAS)

The company capitalizes all interest costs incurred in connection with its construction program that theoretically could have been avoided if expenditures for the assets had not been made.

Extract 35.8 *Borrowing costs capitalised during the period and capitalisation rate*

Stora Enso, Finland, 31 December 2001 (IAS)

The Group has capitalised interest on the construction of qualifying assets using interest rates ranging from 6% to 11%. The amount of interest capitalised for the year ended 31 December 2001 totalled EUR 7.9 (EUR 3.3) million with a corresponding amortisation charge amounting to EUR 10.8 (EUR 16.6) million.

Extract 35.9 *Borrowing costs capitalised during the period and capitalisation rate*

Sinopec Shanghai Petrochemical, People's Republic of China, 31 December 2000 (IAS)

	2000 RMB'000	1999 RMB'000
Interest on bank loans and advances	375,517	482,625
Less: Amount capitalised on construction in progress*	(20,048)	(47,331)
Interest expenses, net	355,469	435,294

*Borrowing costs have been capitalised at a rate of between 5.85% and 8.91% per annum (1999: 5.95%–10.98%) for construction in progress.

CHAPTER 36

Segmental Reporting

36.1 RELEVANT STANDARD

IAS 14 *Segment Reporting*

36.2 HISTORY

IAS 14 *Reporting Financial Information by Segment* (IAS 14 [1981]) was approved in 1981 and required the disclosure of sales, segment result, segment assets employed and the basis of inter-segment pricing for each reported industry and geographical segment.

IAS 14 was included in the original scope of the improvements project. However, in March 1992, the IASC decided to limit the improvements project to those IASs affected by the *Statement of Intent on the Comparability of Financial Statements* which removed IAS 14 from the scope of the project. At the same time, the IASC decided to revise IAS 14 because the topic was of particular importance to securities regulators including IOSCO (*IASC Update*, March 1992, p1).

The project proposal was approved in June 1992. This was the first project on which the IASC chose the members of the steering committee from among the people nominated by board and consultative group organisations and the IASC's member bodies. In view of the importance of this project to IOSCO, the IASC invited IOSCO to appoint a regulator to participate in the work of the steering committee. Somewhat surprisingly, the invitation was not accepted. Following the IASC's 1994 invitation to IOSCO to participate in the work of all steering committees, IOSCO appointed an observer (but not a regulator) to the steering committee.

The project addressed a number of concerns about IAS 14. Some had argued for the clarification and extension of the disclosure requirements and the removal of the implicit or explicit options in the calculation of segment result[1] and the identification of reportable industry and geographic segments (*IASC Insight*, June 1994, p14). One of the aims of the project was, therefore, to 'provide limits to, and guidance for, the use of management judgement in identifying the products and services that should be identified as industry or business segments, and the countries that should be grouped together to form separate geographical segments' (*IASC Insight*, June 1994, p14).

In another 'first' on this project, the IASC published in 1994 a background issues paper, *Reporting Financial Information by Segment*. It was written by Paul Pacter who had recently written the FASB's research report on the same topic[2] and who was later to take over as manager of the IASC project. The issues paper reconsidered the importance of reporting financial information by business and geographical segment. As well as examining international and national standards, regulations and recommendations, it provided an overview of the then segment reporting practices of over 1000 large companies in 32 countries. The paper identified 13 basic issues and 40 sub-issues confronting the IASC and possible approaches to their solution. In yet another 'first', during the comment period on the DSOP, the IASC invited a number of interested organisations, companies and individuals to participate in discussions. Again this was seen as a precedent for similar consultations or public hearings on later IASC proposals.

The IASC's work on this project was carried out in parallel with reviews of the Canadian and US standards on segment reporting. Throughout the project there was close consultation at staff level between the IASC, the CICA and the FASB, and Patricia McConnell, who chaired the IASC steering committee, regularly participated in meetings with those responsible for the Canadian and US projects. This co-operation was a sign of the further evolution of the direct links between the IASC and national standard setting bodies which had become such a feature of the IASC's work by the mid-1990s. While there are a number of important differences between the revised IAS 14 and the virtually identical, revised standards adopted in the Canada and the United States[3], it was felt at the time that a considerable degree of convergence was achieved and that many entities would be able to present segment information which complied with both the revised IAS 14 and the revised Canadian and US standards[4].

The IASC approved the revised IAS 14 in January 1997. However, the IASC decided to delay the final adoption of the revised IAS pending further harmonisation efforts with Canada and the United States (*IASC Update*, January 1997, p1)[5]. IAS 14 *Segment Reporting* was approved finally in July 1997 and applied to accounting periods beginning on or after 1 July 1998. The IASC had been unable to achieve further harmonisation with the Canadian and American standards.

36.3 IOSCO

An adequate international standard on segment reporting had always been important to IOSCO. As a result, IOSCO wrote to the IASC in 1990 setting out its recommendations for improvements to IAS 14 [1981]. Among other changes, IOSCO asked for the disclosure of the following additional items:

- export sales in aggregate and by geographical area;
- infrequently occurring items included in segment data;
- net income, investment, and geographical areas of vertically integrated equity investees by segment;
- sales to major individual customers;
- the nature and effects of financial statement restatements on segment information; and
- depreciation, depletion, amortisation and capital expenditures of segments.

(*Reporting Financial Information by Segment*, p8)

In June 1994, IOSCO advised the IASC that it concurred with the review of IAS 14 and asked the IASC to consider the following issues in addition to those which had been identified in its 1990 letter:

- more definitive guidelines for determining reportable business and geographical segments (this has been done in the revised IAS 14);
- required allocations of the cost of assets used in more than one segment and allocation of income and expenses identifiable with segments (this has been done in the revised IAS 14);
- more definitive guidance on the measurement of segmental profitability (this has been done in the revised IAS 14);
- exemption from disclosure when it would be detrimental to the competitive interests of the entity (such an exemption had been rejected by the IASC in IAS 14 [1981] and was rejected in the revised IAS 14);
- exemption from disclosure when the cost of preparing the information would be prohibitively expensive (such an exemption was rejected by the IASC in both IAS 14 [1981] and the revised IAS 14);
- guidance on the inclusion or exclusion of inter-segment loans and advances, inter-segment investments, and valuation allowances in segment asset totals (this has been done in the revised IAS 14);
- treatment of sales by source or destination (this has been done in the revised IAS 14); and
- disclosure of foreign currency risks in geographical segments.

All the issues raised by IOSCO were considered in the issues paper *Reporting Financial Information by Segment*.

Early in 1997 IOSCO advised the IASC that a majority of its members favoured the IASC's approach in the revised IAS 14 and that all the members of its working party on multinational securities offerings would be prepared to recommend acceptance of the IAS (*IASC Insight*, March 1997, p21). The differences between the revised IAS 14 and the revised US standard may have been a potential obstacle to the SEC's support for the IASC but the SEC staff concluded that the IASC's approach has 'substantial merit' (*IASC Insight*, March 1997, p21). The SEC staff has also suggested that the IASC, the CICA and the FASB should undertake a joint study of the 'resulting quality of segmentation and related disclosures after the [revised] standards have been in use for a period of time, say five years' (*IASC Insight*, March 1997, p21).

IAS 14 is included in 'IAS 2000' endorsed by IOSCO in May 2000. There are five supplemental treatments:

- the need for disclosure of foreign sales, including export sales, by segment for both primary and secondary segments;
- the need for disclosure of the amount of a significant [10%] concentration of revenue from one customer, including disclosure of the segment in which revenue is recognised;
- the need for disclosure of revenue by product or service or by groups of closely related products or services;
- the need for restatement of comparative segment information subsequent to a business combination accounted for as a uniting of interests (the IASB proposes to require that all business combinations should be accounted for as acquisitions); and
- concerns that the definition of segment revenue and segment expense exclude gains or losses on sales of investment property unless the segment's operations involve the operation of investment properties.

In its report, IOSCO also reiterates the view expressed by the SEC immediately after the approval of the revised IAS 14 that the IASB should consider reviewing the quality of segment disclosures after a suitable period (five years) with a view to further convergence with national standard setters (the IASB has identified this as a potential convergence project).

36.4 IAS 14 IN BRIEF

An entity should report information for both business and geographical segments. Segments are determined by reference to the dominant source and nature of the entity's risks and returns and usually reflect the entity's internal reporting and organisational structure. Full segment disclosures are required for the 'primary segments'; less detailed disclosures are required about secondary segments. The main disclosures are summarised in table 36.1.

Table 36.1 *IAS 14 – the main disclosures*

Disclosure	*Segments*	
	Primary	*Secondary*
Sales or other operating revenues	✓	
Sales to external customers	✓	✓
Revenue from transactions with other segments	✓	
Depreciation and amortisation expense	✓	
Other non-cash expenses	✓	
Segment result	✓	
Segment assets	✓	✓
Segment liabilities	✓	
Capital expenditure	✓	✓
Reconciliation to financial statements	✓	
Activities of business segments	✓	✓
Composition of geographical segments	✓	✓
Basis of pricing inter-segment transfers	✓	✓

36.5 SCOPE OF APPLICATION

IAS 14 applies to the financial statements of:

- entities whose equity or debt securities are publicly traded or which are in the process of issuing such securities in public securities markets (IAS 14, 2); and
- any other entity which chooses to disclose segment information in IFRS financial statements (IAS 14, 5).

Segment information needs to be presented only on the basis of the consolidated financial statements (IAS 14, 6). Therefore, segment information is not required in respect of parent financial statements when consolidated financial statements are published. Segment information is required, however, in any financial statements published by a subsidiary if the securities of that subsidiary are publicly traded.

IAS 14 [1981] applied to subsidiaries whose securities were not publicly traded only when the requirements of the IAS were accepted practice for economically significant domestic entities in the same country (IAS 14, 26). The IASC feared that such subsidiaries might be put at a competitive disadvantage if IAS 14 required them to disclose information which was not disclosed by similar entities operating in the same country and which were not expected to disclose segment information under national requirements (*IASC News*, July 1981, p4)[6]. The IASC's decision was made in the context of the possible threat that the United Nations might require the disclosure of segment information by foreign transnationals operating in a particular country and in respect of their activities in that country while not requiring similar disclosures from domestic entities in that country. The IASC removed this limitation on the scope of application in the revised IAS 14.

36.6 SEGMENTS

The IASC gave detailed consideration to two approaches to the identification of segments:

- a 'risks and returns approach' under which segments are defined by reference to the dominant sources of risks faced by, and returns flowing to, the entity; and
- a 'management approach' under which segments are defined by reference to the entity's organisational structure and internal financial reporting system.

Throughout the project, the IASC favoured the 'risks and returns' approach while the Canadian and US standard setters in their project favoured the 'management approach'. However, considerable efforts were made to achieve a convergence of the two ideas. As a result, while IAS 14 continues to favour the 'risks and returns' approach, it acknowledges that the predominant sources of risks affect how most entities are organised and managed and, therefore, that the internal financial reporting structure is normally the basis for identifying the predominant source and nature of risks and differing rates of return (IAS 14, 27). In turn, this means that an entity's primary segments are normally based on the entity's internal financial reporting structure.

In order to apply the new approach, IAS 14 distinguishes between:

- industry and geographical segments;
- reportable segments; and
- primary and secondary segments (to be precise, primary and secondary 'formats' of reporting segment information).

The three stage approach is often confusing as IAS 14 uses 'risks and returns' and 'management structure' arguments to identify both industry and geographical segments and 'primary' and 'secondary' segments. Furthermore, an entity must check that its business and geographical segments are reportable segments and it must ensure that it has identified all the reportable business and geographical segments.

The chapter deals first with the identification of business and geographical segments. It then deals with whether or not those segments are reportable segments and the possibility that further business and geographical segments might have to be disclosed. Having identified the reportable segments, the chapter deals with the distinction between primary and secondary reportable segments, a distinction which is important only if an entity wants to take advantage of the reduced disclosures for secondary segments.

36.7 BUSINESS SEGMENTS

A *business segment* is a distinguishable component of an entity that is engaged in providing an individual product or service or a group of related products or services and which is subject to risks and returns that are different from those of other business segments. Factors which should be considered in determining whether products and services are related include:

- the nature of the products or services;
- the nature of the production processes;
- the type or class of customer for the products or services;
- the methods used to distribute the products or provide the services; and
- the nature of any regulatory environment, for example, banking, insurance, or public utilities.

(IAS 14, 9)

The products and services included in a segment are expected to be similar with respect to the majority of the factors listed above. Therefore, a segment does not include products and services with significantly differing risks and returns (IAS 14, 11). If there are such products and services in a segment, the entity needs to divide further that segment until it includes only those products and services with similar risks and returns.

An entity's business segments should be those organisational units for which information is reported to the board of directors and to the chief executive officer for the purpose of evaluating the unit's past performance and for making decisions about future allocations of resources

(IAS 14, 31). However, two or more internally reported business segments may be combined into a single segment when they are 'substantially similar', that is:

- they exhibit similar long-term financial performance; and
- they are similar in respect of all the factors listed in the definition of a business segment.

(IAS 14, 34)

In rare cases, the segments reported internally to the directors and management do not satisfy the definitions of business segments in IAS 14. In such cases, the entity should look to the next lower level of internal segmentation that reports information along product and service or geographical lines. The entity may need to do this for one or more of its business segments.

Table 36.2 *Examples of business segments for companies reporting under IFRSs*

Pharmaceuticals:

Bayer, Germany	Pharmaceuticals & Biological Products Consumer Care & Diagnostics Crop Protection Animal Health Plastics & Rubber Polyurethanes, Coatings & Colorants Chemicals
Novartis, Switzerland	Pharmaceuticals Generics Consumer Health CIBA Vision Animal Health
Pliva, Croatia	Pharmaceutical OTC DDDI Fine Chemical (+Azithr.) Research (Royalties) Animal Health and Agrochemicals Foodstuffs Cosmetics and Hygiene Products Other

Table 36.2 *Examples of business segments for companies reporting under IFRSs—Continued*

Consumer goods:	
adidas-Salomon, Germany	adidas Salomon TaylorMade – adidas Golf Mavic
Beiersdorf, Germany	Cosmed Medical Tesa
Gucci, Netherlands	Gucci Division Gucci Timepieces YSL Beauté Other Operations
Henkel, Germany	Laundry & Home Care Cosmetics/Toiletries Adhesives Henkel Technologies
Retail:	
Dairy Farm, Hong Kong	Supermarkets/Hypermarkets Convenience Stores Drugstores/Pharmacies Restaurants Other
Jelmoli, Switzerland	Retail Trade Retail Real Estate
Automotive:	
BMW, Germany	BMW Automobiles Rover Automobiles BMW Motorcycles Financial Services Miscellaneous
MAN, Germany	Commercial Vehicles Industrial Services Printing Machines Diesel Engines Industrial Equipment and Facilities MAN Financial Services
Volkswagen, Germany	Automotive Financial Services

Table 36.2 *Examples of business segments for companies reporting under IFRSs—Continued*

Banks:	
Dresdner Bank, Germany	Private Clients Asset Management Corporates & Markets Real Estate
Erste Bank, Austria	Retail and Real Estate Large Corporate Customers Trading and Investment Banking Asset Gathering
UBS, Switzerland	UBS Switzerland UBS Asset Management UBS Warburg
Telecommunications:	
Telia, Sweden	Mobile Carrier & Networks Business Solutions Enterprises
Swisscom, Switzerland	Retail and Network Wholesale and Carrier Services Enterprise Solutions Mobile Debitel Other
Mining:	
Impala, South Africa	Impala Platinum Barplats Impala Refining Services
Xstrata, Switzerland	Metals & Minerals Energy Forestry
Energy:	
CEZ, Czech Republic	Power Production Transmission
EVN, Austria	Electricity Gas Heating and Other Business Areas

Table 36.2 *Examples of business segments for companies reporting under IFRSs—Continued*	
MOL, Hungary	Exploration and Production Gas and Power Refining and Marketing
VA Tech, Austria	Metallurgy Hydro Power Generation Transmission and Distribution Water Systems Infrastructure
Verbund, Austria	Electricity Transmission Others

36.8 GEOGRAPHICAL SEGMENTS

A *geographical segment* is a distinguishable component of an entity that is engaged in providing products or services within a particular economic environment and which is subject to risks and returns that are different from those of components operating in other economic environments. Factors that should be considered in identifying geographical segments include:

- similarity of economic and political conditions;
- relationships between operations in different geographical areas;
- proximity of operations;
- special risks associated with operations in a particular area;
- exchange control regulations; and
- the underlying currency risks.

(IAS 14, 9)

A geographical segment may be a single country, a group of two or more countries, or a region within a country (IAS 14, 12). However, it does not include economic environments with significantly differing risks and returns (IAS 14, 12). If the segment does include such environments, the segment needs to be further divided until each segment includes operations in only those environments with similar risks and returns. The entity may need to do this for one or more of its segments.

IAS 14 allows geographical segments to be based on either:

- the source of its goods and services, that is, the location of its production or service facilities and other assets; or

- the destination of its goods and services, that is, the location of its markets and customers.

The choice is not a free choice. An entity usually looks to its organisational structure to determine whether its geographical segments should be based on the source of sales or the destination of sales (IAS 14, 14). So, for example, if top management receives information based on the destination of goods and services, this may indicate that segment information should also be presented by reference to the destination, rather than the source, of goods and services.

An entity's geographical segments should be those organisational units for which information is reported to the board of directors and to the chief executive officer for the purpose of evaluating the unit's past performance and for making decisions about future allocations of resources (IAS 14, 31). However, two or more internally reported geographical segments may be combined as a single geographical segment when they are 'substantially similar', that is:

- they exhibit similar long-term financial performance; and
- they are similar in respect of all the factors in the definition of a geographical segment.

(IAS 14, 34)

In rare cases, the segments reported internally to the directors and management do not satisfy the definitions of geographical segments in IAS 14. In such cases, the entity should look to the next lower level of internal segmentation that reports information along geographical lines. The entity may need to do this for one or more of its geographical segments.

Table 36.3 *Examples of geographical segments for companies reporting under IFRSs*

Pliva, Croatia	Croatia; North and Latin America; Western Europe; Central and East Europe; Other
Novartis, Switzerland	Europe; The Americas; Asia; Africa; Australia
Bayer, Germany	Europe; North America; Asia; Pacific; Latin America; Africa; Middle East
Beiersdorf, Germany	Germany; Europe (excl. Germany); Americas; Africa; Asia; Australasia

Table 36.3 *Examples of geographical segments for companies reporting under IFRSs—Continued*

Henkel, Germany	Germany; Europe (excl. Germany); Africa; Middle East
adidas-Salomon, Germany	Europe; North America; Asia; Latin America
Gucci, Netherlands	United States; Italy; France; Rest of Europe; Japan; Rest of Asia; Rest of World
Dairy Farm, Hong Kong	North Asia; South Asia; New Zealand
BMW, Germany	Germany; Rest of Europe; America; Africa; Asia/Oceania
Volkswagen, Germany	Germany; Rest of Europe; North America; South America; Africa; Asia; Oceania
MAN, Germany	Germany; Other EU; Other Europe; Asia; Americas; Africa; Australia and Oceania
UBS, Switzerland	Switzerland; Rest of Europe; Americas; Asia/Pacific; Africa; Middle East
Dresdner Bank, Germany	Germany; Europe (excluding Germany); North America; Latin America; Asia; Pacific
Erste Bank, Austria	Austria; Central Europe (Czech Republic, Slovakia, Hungary, Slovenia, Croatia); The Rest of Europe; North America; Central and South America; Asia; Others (including international organisations)
Rostelecom, Russia	Russia; CIS; US; Western Europe; Eastern Europe; Other
Telia, Sweden	Sweden; Other Nordic Countries; Baltic Region; Rest of Europe; Rest of World
Swisscom, Switzerland	Switzerland; Germany; Other international activities

Table 36.3 *Examples of geographical segments for companies reporting under IFRSs—Continued*

Anglogold, South Africa	South Africa; Africa; North America; South America; Australia
Impala, South Africa	North America; Asia; Europe; South Africa
Xstrata, Switzerland	Americas; Africa; Europe; Australasia
VA Tech, Austria	Europe; North America; South America; Asia; Near and Middle East; Africa

36.9 REPORTABLE SEGMENTS

Having made its initial identification of business and geographical segments, the entity must decide whether those segments are reportable segments or whether it needs to identify further segments as reportable segments. A *reportable segment* is a business segment or a geographical segment for which segment information is required to be disclosed by IAS 14 (IAS 14, 9). The identification of reportable segments involves a series of tests set out in paragraph 35 of IAS 14. The tests are applied separately to business and geographical segments.

Test 1

Does the segment earn the majority of its revenue from sales to external customers? If yes, proceed to test 2. If no, then subject to test 5, the segment is not a reportable segment and there is no need to disclose segment information. This test means that the different stages of vertically integrated operations are not reportable segments.

Test 2

Is the segment's revenue from sales to external customers and from transactions with other segments 10% or more of the total revenue, external and internal, of all segments? If yes, the segment is a reportable segment. If no, proceed to test 3.

TEST 3

Is the segment's result, whether profit or loss, 10% or more of the combined segment result of all segments in profit or the combined result of all segments in loss, whichever is the greater in absolute amount? If yes, the segment is a reportable segment. If no, proceed to test 4.

TEST 4

Are the segment's assets 10% or more of the total assets of all segments? If yes, the segment is a reportable segment. If no, then subject to test 5, the segment is not a reportable segment and there is no need to report segment information.

This process should identify the reportable segments. However, an entity must also test to ensure that the four tests have identified all the reportable segments. Test 5 deals with this.

TEST 5

Does the total amount of external revenue attributable to the reportable segments identified in tests 1 to 4 exceed 75% of the total revenue of the entity? If yes, no further segments need to be identified. If no, additional reportable segments should be identified until at least 75% of total revenue is included in reportable segments (IAS 14, 37). This usually means that some of those segments which did not meet any of the thresholds in the first four tests are now treated as reportable segments. It also could mean the identification of further business or geographical segments.

If an internally reported segment is not a reportable segment, that is the answers to tests 1 to 4 are all 'no' and the segment is not an additional reportable segment under test 5, the entity should either:

- treat the internally reported segment as if it were a reportable segment, that is, disclose information about that segment;
- combine the internally reported segment with similar internally reported segments and treat the combined segment as a reportable segment; or
- include the internally reported segment as an unallocated reconciling item.

(IAS 14, 35)

A segment may have been a reportable segment in the prior period but is not a reportable segment in the current period. For example, the segment may no longer pass one of the tests 1 to 4 or other reportable segments may account for more that 75% of the entity's revenue. The entity may continue to treat the segment as a reportable segment. It should do so if it judges the segment to be of 'continuing significance' (IAS 14, 42).

A segment may be a reportable segment in the current period but may not have been a reportable segment in the prior period. For example, the segment may represent a new business or a geographical area which is new to the entity. Alternatively, the entity's internal reporting and management may have changed. The new segment is treated as a reportable segment in the current period. In addition, the entity should restate the segment information for prior periods to reflect the existence of the newly reportable segment unless it is impracticable to do so (IAS 14, 43). This may involve splitting a reportable segment included in the prior period's disclosures.

36.10 PRIMARY AND SECONDARY SEGMENTS

IAS 14 distinguishes between primary and secondary segments (or, to be precise, between primary and secondary reporting formats). It requires more disclosures about primary segments than about secondary segments. However, an entity is free to disclose the same information about secondary segments as it discloses about primary segments.

Primary segments are either business segments or geographical segments; they cannot consist of a mix of business and geographical segments. For most entities, primary segments are business segments. Secondary segments are geographical if the primary segments are business segments; secondary segments are business segments if the primary segments are geographical.

The primary and secondary segments are determined by reference to the dominant source and nature of an entity's risks and returns (IAS 14, 26):

- an entity's primary segments are business segments if its risks and rates of return are affected predominantly by differences in the products and services which it produces; and
- an entity's primary segments are geographical segments if its risks and rates of return are affected predominantly by the fact that it operates in different countries or other geographical areas.

(IAS 14, 26)

The predominant source and nature of an entity's risks and rates are normally based on the entity's internal organisational and management structure and its system of internal financial reporting to its board of directors and its chief executive officer (IAS 14, 27). So, for example, if an entity is organised on business, rather than geographical lines, and the business heads report to the chief executive, the primary segments are business segments. If, on the other hand, the geographical heads report to the chief executive, the primary segments are geographical segments.

When an entity's risks and rates of return are strongly affected by differences in both the products and services it sells and the geographical areas in which it operates, it should use business segments as its primary segments and use geographical segments as its secondary segments (IAS 14, 27). It is, of course, free to present full segment information about both business segments and geographical segments.

An entity's internal organisational and management structure and its system of internal financial reporting may be based neither on products or services nor on geography. For example, they may be based on the legal entities within a group. In such cases, the entity must still determine business and geographical segments and decide which segments are primary and which are secondary based on its exposure to risks and the flow of returns. However, this would be unnecessary if the legal entities were each in different businesses and different geographical locations.

Extract 36.1 *Primary business segments and secondary geographical segments*

Böhler-Uddeholm, Austria, 31 December 2001 (IAS)

Böhler-Uddeholm Group is active in the sectors of Special Steel Long Products, which essentially covers tool steel and high speed steel, Strip Steel, Welding Consumables and Forging Technology. Starting in 2001 the sales and distribution network has been allocated to the individual divisions following the restructured responsibility of the Management Board. This divisional classification also applies to internal reporting and responsibilities, and therefore forms the basis for primary segment reporting. Secondary segment reporting is classified by geographical region.

Extract 36.2 *Primary business segments and secondary geographical segments*

Iscor, South Africa, 30 June 2000 (IAS)

The group is an integrated minerals and metals business. On a primary basis, the business segments are:

- Mining Division, comprising exploration and mining, processing and marketing of iron ore, coal and selected industrial minerals and metals,
- Steel Division, comprising manufacturing and marketing of steel products, and
- Group Division, comprising principally corporate functions and property.

On a secondary segment basis, significant geographic marketing regions have been identified.

The basis of segment reporting is representative of the internal structure used for management reporting.

Extract 36.3 *Primary business segments and secondary geographical segments*

BMW, Germany, 31 December 2001 (IAS)

In accordance with IAS 14, the BMW Group presents segment information using business segments as its primary reporting format and geographical segments as its secondary reporting format. This distinction is based on internal management and financial reporting systems and reflects the risks and earnings structure of the Group.

Extract 36.4 *Single primary business segment and secondary geographical segments*

Anglogold, South Africa, 31 December 2000 (South African GAAP and IAS)

Based on risks and returns the directors consider that the primary reporting format is by business segment. The directors consider that there is only one business segment being mining, extraction and production of gold. Therefore the disclosures for the primary segment have already been given in these financial statements.

The secondary reporting is by geographical analysis by origin and destination.

Extract 36.5 *Primary business segments and secondary geographical segments*

UBS, Switzerland, 31 December 2001 (IAS)

The Group is organized on a worldwide basis into three major Business Groups and the Corporate Center. This organizational structure is the basis upon which the Group reports its primary segment information.

...

The geographical analysis of total assets is based on customer domicile whereas operating income and capital investment is based on the location of the office in which the transactions and assets are recorded. Because of the global nature of the financial markets the Group's business is managed on an integrated basis worldwide, with a view to profitability by product line. The geographical analysis of operating income, total assets, and capital investment is provided in order to comply with International Accounting Standards, and does not reflect the way the Group is managed. Management believes that the analysis by Business Group ... is a more meaningful representation of the way in which the Group is managed.

36.11 SEGMENT INFORMATION

36.11.1 Introduction

Segment revenue, segment expense, segment assets and segment liabilities are the key elements of the information disclosed about segments. All the other disclosures are related to these elements. Segment result is the difference between segment revenue and segment expense. Items such as segment capital expenditure are components of segment assets.

Items are included in the four elements when they are directly attributable to a segment and the amounts can be allocated to a segment on a reasonable basis (IAS 14, 17). An entity looks to its internal financial reporting system as the starting point for identifying those items which can be directly attributed, or reasonably allocated, to segments (IAS 14, 17).

In some cases, an item may have been allocated to a segment for internal financial reporting purposes on a basis which is understood by management but which could be deemed 'subjective, arbitrary or difficult to understand' by external users of financial statements (IAS 14, 18). Such an item is not allocated to a segment for the purposes of IAS 14. Conversely, an entity may choose not to allocate an item for internal financial reporting purposes, even though a reasonable basis for doing so exists. Such an item is allocated for the purposes of IAS 14.

Each of the four elements is determined in a manner consistent with the determination of the other elements. For example revenue is included in segment revenue only when the related assets or liabilities are included in segment assets or segment liabilities (and vice versa). Expenses are included in segment expense only when the related assets or liabilities are included in segment assets or segment liabilities (and vice versa). So, for example:

- depreciation of equipment is included in segment expense when the equipment is included in segment assets, and the equipment is included in segment assets when the depreciation is included in segment expense;
- dividend income is included in segment revenue when the related investments are included in segment assets, and the investments are included in segment assets when the dividends are included in segment revenue; and
- assets which are used jointly by two or more segments are allocated to segments if their related revenues and expenses are allocated to those segments, and the revenue and expenses are allocated to segments only if the assets are allocated to segments (IAS 14, 47).

36.11.2 Segment Revenue

Revenue is the gross inflow of economic benefits during the period arising in the course of the ordinary activities of an entity when those inflows result in increases in equity, other than increases relating to contributions from equity participants (IAS 18, 7). Revenue which arises from the sale of goods, the rendering of services and the use by others of entity assets yielding interest, royalties and dividends is dealt with in accordance with IAS 18. Revenue may also arise from other sources which are outside the scope of IAS 18.

Segment revenue is revenue from sales to external customers or from transactions with other segments of the same entity that either:

- is directly attributable to a segment; or
- can be allocated on a reasonable basis to a segment.

(IAS 14, 16)

While the definition refers to sales, segment revenue also includes revenue arising from the application of the percentage of completion method for the rendering of services to customers or other segments. Such revenue is not necessarily a sale.

Segment revenue includes interest and dividend income but only when the segment's operations are primarily of a financial nature (IAS 14, 16) and the related assets are included in segment assets. For example, for a segment which is a bank, segment revenue includes interest income and segment assets include loans and advances. Similarly, for a segment which is a lessor, segment revenue includes finance income and segment assets includes any finance lease receivables. Segment revenue does not include interest income arising on the short-term investment of surplus funds of an entity which is not a financial institution.

Segment revenue includes gains on sales of investments or gains on the extinguishment of debt when the segment's operations are primarily of a financial nature but not in other cases (IAS 14, 16). For example, for a segment which is a bank, segment revenue includes the realised and unrealised gains arising on dealing in securities and segments assets include those securities. In the case of a manufacturing entity, segment revenue does not include gains arising on the temporary investment of the surplus funds. Segment revenue does not include gains arising on long-term investments or on the settlement of a long-term loan.

Segment revenue includes an entity's share of profits or losses of associates, joint ventures or other investments accounted for under the equity method only if those items are included in the entity's revenue. Such an accounting treatment is unlikely as both IAS 28 and IAS 31 require that the share of profits arising under the equity method should be shown as a separate line item and not included in revenue (this is also the presentation required by IAS 1). Segment revenue does, however, include the share of a jointly controlled entity's revenue which is reported using proportionate consolidation. Under IAS 31, this revenue is included in revenue although it may be shown separately from other revenue of the entity.

Segment revenue does not include extraordinary items (IAS 14, 16). Such items do not meet the definition of revenue; extraordinary items arise from events or transactions that are clearly distinct from the ordinary activities of the entity (IAS 8, 6). Revenue arises in the course of the ordinary activities of an entity (IAS 18, 7).

Extract 36.6 *Segment revenue*

Iscor, South Africa, 30 June 2000 (IAS)

Total segment revenue, which excludes value added tax and sales between group companies, represents the gross value of goods invoiced. Export revenues are recorded at FOB price of product sold. Total segment revenue further includes operating revenues directly and reasonably allocable to the segments. Segment revenue includes sales made between segments. These sales are made on a commercial basis.

36.11.3 Segment Expense

Segment expense is expense resulting from the operating activities of a segment which is directly attributable to the segment and the relevant portion of an expense that can be allocated on a reasonable basis to the segment, including expenses relating to sales to external customers and expenses relating to transactions with other segments of the same entity (IAS 14,16). While the definition refers only to expenses relating to sales, segment expense also includes expense arising from the application of the percentage of completion method for the rendering of services to customers or other segments (such expense does not necessarily relate to a sale).

Segment expense includes any costs incurred at the entity level which relate to the segment's operating activities and which can be directly attributed or allocated to the segment on a reasonable basis. However, segment expense excludes general administrative expenses, head-office expenses and other expenses which relate to the entity as a whole (IAS 14, 16) and which cannot be directly attributed or allocated to the segment on a reasonable basis.

Segment expense includes interest expense but only when the segment's operations are primarily of a financial nature, for example, when the segment carries out banking activities (IAS 14, 16). Similarly, segment expense includes losses on sales of investments or losses on extinguishment of debt only when the segment's operations are primarily of a financial nature, but not in other cases (IAS 14, 16). Therefore, losses on a portfolio of dealing securities are included in segment expense for a segment which carries out banking activities (in practice, such expenses are probably offset against gains on the portfolio of dealing securities). In each of these cases, the relevant assets are also included in segment assets.

Segment expense always excludes an entity's share of losses of associates, joint ventures, or other investments accounted for under the equity method (IAS 14, 16). These losses are reported as a separate line item in the income statements in accordance with IAS 28 and IAS 31. Segment expense does, however, include the share of a jointly controlled entity's expenses which is reported using proportionate consolidation. Such expenses are included in the appropriate line items although they may be shown separately.

Segment expense excludes income tax expense (IAS 14, 16).

Segment expense does not include extraordinary items (IAS 14, 16). Such items do not arise from the operating activities of an entity as they arise from events or transactions that are clearly distinct from the ordinary activities of the entity (IAS 8, 6).

Extract 36.7 *Segment expenses*

Iscor, South Africa, 30 June 2000 (IAS)

Segment expenses represent direct or reasonably allocable operating expenses on a segment basis. Segment expenses exclude interest, losses on investments and income tax expenses, but include head office expense allocation.

Extract 36.8 *Segment expenses*

Swisscom, Switzerland, 31 December 2001 (IAS)

... Costs are allocated among segments based on a variety of factors as determined by management to reflect an appropriate amount of usage. Expenses incurred for services provided by Swisscom's IT division, which is a vertically integrated business, are allocated to the segments based on internal transfer prices.

36.11.4 Segment Result

Segment result is segment revenue less segment expense (IAS 14, 16). It is determined before any adjustments for minority interest.

Extract 36.9 *Segment result*

Pliva, Croatia, 31 December 2001 (IAS)

Each segment's operating profit does not include corporate overheads (administrative expenses of corporate support functions), goodwill depreciation, or certain items of income which are not directly attributable to the reported business segments.

Extract 36.10 *Segment result*

Schindler, Switzerland, 31 December 2001 (IAS)

The results of business segments have been presented on a management reporting basis (Management Approach). They include all revenues and expenses which are directly attributable to a segment plus a Group overhead cost which has been assigned to each segment.

36.11.5 Segment Assets

Segment assets are those operating assets which are employed by a segment in its operating activities and which are either directly attributable to the segment or can be allocated to the segment on a reasonable basis. They include:

- intangible assets;
- goodwill;
- property, plant and equipment;
- assets which are the subject of finance leases;
- inventories, receivables and other current assets used in the operating activities of the segment;
- receivables, loans, investments and other income-producing assets which form part of the operating assets of the segment and for which segment result includes interest, dividends or other income;
- investments accounted for under the equity method when the profit from such investments is included in segment revenue (which would be very unusual);
- the share of the operating assets of a jointly controlled entity which is reported using proportionate consolidation (which is the benchmark treatment in IAS 31); and
- the share of operating assets used by two or more segments if a reasonable basis for allocation exists.

Segment assets do not include:

- assets used for general entity or head-office purposes (unless the related expenses are allocated to the segment);

- receivables, loans, investments and other income-producing assets when segment result excludes the related interest, dividend or other income on those assets;
- investments accounted for under the equity method when segment revenue excludes the profit from such investments (which would be usual); and
- income tax assets.

IAS 14 implies that bank overdrafts may be included in segment assets (IAS 14, 23). Bank overdrafts are liabilities and are presented as such on the balance sheet. Therefore, they are never included in segment assets; they may be included in segment liabilities.

Segment assets are determined after deducting depreciation, amortisation, impairment losses, provisions for bad and doubtful debts, write-downs of inventories to net realisable value, foreseeable losses on construction contracts and similar amounts which are deducted in determining the carrying amounts of assets (IAS 14, 16).

Extract 36.11 *Segment assets*

Ascom, Switzerland, 31 December 2001 (IAS)

The assets of the segments include property, plant and equipment, intangible assets, assets from finance leases, inventories and work in process, accounts receivable, trade and other current assets.

Extract 36.12 *Segment assets*

MAN, Germany, 31 December 2001 (IAS)

Total assets comprise fixed and current assets, as well as deferred tax assets and prepaid expenses and deferred charges.

Extract 36.13 *Segment assets*

Roche, Switzerland, 31 December 2001 (IAS)

Divisional assets consist primarily of property, plant and equipment, goodwill and intangible assets, receivables and inventories. Other segment assets ... consist of assets ... that can be reasonably attributed to reported segments. These include pension assets ... .

36.11.6 Segment Liabilities

Segment liabilities are those operating liabilities which result from the operating activities of a segment and which are either directly attributable to the segment or can be allocated to the segment on a reasonable basis (IAS 14,16).

Segment liabilities include:

- trade and other payables, accrued liabilities, customer advances, provisions and other claims relating to the provision of goods and services;
- the related interest-bearing liabilities, including bank overdrafts, when segment result includes interest expense relating to those liabilities; and
- the share of the liabilities of a jointly controlled entity which is reported using proportionate consolidation (which is the benchmark treatment under IAS 31).

Segment liabilities exclude:

- borrowings, finance lease obligations and other liabilities which are incurred for financing, rather than operating, purposes;
- other interest-bearing liabilities when segment result excludes the related interest expense relating to those liabilities; and
- income tax liabilities.

Extract 36.14 *Segment liabilities*

Ascom, Switzerland, 31 December 2001 (IAS)

The liabilities comprise provisions, customer prepayments, accounts payable, trade and other short-term liabilities as well as liabilities from accruals.

Extract 36.15 *Segment liabilities*

Roche, Switzerland, 31 December 2001 (IAS)

Divisional liabilities consist of trade accounts payable. Other segment liabilities ... consist of liabilities ... that can be reasonably attributed to reported segments. These include pension ... liabilities and provisions.

36.12 SEGMENT ACCOUNTING POLICIES

Segment accounting policies are the accounting policies adopted for preparing and presenting the financial statements of the entity as well as those policies that relate specifically to segment reporting (IAS 14, 16).

Segment information should be prepared in conformity with the accounting policies adopted for preparing and presenting the financial statements of the entity (IAS 14, 44). These policies are, therefore, determined in accordance with IFRSs. For example:

- inventories should be measured at the lower of cost and net realisable value;
- the measurement of segment assets and liabilities includes fair value adjustments made on a business combination which is an acquisition (IAS 14, 21);
- property, plant and equipment which has been revalued in accordance with the allowed alternative treatment in IAS 16 is included in segment assets on the same basis (IAS 14, 21);
- impairment losses are determined in accordance with IAS 36; and
- goodwill and intangible assets are amortised in accordance with IAS 22 and IAS 36.

Inter-segment transfers should be measured on the basis that the entity actually used to price those transfers (IAS 14, 75).

The use of the accounting policies adopted in the financial statements is a major difference from the new Canadian and US standards, both of which require the use of the same accounting policies as are used in the information reported to management. Therefore, under the Canadian and US standards, segment information could be presented, for example, on a cash basis or a replacement cost basis if those bases are used for internal reporting purposes. Under IAS 14, segment information cannot be presented on a cash basis as such a basis does not comply with IFRSs and it could be presented on a replacement cost basis only if that basis was used in the financial statements (in fact, in such a case, the replacement cost basis should be used in the segment information).

There is, however, one important respect in which the accounting policies used in segment information differ from those used in the financial statements. Segment revenue, segment expense, segment assets, and segment liabilities are determined before the elimination of intra-group balances and intra-group transactions between group entities in different segments (IAS 14, 24). Such balances and transactions are eliminated in preparing consolidated financial statements.

An entity may change the accounting policies adopted for preparing and presenting the financial statements of the entity as well as those policies that relate specifically to segment reporting. If the entity adopts the benchmark treatment in IAS 8, prior period segment information is restated as appropriate. If the entity adopts the allowed alternative treatment in IAS 8, the cumulative adjustment that is included in determining the net profit or loss for the period is included in segment result if it is an operating item that can be attributed or reasonably allocated to segments. For example, if the change relates to the measurement of inventories, the cumulative adjustment is included in the segment result of the segments which hold those inventories.

Some changes in accounting policies relate specifically to segment reporting, for example, changes in identification of segments and changes in the basis for allocating revenues and expenses to segments. Changes in accounting policies adopted for segment reporting that have a material effect on segment information should be disclosed and prior period segment information should be restated unless it is impracticable to do so (IAS 14, 76). Such disclosure should include:

- a description of the nature of the change in accounting policy;
- the reasons for the change;
- the fact that comparative information has been restated (or that it is impracticable to do so); and
- the financial effect of the change, if it is reasonably determinable.

If an entity changes the identification of its segments but is unable to restate prior period segment information on the new basis, the entity should report segment data for both the old and the new bases of segmentation in the year in which it changes the identification of its segments (IAS 14, 76). This allows comparisons to be made with previous periods by using the old basis.

A change in the method used to price inter-segment transfers may affect segment result but it is not a change in accounting policy (any more than a change in pricing policy to external customers is a change in accounting policy).

36.13 DISCLOSURE

36.13.1 Primary Segments

For each reportable segment, an entity should disclose:

- segment revenue (IAS 14, 51);
- segment revenue from sales to external customers (IAS 14, 51);
- segment revenue from transactions with other segments (IAS 14, 51);
- depreciation and amortisation of segment assets included in segment expenses (IAS 14, 58) (this disclosure is not required if the entity discloses cash flows arising from the operating, investing and financing activities of each reported segment);
- significant non-cash expenses, other than depreciation and amortisation, included in segment expense;
- segment result (IAS 14, 52);
- segment assets (IAS 14, 55);

- segment liabilities (IAS 14, 56); and
- capital expenditure (on an accrual basis) (IAS 14, 57).

For each reportable segment, an entity should also disclose the following information for associates, joint ventures and other investments accounted for under the equity method when substantially all their operations are within the segment:

- the aggregate share of the net profit or loss (IAS 14, 64); and
- the aggregate investment (IAS 14, 66).

An entity should present a reconciliation between the information disclosed for reportable segments and the aggregate information in the financial statements (IAS 14, 67). In presenting this reconciliation:

- segment revenue should be reconciled to entity revenue from external customers;
- segment result should be reconciled to a comparable measure of entity operating profit or loss as well as to entity net profit or loss;
- segment assets should be reconciled to entity assets; and
- segment liabilities should be reconciled to entity liabilities.

(IAS 14, 67)

Extracts from company disclosures are at the end of the chapter.

IAS 14 encourages the reporting of measures of segment profitability other than segment result (for example gross margin, profit or loss from ordinary activities or net profit or loss) provided that such amounts can be computed without arbitrary allocations. If such measures are prepared on a basis other than the accounting policies adopted for the financial statements, the basis of measurement must be disclosed (IAS 14, 53).

Both IAS 14 and IAS 7 encourage the disclosure of cash flow information for each reportable industry and geographical segment. IAS 7 encourages the disclosure of cash flows arising from the operating, investing and financing activities of each reported segment (IAS 7, 50). An entity which provides these disclosures need not disclose depreciation and amortisation expense or non-cash expenses (IAS 14, 63). IAS 14 also encourages the disclosure of significant non-cash revenues which are included in segment revenue and segment result.

36.13.2 Secondary Segments

Less disclosure is required of secondary segments than primary segments. The requirements are complex as they depend on which segments are the primary segments. Furthermore, an entity may choose to make the same disclosures for its secondary segments as it makes for its primary segments.

When business segments are the primary segments, an entity should disclose:

- for each reportable geographical segment whose revenue from sales to external customers is 10% or more of total entity revenue from sales to all external customers, segment revenue from external customers based on the location of those customers; and
- for each reportable geographical segment whose segment assets are 10% or more of the total assets of all geographical segments:
  - the total carrying amount of segment assets by the location of those assets; and
  - capital expenditure.

(IAS 14, 69)

When geographical segments are the primary segments, the additional disclosures include disclosures about the secondary (business) segments and further geographical disclosures.

When geographical segments are the primary segments, an entity should disclose the following for each business segment whose revenue from sales to external customers is 10% or more of total entity revenue from sales to all external customers or whose segment assets are 10% or more of the total assets of all business segments:

- segment revenue from external customers;
- segment assets; and
- capital expenditure.

(IAS 14, 70)

If the primary segments are geographical segments and they are based on the location of assets but the location of the entity's customers is different from the location of its assets, the entity should report revenue from sales to external customers for each customer-based geographical segment whose revenue from sales to external customers is 10% or more of total entity revenue from sales to all external customers (IAS 14, 71).

If the primary segments are geographical segments based on the location of customers and if the entity's assets are located in different geographical areas from its customers, the entity should report for each asset-based geographical segment whose revenue from sales to external customers or segment assets are 10% or more of related consolidated or total entity amounts:

- segment assets by geographical location of the assets; and
- capital expenditure by geographical location of the assets.

(IAS 14, 72)

If a business segment or geographical segment for which information is reported to the board of directors and chief executive officer is not a reportable segment because it earns the majority of its revenue from sales to other segments, but its revenue from sales to external customers is 10% or more of total entity revenue from sales to all external customers, the entity should disclose that fact and the amounts of revenue from:

- sales to external customers; and
- internal sales to other segments.

(IAS 14, 74)

Extracts from company disclosures are at the end of the chapter.

36.13.3 Inter-Segment Pricing

An entity should disclose the basis of pricing inter-segment transfers and any change therein (IAS 14, 75).

36.13.4 Other Disclosures

An entity should indicate the types of products and services included in each reported business segment and indicate the composition of each reported geographical segment, both primary and secondary, if not otherwise disclosed in the financial statements or elsewhere in the financial report (IAS 14, 81).

Extract 36.16 *Disclosures for primary business segments and secondary geographical segments*

Bayer, Germany, 31 December 2001 (IAS)

Financial Statements
Key Data by Segment and Region

Segments	*Health Care*		*Agriculture*		*Polymers*
	Pharmaceuticals & Biological Products	*Consumer Care Diagnostics*	*Crop Protection*	*Animal Health*	*Plastics & Rubber*
€ million	*2001*	*2001*	*2001*	*2001*	*2001*
Net sales (external)	5,729	4,104	2,708	988	5,581
• Change in €	−6.7%	+5.6%	+10.3%	−1.1%	−4.0%
• Change in local currencies	−6.7%	+5.0%	+10.7%	−1.1%	−5.0%
Intersegment sales	38	2	102	5	116
Other operating income	62	49	102	13	87
Operating result before exceptionals	383	388	453	172	288
Return on sales before exceptionals	6.7%	9.5%	16.7%	17.4%	5.2%
Exceptional items	(332)	(47)	0	0	(50)
Operating result	51	341	453	172	238
Return on sales	0.9%	8.3%	16.7%	17.4%	4.3%
Gross cash flow	229	534	550	163	587
Capital invested	5,352	3,799	3,884	645	6,405
CFROI	4.2%	14.0%	13.9%	22.8%	8.9%
Equity-method income	0	0	0	0	0
Equity-method investments	16	0	0	0	27
Total assets	5,303	3,956	3,488	734	5,867
Capital expenditures	415	267	215	49	592
Amortization and depreciation	364	291	247	40	482
Liabilities	1,869	1,271	1,130	379	1,339
Research and development expenses	1,242	252	292	98	134
Number of employees (as of Dec 31)	26,800	14,900	10,900	3,900	17,900

Author's note: comparative information for 2000 is not reproduced.

Segments	*Polymers Polyurethanes, Coatings & Colorants*	*Chemicals*	*Reconciliation*	*Continuing operations*	*Discontinuing operations*	*Bayer Group*
€ million	*2001*	*2001*	*2001*	*2001*	*2001*	*2001*
Net sales (external)	5,207	3,749	872	28,938	1,337	30,275
• Change in €	+2.6%	+9.9%		+1.1%		−2.2%
• Change in local currencies	+2.1%	+10.0%		+0.8%		−2.5%
Intersegment sales	138	456	(857)			
Other operating income	51	53	63	480	340	820
Operating result before exceptionals	146	271	(246)	1,855	76	1,931
Return on sales before exceptionals	2.8%	7.2%		6.4%		6.4%
Exceptional items	(100)	(68)	(16)	(613)	293	(320)
Operating result	46	203	(262)	1,242	369	1,611
Return on sales	0.9%	5.4%		4.3%		5.3%
Gross cash flow	614	379	(230)	2,826	97	2,923
Capital invested	8,051	4,774	556	33,466	1,392	34,858
CFROI	7.5%	7.7%		8.3%		8.2%
Equity-method income	0	0	12	12	14	26
Equity-method investments	773	13	158	987	179	1,166
Total assets	7,493	4,216	4,933	35,990	1,049	37,039
Capital expenditures	492	483	40	2,553	64	2,617
Amortization and depreciation	604	334	41	2,403	113	2,516
Liabilities	2,311	1,797	9,616	19,712	307	20,019
Research and development expenses	186	114	170	2,488	71	2,559
Number of employees (as of Dec 31)	15,100	19,500	3,000	112,000	4,900	116,900

Author's note: comparative information for 2000 is not reproduced.

Regions	*Europe*	*North America*	*Asia/Pacific*
€ million	*2001*	*2001*	*2001*
Net sales (external) – by market	11,659	9,473	4,660
Net sales (external) – by point of origin	12,999	9,806	3,817
• Change in €	+0.6%	+1.1%	+1.5%
• Change in local currencies	+0.5%	−1.9%	+7.3%
Interregional sales	3,154	1,927	226
Other operating income	312	70	48
Operating result before exceptionals	1,707	23	241
Return on sales before exceptionals	13.1%	0.2%	6.3%
Exceptional items	(272)	(278)	(14)
Operating result	1,435	(255)	227
Return on sales	11.0%	−2.6%	5.9%
Gross cash flow	2,037	632	312
Capital invested	16,355	12,808	2,711
CFROI	12.5%	4.7%	11.3%
Equity-method income	12	0	0
Equity-method investments	351	618	2
Total assets	17,298	12,652	3,132
Capital expenditures	1,620	560	255
Amortization and depreciation	1,227	918	150
Liabilities	9,769	6,407	1,382
Research and development expenses	1,559	690	68
Number of employees (as of Dec 31)	64,600	23,200	12,600

Author's note: comparative information for 2000 is not reproduced.

Regions	*Latin America/ Africa/Middle East*	*Reconciliation*	*Continuing operations*	*Discontinuing operations*	*Bayer Group*
€ million	*2001*	*2001*	*2001*	*2001*	*2001*
Net sales (external) – by market	3,146		28,938	1,337	30,275
Net sales (external) – by point of origin	2,316		28,938	1,337	30,275
• Change in €	+3.4%		+1.1%		−2.2%
• Change in local currencies	+2.5%		+0.8%		−2.5%
Interregional sales	116	(5,423)			
Other operating income	50		480	340	820
Operating result before exceptionals	219	(335)	1,855	76	1,931
Return on sales before exceptionals	9.5%		6.4%		6.4%
Exceptional items	(30)	(19)	(613)	293	(320)
Operating result	189	(354)	1,242	369	1,611
Return on sales	8.2%		4.3%		5.3%
Gross cash flow	225	(380)	2,826	97	2,923
Capital invested	1,607	(15)	33,466	1,392	34,858
CFROI	14.5%		8.3%		8.2%
Equity-method income	0		12	14	26
Equity-method investments	16		987	179	1,166
Total assets	1,834	1,074	35,990	1,049	37,039
Capital expenditures	118	0	2,553	64	2,617
Amortization and depreciation	104	4	2,403	113	2,516
Liabilities	673	1,481	19,712	307	20,019
Research and development expenses	9	162	2,488	71	2,559
Number of employees (as of Dec 31)	11,000	600	112,000	4,900	116,900

Author's note: comparative information for 2000 is not reproduced.

Extract 36.17 *Disclosures for primary geographical segments and secondary business segments*

HeidelbergCement, Germany, 31 December 2001 (IAS)

Regions (Primary reporting format)

	Central Europe West 2001	*Western Europe 2001*	*Northern Europe 2001*
External turnover	**1,383**	**1,089**	**1,168**
Inter-region turnover	**16**	**4**	**79**
Turnover	**1,399**	**1,093**	**1,247**
Change to previous year in %	*−7.1%*	*−2.4%*	*−6.5%*
Operating income before depreciation (OIBD)	**192**	**240**	**200**
in % of turnover	*13.7%*	*22.0%*	*16.0%*
Depreciation	**124**	**131**	**121**
Operating income	**68**	**109**	**79**
in % of turnover	*4.9%*	*10.0%*	*6.3%*
Results from participations	**60**	**8**	**6**
Non-operating result			
Earnings before interest and income taxes (EBIT)	**128**	**117**	**85**
Investments (1)	**73**	**152**	**68**
Segment assets (2)	**1,147**	**1,604**	**1,439**
OIBD in % of segment assets	*16.7%*	*15.0%*	*13.9%*
Segment liabilities (3)	**756**	**502**	**410**
Employees	**7,644**	**4,406**	**7,203**

Author's note: comparative information for 2000 is not reproduced.

Regions (Primary reporting format)	*Central Europe East*	*North America*	*Africa-Asia-Turkey*	*Group Services*	*Reconciliation*	*Group*
	2001	*2001*	*2001*	*2001*	*2001*	*2001*
External turnover	**501**	**1,990**	**389**	**169**		**6,689**
Inter-region turnover	**13**		**22**	**341**	**–475**	
Turnover	**514**	**1,990**	**411**	**510**	**–475**	**6,689**
Change to previous year in %	*18.4%*	*4.1%*	*–3.1%*	*2.6%*		*–1.8%*
Operating income before depreciation (OIBD)	**131**	**354**	**60**	**8**		**1,185**
in % of turnover	*2.5%*	*17.8%*	*14.6%*	*1.6%*		*17.7%*
Depreciation	**63**	**139**	**39**	**3**		**620**
Operating income	**68**	**215**	**21**	**5**		**565**
in % of turnover	*13.2%*	*10.8%*	*5.1%*	*1.0%*		*8.4%*
Results from participations	**–9**	**7**	**3**	**–5**		**70**
Non-operating result					23	23
Earnings before interest and income taxes (EBIT)	**59**	**222**	**24**		**23**	**658**
Investments (1)	**62**	**420**	**42**		**412**	**1,229**
Segment assets (2)	**732**	**1,890**	**518**	**47**		**7,377**
OIBD in % of segment assets	*17.9%*	*18.7%*	*11.6%*	*17.0%*		*16.1%*
Segment liabilities (3)	**101**	**438**	**119**	**72**	**5,528**	**7,926**
Employees	**7,047**	**6,110**	**2,388**	**48**		**34,846**

Author's note: comparative information for 2000 is not reproduced.

Business lines (Secondary reporting format)

	Cement 2001	*Concrete 2001*	*Building materials 2001*	*Group Services 2001*	*Reconciliation 2001*	*Group 2001*
External turnover	**3,148**	**2,167**	**1,205**	**169**		**6,689**
Inter-business line turnover	**389**	**22**	**39**	**341**	**−791**	
Turnover	**3,537**	**2,189**	**1,244**	**510**	**−791**	**6,689**
Changes to previous year in %	*0.9%*	*0.8%*	*− 10.2%*	*2.6%*		*− 1.8%*
Operating income before depreciation (OIBD)	**800**	**242**	**135**	**8**		**1,185**
in % of turnover	*22.6%*	*11.1%*	*10.9%*	*1.6%*		*17.7%*
Investments (1)	**607**	**136**	**74**		**412**	**1,229**
Segment assets (2)	**5,257**	**1,022**	**1,051**	**47**		**7,377**
OIBD in % of segment assets	*15.2%*	*23.7%*	*12.8%*	*17.0%*		*16.1%*

(1) Investments = in the segment columns: tangible and intangible fixed asset investments; in the reconciliation column: financial fixed asset investments
(2) Segment assets = tangible and intangible fixed assets
(3) Segment liabilities = liabilities and provisions; the financial liabilities are recorded in the reconciliation column.

Notes on segment reporting

Certain principal items of information are presented by regions and business lines in accordance with the segment reporting rules of IAS 14. Segment reporting corresponds with the Group's internal management reporting.

In the business lines, we combine operating lines that are in related markets. The concrete business line, for example, contains the operating lines ready-mixed concrete, concrete products, and aggregates. The building materials business line contains the operating lines building chemicals, lime, dry mortar and sand-lime brick. Group Services include all of the Group's trading activities.

Turnover with other regions or business lines represents the turnover between segments. Transfer prices are established in a market-orientated manner. OIBD is calculated as operating income before depreciation.

Author's note: comparative information for 2000 is not reproduced.

Extract 36.18 *Disclosures for primary geographical segment and single secondary business segment*

Serono, Switzerland, 31 December 2001 (IAS)

Primary reporting format – geographic segment

		Year ended 31 December 2001				
		Europe	*North America*	*Latin America*	*Other*	*Group*
	Notes	*US$000*	*US$000*	*US$000*	*US$000*	*US$000*
Product sales		**542,246**	**390,563**	**130,889**	**185,707**	**1,249,405**
Royalty and licence income		**74,759**	**–**	**–**	**52,306**	**127,065**
Total revenues		**617,005**	**390,563**	**130,889**	**238,013**	**1,376,470**
Allocatable operating income		**338,486**	**247,265**	**50,513**	**96,101**	**732,365**
Corporate R&D expenses						**(282,914)**
Unallocated expenses						**(111,799)**
Operating income						**337,652**
Segment assets		**1,080,711**	**165,401**	**95,407**	**1,677,250**	**3,018,769**
Segment liabilities		**482,396**	**57,793**	**53,729**	**103,247**	**697,165**
Unallocated liabilities						**102,103**
Total liabilities						**799,268**
Capital expenditures	14	**62,916**	**24,819**	**1,590**	**7,806**	**97,131**
Depreciation	14	**52,433**	**3,439**	**5,656**	**5,781**	**67,309**
Amortization	15,16	**26,504**	**79**	**202**	**4,812**	**31,597**

Unallocated expenses represent corporate expenses.

Product sales are based on the country in which the customer is located, while royalty and licence income is based on the country that receives the royalty. Segment assets and capital expenditures are shown by the geographical area in which the assets are located. There are no sales or other transactions between the business segments. Segment assets consist primarily of cash, receivables, inventories, prepayments, property, plant and equipment and intangible and other assets, and exclude investments. Segment liabilities comprise operating liabilities and exclude items such as taxation. Capital expenditures comprise additions to property, plant and equipment and capitalized interest.

Secondary reporting format – business segment
Business segment information is not provided as the company operates in one business, namely the pharmaceutical industry. Within the pharmaceutical business, the company operates two divisions: Pharmaceutical and Bioscience, of which the Pharmaceutical division comprises over 95% of sales and shareholders' equity of the company.

Author's note: comparative information for 1999 and 2000 is not reproduced.

Notes

[1] Many of the commentators on E15, the exposure draft which preceded IAS 14 [1981] had been unhappy about the lack of guidance for determining segment result but the IASC recognised at the time that the appropriate base for determining segment result may vary in differing circumstances (*IASC News*, July 1981, p4).

[2] Paul Pacter, *Reporting Disaggregated Information*, FASB, Norwalk, 1993.

[3] 1701 *Segment Disclosures*, CICA, Toronto, 1997 and FAS 131 *Disclosures About Segments of an Enterprise and Related Information*, FASB, Norwalk 1997.

[4] For a description of the different approaches considered by the IASC, the CICA and the FASB, see for example: 'Defining Business Segments', *IASC Insight*, September 1994, pp15–17, 'Steering Committee Responds to Comments', *IASC Insight*, March 1995, pp7–8, 'Board to Vote on Exposure Draft', *IASC Insight*, September 1995, pp11–12, 'Segment Reporting Exposure Draft Approved', *IASC Insight*, December 1995, pp16–17 and 'Segment Reporting: Some Differences Remain with North America', *IASC Insight*, March 1997, pp20–21.

[5] For the differences which existed at that time and which largely remained after the approval of the revised IAS 14 and the revised Canadian and US standards, see 'Segment Reporting: Some Differences Remain with North America', *IASC Insight*, March 1997, pp20–21. See also Tom Porter, 'Comparative Analysis of IAS 14 .... and Related US GAAP', in *'The IASC – US GAAP Comparison Project: A Report of Similarities and Differences Between IASC Standards and US GAAP'*, 2nd edition, ed Carrie Bloomer, Norwalk, CT FASB, 1999.

[6] Since the early 1980s, the London Stock Exchange has required foreign issuers to comply with IASs if they do not adopt UK standards. In an interesting variation on the theme of creating fairness among different issuers, the Stock Exchange did not require foreign issuers to comply with IAS 14 [1981]. At the time there was no equivalent UK standard on segment disclosures and, furthermore, the Stock Exchange had been a strong opponent of IAS 14 [1981]. Following the adoption of SSAP 25 *Segmental Reporting* in 1990, the Stock Exchange required foreign issuers to comply with IAS 14. However, in a further twist to the story, foreign issuers from other EU member states no longer have to comply with IAS 14. EU directives now require the Stock Exchange to accept, in the case of companies from other EU member states, financial statements prepared in accordance with national requirements. Most, if not all these national requirements, fall short of the requirements of IAS 14 [1981] as well as the revised IAS 14.

CHAPTER 37

Discontinuing Operations

37.1 RELEVANT STANDARD

IAS 35 *Discontinuing Operations*

37.2 HISTORY

As part of the improvements project, the IASC added to IAS 8 a standard and guidance on disclosures about discontinued operations. The IASC decided that recognition and measurement issues for discontinued operations should be dealt with as a separate project (*IASC Insight*, July 1992, p20). The project was included in the programme agreed with IOSCO in July 1995 (*IASC Insight*, September 1995, p1).

IAS 35 switches the emphasis from discontinued to discontinuing operations. The IASC also decided that there was no need for specific recognition and measurement requirements for discontinuing operations as the requirements of other IASs should apply (*IASC Update*, April 1997, p1). However, it should be borne in mind that IAS 36 on the impairment of assets and IAS 37 on provisions are particularly important in the context of discontinuing operations as the decision to discontinue an operation may trigger the recognition of impairment losses and provisions.

IAS 35 *Discontinuing Operations* was approved in 1998 and applied to accounting periods beginning on or after 1 January 1999.

37.3 IOSCO

In June 1994, IOSCO advised the IASC that it approved IAS 8 for the purposes of the core standards but reminded the IASC that a standard on discontinued operations, including recognition and measurement issues, was an IOSCO core standard.

IAS 35 is included in 'IAS 2000' endorsed by IOSCO in May 2000. There are no supplemental treatments.

37.4 IAS 35 IN BRIEF

Following the approval and public announcement of a single plan to dispose of or terminate a component of an entity, the entity should disclose and segregate continuing and discontinuing assets, liabilities, income, expenses and cash flows. The disclosures should be made in the first set of financial statements issued after the entity has both approved and announced the planned discontinuance and should be updated in each subsequent period. Comparative information for prior periods must be restated.

The requirements apply only to components of an entity which are separate major lines of business or geographical areas and which can be distinguished operationally and for financial reporting purposes.

37.5 DISCONTINUING OPERATIONS

A *discontinuing operation* is a component of an entity which:

- the entity, pursuant to a single plan, is:
  - disposing of substantially in its entirety;
  - disposing of piecemeal; or
  - terminating through abandonment;
- represents a separate major line of business or geographical area of operations; and
- can be distinguished operationally and for financial reporting purposes.

(IAS 35, 2)

Discontinuing operations are expected to occur relatively infrequently. Many disposals or terminations are not discontinuing operations because they are too small. They may qualify as restructurings in accordance with IAS 37 (see chapter 27). A restructuring, transaction or event which does not meet the definition of a discontinuing operation, should not be called a discontinuing operation (IAS 35, 43).

The change in terminology from 'discontinued operation' in IAS 8 to 'discontinuing operation' in IAS 35 means that disclosures and reclassification are required from the moment of a binding sale agreement or the announcement of a detailed, formal plan, and then throughout the period of the disposal or termination to the period in which the discontinuance is completed. Under IAS 8 separate disclosure was required only when the operation had been discontinued. No disclosures were required during the period of the disposal or termination.

37.5.1 Discontinuance

The definition of a discontinuing operation deals first with the manner of the discontinuance. The entity may dispose of, or terminate, an operation by means of sale, demerger, spin-off or abandonment. In such a case, there is a single date on which the entity enters into a binding sale agreement although the actual transfer of possession and control of the assets and the receipt of the consideration may occur at a different time. Alternatively, an entity may abandon an operation without substantial sales of assets.

The entity may also dispose of an operation piecemeal by selling off the assets and settling the liabilities individually. There is usually no single date at which an overall binding sale agreement is entered into. Rather, the sales of assets and settlements of liabilities usually occur over a period of time which may cover more than one financial reporting period. In some cases, the discontinuance may involve a sale, demerger or spin-off of one part of the operation and the piecemeal sale of the assets of another part of the operation.

Many disposals and terminations are not discontinuing operations as defined in IAS 35 because there is no 'single plan' to dispose of a separate line of business or geographical area of operation. For example, piecemeal sales of assets or groups of assets are not discontinuing operations if they are not carried out under a 'single plan'. Furthermore, even when there is a single plan, a disposal or termination is not a discontinuing operation when it fails to meet the second part of the definition, that is the operation is a 'major line of business which can be distinguished operationally and for financial reporting purposes'.

37.5.2 Operations

The second part of the definition of a discontinuing operation explains which operations would qualify for separate presentation and disclosure if there is a single plan of disposal or termination. To qualify, the operation must represent a separate line of business or geographical area of operation and must be distinguished operationally and for financial reporting purposes.

An operation can be distinguished for financial reporting purposes if:

- its operating assets and liabilities can be directly attributed to it;
- its income (gross revenue) can be directly attributed to it; and
- at least a majority of its operating expenses can be directly attributed to it.

(IAS 35, 11)

Assets, liabilities, income and expenses are directly attributable to an operation if they would be eliminated when the operation is sold, abandoned or otherwise disposed of (IAS 35, 12). Therefore the operation includes those items which are being sold or abandoned. Interest and other financing costs are attributed to a discontinuing operation only if the related liability is attributed to the operation (IAS 35, 12).

A separate, major line of business or geographical area of operations may be:

- a reportable business segment or geographical segment, as defined in IAS 14;
- part of a segment; or
- for an entity which operates in a single business or geographical segment, a major product or service line.

(IAS 35, 9)

The initial focus on segments emphasises that the 'operation' must be large. Therefore, the discontinuance of a single factory is not a discontinuing operation if the entity, under the same single plan, does not dispose of or terminate all its activities in the same business or geographical segment.

The suggestion that for an entity which operates in a single business or geographical segment, a discontinuing operation may be a 'major product or service line' seems to be demanding and unfair. For example, for an entity which operates several hotels and these hotels form only one of a number of business segments, the disposal of a single hotel is not a discontinuing operation. Therefore the separate disclosure required by IAS 35 need not be made. However, for an entity which operates hotels and has no other activities, the disposal of a single hotel appears to be a discontinuing operation and the entity would have to disclose and segregate the assets, liabilities, income, expenses and cash flows of the hotel.

Extract 37.1 *Discontinuing operation – spin-off of business segment*

Novartis, Switzerland, 31 December 2000 (IAS)

Novartis spun off its Agribusiness sector on 6 November 2000 to its shareholders as part of the transactions necessary to form Syngenta AG.

Author's note: Novartis shows its Agribusiness sector as a separate, discontinuing segment.

Extract 37.2 *Discontinuing operation – IPO for business segment*

Zurich Financial Services, Switzerland, 31 December 2001 (IAS)

Reinsurance – discontinued: in December 2001, the Group exited its third party assumed reinsurance operations, previously managed under the Zurich Re brand name, by way of an Initial Public Offering (IPO) of this business, under the name Coverium. The Reinsurance – discontinued segment reflects the results of this discontinued reinsurance business up to the date of the IPO and the results of the run-off of existing liabilities retained by the Group and not transferred to Coverium.

Extract 37.3 *Discontinuing operation – sale of assets in geographical area*

Dairy Farm International, Hong Kong, 31 December 2001 (IAS)

Chairman's statement

Having decided in April to exit from Australia, a managed sell-down of Franklins was undertaken as the most effective means, among limited options available to us, of realising value. An assessment of Franklins' assets in 2000 led to an impairment charge of US$129 million. During the course of the disposal programme, however, a premium was achieved on the sale of the assets, yielding a net gain in 2001 of US$38 million.

Group Chief Executive's Review

Having been unsuccessful in attracting an offshore purchaser, and being prevented by competition authorities from selling the business in its entirety to a local competitor, we undertook a managed sell-down of Franklins during the second half. A total of 249 stores were sold to national and international chains and independent operators, including 14 stores to former managers. We closed 38 stores as well as 10 distribution centres and administrative offices.

37.6 RECOGNITION AND MEASUREMENT

An entity should apply the recognition and measurement principles in other IASs to the assets, liabilities, income and expenses of a discontinuing operation. The fact of the discontinuance may trigger the need for impairment write-downs of assets under IAS 36 (see chapter 25) and the recognition of provisions under IAS 37 (see chapter 27).

37.7 INITIAL DISCLOSURE EVENT

The special disclosures for discontinuing operations come into effect as soon as there is an 'initial disclosure event'. The *initial disclosure event* is the occurrence of the earlier of:

- the date on which the entity has entered into a binding sale agreement for substantially all the assets of the operation; and
- the date on which the board of directors or similar governing body of the entity has both approved a detailed, formal plan for the discontinuance and made an announcement of that plan.

(IAS 35, 16)

Prior to the occurrence of the initial disclosure event, the operation is treated as continuing and no special disclosures or presentation are required or permitted.

The occurrence of the initial disclosure event means that the discontinuing operation should be segregated from the continuing operation for the whole of the current period and for the prior periods presented (IAS 35, 27 and 45). If the initial disclosure event occurs after the end of the reporting period but prior to the approval of the financial statements for that period, the discontinuing operation should be segregated from the continuing operations for the reporting period and for the prior periods presented (IAS 35, 29 and 45).

Example 37.1 *Initial disclosure event during period*

A prepares its financial statements to 31 December and presents comparative information for one prior period. An initial disclosure event in respect of a discontinuing operation occurs on 1 December 2002. A treats the operation as discontinuing for the whole of 2002 and restates the comparative information for 2001 on the same basis.

Example 37.2 *Initial disclosure event after end of period*

B prepares its financial statements to 31 December and presents comparative information for one prior period. An initial disclosure event in respect of a discontinuing operation occurs on 1 February 2003 which is prior to the approval of the 2002 financial statements. B treats the operation as discontinuing for the whole of 2002 and restates the comparative information for 2001 on the same basis. The operation is also a discontinuing operation in the financial statements for 2003.

37.8 DISCLOSURE

In order to segregate the discontinuing and continuing operations, an entity should disclose the following information relating to each discontinuing operation:

- the carrying amounts of the total assets and the total liabilities to be disposed of;
- the amounts of revenue, expenses, pre-tax profit or loss from ordinary activities and income tax expense of the discontinuing operation for the period; and
- the amounts of net cash flows attributable to the operating, investing, and financing activities of the discontinuing operation for the period.

(IAS 35, 28)

Assets, liabilities, income, expenses and cash flows are attributed to a discontinuing operation if they will be disposed of, settled, reduced or eliminated when the discontinuance is completed (IAS 35, 28). In addition, the entity should disclose:

- a description of the discontinuing operation;
- the business or geographical segment(s) in which the operation is reported in accordance with IAS 14;
- the date and nature of the initial disclosure event; and
- the date or period in which the discontinuance is expected to be completed (if known or determinable).

(IAS 35, 28)

The pre-tax gain or loss recognised on the disposal of assets or settlement of liabilities of the discontinuing operation should be included in the profit or loss of the period and should be shown on the face of the income statement (IAS 35, 39). The other disclosures may be presented either in the notes or on the face of the financial statements.

Extract 37.4 *Net profit on disposal*

Dairy Farm International, Hong Kong, 31 December 2001 (IAS)

During the year, the Group announced and substantially completed the managed sell-down of Franklin's assets in Australia. 249 stores were sold to four major purchasers and various independent operators, and the remaining 38 stores were closed. The transaction realised gross proceeds of US$307.5 million, and a net gain of US$37.5 million after the transfer of US$35.4 million cumulative translation differences.

Author's note: The net gain on the disposal of Franklin's assets is included in operating profit.

When an entity disposes of assets or settles liabilities of the discontinuing operation or enters into binding agreements for the sale of such assets or the settlement of such liabilities, it should disclose:

- the amount of any recognised gain or loss and the income tax expense relating to the gain or loss; and
- the net selling price or range of prices of those net assets, the expected timing of receipt of those cash flows, and the carrying amount of those net assets.

(IAS 35, 31)

The same disclosures are made when the sale or the binding sale agreement is entered into after the balance sheet date but before the approval of the financial statements (IAS 35, 32).

Example 37.3 *Disclosure of discontinuing operation*

In March 2002 the group announced its plans to dispose of its textile manufacturing operation. The operation was sold on 30 June 2002. The operation was reported as a separate business segment and the activities of the operation were included in Europe for the purposes of geographical segment information.

The revenue, expenses and cash flows of the textile operations for the six-month period to 30 June 2002 and for the year to 31 December 2001 were as follows:

(Continued)

(Continued)

	6 months to 30 June 2002	*Year to 31 December 2001*
Revenue	x	x
Expenses	x	x
Profit before tax	x	x
Income tax	x	x
Profit after tax	x	x
Cash flows from operating activities	x	x
Cash flows from investing activities	x	x
Cash flows from financing activities	x	x

The assets and liabilities of the textiles operation were:

	At 30 June 2002	*At 31 December 2001*
Property, plant and equipment	x	x
Inventories	x	x
Total assets	x	x
Total liabilities	x	x
Net assets	x	x
Proceeds from sale	x	
Foreign currency translation differences included in equity	x	
Profit on disposal	x	
Income tax	x	
Profit on disposal after tax	x	

Extract 37.5 *Disclosure of discontinuing operations*

Roche, Switzerland, 31 December 2000 (IAS)

On 8 June 2000, the Group's Fragrances and Flavours Division was spun off as an independent company under the name Givaudan. The shares in Givaudan were distributed on this date as a special dividend to the holders of Roche shares and non-voting equity securities. As a result of the spin-off, assets totalling SFr 3.9 billion and liabilities totalling SFr 1.2 billion were transferred to Givaudan. The results and cash flows of the Fragrances and Flavours Division up until the spin-off in June 2000 are included in the consolidated figures. However, the consolidated balance sheet is shown after the spin-off and does not include this Division's assets and liabilities.

The sales, results, assets, liabilities and net cash flows of the Fragrances and Flavours Division as part of the Roche Group are shown as discontinuing operations in the following table.

	Continuing operations		*Discontinuing operations*		*Group*	*Group*
	2000	*1999*	*2000*	*1999*	*2000*	*1999*
Statement of income						
Sales	27,779	25,799	1,193	2,231	28,972	28,030
Less inter-divisional sales*	(270)	(381)	(30)	(82)	(300)	(463)
Sales to third parties	27,509	25,418	1,163	2,149	28,672	27,567
Operating profit	6,931	6,024	200	397	7,131	6,421
Financial income (expense), net	2,383	1,242	(46)	(108)	2,337	1,134
Result before taxes	9,314	7,266	154	289	9,468	7,555
Income taxes	(2,226)	(1,797)	(46)	(105)	(2,272)	(1,902)
Result after taxes	7,088	5,469	108	184	7,196	5,653
Changes in accounting policies	1,395	29	–	(2)	1,395	27
Minority interests	33	88	–	–	33	88
Share of result of associated companies	23	(4)	–	–	23	(4)
Net income	8,539	5,582	108	182	8,647	5,764
Balance sheet at 31 December						
Property, plant and equipment	13,785	13,304	–	936	13,785	14,240
Intangible assets	15,870	14,492	–	1,180	15,870	15,672
Other long-term assets	5,143	5,577	–	311	5,143	5,888
Current assets	34,737	33,329	–	1,302	34,737	34,631
Total assets	69,535	66,702	–	3,729	69,535	70,431
Long-term debt	16,167	15,948	–	14	16,167	15,962
Other non-current liabilities	7,475	7,730	–	1,882	7,475	9,612
Current liabilities	13,857	13,754	–	1,102	13,857	14,856
Total liabilities	37,499	37,432	–	2,998	37,499	40,430
Net assets	32,036	29,270	–	731	32,036	30,001
Statement of cash flows						
Operating activities	3,726	1,436	190	291	3,916	1,727
Financing activities	(2,727)	(749)	189	(146)	(2,538)	(895)
Investing activities	(743)	(743)	(89)	(124)	(832)	(867)
Net effect of currency translation on cash	(51)	94	15	9	(36)	103
Increase (decrease) in cash	205	38	305	30	510	68

*Transfer prices for inter-divisional sales are set on an arm's length basis.

Extract 37.6 *Disclosure of discontinuing operations*

Dairy Farm International, Hong Kong, 31 December 2001 (IAS)

1. PROFIT AND CASH FLOW FROM CONTINUING OPERATIONS	*2001*			*2000*		
	Continuing operations	*Discontinuing operations*	*Total*	*Continuing operations*	*Discontinuing operations*	*Total*
	US$m	*US$m*	*US$m*	*US$m*	*US$m*	*US$m*
a. Profit and Loss Account						
Sales	3,470.2	1,454.3	4,924.5	3,255.3	2,477.7	5,733.0
Cost of sales	(2,470.0)	(1,122.2)	(3,592.2)	(2,339.7)	(1,895.1)	(4,234.8)
Gross margin	1,000.2	332.1	1,332.3	915.6	582.6	1,498.2
Other operating income	6.2	–	6.2	4.9	–	4.9
Selling and distribution costs	(761.9)	(326.7)	(1,088.6)	(736.6)	(528.8)	(1,265.4)
Administration and other operating expenses	(187.4)	(47.6)	(235.0)	(165.1)	(103.1)	(268.2)
	57.1	(42.2)	14.9	18.8	(49.3)	(30.5)
Net profit on sale of Sims	–	17.3	17.3	–	–	–
Net gain on disposal of Franklin's assets	–	37.5	37.5	–	–	–
Restructuring costs of Wellcome Delivers	(6.6)	–	(6.6)	–	–	–
Impairment of assets	(12.9)	–	(12.9)	–	(129.4)	(129.4)
Operating profit/(loss)	37.6	12.6	50.2	18.8	(178.7)	(159.9)
Net financing charges	(24.7)	(10.5)	(35.2)	(11.9)	(17.3)	(29.2)
Share of results of associates and joint ventures	34.0	–	34.0	36.5	(0.9)	35.6
Profit/(loss) before tax	46.9	2.1	49.0	43.4	(196.9)	(153.5)
Tax	(19.0)	–	(19.0)	(19.2)	1.9	(17.3)
Minority interests	(0.2)	–	(0.2)	(0.7)	–	(0.7)
Net profit/(loss)	27.7	2.1	29.8	23.5	(195.0)	(171.5)
b. Cash Flow Statement						
Operating activities						
Operating profit/(loss)	37.6	12.6	50.2	18.8	(178.7)	(159.9)
Depreciation and amortisation	113.4	16.8	130.2	103.7	66.3	170.0
Other non-cash items	22.4	(53.5)	(31.1)	(9.3)	130.7	121.4
Decrease/(increase) in working capital	75.6	(45.4)	30.2	75.7	(5.4)	70.3
Interest received	18.7	0.3	19.0	22.2	0.6	22.8
Interest and other financing charges paid	(41.9)	(12.9)	(54.8)	(34.1)	(16.1)	(50.2)
Tax paid	(12.0)	(0.1)	(12.1)	(15.6)	0.2	(15.4)
	213.8	(82.2)	131.6	161.4	(2.4)	159.0
Dividends from associates and joint ventures	26.4	–	26.4	32.7	–	32.7
Cash flows from operating activities	240.2	(82.2)	158.0	194.1	(2.4)	191.7

1. PROFIT AND CASH FLOW FROM CONTINUING OPERATIONS (continued)	*2001*			*2000*		
	Continuing operations US$m	*Discontinuing operations US$m*	*Total US$m*	*Continuing operations US$m*	*Discontinuing operations US$m*	*Total US$m*
b. Cash Flow Statement (continued)						
Investing activities						
Purchase of tangible assets	(115.2)	(11.6)	(126.8)	(145.5)	(50.6)	(196.1)
Purchase of subsidiaries	(11.7)	–	(11.7)	(10.0)	–	(10.0)
Store acquisitions	(1.0)	–	(1.0)	(10.0)	(2.7)	(12.7)
Purchase of associates, joint ventures and other investments	(5.9)	–	(5.9)	(0.8)	(0.4)	(1.2)
Sale of tangible assets and leasehold land	27.9	–	27.9	3.3	4.7	8.0
Net proceeds on sale of Sims	–	53.6	53.6	–	–	–
Net proceeds on disposal of Franklin's assets	–	217.3	217.3	–	–	–
Sale of associates and joint ventures	0.1	–	0.1	17.0	1.5	18.5
Cash flows from investing activities	(105.8)	259.3	153.5	(146.0)	(47.5)	(193.5)
Financing activities						
Issue of shares	0.1	–	0.1	–	–	–
Capital contribution from minority shareholders	2.2	–	2.2	–	–	–
Drawdown on borrowings	287.6	5.1	292.7	383.2	147.0	530.2
Repayment of borrowings	(412.5)	(251.4)	(663.9)	(320.5)	(80.7)	(401.2)
Intercompany borrowings	(20.8)	20.8	–	14.9	(14.9)	–
Dividends paid by Company	–	–	–	(72.0)	–	(72.0)
Cash flows from financing activities	(143.4)	(225.5)	(368.9)	5.6	51.4	57.0
Effect of exchange rate charges	(2.3)	(3.2)	(5.5)	(2.8)	(9.7)	(12.5)
Net (decrease)/increase in cash and cash equivalents	(11.3)	(51.6)	(62.9)	50.9	(8.2)	42.7
Cash and cash equivalents at 1st January	492.5	57.1	549.6	441.6	65.3	506.9
Cash and cash equivalents at 31st December	481.2	5.5	486.7	492.5	57.1	549.6

37.9 UPDATING THE DISCLOSURES

For periods subsequent to the one in which the initial disclosure event occurs, an entity should disclose any significant changes in the amount or timing of cash flows relating to the assets and liabilities to be disposed of or settled and the events causing those changes (IAS 35, 33). The disclosures should continue up to, and including, the period in which the discontinuance is completed (IAS 35, 35). A discontinuance is completed when the plan is substantially completed or abandoned, though payments from any buyer(s) to the entity may not yet be completed.

If an entity abandons or withdraws from a plan which was previously reported as a discontinuing operation, that fact and its effect should be disclosed (IAS 35, 36).

Example 37.4 *Updated disclosures*

A prepares its financial statements to 31 December and presents comparative information for one prior period. An initial disclosure event in respect of a discontinuing operation occurs on 1 December 2002. A treats the operation as discontinuing for the whole of 2002 and restates the comparative information for 2001 on the same basis.

The discontinuance is completed in March 2004. Therefore, A continues to treat the operation as a discontinuing operation in both 2003 and 2004.

CHAPTER 38

Related Party Disclosures

38.1 RELEVANT STANDARD

IAS 24 *Related Party Disclosures*

38.2 HISTORY

IAS 24 *Related Party Disclosures* was approved in 1982 and published in 1983. It was included in the original programme for the first improvements project but was excluded from the project when, in March 1992, the IASC decided to restrict the project to those IASs affected by the *Statement of Intent on the Comparability of Financial Statements.* There was some support at that time for a separate revision project for IAS 24 (*IASC Insight*, March 1992, p8) but the IASC decided not to proceed with such a project.

In its May 2002 improvements exposure draft, the IASB proposes several amendments that affect the definition of related parties and the scope of application and disclosures in IAS 24.

38.3 IOSCO

38.3.1 Comments on IAS 24

In June 1994, IOSCO advised the IASC that IAS 24 was acceptable for the purposes of the IOSCO core standards. However, IOSCO did ask the IASC to consider:

- disclosures relating to tax allocation agreements;
- enhanced disclosures or accounting for expenses and liabilities paid by principal shareholders; and
- enhanced disclosures or accounting for stock plans established by a principal shareholder for the entity's benefit.

IOSCO also identified one suspense issue: it did not think that some of the scope exclusions in IAS 24 should apply to securities offerings or filings by a subsidiary, to segment disclosures required by IAS 14, or to privatisations or other securities offering or filings by state-controlled entities. The segment reporting issue was considered at the beginning of the project to revise IAS 14[1] but no changes were incorporated in the revised IAS 14.

IAS 24 is included in 'IAS 2000' endorsed by IOSCO in May 2000. There is one supplemental treatment, enhanced disclosures for:

- expenses and liabilities paid by a principal shareholder; or
- stock plans established by a principal shareholder for the benefit of the entity.

38.3.2 Disclosure Standards

In its 1998 disclosure document[2], IOSCO uses the IAS 24 definition of a related party but requires more disclosures than IAS 24. As well as information about major shareholders, it requires disclosure of:

- the nature and extent of any transactions or proposed transactions which are material to the entity or the related party, or any transactions that are unusual in their nature or conditions, involving goods, services, or tangible or intangible assets, to which the company or any of its parent or subsidiaries was a party; and
- the amount of outstanding loans (including guarantees of any kind) made by the entity or any of its parent or subsidiaries to or for the benefit of a related party – the information given should include:
  - the largest amount outstanding during the period covered;
  - the amount outstanding as of the latest practicable date;
  - the nature of the loan and the transaction in which it was incurred; and
  - the interest rate on the loan.

38.4 IAS 24 IN BRIEF

An entity should disclose:

- related party relationships when control exists irrespective of whether there have been transactions between the entity and the related parties; and

- the nature of the related party relationship, and the types and elements of the transactions, when there have been transactions between the entity and the related parties.

38.5 RELATED PARTIES

Parties are considered to be related if one party has the ability to control, or exercise significant influence over, the other party in making financial and operating decisions (IAS 24, 5). A related party may be another entity, an individual, a government or any other party. IAS 24 deals only with the following related party relationships:

- the parent, subsidiaries and fellow subsidiaries of the entity (IAS 24, 3(a));
- the associates of the entity as defined in IAS 28 (IAS 24, 3(b));
- individuals who own, directly or indirectly, an interest in the voting power of the reporting entity that gives them significant influence over the entity (IAS 24, 3(c));
- close members of the family of such an individual (IAS 24, 3(c));
- key management personnel of the entity who have authority and responsibility for planning, directing and controlling the activities of the entity – this includes the directors and officers of companies (IAS 24, 3(d));
- close members of the families of such personnel (IAS 24, 3(d)); and
- entities in which any individual person described above owns, directly or indirectly, a substantial interest in the voting power or is able to exercise significant influence (IAS 24, 3(e)) – this includes entities owned by directors or major shareholders of the reporting entity and entities that have a member of key management in common with the reporting entity (IAS 24, 3(e)).

Close members of the family of an individual are those who may be expected to influence, or be influenced by, the individual in their dealings with the entity (IAS 24, 3(c)).

IAS 24 deems that the following are not related parties :

- two companies simply because they have a director in common unless it is possible and likely that the director would be able to affect the policies of both companies in their mutual dealings (IAS 24, 6(a));
- providers of finance, trades unions, public utilities and government departments and agencies, in the course of their normal dealings with an entity by virtue only of those dealings (IAS 24, 6(b)); and

- a single customer, supplier, franchiser, distributor, or general agent with whom an entity transacts a significant volume of business merely by virtue of the resulting economic dependence (IAS 24, 6(c)).

Any one of the above is a related party of an entity when it is otherwise able to control or exercise significant influence over the entity. Therefore, for example:

- companies A and B are *not* related parties solely because X is a non-executive director of both A and B or a member of the supervisory boards of A and B;
- companies A and B *are* related parties if X is the chief executive of both companies, notwithstanding that neither A nor B has a shareholding in the other;
- when A borrows from or places a deposit with bank B, A and B are *not* related parties solely as a result of the loan or deposit;
- when A controls or exercises significant influence over bank B, A and B *are* related parties;
- companies A and B are *not* related parties solely because B buys 90% of A's output; and
- agent A and company B are *not* related parties solely because A deals only in goods supplied by B.

IASB improvements project

In its May 2002 improvements exposure draft, the IASB proposes to:

- incorporate the examples of related parties into the definition of a related party;
- extend the definition to include parties with joint control over the entity and joint ventures in which the entity is a venturer (but not other venturers in those joint ventures);
- extend the definition to include post-retirement benefit plans for the benefit of employees of either the entity or any other entity that is a related party of the entity;
- clarify that non-executive directors are key management personnel and are, therefore, related parties of the entity; and
- define close members of the family.

38.6 DISCLOSURE OF RELATED PARTY RELATIONSHIPS

An entity should disclose related party relationships when control exists whether or not there have been transactions between the related parties (IAS 24, 20). Certain aspects of this requirement are covered by other IFRSs; for example, IAS 27 requires the disclosure of a list of subsidiaries and, in certain circumstances, the name of the parent. IAS 1 requires the disclosure of both the parent entity and the ultimate parent entity (IAS 1, 102).

38.7 DISCLOSURE OF RELATED PARTY TRANSACTIONS

A *related party transaction* is a transfer of resources or obligations between related parties, regardless of whether a price is charged (IAS 24, 5). Related party transactions include:

- purchases or sales of goods (finished or unfinished);
- purchases or sales of property and other assets;
- the rendering or receiving of services;
- agency arrangements;
- leasing arrangements;
- the transfer of research and development and licence agreements;
- the provision of finance (including loans and equity contributions in cash or in kind);
- guarantees and collaterals; and
- management contracts.

> ***IASB improvements project***
>
> In its May 2002 exposure draft, the IASB proposes to clarify that the settlement of liabilities on behalf of the entity or by the entity on behalf of another entity may be related party transactions.

For transactions with related parties, an entity should disclose the nature of the related party relationship as well as the types of transactions and the elements of the transactions necessary for an understanding of the financial statements (IAS 24, 22). However, no disclosure is required:

- in consolidated financial statements in respect of intra-group transactions;

- in parent financial statements which are made available or published with the consolidated financial statements;
- in financial statements of a wholly-owned subsidiary if its parent is incorporated in the same country and provides consolidated financial statements in that country; and
- in financial statements of state-controlled entities of transactions with other state-controlled entities (in its May 2002 improvements exposure draft, the IASB proposes to eliminate this exception).

(IAS 24, 4)

According to IAS 24, the elements of transactions necessary for an understanding of the financial statements normally include:

- the amount or appropriate proportion of the transactions;
- amounts or appropriate proportions of outstanding items; and
- pricing policies.

(IAS 24, 23)

Similar items may be aggregated except when separate disclosure is necessary for an understanding of the effects of the transactions on the financial statements (IAS 24, 24).

IASB improvements project

In its May 2002 exposure draft, the IASB proposes to:

- require the disclosure of amounts, rather than amounts or proportions, of transactions or outstanding items;
- require the disclosure of the terms and conditions, guarantees given or received and provisions for doubtful debts for outstanding balances due from or to related parties;
- require the disclosure of bad debt expense in respect of debts due from related parties; and
- require separate disclosures for all items for separate categories of related parties.

The IASB also proposes to remove the requirement to disclose pricing policies. It would allow disclosure that related party transactions are made on terms equivalent to those that prevail on arm's length transactions only if the disclosure can be substantiated.

Extract 38.1 *Loans to directors*

Libertel, The Netherlands, 31 March 2001 (IAS)

Except for the loans granted to acquire shares of Libertel N.V. at the public offering and for the loans to pay personal income taxes as a result of granted stock option rights, no loans have been granted to current and former members of the Management Board during the years ended 31 March 2001 and 2000 respectively. These interest bearing loans, with an expiration date of 30 June 2001, granted to present and former members of the Management Board amounted to EURO 0.1 million at 31 March 2001 (at 31 March 2000: EURO 0.2 million). As at 31 March 2001 the interest rate was 5.25%.

Extract 38.2 *Loans to members of board of management*

MAN, Germany, 31 December 2001 (IAS)

One Supervisory Board member has been granted a housing loan carrying interest at the annual rate of 6% and maturing after an agreed term of 25 years. At December 31, 2001, the residual loan balance came to €0.036 million (down from €0.038 million).

Extract 38.3 *Transactions where executive board member has indirect influence*

Adidas-Salomon, Germany, 31 December 2001 (IAS)

Robert Louis-Dreyfus, Chairman of the Executive Board of adidas-Salomon AG until March 8, 2001, had indirect influence on the French football club Olympique de Marseille and the Belgian football club Standard Liège.

The Company has promotion contracts with both clubs. The terms of these promotion contracts are similar to those with other clubs.

Extract 38.4 *Transactions with companies commonly controlled with management*

Homburg Invest, Canada, 31 December 2000 (IAS)

Related party transactions

> ...
>
> C) The company has entered into agreements with a company commonly controlled by the Chairman and Chief Executive Officer to provide management services at market rates. These agreements are based upon asset management, property management and financial services. In 2000 the amount paid under these agreements was $1,115,211 (1999 – $942,717).

D) During 2000, the company earned rental revenue in the amount of $260,311 (1999 – $203,275) from a company commonly controlled by the Chairman and Chief Executive Officer.

E) In 2000 the company purchased property totalling $NIL (1999 – $14,870,314) from a company commonly controlled by the Chairman and Chief Executive Officer.

F) The company has approved a resolution authorizing the property manager, a company commonly controlled by the Chairman and Chief Executive Officer, to operate trust accounts on its behalf as required to conduct business of the company.

G) The company capitalizes property acquisition costs incurred at the time of purchase. In 2000, the total amount of these costs, paid to a company commonly controlled by the Chairman and Chief Executive Officer, amounted to $125,000 (1999 – $1,378,552).

The above transactions were recorded at the exchange amount which is equivalent to fair market value.

Extract 38.5 *Trading transactions with related companies*

Sinopec, People's Republic of China, 31 December 2000 (IAS)

Most of the transactions undertaken by the Group during the year ended 31 December 2000 have been effected with such counterparties and on such terms as have been determined by Sinopec, the immediate parent company, and other relevant PRC authorities.

Sinopec negotiates and agrees the terms of crude oil supply with suppliers on a group basis, which is then allocated among its subsidiaries, including the Group, on a discretionary basis. During the year ended 31 December 2000, the value of crude oil purchased in accordance with Sinopec's allocation was as follows:

	2000 RMB 000	1999 RMB 000
Purchases of crude oil	11,641,888	5,749,527

Other transactions between the Group and other related parties during the year ended 31 December 2000 were as follows:

	2000 RMB 000	1999 RMB 000
Sales	7,317,930	2,459,739
Net surcharge paid under the oil equalisation scheme	–	36,950
Purchases other than crude oil	312,101	417,062
Repairing charges	102,476	112,450
Insurance premiums paid	73,506	70,757
Interest received and receivable	2,903	2,102
Research and development expenses paid	75,000	72,721

Time deposits in related parties

	2000 RMB 000	1999 RMB 000
Time deposits	386,189	258,826

The directors of the company are of the opinion that the above transactions were entered into in the normal course of business and on normal commercial terms or in accordance with the agreements governing such transactions, and this has been confirmed by the non-executive directors.

Extract 38.6 *Trading transactions with related companies*

Jardine Matheson, Hong Kong, 31 December 2001 (IAS)

In the normal course of business the Group undertakes on an arm's-length basis a wide variety of transactions with certain of its associates and joint ventures. The more significant of such transactions are described below.

Property Services

The Group rents property from Hongkong Land. The gross annual rentals paid by the Group in 2001 to Hongkong Land were US$5 million (2000: US$6 million).

The Group provided property services to Hongkong Land in 2001 in aggregate amounting to U$22 million (2000: US$21 million).

One issue which has been raised with the IASC is whether IAS 24 requires the disclosure of remuneration and other benefits paid to directors and other key management personnel. Such people are related parties and their relationship with the entity is one of the relationships dealt with in IAS 24 (IAS 24, 3 – see 38.5 above). The payment of remuneration or other benefits is clearly a related party transaction. Therefore, the only issue is what disclosures, if any, are required.

The IASC did not resolve the issue when it was raised and, therefore, the need for such disclosures is a judgement which has to be taken in the context of IAS 24. However, in its May 2002 improvements exposure draft, the IASB proposed that IAS 24 should not require the disclosure of management compensation, expense allowances and similar items paid in the ordinary course of an entity's business.

Notes

1 Paul Pacter, *Reporting Financial Information by Segment – A Background Issues Paper*, IASC, 1994, p88.

2 *Disclosure Standards to Facilitate Cross-Border Offerings and Listings by Multinational Issuers*, IOSCO, 1998.

CHAPTER 39

Post Balance Sheet Events

39.1 RELEVANT STANDARD

IAS 10 *Events After the Balance Sheet Date*

IAS 10 requires that an entity should not prepare its financial statements on a going concern basis if management determines after the balance sheet date either that it intends to liquidate the entity or cease trading or that it has no realistic alternative but to do so. This issue is dealt with in chapter 8.

39.2 HISTORY

IAS 10 *Contingencies and Events Occurring After the Balance Sheet Date* (IAS 10 [1978]) was approved in 1978. The IAS was reviewed in 1986 when the IASC decided that it should not be revised.

IAS 37 has replaced that part of IAS 10 which dealt with contingencies. In January 1998, the IASC agreed to revise that part of IAS 10 which dealt with post balance sheet events (*IASC Update*, January 1998, p1). It approved IAS 10 *Events After the Balance Sheet Date* in March 1999. The revised IAS 10 was effective for accounting periods beginning on or after 1 January 2000.

39.3 IOSCO

While IOSCO did not accept IAS 10 in 1994, its concerns related solely to the measurement of contingencies. It did not indicate any concerns or suspense issues about that part of IAS 10 which deals with post balance sheet events.

IAS 10 is included in 'IAS 2000' endorsed by IOSCO in May 2000. IOSCO has two general issues:

- concerns that IAS 10 requires that the financial statements for part of an entity that had been prepared on a liquidation basis should be restated on a going concern basis in the consolidated financial statements (see chapter 8); and
- a concern that the example of the resolution of a court case as an adjusting event in IAS 10 may conflict with IAS 37.

IOSCO has one supplemental treatment, the need for disclosures when a board decision prior to the balance sheet date will give rise to expenditure but there is no obligation, and hence provision, at the balance sheet date. IOSCO suggests that the disclosures should include:

- the nature, expected amount and timing of any related expenditures;
- the conditions supplemental to the board decision necessary to recognise the provision; and
- the fact that the board decision has been confirmed prior to the issuance of the financial statements together with the nature of the confirming event.

39.4 IAS 10 IN BRIEF

Amounts in the financial statements should be adjusted to reflect events after the balance sheet date that provide evidence of conditions at the balance sheet date. Amounts should not be adjusted for the effects of events that are indicative of conditions that arose after the balance sheet date but such events should be disclosed when they are of such importance that their non-disclosure would affect the ability of users to make proper evaluations and decisions.

39.5 DEFINITIONS

Events after the balance sheet date are those events, both favourable and unfavourable, that occur between the balance sheet date and the date on which the financial statements are authorised for issue (IAS 10, 2). The definition encompasses all transactions and events which occur after the balance sheet date and includes ordinary operating transactions as well as those which might be regarded as unusual. The issue addressed by IAS 10 is the extent to which these transactions and events should be reflected or disclosed in the financial statements for the period prior to that in which they occur.

Events after the balance sheet date are either:

- adjusting events; or
- non-adjusting events.

Adjusting events are events that provide evidence of conditions at the balance sheet date (IAS 10, 2). *Non-adjusting events* are events that are indicative of conditions that arose after the balance sheet date (IAS 10, 2).

39.6 ADJUSTING EVENTS

An entity should adjust the amounts recognised in its financial statements to reflect adjusting events after the balance sheet date.

Examples of adjusting events include:

- the resolution of a court case which confirms whether or not the entity already had a present obligation at the balance sheet date;
- the bankruptcy of a customer which confirms that a trade receivable was not recoverable at the balance sheet date;
- the sale of inventory for an amount below cost which confirms that the net realisable value of that inventory was below cost at the balance sheet date;
- the sale of a long-term asset for an amount below its carrying amount which confirms that an impairment had taken place prior to the balance sheet date;
- the receipt of information that determines the cost of an asset acquired prior to the balance sheet date;
- the receipt of information that determines the proceeds from an asset that was disposed of prior to the balance sheet date;
- the determination of profit sharing or bonus payments when there is a legal or constructive obligation to make those payments as at the balance sheet date (see IAS 19, 17); and
- the discovery of fraud or errors that show that the financial statements were incorrect as at the balance sheet date.

Dividends that are proposed or declared after the balance sheet date are not an adjusting event because there is not a legal or constructive obligation to pay the dividend at the balance sheet date. Therefore, such dividends are not recognised as a liability (IAS 10, 11). This requirement is consistent with the recognition principles relating to a present obligation under IAS 37 but is different from the requirements of IAS 10 [1978] which allowed, but did not require, the recognition of such dividends as a liability.

As part of its improvements project, the IASB proposes to clarify that a liability for a dividend payable should not be recognised in the financial statements:

- when the dividend has been proposed before the balance sheet date but declared after the balance sheet date; or
- when the payment of the dividend requires approval by the shareholders after the balance sheet date.

39.7 NON-ADJUSTING EVENTS

An entity should disclose the nature and financial effect of those non-adjusting events which are of such importance that non-disclosure would affect the ability of the users of the financial statements to make proper evaluations and decisions (IAS 10, 20). This requirement is generally understood not to include ordinary operating transactions. Examples of non-adjusting events include:

- the destruction of a major production plant by a fire or some natural disaster after the balance sheet date;
- an acquisition of another entity – unless it is impracticable to do so, IAS 22 requires the disclosure of the same information about a business combination occurring after the balance sheet date as it requires for a business combination occurring during the reporting period;
- the discontinuance of all or part of the operations of the entity – IAS 35 requires the disclosure of the same information about a discontinuing operation for which the initial disclosure event occurs after the balance sheet date as it requires for one in which the initial disclosure event occurs on or before the balance sheet date;
- changes in exchange rates which affect foreign currency monetary items or the financial statements of a foreign operation; and
- changes in the market value of marketable investments.

An entity should disclose:

- the nature of the event; and
- an estimate of its financial effect (or a statement that such an estimate cannot be made).

(IAS 10, 20)

An entity should also update any other disclosures for information received after the balance sheet date about conditions that existed at the balance sheet date (IAS 10, 18).

Extract 39.1 *Natural disaster*

Nestlé, Switzerland, 31 December 1994 (IAS)

On 17 January 1995, the Kobe area of Japan was hit by an earthquake. The head office building rented by Nestlé Japan was badly damaged, however, no material damage was suffered by the factories. The assets of Nestlé Japan which were affected by the earthquake were covered by external insurers.

Extract 39.2 *Change in exchange rates*

TOTAL, France, 31 December 1993 (IAS)

Franc CFA devaluation: The 50% Franc CFA devaluation in January 1994 has not been taken into account in the consolidated financial statements for the year ended 31 December 1993. Its effect on the 1994 financial statements is not considered material.

Extract 39.3 *Commitment of cash resources*

Trans Zambezi, Zimbabwe, 30 September 1996 (IAS)

Since 30 September 1996, the company has made the following commitments from cash reserves amounting to US$7.5 million:

- Purchase of adjoining farms to expand horticultural operations.
- Purchase of additional shareholdings in existing financial services investments.
- Funding for purchase of partner's share of assets on dissolution of a manufacturing and marketing joint venture.
- Investment in 50% of a distribution joint venture through an existing subsidiary.

An entity should disclose the date on which the financial statements are authorised for issuance and who gave the authorisation (IAS 10, 16). The financial statements do not reflect adjusting or non-adjusting events after this date (but regulators may require other forms of disclosure about such events).

In some countries, the shareholders are required to approve the financial statements. The date of authorisation is the date on which the financial statements are authorised for original issuance and not the date of shareholder approval (IAS 10, 4).

The disclosure requirement can be satisfied by either a simple statement or by the dated signatures of management.

Extract 39.4 *Date of authorisation for issue of financial statements*

Batelco, Bahrain, 31 December 2001 (IAS)

The consolidated financial statements were approved by the board of directors on 6 February 2002 ...

Extract 39.5 *Date of authorisation for issue of financial statements*

Syngenta, Switzerland, 31 December 2001 (IAS)

No events occurred between the balance sheet date and the date on which these consolidated financial statements were approved by the board of directors that would require adjustment to or disclosure in the consolidated financial statements.

These financial statements were approved by the board of directors on 27 February 2002.

CHAPTER 40

Earnings Per Share

40.1 RELEVANT STANDARDS AND INTERPRETATION

IAS 33 *Earnings per Share*
SIC 24 *Earnings Per Share – Financial Instruments and Other Contracts That May be Settled in Shares*

40.2 HISTORY

40.2.1 IAS 33

The IASC added the project on earnings per share to its work programme in March 1990. The steering committee included four financial analysts (*IASC News*, July 1990, p2). As part of the initial work on the project, the staff compared requirements in over 30 countries and consulted statistical organisations which included earnings per share on their databases (*IASC News*, October 1990, p2).

The IASC approved a point outline in November 1990 but work on the project was then deferred pending completion of the comparability and improvements project. Work restarted in 1993 and the IASC published a DSOP in October 1993 (its first public DSOP).

When it developed its first international plan in 1991, the FASB identified the denominator of the earnings per share calculation as a project which had 'promise for reaching broad international agreement in a relatively short period of time' (FASB *Status Report*, September 1991). As a result, the FASB later started a project on earnings per share 'to be pursued concurrently with the IASC' with two objectives:

- to simplify existing procedures for the computation of earnings per share by US companies; and

- to make US standards on earnings per share compatible with international standards.

(FASB *Status Report*, 11 April 1994)

On many occasions, FASB officials made clear that the FASB would not continue with the project unless these objectives could be achieved.

The IASC approved the main thrust of the DSOP in June 1994. The first joint meeting of the IASC steering committee and the FASB took place in September 1994. The joint meeting of the board of the FASB and the IASC steering committee was probably the first occasion on which the IASC had participated in a public standard setting meeting.

There was substantial agreement between the IASC and the FASB from the outset on the denominator of the calculation. That agreement involved the FASB eliminating the notion of 'primary earnings per share' in favour of the internationally accepted 'basic earnings per share'. There were differences in the detail, in particular the IASC and the FASB initially disagreed on the objectives of the disclosure of diluted earnings per share. The IASC steering committee placed the emphasis on the predictive nature of diluted earnings per share while the FASB had tentatively concluded that diluted earnings per share provided information about performance over the period (*IASC Insight*, September 1994, p8). The disagreement had implications for some aspects of the calculations. The IASC was later persuaded that the performance measure objective was as important as providing a warning signal about the potential variability of basic earnings per share (*IASC Insight*, December 1995, p6).

Resolving this and other minor differences between the IASC and the FASB took some time and it was not until November 1995 that the IASC approved E52. The FASB issued its exposure draft at the same time. The result of the 'shared research and ongoing discussions' was that the IASC and FASB exposure drafts 'generally reach[ed] the same conclusions on the same issues' (*IASC Insight*, December 1995, p6).

After reviewing the comments on E52 and the FASB's exposure draft, IAS 33 *Earnings Per Share* was approved in January 1997 and applied to accounting periods beginning on or after 1 January 1998. The FASB approved FAS 128 *Earnings per Share* in February 1997. Both standards call for the same two main disclosures: basic and diluted earnings per share. During the final discussions the IASC and the FASB reached common conclusions on a number of outstanding differences but one difference remained: FAS 128 requires, while IAS 33 only encourages, the disclosure of additional per share amounts (the cause of the difference is that IFRSs do not require disclosure of the relevant line items in the income statement)[1].

Following the adoption of IAS 33, the United Kingdom decided to bring SSAP 3 *Earnings Per Share* into line with the consensus reached by the IASC and the FASB. This move was significant in two respects. First, the IASC's initial ideas on earnings per share had been influenced by SSAP 3 and similar national requirements. Second, the UK's decision to revise its standard was made solely in order to comply with the international consensus; without that consensus it would not have revised its standard.

The IASB is proposing several changes to IAS 33 in its May 2002 improvements exposure draft that deal with:

- contracts that may be settled either in ordinary shares or cash;
- preferred shares classified as equity;
- contingently issuable shares;
- potential ordinary shares of subsidiaries, joint ventures or associates;
- participating securities;
- written put options; and
- purchased put and call options.

The proposed revised IAS includes an extensive appendix of examples.

40.2.2 Earnings

The main focus of IAS 33 is on the determination of the denominator of the earnings per share, that is, the number of shares. The consensus reached by the IASC and the FASB, and subsequently shared by the UK and others, relates solely to the number of shares. Earnings in each case are determined by reference to the relevant accounting standards (IFRSs in the case of IAS 33, US GAAP in the case of FAS 128 and so on). The harmonisation of the amount of earnings depends on much greater harmonisation of accounting standards.

Financial analysts have, from time to time, expressed reservations about the measure of earnings derived from financial statements. Most notably German analysts, through their professional organisation, have developed the notion of DVFA earning which eliminates the effects of taxation influences on German accounting and some non-recurring items.

The banning of extraordinary items in the United Kingdom led to the development by the Institute of Investment Management and Research of a notion of 'headline earnings'[2], which is now used as a benchmark figure for the trading outcome of a period and reported in the financial columns of British newspapers. The UK's definition of headline earnings includes:

- all trading profits and losses;
- interest;
- abnormal trading items (they should be prominently displayed); and

- profits and losses on operations discontinued or acquired during the period.

Most significantly, headline earnings exclude the following amounts which are included in the net profit or loss for the period whether reported under UK GAAP or IFRSs:

- profits or losses on the sale or termination of a discontinued operation;
- profits or losses on the sale of fixed assets and businesses; and
- impairment losses on fixed assets and businesses.

Similar requirement have been adopted in South Africa.

In June 1994, the financial analysts on the IASC board announced that they had set up a worldwide committee to review the question of the amount of earnings which should be used in the determination of earnings per share. The committee would consider, among other things, the UK's notion of headline earnings (*IASC Insight*, September 1994, p7). A consensus had not been reached by the time the IASC approved IAS 33 (*IASC Insight*, March 1997, p15) and has yet to emerge. If a consensus does emerge, it is likely that the analysts will ask the IASB to consider amending its definition of earnings[3].

40.3 IOSCO

IAS 33 is included in 'IAS 2000' endorsed by IOSCO in May 2000. There are six supplemental treatments:

- concerns about the definition of contingently issuable shares and its consistency with standards developed jointly with national standard setters (this issue is dealt with in the IASB's improvements project);
- concerns about how participating securities should be considered in the EPS computation – it should also be clarified that the two-class method used when there are two classes of ordinary shares should not be used for securities convertible into the other class;
- concerns about whether redemption premiums (or discounts) on the conversion of preferred shares and a dividend stream calculated using an effective interest method for increasing rate preference shares classified as equity should be included in the computation of basic EPS (these issues are dealt with in the IASB's improvements project);
- concerns about whether the vesting of fixed employee stock options is a contingent condition that must be met before such options are considered in the computation of diluted EPS;

- concerns about the need for disclosure of EPS amounts for discontinued operations, extraordinary items, accounting changes and fundamental errors (the disclosure of these amounts is not required by IAS 33); and
- concerns about the need for disclosure of securities that potentially could dilute basic EPS in the future that were not included in the computation of diluted EPS because they were anti-dilutive (IAS 32 requires the disclosure of the nature and terms of such securities).

40.4 IAS 33 IN BRIEF

IAS 33 requires the disclosure of basic and diluted earnings per share. The main focus is on the determination of the denominator of the earnings per share calculation. Earnings are determined in accordance with IFRSs.

40.5 SCOPE

IAS 33 applies to:

- entities whose ordinary shares or potential ordinary shares are publicly traded;
- entities which are in the process of issuing ordinary shares or potential ordinary shares in public securities markets; and
- other entities which disclose earnings per share in IFRS financial statements.

(IAS 33, 1 and 4)

The third category is new and a similar requirement is now included in IAS 14. It means that an unlisted entity cannot claim that its financial statements comply with IFRSs if the earnings per share (and segments) disclosures do not comply with IAS 33 (and IAS 14).

40.6 BASIC EARNINGS PER SHARE

Basic earnings per share should be calculated by dividing earnings – the net profit or loss for the period attributable to ordinary shareholders – by the weighted average number of ordinary shares outstanding during the period (IAS 33, 10).

40.6.1 Earnings

Earnings, for the purpose of calculating basic earnings per share, are the net profit or loss for the period attributable to ordinary shareholders, that is, the net profit or loss for the period after deducting preference dividends. The net profit or loss is determined in accordance with IFRSs and is the final line item required on the face of the income statement (IAS 1, 75(i)). Therefore earnings are determined after deducting tax expense, extraordinary items and minority interest.

Earnings are also determined after deducting preference dividends. Preference dividends may be non-cumulative, that is, the right to the dividend lapses if the entity lacks the profits to pay the dividend. Alternatively, they may be cumulative, that is, unpaid dividends accumulate and are paid when the entity has sufficient profits to make the payment.

In the case of non-cumulative preference shares, the amount of dividends declared in respect of the period are deducted from the net profit for the period irrespective of whether those dividends have been paid during the period.

In the case of cumulative preference shares, the full amount of the required preference dividends for the period is deducted from the net profit for the period irrespective of whether the dividends have been declared. Any dividends which are paid or declared during the period in respect of previous periods are not deducted from earnings; they have already been deducted from the net profit of the period to which they relate.

IASB improvements project

In its May 2002 improvements exposure draft, the IASB proposes to clarify the need for adjustments to earnings for amounts relating to preferred shares classified as equity in accordance with IAS 32.

40.6.2 Per Share

An *ordinary share* is an equity instrument which is subordinate to all other classes of equity instruments (IAS 33, 6). Ordinary shares participate in the net profit for the period only after other types of shares such as preference shares. An entity may have more than one class of ordinary shares, in which case earnings per share may need to be computed either separately for each class or on a combined basis.

Extract 40.1 *Two classes of shares*

Nokia, Finland, 31 December 1997 (IAS)

The weighted average number of K shares and A shares used in calculating earnings per share was 283,282,000 shares for 1997 and 283,561,000 for 1996.

[Author's note: Nokia discloses a combined earnings per share amount for the two classes of shares. A shares are participating cumulative preference shares; the dividend per share on K shares cannot exceed the dividend per share on A shares. For at least the past five years, profit levels have been such that the same dividend has been paid on both classes of shares.]

Extract 40.2 *Two classes of shares*

Amadeus, Spain, 31 December 2000 (IAS)

The General Meeting of Shareholders of 11 August 1999 approved the creation of two different classes of shares with different nominal value, and to split the existing capital. After the split of shares the share capital consisted of 505,196,030 Class 'A' shares, of par value 0.01 EURs and 314,383,557 class 'B' shares of par value 0.10 EURs. Each class 'A' share carries the right of one vote, whilst each class 'B' share carries the right of 10 votes. Economical rights are greater for class 'A' shares in respect of any future distribution of dividends. The right to receive a dividend for class 'B' shares is calculated as the lesser of 1% of total dividends or 1% of the par value of class 'B' shares. In the event of liquidation of the assets of the Group, class 'A' shares have greater economic rights than class 'B', as the Group would pay out the par value of class 'A' shares and in case of any outstanding amounts they would be distributed among class 'B' shares for their par value; further remaining amounts would be distributed among class 'A' shares.

...

For the purposes of allocating earnings between 'A' and 'B' shares, the assumption is made that the maximum economic rights attributable to the 'B' shares would be via the divided calculation described in note 11 [above]. Additionally, the assumption is made that 100% of the profits are paid-out as dividends and the respective portion is allocated to the 'B' shares first and the remainder to the 'A' shares.

[Author's note: the calculation of the earnings per class 'B' share in EURs results in a distribution, which when rounded to two significant digits gives a nil earnings per share.]

The weighted average number of ordinary shares outstanding during the period is the number of ordinary shares outstanding at the beginning of the period, adjusted by the number of ordinary shares bought back or issued during the period multiplied by a time-weighting factor. The time-weighting factor is the number of days that the specific shares are outstanding as a proportion of the total number of days in the period. For example: if 100,000 shares were issued at the mid-point in a year, those shares add 50,000 to the weighted average. A reasonable approximation of the weighted average is adequate in many circumstances (for example, months rather than days) but a large issue or redemption of shares needs to be dealt with in terms of days.

Example 40.1 *Weighted average number of shares*

		Shares issued	*Treasury shares*	*Shares outstanding*
1 January 2002	Balance at beginning of year	1,000,000	150,000	850,000
31 May 2002	Issue of new shares for cash	400,000	–	1,250,000
1 December 2002	Purchase of treasury shares for cash	–	125,000	1,125,000
31 December 2002	Balance at end of year	1,400,000	275,000	1,125,000

The weighted average is computed either on a cumulative basis or on a tranche by tranche basis as follows:

Cumulative number of shares in issue multiplied by the number of months in issue

(850,000 × 5/12) + (1,250,000 × 6/12) + (1,125,000 × 1/12) = 1,072,917 shares

Tranche of shares multiplied by number of months in issue

(850,000 × 12/12) + (400,000 × 7/12) – (125,000 × 1/12) = 1,072,917 shares

Shares are usually included in the weighted average from the date on which the consideration is receivable (which is generally the date of their issue), for example:

- ordinary shares issued in exchange for cash are included in the weighted average from the date when the cash is receivable;

- ordinary shares issued on the reinvestment of dividends are included in the weighted average from the date on which the dividend payment is due;
- ordinary shares issued on the conversion of a debt instrument to ordinary shares are included in the weighted average from the date of the conversion (this is also usually the date on which interest ceases accruing on the debt instrument); and
- ordinary shares issued as consideration for the acquisition of an asset other than cash are included in the weighted average from the date on which the acquisition of the asset is recognised.

Extract 40.3 *Weighted average number of shares*

Technotrans, Germany, 31 December 2001 (IAS)

Calculation of the weighted average number of shares: (2,060,000 × 12/12) + (17,000 × 12/12) + (41,000 × 11/12) + (82,000 × 8/12) = 2,169,250 shares (previous year 2,045,000 shares). Where shares are issued as a component of the purchase price of an acquisition, they are included in the calculation at the weighted average at the time of the takeover of the company, or otherwise at the date on which they are first traded.

Extract 40.4 *Disclosure of weighted average number of shares*

EVN, Austria, 30 September 2001 (IAS)

Subsequent to the successful completion of the capital increase during the year under review, the number of shares issued totalled 37,581,455. Following the deduction of own shares, the weighted number of shares outstanding was 34,340,381. The earnings per share calculated on the basis of a net result for the year of TEUR 87,826.2 (previous year: TEUR 94,545.8) amounted to EUR 2.56 (previous year: EUR 2.78).

Ordinary shares issued as part of the purchase consideration of a business combination which is an acquisition are included in the weighted average number of shares as of the date of the acquisition which is the date on which control of the net assets and operations of the acquiree passes to the acquirer (IAS 22, 9). This is the date from which the acquirer incorporates the results of the operations of the acquiree into its income statement. However, the shares are measured at their fair value as at the date of the exchange transaction (IAS 22, 22 and 25) which may be different from the date of acquisition.

Ordinary shares issued as part of a business combination which is a uniting of interests are included in the calculation of the weighted average number of shares for all periods presented because the financial statements of the combined entity are prepared as if the combined entity had always existed.

Extract 40.5 *Number of ordinary shares in uniting of interests*

Novartis, Switzerland, 31 December 1997 (IAS)

Earnings per share are calculated by dividing the Group net income by the average outstanding number of shares. The average number of shares outstanding for 1997, minus treasury shares, was 69,671,193 (1996 68,825,219 assuming that the 1996 capital increases to facilitate the share exchange [to create Novartis] had been effected retroactively at 1 January 1996).

[Author's note: Novartis was created by a merger between Sandoz and Ciba at the end of 1996; the merger was accounted for under the pooling interests method.]

Ordinary shares which are issued in partly paid form are treated as a fraction of an ordinary share to the extent that they were entitled to participate in dividends relative to a fully paid ordinary share during the financial period (IAS 33, 18). For example, $1 shares issued 50c paid are treated as if each share is a half share.

Ordinary shares which are issuable upon the satisfaction of certain conditions (contingently issuable shares) are included in the weighted average as from the date on which all necessary conditions have been satisfied (IAS 33, 19). In effect, the shares are included in the weighted average when the issue is no longer contingent, that is there are no circumstances in which the shares will not be issued. Contingently issuable shares are, of course, potential ordinary shares and are therefore considered for inclusion in the weighted average number of shares used for the calculation of diluted earnings per share (see below). Ordinary shares which have been issued but which are contingently returnable (that is subject to recall) are treated as contingently issuable shares (IAS 33, 19). Therefore, they are included in the weighted average only when there are no longer any circumstances in which the shares will be returned.

When an entity issues shares for no consideration, the weighted average is adjusted for all periods presented (IAS 33, 21), that is the weighted average assumes that the shares had been in issue throughout all periods presented. For example, the weighted average is adjusted for the current and prior periods for any of the following events in the reporting period:

- a capitalisation or bonus issue or stock dividend;
- the bonus element in any other issue, for example a rights issue to existing shareholders;
- a share split; and
- a reverse share split (consolidation of shares).

In a capitalisation or bonus issue or a share split, ordinary shares are issued to existing shareholders for no consideration. The number of ordinary shares outstanding before the issue or split is adjusted for the proportionate change in the number of ordinary shares outstanding as if the event had occurred at the beginning of the earliest period reported.

Example 40.2 *Bonus issue*

Ordinary shares outstanding from 1 January 2001 to 30 September 2002	1,000,000
Bonus issue on 1 October 2002 of 2 ordinary shares for each ordinary share outstanding at 30 September 2002	
Ordinary shares issued on bonus issue	2,000,000
Ordinary shares outstanding from 1 October	3,000,000

The entity publishes comparative information for the prior period.

Since the bonus issue is an issue without consideration, the issue is treated for the purpose of calculating the weighted average number of shares as if it had occurred as at the beginning of 2001, the earliest period reported. Therefore, assuming that there were no other transactions affecting the number of ordinary shares in 2001 and 2002, the weighted average number of ordinary shares for both 2001 and 2002 is 3,000,000.

A rights issue usually includes a bonus element, that is the exercise price is usually less than the fair value of the shares (otherwise there is no incentive for the shareholders to take up their rights). The effect of the bonus element is calculated by multiplying the number of ordinary shares outstanding prior to the issue by the following factor:

$$\frac{\text{Fair value per share immediately prior to the exercise of rights}}{\text{Theoretical ex-rights fair value per share}}$$

The theoretical ex-rights fair value per share is the aggregate fair value of the shares immediately prior to the exercise of the rights plus the proceeds from the exercise of the rights, divided by the number of shares outstanding after the exercise of the rights. For example, if the aggregate fair value of the shares immediately before the rights issue is $2m and the proceeds of the rights issue are $500,000, the theoretical ex-rights fair value is $2,500,000 divided by the number of shares outstanding after the rights issue.

When the rights themselves are publicly traded separately from the shares prior to the exercise date, the fair value of the shares for the purposes of this calculation is their market value at the close of the last day on which the shares were traded together with the rights.

Example 40.3 *Rights Issue*

Shares outstanding from 1 January 2001 until rights issue on 1 March 2002	1,000,000
Rights issue on 1 March 2002 of one ordinary share for each five ordinary shares outstanding at a price of $5.00	
Fair value of one ordinary share immediately prior to the exercise of the rights	$11.00
Aggregate fair value of all shares outstanding immediately prior to the exercise of rights	$11,000,000
Total amount received from exercise of rights	$1,000,000
Theoretical ex-rights value per share	

$$\frac{11{,}000{,}000 + 1{,}000{,}000}{1{,}000{,}000 + 200{,}000} = \frac{12{,}000{,}000}{1{,}200{,}000} = \$10$$

Adjustment factor =

$$\frac{\text{Fair value per share immediately prior to exercise of rights}}{\text{Theoretical ex-rights fair value per share}} \quad \frac{11.00}{10.00} = 1.1$$

Therefore, assuming that there were no other transactions affecting the number of ordinary shares in 2001 and 2002, the number of shares outstanding from 1 January 2001 to 1 March 2002 is adjusted to 1,100,000. Therefore, for the purpose of recomputing basic earnings per share for 2001, the weighted average number of shares is 1,100,000. The weighted average for 2002 is 1,183,333 (1,100,000 for two months and 1,200,000 for ten months).

40.7 DILUTED EARNINGS PER SHARE

Diluted earnings per share is the amount of earnings which would have been attributable to each ordinary share if all dilutive potential ordinary shares had been converted into ordinary shares.

A *potential ordinary share* is a financial instrument or other contract which may entitle its holder to ordinary shares (IAS 33, 6). Examples of potential ordinary shares include:

- equity instruments, including preference shares, which are convertible into ordinary shares;
- debt instruments which are convertible into ordinary shares, for example, convertible loan stock;
- share warrants and options;
- employee plans which allow employees to receive ordinary shares as part of their remuneration;
- other share purchase plans; and
- shares which would be issued upon the satisfaction of certain conditions resulting from contractual arrangements, such as the purchase of a business or other assets.

Warrants or *options* are financial instruments which give the holder the right to purchase ordinary shares (IAS 33, 6).

Extract 40.6 *Potential ordinary shares*

Novartis, Switzerland, 31 December 2001 (IAS)

For the diluted earnings per share the weighted average number of shares outstanding is adjusted to assume conversion of all potential dilutive shares. The Group's convertible debt represents a potential dilution in the earnings per share to the extent that it is not covered by a hedge with non-consolidated employee share participation and employee benefit foundations to deliver the required number of shares on conversion.

The diluted EPS calculation takes into account all potential dilutions to the earnings per share arising from the convertible debt and call options on Novartis shares. Net income is adjusted to eliminate the applicable convertible debt interest expense less the tax effect.

Extract 40.7 *Potential ordinary shares*

Preussag, Germany, 31 December 2001 (IAS)

A dilution of earnings per share occurs when the average number of shares is increased by adding the issue of potential shares from warrants and conversion options issued by Preussag AG. As a rule, warrants and conversion options have a diluting effect on earnings if they lead to the issue of shares at a price below the average stock market share price.

As with basic earnings per share, diluted earnings per share is calculated by dividing earnings by the weighted average number of shares. However, both earnings – the net profit attributable to ordinary shareholders – and the weighted average number of shares outstanding should be adjusted for the effects of all dilutive potential ordinary shares (IAS 33, 24).

40.7.1 Earnings

Earnings are the net profit or loss for the period attributable to ordinary shareholders, as calculated for basic earnings per share, adjusted by the after-tax effect of :

- any dividends on dilutive potential ordinary shares which have been deducted in arriving at the net profit attributable to ordinary shareholders;
- any interest recognised as an expense in the period on the dilutive potential ordinary shares; and
- any other changes in income or expense that would result from the conversion of the dilutive potential ordinary shares into ordinary shares.

(IAS 33, 26)

After potential ordinary shares are converted into ordinary shares, the dividends, interest and other income or expense associated with them will no longer be incurred. Instead, the new ordinary shares will be entitled to participate in the net profit attributable to ordinary shareholders. Therefore, for the purpose of calculating diluted earnings per shares, the net profit for the period attributable to ordinary shareholders is increased by the amount of dividends, interest and other income or expense which will be saved on the conversion of the dilutive potential ordinary shares into ordinary shares. The expenses or income added back include fees and discounts or premiums which are accounted for as yield adjustments on the potential ordinary shares.

The amounts of dividends, interest and other income or expense added back are adjusted for any taxes which are attributable to them.

Example 40.4 *Impact of convertible bonds on the computation of earnings*

A has issued $1m convertible bonds which are convertible into 300,000 ordinary shares. Interest expense (including the amortisation of a discount) for the current period relating to the liability component of the convertible bond is $100,000. Current and deferred tax relating to that interest expense is $40,000.

For the purposes of calculating diluted earnings per share, the net profit attributable to ordinary shareholders is increased by $60,000, that is by the after-tax amount of the interest expense (including the amortisation of discount) recognised in the period.

The net profit or loss for the period is also adjusted for any consequential changes in income or expense resulting from the conversion of potential ordinary shares (IAS 33, 28). For example, the reduction of interest expense resulting from the conversion of potential ordinary shares increases net profit which may, in turn, increase the expense relating to a non-discretionary profit-sharing plan. This additional expense is deducted from the net profit attributable to ordinary shareholders.

40.7.2 Per Share

The weighted average number of ordinary shares should be the weighted average number of ordinary shares calculated for basic earnings per share plus the weighted average number of ordinary shares which would have been issued on the conversion of all the dilutive potential ordinary shares into ordinary shares (IAS 33, 29). Dilutive potential ordinary shares should be deemed to have been converted into ordinary shares at the beginning of the period or the date of their issue, whichever was later.

Potential ordinary shares are treated as dilutive only when their conversion to ordinary shares would decrease the net profit per share from continuing ordinary operations (IAS 33, 38). For example, the convertible bond in example 40.4 is dilutive if the combined effect of increasing the profit by $60,000 and the number of shares by 300,000 reduces earnings per share which it will if net profit per share from continuing ordinary operations is more than 20c. Potential ordinary shares are anti-dilutive when their conversion to ordinary shares would increase earnings per share from continuing ordinary operations or decrease loss per share from continuing ordinary operations – in the example, this would be the case if net profit per share from continuing ordinary operations is less than 20c. Anti-dilutive potential ordinary shares are ignored in calculating diluted earnings per share.

The net profit from continuing ordinary activities is the net profit from ordinary activities as defined in IAS 8 but excluding items relating to discontinuing operations, extraordinary items and the effects of changes in accounting policies and of corrections of fundamental errors (IAS 33, 39). This amount of net profit is a control number for determining whether or not potential ordinary shares are dilutive, it is not used for disclosure purposes. The IASB's May 2002 improvements exposure draft proposes to replace the reference to discontinued operations in the existing text of IAS 33 with discontinuing operations (under IAS 35).

In considering whether potential ordinary shares are dilutive or anti-dilutive, each issue or series of potential ordinary shares is considered separately rather than in aggregate. The sequence in which potential ordinary shares are considered may affect whether or not they are dilutive. Therefore, in order to maximise the dilution of basic earnings per share, each issue or series of potential ordinary shares is considered in sequence from the most dilutive to the least dilutive.

The computation of the number of ordinary shares which would have been issued on the conversion of dilutive potential ordinary shares is determined by reference to the terms of the potential ordinary shares. When necessary, it assumes the most advantageous conversion rate or exercise price from the standpoint of the holder of the potential ordinary shares (IAS 33, 30).

Ordinary shares which are issuable on the satisfaction of certain conditions (contingently issuable shares) are included in the computation of the weighted average for basic and, hence, diluted earnings per share if the conditions for issuance have been met. If the conditions for issuance have not been met, the number of contingently issuable shares is not included in the computation of the weighted average for basic earnings per share. If, however, the shares are dilutive, they are included in the weighted average for diluted earnings per share. If the conditions for issuance are not met when the contingency period expires, prior periods are not restated.

Instruments that will be settled in cash are not potential ordinary shares because they do not give the right to ordinary shares. Some instruments may be settled in either cash or ordinary shares of the entity at the option of either the issuer or the holder. Such instruments are treated as potential ordinary shares (SIC 24, 4).

IASB improvements project

In its May 2002 improvements exposure draft, the IASB proposes that those instruments that can be settled in cash or ordinary shares at the option of the issuer should be treated as potential ordinary shares based on a rebuttable assumption that they will be settled by the issuance of shares. SIC 24 will be withdrawn.

A subsidiary, joint venture or associate may issue potential ordinary shares which are convertible into either ordinary shares of the subsidiary, joint venture or associate, or ordinary shares of the reporting entity. If these potential ordinary shares of the subsidiary, associate or joint venture have a dilutive effect on the consolidated earnings per share of the reporting entity itself, they are potential ordinary shares of the reporting entity. In such circumstances, they are included in the weighted average number of shares.

The exercise of many dilutive potential ordinary shares will result in the receipt of proceeds by the entity. These proceeds should be considered to have been received from the issue of shares at fair value (IAS 33, 33). The difference between the number of shares issued and the number of shares which would have been issued at fair value should be treated as an issue of ordinary shares for no consideration (IAS 33, 33). Fair value is calculated on the basis of the average price of the ordinary shares during the period (IAS 33, 34).

Options and other share purchase arrangements are dilutive when they would result in the issue of ordinary shares for less than fair value. The amount of the dilution is the fair value of the shares less the issue price. Therefore, in order to calculate diluted earnings per share, each such arrangement is treated as consisting of:

- a contract to issue a certain number of ordinary shares at their average fair value during the period – these shares are assumed to be neither dilutive nor anti-dilutive; and
- a contract to issue the remaining ordinary shares for no consideration – these shares are dilutive.

Example 40.5 *Effects of share options on diluted earnings per share*

Net profit for year 2001	$2,400,000
Weighted average number of ordinary shares outstanding during year 2001	1,000,000
Average fair value of one ordinary share during 2001	$20

Throughout 2001, options existed to issue 200,000 shares at $15.
The number of shares which would have been issued at fair value is 150,000, that is (200,000 × 15.00)/20.00.
Basic earnings per share is $2.40. Diluted earnings per share is $2.29, that is $2,400,000 divided by (1,000,000 + 200,000 − 150,000).

This method of dealing with options and other share purchase arrangements is sometimes referred to as the treasury stock method. When developing IAS 33, the IASC rejected an alternative approach under which imputed income from the proceeds of the options and other arrangements is added to earnings.

Extract 40.8 *Diluted earnings per share*

Holcim, Switzerland, 31 December 2001 (IAS)

The fully diluted Earnings per Share (EPS) factor takes into account the potential dilution effects should the conversion options on the zero coupon convertible bonds (1999 to 2014), the 1% convertible bonds (1998 to 2004) and the share option plan be exercised. The fully diluted EPS is based on a weighted average number of 29,336,537 (2000: 28,161,560) bearer shares – the two bonds may be converted into 1,908,332 (2000: 1,908,332) bearer shares – and 54,304,240 (2000: 52,519,810) registered shares. It amounts to CHF 20.85 (2000: 23.60) per bearer and CHF 4.17 (2000: 4.72) per registered share. The prior year figures were restated based on the 5-for-1 share split which took place in May 2001.

To the extent that partly paid shares are not entitled to participate in dividends during the financial period they are considered the equivalent of warrants or options (IAS 33, 37). For example, $1 shares issued 50c paid which are not entitled to participate in dividends during the period are treated as if they were options or warrants carrying the right to a half share each at a price of 50c.

Potential ordinary shares which have been cancelled or allowed to lapse during the period are included in the computation of the weighted average number of shares for the period during which they were outstanding. They are excluded from the computation in respect of subsequent periods.

Potential ordinary shares which have been converted into ordinary shares during the reporting period are included in the calculation of diluted earnings per share from the beginning of the period to the date of conversion; from the date of conversion, the resulting ordinary shares are included in both basic and diluted earnings per share. For example, the potential number of ordinary shares issuable on the conversion of a convertible bond is included in the weighted average for the purposes of diluted earnings per share up to the date of conversion. As from the date of conversion, the number of shares issued on the conversion is included in the weighted average for basic earnings per share, and hence, diluted earnings per share.

An entity does not restate diluted earnings per share of any prior period presented for changes in the assumptions used or for the conversion of potential ordinary shares into ordinary shares outstanding. However, if the number of ordinary or potential ordinary shares outstanding increases as a result of a capitalisation or bonus issue or

IASB improvements project

In its May 2002 improvements exposure draft, the IASB proposes to add further guidance and illustrative examples to IAS 33 dealing with: contingently issuable shares; potential ordinary shares of subsidiaries, joint ventures or associates; participating securities; written put options; and purchased put and call options.

share split or decreases as a result of a reverse share split, the calculation of diluted earnings per share for all periods presented should be adjusted retrospectively (IAS 33, 43).

40.8 EVENTS AFTER THE BALANCE SHEET DATE

If the number of ordinary shares or potential ordinary shares outstanding increases as a result of a capitalisation or bonus issue or share split or decreases as a result of a reverse share split after the balance sheet date but before the issuance of the financial statements, the per share calculations for those and any prior period financial statements presented should be based on the new number of shares (IAS 33, 43). When earnings per share disclosures reflect such changes that fact should be disclosed.

Example 40.6 *Bonus issue after the balance sheet date*

Ordinary shares outstanding from 1 January 1998 to 31 January 2000	1,000,000
Bonus issue on 1 February 2000 of 2 ordinary shares for each ordinary share outstanding at 31 January 2000	
Ordinary shares issued on bonus issue	2,000,000
Ordinary shares outstanding from 1 February 2000	3,000,000

The entity approves its financial statements for the year ended 31 December 1999 in April 2000. It publishes comparative information for the prior period.

Since the bonus issue is an issue without consideration, the issue is treated for the purpose of calculating the weighted average number of shares as if it had occurred as at the beginning of 1998, the earliest period reported. Therefore, assuming that there were no other transactions affecting the number of ordinary shares in 1998 and 1999, the weighted average number of ordinary shares for both 1998 and 1999 is 3,000,000.

Basic and diluted earnings per share of all periods presented should also be adjusted for:

- the effects of fundamental errors, and adjustments resulting from changes in accounting policies, dealt with in accordance with the benchmark treatment in IAS 8; and

- the effects of a business combination which is a uniting of interests.

(IAS 33, 43)

Ordinary share or potential ordinary share transactions which occur after the balance sheet date and which are of such importance that their non-disclosure would affect the ability of the users of the financial statements to make proper evaluations and decisions should be disclosed (see IAS 10, 28). In deciding whether such transactions should be disclosed consideration is given to their impact on basic and diluted earnings per share as well as on financial position, performance and cash flows. In practice, however, stock exchanges require the disclosure of such events and their disclosure in the financial statements is not onerous. Earnings per share amounts are not adjusted for such transactions because they do not affect the amount of capital used to produce the net profit or loss for the period.

40.9 PRESENTATION

An entity should present basic and diluted earnings per share on the face of the income statement for each class of ordinary shares which has a different right to share in the net profit for the period. An entity should present basic and diluted earnings per share with equal prominence for all periods presented (IAS 33, 47).

40.10 DISCLOSURE

An entity should disclose:

- the amounts used as the numerators in calculating basic and diluted earnings per share, and a reconciliation of those amounts to the net profit or loss for the period; and
- the weighted average number of ordinary shares used as the denominator in calculating basic and diluted earnings per share, and a reconciliation of these denominators to each other.

Extract 40.9 *Disclosure of earnings per share*

Novartis, Switzerland, 31 December 2001 (IAS)

Basic earnings per share is calculated by dividing the net income attributable to shareholders by the weighted average number of shares outstanding during the year, excluding from the issued shares the average number of shares purchased by the Group and held as treasury shares.

	2001	*2000*
Net income attributable to shareholders (CHF millions)	7,024	7,210
Weighted average number of shares outstanding	2,571,673,365	2,613,547,597
Basic earnings per share (expressed in CHF)	2.73	2.75

For the diluted earnings per share the weighted average number of shares outstanding is adjusted to assume conversion of all potential dilutive shares. The Group's convertible debt represents a potential dilution in the earnings per share to the extent that it is not covered by a hedge with non-consolidated employee share participation and employee benefit foundations to deliver the required number of shares on conversion.

The diluted EPS calculation takes into account all potential dilutions to the earnings per share arising from the convertible debt and call options on Novartis shares. Net income is adjusted to eliminate the applicable convertible debt interest expense less the tax effect.

	2001	*2000*
Net income attributable to shareholders (CHF millions)	7,024	7,210
Elimination of interest expense on convertible debt (net of tax effect)	3	2
Net income used to determine diluted earnings per share	7,027	7,212
Weighted average number of shares outstanding	2,571,673,365	2,613,547,597
Adjustment for assumed conversion of convertible debt	1,507,027	1,608,676
Call options on Novartis shares	4,574,401	–
Adjustment for dilutive stock options	1,010,963	982,560
Weighted average number of shares for diluted earnings per share	2,578,765,756	2,616,138,833
Diluted earnings per share (expressed in CHF)	2.72	2.75

Extract 40.10 *Disclosure of earnings per share*

Schering, Germany, 31 December 2001 (IAS)

Basic earnings per share are calculated by dividing net income by the weighted average number of shares outstanding.

	2001	*2000*
Net income (€m)	418	336
Weighted average number of shares outstanding	198,000,000	198,000,000
Basic earnings per share (€)	2.11	1.70

For the calculation of diluted earnings per share, the weighted average number of shares outstanding is adjusted for all potential dilutive shares. The Group's stock option plans represent a potential dilution in the earnings per share.

The plans grant Schering AG share options to management in leading positions. Whether the options can be exercised depends on certain performance criteria relating to the Schering share price which are laid down in the stock option plans (see note (34)).

	2001	*2000*
Net income (€m)	418	336
Weighted average number of shares outstanding	198,000,000	198,000,000
Adjustment for potential dilutive shares	926,418	1,586,700
Weighted average number of shares (including potential dilutive shares)	198,926,418	199,586,700
Diluted earnings per share (€)	2.10	1.68

The terms of the stock option plans reserve Schering AG the right to settle claims relating to the exercise of option rights in the form of cash payments instead of issuing shares.

If an entity discloses, in addition to basic and diluted earnings per share, per share amounts for other components of net profit, such amounts should be calculated using the weighted average number of ordinary shares determined in accordance with IAS 33 (IAS 33, 51). If a component of net profit is used which is not reported as a line item in the income statement, for example DVFA earnings of German companies or headline earnings, a reconciliation should be provided between the component used and a line item in the income statement (IAS 33, 51). Basic and diluted per share amounts should be disclosed with equal prominence (IAS 33, 51).

It can be argued that dividends are a component of the net profit and therefore that IAS 33 requires that the disclosure of dividends per share (required by IAS 1) should be calculated using the weighted average number of shares. Such a presentation would be rather meaningless and it is suggested that dividend per share disclosures should be calculated using the number of shares which are entitled to the dividend.

Extract 40.11 *Disclosure of component of profit per share*

Dairy Farm International, Hong Kong, 31 December 2001 (IAS)

Basic earnings/(loss) per share are calculated on the net profit of US$29.8 million (2000: net loss of US$171.5 million) and on the weighted average number of 1,655.7 million (2000: 1,655.7 million) ordinary shares in issue during the year. The weighted average number excludes the Company's shares held by Trustee under the Senior Executive Shares Schemes (note 22).

... Basic and diluted earnings per share reflecting the revaluation of leasehold properties are also calculated on net profit of US$30.1 million (2000: net loss of US$194.5 million) as shown in the supplementary financial information.

Additional basic and diluted earnings per share are also calculated based on underlying earnings. The difference between underlying net profit and net profit/(loss) is reconciled as follows:

	2001 US$m	*2000 US$m*
Net profit/(loss)	**29.8**	(171.5)
Discontinuing operations (note 1)	**(2.1)**	195.0
Restructuring costs of Wellcome Delivers	**6.6**	–
Impairment of assets, Hong Kong	**12.9**	–
Net profit on sale of leasehold land	**–**	(23.3)
Underlying net profit – IAS basis	**47.2**	0.2
Additional amortisation of leasehold land payments	**0.3**	0.3
Underlying net profit – IAS modified basis	**47.5**	0.5

Extract 40.12 *Operating cash flows per share*

Hongkong Land, Hong Kong, 31 December 2001 (IAS)

Cash flow per share is based on cash flows from operating activities less major renovations expenditure amounting to US$180.5 million (2000: US$198.2 million) and is calculated on the weighted average number of 2,379.1 million (2000: 2,519.2 million) shares in issue during the year, which excludes 69.6 million shares in which the Company held by a wholly-owned subsidiary (see note 21 [share capital]).

Notes

[1] A more extensive comparison of IAS 33 and FAS 128 can be found in Kimberly Petrone, 'Comparative Analysis of IAS 33 ... and Related US GAAP', in *'The IASC – US GAAP Comparison Project: A Report of Similarities and Differences Between IASC standards and US GAAP'*, 2nd edition, ed Carrie Bloomer, Norwalk, CT FASB, 1999.

[2] Institute for Investment Management and Research, Statement of Investment Practice, *The Definition of IIMR Headline Earnings*, 1993.

[3] Rolf Rundfeldt, 'What Do We Mean by Earnings', *IASC Insight*, September 1996, p4.

CHAPTER 41

Interim Reporting

41.1 RELEVANT STANDARD

IAS 34 *Interim Reporting*

41.2 HISTORY

The IASC included a standard on interim reporting in the programme agreed with IOSCO in July 1995 (*IASC Insight*, September 1995, p1). The IASC published an issues paper, *Interim Financial Reporting*, in April 1996 which identified 27 basic issues and 28 subsidiary issues. The DSOP was published in September 1996 and the exposure draft, E57, in July 1997.

IAS 34 *Interim Financial Reporting* was approved in 1998 and applied to financial statements (not interim financial reports) for accounting periods beginning on or after 1 January 1999.

41.3 IOSCO

Interim reporting is one of IOSCO's core standards. The IASC had not addressed the topic when IOSCO considered the existing IASs in June 1994.

IAS 34 is included in 'IAS 2000' endorsed by IOSCO in May 2000. There are 14 supplemental treatments. Three supplemental treatments suggest further guidance on:

- the practical issues arising from the effect of different legal environments on the concept of 'authorised for issue', particularly as it relates to interim financial statements;

- the determination of 'estimated average annual effective rate', particularly as regards the changes in deferred taxes; and
- the clarity and consistency of content in interim financial reports – specific line items in the balance sheet, income statement and statement of cash flows should correspond to those in IAS 1, together with any additional significant line items that appeared in the entity's most recent annual balance sheet.

The remaining 11 supplemental treatments ask for additional disclosures as follows:

- whether the interim financial statements comply with the recognition and measurement principles of IAS 34 and information required by securities regulators;
- amounts used in the computation of the numerator and denominator of EPS and a reconciliation of the numerator to the net profit or loss for the period;
- an explicit statement of the limited nature of the information provided;
- the effects of changes in the composition of the reporting entity together with the major assumptions used in measuring the effect;
- error corrections and changes in accounting policy;
- contingencies and major uncertainties, particularly when a going concern is in question;
- the nature and amount of significant changes in the components of the minimum line items since the last annual report;
- dispositions not considered discontinued operations under IAS 35;
- EPS and income tax amounts for accounting changes, fundamental errors, discontinued operations and extraordinary items;
- the reasons for any significant changes since the last annual period in total assets and segment result for each segment; and
- items whose measurement is based on annual data or data related to several interim periods.

41.4 IAS 34 IN BRIEF

An interim financial report should include (as a minimum) condensed financial statements including an explanation of the events and transactions which are significant to an understanding of those statements. The condensed financial statements should be prepared using the same accounting policies as the annual financial statements and using the same recognition and measurement judgements as would apply in annual financial statements.

41.5 PUBLICATION OF INTERIM FINANCIAL REPORTS

An *interim period* is a financial reporting period shorter than a full financial year (IAS 34, 4). The IASB cannot mandate the publication of financial reports for such periods or the frequency or timeliness of interim reports. It also cannot mandate the publication of an interim report prepared in accordance with IAS 34 by those entities which publish annual IFRS financial statements. IAS 34 applies only to those interim financial reports which are published and which themselves purport to conform with IFRSs.

Governments, securities regulators and stock exchanges often require entities whose debt or equity securities are publicly traded to publish interim financial reports. Most countries require half-yearly reports while a few, notably the United States, require quarterly reports. It is likely that governments or regulators will identify those entities which are required to publish IFRS interim financial reports or are allowed to publish IFRS interim reports in place of reports prepared in accordance with national standards.

41.6 CONTENT OF AN INTERIM FINANCIAL REPORT

An *interim financial report* is a financial report containing either a complete set of financial statements (as described in IAS 1) or a set of condensed financial statements (as described in IAS 34) for an interim period. There is nothing to stop an entity publishing a complete set of financial statements in its interim report. However, in practice, few are required to do so and even fewer opt to do so by choice.

IAS 34 takes the same approach as national standards and regulations. In most national standards and regulations, interim reports are condensed reports (although those published by Italian listed companies are lengthy, many being longer than the annual reports of companies in other countries).

If an entity is required to publish information for only one interim period (for example, the first half of a year), the interim financial report should include, as a minimum:

- a condensed balance sheet as at the end of the interim period;
- a condensed income statement for the interim period;
- a condensed statement of changes in equity for the interim period, adopting either of the presentations permitted by IAS 1;
- a condensed cash flow statement for the interim period; and
- selected explanatory notes.

If an entity is required to publish information for more than one interim period (for example, quarterly), the interim financial report should include, as a minimum:

- a condensed balance sheet as at the end of the interim period;
- condensed income statements for the interim period *and* the year to date;
- a condensed statement of changes in equity for the year to date (rather than the interim period) again adopting either of the presentations permitted by IAS 1;
- a condensed cash flow statement for the year to date (rather than the interim period); and
- selected explanatory notes.

41.6.1 Condensed Statements

The condensed statements should include, at a minimum, each of the headings and sub-totals which were included in the most recent annual financial statement (IAS 34, 10). Additional line items should be included if their omission would make the interim financial statements misleading (IAS 34, 10). IAS 1 specifies the minimum line items for the balance sheet and the income statement. IAS 7 does not specify the format of the cash flow statement or its headings and sub-totals although most entities follow a similar format to that in the appendix of IAS 7.

Basic and diluted earnings per share for the interim period should be presented on the face of the income statement (IAS 34, 11). These amounts are calculated in accordance with IAS 33 (see chapter 40). The weighted average number of shares and the effects of dilutive securities are determined for the interim period; the entity does not project what the weighted average or the dilutive effects will be for the full year.

41.6.2 Comparative Information

The comparative information for the income statement, cash flow statement and statement of changes in equity (but not the balance sheet) corresponds with the information for the current period. When an entity is required to publish information for only one interim period (for example, the first half of a year), the following comparative information in respect of the preceding year should be included in the interim report:

- a balance sheet as of the end of the preceding financial year (but not at the end of the equivalent interim period);
- an income statement for the equivalent interim period;

- a statement of changes in equity for the equivalent period; and
- a cash flow statement for the equivalent period.

(IAS 34, 20)

The requirements are slightly more complex when an entity publishes more than one interim report for an annual period. In this case, a distinction is drawn between comparative information for the equivalent interim period and comparative information for the equivalent year to date. An entity should publish the following comparative information in each interim report:

- a balance sheet as of the end of the preceding financial year;
- income statements for both the equivalent interim period and the equivalent period to date;
- a statement of changes in equity for the equivalent period to date; and
- a cash flow statement for the equivalent period to date.

(IAS 34, 20)

Example 41.1 *Comparative information in half-yearly interim financial reports*

A is required to publish an annual report and an interim report for the first half of the year. Its year end is 31 December. In its interim report for the six months to 30 June 2002, it must publish:

- a balance sheet as at 30 June 2002 and a comparative balance sheet as at 31 December 2001;
- an income statement for the six months to 30 June 2002 and a comparative income statement for the six months to 30 June 2001;
- a statement of changes in equity for the six months to 30 June 2002 and a comparative statement for the six months to 30 June 2001; and
- a cash flow statement for the six months to 30 June 2002 and a comparative cash flow statement for the six months to 30 June 2001.

Example 41.2 *Comparative information in quarterly interim financial reports*

B is required to publish an annual report and quarterly interim reports. Its year end is 31 December. In its interim report for the three months to 31 March, the interim period and the year to date are identical. For the second and third quarters, the interim period is three months but the year to date is six months and nine months respectively. For the interim period to 30 June 2002 (the second quarter) B must publish:

- a balance sheet as at 30 June 2002 and a comparative balance sheet as at 31 December 2001;
- an income statement for the three months to 30 June 2002 and the six months to 30 June 2002 and comparative income statements for the three months to 30 June 2001 and the six months to 30 June 2001;
- a statement of changes in equity for the six months to 30 June 2002 and a comparative statement for the six months to 30 June 2001; and
- a cash flow statement for the six months to 30 June 2002 and a comparative cash flow statement for the six months to 30 June 2001.

41.6.3 Explanatory Notes

The notes are designed to explain events and transactions which are significant to an understanding of the changes in financial position and performance of the entity since the last annual reporting date. Therefore, the notes should include:

- a statement that the same accounting policies and methods of computation have been used as were used in the most recent annual financial statements; and
- a description of the nature and effect of any changes in the accounting policies and methods of computation since the most recent annual financial statements.

Extract 41.1 *Accounting policies*

Hongkong Land Holdings, Hong Kong, six months to 30 June 2000 (IAS)

The accounting policies used in the preparation of the interim financial statements are consistent with those used in the annual financial statements for the year ended 31st December 1999.

Extract 41.2 *Accounting policies*

Hongkong Land Holdings, Hong Kong, six months to 30 June 2001 (IAS)

In accordance with IAS 40 ...., leasehold land and buildings which are investment properties are carried at depreciated historical cost. Similarly leasehold interests in land in respect of other leasehold properties are carried at depreciated cost. This is a change in accounting policy as in previous years the Group had reflected the fair value of leasehold investment properties in the financial statements and recorded fair value changes in property revaluation reserves, except for movements on individual properties below cost which were dealt with in the consolidated profit and loss account. The effect of this change has been to decrease net profit for the six months ended 30 June and for the year ended 31 December 2000 by US$9.9 million and US$21.3 million respectively, and shareholders' funds at 1 January 2000 and 2001 by US$4,217.0 million and US$6,115.0 million respectively.

The notes should also include

- an explanation of seasonality or cyclicality of interim operations;
- the nature and amount of items affecting assets, liabilities, equity, net income or cash flows which are unusual because of their nature, size or incidence;
- the nature and amount of changes in estimates of amounts reported in prior interim periods of the current year if those changes have a material effect in the current interim period;
- the nature and amount of or changes in estimates of amounts reported in prior financial years if those changes have a material effect in the current interim period;
- issuances, repurchases, and repayments of debt and equity securities;
- dividends paid (aggregate or per share) for ordinary shares and separately for other shares;
- segment revenue and segment result for business segments or geographical segments, whichever is the entity's primary basis of segment reporting in accordance with IAS 14;
- material events subsequent to the end of the interim period which have not been reflected in the financial statements for the interim period;
- the effect of changes in the composition of the entity during the interim period, including business combinations, the acquisition or disposal of subsidiaries and long-term investments, restructuring and discontinuing operations; and
- changes in contingent liabilities or contingent assets since the last annual balance sheet date.

(IAS 34, 16)

Examples of the kinds of disclosures that are required include:

- the write-down of inventories to net realisable value and the reversal of such a write-down;
- recognition of a loss from the impairment of property, plant and equipment, intangible assets, or other assets, and the reversal of such an impairment loss;
- the reversal of any provisions of the costs of restructuring;
- acquisitions and disposals of items of property, plant and equipment;
- commitments for the purchase of property, plant and equipment;
- litigation settlements;
- corrections of fundamental errors;
- extraordinary items;
- any debt default or breach of a debt covenant that has not been corrected subsequently; and
- related party transactions.

When an entity publishes more than one interim report for an annual period, the information should normally be reported on a financial year-to-date basis. However, the entity should also disclose any events or transactions that are material to an understanding of the current interim period.

41.6.4 Compliance with IFRSs

The entity should disclose that its interim financial report is in compliance with IAS 34 (IAS 34, 19) but as with the similar requirement in IAS 1 there is no sanction against an entity which does not comply with this requirement.

Extract 41.3 *Compliance with IAS 34*

MAN, Germany, three months to 31 March 2001 (IAS)

The interim financial statements have been prepared according to IAS 34 and are based on the accounting and valuation methods used for the previous consolidated financial statements as of 31 December 2000. IAS 39 *Accounting and Valuation of Financial Instruments* has been applied for the first time. The interim financial statements have not been audited.

An interim financial report should not be described as complying with IFRSs unless it complies with all of the requirements of each IFRS and each interpretation (IAS 34, 19). This is a similar requirement to that in IAS 1 for annual financial statements (see chapter 8). Confusion may arise if the interim report refers to compliance with IFRSs but not specifically to compliance with IAS 34. It seems appropriate, therefore, that there should not be any reference to compliance with IFRSs in an interim report which does not comply with IAS 34.

41.6.5 Materiality

Materiality should be assessed in relation to the interim period but in making assessments of materiality, an entity should recognise that interim measurements may rely on estimates to a greater extent than measurements of annual financial data (IAS 34, 23).

41.6.6 Annual Financial Statements

An entity may not be required to publish an interim report for the final interim period in a year, that is, the second half of the year for an entity which reports twice a year and the fourth quarter for an entity which reports quarterly. If an estimate made in an earlier interim period of the same year is changed significantly during the final interim period, the nature and amount of the change in the estimate should be disclosed in the annual financial statements (IAS 34, 26). The amounts reported in the interim report for the earlier period are not adjusted retrospectively.

For an entity which reports more frequently than half-yearly, income and expenses reported in the current interim period reflect any changes in estimates of amounts reported in any prior interim periods of the same financial year. So, for example, the third and fourth quarter may include adjustments relating to estimates made in the first quarter. The amounts reported in the first quarter are not adjusted retrospectively but the adjustments may need to be disclosed in the later interim periods or the annual financial statements.

41.7 RECOGNITION AND MEASUREMENT

An entity should apply the same accounting policies in its interim financial statements as are applied in its annual financial statement, except for accounting policy changes which will be reflected in the next annual financial statements (IAS 34, 28).

41.7.1 Changes in Accounting Policies

A change in accounting policy should be made in annual financial statements only if:

- it is required by statute or an accounting standard setting body; or
- it will result in more relevant or reliable information about the financial position, performance or cash flows of the entity.

(IAS 8, 42 and 43)

In the context of IFRS financial statements, interim financial statements for annual accounting periods beginning on or after 1 January 1999 (for example, those for interim reports for the six months to 30 June 1999) should apply any revised accounting policies resulting from the adoption of the revised IAS 17 and IAS 19. Interim financial statements for annual accounting periods beginning on or after 1 July 1999 (for example, those for interim reports for the six months to 31 December 1999) should apply any revised accounting policies resulting from the adoption of the revised IAS 22, IAS 36 (and the consequential revisions to IAS 16, IAS 28 and IAS 31), IAS 37 and IAS 38.

A change in accounting policy should be accounted for in accordance with IAS 8 (IAS 34, 43). If an entity adopts the benchmark treatment in IAS 8, the prior interim periods are restated. Prior interim periods in the same financial year should also be restated when the allowed alternative treatment is used (IAS 34, 43(b)), otherwise two different accounting policies would have been applied to like transactions or events within the same financial year.

41.7.2 Measurement of Results

The frequency of an entity's reporting (annual, half-yearly, or quarterly) should not affect the measurement of its annual results. Therefore, measurements in interim reports should be made on a year-to-date basis (IAS 34, 28). These requirements have two consequences:

- the principles for the recognition of assets, liabilities, income, and expenses for interim periods are the same as those which are used in annual financial statements; and
- estimates made in earlier interim periods of a financial year may need to be changed in a later interim period (or the annual financial statements) for the same financial year.

For assets, the same tests of control over future economic benefits apply at interim dates as apply at the end of the financial year. Costs that would not qualify as assets at the financial year end do not qualify as assets at interim dates. Similarly, for liabilities, a present or constructive obligation must exist at the end of the interim period.

For example:

- inventories are written down to net realisable value in interim periods in accordance with the requirements of IAS 2 – if the estimate of net realisable value changes later during the same financial year, the amount of the write-down is changed in a subsequent interim period or in the full financial statements if information for a subsequent interim period is not presented (the same principles apply to any other asset impairments);

- the revenues, costs, the stage of completion and the outcome of a construction contract are determined in each interim period in accordance with the requirements of IAS 11 – if the estimates change later during the same financial year, the amount of revenue, costs and (if appropriate) expected losses is adjusted in a subsequent interim period or in the full financial statements if information for a subsequent interim period is not presented (the same principles apply to the supply of any other services under IAS 18);
- a provision for a restructuring is recognised in an interim period if it meets the recognition criteria in IAS 37 by the end of the period – if the estimate of the provision changes later during the same financial year, the amount of the provision is changed in a subsequent interim period or in the full financial statements if information for a subsequent interim period is not presented;
- a provision for a restructuring is *not* recognised in an interim period if it does not meet the recognition criteria in IAS 37 – if the provision meets the criteria later during the same financial year, the provision is recognised in a subsequent interim period or in the full financial statements if information for a subsequent interim period is not presented;
- development costs are recognised as an asset when they meet the recognition criteria in IAS 38 during an interim period – any such costs which fail to meet the criteria later during the same financial year are dealt with under the impairment requirements in IAS 36 in a subsequent interim period or in the full financial statements if information for a subsequent interim period is not presented; and
- development costs are *not* recognised as an asset when they do not meet the recognition criteria in IAS 38 during an interim period – they are not deferred either to await future information as to whether they have met the definition of an asset or to smooth earnings over interim periods.

Revenues which are earned seasonally, cyclically or occasionally within a financial year should not be anticipated in a period prior to that in which they are earned or deferred into a later period from that in which they are earned if anticipation or deferral would not be appropriate at the end of the entity's financial year (IAS 34, 37). Similarly, costs which are incurred unevenly during the financial year should not be anticipated in a period prior to that in which they are incurred or deferred into a later period from that in which they are incurred unless it is also appropriate to anticipate or defer that type of cost at the end of the financial year (IAS 34, 39).

For example, an entity which grows and sells seasonal produce does not include any revenues for the sale of produce in periods prior to those in which the sale would meet the recognition criteria in IAS 18. The entity does not defer any costs in periods prior to those in which the sales are recognised unless those costs are included in inventories in accordance with IAS 2 or are deferred in accordance with IAS 38. Similarly, an entity which sells holiday package tours does not recognise revenue on tours until the interim period in which the revenue would be recognised under IAS 18 and does not defer any costs into later interim periods unless those costs meet the relevant criteria in IAS 38 or are implied by the application of the percentage of completion method in IAS 18.

IAS 34 includes guidance on a number of practical issues which are likely to arise in applying these requirements:

- year-end bonuses are recognised as a liability and an expense in an interim period report, if payment of the bonus is either a legal or constructive obligation at the end of the interim period and the entity can estimate reliably the amount of the obligation;
- retirement benefit costs for an interim period are calculated by using the actuarially determined pension cost rate at the end of the prior financial year, adjusted for significant market fluctuations since that time and for significant curtailments, settlements, or other significant one-time events;
- volume rebates or discounts and other contractual changes in the prices of raw materials, labour, or other purchased goods and services are anticipated in interim periods, by both the payer and the recipient, if it is probable that they have been earned or will take effect;
- depreciation and amortisation are based only on assets recognised during that interim period;
- foreign currency gains and losses are determined in accordance with IAS 21 using the same principles as at the financial year end – the closing rate is the rate at the end of the interim period (not a forecast rate for the end of the financial year); and
- entities reporting in the currency of a hyperinflationary economy apply IAS 29 by expressing all amounts in terms of the measuring unit as at the end of the interim period.

41.7.3 Income Tax Expense

Income tax expense in each interim period is measured using the expected weighted average annual income tax rate for the full financial year (IAS 34, 30(c)). No practical problems arise for an entity which operates in a jurisdiction in which there is only one rate of tax. Practical problems do arise, however, for entities which operate in jurisdictions with progressive rates of tax. In such cases, the estimated weighted average annual rate reflects a blend of the progressive tax rate structure expected to apply to the full year's profits. To the extent practicable, a separate estimated average annual effective income tax rate is determined for each jurisdiction in which the entity is subject to tax.

The expected average annual income tax rate is re-estimated at the end of each interim period. Any adjustments in respect of prior periods is included in the current interim period.

Changes in tax rates are dealt with in accordance with IAS 12, that is, their effects are recognised when they have been enacted or substantively enacted. When the changes affect the whole period, they are reflected in the weighted average rate for the period. When they affect only the later interim periods, for example when a government decides that new rates will apply only to profits earned after a specified date, a different weighted average rate for the earlier period is based on the old rates and the weighted average for the later period is based on the new rates.

The requirements of IAS 12 are applied in dealing with temporary differences, tax losses and unused tax credits.

Example 41.3 *Expected average annual income tax rate*

Company A publishes interim financial statements quarterly and operates in a jurisdiction in which the following tax rates apply:

	%
First $2 million of taxable profits	40
From $2 million to $5 million profits	50
Profits in excess of $5m	60

A earns profits of $1.2 million in the first quarter of 2002. Annual profits of $1.2 million would be taxed at 40% but A must estimate its annual profits and, hence, its expected weighted average income tax rate for the whole of 2002. A estimates that it will earn profits of $6m in 2002. Its weighted average income tax rate is calculated as follows:

	%	*Profits* $	*Tax* $
First $2 million of taxable profits	40	2,000,000	800,000
From $2 million to $5 million profits	50	3,000,000	1,500,000
Profits in excess of $5m	60	1,000,000	600,000
Total		6,000,000	2,900,000

A's weighted average rate of tax is 48.33%. Therefore, A recognises income tax expense of $580,000 in the first quarter.

Example 41.4 *Revised estimate of expected average annual income tax rate*

The facts are the same as example 41.3. In the second quarter of 2002, company A also earns profits of $1.2 million. A now estimates that it will earn profits of $5.5m in 2002. Its weighted average income tax rate is revised as follows:

	%	*Profits* $	*Tax* $
First $2 million of taxable profits	40	2,000,000	800,000
From $2 million to $5 million profits	50	3,000,000	1,500,000
Profits in excess of $5m	60	500,000	300,000
Total		5,500,000	2,600,000

A's weighted average rate of tax is 47.27%. As of the end of the second quarter, A has earned profits of $2.4 million and, therefore, recognises total income tax expense for the first two quarters of $1,134,545. It has already recognised $580,000 in the first quarter; it recognises $554,545 in the second quarter.

Example 41.5 *Change in enacted tax rate*

The facts are the same as examples 41.3 and 4. Shortly before the end of the second quarter, the government passes legislation which increases the rates of tax as follows:

	Old rate %	*New rate* %
First $2 million of taxable profits	40	45
From $2 million to $5 million profits	50	55
Profits in excess of $5m	60	70

The new rates apply to profits earned after 1 July 2002 and the bands for six months are half those for a full year. Profits earned in the six months to 30 June are taxed at the old rates but the bands are reduced by 50%. A separate weighted average rate of tax is computed for the first six months based on the profits of $2.4 million earned in the six months to 30 June as follows:

(Continued)

(Continued)

	%	*Profits* $	*Tax* $
First $1 million of taxable profits	40	1,000,000	400,000
From $1 million to $2.5 million profits	50	1,400,000	700,000
		2,400,000	1,100,000

A's weighted average rate of tax is 45.83%. A recognises total income tax expense for the first two quarters of $1,100,000. It has already recognised $580,000 in the first quarter; it recognises $520,000 in the second quarter.

Extract 41.4 *Interim financial statements*

Stora Enso, Sweden, nine months to 30 September 2001 (IAS)

Condensed Consolidated Income Statement			
EUR million	*2000*	*Jan–Sept 2000*	*Jan–Sept 2001*
Sales	13,017.0	9,339.0	10,225.9
Expenses and other operating income	−7,520.6	−5,157.0	−6,373.5
Personnel expenses	−1,995.7	−1,402.0	−1,690.6
Depreciation, amortization and impairment charges	−1,129.4	−739.3	−945.0
Operating profit	2,371.3	2,040.7	1,216.8
Share of results of associated companies	20.6	12.9	67.9
Net financial items	−292.9	−204.7	−310.9
Profit before tax and minority interests	2,099.0	1,848.9	973.8
Income tax expense	−650.3	−577.2	−322.1
Profit after tax	1,448.7	1,271.7	651.7
Minority interests	−13.7	−12.5	0.1
Profit for the period	1,435.0	1,259.2	651.8
Key ratios			
Basic earnings per share, EUR	1.77	1.62	0.72
Diluted earnings per share, EUR	1.76	1.61	0.72

Extract 41.4 *Interim financial statements (continued)*

Condensed Consolidated Cash Flow Statement			
EUR million	*2000*	*Jan–Sep 2000*	*Jan–Sep 2001*
Cash flow from operating activities			
Operating profit	2,371.3	2,040.7	1,216.8
Adjustments	531.9	142.7	910.8
Change in working capital	42.1	−371.4	−199.4
Change in short-term interest-bearing receivables	54.5	59.1	−379.2
Cash flow generated by operations	2,999.8	1,871.1	1,549.0
Net financial items	−285.9	−194.4	−296.3
Income taxes paid	−553.3	−312.3	−477.8
Net cash provided by operating activities	2,160.6	1,364.4	774.9
Acquisitions	−2,841.9	−2,355.5	−28.0
Proceeds from sale of fixed assets or shares	720.8	700.8	55.8
Capital expenditure	−769.3	−502.9	−572.9
Proceeds from long-term receivables, net	−20.6	−182.1	−41.9
Net cash used in investing activities	−2911.0	−2,339.7	−587.0
Cash flow from financing activities			
Change in long-term liabilities	2,077.8	1,755.3	−108.6
Change in short-term borrowings	−744.8	−255.6	−25.4
Dividends paid	−303.9	−303.9	−407.4
Proceeds from issuance of share capital	–	–	18.9
Purchase of own shares	−173.7	−0.8	−177.4
Other change in shareholders'equity	−2.4	−6.5	–
Net cash used in financing activities	853.0	1,188.5	−699.9
Net increase in cash and cash equivalents	102.6	213.2	−512.0
Translation differences on cash holdings	−0.4	7.3	42.6
Cash and bank at the beginning of period	642.2	642.2	744.4
Cash and cash equivalents at end of period	744.4	862.7	275.0

Extract 41.4 *Interim financial statements (continued)*

Condensed Consolidated Balance Sheet

Assets *EUR million*	*31 Dec 2000*	*30 Sep 2000*	*30 Sep 2001*
Fixed assets and other long-term investments			
Property, plant and equipment, intangible assets and goodwill	15,103.4	15,710.1	14,295.4
Investment in other companies	177.2	246.8	177.1
Investment in associated companies	213.6	230.1	356.6
Investments	132.3	55.3	173.4
Non-current loan receivables	486.3	705.6	492.5
Deferred tax assets	11.7	5.9	21.2
Other non-current assets	254.5	76.4	244.1
	16,379.0	17,030.2	15,760.3
Current assets			
Inventories	1,589.5	1,628.7	1,651.2
Tax receivables	153.0	213.7	159.5
Short-term receivables	2,360.7	2,570.8	2,209.0
Current portion of loan receivables	96.2	154.7	541.9
Cash and cash equivalents	744.4	862.7	275.0
	4,943.8	5,430.6	4,836.6
Total assets	21,322.8	22,460.8	20,596.9

Shareholders' Equity and Liabilities *EUR million*	*31 Dec 2000*	*30 Sep 2000*	*30 Sep 2001*
Shareholders' equity	8,570.8	8,735.8	8,631.8
Minority interests	149.4	150.0	124.8
Long-term liabilities			
Pension provisions	771.8	592.0	781.7
Deferred tax liabilities	2,247.5	2,404.7	2,120.6
Other provisions	173.4	192.1	140.1
Long-term debt	5,514.7	5,703.7	5,352.8
Other long-term liabilities	92.6	281.0	49.6
	8,800.0	9,173.5	8,444.8
Current liabilities			
Interest-bearing liabilities	1,340.8	1,860.8	1,285.6
Tax liabilities	571.2	613.6	429.6
Other current liabilities	1,890.6	1,927.1	1,680.3
	3,802.6	4,401.5	3,395.5
Total liabilities	12,602.6	13,575.0	11,840.3
Total shareholders' equity and liabilities	21,322.8	22,460.8	20,596.9

Extract 41.4 *Interim financial statements (continued)*

Equity Reconciliation
EUR million

	Share capital	*Share issue*	*Share issue premium*	*Treasury shares*	*Other comprehensive income*	*Cumulative translation adjustment*	*Retained earnings*	*Total*
Balance at 31 Dec 1999, as previously reported	1,277.6		379.6			12.7	4,283.3	5,953.2
Change in accounting policy with respect to forest accounting (net of deferred tax)						3.0	0.3	3.3
Balance at 31 Dec 1999, restated	1,277.6	—	379.6	—	—	15.7	4,283.6	5,956.5
Dividends paid (EUR 0.40 per share)							−303.9	−303.9
To be placed at the disposal of the Board of Directors							−1.0	−1.0
Share issue	0.4		−0.4					0.0
Share issue (Consolidated Papers)	284.5		1,432.7					1,717.2
Conversion of share capital from FIM to EUR	13.8		−13.8					0.0
Acquisition of Stora Enso Oyj shares				−173.7				−173.7
Options issued (Consolidated Papers)			25.1				0.9	26.0
Net profit for the period							1,435.0	1,435.0
Translation adjustment						−85.3		−85.3
Balance at 31 Dec 2000	1,576.3	—	1,823.2	−173.7	—	−69.6	5,414.6	8,570.8
Effect of adopting IAS 39					75.7		−26.5	49.2
Balance at 31 Dec 2000, restated	1,576.3	—	1,823.2	−173.7	75.7	−69.6	5,388.1	8,620.0
Repurchase of Stora Enso Oyj shares				−177.4				−177.4
Cancellation of Stora Enso Oyj shares	−39.4		−208.6	248.0				0.0
Dividends paid (EUR 0.45 per share)							−407.4	−407.4
Share issue	3.9	1.8	13.2					18.9
Net profit for the period							651.8	651.8
Change in other comprehensive income entries					−28.1			−28.1
Translation adjustment						−46.0		−46.0
Balance at 30 Sep 2001	1,540.8	1.8	1,627.8	−103.1	47.6	−115.6	5,632.5	8,631.8

Other comprehensive income comprises hedging reserve of cash flow derivatives and available-for-sale reserve.

Extract 41.4 *Interim financial statements (continued)*

Accounting principles

This interim report is in compliance with IAS 34 Interim Financial Reporting.

The accounting policies and methods of computation used in this interim report are the same as used in the last annual report, except that as of 1 January 2001 the Group adopted IAS 39, Financial Instruments: Recognition and Measurement, which has resulted in the following adjustments in the opening balance.

In accordance with the transitional provisions of IAS 39, Stora Enso recorded a cumulative adjustment of EUR 15.6 million net of taxes in retained earnings to recognize at fair value all derivatives that are designated as fair value hedging instruments. Stora Enso also recorded a cumulative adjustment of EUR –27.8 million in the retained earnings to recognize the difference between the carrying values and fair values of related hedged assets and liabilities.

Stora Enso recorded an adjustment of EUR 23.0 million in interest-bearing assets and an adjustment of EUR 3.2 million in interest-bearing liabilities to recognize at fair value all derivatives that are designated as cash flow hedging instruments. Stora Enso also recorded a corresponding cumulative adjustment of EUR 13.8 million net of taxes in the hedging reserve (equity) to recognize the difference between the carrying values and fair values of these derivatives.

Upon adoption of IAS 39 Stora Enso also recognized in its balance sheet other derivatives, either as assets or liabilities, and measured them at fair value. This recognition resulted in the adjustments of EUR 5.0 million in interest-bearing assets and EUR 25.2 million in interest-bearing liabilities. Stora Enso recorded a corresponding cumulative adjustment of EUR –14.3 million net of taxes in retained earnings to recognize the difference between the carrying values and fair values of these derivatives.

Stora Enso classified its investments as available-for-sale. Stora Enso measured these securities at fair value and recorded a cumulative adjustment of EUR 61.9 million net of taxes in the available-for-sale reserve (equity).

This report is unaudited.

Key exchange rates for the euro

One euro is	*Closing rate*		*Average rate*	
	31 Dec 2000	*30 Sep 2001*	*31 Dec 2000*	*30 Sep 2001*
SEK	8.8313	9.7321	8.4416	9.1747
USD	0.9305	0.9131	0.9242	0.8961
GBP	0.6241	0.6220	0.6088	0.6222
CAD	1.3965	1.4418	1.3711	1.3781

Extract 41.4 *Interim financial statements (continued)*

Capital Expenditure and Commitments			
EUR million	*2000*	*Jan–Sep. 2000*	*Jan–Sep. 2001*
Opening net book amount	11,248.1	11,248.4	15,103.4
Acquisition of subsidiary	5,830.3	5,810.9	28.0
Additions	769.3	502.9	572.9
Disposals	−1,315.3	−1,385.9	−254.4
Depreciation, amortization, impairment and translation differences	−1,429.3	−466.2	−1,154.5
Closing net book amount	15,103.4	15,710.1	14 295.4
Borrowings			
Current	1,340.8	1,860.8	1,285.6
Non-current	5,514.7	5,703.7	5,352.8
Total	6,855.5	7,564.5	6,638.4
Opening amount, borrowings	5,769.5	6,345.0	6,855.5
Acquisition of subsidiary	1,204.9	1,442.4	–
Proceeds from (payments of) borrowings, net	76.8	−303.9	−202.1
Translation difference	−195.7	81.0	−15.0
Closing amount	6,855.5	7564.5	6,638.4
Acquisition			
Property, plant and equipment	3,897.3	4,090.0	28.0
Borrowings	−1,204.9	−1,442.4	–
Other assets, less liabilities	−66.3	−367.8	–
Fair value of net assets	2,626.1	2,279.8	28.0
Goodwill	1,933.0	1,720.9	–
Total purchase consideration	4,559.1	4,000.7	28.0

Extract 41.4 *Interim financial statements (continued)*

Commitments and Contingent Liabilities

EUR million	*31 Dec 2000*	*30 Sep 2000*	*30 Sep 2001*
On own behalf			
Pledges given	38.9	71.2	18.1
Mortgages	400.8	649.0	388.6
On behalf of associated companies			
Mortgages	1.0	1.0	1.0
Guarantees	14.5	11.0	44.2
On behalf of others			
Pledges given	0.4	3.0	1.0
Guarantees	102.8	207.2	100.6
Other commitments, own			
Leasing commitments, in next 12 months	30.3	23.4	36.5
Leasing commitments, after next 12 months	106.9	89.0	214.4
Pension liabilities	2.9	4.7	2.4
Other contingencies	87.2	35.6	89.3
Total			
Pledges given	39.3	74.2	19.1
Mortgages	401.8	650.0	389.6
Guarantees	117.3	218.2	144.8
Leasing commitments	137.2	112.4	250.9
Pension liabilities	2.9	4.7	2.4
Other commitments	87.2	35.6	89.3
Total	785.7	1,095.1	896.1

Extract 41.4 *Interim financial statements (continued)*

Derivative Financial Instruments			
EUR million	*31 Dec 2000*	*30 Sep 2000*	*30 Sep 2001*
Fair value			
Interest rate derivatives	16.7	2.7	73.2
Foreign exchange derivatives	113.8	–19.6	85.8
Commodity derivatives	5.0	5.4	35.6
Equity swaps	–	–	–41.8
Nominal value			
Interest rate derivatives	737.5	950.1	1,777.3
Foreign exchange derivatives	4,801.9	5,236.8	8,287.8
Commodity derivatives	175.9	193.1	259.3
Equity swaps	–	–	131.0

Sales by Product Area								
EUR million	*I/00*	*II/00*	*III/00*	*IV/00*	*2000*	*I/01*	*II/01*	*III/01*
Magazine	562.5	590.0	729.1	937.2	2,818.8	910.2	847.6	831.7
Newsprint	416.0	417.0	449.6	484.1	1,766.7	501.7	490.7	471.9
Fine paper	758.5	768.1	883.5	1,063.1	3,473.2	1,021.3	904.1	838.6
Packaging boards	719.2	746.9	753.0	755.9	2,975.0	701.9	704.2	672.8
Timber products	298.1	334.8	293.7	315.5	1,242.1	307.3	311.8	266.2
Merchants	225.4	221.4	212.9	230.9	890.6	231.4	211.5	188.9
Forest	508.1	452.2	426.4	490.7	1,877.4	511.5	442.3	410.3
Other	–522.8	–449.5	–494.8	–599.4	–2,066.5	–548.3	–523.8	–479.9
Continuing operations total	2,965.0	3,080.9	3,253.4	3,678.0	12,977.3	3,637.0	3,388.4	3,200.5
Divested paper units	–	–	–	–	–	–	–	–
Discontinuing operations, Energy	46.4	23.9	–	–	70.3	–	–	–
Internal sales, Energy	–19.7	–10.9	–	–	–30.6	–	–	–
Total	2,991.7	3,093.9	3,253.4	3,678.0	13,017.0	3,637.0	3,388.4	3,200.5

CHAPTER 42

Changing Prices

42.1 RELEVANT STANDARDS AND INTERPRETATION

IAS 15 *Information Reflecting the Effects of Changing Prices*
IAS 29 *Financial Reporting in Hyperinflationary Economies*
SIC 19 *Reporting Currency – Measurement and Presentation of Financial Statements Under IAS 21 and IAS 29*

An entity which restates its financial statements in accordance with IAS 29 automatically presents the information required by IAS 15.

42.2 HISTORY

IAS 15

Inflation accounting was one of the major issues on the IASC's work programme in its early years. This reflected the relatively high level of inflation at that time in a number of developed economies. The IASC's deliberations mirrored those in a number of national standard setting bodies and the IASC found it no easier than any other body to reach consensus.

In 1977, the IASC published a discussion paper *Proposals for the Accounting Treatment of Changing Prices* which summarised the proposals which had been made in IASC member countries. In 1977, the IASC also approved IAS 6 *Accounting Responses to Changing Prices* which required the disclosure of the impact of any procedures applied to reflect the impact of specific or general price changes. If no such procedures had been applied, IAS 6 required that fact to be disclosed. The IASC believed that the IAS 6 disclosures would 'encourage the formation of an international consensus on this subject' (*IASC News*, March 1977, p1).

In 1978, the IASC commenced work on an IAS dealing with the disclosure of supplementary information reflecting the impact of changing prices on financial statements (*IASC News*, March 1978, p3). IAS 15, which requires such disclosures and which replaced IAS 6, was approved in 1981.

By the mid-1980s inflation levels in developed economies had fallen and the support for national standards on various forms of inflation accounting had largely evaporated. After much deliberation, in October 1989, the IASC agreed that the following statement should be added to IAS 15:

> The international consensus on the disclosure of information reflecting the effects of changing prices that was anticipated when IAS 15 was issued has not been reached. As a result, the Board of the IASC has decided that entities need not disclose the information required by IAS 15 in order that their financial statements conform with IASs. However, the Board encourages entities to present such information and urges those that do to disclose the items required by IAS 15.
> (*International Accounting Standards* 1998, p293)

In its May 2002 improvements exposure draft, the IASB proposes to withdraw IAS 15 for three reasons:

- as a result of the October 1989 statement, entities do not have to comply with IAS 15;
- few entities, if any, are using IAS 15; and
- entities should not be required to disclose information about the effects of changing prices in the current economic environment.

In view of this decision, IAS 15 is not dealt with in any detail.

IAS 29

IAS 29 was approved in 1989 and has not subsequently been reviewed. The project was carried out at the request of countries suffering from very high inflation and involved a number of people from such countries.

The requirements of IAS 29 are based on national standards which have existed and been applied in such countries as Argentina, Brazil, Iceland, Israel, Mexico and Peru. The procedures are also similar to those which have been followed in other countries which have adopted requirements based on a current purchasing power or constant purchasing power.

In 1989 the UN ISAR group adopted a similar approach to that required by IAS 29 as part of its agreed conclusions on accounting and reporting by transnational corporations[1].

The IASC had no plans to review IAS 29 although it acknowledged that the application of the IAS had caused some practical difficulties in the emerging economies in central and eastern Europe.

In its May 2002 improvements exposure draft, the IASB proposes to make consequential amendments to IAS 29 as a result of its proposed amendments to IAS 21 (see chapter 19).

42.3 IOSCO

IAS 15

IOSCO did not consider IAS 15 in the context of its core standards.

IAS 29

In June 1994, IOSCO advised the IASC that IAS 29 was acceptable for the purpose of the IOSCO core standards. IOSCO also approved IAS 21 which requires certain financial statements to be restated in accordance with IAS 29 before they are translated (see chapter 19).

The American SEC, which is a member of IOSCO, also allows foreign issuers to adopt an IAS 21/IAS 29 approach for subsidiaries reporting in the currency of a highly inflationary economy.

IAS 29 is included in 'IAS 2000' endorsed by IOSCO in May 2000. IOSCO identifies one possible future IASB project, the accounting treatment on the initial adoption of IAS 29 of accumulated changes in value included in equity in accordance with IAS 39. The revaluation reserve should be eliminated as part of the initial adjustments to equity (IAS 29, 24) but this may not be an appropriate accounting treatment for value changes arising from the application of IAS 39.

42.4 IAS 15 IN BRIEF

An entity should disclose either:

- depreciation, cost of sales, any gain or loss on monetary items and the carrying amount of property, plant and equipment and inventories computed using the current cost approach; or
- depreciation, cost of sales and any gain or loss on monetary items computed using the general purchasing power approach.

IAS 15 applied to entities whose levels of revenues, profit, assets or employment were significant in the economic environment in which they operated (IAS 15, 3). Other entities were encouraged, but not required, to provide the same information.

The general (or constant) purchasing power approach involves the restatement of some or all of the items in the financial statements for changes in the general price level. The approach changes the measuring unit but not the underlying bases used to measure assets and liabilities. Profit normally reflects adjustments to depreciation and cost of sales and in respect of net monetary items. The approach is based on the maintenance of financial capital in terms of general purchasing power. The approach is identical to that adopted when historical cost financial statements are restated in accordance with IAS 29.

The current cost approach generally uses replacement costs, in place of historical costs, as the primary measurement basis. Profit normally reflects adjustments to depreciation and cost of sales. The approach is based on the maintenance of physical capital usually in terms of monetary units.

Some current cost methods require some form of adjustment reflecting the effects of changing prices on monetary items or monetary items included in working capital. Some methods limit the adjustments to depreciation and cost of sales by the extent to which they are financed by borrowing. Some current cost methods apply a general price level index to the amount of shareholders' interests so that they report profit based on the maintenance of physical capital expressed in terms of general purchasing power. This approach is identical to that adopted when current cost financial statements are restated in accordance with IAS 29.

42.5 IAS 29 IN BRIEF

The primary financial statements of an entity which reports in the currency of a hyperinflationary economy should be stated in terms of the measuring unit current at the balance sheet date. The financial statements may be based on either a historical cost approach or a current cost approach. Corresponding figures for the previous reporting period (and other historical data) should also be restated.

The requirements of IAS 29 do not apply to an entity which operates in a hyperinflationary economy but which reports in a relatively stable foreign currency. For example, many entities in countries in Latin America which have experienced high rates of inflation report in US dollars. IAS 29 does not apply to the US dollar financial statements of such entities.

However, SIC 19 requires that the measurement currency for financial statements of an entity should reflect the economic substance of the underlying events and circumstances relevant to the entity. This interpretation may preclude the use of a stable currency as the measurement currency by an entity that operates in a hyperinflationary economy. The IASB reinforces this message in its May 2002 improvements exposure draft which emphasises that an entity cannot avoid the requirements of IAS 29 by adopting a stable currency as its functional (measurement) currency.

42.6 HYPERINFLATION

Hyperinflation is very high inflation. IAS 29 does not establish an absolute rate at which hyperinflation is deemed to arise. Instead, it identifies a number of characteristics which are indicative of hyperinflation:

- the general population prefers to keep its wealth in non-monetary assets or in a relatively stable foreign currency;
- the general population regards monetary amounts not in terms of the local currency but in terms of a relatively stable foreign currency;
- sales and purchases on credit take place at prices that compensate for the expected loss of purchasing power during the credit period, even if the period is short;
- interest rates, wages and prices are linked to a price index; and
- the cumulative inflation rate over three years is approaching, or exceeds, 100%.

(IAS 29, 3)

The 100% rate in IAS 29 is a compound rate which is equivalent to an annual rate of just over 25%.

The IASC believes that the reporting of operating results and financial position in the local currency of such an economy is not useful as money loses purchasing power at such a rate that comparison of money amounts from transactions and other events that have occurred at different times is misleading. Therefore, IAS 29 requires that the financial statements of entities reporting in the local currency should be restated and expressed in terms of the measuring unit current at the balance sheet date (IAS 29, 8). IAS 29 does not permit presentation of the restated financial statements as a supplement to unrestated financial statements and discourages the separate presentation of the financial statements before restatement (IAS 29, 7).

IAS 29 applies from the beginning of any reporting period in which an entity identifies the existence of hyperinflation in the country in whose currency it reports (IAS 29, 4). It is preferable that all entities that report in the same currency apply IAS 29 from the same date.

When an economy ceases to be hyperinflationary an entity may discontinue the preparation of financial statements prepared in accordance with IAS 29. It should treat the amounts determined in accordance with IAS 29 as the basis for the carrying amounts in its subsequent financial statements (IAS 29, 38). So, for example, the cost and accumulated depreciation of property, plant and equipment in subsequent periods is based on the restated amounts determined while IAS 29 was applied.

42.7 PRICE INDEX

The restatement of the financial statements requires the use of a general price index that reflects changes in general purchasing power in the economy concerned. It is preferable that all entities that report in the currency of the same economy use the same index (IAS 29, 37). When no suitable general price index is available, it may be necessary to use an estimate based, for example, on the movements in the exchange rate between the reporting currency and a relatively stable foreign currency.

42.8 THE RESTATEMENT OF HISTORICAL COST FINANCIAL STATEMENTS

42.8.1 Balance Sheet

The following approach should be adopted:

- balance sheet amounts already expressed in terms of the measuring unit current at the balance sheet date are *not* restated; and
- balance sheet amounts *not* already expressed in terms of the measuring unit current at the balance sheet date are restated by multiplying by the general price index at the balance sheet date and dividing by the general price index at the date of acquisition or subsequent valuation of the asset (IAS 29, 11).

Balance sheet amounts already expressed in terms of the measuring unit current at the balance sheet date include monetary items. Monetary items include money held and items to be received or paid in money; therefore they include virtually all liabilities. They are not restated (IAS 29, 12).

Some monetary assets and liabilities are linked by agreement to changes in prices, for example, index-linked bonds and loans. These items are adjusted in accordance with the agreement and are carried at this adjusted amount in the restated balance sheet (IAS 29, 13). No further adjustment is required for these items.

Non-monetary items based on historical costs are not usually expressed in terms of the measuring unit current at the balance sheet date. Therefore, such items are restated. The restated cost, or cost less depreciation, of each non-monetary item is determined by applying to its historical cost and accumulated depreciation the change in a general price index from the date of acquisition to the balance sheet date (IAS 29, 15). The restated amount of property, plant and equipment is reduced to recoverable amount when appropriate and the restated amount of inventories is reduced to net realisable value when appropriate.

Some non-monetary items in historical cost financial statements are carried at amounts which are current at dates other than that of their acquisition. This includes property, plant and equipment which has been revalued in accordance with the allowed alternative treatment in IAS 16 and financial assets which are carried at fair value in accordance with IAS 39. Such assets are restated from the date of the revaluation (IAS 29, 18) by applying to their carrying amounts the change in the general price index from the date of valuation to the balance sheet date. Non-monetary items which are carried at fair value or market value at the balance sheet date do not require restatement.

IAS 23 allows an entity to capitalise borrowing costs on qualifying assets (see chapter 35). The impact of inflation is invariably recognised in borrowing costs. Therefore, it is inappropriate both to restate the expenditure on an asset financed by borrowing and to capitalise that part of the borrowing costs that compensates for the inflation during the same period. This part of the borrowing costs is recognised as an expense in the period in which the costs are incurred (IAS 29, 21); only that part of the borrowing costs which does not compensate for inflation may be capitalised.

Under the allowed alternative treatment in IAS 21, an entity may include certain foreign exchange differences arising on liabilities in the carrying amount of assets following a severe and recent devaluation. Again, such a practice is inappropriate when the carrying amount of the asset is restated by the changes in the general price index from the date of its acquisition (IAS 29, 22) as the devaluation usually reflects the high rate of inflation. The exchange differences should be recognised as an expense in the income statement. In its May 2002 improvements exposure draft, the IASB proposes to remove the allowed alternative treatment in IAS 21 (see chapter 19).

The components of owners' equity, except retained earnings and any revaluation surplus, are restated at the beginning of the first period of application of IAS 29 by applying a general price index from the dates on which the components were contributed or otherwise arose. Any revaluation surplus is eliminated. This may not be appropriate, however, for accumulated value changes arising from the application of IAS 39, for example gains on available-for-sale financial assets and cash flow hedges, which are likely to be included in the income statement in a future period. Restated retained earnings at the beginning of the first period are derived from all the other amounts in the restated balance sheet (IAS 29, 24). In subsequent periods, all components of owners' equity are restated by applying a general price index from the beginning of the period or the date of contribution, if later (IAS 29, 25).

42.8.2 Income Statement

All items in the income statement should be expressed in terms of the measuring unit current at the balance sheet date (IAS 29, 8). Therefore, all amounts are restated by multiplying by the general price index at the balance sheet date and dividing by the general price index at the dates when the items of income and expenses were initially recorded in the financial statements. So, for example, sales are restated from the date of sale and purchases from the date of acquisition. Depreciation is based on the restated carrying amounts of property, plant and equipment. Opening inventories are restated from the opening balance sheet date and closing inventories are restated from the date of purchase.

In a period of inflation, an entity holding net monetary assets loses, and one with net monetary liabilities gains, purchasing power to the extent the monetary assets and liabilities are not linked to a price level. This gain or loss on the net monetary position may be estimated by applying the change in a general price index to a weighted average of the net monetary assets for the period. It should be included in the profit or loss for the period and separately disclosed (IAS 29, 9).

The adjustment to those assets and liabilities linked by agreement to changes in prices is offset against the gain or loss on net monetary position. The gain or loss on net monetary position may be presented in the income statement with other income and expenses, such as interest income and expense, and foreign exchange differences related to invested or borrowed funds, which are also associated with the net monetary position.

42.9 THE RESTATEMENT OF CURRENT COST FINANCIAL STATEMENTS

42.9.1 Balance Sheet

The same procedures apply to the restatement of current cost financial statements as apply to the restatement of historical cost financial statements.

Monetary items are not restated. Non-monetary items stated at current cost or fair value/market value at the balance sheet date are not restated because they are already expressed in terms of the measuring unit current at the balance sheet date (IAS 29, 29). Any non-monetary items which are not stated in terms of current costs at the balance sheet date are restated in the same way as for the restatement of a historical cost balance sheet.

42.9.2 Income Statement

The current cost income statement, before restatement, generally reports costs current at the time at which the underlying transactions or events occurred. All amounts need to be restated into the measuring unit current at the balance sheet date by applying the change in the general price index from the date of the transactions to the date of the balance sheet.

Some current cost methods require an adjustment reflecting the effects of changing prices on net monetary items. Where the current cost income statement already includes such an adjustment, this forms part of the gain or loss on net monetary position.

42.10 DISCLOSURES

An entity should disclose:

- the fact that the financial statements and the corresponding figures for previous periods have been restated for the changes in the general purchasing power of the reporting currency and, as a result, are stated in terms of the measuring unit current at the balance sheet date (IAS 29, 39(a));
- whether the financial statements are based on a historical cost approach or a current cost approach (IAS 29, 39(b)); and
- the identity and level of the price index at the balance sheet date and the movement in the index during the current and the previous reporting periods (IAS 29, 39(c)).

Extract 42.1 *Disclosure of restatement of financial statements*

Delta Corporation, Zimbabwe, 31 March 2001 (IAS)

Basis of Presentation

The financial statements of the company and of the Group are prepared under the historical cost convention. For the purpose of fair presentation in accordance with IAS 29 *Financial Reporting in Hyperinflationary Economies,* this historical information has been restated for changes in the general purchasing power of the Zimbabwe Dollar and appropriate adjustments and reclassifications have been made. Accordingly, the inflation adjusted financial statements represent the primary financial statements of the Group. The historical cost financial statements have been provided by way of supplementary information.

Inflation Adjustment

IAS 29 requires that financial statements prepared in the currency of a hyperinflationary economy be stated in terms of a measuring unit current at the balance sheet date, and that corresponding figures for previous periods be stated in the same terms to the latest balance sheet date. The restatement has been calculated by means of conversion factors derived from the consumer price index (cpi) prepared by the Zimbabwe Central Statistical Office. The conversion factors used to restate the financial statements at 31 March 2001 are as follows:

	Index	*Conversion Factor*
31 March 2001	2,178.9	1.000
31 March 2000	2,398.5	1.558
31 March 1999	927.4	2.349

All items in the income statements are restated by applying the relevant monthly conversion factors.

The application of the IAS 29 restatement procedures has the effect of amending certain accounting policies which are used in the preparation of the financial statements under the historical cost convention. The policies affected are:

Borrowing costs: capitalisation during construction of qualifying assets is considered to be a partial recognition of inflation and is reversed to the income statement and replaced by indexation of cost.

Inventories: these are carried at the lower of indexed cost and net realisable value.

Donated assets: these are fair valued at the time of receipt, and the resultant gain is treated in the same way as any restatement gain.

Container valuation: subsequent revaluations of containers are not applied in reducing the value of deferred container expenditure.

Deferred tax: this is provided in respect of temporary differences arising from the restatement of assets and liabilities.

Fixed assets: are stated at indexed cost less applicable indexed depreciation and impairment losses.

Extract 42.2 *Disclosure of restatement of financial statements*

Buenaventura, Peru, 31 December 2001 (IAS)

The consolidated financial statements have been prepared from the company's accounting records that are carried out in nominal monetary terms adjusted to reflect the changes in the National Wholesale Price Level index (IPM). The IPM decreased by 2.2% in the year 2001 (increased 3.8% in the year 2000).

Non-monetary accounts in the consolidated balance sheets were adjusted using coefficients determined from the IPM, according to the original date. Monetary accounts were not adjusted, as the book balances represent the monetary value of their components at the date of the consolidated balance sheets. Income statement accounts were adjusted on a monthly basis by applying average coefficients; exchange differences were excluded. Depreciation and amortization were determined from the adjusted amounts of the related assets. The net result from exposure to inflation arising from such adjustments is shown in the consolidated statements of income.

42.11 APPLYING IAS 29

In many countries which have experienced very high inflation, the procedures required by IAS 29 are usually incorporated in the accounting records of an entity. There are a number of computer programs available which can make the necessary restatements on a regular basis. In other cases, it is necessary to prepare the restated financial statements from the underlying historical cost (or current cost) accounting records. In such cases, some form of worksheet is used.

Note

1 *Conclusions on Accounting and Reporting by Transnational Corporations*, United Nations, Geneva and New York, 1994, p14–15.

CHAPTER 43

Banks and Similar Financial Institutions

Given the specialist nature of banking and the general nature of this guide, it is not possible to deal in detail with all the issues which arise in the financial statements of banks and similar financial institutions. Therefore, this chapter seeks to do four things:

- summarise the requirements of IAS 30 and the background to those requirements;
- explain the inter-relationship between IAS 30 and other IASs, in particular IAS 32 and IAS 39;
- indicate those other IASs which are particularly important for banks; and
- provide a number of extracts from the IFRS financial statements of banks from several countries around the world.

43.1 RELEVANT STANDARD

IAS 30 *Disclosures in the Financial Statements of Banks and Similar Financial Institutions*

IAS 32 and IAS 39 also have considerable relevance to the financial statements of banks and similar financial institutions. In November 1994, the IASC agreed that it would consider the consequential implications for IAS 30 of the approval of a financial instruments standard (*IASC Insight*, December 1994, p13). The IASB has taken over this project and is currently developing an exposure draft covering all deposit-taking, lending and securities activities which will eventually replace IAS 30. The IASB intends that the resulting IFRS will apply both to banks and to the similar activities, including treasury activities, of other entities. The exposure draft is unlikely to be approved before mid-2003.

43.2 HISTORY

IAS 30 was the outcome of one of the IASC's longest projects. The project was started in 1977 as a result of the IASC's discussions with the Committee on Banking Regulations and Supervisory Practices of the Group of Ten major industrialised countries and Switzerland (the Basel Committee of Banking Supervisors). The Committee and the IASC thought that it would be helpful to prepare a paper dealing with classifications and disclosures in the financial statements of banks. Accordingly, the IASC agreed to undertake this project. Both the IASC and the Basel Committee recognised that harmonisation of methods of valuation and income measurement of banks would require further study, but they agreed that a first step was that of the extent of disclosures in the financial statements of banks. The Basel Committee also agreed to provide some of the funding for the project.

A discussion paper *Disclosures in Financial Statements of Banks* was published by the IASC in 1980. The paper was welcomed by the Basel Committee in recognition of the benefits that it believed would be derived from the harmonisation of the financial reporting practices of banks throughout the world. The IASC published a summary of the responses to that discussion paper in 1982. In those responses, the IASC concluded: 'Because of the many present developments, not least the proposed EEC banking directive, the IASC does not intend currently to issue an exposure draft relating to financial statement disclosure by banks. It will, however, review the position from time to time in the light of the developments and of the application of other International Accounting Standards to banks.'

The IASC restarted the project in 1984 'in view of the progress on the proposed EEC Directive on Banks and the increasing interest of other international bodies' (*IASC News*, November 1984, p1). At the same time, the IASC also decided to begin work on recognition and measurement issues associated with the financial statements of banks.

Two exposure drafts E29 and E34, were issued dealing with disclosure issues before IAS 30 was approved in 1990. The development of IAS 30 involved extensive consultations with bankers and bank regulators, the users of the financial statements of banks and the European Commission. The steering committee for the project included a bank regulator and representatives of American and European bankers.

Work on recognition and measurement issues was deferred in 1990 pending completion of the financial instruments project.

The Basel Committee has subsequently issued recommendations on loan accounting and disclosure in the financial statements of banks[1]. They deal with:

- the recognition, derecognition and measurement of loans;

- impairment – recognition and measurement;
- the adequacy of the specific and general allowances for credit losses;
- income recognition; and
- disclosure.

The recommendations are consistent with IAS 30, IAS 32 and IAS 39 and include a table of concordance with these IASs.

The Basel Committee and IOSCO have also issued recommendations on disclosures about trading and derivatives activities by banks[2]. The Basel Committee also publishes an annual survey of bank disclosures[3].

Islamic financial institutions sometimes find it difficult to match the accounting treatments in IASs with the *sharia* characteristics of their transactions. The Accounting and Auditing Organization for Islamic Financial Institutions (AAOIFI) was established in 1991 to set accounting standards for such financial institutions based on *sharia* precepts. The IASC participated in AAOIFI meetings in 1992 to discuss EDs of its conceptual framework and its general presentation standard. Subsequently, the AAOIFI has approved a number of standards and is currently comparing those standards with IASs.

43.3 IOSCO

IOSCO has not considered IAS 30 in the context of its core standards. IAS 30 is not included in 'IAS 2000'.

43.4 SCOPE

IAS 30 applies to both the separate financial statements and the consolidated financial statements of a bank (IAS 30, 5). IAS 30 also applies to the banking operations of any group that undertakes such operations (IAS 30, 5). Therefore, an entity which combines both insurance and banking activities should apply IAS 30 in respect of its banking operations, but not necessarily its insurance operations, in any IFRS financial statements.

A bank is any financial institution which:

- among its principal activities, takes deposits and borrows with the objective of lending and investing; and
- is within the scope of banking or similar legislation.

(IAS 30, 2)

IAS 30 is relevant to such an entity whether or not it has the word 'bank' in its name.

43.5 ACCOUNTING POLICIES

As with any other entity, a bank should disclose the specific accounting policies selected and applied for significant events and transactions (IAS 1, 91(a)). The policies should be selected and applied so that the financial statements comply with all IFRSs and interpretations (IAS 1, 20).

IAS 30 suggests that a bank may need to disclose accounting policies dealing with the following items:

- the recognition of the principal types of revenue, for example, interest income, fees, commissions etc;
- the valuation of investment and dealing securities;
- the distinction between those transactions and other events that result in the recognition of assets and liabilities on the balance sheet and those transactions and other events that only give rise to contingencies and commitments;
- the basis for the determination of losses on loans and advances and for writing off uncollectable loans and advances; and
- the basis for the determination of charges for general banking risks and the accounting treatment of such charges.

(IAS 30, 8)

This guidance overlaps with the suggested accounting policy disclosures in IAS 32 (see chapter 20).

43.6 INCOME STATEMENT

A bank should present an income statement which groups income and expenses by nature and discloses the amounts of the principal types of income and expenses (IAS 30, 9).

In addition to the requirements of other IFRSs, the disclosures in the income statement or the notes should include the items set out in table 43.1 (IAS 30, 10 and IAS 1, 75 and 76).

Income and expense items should not be offset except for those relating to hedges and to assets and liabilities which have been offset in accordance with IAS 30 (IAS 30, 13 and IAS 1, 34(a)). Gains and losses arising from each of the following are normally reported on a net basis:

- disposals and changes in the carrying amount of dealing securities;
- disposals of investment securities; and
- dealings in foreign currencies.

(IAS 30, 15 and IAS 1, 34(bb))

Table 43.1 *Income statement of a bank*

Interest and similar income
Interest expense and similar charges
Dividend income
Fee and commission income
Fee and commission expense
Gains less losses arising from dealing securities
Gains less losses arising from investment securities
Gains less losses arising from dealing in foreign currencies
Other operating income
Losses on loans and advances
General administrative expenses
Other operating expenses
Results of operating activities
Share of profits and losses of associates and joint ventures
Tax expense
Profit or loss from ordinary activities
Extraordinary items
Minority interest
Net profit or loss for period

Extract 43.1 *Income statement*

Gulf International Bank, Bahrain, 31 December 2001 (IAS)

Consolidated Statement of Income	*Note*	***Year ended 31.12.01 US$ millions***	*Year ended 31.12.00 US$ millions*
Interest revenue			
Interest on securities		**434.0**	424.3
Interest and fees on loans		**224.4**	319.2
Interest on placements and other liquid assets		**127.7**	230.6
		786.1	974.1
Interest expense		**590.7**	804.4
Net interest income		**195.4**	169.7
Provisions for securities	6	**69.9**	13.8
Provisions for loans and advances	7	**(17.8)**	22.4
Net interest income after provisions		**143.3**	133.5
Other income	18	**68.3**	127.3
Net interest and other income		**211.6**	260.8
Operating expenses			
Staff		**66.5**	83.5
Premises		**9.7**	10.8
Restructuring costs	19	**8.4**	–
Other		**33.5**	38.0
		118.1	132.3
Net income before tax		**93.5**	128.5
Taxation (credit)/charge on overseas activities	20	**(7.0)**	10.4
Net income after tax		**100.5**	118.1

Extract 43.2 *Income statement*

UBS, Switzerland, 31 December 2001 (IAS)

UBS Group Income Statement *CHF million, except per share data* For the year ended	*31.12.01*	*31.12.00*	*31.12.99*	*% change from 31.12.00*
Operating income				
Interest income	**52,277**	51,745	35,604	1
Interest expense	**(44,236)**	(43,615)	(29,695)	1
Net interest income	**8,041**	8,130	5,909	(1)
Credit loss expense/recovery	**(498)**	130	(956)	
Net interest income after credit loss expense/recovery	**7,543**	8,260	4,953	(9)
Net fee and commission income	**20,211**	16,703	12,607	21
Net trading income	**8,802**	9,953	7,719	(12)
Other income	**558**	1,486	3,146	(62)
Total operating income	**37,114**	36,402	28,425	2
Operating expenses				
Personal expenses	**19,828**	17,163	12,577	16
General and administrative expenses	**7,631**	6,765	6,098	13
Depreciation of property and equipment	**1,614**	1,608	1,517	0
Amortization of goodwill and other intangible assets	**1,323**	667	340	98
Total operating expenses	**30,396**	26,203	20,532	16
Operating profit before tax and minority interests	**6,718**	10,199	7,893	(34)
Tax expense	**1,401**	2,320	1,686	(40)
Net profit before minority interests	**5,317**	7,879	6,207	(33)
Minority interests	**(344)**	(87)	(54)	295
Net profit	**4,973**	7,792	6,153	(36)

43.7 BALANCE SHEET

A bank should present a balance sheet which groups assets and liabilities by nature and lists them in an order that reflects their relative liquidity; this may equate broadly to their maturities (IAS 30, 20 and IAS 1, 53). Current and non-current items are not presented separately (IAS 30, 20).

In addition to the requirements of other IFRSs, the disclosures in the balance sheet or the notes to the financial statements should include the assets and liabilities set out in table 43.2 (IAS 30, 19 and IAS 1, 66 and 68). In addition, a bank discloses separately either on the face of the balance sheet or in the notes:

- balances with the central bank (IAS 30, 21);
- placements with other banks (IAS 30, 21);
- other money market placements (IAS 30, 21);
- deposits from other banks (IAS 30, 21);
- other money market deposits (IAS 30, 21);
- other deposits (IAS 30, 21); and
- deposits that have been obtained through the issue of its own certificates of deposit or other negotiable paper (IAS 30, 22).

IAS 1 requires that assets and liabilities should not be offset except when offsetting is required or permitted by another IAS (IAS 1, 33). In the case of a bank, the amount at which any asset or liability is stated in the balance sheet should not be offset by the deduction of another liability or asset unless a legal right of set-off exists and the offsetting represents the expectation as to the realisation or settlement of the asset or liability (IAS

Table 43.2 *Balance sheet of a bank*

Assets
Cash and balances with the central bank
Treasury bills and other bills eligible for rediscounting with the central bank
Government and other securities held for dealing purposes
Placements with, and loans and advances to, other banks
Other money market placements
Loans and advances to customers
Investment securities
Investments accounted for under the equity method
Property, plant and equipment
Intangible assets
Trade and other receivables
Tax assets

Liabilities
Deposits from other banks
Other money market deposits
Amounts owed to other depositors
Certificates of deposits
Promissory notes and other liabilities evidenced by paper
Other borrowed funds
Tax liabilities
Trade and other payables
Provisions
Minority interest
Issued capital and reserves

30, 23) – therefore offsetting is allowed only when there is both a legal right to, and the expectation of, offsetting. IAS 32 requires, rather than allows, offsetting when the bank:

- has a legally enforceable right to set off the recognised amounts; and
- intends to settle on a net basis, or to realise the asset and settle the liability simultaneously.

(IAS 32, 33)

A master netting arrangement does not provide a basis for offsetting unless both the criteria in IAS 32, 33 are met (IAS 32, 41). While such an arrangement may establish a legally enforceable right to set off, it is often not the intent, in the ordinary course of business, to settle on a net basis or realise the asset and settle the liability simultaneously.

Extract 43.3 *Balance sheet*

Gulf International Bank, Bahrain, 31 December 2001 (IAS)

	Note	*At 31.12.01 US$ millions*	*At 31.12.00 US$ millions*
Assets			
Cash and other liquid assets	3	**91.2**	137.3
Placements with banks	4	**2,693.6**	3,065.0
Trading securities	5	**1,006.7**	465.8
Available-for-sale securities	6	**7,641.7**	7,062.1
Loans and advances	7	**3,309.4**	3,923.1
Fixed assets	8	**22.5**	27.2
Other assets	9	**466.9**	439.0
Total assets		**15,232.0**	15,119.5
Liabilities			
Deposits from banks	11	**6,191.0**	6,514.5
Deposits from customers	11	**4,758.7**	4,900.0
Securities sold under agreements to repurchase		**1,422.4**	1,164.6
Securities sold but not yet purchased		**122.6**	44.5
Other liabilities	12	**563.6**	440.1
Senior term financing	13	**830.0**	850.0
Subordinated term loans	14	**150.0**	–
Total liabilities		**14,038.3**	13,913.7
Shareholders' equity			
Share capital	15	**1,000.0**	1,000.0
Share premium		**7.6**	7.6
Reserves	16	**134.3**	93.7
Retained earnings		**51.8**	104.5
Shareholders' equity		**1,193.7**	1,205.8
Total liabilities and shareholders' equity		**15,232.0**	15,119.5

Extract 43.4 *Balance sheet*

UBS, Switzerland, 31 December 2001 (IAS)

UBS Group Balance Sheet *CHF million*	*31.12.01*	*31.12.00*	*% change from 31.12.00*
Assets			
Cash and balances with central banks	**20,990**	2,979	605
Due from banks	**27,526**	29,147	(6)
Cash collateral on securities borrowed	**162,938**	177,857	(8)
Reverse repurchase agreements	**269,256**	193,801	39
Trading portfolio assets	**397,886**	315,588	26
Positive replacement values	**73,447**	57,875	27
Loans, net of allowance for credit losses	**226,545**	244,842	(7)
Financial investments	**28,803**	19,583	47
Accrued income and prepaid expenses	**7,554**	7,062	7
Investments in associates	**697**	880	(21)
Property and equipment	**8,695**	8,910	(2)
Goodwill and other intangible assets	**19,085**	19,537	(2)
Other assets	**9,875**	9,491	4
Total assets	**1,253,297**	1,087,552	15
Total subordinated assets	***407***	*475*	*(14)*
Liabilities			
Due to banks	**106,531**	82,240	30
Cash collateral on securities lent	**30,317**	23,418	29
Repurchase agreements	**368,620**	295,513	25
Trading portfolio liabilities	**105,798**	82,632	28
Negative replacement values	**71,443**	75,923	(6)
Due to customers	**333,781**	310,679	7
Accrued expenses and deferred income	**17,289**	21,038	(18)
Debt issued	**156,218**	129,635	21
Other liabilities	**15,658**	18,756	(17)
Total liabilities	**1,205,655**	1,039,834	16
Minority interests	**4,112**	2,885	43
Shareholders' equity			
Share capital	**3,589**	4,444	(19)
Share premium account	**14,408**	20,885	(31)
Gains/(losses) not recognized in the income statement	**(193)**	(687)	(72)
Retained earnings	**29,103**	24,191	20
Treasury shares	**(3,377)**	(4,000)	(16)
Total shareholders' equity	**43,530**	44,833	(3)
Total liabilities, minority interests and shareholders' equity	**1,253,297**	1,087,552	15
Total subordinated liabilities	***13,818***	*13,996*	*(1)*

43.8 CASH FLOW STATEMENT

A bank is required to present a cash flow statement in accordance with IAS 7 notwithstanding that some banks questioned the usefulness of such a statement. The presentation of cash flow statements by financial institutions is dealt with in chapter 12.

43.9 FINANCIAL INSTRUMENTS AND INVESTMENTS

IAS 32 and IAS 39 have considerable relevance to banks because most of their assets are financial assets and most of their liabilities are financial liabilities (table 43.3). These two IASs are dealt with in chapter 20.

Table 43.3 *Financial assets and financial liabilities of a bank*

	Financial asset	*Financial liability*
Assets		
Cash and balances with the central bank	✓	
Treasury bills and other bills eligible for rediscounting with the central bank	✓	
Government and other securities held for dealing purposes	✓	
Placements with, and loans and advances to, other banks	✓	
Other money market placements	✓	
Loans and advances to customers	✓	
Investment securities	✓	
Liabilities		
Deposits from other banks		✓
Other money market deposits		✓
Amounts owed to other depositors		✓
Certificates of deposits		✓
Promissory notes and other liabilities evidenced by paper		✓
Other borrowed funds		✓

43.10 REVENUE

The revenue of a bank includes:

- interest income;
- finance income on finance leases;
- dividend income;
- fees and commissions;
- gains on dealing securities;
- gains on investment securities;
- gains on foreign currency dealing; and
- gains on dealing in other financial instruments.

Existing IASs deal with various aspects of the recognition and measurement of such income.

43.10.1 Interest Income

The recognition of interest income is currently dealt with in IAS 18 which requires that interest income should be recognised when:

- it is probable that the interest will flow to the bank; and
- the amount of the interest can be measured reliably.

(IAS 18, 29 and 30)

Interest income should be recognised on a time proportion basis that takes into account the effective yield on the asset (IAS 18, 30(a)). The effective yield is the rate of interest required to discount the stream of future cash receipts expected over the asset's life to equate to the initial carrying amount of the asset (IAS 18, 31). Therefore, interest income includes the amount of amortisation of any discount, premium or other difference between the initial carrying amount of the asset and its amount at maturity.

The same approach is required by IAS 39 (see chapter 20). In particular, any discount or premium on issue and fees associated with their issue or acquisition of financial assets carried on on an amortised cost basis are treated as yield adjustments. Furthermore, any interest recognised on a financial asset that has been written down to its recoverable amount is based on the rate of interest that was used to discount the future cash flows for the purpose of measuring recoverable amount (IAS 39, 116).

43.10.2 Interest on Non-Performing Loans

A bank needs to consider whether to recognise interest income on a loan which is in arrears in respect of payments of interest or principal. Such loans are sometimes referred to as non-performing or non-accrual loans. Different bank regulators define these terms in different ways and may require or allow a bank to deal with the interest in a particular way. For example, some regulators require banks to cease recognising interest income on loans which are six months or more in arrears while other regulators may allow the recognition of interest income in such circumstances provided that an appropriate increase is made in the loan loss provision.

IAS 30 does not give specific guidance on this issue because the IASC recognised the different practices around the world. Therefore a bank may:

- continue to recognise interest income on non-performing loans but also make an appropriate adjustment to the loan loss provision;
- continue to add interest income to non-performing loans and credit the interest to 'interest suspense' which is deducted from loans and advances in the balance sheet; or
- cease adding interest to non-performing loans.

In view of the flexibility allowed by IAS 30, it is desirable that a bank discloses its accounting policy for the accrual of interest on such loans. Furthermore, any interest recognised on a non-performing loan that has been written down to its recoverable amount is based on the rate of interest that was used to discount the future cash flows for the purpose of measuring recoverable amount (IAS 39, 116).

Extract 43.5 *Interest on non-performing loans*

EFG Eurobank Ergasias, Greece, 31 December 2000 (IAS)

Interest income and expense are recognised in the income statement on an accruals basis using the effective yield method. Interest income is suspended when loans are overdue by a maximum of more than 12 months for wholesale loans, 90 days for retail loans and 180 days for mortgage loans and is excluded from interest income until received. Interest income includes coupons earned on fixed income investment securities and accrued discount on treasury bills.

Extract 43.6 *Interest on non-performing loans*

United Saudi Commercial Bank, Saudi Arabia, 31 December 1996 (IAS)

Special commission income and expenses are recognised on an accrual basis. However, special commission income on loans and advances which are classified as non-performing is not recognised after a pre-determined period, but transferred to a suspense account.

Thereafter, it is recognised on a cash basis until the accounts become current, then it is again recognised on the accrual basis.

Accumulated commission in suspense is deducted from loans and advances to customers.

Extract 43.7 *Interest on non-performing loans*

Gulf International Bank, Bahrain, 31 December 2001 (IAS)

Interest income and interest expense are recognised for all interest-bearing financial instruments on an accruals basis using the effective yield method based on the original settlement amount.... Interest income is suspended when interest or principal on a credit facility is overdue by more than 90 days whereupon all unpaid and accrued interest is reversed from income. Interest on non-accrual facilities is included in income only when received. Credit facilities are restored to accrual status only after all delinquent interest and principal payments have been brought current and future payments are reasonably assured.

Extract 43.8 *Interest on non-performing loans*

UBS, Switzerland, 31 December 2001 (IAS)

When principal, interest or commission are overdue by 90 days, loans are classified as non-performing, the recognition of interest or commission income ceases according to the original terms of the loan agreement. Allowances are provided for non-performing loans to reflect their net estimated recoverable amount.

43.10.3 Finance Income On Finance Leases

Many banks act as lessors under finance leases. The recognition of finance income arising on a finance lease is dealt with in IAS 17 (see chapter 32).

Extract 43.9 *Finance lease income*

Dresdner Bank, Germany, 31 December 2001 (German GAAP and IAS)

Interest on finance leases is recognised in interest income over the term of the respective lease so that a constant period yield based on the net investment is attained.

43.10.4 Dividend Income

The recognition of dividend income is currently dealt with in IAS 18 which requires that dividend income should be recognised when the bank's right to receive payment is established, which is when:

- it is probable that the dividends will flow to the bank; and
- the amount of the dividends can be measured reliably.

(IAS 18, 29 and 30)

43.10.5 Fees and Commissions

A bank earns fees and commissions as a result of rendering services to its customers. These fees and commissions should be recognised as income for the rendering of services in accordance with the requirements of IAS 18 *Revenue,* which means that a bank recognises such fees and commissions:

- by reference to the stage of completion of the transaction at the balance sheet date when the outcome of the transaction can be estimated reliably (IAS 18, 20); and
- only to the extent of the expenses recognised that are recoverable when the outcome of the transaction cannot be estimated reliably (IAS 18, 26).

Further guidance on the general application of these requirements is provided in chapter 29.

The appendix to IAS 18 includes a number of examples which show how the requirements of IAS 18 for the rendering of services are applied in the case of financial services fees. The recognition of such fees as revenue depends on the purposes for which the fees are assessed and the basis of accounting for any associated financial instrument.

Fees which are an integral part of the effective yield of a financial instrument are:

- recognised as revenue when the instrument is initially recognised when the financial instrument is to be measured at fair value subsequent to its initial recognition; and
- treated as an adjustment to the effective yield in all other cases.

(IAS 18, appendix 14(a))

Fees which are earned as services are provided are recognised as revenue as the services are provided (IAS 18, appendix 14(b)).

Fees earned on the execution of a significant act, which is much more significant than any other act, are recognised as revenue when the significant act has been completed (IAS 18, appendix 14(c)).

Extract 43.10 *Fees and commissions*

UBS, Switzerland, 31 December 2001 (IAS)

Brokerage fees earned from executing securities transactions are recorded when the service has been provided. Portfolio and other management, advisory and other service fees are recognized based on the terms of the applicable service contracts. Asset management fees related to investment funds are recognized rateably over the period the service is provided. The same principle is applied for fees earned for wealth management, financial planning and custody services that are continuously provided over an extended period of time. Transaction-related fees earned from merger and acquisition and other advisory services, securities underwriting, fund raising, and from other investment banking and similar services that have a non-recurring character, are recognized at the time the service has been completed.

Extract 43.11 *Fees and commissions*

National Bank of Fujairah, United Arab Emirates, 31 December 2001 (IAS)

Commission and fee income are accounted for on the date of the transaction giving rise to that income except where such fees and commission relate to credit exposure exceeding six months' duration, when they are recognised quarterly in advance over the relevant period.

43.10.6 Gains and Losses on Dealing in Other Financial Instruments

The recognition of gains and losses on dealing in other financial instruments, including derivatives, is dealt with by IAS 39 (see chapter 20).

43.11 INVESTMENT AND DEALING SECURITIES

IAS 30 distinguishes between the dealing securities and the investment securities of a bank. *Dealing securities* are marketable securities which are acquired and held with the intention of re-selling them in the short term (IAS 30, 25). Therefore they are financial assets held for trading (IAS 39, 8). *Investment securities* are acquired and held for yield or capital growth purposes and are usually held to maturity (IAS

30, 25); investment securities include both marketable and non-marketable securities. Therefore, investment securities are usually either available-for-sale financial assets or held-to-maturity investments (IAS 39, 8).

The measurement of these securities and the treatment of the resulting gains and losses is dealt with in IAS 39 (see chapter 20).

43.12 LOANS AND ADVANCES

Loans and advances are financial assets and their recognition, derecognition and measurement, including the determination of any loan losses, is determined by reference to the requirements for originated loans and receivables in IAS 39. Therefore, the loan loss is the difference between the carrying amount of the loan or advance and the present value of the expected future cash flows discounted at the original effective yield on that loan or advance (IAS 39, 111). Such losses may be measured on a portfolio basis for loans that are not individually identified as impaired (IAS 39, 112). The IGC relating to paragraphs 110 to 113 of IAS 39 are particularly relevant to banks.

43.12.1 Non-Performing Loans

In view of the flexibility allowed by IAS 30 on non-performing loans, a bank should disclose the aggregate amount included in the balance sheet for loans and advances on which interest is not being accrued and the basis used to determine the carrying amount of such loans and advances (IAS 30, 43(d)).

Extract 43.12 *Non-performing loans*

Gulf International Bank, Bahrain, 31 December 2001 (IAS)

Past due loans

The gross and net book value of loans for which either principal or interest was over 90 days past due were as follows:

	31.12.01		31.12.00	
	Gross	*Net Book Value*	*Gross*	*Net Book Value*
	US$ millions	*US$ millions*	*US$ millions*	*US$ millions*
Sovereign	**405.7**	**0.6**	417.6	0.7
Corporate	**135.0**	**52.2**	132.6	54.5
Financial Institutions	**9.2**	**3.2**	10.8	2.4
	549.9	**56.0**	561.0	57.6

The overdue status of past due loans based on original contractual maturities was as follows:

	31.12.01	*31.12.00*
	US$ millions	*US$ millions*
Within 6 months	**25.4**	60.0
7 months to 1 year	–	6.1
2 to 5 years	**73.8**	30.0
Over 5 years	**450.7**	464.9
	549.9	561.0

At 31 December 2001 uncollected interest-in-suspense on past due loans amounted to US$ 464.2 million (2000: US$ 432.9 million).

Extract 43.13 *Non-performing loans*

UBS, Switzerland, 31 December 2001 (IAS)

When principal, interest or commission are overdue by 90 days, loans are classified as non-performing, the recognition of interest or commission income ceases according to the original terms of the loan agreement. Allowances are provided for non-performing loans to reflect their net estimated recoverable amount.

CHF million	*31.12.01*	*31.12.00*
Non-performing loans	8,639	10,452
Amount of allowance for credit losses related to non-performing loans	5,374	6,329[1]
Average non-performing loans[2]	9,648	11,884

[1] 31 December 2000 figure has been restated to account for an overallocation of allowances to non-performing loans.
[2] Average balances are calculated from quarterly data.

CHF million	*31.12.01*	*31.12.00*
Non-performing loans at beginning of year	10,452	13,073
Net additions/(reductions)	1,111	(290)
Write-offs and disposals	(2,924)	(2,331)
Non-performing loans at the end of the year	8,639	10,452

By type of exposure

CHF million	*31.12.01*	*31.12.00*
Banks	386	172
Loans to customers		
Mortgages	2,659	4,586
Other	5,594	5,694
Total loans to customers	8,253	10,280
Total non-performing loans	8,639	10,452

By geographical region (based on the location of the borrower)

CHF million	*31.12.01*	*31.12.00*
Switzerland	6,531	7,588
Rest of Europe	466	342
Americas	737	1,865
Asia/Pacific	653	307
Africa/Middle East	252	350
Total non-performing loans	8,639	10,452

Extract 43.14 *Non-performing loans*

HVB, Germany, 31 December 2001 (IAS)

Loans put on a non-accrual basis:

Placements with, and loans and advances to, other banks and customers include loans totalling €12.9 billion (2000: €12.3 billion) put on a non-accrual basis. The proportion of loans put on a non-accrual basis to the total lending volume rose 2.63% (2000: 2.55%). Consequently, total provisions of losses on loans and advances amount to 99% (2000: 103%) of the loans put on a non-accrual basis. This resulted in a loss of interest totalling €696 million this year (2000: €586 million).

43.13 HIDDEN RESERVES AND PROVISIONS FOR GENERAL BANKING RISKS

The IASC consistently opposed the use of hidden, secret and inner reserves as well as provisions for general banking risks which exceed the amounts required to cover liabilities, asset write-downs or contingencies as required by IAS 10 [1978]. Statements by the IASC on this topic include the following:

Financial statements cannot present a true and fair view as to financial position or results of operations if there are undisclosed overstatements

of liabilities, undisclosed understatements of assets or undisclosed accrual of amounts for general or unspecified banking risks. An acceptable alternative found in some countries is for part of shareholders' interests to be identified as a disclosed contingency reserve. Charges or credits to such a reserve would form part of net income disclosed in the income statement.
(*Disclosures in Financial Statements of Banks*, 28 and 29).

Amounts set aside in excess of requirements, as reserves, to cover future contingencies and the extent of their use to absorb losses, should be disclosed. While it is recognised that in practice making a distinction between justifiable provisions and excess reserves may be difficult, the user of the financial statements is entitled to expect that management has exercised its judgement and experience in determining its requirements.
(*Summary of Responses to Discussion Paper – Disclosures in the Financial Statements of Banks*, 39).

Financial statements cannot present wholly relevant and reliable information about the financial position or results if such items [reserves for general banking risks, other unforeseeable risks and contingencies] are not disclosed. Hence, charges against income for general banking risks, other unforeseeable risks or additional contingencies and the related balance sheet amounts need to be separately disclosed.
(E29, 32).

The income statement cannot present relevant and reliable information about the performance of a bank if net profit or loss for the period includes the effects of undisclosed amounts set aside for general banking risks or additional contingencies, or undisclosed credits resulting from the reversal of such amounts. Similarly, the balance sheet cannot provide relevant and reliable information about the financial position of a bank if the balance sheet includes overstated liabilities, understated assets or undisclosed accruals and provisions.
(E34, 38 and IAS 30, 52).

The IASC's policy also means that losses on loans and advances, as well as losses on investment and dealing securities, are recognised as expenses in the determination of the net profit or loss for the period. It is inappropriate to deduct such losses from hidden, secret and inner reserves or excess provisions for general banking risks.

In IFRS financial statements any amounts set aside in respect of general banking risks, including future losses and other unforeseeable risks or contingencies, in addition to those which are liabilities under IAS 37 or IAS 39, should be separately disclosed in the income statement as appropriations of retained earnings (IAS 30, 50). Similarly, any credits resulting from the reduction of such amounts are increases in retained earnings; they are not included in the determination of net profit or loss for the period (IAS 30, 50). The resulting provisions are classified as equity, rather than liabilities, on the balance sheet.

43.14 CONTINGENCIES AND COMMITMENTS INCLUDING OFF BALANCE SHEET ITEMS

IAS 30 requires a bank to disclose the following contingencies and commitments under IAS 10 [1978]:

- the nature and amount of commitments to extend credit which are irrevocable because they cannot be withdrawn at the discretion of the bank without the risk of incurring significant penalty or expense; and
- the nature and amount of contingencies and commitments arising from off balance sheet items including those relating to:
  - direct credit substitutes including general guarantees of indebtedness, bank acceptance guarantees and standby letters of credit serving as financial guarantees for loans and securities;
  - certain transaction-related contingencies including performance bonds, bid bonds, warranties and standby letters of credit related to particular transactions;
  - short-term self-liquidating trade-related contingencies arising from the movement of goods, such as documentary credits where the underlying shipment is used as security;
  - those sale and repurchase agreements not recognised in the balance sheet;
  - interest and foreign exchange rate-related items including swaps, options and futures; and
  - other commitments, note issuance facilities and revolving underwriting facilities.

(IAS 30, 26)

The list of off balance sheet items was derived from the capital convergence work of the Basel Committee (E34, 20)[4].

Many of the off balance sheet items are financial instruments and give rise to financial assets or financial liabilities to which the disclosure requirements in IAS 32 and the recognition and measurement requirements in IAS 39 apply (see chapter 20).

43.15 MATURITIES OF ASSETS AND LIABILITIES

All entities should disclose for each asset and liability item the amounts expected to be recovered or settled after more than 12 months (IAS 1, 54) and, for each class of financial asset and financial liability, the contractual re-pricing or maturity dates (IAS 32, 56(a)). The requirements for banks are more extensive. A bank should disclose an analysis of assets and

Extract 43.15 *Maturity analysis*

UBS, Switzerland, 31 December 2001 (IAS)

Maturity analysis of assets and liabilities

CFH billion	On demand	Subject to notice[1]	Due within 3 mths	Due between 3 and 12 mths	Due between 1 and 5 years	Due after 5 years	Total
Assets							
Cash and balances with central banks	21.0						21.0
Due from banks	10.6	0.0	14.7	1.5	0.4	0.3	27.5
Cash collateral on securities borrowed	0.0	0.0	162.5	0.0	0.4	0.0	162.9
Reverse repurchase agreements	0.0	0.0	236.9	31.4	1.0	0.0	269.3
Trading portfolio assets	397.9	0.0	0.0	0.0	0.0	0.0	397.9
Positive replacement values	73.4	0.0	0.0	0.0	0.0	0.0	73.4
Loans, net of allowance for credit losses	0.0	29.7	96.0	36.5	54.7	9.6	226.5
Financial investments	9.3	0.3	3.3	4.8	7.1	4.0	28.8
Accrued income and prepaid expenses	7.6	0.0	0.0	0.0	0.0	0.0	7.6
Investments in associates	0.0	0.0	0.0	0.0	0.0	0.7	0.7
Property and equipment	0.0	0.0	0.0	0.0	0.0	8.7	8.7
Goodwill and other intangible assets	0.0	0.0	0.0	0.0	0.0	19.1	19.1
Other assets	9.9	0.0	0.0	0.0	0.0	0.0	9.9
Total 31.12.2001	**529.7**	**30.0**	**513.4**	**74.2**	**63.6**	**42.4**	**1,253.3**
Total 31.12.2000	351.8	38.8	502.3	87.3	60.8	46.6	1,087.6
Liabilities							
Due to banks	11.1	2.7	87.9	4.2	0.5	0.1	106.5
Cash collateral on securities lent	0.0	0.0	30.3	0.0	0.0	0.0	30.3
Repurchase agreements	0.0	0.0	336.9	31.7	0.0	0.0	368.6
Trading portfolio liabilities	105.8	0.0	0.0	0.0	0.0	0.0	105.8
Negative replacement values	71.5	0.0	0.0	0.0	0.0	0.0	71.5
Due to customers	141.4	3.7	178.9	7.7	1.2	0.9	333.8
Accrued expenses and deferred income	17.3	0.0	0.0	0.0	0.0	0.0	17.3
Debt issued	0.0	0.0	66.0	50.3	27.6	12.3	156.2
Other liabilities	15.7	0.0	0.0	0.0	0.0	0.0	15.7
Total 31.12.2001	**362.8**	**6.4**	**700.0**	**93.9**	**29.3**	**13.3**	**1,205.7**
Total 31.12.2000	283.1	77.2	536.5	84.3	33.3	25.4	1,039.8

[1] Deposits without a fixed term, on which notice of withdrawal or termination has not been given (such funds may be withdrawn by the depositor or repaid by the borrower subject to an agreed period of notice).

Extract 43.16 *Maturity analysis*

Gulf International Bank, Bahrain, 31 December 2001 (IAS)

The maturity profile of assets and liabilities based on the remaining periods to contractual maturity dates was as follows:

	Within 3 months US$ millions	4 months to 1 year US$ millions	Years 2 and 3 US$ millions	Years 4 and 5 US$ millions	Over 5 years and other US$ millions	Total US$ millions
At 31 December 2001						
Cash and other liquid assets	88.2	3.0	–	–	–	91.2
Placements	2,486.4	207.2	–	–	–	2,693.6
Securities	1,220.3	279.4	1,506.9	1,188.1	4,453.7	8,648.4
Loans and advances	948.2	654.1	830.0	391.4	485.7	3,309.4
Fixed and other assets	359.2	79.5	–	–	50.7	489.4
Total assets	5,102.3	1,223.2	2,336.9	1,579.5	4,990.1	15,232.0
Deposits	8,988.1	1,808.9	152.7	–	–	10,949.7
Securities sold under agreements to repurchase	1,222.4	200.0	–	–	–	1,422.4
Securities sold but not yet purchased	122.6	–	–	–	–	122.6
Other liabilities	481.5	60.3	–	–	21.8	563.6
Term financing	–	300.0	100.0	430.0	150.0	980.0
Shareholders' equity	–	–	–	–	1,193.7	1,193.7
Liabilities and shareholders' equity	10,814.6	2,369.2	252.7	430.0	1,365.5	15,232.0
At 31 December 2000						
Total assets	4,811.8	1,822.2	2,082.7	1,792.9	4,609.9	15,119.5
Liabilities and shareholders' equity	11,327.6	1,614.7	486.5	400.0	1,290.7	15,119.5

The asset and liability maturities are based on contractual repayment arrangements and as such do not take acount of the effective maturities of deposits as indicated by the Group's deposit retention records. Counterparties each with deposits over US$10 million at 31 December 2001 had average deposits throughout 2001 amounting to US$ 10,244 million (2000: US$ 8,511 million). Formal liquidity controls are nevertheless based on contractual asset and liability maturities.

liabilities into relevant maturity groupings based on the remaining period at the balance sheet date to the contractual maturity date (IAS 30, 30). Periods commonly used are:

- up to 1 month;
- from 1 month to 3 months;
- from 3 months to 1 year;
- from 1 year to 5 years; and
- over 5 years.

(IAS 30, 33)

IAS 30 emphasises that it is essential that the maturity periods are the same for assets and liabilities. This makes clear the extent to which the maturities are matched and the consequent dependence of the bank on other sources of liquidity.

IAS 30 requires the disclosure of maturities based on contractual repayment dates because these dates reflect the liquidity risks attaching to the bank's assets and liabilities. In many countries, deposits made with a bank may be withdrawn on demand and advances given by a bank may be repayable on demand. In practice, however, these deposits and advances often remain outstanding for long periods without withdrawal or repayment or the amounts outstanding may fluctuate significantly. In such cases, the effective date of repayment is later than the contractual date. IAS 30 suggests that information about effective maturities may be made in the commentary on the financial statements. Some assets of a bank do not have a contractual maturity date. The period in which these assets are assumed to mature is usually taken as the expected date on which the assets will be realised (IAS 30, 37).

For the purposes of IAS 30, maturities may be expressed in terms of either repayment or interest rate re-pricing (IAS 30, 35). Disclosure of maturities based on interest rate re-pricing meets the requirements of IAS 30 and IAS 32 but the disclosure of repayment maturities is necessary to meet the requirements of IAS 1.

Extract 43.17 *Maturity analysis*

Hellenic Bank, Cyprus, 31 December 1996 (IAS)

11. PLACEMENTS WITH OTHER BANKS

	1996	1995
	C£'000	C£'000
On demand	**8.273**	9.782
Not more than three months	**121.046**	23.837
Over three months but not more than one year	**.511**	1.616
	129.830	35.235

12. ADVANCES AND OTHER ACCOUNTS

	The Group		The Bank	
	1996	1995	**1996**	1995
	C£'000	C£'000	**C£'000**	C£'000
Advances				
On demand	**290.649**	165.041	**287.569**	162.135
Not more than three months	**22.577**	15.441	**20.880**	14.901
Over three months but not more than one year	**34.142**	24.277	**31.684**	21.975
Over one year but not more than five years	**87.813**	52.865	**72.445**	40.129
Over five years	**112.512**	49.690	**110.196**	43.672
	547.693	307.314	**522.774**	284.812
Provisions for bad and doubtful debts	**(20.976)**	(9.972)	**(19.173)**	(8.460)
	526.717	297.342	**503.601**	276.352
Other accounts	**6.013**	2.712	**5.453**	1.725
	532.730	300.054	**509.054**	278.077

13. INVESTMENTS

Investments consist of investments in tradeable sovereign bonds and bonds issued by first class international banks, shares and debentures of public companies listed on the Cyprus Stock Exchange and other investments.

	The Group		The Bank	
	1996	1995	**1996**	1995
	C£'000	C£'000	**C£'000**	C£'000
International bonds	**29.961**	26.593	**29.961**	26.593
Securities listed on the Cyprus Stock Exchange	**3.198**	3.317	**1.316**	1.316
Other investments	**.270**	.162	**.125**	.017
	33.429	30.072	**31.402**	27.926
Market value at 31 December	**33.746**	31.376	**31.854**	29.102

Remaining maturity on international bonds:

	1996	1995
	C£'000	C£'000
Not more than three months	**2.531**	–
Over three months but not more than one year	**8.817**	4.264
Over one year but not more than five years	**17.203**	19.818
Over five years	**1.410**	2.511
	29.961	26.593

19. DEPOSITS BY BANKS

	1996	1995
	C£'000	C£'000
On demand	**9.004**	3.718
Not more than three months	–	9.037
Over three months but not more than one year	–	.300
	9.004	13.055

20. DEPOSITS AND OTHER ACCOUNTS

	The Group		The Bank	
	1996	1995	**1996**	1995
	C£'000	C£'000	**C£'000**	C£'000
Deposits				
On demand	**183.566**	69.056	**183.278**	68.398
Not more than three months	**298.076**	156.827	**298.076**	156.827
Over three months but not more than one year	**334.705**	202.210	**332.056**	202.210
	816.347	428.093	**813.410**	427.435
Other accounts	**25.104**	11.645	**24.183**	11.122
	841.451	439.738	**837.593**	438.557

43.16 CONCENTRATIONS OF ASSETS, LIABILITIES AND OFF BALANCE SHEET ITEMS

All entities are required to disclose significant concentrations of credit risk (IAS 32, 66(b)). Again, the requirements for a bank are more extensive. A bank should also disclose:

- any significant concentrations of its assets, liabilities and off balance sheet items; and
- the amount of significant net foreign currency exposures.

(IAS 30, 40)

Disclosures of concentrations may be made in terms of geographical areas, customer or industry groups or other concentrations of risk (IAS 30, 41) or from a single debtor or groups of debtors having a similar characteristic (IAS 32, 75). Geographical areas may comprise individual countries, groups of countries or regions within a country; customer disclosures may deal with sectors such as governments, public authorities, and commercial and business entities. The disclosures are made in addition to any segment information required by IAS 14. The IAS 30 disclosure of significant concentrations of assets usually meets the IAS 32 requirements for those assets.

Extract 43.18 *Concentrations of loans and advances*

Gulf International Bank, Bahrain, 31 December 2001 (IAS)

Net loans and advances at 31 December 2001 included exposure to GCC country governments of US$ 352.2 million (2000: US$ 520.6 million) and OECD country central government and agency risk of US$ 165.7 million (2000: US$ 205.4 million).

There were no significant concentrations by industrial sector at 31 December 2001 and at 31 December 2000.

Extract 43.19 *Geographical concentrations*

EFG Eurobank Ergasias, Greece, 31 December 2000 (IAS)

	Total assets Grd. m.	*Total liabilities Grd. m.*	*Credit commitments Grd. m.*	*Capital expenditure Grd. m.*
At 31 December 2000				
Geographical concentrations of assets, liabilities and off balance sheet items				
– Greece	5,165,469	4,385,048	151,275	9,075
– Other Western European countries	475,507	570,324	117	0
– Canada and USA	80,136	12,969	0	0
– Australasia	3,723	2,248	0	0
– South East Asia	1,585	25	0	0
– Other countries	9,392	35,358	9	0
	5,735,812	5,005,972	151,401	9,075
At 31 December 1999				
Geographical concentrations of assets, liabilities and off balance sheet items				
– Greece	4,574,728	3,906,592	330,693	305
– Other Western European countries	426,293	367,252	45,824	0
– Canada and USA	62,248	13,716	0	0
– Australasia	10,655	1,756	0	0
– South East Asia	13,353	10,976	0	0
– Other countries	7,225	54,441	3	0
	5,094,502	4,354,733	376,520	305

Extract 43.20 *Exposure to Currencies*

UBS, Switzerland, 31 December 2001 (IAS)

Breakdown of assets and liabilities by currencies

	31.12.01				31.12.00			
CHF billion	CHF	USD	EUR	Other	CHF	USD	EUR	Other
Assets								
Cash and balances with central banks	3.0	0.3	0.6	17.1	1.9	0.2	0.5	0.4
Due from banks	5.0	8.6	5.2	8.7	5.8	10.4	8.0	4.9
Cash collateral on securities borrowed	0.1	156.4	2.5	3.9	0.5	169.2	2.4	5.8
Revenue repurchase agreements	5.1	142.9	40.2	81.1	5.3	83.7	37.4	67.4
Trading portfolio assets	9.6	265.2	47.2	75.9	16.1	184.1	38.2	77.2
Positive replacement values	30.6	11.4	1.2	30.2	11.7	6.9	0.6	38.7
Loans, net of allowance for credit losses	151.4	43.1	11.9	20.1	154.2	52.3	7.1	31.2
Financial investments	2.9	7.4	1.5	17.0	6.5	8.3	0.9	3.9
Accrued income and prepaid expenses	0.7	4.9	0.8	1.2	1.6	4.4	0.2	0.9
Investments in associates	0.7	0.0	0.0	0.0	0.7	0.0	0.1	0.1
Property and equipment	6.3	1.5	0.1	0.8	6.9	1.4	0.0	0.6
Goodwill and other intangible assets	0.2	18.5	0.0	0.4	0.3	19.1	0.0	0.1
Other assets	2.1	5.6	0.8	1.4	3.2	3.3	0.6	2.4
Total assets	217.7	665.8	112.0	257.8	214.7	543.3	96.0	233.6
Liabilities								
Due to banks	8.0	68.6	12.9	17.0	6.5	46.5	10.6	18.6
Cash collateral on securities lent	0.0	24.3	3.2	2.8	0.1	12.6	5.0	5.7
Repurchase agreements	12.8	271.1	30.7	54.0	10.0	194.6	16.1	74.9
Trading portfolio liabilities	2.8	65.2	12.5	25.3	2.0	52.4	11.4	16.8
Negative replacement values	25.7	6.5	1.6	37.7	8.6	6.3	2.0	59.0
Due to customers	123.3	138.8	41.5	30.2	118.8	129.7	29.9	32.4
Accrued expenses and deferred income	2.4	10.0	0.9	4.0	3.0	11.8	1.7	4.5
Debt issued	15.7	120.0	8.8	11.7	18.3	90.7	4.4	16.2
Other liabilities	7.2	6.1	0.9	1.5	9.9	3.6	2.5	2.8
Minority interests	0.1	3.9	0.0	0.1	0.2	2.5	0.1	0.1
Shareholders' equity	43.5	0.0	0.0	0.0	44.8	0.0	0.0	0.0
Total liabilities, minority interests and shareholders' equity	241.5	714.5	113.0	184.3	222.2	550.7	83.7	231.0

43.17 ASSETS PLEDGED AS SECURITY

A bank should disclose the aggregate amount of secured liabilities and the nature and carrying amount of the assets pledged as security (IAS 30, 53). IAS 32 suggests, but does not require, that the collateral (security) pledged for financial liabilities may warrant disclosure (IAS 32, 49(g)).

43.18 TRUST ACTIVITIES

Banks commonly act in fiduciary capacities that result in the holding or placing of assets on behalf of individuals, trusts, retirement benefit plans and other institutions. Provided the trustee or similar relationship is legally supported, these assets are not assets of the bank and, therefore, are not included in its balance sheet. If the bank is engaged in significant trust activities, IAS 30 suggests, but does not require, disclosure of that fact and the extent of those activities. Such disclosures warn of the potential liability if the bank fails in its fiduciary duties.

Extract 43.21 *Trust activities*

UBS, Switzerland, 31 December 2001 (IAS)

CHF million	*31.12.01*	*31.12.00*
Placements with third parties	58,466	69,300
Fiduciary credits and other fiduciary financial transactions	1,136	1,234
Total fiduciary transactions	59,602	70,534

Fiduciary placement represents funds which customers have instructed the Group to place in foreign banks. The Group is not liable to the customer for any default by the foreign bank nor do creditors of the Group have a claim on the assets placed.

Extract 43.22 *Trust Activities*

Dresdner Bank, Germany, 31 December 2001 (German GAAP and IAS)

[Accounting policies] Assets and liabilities held by the Group in its own name, but for the account of third parties, are not reported on the balance sheet. Commissions received from such business are shown as net fee and commission income in the income statement.

[Note] The table shown below is a breakdown of trustee business not reported in the balance sheet:

€ mn	*31 Dec 2001*	*31 Dec 2000*
Loans and advances to banks	3,415	2,509
Loans and advances to customers	4,497	4,195
Investment securities	7	7
Other	9	6
Assets held in trust*	**7,928**	**6,717**
Liabilities to banks	300	305
Liabilities to customers	7,628	6,412
Liabilities incurred as a trustee	**7,982**	**6,717**

* Including €5,078 million (2000: €5,967 million) of trustee loans.

Extract 43.23 *Trust activities*

HVB, Germany, 31 December 2000 (IAS)

The following tables show the volume of trust business not stated in the consolidated balance sheet.

Trust assets

In millions of €	*2001*	*2000*
Placements with, and loans and advances to, other banks	1,385	1,182
Loans and advances to customers	2,220	2,114
Equity securities and other variable-yield securities	5	59
Debt securities	5	6
Participating interests	72	61
Property, plant and equipment	144	145
Miscellaneous other assets	4	18
Remaining trust receivables	1	1
Total	**3,836**	**3,586**

Trust liabilities

In millions of €	*2001*	*2000*
Deposits from other banks	538	402
Amounts owed to other depositors	2,809	2,711
Liabilities evidenced by paper	329	308
Miscellaneous other liabilities	160	165
Total	**3,836**	**3,586**

43.19 RELATED PARTY TRANSACTIONS

IAS 24 deals generally with the disclosure of related party relationships and transactions between a reporting entity and its related parties. It requires the disclosure of a related party relationship when one party controls the other and of related party transactions.

A bank and its customer are not deemed to be related parties solely as a result of their normal bank dealings (IAS 24, 6(b)). Similarly, a single customer of a bank is not a related party merely by virtue of the customer's resulting economic dependence on the bank (IAS 24, 6(c)). Therefore, for example, a bank and a customer are not related parties solely as a result of the bank providing substantial finance to the customer or the customer placing substantial deposits with the bank. The bank and the customer are related parties, however, if the bank controls or has significant influence over the customer (other than through normal bank dealings) or the customer controls or has significant influence over the bank (other than through normal bank dealings). So, for example:

- when a bank lends to A in the normal course of business, the bank and A are not related parties by virtue of the loan;
- when A makes a deposit with a bank in the normal course of business, the bank and A are not related parties by virtue of the deposit;
- when A controls the bank or the bank controls A, the bank and A are related parties and the relationship and the elements of any transactions are disclosed in accordance with IAS 24; and
- when A has significant influence over the bank or the bank has significant influence over A, the bank and A are related parties and the elements of any transactions are disclosed in accordance with IAS 24.

Certain transactions between related parties may be effected on different terms from those with unrelated parties. For example, a bank may advance a larger sum or charge a lower interest rate on a loan to a related party than it would to an unrelated party. Advances or deposits may be moved between related parties more quickly and with less formality than is possible when unrelated parties are involved. Even when related party transactions arise in the ordinary course of a bank's business, information about such transactions is relevant to the needs of users and its disclosure is required by IAS 24.

When a bank has entered into transactions with related parties, IAS 24 requires the bank to disclose the nature of the related party relationship, the types of transactions, and the elements of transactions necessary for an understanding of the financial statements of the bank (IAS 24, 22). The elements which would normally be disclosed to conform with IAS 24 include:

- the bank's lending policy to related parties; and
- the amount included in, or the proportion of:
  - each of loans and advances, deposits and acceptances and promissory notes – disclosures may include the aggregate amounts outstanding at the beginning and end of the period, as

well as advances, deposits, repayments and other changes during the period;
- each of the principal types of income, interest expense and commissions paid;
- the amount of the expense recognised in the period for losses on loans and advances and the amount of the provision at the balance sheet date; and
- irrevocable commitments and contingencies and commitments arising from off balance sheet items.

(IAS 30, 58)

Extract 43.24 *Loans and advances to related parties*

UBS, Switzerland, 31 December 2001 (IAS)

Loans and advances receivable from related parties were as follows:

CHF million	*31.12.01*	*31.12.00*
Mortgages at the beginning of the year	36	28
Additions	8	9
Reductions	(12)	(1)
Mortgages at the end of the first year	32	36

Members of the Board of Directors, Group Executive Board and Group Managing Board are granted mortgages at the same terms and conditions as other employees. Terms and conditions are based on third-party conditions adjusted for reduced credit risk.

Loans and advances to significant associated companies were as follows:

CHF million	*31.12.01*	*31.12.00*
Loans and advances at the beginning of the year	0	62
Additions	65	0
Reductions	0	(62)
Loans and advances at the end of the year	65	0

All loans and advances to associated companies are transacted at arm's length. At 31 December 2001, there are trading exposures and guarantees to significant associated companies of CHF 306 million. The Group routinely receives services from associated companies at an arm's length basis. For the year ended 31 December 2001, the amount paid to significant associates was CHF 98 million. Note 36 provides a list of significant associates.

43.20 COMMENTARY ON THE FINANCIAL STATEMENTS

IAS 30 encourages the presentation of a commentary on the financial statements which deals with such matters as the management and control of liquidity and risk (IAS 30, 3). Among the matters which may be dealt with in the commentary are:

- average interest rates, average interest-earning assets and average interest-bearing liabilities for the period (IAS 30, 17);
- the extent of deposits and credit facilities which have been provided by governments at interest rates which are substantially below market rates, and the effect of such deposits and facilities on net income (IAS 30, 17);
- information about interest rate exposure and about the way the bank manages and controls such exposures (IAS 30, 35) – this information is now required by IAS 32; and
- information about the effective maturity periods and the way the bank manages and controls the risks and exposures associated with different maturity and interest rate profiles (IAS 30, 39).

Notes

1 *Sound Practices for Loan Accounting and Disclosure,* Basel Committee on Banking Supervision, 1999.

2 *Public Disclosure of the Trading and Derivatives Activities of Banks and Securities Firms,* Basel Committee on Banking Supervision and IOSCO, 1995.

3 *Public Disclosures by Banks – Results of the 2000 Disclosure Survey,* Basel Committee on Banking Supervision, 2001.

4 *International Convergence of Capital Measurement and Capital Standards,* Basel Committee on Banking Supervision, Basle, 1988 (updated April 1997), annex 3.

CHAPTER 44

Retirement Benefit Plans

44.1 RELEVANT STANDARD

IAS 26 *Accounting and Reporting by Retirement Benefit Plans*

IAS 26 complements IAS 19 which deals with the determination of retirement benefit assets, liabilities, income and expenses in the financial statements of employers.

44.2 HISTORY

IAS 26 was approved in June 1986. It was reformatted in 1994. While IAS 19 has been revised twice, IAS 26 has not been revised and the IASB has no plans to do so.

44.3 IAS 26 IN BRIEF

IAS 26 deals with accounting and reporting by a retirement benefit plan to all participants in the plan as a group.

The report of a defined contribution plan should contain a statement of net assets available for benefits and a description of the funding policy.

The report of a defined benefit plan should disclose the net assets available for benefits, the actuarial present value of promised retirement benefits and the resulting excess or deficit (or a reference to this information in an accompanying actuarial report).

Plan investments should be measured at fair value.

44.4 APPLICATION OF OTHER IFRSs

All IFRSs apply to the reports of retirement benefit plans to the extent that they are not superseded by IAS 26 (IAS 26, 2) or they do not apply to retirement benefit plans. In particular, IAS 26 restricts the choice of measurement bases permitted for the valuation of the financial assets and investment property of a retirement benefit plan.

As IAS 39 does not override IAS 26 (IAS 39, 3), a retirement benefit plan may not be able to use all the options in IAS 39 for the measurement of plan assets that are financial assets. Similarly, a retirement benefit plan is unable to use the cost model for plan assets that are investment property.

44.5 RETIREMENT BENEFIT PLANS

A *retirement benefit plan* is an arrangement whereby an entity provides benefits for its employees on or after termination of service (either in the form of an annual income or as a lump sum) when such benefits, or the employer's contributions towards them, can be determined or estimated in advance of retirement from the provisions of a document or from the entity's practices (IAS 26, 8).

Retirement benefit plans are sometimes referred to as pension schemes, superannuation schemes or retirement benefit schemes. Most retirement benefit plans are based on formal agreements between the employer and the employees either individually or as a group.

Retirement benefit plans may be defined contribution plans or defined benefit plans (or may have characteristics of both – such hybrid plans are considered to be defined benefit plans (IAS 26, 12)). A *defined contribution plan* is a retirement benefit plan under which amounts to be paid as retirement benefits are determined by contributions to a fund together with investment earnings thereon (IAS 26, 8). A *defined benefit plan* is a retirement benefit plan under which amounts to be paid as retirement benefits are determined by reference to a formula usually based on employees' earnings and/or years of service (IAS 26, 8).

The definitions of both types of plan were changed in the revised IAS 19 approved in 1998. The IASC felt that the previous IAS 19 definitions (which mirrored those in IAS 26) were unsatisfactory because they focussed on the benefits receivable by the employee rather than on the cost to the employer. The change to IAS 19 does not affect the application of IAS 26.

Retirement benefit plans may be funded or unfunded. *Funding* is defined as the transfer of assets to an entity (the *fund*) separate from the employer's entity to meet future obligations for the payment of retirement benefits. The financial statements of a retirement benefit plan include any such assets and the earnings on those assets. A defined contribution plan is usually funded whereas a defined benefit plan may be funded or unfunded.

IAS 26 applies to the reports of all such plans but only when the plans publish such a report (IAS 26, 1). IAS 26 does not require the publication of such a report. Publication may be required by law or by the terms of the plan.

The *participants* in a plan are the members of that plan and others who are entitled to benefits under the plan (IAS 26, 8). The participants usually include those employees of the entity who are members of the plan and any dependants who are entitled to benefits under the plan, for example, spouses or children of such employees or former employees.

44.6 DEFINED CONTRIBUTION PLANS

The participants in a defined contribution plan are interested in knowing whether their contributions have been received by the plan, that proper control has been exercised to protect the rights of beneficiaries (usually the participants themselves) and the value of the plan assets. Therefore, the report of a defined contribution plan should contain:

- a statement of the net assets available for benefits (IAS 26, 13 and 35) – see example 44.1;
- a statement of changes in net assets available for benefits (IAS 26, 34 and 35);
- a summary of significant accounting policies (IAS 26, 34);
- a description of the plan and the effect of any changes in the plan during the period (IAS 26, 34 and 36); and
- a description of the funding policy (IAS 26, 13 and 35).

The *net assets available for benefits* are the assets of a plan less its liabilities (IAS 26, 8). The assets include the plan's investments. Financial assets which have a fixed redemption value and which have been acquired to match the obligations of the plan, or specific parts of the plan, may be carried at fair value (market value) or at amounts based on their ultimate redemption value assuming a constant rate of return to maturity – in other words, an amortised cost basis (IAS 26, 33). All other financial assets should be measured at fair value which, in the case of marketable securities, is usually market value (IAS 26, 32). Investment property should be measured at fair value based on the guidance in IAS 40 and IVS 1 and draft IVA 1. When it is not possible to estimate fair value of any plan asset, the plan should disclose the reason why fair value is not used (IAS 26, 32 and 33).

Assets used in the operations of the plan are recognised and measured in accordance with the appropriate IFRSs (IAS 26, 33); for example any property, plant or equipment of a plan is dealt with in accordance with IAS 16.

The report of a defined contribution plan does not include an actuarial valuation because there are no promised benefits. Instead, the benefits are based on the contributions to the plan and the earnings on plan assets. The report may include an actuary's assessment of likely level of benefits based on current contributions and asset values and assumptions about future contributions and earnings on plan assets.

Example 44.1 *Defined Contribution Retirement Benefit Plan*

Statement of Net Assets Available for Benefits

	31 December	
	2002	*2001*
Assets	*£000s*	*£000s*
Financial assets at fair value		
UK government securities	355,833	175,695
UK corporate convertible bonds	555,170	560,916
Non-UK government securities	537,308	481,548
Non-UK corporate and convertible bonds	31,524	14,166
Short-term investments	250,506	398,683
UK equity securities	1,186,089	1,200,275
Non-UK equity securities	2,153,450	2,362,813
Other	477,833	300,358
Total investments	5,547,713	5,494,454
Receivables		
Securities sold	109,099	281,894
Accrued interest and dividends	44,247	48,737
Other receivables	2,840	0
Total receivables	156,186	330,631
Cash	16,202	30,771
Total assets	5,720,101	5,855,856
Liabilities		
Accounts payable		
Securities bought	198,208	267,542
Benefits due but unpaid	388	541
Total liabilities	198,596	268,083
Net assets available for benefits	5,521,505	5,587,773

44.7 DEFINED BENEFIT PLANS

The participants in a defined benefit plan want to assess the relationship between the accumulation of resources and the plan benefits, in other words, whether the plan has sufficient resources to provide the promised benefits. In the case of an unfunded defined benefit plan, the plan's assets are usually limited to the obligation of the employer to provide the promised benefits.

The report of a defined benefit plan should contain either:

- a statement that shows the net assets available for benefits, the actuarial present value of promised retirement benefits (distinguishing between vested benefits and non-vested benefits) and the resulting excess or deficit – this statement is similar to a balance sheet for the plan (see example 44.2); or
- a statement of net assets available for benefits together with either a note disclosing the actuarial present value of promised retirement benefits (distinguishing between vested benefits and non-vested benefits) (see example 44.3) or a reference to this information in an accompanying actuarial report.

(IAS 26, 17)

A statement of net assets available for benefits includes, if applicable:

- the assets at the end of the period suitably classified;
- the basis of valuation of those assets;
- details of any single investment exceeding either 5% of the net assets available for benefits or 5% of any class or type of security;
- details of any investment in the employer of the participants in the plan; and
- any liabilities other than the actuarial present value of promised retirement benefits.

(IAS 26, 35(a))

The *net assets available for benefits* are the assets of a plan less its liabilities other than the actuarial present value of promised retirement benefits (IAS 26, 8). The assets include the plan's investments. Financial assets which have a fixed redemption value and which have been acquired to match the obligations of the plan, or specific parts of the plan, may be carried at fair value (market value) or at amounts based on their ultimate redemption value assuming a constant rate of return to maturity – in other words, an amortised cost basis (IAS 26, 33). All other financial assets should be measured at fair value which, in the case of marketable securities, is usually market value (IAS 26, 32). Investment property should be measured at fair value based on the guidance in IAS 40 and

IVS 1 and draft IVA 1. When it is not possible to estimate fair value of any plan asset, the plan should disclose the reason why fair value is not used (IAS 26, 32 and 33).

Assets used in the operations of the plan are recognised and measured in accordance with the appropriate IFRSs (IAS 26, 33).

The *actuarial present value of promised retirement benefits* is the present value of the expected payments by a retirement benefit plan to existing and past employees, attributable to the service already rendered (IAS 26, 8).

The actuarial present value of promised retirement benefits should be based on the benefits promised under the terms of the plan on service rendered to date using either current salary levels or projected salary levels with disclosure of the basis used (IAS 26, 18). IAS 19 requires the use of projected salary levels when determining costs and liabilities in the financial statements of employers; IAS 26 allows more flexibility in the report of the plan.

IAS 26 gives no guidance on the actuarial method which should be used in the report of a retirement benefit plan. In contrast, the choice of methods for use in the financial statements of the employer has been gradually reduced through the successive revisions of IAS 19. IAS 19 now requires the use of the projected unit credit method but IAS 26 does not require the use of a particular method. IAS 19 requires the use of up-to-date actuarial valuations although some flexibility is allowed (IAS 19, 56–67). IAS 26 acknowledges that actuarial valuations may be carried out only once every three years. When an actuarial valuation has not been prepared as at the date of the report, the most recent valuation is used in the report (IAS 26, 27).

Benefits under a retirement benefit plan may be vested or unvested. *Vested benefits* are benefits, the rights to which, under the conditions of a retirement benefit plan, are not conditional on continued employment (IAS 26, 8). This definition is consistent with IAS 19.

The choice of format reflects a disagreement within the IASC at the time at which IAS 26 was approved about the need for, or wisdom of, disclosing the actuarial present value of promised retirement benefits (or any excess or deficit). Some believed that the quantification of the promised retirement benefits helps users to assess the current status of the plan and the likelihood of the plan's obligations being met. Others believed that such information could give the impression that a liability exists when, in their opinion, the actuarial present value of promised retirement benefits is not a liability.

The report should explain the relationship between the actuarial present value of promised retirement benefits and the net assets available for benefits, and the policy for the funding of promised benefits (IAS 26, 19 and 35). Such explanation may be in the form of information about the adequacy of the planned future funding and of the funding policy based on salary projections. It may be included in the financial information or

Example 44.2 *Defined Benefit Retirement Benefit Plan*

Statement of Net Assets Available for Benefits, Actuarial Present Value of Promised Retirement Benefits and Plan Excess or Deficit.

	31 December	
	2002	*2001*
Assets	*£000s*	*£000s*
Financial assets at fair value		
UK government securities	355,833	175,695
UK corporate convertible bonds	555,170	560,916
Non-UK government securities	537,308	481,548
Non-UK corporate and convertible bonds	31,524	14,166
Short-term investments	250,506	398,683
UK equity securities	1,186,089	1,200,275
Non-UK equity securities	2,153,450	2,362,813
Other	477,833	300,358
Total investments	5,547,713	5,494,454
Receivables		
Securities sold	109,099	281,894
Accrued interest and dividends	44,247	48,737
Other receivables	2,840	0
Total receivables	156,186	330,631
Cash	16,202	30,771
Total assets	5,720,101	5,855,856
Liabilities		
Accounts payable		
Securities bought	198,208	267,542
Benefits due but unpaid	388	541
Total liabilities	198,596	268,083
Net assets available for benefits	5,521,505	5,587,773
Actuarial present value of accumulated plan benefits		
Vested benefits		
Participants currently receiving payments	2,292,757	2,173,915
Other participants	2,482,936	2,452,446
Subtotal	4,775,693	4,626,361
Non-vested benefits	24,834	45,001
Benefits	4,800,527	4,671,362
Excess of net assets available for benefits over actuarial present value of accumulated plan benefits	720,978	916,411

Example 44.3 *Defined Benefit Retirement Benefit Plan*

Statement of Net Assets Available for Benefits

	31 December	
	2002	*2001*
Assets	*£000s*	*£000s*
Investments at fair value		
UK government securities	355,833	175,695
UK corporate convertible bonds	555,170	560,916
Non-UK government securities	537,308	481,548
Non-UK corporate and convertible bonds	31,524	14,166
Short-term investments	250,506	398,683
UK equity securities	1,186,089	1,200,275
Non-UK equity securities	2,153,450	2,362,813
Other	477,833	300,358
Total investments	5,547,713	5,494,454
Receivables		
Securities sold	109,099	281,894
Accrued interest and dividends	44,247	48,737
Other receivables	2,840	0
Total receivables	156,186	330,631
Cash	16,202	30,771
Total assets	5,720,101	5,855,856
Liabilities		
Accounts payable		
Securities bought	198,208	267,542
Benefits due but unpaid	388	541
Total liabilities	198,596	268,083
Net assets available for benefits	5,521,505	5,587,773

Statement of Accumulated Plan benefits

Actuarial present value of accumulated plan benefits		
Vested benefits		
Participants currently receiving payments	2,292,757	2,173,915
Other participants	2,482,936	2,452,446
Subtotal	4,775,693	4,626,361
Non-vested benefits	24,834	45,001
Benefits	4,800,527	4,671,362

in the actuary's report (IAS 26, 26). The explanation should help to overcome any misunderstandings about the relationship between the actuarial present value and the value of plan assets as well as the nature of the obligation.

The report of a defined benefits plan should also contain a statement of changes in net assets available for benefits (IAS 26, 34) – see example 44.4. A statement of changes in net assets available for benefits includes, if applicable:

- employer contributions;
- employee contributions;

Example 44.4 *Defined Benefit Retirement Benefit Plan*

Statement of Changes in Net Assets Available for Benefits

	31 December	
	2002	*2001*
Investment income	*£000s*	*£000s*
Net (depreciation) appreciation in fair value of investments	(327,491)	909,726
Interest and dividends	201,887	195,589
Total investment (loss) income	(125,604)	1,105,315
Contributions		
Contributions by employer	117,659	116,684
Contributions by participants	54,570	51,404
Net (payments) receipts to or from pension plans of other entities on behalf of transferred participants	(2,950)	2,353
Total contributions	169,279	170,441
Total additions to net asset value	43,675	1,275,756
Benefit payments		
Pensions	(81,303)	(72,619)
Commutation payments	(22,994)	(15,077)
Contributions, withdrawal benefits, and interest paid to former participants on withdrawal	(4,953)	(4,145)
Lump sum death benefits	(693)	(608)
Total deductions to asset value	(109,943)	(92,449)
Net (decrease) increase in asset value	(66,268)	1,183,307
Net assets available for benefits		
Beginning of year	5,587,773	4,404,466
End of year	5,521,505	5,587,773

- investment income such as interest and dividends;
- other income;
- benefits paid or payable;
- administrative expenses;
- other expenses;
- income taxes;
- profits and losses on disposal of investments and changes in value of investments; and
- transfers from and to other plans.

(IAS 26, 35(b))

The report of a defined benefit retirement plan should also contain:

- a summary of significant accounting policies (IAS 26, 34) including the method used to calculate the actuarial present value of promised retirement benefits (IAS 26, 35);
- a description of the plan and the effect of any changes in the plan during the period (IAS 26, 34 and 36);
- the date of the actuarial valuation if it has not been prepared at the date of the report (IAS 26, 17);
- a description of the significant actuarial assumptions made (IAS 26, 35); and
- the effect of any changes in actuarial assumptions which have had a significant effect on the actuarial present value of promised retirement benefits (IAS 26, 18).

CHAPTER 45

Agriculture

45.1 RELEVANT STANDARD

IAS 41 *Agriculture*

The adoption of the required fair value model in IAS 41 will result in a major change in the way that many agricultural entities currently account for biological assets and agricultural produce. IAS 41 includes illustrative examples of the application of its accounting, presentation and disclosure requirements. As IAS 41 does not come into effect until 2003, no entities appear to have adopted it in their 2001 financial statements.

45.2 HISTORY

The IASC first considered a project on agriculture in 1985. The project proposal had been developed by the Nigerian board delegation and was one of four proposals considered by the IASC board in June 1985. The board decided not to proceed with the agriculture project and, indeed, the other industry specific proposal which dealt with extractive industries, preferring instead to focus on the components of what was to become the IASC's *Framework*. In 1989, the IASC began a comprehensive project on the financial reporting needs of developing and newly industrialised countries[1]. Among other things, the IASC sought to identify any specific projects that it should undertake in order to meet the diverse needs of the countries under review. While the project did not achieve its planned results, the IASC did identify the need for a project on agriculture.

The project was given added impetus when the World Bank suggested to the author, as the then secretary-general of the IASC, that it would fund an IASC project that was directed at the specific needs of developing countries. After extensive discussions between the Bank and the IASC's secretary-general, the Bank agreed in April 1994 to provide $650,000 funding for a project to develop an IAS on accounting for agriculture. The Bank's contribution was the largest amount of funding that the IASC had received or been promised from a single source. A key part of the proposed project was not only its relevance to developing countries but also the IASC's intention to involve research assistants from countries in which agriculture played an important role in their economies.

All that remained after the agreement between the IASC's secretary-general and the World Bank was for the IASC board to approve the project which it did in June 1994. The IASC published a DSOP in December 1996 and E65 *Agriculture* in July 1999. It approved IAS 41 in December 2000. IAS 41 applies to accounting periods beginning on or after 1 January 2003.

45.3 IOSCO

IAS 41 is not an IOSCO core standard and was not included in 'IAS 2000' endorsed by IOSCO in May 2000.

45.4 IAS 41 IN BRIEF

An entity should:

- measure a biological asset at each balance sheet date at its fair value less estimated point-of-sale costs;
- measure agricultural produce harvested from its biological assets at each balance sheet date at its fair value less estimated point-of-sale costs; and
- include all the resulting gains and losses in the profit or loss for the period.

There is a rebuttable presumption that the fair value of a biological asset can be measured reliably. That presumption can be rebutted but only from initial recognition. If the presumption is rebutted, the biological asset should be measured at cost less depreciation and any impairment losses. This cost approach is not permitted for agricultural produce harvested from the entity's biological assets.

45.5 AGRICULTURE

Agricultural activity is the management by an entity of the biological transformation of biological assets for sale, into agricultural produce or into additional biological assets (IAS 41, 5). A *biological asset* is a living animal or plant (IAS 41, 5), for example, a cow, a pig, a sheep, a tree, a bush or a cane. *Agricultural produce* is the harvested product of an entity's biological assets (IAS 41, 5), for example, milk, meat, hide, wool, rubber, tea, coffee beans, maize, apples or grapes.

Therefore, agricultural activity includes:

- the management of a flock of sheep for sale, for their wool, meat or milk, and for the production of more sheep;
- the management of a plantation for sale, for products such as timber, rubber and fruit or nuts, and the production of more trees; and
- the management of a sugar cane, tea or coffee plantation for the production of sugar, molasses, tea and coffee and the creation of more cane or bushes.

Agricultural activity does not include the storage or processing of agricultural produce after its harvest even when that process is an extension of the agricultural process or represents an ageing or maturation process (IAS 41, B 8-11). After harvest, agricultural produce retained by the entity is dealt with in accordance with IAS 2 (see chapter 26) or other relevant IFRS. The carrying amount of the harvested produce determined in accordance with IAS 41 is its cost for the purposes of IAS 2 or other IFRS. Therefore, if a farm processes milk into cheese, it accounts for the milk up to the point of its production in accordance with IAS 41 and thereafter in accordance with IAS 2. The carrying amount of the milk determined in accordance with IAS 41 is the cost of that milk for the purposes of determining the cost of the cheese under IAS 2.

IAS 41 does not deal with:

- land or other property, plant and equipment used in agricultural activity – these assets are deal with in accordance with IAS 16 (see chapter 21);
- intangible assets related to agricultural activity – these assets are dealt with in accordance with IAS 38 (see chapter 23); or
- the sale of biological assets or agricultural produce – this is dealt with in accordance with IAS 18 (see chapter 29).

IAS 41 does deal with government grants associated with biological assets and agricultural produce and, in some circumstances, requires different accounting from that required by IAS 20 (see chapter 34).

45.6 RECOGNITION OF BIOLOGICAL ASSETS AND AGRICULTURAL PRODUCE

An entity should recognise a biological asset or agricultural produce when:

- it controls the asset as a result of past events;
- it is probable that future economic benefits associated with the asset will flow to the entity; and
- the fair value or cost of the asset can be measured reliably.

(IAS 41, 16)

This is the same recognition requirement that is included in the *Framework* and other IFRS. However, the fair value model in IAS 41 means that biological assets and agricultural produce may be recognised earlier than they would be recognised under other IFRS. For example, IAS 41 requires the immediate recognition of new-born animals or newly harvested agricultural produce notwithstanding that their costs may not be estimated reliably.

45.7 INITIAL AND SUBSEQUENT MEASUREMENT

IAS 41 adopts a fair value model which is broadly the same as the fair value model in IAS 39 for certain financial assets and in IAS 40 for investment property[2]. Unlike IAS 39, however, IAS 40 does not allow some gains and losses to be included in equity. Unlike IAS 40, IAS 41 does not permit the use of a cost model.

An entity should measure a biological asset on initial recognition and at each subsequent balance sheet date at its fair value less estimated point-of-sale costs except in the specific circumstances that IAS 41 allows the use of cost (IAS 41, 12). The carrying amount of biological assets is, therefore, their exit price unlike the entry price approach adopted in IAS 39 for the measurement of financial assets.

An entity should measure agricultural produce harvested from its biological assets at its fair value less estimated point-of-sale costs at the point of harvest (IAS 41, 13). Again, it is an exit price rather than an entry price and there are no exceptions permitted to this requirement. The carrying amount of agricultural produce is not adjusted to fair value less point-of-sale costs at any later balance sheet date. The entity applies IAS 2 or another IFRS to that produce after harvest. As explained earlier, fair value less estimated point-of-sale costs at the point of harvest is cost for the purposes of the application of IAS 2 or another IFRS.

IAS 41 presumes that the fair value of a biological asset can be measured reliably. The presumption can be rebutted only:

- on initial recognition of the biological asset; and
- for a biological asset for which market-determined prices or values are not available and for which alternative estimates of fair value are 'clearly unreliable'.

(IAS 41, 30)

In such a case, and only in this case, the entity should measure the biological asset at cost less any accumulated depreciation and any accumulated impairment losses (IAS 41, 30). Cost is determined by reference to IAS 2 and IAS 16 and impairment losses are determined by reference to IAS 36. An entity that uses this approach must make additional disclosures (see below).

If, at a later date, the fair value of the biological asset becomes reliably measurable, the entity should measure the asset at fair value less estimated point-of-sale costs (IAS 41, 30). It should not continue to use the cost approach after the date at which it can reliably determine fair value. Again, additional disclosures are required (see below).

It is important to acknowledge that there is not a similar exemption from the fair value model for agricultural produce. IAS 41 argues that the fair value of agricultural produce at the point of harvest can always be measured reliably (IAS 41, 32).

45.7.1 Determination of fair value

Fair value is the amount at which the biological asset or agricultural produce could be exchanged between knowledgeable, willing parties in an arm's length transaction (IAS 41, 5 and 8).

When little biological transformation has taken place, cost may be used to approximate fair value. For example, the cost of acquiring animals shortly before the balance sheet date may approximate their fair value at the balance sheet date. Similarly, the cost of acquiring and planting seed may approximate the fair value of maize planted immediately prior to a balance sheet date. The cost of acquiring, planting and nurturing young trees may also approximate the fair value of a plantation that will require many more years to mature and generate agricultural produce. In such cases, cost based measurements may give a reliable estimate of fair value at a subsequent balance sheet date. In all other cases, however, cost is unlikely to provide an adequate basis for the determination of fair value.

In many countries, biological assets and agricultural produce are traded on active markets. An *active market* is a market in which:

- the items traded are homogenous;
- willing buyers and sellers can normally be found at any time; and
- prices are available to the public.

(IAS 41, 8)

When an active market exists for a biological asset or agricultural produce, the quoted price in that market is the appropriate basis for determining the fair value of that asset. The market price may need to be adjusted for transport and other costs for biological assets and agricultural produce that is not physically located at the market. The market price may also need to be adjusted for differences in the attributes of the biological assets or agricultural produce, for example the age and condition of cattle or the quality of coffee beans, barley or picked fruit.

An entity may be able to sell its biological assets or agricultural produce on different active markets. In such circumstances it uses the price from the market that it expects to use to sell the assets or produce (IAS 41, 17). Price differences between active markets may, of course, reflect only differences in transport and similar costs or point-of-sale costs and, therefore, may not affect fair value or fair value less point-of-sale costs.

Living plants are usually physically attached to land. When separate market prices for the plants are not available, an entity may use information about the combined assets (the plants and the land) to determine fair value for the plants. For example, an entity may deduct the fair value of raw land and land improvements from the fair value of the combined assets to determine the fair value of plants attached to that land (IAS 41, 25).

Often agricultural entities enter into contracts to sell their biological assets or agricultural produce at a future date. For example, a farm may have pre-sold its expected wheat harvest prior to its actual harvesting. Contract prices may or may not reflect the fair value of the assets or produce at the balance sheet date because the fair value should reflect the current market and the current condition of the biological assets or agricultural produce at the balance sheet date. Therefore, for example, the fair value of unharvested wheat is based on the current market price of the plants in the field; it is not the current market price of harvested wheat or the contracted price for the sale of the wheat after harvesting.

When an active market does not exist for a biological asset or agricultural produce, an entity should use the following techniques for determining fair value:

- the most recent market transaction price (provided that there has not been a significant change in economic circumstances between the date of that transaction and the balance sheet date);
- market prices for similar assets, adjusted to reflect differences between the assets; and
- sector benchmarks such as the value of an orchard expressed per export tray, bushel, or hectare or the value of cattle expressed per kilogram of meat.

(IAS 41, 18)

If market-determined prices or values are not available for a biological asset (but not agricultural produce) in its present condition, the entity should determine fair value by discounting the expected net cash flows from the asset using a current market-determined, pre-tax rate of interest

(IAS 41, 19). The present condition of a biological asset excludes any increases in value from additional biological transformation, harvesting, and selling. The expected cash flows or the discount rate reflect possible variations in the cash flows. The cash flows do not include those for:

- financing the biological asset;
- taxation; or
- re-establishing the biological asset after harvest, for example, replanting or feeding trees after the harvest of agricultural produce.

(IAS 41, 22)

45.7.2 Point of sale costs

Point-of-sale costs include:

- commissions to brokers and dealers;
- levies by regulatory agencies and commodity exchanges; and
- transfer taxes and duties.

(IAS 41, 14)

Point-of-sale costs exclude transport and other costs necessary to get assets to a market (IAS 41, 14). However, fair value may need to be reduced by such transport and other costs in order to ensure that it reflects the location and condition of the biological asset or agricultural produce. For example, prices at an active market may be for assets or produce physically available at that market, in which case the fair value of the asset or produce at a farm is its market price less the transport and other costs of getting the asset or produce to the market. Similarly, prices for delivery at the farm usually assume that the purchaser will bear the transport and other costs.

While acknowledging the arguments for and against the deduction of point-of-sale costs, the IASC concluded that fair value less point-of-sale costs is a more relevant measurement of biological assets. It also acknowledged that the failure to deduct point-of-sale costs from biological assets or agriculture produce could result in the deferral of losses (IAS 41, B26).

45.8 GAINS AND LOSSES

An entity should include all gains and losses in the net profit or loss for the period in which they arise (IAS 41, 26 and 28). Under the fair value approach in IAS 41, gains and losses may arise both:

- on the initial recognition of a biological asset or agricultural produce at fair value less estimated point-of-sale costs; and
- from a change in the fair value less estimated point-of-sale costs of a biological asset.

For example, a gain or loss may arise when:

- an animal is born and is, therefore, recognised as an asset at its fair value less point-of-sale costs;
- living plants and animals grow and, therefore, their fair value changes;
- living plants are harvested and agricultural produce is recognised at fair value less point-of-sale costs;
- animals generate or are converted into agricultural produce which is recognised at fair value less point-of-sale costs.

A loss may also arise on the initial recognition of a biological asset. For example, the fair value less estimated point-of-sale costs of a newly purchased animal is likely to be less than the cost of acquisition plus transaction costs of the animal. Similarly the harvesting of agricultural produce may result in a decline in the fair value less estimated point-of-sale costs of the related biological asset. For example, the harvesting of wheat results in the recognition of agricultural produce at fair value less point-of-sale costs but also results in a decline in the fair value of the wheat plants.

The immediate recognition of all the gains and losses in the income statement simplifies the accounting for expenses associated with agricultural activity. Under the fair value model, there is no need to consider whether any costs should be capitalised as part of the cost of biological assets or agricultural produce. For example, the fair value model means that all the replanting or harvesting costs associated with plantations or crops such as wheat and barley should be recognised as an expense in the period in which they are incurred. Similarly, all the feed and other costs associated with agricultural animals should be recognised as an expense in which they are incurred. The capitalisation of borrowing costs, while permitted by IAS 23, serves only to reduce borrowing costs and gains on biological assets by matching amounts. The sale of agricultural produce subsequent to its harvest may result in further gains. These gains are recognised on the sale in accordance with IAS 18 (see chapter 29). Similarly, the storage of agricultural produce increases the risk that its cost exceeds its net realisable value.

45.9 GOVERNMENT GRANTS

An unconditional government grant related to a biological asset measured at fair value less point-of-sale costs should be recognised as income when it becomes receivable (IAS 41, 34). If the receipt or the retention of the grant is conditional, the entity should recognise the grant only when the conditions are met (IAS 41, 35).

This approach is different from that required by IAS 20 (see IAS 41, B63-73) in two respects:

- the grant is recognised in income once it is receivable and any conditions are met and not over the life of the asset; and
- when the grant is conditional, it is recognised in income once the conditions are met and not when there is reasonable assurance that they will be met.

For example, a government may subsidise the cost of acquisition of cattle. If the subsidy is unconditional, IAS 41 requires that the grant should be recognised and included in income as soon as it is receivable. In contrast, while IAS 20 requires the recognition of the subsidy on the balance sheet at about the same time, it requires that the grant should be recognised as income over the useful life of the cattle, which may be several years.

In the rare circumstances in which a biological asset is measured at cost less depreciation and impairment losses, any government grant related to that asset must be dealt with in accordance with IAS 20 (IAS 41, 38) (see chapter 34).

IAS 41 does not deal with government grants related to agricultural produce, for example subsidies for meat or milk. Such subsidies are usually payable only on the sale of the produce and are, therefore, recognised as income at the same time as the sale. A subsidy based on production would be recognised as income when it becomes receivable if it is accounted for using the requirements of IAS 40 but when the produce is sold if it is accounted for using the requirements of IAS 20.

45.10 DISCLOSURE

An entity should present the carrying amount of its biological assets separately on the face of its balance sheet (IAS 41, 39) and provide a description of each group of biological assets (IAS 41, 41).

An entity should disclose:

- the aggregate gains or losses during the period on the measurement and re-measurement of biological assets and agricultural produce (IAS 41, 40);
- the gains or losses on the sale of biological assets carried at cost less depreciation and impairment losses (IAS 41, 55);
- the methods and significant assumptions applied in determining the fair value of each group of agricultural produce at the point of harvest (IAS 41, 47);
- the methods and significant assumptions applied in determining the fair value of each group of biological assets (IAS 41, 47);
- the fair value less estimated point-of-sale costs of agricultural produce harvested during the period, determined at the point of harvest (IAS 41, 48);
- the existence and carrying amounts of biological assets whose title is restricted (IAS 41, 49(a));
- the existence and carrying amounts of biological assets pledged as security for liabilities (IAS 41, 49(a));
- the amount of commitments for the development or acquisition of biological assets (IAS 41, 49(b));
- the entity's financial risk management strategies related to agricultural activity (IAS 41, 49(c));
- the nature and extent of government grants recognised in the financial statements and dealt with in accordance with IAS 41 (IAS 41, 57);
- unfulfilled conditions and other contingencies attaching to those government grants (IAS 41, 57); and
- significant decreases expected in the level of government grants dealt with in accordance with IAS 41 (IAS 41, 57).

When an entity measures biological assets at their cost less any accumulated depreciation and any accumulated impairment losses, it should disclose for such biological assets:

- a description of the assets;
- an explanation of why fair value cannot be measured reliably;
- if possible, the range of estimates within which fair value is highly likely to lie;
- the depreciation method used;
- the useful lives or the depreciation rates used; and
- the gross carrying amount and the accumulated depreciation (aggregated with accumulated impairment losses) at the beginning and end of the period.

(IAS 41, 54)

When the fair value of biological assets previously measured at their cost less any accumulated depreciation and any accumulated impairment losses becomes reliably measurable during the current period, an entity should disclose for those assets:

- a description of the assets;
- an explanation of why fair value has become reliably measurable; and
- the effect of the change.

(IAS 41, 56)

An entity should describe:

- the nature of its activities involving each group of biological assets; and
- non-financial measures or estimates of the physical quantities of each group of the enterprise's biological assets at the end of the period and the output of agricultural produce during the period.

(IAS 41, 46)

This disclosure may be made in the financial statement or elsewhere in the entity's annual report.

An entity should present a reconciliation of changes in the carrying amount of biological assets between the beginning and the end of the current period that includes:

- the gain or loss arising from changes in fair value less estimated point-of-sale costs;
- increases due to purchases;
- decreases due to sales;
- decreases due to harvest;
- depreciation (if applicable);
- impairment losses (if applicable);
- reversals of impairment losses (if applicable);
- increases resulting from business combinations;
- net exchange differences arising on the translation of financial statements of a foreign entity; and
- other changes.

(IAS 41, 50 and 55)

Comparative information is not required for this reconciliation.

When an entity measures biological assets at their cost less any accumulated depreciation and any accumulated impairment losses, the reconciliation should disclose amounts related to such biological assets separately (IAS 41, 55). In addition, the reconciliation should include certain amounts related to those biological assets (IAS 41, 55). Specifically, an entity is encouraged to disclose:

- a quantified description of each group of biological assets, distinguishing between consumable and bearer biological assets or between mature and immature biological assets (IAS 41, 43);

- the amount of changes in fair value less estimated point-of-sale costs included in net profit or loss that arise from physical changes in the assets (IAS 41, 51); and
- the amount of changes in fair value less estimated point-of-sale costs included in net profit or loss that arise from price changes (IAS 41, 51).

---

[1] For the background to, the objectives of, and the issues addressed by, this project, see David Cairns, 'Aid for the Developing World', *Accountancy*, March 1990, pp82–3.
[2] The arguments for and against the fair value model and a cost model are set out in IAS 41, B13-21.

APPENDIX 1

Disclosure Checklist

All references are to paragraph numbers in *International Accounting Standards 2002*. The checklist does not deal with the specialised requirements for banks and similar financial institutions in IAS 30 *Disclosures in the Financial Statements of Banks and Similar Financial Institutions* or agriculture in IAS 41 *Agriculture*.

REPORTING ENTITY

Name (IAS 1, 46 (a))
Domicile (IAS 1, 102 (a))
Legal form (IAS 1, 102 (a))
Country of incorporation (IAS 1, 102 (a))
Address of registered office (IAS 1, 102 (a))
Principal place of business (if different from registered office) (IAS 1, 102(a))
Nature of operations and principal activities (IAS 1, 102(b))

GENERAL

Fact that financial statements comply with IASs (IAS 1, 11)
Fact that IAS applied before effective date (IAS 1, 19)
Each material item (IAS 1, 29)
Number of employees at the end of the period or the average for the period (IAS 1, 102(d))
Date when financial statements authorised for issuance and who gave that authorisation (IAS 10, 16)
Fact if owners or others have the power to amend the financial statements after issuance (IAS 10, 16)

COMPARATIVE INFORMATION

For all numerical information (with certain specified exceptions) (IAS 1, 38)
For all narrative and description information when relevant to understanding of current period's financial statements (IAS 1, 38)

REPORTING CURRENCY

Measurement and presentation currencies (IAS 1, 46(d) and SIC 19, 17)
Reason for using a measurement currency different from the currency of the country in which the entity is domiciled (IAS 21, 43 as interpreted by SIC 19, 10(a))
Reason for using a presentation currency different from the measurement currency and the method used in the translation process (IAS 21, 43, SIC 19(c) and SIC 30, 8)
Reason for change in the measurement or presentation currency (IAS 21, 43 as interpreted by SIC 19, 10(b))
Rates of exchange between presentation currency and measurement currency when measurement currency is currency of hyperinflationary economy (SIC 30, 9)
Level of precision (thousands, millions etc.) (IAS 1, 46(e))
Measurement and display currency of convenience translations (SIC 30, 10)

GOING CONCERN

Uncertainties that cast doubt on the entity's ability to remain a going concern (IAS 1, 23)
Fact that going concern assumption not followed (IAS 1, 23)

ACCOUNTING POLICIES

Measurement basis (IAS 1, 97 (a))
Each policy necessary for a proper understanding of the financial statements (IAS 1, 97(b))
Proportions of item to which different policies have been applied in consolidated financial statements (IAS 27, 21)

FAIR PRESENTATION OVERRIDE

Fact that the financial statements fairly present the entity's financial position, financial performance and cash flows (IAS 1, 13)
Fact that the entity has departed from an IAS in order to achieve a fair presentation (IAS 1, 13)
IAS from which departed (IAS 1, 13)
Nature of the departure (IAS 1, 13)
Treatment required by the IAS and reason why would be misleading (IAS 1, 13)
Treatment adopted (IAS 1, 13)
Impact on net profit or loss, assets, liabilities, equity and cash flows (IAS 1, 13)

CHANGES IN ACCOUNTING POLICY

Reasons for change (IAS 8, 53 and 57)
Tax expense relating to changes in accounting policy (IAS 12, 49)

Benchmark Treatment

Adjustment for the current period and each period presented (IAS 8, 53)
Adjustment relating to periods prior to those included in the comparative information (IAS 8, 53)
Fact that comparative information has been restated (IAS 8, 53)
Fact if impracticable to restate comparative information (IAS 8, 53)

Allowed Alternative Treatment

Adjustment recognised in net profit or loss in the current period (IAS 8, 57)
Adjustment included in each period for which pro forma information is presented (IAS 8, 57)
Adjustment relating to periods prior to those included in the financial statements (IAS 8, 57)
Fact if impracticable to present pro forma information (IAS 8, 57)

FUNDAMENTAL ERRORS

Nature of the fundamental error (IAS 8, 37 and IAS 8, 40)
Amount of the correction for the current period (IAS 8, 37 and IAS 8, 40)
Tax expense relating to fundamental errors (IAS 12, 49)

Benchmark Treatment

Amount of the correction for each prior period presented (IAS 8, 37)
Amount of the correction relating to periods prior to those included in the comparative information (IAS 8, 37)
Fact that comparative information has been restated (IAS 8, 37)
Fact if it is impracticable to restate comparative information (IAS 8, 37)

Allowed Alternative Treatment

Amount of the correction included in each period for which pro forma information is presented (IAS 8, 40)
Amount of the correction relating to periods prior to those included in the pro forma information (IAS 8, 40)
Fact if impracticable to present pro forma information (IAS 8, 40)

PROFIT

Profit or loss from ordinary activities (IAS 8, 11)
Nature and amount of income and expense that are of such size, nature or incidence that disclosure is relevant to explain performance (IAS 8, 16)
Nature and amount of a change in an accounting estimate that has a material effect in the current period or which is expected to have a material effect in subsequent periods (or fact that impracticable to quantify the amount) (IAS 8, 30)
Nature and amount of each extraordinary item (IAS 8, 11)

CASH FLOW STATEMENT

Cash flows classified by operating, investing and financing activities (IAS 7, 10)
Cash flows from:

- extraordinary items (IAS 7, 29)
- interest and dividends received and paid (IAS 7, 31)
- income taxes (IAS 7, 35)
- acquisitions and disposals of subsidiaries (IAS 7, 39)

Non-cash investing and financing transactions (IAS 7, 43)

Components of cash and cash equivalents and reconciliation to equivalent items in balance sheet (IAS 7, 45)
Cash and cash equivalents not immediately available for use generally or by the group (IAS 7, 48)

CONSOLIDATED FINANCIAL STATEMENTS

List of significant subsidiaries including:

- name
- country of incorporation or residence
- proportion of ownership interest and, if different, proportion of voting power held

(IAS 27, 32)

Nature of the relationship when parent does not own, directly or indirectly through subsidiaries, more than one half of the voting power of subsidiary (IAS 27, 32)
Name of an entity in which more than one half of the voting power is owned, directly or indirectly through subsidiaries, but which is not a subsidiary (IAS 27, 32)
Reasons for not consolidating a subsidiary (IAS 27, 32)
Name and registered office of parent that publishes consolidated financial statements when consolidated financial statements are not presented because entity is wholly owned or virtually wholly owned subsidiary (IAS 27, 8)

BUSINESS COMBINATIONS

In the period in which the combination has taken place:

- the names and descriptions of the combining entities
- the method of accounting for the combination
- the effective date of the combination for accounting purposes
- any operations resulting from the business combination which the entity has decided to dispose of

(IAS 22, 86)

Same information for a business combination effected after the balance sheet date as for business combination during the period (unless impracticable) (IAS 22, 96)

Acquisitions

In the period in which the acquisition has taken place:

- the percentage of voting shares acquired (IAS 22, 87)
- the cost of acquisition (IAS 22, 87)
- description of the purchase consideration paid or contingently payable (IAS 22, 87)
- fact and reasons if the fair values of the identifiable assets and liabilities or the purchase consideration can only be determined on a provisional basis (IAS 22, 93)
- effect of the acquisition of subsidiaries on financial position, the results for the period and the corresponding amounts for the preceding period (IAS 27, 32)

Same information for provisions for terminating or reducing the activities of the acquiree as for other provisions (see IAS 37) (IAS 22, 92)
Subsequent adjustments to provisional fair values (IAS 22, 93) and to the carrying amounts of identifiable assets or liabilities or goodwill or negative goodwill arising on such adjustments (SIC 22, 8)
When published price of an equity instrument issued as purchase consideration not used as fair value:

- reasons why published price is not the fair value
- the method and significant assumptions applied in determining the fair value
- difference between the published price and fair value

(SIC 28, 7)

When an equity instrument issued as purchase consideration does not have a published price:

- method and significant assumptions applied in determining the fair value

(SIC 28, 8)

Uniting of Interests

In the period in which the uniting of interests has taken place:

- description and number of shares issued
- percentage of each entity's voting shares exchanged
- amounts of assets and liabilities contributed by each entity
- sales revenue, other operating revenues, extraordinary items and the net profit or loss of each entity prior to the date of the combination

which are included in the net profit or loss shown by the combined entity's financial statements

(IAS 22, 94)

ASSOCIATES

List and description of significant associates (IAS 28, 27)
Proportion of ownership interest and, if different, the proportion of voting power held (IAS 28, 27)
Share of the profits or losses (IAS 28, 28)
Share of associates' extraordinary items or fundamental errors (IAS 28, 28)
Share of unrecognised losses for period and cumulatively when recognition of share of losses has been discontinued (SIC 20, 10)

JOINT VENTURES

List and description of interests in significant joint ventures (IAS 31, 48)
Proportion of ownership interest held in jointly controlled entities (IAS 31, 48)
Aggregate amounts of each of current assets, long-term assets, current liabilities, long-term liabilities, income and expenses related to its interests in joint ventures (IAS 31, 48)

FOREIGN OPERATIONS

When there is a change in the classification of a significant foreign operation:

- the nature of the change in classification
- the reason for the change
- the impact of the change in classification on shareholders' equity
- the impact on net profit or loss for each prior period presented had the change in classification occurred at the beginning of the earliest period presented

(IAS 21, 44)

Method used to translate goodwill and fair value adjustments (IAS 21, 45)

PROPERTY, PLANT AND EQUIPMENT

In respect of each class:

- measurement basis (IAS 16, 60)
- gross carrying amount for each basis when more than one measurement basis used (IAS 16, 60)
- gross carrying amount and the accumulated depreciation (aggregated with accumulated impairment losses) at the beginning and end of the period (IAS 16, 60)
- reconciliation of the carrying amount at the beginning and end of the period (IAS 16, 60)
- depreciation method (IAS 16, 60)
- useful lives or depreciation rates (IAS 16, 60)
- net carrying amount subject to finance leases (IAS 17, 23(a))
- gross carrying amounts, accumulated depreciation and accumulated impairment losses of assets subject to operating leases (IAS 17, 48(a))

Exchange differences arising during the period included in carrying amount (IAS 21, 42)
When items stated at revalued amounts:

- basis used to revalue assets
- effective date of the revaluation
- whether an independent valuer was involved
- nature of any indices used to determine replacement cost
- carrying amount of each class if had been carried under the benchmark treatment

(IAS 16, 64)

Accounting policy for restoration costs (IAS 16, 61)
Existence and amounts of restrictions on title (IAS 16, 61)
Property, plant and equipment pledged as security for liabilities (IAS 16, 61)
Property, plant and equipment in course of construction (IAS 16, 61)
Commitments for acquisition of property, plant and equipment (IAS 16, 61)

INVESTMENT PROPERTY

Criteria to distinguish investment property from owner-occupied property and from property held for sale in the ordinary course of business (IAS 40, 66)

Methods and significant assumptions in determining fair value of investment property including whether supported by market evidence or other factors (IAS 40, 66)
Use of professionally qualified valuer to determine fair value (IAS 40, 66)
Amounts included in the income statement for:

- rental income
- direct operating expenses from property that generated rental income
- direct operating expenses from property that did not generate rental income

(IAS 40, 66)

Restrictions on the realisability of investment property or the remittance of income and proceeds of disposal (IAS 40, 66)
Contractual obligations to purchase, construct or develop investment property or for repairs, maintenance or enhancements (IAS 40, 66)

Fair Value Model

Reconciliation of carrying amount at the beginning and end of the period with separate disclosure of investment property carried on IAS 16 cost basis (IAS 40, 67)
For investment property carried on IAS 16 cost basis:

- description
- why fair value cannot be reliably measured
- range of estimates within which fair value is highly likely to lie
- carrying amount and recognised gain or loss on disposals

(IAS 40, 68)

Cost Model

Depreciation methods (IAS 40, 69)
Useful lives or depreciation rates (IAS 40, 69)
Reconciliation of carrying amount at the beginning and end of the period (IAS 40, 69)
Fair value (IAS 40, 69)

INTANGIBLE ASSETS

For each class, distinguishing between internally generated and others:

- useful lives or the amortisation rates
- amortisation methods

- gross carrying amount and the accumulated amortisation (aggregated with accumulated impairment losses) at the beginning and end of the period
- the line item(s) of the income statement in which the amortisation is included
- reconciliation of the carrying amount at the beginning and end of the period

(IAS 38, 107)

Reason if amortised over more than twenty years (IAS 38, 111)
Description, carrying amount and remaining amortisation period of any individual intangible asset which is material to the financial statements as a whole (IAS 38, 111)
For intangible assets acquired by way of a government grant and initially recognised at fair value:

- fair value initially recognised
- carrying amount
- whether carried under the benchmark or the allowed alternative treatment

(IAS 38, 111)

Restrictions on title (IAS 38, 111)
Intangible assets pledged as security for liabilities (IAS 38, 111)
Commitments for the acquisition of intangible assets (IAS 38, 111)
If carried at revalued amounts:

- date of revaluation
- carrying amount of revalued intangible assets
- the carrying amount that would have been included if carried under the benchmark treatment

(IAS 38, 113)

Research and development expenditure recognised as an expense (IAS 38, 115)

GOODWILL

Amortisation period (IAS 22, 88)
Reason if amortised over more than 20 years and factors which played a significant role in determining the useful life (IAS 22, 88)
Amortisation basis used if not straight line and reason (IAS 22, 88)

Line item in the income statement in which amortisation is included (IAS 22, 88)
Reconciliation of the carrying amount at the beginning and end of the period showing:

- the gross amount and the accumulated amortisation (aggregated with accumulated impairment losses) at the beginning of the period
- additional goodwill recognised during the period
- adjustments from subsequent identification or changes in value of identifiable assets and liabilities
- goodwill derecognised on the disposal of all or part of the business to which it relates
- amortisation during the period
- impairment losses during the period
- impairment losses reversed during the period
- other changes in the carrying amount
- the gross amount and the accumulated amortisation (aggregated with accumulated impairment losses) at the end of the period.

(IAS 22, 88)

NEGATIVE GOODWILL

Extent to which recognised as income to match losses and expenses which were identified in the entity's plan for the acquisition, together with a description of and the amount and timing of the losses and expenses (IAS 22, 91)
Amortisation period (IAS 22, 91)
Line item in the income statement in which amortisation is included (IAS 22, 91)
Reconciliation of the carrying amount of goodwill at the beginning and end of the period showing:

- gross amount and the accumulated amortisation at the beginning of the period
- additional negative goodwill recognised during the period
- adjustments resulting from subsequent identification or changes in value of identifiable assets and liabilities
- negative goodwill derecognised on the disposal of all or part of the business to which it relates
- amortisation during the period showing separately the amount recognised as income to match losses and expenses which were identified in the entity's plan for the acquisition
- other changes in the carrying amount

- the gross amount and the accumulated amortisation (aggregated with accumulated impairment losses) at the end of the period.

(IAS 22, 91)

IMPAIRMENT OF ASSETS

For each class of assets:

- amount of impairment losses recognised in the income statement
- amount of reversals of impairment losses recognised in the income statement
- amount of impairment losses recognised directly in equity
- amount of reversals of impairment losses recognised directly in equity

(IAS 36, 113)

If an impairment loss is material to the financial statements as a whole:

- events and circumstances that led to the recognition or reversal of the impairment loss
- amount of the impairment loss recognised or reversed
- for an individual asset, its nature and the primary reportable segment to which it belongs
- for a cash generating unit, a description, amount of impairment loss recognised or reversed by class of assets and primary segment, and (if unit has changed) current and former way of aggregating assets and the reasons for change
- whether the recoverable amount is net selling price or value in use
- basis used to determine net selling price if recoverable amount is net selling price
- discount rate used in the current and previous estimate if recoverable amount is value in use

(IAS 36, 117)

If impairment losses recognised (reversed) during the period are material in aggregate:

- main classes of assets affected
- main events and circumstances that led to the recognition of these impairment losses

(IAS 36, 118)

INVENTORIES

Total carrying amount (IAS 2, 34)
Carrying amount in appropriate classifications (merchandise, production supplies, materials, work in progress and finished goods) (IAS 2, 34)
Carrying amount of inventories at net realisable value (IAS 2, 34)
Carrying amount of inventories pledged as security for liabilities (IAS 2, 34)
When the cost determined using LIFO, difference between the amount of inventories in the balance sheet and either:

- lower of FIFO/weighted average cost and net realisable value, or
- lower of current cost and net realisable value

(IAS 2, 36)

Exchange differences arising during the period included in carrying amount (IAS 21, 42)

CONSTRUCTION CONTRACTS IN PROGRESS

Aggregate costs incurred and recognised profits (less recognised losses) to date (IAS 11, 40)
Advances received (IAS 11, 40)
Retentions (IAS 10, 40)

SERVICE CONCESSIONS

Description, significant terms and details of arrangements (SIC 29, 6)

PROVISIONS

For each class of provision:

- carrying amount at the beginning and end of the period
- additional provisions made in the period, including increases to existing provisions
- amounts used during the period
- unused amounts reversed during the period

- the increase in the discounted amount arising from the passage of time
- effect of any change in the discount rate
- nature of the obligation
- expected timing of any outflows of economic benefits
- uncertainties about the amount or timing of those outflows, including major assumptions
- any expected reimbursement, stating amount of any asset recognised for that expected reimbursement

(IAS 37, 84 and 85)

CONTINGENT LIABILITIES

For each class of contingent liability:

- nature
- estimate of its financial effect
- uncertainties relating to the amount or timing of any outflow
- possibility of any reimbursement

(IAS 37, 86)

Significant financing restrictions, renewal or purchase options, contingent rentals and other contingencies arising from leases in the financia statements of a lessee (IAS 17, 24)
Unfulfilled conditions and other contingencies attaching to government assistance that has been recognised (IAS 20, 39)
Contingencies in relation to interests in joint ventures (IAS 31, 45)
Share in each of the contingencies incurred jointly with other venturers (IAS 31, 45)
Share of the contingencies of the joint ventures themselves for which contingently liable (IAS 31, 45)
Contingencies because contingently liable for the liabilities of the other venturers of a joint venture (IAS 31, 45)

CONTINGENT ASSETS

When an inflow of economic benefits is probable:

- nature
- estimate of financial effect

(IAS 37, 89)

LIABILITIES

Amount of liability excluded from current liabilities when due to be settled within 12 months but intended refinancing (IAS 1, 63)
Security given in respect of liabilities (IAS 2, 34 and IAS 16, 6)

EQUITY

For each class of share capital:

- the number of shares authorised
- number of shares issued and fully paid
- number of shares issued and not fully paid
- par value
- reconciliation of the number of shares outstanding at the beginning and at the end of the year
- rights, preferences and restrictions attaching to class including restrictions on the distribution of dividends and the repayment of capital
- shares in the entity held by the entity itself or by subsidiaries or associates of the entity
- shares reserved for issuance under options and sales contracts, including the terms and amounts

(IAS 1, 74(a))

Amounts of reductions of equity for treasury shares (SIC 16, 6)
Description of the nature and purpose of each reserve (IAS 1, 74(b))
Revaluation surplus (IAS 16, 64 and IAS 25, 49)
Foreign exchange differences classified as equity (IAS 21, 42)
Costs of equity transactions deducted from equity in period (SIC 17, 9)
Amount of dividends which have been proposed but not formally approved for payment (IAS 1, 74(c))
Amount of any cumulative preference dividends not recognised (IAS 1, 74(d))

INCOME

Amount of revenue arising from:

- the sale of goods (IAS 18, 35)
- the rendering of services (IAS 18, 35)
- construction contracts (IAS 11, 39)

- interest (IAS 18, 35 and IAS 25, 49)
- royalties (IAS 18, 35 and IAS 25, 49)
- dividends (IAS 18, 35 and IAS 25, 49)
- rentals (IAS 25, 49)

Amount arising from exchanges of goods or services included in each significant category (IAS 18, 35)
Significant amounts included in income for:

- profits and losses on disposal of current investments
- changes in value of such investments

(IAS 25, 49)

Method used to determine:

- stage of completion of transactions involving the rendering of services (IAS 18, 35)
- stage of completion of contracts in progress (IAS 11, 39)
- contract revenue in period (IAS 11, 39)

EXPENSES

Cost of sales (cost of inventories recognised as an expense during the period) or operating costs (for example, raw materials, labour, other operating costs and the net change in inventories) (IAS 2, 37)
Amount of reversal of any write-down to inventories recognised as income and the circumstances or events that led to the reversal (IAS 2, 34)
Retirement benefit costs (IAS 19, 46 and 120)
Staff costs (IAS 1, 83)
Research and development costs (IAS 38, 115)
Foreign exchange differences (IAS 21, 42)
Nature and the amount of each extraordinary item (IAS 8, 11)

INCOME TAX ASSETS AND LIABILITIES

Amount and expiry date of deductible temporary differences, unused tax losses, and unused tax credits for which no deferred tax asset is recognised (IAS 12, 82)
Aggregate amount of temporary differences associated with investments in subsidiaries, branches and associates and interests in joint ventures, for which deferred tax liabilities have not been recognised (IAS 12, 82)

For each type of temporary difference, unused tax losses and unused tax credits:

- the amount of the deferred tax assets and liabilities
- the amount of the deferred tax income or expense
- in respect of discontinued operations, the tax expense relating to:
  - the gain or loss on discontinuance
  - the profit or loss from the ordinary activities of the discontinued operation

(IAS 12, 81)

Amount of a deferred tax asset and the nature of the evidence supporting recognition when:

- the utilisation of the deferred tax asset is dependent on future taxable profits in excess of the profits arising from the reversal of existing taxable temporary differences
- the entity has suffered a loss in either the current or preceding period in the tax jurisdiction to which the deferred tax asset relates

(IAS 12, 82)

Amount of tax consequences of dividends payable that were proposed or declared before the financial statements were authorised for issue but not recognised as a liability (IAS 12, 81)
When different taxes apply to distributed and retained profits, nature of potential income tax consequences that would result from payment of dividends to shareholders (IAS 12, 82A)
Major components of tax expense (income) (IAS 12, 79)
Aggregate current and deferred tax relating to items that are charged or credited to equity (IAS 12, 82) including amounts attributable to costs of equity transactions (SIC 17, 9)
Tax expense (income) relating to extraordinary items (IAS 12, 82)
Explanation of the relationship between tax expense (income) and accounting profit (IAS 12, 82)
Explanation of changes in the applicable tax rate (IAS 12, 82)

LEASES

Transactions involving the substance of a lease:

- description
- underlying assets and any restrictions on use
- the life and other significant terms of the arrangement

- linked transactions
- the accounting treatment and amounts for any fee received

(SIC 27, 10)

The disclosures required in accordance with the above paragraph are provided individually for each arrangement or in aggregate for each class of arrangement. A class is a grouping of arrangements with underlying assets of a similar nature (e.g. power plants).

Finance Leases – Lessees

Net carrying amount of finance leases (IAS 17, 23(a))
Reconciliation between the total of minimum lease payments at the balance sheet date and present value (IAS 17, 23(b))
Total of the minimum lease payments at the balance sheet date and their present value for each of the following periods:

- not later than one year;
- later than one year and not later than five years
- later than five years

(IAS 17, 23(b))

Contingent rents recognised as expenses for the period (IAS 17, 23(c))
Total of future minimum sublease payments expected to be received under non-cancellable subleases at the balance sheet date (IAS 17, 23(d))
General description of the lessee's significant leasing arrangements (IAS 17, 23(e))

Operating Leases – Lessees

Total of future minimum lease payments under non-cancellable operating leases for each of the following periods:

- not later than one year
- later than one year and not later than five years
- later than five years

(IAS 17, 27(a))

Total of future minimum sublease payments expected to be received under non-cancellable subleases at the balance sheet date (IAS 17, 27(b))
Lease and sublease payments recognised in income for the period, with separate amounts for minimum lease payments, contingent rents, and sublease payments (IAS 17, 27(c))

General description of the lessee's significant leasing arrangements (IAS 17, 27(d))

Finance Leases – Lessors

Reconciliation between the total gross investment in the lease at the balance sheet date, and the present value of minimum lease payments receivable at the balance sheet date (IAS 17, 39(a))
Total gross investment in the lease and the present value of minimum lease payments receivable at the balance sheet date, for each of the following periods:

- not later than one year
- later than one year and not later than five years
- later than five years

(IAS 17, 39(a))

Unearned finance income (IAS 17, 39(b))
Unguaranteed residual values accruing to the benefit of the lessor (IAS 17, 39(c))
Accumulated allowance for uncollectable minimum lease payments receivable (IAS 17, 39(d))
Contingent rents recognised in income (IAS 17, 39(e))
General description of the lessor's significant leasing arrangements (IAS 17, 39(f))

Operating Leases – Lessors

For each class of asset:

- gross carrying amount, the accumulated depreciation and accumulated impairment losses at the balance sheet date
- depreciation recognised as an expense
- impairment losses recognised as an expense
- impairment losses reversed in income for the period
- the future minimum lease payments under non-cancellable operating leases in the aggregate and for each of the following periods:
  - not later than one year
  - later than one year and not later than five years
  - later than five years
- total contingent rents recognised in income
- a general description of the lessor's significant leasing arrangements

(IAS 17, 48)

POST-EMPLOYMENT BENEFITS

Defined Contribution Plans

Amount recognised as an expense (IAS 19, 46)

Defined Benefit Plans:

Accounting policy for recognising actuarial gains and losses (IAS 19, 120(a))
General description of the type of plan (IAS 19, 120(b))
Reconciliation of the assets and liabilities in the balance sheet showing:

- present value of defined benefit obligations that are wholly unfunded
- present value (before deducting the fair value of plan assets) of defined benefit obligations that are wholly or partly funded
- fair value of any plan assets
- net actuarial gains or losses not recognised
- past service cost not yet recognised
- amount not recognised as an asset as a result of asset ceiling test
- fair value of any reimbursement right recognised as an asset, together with link between right and related obligation

(IAS 19, 120(c))

Amounts included in the fair value of plan assets for:

- each category of the reporting entity's own financial instruments
- any property occupied by, or other assets used by, the reporting entity

(IAS 19, 120(d))

Reconciliation showing the movements during the period in the net liability (or asset) recognised in the balance sheet (IAS 19, 120(e))
Total expense recognised in the income statement for each of the following:

- current service cost
- interest cost
- expected return on plan assets
- expected return on any reimbursement right recognised as an asset
- actuarial gains and losses
- past service cost
- the effect of any curtailment of settlement

(IAS 19, 120(h))

Actual return on the plan assets (IAS 19, 120(g))
Principal actuarial assumptions (in absolute terms) used as at the balance sheet date, including:

- discount rates
- expected rates of return on any plan assets for the periods presented
- expected rates of return on any reimbursement right recognised as an asset
- expected rates of salary increases (and of changes in an index or other variable specified in the formal or constructive terms of a plan as the basis for future benefit increases)
- medical cost trend rates
- any other material actuarial assumptions

(IAS 19, 120(h))

EQUITY COMPENSATION BENEFITS

Nature and terms (including any vesting provisions) (IAS 19, 147)
Accounting policy (IAS 19, 147)
Amounts recognised in the financial statements (IAS 19, 147(c))
Number and terms of own equity financial instruments held by equity compensation plans (and in the case of share options, employees) at the beginning and end of the period and extent to which employees' entitlements are vested (IAS 19, 147(d))
Number and terms of equity financial instruments issued by the entity to equity compensation plans (and in the case of share options, employees) at the beginning and end of the period and the extent to which employees' entitlements are vested (IAS 19, 147(e))
Number, exercise dates and exercise prices of share options exercised (IAS 19, 147(f))
Number of share options held by equity compensation plans, or held by employees under such plans, that lapsed during the period (IAS 19, 147(g))
Amount, and principal terms, of any loans or guarantees granted by the reporting entity to, or on behalf of, equity compensation plans (IAS 19, 147(h))
Fair value, at the beginning and end of the period, of the entity's own equity financial instruments (other than share options) held by equity compensation plans (IAS 19, 148)
Fair value, at the date of issue, of the entity's own equity financial instruments (other than share options) issued by the entity to equity compensation plans or to employees, or by equity compensation plans to employees during the period (IAS 19, 148)

Fact that not practicable to determine the fair value of the equity financial instruments (other than share options) (IAS 19, 148)

GOVERNMENT GRANTS

Nature and extent of recognised government grants (IAS 20, 39)
Other forms of government assistance from which benefited (IAS 20, 39)

BORROWING COSTS

Amount capitalised during the period (IAS 23, 29)
Capitalisation rate (IAS 23, 29)

SEGMENT INFORMATION

Basis of pricing inter-segment transfers and any change (IAS 14, 75)
Changes in accounting policies adopted for segment reporting (IAS 14, 76)
Types of products and services in each reported business segment (IAS 14, 81)
Composition of each reported geographical segment (IAS 14, 81)

Primary Segments

Segment revenue (IAS 14, 51)
Segment revenue from sales to external customers (IAS 14, 51)
Segment revenue from transactions with other segments (IAS 14, 51)
Segment result (IAS 14, 52)
Segment assets (IAS 14, 55)
Segment liabilities (IAS 14, 56)
Capital expenditure (IAS 14, 57)
Depreciation and amortisation of segment assets for the period (IAS 14, 58)
Significant non-cash expenses, other than depreciation and amortisation (IAS 14, 61)
Share of the net profit or loss of associates, joint venturers, or other investments accounted for under the equity method if substantially all those associates' operations are within a single segment (IAS 14, 64)

Reconciliation between segment information and aggregate information (IAS 14, 67)
Amount of impairment losses and reversals of impairment losses recognised in the income statement and directly in equity (IAS 36, 116)

Secondary Segments

If primary format is business segments, for each geographical segment whose segment assets are 10% or more of the total assets of all geographical segments:

- segment revenue from external customers by location of customers
- carrying amount of segment assets by location of assets
- capital expenditure by geographical location of assets

(IAS 14, 69)

If primary format is geographical segments, for each business segment whose revenue from sales to external customers is 10% or more of total entity revenue from sales to all external customers or whose segment assets are 10% or more of the total assets of all business segments:

- segment revenue from external customers
- carrying amount of segment assets
- capital expenditure in the period

(IAS 14, 70)

If primary format is geographical segments based on location of assets and if the location of the customers is different from the location of assets, revenue from sales to external customers for each customer-based geographical segment whose revenue from sales to external customers is 10% or more of total entity revenue from sales to all external customers (IAS 14, 71)
If primary format is geographical segments based on location of customers and if the entity's assets are located in different geographical areas from its customers, for each asset-based geographical segment whose revenue from sales to external customers or segment assets is 10% or more of related consolidated or total entity amounts:

- carrying amount of segment assets by geographical location of the assets
- the total cost incurred during the period to acquire property, plant, equipment, and intangible assets by location of the assets

(IAS 14, 72)

If a business segment or geographical segment for which information is reported to the board of directors and chief executive officer is not a reportable segment but its revenue from sales to external customers is 10% or more of total entity revenue from sales to all external customers, amounts of revenue from sales to external customers and internal sales to other segments (IAS 14, 74)

DISCONTINUING OPERATIONS

Effect of the disposal of subsidiaries on:

- the financial position
- the results for the period
- the corresponding amounts for the preceding period

(IAS 27, 32)

Description (IAS 35, 27)
Business or geographical segment in which it is reported (IAS 35, 27)
Date and nature of the initial disclosure event (IAS 35, 27)
Date or period in which the discontinuance is expected to be completed (IAS 35, 27)
Carrying amounts of the assets and liabilities to be disposed of (IAS 35, 27)
Revenue, expenses and pre-tax profit or loss from ordinary activities attributable to the discontinuing operation during the current period, and the income tax expense relating thereto (IAS 35, 27)
Net cash flows attributable to the operating, investing, and financing activities of the discontinuing operation (IAS 35, 27)
Pre-tax gain or loss recognised on the disposal of assets or settlement of liabilities attributable to the discontinuing operation and income tax expense relating to the gain or loss (IAS 35, 31)
Net selling prices or range of prices (after deducting the expected disposal costs) of net assets for which the entity has entered into binding sales agreements, the expected timing of receipt of those cash flows, and the carrying amount of those net assets (IAS 35, 31)
For periods subsequent to that in which the initial disclosure event occurs, a description of any significant changes in the amount or timing of cash flows relating to the assets and liabilities to be disposed of or settled and the events causing those changes (IAS 35, 33)
Fact that plan has been abandoned or withdrawn and effect (IAS 35, 36)

RELATED PARTIES

Related party relationships where control exists (IAS 24, 20)
If there have been transactions with related parties:

- the nature of the related party relationships
- types of transactions
- the elements of the transactions necessary for an understanding of the financial statements

(IAS 24, 22 and 24)

Above disclosures when entity or its subsidiary reacquires its own equity instruments from a related party (SIC 16, 7)

EVENTS OCCURRING AFTER THE BALANCE SHEET DATE

When non-adjusting events occurring after the balance sheet date are of such importance that non-disclosure would affect the ability of the users of the financial statements to make proper evaluations and decisions, for each event:

- nature
- estimate of financial effect or a statement that such an estimate cannot be made

(IAS 10, 20)

Update of disclosures about conditions at balance sheet date when information received after the balance sheet date (IAS 10, 18)

FINANCIAL ASSETS, FINANCIAL LIABILITIES AND EQUITY INSTRUMENTS

Financial risk management objectives and policies including policy for hedging each major type of forecasted transaction for which hedge accounting is used (IAS 32, 43A and IAS 39, 169)
For each class of recognised and unrecognised financial asset, financial liability and equity instrument:

- the extent and nature of the financial instruments, including significant terms and conditions that may affect the amount, timing and certainty of future cash flows

- the accounting policies and methods adopted, including the criteria for recognition and the basis of measurement applied
- methods and significant assumptions applied in estimating fair values of financial assets and financial liabilities that are carried at fair value;
- whether gains and losses of changes in fair value of available-for-sale financial assets are included in net profit or loss or equity
- whether regular way purchases and sales of financial assets are accounted for at trade date or settlement date

(IAS 32, 47 and IAS 39, 167)

For each class of recognised and unrecognised financial asset and financial liability, information about exposure to interest rate risk, including:

- contractual repricing or maturity dates, whichever dates are earlier (IAS 32, 56)
- effective interest rates, when applicable (IAS 32, 56)
- information about fair value unless carried at fair value (IAS 32, 77 and IAS 39, 166)
- fact if not practicable to determine fair value with sufficient reliability, together with information about principal characteristics of the underlying financial instrument (IAS 32, 77)

For each class of recognised and unrecognised financial asset, information about exposure to credit risk, including:

- the amount that best represents maximum credit risk exposure at the balance sheet date, without taking account of the fair value of any collateral, in the event that other parties fail to perform their obligations under financial instruments
- significant concentrations of credit risk

(IAS 32, 66)

For financial assets carried in excess of fair value:

- the carrying amount and the fair value of either the individual assets or appropriate groupings of those individual assets
- the reasons for not reducing the carrying amount, including the nature of the evidence that provides the basis for management's belief that the carrying amount will be recovered

(IAS 32, 88)

For designated fair value hedges, cash flow hedges and hedges of a net investment in a foreign entity:

- description of hedge
- description and fair values of financial instruments designated as hedging instruments
- nature of risks being hedged

(IAS 39, 169)

For hedges of forecasted transactions:

- periods in which transactions are expected to occur and enter into determination of net profit
- description of forecasted transactions for which hedge accounting had previously been used but that are no longer expected to occur

(IAS 39, 169)

For gains and losses on hedging instruments in cash flow hedges recognised in equity:

- amount recognised in equity in current period
- amount removed from equity and included in net profit or loss for current period
- amount removed from equity and added to (deducted from) carrying amount of assets or liabilities in current period

(IAS 39, 169)

Gains or losses on available-for-sale securities recognised in, and removed from, equity in current period (IAS 39, 170)
Fact that, and description of, any available-for-sale financial assets and financial assets held for trading are carried at amortised cost together with:

- carrying amounts
- reason why fair value cannot be reliably measured
- range of estimates within which fair value is highly likely to lie

(IAS 39, 170)

Significant income, expenses, gains and losses resulting from financial assets and financial liabilities whether included in net profit or loss or equity including:

- total interest income
- total interest expense
- realised gains and losses on available-for-sale financial assets
- unrealised gains and losses on available-for-sale financial assets

(IAS 39, 170)

EARNINGS PER SHARE

Numerator for basic and diluted (IAS 33, 49)
Reconciliation to the net profit or loss for the period (IAS 33, 49)
Weighted average number of ordinary shares used in calculating basic and diluted (IAS 33, 49)
Reconciliation to each other (IAS 33, 49(b))

RESTATED FINANCIAL STATEMENTS IN HYPERINFLATIONARY ECONOMIES

Fact that the financial statements and the corresponding figures for previous periods have been restated (IAS 29, 39)
Whether financial statements are based on a historical cost approach or a current cost approach (IAS 29, 39)
Identity and level of the price index at the balance sheet date (IAS 29, 39)
Movement in the index during current and previous reporting period (IAS 29, 39)
Gain or loss on net monetary position (IAS 29, 9)

APPENDIX 2

Further Reading

INTERNATIONAL ACCOUNTING STANDARDS BOARD

Copies of all IASs/IFRSs, exposure drafts and other IASB publications can be obtained from:

Publications Department
International Accounting Standards Board
30 Cannon Street
London EC4M 6XH
United Kingdom
Telephone: +44 (0) 20 7246 6410
Telefax: +44 (0) 20 7246 6411
E-mail: publications @iasb.org.uk
Website: www.iasb.org.uk

International Accounting Standards

International Accounting Standards 2002 includes the full text of IASs, interpretations of IASs and the *Framework for the Preparation and Presentation of Financial Statements* extant at 1 April 2002. The volume also includes the IASCF constitution, the *Preface to International Financial Reporting Standards* and a description of IASB's processes and objectives.

International Accounting Standards on CD-Rom is also available from the IASB. It contains the same contents as the annual volume of IASs plus exposure drafts and a fully-linked glossary of terms.

Draft Statements of Principles

Earnings Per Share, October 1993
Intangible Assets, January 1994

Reporting Financial Information by Segment, September 1994
Presentation of Financial Statements, March 1995
Interim Financial Reporting, September 1996
Discontinuing Operations, November 1996
Provisions and Contingencies, November 1996
Agriculture, December 1996

Comment Letters

Copies of the comment letters on each exposure draft from E32 onwards, all DSOPs and all draft interpretations are available for purchase from the IASB. Comment letters on exposure drafts prior to E32 were not placed on the public record.

Discussion Papers

Disclosures in Financial Statements of Banks, March 1980
Summary of Responses to Discussion Paper, Disclosures in Financial Statements of Banks, March 1982
Report of the International Accounting Standards Foundation Working Party, February 1994
Accounting for Financial Assets and Financial Liabilities, March 1997
Shaping IASC for the Future, November 1998
Recommendations on Shaping IASC for the Future, November 1999

Newsletters

IASB Insight, quarterly
IASB Update, a summary of board decisions published immediately after board meetings
News from the IFRIC, a summary of IFRIC decisions

Issues Papers

Paul Pacter, *Reporting Financial Information by Segment*, April 1994
Retirement Benefit and Other Employee Benefit Costs, August 1995
Interim Financial Reporting, May 1996
Business Reporting on the Internet, November 1999
Extractive Industries, November 2000
Insurance, May 2001 (two volumes)

Survey

Survey of the Use and Application of International Accounting Standards, 1988
Axel Vietze, *Survey on Derivatives*, 1996

SURVEYS OF IAS COMPLIANCE

David Cairns, *International Accounting Standards Survey 2000*, David Cairns, www.cairns.co.uk, 2001
David Cairns, *International Accounting Standards Survey Update 2002*, David Cairns, www.cairns.co.uk, 2002
Donna L. Street and Sydney J. Gray, *Observance of International Accounting Standards: Factors Explaining Non-Compliance,* The Association of Chartered Certified Accountants, London, 2001

G4+1

The members of G4+1 were: Australian Accounting Standards Board; Canadian Accounting Standards Board; New Zealand Financial Reporting Standards Board; United Kingdom Accounting Standards Board; United States Financial Accounting Standards Board plus the International Accounting Standards Committee. Copies of all G4+1 papers are available from each of the members.
Future Events: A Conceptual Study of their Significance for Recognition and Measurement, (principal author L. Todd Johnson), 1994
Major Issues Related to Hedge Accounting, (principal authors J. B. Adams and C. J. Montesi), 1995
Provisions: Their Recognition, Measurement, and Disclosure in Financial Statements, (principal authors A. Lennard, S. Thompson), 1995
Accounting for Leases: A New Approach, (principal author W. McGregor), 1996
International Review of Accounting Standards Specifying a Recoverable Amount Test for Long-Lived Assets, (principal author J. Paul), 1997
Reporting Financial Performance: Current Developments and Future Directions, (principal authors L. Todd Johnson and A. Lennard), 1998
Recommendations for Achieving Convergence on the Methods of Accounting for Business Combinations, 1998
Accounting by Recipients for Non-Reciprocal Transfers, Excluding Contributions by Owners, (principal authors M. Westwood and A. Mackenzie), 1999
Reporting Interests in Joint Ventures and Similar Arrangements, (principal authors J. A. Milburn and P. D. Chant), 1999

Reporting Financial Performance: A Proposed Approach, (principal author K. Cearns), 1999
Leases: Implementation of a New Approach, G4+1 position paper, 2000
Accounting for Share-Based Payments, G4+1 position paper, 2000

JOINT WORKING GROUP OF STANDARD SETTERS

Draft Standard and Basis for Conclusions: Financial Instruments and Similar Items, 2000

EUROPEAN UNION

Directives

Fourth Council Directive on the Annual Accounts of Certain Types of Companies, 25 July 1978 (78/660/EEC), European Commission
Seventh Council Directive on Consolidated Accounts, 13 June 1983 (83/349/EEC), European Commission
Directive on the Annual Accounts and Consolidated Accounts of Banks and Other Financial Institutions, 8 December 1986 (86/635/EEC), European Commission
Directive on the Annual Accounts and Consolidated Accounts of Insurance Undertakings, 19 December 1991 (91/674/EEC), European Commission
Regulation of The European Parliament and The Council on the Application of International Accounting Standards, European Parliament, 1606/2002, 2002

European Commission

The Future of Harmonisation of Accounting Standards Within the European Community, European Commission – the Commission's report on its 1990 conference on future directions, including some useful position papers from important players
The Accounting Harmonisation in the European Communities: Problems of Applying the 4th Directive on the Annual Accounts of Limited Companies, 1990, European Commission
Accounting Harmonisation: A New Strategy vis-à-vis International Harmonisation, 1995, European Commission (COM 95 (508))
An Examination of the Conformity between the International Accounting Standards and the European Accounting Directives, Contact Committee on the Accounting Directives, 1996, European Commission

Interpretative Communication Concerning Certain Articles of the Fourth and the Seventh Council Directives on Accounting, 1997, European Commission
EU Financial Reporting Strategy: The Way Forward, European Commission (COM (2000) 359), 2000

European Commission Accounting Advisory Forum

Government Grants, 1995, European Commission
Accounting for Lease Contracts, 1995, European Commission
Foreign Currency Translation, 1995, European Commission

FÉDÉRATION DES EXPERTS COMPTABLES EUROPÉENS (FEE)

Further information can be obtained from:

Fédération des Experts Comptables Européens
Rue de la Loi 83
1040 Bruxelles
Belgium
Telephone: +32 (2) 285 40 85
Telefax: +32 (2) 231 11 12
E-mail: Secretariat@FEE.be
Website: www.fee.be

Comparison of the European Community Fourth Directive with International Accounting Standards, 1990
Subjects with which the Fourth Directive Deals Insufficiently or Not at All, 1990
Analysis of European Accounting and Disclosure Practices, 1992, London, Routledge
Survey on Legal Mergers in the Context of IASC's E45, Business Combinations, 1993
Seventh Directive Options and Their Implementation, 1993, London, Routledge
Investigation of Emerging Accounting Areas, 1994, London, Routledge
Responsibilities for Financial Reporting by Companies, 1994
The Application of Prudence and Matching in Selected European Countries, 1995
International Accounting Standard for Insurance Undertakings, 1995
Survey of Pensions and Other Retirement Benefits in EU and Non-EU Countries, 1995, London, Routledge
Comparative Study on Conceptual Accounting Frameworks in Europe, 1997
Accounting Treatment of Financial Instruments – A European Perspective, 1997
Review of International Accounting Standards for Environmental Issues, 1998

Towards a Generally Accepted Framework for Environmental Reporting, 1999
Accounting Standard Setting in Europe, 2000
Enforcement Mechanisms in Europe: A Preliminary Investigation of Oversight Systems, 2001
Modernisation of the Accounting Directives, 2001
Enforcement of IFRS Within Europe, 2002

INTERNATIONAL FEDERATION OF ACCOUNTANTS (IFAC)

Copies of all IFAC publications can be obtained from:
International Federation of Accountants
535 Fifth Avenue
26th Floor
New York, NY 10017
United States of America
Telephone: +1 212 286 9344
Telefax: +1 212 286 9570
Website: www.ifac.org

IFAC Bound Volume 2002 includes the full text of all IFAC pronouncements extant at 1 July 2002 including International Standards on Auditing, International Public Sector Guidelines (including *Financial Reporting by Government Business Enterprises*) and International Public Sector Accounting Standards.

International Capital Markets Group

Harmonization of International Accounting Standards, 1992 – this study looks at the likelihood of accounting harmonisation in France, Germany, Japan, the United Kingdom and the United States of America and addresses whether US GAAP should be the international standard.
International Corporate Governance – Who Holds the Reins, 1995

THE INTERNATIONAL VALUATION STANDARDS COMMITTEE (IVSC)

Copies of International Valuation Standards and other IVSC publications can be obtained from:

The International Valuation Standards Committee
12 Great George Street
London SW1P 3AD
United Kingdom
Telephone: +44 (0) 20 7222 7000
Telefax: +44 (0) 20 7222 9430

Further information about the IVSC and copies of its newsletter can also be obtained from www.ivsc.org

INTERNATIONAL ORGANIZATION OF SECURITIES COMMISSIONS (IOSCO)

International Accounting and Auditing Standards, Report of the Technical Committee, November 1990

Public Disclosure of the Trading and Derivatives Activities of Banks and Securities Firms, 1995 (with Basle Committee on Banking Supervision)

Report on the Implementation of IOSCO Resolutions, Report of the General Secretariat, 1998 (includes information on the current status of IOSCO's 1993 endorsement of IAS 7 and its 1992 endorsement of International Standards on Auditing)

Comparative Report on the Requirement of Adjustment for Inflation of the Emerging Markets' Financial Statements, Emerging Markets Committee, updated November 1998

International Disclosure Standards for Cross-Border Offerings and Initial Listings by Foreign Issuers, 1998

IASC Standards, Report of the Technical Committee, 2000

Copies of IOSCO documents, including all papers presented at IOSCO annual meetings, are available from:

International Organization of Securities Commissions (IOSCO)
Plaza de Carlos Trías Bertrán, 7
Planta 3ª
28020 Madrid
Spain
Telephone: +34 (0) 91 417 55 49
Facsimile: +34 (0) 91 555 93 68
Website: www.iosco.org

US SECURITIES AND EXCHANGE COMMISSION

Report on Promoting Global Preeminence of American Securities Markets, www.sec.gov, 1997
International Accounting Standards, Concept Release, 2000, www.sec.gov
International Financial Reporting and Disclosure Issues, Division of Corporate Finance, SEC, Washington DC, 2001, www.sec.gov

BASEL COMMITTEE ON BANKING SUPERVISION

Public Disclosure of the Trading and Derivatives Activities of Banks and Securities Firms, 1995 (with IOSCO)
Sound Practices for Loan Accounting and Disclosure, 1999
Public Disclosures by Banks – Results of the 2000 Disclosure Survey, 2001

ORGANISATION FOR ECONOMIC CO-OPERATION AND DEVELOPMENT (OECD)

Harmonization of Accounting Standards: Achievements and Prospects, 1986, Paris: OECD – this book reports on an OECD conference in 1985 which was probably one of the most significant landmarks in efforts at accounting harmonisation and the future fortunes of IASC
Multinational Enterprises and Disclosure of Information, Paris, OECD, 1988

UNITED NATIONS INTERGOVERNMENTAL WORKING GROUP OF EXPERTS ON INTERNATIONAL STANDARDS OF ACCOUNTING AND REPORTING (UN ISAR GROUP)

Conclusions on Accounting and Reporting by Transnational Corporations, United Nations, 1988

The UN ISAR Group also publishes an annual survey of international accounting and reporting issues.

ACCOUNTING AND AUDITING ORGANIZATION FOR ISLAMIC FINANCIAL INSTITUTIONS (AAOIFI)

More information about the accounting and auditing standards issued by AAOIFI can be obtained from:

Accounting and Auditing Organization for Islamic Financial Institutions
PO Box 1176
Manama, Bahrain
Telephone: +973 244496
Telefax: +973 250194

OTHER USEFUL SOURCES

Achleitner, A-K., *Die Normierung der Rechunglegung*, Zurich: Treuhand-Kammer, 1995, – a comprehensive and up-to-date German study, with an extensive bibliography, of IASC and other organisations involved in accounting harmonisation

Financial Accounting Standards Board, *International Accounting Standards Setting: A Vision for the Future*, FASB, Norwalk, 1999

Financial Accounting Standards Board, *The IASC – US GAAP Comparison Project: A Report of Similarities and Differences Between IASC Standards and US GAAP*, ed Carrie Bloomer, Norwalk, CT FASB, 1999

Harris, T. S., *International Accounting Standards versus US GAAP Reporting: Empirical Evidence Based on Case Studies*, 1995, Cincinnati: South-Western College Publishing – a comparison of the impact of International Accounting Standards, US GAAP and domestic reporting requirements on the financial statements of eight large European and Australian multinationals

Schuetz, W., Biener, H. and Cairns, D., (1994) 'The Politics of Mutual Recognition', *The European Accounting Review* 3 (3): 329–352 – a description and analysis of the attitudes of regulators to harmonisation and mutual recognition

Company Index

Alphabetical list of references to company financial statements of

Index